America

Past and Present

Brief Sixth Edition

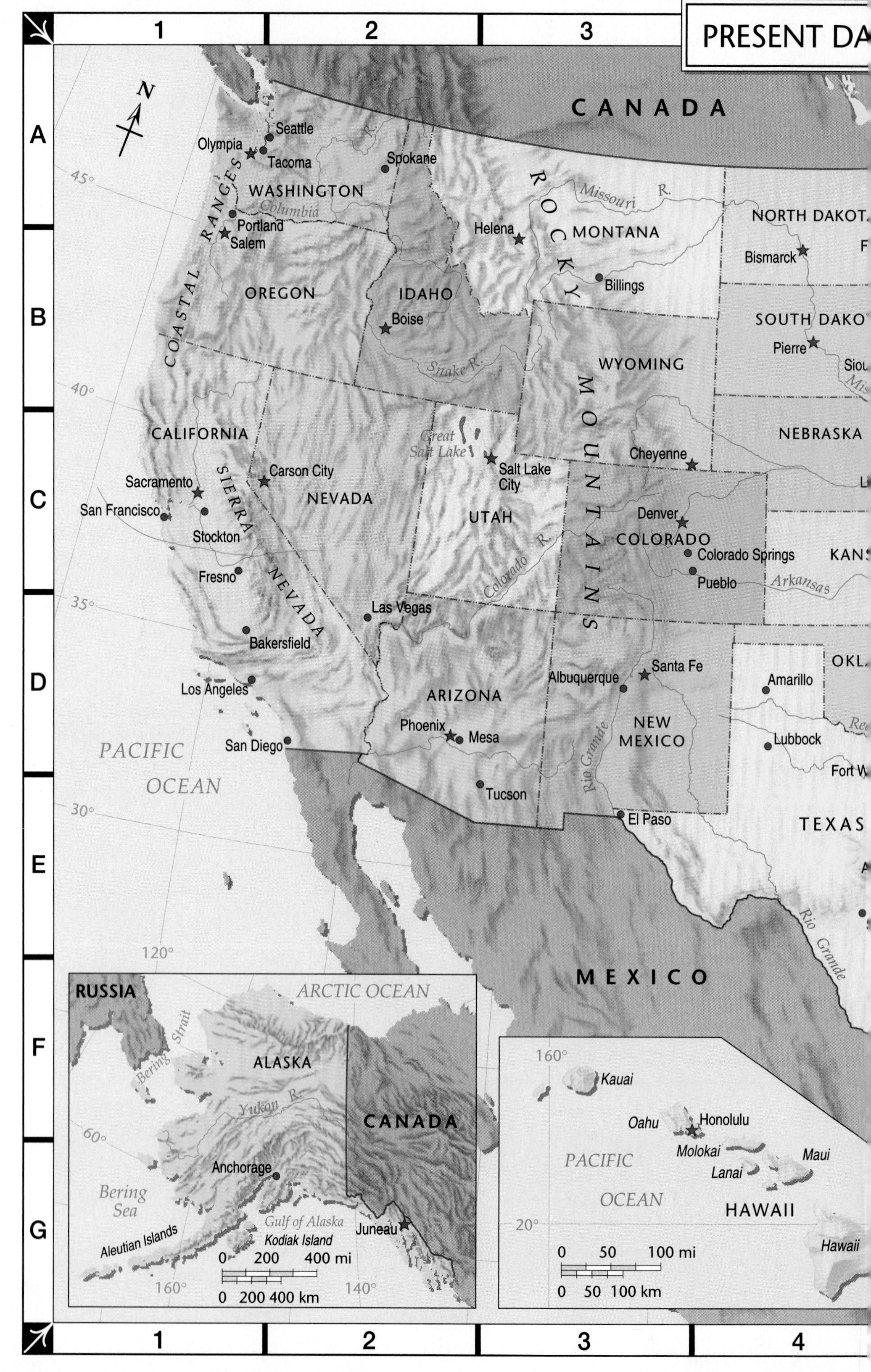
PRESENT DA
1
2
3
4
A
B
C
D
E
F
G
CANADA
WASHINGTON
Seattle
Olympia
Tacoma
Spokane
COASTAL RANGES
Portland
Salem
Columbia
OREGON
IDAHO
Boise
Snake R.
Helena
MONTANA
Billings
Missouri R.
ROCKY MOUNTAINS
NORTH DAKOT
Bismarck
SOUTH DAKO
Pierre
WYOMING
NEBRASKA
Cheyenne
CALIFORNIA
Sacramento
San Francisco
Stockton
SIERRA NEVADA
Fresno
Bakersfield
Los Angeles
San Diego
Carson City
NEVADA
Las Vegas
Great Salt Lake
Salt Lake City
UTAH
Colorado R.
Denver
COLORADO
Colorado Springs
Pueblo
Arkansas
KAN
ARIZONA
Phoenix
Mesa
Tucson
NEW MEXICO
Santa Fe
Albuquerque
Rio Grande
El Paso
OKL
Amarillo
Lubbock
Fort W
TEXAS
PACIFIC OCEAN
MEXICO
45°
40°
35°
30°
120°
RUSSIA
ARCTIC OCEAN
Bering Strait
ALASKA
Yukon R.
CANADA
Anchorage
Bering Sea
Aleutian Islands
Gulf of Alaska
Kodiak Island
Juneau
0 200 400 mi
0 200 400 km
60°
160°
140°
160°
Kauai
Oahu
Honolulu
Molokai
Maui
Lanai
PACIFIC OCEAN
HAWAII
Hawaii
20°
0 50 100 mi
0 50 100 km

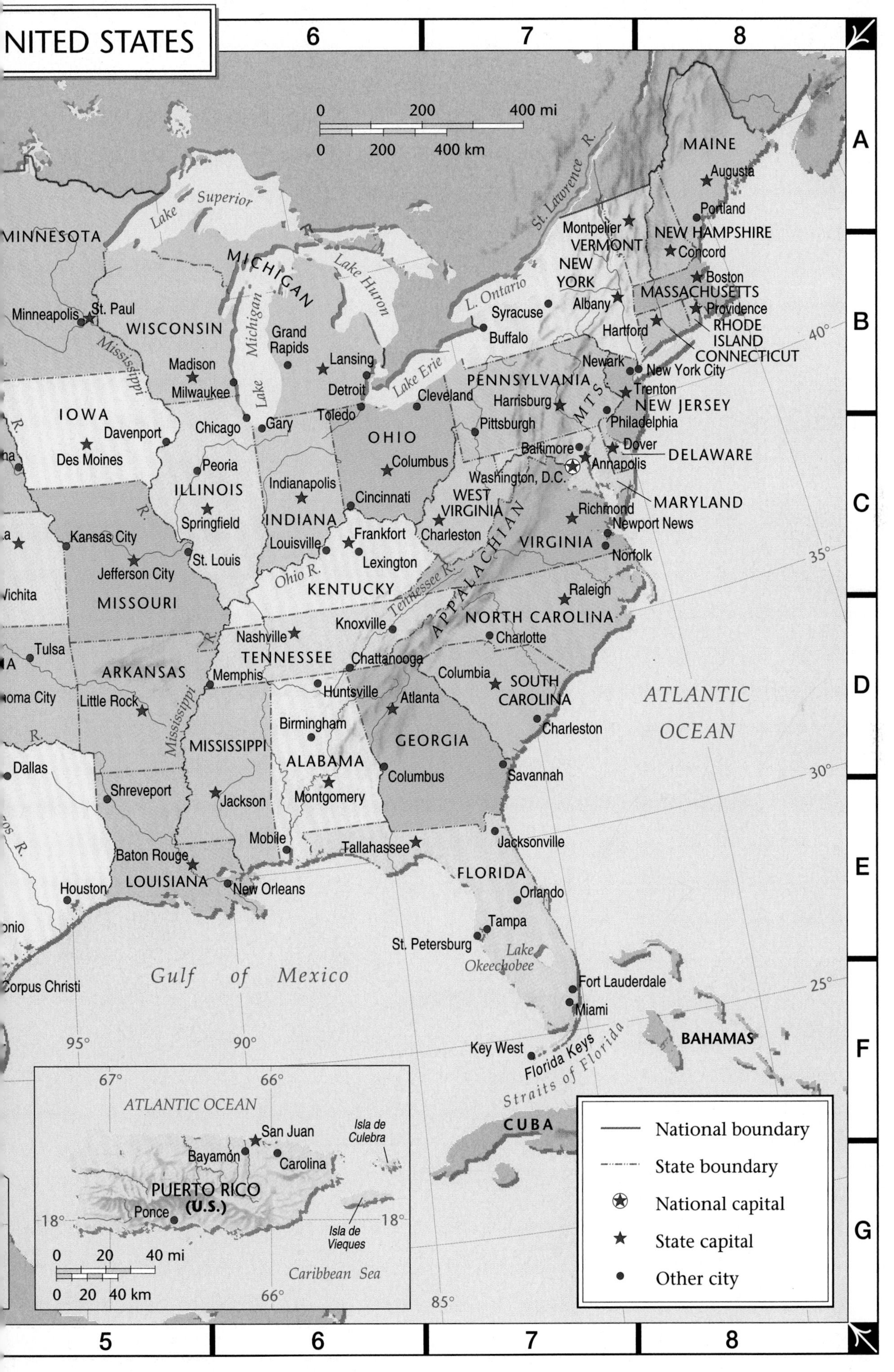

NITED STATES
MINNESOTA
WISCONSIN
MICHIGAN
IOWA
ILLINOIS
INDIANA
OHIO
PENNSYLVANIA
NEW YORK
VERMONT
NEW HAMPSHIRE
MAINE
MASSACHUSETTS
RHODE ISLAND
CONNECTICUT
NEW JERSEY
DELAWARE
MARYLAND
WEST VIRGINIA
VIRGINIA
KENTUCKY
MISSOURI
TENNESSEE
NORTH CAROLINA
SOUTH CAROLINA
ARKANSAS
MISSISSIPPI
ALABAMA
GEORGIA
LOUISIANA
FLORIDA
APPALACHIAN MTS
ATLANTIC OCEAN
Gulf of Mexico
BAHAMAS
CUBA
Straits of Florida
Florida Keys
Lake Superior
Lake Michigan
Lake Huron
Lake Erie
L. Ontario
Lake Okeechobee
St. Lawrence R.
Mississippi R.
Ohio R.
Tennessee R.
Augusta
Portland
Montpelier
Concord
Boston
Providence
Hartford
Albany
Syracuse
Buffalo
New York City
Newark
Trenton
Philadelphia
Harrisburg
Pittsburgh
Dover
Baltimore
Annapolis
Washington, D.C.
Richmond
Newport News
Norfolk
Raleigh
Charlotte
Columbia
Charleston
Savannah
Atlanta
Columbus
Jacksonville
Tallahassee
Orlando
Tampa
St. Petersburg
Fort Lauderdale
Miami
Key West
Minneapolis
St. Paul
Madison
Milwaukee
Chicago
Gary
Grand Rapids
Lansing
Detroit
Toledo
Cleveland
Columbus
Cincinnati
Indianapolis
Peoria
Springfield
Davenport
Des Moines
Kansas City
Jefferson City
St. Louis
Louisville
Frankfort
Lexington
Charleston
Knoxville
Nashville
Chattanooga
Memphis
Huntsville
Birmingham
Montgomery
Little Rock
Tulsa
Wichita
Dallas
Shreveport
Jackson
Mobile
Baton Rouge
New Orleans
Houston
Corpus Christi
0 200 400 mi
0 200 400 km
40°
35°
30°
25°
95°
90°
85°
ATLANTIC OCEAN
San Juan
Bayamón
Carolina
Isla de Culebra
PUERTO RICO (U.S.)
Ponce
Isla de Vieques
Caribbean Sea
67°
66°
18°
0 20 40 mi
0 20 40 km
National boundary
State boundary
National capital
State capital
Other city
6 7 8
A B C D E F G
5 6 7 8

Past and Present

Brief Sixth Edition

ROBERT A. DIVINE
University of Texas

T. H. BREEN
Northwestern University

GEORGE M. FREDRICKSON
Stanford University

R. HAL WILLIAMS
Southern Methodist University

ARIELA J. GROSS
University of Southern California

H. W. BRANDS
Texas A&M University

RANDY ROBERTS
Purdue University

PEARSON
Longman

New York San Francisco Boston
London Toronto Sydney Tokyo Singapore Madrid
Mexico City Munich Paris Cape Town Hong Kong Montreal

Vice President and Publisher: Priscilla McGeehon
Development Manager: Betty Slack
Development Editor: Karen Helfrich
Executive Marketing Manager: Sue Westmoreland
Media Editor: Patrick McCarthy
Supplements Editor: Kristi Olson
Production Manager: Douglas Bell
Project Coordination, Text Design, and Electronic Page Makeup: Elm Street Publishing Services, Inc.
Senior Design Manager/Cover Designer: Nancy Danahy
Cover Image: "The Reconciliation Quilt" made by Lucinda Ward Honstain, dated 1867, Brooklyn, NY.
Copyright © Photo courtesy of the International Quilt Study Center at the University of Nebraska-Lincoln, 2001.011.0001.
Art Studio: Maps.com and Elm Street Publishing Services, Inc.
Photo Research: Photosearch, Inc.
Senior Manufacturing Buyer: Alfred C. Dorsey
Printer and Binder: Quebecor World/Versailles
Cover Printer: The Lehigh Press, Inc.

Text credits: p. 363, Arthur Miller, *The Price.* New York, New York: Viking Penguin, 1968.

Library of Congress Cataloging-in-Publication Data

Divine, Robert A.
America past and present / Robert A. Divine . . . [et al.].—Brief 6th ed.
p. cm.
Includes bibliographical references and index.
ISBN 0-321-18306-1 (set)—ISBN 0-321-18305-3 (v.1)—ISBN 0-321-18304-5 (v. 2)
1. United States—History. I. Title.

E178.A4894 2005
973—dc22

2004044277

Please visit our website at http://www.ablongman.com/divine

ISBN 0-321-18306-1 (Complete Brief Edition)
ISBN 0-321-18305-3 (Volume I)
ISBN 0-321-18304-5 (Volume II)

2 3 4 5 6 7 8 9 10—QWV—07 06 05

Brief Contents

Detailed Contents *ix*
Maps *xix*
Charts, Figures, and Tables *xx*
Features *xxi*
Preface *xxiii*
Acknowledgments *xxix*
About the Authors *xxx*

CHAPTER 1
New World Encounters 1

CHAPTER 2
Conflicting Visions: England's Seventeenth-Century Colonies 21

CHAPTER 3
Putting Down Roots: Opportunity and Oppression in Colonial Society 42

CHAPTER 4
Experience of Empire: Eighteenth-Century America 58

CHAPTER 5
The American Revolution: From Elite Protest to Popular Revolt, 1763–1783 82

CHAPTER 6
The Republican Experiment 103

CHAPTER 7
Democracy in Distress: The Violence of Party Politics, 1788–1800 126

CHAPTER 8
Republican Ascendancy: The Jeffersonian Vision 146

CHAPTER 9
Nation Building and Nationalism 165

CHAPTER 10
The Triumph of White Men's Democracy 184

CHAPTER 11
Slaves and Masters 204

CHAPTER 12
The Pursuit of Perfection 226

CHAPTER 13
An Age of Expansionism 244

CHAPTER 14
The Sectional Crisis 266

CHAPTER 15
Secession and the Civil War 287

CHAPTER 16
The Agony of Reconstruction 310

CHAPTER 17
The West: Exploiting an Empire 331

CHAPTER 18
The Industrial Society 353

CHAPTER 19
Toward an Urban Society, 1877–1900 371

CHAPTER 20
Political Realignments in the 1890s 390

CHAPTER 21
Toward Empire 407

CHAPTER 22
The Progressive Era 426

CHAPTER 23
From Roosevelt to Wilson in the Age of Progressivism 442

CHAPTER 24
The Nation at War 464

CHAPTER 25
Transition to Modern America 486

CHAPTER 26
Franklin D. Roosevelt and the New Deal 503

CHAPTER 27
America and the World, 1921–1945 522

CHAPTER 28
The Onset of the Cold War 543

CHAPTER 29
Affluence and Anxiety 565

CHAPTER 30
The Turbulent Sixties 577

CHAPTER 31
A Crisis in Confidence, 1969–1980 607

CHAPTER 32
The Republican Resurgence, 1980–1992 629

CHAPTER 33
America in Flux 654

Appendix A-1
Credits C-1
Index I-1

Detailed Contents

Maps xix

Charts, Figures, and Tables xx

Features xxi

Preface xxiii

Acknowledgments xxix

About the Authors xxx

CHAPTER 1

New World Encounters 1

Clash of Cultures:
The Meaning of Murder in Early Maryland 1

Native American Histories Before Conquest 2
- The Environmental Challenge: Food, Climate, and Culture 2
- Mysterious Disappearances 3
- Aztec Dominance 4
- Eastern Woodland Cultures 4

A World Transformed 5
- Cultural Negotiations 6
- Threats to Survival: Trade and Disease 7

West Africa: Ancient and Complex Societies 8

Europe on the Eve of Conquest 9
- Building New Nation-States 9

Imagining a New World 10
- Myths and Reality 10
- The Conquistadores: Faith and Greed 11
- From Plunder to Settlement 11

French Exploration and Settlement 13

The English New World 14
- Religious Turmoil and Reformation in Europe 14
- The Protestant Queen 15
- Religion, War, and Nationalism 16

Rehearsal in Ireland for American Colonization 16

An Unpromising Beginning: Mystery at Roanoke 17

Conclusion: Propaganda for Empire 18

CHAPTER 2

Conflicting Visions: England's Seventeenth-Century Colonies 21

Profit and Piety:
Competing Blueprints for English Settlement 21

Breaking Away 22

The Chesapeake: Dreams of Wealth 22
- Entrepreneurs in Virginia 23
- "Stinking Weed" 24
- Time of Reckoning 25
- Maryland: A Troubled Refuge for Catholics 26

Reforming England in America 27
- "The Great Migration" 28
- "A City on a Hill" 29
- Limits of Religious Dissent 31
- Mobility and Division 32

Diversity in the Middle Colonies 32
- Anglo-Dutch Rivalry on the Hudson 32
- Confusion in New Jersey 34

Quakers in America 34

Planting the Carolinas 36

The Founding of Georgia 39

Conclusion: Living with Diversity 40

CHAPTER 3

Putting Down Roots: Opportunity and Oppression in Colonial Society 42

Families in an Atlantic Empire 42

Sources of Stability: New England Colonies of the Seventeenth Century 43
- Immigrant Families and New Social Order 43
- Commonwealth of Families 44
- Women's Lives in Puritan New England 44
- Social Hierarchy in New England 45

The Challenge of the Chesapeake Environment 46
- Family Life at Risk 46
- The Structure of Planter Society 47

Race and Freedom in British America 48
- Roots of Slavery 48
- Constructing African American Identities 50

Rise of a Commercial Empire 50
- Response to Economic Competition 51
- Regulating Colonial Trade 51

Colonial Factions Spark Political Revolt, 1676–1691 53
- Civil War in Virginia: Bacon's Rebellion 53
- The Glorious Revolution in the Bay Colony 54
- Contagion of Witchcraft 55
- The Glorious Revolution in New York and Maryland 55

Conclusion: Local Aspirations Within an Atlantic Empire 56

CHAPTER 4
Experience of Empire: Eighteenth-Century America 58
Constructing an Anglo-American Identity: The Journal of William Byrd 58
Growth and Diversity 60
Scots-Irish and Germans 60
Convict Settlers 61
Native Americans Stake Out a Middle Ground 61
Spanish Borderlands of the Eighteenth Century 62
Conquering the Northern Frontier 63
Peoples of the Spanish Borderlands 63
The Impact of European Ideas on American Culture 64
Provincial Cities 64
American Enlightenment 65
Economic Transformation 66
Birth of a Consumer Society 67
Religious Revivals in Provincial Societies 68
The Great Awakening 68
The Voice of Popular Religion 68
Clash of Political Cultures 70
The Theory and the Reality of British Politics 70
Governing the Colonies: The American Experience 70
Colonial Assemblies 71
Century of Imperial War 72
King William's and Queen Anne's Wars 72
King George's War and Its Aftermath 73
Albany Congress and Braddock's Defeat 74
Seven Years' War 74
Conclusion: Rule Britannia? 77
We Americans
Learning to Live with Diversity in the Eighteenth Century: What Is an American? 80

CHAPTER 5
The American Revolution: From Elite Protest to Popular Revolt, 1763–1783 82
Rethinking the Meaning of Equality 82
Structure of Colonial Society 83
Breakdown of Political Trust 83
No Taxation Without Representation: The American Perspective 84
Eroding the Bonds of Empire 85
Popular Protest 86
Fueling the Crisis 87
Fatal Show of Force 88
Last Days of the Old Order, 1770–1773 89
The Final Provocation: The Boston Tea Party 90
Steps Toward Independence 91
Shots Heard Around the World 91
Beginning "The World Over Again" 91
Fighting for Independence 93
Testing the American Will 94
Victory in a Year of Defeat 95
The French Alliance 96
The Final Campaign 97
The Loyalist Dilemma 98
Winning the Peace 99
Conclusion: Preserving Independence 101

CHAPTER 6
The Republican Experiment 103
A New Moral Order 103
Defining Republican Culture 104
Living in the Shadow of Revolution 105
Social and Political Reform 105
African Americans in the New Republic 106
The Challenge of Women's Rights 107
The States: Experiments in Republicanism 108
Blueprints for State Government 108
Power to the People 109
Stumbling Toward a New National Government 109
Articles of Confederation 110
Western Land: Key to the First Constitution 110
Northwest Ordinance: The Confederation's Major Achievement 112
Strengthening Federal Authority 113
The Nationalist Critique 114
Diplomatic Humiliation 115
"Have We Fought for This?" 116
A Crisis Mentality 116
The Philadelphia Convention 117
Inventing a Federal Republic 117
Compromise Saves the Convention 118
Compromising with Slavery 119
Whose Constitution? Struggle for Ratification 120
Federalists and Antifederalists 120
Adding the Bill of Rights 122
Conclusion: Success Depends on the People 123

CHAPTER 7
Democracy in Distress: The Violence of Party Politics, 1788–1800 126
Partisan Passions 126
Power of Public Opinion 127
Principle and Pragmatism: Establishing a New Government 127
Conflicting Visions: Jefferson and Hamilton 129
Hamilton's Plan for Prosperity and Security 130
Funding and Assumption 130

Interpreting the Constitution: The Bank Controversy 131
Setback for Hamilton 131

Charges of Treason: The Battle over Foreign Affairs 132
The Peril of Neutrality 132
Jay's Treaty Sparks Domestic Unrest 133
Pushing the Native Americans Aside 134

Popular Political Culture 135
Whiskey Rebellion: Charges of Republican Conspiracy 136
Washington's Farewell 136

The Adams Presidency 137
The XYZ Affair and Domestic Politics 137
Crushing Political Dissent 138
Silencing Political Opposition: The Alien and Sedition Acts 139
Kentucky and Virginia Resolutions 139
Adams's Finest Hour 141

The Peaceful Revolution: The Election of 1800 141

Conclusion: Danger of Political Extremism 142

We Americans

Counting the People: The Federal Census of 1790 144

CHAPTER 8
Republican Ascendancy: The Jeffersonian Vision 146

Limits of Equality 146

Regional Identities in a New Republic 147
Westward the Course of Empire 147
Commercial Life in the Cities 148

Jefferson as President 149
Jeffersonian Reforms 150
The Louisiana Purchase 150
The Lewis and Clark Expedition 152
Conflict with the Barbary States 152

Jefferson's Critics 153
Attack on the Judges 153
Politics of Desperation 154
Murder and Conspiracy: The Curious Career of Aaron Burr 154
The Slave Trade 155

Embarrassments Overseas 156
Embargo Divides the Nation 157
A New Administration Goes to War 158
Fumbling Toward Conflict 159

The Strange War of 1812 159
Hartford Convention: The Demise of the Federalists 161
Treaty of Ghent Ends the War 161

Conclusion: Republican Legacy 163

CHAPTER 9
Nation Building and Nationalism 165

A Revolutionary War Hero Revisits America in 1824 165

Expansion and Migration 166
Extending the Boundaries 166
Settlement to the Mississippi 168
The People and Culture of the Frontier 169

A Revolution in Transportation 170
Roads and Steamboats 170
The Canal Boom 171

Emergence of a Market Economy 173
The Beginning of Commercial Agriculture 173
Commerce and Banking 174
Early Industrialism 174

The Politics of Nation Building After the War of 1812 176
The Republicans in Power 176
Monroe as President 177
The Missouri Compromise 177
Postwar Nationalism and the Supreme Court 179
Nationalism in Foreign Policy: The Monroe Doctrine 180
The Troubled Presidency of John Quincy Adams 181

Conclusion: The End of the Era of Good Feelings 182

CHAPTER 10
The Triumph of White Men's Democracy 184

Democratic Space: The New Hotels 184

Democracy in Theory and Practice 185
Democracy and Society 185
Democratic Culture 186
The Democratic Ferment 189

Jackson and the Politics of Democracy 190
The Election of 1824 and J. Q. Adams's Administration 190
Jackson Comes to Power 191
Indian Removal 192
The Nullification Crisis 193

The Bank War and the Second Party System 195
Biddle, the Bank Veto, and the Election of 1832 195
Killing the Bank 197
The Emergence of the Whigs 197
The Rise and Fall of Van Buren 198

Heyday of the Second Party System 200

Conclusion: Tocqueville's Wisdom 201

CHAPTER 11
Slaves and Masters 204

Nat Turner's Rebellion: A Turning Point in the Slave South 204

The Divided Society of the Old South 205

The World of Southern Blacks 205
- Slaves' Daily Life and Labor 206
- Slave Families, Kinship, and Community 207
- African American Religion 208
- Resistance and Rebellion 209
- Free Blacks in the Old South 210

White Society in the Antebellum South 212
- The Planters' World 212
- Planters and Paternalism 213
- Small Slaveholders 214
- Yeoman Farmers 214
- A Closed Mind and a Closed Society 215

Slavery and the Southern Economy 216
- The Internal Slave Trade 216
- The Rise of the Cotton Kingdom 217
- Slavery and Industrialization 219
- The "Profitability" Issue 220

Conclusion: Worlds in Conflict 222

We Americans

Women of Southern Households 224

CHAPTER 12

The Pursuit of Perfection 226

Redeeming the Middle Class 226

The Rise of Evangelicalism 227
- The Second Great Awakening: The Frontier Phase 227
- The Second Great Awakening in the North 228
- From Revivalism to Reform 229

Domesticity and Changes in the American Family 231
- Marriage for Love 231
- The Cult of Domesticity 232
- The Discovery of Childhood 233

Institutional Reform 234
- The Extension of Education 234
- Discovering the Asylum 235

Reform Turns Radical 236
- Divisions in the Benevolent Empire 236
- The Abolitionist Enterprise 237
- Black Abolitionists 238
- From Abolitionism to Women's Rights 239
- Radical Ideas and Experiments 239

Conclusion: Counterpoint on Reform 241

CHAPTER 13

An Age of Expansionism 244

The Spirit of Young America 244

Movement to the Far West 245
- Borderlands of the 1830s 245
- The Texas Revolution 247
- The Republic of Texas 247
- Trails of Trade and Settlement 248
- The Mormon Trek 249

Manifest Destiny and the Mexican-American War 251
- Tyler and Texas 251
- The Triumph of Polk and Annexation 251
- The Doctrine of Manifest Destiny 252
- Polk and the Oregon Question 253
- War with Mexico 254
- Settlement of the Mexican-American War 255

Internal Expansionism 256
- The Triumph of the Railroad 257
- The Industrial Revolution Takes Off 257
- Mass Immigration Begins 259
- The New Working Class 260

Conclusion: The Costs of Expansion 262

We Americans

The Irish in Boston, 1845–1865 264

CHAPTER 14

The Sectional Crisis 266

The Brooks–Sumner Brawl in Congress 266

The Compromise of 1850 267
- The Problem of Slavery in the Mexican Cession 267
- The Wilmot Proviso Launches the Free-Soil Movement 267
- Squatter Sovereignty and the Election of 1848 268
- Taylor Takes Charge 268
- Forging a Compromise 269

Political Upheaval, 1852–1856 270
- The Party System in Crisis 271
- The Kansas-Nebraska Act Raises a Storm 271
- An Appeal to Nativism: The Know-Nothing Episode 273
- Kansas and the Rise of the Republicans 274
- Sectional Division in the Election of 1856 275

The House Divided, 1857–1860 275
- Cultural Sectionalism 276
- The Dred Scott Case 276
- The Lecompton Controversy 277
- Debating the Morality of Slavery 278
- The South's Crisis of Fear 278
- The Election of 1860 280

Conclusion: Explaining the Crisis 281

We Americans

Hispanic America After 1848: A Case Study in Majority Rule 285

CHAPTER 15

Secession and the Civil War 287

The Emergence of Lincoln 287

The Storm Gathers 288
- The Deep South Secedes 288
- The Failure of Compromise 290
- And the War Came 290

Adjusting to Total War 292
- Prospects, Plans, and Expectations 292

Mobilizing the Home Fronts 293
Political Leadership: Northern Success and Southern Failure 295
Early Campaigns and Battles 297
The Diplomatic Struggle 299

Fight to the Finish 300
The Coming of Emancipation 300
African Americans and the War 301
The Tide Turns 301
Last Stages of the Conflict 303
Effects of the War 305

Conclusion: An Organizational Revolution 307

CHAPTER 16
The Agony of Reconstruction 310

Robert Smalls and Black Politicians During Reconstruction 310

The President versus Congress 311
Wartime Reconstruction 312
Andrew Johnson at the Helm 313
Congress Takes the Initiative 314
Congressional Reconstruction Plan Enacted 315
The Impeachment Crisis 316

Reconstructing Southern Society 317
Reorganizing Land and Labor 317
Black Codes: A New Name for Slavery? 318
Republican Rule in the South 319
Claiming Public and Private Rights 320

Retreat from Reconstruction 322
Rise of the Money Question 322
Final Efforts of Reconstruction 323
Spoilsmen versus Reformers 325

Reunion and the New South 326
The Compromise of 1877 326
"Redeeming" a New South 327
The Rise of Jim Crow 328

Conclusion: The "Unfinished Revolution" 329

CHAPTER 17
The West: Exploiting an Empire 331

Lean Bear's Changing West 331

Beyond the Frontier 332

Crushing the Native Americans 332
Life of the Plains Indians 333
"As Long as Waters Run": Searching for an Indian Policy 333
Final Battles on the Plains 335
The End of Tribal Life 335

Settlement of the West 337
Men and Women on the Overland Trail 337
Land for the Taking 338
The Spanish-Speaking Southwest 340

The Bonanza West 340
The Mining Bonanza 341
Gold from the Roots Up: The Cattle Bonanza 343
Sodbusters on the Plains: The Farming Bonanza 345
New Farming Methods 346
Discontent on the Farm 346
The Final Fling 347

Conclusion: The Meaning of the West 347

We Americans

Blacks in Blue: The Buffalo Soldiers in the West 351

CHAPTER 18
The Industrial Society 353

A Machine Culture 353

Industrial Development 354

An Empire on Rails 355
Building the Empire 356
Linking the Nation via Trunk Lines 356
Rails Across the Continent 357
Problems of Growth 357

An Industrial Empire 358
Carnegie and Steel 358
Rockefeller and Oil 359
The Business of Invention 361

The Sellers 362

The Wage Earners 363
Working Men, Working Women, Working Children 363
Culture of Work 364
Labor Unions 365
Labor Unrest 366

Conclusion: Industrialization's Benefits and Costs 368

CHAPTER 19
Toward an Urban Society, 1877–1900 371

The Overcrowded City 371

The Lure of the City 372
Skyscrapers and Suburbs 372
Tenements and the Problems of Overcrowding 373
Strangers in a New Land 373
Immigrants and the City 374
The House That Tweed Built 375

Social and Cultural Change, 1877–1900 376
Manners and Mores 377
Leisure and Entertainment 378
Changes in Family Life 379
Changing Views: A Growing Assertiveness Among Women 380
Educating the Masses 380
Higher Education 381

The Stirrings of Reform 383
New Currents in Social Thought 383
The Settlement Houses 385
A Crisis in Social Welfare 385

Conclusion: The Pluralistic Society 386

We Americans

Ellis Island:
Isle of Hope, Isle of Tears 388

CHAPTER 20
Political Realignments in the 1890s 390

Hardship and Heartache 390

Politics of Stalemate 391
- The Party Deadlock 391
- Experiments in the States 392
- Reestablishing Presidential Power 392

Republicans in Power: The Billion-Dollar Congress 393

The Rise of the Populist Movement 394
- The Farm Problem 394
- The Fast-Growing Farmers' Alliance 395
- The People's Party 396

The Crisis of the Depression 396
- Coxey's Army and the Pullman Strike 397
- The Miners of the Midwest 397
- A Beleaguered President 399
- Breaking the Party Deadlock 399

Changing Attitudes 399
- "Everybody Works But Father" 400
- Changing Themes in Literature 400

The Presidential Election of 1896 401
- The Mystique of Silver 401
- The Campaign and Election 401

The McKinley Administration 403

Conclusion: A Decade's Dramatic Changes 404

CHAPTER 21
Toward Empire 407

Roosevelt and the Rough Riders 407

America Looks Outward 408
- Catching the Spirit of Empire 408
- Foreign Policy Approaches, 1867–1900 409
- The Lure of Hawaii and Samoa 411
- The New Navy 412

War with Spain 413
- A War for Principle 413
- "A Splendid Little War" 415
- "Smoked Yankees" 415
- The Course of the War 416

Acquisition of Empire 418
- Guerrilla Warfare in the Philippines 419
- Governing the Empire 421
- The Open Door 422

Conclusion: Outcome of the War with Spain 424

CHAPTER 22
The Progressive Era 426

Muckrakers Call for Reform 426

The Changing Face of Industrialism 427
- The Innovative Model T 427
- The Burgeoning Trusts 428
- Managing the Machines 428

Society's Masses 429
- Better Times on the Farm 430
- Women and Children at Work 431
- The Niagara Movement and the NAACP 432
- "I Hear the Whistle": Immigrants in the Labor Force 432

Conflict in the Workplace 434

A New Urban Culture 435
- Popular Pastimes 437
- Experimentation in the Arts 438

Conclusion: A Ferment of Discovery and Reform 440

CHAPTER 23
From Roosevelt to Wilson in the Age of Progressivism 442

The Republicans Split 442

The Spirit of Progressivism 443
- The Rise of the Professions 443
- The Social-Justice Movement 444
- The Purity Crusade 445
- Woman Suffrage, Women's Rights 445
- A Ferment of Ideas: Challenging the Status Quo 446

Reform in the Cities and States 448
- Interest Groups and the Decline of Popular Politics 448
- Reform in the Cities 449
- Action in the States 450

The Republican Roosevelt 451
- Busting the Trusts 451
- "Square Deal" in the Coalfields 452

Roosevelt Progressivism at Its Height 453

The Ordeal of William Howard Taft 454
- Party Insurgency 455
- The Ballinger-Pinchot Affair 456
- Taft Alienates the Progressives 456
- Differing Philosophies in the Election of 1912 457

Woodrow Wilson's New Freedom 458
- The New Freedom in Action 458
- Wilson Moves Toward the New Nationalism 459

Conclusion: The Fruits of Progressivism 461

CHAPTER 24
The Nation at War 464

The Sinking of the Lusitania *464*

A New World Power 465
- "I Took the Canal Zone" 465

The Roosevelt Corollary 466
Ventures in the Far East 467

Foreign Policy Under Wilson 468
Conducting Moral Diplomacy 468
Troubles Across the Border 468

Toward War 470
The Neutrality Policy 470
Freedom of the Seas 471
The U-Boat Threat 471
"He Kept Us Out of War" 472
The Final Months of Peace 472

Over There 474
Mobilization 474
War in the Trenches 474

Over Here 476
The Conquest of Convictions 476
A Bureaucratic War 477
Labor in the War 478

The Treaty of Versailles 479
A Peace at Paris 480
Rejection in the Senate 482

Conclusion: Postwar Disillusionment 483

CHAPTER 25
Transition to Modern America 486

Wheels for the Millions 486

The Second Industrial Revolution 487
The Automobile Industry 487
Patterns of Economic Growth 488
Economic Weaknesses 489

City Life in the Jazz Age 490
Women and the Family 490
The Roaring Twenties 491
Flowering of the Arts 492

The Rural Counterattack 493
The Fear of Radicalism 494
Prohibition 495
The Ku Klux Klan 495
Immigration Restriction 496
The Fundamentalist Challenge 497

Politics of the 1920s 498
Harding, Coolidge, and Hoover 498
Republican Policies 499
The Divided Democrats 499
The Election of 1928 500

Conclusion: The Old and the New 501

CHAPTER 26
Franklin D. Roosevelt and the New Deal 503

The Struggle Against Despair 503

The Great Depression 504
The Great Crash 504
Effect of the Depression 505

Fighting the Depression 506
Hoover and Voluntarism 506
The Emergence of Roosevelt 507
The Hundred Days 507
Roosevelt and Recovery 508
Roosevelt and Relief 509

Roosevelt and Reform 511
Challenges to FDR 511
Social Security 512
Labor Legislation 513

Impact of the New Deal 513
Rise of Organized Labor 513
The New Deal Record on Help to Minorities 515
Women at Work 515

End of the New Deal 516
The Election of 1936 516
The Supreme Court Fight 517
The New Deal in Decline 517

Conclusion: Evaluation of the New Deal 518

CHAPTER 27
America and the World, 1921–1945 522

A Pact Without Power 522

Retreat, Reversal, and Rivalry 523
Retreat in Europe 523
Cooperation in Latin America 524
Rivalry in Asia 524

Isolationism 525
The Lure of Pacifism and Neutrality 526
War in Europe 526

The Road to War 528
From Neutrality to Undeclared War 528
Showdown in the Pacific 529

Turning the Tide Against the Axis 531
Wartime Partnerships 532
Halting the German Blitz 532
Checking Japan in the Pacific 534

The Home Front 535
The Arsenal of Democracy 535
A Nation on the Move 536
Win-the-War Politics 538

Victory 538
War Aims and Wartime Diplomacy 539
Triumph and Tragedy in the Pacific 540

Conclusion: The Transforming Power of War 541

CHAPTER 28
The Onset of the Cold War 543

The Potsdam Summit 543

The Cold War Begins 544
The Division of Europe 544
Withholding Economic Aid 545
The Atomic Dilemma 546

Containment 546
- The Truman Doctrine 547
- The Marshall Plan 547
- The Western Military Alliance 548
- The Berlin Blockade 549

The Cold War Expands 550
- The Military Dimension 550
- The Cold War in Asia 551
- The Korean War 552

The Cold War at Home 554
- Truman's Troubles and Vindication 554
- The Loyalty Issue 555
- McCarthyism in Action 556
- The Republicans in Power 557

Eisenhower Wages the Cold War 558
- Entanglement in Indochina 558
- Containing China 559
- Turmoil in the Middle East 560
- Covert Actions 560
- Waging Peace 561

Conclusion: The Continuing Cold War 562

CHAPTER 29

Affluence and Anxiety 565

Levittown: The Flight to the Suburbs 565

The Postwar Boom 566
- Postwar Prosperity 566
- Life in the Suburbs 567

The Good Life? 568
- Areas of Greatest Growth 568
- Critics of the Consumer Society 568
- The Reaction to *Sputnik* 569

Farewell to Reform 570
- Truman and the Fair Deal 570
- Eisenhower's Modern Republicanism 570

The Struggle over Civil Rights 572
- Civil Rights as a Political Issue 572
- Desegregating the Schools 573
- The Beginnings of Black Activism 573

Conclusion: Restoring National Confidence 575

CHAPTER 30

The Turbulent Sixties 577

Kennedy versus Nixon: The First Televised Presidential Candidate Debate 577

Kennedy Intensifies the Cold War 578
- Flexible Response 578
- Crisis over Berlin 579
- Containment in Southeast Asia 579
- Containing Castro: The Bay of Pigs Fiasco 580
- Containing Castro: The Cuban Missile Crisis 581

The New Frontier at Home 582
- The Congressional Obstacle and Economic Advance 582
- Moving Slowly on Civil Rights 583
- "I Have a Dream" 584
- The Supreme Court and Reform 585

"Let Us Continue" 586
- Johnson in Action 586
- The Election of 1964 587
- The Triumph of Reform 588

Johnson Escalates the Vietnam War 589
- The Vietnam Dilemma 590
- Escalation 590
- Stalemate 592

Years of Turmoil 593
- The Student Revolt 593
- Protesting the Vietnam War 594
- The Cultural Revolution 595
- "Black Power" 595
- Ethnic Nationalism 596
- Women's Liberation 597

The Return of Richard Nixon 598
- Vietnam Undermines Lyndon Johnson 598
- Democrats Divided 599
- The Republican Resurgence 601

Conclusion: The End of an Era 601

We Americans

Unintended Consequences:
The Second Great Migration 605

CHAPTER 31

A Crisis in Confidence, 1969–1980 607

The Watergate Break-in 607

Nixon in Power 608
- Reshaping the Great Society 608
- Nixonomics 609
- Building a Republican Majority 610
- In Search of Détente 610
- Ending the Vietnam War 611

The Crisis of Democracy 612
- The Election of 1972 612
- The Watergate Scandal 613

Energy and the Economy 614
- The October War 614
- The Oil Shocks 615
- The Search for an Energy Policy 616
- The Great Inflation 617
- The Shifting American Economy 617

Private Lives—Public Issues 618
- The Changing American Family 618
- Gains and Setbacks for Women 618
- The Gay Liberation Movement 620

Politics After Watergate 622
- The Ford Administration and the 1976 Campaign 622
- Disenchantment with Carter 623

From Détente to Renewed Cold War 624
- Retreat in Asia 624

Accommodation in Latin America 624
The Quest for Peace in the Middle East 625
The Cold War Resumes 626

Conclusion: A Failed Presidency 627

CHAPTER 32
The Republican Resurgence, 1980–1992 629

Reagan and the Rise of Conservatism 629

Reagan in Power 630
The Reagan Victory 631
Cutting Spending and Taxes 632
Limiting the Role of Government 633

Reaganomics 634
Recession and Recovery 634
The Growing Deficit 634
The Rich Grow Richer 635
Reagan Affirmed 636

Reagan and the World 637
Challenging the "Evil Empire" 638
Turmoil in the Middle East 638
Confrontation in Central America 639
Trading Arms for Hostages 641
Reagan the Peacemaker 642

Social Dilemmas 643
The AIDS Epidemic 643
The War on Drugs 645

Passing the Torch to Bush 646
The Changing Palace Guard 646
The Election of 1988 647
Bush's Domestic Agenda 648
The End of the Cold War 649
Waging Peace 650

Conclusion: Republican Economic Woes 652

CHAPTER 33
America in Flux 654

The Buck Starts Here 654

The Changing American Population 655
A People on the Move 656
The Revival of Immigration 657
The Surging Hispanics 657
Advance and Retreat for African Americans 658
Americans from Asia and the Middle East 659
Melting Pot or Multiethnic Diversity? 660

Democratic Revival 661
The Election of 1992 661
Economic Recovery 662
President versus Congress 663
Contract with America 665
The Clinton Rebound 666

Clinton and the World 667
Global Tensions in the Post–Cold War Era 668
Intervening in Somalia and Haiti 669
Halting Civil War in Bosnia 669
Saving Kosovo 671

The End of the Century 672
From Deficit to Surplus 672
Violence in the 1990s 673
Shadow on the White House 675

The New Millennium 676
The Disputed Election of 2000 677
Bush's Domestic Agenda 679
Terrorism: Attack and Counterattack 681
The New American Empire? 684

Conclusion: The American Century? 687

Appendix A-1
Credits C-1
Index I-1

Maps

ii–iii Political and Physical Map of the United States
I-38–I-39 Political Map of the World

PAGE

5 The First Americans: Location of Major Indian Groups and Culture Areas in the 1600s
12 Voyages of Exploration
23 Chesapeake Colonies, 1640
30 New England Colonies, 1650
33 Middle Colonies, 1685
38 The Carolinas and Georgia
49 Origins and Destinations of African Slaves, 1619–1760
59 Distribution of European and African Immigrants in the Thirteen Colonies
64 The Spanish Borderlands, ca. 1770
73 North America, 1750
76 North America After 1763
92 The American Revolution, 1775–1781
98 Loyalist Strongholds
111 Western Land Claims Ceded by the States
122 Ratification of the Constitution
135 Conquest of the West
148 North America in 1800
151 The Louisiana Purchase and the Route of Lewis and Clark
160 The War of 1812
167 North America, 1819
178 The Missouri Compromise, 1820–1821
194 Indian Removal
211 Slave Rebellions and Uprisings, 1800–1831
218 Slave Concentration, 1820
219 Slave Concentration, 1860
240 Utopian Communities Before the Civil War
246 Territorial Expansion by the Mid-Nineteenth Century
249 Western Trails
253 Northwest Boundary Dispute
256 The Mexican-American War
270 The Compromise of 1850
272 The Kansas-Nebraska Act of 1854
289 Secession
293 Overview of Civil War Strategy
296 Civil War, 1861–1862
304 Civil War, 1863–1865
315 Reconstruction
334 Native Americans in the West: Major Battles and Reservations
342 Mining Regions of the West
344 Cattle Trails
367 Labor Strikes, 1870–1890
375 Foreign-born Population, 1890
416 Spanish-American War: Pacific Theater
417 Spanish-American War: Caribbean Theater
420 American Empire, 1900
421 World Colonial Empires, 1900
430 Irrigation and Conservation in the West to 1917
446 Woman Suffrage Before 1920
455 National Parks and Forests
469 Activities of the United States in the Caribbean, 1898–1930s
473 European Alliances and Battlefronts, 1914–1917
475 The Western Front: U.S. Participation, 1918
479 African American Migration Northward, 1910–1920
481 Europe After the Treaty of Versailles, 1919
508 Tennessee Valley Authority
533 World War II in Europe and North Africa
534 World War II in the Pacific
545 Europe After World War II
548 Marshall Plan Aid to Europe, 1948–1952
553 The Korean War, 1950–1953
571 The Interstate Highway System
588 African American Voter Registration Before and After the Voting Rights Act of 1965
591 Southeast Asia and the Vietnam War
620 Voting on the Equal Rights Amendment
639 Trouble Spots in the Middle East, 1979–1992
640 Trouble Spots in Central America and the Caribbean
650 The End of the Cold War
656 Population Shifts, 1970–2000
670 The Breakup of Yugoslavia/Civil War in Bosnia

Charts, Figures, and Tables

PAGE
37 England's Principal Mainland Colonies
75 A Century of Conflict: Major Wars, 1689–1763
99 Chronicle of Colonial-British Tension
112 Land Ordinance of 1785
121 Revolution or Reform? The Articles of Confederation and the Constitution Compared
258 The Age of Practical Invention
294 Resources of the Union and the Confederacy, 1861
306 Casualties of War
316 Reconstruction Amendments, 1865–1870
328 Supreme Court Decisions Affecting Black Civil Rights, 1875–1900
480 Woodrow Wilson's Fourteen Points, 1918: Success and Failure in Implementation
505 Unemployment, 1929–1942
518 Major New Deal Legislation and Agencies
592 U.S. Troop Levels in Vietnam
606 The Second Great Migration: A Theoretical Example

Features

We Americans

PAGE

80 Learning to Live with Diversity in the Eighteenth Century: What Is an American?
144 Counting the People: The Federal Census of 1790
224 Women of Southern Households
264 The Irish in Boston, 1845–1865
285 Hispanic America After 1848: A Case Study in Majority Rule
351 Blacks in Blue: The Buffalo Soldiers in the West
388 Ellis Island: Isle of Hope, Isle of Tears
605 Unintended Consequences: The Second Great Migration

A Look at the Past

PAGE

3 Effigy Jar
25 Armor
45 Freake Portraits
66 Westover
87 Stamp Act Teapot
114 Continental Paper Money
128 Eagle Decoration
152 Buffalo Robe
162 "We Owe Allegiance to No Crown"
173 Merino Sheep
187 Portrait of Andrew Jackson
199 Columbian Star Dishes
213 Slave Clothing
233 Gothic Revival Cottage
234 Manufactured Toy
259 Steel Plow
276 Poster for *Uncle Tom's Cabin*
295 Civil War Rations
324 Cartoon "Worse Than Slavery"
343 Cowboy Clothing
346 Barbed Wire
363 Cash Register
365 Typewriter
376 Toy Bank
391 Ballot Box
409 Trade Card
419 Cartoon "School Begins"
436 Sears Catalog
454 Patent Medicine
470 Sheet Music Cover
488 Radio
489 Glenwood Stove Ad
510 FSA Photos
535 WWII Ration Stamps
537 Service Star
561 Fallout Shelter
567 Western-themed Toys
594 Army Fatigue Jacket
595 Woodstock Brochure
616 Locking Gas Cap
644 AIDS Brochure
673 Handheld Computer

Preface

America Past and Present, Brief Sixth Edition, is derived from the full-length *America Past and Present,* Seventh Edition. The Brief Sixth Edition shares the goal of its parent text: to present a clear, relevant, and balanced history of the United States as an unfolding story of national development, from the days of the earliest inhabitants to the present. The goal of the abridgement is to produce a condensation true to the original in all its dimensions—a miniaturized replica or *bonsai,* as it were—retaining the style and tone, and the interpretations, with their nuances and subtleties intact. This Brief Sixth Edition contains about two-thirds of the text of the full-length book, more than one-half of the maps, charts, and figures, and a commensurate proportion of the illustration program.

Presenting American history as the story of a nation in flux, *America Past and Present,* Brief Sixth Edition, goes beyond recounting the major events that have helped to shape the nation—the wars fought, the presidents elected, the treaties signed. The impact of change on human lives adds a vital dimension to the understanding of history. How did the American Revolution affect the lives of ordinary citizens? What was it like for both blacks and whites to live in a plantation society? How did the shift from an agrarian to an industrial economy affect men and women alike? What impact did technology, in the form of the automobile and the computer, have on patterns of life in the twentieth century? As the narrative explores answers to these and other questions, it blends the excitement and drama of the American experience with insights about the social, political, economic, and cultural issues that underlie it.

America Past and Present, Brief Sixth Edition, espouses no particular ideology or point of view; instead the text encourages readers to explore the American past and reach their own conclusions about its significance in their lives. And yet the text does not avoid examining controversial issues but seeks to offer balanced and reasoned judgments on such morally charged subjects as the nature of slavery and the use of nuclear weapons. Although history may rarely repeat itself, the story of the American past is relevant to the problems and dilemmas facing the American nation and the American people today.

Text Revisions

The principal revisions in *America Past and Present,* Brief Sixth Edition, have been undertaken with the goals of clarifying the prose and sharpening the analysis, taking account of new scholarship, and offering new perspectives. As in previous editions, the roles that women and minority groups have played in the nation's development merit particular attention. These people appear not as passive witnesses to the historical narrative but as active participants in its evolution. New and expanded material throughout the chapters includes the following:

- Chapter 1, expanded coverage of Native Americans before encounter with Europeans.
- Chapter 6, new opening vignette highlighting the search for balance between public morality and private freedom in the new republic; additional coverage of political and social reform.
- Chapter 9, expanded discussion of treaties negotiated with Great Britain following the War of 1812.
- Chapter 11, revised and reorganized to enhance and emphasize coverage of the lives and lifestyles of slaves and their experience of slavery.
- Chapter 12, expanded discussion of black abolitionists and women's rights reformers.
- Chapter 16, restructured and revised to devote greater attention to lives of former slaves during Reconstruction; includes new sections on Black Codes and Jim Crow laws.
- Chapter 17, new opening vignette exploring a Native American's experience of conquest and exploitation of the American West.
- Chapter 26, new opening vignette highlighting personal experiences of hardship during the Great Depression; revised discussion of the stock market crash of 1929.
- Chapter 30, expanded discussion of the student protest movement of the 1960s.

- Chapter 31, shifts in the labor movement in the 1970s, including the rise of public employee unions; the changing American family at the turn of the century.
- Chapter 33, revised and restructured to concentrate on the shifting economy of the 1990s to the present and the role of government policy in shaping American economy; updated with new discussion of foreign policy and homeland defense post-September 11, including new sections on the war on terrorism and war in Iraq.

Format and Features

The more spacious page design of *America Past and Present*, Brief Sixth Edition, allows for larger maps and figures as well as the addition of marginal definitions of key terms in each chapter.

America Past and Present, Brief Sixth Edition, includes eight essays entitled "We Americans," each focusing on some aspect of diversity or multiculturalism in America. Some of the "We Americans" essays explore the roles different ethnic groups have played in shaping the nation; others examine change and constancy in the American population and national ethos. The eight "We Americans" essays are:

- Learning to Live with Diversity in the Eighteenth Century: What Is an American? (Chapter 4)
- Counting the People: The Federal Census of 1790 (Chapter 7)
- Women of Southern Households (Chapter 11)
- The Irish in Boston, 1845–1865 (Chapter 13)
- Hispanic America After 1848: A Case Study in Majority Rule (Chapter 14)
- Blacks in Blue: The Buffalo Soldiers in the West (Chapter 17)
- Ellis Island: Isle of Hope, Isle of Tears (Chapter 19)
- Unintended Consequences: The Second Great Migration (Chapter 30)

A second feature in *America Past and Present,* Brief Sixth Edition, is the "A Look at the Past" photographs. These illustrations of material culture artifacts show students some of the variety of materials historians use to learn about and interpret the past. Captions with the photographs include critical thinking questions that encourage students to reflect on the historical purpose and significance of the object pictured.

Supplements

For Qualified College Adopters: Instructor Supplements

Instructor's Resource Manual

Created for the full version of *America Past and Present,* this Instructor's Resource Manual is appropriate for the Brief Sixth Edition as well. Prepared by James Walsh of Central Connecticut State University, each chapter of this resource manual contains interpretative essays, anecdotes and references to biographical or primary sources, and a comprehensive summary of the text. ISBN: 0-321-21724-1.

Test Bank

This test bank contains notations indicating questions that are particularly relevant to the Brief Sixth Edition. Prepared by Denise Wright of University of Georgia, the test bank contains over 1,200 multiple-choice, true/false, matching, and completion questions. ISBN: 0-321-21721-7.

TestGen-EQ Computerized Testing System

This flexible, easy-to-master computerized test bank on a dual-platform CD includes all of the items in the printed test bank and allows instructors to select specific questions, edit existing questions, and add their own items to create exams. Tests can be printed in several different fonts and formats and can include figures such as graphs and tables. ISBN: 0-321-21720-9.

History Digital Media Archive CD-ROM

The Digital Media Archive CD-ROM contains electronic images and interactive and static maps, along with media elements such as video. These media assets are fully customizable and ready for classroom presentation or easy downloading into your PowerPoint™ presentations or any other presentation software. ISBN: 0-321-14976-9.

Digital Media Archive, Updated Second Edition

Now on two CD-ROMs and with added content, this Digital Media Archive is an encyclopedic collection that contains dozens of narrated vignettes and videos as well as hundreds of photos and illustrations ready for use in your own PowerPoint™ presentations, course web sites, or on-line courses. Free to qualified college adopters.

Companion Web Site, www.ablongman.com/divine

Instructors can take advantage of the Companion Web Site that supports this text. The instructor section of the Web site includes teaching links and links to downloadable versions of all print supplements.

PowerPoint™ Presentations

These presentations contain an average of 15 PowerPoint™ slides for each chapter. These slides may include key points and terms for a lecture on the chapter as well as four-color slides of all maps, graphs, and charts within a particular chapter. The presentations are available for download at www.ablongman.com/suppscentral.

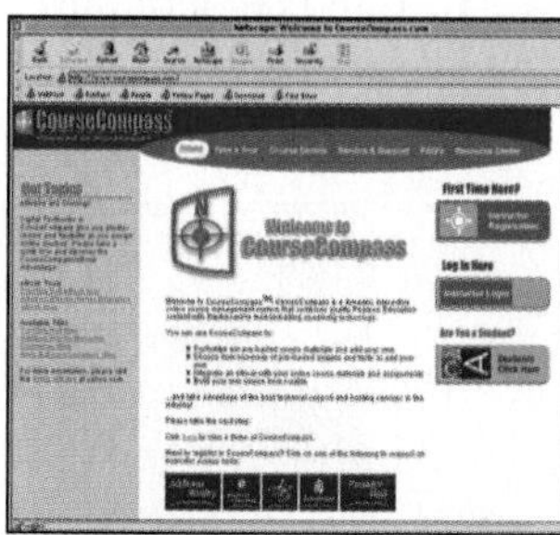

CourseCompass™, www.ablongman.com/coursecompass

Combines the strength of the content from *America Past and Present,* Brief Sixth Edition, with state-of-the-art eLearning tools. CourseCompass™ is an easy-to-use on-line course management system that allows professors to tailor content and functionality to meet individual course needs. Every CourseCompass™ course includes a range of pre-loaded content—all designed to help students master core course objectives. Organized by era, CourseCompass™ allows you to access maps, map exercises, and primary sources as well as test questions from the print test bank and the full text of several of our best-selling supplements. The *America Past and Present* CourseCompass™ site is available at no additional charge for students whose professor has requested that a student Access Kit be bundled with the text.

BlackBoard and WebCT

Longman's extensive American history content is available in these two major course management platforms: BlackBoard and WebCT. All quickly and easily customizable for use with *America Past and Present,* Brief Sixth Edition, the content includes multiple primary sources, maps, and map exercises. Book-specific testing is simply uploaded.

The History Place Premium Web Site, www.ushistoryplace.com

Available at no additional cost when requested as a bundle component by the professor, the site offers extraordinary breadth and depth, featuring unmatched interactive maps, timelines, and activities; hundreds of source documents, images, and audio clips; and much more.

Comprehensive American History Transparency Set

This collection includes more than 200 four-color American history map transparencies on subjects ranging from the first Native Americans to the end of the Cold War, covering wars, social trends, elections, immigration, and demographics. ISBN: 0-673-97211-9.

Text-specific Transparency Set

Created for the full version of *America Past and Present,* this transparency

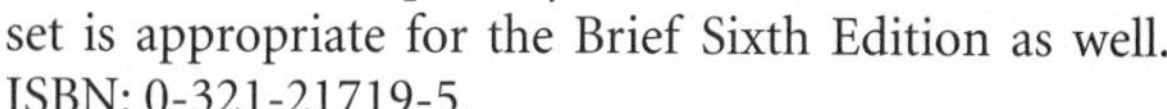

set is appropriate for the Brief Sixth Edition as well. ISBN: 0-321-21719-5.

Video Lecture Launchers

Prepared by Mark Newman, University of Illinois at Chicago, these video lecture launchers (each two to five minutes in duration) cover key issues in American history from 1877 to the present. The launchers are accompanied by an Instructor's Manual. ISBN: 0-321-01869-9.

For Students

Multimedia Edition CD-ROM for *America Past and Present,* Seventh Edition

This unique CD-ROM takes students beyond the printed page, offering them a complete multimedia learning experience. It contains the full annotatable textbook on CD-ROM, with contextually placed media—audio, video, interactive maps, photos, figures, Web links, and practice tests—that link students to additional content directly related to key concepts in the text. The CD also contains the Study Guide, map workbooks, a primary source reader, and more than a dozen supplementary books most often assigned in American history courses. Free to qualified college adopters when packaged with the text. ISBN: 0-321-23477-4.

Study Guide and Practice Tests

Created for the full version of *America Past and Present,* these study guides are appropriate for the Brief Sixth Edition as well. Prepared by Jennifer Lynn Gross of Jacksonville State University and John Walker Davis of University of Georgia. Each of the two-volume study guides begins with an introductory essay, "Skills for Studying and Learning History." Each chapter contains a summary, learning objectives, identification list, map exercises, glossary, and multiple-choice, completion, and essay questions, and critical thinking exercises involving primary sources. Volume One: ISBN: 0-321-21286-X; Volume Two: ISBN: 0-321-21722-5.

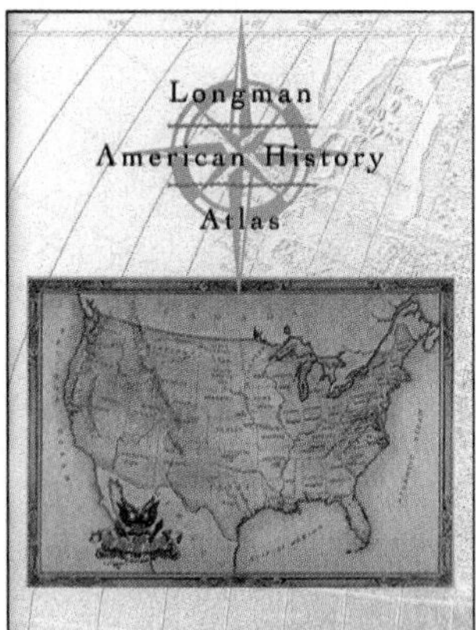

Longman American History Atlas

A four-color reference tool and visual guide to American history that includes almost 100 maps and covers the full scope of history. Atlas overhead transparencies available to qualified college adopters. $3.00 when bundled. ISBN: 0-321-00486-8.

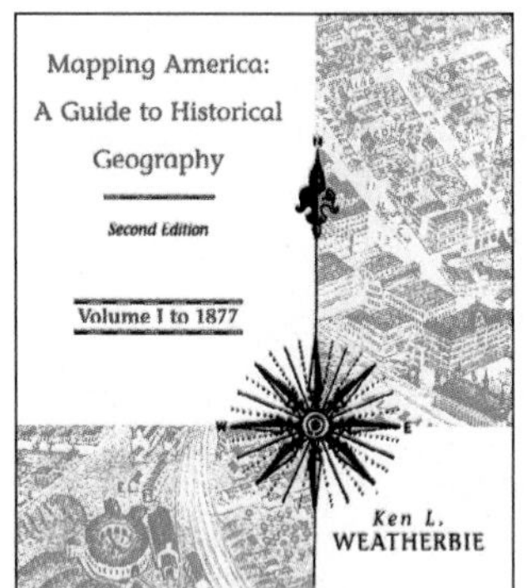

***Mapping America: A Guide to Historical Geography,* Second Edition**

A two-volume workbook by Ken L. Weatherbie, Del Mar College, that presents the basic geography of the United States and helps students place the history of the United States into spatial perspective. Free to qualified college adopters when bundled. Volume One: ISBN: 0-321-00487-6; Volume Two: ISBN: 0-321-00488-4.

Mapping American History

A workbook created by Gerald A. Danzer for use in conjunction with *Discovering American History Through Maps and Views* and designed to teach students to interpret and analyze cartographic materials as historical documents. Free to qualified college adopters when bundled. ISBN: 0-673-53768-4.

Companion Web Site for *America Past and Present,* Brief Sixth Edition, www.ablongman.com/divine

The Companion Web Site provides a wealth of resources for students using the text. Students can access chapter summaries, interactive practice test questions, and Web links for every chapter. The Web site is a comprehensive on-line study guide for students.

Research Navigator Guide

This guidebook includes exercises and tips on how to use the Internet. It also includes an access code for Research Navigator™—the easiest way for students to start a research assignment or research paper. Research Navigator™ is composed of three exclusive databases of credible and reliable source material including EBSCO's ContentSelect™ Academic Journal Database, New York Times Search by Subject Archive, and "Best of the Web" Link Library. This comprehensive site also includes a detailed help section. ISBN: 0-205-40838-9.

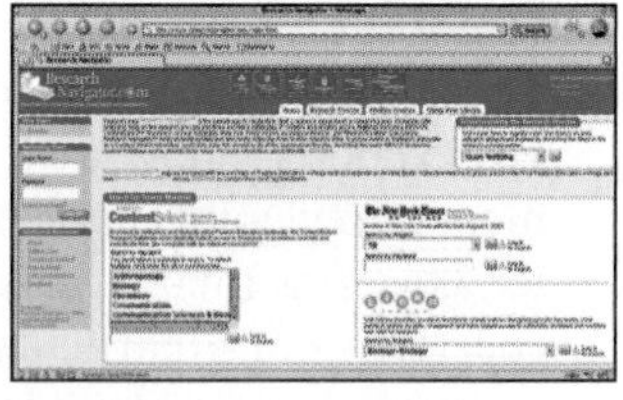

***America Through the Eyes of Its People,* Second Edition**

A comprehensive anthology that makes primary sources widely available in an inexpensive format, balancing social and political history and providing up-to-date narrative material. Free to qualified college adopters when bundled. ISBN: 0-673-97738-2.

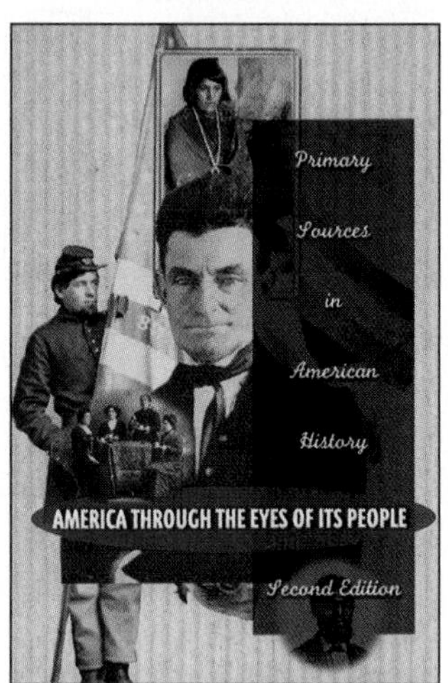

***Sources of the African American Past,* Second Edition**

Edited by Roy Finkenbine, University of Detroit at Mercy, this collection of primary sources covers key themes in the African American experience from the West African background to the present. Balanced between political and social history, it offers a vivid snapshot of the lives of African Americans in different historical periods and includes documents representing women and different regions of the United States. Available to qualified college adopters at a minimum cost when bundled with the text. ISBN: 0-321-16216-1.

***Women and the National Experience,* Second Edition**

Edited by Ellen Skinner, Pace University, this primary source reader contains both classic and unusual documents describing the history of women in the United States. The documents provide dramatic evidence that outspoken women attained a public voice and participated in the development of national events and policies long before they could vote. Chronologically organized and balanced between social and political history, this reader offers a striking picture of the lives of women across American history. Available to qualified college adopters at a minimum cost when bundled with the text. ISBN: 0-321-00555-4.

Reading the American West

Edited by Mitchel Roth, Sam Houston State University, this primary source reader uses letters, diary excerpts, speeches, interviews, and newspaper articles to let students experience how historians research and how history is written. Every document is accompanied by a contextual headnote and study questions. The book is divided into chapters with extensive introductions. Available to qualified college adopters at a minimum cost when bundled with the text. ISBN: 0-321-04409-6.

***A Short Guide to Writing About History,* Fifth Edition**

Richard Marius, Harvard University, Melvin E. Page Eastern Tennessee University. This engaging and practical text helps students get beyond merely compiling dates and facts; it teaches them how to incorporate their own ideas into their papers and to tell a story about history that interests them and their peers. Covering both brief essays and the documented resource paper, the text explores the writing and researching processes, different modes of historical writing including argument, and concludes with guidelines for improving style. ISBN: 0-321-22716-6.

***Constructing the American Past,* Fifth Edition**

Compiled and edited by Elliot Gorn and Randy Roberts of Purdue University, this popular two-volume reader consists of a variety of primary sources, grouped around central themes in American history. Each chapter focuses on a particular problem in American history, providing students with several points of view from which to examine the historical evidence. Introductions and study questions prompt students to participate in interpreting the past and challenge them to understand the problems in relation to the big picture of American history. Volume One ISBN: 0-321-21642-3; Volume Two ISBN: 0-321-21641-5.\

***From These Beginnings: A Biographical Approach to American History,* Seventh Edition**

Written by Roderick Nash of the University of California, Santa Barbara, and Gregory Graves of California State University, Northridge, this collection of biographical essays takes a look at the lives of famous men and women whose contributions helped create a nation and a society. Each biography offers students a uniquely personal and provocative glimpse into the lives of these Americans and shows how their experiences are linked to historical events. Volume One ISBN: 0-321-21640-7; Volume Two ISBN: 0-321-21639-3.

***American Experiences: Readings in American History,* Sixth Edition**

This two-volume collection of secondary readings, compiled and edited by Randy Roberts of Purdue University and James Olson of Sam Houston State University, contains articles that emphasize social history in order to illuminate important aspects of America's past. *American Experiences* addresses the complexity and richness of the nation's past by focusing on the people themselves—how they coped with, adjusted to, or rebelled against America. The readings examine people as they worked and played, fought and loved, lived and died. Volume One ISBN: 0-321-21644-X; Volume Two ISBN: 0-321-21643-1.

American History in a Box

This unique primary source reader offers students the opportunity to experience written documents, visual materials, material culture artifacts, and maps in order to learn firsthand what history is and what historians actually do. It was written and put together by Julie Roy Jeffrey and Peter Frederick; Volume One (to 1877) ISBN: 0-321-30005-2; Volume Two (since 1865) ISBN: 0-321-03006-0.

The History Place Premium Web Site, www.ushistoryplace.com

Available at no additional cost when requested as a bundle component by the professor, the site is a continually updated American history Web site of extraordinary breadth and depth, which features unmatched interactive maps, timelines, and activities; hundreds of source documents, images, and audio clips; and much more.

The Library of American Biography Series

Each of the interpretative biographies in this series focuses on a figure whose actions and ideas significantly influenced the course of American history and national life. Brief and inexpensive, they are ideal for any American history survey course. Available to qualified college adopters at a discount when bundled with this text.

Penguin Books

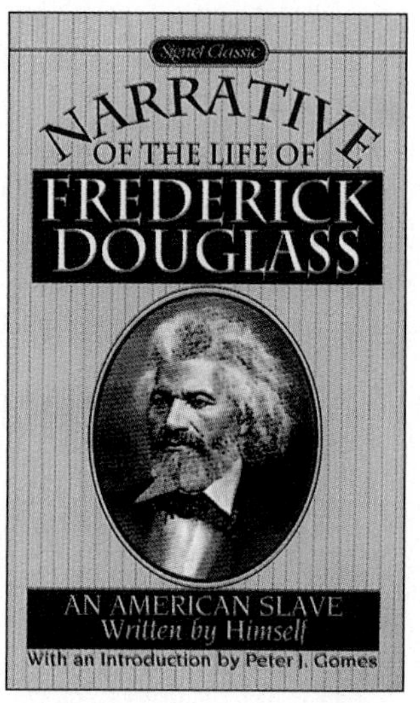

The partnership between Penguin-Putnam USA and Longman Publishers offers students a discount on many titles when you bundle them with any Longman survey. Among these include

- Frederick Douglass, *Narrative of the Life of Frederick Douglass*
- L. Jesse Lemisch (Editor), *Benjamin Franklin: The Autobiography & Other Writings*
- Upton Sinclair, *The Jungle*
- Harriet Beecher Stowe, *Uncle Tom's Cabin*

Acknowledgments

We extend special thanks to Professor Jeanne Whitney of Salisbury State University for her contribution in selecting images for many of the "Look at the Past" illustrations and writing the informative and thought-provoking captions to accompany them. We also express our gratitude to the following reviewers who gave generously of their time and knowledge to provide thoughtful evaluations and suggestions for revision:

Albert Berger, *University of North Dakota*
John P. Boubel, *Bethany Lutheran College*
John Braeman, *University of Nebraska*
Howard Jablon, *Purdue University North Central*
Ted Kallman, *San Joaquin Delta College*
Lawrence F. Kohl, *University of Alabama*
Armand S. LaPotin, *State University College*
Margaret Lowe, *Bridgewater State College*
Jonathan Lurie, *Rutgers University*
Rob Schorman, *Miami University–Middletown*
Kenneth Townsend, *Coastal Carolina University*

We also acknowledge with gratitude the contributions of reviewers of previous editions of this text. Their suggestions, too, have helped shape this book.

Gisela R. Ables, *Houston Community College*
James Barringer, *Hillsborough Community College*
Vincent F. Bonelli, *Bronx Community College*
Susan Meyer Butler, *Cerritos College*
William R. Cario, *Concordia University*
Simon Cordery, *Monmouth College*
Sandra McGee Deutsch, *University of Texas, El Paso*
Alan L. Golden, *Lock Haven University*
Gregory L. Goodwin, *Bakersfield College*
James Graham, *Carl Sandburg College*
Robert Hilderbrand, *University of South Dakota*
Chana Kai, *Indiana University*
James E. McMillan, *New Mexico State University*
Manuel F. Medrano, *University of Texas, Brownsville*
Douglas C. Oliver, *Skyline College*
Marguerite Renner, *Glendale Community College*
John Ricks, *Middle Georgia College*
Megan Seaholm, *University of Texas*
Charles J. Shindo, *Louisiana State University*
William P. Short, Jr., *Cecil Community College*
Sheila Skemp, *University of Mississippi*
Grant W. Smart, *Salt Lake Community College*
Kay C. Starnes, *University of North Carolina, Charlotte*
Roger Tate, *Somerset Community College*
Jason Tetzloff, *Defiance College*
Dean Wolfe, *Kingwood College*

The Authors

About the Authors

ROBERT A. DIVINE

Robert A. Divine, George W. Littlefield Professor Emeritus in American History at the University of Texas at Austin, received his Ph.D. from Yale University in 1954. A specialist in American diplomatic history, he taught from 1954 to 1996 at the University of Texas, where he was honored by both the student association and the graduate school for teaching excellence. His extensive published work includes *The Illusion of Neutrality* (1962); *Second Chance: The Triumph of Internationalism in America During World War II* (1967); and *Blowing on the Wind* (1978). His most recent work is *Perpetual War for Perpetual Peace* (2000), a comparative analysis of twentieth-century American wars. He is also the author of *Eisenhower and the Cold War* (1981) and editor of three volumes of essays on the presidency of Lyndon Johnson. His book *The Sputnik Challenge* (1993) won the Eugene E. Emme Astronautical Literature Award for 1993. He has been a fellow at the Center for Advanced Study in the Behavioral Sciences and has given the Albert Shaw Lectures in Diplomatic History at Johns Hopkins University.

T. H. BREEN

T. H. Breen, William Smith Mason Professor of American History at Northwestern University, received his Ph.D. from Yale University in 1968. He has taught at Northwestern since 1970. Breen's major books include *The Character of the Good Ruler: A Study of Puritan Political Ideas in New England* (1974); *Puritans and Adventurers: Change and Persistence in Early America* (1980); *Tobacco Culture: The Mentality of the Great Tidewater Planters on the Eve of Revolution* (1985); and, with Stephen Innes of the University of Virginia, *"Myne Owne Ground": Race and Freedom on Virginia's Eastern Shore* (1980). His *Imagining the Past* (1989) won the 1990 Historic Preservation Book Award. His most recent book is *Common Goods: Revolutionary Markets on the Eve of American Independence* (2003). In addition to receiving several awards for outstanding teaching at Northwestern, Breen has been the recipient of research grants from the American Council of Learned Societies, the Guggenheim Foundation, the Institute for Advanced Study (Princeton), the National Humanities Center, and the Huntington Library. For his article "Narrative of Commercial Life: Consumption, Ideology, and Community on the Eve of the American Revolution," which appeared in the July 1993 issue of *William and Mary Quarterly,* Breen received an award from the National Society, Daughters of Colonial Wars, for best article published in the quarterly in 1993, and the Douglass Adair Memorial Prize for best article published in the quarterly during the 1988–1993 period. He has served as the Fowler Hamilton Fellow at Christ Church, Oxford University (1987–1988), the Pitt Professor of American History and Institutions, Cambridge University (1990–1991), and the Harmsworth Professor of American History at Oxford University (2000–2001). He is currently working on an opera based on an essay he wrote on the wrongful execution of an African American in 1768.

GEORGE M. FREDRICKSON

George M. Fredrickson is Edgar E. Robinson Professor Emeritus of United States History at Stanford University. He is the author or editor of several books, including *The Inner Civil War* (1965), *The Black Image in the White Mind* (1971), and *White Supremacy: A Comparative Study in American and South African History* (1981), which won both the Ralph Waldo Emerson Award from Phi Beta Kappa and the Merle Curti Award from the Organization of American Historians. His most recent books are *Black Liberation: A Comparative History of Black Ideologies in the United States and South Africa* (1995), *The Comparative Imagination: Racism, Nationalism, and Social Movements* (1997), and *Racism: A Short History* (2002). He received his A.B. and Ph.D. from Harvard and has been the recipient of a Guggenheim Fellowship, two National Endowment for the Humanities Senior

Fellowships, and a Fellowship from the Center for Advanced Studies in the Behavioral Sciences. Before coming to Stanford in 1984, he taught at Northwestern. He has also served as Fulbright lecturer in American History at Moscow University and as the Harmsworth Professor of American History at Oxford. He served as president of the Organization of American Historians in 1997–1998.

R. HAL WILLIAMS

R. Hal Williams is Professor of History at Southern Methodist University. He received his A.B. from Princeton University in 1963 and his Ph.D. from Yale University in 1968. His books include *The Democratic Party and California Politics, 1880–1896* (1973); *Years of Decision: American Politics in the 1890s* (1978); and *The Manhattan Project: A Documentary Introduction to the Atomic Age* (1990). A specialist in American political history, he taught at Yale University from 1968 to 1975 and came to SMU in 1975 as chair of the Department of History. From 1980 to 1988, he served as dean of Dedman College, the school of humanities and sciences, at SMU. In 1980, he was a visiting professor at University College, Oxford University. Williams has received grants from the American Philosophical Society and the National Endowment for the Humanities, and he has served on the Texas Committee for the Humanities. He is currently working on a biography of James G. Blaine, the late-nineteenth-century speaker of the House, secretary of state, and Republican presidential candidate.

ARIELA J. GROSS

Ariela J. Gross is professor of law and history at the University of Southern California. She received her B.A. from Harvard University, her J.D. from Stanford Law School, and her Ph.D. from Stanford University. She is the author of *Double Character: Slavery and Mastery in the Antebellum Southern Courtroom* (2000) and numerous law review articles and book chapters. Her current work in progress, a history of racial identity on trial in the United States to be published by Farrar, Straus & Giroux, is supported by fellowships from the Guggenheim Foundation, the National Endowment for the Humanities, and the American Council for Learned Societies.

H. W. BRANDS

H. W. Brands is University Distinguished Professor and Melbern G. Glasscock Chair in American History at Texas A&M University, where he has taught since 1987. He is the author of numerous works of history and international affairs, including *The Devil We Knew: Americans and the Cold War* (1993), *What America Owes the World: The Struggle for the Soul of Foreign Policy* (1998), *Into the Labyrinth: The United States and the Middle East* (1994), *The Reckless Decade: America in the 1890s* (1995), *TR: The Last Romantic* (a biography of Theodore Roosevelt) (1997), *The First American: The Life and Times of Benjamin Franklin* (2000), *The Strange Death of American Liberalism* (2001), *The Age of Gold: The California Gold Rush and the New American Dream* (2002), and *Woodrow Wilson* (2003). His writing has received critical and popular acclaim; *The First American* was a finalist for the Pulitzer Prize and a national best-seller. He lectures frequently across North America and in Europe. His essays and reviews have appeared in the *New York Times*, the *Wall Street Journal*, the *Washington Post*, the *Los Angeles Times*, and *Atlantic Monthly*. He is a regular guest on radio and television, and has participated in several historical documentary films.

RANDY ROBERTS

Randy Roberts earned his Ph.D. from Louisiana State University. His areas of special interest include modern U.S. history and the history of sports and films in America. He is a faculty member at Purdue University where he has won the Murphy Award for outstanding teaching, the Teacher of the Year Award, and the Society of Professional Journalists Teacher of the Year Award. The books he has authored or co-authored include *Jack Dempsey: The Manassa Mauler* (1979, expanded ed., 1984); *Papa Jack: Jack Johnson and the Era of White Hopes* (1983); *Heavy Justice:* The State of Indiana *vs.* Michael G. Tyson (1994); *My Lai: A Brief History with Documents* (1998); *John Wayne: American* (1995); *Where the Domino Fell: America in Vietnam, 1945–1990* (1990, rev. ed., 1996); *Winning Is the Only Thing: Sports in America Since 1945* (1989); *Pittsburg Sports: Stories from the Steel City* (2000); and *A Line in the Sand: The Alamo in Blood and Memory* (2001). Roberts serves as co-editor of the Sports and Society series, University of Illinois Press, and is on the editorial board of the *Journal of Sports History.*

Chapter 1

New World Encounters

Clash of Cultures: Interpreting Murder in Early Maryland

New World conquest sparked unexpected, often embarrassing contests over the alleged superiority of European culture. Not surprisingly, the colonizers insisted they brought the benefits of civilization to the primitive and savage peoples of North America. Native Americans never shared that perspective, voicing a strong preference for their own values and institutions. In early seventeenth-century Maryland the struggle over cultural superiority turned dramatically on how best to punish the crime of murder, an issue about which both Native Americans and Europeans had firm opinions.

The actual events that occurred at Captain William Claiborne's trading post in 1635 may never be known. Surviving records indicate that several young Native American males identified as Wicomesses apparently traveled to Claiborne's on business, but to their great annoyance, they found the proprietor entertaining Susquehannocks, their most hated enemies. The situation deteriorated rapidly after the Susquehannocks ridiculed the Wicomesses. Unwilling to endure public humiliation, the Wicomesses later ambushed the Susquehannocks, killing five, and then returned to the trading post where they murdered three Englishmen.

Wicomess leaders realized immediately that something had to be done. They dispatched a trusted messenger to inform the governor of Maryland that they intended "to offer satisfaction for the harm . . . done to the English." The murder of the Susquehannocks was another matter, best addressed by the Native Americans themselves. The governor praised the Wicomesses for coming forward, announcing that "I expect that those men, who have done this outrage, should be delivered unto me, to do with them as I shall think fit." The Wicomess spokesman was dumbfounded. The governor surely did not understand basic Native American legal procedure. "It is the matter amongst us Indians, that if any such like accident happens," he explained, "we do redeem the life of a man that is so slain with 100 Arms length of *Roanoke* (which is a sort of Beads that they make, and use for money.)" The governor's demand for prisoners seemed doubly impertinent, "since you [English settlers] are here strangers, and coming into our Country, you should rather conform your selves to the Customs of our Country, than impose yours upon us." At this point the governor hastily ended the conversation, perhaps uncomfortably aware that if the legal tables had been turned and the murders had been committed in England, he would be the one loudly defending "the Customs of our Country."

EUROPEANS SAILING IN THE WAKE of Admiral Christopher Columbus constructed a narrative of superiority that survived long after the Wicomesses had been dispersed—a fate that befell them in the late seventeenth century. The story recounted first in Europe and then in the United States depicted heroic adventurers,

Outline

Native American Histories Before Conquest

A World Transformed

West Africa: Ancient and Complex Societies

Europe on the Eve of Conquest

Imagining a New World

French Exploration and Settlement

The English New World

Rehearsal in Ireland for American Colonization

An Unpromising Beginning: Mystery at Roanoke

Conclusion: Propaganda for Empire

missionaries, and soldiers sharing Western civilization with the peoples of the New World and opening a vast virgin land to economic development. The familiar tale celebrated material progress, the inevitable spread of European values, and the taming of frontiers.

That narrative of events no longer provides an adequate explanation for European conquest and settlement. It is not so much wrong as partisan, incomplete, and even offensive. History recounted from the perspective of the victors inevitably silences the voices of the victims, the peoples who, in the victors' view, foolishly resisted economic and technological progress. Heroic tales of the advance of Western values only serve to deflect modern attention away from the rich cultural and racial diversity that characterized North American societies. More disturbing, traditional tales of European conquest also obscure the sufferings of the millions of Native Americans, as well as huge numbers of Africans sold as slaves in the New World.

By placing these complex, often unsettling, experiences within an interpretive framework of *creative adaptations*—rather than of *exploration* or *settlement*—progress is made in recapturing the full human dimensions of conquest and resistance. While the New World often witnessed tragic violence and systematic betrayal, it allowed ordinary people of three different races and many different ethnic identities opportunities to shape their own lives as best they could within diverse, often hostile environments. It should be remembered that neither Native Americans nor Africans were passive victims of European exploitation. Within their own families and communities they made choices, sometimes rebelling, sometimes accommodating, but always trying to make sense in terms of their own cultures of what they were experiencing. Of course, that was precisely what the Wicomess messenger tried to tell the governor of Maryland.

Native American Histories Before Conquest

The peopling of North America did not begin with Columbus's arrival in 1492. Although Spanish invaders proclaimed the discovery of a "New World," they really brought into contact three worlds—Europe, Africa, and America—that in the fifteenth century were already old. Indeed, the first migrants reached the North American continent some fifteen to twenty thousand years ago.

Environmental conditions played a major role in this story. Twenty thousand years ago, the earth's climate was considerably colder than it is today. Huge glaciers, often more than a mile thick, extended as far south as the present states of Illinois and Ohio and covered broad sections of western Canada. Much of the world's moisture was transformed into ice, and the oceans dropped hundreds of feet below their current level. The receding waters created a land bridge connecting Asia and North America, a region now submerged beneath the Bering Sea that modern archaeologists have named Beringia.

Even at the height of the last Ice Age, much of the far North remained free of glaciers. Small bands of spear-throwing Paleo-Indians pursued giant mammals—woolly mammoths and mastodons, for example—across Beringia. Because these migrations took place over a long period of time and involved small, independent bands of highly nomadic people, the Paleo-Indians never developed a common identity. Each group focused on its own immediate survival, adjusting to the opportunities presented by various microenvironments.

The Environmental Challenge: Food, Climate, and Culture

Some twelve thousand years ago global warming substantially reduced the glaciers, allowing nomadic hunters to pour into the heart of North America. Within just a few thousand years, Native Americans had reached the southern tip of South America. Blessed with a seemingly inexhaustible supply of meat, the early migrants experienced rapid population growth. Archaeologists have discovered that this sudden expansion of human population coincided with the loss of scores of large mammals. Some archaeologists have suggested that the Paleo-Indian hunters bear responsibility for the mass extinction of so many animals. It is more probable that climatic warming put the large animals under severe stress, and the early humans simply contributed to an ecological process over which they had little control.

The Indian peoples adjusted to the changing environmental conditions. Dispersing across the North American continent, they found new food sources, such as smaller mammals, fish, nuts, and berries. About five thousand years ago, they discovered how to cultivate certain plants. The peoples living in the Southwest acquired cultivation skills long before the bands living along the Atlantic coast as knowledge of maize (corn), squash, and beans spread north from central Mexico. The shift to basic crops—a transformation that is sometimes termed the **Agricultural Revolution**—profoundly altered Native American societies. Freed from the insecurity of an existence based solely on hunting and gathering, Native Americans began settling in permanent villages. They also began to produce ceramics, a valuable technology for the storage of grain. As the food supply increased, the Native American population greatly expanded, especially in the Southwest and in the Mississippi Valley.

Agricultural Revolution The gradual shift from hunting and gathering to cultivating basic food crops that occurred worldwide from 7,000 to 9,000 years ago.

Mysterious Disappearances

Several magnificent sites in North America provide powerful testimony to the cultural and social achievements of native peoples before European conquest. One of the more impressive is Chaco Canyon on the San Juan River in present-day New Mexico. The massive pueblo was the center of Anasazi culture, serving both political and religious functions, and it is estimated that its complex structures may have housed as many as fifteen thousand people. The Anasazi sustained their agriculture through a huge, technologically sophisticated network of irrigation canals that carried water long distances. They also constructed a transportation system connecting Chaco Canyon by road to more than seventy outlying villages.

Equally impressive urban centers developed throughout the Ohio and Mississippi Valleys. In present-day Ohio, the Adena and Hopewell peoples—names assigned by archaeologists to distinguish differences in material culture—built large ceremonial mounds, where they buried the families of local elites. Around A.D. 1000, the groups gave way to the Mississippian culture, a loose collection of communities along the Mississippi River from Louisiana to Illinois that shared similar technologies and beliefs. Cahokia, a huge fortification and ceremonial site in Illinois that originally rose high above the river and supported a population of almost twenty thousand, represented the greatest achievement of the Mississippian peoples.

Recent research reveals that Native American peoples did not isolate themselves in their own communities. Over the millennia they developed different cultural and social practices, and more than three hundred separate languages had evolved in North America before European conquest. Members of different groups traded goods over extremely long distances. Burial mounds in the Ohio Valley, for example, have yielded obsidian from

❖ A Look at the Past ❖

Effigy Jar

Clay effigy jars reveal the complexity of Mississippian culture. Members of the culture built large earthen temple mounds, practiced elaborate burials, and made clay jars depicting the faces of respected dead members. What do these customs, particularly the effigy jars, reveal about the Mississippian attitude toward death?

western Wyoming, shells from Florida, mica quarried in North Carolina and Tennessee, and copper from near Lake Superior.

Yet however advanced the Native American cultures of the southwest and Mississippi Valley may have been, both cultures disappeared rather mysteriously just before the arrival of the Europeans. No one knows what caused the disappearances. Some scholars have suggested that climatic changes and continuing population growth affected food supplies; others insist that chronic warfare destabilized the social order. Still others argue that diseases carried to the New World by the first European adventurers ravaged the cultures. No matter what the explanation, modern commentators agree that the breakdown of Mississippian culture caused smaller bands to disperse, construct new identities, and establish different political structures. These were the peoples who encountered the first European arrivals along the Atlantic Coast.

Aztec Dominance

The stability resulting from the Agricultural Revolution allowed the Indians of Mexico and Central America to structure their societies in more complex ways. Like the Incas who lived in what is now Peru, the Mayan and Toltec peoples of Central Mexico built vast cities, formed government bureaucracies that dominated large tributary populations, and developed hieroglyphic writing as well as an accurate solar calendar.

Not long before Columbus began his voyage across the Atlantic, the Aztecs, an aggressive, warlike people, swept through the Valley of Mexico, conquering the great cities of their enemies. Aztec warriors ruled by force, reducing defeated rivals to tributary status. In 1519, the Aztecs' main ceremonial center, Tenochtitlán, contained as many as 250,000 people as compared with only 50,000 in Seville, the port from which the early Spaniards had sailed. Elaborate human sacrifice associated with Huitzilopochtli, the Aztec sun god, horrified Europeans, who apparently did not find the savagery of their own civilization so objectionable. The Aztec ritual killings were connected to the agricultural cycle, and the Indians believed the blood of their victims possessed extraordinary fertility powers.

Eastern Woodland Cultures

Indians living in the northeast region along the Atlantic coast, who numbered less than a million at the time of conquest, generally supplemented farming with seasonal hunting and gathering. Most belonged to what ethnographers term the Eastern Woodland Cultures. Small bands formed villages during the warm summer months. The women cultivated maize and other crops while the men hunted and fished. During the winter, difficulties associated with feeding so many people forced the communities to disperse. Each family lived off the land as best it could.

Seventeenth-century English settlers were most likely to have encountered the Algonquian-speaking peoples who occupied much of the territory along the Atlantic Coast from North Carolina to Maine. Included in this large linguistic group were the Powhatan of Tidewater Virginia, the Narragansett of Rhode Island, and the Abenaki of northern New England.

Despite common linguistic roots, the scattered Algonquian communities would have found communication extremely difficult because they had developed very different dialects. Furthermore, linguistic ties had little effect on Indian politics. Algonquian groups who lived in different regions, exploited different resources, and spoke different dialects did not develop strong ties of mutual identity. When their own interests were involved, they were more than willing to ally themselves with Europeans against other Algonquian speakers. Divisions among Indian groups would in time facilitate European conquest.

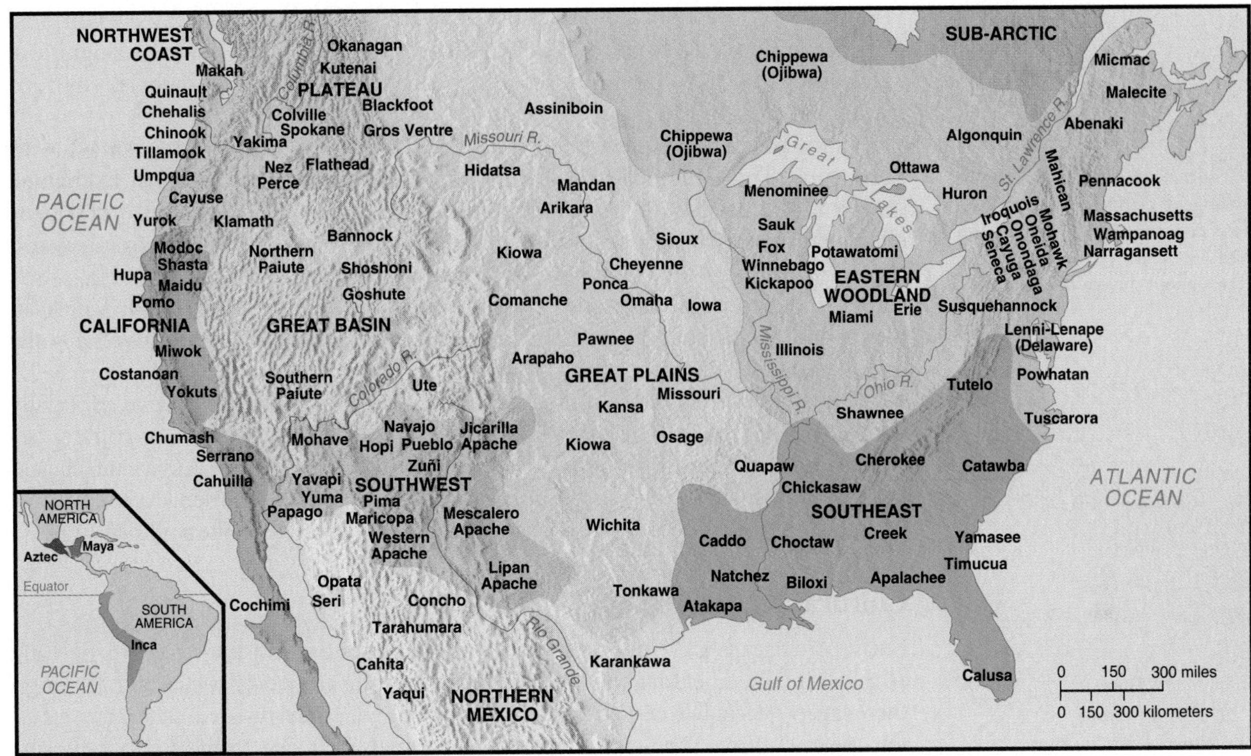

THE FIRST AMERICANS: LOCATION OF MAJOR INDIAN GROUPS AND CULTURE AREAS IN THE 1600s *Native Americans had complex social structures and religious systems and a well-developed agricultural technology when they came into initial contact with Europeans.* ❖

However divided the Indians of eastern North America may have been, they shared many cultural values and assumptions. Most Native Americans, for example, defined their place in society through kinship. Such personal bonds determined the character of economic and political relations. The farming bands living in areas eventually claimed by England were often matrilineal, which meant in effect that women owned the planting fields and houses, maintained tribal customs, and had a role in tribal government. The native communities of Canada and the northern Great Lakes were more likely to be patrilineal. In these groups, men owned the hunting grounds that the family needed to survive.

Eastern Woodland communities organized diplomacy, trade, and war around reciprocal relationships that impressed Europeans as being remarkably democratic. Chains of native authority were loosely structured. Native leaders were accomplished public speakers because persuasive rhetoric was often their only effective source of power. It required considerable oratorical skill for an Indian leader to persuade independent-minded warriors to support a certain policy.

Before the arrival of the Europeans, Indian wars were seldom very lethal. Fatalities, when they did occur, sparked cycles of revenge. Young warriors attacked neighboring bands largely to exact revenge for a previous insult or the death of a relative, or to secure captives. Some captives were tortured to death; others were adopted into the community as replacements for fallen relatives.

A World Transformed

The arrival of Europeans on the North American continent profoundly altered Native American cultures. Indian villages located on the Atlantic Coast came under severe pressure almost immediately; inland groups had more time to adjust.

Wherever they lived, however, Indians discovered that conquest strained traditional ways of life, and as daily patterns of experience changed almost beyond recognition, native peoples had to devise new ways to survive in physical and social environments that eroded tradition.

Columbian Exchange The exchange of plants, animals, culture, and diseases between Europe and the Americas from first contact throughout the era of exploration.

Cultural change was not the only effect of Native Americans' contact with Europeans. The ecological transformation, known as the **Columbian Exchange,** profoundly affected both groups of people. Some aspects of the exchange were beneficial. Europeans introduced into the Americas new plants—bananas, oranges, and sugar, for example—and animals—pigs, sheep, cattle, and especially horses—that altered the diet, economy, and way of life for the native peoples. Native American plants and foods, such as maize, squash, tomatoes, and potatoes, proved equally transforming in Europe.

Other aspects of the Columbian Exchange were far more destructive, especially for Native Americans. The most immediate biological consequence of contact between Europeans and Indians was the transfer of disease. Native Americans lacked natural immunity to many common European diseases and when exposed to influenza, typhus, measles, and especially smallpox, they died by the millions.

Cultural Negotiations

Native Americans were not passive victims of forces beyond their control. So long as they remained healthy, they held their own in the early exchanges, and although they eagerly accepted certain trade goods, they generally resisted other aspects of European cultures. The earliest recorded contacts between Indians and explorers suggest curiosity and surprise rather than hostility. A Southeastern Indian who encountered Hernando de Soto in 1540 expressed awe (at least that is what a Spanish witness recorded): "The things that seldom happen bring astonishment. Think, then, what must be the effect on me and mine, the sight of you and your people, whom we have at no time seen . . . things so altogether new, as to strike awe and terror to our hearts."

What Indians desired most was peaceful trade. The earliest French explorers reported that natives waved from shore, urging the Europeans to exchange metal items for beaver skins. In fact, the Indians did not perceive themselves at a disadvantage in these dealings. They could readily see the technological advantage of guns over bows and arrows. Metal knives made daily tasks much easier. To acquire such goods they traded pelts, which to them seemed in abundant supply. "The English have no sense," one Indian informed a French priest. "They give us twenty knives like this for one Beaver skin."

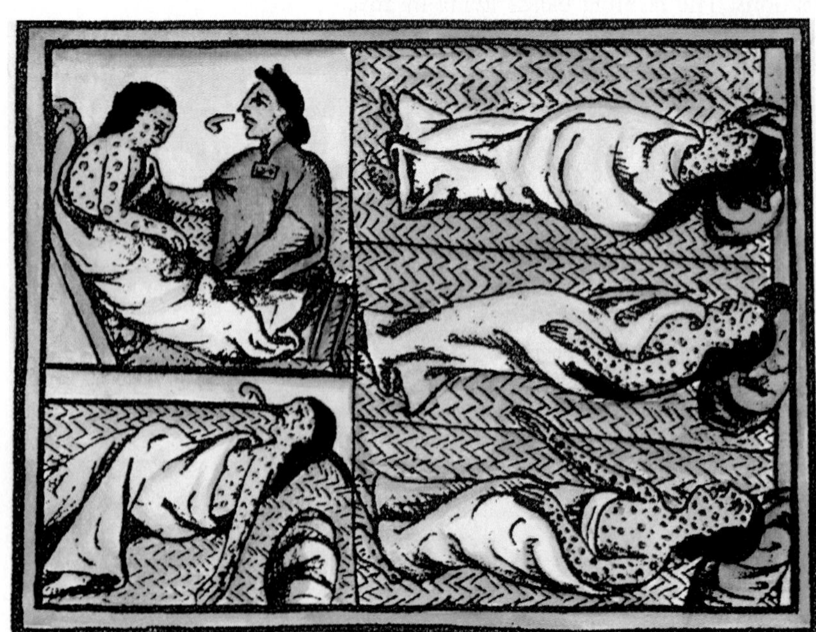

As Native Americans were exposed to common Old World diseases, particularly smallpox, they died by the millions. ❖

Trading sessions along the eastern frontier were really cultural seminars. The Europeans tried to make sense out of Indian cultures, and although they may have called the natives "savages," they quickly discovered that the Indians drove hard bargains. They demanded gifts; they set the time and place of trade. Indians used the occasions to study the newcomers. They formed opinions about the Europeans, some flattering, some less so, but they never concluded from their observations that Indian culture was inferior to that of the colonizers.

For Europeans, communicating with the Indians was always an ordeal. The invaders reported having gained deep insight into Native American cultures through sign languages. How much accurate information explorers and traders took from these crude improvised exchanges is a matter of conjecture. In the absence of meaningful conversation, Europeans often concluded that the Indians held them in high regard, perhaps seeing the newcomers as gods. Sometimes the adventurers did not even try to communicate, assuming from superficial observation—as did the sixteenth-century explorer Giovanni da Verrazzano—"that they have no religion, and that they live in absolute freedom, and that everything they do proceeds from Ignorance."

Ethnocentric Europeans tried repeatedly to "civilize" the Indians. In practice that meant persuading natives to dress like the colonists, attend white schools, live in permanent structures, and, most important, accept Christianity. The Indians listened more or less patiently, but in the end they usually rejected European values. Although some Indians accepted Christianity, most paid it lip service or found it irrelevant to their needs. As one Huron told a French priest, "It would be useless for me to repent having sinned, seeing that I never have sinned."

Among some Indian groups, gender figured prominently in a person's willingness to convert to Christianity. Native men who traded pelts for European goods had more frequent contact with Europeans, and they proved more receptive to the arguments of missionaries. But native women jealously guarded traditional culture, a system that often sanctioned polygamy—a husband having several wives—and gave women substantial authority over the distribution of food within the village. French Jesuit missionaries insisted on monogamous marriages, an institution based on Christian values but that made little sense in Indian societies where constant warfare killed off large numbers of young males and increasingly left native women without sufficient marriage partners.

Even matrimony seldom eroded the Indians' attachment to their own customs. When Native Americans and Europeans married, the European partner usually chose to live among the Indians. Impatient settlers who regarded the Indians simply as an obstruction to progress sometimes developed more coercive methods, such as enslavement, to achieve cultural conversion. Again, from the European perspective, the results were disappointing. Indian slaves ran away or died. In either case, they did not become European.

Threats to Survival: Trade and Disease

Over time, cooperative encounters between Native Americans and Europeans became less frequent. The Europeans found it almost impossible to understand the Indians' relation to the land and other natural resources. English planters cleared the forests and fenced the fields and, in the process, radically altered the ecological systems on which the Indians depended. The European system of land use inevitably reduced the supply of deer and other animals essential to traditional native cultures.

Trade, too, came to threaten Native Americans' survival. The Indians welcomed European commerce, but like so many consumers throughout recorded history, they discovered that the objects they most desired led them into debt. To pay for the goods, the Indians hunted more aggressively and so further reduced the population of fur-bearing animals.

Commerce affected Indian survival in other ways. After several disastrous wars—the Yamasee War in South Carolina in 1715, for example—the natives learned that demonstrations of force usually resulted in the suspension of normal trade, on which the Indians had grown quite dependent for guns and ammunition, among other things.

It was disease, however, that ultimately brought disaster to many North American tribes. European adventurers exposed Indians to bacteria and viruses to which they had no natural immunity. Smallpox, measles, and influenza decimated the Native American population. Other diseases such as alcoholism took a terrible toll.

Within a generation of initial contact with Europeans, the Carib, who gave the Caribbean its name, were virtually extinct. The Algonquian communities of New England experienced appalling rates of death. Historical demographers now estimate that some tribes suffered a 90 to 95 percent population loss within the first century of European contact. The death of so many Indians decreased the supply of indigenous laborers, whom the Europeans needed to work the mines and cultivate staple crops such as sugar and tobacco. The decimation of native populations may have persuaded colonists throughout the New World to seek a substitute labor force in Africa. Indeed, the enslavement of blacks has been described as an effort by Europeans to "repopulate" the New World.

Some native peoples, such as the Iroquois, who lived a long way from the coast and thus had more time to adjust to the challenge, withstood the crisis better than did those who immediately confronted the Europeans. Refugee Indians from the hardest hit eastern communities were absorbed into healthier western groups. However horrific the crisis may have been, it demonstrated how much the environment—a source of opportunity as well as devastation—shaped human encounters throughout the New World.

West Africa: Ancient and Complex Societies

During the era of the European slave trade, a number of myths about sub-Saharan Africa were propagated. Europeans maintained that the sub-Saharan Africans lived simple, isolated lives. Indeed, some scholars still depict the vast region stretching from the Senegal River south to modern Angola as a single cultural unit, as if at one time all the men and women living there had shared a common set of political, religious, and social values.

Such was not the case. Sub-Saharan West Africa was rich in political, religious, and cultural diversity. Centuries earlier, the Muslim religion had slowly spread into black Africa, and although many West Africans resisted the Islamic faith, it was widely accepted in the Senegal Valley. The Muslim traders from North Africa and the Middle East who introduced their religion to West Africans also established sophisticated trade networks that linked the villagers of Senegambia with the urban centers of northwestern Africa—Tangier, Algiers, Tunis, and Tripoli. Great camel caravans regularly crossed the Sahara carrying trade goods, which were exchanged for gold and slaves.

West Africans spoke many languages and organized themselves into diverse political systems. As in Europe, kingdoms rose and fell, and when the first European traders arrived, Mali, Benin, and Kongo were among the major states. Other Africans lived in stateless societies organized along lineage structures. But whatever the form of government, men and women found their primary social identity within well-defined lineage groups, which consisted of persons claiming descent from a common ancestor. In these lineage groups, the clan elders made the important economic and social decisions, from who should receive land to who might take a wife. These communities were usually self-sufficient, producing both food and trade goods.

The first Europeans to reach the West African coast by sail were the Portuguese. In the fifteenth century, they journeyed to Africa in search of gold and slaves. Africans were willing partners in the commerce but insisted that Europeans respect their trade regulations. They required the Europeans to pay tolls and other fees and restricted the foreign traders to conducting their business in small forts or castles located at the mouths of the major rivers. Local merchants acquired slaves and gold in the interior and transported them to the coast, where they were exchanged for European goods. Strong African armies and deadly diseases prevented Europeans from moving into the interior regions of Africa.

Even before Europeans colonized the New World, the Portuguese were purchasing almost a thousand slaves a year on the West African coast and sending them to Portuguese and Spanish island plantations across the Atlantic. Current estimates are that approximately 10.7 million Africans were taken to the New World as slaves. The slave trade was so extensive that during every year between 1650 and 1831, more Africans than Europeans relocated to the Americas. As one historian noted, "In terms of immigration alone . . . America was an extension of Africa rather than Europe until late in the nineteenth century."

Local African rulers allowed European traders to build compounds along the West African coast. Constructed to expedite the slave trade, each of these so-called "slave factories" served a different European interest. Cape Coast Castle, which changed hands several times as rival nations fought for its control, became one of the largest slave trading posts in the world after the British captured and reinforced it in 1665. ❖

Europe on the Eve of Conquest

In ancient times, points west had an almost mythical appeal among people living along the shores of the Mediterranean Sea. Classical writers speculated about the fate of the legendary Atlantis, a great civilization that had mysteriously sunk beneath the ocean waves. In the fifth century A.D., an intrepid Irish monk, Saint Brendan, reported finding enchanted islands far out in the Atlantic where he also met a talking whale. Such stories aroused curiosity but proved difficult to verify.

About A.D. 1000, Scandinavian seafarers known as Norsemen or Vikings actually established settlements in the New World. In the year 984, a band of Vikings led by Eric the Red sailed west from Iceland to a large island in the North Atlantic, which Eric inappropriately named Greenland in an effort to attract colonists to the icebound region. A few years later, Eric's son, Leif, pushed even farther west to northern Newfoundland. Poor communications, hostile natives, and political upheavals at home, however, made maintenance of these distant outposts impossible. The Vikings' adventures were not widely known; when Columbus set out on his great voyage in 1492, he was most likely unaware of these earlier exploits.

Building New Nation-States

The Viking achievement went unnoticed partly because other Europeans were not prepared to sponsor transatlantic exploration and settlement. Medieval kingdoms were loosely organized, and for several centuries, fierce provincial loyalties, widespread ignorance of classical learning, and dreadful plagues such as the Black Death discouraged people from thinking about the world beyond their villages.

In the fifteenth century, these conditions began to change. The expansion of commerce, a more imaginative outlook fostered by the European cultural awakening and humanistic movement known as the **Renaissance,** and population growth after 1450 contributed to the exploration impulse. Land became more expensive, and landowners prospered. Demands from wealthy landlords for such luxury goods

Renaissance A cultural awakening that began in Italy and spread throughout Europe in the fifteenth and sixteenth centuries.

as spices and jewels, obtainable only in distant ports, introduced powerful new incentives for exploration and trade.

This period also witnessed the victory of the "new monarchs" over feudal nobles; political authority was centralized. The changes came slowly—and in numerous areas, violently—but wherever they occurred, the results altered traditional political relationships between the nobility and the crown, between the citizen and the state. The new rulers recruited national armies and paid for them with national taxes. These rulers could be despotic, but they usually restored a measure of peace to communities tired of chronic feudal war.

The story was the same throughout most of western Europe. Henry VII in England, Louis XI in France, and Ferdinand of Aragon and Isabella of Castile in Spain forged strong nations from weak kingdoms. If these political changes had not occurred, the major European countries could not possibly have generated the financial and military resources necessary for worldwide exploration. Indeed, the formation of aggressive nation-states prepared the way for the later wars of empire.

During this period, naval innovators revolutionized ship design and technology. Before the fifteenth century, the ships that plied the Mediterranean were clumsy and slow. But by the time Columbus sailed from Spain, they were faster, more maneuverable, and less expensive to operate. Most important of all was a new type of rigging developed by the Arabs, the lateen sail, which allowed large ships to sail into the wind, permitting transatlantic travel and difficult maneuvers along the rocky, uncharted coasts of North America. By the end of the fifteenth century, seafarers set sail with a new sense of confidence.

The final prerequisite to exploration was knowledge. The rediscovery of classical texts and maps in the humanistic Renaissance of the fifteenth century helped stimulate fresh investigation of the globe. And because of the invention of the printing press in the 1430s, this new knowledge could spread across Europe. The printing press opened the European mind to exciting possibilities that had only been dimly perceived when the Vikings sailed the North Atlantic.

Imagining a New World

In the early fifteenth century, Spain was politically divided, its people were poor, and its harbors were second-rate. There was little to indicate that this land would take the lead in conquering the New World. But in the early sixteenth century, Spain came alive. The union of Ferdinand and Isabella sparked a drive for political consolidation that, owing to the monarchs' militant Catholicism, took on the characteristics of a religious crusade. The new monarchs waged a victorious war against the Muslim states in southern Spain, which ended in 1492 when Granada, the last Muslim stronghold, fell. Out of this volatile political and social environment came the **conquistadores,** explorers eager for personal glory and material gain, uncompromising in matters of religion, and unswerving in their loyalty to the crown. These were the men who first carried European culture to the New World.

conquistadores Sixteenth-century Spanish adventurers, often of noble birth, who subdued the Native Americans and created the Spanish empire in the New World.

Myths and Reality

If it had not been for Christopher Columbus (Cristoforo Colombo), Spain might never have gained an American empire. Born in Genoa, Italy, in 1451 of humble parentage, Columbus devoured classical learning and became obsessed with the idea of sailing west across the Atlantic Ocean to reach Cathay, as China was then known. In 1484, he presented his plan to the king of Portugal, who was also interested in a route to Cathay. But the Portuguese were more interested in the route that went around the tip of Africa. After a polite audience, Columbus was refused support.

Undaunted by rejection, Columbus petitioned Isabella and Ferdinand for financial backing. They initially were no more interested in his grand design than the

Portuguese had been. But fear of Portugal's growing power, as well as Columbus's confident talk of wealth and empire, led the new monarchs to reassess his scheme. Finally, the two sovereigns provided the supremely self-assured navigator with three ships, named *Niña, Pinta,* and *Santa Maria.* The indomitable admiral set sail for Cathay in August 1492, the year of Spain's unification.

Educated Europeans in the fifteenth century knew without question that the world was round. The question was size, not shape. Columbus estimated the distance to the mainland of Asia to be about 3000 nautical miles, a voyage that his small ships would have had no difficulty completing. The actual distance is 10,600 nautical miles, however, and had he not bumped into the New World along the way, he and his crew would have run out of food and water long before they reached China.

After stopping in the Canary Islands for ship repairs and supplies, Columbus crossed the Atlantic in thirty-three days, landing on an island in the Bahamas. He searched for the fabled cities of Asia, never considering that he had come upon a landmass completely unknown in Europe. Since his mathematical calculations had been correct, it didn't occur to him that he had come upon a new world, where he met friendly, though startled, Native Americans, whom he called Indians.

Three more times Columbus returned to the New World in search of fabled Asian riches. He died in 1506, a frustrated but wealthy entrepreneur, unaware that he had reached a previously unknown continent. The final blow came in December 1500 when an ambitious falsifier, Amerigo Vespucci, published a sensational travel account that convinced German mapmakers that he had beaten Columbus to the New World. By the time the deception was discovered, *America* had gained general acceptance throughout Europe as the name for the newly discovered continent.

The Conquistadores: Faith and Greed

Under the **Treaty of Tordesillas** (1494), Spain and Portugal divided the New World between themselves. Portugal got Brazil, and Spain laid claim to all the remaining territories. Spain's good fortune unleashed a horde of conquistadores on the Caribbean. They came not as colonists but as fortune hunters seeking instant wealth, preferably gold, and they were not squeamish about the means they used to obtain it. The primary casualties of their greed were the Native Americans. In less than two decades, the tribes that had inhabited the Caribbean islands had been exterminated, victims of exploitation and disease.

Treaty of Tordesillas Treaty negotiated by the pope in 1494 to resolve competing land claims of Spain and Portugal in the New World. It divided the world along a north-south line in the middle of the Atlantic Ocean, granting to Spain all lands west of the line and to Portugal lands east of the line.

Around then, rumors of fabulous wealth in Mexico began to lure the conquistadores from the islands Columbus had found to the mainland. On November 18, 1518, Hernán Cortés, a minor government functionary in Cuba, and a small army set sail for Mexico. There Cortés soon demonstrated that he was a leader of extraordinary ability, a person of intellect and vision who managed to rise above the goals of his avaricious followers.

His adversary was the legendary Aztec emperor Montezuma. It was a duel of powerful personalities. After burning his ships to cut off his army from a possible retreat, Cortés led his band of six hundred followers across difficult mountain trails toward the Valley of Mexico. The sound of gunfire and the sight of armor-clad horses, both unknown to Native Americans, frightened them. Added to the technological advantages was a potent psychological factor. At first Montezuma thought that the Spaniards were gods, representatives of the fearful plumed serpent, Quetzalcoatl. By the time the Aztec ruler realized his error, it was too late to save his empire.

From Plunder to Settlement

Cortés's victory in Mexico, coupled with other Spanish conquests, notably in Peru, transformed the mother country into the wealthiest nation in Europe. But the

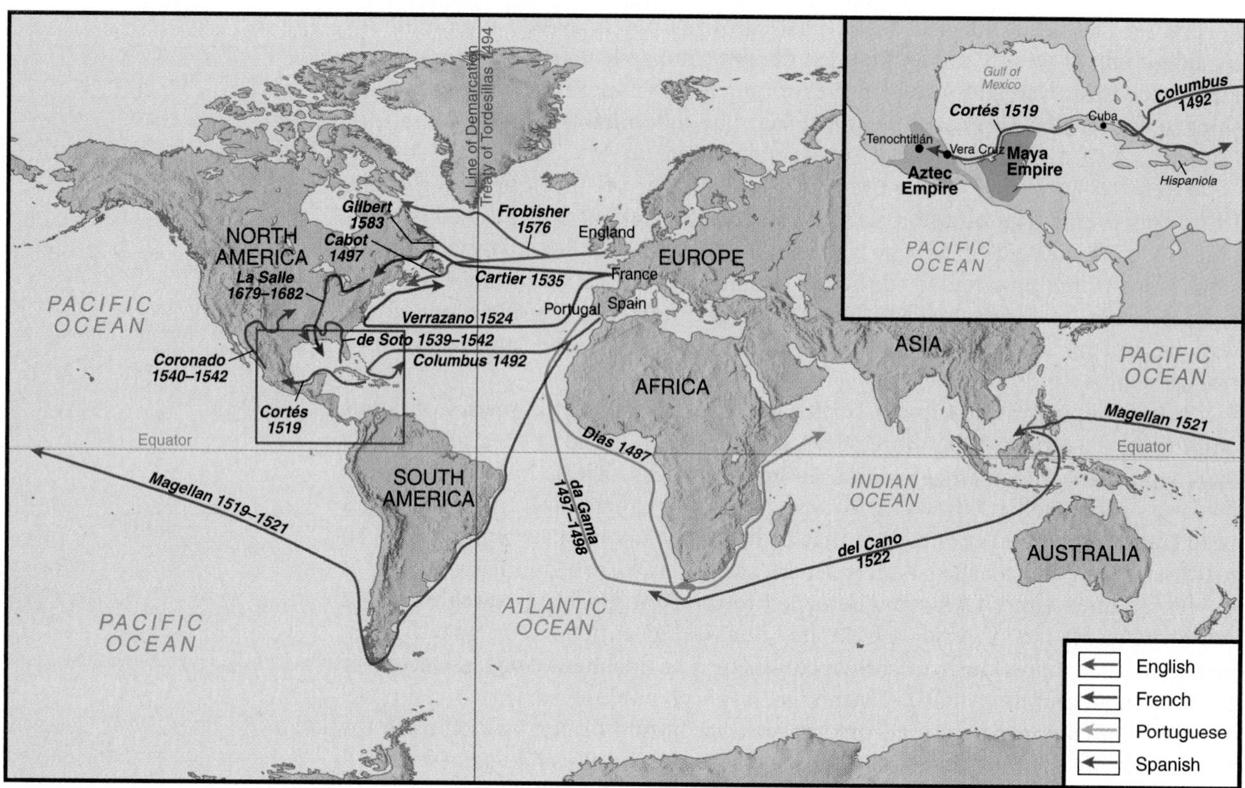

VOYAGES OF EXPLORATION *The routes of the major voyages in the Age of Exploration. The great explorers and navigators established land claims for the European nations.*

encomienda An exploitative labor system designed by Spanish rulers to reward conquistadores in the New World by granting them local villages and control over native labor.

Spanish crown soon faced new difficulties. The conquistadores had to be brought under royal authority. Adventurers like Cortés were stubbornly independent, quick to take offense, and thousands of miles from the seat of government. One solution was the ***encomienda*** system. Conquistadores were rewarded with local villages and control over native labor. They also had the responsibility of protecting the Indians, who suffered terribly under this cruelly exploitative system of labor tribute. The system did make the colonizers very dependent on the king, however, for it was he who legitimized their title. As one historian noted, the system transformed "a frontier of plunder into a frontier of settlement."

Bureaucrats dispatched directly from Spain soon replaced the aging conquistadores. Unlike the governing system that later existed in England's mainland American colonies, Spain's rulers maintained tight control over their American possessions through their government officials. After 1535, a viceroy, a nobleman appointed to oversee the king's colonial interests, ruled the people of New Spain. Working independently of the viceroy, an *audiencia,* the supreme judicial body, brought a measure of justice to the Indians and Spaniards and made certain that the viceroys did not slight their responsibilities to the king. Finally, the Council of the Indies in Spain handled colonial business. Although cumbersome and slow, somehow the rigidly controlled system worked.

The Spanish also brought Catholicism to the New World. The Dominicans and Franciscans, the two largest religious orders, established Indian missions throughout New Spain, and some barefoot friars protected the Native Americans from the worst forms of exploitation. One courageous Dominican, Fra Bartolomé de Las Casas, even published an eloquent defense of Indian rights, *Historia de las Indias,* that among other things questioned the European conquest of the New World. The book led to reforms designed to bring greater "love and moderation" to Spanish-Indian relations.

About 750,000 people migrated to the New World from Spain. Most of the colonists were impoverished, single males in their late twenties in search of economic opportunities. They generally came from the poorest agricultural regions of southern Spain. Since few Spanish women migrated, especially in the sixteenth century, the men often married Indians and, later, blacks, unions that produced offspring known, respectively, as *mestizos* and *mulattoes.* The frequency of interracial marriage created a society of more fluid racial categories than there were in the English colonies, where the sex ratio of the settlers was more balanced and the racially mixed population comparatively small.

The lure of gold drew Spanish conquistadores to the unexplored lands to the north of Mexico. Between 1539 and 1541, Hernando de Soto trekked across the Southeast from Florida to the Mississippi River looking for gold and glory, and at about the same time, Francisco Vásquez de Coronado set out from New Spain in search of the fabled Seven Cities of Cíbola. Neither conquistador found what he was searching for. In the seventeenth century, when Juan de Oñate established outposts in the Southwest, the Spanish came into open conflict with Native Americans in that region. In 1680, the Indians drove the invaders completely out of the territory. Thereafter, the Spanish decided to maintain only a token presence in present-day Texas and New Mexico in order to discourage French encroachment on Spanish lands. For the same reason, the Spanish colony of St. Augustine was established in Florida in 1565. Spanish authorities showed little interest in California, a land of poor Indians and even poorer natural resources. Had it not been for the work of a handful of priests, Spain would have had little claim to California.

Even so, Spain claimed far more of the New World than it could possibly manage. After the era of the conquistadores, Spain's rulers regarded the American colonies primarily as a source of precious metal, and between 1500 and 1650 an estimated 200 tons of gold and 16,000 tons of silver were shipped back to the Spanish treasury in Madrid. The resulting inflation hurt the common people in Spain and prevented the growth of Spanish industry. Unimaginative leadership and debilitating wars hastened the Spanish decline. As one insightful observer declared in 1603, "The New World conquered by you has conquered you in its turn." Nonetheless, Spain's great cultural contribution to the American people is still very much alive today.

French Exploration and Settlement

French interest in the New World developed more slowly. In 1534, Jacques Cartier first sailed to the New World in search of a northwest passage to China. At first he was depressed by the rocky, barren coast of Newfoundland. He grumbled, "I am rather inclined to believe that this is the land God gave to Cain." But the discovery of a large, promising waterway raised Cartier's spirits. He reconnoitered the Gulf of St. Lawrence, traveling up the river as far as Montreal, but he did not discover a northwest passage, nor did he find gold or other precious metals. After several voyages to Canada, Cartier became discouraged by the harsh winters and meager findings; he returned home for good in 1542. Not until seventy-five years later did the brilliant navigator Samuel de Champlain rediscover the region for France. He founded Quebec in 1608.

In Canada, the French developed an economy based primarily on the fur trade, a commerce that required close cooperation with the Native Americans. They also explored the heart of the continent. In 1673, Père Jacques Marquette journeyed down the Mississippi River, and nine years later, Sieur de La Salle traveled all the way to the Gulf of Mexico. In the early eighteenth century, the French established small settlements in Louisiana, the most important being New Orleans.

Although the French controlled the region along the Mississippi and its tributaries, their dream of a vast American empire suffered from several serious flaws.

From the first, the king remained largely indifferent to colonial affairs. An even greater problem was the nature of the land and climate. Few rural peasants or urban artisans wanted to venture to the inhospitable northern country, and throughout the colonial period, New France was underpopulated. By the first quarter of the eighteenth century, the English settlements had outstripped their French neighbors in population as well as in volume of trade.

The English New World

The earliest English visit to North America remains something of a mystery. Fishermen working out of the western English ports may have landed in Nova Scotia and Newfoundland as early as the 1480s. John Cabot (Giovanni Caboto), a Venetian sea captain, completed the first recorded transatlantic voyage by an English vessel in 1497. Henry VII had rejected Columbus's enterprise for the Indies, but the first Tudor monarch apparently experienced a change of heart after hearing of Spain's success.

Like other explorers of that time, Cabot believed that he could find a northwest passage to Asia. He doggedly searched the northern waters for a likely opening, but a direct route to Cathay eluded him. Cabot died during a second attempt in 1498. Although Sebastian Cabot continued his father's explorations in the Hudson Bay region in 1508–1509, English interest in the New World waned. For the next three-quarters of a century, the English people were preoccupied with more pressing domestic and religious concerns. The Cabot voyages did, however, establish an English claim to American territory.

Religious Turmoil and Reformation in Europe

The reign of Henry VII was plagued by domestic troubles. England possessed no standing army, a small, weak navy, and many strong and independent local magnates. During the sixteenth century, however, the next Tudor king, Henry VIII, and his daughter, Elizabeth I, developed a strong central government and transformed England into a Protestant nation. These changes propelled England into a central role in European affairs and were crucial to the creation of England's North American empire.

The Protestantism that eventually stimulated colonization was definitely not of English origin. In 1517, a relatively obscure German monk, Martin Luther, publicly challenged certain tenets and practices of Roman Catholicism, and within a few years, the religious unity of Europe was forever shattered. Luther's message was straightforward. God spoke through the Bible, Luther maintained, not through the pope or priests. Pilgrimages, fasts, alms, indulgences—none of these traditional acts could ensure salvation. Luther's radical ideas spread rapidly across northern Germany and Scandinavia.

Other Protestant reformers soon spoke out against Catholicism. The most important of these was John Calvin, a lawyer turned theologian, who lived in the Swiss city of Geneva. Calvin stressed God's omnipotence over human affairs. The Lord, he maintained, chose some persons for "election," the gift of salvation, while condemning others to eternal damnation. Human beings were powerless to alter this decision by their individual actions.

Common sense suggests that such a bleak doctrine might lead to fatalism or hedonism. After all, why not enjoy worldly pleasures if they have no effect on God's judgment? But common sense would be wrong. Indeed, the Calvinists constantly were busy searching for signs that they had received God's gift of grace. The uncertainty of their eternal state proved a powerful psychological spur, for as long as people did not know whether they were scheduled for heaven or hell, they worked diligently to demonstrate that they possessed at least the seeds of grace. This doctrine of "predestination" became the distinguishing mark of Calvin's followers throughout northern Europe. In the seventeenth century, they were known in France as Huguenots and in England and America as Puritans.

Popular anticlericalism was the basis for the **Protestant Reformation** in England. Although they observed traditional Catholic ritual, the English people had long resented paying monies to a distant pope. Early in the sixteenth century, opposition to the clergy grew increasingly vocal. Cardinal Thomas Wolsey, the most powerful prelate in England, flaunted his immense wealth and became a symbol of spiritual corruption. Parish priests were ridiculed for their ignorance and greed. Anticlericalism did not run as deep in England as in Germany, but by the late 1520s, the Roman Catholic clergy had strained the allegiance of the great mass of the population. Ordinary men and women throughout the kingdom were ready to leave the institutional church.

Protestant Reformation
Sixteenth-century religious movement to reform and challenge the spiritual authority of the Roman Catholic Church, associated with figures such as Martin Luther and John Calvin.

The catalyst for the Reformation in England was Henry VIII's desire to end his marriage to Catherine of Aragon, daughter of the king of Spain. Their union in 1509 had produced a daughter, Mary, but no son. The need for a male heir obsessed Henry. He and his counselors assumed that a female ruler could not maintain domestic peace and that England would fall once again into civil war. Henry petitioned Pope Clement VII for a divorce. Unwilling to tolerate the public humiliation of Catherine, Spain forced the pope to procrastinate. In 1527, time ran out. Henry fell in love with Anne Boleyn, who later bore him a daughter, Elizabeth. The king divorced Catherine without papal consent.

The final break with Rome came swiftly. Between 1529 and 1536, the king, acting through Parliament, severed all ties with the pope, seized church lands, and dissolved many of the monasteries. In March 1534, the Act of Supremacy boldly named Henry VIII "supreme head of the Church of England." Land formerly owned by the Catholic Church passed quickly into private hands, and property holders acquired a vested interest in Protestantism. In 1539, William Tyndale and Miles Coverdale issued an English edition of the Bible, which made it possible for the common people to read the Scriptures in their own language rather than Catholicism's Latin. The separation was complete.

When Henry died in 1547, his young son Edward VI came to the throne. But Edward was a sickly child. Militant Protestants took advantage of the political uncertainty to introduce Calvinism into England. In breaking with the papacy, Henry had shown little enthusiasm for theological change; most Catholic ceremonies remained. But opponents now insisted that the Church of England remove every trace of its Catholic origins. Edward died in 1553, and these ambitious efforts came to a sudden halt. Henry's eldest daughter, Mary I, ascended the throne. Fiercely loyal to the Catholic faith, she vowed to return England to the pope. Hundreds of Protestants were executed; others scurried off to Geneva and Frankfurt, where they absorbed the radical Calvinist doctrines. When Mary died in 1558 and was succeeded by Elizabeth I, these "Marian exiles" returned, more eager than ever to purge the Tudor church of Catholicism. Mary had inadvertently advanced the cause of Calvinism by creating so many Protestant martyrs. The Marian exiles now controlled the Elizabethan church, which remained fundamentally Calvinist until the end of the sixteenth century.

The Protestant Queen

Elizabeth was a woman of extraordinary talent. She governed England from 1558 to 1603, an intellectually exciting period during which some of her subjects took the first halting steps toward colonizing the New World.

Elizabeth's most urgent duty was to end the religious turmoil that had divided the country for a generation. She had no desire to restore Catholicism. After all, the pope openly referred to her as a woman of illegitimate birth. Nor did she want to recreate the church exactly as it had been in the final years of her father's reign. Rather, Elizabeth established a unique church, near-Catholic in ceremony but Protestant in doctrine. The examples of Edward and Mary had demonstrated that neither radical change nor widespread persecution gained a monarch lasting popularity.

Elizabeth still faced serious religious challenges. Catholicism and Protestantism were warring faiths; each was an ideology, a body of deeply held beliefs that influenced the way that average men and women interpreted the experiences of everyday life. The confrontation between Protestantism and Catholicism affected Elizabeth's entire reign.

Militant Calvinists urged her to drop all Catholic rituals, and fervent Catholics wanted her to return to the Roman church. Pope Pius V excommunicated her in 1570. Spain, the most intensely Catholic state in Europe, vowed to restore England to the "true" faith, and the Catholic terrorists plotted to overthrow the Tudor monarchy.

Religion, War, and Nationalism

English Protestantism and English nationalism slowly merged. A loyal English subject in the late sixteenth century loved the monarch, supported the Church of England, and hated Catholics, especially those who happened to live in Spain. Elizabeth's subjects adored their Virgin Queen, and they applauded when her famed "Sea Dogs"—dashing naval commanders such as Sir Francis Drake and Sir John Hawkins—seized Spanish treasure ships in American waters. The English naval raids were little more than piracy, but they passed for grand victories. With each engagement, each threat, each plot, English nationalism took deeper root. By the 1570s, the English people were driven by powerful ideological forces similar to those that had moved the subjects of Isabella and Ferdinand almost a century earlier.

In the mid-1580s, Philip II of Spain constructed a mighty fleet carrying thousands of Spain's finest infantry. The Armada was built to cross the English Channel and destroy the Protestant queen. When one of Philip's lieutenants viewed the Armada at Lisbon in May 1588, he described it as *la felicissima armada,* the invincible fleet. The king believed that with the support of England's oppressed Catholics, Spanish troops would sweep Elizabeth from power.

It was a grand scheme; it was an even grander failure. In 1588, a smaller, more maneuverable English navy dispersed the Armada and revealed Spain's vulnerability. Philip's hopes for a Catholic England lay wrecked along the rocky coasts of Scotland and Ireland. Elizabeth's subjects remained loyal throughout the crisis. Inspired by success in the Channel, bolder personalities dreamed of acquiring riches and planting colonies across the North Atlantic. Spain's American monopoly had been broken.

Rehearsal in Ireland for American Colonization

England's first colony was Ireland. On that island, enterprising Englishmen first learned to subdue a foreign population and seize its lands. Ireland's one million inhabitants were scattered mainly along the coast, and there were few villages. To the English, the Irish seemed wild and barbaric. They were also fiercely independent. The English dominated a small region around Dublin, but much of Ireland remained in the hands of Gaelic-speaking Catholics who presumably lived beyond the reach of civilization.

During the 1560s and 1570s, the English decided that money could be made in Ireland, despite the hostility of the Irish. English colonists moved in and forced the Irish either into tenancy or off the land altogether. Semimilitary colonies were planted in Ulster and Munster.

Colonization brought about severe cultural strains. The English settlers, however humble their own origins, felt superior to the Irish. After all, the English had championed the Protestant religion, constructed a complex market economy, and created a powerful nation-state. To the English, the Irish appeared lazy, lawless, superstitious, and often stupid. Even educated representatives of the two cultures found communication virtually impossible. English colonists, for example, criticized Ireland's pastoral farming methods. It seemed perversely wasteful for the Irish to be forever moving about because this practice retarded the development of towns. Sir John Davies, a leading English colonist, declared that if the Irish were left to themselves, they would "never . . . build houses, make townships or villages or manure or improve the land *as it ought to be.*" Such wastefulness became the standard English justification for seizing more land. No matter what the Irish did, they could never be sufficiently English to please their new masters.

English ethnocentrism was relatively benign so long as the Irish accepted subservient roles. But they rebelled frequently, and English condescension turned quickly to violence. Resistance smacked of disrespect, and for the good of the Irish and the safety of the English, it had to be crushed. Sir Humphrey Gilbert was especially brutal. A talented man who wrote treatises on geography, Gilbert explored the coast of North America and entertained Queen Elizabeth with witty conversation. But as military governor in Ireland, he tolerated no opposition.

In 1569, when the Irish rose up in Munster, he executed everyone he could catch, "man, woman, and child." He cut off the heads of many enemy soldiers killed in battle, and in the words of one contemporary, Gilbert laid his macabre trophies "on the ground by each side of the way leading into his tent, so that none should come into his tent for any cause but commonly he must pass through a lane of heads." Instead of bringing peace and security, such behavior generated a hatred so deep that it continues to this day.

The Irish experiments served as models for later English colonies in the New World, shaping the English view of America and its people. English adventurers in the New World compared Native Americans to the "wild" Irish. This ethnocentrism was a central element in the transfer of English culture to America. The English, like the Spanish and the French, did not perceive America in objective terms. They had already constructed an image of America, and the people and objects that greeted them on the other side of the Atlantic were forced into Old World categories, some of them Irish.

An Unpromising Beginning: Mystery at Roanoke

By the 1570s, England was ready to challenge Spain and reap the profits of Asia and America. Only dimly aware of Cabot's voyages and with very limited colonization experience in Ireland, the English adventurers made almost every mistake that one could possibly imagine between 1575 and 1600. They did, however, acquire valuable information about winds and currents, supplies, and finance that laid the foundation for later, more successful ventures.

Sir Walter Raleigh's experience provided all English colonizers with a sobering example of the difficulties that awaited them in America. In 1584, he dispatched two captains to the coast of present-day North Carolina to claim land granted to him by Elizabeth. The men returned with glowing reports about the fertility of the

John White depicts several fishing techniques practiced by the Algonquian Indians of the modern Carolinas. Riders in the canoe use dip nets and multipronged spears. In the background, Indians stab at fish with long spears. At left, a weir traps fish by taking advantage of the river current's natural force. ❖

soil. Diplomatically, Raleigh renamed this marvelous region Virginia, in honor of his patron, the Virgin Queen.

Raleigh's enterprise seemed ill-fated from the start. Though encouraged by Elizabeth, he received no financial backing from the crown, and despite careful planning, everything went wrong. In 1585, Sir Richard Grenville transported a group of men to Roanoke Island, but the colonists did not arrive in Virginia until nearly autumn. The settlement was also poorly located, and even experienced navigators found it dangerous to reach. Finally, Grenville alienated the local Indians when he senselessly destroyed an entire Indian village in retaliation for the theft of a silver cup.

Grenville hurried back to England in the autumn of 1585, leaving the colonists to fend for themselves. They performed quite well. But when an expected shipment of supplies failed to arrive on time, the colonists grew discontented. In the spring of 1586, Sir Francis Drake unexpectedly landed at Roanoke, and the colonists impulsively decided to return home with him.

In 1587, Raleigh launched a second colony. The new settlement was more representative, containing men, women, and even children. The settlers feasted on Roanoke's fish and game and bountiful harvests of corn and pumpkin. Yet within weeks after arriving, the leader of the settlement, John White, returned to England at the colonists' urging to obtain additional food and clothing and to recruit new immigrants.

Once again, Raleigh's luck turned sour. War with Spain pressed every available ship into military service. When rescuers eventually reached the island in 1590, they found the village deserted. The fate of the "lost" colonists remains a mystery. The best guess is that they were absorbed by neighboring groups of natives, some from as far as the southern shore of the James River.

Conclusion: Propaganda for Empire

Richard Hakluyt, a supremely industrious man, never saw America. Nevertheless, his vision of the New World powerfully shaped public opinion. He interviewed captains and sailors and carefully collected their travel stories in a massive book titled *The Principall Navigations, Voyages, and Discoveries of the English Nation* (1589). Although each tale appeared to be a straightforward narrative, Hakluyt edited each piece to drive home the book's central point: England needed American colonies. English settlers, he argued, would provide the mother country with critical natural resources, and in the process they would grow rich themselves.

As a salesperson for the New World, Hakluyt was as misleading as he was successful. He failed to mention the rich cultural diversity of the Native Americans and the varied backgrounds of the Europeans. Nor did he say a word about the sufferings of Africans in America. Instead he led many ordinary men and women who traveled to America to expect nothing less than a paradise on earth. As the history of Jamestown was soon to demonstrate, the harsh realities of America bore little relation to those golden dreams.

CHRONOLOGY

30,000–20,000 B.C.	Settlers cross the Bering Strait land bridge into North America
2000–1500 B.C.	Agricultural Revolution transforms Native American life
A.D. 1001	Norsemen establish a small settlement in Vinland (Newfoundland)
1438	Printing method using movable type is invented
1492	Marriage of Isabella and Ferdinand leads to the unification of Spain
1492	Columbus lands at San Salvador
1497	Cabot leads first English exploration of North America
1502	Montezuma becomes emperor of the Aztecs
1506	Columbus dies in Spain after four voyages to America
1517	Martin Luther's protests set off the Reformation in Germany
1521	Cortés achieves victory over the Aztecs at Tenochtitlan
1529–1536	Henry VIII provokes the English Reformation
1534	Cartier claims Canada for France
1536	Calvin's *Institutes* is published
1540	Coronado explores the North American Southwest for Spain
1558	Elizabeth becomes queen of England
1583	Sir Humphrey Gilbert dies
1585	First Roanoke settlement is established on the coast of North Carolina
1588	Spanish Armada is defeated by the English
1603	Elizabeth I dies
1608	Champlain founds Quebec
1682	La Salle travels the length of the Mississippi River

KEY TERMS

Agricultural Revolution, p. 3
Columbian Exchange, p. 6
Renaissance, p. 9
conquistadores, p. 10
Treaty of Tordesillas, p. 11
encomienda, p. 12
Protestant Reformation, p. 15

RECOMMENDED READING

The histories of three different peoples coming together for the first time in the New World has sparked innovative scholarship. Many interdisciplinary works explore diverse patterns of cultural adaptation. Some of the best titles bring fresh insights to the Native Americans' response to radical environmental and social change. Among these are Inga Clendinnen, *Aztecs: An Interpretation* (1991); James H. Merrell, *The Indians' New World: Catawbas and Their Neighbors From European Contact Through the Era of Removal* (1989); and James F. Brooks, *Captives and Cousins: Slavery, Kinship and Community in the Southwest Borderlands* (2002). Other broad-ranging volumes examine how early European invaders imagined the New World and how they translated what they thought they had seen into a familiar and unthreatening language: Stephen Greenblatt, *Marvelous Possessions: The Wonder of the New World* (1991), and Anthony Pagden, *European Encounters with the New World: From Renaissance to Romanticism* (1992). The impact of the environment—a major theme of this chapter—is the topic of three pioneering investigations: A. W. Crosby, *The Columbian Voyages, The Columbian Exchange, and Their Historians* (1987); William Cronon, *Changes in the Land: Indians, Colonists, and the*

Ecology of New England (1983); and Shepard Krech III, *The Ecological Indian: Myth and History* (1999). The best overview of the European response to the Conquest is John H. Elliott, *The Old World and New, 1492–1650* (1970). For the Irish experience one should consult Nicholas Canny, *Making Ireland British 1580–1650* (2001). Two outstanding interpretations of the English Reformation are Ethan H. Shagan, *Popular Politics and the English Reformation* (2003) and Eamon Duffy, *The Stripping of the Altars: Traditional Religion in England 1400–1580* (1992). Books that offer boldly original interpretations of the Conquest are Kirkpatrick Sale, *The Conquest of Paradise: Christopher Columbus and the Columbian Legacy* (1990); and Kathleen M. Brown, *Good Wives, Nasty Wenches, and Anxious Patriarchs: Gender, Race, and Power in Colonial Virginia* (1996).

For a list of additional titles related to this chapter's topics, please see http://www.ablongman.com/divine.

Suggested Web Sites

Vikings in the New World

http://emuseum.mnus.edu/prehistory/vikings/vikhome.html
This site explores the history of some of the earliest European visitors to America.

Sir Francis Drake

http://www.mcn.org/2/oseeler/drake.htm
This comprehensive site covers much of Drake's life and voyages.

Ancient Mesoamerican Civilizations

http://www.angelfire.com/ca/humanorigins/index.html
Kevin L. Callahan of the University of Minnesota Department of Anthropology maintains this page regarding Mesoamerican civilizations with well-organized essays and photos.

National Museum of the American Indian

http://www.si.edu/nmai
The Smithsonian Institution maintains this site, providing information about the museum, which is dedicated to everything about Native Americans.

1492: An Ongoing Voyage

http://www.loc.gov/exhibits/1492
An exhibit of the Library of Congress, Washington, D.C., with brief essays and images about early civilizations and contact in the Americas.

The Computerized Information Retrieval System on Columbus and the Age of Discovery

http://muweb.millersv.edu/~columbus/
The History Department and Academic Computing Services of Millersville University of Pennsylvania provide this text retrieval system containing more than one thousand text articles from various magazines, journals, newspapers, speeches, official calendars, and other sources relating to various encounter themes.

Cahokia Mounds

http://medicine.wustl.edu/~mckinney/cahokia/cahokia.html
The Cahokia Mounds State Historical Site gives information about a fascinating pre-Columbian culture in North America.

Mexico Pre-Columbian History

http://www.mexonline.com/precolum.htm
This site "provides information on the Aztecs, Maya, Mexica, Olmecs, Toltec, Zapotecs, and other Pre-European cultures, as well as information on museums, archeology, language and education."

White Oak Fur Post

http://www.whiteoak.org/
This site documents an eighteenth-century fur trading post among the Indians in what would become Minnesota.

La Salle's Shipwreck Project

http://www.thc.state.tx.us/belle/lasbelle.html
Texas Historical Commission site about this archaeological dig to recover the ship of one of America's famous early explorers.

The Discoverer's Web

http://www.win.tue.nl/cs/fm/engels/discovery/
Andre Engels maintains this most complete collection of information on the various efforts at exploration.

Chapter 2

Conflicting Visions: England's Seventeenth-Century Colonies

Profit and Piety: Competing Blueprints for English Settlement

In the spring of 1644, John Winthrop, governor of Massachusetts Bay, learned that Native Americans had overrun the scattered tobacco plantations of Virginia, killing as many as five hundred colonists. Winthrop never thought much of the Chesapeake settlements. He regarded the people who had migrated to that part of America as grossly materialistic, and because Virginia had recently expelled several Puritan ministers, Winthrop decided that the hostilities were God's way of punishing the tobacco planters for their worldliness. He gave the Virginians neither help nor sympathy.

In 1675, Native Americans declared all-out war against the New Englanders, and reports of the destruction of Puritan communities were soon circulating in Virginia. Sir William Berkeley, Virginia's royal governor, was not displeased by the news of New England's adversity. He and his friends held the Puritans in contempt. Indeed, the New Englanders reminded them of the religious fanatics who had provoked civil war in the mother country and who, in 1649, had executed Charles I. In reasoning that echoed Winthrop's, Berkeley concluded that the Native American attacks were God's revenge on the Puritans. He, in turn, declined to send the New Englanders the necessary supplies or sympathy.

UNITY AND NATIONALISM WERE NOT PART of Winthrop's and Berkeley's America. English colonization in the seventeenth century did not spring from a desire to build a centralized empire in the New World similar to that of Spain or France. Instead, the English crown awarded colonial charters to a wide variety of people including merchants, religious idealists, and aristocratic adventurers, all of whom established separate and profoundly different colonies.

OUTLINE

Breaking Away

The Chesapeake: Dreams of Wealth

Reforming England in America

Diversity in the Middle Colonies

Quakers in America

Planting the Carolinas

The Founding of Georgia

Conclusion: Living with Diversity

Breaking Away

Changes in the mother country occurring throughout the period of settlement help explain the diversity of English colonization. Far-reaching economic, political, and religious transformations swept seventeenth-century England. Many people left the villages where they were born in search of fresh opportunities. Thousands traveled to London, by 1600 a city of several hundred thousand inhabitants. A large number of English settlers migrated to Ireland; lucrative employment and religious freedom attracted others to Holland. Others set out for more exotic destinations. The most adventurous individuals went to the New World—to Caribbean islands such as Barbados or to the mainland colonies.

Various reasons drew the colonists across the Atlantic. The quest for a purer form of worship motivated many, while the dream of owning land attracted others. And a few came to escape bad marriages, jail terms, and poverty. But whatever their reasons for crossing the ocean, English men and women who emigrated to America in the seventeenth century left a mother country wracked by recurrent and often violent political and religious controversies. During the 1620s, the Stuart monarchs—James I (ruled 1603–1625) and his son Charles I (1625–1649)—fought constantly with the elected members of Parliament. In 1640, the conflict escalated into a bloody civil war between the king and supporters of Parliament. Finally, in 1649, the victorious parliamentarians beheaded Charles, and for almost a decade Oliver Cromwell, a brilliant general and religious reformer, governed England as Lord Protector.

The unrest did not end with the death of Charles I. After Cromwell's death, the Stuarts were restored to the throne (1660). But through the reigns of Charles II (1660–1685) and James II (1685–1688), the political turmoil continued. When the authoritarian James openly favored his fellow Catholics, the nation rose up in the so-called **Glorious Revolution** (1688), sent him into permanent exile, and placed his staunchly Protestant daughter, Mary, and son-in-law, William, on the throne.

Glorious Revolution Replacement of James II by William and Mary as English monarchs in 1688, marking the beginning of constitutional monarchy in Britain. American colonists celebrated this moment as a victory for the rule of law over despotism.

Political turmoil, religious persecution, and economic insecurity determined the flow of emigration. Men and women thought more seriously about living in the New World at such times. Ever-changing conditions in England help explain the diversity of American settlement.

Regardless of when they came, the colonists carried with them a bundle of ideas, beliefs, and assumptions that shaped the way they viewed their new environment. The New World tested and sometimes transformed their values but never destroyed them. The different subcultures that emerged in America were determined largely by the interaction between these values and such physical elements as climate, crops, and soil. The Chesapeake, the New England Colonies, the Middle Colonies, and the Carolinas formed distinct regional identities that persisted long after the first settlers had passed from the scene.

The Chesapeake: Dreams of Wealth

The Roanoke debacle raised questions about America's promise, but with the aid of visionaries such as Richard Hakluyt, the dream persisted. Writers insisted that there were profits to be made in the New World. In addition, goods from America would supply England with raw materials that it would otherwise be forced to purchase from European rivals—Holland, France, and Spain. The three motives of making money, helping England, and annoying Catholic Spain constituted a powerful incentive. Shortly after James I ascended the throne, the settlers were given an opportunity to test their theories in the Chesapeake colonies of Virginia and Maryland.

Entrepreneurs in Virginia

Money had been an early obstacle to colonization. The **joint-stock company** removed the barrier. A business organization in which scores of people could invest without fear of bankruptcy, it proved very successful. A person could purchase a share of stock at a stated price and at the end of several years could anticipate recovering the initial investment plus a portion of whatever profits the company had made. Within a very short time, some of the enterprises were able to amass large amounts of capital, enough to finance a new colony. Virginia was the first such venture.

joint-stock company Business enterprise that enabled investors to pool money for commercial trading activity and funding for sustaining colonies.

On April 10, 1606, James I issued a charter authorizing the London Company under the dynamic leadership of Sir Thomas Smythe to establish plantations in Virginia. Although the boundaries mentioned in the charter were vague, the London Company promptly renamed itself the Virginia Company and set out to find the treasure that Hakluyt had promised. In December 1606, under the command of Captain John Smith, the *Susan Constant,* the *Godspeed,* and the *Discovery,* with 104 men and boys aboard, sailed for America. The land the voyagers found was lush and well watered, with "faire meadowes and goodly tall trees."

They soon found something else—death and dissension. The low-lying ground on which they set up their base was 30 miles up the James River on a marshy peninsula they named Jamestown. It proved to be a disease-ridden death trap; even the

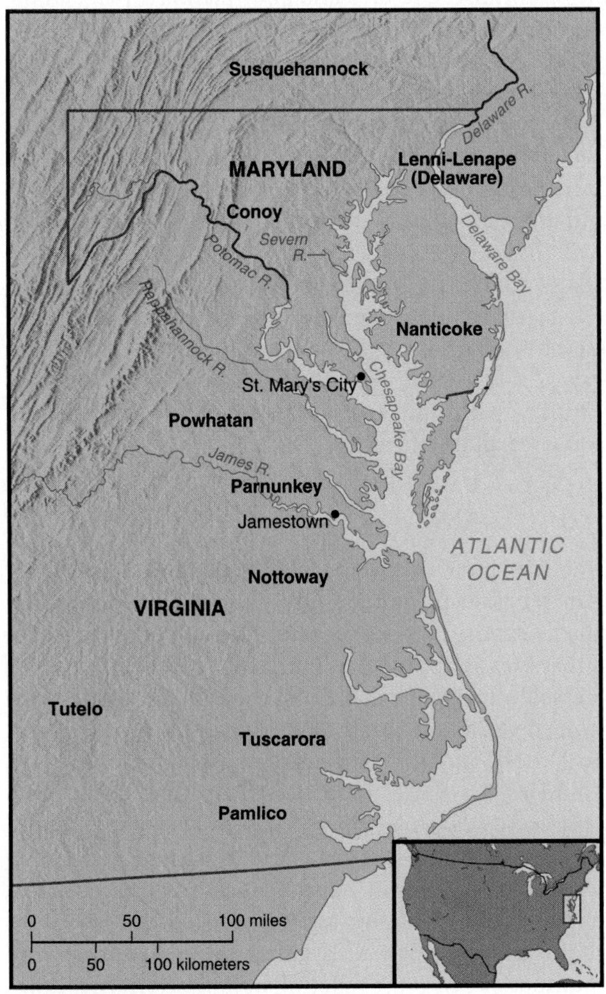

CHESAPEAKE COLONIES, 1640 *The many deep rivers that flowed into the Chesapeake Bay provided scattered English planters with a convenient transportation system, linking them directly to European markets.* ❖

drinking water was contaminated with salt. However, a peninsula was easier to defend, and they feared a surprise attack more than sickness.

Almost instantly, the colonists began quarreling. Tales of beaches strewn with rubies and diamonds had lured them to Virginia. Once there, instead of cooperating for the common good—guarding the palisade or farming—each individual pursued personal interests. Meanwhile, disease, hostile Indians, and then starvation ravaged the hapless settlers.

Had it not been for Captain John Smith, Virginia might have gone the way of Roanoke. Smith told tales of fighting the Turks and being saved from certain death by various beautiful women, claims that modern historians have largely verified. In Virginia, Smith brought order out of anarchy. He traded with the Indians for food, mapped the Chesapeake Bay, and was even rescued from execution by a precocious Indian princess, Pocahontas. After seizing control of the ruling council in 1608, he instituted a tough military discipline, forcing the lazy to work and breathing life back into the dying colony.

Leaders of the Virginia Company in London soon recognized the need to reform the entire enterprise. A new charter in 1609 granted the company the right to make all commercial and political decisions affecting the colonists. Moreover, in an effort to obtain scarce capital, the original partners opened the joint-stock company to the general public. The company sponsored a spirited publicity campaign; pamphlets and sermons extolled the colony's potential and exhorted patriotic English citizens to invest in the enterprise.

This burst of energy came to nothing. Bad luck and poor planning plagued the Virginia Company. A ship carrying settlers and supplies went aground in the Caribbean; the governor, Lord De La Warr, postponed his departure for America; and Captain Smith suffered a debilitating accident and had to return to England. As a result, between 1609 and 1611, the remaining settlers lacked capable leadership. Food supplies grew short. The terrible winter of 1609–1610—termed the "starving time"—drove a few desperate colonists to cannibalism. Smith reported that one crazed settler killed, salted, and ate parts of his wife before the murder was discovered. Many people lost their will to live.

Governor De La Warr finally arrived in June 1610. He and the deputy governors who succeeded him ruled by martial law. Men and women marched to work by the beat of the drum. These extreme measures saved the colony, but Virginia did not flourish. In 1616, the year profits were to be distributed to shareholders, the company hovered near bankruptcy, with only a vast expanse of unsurveyed land 3000 miles from London to show for all its efforts.

"Stinking Weed"

The solution to Virginia's problems grew in the vacant lots of Jamestown. Only Indians cultivated tobacco—for religious purposes—until John Rolfe realized that this local weed might be a valuable export crop. Rolfe, who married Pocahontas, developed a milder tobacco leaf that greatly appealed to European smokers.

Virginians suddenly possessed a means to make money. Tobacco was easy to grow, and settlers who had avoided work now threw themselves into its production with single-minded diligence. James I initially considered smoking immoral and unhealthy; he changed his mind as the duties he collected on tobacco imports mounted.

House of Burgesses An elective representative assembly in colonial Virginia. It was the first example of representative government in the English colonies.

The Virginia Company in 1618 launched one last effort to transform Virginia into a profitable enterprise, promising a series of reforms, including relaxation of martial law and establishment of a representative assembly called the **House of Burgesses.** Sir Edwin Sandys (pronounced Sands), a gifted entrepreneur, led the faction of stockholders who pumped life into the faltering organization, encouraging private investors to develop their own estates in Virginia. Sandys even intro-

❖ A Look at the Past ❖

Armor

The earliest English settlers to Virginia may have come with insufficient food and too few practical tools, but they did supply themselves with arms and armor. Colonizing North America provided opportunity for individual success as well as a way to advance England's imperial and strategic interests. Armor like this breastplate recovered from James Fort reveals how carefully the settlers prepared in advance for military combat. Could the anticipated enemy have been other Europeans such as the Spanish? If so, why might they have attacked Jamestown in its infancy? Would such heavy armor have offered much protection against the weapons of Indian warriors?

duced a new method for distributing land. Colonists who paid their own way to Virginia were guaranteed a **headright,** a 50-acre lot for which they paid only a small annual rent. Additional headrights were granted to the adventurers for each servant that they brought to the colony. This procedure enabled planters to build up huge estates with dependent labor, a land system that persisted long after the company's collapse. Headrights were awarded not to the newly freed servant, but to the great planters who had borne the cost of the servant's transportation to the New World and paid for food and clothing during the indenture. And even though **indentured servants** were promised their own land at the moment of freedom, they were most often cheated, becoming members of a growing, disaffected landless class in seventeenth-century Virginia.

headright System of land distribution through which settlers were granted a 50-acre plot of land from the colonial government for each servant or dependent they transported to the New World. The system encouraged the recruitment of a large servile labor force.

indentured servants Individuals who agreed to serve a master for a set number of years in exchange for the cost of boat transport to America. Indentured servitude was the dominant form of labor in the Chesapeake colonies before slavery.

Sandys had only just begun. He also urged the settlers to diversify their economy. He envisioned colonists busily producing iron and tar, silk and glass, sugar and cotton, as well as tobacco. To finance such a huge project, Sandys relied on a lottery. The final element in the grand scheme was people. Sandys sent thousands of hopeful settlers to Virginia, newcomers swept up by the same hopes as the original colonists of 1607.

Time of Reckoning

Between 1619 and 1622, colonists arrived in Virginia in record numbers. Most of the 3570 individuals who emigrated to the colony during those years were single males in their teens or early twenties. Most of them came as indentured servants. In exchange for transportation across the Atlantic, they agreed to serve a master for a stated number of years. The younger the servant, the longer he or she was expected to serve. In return, the master promised to give the laborers proper care and, at the

This tobacco label advertises Virginia's valuable export—tobacco. Despite King James's initial attitude toward the "stinking weed," once the government saw that tobacco made a profit, it dropped its moral criticism of the American crop. ❖

conclusion of their contracts, to provide them with tools and clothes according to "the custom of the country."

Since the Virginia masters needed strong servants able to do heavy field work, young males were preferred. Thus the gender ratio in Virginia was dramatically skewed. In the early decades, men outnumbered women by as much as six to one. Even if a man lived to the end of his indenture, he could not realistically expect to start a family of his own. Moreover, servants were often treated harshly. They were sold, traded, even gambled away in games of chance. It does not require much imagination to see that a society that tolerated such an exploitative labor system might later embrace slavery.

Most Virginians did not live long enough to worry about marrying and starting a family. Between 1618 and 1622, perhaps three out of every four persons in Virginia died. Contagious diseases killed the most. Salt poisoning also took a toll. And on Good Friday, March 22, 1622, the local Indians slew 347 settlers in a well-coordinated surprise attack. Those who survived must have lived with a sense of impermanence and a desire to escape Virginia with a little money before they, too, met an early death.

On both sides of the Atlantic, people wondered who should be blamed for the debacle. The burden of responsibility lay with the Virginia Company. Neither food nor shelter awaited the settlers when they arrived in Virginia. Weakened by the long sea voyage, the malnourished colonists quickly succumbed to contagious diseases.

Officials in Virginia also shared the guilt. Their greed caused them to overlook both the common good and the public defenses. Jamestown took on the characteristics of a boom town. Unrestrained self-advancement was the dominant feature of this highly individualistic, competitive society.

In 1624, King James took charge, dissolving the bankrupt enterprise and finally transforming Virginia into a royal colony. He appointed a governor and a council but made no provision for the continuation of Virginia's representative assembly. Even without the king's authorization, however, the House of Burgesses gathered annually, and in 1639, James's successor, Charles I, belatedly recognized its existence.

Charles had no choice. The colonists who served on the council or in the assembly were strong-willed, ambitious men. Having survived privation, disease, and Native American attacks, they were single-mindedly determined to get rich and had no intention of surrendering their control over local affairs. Governors who opposed the council did so at considerable personal risk. Nor was Charles, encountering his own problems at home, much disposed to intervene. In 1634, the assembly divided the colony into eight counties, each of which was governed by a justice of the peace. The "county court"—as these officers were called—remained the center of Virginia's social, political, and commercial life long after the American Revolution.

The changes in government had little impact on the character of daily life in Virginia. The isolated tobacco plantations that dotted Virginia's many navigable rivers were the focus of the settlers' lives. This dispersed pattern of settlement retarded the development of institutions such as schools and churches. And for more than a century, Jamestown was the only place that could reasonably be called a town.

Maryland: A Troubled Refuge for Catholics

Maryland's roots lay not in a wild scramble for wealth but in a nobleman's desire to create a sanctuary for England's persecuted Catholics. The driving force behind the settlement of Maryland was Sir George Calvert, later known as Lord Baltimore. Well educated, charming, ambitious, and from an excellent family, he became a favorite of James I. Although for a time he kept his religious beliefs private, he showed great interest in the progress of Virginia and New England. By the late 1620s, after publicly declaring himself a Catholic, Calvert longed to establish a colony of his own.

On June 30, 1632, Charles I granted George Calvert's son, Cecilius, a charter for a colony to be located on the Chesapeake Bay, north of Virginia. George died while the negotiations were in progress, but his vision shaped the character of the new settlement, named "Mariland, in honor of the Queene." For his part, Charles wanted to halt the southward spread of Dutch influence from New Netherland and regarded Baltimore's project as a cheap and convenient way to do so.

The charter itself is an odd document, part medieval and part modern. Lord Baltimore held absolute authority over the colonists. He was as powerful in his colony as a lord on a feudal estate. As proprietor, Baltimore owned the land outright, but he subdivided it into manors where landed aristocrats could establish their own courts of law. The more land a person owned, the more privileges that person enjoyed in the government.

Embedded in this feudal scheme was a concept that broke boldly with the past. Unlike the European leaders of his day, Baltimore championed religious freedom for all people who accepted the divinity of Christ. Even though Maryland's early settlers—Catholics as well as Protestants—occasionally persecuted each other, Baltimore's commitment to toleration never flagged.

In 1634, the first of Maryland's immigrants landed at St. Mary's, near the mouth of the Potomac River. As noted, Maryland attracted both Catholics and Protestants, and for a brief period, the two groups seemed capable of living in peace. Unlike the Virginia settlers, these early colonists were not threatened by starvation, and they maintained friendly relations with the local Indians.

Lord Baltimore's feudal system never took root in Chesapeake soil. People simply refused to play the social roles that he had assigned. Most important, the elected assembly, which first met in 1635, insisted on exercising traditional parliamentary privileges that eventually undermined Baltimore's authority. With each passing year, the proprietor's absolute control over the men and women of Maryland progressively weakened.

Despite Lord Baltimore's efforts to establish liberty of conscience, Maryland's gravest problems grew out of the colonists' religious intolerance. Aggressive Jesuits frightened Protestants, who in turn tried to unseat the proprietor on the grounds that he and his chief advisers were Catholic. In fact, Baltimore's experiment led to chronic instability during the first thirty years after settlement. Violence, not toleration, resulted from his efforts to put freedom of conscience into practice.

In this troubled sanctuary, planters cultivated tobacco on dispersed riverfront plantations. No towns developed. The tobacco culture permeated every aspect of society. A steady stream of indentured servants supplied the plantations with dependent laborers until they were replaced, at the end of the seventeenth century, by slaves. Both Maryland and Virginia were peopled by settlers occupied primarily by their own personal concerns.

Reforming England in America

Legend surrounds the Pilgrims. These brave refugees crossed the cold Atlantic in search of religious liberty, signed a democratic compact aboard the *Mayflower*, landed at Plymouth Rock, and gave us our Thanksgiving Day. As with most mythic accounts, this one contains only a core of truth.

The Pilgrims were not crusaders who set out to change the world. They were humble English farmers from Scrooby Manor. They believed that the Church of

England retained too many traces of its Catholic origin, that its very rituals compromised God's true believers. And so, in the early years of the reign of James I, the Scrooby congregation formally left the state church. Like others who followed this logic, they were called Separatists. Because English statute required citizens to attend established Church of England services, the Scrooby Separatists moved to Holland in 1608–1609 rather than compromise their souls.

The Netherlands provided the Separatists with a good home—too good. They feared that their distinct identity was threatened, that their children were becoming Dutch. By 1617, a portion of the Scrooby congregation vowed to sail to America. A group of English investors who were only marginally interested in Separatism underwrote their trip. In 1620, they sailed for Virginia aboard the *Mayflower.*

Hardship soon shattered the voyagers' optimism. Because of an error in navigation, the Pilgrims landed not in Virginia but in New England, where their land patent from the Virginia Company had no validity. Without a patent, the colonists possessed no authorization to form a civil government, a serious matter, in that some of the sailors who were not Pilgrims threatened mutiny. To preserve the struggling community from anarchy, forty-one men signed an agreement to "covenant and combine our selves together into a civil body politick."

Mayflower Compact Agreement among the Pilgrims aboard the Mayflower in 1620 to create a civil government at Plymouth Colony.

Unfortunately, this **Mayflower Compact,** as the voluntary agreement was called, could not ward off disease and hunger. During the first months at Plymouth, death claimed approximately half of the 102 people who had initially set out from England. Moreover, debts contracted in the mother country severely burdened the new colony. Through strength of will and self-sacrifice, their elected leader, William Bradford, persuaded frightened men and women that they could survive in America.

Bradford had a lot of help. Almost anyone who has heard of the Plymouth Colony knows of Squanto, a Patuxt Indian who welcomed the first Pilgrims in excellent English. In 1614, unscrupulous adventurers had kidnapped Squanto and sold him in Spain as a slave. Somehow this resourceful man escaped bondage, making his way to London, where a group of merchants who owned land in Newfoundland taught him to speak English. They apparently hoped that he would deliver moving public testimonials about the desirability of moving to the New World. In any case, Squanto returned to the Plymouth area just before the Pilgrims arrived. Squanto joined Massasoit, a local Native American leader, in teaching the Pilgrims much about hunting and agriculture, a debt that Bradford freely acknowledged. Although evidence for the so-called "First Thanksgiving" is extremely sketchy, it is certain that without Native American support the Europeans would have starved.

The Pilgrims never became very prosperous, but they did build a humble farm community and practice their Separatist beliefs. Although they experimented with commercial fishing and the fur trade, most families relied on mixed husbandry, raising grain and livestock. Never a populous colony, in 1691, Plymouth was absorbed into its thriving, larger neighbor, Massachusetts Bay.

"The Great Migration"

Puritan Member of a reformed Protestant sect in Europe and America that insisted on removing all vestiges of Catholicism from popular religious practice.

During the seventeenth century, Puritan zeal transformed the face of England and America. The popular image of a **Puritan**—a carping critic who condemned liquor and sex, dressed in drab clothes, and minded the neighbors' business—is based on a fundamental misunderstanding of the actual nature of Puritanism. Puritans were radical reformers committed to far-reaching institutional change, not Victorian-type prudes. Not only did they found several American colonies, but they also sparked the English civil war and the bold new thinking about popular representation that accompanied it.

The Puritan movement came out of the Protestant Reformation. It accepted the notion that an omnipotent God predestined some people to salvation and damned others throughout eternity (see Chapter 1). Puritans constantly monitored themselves for signs of grace, hints that God had in fact placed them among his "elect." And their attempt to live as if they *were* saved—that is, according to the Scriptures—became the driving engine for reform on this earth.

They saw their duty clearly: to eradicate unscriptural elements and practices from the Church of England; to campaign vigorously against the sins of sexual license and drunkenness; and to inveigh against alliances with Papist (Catholic) states. Puritans were more combative than the Pilgrims had been. They wanted to purify the English Church from within, and Separatism held little appeal for them.

From the Puritan perspective, the early Stuarts, James I and Charles I, seemed unconcerned about the spiritual state of the nation. The monarchs, Puritans believed, courted Catholic alliances and showed no interest in purifying the Church of England. As long as Parliament met, Puritan voters in the various boroughs and counties throughout the nation elected men sympathetic to their point of view. These outspoken representatives criticized royal policies. And because of their defiance, Charles decided in 1629 to rule England without Parliament. Four years later, he named as archbishop of Canterbury the Puritans' most conspicuous clerical opponent, William Laud. The last doors of reform slammed shut; the corruption remained.

John Winthrop, the future governor of Massachusetts Bay, was caught up in these events. A man of modest wealth and education, he believed that God would punish England, although he was confident that the Lord would provide shelter somewhere for his Puritan flock. Other Puritans, some wealthier and better connected than Winthrop, reached similar conclusions about England's future. They turned their attention to the possibility of establishing a colony in America. On March 4, 1629, their Massachusetts Bay Company obtained a charter directly from the king.

The king may have believed that Massachusetts Bay would be simply another commercial venture, but Winthrop and his associates knew better. In the Cambridge Agreement (August 1629), they pledged to emigrate, knowing that their charter allowed the company to hold meetings wherever the stockholders desired, *even in America.* And if they were in America, the king could not easily interfere in their affairs.

"A City on a Hill"

The Winthrop fleet departed England in March 1630. By the end of the year, almost two thousand people had arrived in Massachusetts Bay, and before the Great Migration concluded in the early 1640s, almost sixteen thousand men and women would arrive in the new Puritan colony.

Unlike the early immigrants to Virginia and Maryland, they moved to Massachusetts Bay as nuclear families: fathers, mothers, and their dependent children. This guaranteed a more balanced gender ratio than in the Chesapeake colonies. Most significantly, these colonists thrived. In fact, their life expectancy compares favorably to that of modern Americans. This remarkable phenomenon alleviated the emotional shock of long-distance migration.

Their common sense of purpose provided another source of strength and stability. God, they insisted, had formed a special covenant with them. On his part, the Lord expected them to live according to Scripture, to reform the church—in other words, to create a "city on a hill" that would stand as a beacon of righteousness for the rest of the Christian world. If everyone kept the covenant, the colonists could expect peace and prosperity. They had no doubt that they would transform their religious vision into a social reality.

They arrived in Massachusetts Bay without a precise plan for their church, other than that they refused to separate formally from the Church of England.

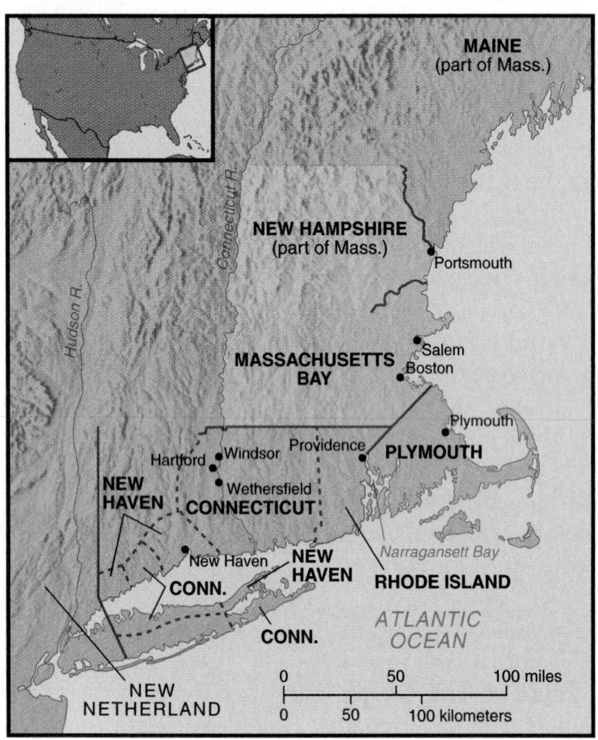

NEW ENGLAND COLONIES, 1650 *The early settlers quickly carved up New England. New Haven briefly flourished as a separate colony before being taken over by Connecticut in 1662. Long Island later became part of New York; Plymouth was absorbed into Massachusetts, and in 1677 New Hampshire became a separate colony.* ❖

Reform, not separation, was their mission. Gradually, they came to accept a form of church government known as Congregationalism. Under this system, each congregation was independent of outside interference. The people (known as "saints") *were* the church. They pledged as a body to uphold God's law. In Congregational churches, full members—men and women who testified that they were among the Lord's elect—selected a minister, punished errant members, and determined matters of theology. This loose structure held together for more than a century.

In creating a civil government, the Bay Colony faced a particularly difficult challenge. Its charter allowed the investors in a joint-stock company to set up a business organization. When the settlers arrived in America, however, company leaders—men like Winthrop—moved quickly to transform the commercial structure into a colonial government. In 1631, they expanded the franchise to include all adult males who had become members of a Congregational church. During the 1630s, at least 40 percent of the adult male population could vote in elections—a percentage far above the standards in England. These "freemen" elected their own governor, magistrates, local representatives, and even military officers.

Two popular misconceptions about the government should be dispelled. It was neither a democracy nor a theocracy. Magistrates ruled in the name of the electorate but believed that their responsibilities as rulers were to God. And Congregational ministers possessed no formal political authority; they could not even hold civil office.

Unlike in Virginia, the town, rather than the county, became the center of public life in the Bay Colony. Groups of men and women voluntarily covenanted together to live by certain rules. They constructed their communities around a meetinghouse where church services and town meetings were held. Each townsman received land sufficient to build a house and to support a family. The house lots were clustered around the meetinghouse; the fields were located on the village perimeter. Land was free, but villagers were obliged to contribute to the minister's salary, to pay local and colony taxes, and to serve in the town militia.

Limits of Religious Dissent

The settlers of Massachusetts Bay managed to live in peace. When differences arose, as they often did, the courts settled matters. People believed in a rule of law, as was illustrated in 1648 when the colonial legislature drew up the *Laws and Liberties,* the first alphabetized code of law printed in English. This code clearly stated the colonists' rights and responsibilities as citizens of the commonwealth. It engendered public trust in government and discouraged magistrates from the arbitrary exercise of authority.

The most serious challenges to Puritan orthodoxy in Massachusetts Bay came from two remarkable individuals. The first, Roger Williams, arrived in 1631. He was well liked and immediately attracted a body of loyal followers. But he preached extreme Separatism. Moreover, he questioned the validity of the colony's charter, since the king had not first purchased the land from the Indians. Williams also insisted that the civil rulers of Massachusetts had no business punishing settlers for their religious beliefs. The magistrates believed that Williams threatened the social and religious foundation of the colony, and in 1636, they banished him. Williams then bought a tract of land from the Narragansett Indians and founded the Providence settlement in Rhode Island.

The magistrates of the Bay Colony rightly concluded that Anne Hutchinson posed an even greater threat to the peace of the commonwealth. Intelligent and outspoken, she questioned the authority and theology of some of the most respected ministers of the colony. As justification for her own views, known as **Antinomianism,** she cited divine inspiration, rather than the Bible or the clergy. In other words, Hutchinson's teachings could not be tested by Scripture, a position that Puritan leaders regarded as dangerously subjective. Without clear, external standards, one person's truth was as valid as that of anyone else's, and from Winthrop's perspective, Hutchinson's teachings invited civil and religious anarchy. But her challenge to authority was not simply theological. As a woman, her aggressive speech sparked a deeply misogynist response from the colony's male leaders.

Antinomianism Religious belief rejecting traditional moral law as unnecessary for Christians who possess saving grace and affirming that an individual could experience divine revelation and salvation without the assistance of formally trained clergy.

One early Puritan meetinghouse was the Old Ship Meetinghouse in Hingham, Massachusetts. Its name derives from its interior design, which resembles the hull of a ship. The oldest wooden church in the United States, it could accommodate about seven hundred people, nearly the entire population of seventeenth-century Hingham. Members of the congregation would have sat on backless wooden benches in the unheated building, listening to the preacher address them, not from an altar but from an undecorated square speaking box. ❖

When she described some of the leading ministers as unconverted men, the General Court intervened. Hutchinson was cross-examined for two days in 1637, but she knew Scripture too well to be easily tripped up. Then she made a slip that led to her undoing. She stated that what she knew of God came "by an immediate revelation." She had heard a voice. This "heretical" declaration fulfilled the worst fears of the colony's rulers, and they were relieved to exile Hutchinson and her followers to Rhode Island.

Mobility and Division

Massachusetts Bay spawned four new colonies, three of which survived to the American Revolution. New Hampshire became a separate colony in 1677, although its population grew slowly, and for much of the colonial period it remained economically dependent on Massachusetts.

Far more people were drawn to the fertile lands of the Connecticut River Valley. Populated by settlers from the Bay Colony under the ministry of Thomas Hooker, the valley took on the religious and cultural characteristics of Massachusetts. In 1639, representatives from the Connecticut towns drafted the Fundamental Orders, a blueprint for civil government; in 1662, Charles II awarded the colony a charter of its own. That same year, Connecticut absorbed the New Haven colony, a struggling Puritan settlement on Long Island Sound.

Rhode Island experienced a wholly different history. From the beginning, it drew people of a highly independent turn of mind. One Dutch visitor uncharitably characterized it as "the receptacle of all sorts of riff-raff people." However, the colony's broad toleration attracted many men and women who held unorthodox religious beliefs.

Toleration, however, did not mean cooperation. Villagers fought over land and schemed with outside speculators to divide the tiny colony into even smaller pieces. Even a royal charter obtained in 1663 did not calm the political turmoil. For most of the seventeenth century, colonywide government existed in name only. But despite all the bickering, Rhode Island's population grew, and the colony's commerce flourished.

Diversity in the Middle Colonies

New York, New Jersey, Pennsylvania, and Delaware were founded for quite different reasons. William Penn, for example, envisioned a Quaker sanctuary; the duke of York worried chiefly about his own income. Despite the founders' intentions, however, some common characteristics emerged. Each colony developed a strikingly heterogeneous population of men and women of different ethnic and religious backgrounds. This cultural diversity became a major influence on the economic, political, and ecclesiastical institutions of the Middle Colonies and foreshadowed later American society.

Anglo-Dutch Rivalry on the Hudson

By the early decades of the seventeenth century, the Dutch had established themselves as Europe's most aggressive traders. Holland's merchant fleet was second to none, trading in Asia, Africa, and America. While searching for the elusive Northwest Passage in 1609, Henry Hudson, an English explorer employed by a Dutch company, sailed up the river that bears his name and claimed the area for Holland. Hudson's sponsors, the Dutch West India Company, established two permanent settlements, Fort Orange (Albany) and New Amsterdam (New York City) in the colony of New Netherland.

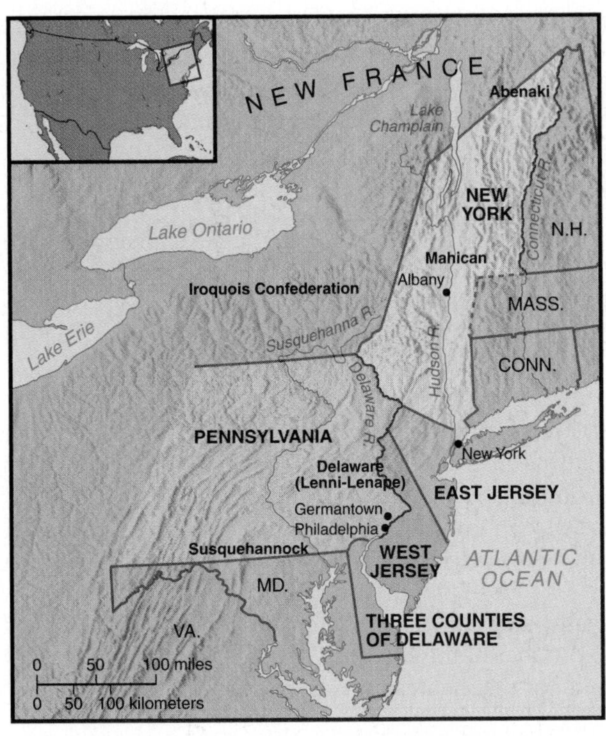

MIDDLE COLONIES, 1685 *Until the Revolution, the Iroquois blocked European expansion into western New York. The Jerseys initially attracted English and Irish Quakers, who soon were joined by thousands of Protestant Irish and Germans.* ❖

The first Dutch settlers in New Netherland were not actually colonists. Rather they were salaried employees of the company, who were expected to spend most of their time gathering animal fur pelts. They received no land for their efforts. Needless to say, this arrangement attracted relatively few Dutch immigrants.

Although the colony's population was small, only 270 in 1628, it contained an extraordinary ethnic mix. By the 1640s, Finns, Germans, and Swedes lived there, along with a sizable community of free blacks. Another contribution to the cacophony of languages was added by New England Puritans who moved to New Netherland to stake out farms on Long Island.

The company sent a succession of directors-general to oversee and govern. Without exception, these men were temperamentally unsuited to govern an American colony. They were autocratic, corrupt, and, above all, inept. The Long Island Puritans complained bitterly about the absence of any sort of representative government, and none of the colonists felt much loyalty to the trading company.

In August 1664, the Dutch lost their tenuous hold on New Netherland. The English crown, eager to score an easy victory over a commercial rival, dispatched a fleet of warships to New Amsterdam (renamed New York City). No real fighting was needed. Although the last director-general, Peter Stuyvesant (1647–1664), urged resistance, the settlers decided otherwise. They accepted the Articles of Capitulation, a generous agreement that allowed Dutch nationals to remain in the province and to retain their property.

Charles II had already granted his brother, James, the duke of York, a charter for the newly captured territory and much else besides. He became absolute proprietor of Maine, Nantucket, Martha's Vineyard, and land extending from the Connecticut River to Delaware Bay. The duke was no more receptive to the idea of a representative government than the Dutch trading company had been; to appease the complaining colonists, the governor, Colonel Richard Nicolls, drew up a legal code known as the Duke's Laws. It guaranteed religious toleration and created local governments.

There was no provision, however, for an elected assembly. Nor was there much harmony in the colony. The Dutch, for example, continued to speak their own language, worship in their own churches (as Dutch Reformed Calvinists), and eye their English neighbors with suspicion. In fact, the colony seemed little different from what it had been under the Dutch West India Company: a loose collection of independent communities ruled by an ineffectual central government.

Confusion in New Jersey

Only three months after receiving a charter for New York, the duke made a terrible mistake—something this stubborn, humorless man was quite prone to do. He awarded the land situated between the Hudson and Delaware Rivers to two courtiers, John, Lord Berkeley, and Sir George Carteret. This colony was named New Jersey in honor of Carteret's birthplace, the isle of Jersey in the English Channel.

The duke's impulsive act bred confusion. Before learning of James's decision, the governor of New York allowed migrants from New England to take up farms west of the Hudson River, promising them an opportunity to establish an elected assembly and liberty of conscience in exchange for the payment of a small annual quitrent to the duke. Berkeley and Carteret recruited colonists on similar terms. The new proprietors assumed, of course, that they would receive the rent money.

The result was chaos. Legally, only James could set up a colonial government or authorize an assembly. But knowledge of the law failed to quiet the controversy, and through it all, the duke showed not the slightest interest in the peace and welfare of the people of New Jersey.

Matters were further complicated in 1674 when Berkeley tired of the venture and sold his proprietary rights to a group of surprisingly quarrelsome Quakers. The colony was legally divided into East and West Jersey, but neither half prospered. When the West Jersey proprietors went bankrupt in 1702, the crown mercifully reunited the two Jerseys into a single royal colony.

In 1700, the population of New Jersey amounted to approximately fourteen thousand. Its residents lived on scattered, often isolated farms; villages of more than a few hundred people were rare. And as in New York, the ethnic and religious diversity of the settlers was striking. Yet the colonists of New Jersey somehow managed to live together peaceably.

Quakers in America

Quakers Members of a radical religious group, formally known as the Society of Friends, that rejected formal theology and stressed each person's "Inner Light," a spiritual guide to righteousness.

Quakers founded Pennsylvania. This radical religious group, formally known as the Society of Friends, gained its informal name from the English civil authorities' disparaging observation that its members "tremble at the word of the Lord." George Fox (1624–1691) was the tireless spokesman of the Society of Friends. He preached that every man and woman possessed a powerful, consoling "Inner Light." This was a wonderfully liberating message, especially for persons of lower-class origin. Gone was the stigma of original sin; discarded was the notion of eternal predestination. Everyone could be saved.

Quakers practiced humility. They wore simple clothes and employed old-fashioned terms of address that set them apart from their neighbors. They were also pacifists. According to Fox, all persons were equal in the sight of the Lord, a belief that annoyed people of rank and achievement. Moreover, they refused to keep their thoughts to themselves, spreading the light throughout England, Ireland, and America. Harassment, imprisonment, and even execution failed to curtail their activities. In fact, such measures proved counterproductive, for persecution only inspired the Quakers to redouble their efforts.

William Penn lived according to the Inner Light, a commitment that led eventually to the founding of Pennsylvania. He was a complex man: an athletic person interested in intellectual pursuits, a visionary capable of making pragmatic decisions, and an aristocrat whose religious beliefs involved him with the lower classes. Penn's religious commitment irritated his father, who hoped William would become a favorite at the Stuart court. Instead, Penn was expelled from Oxford University for holding unorthodox religious views, moved to the forefront of the Quaker movement, and even spent two years in an English jail for his beliefs.

Precisely when Penn's thoughts turned to America is not known, but in 1681, he negotiated one of the most impressive deals in the history of American real estate. Charles II awarded Penn a charter making him the sole proprietor of a vast area called Pennsylvania (literally, "Penn's woods"), a name that embarrassed the modest Quaker. The next year, Penn purchased from the duke of York the so-called Three Lower Counties that eventually became Delaware. This astute move guaranteed that Pennsylvania would have open access to the Atlantic and determined even before Philadelphia had been established that it would become a great commercial center.

Penn lost no time in launching his "Holy Experiment." His plan blended traditional notions about the privileges of a landed aristocracy with daring concepts of personal liberty. Penn guaranteed that the settlers would enjoy, among other things, liberty of conscience, freedom from persecution, no taxation without representation, and due process of law. He believed that both rich and poor had to have a voice in political affairs; neither should be able to overrule the legitimate interests of the other class. In his Frame of Government (1682), he envisioned a governor appointed by the proprietor, a provisional council responsible for initiating legislation, and an assembly that could accept or reject the bills presented to it. Penn apparently thought that the council would be filled by the colony's richest landholders and that the assembly would be peopled by the smaller landowners. It was a fanciful, clumsy structure, and the entire edifice crumbled ultimately under its own weight.

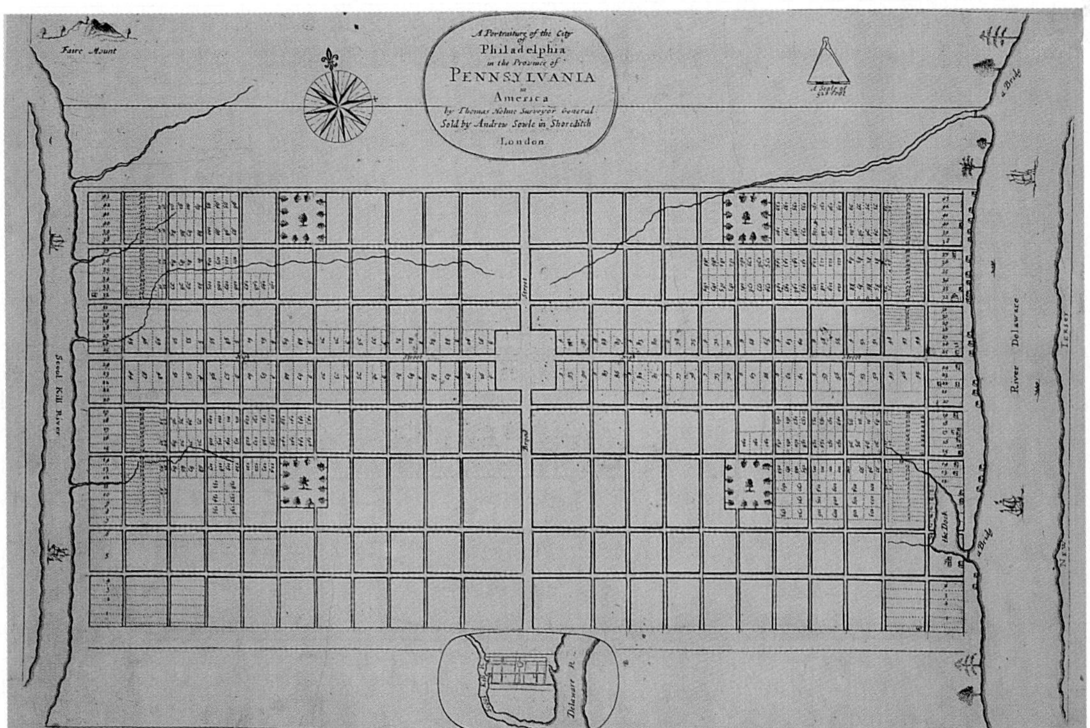

Penn's plan for Philadelphia shows the city laid out where the Scool Kill (Schuylkill) and Delaware rivers parallel each other. Four of the five public squares were intended to be parks while the fifth (at the center) was designated for public buildings. Today it is the site of Philadelphia's city hall. ❖

Penn promoted his colony aggressively throughout England, Ireland, and Germany. The response was overwhelming. People poured into Philadelphia and the surrounding area. Most of the early settlers were Quakers—Irish, Welsh, and English. But men and women from other lands soon joined the Quaker surge toward Penn's woods. One newcomer called the vessel that brought him to Philadelphia a "Noah's ark" of nationalities and religions.

Penn himself emigrated to America in 1682. His stay, however, was unexpectedly short and unhappy. The council and assembly fought over the right to initiate legislation. Wealthy Quaker merchants dominated the council, and rural settlers unconcerned about the Holy Experiment controlled the assembly. Many colonists refused to pay quitrents, and the Baltimore family claimed that much of Pennsylvania actually lay in Maryland. In 1684, to defend his charter against Baltimore's attack, Penn returned to London.

Penn did not see his colony again until 1699. By that time, the settlement had changed considerably. Although it had prospered, a contentious quality pervaded its politics. Even the Quakers split into hostile factions. As the seventeenth century closed, few colonists still shared the founder's desire to create a godly, paternalistic society.

In 1701, legal challenges in England again forced Penn to depart for the mother country. Just before he sailed, Penn signed the Charter of Liberties, a new framework of government that established a unicameral, or one-house, legislature (the only one in colonial America) and gave the representatives the right to initiate legislation. The charter also provided for the political separation of the Three Lower Counties (Delaware) from Pennsylvania, something people living in the area had demanded for years. This hastily drafted document served as Pennsylvania's constitution until the American Revolution.

His experience in America must have depressed Penn, now old and sick. In England, Penn was imprisoned for debts incurred by dishonest colonial agents, and in 1718, Pennsylvania's founder died a broken man.

Planting the Carolinas

In some ways, Carolina society seemed very similar to the one that had developed in Virginia and Maryland. In both areas, white planters forced unfree laborers to produce staple crops for a world market. But such superficial similarities masked substantial regional differences. In fact, "the South"—certainly the fabled solid South of the early nineteenth century—did not exist during the colonial period. The Carolinas, joined at a much later date by Georgia, stood apart from their Chesapeake neighbors.

Carolina owed its establishment to the restoration of the Stuarts to the English throne. Court favorites who had followed the Stuarts into exile during the civil war demanded tangible rewards for their loyalty. New York and New Jersey were obvious plums. So, too, was Carolina. On March 24, 1663, King Charles II granted Sir John Colleton and seven other courtiers a charter to the vast territory between Virginia and Florida and running west "as far as the South Seas."

Unlike so many Englishmen before them, the eight proprietors did not think of America in terms of instant wealth. Their plan involved luring settlers from established American colonies by means of an attractive land policy and such other incentives as a representative assembly, liberty of conscience, and a liberal headright system. In exchange for their privileges, they demanded only a small annual quitrent.

After dividing their grant into three distinct jurisdictions—Albermarle, Cape Fear, and Port Royal—proprietors waited for the money to roll in; to their dismay, no one seemed particularly interested in moving to the Carolina frontier. Plans for

England's Principal Mainland Colonies

Name	Original Purpose	Date of Founding	Principal Founder	Major Export	Estimated Population ca. 1700
Virginia	Commercial venture	1607	Captain John Smith	Tobacco	64,560
New Amsterdam (New York)	Commercial venture	1613 (made English colony, 1664)	Peter Stuyvesant, Duke of York	Furs, grain	19,107
Plymouth	Refuge for English Separatists	1620 (absorbed by Massachusetts, 1691)	William Bradford	Grain	Included with Massachusetts
New Hampshire	Commercial venture	1623	John Mason	Wood, naval stores	4,958
Massachusetts	Refuge for English Puritans	1628	John Winthrop	Grain, wood	55,941
Maryland	Refuge for English Catholics	1634	Lord Baltimore (George Calvert)	Tobacco	34,100
Connecticut	Expansion of Massachusetts	1635	Thomas Hooker	Grain	25,970
Rhode Island	Refuge for dissenters from Massachusetts	1636	Roger Williams	Grain	5,894
New Sweden (Delaware)	Commercial venture	1638 (included in Penn grant, 1681; given separate assembly, 1703)	Peter Minuit, William Penn	Grain	2,470
North Carolina	Commercial venture	1663	Anthony Ashley Cooper	Wood, naval stores, tobacco	10,720
South Carolina	Commercial venture	1663	Anthony Ashley Cooper	Naval stores, rice, indigo	5,720
New Jersey	Consolidation of new English territory, Quaker settlement	1664	Sir George Carteret	Grain	14,010
Pennsylvania	Refuge for English Quakers	1681	William Penn	Grain	18,950
Georgia	Discourage Spanish expansion; charity	1733	James Oglethorpe	Rice, wood, naval stores	5,200 (in 1750)

Sources: U.S. Bureau of the Census, *Historical Statistics of the United States: Colonial Times to 1970,* Washington, D.C., 1975; John J. McCusker and Russell R. Menard, *The Economy of British America, 1607–1789,* Chapel Hill, 1985.

the settlement of Cape Fear and Port Royal fell through, and the majority of the surviving proprietors gave up on Carolina.

Anthony Ashley Cooper, later known as the earl of Shaftesbury, was an exception. In 1669, he persuaded the remaining proprietors to invest their own capital in the colony. He then dispatched more than three hundred English colonists to Carolina. After a rough voyage that saw one ship destroyed by Atlantic gales, the settlers arrived at the Ashley River. Later the colony's administrative center, Charles Town (it did not become Charleston until 1783), was established at the junction of the Ashley and Cooper Rivers.

Ashley also wanted to bring order to the new society. With assistance from John Locke, the famous English philosopher (1632–1704), Ashley devised the Fundamental Constitutions of Carolina. His goal was to create a landed aristocracy that governed the colony through the Council of Nobles, a body designed to administer justice, oversee civil affairs, and initiate legislation. A parliament in which smaller landowners had a voice could accept or reject bills drafted by the council. The very poor were excluded from political activity altogether. Ashley's plans for a "balance of government" between aristocracy and democracy, however, never conformed to the realities of Carolina society, and his Council of Nobles remained a paper dream.

Before 1680, almost half the men and women who settled in the Port Royal area came from Barbados. This small Caribbean island, which produced an annual fortune in sugar, depended on slave labor. By the third quarter of the seventeenth century, Barbados had become overpopulated, and Barbadians looked to Carolina for relief. These migrants, many of whom were quite wealthy, traveled to Carolina both as individuals and as family groups. Some brought slave gangs with them. The Barbadians carved out plantations on the tributaries of the Cooper River and established themselves immediately as the colony's most powerful political faction. The society they created was closer to the slave-based plantation society they left than to any of the other English colonies.

Much of the planters' time was taken up with the search for a profitable crop. They experimented with a number of plants—tobacco, cotton, silk, and grapes. The most successful items in the early years turned out to be beef, cattle, furs, and naval stores (especially tar, used to maintain ocean vessels). It was not until the 1690s that the planters came to appreciate fully the value of rice, but once they had done so, it quickly became the colony's main staple.

Proprietary Carolina was in a constant political uproar. Barbadian settlers resisted the proprietors' policies, and the proprietors appointed a series of utterly incompetent governors. By the end of the century, the lower houses of assembly had assumed the right to initiate legislation. In 1719, the colonists overthrew the last proprietary government, and in 1729, the king created separate royal governments in North and South Carolina.

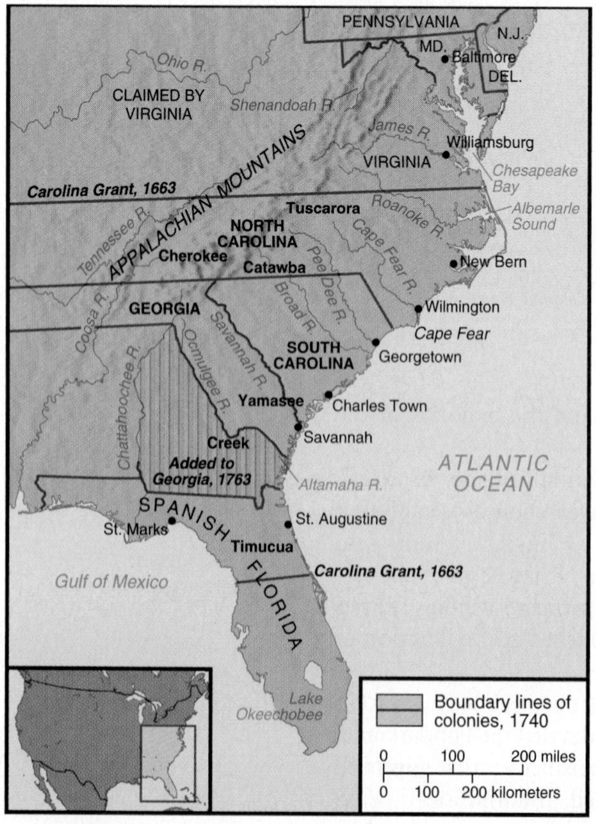

THE CAROLINAS AND GEORGIA *Caribbean sugar planters migrated to the Goose Creek area where, with knowledge supplied by African slaves, they eventually mastered rice cultivation. Poor harbors in North Carolina retarded the spread of European settlement in that region.* ❖

The Founding of Georgia

The early history of Georgia was strikingly different from that of Britain's other mainland colonies. Its settlement was really an act of aggression against Spain, a country that had as good a claim to the area as the English did. During the eighteenth century, the two nations were often at war (see Chapter 4), and South Carolinians worried that the Spaniards moving up from bases in Florida would occupy the disputed territory between Florida and the Carolina grant.

The colony owed its existence primarily to James Oglethorpe, a British general and member of Parliament who believed that he could thwart Spanish designs on the area south of Charles Town while providing a fresh start for London's debtors. Although Oglethorpe envisioned Georgia as an asylum as well as a garrison, the military aspects of his proposal were especially appealing to the leaders of the British government. In 1732, the king granted Oglethorpe and a board of trustees a charter for a new colony. The trustees living in the mother country were given complete control over Georgia politics, a condition the settlers soon found intolerable.

At first, the colony did not fare very well. Few English debtors showed any desire to move there, and the trustees provided little incentive for emigration. No settler could amass more than 500 acres of land. Moreover, land could be passed only to an eldest son, and if a planter died without a son, the holding reverted to Oglethorpe and the trustees. Slavery and rum were prohibited.

The settlers wanted more—slaves, a voice in local government, unrestricted land ownership. Oglethorpe met their demands with angry rebuffs. Eventually, however, Oglethorpe lost interest in his colonial experiment, and the trustees were

CHRONOLOGY	
1607	First English settlers arrive at Jamestown
1608–1609	Scrooby Congregation (Pilgrims) leaves England for Holland
1609–1611	"Starving time" in Virginia threatens survival of the colonists
1619	Virginia assembly, called House of Burgesses, meets for the first time ❖ First slaves sold at Jamestown
1620	Pilgrims sign the Mayflower Compact
1622	Surprise attack by local Indians devastates Virginia
1624	Dutch investors create permanent settlements along the Hudson River ❖ James I, king of England, dissolves the Virginia Company
1625	Charles I ascends the English throne
1630	John Winthrop transfers Massachusetts Bay charter to New England
1634	Colony of Maryland is founded
1638	Anne Hutchinson is exiled to Rhode Island
1639	Connecticut towns accept Fundamental Orders
1649	Charles I is executed during the English civil war
1660	Stuarts are restored to the English throne
1663	Rhode Island obtains royal charter ❖ Proprietors receive charter for Carolina
1664	English soldiers conquer New Netherland
1677	New Hampshire becomes a royal colony
1681	William Penn granted patent for his Holy Experiment

then forced to compromise their principles. In 1738, they eliminated all restrictions on the amount of land a person could own and allowed women to inherit land. Slaves came next, then rum. In 1751, the trustees gave up on what had become a hard-drinking, slave-holding plantation society and returned Georgia to the king. That same year, the king authorized an assembly. But even with these social and political changes, Georgia attracted very few new settlers.

Conclusion: Living with Diversity

The seventeenth-century English colonies had little in common beyond their allegiance to the king. A contemporary visitor could find along the Atlantic Coast a spectrum of settlements, from the almost feudal hierarchy of Carolina to the visionary paternalism of Pennsylvania to the Puritan commonwealth of Massachusetts Bay. The diversity of English colonization needs to be emphasized precisely because it is so easy to overlook. Even though the colonists eventually banded together and fought for independence and established a federal government, persistent differences separated New Englanders from Virginians, Pennsylvanians from Carolinians.

Key Terms

Glorious Revolution, p. 22
joint-stock company, p. 23
House of Burgesses, p. 24
headright, p. 25
indentured servants, p. 25
Mayflower Compact, p. 28
Puritan, p. 28
Antinomianism, p. 31
Quakers, p. 34

Recommended Reading

The literature of seventeenth-century English settlement in North America is immense. To comprehend better the diversity of American colonial experience, it is wise to start with the society from which the settlers migrated. Two good introductions to England's participation in an Atlantic World are David Armitage and Michael J. Braddick, eds., *The British Atlantic World, 1500–1800* (2002) and Nicholas Canny, ed., *The Oxford History of the British Empire, vol. 1, The Origins of Empire: English Overseas Enterprise from the Beginning to the Close of the Seventeenth Century* (1998). The best single work on Puritanism remains Perry Miller, *The New England Mind: From Colony to Province* (1956). David D. Hall explores popular religious practice in New England in *Worlds of Wonder, Days of Judgment: Popular Religious Belief in Early New England* (1989). Also valuable is Michael P. Winship, *Making Heretics: Militant Protestantism and Free Grace in Massachusetts, 1636–1641* (2002). On the challenge of creating new social and political institutions in early Massachusetts, see Kenneth A. Lockridge, *A New England Town: The First Hundred Years* (1970). Two brilliantly original studies of the founding of Virginia are Edmund S. Morgan, *American Slavery, American Freedom: The Ordeal of Colonial Virginia* (1975) and Kathleen M. Brown, *Good Wives, Nasty Wenches, and Anxious Patriarchs: Gender, Race, and Power in Colonial Virginia* (1996). T. H. Breen compares the development of seventeenth-century New England and the Chesapeake in *Puritans and Adventurers: Change and Persistence in Early America* (1980). The forces that drove migration to the New World during this period are the subject of David Cressy's *Coming Over: Migration and Communication Between England and New England in the Seventeenth Century* (1987) and James Horn's, *Adapting to a New World: English Society in the Seventeenth-Century Chesapeake* (1994). On the rituals of public execution, see Daniel A. Cohen, *Pillars of Salt, Monuments of Grace: New England Crime Literature and the Origins of American Popular Culture, 1674–1860* (1993). Useful investigations of the founding of New York and Pennsylvania are Gary B. Nash, *Quakers and Politics: Pennsylvania 1681–1726* (1968); Richard S. Dunn and Mary Maples Dunn, eds., *The World of William Penn* (1986); and Joyce D. Goodfriend, *Before the Melting Pot: Society and Culture in Colonial New York City, 1664–1730* (1995).

For a list of additional titles related to this chapter's topics, please see http://www.ablongman.com/divine.

Suggested Web Sites

The Plymouth Colony Archive Project at the University of Virginia

http://etext.virginia.edu/users/deetz
This site contains comprehensive and fairly extensive information about late seventeenth-century Plymouth Colony.

Jamestown Rediscovery

http://www.apva.org.
This site, mounted the Association for the Preservation of Virginia Antiquity, has excellent material on archaeological excavations at Jamestown.

Georgia Before Oglethorpe

http://www.spanishflorida.net/gboindex.htm
This resources guide informs the viewer about Native American Georgia in the seventeenth century.

William Penn, Visionary Proprietor

http://xroads.virginia.edu/~CAP/PENN/pnhome.html
William Penn had an interesting life, and this site is a good introduction to the man and some of his achievements.

LVA Colonial Records Project—Index of digital facsimiles of documents on early Virginia

http://eagle.vsla.edu/colonial/
This site contains numerous early documents, but it is unguided and a little difficult to use.

Chapter 3

Putting Down Roots: Opportunity and Oppression in Colonial Society

Families in an Atlantic Empire

The Witherspoon family moved from Great Britain to the South Carolina backcountry early in the eighteenth century. Their son, Robert, who was only a small child when his family moved to America, later produced an exceptional and candid account of their pioneer life. On arrival in South Carolina, the Witherspoons experienced a wave of despondency. Where they expected to find a fine-timbered house and the comforts of England, they discovered acres of wilderness and "a very mean dirt house." For many years, the Witherspoons feared that they would be killed by Indians, become lost in the woods, or be bitten by snakes.

The Witherspoons managed to survive the early difficult years on the Black River. Although the Carolina backcountry did not look very much like the world they had left behind, Robert's father remained optimistic about the future. He assured his family that soon the trees would be cut down and the land would be populated by neighbors.

ROBERT WITHERSPOON'S ACCOUNT SERVES as a reminder that early American history was created by families and not, as some commentators would have people believe, by individuals. Neither the peopling of the Atlantic frontier, the cutting down of the forests, nor the creation of communities was part of what would be considered state policy today. Families determined much of the character of the American colonies. It was within this primary social unit that most colonists earned their livelihoods, educated their children, defined gender roles, sustained religious traditions, and nursed each other in sickness.

Early colonial families did not exist in isolation. They were part of larger societies. The characteristics of the first English settlements in the New World varied substantially (see Chapter 2), and these initial differences grew stronger during the seventeenth century as each region responded to different environmental conditions and developed its own traditions. The characteristics of the local societies reflected their supply of labor, abundance of land, and commercial ties with European markets.

By 1660, the regional differences had nearly undermined any possibility of a unified English empire in America. During the reign of King Charles II, however, a trend toward cultural convergence began. Such unifying forces as a common language and a common religion began to overcome the economic and cultural differences and pull the English colonists together. Parliament took advantage of this

OUTLINE

- **Sources of Stability: New England Colonies of the Seventeenth Century**
- **The Challenge of the Chesapeake Environment**
- **Race and Freedom in British America**
- **Rise of a Commercial Empire**
- **Colonial Factions Spark Political Revolt, 1676–1691**
- **Conclusion: Local Aspirations Within an Atlantic Empire**

trend and began to establish a uniform set of rules for the expanding American empire. The process was slow and uneven, often sparking violent colonial resistance. By the end of the seventeenth century, England had made significant progress toward transforming New World provinces into an empire that produced raw materials and purchased manufactured goods. If a person was black and enslaved, however, he or she was more apt to experience oppression rather than opportunity in British America.

Sources of Stability: New England Colonies of the Seventeenth Century

Seventeenth-century New Englanders successfully replicated in America a traditional social order they had known in England. The transfer of a familiar way of life to the New World seemed less difficult for these Puritan migrants than it did for the many English men and women who settled in the Chesapeake colonies. Their contrasting experiences, fundamental to an understanding of the development of both cultures, can be explained, at least in part, by the extraordinary strength and resilience of New England families.

Immigrant Families and New Social Order

Early New Englanders believed that God ordained the family for human benefit. It was essential to the maintenance of social order, since outside the family, men and women succumbed to carnal temptation. Such people had no one to sustain them, no one to remind them of Scripture. And just as Scripture taught obedience to the Lord, the godly seventeenth-century family required obedience to the patriarch at its head.

Familial experience exercised a powerful influence on early New England life. Mature adults who migrated to America within nuclear families preserved local English customs more fully than did the youths who traveled to other parts of the continent as single men and women. Not only did traveling with one's family help reduce the shock of migration, but it also ensured that the ratio between men and women would be fairly well balanced. Persons who had not already married in England could expect to form nuclear families of their own.

The great migration of the 1630s and early 1640s brought approximately twenty thousand persons to New England. The English civil war reduced this flood to a trickle, but by the end of the century, the population of New England had reached almost 120,000, an amazing increase considering the small number of original immigrants. Historians have long searched for the reason. Men and women in New England married no earlier than they did in England: for a first marriage, men's average age was in the mid-twenties; women wed in their early twenties. Nor were Puritan families unusually large by the standards of the period.

The reason turned out to be longevity. Put simply, people who, under normal conditions, would have died in contemporary Europe survived in New England. Indeed, the life expectancy of seventeenth-century settlers was not very different from that of Americans today. Males who survived infancy could expect to see their seventieth birthday. The figures for women were only slightly lower. No one is sure why they lived longer, but pure drinking water, a cool climate that retarded the spread of fatal contagious disease, and a dispersed population promoted general good health.

Longer life altered family relations. New England may have been one of the first societies in recorded history in which a person could reasonably anticipate knowing his or her grandchildren. The traditions of particular families and communities therefore remained alive, literally, in the memories of the colony's oldest citizens.

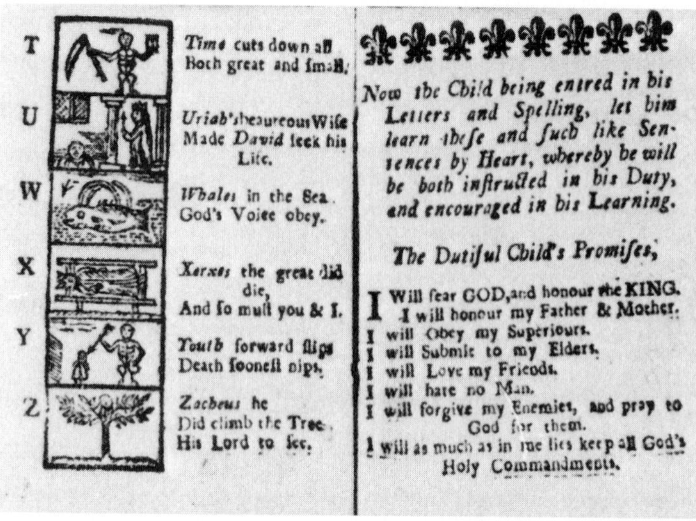

T Time cuts down all
Both great and ſmall.

U Uriah's beauteous Wife
Made David ſeek his
Life.

W Whales in the Sea.
God's Voice obey.

X Xerxes the great did
die,
And ſo muſt you & I.

Y Youth forward ſlips
Death ſooneſt nips.

Z Zacheus he
Did climb the Tree,
His Lord to ſee.

Now the Child being entred in his Letters and Spelling, let him learn theſe and ſuch like Sentences by Heart, whereby he will be both inſtructed in his Duty, and encouraged in his Learning.

The Dutiful Child's Promiſes,

I Will fear GOD, and honour the KING.
I will honour my Father & Mother.
I will Obey my Superiours.
I will Submit to my Elders.
I will Love my Friends.
I will hate no Man.
I will forgive my Enemies, and pray to God for them.
I will as much as in me lies keep all God's Holy Commandments.

New England parents took seriously their responsibility for the spiritual welfare of their children. To seek the word of God, young people had to learn to read. The New England Primer, *shown here, was their primary vehicle.* ❖

Commonwealth of Families

The life cycle of the family in New England began with marriage. Young men and women generally selected their own partners, usually a neighbor. Prospective brides were expected to possess a dowry worth approximately one-half what the bridegroom brought to the union. The overwhelming majority of the region's population married, for in New England, the single life was not only physically difficult but also morally suspect.

The household was primarily a place of work—very demanding work. The primary goal, of course, was to clear enough land to feed the family. But a family also needed a surplus crop to pay for items that could not be manufactured at home—metal tools, for example. The belief that early American farmers were self-sufficient is a misconception.

During the seventeenth century, men and women generally lived in the communities of their parents and grandparents. Towns, in fact, were collections of families, not individuals. Over time, the families intermarried, so that the community became an elaborate kinship network. In many towns, the original founders dominated local politics and economic affairs for several generations. Not surprisingly, newcomers who were not absorbed into the family system tended to move away from the village with greater frequency than the sons and daughters of the established lineage groups.

Congregational churches were also built on a family foundation. During the earliest years of settlement, the churches accepted persons who could demonstrate that they were among God's "elect." But when the sons and daughters of the elect failed to experience saving grace, a synod in 1662 adopted the so-called Half-Way Covenant. The compromise allowed the grandchildren of persons in full communion to be baptized even though their own parents could not demonstrate conversion. Obsession with family meant that by the end of the century, Congregational churches often failed to meet the religious needs of New Englanders who were not members of the select families.

Colonists regarded education as primarily a family responsibility. The ability to read was considered essential for learning the principles of Christianity. For this reason, the Massachusetts legislature ordered towns containing at least fifty families to open elementary schools supported by local taxes. Larger towns supported more advanced grammar schools, which taught a basic knowledge of Latin. After 1638, young men could attend Harvard College, the first institution of higher learning founded in England's mainland colonies.

This family-based education system worked. A majority of the region's adult males could read and write, an accomplishment not achieved in the Chesapeake colonies for another century. The literacy rate for women was somewhat lower, but by the standards of the period, it was still impressive.

Women's Lives in Puritan New England

The status of women in colonial New England was complex. Although subordinate to men by law and custom, their productive labor was essential to the survival of most households. They cooked, washed, made clothes, milked cows, gardened, and raised poultry. Sometimes, by selling surplus food, wives achieved some economic independence. Women also joined churches in greater numbers than men did, and it is possible that their involvement in these institutions encouraged them to express their ideas.

In both political and legal matters, society sharply curtailed the rights of colonial women. According to common law practice, a wife exercised no control over property. And since a divorce was extremely difficult to obtain, a woman married to a cruel or irresponsible spouse had little recourse but to run away or accept the unhappy situation.

Yet most women were neither prosperous entrepreneurs nor abject slaves. Like men, they generally accepted the roles that they thought God had ordained. Although Puritan couples worried that the affection they felt for a husband or a wife might turn their thoughts away from God's perfect love, this was a danger they were willing to risk.

Social Hierarchy in New England

During the seventeenth century, the New England colonies attracted neither noblemen nor paupers, an incomplete social structure by contemporary European standards. The lack of very wealthy, titled persons was particularly troublesome.

❖ A Look at the Past ❖

Freake Portraits

Bright colors, lace, embroidery, and other lavish details on the clothing John and Elizabeth Freake wore for their portraits, painted by an unknown artist in the 1670s, refute the notion that Puritans wore only somber clothes. The Freakes's attire also reveals attitudes about children and gender roles. Elizabeth is holding her son, dressed in a gown as both male and female babies were at the time. Note how similar their gowns are; her son's is nearly a miniaturized version of Elizabeth's. If babies wore miniaturized adult clothing, what does that suggest about the lives of children? Was childhood a distinctive developmental stage to be relished?

According to the prevailing hierarchical view of the structure of society, well-placed individuals were *natural rulers*, people intended by God to exercise political authority over the rank and file. Migration forced the colonists, however, to choose their rulers from men of more modest status, ignoring the "ordinariness of their persons."

The colonists gradually sorted themselves out into distinct social groupings. To become part of the ruling elite, it helped to possess at least moderate wealth and education; it was also expected that leaders would belong to a Congregational church and defend religious orthodoxy. The Winthrops, Dudleys, and Pynchons fulfilled these expectations, and in public affairs they assumed dominant roles. They took their responsibility quite seriously and certainly did not look kindly on anyone who spoke of their "ordinariness."

The problem was that while most New Englanders accepted a hierarchical view of society, they disagreed over their assigned places. Both Massachusetts Bay and Connecticut enacted sumptuary laws—statutes that restricted the wearing of fine apparel to the wealthy and prominent—designed to curb the pretensions of lower-status individuals. By the end of the century, the character of the ruling class in New England had changed, and personal piety figured less importantly in social ranking than family background and a large estate.

Most northern colonists were yeomen (independent farmers), few of whom became rich and even fewer of whom fell hopelessly into debt. Possession of land gave agrarian families a sense of independence from external authority, but during the seventeenth century, this independence was balanced by an equally strong feeling of local identity. Not until the late eighteenth century, when a large number of New Englanders left their familial villages in search of new land, did many northern yeomen place personal material ambition above traditional community bonds.

It was not unusual for northern colonists to work as servants among their neighbors at some point in their lives. New Englanders recruited few servants from the Old World. Their forms of agriculture, which mixed cereal with dairy farming, made employment of large gangs of dependent workers uneconomical. New England servants more resembled apprentices than anything else, and servitude was more a vocational training program than an exploitative system. This was vastly different from the institutions that developed in the Southern Colonies.

By the end of the seventeenth century, the New England Puritans had developed a compelling story about their own history in the New World. The founders had been extraordinarily godly men and women, and in a heroic effort to establish a purer form of religion, pious families had passed "over the vast ocean into this vast and howling wilderness." Although the children and grandchildren of the first generation sometimes questioned their own ability to please the Lord, they recognized the mission to the New World as a success.

The Challenge of the Chesapeake Environment

An entirely different regional society developed in England's Chesapeake colonies, Virginia and Maryland. Although the two areas were founded at roughly the same time by Protestant Englishmen, the regions were worlds apart in terms of environmental conditions, labor systems, and agrarian economies. The most important reason for the distinctiveness of these early southern plantation societies, however, turned out to be the Chesapeake's death rate, a frighteningly high mortality that tore at the very fabric of family life.

Family Life at Risk

Unlike the New England settlers, the men and women who migrated to the Chesapeake region did not move in family units. Nor were most entirely free when they arrived. Between 70 and 85 percent of the white colonists who went to Virginia and Maryland during the seventeenth century owed four or five years' labor in exchange for the cost of passage to America. Most of these indentured servants were men, and although more women made the voyage after 1640, the gender ratio in the Chesapeake was never as balanced as it had been in early Massachusetts.

Most immigrants to the Chesapeake region died soon after arriving. Malaria and other diseases took a frightful toll, and drinking water contaminated with salt killed many colonists living in low-lying areas. Life expectancy for Chesapeake males was about 43, some ten to twenty years less than for men born in New England! For women, life expectancy was even shorter. A full 25 percent of all children died in infancy. Another 25 percent did not see their twentieth birthday. The survivors were often weak or ill, unable to perform hard physical labor.

These demographic conditions retarded normal population increase. Young women who might have become wives and mothers could not do so until they had completed their terms of servitude. They thus lost several reproductive years, and in a society in which so many children died in infancy, late marriages greatly restricted family size. Moreover, the unbalanced gender ratio meant that many men could not find wives. Without a constant flow of immigrants, the population of Virginia and Maryland would have actually declined.

High mortality compressed the family cycle into a few short years. Marriages were extremely fragile, and one partner usually died within seven years. Not only did children not meet grandparents, but they also often did not even know their own parents. Widows and widowers quickly remarried, and children frequently grew up with persons to whom they had no blood relation. People had to adjust to the impermanence of family life and to cope with a high degree of personal insecurity.

The unbalanced gender ratio in the Chesapeake may have provided women with the means to improve their social status. Because of the uneven numbers, women could be confident of finding husbands, regardless of their abilities, attractiveness, or moral character. Despite liberation from some traditional restraints, however, women as servants were still vulnerable to sexual exploitation by their masters. Moreover, childbearing was extremely dangerous; women in the Chesapeake usually died twenty years earlier than their New England counterparts.

The Structure of Planter Society

Tobacco cultivation formed the basis of the Chesapeake economy. Although anyone with a few acres of cleared land could grow leaves for export, cultivation of the Chesapeake staple did not produce a society of individuals roughly similar in wealth and status. To the contrary, it generated inequality. The amassing of a large fortune involved the control of a large labor force. More workers in the fields meant larger harvests and, of course, larger profits. Since free persons showed no interest in toiling away in another man's fields of tobacco, not even for wages, wealthy planters relied on laborers who were not free as well as on slaves. The social structure that developed in the seventeenth-century Chesapeake reflected a wild, often unscrupulous scramble to bring men and women of three races—black, white, and Indian—into various degrees of independence.

Great planters dominated Chesapeake society. The group was small and, during the early decades of the seventeenth century, constantly changing. Not until the 1650s did the family names of those who would become famous eighteenth-century gentry appear on the records. These ambitious men arrived in America with capital. They invested immediately in laborers, and one way or another, they obtained huge tracts of the best tobacco-growing land. Though not aristocrats, but rather the younger sons of English merchants and artisans, they soon acquired political and social power. Over time, these gentry families—including the Burwells, Byrds, Carters, and Masons—intermarried so extensively that they created a vast network of cousins. During the eighteenth century, it was not uncommon to find a half dozen men with the same surname sitting simultaneously in the Virginia House of Burgesses.

Freemen formed the largest class in Chesapeake society. Most came as indentured servants, unlike New England's yeomen farmers, and by sheer good fortune managed to stay alive to the end of their contracts. When their period of indenture was over, many freemen lived on the edge of poverty, although a few lived better than they might have in England.

Below the freemen came indentured servants. Membership in this group was not demeaning; after all, servitude was a temporary status. But servitude in the Chesapeake colonies was not the benign institution it was in New England. Great planters took on servants to grow tobacco, and they were not overly concerned with the well-being of the laborers. The unhappy servants regarded their servitude as a form of slavery, while the planters worried that discontented servants and impoverished freemen would rebel at the slightest provocation. Later events would justify these fears.

Social mobility changed during the seventeenth century. Before the 1680s, movement into the planter elite by newcomers who possessed capital was relatively easy. After the 1680s, however, life expectancy rates improved in the Chesapeake colonies, and the sons of great planters replaced their fathers in powerful government positions. The key to success was possession of slaves. Planters who owned more slaves could grow more tobacco and thus purchase additional laborers. Over time, the rich not only became richer, but they also formed a distinct ruling elite that newcomers found increasingly difficult to enter.

Opportunities for advancement also decreased for the region's freemen. As the gentry consolidated its hold on political and economic institutions, ordinary people discovered that it was much harder to rise in Chesapeake society. Men and women with more ambitious dreams headed for Pennsylvania, North Carolina, and western Virginia.

Social institutions that figured importantly in the New Englanders' daily lives were either weak or nonexistent in the Chesapeake, partly due to the high infant mortality rates. There was little incentive to build elementary schools, for example, since only half the children would reach adulthood. The development of higher education languished, similarly, and the great planters sent their sons to English or Scottish schools through much of the colonial period.

Tobacco also inhibited the growth of towns in this region. Owners of isolated plantations along the riverbanks traded directly with English merchants and had little need for local markets. People met sporadically at scattered churches, courthouses, and taverns. Seventeenth-century Virginia could not boast of even one printing press.

Race and Freedom in British America

Many people who landed in the colonies had no desire to come to the New World; they were brought from Africa as slaves to cultivate rice, sugar, and tobacco. As the Native Americans were exterminated and the supply of white indentured servants dried up, white planters demanded ever more African laborers.

Roots of Slavery

Between the sixteenth and nineteenth centuries, slave traders carried almost eleven million blacks from Africa to the New World, mainly to Brazil and the Caribbean. Only a small part of this commerce involved British North America. Young black males predominated in the human cargo; the planters preferred this group for the hard physical labor of the plantations. In many early slave communities, black men outnumbered women by a ratio of two to one.

English colonists did not hesitate to enslave black people; the decision to import African slaves to the British colonies was based primarily on economic consid-

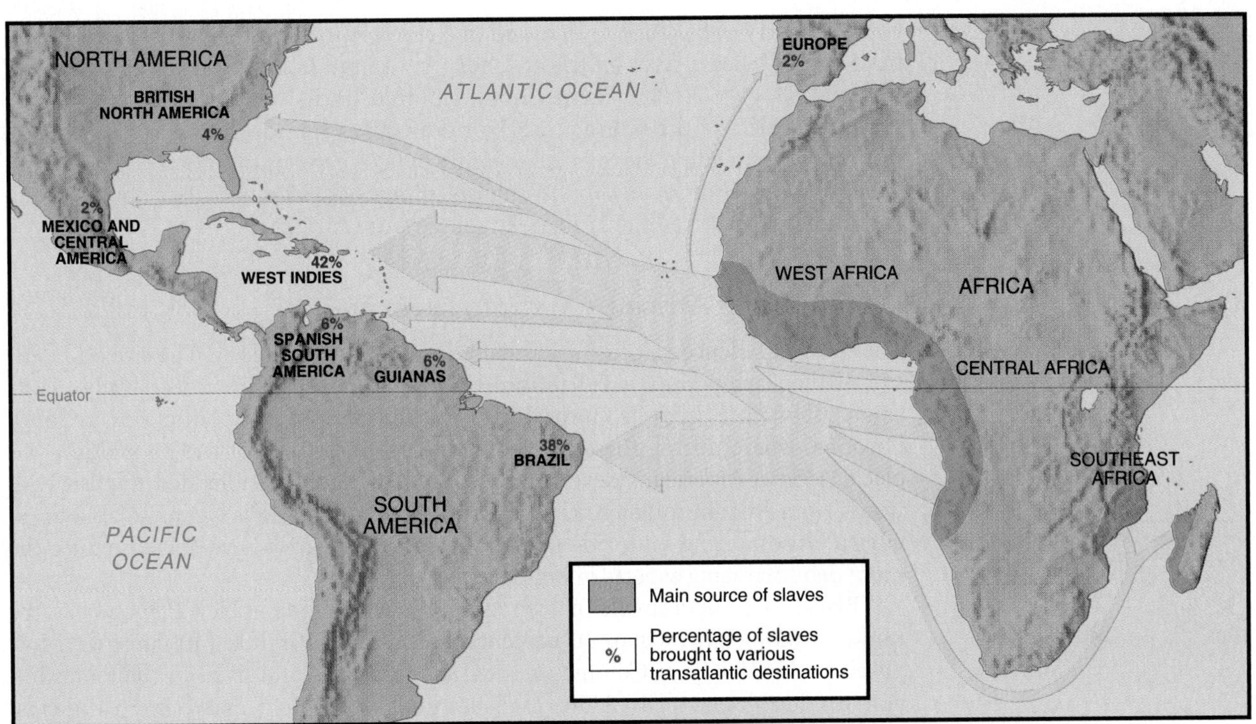

ORIGINS AND DESTINATIONS OF AFRICAN SLAVES, 1619–1760 *Although many African slaves were transported to Britain's North American colonies, far more slaves were sold in the Caribbean sugar colonies and Brazil, where because of horrific health conditions, the death rate far exceeded that of the British mainland colonies.* ❖

erations. But English masters never justified the practice purely in terms of planter profits. They associated blacks in Africa with heathen religion, barbarous behavior, sexual promiscuity—in fact, with evil itself. From such a perspective, the enslavement of African men and women seemed unobjectionable. Planters avowed that loss of freedom was a small price for the civilizing benefits of conversion to Christianity.

Africans first landed in Virginia in 1619. For the next fifty years, their status remained unclear. English settlers classified some black laborers as slaves for life, others as indentured servants. A few blacks purchased their freedom. Several seventeenth-century Africans even became successful Virginia planters.

One reason that Virginia lawmakers tolerated such confusion was that the black population remained very small. Planters wanted more African slaves, but during this period, slave traders sold their cargoes on Barbados or the other sugar islands of the West Indies, where they fetched a higher price than Virginians could afford. In fact, before 1680, most blacks who reached England's colonies on the North American mainland came from Barbados or through New Netherland rather than directly from Africa.

By the end of the seventeenth century, the status of Virginia's black people was no longer in doubt. They were slaves for life, as were their children after them. Slavery was unequivocally based on skin color alone. This transformation reflected an increase in the supply of Africans to British North America. After 1672, the Royal African Company undertook to meet the colonial planters' rising demands for black laborers, and during the eighteenth century, many American merchants entered the lucrative trade.

The expanding black population apparently frightened white colonists, and lawmakers drew up ever stricter slave codes. The white planter could deal with his black property as he alone saw fit, and one extraordinary Virginia statute excused a master who killed a slave on the grounds that no rational person would purposely "destroy his own estate." Furthermore, children born to a slave woman became slaves regardless of the father's race. Nor did conversion to Christianity free blacks from bondage. Unlike the Spanish colonies, where persons of lighter color enjoyed greater privileges in society, in the English colonies, racial mixing was not tolerated, and mulattoes received the same treatment as pure Africans.

Constructing African American Identities

The slave experience varied substantially from colony to colony. The size and density of the slave population determined in large measure how successfully blacks could maintain a separate cultural identity. On isolated rice plantations in South Carolina, where during the eighteenth century 60 percent of the population was black, African Americans developed creoles, languages that blended English with words from African tongues. Slaves on these large plantations were also able to establish elaborate and enduring kinship networks that may have helped reduce the more dehumanizing aspects of bondage.

Blacks made up a smaller percentage of the population in New England and the Middle Colonies (less than 10 percent) and even in Virginia (40 percent). Most slaves in the Northern Colonies worked as domestics and lived in their masters' homes. Close contact with whites made it more difficult to preserve and reaffirm an African heritage and identity.

In eighteenth-century Virginia, native-born blacks had learned to cope with whites on a daily basis. They looked with disdain on slaves who had just arrived from Africa. Blacks as well as whites pressed these "outlandish" newcomers to accept elements of English culture, especially to speak the English language.

Despite their wrenching experiences, black slaves did establish cultural traditions that involved an imaginative reshaping of African and European customs into something that was neither African nor European; it was African American. For example, slaves embraced Christianity but transformed it into an expression of religious feeling in which an African element remained vibrant.

During the early decades of the eighteenth century, blacks living in England's mainland colonies began to experience reproductive success as live births exceeded deaths. This demographic milestone was not reached in the Caribbean or South American colonies until a much later date. Historians surmise that North American blacks enjoyed a healthier climate and a better diet than other New World slaves.

But longer lives did not make them any less slaves. Nor did it prevent slave protests, including organized revolt. The most serious slave rebellion of the colonial period was the Stono Uprising, which took place in September 1739. One hundred and fifty South Carolina blacks rose up and murdered several whites. They marched toward Florida and the promise of freedom, but the local militia overtook and crushed the revolt. Such rebellions were rare; in fact, the level of interracial violence in colonial North America was quite low. But the fear of slave rebellions was pervasive, prompting whites to take drastic defensive measures.

Rise of a Commercial Empire

Just as the status of slaves changed during the seventeenth century, so did the status of white colonists. Until the middle of the seventeenth century, English political leaders largely ignored the American colonists. After the restoration of Charles II to the throne in 1660, however, intervention replaced indifference. The crown, Parliament, and the mercantile interests decided that the colonies should be brought more tightly under the control of the mother country. Regulatory policies

Old Plantation, *a watercolor by an unknown artist (about 1800), shows that African customs survived plantation slavery. The man and women in the center dance (possibly to celebrate a wedding) to the music of drum and banjo. Instruments, turbans, and scarves reflect a distinctive African American culture in the New World.* ❖

that evolved during this period formed a framework for empire that survived with only minor adjustments until 1765.

Response to Economic Competition

The famous eighteenth-century Scottish economist Adam Smith coined the term **mercantilism** to describe the system on which England based its commercial regulations. An advocate of free trade, Smith argued that it made no sense for European states to exclude commercial competitors from their own colonial markets. More trade increased general prosperity. Smith's specific term, however, is misleading. "Mercantilist system" as administered by the policymakers of the late seventeenth century was not nearly as well thought out or organized as Smith suggested. Rather, it represented a series of individual responses to the needs of several powerful interest groups.

mercantilism An economic theory that shaped imperial policy throughout the colonial period, mercantilism was built on the assumption that the world's wealth was a fixed supply. In order to increase its wealth, a nation needed to export more goods than it imported. Favorable trade and protective economic policies, as well as new colonial possessions rich in raw materials, were important in achieving this balance.

Each group looked to colonial commerce to solve a different problem. Charles wanted money to pay his enormous debts. English merchants were eager to exclude Dutch rivals from lucrative American markets, but without government assistance, they could not compete successfully with the Dutch merchant marine. Parliament wanted to strengthen England's navy, and the expansion of the domestic shipbuilding industry was a fine starting place. And almost everyone agreed with the mercantilist view that the mother country should establish a more favorable balance of trade—that is, increase exports, decrease imports, and grow richer at the expense of other European states. Together, these ideas provided a blueprint for England's first empire, a complex set of regulations that shaped the character of Anglo-American cultural and economic relations until the American Revolution.

Regulating Colonial Trade

In 1660, Parliament passed the first Navigation Act, the most important piece of imperial legislation drafted before the American Revolution. Colonists from Maine to Georgia paid close attention to the act, which stated (1) that no ship could trade in the colonies unless it had been constructed in either England or America and carried a crew that was at least 75 percent English and (2) that certain **enumerated goods** of great value that were not produced in England—tobacco, sugar, cotton,

enumerated goods Certain essential raw materials produced in the North American colonies, such as tobacco, sugar, and rice, specified in the Navigation Acts, which stipulated that these goods could be shipped only to England or its colonies.

indigo, dye, wool, ginger—could be transported from the colonies *only* to an English or colonial port. Early in the next century, Parliament added rice, molasses, wood resins, tars, and turpentines to the enumerated list.

The Navigation Act of 1660 was masterfully conceived. It encouraged the development of domestic shipbuilding, prohibited European rivals from obtaining enumerated goods anywhere except in England, and provided the crown with added revenue. Parliament supplemented the act in 1663 with the second Navigation Act, known as the Staple Act, that closed off nearly all direct trade between European nations and the American colonies. With a few noted exceptions, nothing could be imported into America unless it had first been transshipped through the mother country, a process that greatly added to the price paid by colonial consumers.

During the 1660s, Virginians showed little enthusiasm for the new imperial regulation. Not only did the collection of customs on tobacco greatly reduce profits, but with the exclusion of the Dutch as the middlemen in American commerce, tobacco planters had to sell their crops to English merchants at artificially low prices. Virginia's loss (£100,000 in import duties collected for the crown by 1670) was Charles II's gain. At first, New England merchants ignored or cleverly circumvented the commercial restrictions. The crafty traders picked up cargoes of enumerated goods such as sugar or tobacco, sailed to another colonial port (thereby technically fulfilling the letter of the law), and then made directly for Holland or France. Along the way, they paid no customs duties.

To plug this loophole, Parliament passed another Navigation Act in 1673. This statute established a plantation duty to be collected at the various colonial ports. New Englanders could no longer escape paying customs fees. And in 1675, as part of the new imperial firmness, the Privy Council formed a powerful subcommittee, the Lords of Trade, whose members monitored colonial affairs.

Despite the legal reforms, serious obstacles impeded the execution of imperial policy. The customs service did not have enough effective agents in American ports to enforce the **Navigation Acts** fully, and imperial officials of various independent agencies often worked at cross-purposes.

Navigation Acts A series of commercial restrictions passed by Parliament intended to regulate colonial commerce in such a way to favor England's accumulation of wealth.

Parliament passed the last major piece of imperial legislation in 1696. Among other things, the statute tightened enforcement procedures, putting pressure specifically on the colonial governors to keep England's competitors out of American ports. The Navigation Act of 1696 also expanded the American customs service and for the first time set up vice-admiralty courts in the colonies. This decision particularly rankled the colonists. Established to settle disputes that occurred at sea, vice-admiralty courts required neither juries nor oral cross-examination, both traditional elements of common law. On the eve of the American Revolution, a sudden expansion of the admiralty system raised a storm of protest.

The year 1696 witnessed one other significant change in the imperial system. William III replaced the ineffective Lords of Trade with a body of policy advisers that came to be known as the Board of Trade. This group was expected to monitor colonial affairs closely, and for several decades, at least, it energetically carried out its responsibilities.

The members of Parliament believed that these reforms would belatedly compel the colonists to accept the Navigation Acts, and in large measure they were correct. By 1700, American goods transshipped through the mother country accounted for a quarter of *all* English exports, an indication that the colonists found it profitable to obey the commercial regulations. In fact, during the eighteenth century, smuggling from Europe to America dried up almost completely.

The Navigation Acts of the seventeenth century also shaped the colonists' material culture. Over time, Americans grew increasingly accustomed to purchasing British goods; they established close ties with specific merchant houses in London, Bristol, or Glasgow. Thus it is not surprising that by the mid-eighteenth century, the colonists preferred the manufactures of the mother country over those of England's commercial rivals. In other words, the Navigation Acts affected the development of consumer habits throughout the empire, and it is not an exaggeration to suggest that this regulatory system was in large part responsible for the Anglicization of eighteenth-century American culture (see Chapter 4).

Colonial Factions Spark Political Revolt, 1676–1691

The Navigation Acts created an illusion of unity; the imperial statutes superimposed a system of commercial regulations on all the colonies. But within each society, men and women struggled to bring order out of disorder, to establish stable ruling elites, to defuse ethnic and racial tensions, and to cope with population pressures that imperial planners only dimly understood. During the final decades of the seventeenth century, these efforts sometimes sparked revolt between factions of the local gentry, usually the "outs" versus the "ins," for political power.

Civil War in Virginia: Bacon's Rebellion

Virginia was the first colony to experience this political unrest. After 1660, the Virginia economy suffered a prolonged depression. Returns from tobacco had not been good for some time, and the Navigation Acts reduced profits even further. Into this unhappy environment came thousands of ambitious indentured servants.

The reality bore little relation to their dreams. A hurricane destroyed one entire tobacco crop, and in 1667, Dutch warships captured the tobacco fleet just as it was about to sail for England. Indentured servants complained about lack of food and clothing. No wonder that Virginia's governor, Sir William Berkeley, despaired of ever ruling "a People where six parts of seven at least are Poor, Endebted, Discontented and Armed." In 1670, he and the House of Burgesses disfranchised all landless freemen, persons they regarded as troublemakers, but the threat of social violence remained.

Enter Nathaniel Bacon. This ambitious young man arrived in Virginia in 1674. He came from a respectable English family and set himself immediately as a substantial planter. But he wanted more. Bacon envied the government patronage monopolized by Berkeley's cronies, a group known locally as the Green Spring faction. When Bacon attempted to obtain a license to engage in the fur trade, he was rebuffed. This lucrative commerce was reserved for the governor's friends. If Bacon had been willing to wait, he would probably have been accepted into the ruling clique, but as subsequent events would demonstrate, Bacon was not a man of patience.

In 1675, Indian attacks on outlying plantations thrust Bacon suddenly into the center of Virginia politics. Virginians expected the governor to send an army to retaliate. Instead, Berkeley called for the construction of a line of defensive forts. Settlers suspected that the governor was simply trying to protect his own fur interests and was rewarding his friends with contracts to build useless forts.

In response, Bacon boldly offered to lead a volunteer army against the Indians at no cost to the hard-pressed Virginia taxpayers. All he demanded was an official commission from Berkeley giving him military command. The governor steadfastly refused.

What followed, known as **Bacon's Rebellion,** would have been comic had not so many people died. Bacon thundered against the governor's treachery; Berkeley labeled Bacon a traitor. Bacon led several campaigns against the Indians, failing to kill any enemies but managing to massacre some friendly Indians. Bacon also burned Jamestown to the ground, forcing Berkeley to flee to the colony's eastern shore. Charles II sent troops to aid the governor, but by the time they arrived, Berkeley had gained full control of the colony's government. In October 1676, Bacon died after a brief illness, and his band of rebels dispersed within a few months.

Bacon's Rebellion An armed rebellion in Virginia (1675–1676) led by Nathaniel Bacon against the colony's royal governor, Sir William Berkeley. Although some of his followers called for an end of special privilege in government, Bacon was chiefly interested in gaining a larger share of the lucrative Indian trade.

Order was soon restored, and in 1677, the crown recalled the embittered Berkeley. The governors who followed were unusually greedy, and the local gentry formed a united front against them.

The Glorious Revolution in the Bay Colony

During John Winthrop's lifetime, the settlers of Massachusetts developed an inflated sense of their independence from the mother country. After the Restoration in 1660, however, the crown put an end to that illusion. Royal officials demanded full compliance with the Navigation Acts, which were constant reminders of New England's colonial status. The growth of commerce attracted new merchants who were there to make money and were restive under the Puritan strictures. These developments divided Bay Colony leaders. A few Puritan ministers and magistrates regarded compromise with England as treason, a breaking of the Lord's covenant. Other spokesmen recognized the changing political realities within the empire and urged a more moderate course.

In 1675, the Indians dealt the New Englanders a terrible setback. Metacomet, a Wampanoag chief whom the whites called King Philip, declared war against the colonists; he was joined by the powerful Narragansetts. In little more than a year of fighting, the Indians destroyed scores of frontier villages, killed hundreds of colonists, and disrupted the entire regional economy. "In proportion to population, King Philip's War inflicted greater casualties upon the people than any other war in our history," wrote historian Douglas Leach.

Metacomet, the Wampanoag chief known to the English colonists as King Philip, led Native Americans in a major war designed to remove the Europeans from New England. ❖

Another shock followed. In 1684, the Court of Chancery, sitting in London and acting under a petition from King James II, annulled the charter of the Massachusetts Bay Company. The decision forced even the most stubborn Puritans to recognize that they were part of an empire run by people who did not share their particular religious vision.

In the place of representative governments, James II created the Dominion of New England. In various stages from 1686 to 1689, it incorporated Massachusetts, Connecticut, Rhode Island, Plymouth, New York, New Jersey, and New Hampshire under a single appointed royal governor. For this demanding position, James selected Sir Edmund Andros (pronounced Andrews), a military veteran of tyrannical temperament. He quickly abolished elective assemblies and town meetings and enforced the Navigation Acts so rigorously that he brought about a commercial depression. His high-handed methods alienated almost all the colonists.

Early in 1689, news of the Glorious Revolution reached Boston. The English people had deposed James II, an absolutist monarch who openly espoused Catholicism. His Protestant daughter, Mary, and her husband, William of Orange, ascended the throne as joint monarchs in James's place. William and Mary had accepted a "bill of rights" that set out the constitutional rights of their subjects. Almost immediately, the Bay colonists overthrew the hated Andros regime and jailed the governor. No one came to Andros's defense.

However united they were, the Bay colonists could not take the newly crowned monarchs' support for granted. But thanks largely to the tireless lobbying of Increase Mather, a Congregational minister and father of Cotton Mather, who pleaded the colonists' case in London, King William abandoned the Dominion of New England and in 1691 conferred a new royal charter on Massachusetts. This document provided for a crown-appointed governor and a franchise based on property ownership rather than church membership. On the local level, town government remained much as it had been in Winthrop's time.

Contagion of Witchcraft

During these politically troubled times, excessively fearful men and women living in Salem Village, a small, struggling farming community, created panic in Massachusetts Bay. In late 1691, during a very cold winter, several adolescent girls began to behave in strange ways. They cried for no apparent reason; they twitched on the ground. The girls attributed their suffering to the work of witches. The arrest of several alleged witches did not relieve the girls' "fits," and other arrests followed. At least one person confessed, providing a frightening description of the devil as "a thing all over hairy, all the face hairy, and a long nose." By the end of the summer, a specially convened court had hanged nineteen individuals; another was pressed to death. Many more suspects were in jail awaiting trial.

Then suddenly, the storm was over. Led by Increase Mather, a group of prominent Congregational ministers urged leniency and restraint. Especially troubling to the clergymen was the court's decision to accept **spectral evidence,** reports of dreams and visions in which the accused appeared as the devil's agent. The colonial government accepted the minister's advice and convened a new court, which promptly acquitted, pardoned, or released the remaining suspects.

spectral evidence In the Salem witch trials, the court allowed reports of dreams and visions in which the accused appeared as the devil's agent to be introduced as testimony. The accused had no defense against this kind of evidence. When the judges later disallowed this testimony, the executions for witchcraft ended.

No one knows exactly what sparked the terror in Salem Village. The community had a history of discord, and during the 1680s, the people split into angry factions over the choice of a minister. Jealousy and bitterness apparently festered to the point that adolescent girls who would normally have been disciplined were allowed to incite judicial murder. As often happens in incidents like this one, the accusers later came to their senses and apologized for the cruel suffering that they had inflicted.

The Glorious Revolution in New York and Maryland

When news of the Glorious Revolution reached New York City in May 1689, Jacob Leisler, a German immigrant with mercantile ties to the older Dutch elite, raised a group of militiamen and seized a local fort in the name of William and Mary. For a short time, he controlled the city. But English newcomers and powerful Anglo-Dutch families who had recently risen to prominence opposed the older Dutch group to which he was allied, and Leisler was never able to construct a secure political base.

In 1691, a new royal governor, Henry Sloughter, arrived in New York and ordered Leisler to surrender his authority. Leisler hesitated; he may have feared the vengeance of rival factions. The pause cost Leisler his life. He was declared a rebel, promptly tried, and executed in grisly fashion. Four years later, Parliament officially pardoned him, but the decision came a bit late. The bitter political factionalism that engendered this unfortunate episode plagued New York throughout the next century.

Tensions in Maryland between Protestants and Catholics ran high during the last third of the seventeenth century. When news of James's overthrow reached Maryland early in 1689, pent-up antiproprietary and anti-Catholic sentiment exploded. John Coode, a member of the assembly and an outspoken Protestant,

CHRONOLOGY	
1619	First blacks arrive in Virginia
1638	Harvard College is established
1660	Charles II is restored to the English throne ❖ First Navigation Act is passed by Parliament
1663	Second Navigation (Staple) Act is passed
1673	Plantation duty is imposed to close loopholes in commercial regulations
1675	King Philip's War devastates New England
1676	Bacon's Rebellion threatens Governor Berkeley's government in Virginia
1684	Charter of Massachusetts Bay Company is revoked
1685	Duke of York becomes James II
1686	Dominion of New England is established
1688	James II is driven into exile during the Glorious Revolution
1689	Rebellions break out in Massachusetts, New York, and Maryland
1691	Jacob Leisler is executed
1692	Salem Village is wracked by witch trials
1696	Parliament establishes the Board of Trade
1739	Stono Uprising of South Carolina slaves terrifies white planters

formed a group called the Protestant Association, which forced the governor appointed by Lord Baltimore to resign.

The Protestant Association petitioned the newly crowned Protestant monarchs to transform Maryland into a royal colony, alleging many wrongs suffered at the hands of the Catholic-dominated upper house. William complied, sending a royal governor in 1691. The new assembly then proclaimed the Church of England as the established religion and excluded Catholics from public office. Baltimore lost control of the colony's government. In 1715, however, the fourth Lord Baltimore, who had been raised a member of the Church of England, regained full proprietorship from the crown. Maryland remained in the hands of the Calvert family until 1776.

Conclusion: Local Aspirations Within an Atlantic Empire

"It is no little Blessing of God," Cotton Mather announced proudly in 1700, "that we are part of the *English* nation." A half century earlier, John Winthrop would not have spoken these words, at least not with such enthusiasm. The two men were products of different political cultures. It was not so much that the character of Massachusetts society had changed. In fact, the Puritan families of 1700 were much like those of the founding generation. Rather, the difference was in England's attitude toward the colonies. Rulers living more than three thousand miles away now made political and economic demands that Mather's contemporaries could not ignore.

The creation of a new imperial system did not, however, erase profound sectional differences. By 1700, for example, the Chesapeake colonies were more, not less, committed to the cultivation of tobacco and slave labor. Although the separate regions were being pulled slowly into England's commercial orbit, they did not have much to do with each other. The elements that sparked a powerful sense of nationalism among colonists dispersed over a huge territory would not be evident for a very long time. It would be a mistake, therefore, to anticipate the coming of the American Revolution.

Key Terms

mercantilism, p. 51
enumerated goods, p. 51
Navigation Acts, p. 52
Bacon's Rebellion, p. 53
spectral evidence, p. 55

Recommended Reading

The most innovative research of chapters covered in this chapter explores the history of New World slavery during the period before the American Revolution. Much of this literature is boldly interdisciplinary, providing not only a fresh comparative interpretation of the creation and development of African American cultures in the New World, but also splendid insight into how imaginative scholars reconstruct the pasts of peoples who for a very long time have been denied a voice in mainstream histories. Among the more impressive contributions are Ira Berlin, *Many Thousands Gone: The First Two Centuries of Slavery in North America* (2000); Philip Morgan, *Slave Counterpoint: Black Culture in the Eighteenth-Century Chesapeake and Lowcountry* (1998); and Robin Blackburn, *The Making of New World Slavery, 1492–1800* (1997). A pioneering work of high quality is Winthrop D. Jordan, *White Over Black: American Attitudes Toward the Negro, 1550–1812* (1968). Peter Wood provides an original interpretation of the evolution of race relations in *Black Majority: Negroes in Colonial South Carolina from 1670 Through the Stono Rebellion* (1974). The world of Anthony Johnson, a free black planter in early Virginia, is reconstructed in T. H. Breen and Stephen Innes, *"Myne Owne Ground": Race and Freedom on Virginia's Eastern Shore, 1640–1676* (1980). The most recent account of the Salem witch trials can be found in Mary Beth Norton, *In the Devil's Snare: The Salem Witchcraft Crisis of 1692* (2002). Richard Godbeer offers a solid account of the Puritans' intimate lives in *Sexual Revolution in Early America* (2002), but one should also consult Laurel T. Ulrich, *Good Wives: Image and Reality in the Lives of Women in Northern New England, 1650–1750* (1982), and a path-breaking essay by Lois G. Carr and Lorena Walsh, "The Planter's Wife: The Experience of White Women in Seventeenth-Century Maryland," *William and Mary Quarterly*, 3rd ser., 34 (1977): 542–571. A provocative discussion of cultural tensions within the British Empire can be found in Linda Colley, *Captives: The Story of Britain's Pursuit of Empire and How its Soldiers and Civilians Were Held Captive by the Dream of Global Supremacy, 1600–1850* (2002).

For a list of additional titles related to this chapter's topics, please see http://ww.ablongman.com/divine.

Suggested Web Sites

DPLS Archive: Slave Movement During the Eighteenth and Nineteenth Centuries (Wisconsin)

http://dpls.dacc.wisc.edu/slavedata/index.html
This site explores the slave ships and the slave trade that carried thousands of Africans to the New World.

Excerpts from Slave Narratives

http://vi.uh.edu/pages/mintz/primary.htm
The seventeenth- through nineteenth-century accounts of slavery in this site speak volumes about the many impacts of slavery.

Salem Witch Trials: Documentary Archive and Transcription Project

http://etext.virginia.edu/salem/witchcraft/
Extensive archive of the 1692 trials and life in late seventeenth-century Massachusetts.

Salem Witchcraft Trials (1692)

http://www.law.umkc.edu/faculty/projects/ftrials/salem/salem.htm
Images, chronology, court and official documents by Dr. Doug Linder at University of Missouri–Kansas City Law School.

Colonial Documents

http://www.yale.edu/lawweb/avalon/18th.htm
The key documents of the Colonial Era are reproduced here, as are some of the important documents from earlier and later time periods in American history.

LVA Colonial Records Project—Index of digital facsimiles of documents on early Virginia.

http://eagle.vsla.edu/colonial/
This site contains numerous early documents, but it is unguided and a little difficult to use.

Chapter 4

Experience of Empire: Eighteenth-Century America

Constructing an Anglo-American Identity: The Journal of William Byrd

William Byrd II (1674–1744) was a type of English American that would not have been encountered during the earliest years of settlement. This successful Tidewater planter was a product of a new, more cosmopolitan environment, as much at home in London as in his native Virginia. In 1728, at the height of his political influence in Williamsburg, the capital of colonial Virginia, Byrd accepted a commission to help survey a disputed boundary between North Carolina and Virginia. During his long journey into the distant backcountry, Byrd kept a detailed journal, a satiric, often bawdy chronicle of daily events.

On his trip into the wilderness, Byrd met many different people. No sooner had he departed a familiar world of tobacco plantations than he came across a self-styled hermit, an Englishman who apparently preferred the freedom of the woods to the constraints of society. As the boundary commissioners pushed farther into the backcountry, they encountered more highly independent men and women of European descent, small frontier families that Byrd regarded as living no better than savages. He attributed their uncivilized behavior to a diet of too much pork. The pork, he thought, made them "extremely hoggish in their Temper, & many of them seem to Grunt rather than Speak in their ordinary conversation." The wilderness journey also brought Byrd's party of surveyors into regular contact with Native American tribes.

Outline

Growth and Diversity

Spanish Borderlands of the Eighteenth Century

The Impact of European Ideas on American Culture

Religious Revivals in Provincial Societies

Clash of Political Cultures

Century of Imperial War

Conclusion: Rule Britannia?

We Americans

Learning to Live with Diversity in the Eighteenth Century: What Is an American?

BYRD'S JOURNAL INVITES READERS to perceive the rapidly developing eighteenth-century backcountry from a fresh perspective. It was not a vast empty territory awaiting the arrival of European settlers. Maps often sustain this erroneous impression. They depict cities and towns, farms and plantations clustered along the Atlantic Coast; they suggest a "line of settlement" steadily pushing outward into a huge blank area with no mark of civilization. The people Byrd met on his journey into the backcountry would not have understood such maps. After all, the empty space on the maps was their home. They experienced the frontier as populous zones of

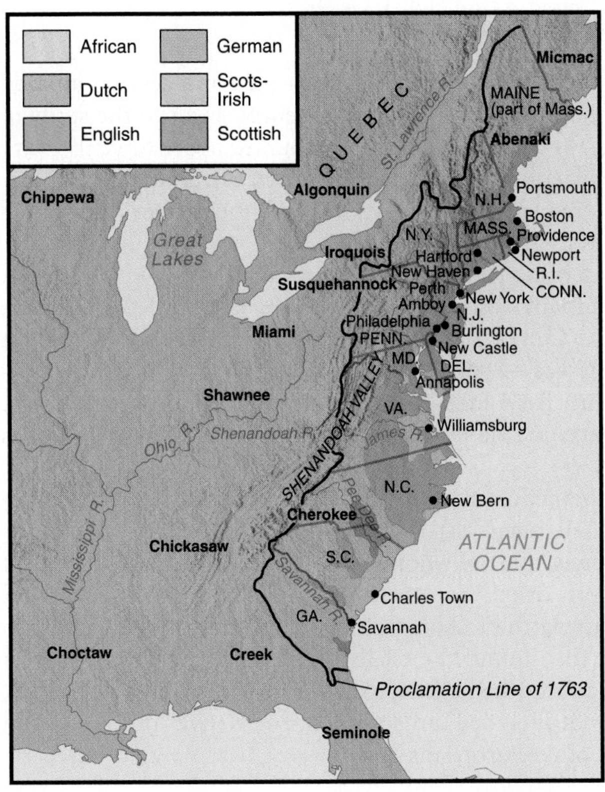

DISTRIBUTION OF EUROPEAN AND AFRICAN IMMIGRANTS IN THE THIRTEEN COLONIES *A flood of non-English immigrants swept the British colonies between 1700 and 1775.* ❖

many cultures stretching from the English and French settlements in the north all the way to the Spanish borderlands in the far southwest.

The point is not to discount the significance of the older Atlantic settlements. During the eighteenth century, Britain's thirteen colonies underwent a profound transformation. The population in the colonies grew at unprecedented rates. German and Scots-Irish immigrants arrived in huge numbers. So, too, did African slaves. Wherever they lived, colonial Americans of this period found they were not as isolated from each other as they had been during most of the seventeenth century. Indeed, after 1690, men and women expanded their cultural horizons, becoming part of a larger Anglo-American empire. The change was striking. Colonists whose parents or grandparents had come to the New World to confront a "howling wilderness" now purchased imported European manufactures, read English journals, participated in imperial wars, and sought favors from a growing number of resident royal officials. No one could escape the influence of Britain. The cultural, economic, and political links connecting the colonists to the imperial center in London grew stronger with time.

This surprising development raises a difficult question for the modern historian. If the eighteenth-century colonists were so powerfully attracted to Great Britain, why did they ever declare independence? The answer may well be that as the colonists became more British, they inevitably became more American as well. This development helps explain the appearance after midcentury of a genuine nationalist sentiment. Political, commercial, and military links that brought the colonists into more frequent contact with Great Britain also made them more aware of other colonists. It was within an expanding, prosperous empire that they first began seriously to consider what it meant to be American.

Growth and Diversity

The phenomenal growth of British America during the eighteenth century amazed Benjamin Franklin, one of the first persons to bring scientific rigor to the study of demography. The population of the English colonies doubled approximately every twenty-five years, and if the expansion continued at such an extraordinary rate, according to calculations Franklin made in 1751, in another century more Englishmen would live in America than in England.

Few societies in recorded history have expanded so rapidly, and if the growth rate had not dropped substantially during the nineteenth and twentieth centuries, the current population of the United States would stand at more than one billion people. Natural reproduction was responsible for most of the growth. More families bore children who in turn lived long enough to have children of their own. Because of this sudden expansion, the population of the late colonial period was strikingly young.

Not only was the total population increasing at a very rapid rate, it also was becoming more dispersed and heterogeneous. Each year witnessed the arrival of thousands of non-English Europeans, most of whom soon moved to the **backcountry** of Pennsylvania and the southern colonies in the hope of obtaining their own land and setting up as independent farmers. Although they planned to follow customs they had known in Europe, they found the challenge of surviving on the British frontier more demanding than they had anticipated. They plunged into a complex, fluid, often violent society that included large numbers of Native Americans and African Americans as well as other Europeans.

backcountry In the eighteenth century, the edge of settlement extending from western Pennsylvania to Georgia. This region formed the second frontier as settlers moved westward from the Atlantic coast into the nation's interior.

Scots-Irish and Germans

Non-English colonists poured into American ports throughout the eighteenth century, creating rich ethnic diversity in areas originally settled by Anglo-Saxons. The largest group of newcomers was the Scots-Irish. The experiences of these people in Britain influenced not only their decision to move to the New World but also their behavior once they arrived. During the seventeenth century, English rulers thought they could thoroughly dominate Catholic Ireland by transporting thousands of lowland Scottish Presbyterians to the northern region of that war-torn country. The plan failed, and after a short time, many of the Scots-Irish elected to emigrate to America, where they hoped to find the freedom and prosperity that had been denied them in Ireland. Often entire Presbyterian congregations followed charismatic ministers to the New World, intent on replicating a distinctive, fiercely independent culture on the frontier. It is estimated that about 150,000 Scots-Irish migrated to the colonies before the American Revolution.

Most Scots-Irish immigrants landed initially in Philadelphia, but they soon moved west and carved out farms on Pennsylvania's western frontier. The colony's proprietors welcomed the influx of new settlers, for it seemed they would form an ideal barrier between the Indians and the older, coastal communities. The Penn family soon had second thoughts, however. The Scots-Irish settled wherever they found unoccupied land, regardless of who owned it, and challenged the established order.

A second large body of non-English settlers, more than 100,000 people, came from the upper Rhine Valley, the German Palatinate. Some of the migrants belonged to small pietistic Protestant sects, and they came to America in search of religious toleration. Most Germans, however, sought the peace and good lands of the colonies. The German migrants—mistakenly called Pennsylvania Dutch because the English confused *Deutsch* (German) with *Dutch* (from Holland)—began reaching Philadelphia in large numbers after 1717, and by 1766, persons of German stock accounted for more than one-third of Pennsylvania's total population. Even their most vocal detractors admitted that the Germans were the best farmers in the colony.

Ethnic differences in Pennsylvania bred disputes. The Scots-Irish as well as the Germans preferred to live with people of their own background, and they sometimes fought to keep members of the other nationality out of their areas. The English were suspicious of both groups. Indeed, many Pennsylvanians shared Franklin's opinion that the Germans posed a threat to the primacy of the English language and government in that colony.

Such prejudice may have persuaded members of both groups to search for new homes. After 1730, Germans and Scots-Irish pushed southward from western Pennsylvania into the Shenandoah Valley, thousands of them settling in the back-country of Virginia and the Carolinas. The Germans usually remained wherever they found unclaimed fertile land. By contrast, the Scots-Irish often moved two or three times. But wherever the newcomers settled, they often found themselves living beyond the effective authority of the various colonial governments. These conditions heightened the importance of religious institutions within the small ethnic communities. Although the original stimulus for coming to America may have been a desire for economic independence and prosperity, backcountry families—especially the Scots-Irish—flocked to evangelical Protestant preachers, to Presbyterian and later to Baptist and Methodist ministers who not only fulfilled the settlers' spiritual needs but also gave these scattered backcountry communities a pronounced moral character that survived long after the colonial period.

This folk art painting from the cover of a clothes box depicts a well-dressed German-American farmer. The stock around the farmer's neck, his coat, and walking stick indicate that he enjoyed a middling to high status. ❖

Convict Settlers

Since the story of European migration tends to be upbeat—men and women engaged in a largely successful quest for a better material life—it often is forgotten that British courts compelled many people to come to America. Indeed, the African slaves were not the only large group of people coerced into moving to the New World. In 1718, Parliament passed the Transportation Act, allowing judges in England, Scotland, and Ireland to send convicted felons to the American colonies. Between 1718 and 1775, the courts shipped approximately fifty thousand convicts across the Atlantic, with the majority seemingly having committed only minor crimes against property. Although transported convicts—almost 75 percent of whom were young males—escaped the hangman, they found life difficult in the colonies. Sold primarily in the Chesapeake colonies as indentured servants, they faced an uncertain future, and few prospered.

Although Americans contracted with the convict servants, they expressed fear that the men and women would create a dangerous criminal class. In one irate essay, Benjamin Franklin asked his readers to consider just how the colonists might repay the leaders of Great Britain for shipping so many felons to America. He suggested that rattlesnakes, distributed liberally in the gardens throughout England, might be the appropriate gift. The Revolution forced the British courts to redirect the flow of convicts to another part of the world; an indirect result of American independence was the founding of Australia by transported felons.

Native Americans Stake Out a Middle Ground

In some histories of the colonial period, Native Americans make only a brief appearance, usually during the earliest years of conquest and settlement. After initial contact with the first European invaders, the Indians seem mysteriously to disappear from the central narrative of colonization, and it is not until the nineteenth century that they turn up again, this time to wage a last desperate battle against the encroachment of white society.

This obviously inadequate account slights one of the richest chapters of Native American history. To be sure, during much of the seventeenth century, various Indian groups that contested the English settlers for control of coastal lands suffered terribly, sometimes from war but more often from the spread of contagious diseases such as smallpox. The two races found it very difficult to live in close proximity. But the Indians managed to survive. By the eighteenth century, the site of the most intense and creative contact between the races had shifted to the huge territory between the Appalachian Mountains and the Mississippi River, where several hundred thousand Native Americans made their homes.

Many Indians had only recently migrated to the area. Some moved to escape confrontation with European invaders; others were refugees of lost wars. These survivors joined with other Indians to establish new multiethnic communities. In this respect, the Native American villages may not have seemed all that different from the mixed European settlements of the backcountry.

Stronger groups of Indians such as the Creek, Choctaw, Chickasaw, Cherokee, and Shawnee generally welcomed the refugees. Strangers were formally adopted to take the places of family members killed in battle or overcome by sickness, and it should be appreciated that many seemingly traditional Indian villages of the eighteenth century actually represented innovative responses to rapidly shifting external conditions.

The concept of a *middle ground* helps us comprehend more fully how eighteenth-century Indians held their own in the backcountry beyond the Appalachian Mountains. The Native Americans never intended to isolate themselves completely from European contact. They relied on white traders, French as well as English, to provide essential metal goods and weapons. The goal of the Indian confederacies rather was to maintain a strong independent voice in these commercial exchanges, playing the French off against the British whenever possible. So long as the confederacies had sufficient military strength, they compelled everyone who came to negotiate in the "middle ground" to give them proper respect. It would be incorrect, therefore, to characterize their relations with the Europeans as a stark choice between total war or abject surrender. Native Americans took advantage of rivals when possible; they compromised when necessary. It is best to imagine the Indians' middle ground as an open, dynamic process of creative interaction.

The survival of the middle ground depended ultimately on factors over which the Native Americans had little control. Imperial competition between France and Britain enhanced the Indians' bargaining position, but after the British defeated the French in 1763, the Indians no longer received the same solicitous attention as they had in earlier times. Keeping old allies happy seemed to the British a needless expense. Moreover, contagious disease continued to take a fearful toll. In the southern backcountry between 1685 and 1790, the Indian population dropped an astounding 72 percent. In the Ohio Valley, the numbers suggest similar rates of decline. In fact, there is some evidence that British military officers consciously practiced germ warfare against the Native Americans, giving them blankets contaminated by smallpox. By the time the United States took control of this region, the middle ground itself had become a casualty of history.

SPANISH BORDERLANDS OF THE EIGHTEENTH CENTURY

In many traditional histories of North America, the Spanish make only a brief appearance, usually as fifteenth-century conquistadores. But as soon as they have conquered Mexico, they are dropped from the story as if they had no serious part to play in the ongoing development of the continent. This is, of course, a skewed perspective that masks the roots of ethnic diversity in this country. The Spanish empire did not disappear. Indeed, it continued to shape the character of borderlands societies well into the eighteenth century. As anyone who visits the modern American Southwest quickly discovers, Spanish administrators and priests—not to mention ordinary settlers—left a lasting imprint on the cultural landscape of the United States.

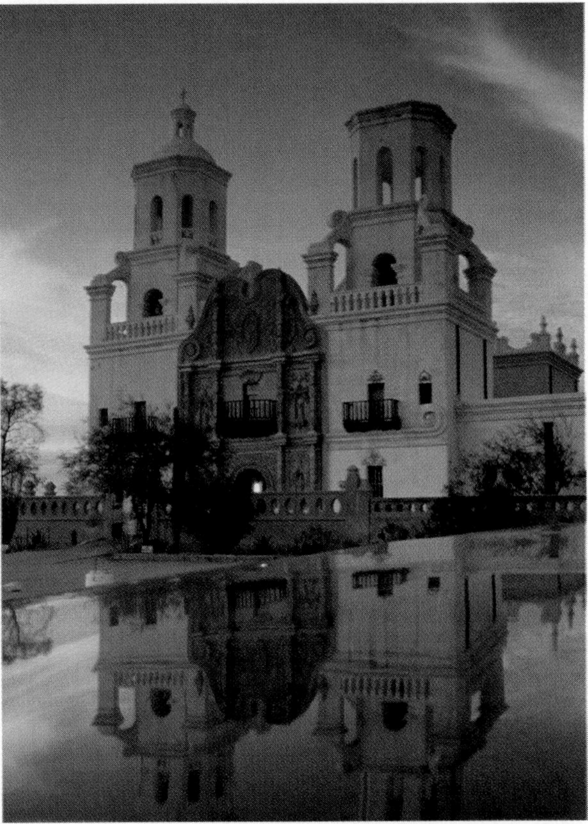

Baroque-style eighteenth-century Spanish mission at San Xavier del Bac in present-day Arizona. Spanish missions dotted the frontier of northern New Spain from Florida to California. ◆

Conquering the Northern Frontier

Spanish settlers established no communities north of the Rio Grande until late in the sixteenth century. The local Pueblo tribes resisted the invasion of colonists, soldiers, and missionaries, and in a major rebellion in 1680, the native peoples drove the whites completely out of New Mexico. Not until 1692 were the Spanish able to reconquer this fiercely contested area. By then, Native American hostility, coupled with the settlers' failure to find precious metal, had cooled Spain's enthusiasm for the northern frontier.

Concern over French encroachment in the Southeast led Spain to colonize St. Augustine in Florida in 1565. Although this enterprise never flourished, it claims attention as the first permanent European settlement established in what would become the United States, predating the founding of Jamestown and Plymouth by several decades. Pedro Menéndez de Avilés brought some fifteen hundred soldiers and settlers to St. Augustine, where they constructed an impressive fort, but the colony failed to attract additional Spanish migrants.

California never figured prominently in Spain's plans for the New World. Early explorers reported finding only impoverished Indians living along the Pacific Coast. Adventurers saw no natural resources worth mentioning, and since the area proved extremely difficult to reach from Mexico City, California received little attention. Fear that the Russians might seize the entire region belatedly sparked Spanish activity, however, and after 1769, two indomitable servants of empire, Fra Junípero Serra and Don Gaspar de Portolá, organized permanent missions and presidios (forts) at San Diego, Santa Barbara, Monterey, and San Francisco.

Peoples of the Spanish Borderlands

In sharp contrast to the English frontier settlements of the eighteenth century, the Spanish outposts in North America grew very slowly. A few Catholic priests and imperial administrators traveled to the northern provinces, but the danger of Indian attack and the harsh physical environment discouraged ordinary colonists. The European migrants were overwhelmingly male, most of them soldiers in the pay of the empire. Although some colonists came directly from Spain, most had been born in other Spanish colonies such as Minorca, the Canaries, or New Spain, and because European women rarely appeared on the frontier, Spanish males formed relationships with Indian women, fathering large numbers of mestizos, children of mixed race.

As in other European frontiers of the eighteenth century, encounters with Spanish soldiers, priests, and traders altered Native American cultures. The experience here was markedly different from that of the whites and Indians in the British

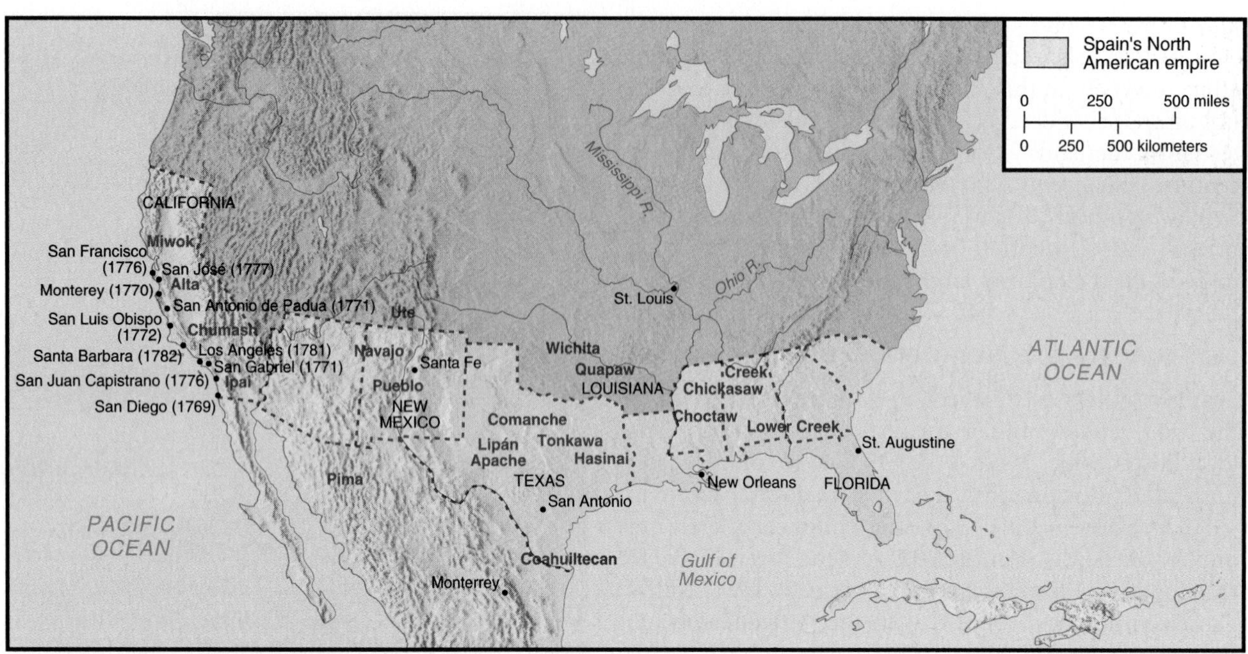

THE SPANISH BORDERLANDS, CA. 1770 *In the late eighteenth century, Spain's North American empire stretched across what is now the southern United States from Florida through Texas and New Mexico to California.* ❖

backcountry. The Spanish exploited Native American labor, reducing entire Indian villages to servitude. Many Indians moved to the Spanish towns, and although they lived in close proximity to the Europeans—something rare in British America—they were consigned to the lowest social class, objects of European contempt. However much their material conditions changed, the Indians of the Southwest resisted strenuous efforts to convert them to Catholicism. The Pueblos maintained their own religious forms—often at great personal risk—and they sometimes murdered priests who became too intrusive.

The Spanish empire never had the resources necessary to secure the northern frontier fully. It would be misleading, however, to stress the fragility of Spanish colonization. The urban design and public architecture of many southwestern cities still reflect the vision of the early Spanish settlers, and to a large extent, the old borderlands remain Spanish-speaking to this day.

The Impact of European Ideas on American Culture

The character of the older, more established British colonies changed almost as quickly as that of the backcountry. The rapid growth of an urban cosmopolitan culture impressed eighteenth-century commentators, and even though most Americans still lived on scattered farms, they had begun to participate aggressively in an exciting consumer marketplace that expanded their imaginative horizons.

Provincial Cities

Despite the rate of population growth, few eighteenth-century Americans lived in cities. Boston, Newport, New York, Philadelphia, and Charles Town—the five largest cities—contained only about 5 percent of the colonial population. In 1775, none held more than forty thousand persons. The explanation for the dearth of city dwellers can be found in the highly specialized nature of colonial commerce. Port towns served as intermediary trade and shipping centers in which bulk cargoes were broken up for inland distribution; they did not support large-scale manufacturing. Moreover, men who worked for wages in Europe usually became farmers in America.

Yet American cities profoundly affected colonial culture, for it was in the cities that the English influence was most pronounced. Wealthy merchants and lawyers tried to emulate the culture of the mother country. They went to the theater, attended concerts, and dressed in the high fashion of London society. The architectural splendor was especially noticeable. Homes of enduring beauty, modeled on English country houses, were constructed during the reign of Britain's early Hanoverian kings. Since all these kings were named George, the term *Georgian* was applied to this style of architecture.

Their owners filled the houses with fine furniture. Each city patronized certain skilled craftsmen, but the artisans of Philadelphia were known for producing magnificent copies of the works of Thomas Chippendale, Great Britain's most renowned furniture designer. These developments gave American cities an elegance they had not possessed in the previous century.

American Enlightenment

European historians often refer to the eighteenth century as the Age of Reason. During this period, a body of new ideas, collectively called the **Enlightenment,** altered the way that educated Europeans thought about God, nature, and society. Enlightenment philosophers replaced the concept of original sin with a far more optimistic view of human nature. A benevolent God, they argued, having set the universe in motion, gave human beings the power of reason to enable them to comprehend the orderly workings of his creation. Everything, even human society, operated according to these mechanical laws. It was the duty of men and women, therefore, to make certain that institutions such as church and state conformed to self-evident natural laws. Through the use of reason, they asserted, human suffering could be eliminated and perfection achieved.

Enlightenment Philosophical and intellectual movement that began in Europe during the eighteenth century. It stressed the application of reason to solve social and scientific problems.

The American Enlightenment was a rather tame affair compared to its European counterpart. Colonists welcomed the advent of experimental science but stoutly defended the tenets of traditional Christianity. Americans emphasized the search for useful knowledge, ideas, and inventions. What mattered was practical experimentation, and the Enlightenment spawned scores of earnest scientific tinkerers, people who dutifully recorded changes in temperature, the appearance of strange plants or animals, and the particulars of astronomical phenomena.

The greatest of all these American experimenters was Benjamin Franklin (1706–1790). As a young man working in his brother's Boston print shop, he discovered a copy of a new British journal, the *Spectator.* It was like a breath of fresh air to a boy growing up in Puritan New England. In August 1721, he and his brother founded the *New-England Courant,* a weekly newspaper that satirized Boston's political and religious leaders in the manner of the contemporary British press. Proper Bostonians were not prepared for such a critical journal, and in 1723, Franklin left Massachusetts in search of a less antagonistic intellectual environment.

He settled in Philadelphia. There he devoted himself to the pursuit of useful knowledge. Franklin never denied the existence of God. Rather he pushed the Lord aside, making room for the free exercise of reason. A naturally curious man, he was constantly experimenting and broadening his understanding of science, always with some practical end in mind. The lightning rod and a marvelously efficient stove are only two of Franklin's important contributions to material progress through human ingenuity.

Franklin energetically promoted the spread of Enlightenment ideas. In Philadelphia, he formed "a club for mutual Improvement, which we call'd the Junto" and a library association to discuss literature, philosophy, and science. The members of these groups communicated with Americans living in other colonies, providing them not only with the latest information from Europe but also with models for their own clubs and associations. Such efforts broadened the intellectual horizons of many colonists, especially city dwellers.

Economic Transformation

The colonial economy kept pace with the stunning growth in population. Per capita income never fell behind the population explosion. An abundance of land and the extensive growth of agriculture accounted for this economic success. Each year, more Americans produced more tobacco, wheat, and rice—just to cite the major export crops—and by this means, they maintained a high level of individual prosperity without developing an industrial base.

Half of the American goods produced for export went to Great Britain. The Navigation Acts (see Chapter 3) were still in effect, and enumerated items such as

❖ A Look at the Past ❖

Westover

By the mid-eighteenth century a native-born elite class took shape in Virginia and other colonies. Many constructed houses to signify their status and power. Few houses were as grand as Westover in Virginia, probably built by William Byrd III around 1750, but all "great houses" impressed visitors with their size and level of interior decorations. Such houses required vast sums of money as well as knowledge of the latest European styles to construct, maintain, and furnish. The funds needed to maintain these estates often came from the production of export crops such as tobacco and rice, crops cultivated by an unfree black labor force. How do you think the typical Virginian, who lived in a one-room house, reacted to houses such as this one? What did the difference between great houses like Westover and the typical one-room house suggest about eighteenth-century Virginia society? How did building large, elaborate, and fashionable houses contribute to cementing gentry power?

tobacco and furs had to be landed first at a British port. Over the years, specific legislation brought white pine trees, molasses, hats, and iron under imperial control as England regulated colonial trade to its advantage.

The statutes might have created tensions between the colonists and the mother country had they been rigorously enforced. Crown officials, however, generally ignored the new laws. But even without the Navigation Acts, a majority of colonial exports would have been sold on the English markets. The emerging consumer society in Great Britain was beginning to create a generation that possessed enough income to purchase American goods, especially sugar and tobacco. This rising demand was the major market force shaping the colonial economy.

Roughly one-fourth of all American exports went to the West Indies. Colonial ships carrying food sailed for the Caribbean and returned immediately to the Middle Colonies or New England with cargoes of molasses, sugar, and rum. "Triangular trade," crossing first to the west coast of Africa, was insignificant. In addition, the West Indies played a vital role in preserving American credit. Without this source of income, colonists would not have been able to pay for the manufactured items that they purchased in the mother country. The cost of goods imported from Great Britain normally exceeded the revenues collected on American exports to the mother country. To cover this small but recurrent deficit, colonial merchants relied on profits made in the West Indies.

Birth of a Consumer Society

After midcentury, however, the balance of trade turned dramatically against the colonists. Americans began buying more English goods than their parents and grandparents had done. Between 1740 and 1770, English exports to the American colonies increased by an astounding 360 percent.

In part, this shift reflected the increased production of British industries. Because of technological advancements in manufacturing, Great Britain was able to produce certain goods more efficiently and more cheaply than the colonists could. Americans started to buy as never before; Staffordshire china and imported cloth replaced crude earthenware and rough homespun. In this manner, British industrialization undercut American handicrafts and folk art.

To help Americans purchase manufactured goods, British merchants offered generous credit. For many people, the temptation to acquire English finery blinded them to hard economic realities. Colonists deferred settlement by agreeing to pay interest on their debts, and by 1760, the total indebtedness had reached £2 million. Colonial governments could delay the balance-of-payments crisis for a time by issuing paper money, but the problem was not resolved.

The eighteenth century brought a substantial increase in intercoastal trade. Southern planters sent tobacco and rice to New England and the Middle Colonies, where these staples were exchanged for meat and wheat as well as for goods imported from Great Britain. By 1760, approximately 30 percent of the colonists' total tonnage capacity was involved in this extensive "coastwise" commerce. In addition, American colonists carried on a substantial amount of commerce over the rough, backcountry highway known as the Great Wagon Road, which stretched 735 miles along the Blue Ridge Mountains from Pennsylvania to South Carolina. The long, gracefully designed Conestoga wagon was vital to this overland trade.

The shifting patterns of trade had an immense effect on the development of an American culture. First, the flood of British imports eroded local and regional identities. Deep sectional differences remained, of course, but Americans from New Hampshire to Georgia were increasingly drawn into a sophisticated economic network centered in London.

Second, the expanding coastwise and overland trade brought colonists of different backgrounds into more frequent contact, exchanging ideas and experience as well as tobacco and wheat. New journals and newspapers appeared. Americans were kept abreast of the latest news in the colonies as well as in London. Americans were expanding their horizons, and slowly, sometimes painfully, a distinct culture was emerging.

Religious Revivals in Provincial Societies

Great Awakening Widespread evangelical religious revival movement of the mid-1700s. The movement divided congregations and weakened the authority of established churches in the colonies.

A sudden, spontaneous series of Protestant revivals known as the **Great Awakening** had a far greater impact than the Enlightenment on the lives of the common people. This unprecedented evangelical outpouring caused men and women to rethink basic assumptions about society, church, and state. In our own time, we have witnessed the forces of religious revival in different regions of the world. It is no exaggeration to claim that a similar revolution took place in mid-eighteenth-century America.

The Great Awakening

Only with hindsight does the Great Awakening seem a unified religious movement. Revivals occurred in different places at different times. The first signs of a spiritual awakening appeared in New England during the late 1730s. The intensity of the event varied from region to region. Revivals were most important in Massachusetts, Connecticut, Rhode Island, Pennsylvania, New Jersey, and, in the 1750s and 1760s, Virginia. No single religious denomination or sect monopolized the Awakening; mainly Congregationalist churches were affected in New England, but elsewhere revivals involved Presbyterians, Methodists, and Baptists.

The evangelism of the Great Awakening infused a new sense of vitality into religions that had lost their fervor. People in New England complained that Congregational ministers seemed obsessed with dull, scholastic matters; their sermons no longer touched the heart. And in the Southern Colonies, there were simply not enough ordained ministers to tend to the religious needs of the population.

The Great Awakening began unexpectedly in Northampton, a small farm community in western Massachusetts, sparked by the preaching of Jonathan Edwards, the local Congregationalist minister. With fervent zeal, Edwards reminded the members of his flock that their fate had been determined for all eternity by an omnipotent God. He thought his fellow ministers had grown soft and were preaching easy salvation. Edwards disabused his congregation of that false comfort. With calm self-assurance, he described in vivid detail the torments of the damned, those whom God had not elected to receive divine grace.

Why this uncompromising Calvinist message set off religious revivals during the late 1730s is not known. Whatever the explanation for the sudden popular response to Edwards's preaching, young people began flocking to church. They experienced a searing conversion, a sense of "new birth" and utter dependence on God. The excitement spread, and evangelical ministers concluded that God must be preparing Americans, his chosen people, for the millennium.

The Voice of Popular Religion

The best-known figure of the Great Awakening was George Whitefield, a young, inspiring preacher from England who toured the colonies from Georgia to New Hampshire. He was an extraordinary public speaker who cast a spell over the throngs who came to see and hear him.

Whitefield's audience came from all groups of American society, rich and poor, young and old, rural and urban. Though Whitefield described himself as a Calvinist, he welcomed all Protestants, and he spoke from any pulpit that was available.

"Don't tell me you are a Baptist, an Independent, a Presbyterian, a dissenter," he thundered. "Tell me you are a Christian, that is all I want."

American-born **itinerant preachers** followed Whitefield's example. The most famous was Gilbert Tennent, a Presbyterian of Scots-Irish background who had been educated in the Middle Colonies. He and other revivalists of like mind traveled from town to town, colony to colony, challenging local clergymen who seemed hostile to evangelical religion. Many ministers remained suspicious of the itinerants and their methods. Some complaints may have amounted to little more than jealousy. Others raised serious questions: How could the revivalists be certain that God had sparked the Great Awakening? And how could the revivalists be certain that the "dangers of enthusiasm" would not lead them astray? During the 1740s and 1750s, many congregations split between defenders of the new emotional preaching, the New Lights, and those who regarded the entire movement as dangerous nonsense, the Old Lights.

itinerant preachers Traveling revivalist ministers of the Great Awakening movement. These charismatic preachers spread revivalism throughout America.

Although Tennent did not condone the excesses of the Great Awakening, his direct attacks on formal learning invited the crude anti-intellectualism of such deranged revivalists as James Davenport. Davenport preached under the light of smoky torches; he danced and stripped, shrieked and laughed. He also urged people to burn books written by anyone who had not experienced the "new light."

To focus on occasional anti-intellectual outbursts is to obscure the positive ways in which this vast revival changed American society. First, the New Lights founded several important centers of higher education. They wanted to train young men who would carry on the good works of Edwards, Whitefield, and Tennent. Princeton (1747), Brown (1764), Rutgers (1766), and Dartmouth (1769) were all colleges founded by revivalist leaders.

Second, the Great Awakening encouraged men and women who had been taught to remain silent before traditional figures of authority to take an active role in their own salvation. They could no longer rely on ministers or institutions. The individual alone stood before God. This emphasis on personal religious choices shattered the old harmony that existed among Protestant sects and in its place introduced a boisterous, often bitterly fought competition.

With religious contention, however, came an awareness of a larger community, a union of fellow believers that extended beyond the boundaries of town and colony. In fact, evangelical religion was one of several forces at work during the mid-eighteenth century that brought scattered colonists into contact with one another for the first time. In this sense, the Great Awakening was a "national" event long before a nation actually existed.

People who had been touched by the Great Awakening saw America as "an instrument of Providence." With God's help, social and political progress was achievable, and from this perspective, of course, the New Lights did not sound much different from the mildly rationalist American spokesmen of the Enlightenment.

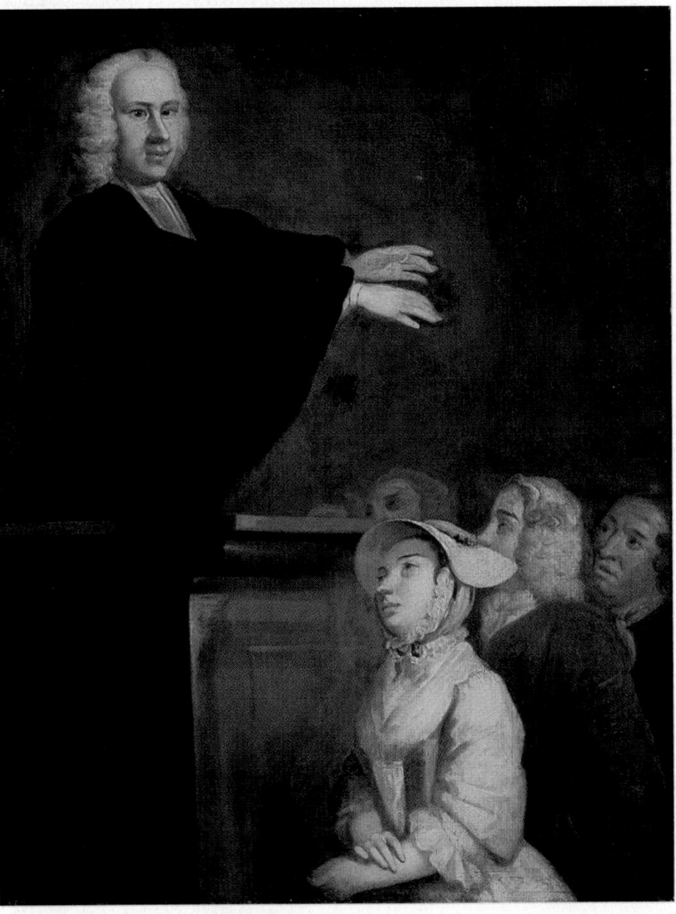

The fervor of the Great Awakening was intensified by the eloquence of itinerant preachers such as George Whitefield, the most popular evangelical of the mid-eighteenth century. ❖

Both groups prepared the way for the development of a revolutionary mentality in colonial America.

Clash of Political Cultures

The political history of this period illuminates a growing tension within the empire. Americans of all regions repeatedly stated their desire to replicate British political institutions. Parliament, they claimed, provided a model for the American assemblies. They revered the English constitution. According to its defenders, the balanced constitution of Great Britain protected life, liberty, and property better than any other contemporary government. However, the more colonists studied British political theory and practice—in other words, the more they attempted to become British—the more aware they became of major differences. By trying to copy Great Britain, they unwittingly discovered something about being American.

The Theory and the Reality of British Politics

The English constitution incorporated three distinct parts: the monarch, the House of Lords, and the House of Commons. Thus, in theory, the government represented the socioeconomic interests of the king, the nobility, and the common people. Acting alone, each body would run to excess, even tyranny, but operating within a mixed system, each automatically checked the others' ambitions, for the common good.

The reality of daily political life, however, bore little relation to theory. The three elements of the constitution did not, in fact, represent distinct socioeconomic groups. Men elected to the House of Commons often came from the same social background as those who served in the House of Lords. All represented the interests of Britain's landed elite. Moreover, there was no attempt to maintain strict constitutional separation. The king exerted considerable influence, for example, in the House of Commons.

The claim that the members of the House of Commons represented all the people of England also seemed farfetched. In 1715, only about 20 percent of English adult males had the right to vote, and there was no standard size for electoral districts. Some representatives to Parliament were chosen by several thousand voters, others by only a handful of electors.

Before 1760, few people in England spoke out against these constitutional abuses. The main exception was a group of radical publicists whom historians have labeled the "Commonwealthmen." These writers decried the corruption of political life, warning that the nation that compromised its civic virtue deserved to lose its liberty and property. The most famous Commonwealthmen were John Trenchard and Thomas Gordon, who penned a series of essays titled *Cato's Letters* between 1720 and 1723. They warned the nation to be vigilant against tyranny by England's rulers.

But however shrilly these writers protested, however many newspaper articles they published, the Commonwealthmen won little support for their potential reforms. Englishmen were not willing to tamper with a system of government that had so recently survived a civil war and a Glorious Revolution. Americans, however, took Trenchard and Gordon to heart.

Governing the Colonies: The American Experience

The colonists assumed—perhaps naively—that their governments were modeled on the balanced constitution of Great Britain. They argued that within their political systems, the governor corresponded to the king, the governor's council to the House of Lords, and the colonial assemblies to the House of Commons. As the colonists discovered, however, English theories about the mixed constitution were no more relevant in America than they were in the mother country.

By midcentury, royal governors appointed by the crown ruled a majority of the mainland colonies. Many of the appointees were career army officers who through luck, charm, or family connection had gained the ear of someone close to the king. These patronage posts did not generate income sufficient to interest the most powerful or talented personalities of the period, but they did draw middle-level bureaucrats who were ambitious or desperate (or both).

Before departing for the New World, royal governors received an elaborate set of instructions drafted by the Board of Trade. The document dealt with almost every aspect of colonial life—political, economic, and religious—and no one knew for certain that these orders even possessed the force of law.

About the governors' powers, however, there was no doubt; they were enormous. In fact, royal governors could do certain things in America that a king could not do in eighteenth-century England. Among these were the right to veto legislation and to dismiss judges. The governors also served as commanders in chief in each province.

Royal governors were advised by a council, usually a body of about twelve wealthy colonists selected by the Board of Trade in London on the recommendation of the governor. By the eighteenth century, however, the council had lost most of its power. This body was certainly no House of Lords.

Nor were the colonial assemblies much like the House of Commons. A far greater proportion of men could vote in America than in Britain. In most colonies, adult white males who owned a small amount of land could vote in countywide elections. Although participation in government was not high, and most colonists were content to let gentry represent them in the assemblies, the potential for throwing the rascals out was always present.

Colonial Assemblies

Members of the assemblies were convinced that they had a special obligation to preserve colonial liberties. Any attack on the legislature was perceived as an assault on the rights of Americans. So aggressive were these bodies in seizing privileges, determining procedures, and controlling money bills that some historians refer to the political developments of eighteenth-century America as "the rise of the assemblies."

This political system seemed designed to generate hostility. There was simply no reason for the colonial legislature to cooperate with appointed royal governors. A few governors managed briefly to create in America a political culture of patronage akin to what they knew in England. But usually such efforts clashed with the colonists' perceptions of politics. They truly believed in the purity of the balanced constitution, and attempts to revert to a patronage system were met by loud protests in language that seemed to be directly lifted from the pages of *Cato's Letters*.

The major source of shared political information was the weekly journal, a new and vigorous institution in American life. In New York and Massachusetts especially, weekly newspapers urged readers to preserve civic virtue and to exercise extreme vigilance against the spread of privileged power. Through such journals, a pattern of political rhetoric that in Britain had gained only marginal respectability became after 1765 America's normal form of political discourse.

The rise of the assemblies shaped American culture in other, subtler ways. Over the course of the century, the language of the law became increasingly Anglicized. Varying local legal practices that had been widespread during the seventeenth century became standardized. Indeed, by 1750, there was little difference between the colonial legal system and that of the mother country. Not surprisingly, a number of men who served in colonial assemblies were lawyers or others who had received legal training. When Americans from different regions met, they discovered that they shared a commitment to the preservation of the English common law.

But if eighteenth-century political developments drew the colonists closer to the mother country, they also brought Americans a greater awareness of one another. As their horizons widened, they learned that they operated within the same general imperial system and that they shared similar problems. Like the revivalists and merchants—people who crossed old boundaries—colonial legislators laid the foundation for a broader cultural identity.

Century of Imperial War

The scope and style of warfare in the colonies changed radically during the eighteenth century. Local conflicts with the Indians, such as King Philip's War (1675–1676) in New England, gave way to hostilities that originated on the other side of the Atlantic, in rivalries between Great Britain and France over geopolitical considerations and commercial ambitions. The external threat to security forced people in different colonies to devise unprecedented measures of military and political cooperation.

On paper, at least, the British settlements enjoyed military superiority. Nonetheless, for most of the first half of the eighteenth century, their advantage proved more apparent than real. While the British settlements possessed a larger and more prosperous population than the French—1,200,000 to 75,000—they were divided into separate governments that sometimes seemed more suspicious of each other than of the French. When war came, French officers and Indian allies exploited these jealousies with considerable skill. Moreover, the small population of New France was concentrated along the St. Lawrence, and it could easily mass the forces needed to defend Montreal and Quebec.

King William's and Queen Anne's Wars

Colonial involvement in imperial war began in 1689, when England's new king, William III, declared war on France's Louis XIV. Europeans called this struggle the War of the League of Augsburg, but to the Americans, it was simply King William's War. Canadians raided the northern frontiers of New York and New England, and although they made no territorial gains, they caused considerable suffering among the civilian population of Massachusetts and New York.

The war ended with the Treaty of Ryswick (1697), but the colonists were drawn almost immediately into a new conflict, Queen Anne's War, a dynastic conflict known in Europe as the War of the Spanish Succession (1702–1713). Colonists in South Carolina as well as New England battled against the French and their Indian allies. The bloody combat along the American frontier was formally terminated in 1713 when Great Britain and France signed the Treaty of Utrecht. European concerns were paramount in the peace negotiations. Although two decades of fighting had taken a fearful toll in North America, neither France nor the English colonists had much to show for their sacrifice.

When George I, the first Hanoverian king of Great Britain, replaced Queen Anne in 1714, parliamentary leaders were determined to preserve peace. But on the American frontier, hostilities continued. At stake was the entire West, including the Mississippi Valley. English colonists believed that the French planned to "encircle" them, to confine them to a narrow strip of land along the Atlantic Coast. As evidence, they pointed to the French forts that had been constructed through the heart of America. On their part, the French suspected that their rivals intended to seize all

NORTH AMERICA, 1750 *By 1750, the French had established a chain of settlements southward through the heart of the continent from Quebec to New Orleans. The English saw this development as a threat to their own seaboard colonies, which were expanding westward.* ❖

of North America. They noted that land speculators and Indian traders were pushing aggressively into territory claimed by France. And so the two sides lined up their Indian allies and made ready for war.

King George's War and Its Aftermath

In 1743, the Americans were dragged once again into the imperial conflict. During King George's War (1743–1748), known in Europe as the War of the Austrian Succession, the colonists scored a magnificent victory over the French. In June 1745, an army of New England troops under the command of William Pepperrell captured Louisbourg, a gigantic fortress on Cape Breton Island guarding the approaches to the Gulf of St. Lawrence and Quebec. The Americans, however, were in for a shock. When the war ended with the signing of the Treaty of Aix-la-Chapelle in 1748, the British government handed Louisbourg back to the French in exchange for concessions elsewhere. New Englanders saw this as an insult, one they did not soon forget.

By the conclusion of King George's War, the goals of the conflict had clearly changed. Americans no longer aimed simply at protecting their territory from attack. They now wanted to gain complete control over the West, a region obviously

Native Americans often depended on trade goods supplied by the British and sometimes adopted British dress. Here the Mohawk chief Theyanoguin, called King Hendrick by the British, wears a cloak he received from Queen Anne during a visit to London in 1710. During the Seven Years' War, Theyanoguin mobilized Mohawk support for the British. ❖

rich in economic opportunity. Vast tracts of land and lucrative trade with the Indians awaited ambitious colonists.

The French were not prepared to surrender an inch. But time was running against them. Not only were the English colonies growing more populous, but they also possessed a seemingly inexhaustible supply of manufactured goods to trade with the Indians. The French decided in the early 1750s, therefore, to seize the Ohio Valley before their rivals could do so. They established forts throughout the region, the most formidable being Fort Duquesne, located at the strategic fork in the Ohio River near the modern city of Pittsburgh.

Although France and England had not officially declared war, British officials advised the governor of Virginia to "repel force by force." The Virginians, who had their eyes on the Ohio Valley, needed no encouragement. In 1754, several militia companies, under the command of a promising young officer named George Washington, constructed Fort Necessity not far from Fort Duquesne. The plan failed. French and Indian troops overran the badly exposed outpost (July 3, 1754). Among other things, this humiliating setback revealed that a single colony could not defeat the French.

Albany Congress and Braddock's Defeat

Benjamin Franklin, for one, understood the necessity for intercolonial cooperation. When British officials invited representatives from the Northern Colonies to Albany (June 1754) to discuss relations with the Iroquois, Franklin used the occasion to present a bold blueprint for colonial union. His so-called **Albany Plan** envisioned the formation of a Grand Council, made up of elected delegates from the various colonies, to oversee matters of common defense, western expansion, and Indian affairs. Most daring of all, he wanted to give the council the power of taxation.

First reaction to the Albany Plan was enthusiastic, but ultimately neither the separate colonial assemblies nor Parliament approved the plan. The assemblies were jealous of their fiscal authority, whereas the English thought the scheme undermined the crown's power in the colony.

Even though there was still no formal declaration of war, the British resolved to destroy Fort Duquesne, and to that end, in 1755 they dispatched units of the regular army to the Ohio Valley under the command of Major General Edward Braddock. A poor leader who inspired no respect, on July 9, Braddock led his force of British "redcoats" and colonists into one of the worst defeats in British military history. The French and Indians opened fire as Braddock's forces were wading across the Monongahela River, about 8 miles from Fort Duquesne. Enraged, Braddock ordered a senseless counterattack. In the end, nearly 70 percent of Braddock's troops were either killed or wounded, and Braddock himself was dead. The French remained in firm control of the Ohio Valley.

Albany Plan Plan of intercolonial cooperation proposed by prominent colonists including Benjamin Franklin at a conference in Albany, New York, in 1754. The plan envisioned the formation of a Grand Council of elected delegates from the colonies that would have powers to tax and provide for the common defense. It was rejected by the colonial and British governments but was a prototype for colonial union.

Seven Years' War

Britain's imperial war effort had hit rock bottom. No one in England or America seemed to possess the leadership necessary to drive the French from the Mississippi Valley. Still, on May 18, 1756, Great Britain declared war on France, a conflict called the French and Indian War in America and the **Seven Years' War** in Europe.

William Pitt, the most powerful minister in the cabinet of George II, finally provided Great Britain with what it needed most, a forceful leader. Arrogant and conceited, Pitt nevertheless offered a bold, new imperial policy. Rather than fight great battles in Europe, where France had the advantage, Pitt decided that the critical theater of the war would be North America, where Britain and France were struggling for control of colonial markets and raw materials. His goal was clear: to expel the French from the continent, however great the cost.

Seven Years' War Worldwide conflict (1756–1763) that pitted Britain against France for control of North America. With help from the American colonists, the British won the war and eliminated France as a power on the North American continent. Also known in America as the French and Indian War.

To effect this ambitious scheme, Pitt took personal command of the army and navy. He mapped out strategy; he promoted promising young officers over the heads of their superiors. He convinced Parliament to pour millions of pounds into his imperial efforts, thus creating an enormous national debt that would soon haunt both Britain and its colonies.

To direct the grand campaign, Pitt selected two relatively obscure colonels, Jeffrey Amherst and James Wolfe. It was a masterful choice that soon proved sound. Forces under their direction captured Louisbourg on July 26, 1758, effectively severing the Canadians' main supply line with France. Time was now on the side of the British. Two poor harvests, in 1756 and 1757, and a population too small to meet the military demands of the accelerated conflict led to a desperate situation for the French empire in North America. Frontier forts began to fall; Fort Duquesne was abandoned in 1758. French and Indian troops retreated to Quebec and Montreal, surrendering key outposts at Ticonderoga, Crown Point, and Niagara as they withdrew.

The climax to a century of war came dramatically in September 1759. Wolfe, now a major general, assaulted Quebec, held by a brilliant French commander, the marquis de Montcalm. The remarkable campaign saw Wolfe's men scale a cliff under the cover of darkness and launch a successful surprise attack at dawn on September 13, 1759. Both Wolfe and Montcalm were mortally wounded. When an

A Century of Conflict: Major Wars, 1689–1763

Dates	European Name	American Name	Major Allies	Issues	Major American Battle	Treaty
1689–1697	War of the League of Augsburg	King William's War	Britain, Holland, Spain, their colonies, and Native American allies against France, its colonies, and Native American allies	Opposition to French bid for control of Europe	New England troops assault Quebec under Sir William Phips (1690)	Treaty of Ryswick (1697)
1702–1713	War of the Spanish Succession	Queen Anne's War	Britain, Holland, their colonies, and Native American allies against France, Spain, their colonies, and Native American allies	Austria and France hold rival claims to Spanish throne	Attack on Deerfield (1704)	Treaty of Utrecht (1713)
1743–1748	War of the Austrian Succession (War of Jenkin's Ear)	King George's War	Britain, its colonies, and Native American allies, and Austria against France, Spain, their Native American allies, and Prussia	Struggle among Britain, Spain, and France for control of New World territory; among France, Prussia, and Austria for control of central Europe	New England forces capture of Louisbourg under William Pepperrell (1745)	Treaty of Aix-la-Chapelle (1748)
1756–1763	Seven Years' War	French and Indian War	Britain, its colonies, and Native American allies against France, its colonies, and Native American allies	Struggle among Britain, Spain, and France for worldwide control of colonial markets and raw materials	British and Continental forces capture Quebec under Major General James Wolfe (1759)	Peace of Paris (1763)

NORTH AMERICA AFTER 1763 *The Peace of Paris (1763) redrew the map of North America. Great Britain received all the French holdings except for a few islands in the Atlantic and some sugar-producing islands in the Caribbean.* ❖

aide informed Wolfe that the French had been routed, he sighed, "Now, God be praised, I will die in peace." One year later, Amherst accepted the final surrender of the French army at Montreal.

The Peace of Paris, signed on February 10, 1763, almost fulfilled Pitt's grandiose dreams. Great Britain took possession of an empire that stretched around the globe. After a century-long struggle, the French had been driven from America, retaining only their sugar islands in the Caribbean. The treaty gave Britain title to Canada, Florida, and all the land east of the Mississippi River. The colonists were overjoyed. It was a time of good feelings and imperial pride.

The Seven Years' War made a deep impression on American society. The military struggle had forced the colonists to cooperate on an unprecedented scale. It also drew them into closer contact with the mother country. They became aware of being part of a great empire, but in the very process of waging war, they acquired a more intimate sense of an America that lay beyond the plantation and the village. Moreover, the war trained a corps of American officers, people such as George Washington, who learned from firsthand experience that the British were not invincible.

British officials later accused the Americans of ingratitude. The English charged that they had sent troops and provided funds to liberate the colonists from the threat of French attack, but the Americans had refused to shoulder their fair share of the costs. The British used this argument to justify parliamentary taxation in America. In fact, the Americans had been slow in providing men and materials needed to fight the French, but in the end, they did contribute to the defense of the empire. The colonies supplied almost twenty thousand soldiers and spent well over £2 million. Americans believed they had played a vital role.

Conclusion: Rule Britannia?

James Thomson, an Englishman, understood the hold of empire on the popular imagination of the eighteenth century. In 1740, he composed words that British patriots have sung proudly ever since:

> Rule Britannia, rule the waves
> Britons never will be slaves

Colonial Americans of British background joined the chorus. By midcentury, they took their political and cultural cues from Great Britain. They fought its wars, purchased its consumer goods, flocked to hear its evangelical preachers, and read its many publications. Without question, the empire provided the colonists with a compelling source of identity.

An editor justified the establishment of New Hampshire's first newspaper in precisely these terms. "By this Means," the publisher observed, "the spirited *Englishman*, the mountainous *Welshman*, the brave *Scotchman*, and *Irishman*, and the loyal *American*, may be firmly united and mutually RESOLVED to guard the glorious Throne of BRITANNIA . . . as *British Brothers*, in defending the Common Cause." Even new immigrants, the Germans, Scots-Irish, and Africans, who felt no political loyalty to Great Britain or affinity for British ways, had to assimilate to some degree to the dominant English culture of the colonies.

CHRONOLOGY	
1689	William and Mary accede to the English throne
1702	Anne becomes queen of England
1706	Benjamin Franklin is born
1714	George I of Hanover becomes monarch of Great Britain
1727	George II accedes to the British throne
1732	Colony of Georgia is established ❖ George Washington is born
1734–1736	First expression of the Great Awakening appears at Northampton, Massachusetts
1740	George Whitefield electrifies his listeners at Boston
1745	Colonial troops capture Louisbourg
1754	Albany Congress meets
1755	Braddock is defeated by the French and Indians in western Pennsylvania
1756	French and Indian War (Seven Years' War) is formally declared
1759	British are victorious at Quebec ❖ Wolfe and Montcalm are killed in battle
1760	George III becomes king of Great Britain
1763	Peace of Paris ending French and Indian War is signed

Americans hailed Britannia. In 1763, they were the victors, the conquerors of the backcountry. In their moment of glory the colonists assumed that Britain's rulers saw the Americans as "brothers," as equal partners in the business of empire. Only slowly would they realize that the British had a different perception. For them, "American" was a way of saying "not quite English."

Key Terms

backcountry, p. 60
Enlightenment, p. 65
Great Awakening, p. 68
itinerant preachers, p. 69
Albany Plan, p. 74
Seven Years' War, p. 75

Recommended Reading

The central theme of this chapter has been the re-integration of the American colonies into an increasingly powerful and prosperous British Empire. A good introduction to the imperial dimension of eighteenth-century experience is P. J. Marshall, ed., *The Oxford History of the British Empire, vol. 2, The Eighteenth Century* (1998). In *Britons: Forging the Nation, 1707–1837* (1992), Linda Colley provides an excellent discussion of the aggressive spirit of the British nationalism that the Americans came to celebrate. The arrival of new ethnic groups is examined in Eric Hinderaker and Peter C. Mancall, *At the Edge of Empire: The Backcountry in British North America* (2003); Patrick Griffin, *The People with No Name: Ulster's Presbyterians in a British Atlantic World, 1688–1763* (2001); Bernard Bailyn, *The Peopling of British North America: An Introduction* (1988); and Bernard Bailyn and Philip D. Morgan, eds., *Strangers Within the Realm: Cultural Margins of the First British Empire* (1991). Richard White has transformed how we think about Native American resistance during this period in *The Middle Ground: Indians, Empires, and Republics in the Great Lakes Region* (1991). Two other fine books explore the Indians' response to the expanding European empires: Timothy Shannon, *Indians and Colonists at the Crossroads of Empire: The Albany Congress of 1754* (2000) and Gregory Evans Dowd, *War Under Heaven: Pontiac, The Indian Nations and the British Empire* (2002). The complex story of Spanish colonization of the Southwest is told masterfully in David J. Weber, *The Spanish Frontier in North America* (1992). Fred Anderson offers the most complete treatment of war and empire in *Crucible of War: The Seven Years' War and the Fate of Empire in British North America, 1754–1766* (2000). A splendid examination of Benjamin Franklin as a colonial voice of the Enlightenment is Edmund S. Morgan, *Benjamin Franklin* (2002). The extraordinary impact of evangelical religion on colonial life is addressed in Mark A. Noll, *America's God: From Jonathan Edwards to Abraham Lincoln* (2002); Frank Lambert, *"Pedlar of Divinity": George Whitefield and the Transatlantic Revivals, 1734–1770* (1994); and Timothy D. Hall, *Contested Boundaries: Itinerancy and the Reshaping of the Colonial Religious World* (1994). The cultural concerns of a rising Anglicized colonial middle class are analyzed in David S. Shields, *Civil Tongues and Polite Letters in British America* (1997).

For a list of additional sites related to this chapter's topics, please see http://www.ablongman.com/divine.

Suggested Web Sites

History Buff's—American History Library

http://www.historybuff.com/library

Brief journalistic essays on newspaper coverage of sixteenth- to eighteenth-century American history.

Benjamin Franklin Documentary History Web Site

http://www.english.udel.edu/lemay/franklin/

University of Delaware professor J. A. Leo Lemay tells the story of Franklin's varied life in seven parts on this intriguing site.

Jonathan Edwards

http://www.jonathanedwards.com/

Speeches by this famous preacher of the Great Awakening are on this site.

Religion and the Founding of the American Republic

http://lcweb.loc.gov/exhibits/religion/religion.html

This Library of Congress site is an on-line exhibit about religion and the creation of the United States.

Smithsonian Institution: You Be the Historian

http://www.americanhistory.si.edu/hohr/springer
Part of the Smithsonian's on-line museum, this exhibit enables students to examine artifacts from the home of New Castle, Delaware, residents Thomas and Elizabeth Springer and interpret the lives of a late eighteenth-century American family.

National Museum of the American Indian

http://www.si.edu/nmai
The Smithsonian Institution maintains this site, providing information about the museum. The museum is dedicated to everything about Native Americans.

The French and Indian War

http://web.syr.edu/~laroux/
This site is about French soldiers who came to New France between 1755 and 1760 to fight in the French and Indian War.

DoHistory, Harvard University Film Study Center

http://www.dohistory.org/
Focusing on the life of Martha Ballard, a late eighteenth-century New England woman, this site employs selections from her diary, excerpts from a book and film of her life, and other primary documents to enable students to conduct their own historical investigation.

Learning to Live with Diversity in the Eighteenth Century

What Is an American?

Americans have had a hard time dealing with difference. It is only recently that some commentators have begun to describe social diversity as a positive good. For most of our history, attempts to define national identity have inevitably excluded members of minority groups or newcomers whose language and culture were not English. Over the past two centuries those in authority have devised various strategies for accommodating ethnic and racial diversity, some more successful than others, but all of them at any moment are as likely to produce anger and violence as mutual understanding. These explosive issues first sparked public debate during the eighteenth century, long before Americans advocated independence.

The sudden arrival of thousands of men and women born in Ireland and Germany worried colonial leaders who assumed that being British meant that a person spoke English and accepted the basic traditions of English law and politics. Problems related to ethnic diversity seemed most pressing in the Middle Colonies such as Pennsylvania, for after the 1720s poor people from the German Palatinate and the area around Belfast, Ireland, flocked to America in search of economic opportunity. James Logan, the provincial secretary of Pennsylvania, sounded the alarm, warning those of English stock of the "foreigners" who threatened to transform the local culture. Because of the number of Germans entering the colony, Logan argued, "these colonies will in time be lost to the Crown." The Scots-Irish were even more menacing. These Protestant migrants who fled the north of Ireland to escape chronic poverty appeared intent on making "themselves Proprietors of the Province."

It might have been predicted that English colonists would have welcomed so many able workers, people who could pay taxes and defend the frontiers. But such was not the case. Benjamin Franklin, often depicted as the voice of reason, almost panicked when he contemplated the growing diversity. Why, he demanded, should the Germans be allowed "to swarm into our Settlements, and by herding together establish their Language and Manners to the Exclusion of ours? Why should Pennsylvania, founded by the English, become a Colony of *Aliens?*" In fact, Franklin predicted that "Instead of their Learning our Language, we must learn theirs, or live as in a foreign Country." As in so many cultural confrontations of this sort, the representatives of the dominant group defined difference as a contest in which one either won or lost. Accommodation had little appeal for those so anxious to preserve the purity of their own heritage.

The question for people such as Franklin was how best to make the Germans and the Scots-Irish more like the English. It was thought that education might save the day. After all, the "foreigners" could be taught to accept a common set of values that obviously served as the foundation for society. Pennsylvania leaders contended that these standards rested ultimately on "the noble Privilege or Birth-Right of an *English Subject.*" As anyone could see, English identity meant developing a deep respect for the law, property, and institutions originally erected by migrants from England and their descendants. During the years of heaviest immigration, those who claimed to speak for the cultural mainstream, extolled the "sober and prudent conduct of the ancient Settlers and their Successors," in other words, those who understood that "the Rights and Privileges of this Colony, [rested] on the true basis of English *Liberty and Property.*" Some enthusiasts even encouraged the colonial legislature to pass laws for the encouragement of "Virtue, Sobriety, and Industry . . . [to] prevent an English Plantation from Being turned into a Colony of Aliens."

The key to preserving social order in the face of growing diversity was Anglicization, a process of transforming Germans and Scots-Irish into people who at least seemed English. Success was just a matter of time. Strange languages, customs, and beliefs could be made to disappear under a veneer of Englishness. Thomas Penn, whose family actually owned Pennsylvania, predicted that the Germans would "certainly by degrees loose their attachment to their Language, and become English, and as they acquire property I dare prophecy will become good Subjects." Indeed, so confident was his brother John of the ability of the Germans to acculturate that he concluded "we ought by no Means to Debar their coming over," because "when settled these [people] will Esteem themselves Pennsylvanians." To accomplish this goal, "Foreigners imported, should not be allowed to settle in large separate Districts . . . because for many Generations they may continue, as it were, a separate People in Language, Modes of Religion, Customs and Manners." The newcomers, therefore, were best "intermixed with the *British* settlers." But one had to be on guard. By "distinguishing themselves" from the dominant culture the members of these groups showed contempt for English traditions. After all, asked a colonial official, "How far is it consistent with the Peace, Honour or Security of an English Government that they, who . . . have had the utmost Protection, should upon Occasions, be thus nationally distinguished?"

All the advice apparently fell on deaf ears. The migrants failed to measure up to English standards, and differences came to be seen as rejection and hostility. To the chagrin of fully Anglicized Pennsylvanians, the German settlers could not be "restrained" from forming tight-knit ethnic communities. They refused to abandon the culture they had known in Europe. Moreover, they did not intermarry with those from other groups, established newspapers in their own language, and set up German-speaking schools. The Scots-Irish raised even more hackles. Although they had demonstrated their loyalty to the British crown in the Old World, they seemed in the New to "have little Honesty and less Sense." An unruly people, they squatted on lands owned by the Penn family or by Native Americans. What is more, they showed no desire to mix with neighbors of different ethnicity. The Scots-Irish held that "no strangers should be admitted to settle within [their] Bounds," and instead of taking their legal disputes to the province's official courts—as any proper Englishman would do—they relied on church elders. To make matters worse for critics such as Franklin, they often reacted to minor insults with violence and were "generally rough" with the Indians. When some Scots-Irish murdered twenty Native Americans in 1763, Franklin called them "Christian white savages," while another colonial official dubbed them "the very scum of mankind."

As has been so often the case with cultural tensions of this sort, the various participants gradually reached an accommodation, often perhaps without even realizing how much they had adjusted to changing conditions. The "foreigners" did not in fact destroy Pennsylvania. Indeed, political leaders who identified themselves as English were soon soliciting the votes of the migrant population, and over time, it became clear that the colony's prosperity in the Atlantic World owed a lot to hardworking aliens. And on the eve of revolution, some Americans had come to realize that diversity was not all that objectionable. As one patriot who called himself "A Son of Liberty" observed in 1768, "It is true that the first emigrations were from *England;* but upon the whole, more settlers have come from *Ireland, Germany,* and other parts of *Europe,* than from *England.*"

The Donegal Presbyterian Church in Lancaster County, Pennsylvania, recalls the cultural heritage of the Scots-Irish settlers of the region. ❖

Chapter 5

The American Revolution: From Elite Protest to Popular Revolt, 1763–1783

Rethinking the Meaning of Equality

During the Revolutionary War, a captured British officer spent some time at the plantation of Colonel Thomas Mann Randolph, a leader of Virginia's gentry. The Englishman described with a note of disgust the arrival of three ordinary farmers who were members of the local militia—the way the militiamen drew chairs up to the fire, pulled off their muddy boots, and began spitting. Randolph explained that such behavior demonstrated "the spirit of independency" in America. Indeed, every American who "bore arms" during the Revolution considered himself as good as his neighbors.

This chance encounter illuminates the character of the American Revolution. The initial stimulus for rebellion came from the gentry—from the rich and well-born. They pronounced their unhappiness in public statements and in speeches before elected assemblies. However, they soon lost control as the revolutionary movement generated a momentum of its own. As relations with the mother country deteriorated, the traditional leaders of colonial society were forced to invite the common folk to join the protest—as rioters, as petitioners, and finally as soldiers. What had started as a squabble among the gentry had been transformed into a mass movement, and as Randolph learned, once the common people had become involved in shaping the nation's destiny, they could never again be excluded.

THE INCIDENT AT RANDOLPH'S PLANTATION reveals a second, often overlooked, aspect of the American Revolution. It involved a massive military commitment. If mud-covered Virginia militiamen had not been willing to stand up to seasoned British troops, to face the terror of the bayonet charge, independence would have remained a dream of intellectuals. Proportionate to the population, a greater percentage of Americans died in military service during the Revolution than in any war in American history, with the exception of the Civil War. Liberty to them was more than an abstraction studied by political theorists, and those Americans who risked death and survived the ordeal saw new meaning in the concept of equality as well.

Outline

Structure of Colonial Society

Eroding the Bonds of Empire

Steps Toward Independence

Fighting for Independence

The Loyalist Dilemma

Winning the Peace

Conclusion: Preserving Independence

Structure of Colonial Society

Only with hindsight can one see the coming of the American Revolution. The lives of most free colonists were filled with economic and political expectations. It was a period of optimism. The population continued to grow, and the standard of living continued to improve. To be sure, wealth was not evenly distributed. The southern colonies were richer than the northern colonies. But even the poorest colonists benefited from the rising standard of living. Economic and political discontent was out of step with the tempo of the age.

No one consciously set out in 1763 to achieve independence. The bonds of loyalty that had cemented the British empire dissolved slowly. At several points, the British rulers and American colonists could have compromised. Their failure to do so was the result of thousands of separate decisions, errors, and misunderstandings. The Revolution was, in fact, a complex series of events, full of unexpected turns, extraordinary creativity, and great personal sacrifice.

Breakdown of Political Trust

Ultimate responsibility for preserving the empire fell to George III, whose reign began in 1760. He was only 22 years old and poorly educated, the product of a sheltered and loveless upbringing. He displayed little understanding of the larger implications of government policy, and many people who knew him considered him dull-witted. Unfortunately, the king could not be ignored, and during a difficult period that demanded imagination, generosity, and wisdom, George muddled along as best he could.

Unlike the preceding Georges, George III decided to play an aggressive role in government. He selected as his chief minister the earl of Bute, a Scot whose only qualification for office appeared to be his friendship with the young king and the young king's mother. The **Whigs,** a political faction that dominated Parliament, believed that George was attempting to turn back the clock to the time before the Glorious Revolution; in other words, attempting to reestablish a monarchy free from traditional constitutional restraints. George did not, in fact, harbor such arbitrary ambitions, but his actions threw customary political practices into doubt.

Whigs In the mid-eighteenth century, the Whigs were a political faction that dominated Parliament. Generally they were opposed to royal influence in government and wanted to increase the control and influence of Parliament. Later they were associated with parliamentary reform.

In 1763, Bute left office. What followed was a seven-year period of confusion during which ministers came and went, often for no other reason than George's personal dislike. Because of this chronic instability, subministers, the minor bureaucrats who directed routine colonial affairs, did not know what was expected of them. In the absence of a long-range policy, the ministers showed more concern for their own future than for coping with the problems of empire building.

The king does not bear the sole responsibility for England's loss of empire in the American colonies. The members of Parliament, the men who actually drafted the statutes that drove a wedge between the colonies and the mother country, failed to respond creatively to the challenge of events. They clung doggedly to the principle of **parliamentary sovereignty,** and when Americans questioned whether that legislative body in London should govern colonial affairs, parliamentary spokesmen provided no constructive basis for compromise. They refused to see a middle ground between the preeminent authority of Parliament and complete American independence.

parliamentary sovereignty Principle that emphasized the power of Parliament to govern colonial affairs as the preeminent authority.

Parliament's attitude was in part a result of ignorance. Few men active in English government had visited America. For those who attempted to follow colonial affairs, accurate information proved extremely difficult to obtain. One could not expect to receive an answer from America to a specific question in less than three months. As a result of the lag in communication between England and America, rumors sometimes passed for true accounts, and misunderstanding influenced the formulation of colonial policy.

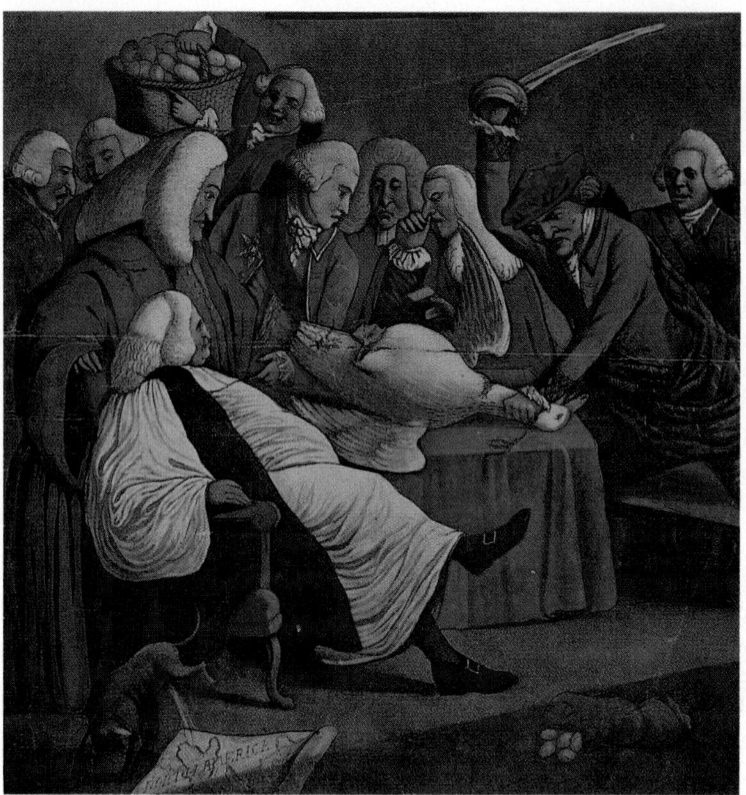

Cartoons became a popular means of criticizing the government during this period. Here, King George III watches as the kilted Lord Brute slaughters the goose America. A cabinet member holds a basket of golden eggs at the rear. At front left, a dog relieves itself on a map of North America. ❖

But failure of communication alone was not to blame for the widening gap between the colonies and England. Even when complete information was available, the two sides were often unable to understand each other's positions. The central element in this Anglo-American debate was a concept known as parliamentary sovereignty. The English ruling classes viewed the role of Parliament from a historical perspective that most colonists never shared. They insisted that Parliament was the dominant element within the constitution. Indeed, this elective body protected rights and property from an arbitrary monarch. During the reign of the Stuarts, especially under Charles I (r. 1625–1649), the authority of Parliament had been challenged, and it was not until the Glorious Revolution of 1688 that the English crown formally recognized Parliament's supreme authority in matters such as taxation.

Such a constitutional position did not leave much room for compromise. Most members of Parliament took a hard line on this issue. The notion of dividing or sharing sovereignty simply made no sense to the English ruling class. As Thomas Hutchinson, royal governor of Massachusetts, explained, no middle ground existed "between the supreme authority of Parliament and the total dependence of the colonies." The logic of this argument seemed self-evident to the British. In fact, parliamentary leaders could never quite understand why the colonists were so difficult to persuade.

No Taxation Without Representation: The American Perspective

At the conclusion of the Seven Years' War (French and Indian War), it seemed inconceivable that the colonists would challenge the supremacy of Parliament. But the crisis in imperial relations that soon developed impelled the Americans first to define and then to defend principles that were rooted deeply in the colonial political culture.

For more than a century, the colonists' ideas about their role within the British empire had remained a vague, untested bundle of assumptions about personal liberties, property rights, and representative institutions. But by 1763, certain fundamental beliefs had become clear. Americans accepted the authority of representative local assemblies to tax their constituents, but to declare that the House of Commons in London enjoyed the same right made no sense to them. Moreover, the colonists rejected the distinction that the British officials sometimes made between taxes imposed directly on a person's estate and taxes on trade that could be passed on to consumers. Americans firmly believed that a tax was a tax by whatever name and that Parliament had no right to collect taxes on the American side of the Atlantic, especially since no Americans sat in Parliament.

Political thought in the colonies contained a strong moral component, one that British rulers and American **Loyalists** (people who sided with the king during the Revolution) never fully understood. The origins of this perspective on civil government are difficult to pinpoint, but certainly the moral fervor of the Great Awakening and the reformist writings of the Commonwealthmen played a part (see Chapter 4). Whatever the intellectual sources may have been, colonists viewed *power* as extremely dangerous, unless it was countered by *virtue.*

Loyalists Throughout the conflict with Great Britain, many colonists sided with the king and Parliament. Also called Tories, these people feared that American liberty might promote social anarchy.

Insistence on civic virtue—sacrifice of self-interest to the public good—became the dominant theme of revolutionary political writing. American pamphleteers shared the outlook of those who regarded bad government not as human error but as sin. They saw a host of external threats and plots—arbitrary taxation, standing armies, bishops sent over by the Church of England—all designed to crush American liberty. Popular writers seldom took a dispassionate, legalistic approach in their analysis of Anglo-American relations. They described events in conspiratorial terms, using language charged with emotion.

Colonial newspapers spread these ideas through a large, dispersed population. A majority of adult white males—a great majority in the northern colonies—were literate, and the number of journals in the country increased dramatically during the revolutionary period. The newspaper united the colonies, informing each colony about the political activities in the others, and provided the rhetoric that successfully roused ordinary folk to take up arms against Britain.

Eroding the Bonds of Empire

Following the Seven Years' War, more than seven thousand British troops, members of the regular army, remained in North America. Their alleged purpose was to provide a buffer between Indians and frontiersmen and to preserve order in the newly conquered territories of Florida and Quebec. But not one person in the British government actually made the decision to keep an army in the colonies. The army was not recalled simply because of bureaucratic confusion and inertia.

The war had saddled Britain with a national debt so huge that more than one-half of the annual budget went to interest payments. Maintaining a peacetime army so far from the mother country fueled the budgetary crisis. The growing financial burden weighed heavily on restive English taxpayers and sent the government leaders scurrying in search of new sources of revenue.

For their part, colonists doubted the value of this very expensive army. First, the British troops did not maintain peace effectively. This was demonstrated in 1763 when Ottawa Chief Pontiac, who had been allied with the French and hated the British, organized a general uprising along the western frontier. His warriors easily slipped by the redcoats and slew several thousand settlers. In fact, relations between whites and Indians deteriorated. Unable to play the British off against the French, the Indians suffered terribly from the imperial reorganization. Second, the colonists resented the Proclamation of 1763, which attempted unsuccessfully to restrain Americans from moving onto Indian lands west of the Appalachian Mountains, and they identified the hated policy with the British troops who guarded the frontier.

The task of reducing England's debt fell to George Grenville, the somewhat unimaginative chancellor of the exchequer who replaced Bute in 1763 as the king's first minister. Grenville decided that the colonists would have to contribute to the maintenance of the army. The first bill he steered through Parliament was the Revenue Act of 1764, known as the Sugar Act.

This legislation placed a new burden on the Navigation Acts, which had governed the flow of colonial commerce for almost a century (see Chapter 3). Their primary purpose was not to raise money but to force Americans to trade with the mother country. The Sugar Act, by contrast, was specifically designed to generate revenue. It imposed new import duties on sugar, coffee, wines, and other imports; instituted tougher customs collection methods; and expanded the jurisdiction of the vice-admiralty courts. The act also included provisions aimed at curbing colonial smuggling of molasses and bribery of customs officials.

American reaction came swiftly. James Otis, a fiery orator from Massachusetts, exclaimed that the legislation deprived Americans of "the rights of assessing their own taxes." Petitions of protest involved no violence, but to Grenville and persons of his temperament, even petitions smacked of ingratitude. After all, they reasoned, had not the mother country saved the Americans from the French? But Grenville's perspective overlooked the contribution of colonial staples such as rice and tobacco to the prosperity of the mother country. Moreover, American markets helped sustain British industry (see Chapter 4). The colonists saw no justification for Grenville's aggressive new policy now that the military emergency had passed.

Popular Protest

Even before the Sugar Act had gone into effect, Grenville put the final touches on a second revenue measure, the Stamp Act. Although a few members of Parliament warned that the Americans would bitterly resent the act, the majority of the House of Commons supported the legislation. Specifically, the Stamp Act required printed documents—such as newspapers, legal contracts, and marriage licenses—to bear revenue stamps purchased from royal stamp distributors. The act was to go into effect November 1, 1765.

Word of the Stamp Act reached America by May, and the colonial reaction against it was swift. In Virginia's House of Burgesses, eloquent young Patrick Henry introduced five resolutions protesting the act. He timed his move carefully. It was late in the session; many of the more conservative burgesses had already departed for their plantations. Even then, Henry's resolves declaring that Virginians had the right to tax themselves as they alone saw fit passed by narrow margins.

The Virginia Resolves might have remained a local matter had it not been for the colonial press. Newspapers throughout America printed Henry's resolutions. The newspaper accounts, however, were not always accurate. Some accounts said that all five of Henry's resolutions had passed when in fact the fifth resolution, which announced that Britain's actions were "illegal, unconstitutional, and unjust," had been stricken from the legislative record. Several newspapers even printed two resolutions that Henry had not dared to introduce. The result of this misunderstanding, of course, was that the Virginians appeared to have taken an extremely radical position on the issue of the supremacy of Parliament, one that other Americans now trumpeted before their own assemblies.

Not to be outdone by Virginia, the Massachusetts assembly in June proposed a general meeting to protest Grenville's policy. Nine colonies sent representatives to the **Stamp Act Congress,** which convened in New York City in October 1765. The delegates drafted petitions to the king and Parliament that restated the colonists' belief "that no taxes should be imposed on them, but with their own consent, given personally, or by their representatives." There was no mention of independence or disloyalty to the crown.

Stamp Act Congress Meeting of colonial delegates in New York City in October 1765 to protest the Stamp Act, a law passed by Parliament to raise revenue in America. The delegates drafted petitions denouncing the Stamp Act and other taxes imposed on Americans without colonial consent.

Resistance to the Stamp Act soon moved from assembly petitions to mass protests in the streets. In Boston, a mob calling itself the Sons of Liberty burned the local stamp distributor in effigy. The violent outbursts frightened colonial leaders; yet the evidence suggests that they encouraged the lower classes to intimidate royal officials. After 1765, it was impossible for either royal governors or patriot leaders to take for granted the support of ordinary men and women.

By November 1, 1765, stamp distributors in almost every American port had publicly resigned, and without distributors, the hated revenue stamps could not be

A Look at the Past

Stamp Act Teapot

Colonists could celebrate the repeal of the hated Stamp Act by purchasing goods decorated like this teapot. Because no manufacturers of fine ceramics existed in British America, the teapot came from England. As this piece indicates, English manufacturers readily produced goods suited to colonial tastes. British merchants and manufacturers had good reason to celebrate the repeal of the Stamp Act as it meant that colonists resumed purchasing English goods. What does this teapot suggest about the economic and cultural connections between England and the colonies? Why would some individuals in England regard imperial actions as unfavorably as some colonists did?

sold. The Sons of Liberty convinced colonial merchants to boycott British goods. What most Americans did not yet know—communication with the mother country took months—was that in July, Grenville had fallen from power. His replacement as first lord of the treasury, Lord Rockingham, envisioned a prosperous empire founded on an expanding commerce, with local government under the gentle guidance of Parliament. Grenville, now simply a member of Parliament, urged a tough policy toward America, but important men, such as William Pitt, defended the colonists' position. Finally, Rockingham called for the repeal of the Stamp Act. On March 18, 1766, the Act was repealed.

Repeal failed to restore imperial harmony. Lest its retreat on the Stamp Act be interpreted as weakness, the House of Commons passed the Declaratory Act (March 1766), a shrill defense of parliamentary supremacy over the Americans "in all cases whatsoever." The colonists' insistence on no taxation without representation failed to impress British rulers. Clearly, if America thought it won the Stamp Act battle, Parliament was announcing that it fully expected to win the war.

In America, too, attitudes hardened. Respect for imperial officeholders as well as Parliament had diminished. Suddenly, royal governors, customs collectors, and military personnel appeared alien, as if their interests were not those of the people over whom they exercised authority. Indeed, it is testimony to the Americans' lingering loyalty to the British crown and constitution that rebellion did not occur in 1765.

Fueling the Crisis

Rockingham's ministry soon gave way to a government headed once again by William Pitt, now the earl of Chatham. The aging Pitt suffered horribly from gout, and during his long absences from London, Charles Townshend, his chancellor of the exchequer, made important political decisions. Townshend's mouth often outran his mind, and in January 1767, he pleased the House of Commons by announcing that he knew a way to obtain revenue from the Americans.

His plan turned out to be a grab bag of duties on American imports of paper, glass, paint, and tea, collectively known as the Townshend Revenue Acts (June 1767). To collect these duties, he created the American Board of Customs Commissioners, a body based in Boston and supported by reorganized vice-admiralty courts in port cities.

Americans were no more willing to pay Townshend's duties than they had been to buy Grenville's stamps. In major ports, the Sons of Liberty organized boycotts of

British goods. Imported finery came to symbolize England's political corruption. Americans prided themselves on wearing homespun clothes as a badge of simplicity and virtue. Women were ardent supporters of the boycott, holding public spinning bees to produce more homespun.

On February 11, 1768, the Massachusetts House of Representatives drafted a circular letter, a provocative appeal that it sent directly to the other colonial assemblies. The letter requested suggestions on how best to thwart the Townshend Acts. Although the letter was mild, Lord Hillsborough, England's secretary for American affairs, took offense. He called the letter a "seditious paper" and ordered the Massachusetts representatives to rescind it; the legislators refused.

Suddenly, the circular letter became a cause célèbre. When the royal governor of Massachusetts dissolved the House of Representatives, the other colonies demonstrated their support of the Bay Colony by taking up the circular letter in their assemblies. Hillsborough promptly dissolved more colonial legislatures. Parliament's challenge had brought about the very results it most wanted to avoid: a basis for intercolonial communication and a growing sense among the colonists of the righteousness of their position.

Fatal Show of Force

In October 1768, British rulers made another critical mistake. The issue was the army. In part to intimidate colonial troublemakers, the ministry stationed four thousand regular troops around Boston. The armed strangers camped on Boston Commons, sometimes shouting obscenities at citizens passing the site. To make relations worse, the redcoats, ill-treated and underpaid, competed in their spare time for jobs with local dockworkers and artisans.

When citizens questioned why the army had been sent to a peaceful city, pamphleteers claimed that the soldiers in Boston were simply another phase of a conspiracy originally conceived by the earl of Bute to oppress Americans, to take away their liberties, and to collect illegal revenues. Grenville, Hillsborough, and Townshend were all, supposedly, part of the plot. To Americans raised on the political theories of the Commonwealthmen, the pattern of tyranny seemed obvious.

Colonists had no difficulty interpreting the violence that erupted in Boston on March 5, 1770. In the gathering dusk of that afternoon, young boys and street toughs used rocks and snowballs to bombard a small isolated patrol outside the offices of the hated customs commissioners in King Street. The details of the incident are obscure, but it appears that as the mob grew and became more threatening, the troops panicked and fired, leaving five Americans dead.

Boston Massacre A violent confrontation between British troops and a Boston mob on March 5, 1770. Five citizens were killed when the troops fired into the crowd. The incident inflamed anti-British sentiment in Massachusetts.

Pamphleteers promptly labeled the incident a "massacre," its victims cast as martyrs. To the propagandists, what actually happened during the **Boston Massacre** mattered little. Their job was to inflame emotions; they performed their work well. Confronted with such an intense reaction and with the possibility of massive armed resistance, crown officials wisely moved the army to an island in Boston harbor.

At this critical moment, the king's new first minister restored a measure of tranquillity. Lord North, congenial, well meaning, but not very talented, was appointed the first minister in 1770, and for the next twelve years—indeed, throughout most of the American crisis—he managed to retain his office. His secret formula seems to have been an ability to get along with George III and to build an effective majority in Parliament.

One of North's first recommendations to Parliament was the repeal of the ill-conceived Townshend duties. Not only had the duties enraged Americans, but they also hurt British manufacturers by encouraging Americans to develop their own industries. Parliament responded by dropping all the duties, with the exception of the tax on tea. But Parliament still maintained that it held total supremacy over the

Outrage over the Boston Massacre was fanned by propaganda, such as this etching by Paul Revere, which showed British redcoats firing on ordinary citizens. In subsequent editions of the print, the blood spurting from the dying Americans became more conspicuous. ❖

colonies. For a time, Americans drew back from the precipice of confrontation, frightened by the events of the past two years.

Last Days of the Old Order, 1770–1773

For a brief moment, the American colonists and British officials put aside their recent animosities. Merchants returned to familiar patterns of trade, and American indebtedness grew. Even in Massachusetts, the people decided that they could accept their new royal governor, an American, Thomas Hutchinson.

But appearances were deceiving. The bonds of imperial loyalty remained fragile, and even as Lord North attempted to win the colonists' trust, crown officials in America created new strains. Customs commissioners abused their powers of search and seizure and in the process lined their own pockets. Any failure to abide by the Navigation Acts, no matter how minor, could bring confiscation of ship and cargo.

The commissioners were not only corrupt but also foolish. They harassed the wealthy and powerful as well as the common folk. The commissioners' actions drove members of the colonial ruling class, men such as John Hancock of Boston, into opposition to the king's government. Eventually, the commissioners' greed brought the colonists closer together.

Samuel Adams (1722–1803) refused to accept the notion that the repeal of the Townshend duties had secured American liberty. During the early 1770s, while colonial leaders turned to other matters, Adams kept the cause alive with a drumfire of publicity. He never allowed the people of Boston to forget the many real and alleged wrongs perpetrated by the crown. Adams was a genuine revolutionary, seemingly obsessed with the need to preserve civic virtue and moral values in the conduct of public affairs. With each new attempt by Parliament to assert its supremacy over the colonists, more and more Bostonians listened to what Adams had to say. By 1772, Adams had attracted broad support for the formation of a **committee of correspondence** to communicate grievances to villagers throughout Massachusetts. People in other colonies soon copied his idea and established intercolonial committees as well. It was a brilliant stroke; Adams developed a structure of political cooperation completely independent of royal government.

committee of correspondence Vast communication network formed in Massachusetts and other colonies to communicate grievances and provide colonists with evidence of British oppression.

The Final Provocation: The Boston Tea Party

In May 1773, Parliament resumed its old tricks. It passed the Tea Act, a strange piece of legislation that Parliament thought the colonists would welcome. The statute was designed to save the floundering East India Company, not to raise revenue. It allowed the company to ship tea directly to America, thereby eliminating the colonial middlemen and permitting Americans to purchase tea at bargain rates. The plan, however, was flawed. First, since the Townshend duty on tea remained in effect, the new arrangement seemed to be a devious way to win popular support for Parliament's right to tax the colonists without representation. Second, the act threatened to undercut tea smugglers and the powerful mercantile groups operating in Boston.

Americans soon registered their protest. Boston took the most dramatic stand. Although colonists in Philadelphia and New York City turned back tea ships before they could unload, in Boston, Governor Hutchinson would not permit the vessels to return to England. Local patriots would not let them unload. So the ships sat in Boston harbor crammed with tea until the night of December 16, 1773, when a group of men in Indian garb boarded the ships and pitched 340 chests of tea worth £10,000 into the water.

When news of the "Tea Party" reached London in January 1774, the North ministry was stunned. The people of Boston had treated parliamentary supremacy with utter contempt, and British rulers saw no humor whatsoever in the destruction of private property by subjects of the crown dressed in costume. To quell such rebelliousness, Parliament passed a series of laws called the **Coercive Acts.** (In America, they were referred to as the Intolerable Acts.) The legislation (1) closed the port of Boston until the city fully compensated the East India Company for the lost tea; (2) restructured the Massachusetts government by transforming the upper house from an elective to an appointed body and restricting the number of legal town meetings to one a year; (3) allowed the royal governor to transfer British officials arrested for offenses committed in the line of duty to England or Canada, where there was little likelihood they would be convicted; and (4) authorized the army to quarter troops wherever they were needed, even if this required the compulsory requisition of uninhabited private buildings. George III enthusiastically supported the tough policy; he appointed General Thomas Gage to serve as the colony's new royal governor.

Coercive Acts Also known as the Intolerable Acts, the four pieces of legislation passed by Parliament in 1774 in response to the Boston Tea Party were meant to punish the colonies.

The sweeping series of laws confirmed the colonists' worst fears. The vindictiveness of the acts strengthened the influence of men such as Samuel Adams and undermined the influence of colonial moderates. In Parliament, a saddened Edmund Burke, one of America's few remaining friends, warned his countrymen that the acts could lead to war.

In the midst of this constitutional crisis, Parliament announced plans to establish a new civil government for the Canadian province of Quebec. The Quebec Act (June 22, 1774) also extended the province's boundaries all the way south to the Ohio River and west to the Mississippi. The act made no provision for an elective assembly, but it granted French-speaking Roman Catholics religious and political rights and a large voice in local affairs. These measures were seen by Americans as a denial of *their* rights to settle and trade in this fast-developing region.

Americans everywhere rallied to Massachusetts's defense. Few persons advocated independence, but they could not remain passive while Boston was destroyed.

They sent food and money and, during the autumn of 1774, reflected more deeply than ever on what it meant to be a colonist in the British empire. And the more they reflected, the more they objected to the idea of the sovereignty of Parliament.

Steps Toward Independence

Samuel Adams had prepared Americans for this moment. Something had to be done. But what? The committees of correspondence endorsed a call for a continental congress, a gathering of fifty-five elected delegates from twelve colonies (Georgia sent none but agreed to support the action taken). The **First Continental Congress** convened in Philadelphia on September 5, 1774, and included such respected leaders as John Adams, Samuel Adams, Patrick Henry, Richard Henry Lee, and George Washington.

First Continental Congress Meeting of delegates from twelve colonies in Philadelphia in 1774. The Congress denied Parliament's authority to legislate for the colonies, condemned British actions toward the colonies, created the Continental Association, and endorsed a call to take up arms.

But the delegates were strangers to one another. They knew little about the customs and values, geography, and economy of Britain's other American provinces. Differences of opinion soon surfaced. Delegates from the middle colonies wanted to proceed with caution, but before they knew what had happened, Samuel Adams maneuvered these moderates into a position far more radical than they found comfortable. Boston's master politician engineered congressional commendation of the Suffolk Resolves, a bold statement drawn up in Suffolk County, Massachusetts, that encouraged Americans to resist the Coercive Acts forcibly.

The tone of the meeting was set. The more radical delegates carried the day. They agreed to form an "association" to halt all commerce with the mother country until Parliament repealed the Intolerable Acts. They also agreed to meet in the coming year. Meanwhile, in London, George III told his confidants, "Blows must decide whether [New England governments] are to be subject to this country or independent."

Shots Heard Around the World

Before Congress reconvened, "blows" fell at Lexington and Concord, two small farm villages in eastern Massachusetts. On the evening of April 18, 1775, General Gage dispatched troops from Boston to seize rebel supplies. Paul Revere, a renowned silversmith and active patriot, with the help of William Dawes and Samuel Prescott, warned the colonists that the redcoats were coming. The militia of Lexington, a collection of ill-trained farmers, decided to stand on the village green the following morning, April 19, as the British soldiers passed on the road to Concord. No one planned to fight, but in a moment of confusion someone (probably a colonist) fired; the redcoats discharged a volley, and eight Americans lay dead.

Word of the incident spread rapidly. "Minutemen," special companies of Massachusetts militia prepared to respond instantly to military emergencies, went into action. The redcoats found nothing of significance in Concord and turned back to Boston. The long march back became a rout; the minutemen swarmed all over the redcoats. On June 17, colonial militiamen again held their own against seasoned troops at the battle of Bunker Hill (actually Breed's Hill). The British finally captured the hill, but after this costly "victory" in which he lost 40 percent of his troops, Gage took the American militiamen more seriously.

Beginning "The World Over Again"

Members of the **Second Continental Congress** gathered in Philadelphia in May 1775. They faced an awesome responsibility. British government in the mainland colonies had almost ceased to function, Americans were fighting redcoats, and the country desperately needed strong central leadership. Congress provided that leadership. The

Second Continental Congress This meeting took place in Philadelphia in May 1775, in the midst of rapidly unfolding military events. It organized the Continental Army and commissioned George Washington to lead it, then began requisitioning men and supplies for the war effort.

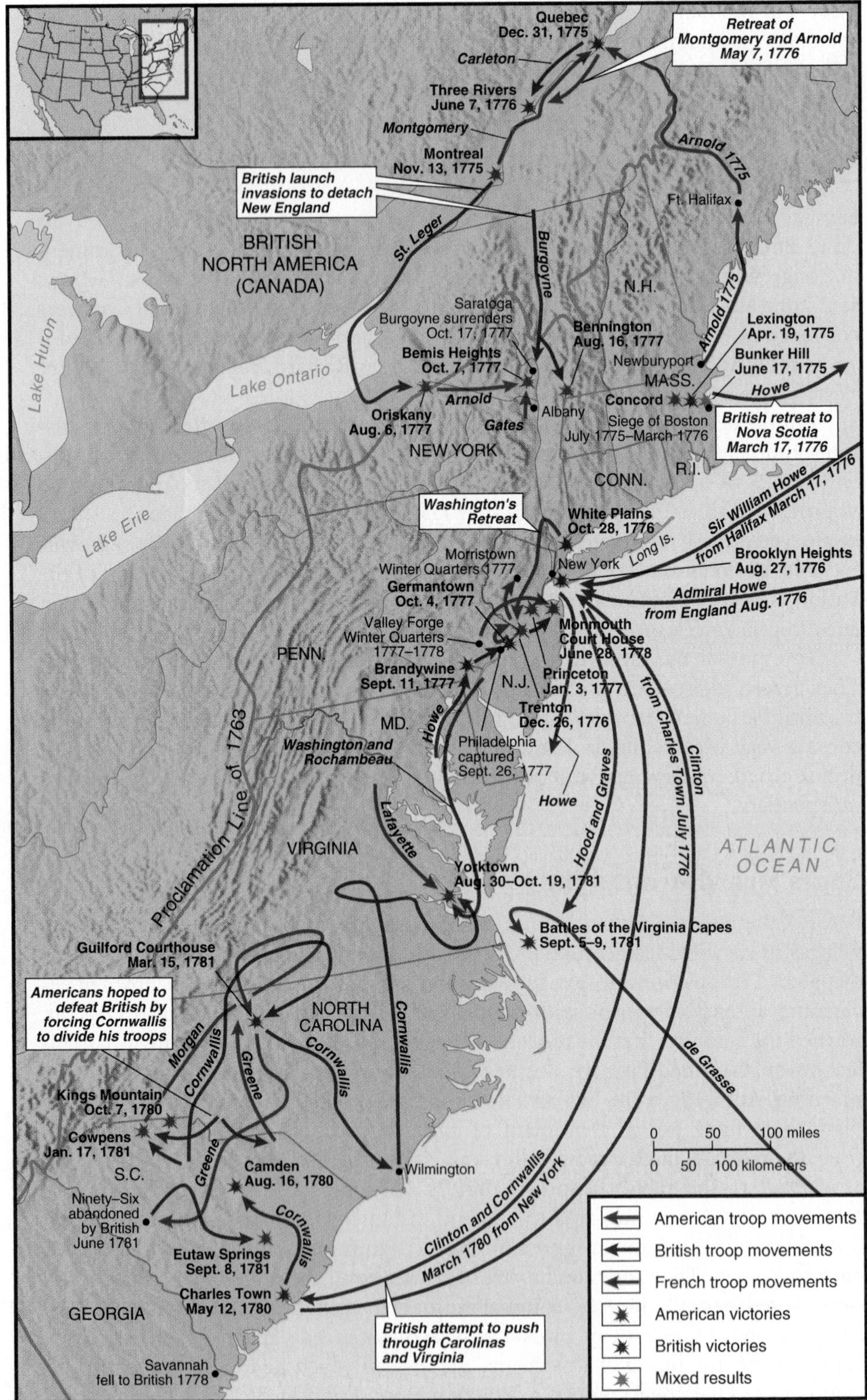

THE AMERICAN REVOLUTION, 1775–1781 *The War for Independence ranged over a huge area. Battles were fought in the colonies, north and south, on the western frontier, and along the Gulf of Mexico. The major battles of the first years of the war, from the spontaneous rising at Concord in 1775 to Washington's well-coordinated attack on Trenton in December 1776, were fought in the northern colonies. In the middle theater of war, Burgoyne's attempt in 1777 to cut off New England from the rest of the colonies failed when his army was defeated at Saratoga. Action in the final years of the war, from the battles at Camden, Kings Mountain, Cowpens, and Guilford Courthouse to the final victory at Yorktown, occurred in the southern theater of war.* ❖

delegates formed a Continental Army, appointed George Washington its commander, purchased military supplies, and, to pay for them, issued paper money. But they refused to take the final step—independence.

Indecision drove John Adams nearly mad with frustration. He and other like-minded delegates ranted against their timid colleagues. Haste, however, would have been a terrible mistake, for many Americans were not convinced that independence was either necessary or desirable. If Congress had moved too quickly, it might have faced charges of extremism and thereby lost mass support for its cause.

The British government appeared intent on transforming colonial moderates into angry rebels. In December 1775, Parliament passed the Prohibitory Act, declaring war on American commerce. The British navy blockaded colonial ports and seized American ships on the high seas. Lord North also hired German mercenaries to put down the rebellion. And in America, royal governors such as Lord Dunmore further undermined the possibility of reconciliation by urging Virginia's slaves to take up arms against their masters.

Thomas Paine (1737–1809) pushed the colonists even closer to independence. In January 1776, Paine, a recent arrival from England, published a pamphlet titled ***Common Sense.*** In this powerful democratic manifesto, Paine urged the colonists to resist "tyranny and false systems of government." The essay became an instant best-seller. More than 120,000 copies were sold in the first three months after publication. *Common Sense* systematically stripped kingship of historical and theological justification. Contrary to traditional English belief, Paine said, monarchs could and did commit many wrongs. George III was simply a "royal brute" who by his arbitrary behavior had surrendered his claim to the colonists' obedience.

Common Sense Revolutionary tract written by Thomas Paine in January 1776. It called for independence and the establishment of a republican government in America.

Paine's greatest contribution to the revolutionary cause was persuading ordinary folk to sever their ties with Great Britain. "Europe, and not England," he exclaimed, "is the parent country of America. This new world hath been the asylum for the persecuted lovers of civil and religious liberty from *every part* of Europe." The time had come for the colonists to form an independent republic. "We have it in our power," Paine wrote in one of his most moving statements, "to begin the world over again . . . . The birthday of a new world is at hand."

On July 2, 1776, after a long and tedious debate, Congress finally voted for independence. The motion passed: twelve states for, none against. Thomas Jefferson, a young Virginia lawyer and planter who enjoyed a reputation as a graceful writer, drafted a formal declaration that was accepted two days later with only minor alterations. Much of the Declaration of Independence consisted of a list of specific grievances against George III and his government. But the document's enduring fame rests on statements of principle that are tested anew in each generation of Americans: that "all men are created equal"; that they are endowed with certain rights, among which are "life, liberty, and the pursuit of happiness"; and that governments are formed to protect these rights.

Fighting for Independence

Only fools and visionaries expressed optimism about America's prospects of winning independence in 1776. The Americans had taken on a formidable military power whose population was perhaps four times greater than their own. Britain also possessed a strong industrial base, a well-trained regular army supplemented by thousands of hired German (Hessian) troops, and a navy that dominated the world's oceans. Many British officers had battlefield experience. They already knew what the Americans would slowly learn—that waging war requires great discipline, money, and sacrifice.

The British government entered the conflict fully confident that it could beat the Americans. Lord North and his colleagues regarded the war as a police action.

They anticipated that a mere show of armed force would intimidate the upstart colonists. Humble the rebels in Boston, they reasoned, and Americans will abandon independence like rats fleeing a burning ship.

As later events demonstrated, of course, Britain had become involved in an impossible military situation, somewhat analogous to that in which the United States found itself in Vietnam. Three separate elements neutralized advantages held by the larger power over its adversary. First, the British had to transport men and supplies across the Atlantic, a logistic challenge of unprecedented complexity. Second, America was too vast to be conquered by conventional military methods. Redcoats might gain control over the major port cities, but as long as the Continental Army remained intact, the rebellion continued. And third, British strategies never appreciated the depth of the Americans' commitment to a political ideology. European troops before the French Revolution served because they were paid or because they were professional soldiers but not because they hoped to advance a set of constitutional principles. Americans were different. Although some joined the army for the bounty money or to escape unhappy families or because they were drafted, a remarkable number of American troops were committed to republican ideals.

During the earliest months of rebellion, American soldiers—especially those of New England—suffered no lack of confidence. Indeed, they interpreted their engagements at Concord and Bunker Hill as evidence that brave, yeoman farmers could lick British regulars on any battlefield. George Washington spent the first years of the war disabusing the colonists of this foolishness. As he had learned during the French and Indian War, military success depended on careful planning, endless drill, and tough discipline.

Washington insisted on organizing a regular, well-trained field army. He rejected the idea of waging a guerrilla war. He recognized that the Continental Army served not only as a fighting force but also as a symbol of the republican cause. Its very existence would sustain American hopes, and so long as the army survived, American agents could plausibly solicit foreign aid. This thinking shaped Washington's cautious wartime strategy; he studiously avoided any "general actions" in which the Continental Army might be destroyed.

If the commander in chief was correct about the army, however, he failed to comprehend the political importance of local militias. These scattered, almost amateur military units seldom altered the outcome of a battle, but they did maintain control over large areas of the country not directly affected by the British army. Throughout the war, they compelled men and women who would rather have remained neutral to support the American effort actively. Without the local militias' political coercion, Washington's task would have been considerably more difficult.

For the half million African American colonists, most of them slaves, the fight for independence took on special poignancy. After all, they wanted to achieve personal as well as political freedom, and many African Americans supported those who seemed most likely to deliver them from bondage. It is estimated that some five thousand African Americans took up arms to fight against the British. In 1778, the legislature of Rhode Island voted to free any slave who volunteered to serve, since, according to the lawmakers, history taught that "the wisest, the freest, and bravest nations . . . liberated their slaves, and enlisted them as soldiers to fight in defence of their country." In the South, especially in Georgia and South Carolina, more than ten thousand African Americans supported the British, and after the patriots had won the war, most of these men and women left the United States, relocating to Nova Scotia, Florida, and Jamaica, with some eventually resettling in Africa.

Testing the American Will

After the embarrassing losses in Massachusetts, the king appointed General Sir William Howe to replace the ill-fated Gage. British rulers now understood that a simple police action would not be sufficient to crush the American rebellion. Howe promptly evacuated Boston—an untenable strategic position—and on July 3, 1776, his forces stormed Staten Island in New York harbor. From this central position, he hoped to cut off New Englanders from the rest of America.

When Washington learned that the British were digging in at New York, he transferred many of his inexperienced soldiers to Long Island, where they suffered a serious defeat (August 26, 1776). Howe drove the Continental Army across the Hudson River into New Jersey, but he failed to annihilate Washington's entire army. Nevertheless, the Americans were on the run, and in the fall of 1776, contemporaries predicted that the rebels would soon capitulate.

His swift victories in New York and New Jersey persuaded General Howe that few Americans enthusiastically supported independence. He issued a general pardon, therefore, to anyone who would swear allegiance to George III. More than three thousand Americans responded to Howe's peaceful overtures. However, the pardon plan eventually failed, partly because Howe's soldiers and officers regarded loyal Americans as inferior provincials, an attitude that did little to promote good relations, and partly because the rebel militias often retaliated against Americans who had deserted the patriots' cause.

In December 1776, Washington's bedraggled forces retreated across the Delaware River into Pennsylvania. American prospects appeared bleaker than at any other time during the war. "These are the times that try men's souls," Tom Paine wrote in a pamphlet titled *American Crisis.* "The summer soldier and the sunshine patriot will, in this crisis, shrink from the service of their country, but he that stands it *now* deserves . . . love and thanks of man and woman." Before winter, Washington determined to attempt one last desperate stroke.

Howe played into Washington's hands. The British army was strung out across New Jersey. On the night of December 25, Continental soldiers slipped over the ice-covered Delaware River and at Trenton took nine hundred sleeping Hessian mercenaries by complete surprise. Cheered by success, Washington returned a second time to Trenton, but on this occasion a large British force headed by Lord Cornwallis trapped the Americans. Washington secretly, by night, marched his little army around Cornwallis's left flank. On January 3, 1777, the Americans surprised a British garrison at Princeton. Having regained their confidence, Washington's forces then went into winter quarters. The British, fearful of losing any more outposts, consolidated their troops, thus leaving much of the state in the hands of the patriot militias.

Victory in a Year of Defeat

In 1777, England's chief military strategist, Lord George Germain, still perceived the war in conventional European terms. He believed that England could achieve a complete victory by crushing Washington's army in a major battle. Unfortunately, the Continental forces proved extremely elusive, and while one British army vainly tried to corner Washington in Pennsylvania, another was forced to surrender in the forests of upstate New York.

In the summer of 1777, General John Burgoyne marched south from Canada determined to clear the Hudson Valley of rebel resistance. He intended to join Howe's army, which was to come up to Albany, thereby cutting New England off from the other states. Burgoyne moved slowly, weighed down by a German band, thirty carts filled with the general's liquor and belongings, and two thousand dependents and camp followers. The campaign was a disaster. American military units cut the enemy force apart in the deep woods north of Albany and overwhelmed Burgoyne's German mercenaries at Bennington. After it became clear that Howe could provide no relief, the haughty Burgoyne was forced to surrender 5,800 men to the American General Horatio Gates at Saratoga (October 17).

Defeat of the British at the Battle of Princeton, *oil painting by William Mercer, ca. 1786–1790. The painting shows George Washington (left, on horseback) directing cannon fire with his sword. Often risking his own life, Washington led the American troops into battle. The artist's father was mortally wounded in the battle.* ❖

General Howe could provide no support to Burgoyne because about the time Burgoyne left Canada, Howe unexpectedly decided to move his main army from New York City to Philadelphia, trying to devise a way to destroy Washington's forces. The British troops sailed to the head of the Chesapeake Bay and then marched north to Philadelphia. Washington's troops obstructed the enemy's progress, but they could not stop the British from entering the city on September 26, 1777.

Lest these defeats discourage Congress and the American people, Washington attempted one last battle before the onset of winter. In a curious engagement at Germantown (October 4), beset by bad luck and confusion, the Americans launched a major counterattack on a fog-covered battlefield, but just at the moment when success seemed assured, the Americans broke off the fight. The discouraged Continental Army dug in for the winter at Valley Forge, 20 miles outside of Philadelphia, where camp diseases took 2,500 American lives.

The French Alliance

Even before the Americans declared their independence, agents of the government of Louis XVI began to explore ways to aid the colonists, not so much because the French monarchy favored the republican cause but because it hoped to avenge its defeat in the Seven Years' War and lessen the power of Britain. During the early months of the Revolution, the French covertly sent tons of essential military supplies to the Americans but refused to recognize American independence or sign an outright military alliance with the rebels. The international stakes were too great for the king openly to back a cause that had little chance of success.

The American victory at Saratoga convinced the French that the rebels had formidable forces and were serious in their resolve. Meanwhile, in Paris, American representative Benjamin Franklin hinted that Congress might accept a recently tendered British peace overture. Hence, if the French wanted the war to continue and if they really wanted to strike at their old rival, they formally had to recognize the independence of the United States.

The stratagem paid off handsomely. On February 6, 1778, the French presented American representatives with two separate treaties. The first, called the Treaty of Amity and Commerce, established commercial relations between France and the United States. It tacitly accepted the existence of a new, independent republic. The Treaty of Alliance was even more generous. In the event that France and England went to war (they did so on June 14), the French agreed to reject any peace initiative until Britain recognized American independence. The Americans pledged that they would not sign a separate peace with Britain without first informing their new ally. Amazingly, France made no claim to Canada or any territory east of the Mississippi River.

French intervention instantly transformed British military strategy. What had been a colonial rebellion suddenly became a world conflict, a continuation of the great wars for empire of the late seventeenth century (see Chapter 4). Scarce military resources, especially newer fighting ships, had to be diverted from the American theater to guard the English Channel. England realized that the French navy posed a serious challenge to the overextended British fleet.

The Final Campaign

British General Henry Clinton replaced Howe, who resigned after the battle of Saratoga. As a subordinate officer, Clinton was imaginative, but as commander of British forces in America, his resolute self-confidence suddenly dissolved. Perhaps he feared failure. Whatever the explanation for his vacillation, Clinton's record in America was little better than Howe's or Gage's.

Military strategists calculated that Britain's last chance of winning the war lay in the southern colonies, a region largely untouched in the early years of fighting. They believed that with proper support and encouragement, the Loyalists in Georgia and South Carolina would take up arms for the crown. The southern strategy devised by Germain and Clinton in 1779 turned the war into a bitter guerrilla conflict, and during the last months of battle, British officers worried that their search for an easy victory had inadvertently opened a Pandora's box of uncontrollable partisan furies.

The southern campaign opened in the spring of 1780. Savannah had already fallen, and Clinton reckoned that if the British could take Charles Town, they would be able to control the entire South. Clinton and his second in command, General Cornwallis, gradually encircled the city, and on May 12, the six-thousand-man American army in Charles Town surrendered.

The defeat took Congress by surprise, and without making the proper preparations, it dispatched a second army to South Carolina under Horatio Gates, the hero of Saratoga. He, too, failed. At Camden, Cornwallis outmaneuvered the raw American recruits (August 16). Gates galloped from the scene and did not stop until he reached Hillsboro, North Carolina, 200 miles away.

Even at this early stage of the southern campaign, the savagery of partisan warfare had become evident. Loyalist raiders plundered or occasionally killed neighbors against whom they harbored ancient grudges. Men who supported independence or who had merely fallen victim to the Loyalist guerrillas bided their time. On October 7 at Kings Mountain, North Carolina, they struck back against a force of Loyalists and British regulars who had strayed too far from base. This was the most vicious fighting of the Revolution; the Americans gave no quarter.

Cornwallis, badly confused and poorly supported, proceeded to squander his strength, senselessly chasing American forces across the Carolinas in the winter and early spring of 1781. When he did engage a freshly formed army under the command of Nathanael Greene, the most capable general on Washington's staff, Cornwallis was outmaneuvered and outfought at Cowpens and Guilford Courthouse. His army's strength sapped, Cornwallis pushed north into Virginia, planning apparently to establish a base of operations on the coast.

He selected Yorktown, a sleepy tobacco market located on a peninsula bounded by the York and James Rivers. Washington watched the maneuvers closely. The canny Virginia planter knew the territory intimately, and he sensed that Cornwallis had made a serious blunder. When Washington learned that the French fleet could attain temporary dominance in the Chesapeake Bay, he rushed south from New Jersey. With him marched thousands of well-trained French troops commanded by Comte de Rochambeau; they were joined along the way by a sizable contingent of forces led by the marquis de Lafayette. All the pieces fell into place. The French admiral, Comte de Grasse, cut Cornwallis off from the sea, while Washington and his lieutenants encircled the British on the land. On October 19, 1781, Cornwallis surrendered his entire army of six thousand men. The Continental Army had completed its mission; the task of securing independence now rested in the hands of American diplomats.

The Loyalist Dilemma

The war lasted longer than anyone had predicted in 1776. The nation had won its independence, but its people had paid a terrible price. Indeed, a great many men and women decided that no matter how much they had loved living in America, they could not accept the new government.

No one knows for certain how many Americans supported the crown during the Revolution. But more than 100,000 men and women permanently left America. Although a number of these exiles had served as British officeholders, they came

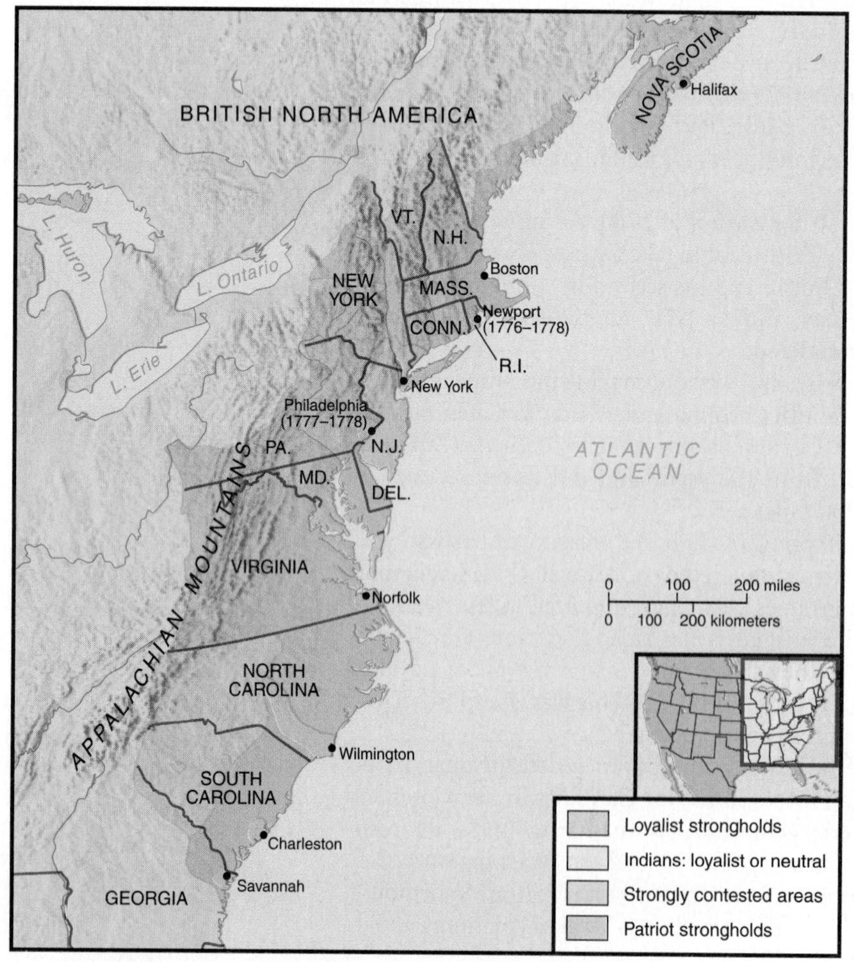

LOYALIST STRONGHOLDS
The highest concentrations of Loyalists were in the colonies of New York, North Carolina, South Carolina, and Georgia, especially in the areas around port cities such as New York City, Wilmington, Charleston, and Savannah.

Chronicle of Colonial–British Tension

Legislation	Date	Provisions	Colonial Reaction
Sugar Act	April 5, 1764	Revised duties on sugar, coffee, tea, wine, other imports; expanded jurisdiction of vice-admiralty courts	Several assemblies protest taxation for revenue
Stamp Act	March 22, 1765; repealed March 18, 1766	Printed documents (deeds, newspapers, marriage licenses, etc.) issued only on special stamped paper purchased from stamp distributors	Riots in cities; collectors forced to resign; Stamp Act Congress (October 1765)
Quartering Act	May 1765	Colonists must supply British troops with housing, other items (candles, firewood, etc.)	Protest in assemblies; New York Assembly punished for failure to comply, 1767
Declaratory Act	March 18, 1766	Parliament declares its sovereignty over the colonies "in all cases whatsoever"	Ignored in celebration over repeal of the Stamp Act
Townshend Revenue Acts	June 26, 29, July 2, 1767; all repealed—except duty on tea, March 1770	New duties on glass, lead, paper, paints, tea; customs collections tightened in America	Nonimportation of British goods; assemblies protest; newspapers attack British policy
Tea Act	May 10, 1773	Parliament gives East India Company right to sell tea directly to Americans; some duties on tea reduced	Protests against favoritism shown to monopolistic company; tea destroyed in Boston (December 16, 1773)
Coercive Acts (Intolerable Acts)	March–June 1774	Closes port of Boston; restructures Massachusetts government; restricts town meetings; troops quartered in Boston; British officials accused of crimes sent to England or Canada for trial	Boycott of British goods; First Continental Congress convenes (September 1774)
Prohibitory Act	December 22, 1775	Declares British intention to coerce Americans into submission; embargo on American goods; American ships seized	Drives Continental Congress closer to decision for independence

from all ranks and sections of society—farmers, merchants, tradesmen. The wealthier exiles went to London and begged for pensions from the king. Others relocated to Canada or the West Indies.

The Loyalists, or Tories, were caught in a difficult squeeze. The British did not trust them; they were, after all, Americans. Nor could they trust the British, who, after urgently soliciting their support, left them exposed to rebel retaliation. In England, the exiles found themselves treated as second-class citizens. Embittered and unwanted in America, they often found themselves just as embittered and unwanted in London.

Americans who actively supported independence saw these people as traitors. According to one patriot, "A Tory is a thing whose head is in England, its body in America, and its neck ought to be stretched." In many states, revolutionary governments confiscated Loyalist property. Some Loyalists were beaten, and a few were even executed. Long after the victorious Americans turned their attentions to the business of building a new republic, Loyalists remembered a comfortable, ordered world that had been lost forever at Yorktown. Theirs was a sad, often lonely fate.

Winning the Peace

Congress appointed a skilled delegation to negotiate a peace treaty: Benjamin Franklin, John Adams, and John Jay. According to their official instructions, they were to insist only on the recognition of the independence of the United States. On other issues, Congress ordered its delegates to defer to the counsel of the French government.

But in Paris there were grave problems. The French had formed a military alliance with Spain, and French officials announced that they could not consider the details of an American settlement until after the Spanish had recaptured Gibraltar from the British. The prospects for a Spanish victory were not good. More than anything, the American representatives feared that some European intrigue might cost the United States its independence.

While the three American delegates publicly paid their respects to French officials, they secretly entered into negotiations with an English agent. These actions—in violation of the men's instructions—did not fool the French for a moment. French spies reported what transpired at these meetings, and though the French could have protested the American breach of faith, they did not do so.

The negotiators drove a remarkable bargain. The preliminary agreement, signed on September 3, 1783, not only guaranteed the independence of the United States but also transferred all the territory east of the Mississippi River—except Florida, which remained under Spanish sovereignty—to the new republic. The treaty established generous boundaries on the north and south and gave the Americans important fishing rights in the North Atlantic. In exchange, Congress

CHRONOLOGY

1763	Peace of Paris ends the Seven Years' War (February)
1764	Parliament passes the Sugar Act to collect American revenue (April)
1765	Stamp Act receives support of the House of Commons (March) ❖ Stamp Act Congress meets in New York City (October)
1766	Stamp Act is repealed the same day as the Declaratory Act becomes law (March 18)
1767	Townshend Revenue Acts stir American anger (June–July)
1768	Massachusetts assembly refuses to rescind circular letter (February)
1770	British troops "massacre" Boston civilians (March) ❖ Parliament repeals all Townshend duties except the duty on tea (March)
1772	Samuel Adams forms committee of correspondence (October–November)
1773	Lord North's government passes the Tea Act (May) ❖ Bostonians hold the Tea Party (December)
1774	Parliament punishes Boston with the Coercive Acts (March–June) ❖ First Continental Congress convenes (September)
1775	Patriots take a stand at Lexington and Concord (April) ❖ Second Continental Congress gathers (May) ❖ Americans hold their own at Bunker Hill (June)
1776	Congress votes for independence; Declaration of Independence is signed (July) ❖ British defeat Washington off Long Island (August) ❖ Americans score a victory at Trenton (December)
1777	General Burgoyne surrenders at Saratoga (October)
1778	French treaties recognize independence of the United States (February)
1780	British take Charles Town (May), later renamed Charleston
1781	Washington forces Cornwallis to surrender at Yorktown (October)
1783	Peace treaty is signed (September) ❖ British evacuate New York City (November)

promised to help British merchants collect debts contracted before the Revolution and to compensate Loyalists whose land had been confiscated by the various state governments. The preliminary treaty did not take effect until after the French reached their own agreement with Great Britain, thus formally honoring the Franco-American alliance. It is hard to imagine how Franklin, Adams, and Jay could have negotiated a more favorable conclusion to the war. In the fall of 1783, the last redcoats sailed from New York City, ending 176 years of colonial rule.

Conclusion: Preserving Independence

The American people had waged war against the most powerful nation in Europe and emerged victorious. The treaty marked the conclusion of a colonial rebellion, but it remained for the men and women who had resisted taxation without representation to work out the full implications of republicanism. What would be the scope of the new government? What powers would be delegated to the people, the states, the federal authorities? How far would the wealthy, well-born leaders of the rebellion be willing to extend political, social, and economic rights? The war was over, but the drama of the American Revolution was still unfolding.

Key Terms

Whigs, p. 83
parliamentary sovereignty, p. 83
Loyalists, p. 85
Stamp Act Congress, p. 85
Boston Massacre, p. 88
committee of correspondence, p. 90
Coercive Acts, p. 90
First Continental Congress, p. 91
Second Continental Congress, p. 91
Common Sense, p. 93

Recommended Reading

Several books have had a profound impact on how historians think about the ideas that energized the Revolution. In a moving narrative account, Edmund S. Morgan and Helen M. Morgan explore how Americans interpreted the first great imperial controversy: *The Stamp Act Crisis: Prologue to Revolution* (1953). In his classic study, *The Ideological Origins of the American Revolution* (1967), Bernard Bailyn maps an ideology of power that informed colonial protest. Gordon Wood extends this argument in *The Radicalism of the American Revolution* (1992). In *Marketplace of Revolution: How Consumer Politics Shaped American Independence* (2004), T. H. Breen attempts to integrate more fully the experiences of ordinary men and women into the analysis of popular mobilization. Alfred F. Young demonstrates that it is possible to write about revolution from the perspective of working class colonists in *The Shoemaker and the Tea Party: Memory and the American Revolution* (2000). Works that focus productively on popular mobilization in specific colonies include Rhys Isaac, *The Transformation of Virginia, 1740–1790* (1983); Robert A. Gross, *The Minutemen and Their World* (1976); Woody Holton, *Forced Founders: Indians, Debtors, Slaves and the Making of the American Revolution in Virginia* (1999); and T. H. Breen, *Tobacco Culture: The Mentality of the Great Tidewater Planters on the Eve of Revolution* (1985). The tragedy that visited the Native Americans is examined in Colin C. Calloway, *American Revolution in Indian Country: Crisis and Diversity in Native American Communities* (1995), and Gregory Evans Dowd, *War Under Heaven: Pontiac, The Indian Nations and the British Empire* (2002). A useful study of the aspirations and disappointments of American women during this period is Linda Kerber, *Women of the Republic: Intellect and Ideology in Revolutionary America* (1980). Charles Royster investigates the changing attitudes of the American people about the Continental Army in *A Revolutionary People at War: The Continental Army and American Character, 1775–1783* (1979). Also valuable is John W. Shy, *A People Numerous and Armed: Reflections on the Military Struggle for American Independence*, rev. ed. (1990). Sidney Kaplan, *The Black Presence in the Era of the American Revolution* (1973), documents the hopes of African Americans during a period of radical political change.

For a list of additional titles related to this chapter's topics, please see http://www.ablongman.com/divine.

SUGGESTED WEB SITES

Canada History

http://www.civilization.ca/indexe.asp

Canada and the United States shared a colonial past but developed differently in the long run. This site is a part of the virtual museum of the Canadian Museum of Civilization Corporation.

Georgia's Rare Map Collection

http://scarlett.libs.uga.edu/darchive/hargrett/maps/colamer.html

http://scarlett.libs.uga.edu/darchive/hargrett/maps/revamer.html.

These two sites contain maps for Colonial and Revolutionary America.

Maryland Loyalism and the American Revolution

http://users.erols.com/candidus/index.htm

This look at Maryland's loyalists promotes the author's book, but it has good information about an underappreciated phenomenon, including loyalist songs and poems.

The American Revolution

http://revolution.h-net.msu.edu/

This site accompanies the PBS *Revolution* series with essays and resource links.

Chapter 6

The Republican Experiment

A New Moral Order

In 1788, Lewis Hallam and John Henry petitioned the General Assembly of Pennsylvania to open a theater. Although a 1786 state law banned the performance of stage plays and other "disorderly sports," many Philadelphia leaders favored the request to hold "dramatic representation" in their city. A committee appointed to study the issue concluded that a theater would contribute to "the general refinement of manners and the polish of society." Some supporters even argued that the sooner the United States had a professional theater the sooner the young republic would escape the "foreign yoke" of British culture.

The Quakers of Philadelphia dismissed such claims out of hand. They warned such "seminaries of lewdness and irreligion" would quickly undermine "the virtue of the people." They pointed out that "no sooner is a playhouse opened than it becomes surrounded with . . . brothels." Since Philadelphia was already suffering from a "stagnation of commerce [and] a scarcity of money"—unmistakable signs of God's displeasure—it seemed to them unwise to risk divine punishment by encouraging new "hot-beds of vice."

Such rhetoric did not sit well with other citizens who interpreted the revolutionary experience from an entirely different perspective. At issue, they insisted, was not popular morality, but state censorship. If the government silenced the stage, then "the same authority . . . may, with equal justice, dictate the shape and texture of our dress, or the modes and ceremonies of our worship." Depriving those who wanted to see plays of an opportunity to do so, they argued, "will abridge the natural right of every freeman, to dispose of his time and money, according to his own tastes and dispositions."

THROUGHOUT POST-REVOLUTIONARY AMERICA apparently trivial matters such as the opening of a new playhouse provoked passionate public debate. These divisions were symptomatic of a new, uncertain political culture struggling to find the proper balance between public morality and private freedom. During the long fight against Great Britain, Americans had defended individual rights. The problem was that the same people also believed that a republic that compromised its virtue could not long preserve liberty and independence. During the 1780s Americans understood their responsibility not only to each other, but also to history. They worried, however, that they might not successfully meet the challenge.

OUTLINE

Defining Republican Culture

Living in the Shadow of Revolution

The States: Experiments in Republicanism

Stumbling Toward a New National Government

Strengthening Federal Authority

"Have We Fought for This?"

Whose Constitution? Struggle for Ratification

Conclusion: Success Depends on the People

Defining Republican Culture

Today, the term *republican* no longer possesses the evocative power it did for most eighteenth-century Americans. For them, it defined an entire political culture. After all, they had done something that no other people had achieved for a very long time. They founded a national government without a monarch or aristocracy; in other words, a genuine republic. Making the new system work was a daunting task. Those Americans who read deeply in ancient and renaissance history knew that most republics had failed, often within a few years, only to be replaced by tyrants who cared not at all what ordinary people thought about the public good. To preserve their republic from such a fate, victorious revolutionaries such as Samuel Adams recast fundamental political values. For them, **republicanism** represented more than a particular form of government. It was a way of life, a core ideology, an uncompromising commitment to liberty and equality.

republicanism Concept that ultimate political authority is vested in the citizens of the nation. The character of republican government was dependent on the civic virtue of its citizens to preserve the nation from corruption and moral decay.

Adams and his contemporaries certainly believed that creating a new nation-state involved more than simply winning independence from Great Britain. More than did any other form of government, they insisted, a republic demanded an exceptionally high degree of public morality. If American citizens substituted "luxury, prodigality, and profligacy" for "prudence, virtue, and economy," then their revolution surely would have been in vain. Maintaining popular virtue was crucial to success. An innocent stage play, therefore, set off alarm bells. Such "foolish gratifications" seemed to compromise republican goals.

White Americans came out of the Revolution with an almost euphoric sense of the nation's special destiny. This expansive outlook, encountered among so many ordinary men and women, owed much to the spread of Protestant evangelicalism. However skeptical Jefferson and Franklin may have been about revealed religion, the great mass of American people subscribed to an almost utopian vision of the country's future. To this new republic, God had promised progress and prosperity. The signs were visible for everyone.

Such experience did not translate easily or smoothly into the creation of a strong central government. Modern Americans tend to take for granted the acceptance of the Constitution. Its merits seem self-evident largely because it has survived for two centuries. But in the early 1780s, no one could have predicted that the Constitution as we know it would have been written, much less ratified. It was equally possible that the Americans would have supported a weak confederation or perhaps allowed the various states and regions to go their separate ways.

In this uncertain political atmosphere, Americans divided sharply over the relative importance of *liberty* and *order*. The revolutionary experience had called into question the legitimacy of any form of special privilege. A legislative leader in Pennsylvania put the point bluntly: "No man has a greater claim of special privilege for his $100,000 than I have for my $5." The man who passionately defended social equality for those of varying economic status, however, may still have resisted the extension of civil rights to women or blacks. Nevertheless, liberty was contagious, and Americans of all backgrounds began to make new demands on society and government. For them, the Revolution had suggested radical alternatives, and in many forums throughout the nation—especially in the elected state assemblies—they insisted on being heard.

In certain quarters, the celebration of liberty met with mixed response. Some Americans—often the very men who had resisted British tyranny—worried that the citizens of the new nation were caught up in a wild, destructive scramble for material wealth. Democratic excesses seemed to threaten order, to endanger the rights of property. Surely a republic could not long survive unless its citizens showed greater self-control. For people concerned about the loss of order, the state assemblies appeared to be the greatest source of instability. Popularly elected representatives lacked what men of property defined as real civic virtue, an ability to work for the common good rather than their private interests.

Working out the tensions between order and liberty, between property and equality, generated an outpouring of political genius. At other times in American history, persons of extraordinary talent have been drawn to theology, commerce, or science, but during the 1780s, the country's intellectual leaders—Thomas Jefferson, James Madison, Alexander Hamilton, and John Adams, among others—focused their creative energies on the problem of how republicans ought to govern themselves.

Living in the Shadow of Revolution

If America's revolution seems less radical than that of other nations, particularly France, it may be because eighteenth-century Americans had fewer entrenched barriers to overcome in the first place. Indeed, the American Revolution confirmed many rights that colonial Americans had long enjoyed—broad suffrage, religious toleration, freedom of movement. Although the Revolution did not bring about massive changes in American society, it did raise issues of immense importance for the later history of the United States. Republican spokesmen, such as Samuel Adams and Thomas Jefferson, insisted that equality, however narrowly defined, was an essential element of republican government. Even though they failed to institute universal manhood suffrage, abolish slavery, or apply equality to women, they vigorously articulated a set of assumptions about people's rights and liberties that challenged future generations of Americans to make good on the promise of the Revolution.

Social and Political Reform

Following the war, Americans aggressively ferreted out and, with republican fervor, denounced any traces of aristocratic pretense. As colonists, they had long resented the claims of certain Englishmen to special privilege simply because of noble birth. A society based on artificial status was contrary to republican principles.

The appearance of equality was as important as its actual achievement. In fact, the distribution of wealth in postwar America was more uneven than it had been a few decades earlier. Yet Americans attempted to root out the notion of a privileged class. States abolished laws of primogeniture and entail, which in colonial times allowed a landholder to pass his entire estate to his eldest son or to declare that his property could never be divided, sold, or given away. Although America had never been affected greatly by such customs, their abolition was an important symbolic blow against the idea of a landed aristocracy.

Republican ferment also encouraged many states to lower property requirements for voting. After the revolutionary experience, such a step seemed logical. The concept of a representative government was well accepted in America. These reforms, however, did not significantly expand the American electorate. Long before the Revolution, an overwhelming percentage of free males had owned enough land to vote, and few leaders at that time were willing to entertain the idea of universal manhood suffrage.

The most important changes in voting patterns were the result of western migration. As Americans moved to the frontier, they received full political representation in their state legislatures, and because new districts tended to be poorer than established coastal settlements, their inhabitants selected representatives who seemed less cultured and less well trained than those sent by eastern voters. Moreover, western delegates resented traveling so far to attend legislative meetings, and they lobbied successfully to transfer state capitals to more convenient locations.

After independence, Americans also reexamined the relationship between church and state. Republican spokesmen such as Thomas Jefferson argued in favor of the disestablishment of state churches. They insisted that rulers had no right to interfere with the free expression of an individual's religious beliefs. Nor did they believe that churches should be supported with taxpayers' monies. Massachusetts and Connecticut did not alter the status of their Congregational churches, but most of the southern states did disestablish the Anglican Church. Americans championed religious toleration, though few favored irreligion or secularism.

African Americans in the New Republic

Revolutionary fervor forced Americans to confront the most appalling contradiction to republican principles—slavery. During the 1780s, abolitionist sentiment spread. Both in private and in public, people began to criticize slavery in other than religious language. No doubt, the double standard of their own political rhetoric embarrassed many white Americans. They hotly demanded liberation from British enslavement at the same time that they held several hundred thousand blacks in bondage.

By keeping the issue of slavery before the public through writing and petitioning, African Americans powerfully undermined arguments advanced in favor of human bondage. They demanded freedom, reminding white lawmakers that African American men and women had the same natural right to liberty as did other Americans. In 1779, for example, a group of African Americans asked the members of the Connecticut assembly "whether it is consistent with the present Claims, of the United States, to hold so many Thousands, of the Race of Adam, our Common Father, in perpetual Slavery."

The scientific accomplishments of Benjamin Banneker (1731–1806), Maryland's African American astronomer and mathematician, and the international fame of Phillis Wheatley (1753–1784), Boston's celebrated "African muse," made it increasingly difficult for white Americans to maintain credibly that African Americans could not hold their own in a free society. Wheatley's poems went through many editions, and after reading her work, the French philosopher Voltaire rebuked a friend who had claimed "there never would be Negro poets." Banneker, like Wheatley, enjoyed a well-deserved reputation, in his case for contributions as a scientist. After receiving a copy of an almanac that Banneker had published in Philadelphia, Thomas Jefferson concluded "that nature has given to our black brethren, talents equal to those of the other colors of men."

In the northern states, where there was no economic justification for slavery, white laborers resented having to compete in the workplace against slaves. This economic situation, combined with the acknowledgment of the double standard represented by slavery, contributed to the establishment of antislavery societies, groups that included such prominent figures as Alexander Hamilton, John Jay, and Benjamin Franklin. By 1792, antislavery societies meeting from Virginia to Massachusetts put slaveholders on the intellectual defensive for the first time in American history.

In several states north of Virginia, the attack on slavery took a number of different forms. The Vermont constitution of 1777 specifically prohibited slavery. In 1780, the Pennsylvania legislature abolished the practice. Other states followed suit. By 1800, slavery was well on the road to extinction in the North.

These developments did not mean that white people accepted blacks as equals. In the very states that outlawed slavery, African Americans still faced systematic discrimination. Free blacks were generally excluded from voting, juries, and militia duty—rights and responsibilities usually associated with full citizenship. They rarely enjoyed access to education, and in cities such as Philadelphia and New York, where African Americans went to look for work, they ended up living in segregated wards or neighborhoods. Even in the churches—institutions that had often spoken out against slavery—free African Americans were denied equal standing with white worshipers. Humiliations of this sort persuaded African Americans to form their own churches. In Philadelphia, Richard Allen, a former slave, founded the Bethel

Church for Negro Methodists (1793) and later organized the African Methodist Episcopal Church (1814), an institution of great cultural as well as religious significance for nineteenth-century American blacks.

Even in the South, where African Americans made up a large percentage of the population, slavery disturbed thoughtful white republicans. Some planters simply freed their slaves, and by 1790, the number of free blacks living in Virginia was 12,766. By 1800, the figure had reached 30,750. Most southern slaveholders rejected this course of action. Perhaps more significant, however, is the fact that no southern leader during the era of republican experimentation defended slavery as a positive good. Such overtly racist rhetoric did not become part of the public discourse until the nineteenth century.

Despite promising starts in that direction, the southern states did not abolish slavery. The economic incentives to maintain a servile labor force, especially after the invention of the cotton gin in 1793 and the opening up of the Alabama and Mississippi frontier, overwhelmed the initial abolitionist impulse. An opportunity to translate the principles of the American Revolution into social practice had been lost, at least temporarily.

The Challenge of Women's Rights

The revolutionary experience accelerated changes in how ordinary people viewed the family. At the beginning of the eighteenth century, fathers claimed absolute authority over other members of their families simply on the grounds that they were fathers. At the time of the American Revolution, however, few seriously accepted the notion that fathers—be they tyrannical kings or heads of ordinary families—enjoyed unlimited powers over women and children. Indeed, people in England as well as America increasingly described the family in terms of love and companionship. Instead of duties, they spoke of affection. This transformation in the way men and women viewed relations of power within the family was most evident in the popular novels of the period. Americans devoured *Pamela* and *Clarissa,* stories by the English writer Samuel Richardson about women who were the innocent victims of unreformed males, usually deceitful lovers and unforgiving fathers.

In this changing intellectual environment, American women began making new demands not only on their husbands but also on republican institutions. Abigail Adams, one of the generation's most articulate women, instructed her husband, John, as he set off for the opening of the Continental Congress: "I desire you would Remember the Ladies, and be more generous and favourable to them than your ancestors. Do not put such unlimited power into the hands of the Husbands." John responded in a condescending manner. The "Ladies" would have to wait until the country achieved independence.

In fact, women justified their assertiveness largely on the basis of political ideology. If survival of republics really depended on the virtue of their citizens, they argued, then it was the special responsibility of women as mothers to nurture the right values in their children and as wives to instruct their husbands in proper behavior.

Questions of equality in the new republic extended to the rights of women. In this illustration, which appeared as the frontispiece in the 1792 issue of The Lady's Magazine and Repository of Entertaining Knowledge, *the "Genius of the Ladies Magazine" and the "Genius of Emulation" (holding in her hand a laurel crown) present to Liberty a petition for the rights of woman.* ❖

Ill-educated women could not possibly fulfill these high expectations. They required education that was at least comparable to what men received. Scores of female academies were established during this period to meet what many Americans, men as well as women, now regarded as a pressing social need. The schools may have received widespread encouragement precisely because they did not radically alter traditional gender roles. After all, the educated republican woman of the late eighteenth century did not pursue a career; she returned to the home, where she followed a familiar routine as wife and mother.

During this period, women petitioned for divorce on new grounds. One case is particularly instructive concerning changing attitudes toward women and the family. In 1784, John Backus, an undistinguished Massachusetts silversmith, was hauled before a local court and asked why he beat his wife. He responded that "it was Partly owing to his Education for his father treated his mother in the same manner." The difference was that Backus's wife refused to tolerate such abuse, and she sued successfully for divorce. Studies of divorce patterns in Connecticut and Pennsylvania show that after 1773 women divorced on about the same terms as men.

The war itself presented some women with fresh opportunities. In 1780, Ester DeBerdt Reed founded a large volunteer women's organization in Philadelphia—the first of its kind in the United States—that raised more than $300,000 for Washington's army. Other women ran family farms and businesses while their husbands fought the British. And in 1790, the New Jersey legislature explicitly allowed women who owned property to vote.

Despite these scattered gains, republican society still defined women's roles exclusively in terms of mother, wife, and homemaker. Other pursuits seemed unnatural, even threatening, and it is perhaps not surprising, therefore, that in 1807, New Jersey lawmakers—angry over a close election in which women voters may have determined the result—repealed female suffrage in the interests of "safety, quiet, and good order and dignity of the state."

The States: Experiments in Republicanism

In May 1776, the Second Continental Congress urged the states to adopt constitutions. Rhode Island and Connecticut already had republican governments by virtue of their unique charters, and the rest of the new states soon complied. Several constitutions were frankly experimental, and some states later rewrote documents that had been drafted in the first flush of independence. But if these early constitutions were provisional, they nevertheless provided the framers of the federal Constitution of 1787 with valuable insights into the strengths and weaknesses of government based on the will of the people.

Blueprints for State Government

Despite disagreements over details, Americans who wrote the various state constitutions shared certain political assumptions. First, they insisted on preparing *written* documents. As colonists, they had lived under royal charters, documents that described the workings of local government in detail, and they felt comfortable with the contractual language of legal documents.

However logical the decision to produce written documents may have seemed to the Americans, it represented a major break with English practice. Political philosophers in the mother country had long boasted of Britain's unwritten constitution, a collection of judicial reports and parliamentary statutes. Yet this highly vaunted system had not protected the colonists from oppression. It is understandable, then, why, after declaring independence, Americans demanded that their state constitutions explicitly define the rights of the people as well as the powers of their rulers. They desired more from public officials than simply assurances of good faith.

The authors of the state constitutions believed that men and women possessed certain **natural rights** over which government exercised no control whatsoever. So that future rulers—potential tyrants—would know the exact limits of their authority, these fundamental rights were carefully spelled out.

natural rights Fundamental rights over which the government could exercise no control. An uncompromising belief in such rights energized the popular demand for a formal bill of rights in 1791.

Eight state constitutions contained specific declarations of rights. In general, they affirmed three fundamental freedoms: of religion, of speech, and of the press. They protected citizens from unlawful searches and seizures; they upheld trial by jury. Ultimately, the best expression of this impulse is contained in the famed Bill of Rights, the first ten amendments to the federal Constitution.

In almost every state, delegates to constitutional conventions drastically reduced the power of the governor. He was allowed to make almost no political appointments, and while the state legislators closely monitored his activities, he possessed no veto over their decisions (Massachusetts being the lone exception). Most early constitutions lodged nearly all effective power in the legislature. In fact, the writers of the state constitutions were so fearful of the concentration of power in the hands of one person that they failed to recognize that governors, like the representatives, were servants of a free people.

The legislature dominated early state government. Some states even questioned the need for a senate or upper house, and Pennsylvania and Georgia instituted a unicameral, or one-house, system. Many Americans believed that the lower house could handle all the state's problems. The two-house form survived the Revolution largely because it was familiar and because some persons had already begun to suspect that certain checks on the popular will, however arbitrary they might appear, were necessary to preserve minority rights.

Power to the People

Perhaps the most significant state constitution was the one adopted by the people of Massachusetts because they hit upon a remarkable political innovation. Their state constitution was drafted by a specifically elected convention of delegates, not ordinary officeholders.

John Adams served as the chief architect of the governmental framework of the state. It included a house and a senate, a popularly elected governor who possessed a veto over legislative bills, and property qualifications for officeholders as well as voters. The most striking aspect of the 1780 constitution, however, was its opening sentence: "We . . . the people of Massachusetts . . . agree upon, ordain, and establish . . ." This powerful vocabulary would be echoed in the federal Constitution.

The state constitutions ushered a different type of person into public office. When one Virginian surveyed the newly elected House of Burgesses in 1776, he discovered that it was "composed of men not quite so well dressed, not so politely educated, nor so highly born as some Assemblies I have formerly seen." They were indeed the people's people, representative republicans. Whether this new breed of representative would be virtuous enough to safeguard the fledgling republic remained a hotly debated question.

Stumbling Toward a New National Government

When the Second Continental Congress convened in 1775, the delegates found themselves waging war in the name of a country that did not yet exist. As the military crisis deepened, Congress gradually—though often reluctantly—assumed greater authority over national affairs, but everyone agreed that such narrowly conceived measures were a poor substitute for a legally constituted government. The separate states could not possibly deal with the range of issues that now confronted the American people. Indeed, if independence meant anything in a world of sovereign nations, it implied the creation of a central authority capable of conducting war, borrowing money, regulating trade, and negotiating treaties.

Articles of Confederation

The first attempt to produce a framework for national government failed miserably. Congress appointed a committee headed by John Dickinson, a lawyer who had written an important revolutionary pamphlet titled *Letters from a Farmer in Pennsylvania.* Dickinson's plan for creating a strong central government shocked the delegates, who had assumed that the constitution would authorize a loose confederation of states.

Dickinson's plan called for equal state representation in Congress. This upset states such as Virginia and Massachusetts that were more populous than others and fueled tensions between large and small states. Also unsettling was Dickinson's recommendation that taxes be paid to Congress on the basis of a state's total population, black as well as white, a formula that angered Southerners.

Not unexpectedly, the draft that Congress finally approved in November 1777 bore little resemblance to Dickinson's original plan. The **Articles of Confederation** jealously guarded the sovereignty of the states. The delegates who drafted this framework shared a general republican conviction that power—especially power so far removed from the people—was inherently dangerous and that the only way to preserve liberty was to place as many constraints as possible on federal authority.

Articles of Confederation Ratified in 1781, this document was the United States' first constitution, providing a framework for national government. The articles sharply limited central authority by denying the national government any taxation or coercive powers.

They succeeded marvelously; Congress created a government that many people regarded as powerless. The Articles provided for a single legislative body, consisting of representatives selected annually by the state legislatures. Each state possessed a single vote in Congress. There was no independent executive and, of course, no veto over legislative decisions. The Articles also denied Congress the power of taxation, a serious oversight in time of war. The national government could obtain funds only by asking the states for contributions, called requisitions. If a state failed to cooperate—and many did—Congress limped along without financial support. Amendments to this constitution required unanimous assent by all thirteen states. The authors of the new system apparently expected a powerless national government to handle foreign relations, military matters, Native American affairs, and interstate disputes. They most emphatically did not award Congress ownership of the lands west of the Appalachian Mountains.

Western Land: Key to the First Constitution

Once the new constitution had been sent to the states for ratification, the major bone of contention became the disposition of the vast, unsurveyed territory west of the Appalachians that everyone hoped the British would soon surrender. Although the region was claimed by the various states, most of it actually belonged to the Native Americans. In a series of land grabs that federal negotiators called treaties, the United States government took the land comprising much of modern Ohio, Indiana, Illinois, and Kentucky. Since the Indians had put their faith in the British during the war, they could do little to resist the humiliating treaty agreements at Fort McIntosh (1785), Fort Stanwix (1784), and Fort Finney (1786).

Some states, such as Virginia and Georgia, claimed land all the way from the Atlantic Ocean to the elusive "South Sea" by virtue of royal charters. People who lived in those states not blessed with vague or ambiguous royal charters seemed to

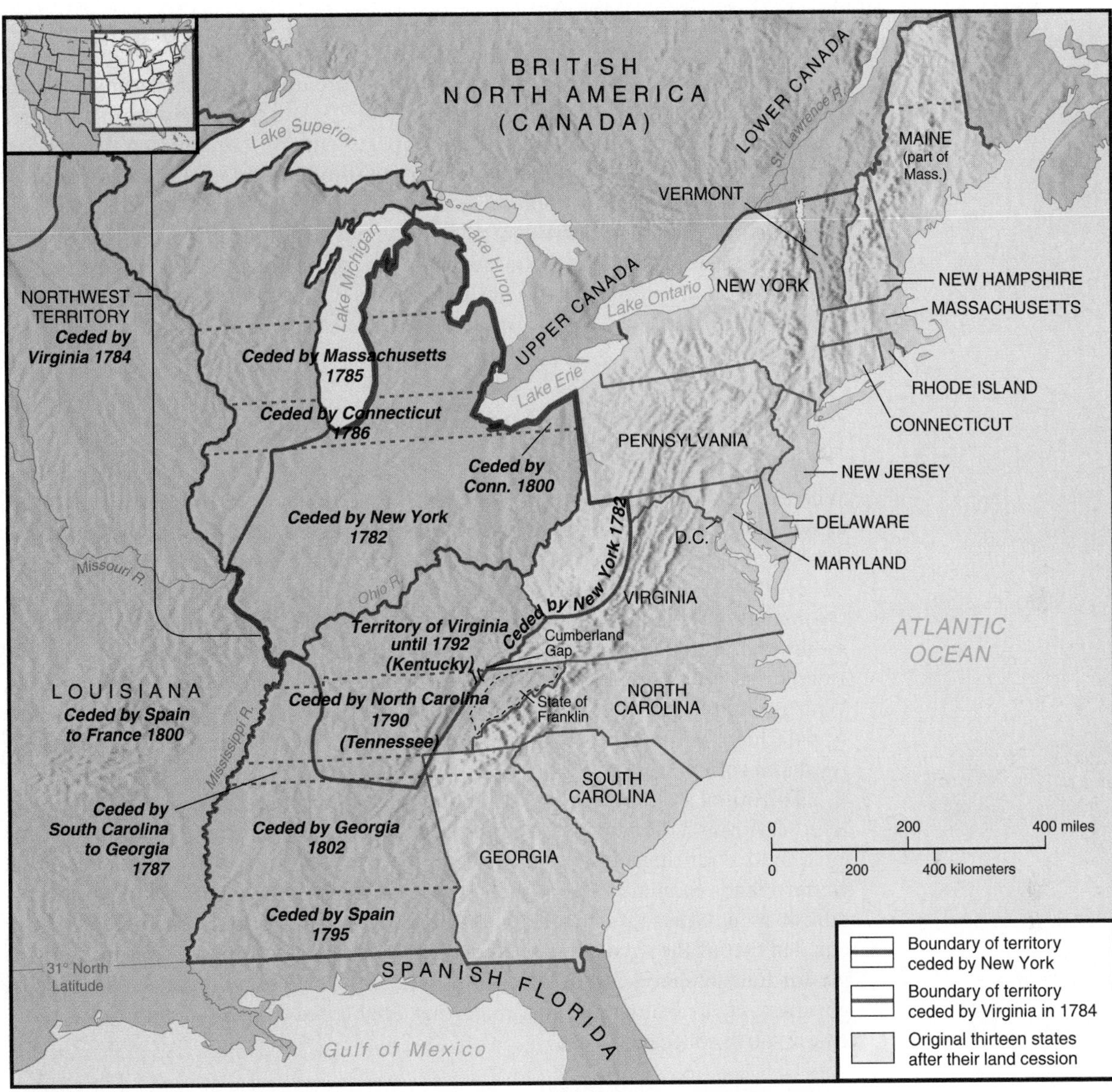

WESTERN LAND CLAIMS CEDED BY THE STATES *After the Revolution, the major issue facing the Continental Congress under the Articles of Confederation was mediating conflicting states' claims to rich western land. By 1802, the states had ceded all rights to the federal government.* ❖

be in danger of being permanently cut off from the anticipated bounty. In protest, the "landless" states stubbornly refused to ratify the Articles of Confederation. All states had sacrificed during the Revolution, they reasoned, and so all states should profit from the fruits of victory—in this case, from the sale of western lands. Marylanders were particularly vociferous, fearing depopulation by settlers in search of cheap farmland.

The states resolved this bitter controversy in 1781 as much by accident as by design. Virginia, a landed state, realized the problems inherent in the situation. If the state were to extend beyond the mountains, poor transportation links would make it difficult or even impossible to govern such a large territory effectively from Richmond. The western settlers might even come to regard Virginia as a colonial power insensitive to their needs. Virginia therefore opted to cede its western land claims to Congress, and the other landed states soon followed suit. These transfers established an important principle, for after 1781 there was no question that the West belonged not to the states but to the United States.

No one greeted ratification of the Articles with jubilation. Americans were still fully occupied with winning independence. In 1781, the new government began setting up a bureaucracy. It created the Departments of War, Foreign Affairs, and Finance. By far the most influential presence within the Confederation government was Robert Morris (1734–1806), a freewheeling Philadelphia merchant who was appointed the first superintendent of finance. His decisions provoked controversy. Contemporaries who feared the development of a strong national government identified Morris with efforts to undermine the authority of the states and to seize the power of taxation; at least one congressional critic labeled him a "pecuniary dictator."

Northwest Ordinance: The Confederation's Major Achievement

Whatever the weaknesses of Congress, it scored one impressive triumph. Congressional action brought order to western settlement, especially in the Northwest Territory, and incorporated frontier Americans into an expanded federal system.

In 1781, however, the prospects for success did not seem promising. For years, colonial authorities had ignored people who migrated far inland, sending neither money nor soldiers to protect them from Indian attack. Tensions between the seaboard colonies and the frontier regions had occasionally flared into violence. With thousands of men and women, most of them squatters, pouring across the Appalachian Mountains, Congress had to act quickly to avoid the past errors of royal and colonial authorities.

The initial attempt to deal with this explosive problem came in 1784. Jefferson, then serving as a member of Congress, drafted an ordinance that became a basis for later, more enduring legislation. He recommended carving ten new states out of the western lands located north of the Ohio River. He specified that each new state establish a republican form of government. When the population of a territory equaled that of the smallest state already in the Confederation, the region could apply for full statehood. In the meantime, free adult males could participate in local government, a democratic guarantee that frightened several of Jefferson's more conservative colleagues.

LAND ORDINANCE OF 1785

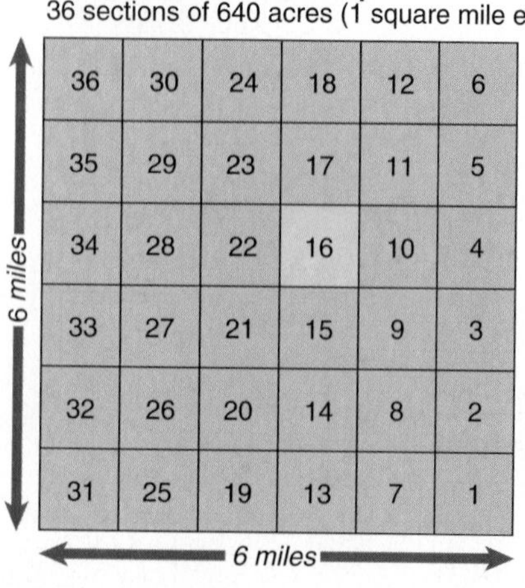

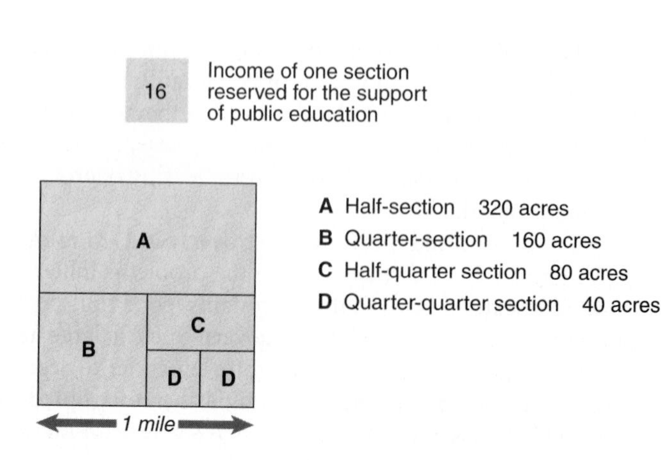

The impoverished Congress was eager to sell off the western territory as quickly as possible. After all, the frontier represented a source of income that did not depend on the unreliable generosity of the states. A second ordinance, passed in 1785 and called the Land Ordinance, established an orderly process for laying out new townships and marketing public lands. After surveying and subdividing various regions, the government planned to auction off its holdings in 640-acre (1-square-mile) sections at prices of not less than $1 an acre, payable in coin only. Section 16 was set aside for the support of public education, and four other sections were held for the government.

Public response disappointed Congress. Surveying the lands took far longer than anticipated, and few persons possessed enough hard currency to make even the minimum purchase of 640 acres. Finally, a solution to the problem came from Manasseh Cutler, a land speculator and congressional lobbyist. He and his companions offered to purchase more than 6 million unsurveyed acres of land located in present-day southeastern Ohio by persuading Congress to accept at full face value government loan certificates that had been issued to soldiers during the Revolution. The speculators could pick up these certificates on the open market for as little as 10 percent of their face value. Like so many other get-rich-quick schemes, however, this one failed to produce the anticipated millions.

Congress also had reservations about frontier democracy. In the 1780s, the West seemed to be filling up with people who, by eastern standards, were uncultured. The attitude was as old as the frontier itself. Indeed, seventeenth-century Englishmen had felt the same way regarding the earliest Virginians. The belief that the westerners were lawless, however, persisted, and even a sober observer like Washington insisted that the West crawled with "banditti." The Ordinance of 1784 placed the government of the territories in the hands of people about whom congressmen and speculators had second thoughts.

These various currents shaped the Ordinance of 1787, one of the final acts passed under the Confederation. This bill, also called the **Northwest Ordinance,** provided a new structure for government of the Northwest Territory. The plan authorized the creation of between three and five territories, each to be ruled by a governor, a secretary, and three judges appointed by Congress. When the population reached five thousand, voters who owned property could elect an assembly, but the decisions were subject to the governor's absolute veto. Once sixty thousand persons resided in a territory, they could write a constitution and petition for full statehood. Although the procedures represented a retreat from Jefferson's original proposal, the Ordinance of 1787 contained several significant features. A bill of rights guaranteed the settlers trial by jury, freedom of religion, and due process of law. In addition, the act outlawed slavery, a prohibition that freed the future states of Ohio, Indiana, Illinois, Michigan, and Wisconsin from the curse of human bondage.

Northwest Ordinance Legislation that formulated plans for governments in America's northwestern territories, defined a procedure for the territories' admission to the Union as states, and prohibited slavery north of the Ohio River.

By contrast, the growing settlements south of the Ohio River seemed chaotic. Between 1775 and 1784, for example, the population of what was to become Kentucky jumped from around one hundred to thirty thousand. In this and other southwestern regions, land speculators were an ever-present problem. By 1796, the entire region south of the Ohio River had been transformed into a crazy quilt of claims and counterclaims that generated lawsuits for many years thereafter.

Strengthening Federal Authority

Throughout the country, Americans became increasingly critical of the Articles of Confederation. Complaints varied from region to region and from person to person, but most disappointment reflected economic frustration. Americans had assumed that peace would restore prosperity. When such was not the case, they searched the political horizon for a reason.

The Nationalist Critique

Renewed trade with Great Britain on a large scale undermined the stability of the American economy. Specie (coins) flowed eastward across the Atlantic, leaving the United States desperately short of hard currency. When British merchants called in their debts, thriftless American buyers often fell into bankruptcy. Critics also pointed to the government's inability to regulate trade. Southerners in particular resisted any such attempts. They protested that any controls on the export of tobacco, rice, and cotton smacked of the Navigation Acts.

To blame the Confederation alone for the economic depression would be unfair. Nevertheless, during the 1780s, many people agreed that a stronger government could somehow have softened the blow. In their rush to acquire imported luxuries, Americans seemed to have deserted republican principles, and a weak Congress was helpless to restore national virtue.

The country's chronic fiscal instability increased public anxiety. During the war, Congress printed more than $200 million in paper currency, but because of an extraordinarily high rate of inflation, the rate of exchange for Continental bills soon declined to a fraction of their face value. In 1781, Congress turned to the states for help, asking them to retire the worthless money. Instead, several states not only recirculated the Continental bills but also issued worthless currency of their own.

A heavy burden of state and national debt compounded the general sense of economic crisis. Revolutionary soldiers had yet to be paid, and the government owed money to domestic and foreign creditors. The pressure to pay the debts grew, but Congress was unable to respond. Since Congress was prohibited from taxing the American people, it required little imagination to see that the Confederation would soon default on its legal obligations unless something was done quickly.

❖ A Look at the Past ❖

Continental Paper Money

Fighting the American Revolution cost a lot of money. The new government of the United States simply did not have sufficient gold and silver—called specie—to pay the troops and buy weapons. Pressed on all sides by creditors, the fledgling government issued huge quantities of paper money, such as these bills issued from the colony of New Jersey in 1776 and the Continental Congress in 1778. The flood of Continental currency sparked massive inflation, as nearly worthless money chased a finite supply of consumer goods. Considering the threat of economic stability, should the Continental Congress have printed so much paper money? Did it have other realistic alternatives? What sorts of people in this society were most harmed by hyperinflation?

In response, an aggressive group of men announced that they knew how to save the Confederation. The **nationalists**—led by Alexander Hamilton, James Madison, and Robert Morris—called for major constitutional reforms, the chief of which was an amendment allowing Congress to collect a 5 percent tax on imported goods. Revenues generated by the proposed Impost of 1781 would be used by the Confederation to reduce the national debt. Twelve states accepted the impost, but Rhode Island resolutely refused to cooperate. One negative vote on this proposed constitutional change was enough to kill the taxing plan; amending the Articles required unanimous consent.

nationalists Group of leaders who favored replacing the Articles of Confederation with a stronger national government.

The nationalists sparked fierce opposition. Many Americans were apprehensive of their plans. The nationalists, for their part, regarded their opponents as economically naive and argued that a country with the potential of the United States required a complex, centralized fiscal system. But for all their pretensions to realism, the nationalists of the early 1780s were politically inept. They underestimated the depth of republican fears, and in their rush to strengthen the Articles, they overplayed their hand.

A group of extreme nationalists even appealed to the army for support. To this day, no one knows the full story of the Newburgh Conspiracy of 1783. Officers of the Continental army stationed at Newburgh, New York, worried that Congress would disband them without funding their pensions and began to lobby intensively for relief. The officers' initial efforts were harmless enough, but frustrated nationalists such as Morris and Hamilton decided that if the army exerted sufficient pressure on the government, perhaps even threatened a military takeover, stubborn Americans might be compelled to amend the Articles.

The conspirators failed to take George Washington's integrity into account. In a surprise visit, he confronted the officers directly at Newburgh. So great was his personal influence that a few words from him ended any chance of rebellion. Washington, indeed, deserves credit for preserving civilian rule in this country. He refused to consider any scheme that contemplated using the army as a political instrument.

In April 1783, Congress proposed a second impost, but it, too, failed to win unanimous ratification. Even a personal appeal by Washington could not save the amendment. With this defeat, nationalists gave up on the Confederation. Morris retired from government, and Madison returned to Virginia utterly depressed by what he had witnessed.

Diplomatic Humiliation

In foreign affairs, Congress endured further embarrassment. American negotiators had promised Great Britain that its citizens could collect debts contracted before the Revolution. The states, however, dragged their heels, and several even passed laws obstructing the settlement of legitimate prewar claims. Congress was powerless to force compliance. The British responded to this apparent provocation by refusing to evacuate troops from posts located in the Northwest Territory. A strong central government would have driven the redcoats out, but without adequate funds, the weak Congress was powerless to act.

Congress's postrevolutionary dealings with Spain were equally humiliating. That nation refused to accept the southern boundary of the United States established by the Treaty of Paris. Spanish agents schemed with southern Indian tribes to resist American expansion, and on July 21, 1784, Spain added a further insult by closing the lower Mississippi River to citizens of the United States. This last event devastated western farmers, who needed unrestricted use of the Mississippi to send their crops to the world's markets. Without the river, the economic development of the entire Ohio Valley was in jeopardy.

In 1786, a Spanish official, Don Diego de Gardoqui, opened talks with John Jay, a New Yorker appointed by Congress to obtain rights to navigation on the Mississippi. Jay soon discovered that Gardoqui would not compromise, but he pressed on, attempting to win concessions that would have commercially linked the United States to Spain and benefited northern traders while forgoing free navigation of the Mississippi for twenty-five years. When Congress learned of Jay's plans, it wisely terminated the negotiations with Spain.

By the mid-1780s, Congress had squandered whatever respect it may once have enjoyed. It met irregularly, and some states did not even bother to send delegates. The nation lacked a permanent capital, and Congress thus drifted from Philadelphia to Princeton to Annapolis to New York City, prompting one humorist to suggest that the government purchase an air balloon to allow members of Congress to "float along from one end of the continent to the other" and "suddenly pop down into any of the states they please."

"Have We Fought for This?"

Thoughtful Americans, especially those who had provided leadership during the Revolution, agreed that something had to be done. By 1785, the country seemed to be drifting; the buoyant optimism that had sustained revolutionary patriots had dissolved into pessimism and doubt. Washington was soon asking his countrymen exactly why they had fought the Revolution.

A Crisis Mentality

The country's problems could be traced in part to the republicans' own ideology. More than anything else, they feared the concentration of power in the hands of unscrupulous rulers. They therefore created governments—national and state—with weak chief executives and strong assemblies. However, too many of the people who manned the state assemblies and Congress were not up to the task. The result was a government of excessive individualism where legitimate minority rights took a backseat to the desires of the majority.

Facing economic chaos, many states blithely churned out worthless currency, while others passed laws impeding the collection of debts. In Rhode Island, the situation became absurd. State legislators made it illegal for merchants to reject Rhode Island money even though everyone knew it had no value. As Americans tried to interpret these experiences within a republican framework, they were checked by the most widely accepted political wisdom of the age. Baron de Montesquieu (1689–1755), a French political philosopher of immense international reputation, declared flatly that a republican government could not flourish in a large territory. For such a government to function properly, the people had to be able to keep a close eye on their representatives. Americans treated Montesquieu's theories as self-evident truths, and they were thus nervous about tampering with the sovereignty of the states.

James Madison rejected Montesquieu's argument and in so doing helped Americans think of republican government in exciting new ways. This soft-spoken, rather unprepossessing Virginian was the most brilliant American political thinker of his generation. Based on his reading of the Scottish philosopher David Hume and others, Madison became convinced that Americans need not fear a greatly expanded republic. In fact, he believed that a republican form of government would work better in a large country than in a small one. In small states such as Rhode Island, for example, legislative majorities tyrannized the propertied minority. In a large republic, these injustices could be avoided. With so many people scattered over a huge area, no one faction would be able to form an effective majority, and one powerful interest would be checked by some other equally powerful interest.

Madison did not, however, advocate a modern "interest group" model of political behavior. Rather he thought that the competing selfish factions would neutralize each other, leaving the business of governing the republic to the ablest, most virtuous persons that the nation could produce. In other words, the government Madison envisioned would be based on the will of the people and yet detached from their narrowly based demands. This thinking formed the foundation of Madison's most famous political essay, *The Federalist* No. 10.

A concerted movement to overhaul the Articles of Confederation developed in the mid-1780s. The Massachusetts legislature asked Congress to call a convention for the purpose of revising the entire constitution. Nothing came of the suggestion until 1786, when Madison and his friends persuaded the Virginia assembly to recommend a convention to explore the creation of a unified system of "commercial regulation." Congress supported the idea. However, only five states sent delegates to the Annapolis convention. Rather than try to conduct any business, the Annapolis delegates advised Congress to hold a second meeting in Philadelphia to consider constitutional changes. Congress authorized a grand convention to gather in May 1787.

Events played into Madison's hands. Soon after the Annapolis meeting, an uprising known as **Shays's Rebellion,** involving several thousand impoverished farmers, shattered the peace of western Massachusetts. The farmers complained of high taxes, of high interest rates, and of a state government insensitive to their economic problems. In 1786, Daniel Shays, a veteran of the battle of Bunker Hill, and his armed neighbors closed a county courthouse where creditors were suing to foreclose farm mortgages. His band then marched to Springfield, site of a federal arsenal, but the state militia soon put down the rebellion.

Shays's Rebellion Armed insurrection of farmers in western Massachusetts led by Daniel Shays, a veteran of the Continental Army. Intended to prevent state courts from foreclosing on debtors unable to pay their taxes, the rebellion was put down by the state militia. Nationalists used the event to justify the calling of a constitutional convention to strengthen the national government.

Nationalists throughout the United States overreacted to news of Shays's Rebellion. From their perspective, the incident symbolized the breakdown of law and order that they had long predicted. Even more important, the event persuaded persons who might otherwise have ignored the Philadelphia meeting to participate in drafting a new constitution.

The Philadelphia Convention

In the spring of 1787, fifty-five men representing twelve states traveled to Philadelphia. Only Rhode Island refused to take part in the proceedings. The delegates were practical men: lawyers, merchants, and planters, many of whom had fought in the Revolution and served in the Congress of the Confederation. The majority were in their thirties and forties. The gathering included George Washington, James Madison, George Mason, Robert Morris, John Dickinson, Benjamin Franklin, and Alexander Hamilton. Absent were John Adams and Thomas Jefferson, who were conducting diplomacy in Europe; Patrick Henry stayed home in Virginia because he "smelled a rat."

As soon as the convention opened on May 25, the delegates made several procedural decisions of utmost importance. First, they ruled that their discussions would be kept absolutely secret. This determination allowed delegates to speak their minds freely without fear of criticism from people who had not actually witnessed the debates. The delegates also decided to vote by state, but to avoid the kinds of problems that had plagued the Confederation, they ruled that key proposals needed the support of only a majority instead of the nine states required in the Articles.

Inventing a Federal Republic

Madison understood that whoever sets the agenda controls the meeting. Even before the delegates had arrived, he drew up a framework for a new federal system known as the **Virginia Plan.** He wisely persuaded Edmund Randolph, Virginia's popular governor, to present this scheme to the convention on May 29. In his plan,

Virginia Plan Offered by James Madison and the Virginia delegation at the Constitutional Convention, this proposal called for a new government with a strong executive office and two houses of Congress, each with representation proportional to a state's population.

Madison advocated a strong central government, one that could override the shortsighted local legislatures.

The Virginia Plan envisioned a national legislature consisting of two houses, one elected directly by the people, the other chosen by the first house from nominations made by the state assemblies. Representation in both houses was proportional to the state's population. The Virginia Plan provided for an executive elected by Congress. To the surprise of the states' rights supporters, the entire package carried easily, and the convention found itself discussing the details of "a *national* Government . . . consisting of a *supreme* Legislature, Executive, and Judiciary."

New Jersey Plan Proposal of the New Jersey delegation at the Constitutional Convention that called for a strong government with one house of Congress in which all states would have equal representation.

On June 15, William Paterson, a New Jersey lawyer, presented a counterproposal. The **New Jersey Plan** preserved the fundamental spirit of the Articles of Confederation, including the retention of a unicameral legislature. Paterson argued that his revisions, though more modest than Madison's plan, would have greater appeal for the American people. The delegates listened politely to his plan, which would have given Congress extensive new powers to tax and regulate trade, and then they soundly rejected it on June 19.

Rejection of the New Jersey Plan, however, did not clear the way for a final vote. Delegates from small states feared that Madison's plan would hurt their states. These men maintained that unless each state possessed an equal vote in Congress, the small states would find themselves at the mercy of their larger neighbors. Countering this claim, delegates from the large states argued that it was absurd to assert that Rhode Island, with only 68,000 people, should have the same voice in Congress as Virginia's 747,000 inhabitants.

Compromise Saves the Convention

The mood of the convention was tense. Hard work and frustration, coupled with Philadelphia's sweltering summer heat, frayed nerves. Although some members predicted that the meeting would accomplish nothing of significance, the gathering did not break up; the delegates desperately wanted to produce a constitution. On July 2, a "grand committee" of one person from each state was elected by the convention to resolve persistent differences between the large and small states.

The grand committee did just that. It recommended that the states be equally represented in the upper house of Congress and proportionately by population in the lower house. Only the lower house could initiate money bills. The committee also decided that one member of the lower house should be selected for every forty thousand inhabitants of a state, and for this purpose, a slave was to be counted as three-fifths of a freeman. This compromise overcame the impasse between large and small states.

On July 26, the convention formed a "committee of detail," a group that prepared a rough draft of the Constitution. When its work was done, the delegates debated each article. The task required the better part of a month.

During the sessions, the members of the convention concluded that the president, as they now called the executive, should be selected by an electoral college, a body of prominent men in each state chosen by local voters. The number of electoral votes held by each state equaled its number of representatives and senators. Whoever received the second-largest number of votes in the electoral college automatically became vice president. In the event that no person received a majority of the votes, the election would be decided by the lower house—the House of Representatives—with each state casting a single vote.

Delegates also armed the chief executive with a veto power over legislation as well as the right to nominate judges. Both privileges would have been unthinkable a decade earlier, but the state experiences revealed the importance of having an independent executive to maintain a balanced system of republican government. The Philadelphia convention thus telescoped into four months the process of constitutional education that had taken more than four years to learn at the state level.

Compromising with Slavery

During the final days of August, two new issues suddenly disrupted the convention. One was a harbinger of the great sectional crisis of the nineteenth century. Many northern representatives detested the slave trade and wanted to end it immediately. In order to win southern support for the Constitution, however, the northern delegates promised that the legislature would not interfere with the slave trade until 1808 (see Chapter 8).

The second issue was the absence in the Constitution of a bill of rights. Such declarations had been included in most state constitutions. Virginians such as George Mason insisted that the states and their citizens needed explicit protection from possible excesses by the federal government. Though many delegates sympathized with Mason's appeal, they insisted that the proposed constitution provided sufficient security for individual rights. During the hard battle over ratification, the delegates to the convention may have regretted passing over the issue so lightly.

The delegates adopted an ingenious procedure for ratification. Instead of submitting the Constitution to the various state legislatures, all of which had a vested interest in maintaining the status quo, they called for the election of thirteen state conventions especially chosen to review the new federal government. Moreover, the Constitution would take effect after the assent of only nine states. There was no danger, therefore, that the proposed system would fail simply because a single state such as Rhode Island withheld approval.

The convention asked Gouveneur Morris, a delegate from Pennsylvania noted for his urbanity, to make final stylistic changes in the wording of the Constitution. Since the wording of the working draft spoke of the collection of states forming a new government, a strong possibility existed that several New England states would reject the document. Morris's brilliant phrase, "We, the People of the United States," eliminated this difficulty. The new nation was a republic of people, not of states.

On September 17, thirty-nine men signed the Constitution. A few members of the convention, like Mason, could not support the document. Others had already

Although the words slave *and* slavery *do not appear in the U.S. Constitution, debate over slavery and the slave trade resulted in a compromise in which both institutions persisted in the new Republic. Not everyone was pleased with the compromise. The Library Company of Philadelphia commissioned this painting* Liberty Displaying the Arts and Sciences *(1792) by Samuel Jennings. The broken chain at the feet of the goddess Liberty is meant to demonstrate her opposition to slavery.* ◆

gone home. Out of the three months of heat and effort, a new form of government had emerged.

Whose Constitution? Struggle for Ratification

Supporters of the Constitution recognized that ratification would not be easy. After all, the convention had been authorized only to revise the Articles. Instead it produced a radical new plan that fundamentally altered relations between the states and the central government. The delegates dispatched a copy of the document to the Congress of Confederation, which in turn referred it to the separate states. The fight for ratification had begun.

Federalists and Antifederalists

Federalists Supporters of the Constitution who advocated its ratification.

Antifederalists Critics of the Constitution who expressed concern that it seemed to possess no specific provision for the protection of natural and civil rights.

The Federalist A series of essays penned by Alexander Hamilton, James Madison, and John Jay that explained and defended the stronger national government created by the Constitutional Convention of 1787.

Proponents of the Constitution enjoyed great advantages over the unorganized opposition. In the contest for ratification, however, they took no chances. Their most astute move was the adoption of the label **Federalists,** a term that cleverly suggested that they stood for a confederation of states rather than for the creation of a supreme national authority. Critics of the Constitution—who tended to be somewhat poorer, less urban, and less well educated than their opponents—cried foul, but there was little they could do. They were stuck with the name **Antifederalists,** an awkward term that made their cause seem far more obstructionist than it actually was.

The Federalists recruited the most prominent public figures of the day. In every state convention, speakers favoring the Constitution were more polished, better educated, and more fully prepared than their opponents. In New York, the campaign to win ratification sparked publication of ***The Federalist,*** a remarkable series of essays written by Madison, Hamilton, and Jay during the fall and winter of 1787–1788. The nation's newspapers threw themselves overwhelmingly behind the new government. Few journals even bothered to carry Antifederalist writings. Nor were the Federalists above using threats and even strong-arm tactics. They were determined to win. A nation was at stake.

With so many factors working against them, the Antifederalists still came very near victory. Voting was exceptionally close in three large states: Massachusetts, New York, and Virginia. Apparently those who resisted ratification were not so far removed from the political mainstream as has sometimes been suggested by scholars who dismiss the Antifederalists as "narrow-minded local politicians."

The Antifederalists spoke in the language of the Commonwealthmen (see Chapter 4). Like the extreme republicans who wrote the first state constitutions, the Antifederalists were deeply suspicious of political power. During the debates over ratification, they warned that public officials, however selected, would be constantly scheming to expand their authority. It seemed obvious to these critics of the Constitution that the larger the republic, the greater the opportunity for political corruption. Local voters could not possibly know what their representatives in a distant capital were doing. Antifederalists possessed a narrow view of representation. They argued that elected officials should reflect the character of their constituents as closely as possible. They feared that in large congressional districts, representatives would lose touch with the people, and the wealthy would win the elections. Older on the average than their opponents, they recalled how aristocrats in Britain had abused their power.

Federalist speakers mocked their opponents' limited perspective. The Constitution deserved general support precisely because it ensured that future Americans would be represented by "natural aristocrats," individuals possessing greater insights, skills, and training than the average citizen. These talented leaders,

Revolution or Reform?
The Articles of Confederation and the Constitution Compared

Political Challenge	Articles of Confederation	Constitution
Mode of ratification or amendment	Require confirmation by every state legislature	Requires confirmation by three-fourths of state conventions or legislatures
Number of houses in legislature	One	Two
Mode of representation	One to seven delegates represent each state; each state holds only one vote in Congress	Two senators represent each state in upper house; each senator holds one vote. One representative to lower house represents every 30,000 people (in 1788) in a state; each representative holds one vote
Mode of election and term of office	Delegates appointed annually by state legislatures	Senators chosen by state legislatures for six-year term (direct election after 1913); representatives chosen by vote of citizens for two-year term
Executive	No separate executive: delegates annually elect one of their number as president, who possesses no veto, no power to appoint officers or to conduct policy. Administrative functions of government theoretically carried out by Committee of States, practically by various single-headed departments	Separate executive branch: president elected by electoral college to four-year term; granted veto, power to conduct policy and to appoint ambassadors, judges, and officers of executive departments established by legislation
Judiciary	Most adjudication left to state and local courts; Congress is final court of appeal in disputes between states	Separate branch consisting of Supreme Court and inferior courts established by Congress to enforce federal law
Taxation	States alone can levy taxes; Congress funds the Common Treasury by making requisitions for state contributions	Federal government granted powers of taxation
Regulation of commerce	Congress regulates foreign commerce by treaty but holds no check on conflicting state regulations	Congress regulates foreign commerce by treaty; all state regulations must obtain congressional consent

Federalists insisted, could discern the interests of the entire population. They were not tied to the selfish needs of local communities. The first ten amendments to the Constitution are the major legacy of the Antifederalist argument. The absence of a bill of rights troubled many people. In almost every state convention, opponents of the Constitution pointed to the need for greater protection of individual liberties and rights that people presumably possessed naturally, such as freedom of religion and the right to a jury trial. To counter this complaint, Federalists pledged to present a bill of rights to Congress as soon as the Constitution was ratified.

The Constitution drew support from many different types of people. In fact, historians have been unable to discover sharp correlations between wealth and occupation on the one hand and attitudes toward the proposed system of government on the other. In general, Federalists lived in more commercialized areas than their opponents did. Men involved in commerce—artisans as well as merchants—tended to vote for ratification, while farmers only marginally involved in commercial agriculture frequently voted Antifederalist.

Despite passionate pleas from Patrick Henry and other Antifederalists, most of the state conventions quickly adopted the Constitution. Although the battle was close in several states, and although it took almost three years for Rhode Island to ratify, all the states eventually ratified the Constitution. And once the ratification process was over, Americans soon closed ranks behind the new government.

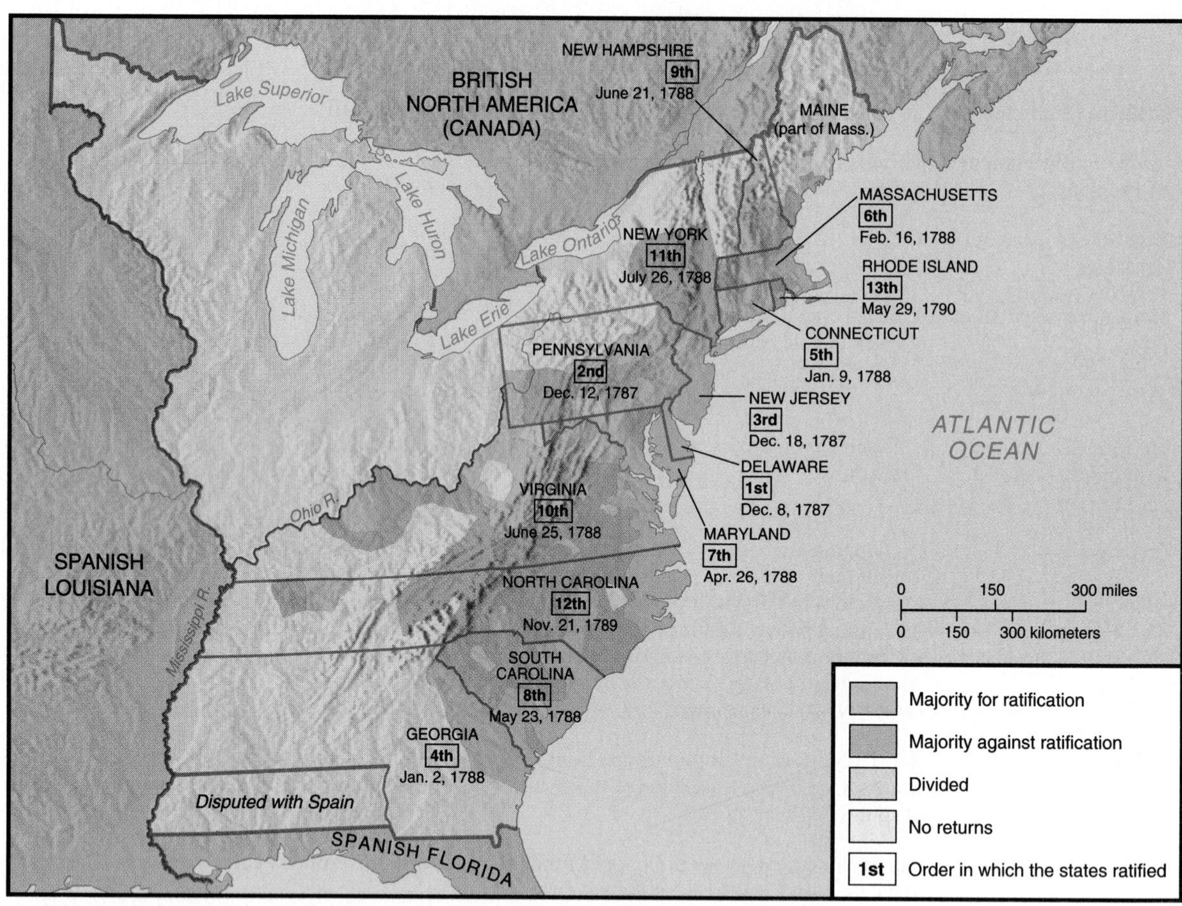

RATIFICATION OF THE CONSTITUTION *Advocates of the new Constitution called themselves Federalists, and those who opposed its ratification were known as Antifederalists.* ❖

Adding the Bill of Rights

The first ten amendments to the Constitution are the major legacy of the Antifederalist argument. In almost every state convention, opponents of the Constitution pointed to the need for greater protection of individual liberties, rights that people presumably had possessed in a state of nature and that protected the minority from the majority. The list of fundamental rights varied from state to state, but most Antifederalists demanded specific guarantees for jury trial and freedom of religion. They wanted prohibitions against cruel and unusual punishments. There was also considerable, though not universal, support for freedom of speech and freedom of the press.

Madison and others regarded the proposals with little enthusiasm. But after the adoption of the Constitution had been assured, Madison moderated his stand. If nothing else, passage of a bill of rights would appease able men such as George Mason and Edmund Randolph, who might otherwise remain alienated from the new federal system.

The crucial consideration was caution. A number of people throughout the nation advocated calling a second constitutional convention, one that would take Antifederalist criticism into account. Madison wanted to avoid such a meeting, and he feared that some members of the first Congress might use a bill of rights as an excuse to revise the entire Constitution or to promote a second convention.

Madison carefully reviewed the state recommendations as well as the various declarations of rights that had appeared in the early state constitutions, and on June

CHRONOLOGY

1776	Second Continental Congress authorizes colonies to create republican governments ❖ Eight states draft new constitutions; two others already enjoy republican government by virtue of former colonial charters
1777	Congress accepts Articles of Confederation after long debate
1780	Massachusetts ratifies state constitution
1781	States ratify Articles of Confederation following settlements of Virginia's western land claims ❖ British army surrenders at Yorktown
1782	States fail to ratify proposed impost tax
1783	Newburgh Conspiracy thwarted ❖ Treaty of Peace signed with Great Britain
1785	Land Ordinance for Northwest Territory passed by Congress
1786	Jay-Gardoqui negotiations over Mississippi navigation anger southern states ❖ Annapolis Convention suggests second meeting to revise the Articles of Confederation ❖ Shays's Rebellion frightens American leaders
1787	Constitutional Convention convenes in Philadelphia ❖ Northwest Ordinance passed by Congress; restructures territorial government
1787–1788	Federal Constitution is ratified by all states except North Carolina and Rhode Island
1791	Bill of Rights (first ten amendments of the Constitution) ratified by states

8, 1789, he placed before the House of Representatives a set of amendments designed to protect individual rights from government interference. Madison told the members of Congress that the greatest dangers to popular liberties came from "the majority [operating] against the minority." A committee compressed and revised his original ideas into twelve amendments, ten of which were ratified and became known collectively as the **Bill of Rights.**

Bill of Rights The first ten amendments to the U.S. Constitution, adopted in 1791 to preserve the rights and liberties of individuals.

The Bill of Rights protects the freedoms of assembly, speech, religion, and the press; guarantees speedy trial by an impartial jury; preserves the people's right to bear arms; and prohibits unreasonable searches. Other amendments deal with legal procedure. Only the Tenth Amendment addresses the states' relation to the federal system. This crucial article, designed to calm Antifederalists' fears, specifies that all "powers not delegated to the United States by the Constitution, nor prohibited by it to the States, are reserved to the States respectively, or to the people."

On September 25, 1789, the Bill of Rights passed both houses of Congress, and by December 15, 1791, these amendments had been ratified by more than the requisite three-fourths of the states. Madison was justly proud of his achievement. He had effectively secured individual rights without undermining the Constitution.

Conclusion: Success Depends on the People

By 1789, one phase of American political experimentation had come to an end. During these exciting years, the people gradually, often haltingly, learned that in a republican society, they themselves were sovereign. They could no longer blame the failure of government on inept monarchs or greedy aristocrats. They bore a great responsibility. Americans had demanded a government of the people only to discover during the late 1780s that in some situations the people cannot be trusted with power, that majorities can tyrannize minorities, that the best government can abuse individual rights. They had the good sense, therefore, to establish an effective system of checks and balances that protected the people from themselves.

The country's prospects seemed brighter. Benjamin Franklin captured the national mood during the final moments of the constitutional convention. As the delegates came forward to sign the document, he observed that there was a sun carved on the back of Washington's chair. "I have . . . often in the course of the session . . . looked at the sun behind the President without being able to tell whether it was rising or setting: but now at length I have the happiness to know that it is a rising and not a setting sun."

Key Terms

republicanism, p. 104
natural rights, p. 109
Articles of Confederation, p. 110
Northwest Ordinance, p. 113
nationalists, p. 115
Shays's Rebellion, p. 117
Virginia Plan, p. 117
New Jersey Plan, p. 118
Federalists, p. 120
Antifederalists, p. 120
The Federalist, p. 120
Bill of Rights, p. 123

Recommended Reading

The best way to comprehend the major issues debated at the Philadelphia Convention and then later at the separate state ratifying conventions is to examine the key documents of the period. One could do no better than reading James Madison, *Journal of the Federal Constitution* (reprinted in many modern editions), our only detailed account of what actually occurred during the closed debates in Philadelphia. A good introduction to the contest between the Federalists and Antifederalists over ratification is Bernard Bailyn, ed., *The Debate on the Constitution: Federalist and Antifederalist Speeches, Articles, and Letters During the Struggle Over Ratification* (1993). Gordon S. Wood analyzes late-eighteenth-century republican political thought in *The Creation of the American Republic, 1776–1787* (1969). Three recent titles interpret the complex political experience of the 1780s: Jack N. Rakove, *The Beginnings of National Politics: An Interpretive History of the Continental Congress* (1979) and *Original Meanings: Politics and Ideas in the Making of the Constitution* (1996); and Peter Onuf, *Statehood and Union: A History of the Northwest Ordinance* (1987). For a thoughtful investigation of the many different meanings of "republicanism," see Richard Beeman et al., eds., *Beyond Confederation: Origins of the Constitution and American National Identity* (1987) and Daniel T. Rodgers, "Republicanism: The Career of a Concept," *Journal of American History*, Vol. 79 (June 1992), 1–38. On the expectations of African Americans and women during this period, see the final sections of Winthrop Jordan, *White Over Black: American Attitudes Toward the Negro, 1550–1812* (1968); T. H. Breen, "Making History: The Force of Public Opinion and the Last Years of Slavery in Revolutionary Massachusetts," in Ronald Hoffman, et al., eds., *Through a Glass Darkly: Reflections on Personal Identity in Early America* (1997), 67–95; and Ronald Hoffman and Peter J. Albert, eds., *Women in the Age of the American Revolution* (1990). The Newburgh Conspiracy is explored in Richard H. Kohn, *Eagle and Sword: The Federalists and the Creation of the Military Establishment in America, 1783–1802* (1975). On Shays's Rebellion, see Robert A. Gross, ed., *In Debt to Shays: The Bicentennial of an Agrarian Rebellion* (1993).

For a list of additional titles related to this chapter's topics, please see http://www.ablongman.com/divine.

Suggested Web Sites

The Leslie Brock Center for the Study of Colonial Currency

http://etext.lib.virginia.edu/users/brock

This site includes both useful primary and secondary documents on early American currency.

Northwest Territory Alliance

http://www.nwta.com/main.html

This Revolutionary Era reenactment organization site contains several links and is an interesting look at historical reenactment.

Independence Hall National Historical Park

http://www.nps.gov/inde/visit.html

This site includes images and historical accounts of Independence Hall and other Philadelphia buildings closely associated with the nation's founding.

Biographies of the Founding Fathers

http://www.colonialhall.com/

This site provides interesting information about the men who signed the Declaration of Independence and includes a trivia section.

The Federalist Papers

http://www.law.emory.edu/FEDERAL/federalist/
A collection of the most important Federalist Papers, a series of documents designed to convince people to support the new Constitution and the Federal party.

The Constitution and the Amendments

http://www.law.emory.edu/FEDERAL/usconst.html
A searchable site to the Constitution, especially useful for its information about the Bill of Rights and other constitutional amendments.

Documents from the Continental Congress and the Constitutional Convention, 1774–1789

http://memory.loc.gov/ammem/bdsds/bdsdhome.html
The Continental Congress Broadside Collection (253 titles) and the Constitutional Convention Broadside Collection (21 titles) contain 274 documents relating to the work of Congress and the drafting and ratification of the Constitution. Items include extracts of the journals of Congress, resolutions, proclamations, committee reports, treaties, and early printed versions of the United States Constitution and the Declaration of Independence.

Chapter 7

Democracy in Distress: The Violence of Party Politics, 1788–1800

OUTLINE

- Power of Public Opinion
- Principle and Pragmatism: Establishing a New Government
- Conflicting Visions: Jefferson and Hamilton
- Hamilton's Plan for Prosperity and Security
- Charges of Treason: The Battle over Foreign Affairs
- Popular Political Culture
- The Adams Presidency
- The Peaceful Revolution: The Election of 1800
- Conclusion: Danger of Political Extremism

WE AMERICANS

- Counting the People: The Federal Census of 1790

Partisan Passions

While presiding over the first meeting of the United States Senate in 1789, Vice President John Adams raised a pressing procedural question: How should the senators address George Washington, the newly elected president? Adams insisted that Washington deserved an impressive title, a designation that would lend dignity and weight to his office. Adams recommended "His Highness, the President of the United States, and Protector of their Liberties," but some senators favored "His Elective Majesty" or "His Excellency."

Washington and many other people regarded the entire debate as ridiculous. Madison believed that such a discussion befit European aristocrats more than American republicans. When the senators learned that their efforts embarrassed Washington, they dropped the topic. The leader of the new Republic would be called President of the United States. One wag, however, dubbed the portly Adams "His Rotundity."

THE COMIC-OPERA QUALITY of the debate about Washington's title should not obscure the participants' seriousness. During the 1790s, decisions about the use of power, about actual governmental policies and positions, had the potential to set a lasting precedent and thus to reinforce or imperil the Revolution itself. But the question of how best to put widely shared republican principles into practice divided Americans. Pressured by Great Britain and France, and unsure about how to transform their country into an economically strong and commercially viable nation, Americans advanced different solutions. Public figures increasingly gravitated to Alexander Hamilton or Thomas Jefferson, the two most powerful personalities of the decade, and before Washington retired from the presidency, these loose political affiliations had hardened into open party identification, either Federalist or Republican, a development that no one in 1787 had anticipated or desired.

Power of Public Opinion

Although no one welcomed them, political parties gradually took shape during this period. Neither the Jeffersonians nor the Federalists—as the two major groups were called—doubted that the United States would one day become a great commercial power. They differed, however, on how best to manage the transition from an agrarian household economy to an international system of trade and industry. The Federalists encouraged rapid integration of the United States into a world economy, but however enthusiastic they were about capitalism, they did not trust the people or local government to do the job effectively. A modern economy, they insisted, required strong national institutions that would be directed by a social elite that understood the financial challenge and that would work in the best interests of the people.

Such claims frightened persons who came to identify themselves as Jeffersonians. Strong financial institutions, they thought, had corrupted the government of Great Britain from which they had just separated themselves. They searched for alternative ways to accommodate the needs of commerce and industry. Unlike the Federalists, the Jeffersonians put their faith in the people, defined for the most part politically as white yeoman farmers. The Jeffersonians insisted that ordinary entrepreneurs, if they could be freed from intrusive government regulations, could be trusted to resist greed and crass materialism and to sustain the virtue of the republic.

During the 1790s, former allies were surprised to discover themselves at odds over such basic political issues. One person—Hamilton, for example—would stake out a position. Another, such as Jefferson or Madison, would respond, perhaps speaking a little more extravagantly than a specific issue demanded, goaded by the rhetorical nature of public debate. The first in turn would rebut passionately the new position. By the middle of the decade, this dialectic had almost spun out of control, taking the young republic to the brink of political violence.

Leaders of every persuasion had to learn to live with "public opinion." The revolutionary gentry had invited the people to participate in government, but the gentlemen assumed that ordinary voters would automatically defer to their social betters. Instead, the Founders discovered they had created a rough-and-tumble political culture, a robust public sphere of cheap newspapers and street demonstrations. The newly empowered "public" followed the great debates of the period through articles they read in hundreds of highly partisan journals and magazines.

Just as television did in the twentieth century, print journalism opened politics to a large audience that previously might have been indifferent to the activities of elected officials. By the time John Adams left the presidency in 1800, he had learned this lesson well. The ordinary workers and farmers of the United States, feisty individuals who thought they were as good as anyone else and who were not afraid to let their political opinions be known, were not likely to let their president become an "Elective Majesty."

Principle and Pragmatism: Establishing a New Government

In 1788, George Washington enjoyed great popularity throughout the nation. In America's first presidential election, he received the unanimous support of the electoral college, an achievement that no subsequent president has duplicated. John Adams was elected vice president.

The responsibility Washington bore was as great as his popularity. The political stability of the young republic depended in large measure on how he handled himself in office. In the eyes of his compatriots, he had been transformed into a living

❖ A Look at the Past ❖

Eagle Decoration

Following the American Revolution, patriotic symbols and themes became common in decorative arts. Eagles, a traditional symbol of strength, enjoyed special popularity. English manufacturers printed eagles on ceramics and textiles. Women embroidered eagles and appliqued them onto quilts and coverlets like the one pictured here. Such objects reflected pride in a new, untested nation. Why would consumers want patriotic emblems on their fine fabrics and furniture? Could the popularity of patriotic symbols reveal something besides pride?

symbol of the new government, and during his presidency (1789–1797), he carried himself with studied dignity and reserve—never ostentatious, he was the embodiment of classical republican values. A French diplomat who witnessed Washington's first inauguration reported in awe: "He has the soul, look and figure of a hero united in him." But the adulation of Washington, however well meant, seriously affected the conduct of public affairs, for criticism of his administration was regarded as an attack on the president and, by extension, on the republic itself. During the early years of Washington's presidency, therefore, American public opinion discouraged partisan politics.

Washington created a strong, independent presidency. Though he discussed pressing issues with the members of his cabinet, he left no doubt that it was ultimately he who made policy. Moreover, the first president resisted congressional efforts to restrict executive authority, especially in foreign affairs.

The first Congress quickly established executive departments. Each department was headed by a secretary nominated by the president and serving at the president's pleasure. For the Departments of War, State, and the Treasury, Washington nominated Henry Knox, Thomas Jefferson, and Alexander Hamilton, respectively. Edmund Randolph served as part-time attorney general, a position that ranked slightly lower in prestige than the head of a department. As head of the Treasury, which oversaw the collection of customs and other federal taxes, Hamilton could anticipate having several thousand political patronage jobs to dispense.

To modern Americans accustomed to a huge federal bureaucracy, the size of Washington's government seems amazingly small. Jefferson, for example, ran the entire State Department with a staff of two chief clerks, two assistants, and a part-time translator. The situation in most other departments was similar. Overworked clerks scribbled madly just to keep up with the press of correspondence. Considering the workloads of men such as Jefferson, Hamilton, and Adams, it is no wonder that the president had difficulty persuading able people to accept positions in the new government.

Congress also provided for a federal court system. The Judiciary Act of 1789 created a Supreme Court staffed by a chief justice and five associate justices. In addition, the statute set up thirteen district courts authorized to review the decisions of the state courts. John Jay, a leading figure in New York politics, agreed to serve as chief justice, but since federal judges in the 1790s were expected to travel hundreds of miles over terrible roads to attend sessions of the inferior courts, few persons of outstanding talent and training joined Jay on the federal bench.

Remembering the financial insecurity of the old Confederation government, the newly elected congressmen passed the tariff of 1789, a tax of approximately 5 percent on imports. The act generated considerable revenue, but it also sparked controversy. Southern planters, who relied heavily on European imports, claimed the tariff discriminated against their interests in favor of those of northern merchants. These battle lines would form again and again in the years to come.

Conflicting Visions: Jefferson and Hamilton

Washington's first cabinet included two extraordinary personalities, Alexander Hamilton and Thomas Jefferson. Both had served the country with distinction during the Revolution, were recognized by contemporaries as men of special genius as well as high ambition, and brought to public office a powerful vision of how the American people could achieve greatness. The story of their opposing views during the decade of the 1790s provides insight into the birth and development of political parties. It also reveals how a common political ideology, republicanism, could be interpreted in two vastly different ways, turning former friends into bitter adversaries. Indeed, the falling out of Hamilton and Jefferson reflected deep and potentially explosive political divisions within American society.

Hamilton was a brilliant, dynamic young lawyer who had distinguished himself as Washington's aide-de-camp during the Revolution. Born in the West Indies, the child of an adulterous relationship, Hamilton employed charm, courage, and intellect to fulfill his inexhaustible ambition. He strove not for wealth but for reputation. Men and women who fell under his spell found him almost irresistible, but to enemies, Hamilton appeared a dark, calculating, even evil genius. He advocated a strong central government and refused to be bound by the strict wording of the Constitution. He loved America, but he admired English culture, and during the 1790s, he advocated closer commercial and diplomatic ties with Britain.

Jefferson possessed a profoundly different temperament. More reflective, he shone less brightly in society than Hamilton did. He thirsted not for power or wealth but for an opportunity to advance the democratic principles that he had stated so eloquently in the Declaration of Independence. He became secretary of state just after returning from Paris, where he had witnessed the first exhilarating moments of the French Revolution. He believed that republicanism would everywhere replace absolute monarchy and aristocratic privilege. His European experiences biased Jefferson in favor of France over Great Britain when the two nations clashed.

Both Hamilton and Jefferson insisted that they were working for the creation of a strong, prosperous republic. Rather than seeing them as spokesmen for competing ideologies, Hamilton and Jefferson should be viewed as different kinds of republicans who during the 1790s attempted as best they could to cope with unprecedented political challenges.

The two men did seriously disagree on precisely how the United States should fulfill its destiny. As head of the Treasury Department, Hamilton urged his fellow citizens to think in terms of bold commercial development, of farms and factories embedded within a complex financial network that would reduce the nation's reliance on foreign trade. Because Great Britain had already established an elaborate system of banking and credit, the secretary looked to that country for economic models that might be reproduced on this side of the Atlantic.

Hamilton's pessimistic view of human nature caused him to fear democratic excess. Anarchy, not monarchy, was his nightmare. The best hope for the survival of the republic, Hamilton believed, lay with the country's monied classes. If the wealthiest people could be persuaded that their economic self-interest could be advanced by the central government, they would strengthen it and, by so doing, bring a greater measure of prosperity to the common people. From Hamilton's perspective, there was no conflict between private greed and public good; one was the source of the other.

In almost every detail, Jefferson challenged Hamilton's analysis. The secretary of state assumed that the strength of the American economy lay not in its industrial potential but in its agricultural productivity. He recognized the necessity of change, and because he thought that persons who worked the soil were more responsible citizens than those who labored in factories for wages, he encouraged the nation's farmers to participate in an expanding international market.

Unlike Hamilton, Jefferson expressed faith in the ability of the American people to shape policy. He had a boundless optimism in the judgment of the common folk. He instinctively trusted the people, feared that uncontrolled government power might destroy their liberties, and insisted that public officials follow the letter of the Constitution. The greatest threat to the young republic, he argued, came from the corrupt activities of pseudo aristocrats, persons who placed the protection of property and civil order above the preservation of liberty. Under no circumstances did he want to mortgage the nation's future—through the creation of a large national debt—to the selfish interests of bankers, manufacturers, and financial speculators.

Hamilton's Plan for Prosperity and Security

The unsettled state of the nation's finances presented a staggering challenge to the new government. Congress turned to Hamilton for a policy, and he eagerly accepted the assignment. He read deeply in abstruse economic literature, but the reports he wrote bore the unmistakable stamp of his own creative genius. The secretary synthesized a vast amount of information into an economic blueprint so complex and so innovative that even his allies were slightly baffled. Certainly, Washington never fully grasped the subtleties of Hamilton's plan.

The secretary presented his *Report on the Public Credit* to Congress on January 14, 1790. His research revealed that the nation's outstanding debt stood at approximately $54 million. This sum represented various foreign and domestic obligations that the United States government had incurred during the Revolutionary War. But that was not all. The states still owed creditors approximately $25 million. During the 1780s, Americans desperate for cash had been forced to sell government loan certificates to speculators at greatly discounted prices, and it was estimated that approximately $40 million of the nation's debt was owed to twenty thousand people, only 20 percent of whom were the original creditors.

Funding and Assumption

Hamilton's report contained two major recommendations covering the areas of funding and assumption. First, under his plan, the United States promised to fund its foreign and domestic obligations at full face value. Current holders of loan certificates, whoever they were and no matter how they obtained the documents, could exchange the old certificates for new government bonds bearing a moderate rate of interest. Second, the secretary urged the federal government to assume responsibility for paying the remaining state debts.

Hamilton reasoned that his credit system would accomplish several desirable goals. It would significantly reduce the power of the individual states to shape national economic policy, something Hamilton regarded as essential in maintaining a strong federal government. Moreover, the creation of a fully funded national debt signaled to investors throughout the world that the United States was now solvent, that its bonds represented a good risk. Hamilton hoped that American investment capital would remain in America, providing a source of money for commercial and industrial growth, rather than flow to Europe. In short, Hamilton invited the country's wealthiest citizens to invest in the future of the United States.

To Hamilton's great surprise, his friend Madison attacked the funding scheme in the House of Representatives. He, too, wanted the United States to pay its debts, but he was more concerned with the original buyers of the certificates than with the speculators who had purchased them from the hard-pressed patriots. However, far too many records had been lost since the Revolution for the Treasury Department to be able to identify all the original holders. In the end, Congress sided with Hamilton's more practical position.

Assumption unleashed even greater criticism. Hamilton's program seemed designed to reward states that had not paid their debts. In addition, the secretary's opponents in Congress became suspicious that assumption was only a ploy to increase the power and wealth of Hamilton's immediate friends. On April 12, 1790, a rebellious House, led by Madison, defeated assumption.

The victory was short-lived. Hamilton and congressional supporters resorted to legislative horse trading to revive his foundering program. In exchange for locating the new federal capital on the Potomac River, a move that would stimulate the depressed economy of northern Virginia, several key congressmen who shared Madison's political philosophy changed their votes on assumption. In August, Washington signed assumption and funding into law. The first element of Hamilton's design was now securely in place.

Interpreting the Constitution: The Bank Controversy

The persistent Hamilton submitted his second report to Congress in January 1791. He proposed that the United States government charter a national bank. This privately owned institution would be funded in part by the federal government. The **Bank of the United States** not only would serve as the main depository of the United States government but also would issue currency acceptable in payment of federal taxes. Because of that guarantee, the money would maintain its value while in circulation.

Bank of the United States National bank proposed by Secretary of the Treasury Alexander Hamilton and established in 1791. It served as a central depository for the U.S. government and had the authority to issue currency.

Madison and others in Congress immediately raised a howl of protest. They feared that banks might "perpetuate a large monied interest" in America. And what about the Constitution? That document said nothing specifically about chartering financial corporations, and they warned that if Hamilton and his supporters were allowed to stretch fundamental law on this occasion, they could not be held back in the future. On this issue, Hamilton stubbornly refused to compromise.

The intense controversy involving his closest advisers worried the president. Even though the bank bill passed Congress (February 8), Washington seriously considered vetoing the legislation on constitutional grounds. Before doing so, however, he requested written opinions from the members of his cabinet. Jefferson's rambling attack on the bank was wholly predictable; Hamilton's defense was masterful. He boldly articulated a doctrine of *implied powers*—that the "necessary and proper" clause of the Constitution (Article I, Section 8) gave Congress more power than it specified. Neither Madison nor Jefferson had anticipated this interpretation of the Constitution. Hamilton's so-called loose construction carried the day, and on February 25, 1791, Washington signed the bank act into law.

Hamilton triumphed in Congress, but the general public regarded his actions with growing fear and hostility. Many persons associated huge national debts and privileged banks with the decay of public virtue. They believed that Hamilton was intent on turning the future of America over to corrupt speculators. To backcountry farmers, making money without actually engaging in physical labor appeared immoral, unrepublican, and un-American. When the greed of a former Treasury Department official led to several serious bankruptcies in 1792, people began to listen more closely to what Madison, Jefferson, and their associates were saying about growing corruption in high places.

Setback for Hamilton

In his third major report, *Report on Manufactures,* submitted to Congress in December 1791, Hamilton revealed the final details of his grand design for the economic future of the United States. The lengthy document suggested ways by which the federal government might stimulate manufacturing and thus free itself from dependence on European imports. What was needed was direct government intervention. Hamilton argued that protective tariffs and special industrial bounties would greatly accelerate the growth of a balanced economy, and with proper planning, the United States would soon hold its own with England and France.

In Congress, the battle lines were clearly drawn. Hamilton's opponents ignored his economic arguments and instead engaged him on moral and political grounds. Madison took a states' rights position and railed against the dangers of "consolidation," a process that threatened to concentrate all power in the federal government, leaving the states defenseless. Jefferson argued that the development of manufacturing entailed urbanization, and cities bred every sort of vice. Other southern congressmen saw tariffs and bounties as vehicles for enriching Hamilton's northern friends at the planters' expense. The recommendations in the *Report on Manufactures* were soundly defeated in the House of Representatives.

Washington detested political squabbling. In August 1792, he begged Hamilton and Jefferson to rise above their differences. The appeal came too late. Hamilton's reports eroded the goodwill of 1788, and by the conclusion of Washington's term, neither secretary trusted the other's judgment. Their sparring had produced congressional factions, but as yet no real parties with permanent organizations that engaged in campaigning had come into existence.

Charges of Treason: The Battle over Foreign Affairs

During Washington's second presidential term (1793–1797), war in Europe dramatically thrust foreign affairs into the forefront of American life. Officials who had disagreed over Hamilton's economic policies now were divided by the fighting between France and Britain. Bitter feelings, inflamed emotions, and accusations of treason were common. This poisonous atmosphere spawned the formation of formal political organizations—the Federalists and the Republicans. The clash between the groups developed over how best to preserve the new republic. The Republicans advocated states' rights, strict interpretation of the Constitution, friendship with France, and vigilance against "the avaricious, monopolizing Spirit of Commerce and Commercial Man." The Federalists urged a strong national government, central economic planning, closer ties with Great Britain, and maintenance of public order, even if that meant calling out federal troops.

The Peril of Neutrality

Great Britain treated the United States with arrogance. Contrary to the instructions of the Treaty of 1783, British troops continued to occupy military posts in the Northwest Territory. Moreover, even though 75 percent of American imports came from Great Britain, that country refused to grant the United States full commercial reciprocity.

French Revolution A social and political revolution in France (1789–1799) that toppled the monarchy.

France presented a very different challenge. In the spring of 1789, the **French Revolution** began, and Louis XVI was dethroned. The men who seized power were militant republicans, ideologues eager to liberate all Europe from feudal institutions. Once the French Revolution was set in motion, however, the leaders lost control. Constitutional reform turned into bloody purges, and one radical group, the Jacobins, guillotined thousands of people during the so-called Reign of Terror (October 1793–July 1794). These horrific events left Americans confused. While those who shared Jefferson's views celebrated the spread of republicanism, those who sided with Hamilton condemned French expansionism and political excess.

In the face of growing international tension, neutrality seemed the most prudent course for the United States. But the policy was easier for a weak country to proclaim than to defend. In February 1793, France declared war on Great Britain, and both countries immediately challenged the official American position on shipping: "free ships make free goods," meaning that belligerents should not interfere with the shipping of neutral carriers. To make matters worse, no one was certain whether the Franco-American treaties of 1778 (see Chapter 5) legally bound the United States to support its old ally against Great Britain.

Both Hamilton and Jefferson wanted to avoid war. Jefferson believed that if Great Britain refused to honor America's neutrality and observe neutral shipping rights—in other words, if the Royal Navy seized American sailors—then the United States should award France special trade advantages. Hamilton thought Jefferson's scheme insane. He pointed out that Britain possessed the largest navy in the world and was not likely to be coerced by American threats. The United States, he advised, should appease the former mother country, even if that meant swallowing national pride.

A newly appointed French minister to the United States, Edmond Genêt, precipitated the first major diplomatic crisis. This incompetent young man arrived in Charleston, South Carolina, in April 1793. He found considerable popular enthusiasm for the French Revolution, and heartened by this reception, he authorized privately owned American vessels to seize British ships in the name of France. Such actions clearly violated United States neutrality and invited British retaliation. When government officials warned Genêt to desist, he threatened to take his appeal directly to the American people, who presumably loved France more than the Washington administration did.

The confrontation particularly embarrassed Jefferson, the most outspoken pro-French member of the cabinet. He condemned Genêt's imprudent actions. Washington did not wait to determine if the treaties of 1778 were still in force. Even before he had formally received the French minister, the president issued a proclamation of neutrality (April 22).

Jay's Treaty Sparks Domestic Unrest

Great Britain failed to take advantage of Genêt's insolence. Instead, it pushed the United States to the brink of war. British forts on U.S. soil in the Northwest Territory remained a constant source of tension. In June 1793, a new element was added. The London government closed French ports to neutral shipping, and in November, its navy captured several hundred American vessels trading in the French West Indies. Outraged members of Congress, especially those who identified with Jefferson and Madison, demanded retaliation, an embargo, a stoppage of debt payment, even war.

Before the rhetoric produced violence, Washington made one final effort to preserve peace. In May 1794, he sent Chief Justice John Jay to London to negotiate a formidable list of grievances. Jay's major objectives were removal of the British forts on U.S. territory, payment for ships taken in the West Indies, improved commercial relations, and acceptance of the American definition of neutral rights.

Jay's mission had little chance of success, partly because Hamilton had secretly informed British officials that the United States would compromise on most issues. Jay did persuade the British to abandon their frontier posts and to allow small American ships to trade in the British West Indies, but they rejected out of hand the United States' position on neutral rights. The British would continue to search American vessels on the high seas for contraband and to seize sailors suspected of being British citizens. Moreover, there would be no compensation for the ships seized in 1793 until the Americans paid British merchants for debts contracted before the Revolution. And to the particular annoyance of Southerners, not a word was said about the slaves that the British army had carried off at the conclusion of the war. Jay may have salvaged the peace, but only by betraying the national interest.

Jay's Treaty Controversial treaty with Britain negotiated by Chief Justice John Jay in 1794 to settle American grievances and avert war. Though the British agreed to surrender forts on U.S. territory, the treaty failed to realize key diplomatic goals and provoked a storm of protest in America.

News of **Jay's Treaty** produced an angry outcry in the nation's capital. Even Washington was apprehensive. He submitted the document to the Senate without recommending ratification. After an extremely bitter debate, the upper house, controlled by Federalists, narrowly accepted a revised version of the treaty (June 1795).

The details of the Jay agreement soon leaked to the press. Throughout the country, Jay was burned in effigy. Southerners made known that they would not pay prewar debts to British merchants. And when news of the treaty reached the House of Representatives, a storm of protest broke out. Followers of Jefferson—now calling themselves Republicans—thought they could stop Jay's Treaty in Congress by withholding funds for its implementation.

But the president still had a trump card to play. He raised the possibility that the House was really contemplating his impeachment. Such an action was, of course, unthinkable, and public support quickly swung toward Washington and the Federalists, as the followers of Hamilton were now known. Jay's Treaty was saved, but the division between the two parties was beyond repair.

By the time that Jay's Treaty became law (June 14, 1795), the two giants of Washington's first cabinet had retired. Late in 1793, Jefferson returned to his Virginia plantation, Monticello, where despite his separation from day-to-day political affairs, he remained the chief spokesman for the Republican party. His rival, Hamilton, left the Treasury in January 1795 to return to private life in New York City. He maintained close ties with important Federalist officials, however, and even more than Jefferson, Hamilton concerned himself with the details of party organization.

Pushing the Native Americans Aside

Before Great Britain finally withdrew its troops from the western forts in 1796, its military officers encouraged local tribes to attack settlers and traders from the United States. The Indians won several impressive victories over federal troops in the area that would become western Ohio and Indiana. But the tribes were actually more vulnerable than they realized, for when they met up with the United States army under the command of General Anthony Wayne, they received no support from their British allies. At the battle of Fallen Timbers (August 20, 1794), Wayne's forces crushed Indian resistance in the Northwest Territory, and the tribes were compelled to sign the Treaty of Greenville, formally ceding to the United States government much of the land that became Ohio.

Shrewd negotiations mixed with pure luck helped secure the nation's southwestern frontier. For complex reasons having to do with the state of European diplomacy, Spanish officials in 1795 encouraged the United States' representative in Madrid to discuss navigation on the Mississippi River. Before this initiative, the Spanish government had not only closed the river to American commerce but also incited the Indians of the region to harass U.S. settlers (see Chapter 6). Relations between the two countries would probably have deteriorated further had the United States not signed Jay's Treaty. The Spanish assumed—quite erroneously—that Great Britain and the United States had formed an alliance to strip Spain of its North American possessions.

To avoid the imagined disaster, officials in Madrid offered the American envoy, Thomas Pinckney, extraordinary concessions: the opening of the Mississippi, the right to deposit goods in New Orleans without paying duties, a secure southern boundary on the 31st parallel, and a promise to stay out of Indian affairs. An amazed Pinckney signed the Treaty of San Lorenzo (also called Pinckney's Treaty) on October 27, 1795, and in March, the Senate ratified the document without a single dissenting vote.

Popular Political Culture

Ratification of Jay's Treaty generated intense political strife during Washington's administration. It divided Americans along party lines at a time when parties were viewed as subversive. Party conflict also suggested that Americans had lost the sense of common purpose that had united them during the Revolution. Politicians agreed that opposition smacked of disloyalty and therefore should be eliminated by any means, fair or foul. But who should eliminate whom? That was the question that occupied both Federalists and Republicans.

More than any other single element, newspapers transformed the political culture of the United States. Americans were voracious readers, and they were well supplied with newspapers. Most of the journals were fiercely partisan. Rumor and opinion were presented as fact, and public officials were regularly dragged through the rhetorical mud. Jefferson, for example, was accused of cowardice, and Hamilton was vilified as an adulterer.

Even poets and essayists were caught up in the political fray. The better writers often produced party propaganda. American writers sometimes complained that the culture of the young republic was too materialistic, too unappreciative of the subtler forms of art then popular in Europe. But it was clear that poets who ignored patriotism and politics simply did not sell well in the United States.

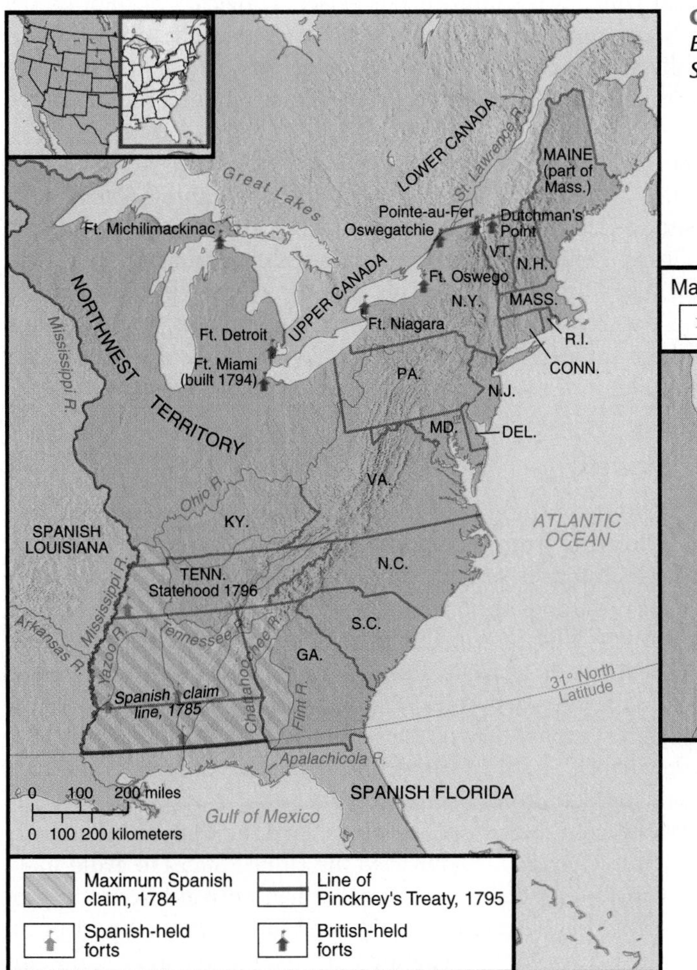

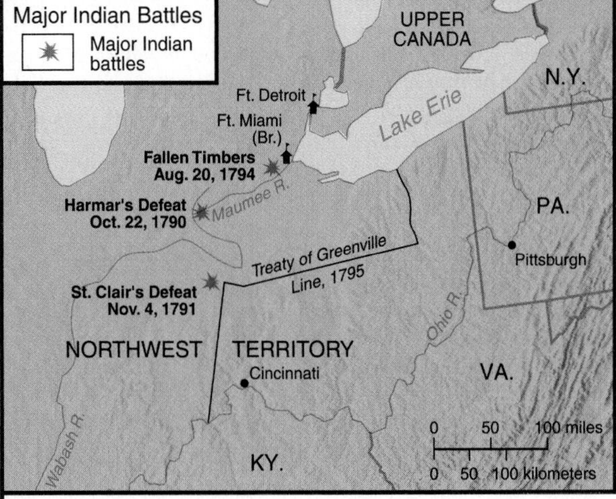

CONQUEST OF THE WEST *Withdrawal of the British, defeat of Native Americans, and negotiations with Spain secured the nation's frontiers.*

The decade also witnessed the birth of political clubs. Modeled on the political debating societies that sprang up in France during the early years of the French Revolution, the clubs emphasized political indoctrination. By 1794, at least twenty-four clubs were holding regular meetings. Along with newspapers, they provided the common people with highly partisan political information.

Whiskey Rebellion: Charges of Republican Conspiracy

Political tensions became explosive in 1794. The Federalists convinced themselves that the Republicans were actually prepared to employ violence against the U.S. government. Though the charge was without foundation, it took on plausibility in the context of growing party strife.

The crisis developed when a group of farmers living in western Pennsylvania protested a federal excise tax on distilled whiskey that Congress had originally passed in 1791. These men did not relish paying any taxes, but this tax struck them as particularly unfair. They made a good deal of money distilling their grain into whiskey, but the excise could seriously reduce the profits.

Largely because the Republican governor of Pennsylvania refused to suppress the angry farmers, Washington and other leading Federalists assumed that the insurrection represented a direct political challenge. The president called out fifteen thousand militiamen, and accompanied by Hamilton, he marched against the rebels. The expedition was an embarrassing fiasco. The distillers disappeared, and, predictably enough, no one living in the Pittsburgh region seemed to know where the troublemakers had gone. Two supposed rebels were convicted of high crimes against the United States, one reportedly a "simpleton" and the other insane. Washington eventually pardoned both men. As peace returned to the frontier, Republicans gained much electoral support from voters whom Federalists had alienated.

Whiskey Rebellion Protests in 1794 by western Pennsylvania farmers resisting payment of a federal tax on whiskey. The uprising was forcibly suppressed when President George Washington called an army of 15,000 troops to the area, where they encountered almost no resistance.

In the national political forum, however, the **Whiskey Rebellion** had just begun. Washington blamed the "Republican" clubs for promoting civil unrest. Jefferson labeled the entire episode a Hamiltonian device to create an army for the purpose of intimidating Republicans. How else could one explain the administration's gross overreaction to a few disgruntled farmers? The response of both parties reveals a pervasive fear of some secret, evil design to destroy the republic. The clubs and newspapers fanned these anxieties, convincing many government officials that the First Amendment should not be interpreted as protecting political dissent.

Washington's Farewell

Farewell Address In this 1796 speech, President George Washington announced his intention not to seek a third term in office. He also stressed federalist interests and warned the American people to avoid political factions and foreign entanglements that could sacrifice U.S. security.

In September 1796, Washington published his famed **Farewell Address,** formally declaring his intention to retire from the presidency. Written largely by Hamilton, drawing on a draft by Madison, it sought to advance the Federalist cause in the forthcoming election. By waiting until September to announce his retirement, Washington denied the Republicans valuable time to organize an effective campaign. There was an element of irony in this initiative. Washington had always maintained that he stood above party lines. Though he may have done so in the early years of his presidency, events such as the signing of Jay's Treaty and the suppression of the Whiskey Rebellion transformed him in the eyes of many Americans into a spokesman solely for Hamilton's Federalist party.

In the address, Washington issued two warnings. First, he warned his country against all political factions. Second, he counseled the United States to avoid making any permanent alliances with distant nations that had no real interest in promoting American security. If few Americans paid attention to the first part of his message, the second part guided foreign relations for many years and became the credo of later American isolationists.

The Adams Presidency

The election of 1796 took place in an atmosphere of mutual distrust. Jefferson, candidate of the Republicans, believed he was running against American representatives of the British aristocracy. The Federalists were convinced that their Republican opponents wanted to hand the government over to French radicals. By modern standards, the structures of both parties and the campaign methods employed were still primitive.

During the campaign, the Federalists sowed the seeds of their eventual destruction. Party stalwarts agreed that John Adams should run against Jefferson. Hamilton, however, could not leave well enough alone. From his law office in New York City, he schemed to deprive Adams of the presidency. He apparently feared that an independent-minded Adams would be difficult to manipulate. He was correct.

Hamilton exploited an awkward feature of the electoral college. In accordance with the Constitution, each elector cast two ballots, and the person who gained the most votes became president. The runner-up, regardless of party affiliation, served as vice president. Ordinarily, the Federalist electors would have cast one vote for Adams and one for Thomas Pinckney, the party's choice for vice president. Everyone hoped, of course, that there would be no tie. Hamilton secretly urged southern Federalists to support Pinckney with their first vote, which meant throwing away an elector's second vote. The strategy backfired when New Englanders loyal to Adams heard of Hamilton's maneuvering. They dropped Pinckney, and when the votes were counted, Adams had 71, Jefferson 68, and Pinckney 59. Hamilton's treachery not only angered the new president but also heightened tensions within the Federalist party.

Adams assumed the presidency under intolerable conditions. He found himself saddled with the members of Washington's old cabinet, who regularly consulted with Hamilton behind Adams's back. But to have dismissed them summarily would have called Washington's judgment into question, and Adams was not prepared publicly to take that risk. Adams also had to work with a Republican vice president. Adams hoped that he and Jefferson could cooperate, but partisan pressures soon overwhelmed the president's good intentions. After a short time, Adams stopped consulting Jefferson.

The XYZ Affair and Domestic Politics

Foreign affairs immediately occupied Adams's full attention. The French government regarded Jay's Treaty as an affront. By allowing Great Britain to define the condition for neutrality, the United States had in effect sided with that nation against the interest of France.

Relations between the two countries steadily deteriorated. The French dismissed Charles Cotesworth Pinckney, the United States' representative in Paris, and the French minister in Philadelphia openly supported Jefferson for president in 1796. In 1797, French privateers began seizing American ships. During this period, neither country bothered to declare war, and for that reason the hostilities came to be known as the Quasi-War.

Hamilton and his friends welcomed the popular outpouring of anti-French sentiment. They counseled the president to prepare for all-out war, hoping that war would purge the United States of French influence. Adams was not persuaded to escalate the conflict. Instead he sent a three-member commission—Charles Pinckney, John Marshall, and Elbridge Gerry—to Paris in a final attempt to remove the sources of antagonism. They were instructed to obtain compensation for the ships seized by French privateers as well as release from the treaties of 1778. In exchange, the commission offered France the same commercial privileges granted to Great Britain in Jay's Treaty.

This cartoon, Property Protected à la Françoise *(1798), captures the anti-French sentiment many Americans felt after President Adams disclosed the papers of the XYZ Affair. America—depicted as a young maiden—is being plundered by five Frenchmen, who represent the five directors of the French government.* ◆

The commission was shocked by the outrageous treatment it received in France. Instead of dealing directly with Talleyrand, the French minister of foreign relations, they met with obscure intermediaries who reported that Talleyrand would not open negotiations unless he was given $250,000. In addition, the French government expected a "loan" of millions of dollars. The Americans refused to play the insulting game.

The event set off a domestic political explosion. When Adams presented the commission's official correspondence before Congress—the names of Talleyrand's lackeys were disguised as X, Y, and Z—the Federalists burst out with a war cry. At last, because of the **XYZ Affair** they would be able to even old scores with the Republicans. So tense was the atmosphere that old friendships between Federalists and Republicans were shattered. As Jefferson wrote to an old colleague: "Men who have been intimate all their lives, cross the streets to avoid meeting, and turn their heads another way, lest they should be obliged to touch their hats."

XYZ Affair A diplomatic incident in which American peace commissioners sent to France by President John Adams in 1797 were insulted with bribe demands from their French counterparts, dubbed X, Y, and Z in American newspapers. The incident heightened war fever against France.

Crushing Political Dissent

In the spring of 1798, the followers of Hamilton—called High Federalists—assumed that it was just a matter of time until Adams asked Congress for a formal declaration of war. In the meantime, they pushed for a general rearmament, new fighting ships, additional harbor fortifications, and a greatly expanded U.S. army. About the need for land forces, Adams remained understandably skeptical. He saw no likelihood of a French invasion.

The president missed the political point. The army the Federalists wanted was intended not to thwart French aggression but to stifle internal opposition. Indeed, militant Federalists used the XYZ Affair as the occasion to institute what Jefferson termed the "reign of witches." Jefferson was right; the threat to Republicans was real.

During the summer of 1798, a provisional army gradually came into existence. George Washington agreed to lead the troops, but he would do so only on condition that Adams appoint Hamilton as second in command. Although Adams did not want to promote Hamilton to the command over others who outranked him and were more agreeable, he was not about to refuse Washington's request.

The chief of the High Federalists threw himself into the task of recruiting and supplying the troops. No detail escaped his attention. Only loyal Federalists received a commission—even Adams's son-in-law was denied a post—as Hamilton put the finishing touches on his plan to restore domestic order. The mood of the nation grew tense, and many politicians predicted that a civil war would soon erupt.

Hamilton should not have treated Adams with such open contempt. After all, without presidential cooperation, Hamilton could not fulfill his grand military ambitions. Whenever pressing questions concerning the army arose, Adams was nowhere to be found. He delayed Hamilton at every step, making it quite clear that his first love was the navy. In May 1798, the president even persuaded Congress to establish the Navy Department. Moreover, Adams steadfastly refused to ask Congress for a formal declaration of war. As the weeks passed, the American people increasingly regarded the idle army as an expensive extravagance.

Silencing Political Opposition: The Alien and Sedition Acts

The Federalists did not rely solely on the army to crush political dissent. During the summer of 1798, the party's majority in Congress passed a group of bills known collectively as the **Alien and Sedition Acts.** The legislation authorized the use of federal courts and the powers of the presidency to silence the Republicans. The acts were born of fear and vindictiveness, and in their efforts to punish the followers of Jefferson, the Federalists created the nation's first major crisis over civil liberties.

Alien and Sedition Acts Collective name given to four laws passed in 1798 designed to suppress criticism of the federal government and to curb liberties of foreigners living in the United States.

Congress drew up three separate Alien Acts. The first, the Alien Enemies Law, vested the president with extraordinary wartime powers. On his own authority, he could detain or deport foreigners who behaved in a manner he thought suspicious. Due to the fact that Adams refused to ask for a declaration of war, this legislation never went into effect. The second act, the Alien Law, empowered the president to expel any foreigner from the United States simply by executive decree. Though Adams did not attempt to enforce the act, the mere threat of arrest caused some Frenchmen to flee the country. The third act, the Naturalization Law, was the most flagrantly political of the group. The act established a fourteen-year probationary period before foreigners could apply for full U.S. citizenship. This act was designed to limit the "hordes of wild Irishmen" and other immigrants who voted Republican.

The Sedition Law struck at the heart of free political exchange. It defined criticism of the U.S. government as criminal libel; citizens found guilty by a jury were subject to fines and imprisonment. Republicans were justly worried that the Sedition Law undermined rights guaranteed by the First Amendment. As far as the Federalists were concerned, if their opposition could be silenced, they were willing to restrict freedom of speech.

Americans living in widely scattered regions of the country soon witnessed political repression firsthand. District courts staffed by Federalist appointees indicted seventeen people for criticizing the government. The most celebrated trial occurred in Vermont. A Republican congressman, Matthew Lyon, who was running for reelection, publicly accused the Adams administration of mishandling the Quasi-War. Lyon, an Irish immigrant, had earlier angered Federalists by spitting in the eye of a Federalist congressman during a heated exchange. Now a Federalist court was pleased to have the opportunity to convict him of libel. But Lyon enjoyed the last laugh. While he served his term in jail, his constituents reelected him to Congress.

As this and other cases demonstrated, the federal courts had become political tools. Although the fumbling efforts at enforcement of the Sedition Law did not silence opposition—indeed, they sparked even greater criticism and created martyrs—the actions of the administration persuaded Republicans that the survival of free government was at stake.

Kentucky and Virginia Resolutions

By the fall of 1798, Jefferson and Madison were convinced that the Federalists envisioned the creation of a police state. Some extreme Republicans such as John Taylor

In the early years of the republic, political dissent sometimes escalated to physical violence. This fistfight took place on the floor of Congress, February 15, 1798. The combatants are Republican Matthew Lyon and Federalist Roger Griswold. ❖

of Virginia recommended secession from the Union; others advocated armed resistance. But Jefferson wisely counseled against such extreme strategies. Instead he turned to the state legislatures for help.

Kentucky and Virginia Resolutions Statements penned by Thomas Jefferson and James Madison to mobilize opposition to the Alien and Sedition Acts, which they argued were unconstitutional. Jefferson's statement (the Kentucky Resolution) suggested that states should have the right to declare null and void congressional acts they deemed unconstitutional. Madison produced a more temperate resolution, but most Americans rejected such an extreme defense of states' rights.

As the crisis deepened, Jefferson and Madison drafted separate protests known, respectively, as the **Kentucky and Virginia Resolutions.** Both statements vigorously defended the right of individual state assemblies to interpret the constitutionality of federal law. Jefferson wrote the Kentucky Resolutions in November 1798, and in an outburst of partisan anger, he flirted with a doctrine as dangerous to the survival of the United States as anything advanced by Hamilton and his High Federalist friends.

In the Kentucky Resolutions, Jefferson described the federal union as a compact. The states transferred certain explicit powers to the national government, but in his opinion, they retained full authority over all matters not specifically mentioned in the Constitution. Jefferson rejected Hamilton's broad interpretation of the "general welfare" clause. He believed that individual states had the right to nullify any law that was not specifically within the charter of the Constitution. Carried to an extreme, Jefferson's logic could have led to the breakup of the federal government. Although Madison agreed that the Alien and Sedition Acts were unconstitutional, his Virginia Resolutions were more moderate than Jefferson's Kentucky Resolutions.

The Kentucky and Virginia Resolutions must be viewed in proper historical context. They were not intended as statements of abstract principles and most certainly not as a justification for southern secession. They were pure political party propaganda. Jefferson and Madison were simply reminding American voters during a period of severe domestic tension that the Republicans offered a clear alternative to Federalist rule.

Adams's Finest Hour

In February 1799, President Adams belatedly declared his independence from the Hamiltonian wing of the Federalist party. Throughout the confrontation with France, Adams had shown little enthusiasm for war, and after the XYZ Affair, the French changed their tune. Talleyrand now sent word that he was ready to negotiate in good faith. The High Federalists ridiculed this report, but Adams decided to accept the peace initiative. In February, he asked the Senate to confirm William Vans Murray as the United States' representative to France.

In November 1799, Murray and several other negotiators arrived in France. By then, Napoleon Bonaparte had come to power, but he cooperated with the Americans. Together, they drew up an agreement known as the Convention of Mortefontaine. The French refused to compensate the Americans for vessels taken during the Quasi-War, but they did declare the treaties of 1778 null and void. Moreover, the convention removed annoying French restrictions on United States commerce. Not only had Adams avoided war, but he had also created an atmosphere of mutual trust that paved the way for the purchase of the Louisiana Territory. The negotiations brought Adams personal satisfaction, but they cost him reelection.

The Peaceful Revolution: The Election of 1800

On the eve of the election of 1800, the Federalists were fatally divided between the followers of both Adams and Hamilton. Once again, the former secretary of the treasury attempted to rig the voting in the electoral college so that the party's vice presidential candidate, Charles Cotesworth Pinckney, would receive more ballots than Adams did. Again the conspiracy backfired, and the Republicans carried the election.

But to everyone's surprise, the election was not resolved in the electoral college. When the ballots were counted, Jefferson and his running mate, Aaron Burr, had tied. This accident—a Republican elector should have thrown away his second vote—sent the selection of the next president to the House of Representatives, a body still controlled by members of the Federalist party.

As the House began its work on February 27, 1801, excitement ran high. Each state delegation cast a single vote, with nine votes needed to be elected. The drama dragged on for days. To add to the confusion, the ambitious Burr refused to withdraw. Finally, leading Federalists decided that Jefferson, whatever his faults, would make a more responsible president than the shifty Burr. On the thirty-sixth ballot, Jefferson was elected. The Twelfth Amendment, ratified in 1804, saved the American people from repeating this potentially dangerous turn of events. Henceforth, the electoral college cast separate ballots for president and vice president.

During the final days of his presidency, Adams appointed as many Federalists as possible to the federal bench. Jefferson protested the hasty manner in which these "midnight judges" were selected. One of them, John Marshall, became chief justice of the United States, a post he held with distinction for thirty-four years. But behind the last-minute flurry of activity lay bitterness and disappointment. On the morning of Jefferson's inauguration, Adams slipped away from the capital—now located in Washington—unnoticed and unappreciated.

In the address that Adams missed, Jefferson attempted to quiet partisan fears. "We are all Republicans; we are all Federalists," he declared. He did not mean that there were no longer any party differences, only that all politicians shared a deep commitment to a federal union based on republican ideals. Indeed, the president interpreted the election of 1800 as a fulfillment of the principles of 1776.

CHRONOLOGY

1787	Constitution of the United States signed (September)
1789	George Washington inaugurated (April) ❖ Louis XVI of France calls meeting of the Estates General (May)
1790	Congress approves Hamilton's plan for funding and assumption (July)
1791	Bank of the United States is chartered (February) ❖ Hamilton's *Report on Manufactures* is rejected by Congress (December)
1793	France's revolutionary government announces a "war of all people against all kings" (February) ❖ Genêt affair strains relations with France (April) ❖ Washington issues Proclamation of Neutrality (April) ❖ Spread of "democratic" clubs alarms Federalists ❖ Jefferson resigns as secretary of state (December)
1794	Whiskey Rebellion is put down by the United States Army (July–November) ❖ General Anthony Wayne defeats Indians at the battle of Fallen Timbers (August)
1795	Hamilton resigns as secretary of the treasury (January) ❖ Jay's Treaty divides the nation (June) ❖ Pinckney's Treaty with Spain is a welcome surprise (October)
1796	Washington publishes his Farewell Address (September) ❖ John Adams is elected president (December)
1797	XYZ Affair poisons U.S. relations with France (October)
1798	Quasi-War with France begins ❖ Congress passes the Alien and Sedition Acts (June, July) ❖ Provisional army is formed ❖ Kentucky and Virginia Resolutions protest the Alien and Sedition Acts (November, December)
1799	George Washington dies (December)
1800	Convention of Mortefontaine is signed with France, ending the Quasi-War (September)
1801	House of Representatives elects Thomas Jefferson president (February)

Conclusion: Danger of Political Extremism

From a broader historical perspective, the election of 1800 seems noteworthy for what did not occur. There were no riots in the streets, no attempted coup by military officers, no secession from the Union, nothing except the peaceful transfer of government from the leaders of one political party to those of the opposition.

Americans had weathered the Alien and Sedition Acts, the meddling by predatory foreign powers in domestic affairs, the shrilly partisan rhetoric of hack journalists, and now, at the start of a new century, they were impressed with their own achievement. As one woman who attended Jefferson's inauguration noted, "The changes of administration which in every government and in every age have most generally been epochs of confusion, villainy and bloodshed, in this our happy country take place without any species of distraction, or disorder." But as she well understood—indeed, as modern Americans must constantly relearn—extremism in the name of partisan political truth can easily unravel the delicate fabric of representative democracy and leave the republic at the mercy of those who would manipulate the public for private benefit.

Key Terms

Bank of the United States, p. 131
French Revolution, p. 132
Jay's Treaty, p. 134
Whiskey Rebellion, p. 136
Farewell Address, p. 136
XYZ Affair, p. 138
Alien and Sedition Acts, p. 139
Kentucky and Virginia Resolutions, p. 140

Recommended Reading

The sudden development of deeply partisan politics on the national level dominated public life during the 1790s. Several recent accounts capture the sense of anger and disappointment that informed the political culture: Joanne B. Freeman, *Affairs of Honor: National Politics in the New Republic* (2001) and Joseph J. Ellis, *Founding Brothers: The Revolutionary Generation* (2000). Joyce Appleby provides useful insights into the ideological tensions that divided former allies in *Liberalism and Republicanism in the Historical Imagination* (1992). Jack N. Rakove offers a fine short introduction to James Madison's political thought in *James Madison and the Creation of the American Republic* (1990). An excellent discussion of the conflicting economic visions put forward by Hamilton and Jefferson can be found in Drew McCoy, *The Elusive Republic: The Political Economy in Jeffersonian America* (1980). Anyone curious about the controversial rise of political parties should consult Richard Hofstadter, *The Idea of a Party System: The Rise of Legitimate Opposition in the United States, 1780–1840* (1997) and Stanley Elkins and Eric McKitrick, *The Age of Federalism: The Early Republic* (1993). One can obtain many useful and readable biographies of the dominant leaders of the period. Two more analytic studies are Peter Onuf, ed., *Jeffersonian Legacies* (1993) and Paul K. Longmore, *The Invention of George Washington* (1999). How Americans constructed a convincing sense of national identity is examined in David Waldstreicher, *In the Midst of Perpetual Fetes: The Making of American Nationalism, 1776–1820* (1997). Two regional studies suggest how republican values worked themselves out among ordinary people: Alan Taylor, *Liberty Men and Great Proprietors: The Revolutionary Settlement of the Maine Frontier, 1760–1820* (1990) and Andrew Cayton, *Frontier Republic: Ideology and Politics in Ohio Country, 1780–1825* (1986). Conor Cruise O'Brien helps explain why foreign affairs, especially with the leaders of the French Revolution, disrupted domestic politics: *The Long Affair: Thomas Jefferson and the French Revolution, 1785–1800* (1996). A scientific debate driven by nationalism is the subject of Gordon S. Wood, "The Bigger the Beast the Better," *American History Illustrated*, Vol. 17 (1982), 30–37.

For a list of additional titles related to this chapter's topics, please see http://www.ablongman.com/divine.

Suggested Web Sites

Temple of Liberty—Building the Capitol for a New Nation

http://www.lcweb.loc.gov/exhibits/us.capitol/s0.html
Compiled from holdings in the Library of Congress, this site contains detailed information on the design and early construction of the Capitol building in Washington, D.C.

U.S. Electoral College

http://www.nara.gov/fedreg/elctcoll/index.html
This National Archives and Records Administration site explains how the electoral college works.

George Washington Papers

http://www.virginia.edu/gwpapers/
Information on the publishing project, with selected documents, essays, and an index of the published volumes.

George Washington's Mount Vernon

http://www.mountvernon.org/
Pictures and documents of Mount Vernon, the home of the first president, George Washington.

George Washington Papers at the Library of Congress, 1741–1799

http://memory.loc.gov/ammem/gwhtml/gwhome.html
This site is described as follows: "The complete George Washington Papers from the Manuscript Division at the Library of Congress consists of approximately 65,000 documents. This is the largest collection of original Washington documents in the world."

Archiving Early America

http://earlyamerica.com/
Old newspapers are excellent windows into the issues of the past. This site includes the Keigwin and Matthews collection of historic newspapers.

John Adams

http://www.ipl.org/div/potus/jadams.html
This Internet Public Library page contains biographical information about the second president, his inaugural address, and links to more information.

Counting the People

The Federal Census of 1790

Modern Americans have more or less come to take the federal census for granted. During the early days of the new national government, however, no one had much experience in counting the people. The various imperial administrators who ruled before the Revolution had only a very rough sense of how many men and women lived in Great Britain's mainland colonies, and population estimates advanced by able mathematicians such as Benjamin Franklin amounted to little more than informed speculation. But the creation of a representative republic, one that boldly claimed to reflect the will of "We the People of the United States," demanded much greater precision.

As they struggled to organize a new federal government, the delegates to the Constitutional Convention had to figure out how to apportion "representation and direct taxation" among the states. The ineffectual Articles of Confederation provided no practical solution for determining either, stipulating simply that each state—regardless of size—have a single vote in Congress. Moreover, during the 1780s the states had the responsibility of levying and collecting federal taxes, leading their assemblies to try any connivance to lighten the local tax burden.

The framers of the Constitution solved both problems by basing taxation and representation on a state's population. "It is of great importance," James Madison argued, "that the State should feel as little bias as possible to swell or reduce the amount of their numbers." Madison believed that "were their share of representation alone to be governed by this rule, they would have an interest in exaggerating their inhabitants. Were the rule to decide their share of taxation alone, a contrary temptation would prevail." In article 1, section 2, the Constitution called for the federal government to conduct a census every ten years. In counting the people, the framers considered white inhabitants as "whole numbers." Indians, who were neither taxed nor represented, would be "excluded" from the count. Slaves, referred to as "all other persons," were neither fully people nor wholly property and were counted as three-fifths of the white population in determining a state's representation in Congress.

The First Congress faced the challenge of putting the admittedly racist principles into practice. Madison lobbied for a schedule that would "embrace some other objects besides the bare enumeration of the inhabitants." The House of Representatives passed an enumeration bill that empowered the federal government to distinguish white males over sixteen years of age from those younger, heads of households from dependents, slaves from free citizens, and men from women. Madison also proposed tallying the occupations of the people so that Congress "might proceed to make property provisions for the agricultural, commercial, and manufacturing interests." Senators modified the bill, voting for an enumeration act that did not require inhabitants to list their occupations. Asking for too many details about personal matters, some suggested, "might excite some disagreeable ideas in the minds of the people," leading to charges "that the Government was too particular, in order to learn their ability to bear the burden of direct or other taxes." After more than two centuries, suspicion about the use of private data still agitates many Americans, who see the census as potentially compromising their right of privacy.

The first official count began on August 2, 1790. President George Washington appointed Thomas Jefferson, his secretary of state, to administer the census and to oversee the federal marshals who would carry it out. Marshals hired a total of 650 enumerators, each to survey a distinct district or county and to report the findings within nine months. Beyond this charge, they received few instructions. The government agreed to pay enumerators who canvassed cities and towns $1 for every 300 inhabitants they listed. In rural areas, where travel proved difficult and the people scattered, census takers received $1 for every 150 entries they registered.

In some areas of the country, the census progressed smoothly. Boston's enumerator began his work on August 2 and within three weeks had counted each of the city's 18,000 inhabitants. Virginia's federal marshal, Edward Carrington, anticipated similar results as his assistants began their work. "There exists throughout every part of the Country," he declared, "so favorable a disposition upon this subject that I am confident the business will be done with greater accuracy than any person at first expected." Simple

This Liverpool Ware jug records the results of the nation's first census in 1790. Symbols of prosperity surround the census figures, even though the results disappointed many people who hoped the final count would show a population of more than four million people. ❖

entries hastened the process. In the South, for example, enumerators listed slaves as "Peter negro (Chas. Wells property)," and free African Americans as "Ruth Free negro." As returns accumulated, Jefferson exclaimed "The census has made considerable progress." Based on early estimates, "our numbers," he insisted, "will be between 4 and 5 millions." Larger totals were seen as an indication of the nation's commercial prospects and military strength.

Optimism about the first census was short-lived. Assistants faced considerable challenges in reaching a reliable count. In Maine—then still part of Massachusetts—"natural obstacles of woods, hills" as well as "the want of roads" slowed enumerators. "Where the habitations are as scattered as they are in Kentucky," one Congressman warned, marshals "would be obliged to hire a man on purpose to travel over a tract of land of 160 or 170 miles." With uncertain boundaries, poor transportation, and a mobile citizenry, census takers made mistakes. In some regions, they counted inhabitants two or three times. In others, not at all.

Enumerators also encountered men and women who rejected the entire notion of counting the people. A failure to cooperate with the census could result in a $20 fine. Nonetheless, as Washington complained, "the religious scruples of some, would not allow them to give their lists." A number of New Yorkers, who remembered an epidemic that followed an earlier colonial census, refused to participate in 1790 because of "the Sin of David." According to the Old Testament, King David had incurred God's wrath by ordering a head count of the nation of Israel. Although Carrington encountered similar beliefs in Virginia, especially among "old people," he found a way to alleviate the problem. "The assistants, who are truly respectable characters," he argued, "will be able to come at the Numbers in a variety of ways," including interrogating neighbors. Suspicion of federal authority also thwarted an accurate count. Washington believed that a widespread "fear" that the census "was intended as the foundation of a tax" encouraged inhabitants "to conceal" the truth. A North Carolina enumerator, "after Riding horses almost to Death," could not complete his circuit. No citizen, he found, "that understands will have anything to do with it." In South Carolina, where the census dragged on for eighteen months, the government brought charges against a number of frontier settlers who refused to provide information.

As the final numbers arrived, federal officials could hardly conceal their disappointment. They wanted to demonstrate to European nations the power of the United States, but as Washington conceded, "we shall hardly reach four millions." The final tally of 3,929,214, including 700,000 enslaved African Americans, confirmed the president's fears. Jefferson issued copies to his ministers abroad with two sets of numbers, an actual count in black ink, another in red reflecting his estimate of a more accurate number. Yet for a cost of $44,377.28 the census proved a bargain. After the count of 1790, Congress increased the number of representatives in the House from 65 to 105 and gained a more certain idea of a proper apportionment of taxation. The count also brought legitimacy to the struggling young government. "The authenticated number," Washington declared, "is far greater . . . than has ever been allowed in Europe, and will have no small influence in enabling them to form a more just opinion of our present and growing importance than has yet been entertained there."

Chapter 8

Republican Ascendancy: The Jeffersonian Vision

Limits of Equality

British visitors often disliked Jeffersonian society. Wherever they traveled in the young republic, they met ill-mannered people inspired with a ruling passion for liberty and equality. Charles William Janson, an Englishman who lived in the United States for thirteen years, was particularly upset by the lack of deference in American society. He remembered one woman who worked for an acquaintance of his and who refused to acknowledge that any person was her master. She told Janson: "I'd have you know, *man,* that I am no *sarvant* [sic]; none but *negers* [sic] are *sarvants.*"

This was the authentic voice of Jeffersonian republicanism—self-confident, assertive, blatantly racist, and having no intention of being relegated to low social status. The maid believed that she was her employer's equal. She may even have fostered dreams of having employees of her own some day. After all, for the men and women who believed in the vision that Jefferson and other Republicans offered, America was a land of boundless opportunity.

Yet the limits of the Jeffersonian vision were obvious even to contemporaries. The people who spoke most nobly about equality often owned slaves. Little had changed since the Revolution. African Americans, who represented one-fifth of the population of the United States, were totally excluded from the new opportunities opening up in the cities and the West. Indeed, the maid in the incident just described insisted—with no apparent sense of inconsistency—that her position was superior to that of blacks, who were brought involuntarily to lifelong servitude.

Outline

Regional Identities in a New Republic

Jefferson as President

Jefferson's Critics

Embarrassments Overseas

The Strange War of 1812

Conclusion: Republican Legacy

IT IS NOT SURPRISING THAT in this highly charged racial climate leaders of the Federalist Party accused the Republicans, especially those who lived in the South, of hypocrisy. The race issue simply would not go away. Beneath the political maneuvering over the acquisition of the Louisiana Territory and of the War of 1812 lay fundamental disagreement about the spread of slavery to the western territories.

In other areas, the Jeffersonians did not fulfill even their own high expectations. As members of the opposition party during the presidency of John Adams, they insisted on a strict interpretation of the Constitution, peaceful foreign relations, and a reduction of the role of the federal government in the lives of the average citizen. But following the election of 1800, Jefferson and his supporters discovered that unanticipated pressures, foreign and domestic, forced them to moderate these goals. Before he retired from public office, Jefferson interpreted the Constitution in a way that permitted the government to purchase the Louisiana Territory when the opportunity arose; he regulated the national economy with a rigor that would have made Alexander Hamilton blush; and he led the country to the brink of war. Some Americans praised the president's pragmatism; others felt betrayed.

Regional Identities in a New Republic

During the early decades of the nineteenth century, the population of the United States experienced substantial growth, more the result of natural reproduction than immigration. The 1810 census counted 7,240,000 Americans, a jump of almost 2 million in just ten years. Of this total, approximately 20 percent were blacks. It was a young population. The largest single group in the society was children, boys and girls who were born after Washington's administration and who came of age at a time when the nation's boundaries were rapidly expanding.

Even as Americans defended the rights of individual states, they were forming strong regional identifications. In commerce and politics they perceived themselves as representatives of distinct subcultures, as Southerners, New Englanders, or Westerners. Pride and defensiveness mingled together to produce sectional identities, which in time became stronger than even state loyalties.

This shifting focus of attention resulted not only from an awareness of shared economic interests but also from a sensitivity to outside attacks on slavery. Long before Jefferson died in 1826, Southerners raised the specter of secession and showed how fragile national unity was.

Westward the Course of Empire

The most striking changes occurred in the West. Before the end of the American Revolution, only Indian traders and a few hardy settlers had ventured across the Appalachians. After 1790, however, a flood of people poured west to stake out farms on the rich soil. Pittsburgh and Cincinnati, both strategically located on the Ohio River, became important commercial ports. Congress rapidly formed new territories and admitted new states. Wherever they located, Westerners depended on water transportation. Riverboats represented the cheapest and fastest way to get crops to market. The Mississippi River was the crucial commercial link for the entire region.

Families who moved west attempted to transplant familiar Eastern customs to the frontier. In some areas such as the Western Reserve, a narrow strip of land along Lake Erie in northern Ohio, the influence of New England remained strong. In general, however, a creative mixing of peoples of different backgrounds in a strange environment generated distinctive folkways. They developed their own heroic figures and prided themselves on their toughness, ambition, and self-confidence. Restless and excited by the challenges and opportunities of the frontier, these settlers thought little about packing up their belongings and moving farther west.

Only one obstacle barred the way—Indians. Native Americans still lived in the greater Ohio valley, and they insisted that they owned the land. The tragedy was that the Indians, many of them dependent on trade with whites and ravaged by disease and alcohol, lacked unity. Small groups allegedly representing the interests of an entire tribe sold off huge pieces of land, often for whiskey or trinkets.

These fraudulent transactions disgusted the brilliant Shawnee leaders, Tecumseh, and his brother, Tenskwatawa (known as the Prophet). These men desperately tried to revitalize tribal culture, encouraging Indians to avoid contact with whites, to resist alcohol, and to hold on to their land. The frontiersmen saw Tecumseh as a threat to progress, and during the War of 1812, they shattered the Indians' dream of a cultural renaissance. American settlers pushing west swept away the Indian barrier.

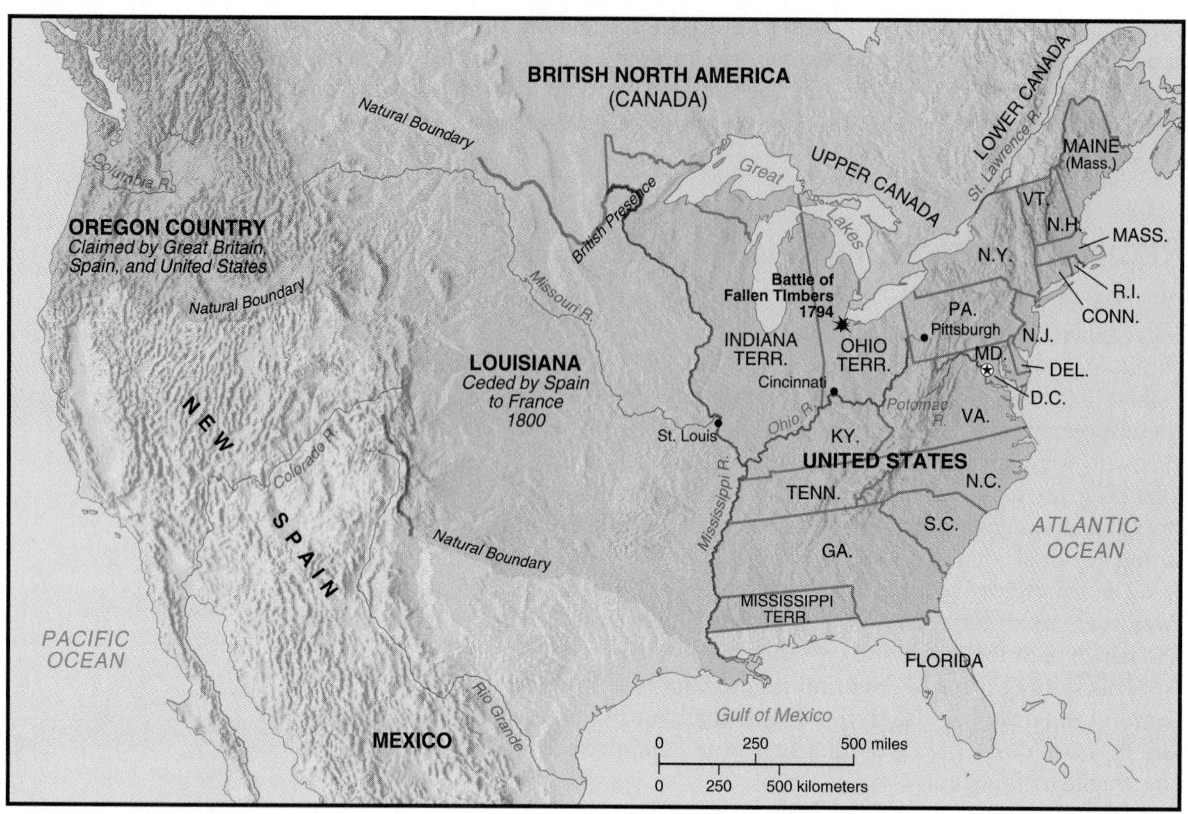

NORTH AMERICA IN 1800 *In the 1790s, diplomatic agreements with Britain and Spain and defeat of the Native Americans at the battle of Fallen Timbers opened the way to U.S. settlement of the land beyond the Appalachian Mountains.* ❖

Well-meaning Jeffersonians did not intend to exterminate the Indians. The president talked about creating a vast reservation beyond the Mississippi River. He planned to turn the Indians into yeoman farmers. But even the most enlightened thinkers of the day did not believe that the Indians possessed a culture worth preserving.

Commercial Life in the Cities

Before 1820, the prosperity of the United States depended primarily on its agriculture and trade. Jeffersonian America was by no stretch of the imagination an industrial economy. Except for the cotton gin, important mechanical and chemical inventions did not appear for another generation. Southerners concentrated on staple crops—tobacco, rice, and cotton. In the North, people generally raised livestock and cereal crops. Regardless of location, however, the nation's farmers, who represented 84 percent of the population, followed a backbreaking work routine that did not differ substantially from that of their parents and grandparents. Probably the major innovation of this period was the agricultural fair, which was first introduced in the hope of improving animal breeding.

The merchant marine represented an equally important element in America's preindustrial economy. At the turn of the century, ships flying the Stars and Stripes transported a large share of the world's trade. Merchants in Boston, New York, and Philadelphia received handsome profits from this commerce. Their vessels provided essential links between European countries and their Caribbean colonies. This trade, along with the export of domestic staples, especially cotton, generated great fortunes. Unfortunately, the boom did not last. The success of the "carrying trade" depended in large measure on friendly relations between the United States and the major European powers. When England and France began seizing American ships—as both did after 1805—national prosperity suffered.

The cities of Jeffersonian America functioned chiefly as depots for international trade. Only about 7 percent of the nation's population lived in urban centers, which were densely inhabited, and most of these people owed their livelihoods either directly or indirectly to the carrying trade. Shipbuilders, stevedores, and artisans, as well as merchants, contributed to the shipping business. As the merchant families grew wealthy, their demand for luxury items drew a group of master craftsmen whose beautiful and intricate pieces—such as New England clocks—were perhaps the highest artistic achievement of the period.

American cities had only a marginal economic influence on the nation's vast hinterland. Because of the high cost of land transportation, urban merchants seldom purchased goods for export—flour and meat, for example—from more than 150 miles away. The separation between rural and urban Americans was far more pronounced during Jefferson's presidency than it was after the development of canals and railroads a few decades later.

The booming carrying trade may have in effect retarded the industrialization of the United States. The lure of large profits drew investment capital—a scarce resource in a developing society—into commerce. By contrast, manufacturing seemed too risky.

Industry was not entirely forgotten, however. Samuel Slater, an English-born designer of textile machinery, did establish several cotton-spinning mills in New England, but before the 1820s, these plants employed only a small number of workers. Another farsighted inventor, Robert Fulton, sailed the first American steamship up the Hudson River in 1807. In time, this marvelous innovation opened new markets for domestic manufacturers, especially in the West.

Jefferson as President

The District of Columbia seemed an appropriate capital for a Republican president. At the time of Jefferson's first inauguration, Washington was still an isolated rural village. Jefferson fit comfortably into Washington society. He despised formal ceremony and sometimes shocked foreign dignitaries by meeting them in his slippers or a threadbare jacket. Reading and reflection were his primary escapes from official duties.

The president was a poor public speaker. He wisely refused to deliver annual addresses before Congress. In personal conversation, however, Jefferson exuded considerable charm. His dinner parties were major social events, and in this forum, Jefferson regaled politicians with his knowledge of literature, philosophy, and science.

Notwithstanding his commitment to the life of the mind, Jefferson was a politician to the core. He ran for the presidency in order to achieve specific goals: reduction of the size and cost of federal government, repeal of Federalist legislation such as the Alien Acts, and the maintenance of international peace. Jefferson realized that he required the full cooperation of congressional Republicans, some of whom were fiercely independent men. To accomplish his program, Jefferson developed friendships, wrote memoranda, and held intimate meetings with key Republicans. In two terms as president, Jefferson never had to veto a single act of Congress.

Jefferson carefully selected the members of his cabinet. During Washington's administration, he had witnessed—even provoked—severe infighting; as president, he nominated only men who enthusiastically supported his programs. James Madison became secretary of state, and Albert Gallatin, a Swiss-born financier who understood the complexities of the federal budget, accepted Jefferson's appointment as secretary of the treasury. Henry Dearborn, Levi Lincoln, and Robert Smith, all loyal to Jefferson, filled the other cabinet posts.

Jeffersonian Reforms

A top priority of the new government was cutting the national debt. Throughout American history, presidents have advocated such reductions, but into the twenty-first century, few have achieved them. Jefferson succeeded. Both he and Gallatin associated debt with Alexander Hamilton's Federalist financial programs, measures they considered harmful to republicanism. Jefferson claimed that legislators elected by the current generation did not have the right to mortgage the future of unborn Americans.

Jefferson also wanted to diminish the activities of the federal government. He urged Congress to repeal all direct taxes. Gallatin linked federal income to the carrying trade. He calculated that the entire cost of national government could be borne by customs receipts. The only problem with Gallatin's plan was that it depended on peaceful international relations, a factor that was not predictable.

To help pay the debt inherited from the Adams administration, Jefferson ordered substantial cuts in the national budget. He closed several embassies in Europe, slashed military spending, and during his first term reduced the size of the army by 50 percent. In addition, he retired a majority of the navy's warships, a move he claimed promoted peace.

More than just budgetary considerations prompted Jefferson's military reductions. A product of the revolutionary experience, he was deeply suspicious of standing armies. In the event of foreign attack, he reasoned, the militia would rise in defense of the republic. To ensure that the citizen soldiers would receive professional leadership in battle, Jefferson created the Army Corps of Engineers and the military academy at West Point in 1802.

Political patronage greatly annoyed the new president. Although he controlled several hundred jobs, he refused to dismiss all the Federalists. To transform federal hiring into an undisciplined spoils system, especially at the highest levels of the federal bureaucracy, struck Jefferson as shortsighted. Moderate Federalists might be converted to the Republican party, and in any case, there was a good chance that they possessed the expertise needed to run the government.

Jefferson's political moderation helped hasten the demise of the Federalist party. But the Federalists also contributed to their own decline. The party's organization was loose, and Federalist leaders refused to adopt the popular forms of campaigning that the Republicans had developed so successfully during the late 1790s. The mere prospect of flattering the common people was odious enough to drive some Federalists into political retirement.

Many of them also sensed that national expansion worked against their interests. Western states inevitably seemed to send Republican representatives to Washington. By 1805, the Federalists retained only Delaware and a few states in New England.

Faced with the imminent death of their party, younger Federalists belatedly attempted to pump life into their organization. They experimented with popular election techniques, tightened party organization, held nominating conventions, and campaigned energetically for office. But the results of these activities were disappointing. Even the younger Federalists thought it was demeaning to appeal to voters.

The Louisiana Purchase

When Jefferson first took office, he was confident that Louisiana and Florida would eventually become part of the United States. He hoped to persuade the notoriously weak Spanish rulers to sell the territory, but failing in this, he was prepared to threaten forcible occupation.

In May 1801, however, prospects for the easy or inevitable acquisition of Louisiana suddenly darkened. Jefferson learned that Spain had secretly transferred title of the entire region to France. To make matters worse, the French ruler, Napoleon Bonaparte, seemed intent on reestablishing an empire in North America. Napoleon dispatched a large army to put down a rebellion in France's sugar-rich Caribbean colony, Santo Domingo. From that island stronghold in the West Indies, French troops could seize New Orleans and close the Mississippi River to American trade.

A sense of crisis enveloped Washington. Tensions increased when the Spanish officials who still governed New Orleans announced the closing of that port to American commerce (October 1802). Jefferson and his advisers assumed that the Spanish had acted on orders from France, but despite this serious provocation, the president preferred negotiations to war. In January 1803, he asked James Monroe, a loyal Republican from Virginia, to join the American minister, Robert Livingston, in Paris. The president instructed the two men to explore the possibility of purchasing the city of New Orleans. If Livingston and Monroe failed, Jefferson realized that he would be forced to turn to Great Britain for military assistance.

By the time Monroe joined Livingston in France, Napoleon's army in Santo Domingo had succumbed to tropical disease, and he had lost interest in establishing an American empire. Knowing nothing of these developments, the American diplomats were taken by surprise when they were offered the entire Louisiana Territory for only $15 million. At one stroke, the Americans doubled the size of the United States, although the boundaries were vague.

The American people responded enthusiastically to news of the treaty that formalized the **Louisiana Purchase** (May 1803). Jefferson, of course, was relieved that the nation had avoided war with France, but he worried that the agreement might

Louisiana Purchase U.S. acquisition of the Louisiana Territory from France in 1803 for $15 million. The purchase secured American control of the Mississippi River and doubled the size of the nation.

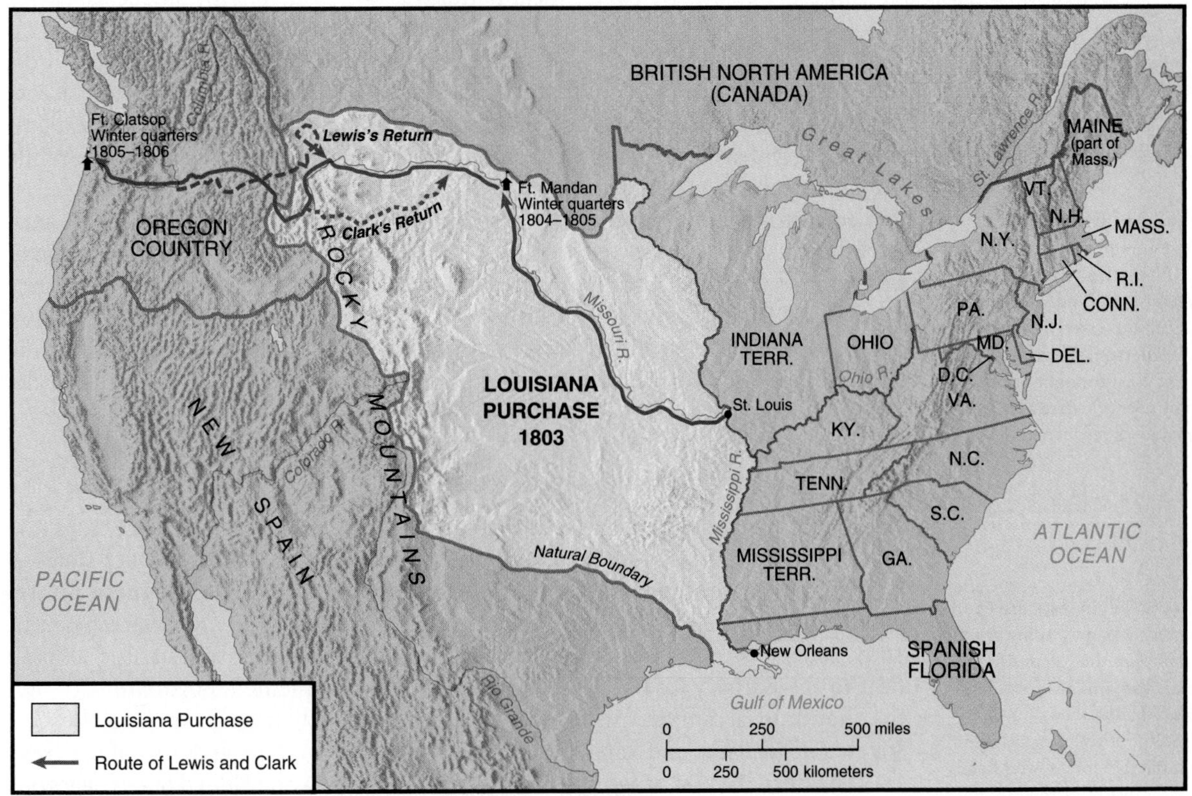

THE LOUISIANA PURCHASE AND THE ROUTE OF LEWIS AND CLARK *Not until Lewis and Clark had explored the Far West did citizens of the United States realize just how much territory Jefferson had acquired through the Louisiana Purchase.* ❖

❖ A Look at the Past ❖

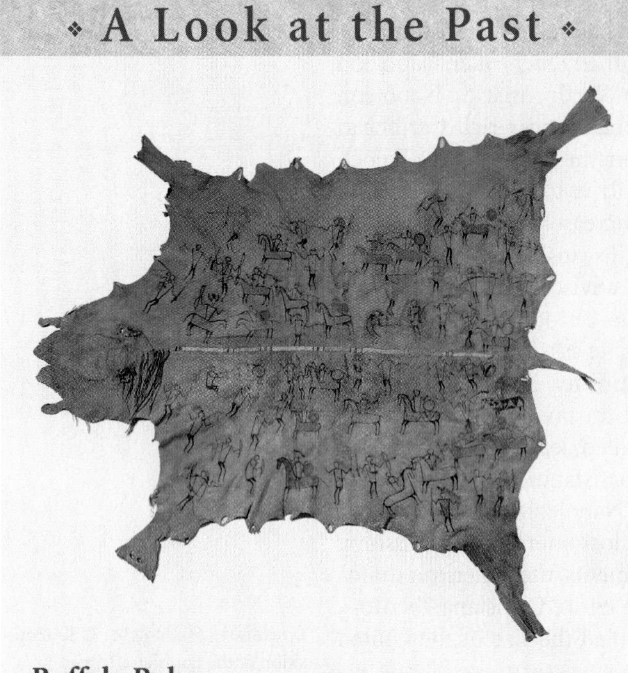

Buffalo Robe

Lewis and Clark collected Native American artifacts, including this Mandan buffalo robe. They sent the robe to Jefferson following a winter spent with the Mandans. Why do you think the Mandans gave Lewis and Clark a robe that depicted a recent battle with their traditional enemy, the Sioux? Why did Lewis and Clark send the robe to Jefferson?

be unconstitutional. The president pointed out that the Constitution did not specifically authorize the acquisition of vast new territories and the incorporation of thousands of foreign citizens. To escape this apparent legal dilemma, Jefferson proposed an amendment to the Constitution, but Napoleon's impatience for money convinced the president to forgo the amendment and act quickly.

Jefferson's fears about the incorporation of the new territory were not unwarranted. The Spanish and French people who lived in the region were unfamiliar with America's customs, government, and laws. Jefferson frankly questioned whether these people would be loyal to the United States. He therefore recommended to Congress a transitional government consisting entirely of appointed officials. Some congressmen attacked the bill as antirepublican because it imposed taxes on the citizens of Louisiana without their consent. By a narrow margin the bill passed.

The Lewis and Clark Expedition

In the midst of the Louisiana controversy, Jefferson dispatched a secret message to Congress requesting $2,500 for the exploration of the Far West. How closely this decision was connected to the Paris negotiations is not clear. The president asked his talented private secretary, Meriwether Lewis, to discover whether the Missouri River offered a direct and practical "water communication across this continent for the purposes of commerce." Jefferson also regarded the expedition as a wonderful opportunity to collect precise data about flora and fauna. While preparing for this great adventure, Lewis's second in command, William Clark, assumed such a prominent role that the effort became known as the **Lewis and Clark expedition.** The effort owed much of its success to a young Shoshoni woman known as Sacagawea. Setting out from St. Louis in May 1804, the exploring party reached the Pacific Ocean in November 1805. The group returned safely the following September. The results of this expedition not only fulfilled Jefferson's scientific expectations but also reaffirmed his faith in the future economic prosperity of the United States.

Lewis and Clark expedition Overland expedition to the Pacific coast (1804–1806) led by Meriwether Lewis and William Clark. Commissioned by President Thomas Jefferson, the exploration of the Far West brought back a wealth of scientific data about the country and its resources.

Conflict with the Barbary States

During this period, Jefferson dealt with another problem. For several decades, the North African states of Morocco, Algiers, Tripoli, and Tunis—the Barbary states—had preyed on commercial shipping. Most European nations paid these pirates tribute, hoping in this way to protect merchants trading in the Mediterranean. In 1801, Jefferson responded to a demand for more tribute by dispatching a small fleet to the Barbary Coast to, as one commander commented, negotiate "through the mouth of a cannon." In the fighting that followed, Tripoli captured the U.S. frigate *Philadelphia,* and Jefferson had to pay $60,000 for the safe return of the crew.

The **Barbary War** dragged on for four years. By 1805, the United States' vigorous naval blockade helped end the war. One diplomat observed that the war demonstrated to Europe the proper way to negotiate with pirates.

Barbary War In response to constant attacks on trading vessels by pirates from the North African Barbary states, in 1801 President Thomas Jefferson sent a naval squadron to resolve the problem through military force. After failing to achieve most of its military objectives, the administration signed an 1805 treaty ending the war.

Jefferson concluded his term on a wave of popularity. He had maintained the peace, reduced taxes, and expanded the boundaries of the United States. He overwhelmed Federalist Charles Cotesworth Pinckney in the election of 1804. So far, Jefferson's "revolution" had been successful.

Jefferson's Critics

At the moment of Jefferson's greatest electoral victory, a perceptive person might have seen signs of serious division within the Republican party and within the country. The president's heavy-handed attempts to reform the federal courts stirred deep animosities. Republicans had begun sniping at other Republicans, and one leading member of the party, Aaron Burr, became involved in a bizarre plot to separate the West from the rest of the nation. Congressional debates over the future of the slave trade revealed the existence of powerful sectional loyalties and profound disagreement on the issue.

Attack on the Judges

Jefferson's controversy with the federal bench commenced the moment he became president. The Federalists, realizing that they would soon lose control over the executive branch, passed the Judiciary Act of 1801, which expanded the federal court system. Through his "midnight" appointments, Adams filled the posts with loyal Federalists. Jefferson opposed the attempt by Federalists to maintain their political control. Even more infuriating was Adams's appointment of John Marshall as the new chief justice. Marshall was one of the few men in the country who could hold his own against Jefferson.

In January 1802, Jefferson's congressional allies called for repeal of the Judiciary Act. Although they avoided the political issues, no one doubted that their attack was politically motivated. But the Constitution held that judges could be removed only when they were found guilty of high crimes and misdemeanors. By repealing the Judiciary Act, Congress would in effect be dismissing judges without a trial, a clear violation of their constitutional rights. Unimpressed by this argument, in March, Congress voted for repeal.

While Congress debated the Judiciary Act, another controversy suddenly erupted. One of Adams's midnight appointees, William Marbury, complained that the new administration would not give him his commission for the office of justice of the peace for the District of Columbia. He sought redress before the Supreme Court, demanding that the federal justices compel James Madison, the secretary of state, to deliver the necessary papers. In his celebrated ***Marbury* v. *Madison*** decision (February 1803), Marshall berated the secretary of state for withholding Marbury's commission. Nevertheless, he concluded that the Supreme Court did not possess jurisdiction over such matters. Poor Marbury was out of luck. The Republicans proclaimed victory. However, they failed to examine the logic of Marshall's decision. He had ruled that part of the earlier judiciary act on which Marbury based his appeal, the one Congress passed in 1789, was unconstitutional. Thus *Marbury* v. *Madison* set an important precedent for judicial review of federal statutes.

Marbury v. *Madison* In this 1803 landmark decision, the Supreme Court first asserted the power of judicial review by declaring an act of Congress, the Judiciary Act of 1789, unconstitutional.

Neither Marbury's defeat nor repeal of the Judiciary Act placated extreme Republicans. They insisted that federal judges should be made more responsible to the will of the people. One solution, short of electing federal judges, was impeachment. Early in 1803, John Pickering, an incompetent judge from New Hampshire, presented the Republicans with a curious test case. This Federalist appointee suffered from alcoholism as well as insanity. However, Pickering had not committed any high crimes against the federal government. Ignoring such legal niceties,

Jefferson's allies in the Senate impeached Pickering (March 1804), and he was removed from the bench.

Jefferson had his sights set on bigger game even before Pickering's impeachment. In the spring of 1803, he accused Samuel Chase, a justice of the Supreme Court, of delivering a treasonous speech. Republican congressmen took the hint, agreeing that Chase, who had frequently attacked Republican policies, had committed an indictable offense.

At this stage, some members of Congress expressed uneasiness. The charges drawn up against the judge were purely political. No one denied that Chase had been indiscreet, accusing Republicans of threatening "peace and order, freedom and property." But his attack on the Jefferson administration hardly seemed criminal. It was clear that if the Senate convicted Chase, every member of the Supreme Court, including Marshall, might also be dismissed.

Chase's impeachment trial before the Senate was one of the most dramatic events in American legal history. Aaron Burr, the vice president, organized the proceeding, and he redecorated the Senate chamber for the event. In this luxurious setting, Chase and his lawyers conducted a masterful defense. By contrast, John Randolph, the congressman who served as chief prosecutor, behaved in an erratic manner, betraying repeatedly his ignorance of relevant points of law. On March 1, 1805, the Senate acquitted the justice of all charges. This trial, too, set a valuable precedent: even though most Republican senators personally disliked the arrogant Chase, they refused to expand the constitutional definition of impeachable offenses.

Politics of Desperation

The collapse of the Federalists on the national level encouraged dissension within the Republican party. Extremists in Congress insisted on monopolizing the president's ear, and when he listened to political moderates, they rebelled. During Jefferson's second term, these critics, labeled "Tertium Quids" ("third sorts," at neither extreme), argued that the president's policies, foreign and domestic, sacrificed virtue for pragmatism. Their chief spokesmen were two members from Virginia, John Randolph and John Taylor. They both despised commercial capitalism and urged Americans to return to a simple agrarian way of life.

The Yazoo controversy raised the Quids from political obscurity. A complex legal battle began in 1795 when a thoroughly corrupt Georgia assembly sold 35 million acres of western land, known as the Yazoo claims, to private companies at bargain prices. It soon became apparent that every member of the legislature had been bribed, and in 1796, state lawmakers rescinded the entire agreement. Unfortunately, some land had already changed hands. Jefferson inherited the entire mess when he became president. The special commission he appointed to look into the matter recommended that Congress set aside 5 million acres for buyers who had unwittingly purchased land from the discredited companies.

Randolph immediately cried foul. Such a compromise, however well-meaning, condoned fraud. Republican virtue hung in the balance. Finally, the Marshall Supreme Court ruled in *Fletcher* v. *Peck* (1810) that legislative fraud did not impair private contracts and that the Georgia assembly of 1796 did not have the authority to take away lands already sold to innocent buyers. This important case upheld the Supreme Court's authority to rule on the constitutionality of state laws.

Murder and Conspiracy: The Curious Career of Aaron Burr

Vice President Aaron Burr created far more serious difficulties for the president. The two men had never been close, and Burr's refusal to bow out during the election of 1800 further strained the relationship. During Jefferson's first term, the ambitious Burr played a distinctly minor role in shaping policy.

In the spring of 1804, Burr decided to run for the governorship of New York. Although he was a Republican, he curried the favor of High Federalists who were plotting the secession of New England and New York from the Union. Alexander Hamilton frustrated Burr's efforts, however, when he described the Republican as "a dangerous man . . . who ought not to be trusted with the reins of government." Burr blamed Hamilton for his subsequent defeat and challenged his tormentor to a duel. On July 11, 1804, at Weehawken, New Jersey, the vice president shot and killed the former secretary of the treasury. Both New York and New Jersey indicted Burr for murder. His political career lay in shambles.

In his final weeks as vice president, Burr hatched a scheme so audacious that the people with whom he dealt could not decide whether he was a genius or a madman. Although he told different stories to different men, he evidently planned a filibustering campaign against a Spanish colony, perhaps Mexico, and he envisioned separating the western states and territories from the Union. The persuasive Burr convinced a handful of politicians and adventurers to follow him. Even James Wilkinson, commander of the U.S. Army in the Mississippi Valley, joined Burr.

Late in the summer of 1806, Burr put his ill-defined plan into action. It ended almost before it started. Wilkinson had a change of heart and denounced Burr to Jefferson. This started a general stampede, as conspirators rushed pell-mell to save their own skins. Federal authorities arrested Burr in February 1807 and took him to Richmond to stand trial for treason. Even before a jury had been called, Jefferson announced publicly that Burr's guilt was beyond question.

Jefferson spoke prematurely. The trial judge was John Marshall, who insisted on a narrow constitutional definition of treason. He refused to hear testimony regarding Burr's supposed intentions and demanded two witnesses to each overt act of treason.

Burr, of course, had been too clever to leave this sort of evidence. While Jefferson complained bitterly about the miscarriage of justice, the jurors declared on September 1, 1807, that the defendant was "not proved guilty by any evidence submitted to us." Although Marshall had acted in an undeniably partisan manner, his actions inadvertently helped protect the civil rights of all Americans. If the chief justice had admitted circumstantial evidence into the Richmond courtroom, if he had listened to rumor and hearsay, he would have made it much easier for later presidents to use trumped-up conspiracy charges to silence legitimate political opposition.

The Slave Trade

Slavery sparked angry debate at the Constitutional Convention of 1787. If delegates from the northern states had refused to compromise on this issue, Southerners would not have supported the new government. At the convention, the South agreed that after 1808, Congress *might consider* banning the importation of slaves into the United States. In return, the North agreed to count a slave as three-fifths of a free white male, which increased southern representatives in Congress and accounted for Jefferson's 1800 presidential victory.

In an annual message sent to Congress in December 1806, Jefferson urged the representatives to prepare legislation outlawing the slave trade. During the early months of 1807, congressmen debated various ways of ending the embarrassing commerce. Although northern representatives generally favored a strong bill, southern congressmen responded with threats and ridicule. They explained to their northern colleagues that no one in the South regarded slavery as evil. It appeared naive, therefore, to expect local planters to enforce a ban on the slave trade or to inform federal agents when they spotted a smuggler.

The bill that Jefferson finally signed in March 1807 probably pleased no one. The law prohibited the importation of slaves into the United States after the new

Although the external slave trade was officially outlawed in 1808, the commerce in humans persisted. An estimated 250,000 African slaves were brought illicitly to the United States between 1808 and 1860. The internal slave trade continued as well. Folk artist Lewis Miller sketched this slave coffle marching from Virginia to new owners in Tennessee under the watchful eyes of mounted white overseers. ❖

year. Whenever customs officials captured a smuggler, the slaves were turned over to state authorities and disposed of according to local custom. Southerners did not cooperate, and for many years African slaves continued to pour into southern ports. Undoubtedly Great Britain, which outlawed the slave trade in 1807, was the greatest single force in limiting the number of African slaves shipped to the United States. Ships of the Royal Navy took British—and in this case, American—laws seriously.

Embarrassments Overseas

During Jefferson's second term (1805–1809), the United States found itself in the midst of a world at war. A brief peace in Europe ended abruptly in 1803, and the two military giants of the age, France and Great Britain, fought for supremacy on land and sea. It was a total war, an ideological war, a type of war unknown in the eighteenth century. Britain was the master of the seas, but France held supremacy on land.

During the early stages of the war, the United States profited from European adversity. As "neutral carriers," the American ships transported goods to any port in the world where they could find a buyer, and American merchants grew wealthy serving Britain and France.

Napoleon's successes on the battlefield, however, quickly strained Britain's economic resources. In response, Britain tightened its control over the seas. British warships seized American vessels engaged in trade beneficial to France, and British captains stepped up impressment of sailors on ships flying the United States flag. Then in 1806, the British government issued a series of trade regulations known as Orders in Council. These proclamations forbade neutral commerce with the European Continent and threatened with seizure any ship that violated the orders. The declarations created what were in effect "paper blockades," for even the powerful British navy could not monitor the activities of every continental port.

Napoleon responded to Britain's commercial regulations with his own paper blockade, called the Continental System. In the Berlin Decree of November 1806 and the Milan Decree of December 1807, he announced the closing of all continental ports to British trade and decreed that neutral vessels carrying British goods were subject to seizure. Since French armies occupied most of the territory between

Spain and Germany, the decrees cut the British out of a large market. Americans were caught between two conflicting systems. To please one power was to displease the other.

The unhappy turn of international events baffled Jefferson. He had assumed that civilized countries would respect neutral rights; justice obliged them to do so. Appeals to reason, however, made little impression on states at war. Jefferson tried to negotiate with Britain, but the agreement that resulted was unacceptable to the president.

The United States soon suffered an even greater humiliation. A ship of the Royal Navy, the *Leopard,* sailing off the coast of Virginia, commanded an American warship to submit to a search for deserters (June 21, 1807). When the captain of the *Chesapeake* refused to cooperate, the *Leopard* opened fire, killing three men and wounding eighteen. The attack clearly violated the sovereignty of the United States. The American people demanded revenge.

Despite the pressure of public opinion, Jefferson played for time. He recognized that the United States was unprepared for war against a powerful nation such as Great Britain. The president worried that an expensive conflict with Great Britain would quickly undo the fiscal reforms of his first term. For Jefferson, war entailed deaths, debts, and taxes, none of which he particularly relished.

Embargo Divides the Nation

Jefferson found what he regarded as a satisfactory way to deal with European predators with a policy he called "peaceable coercion." If Britain and France refused to respect the rights of neutral carriers, then the United States would keep its ships at home. Not only would this action protect them from seizure, but it would also deprive the European powers of much-needed American goods, especially food. Jefferson predicted that a total embargo of American commerce would soon force Britain and France to negotiate with the United States in good faith. Congress passed the **Embargo Act** on December 22, 1807.

Embargo Act In response to a British attack on an American warship off the coast of Virginia, this 1807 law prohibited foreign commerce.

Peaceable coercion turned into a Jeffersonian nightmare. Americans objected strenuously to the legislation, and Jefferson had to push through a series of acts to force compliance. By the middle of 1808, Jefferson and Gallatin were involved in the regulation of the smallest details of American economic life. The federal government supervised the coastal trade and regulated the overland trade with Canada. When violations still occurred, Congress gave customs collectors the right to seize a vessel merely on suspicion of wrongdoing. Jefferson's eagerness to pursue a reasonable foreign policy blinded him to the fact that he and a Republican Congress would have to establish a police state to make it work.

Northerners hated the embargo and regularly engaged in smuggling. Persons living near Lake Champlain in upper New York State simply ignored the regulations, and they roughed up collectors who interfered with the Canadian trade. Jefferson was so determined to stop the illegal activity that he even urged the governor of New York to call out the militia. In a decision that George III might have applauded, Jefferson dispatched federal troops to overawe the citizens of New York.

New Englanders regarded the embargo as lunacy. Merchants preferred to take their chances on the high seas. Sailors and artisans were thrown out of work. The popular press maintained a constant howl of protest. One writer observed that embargo in reverse spelled "O grab me!" Opposition to the embargo caused a brief revival of the Federalist party in New England, and a few extremists suggested the possibility of state assemblies' nullifying federal laws.

By 1809, the bankruptcy of Jefferson's foreign policy was obvious. The embargo never seriously damaged the British economy. Napoleon liked the embargo because it seemed to harm Great Britain more than it did France. Finally, Republicans in

The Ograbme (embargo *spelled backward) snapping turtle, created by cartoonist Alexander Anderson, is shown here biting an American tobacco smuggler who is breaking the embargo.* ❖

Congress panicked and repealed the embargo a few days before James Madison's inauguration. Relations between the United States and the great European powers were much worse in 1809 than they had been in 1805.

A New Administration Goes to War

Madison followed his good friend Jefferson into the White House. As president, Madison suffered from several personal and political handicaps. Although his intellectual abilities were great, he lacked the qualities necessary for effective leadership. His critics argued that his modest and unassuming manner indicated a weak and vacillating character.

During the election of 1808, Randolph and the Quids tried unsuccessfully to persuade James Monroe to challenge Madison's candidacy. Jefferson favored his old friend Madison. In the end, a caucus of Republican congressmen gave the official nod to Madison, the first time in American history that such a congressional group controlled a presidential nomination. Although Madison won the presidency, the Federalists made impressive gains in the House of Representatives. Madison compounded his difficulties by appointing cabinet members who actively opposed his policies.

The new president inherited Jefferson's foreign policy problems. Neither Britain nor France showed the slightest interest in respecting American neutral rights. Madison's solution was to implement the weak and clumsy Non-Intercourse Act (March 1, 1809), which Congress passed at the same time it repealed the embargo. The new bill authorized the resumption of trade between the United States and all nations of the world *except* Britain and France. Either of these countries could restore full commercial relations simply by promising to observe the rights of neutral carriers.

The British immediately took advantage of the offer. Their minister to the United States, David M. Erskine, informed Madison that the British government had modified its position on a number of sensitive commercial issues. Encouraged by these talks, Madison announced that trade with Great Britain could resume on June 10, 1809. Unfortunately, Erskine had not conferred with his superiors, who rejected the agreement out of hand. While an embarrassed Madison fumed in Washington, the Royal Navy seized the American ships that had already put to sea.

Britain's apparent betrayal led the artless Madison straight into a French trap. In May 1810, Congress passed Macon's Bill Number Two. In a complete reversal of strategy, this poorly drafted legislation reestablished trade with *both* England and France. It also contained a curious carrot-and-stick provision. As soon as either of these European states repealed restrictions on neutral shipping, the U.S. government promised to halt all commerce with the other.

Napoleon spotted a rare opportunity. He announced that he would respect American neutral rights. Again, Madison acted impulsively, announcing that unless Britain repealed the Orders in Council by November, the United States would cut off all commercial relations. Only later did Madison learn that Napoleon had no intentions of living up to his side of the bargain. But humiliated by the Erskine experience, Madison decided to ignore French provocations and to pretend that the emperor was behaving in an honest manner.

Events unrelated to international commerce fueled anti-British sentiment in the newly settled parts of the United States. Westerners believed—incorrectly, as it turned out—that British agents operating out of Canada had persuaded Tecumseh's warriors to resist the spread of American settlement. General William Henry Harrison, governor of the Indian Territory, marched an army to the edge of a large Shawnee village at the mouth of Tippecanoe Creek near the banks of the Wabash River. On the morning of November 7, 1811, the American troops bested the Indians at the battle of Tippecanoe. The incident forced Tecumseh to seek British military assistance, something he probably would not have done had Harrison left him alone.

Fumbling Toward Conflict

In 1811, the anti-British mood of Congress intensified. A group of militant representatives, some of them elected to Congress for the first time in the election of 1810, announced that they would no longer tolerate national humiliation. These aggressive nationalists, many from the South and West, have sometimes been labeled the **War Hawks.** Men such as Henry Clay and John C. Calhoun spoke about honor and pride, as if foreign relations were some sort of duel between gentlemen. Although Republicans themselves, the War Hawks repudiated Jefferson's policy of peaceful coercion.

War Hawks **Congressional leaders who, in 1811 and 1812, called for war against Britain to defend the national honor and force Britain to respect America's maritime rights.**

Madison surrendered to the War Hawks. On June 1, 1812, he sent Congress a message requesting a declaration of war against Great Britain. The timing of his action was peculiar. Over the preceding months, tensions between the two countries had relaxed, and the British government was suspending the Orders in Council.

However inadequately Madison communicated his goals, he was able to enforce a plan. His major aim was to force the British to respect American maritime rights, especially in Caribbean waters. The president's problem was to figure out how a nation as small and as militarily weak as the United States could bring effective pressure on Great Britain. The answer—at least Madison's answer—seemed to be Canada. This colony supplied Britain's Caribbean possessions with much-needed foodstuffs. The president therefore reasoned that by threatening to seize Canada, the Americans might compel the British to make concessions on maritime issues. It was this logic that Secretary of State James Monroe had in mind when he explained in June 1812 that "it might be necessary to invade Canada, not as an object of the war, but as a means to bring it to a satisfactory conclusion."

Even contemporaries expressed confusion about the causes of the War of 1812. Madison's formal message to Congress listed Great Britain's violation of maritime rights, impressment of American seamen, and provocation of Indians. The War Hawks wanted war for other reasons. Some probably hoped to conquer Canada. For others, the whole affair may have truly been a matter of national pride. Surprisingly, New Englanders, in whose commercial interests the war would supposedly be waged, ridiculed such chauvinism. Although Congress voted for war, the nation was clearly divided about the need to fight Britain. Madison's slim victory over De Witt Clinton, nominated by a faction of antiwar Republicans, in the election of 1812 indicated this split in America.

The Strange War of 1812

Optimism among the War Hawks ran high. However, they failed to appreciate how unprepared the country was for war, and they also refused to mobilize needed resources. The House rejected proposals for direct taxes and authorized naval appropriations only with the greatest reluctance. They did not seem to understand that a weak, highly decentralized government—the one that Jeffersonians championed—was incapable of waging an expensive war against the world's greatest sea power.

War of 1812 **War between Britain and the United States. U.S. justifications for war included British violations of American maritime rights, impressment of seamen, provocation of the Indians, and defense of national honor.**

New Englanders refused to cooperate with the war effort. Throughout the **War of 1812,** they carried on a lucrative, though illegal, commerce with the enemy. The British government apparently believed that the New England states might

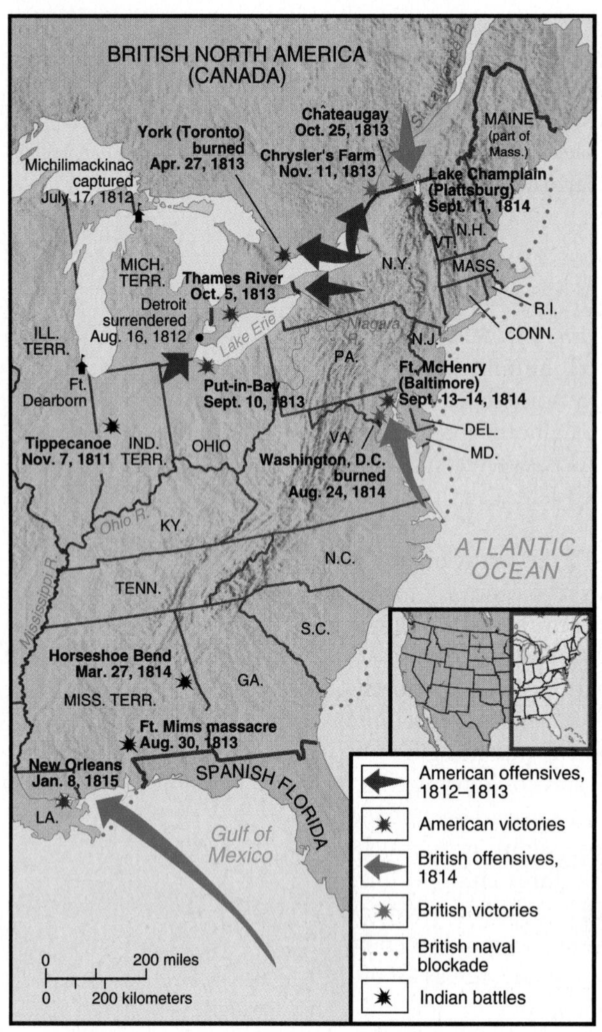

THE WAR OF 1812 *Major battles of the War of 1812 brought few lasting gains to either the British or the Americans.*

negotiate a separate peace, and during the first year of the war, the Royal Navy did not bother to blockade the major northern ports.

American military operations focused initially on the western forts, but the battles in the region demonstrated that the militia, no matter how enthusiastic, was no match for well-trained European veterans. American forces surrendered Detroit and Michilimackinac to the enemy, and poorly coordinated marches on Niagara and Montreal accomplished nothing. On the sea, the United States did much better. In August, Captain Isaac Hull's *Constitution* defeated HMS *Guerrière* in a fierce battle, and American privateers destroyed or captured a number of British merchantmen. These victories, however, indicate that Britain was more concerned with Napoleon than the United States. As soon as peace returned to Europe in the spring of 1814, Britain redeployed its fleet and easily blockaded the tiny U.S. Navy.

The campaigns of 1813 revealed that conquering Canada would be more difficult than the War Hawks ever imagined. Both sides in this war recognized that whoever controlled the Great Lakes controlled the West. On Lake Erie, the Americans won the race for naval superiority. Oliver Hazard Perry won an important naval battle at Put-in-Bay, and General Harrison overran an army of British troops and Indian warriors at the battle of Thames River. During this engagement, Tecumseh was killed. On the other fronts, however, the war went badly for the Americans.

In 1814, the British took the offensive. Following their victory over Napoleon, British strategists planned to increase pressure on three separate American fronts:

the Canadian frontier, Chesapeake coastal settlements, and New Orleans. In the Canadian theater, the British suffered a setback. The American victory off Plattsburg on Lake Champlain accelerated peace negotiations, for after news of the battle reached London, the British government concluded that major land operations along the Canadian border were futile.

Throughout the year, British warships harassed the Chesapeake coast. To their surprise, the British found the region almost totally undefended, and on August 24, 1814, a small force of British marines burned the nation's capital, a victory more symbolic than strategic. Encouraged by their easy success, the British launched a full-scale attack on Baltimore (September 14). To everyone's surprise, the fort guarding the harbor held out against a heavy bombardment, and the British gave up the operation. The survival of Fort McHenry inspired Francis Scott Key to write "The Star-Spangled Banner."

The battle of New Orleans should never have occurred: it took place after the diplomats in Europe had concluded their peace negotiations. But General Edward Pakenham, the commander of the British forces, was not aware of the negotiations, and on January 8, 1815, he foolishly ordered a frontal attack against General Andrew Jackson's well-defended positions. In a matter of hours, the entire British force had been destroyed. The victory not only transformed Jackson into a national folk hero but also provided the people of the United States with a much needed source of pride. Even in military terms, the battle was significant, for if the British had managed to occupy New Orleans, they would have been difficult to dislodge regardless of the specific provisions of the peace treaty.

Hartford Convention: The Demise of the Federalists

In the fall of 1814, a group of leading New England politicians, most of them moderate Federalists, gathered in Hartford to discuss relations between the people of their region and the federal government. The **Hartford Convention** delegates were angered and hurt by the Madison administration's seeming insensitivity to the economic interests of the New England states.

Hartford Convention An assembly of New England federalists who met in Hartford, Connecticut, in December 1814 to protest Madison's foreign policy in the War of 1812, which had undermined commercial interests in the North. They proposed amending the Constitution to prevent future presidents from declaring war without a two-thirds majority in Congress.

The men who met at Hartford on December 15 did not advocate secession from the Union. Although people living in other sections of the country cried treason, the convention delegates only recommended changes in the Constitution. Frustrated by the three-fifths clause that gave southern slaveholders a disproportionately large voice in the House, delegates proposed that congressional representation should be calculated on the basis of the number of white males living in a state. The convention also wanted to limit each president to a single term in office, a reform that New Englanders hoped might end Virginia's monopoly of the executive mansion. Finally, to protect their region from what they saw as the tyranny of southern Republicans, the delegates insisted that a two-thirds majority should be necessary before Congress could declare war, pass commercial regulations, or admit new states to the Union.

The convention's recommendations arrived in Washington at the same time as news of the battle of New Orleans. Republican leaders in Congress accused the hapless New Englanders of disloyalty, and people throughout the country were persuaded that a group of wild secessionists had attempted to destroy the Union. The Hartford Convention accelerated the demise of the Federalist party.

Treaty of Ghent Ends the War

In August 1814, the United States dispatched a distinguished negotiating team to Ghent, a Belgian city where the Americans opened talks with their British counterparts. During the early weeks of discussion, the British made impossible demands. They insisted on territorial concessions from the United States, the right to navigate

❖ A Look at the Past ❖

"We Owe Allegiance to No Crown"

Patriotic symbols abound in this print by John Archibald Woodside, Jr. Carrying a liberty cap on a pole, Miss Liberty crowns an American sailor with a laurel wreath, signifying that American liberty is victorious. The sentiment expressed visually and emphatically, "We Owe Allegiance to No Crown," seems appropriate for the revolutionary era, but in fact this print dates much later, to the early nineteenth century, when the War of 1812 sparked nationalism. What does this print suggest about American confidence at that time? Does it raise questions about United States–British relations following the American Revolution?

the Mississippi River, and the creation of a large Indian buffer state in the Northwest Territory. The Americans listened to the presentation, more or less politely, and then rejected the entire package. In turn, they lectured their British counterparts about maritime rights and impressments.

Fatigue finally broke the diplomatic deadlock. The British government realized that no amount of military force could significantly alter the outcome of hostilities in the United States. Weary negotiators signed the Treaty of Ghent on Christmas Eve in 1814. The document dealt with virtually none of the topics contained in Madison's original war message. Neither side surrendered territory; Great Britain

CHRONOLOGY	
1801	Thomas Jefferson is elected president ❖ Adams makes "midnight" appointments of federal judges (March)
1802	Judiciary Act is repealed (March)
1803	Chief Justice John Marshall rules on *Marbury* v. *Madison,* setting precedent for judicial review (February) ❖ Louisiana Purchase is concluded with France (May)
1804–1806	Lewis and Clark explore the Northwest
1804	Aaron Burr kills Alexander Hamilton in a duel (July) ❖ Jefferson is elected to a second term (November)
1805	Justice Samuel Chase is acquitted by the Senate (March)
1807	American warship *Chesapeake* is fired on by the British *Leopard* (June) ❖ Burr is tried for conspiracy (August–September) ❖ Embargo Act is passed (December)
1808	Slave trade is ended (January) ❖ Madison is elected president (November)
1809	Embargo is repealed; Non-Intercourse Act is passed (March)
1810	Macon's Bill Number Two reestablishes trade with Britain and France (May)
1811	Harrison defeats Indians at Tippecanoe (November)
1812	War is declared against Great Britain (June) ❖ Madison is elected to a second term, defeating De Witt Clinton of New York (November)
1813	Perry destroys the British fleet at Put-in-Bay (September) ❖ Harrison wins again at Thames River (October)
1814	Jackson crushes Creek Indians at Horseshoe Bend (March) ❖ British burn Washington, D.C. (August) ❖ Americans turn back the British at Plattsburg (September) ❖ Hartford Convention meets to recommend constitutional changes (December) ❖ Treaty of Ghent ends War of 1812 (December)
1815	Jackson routs the British at New Orleans (January)

refused even to discuss the topic of impressment. In fact, the treaty was simply an agreement to stop fighting. The Senate apparently concluded that stalemate was preferable to continued conflict and ratified the treaty 35 to 0.

Most Americans thought the War of 1812 an important success. Even though the country's military accomplishments had been unimpressive, the people of the United States had been swept up in a contagion of nationalism. For many Americans, this "second war of independence" reaffirmed their faith in themselves and the revolutionary experience.

Conclusion: Republican Legacy

A remarkable coincidence occurred on July 4, 1826, the fiftieth anniversary of the Declaration of Independence. On that day, Thomas Jefferson died at Monticello. His last words were, "Is it the Fourth?" On the same day several hundred miles to the north, John Adams also passed his last day on earth. His mind was on his old friend and sometime adversary, and during his final moments, Adams found comfort in the assurance that "Thomas Jefferson still survives." The political battles that occupied both men during their presidencies had already passed into history and were largely forgotten. But the spirit of the Declaration of Independence survived, and Jefferson's vision of a society in which "all men are created equal" challenged later Americans to make good on the promise of 1776.

Key Terms

Louisiana Purchase, p. 151
Lewis and Clark expedition, p. 152
Barbary War, p. 152
Marbury v. *Madison,* p. 153
Embargo Act, p. 157
War Hawks, p. 159
War of 1812, p. 159
Hartford Convention, p. 161

Recommended Reading

A challenge for historians of this period is explaining how Thomas Jefferson and his followers managed to reconcile Republican theories of government with the practical responsibilities of the presidency. The fullest account of his administration can be found in Merrill D. Peterson, *Thomas Jefferson and the New Nation: A Biography* (1970). Three more recent books examine Jefferson's complex character as well as the impact of Republican policies on the larger society: Peter S. Onuf, *Jeffersonian America* (2001); Joseph J. Ellis, *American Sphinx: The Character of Thomas Jefferson* (1997); and James Horn, et al., eds., *The Revolution of 1800: Democracy, Race, and the New Republic* (2002). The tensions that made this political culture so explosive are treated in Roger Sharp, *American Politics in the Early Republic: The New Nation in Crisis* (1993) and Bernard A. Weisberger, *America Afire: Jefferson, Adams, and the Revolutionary Election of 1800* (2000). The controversies over how best to interpret the Constitution and the politics of the Supreme Court are explored in Jean Edward Smith, *John Marshall: Definer of a Nation* (1996). Also valuable for understanding difficult legal issues are Richard E. Ellis, *The Jeffersonian Crisis: Courts and Politics in the Young Republic* (1971); Leonard W. Levy, *Emergence of a Free Press* (1985); and Morton J. Horowitz, *The Transformation of American Law, 1780–1860* (1977). The Louisiana Purchase is the subject of Alexander DeConde, *The Affair of Louisiana* (1976). On the Lewis and Clark Expedition, see James P. Ronda, *Lewis and Clark Among the Indians* (1984) and Donald Jackson, *Thomas Jefferson and the Stony Mountains: Exploring the West from Monticello* (1981). Several fine studies chronicle the politics of slavery and Jefferson's own problems with freeing African Americans; Henry Wiencek tells how Washington confronted the problem in *An Imperfect God: George Washington, His Slaves, and the Creation of America* (2003). On foreign relations, see Peter S. Onuf, ed., *America and the World: Diplomacy, Politics, and War* (1991); J. C. A. Stagg, *Mr. Madison's War: Politics, Diplomacy, and Warfare in the Early American Republic* (1983); James E. Lewis, Jr., *The American Union and the Problem of Neighborhood: The United States and the Collapse of the Spanish Empire, 1783–1829* (1998); and Paul Baepler, ed., *White Slaves, African Masters: An Anthology of American Barbary Captivity Narratives* (1999). Two splendid works demonstrate how Evangelical Protestantism shaped early nineteenth-century public culture: Nathan O. Hatch, *The Democratization of American Christianity* (1989) and Mark A. Noll, *America's God: From Jonathan Edwards to Abraham Lincoln* (2002).

For a list of additional titles related to this chapter's topics, please see http://www.ablongman.com/divine.

Suggested Web Sites

Thomas Jefferson

http://www.pbs.org/jefferson/

A companion site to the Public Broadcasting Service series on Jefferson, especially important because it contains a fine collection of other people's views of Jefferson.

White House Historical Association

http://www.whitehousehistory.org/

This site contains a timeline of the history of the White House and several interesting photos and links.

Thomas Jefferson Digital Archive at the University of Virginia

http://etext.virginia.edu/jefferson/

Mr. Jefferson's University—the University of Virginia—houses this site with numerous on-line resources about Jefferson and his times, including electronic versions of texts by Jefferson, a page of selected quotations, and a comprehensive annotated bibliography of works on Jefferson from 1826 to 1997.

Lewis and Clark: The Maps of Exploration 1507–1814

http://www.lib.virginia.edu/speccol/exhibits/lewisclark/home.html

Maps and charts reveal knowledge and conceptions about the known and the unknown. This site includes a number of eighteenth-century maps.

PBS Online—Lewis and Clark

http://www.pbs.org/lewisandclark/

This is a companion site to Ken Burns's documentary on Lewis and Clark containing a timeline of the expedition, a collection of related links, a bibliography, and more than eight hundred minutes of unedited, full-length RealPlayer interviews with seven experts featured in the film.

The War of 1812

http://members.tripod/com/~war1812/index.html

In-depth and varied information about the War of 1812.

Chapter 9

Nation Building and Nationalism

A Revolutionary War Hero Revisits America in 1824

When the Marquis de Lafayette returned to the United States in 1824, he marveled at how the country had changed in the more than forty years since he had served with George Washington. The country had grown remarkably, and steam-powered boats now united the various western outposts. Everywhere Lafayette was greeted with patriotic oratory celebrating the liberty, prosperity, and progress of the new nation. Always the diplomat, Lafayette told Americans what they wanted to hear. He hailed the "immense improvements" and "admirable communications" that he had witnessed and declared himself deeply moved by "all the grandeur and prosperity of these happy United States, which, at the same time they nobly seem the complete assertion of American independence, reflect on every part of the world the light of a far superior political civilization."

There were good reasons why Americans made Lafayette's return visit the occasion for patriotic celebration and reaffirmation. Free from foreign threats, America was growing rapidly in population, size, and wealth. Its republican form of government was apparently working well. In his first inaugural address, James Monroe had anticipated Lafayette's observations. It was a speech full of national self-satisfaction. "No country was ever happier with respect to its domain," Monroe said. As for the government itself, it was so near to perfection that "in respect to it we have no essential improvements to make."

Beneath the optimism and self-confidence, however, there were undercurrents of doubt and anxiety about the future. Almost all the Founders were dead. Could their example of republican virtue and self-sacrifice be maintained in an increasingly prosperous and materialistic society? Many Americans feared the answer. And what about the place of slavery in a "perfect" democratic republic? Lafayette himself wondered why the United States had not yet extended freedom and equality to the slaves.

But the peace following the War of 1812 did open the way for a great surge of nation building. Transportation improvements created new markets, and advances in the processing of raw materials led to the first stirrings of industrialization. Political leadership provided little active direction for the process of growth and expansion, but an active judiciary took up part of the slack in a series of decisions that served to promote economic development and assert the priority of national over state

Outline

Expansion and Migration

A Revolution in Transportation

Emergence of a Market Economy

The Politics of Nation Building After the War of 1812

Conclusion: The End of the Era of Good Feelings

and local interests. To guarantee the peace and security essential for internal progress, statesmen proclaimed a foreign policy designed to insulate America from external involvements. A new nation of great potential wealth and power was emerging.

Expansion and Migration

The new peaceful relations with Great Britain in 1815 allowed the American people to shift their attention from Europe and the Atlantic to the vast lands of North America that lay before them. Two treaties negotiated with Great Britain dealt with northern borders. The Rush-Bagot Agreement (1817) limited U.S. and British naval forces on the Great Lakes and Lake Champlain and guaranteed that the British would never try to invade the United States from Canada and that the United States would never try to take Canada from the British. The Anglo-American Convention of 1818 set the border between the lands of the Louisiana Purchase and Canada at the 49th parallel and provided for joint U.S. and British occupation of Oregon.

Between the Appalachians and the Mississippi, settlement already had begun, especially in the new states of Ohio, Kentucky, and Tennessee. In the lower Mississippi Valley, the former French colony of Louisiana had been admitted as a state in 1812, and a thriving settlement existed around Natchez in the Mississippi Territory. Elsewhere in the trans-Appalachian west, white settlement was sparse and much land remained in Indian hands. Diplomacy, military action (or at least the threat of it), and massive westward migration and settlement were needed before the continent would yield up its wealth to its white inhabitants.

Extending the Boundaries

The first goal of postwar expansionists was to obtain Florida from Spain. In the eyes of the Spanish, their possession extended along the Gulf Coast to the Mississippi, but in 1812, the United States had annexed the area between the Mississippi and Perdido Rivers in what became Alabama. The remainder, known as East Florida, became the prime object of territorial ambition for President James Monroe and his energetic secretary of state, John Quincy Adams. Spanish claims west and east of the Mississippi blocked Adams's grand design for continental expansion.

General Andrew Jackson provided Adams with an opportunity to acquire the land. In 1816, United States troops touched off a conflict when they went into East Florida in pursuit of hostile Seminole Indians and the fugitive slaves that they were harboring. In April and May 1818, Jackson exceeded his official orders and occupied East Florida. In addition, he court-martialed and executed two British subjects whom he accused of being enemy agents. Although his actions were widely criticized by government officials, no disciplinary action was taken.

Secretary Adams informed the Spanish government that the United States had acted in self-defense and that further conflict could be avoided only if East Florida was ceded to the United States. Weakened by Latin American revolutions and liberation movements, Spain was in no position to resist American bullying. Spanish minister Luis de Onís acceded. In addition to relinquishing Florida, de Onís agreed to a dividing line between Spanish and American territory that ran all the way to the Pacific, thus giving up Spain's claim to Pacific coastal areas north of California and opening a path for future American expansion. These understandings were formalized in the **Adams-Onís Treaty** (1819), also known as the Transcontinental Treaty. Great Britain and Russia still had competing claims to the Pacific Northwest, but the United States was now poised to acquire some frontage on a second ocean. Secretary Adams described the agreement on a definite boundary to the Pacific as "forming a great epoch in our history."

Adams-Onís Treaty Signed by Secretary of State John Quincy Adams and Spanish minister Luis de Onís in 1819, this treaty allowed for American annexation of Florida.

Interest in exploitation of the Far West continued to grow between 1810 and 1830. In 1811, a New York merchant, John Jacob Astor, founded the fur-trading post

NORTH AMERICA, 1819 *Treaties with Britain following the War of 1812 setting the border between the United States and Canada (British North America) made this border the longest unfortified boundary line in the world.* ❖

of Astoria at the mouth of the Columbia River in the Oregon country. In the 1820s and 1830s, fur traders operating out of St. Louis worked their way up the Missouri to the northern Rockies and beyond. First they limited themselves to trading for furs with the Indians, but eventually the "mountain men" went after game on their own and sold the furs to agents of the Rocky Mountain Fur Company at an annual meeting or "rendezvous."

These colorful characters, who included such legendary figures as Jedediah Smith, Jim Bridger, Kit Carson, and Jim Beckwourth, accomplished prodigious feats of survival under harsh natural conditions. Although they actually depleted the animal resources on which the Indians depended, the mountain men projected an image of being part of their environment rather than destroyers of it. To later generations, they typified a romantic ideal of lonely self-reliance in harmony with unspoiled nature.

The reports of military expeditions provided better information about the Far West than the tales of the mountain men, most of whom were illiterate. The most notable of the postwar expeditions was mounted by Major Stephen S. Long in 1819–1820. Long mapped some of the rivers of the Great Plains and endorsed the somewhat misleading view that the plains beyond the Missouri were a "great American desert" unfit for cultivation or settlement. The real focus of attention between 1815 and the 1840s, therefore, was the nearer West, the rich agricultural lands between the Appalachians and the Mississippi that were being opened up for settlement.

Settlement to the Mississippi

Complete occupation and exploitation of the trans-Appalachian interior required displacing the many Indian communities still inhabiting that region in 1815. In the Ohio Valley and the Northwest Territory, the Indians had already been defeated. Consigned by treaty to reservations outside the main lines of white advance, most of the tribes were eventually forced west of the Mississippi. In 1831–1832, a faction of the confederated Sac and Fox Indians under Chief Black Hawk attempted to reoccupy lands east of the Mississippi previously ceded by another tribal faction. Federal troops and Illinois state militia routed the Indians. It was the last stand of the woodland Indians of the Midwest.

Uprooting the once populous Indian communities of the Old Northwest was part of a national program for removing Indians of the eastern part of the country to an area beyond the Mississippi. Not everyone agreed with Thomas Jefferson's belief that Indians, unlike blacks, had the natural ability to adopt white ways and become useful citizens of the republic. People living on the frontier who coveted Indian land and risked violent retaliation for trying to take it, were more likely to think of Native Americans as irredeemable savages, or even as vermin to be exterminated if necessary. Whites also believed that Indians impeded "progress." Furthermore, Indians held land communally and not in private parcels; white settlers regarded this practice as an insuperable obstacle to economic development. During the Monroe era, it became clear that white settlers wanted the removal of all Indians. The issue was particularly pressing in the South, where greed combined with racism to doom the Indian tribes.

In the South, as in the Old Northwest, a series of treaties negotiated between 1815 and 1830 reduced tribal holdings and provided for the eventual removal of most Indians to the trans-Mississippi West. Not all tribes left quietly. The so-called five civilized tribes—the Cherokee, Creek, Seminole, Choctaw, and Chickasaw—had become settled agriculturists, and they owned good land in the South. Pressure continued to mount. When deception, bribery, and threats by the federal government failed to induce land cessions, state governments took matters into their own hands. The stage was thus set for the forced removal of the five civilized tribes to Oklahoma during the 1830s. (For further discussion of the Indian removal, see Chapter 10.)

While the Indians were being driven beyond the Mississippi, settlers poured into the agricultural heartland of the United States. This movement was the most dramatic and significant phase of the great westward expansion of population and settlement that began in the early colonial period and lasted until the 1880s. In 1810, only about one-seventh of the American population lived beyond the Appalachians; by 1840, more than one-third did. Eight new states were added to the Union during this period. The government took care of Indian removal, but the settlers faced the difficult task of gaining a livelihood from the land.

Much of the vast acreage opened up by the western movement passed through the hands of land speculators before it reached those of the farmers and planters. After a financial panic in 1819 brought ruin to many who had purchased tracts on credit, the minimum price was lowered from $2.00 to $1.25 an acre, but full payment was required in cash. This change favored wealthy speculators, who bought land in massive quantities.

Eventually, most of the land did find its way into the hands of actual cultivators. In some areas, squatters arrived before the official survey and formed claims associations that policed land auctions to prevent "outsiders" from bidding up the price and buying their farms out from under them. Squatters also insisted that they

View of the Great Treaty Held at Prairie du Chien *(1825). Representatives of eight Native American tribes met with government agents at Prairie du Chien, Wisconsin, in 1825 to define the boundaries of their respective land claims. The United States claimed the right to make "an amicable and final adjustment" of the claims. Within twenty-five years, most of the tribes present at Prairie du Chien had ceded their land to the U.S. government.* ❖

had the right to buy the land that they had already improved at the minimum price, a program called "preemption." In 1841, Congress formally acknowledged the right to farm on public lands with assurance of a *future* preemption right.

Settlers who arrived after speculators had secured title had to deal with land barons. Fortunately for the settlers, most speculators operated on credit and were forced to obtain a quick return on their investment. They did this by selling land at a profit to settlers who had some capital and by arranging finance plans for tenants who did not. Thus the family farm or owner-operated plantation quickly became the typical unit of western agriculture.

Since debt was common in the West, most farmers found it necessary to do more than simply raise enough food to subsist; they had to produce something for market. Most of the earliest settlement was along rivers, which provided cheap transportation. But even in more remote areas, farmers managed to get their corn, wheat, cotton, or cured meat to market. To meet the needs of the farmers, local marketing centers quickly sprang up, usually at river junctions. Cities emerged seemingly overnight, and they in turn accelerated regional development.

The People and Culture of the Frontier

Most of the hundreds of thousands of settlers who populated the West were farmers from the seaboard states. They migrated for all sorts of reasons, but prominent among them were overpopulation, rising land prices, and declining fertility of the soil in the older regions. Most moved as family units and tried to recreate their former way of life as soon as possible. Women were often reluctant to migrate in the first place, and when they arrived in new areas, they strove valiantly to recapture the comfort and stability that they had left behind.

New Englanders carried with them their churches, schools, notions of community uplift, and Puritan ideals of hard work and self-denial. Similarly, settlers from

Virginia and the Carolinas retained their devotion to family honor, personal independence, and ideas of white supremacy. In the West, differences between the North and South soon emerged.

In general, the pioneers sought out the kind of terrain and soil with which they were already familiar. People from the eastern uplands favored the hill country of the West. Piedmont and tidewater farmers and planters usually made for the lower and flatter areas. Both groups avoided the fertile but unfamiliar prairies. Rather than being the bold and deliberate innovators of myth, the typical agricultural pioneers were deeply averse to changing their traditional habits.

Yet some adjustments were necessary simply to survive under frontier conditions. Initially, at least, an isolated homestead required a high degree of self-sufficiency. The settlers built their own homes and raised their own crops; they made their own clothes and manufactured their own household necessities, such as soap and candles.

But this picture of frontier self-reliance is not the whole story. Most settlers in fact found it extremely difficult to accomplish all the tasks using only family labor. A more common practice was the sharing of work by a number of pioneer families. Assembling the neighbors to raise a house, harvest wheat, or sew quilts helped turn collective work into rare festive occasions. The jug was passed, and various contests sped the work along. Sharing the work was a creative response to the shortage of labor that also provided a source for communal solidarity. These events probably tell us more about the "spirit of the frontier" than the conventional image of the pioneer as a lonely individualist.

Restlessness and geographic mobility also characterized many of the settlers. The wandering of young Abraham Lincoln's family from Kentucky to Indiana and finally to Illinois between 1816 and 1830 was fairly typical. Improved land could be sold at a profit and the proceeds used to buy new acreage beyond the horizon where the soil was reportedly richer. Hence few early-nineteenth-century American farmers developed the kind of attachment to the land that is often associated with rural populations in other parts of the world.

A Revolution in Transportation

It took more than the spread of settlement to bring prosperity to new areas and ensure that they would identify with older regions or with the country as a whole. Along the eastern seaboard, land transportation was so primitive that in 1813 it took seventy-five days for one wagon of goods drawn by four horses to make a trip of 1,000 miles, and traveling west over the mountains meant months on the trail.

After the War of 1812, political leaders realized that national security, economic progress, and political unity were all more or less dependent on binding the nation together through a greatly improved transportation network. Accordingly, President Monroe called for a federally supported program of "internal improvements" in 1815. In the ensuing decades, the nationalist's vision of a transportation revolution was realized to a considerable extent, although the direct role of the federal government turned out to be less important than anticipated.

Roads and Steamboats

Americans who wanted to get from place to place rapidly and cheaply needed new and improved roads. The first great federal transportation project was the building between 1811 and 1818 of the National Road between Cumberland, Maryland, on the Potomac, and Wheeling, Virginia, on the Ohio. This impressive, gravel-surfaced toll road was subsequently extended and reached Vandalia, Illinois, in 1838. Soon state governments promoted the building of other "turnpikes," as these privately owned toll roads chartered by the states were called. By about 1825, thousands of miles of turnpikes crisscrossed southern New England, upstate New York, much of Pennsylvania, and northern New Jersey.

But the toll roads benefited travelers more than they did transporters of bulky freight. The latter usually found that total expenses—toll plus the cost and maintenance of heavy wagons and great teams of horses—were too high to guarantee a satisfactory profit from haulage. Hence traffic was less than anticipated, and investors were disappointed with returns. In the final analysis, turnpikes failed to link up the settled seaboard areas with the new West. What was desperately needed was a form of transportation that could inexpensively haul freight over long distances.

The fact that the United States had a great natural transportation system in its river network was one of the most significant reasons for the country's rapid economic development. The Ohio-Mississippi system in particular provided ready access to the rich agricultural areas of the interior and a natural outlet for their products. By 1815, flatboats loaded with wheat, flour, salt pork, and cotton were floating toward New Orleans. Even after the coming of the steamboat, flatboats continued to carry a major share of the downriver trade.

But the flatboat trade was necessarily a one-way traffic. A farmer from Ohio or Illinois, or someone hired to do the job, could float down to New Orleans easily enough, but there was generally no way to get back except by walking overland through rough country. Until the problem of upriver navigation was solved, the Ohio and Mississippi could not carry the manufactured goods that farmers desired in exchange for their crops.

Fortunately, a solution was readily at hand—the use of steam power for river transportation. Inventor Robert Fulton improved on an idea that many men had toyed with for years. In 1807, he successfully propelled the *Clermont* 150 miles up the Hudson River. The first steamboat launched in the West was the *New Orleans,* which made the trip from Pittsburgh to New Orleans in 1811–1812. The steamboat revolutionized the commerce of the West. By 1820, sixty-nine steamboats with a total capacity of 13,890 tons were plying western waters.

Steam transport was a great boon for farmers and merchants. It reduced costs, increased the speed of moving goods and people, and allowed two-way commerce on the Mississippi and Ohio Rivers. Eastern manufacturers and merchants were now much more firmly linked to the interior markets.

The steamboat quickly captured the American imagination. The great paddle wheelers became luxurious floating hotels, the natural habitats of gamblers and confidence men. But the boats also had a lamentable safety record, frequently running aground, colliding, or blowing up. As a result of such accidents, the federal government began in 1838 to regulate steamboats and monitor their construction and operation. This legislation stands as the only instance in the pre–Civil War period of direct federal regulation of domestic transportation.

The Canal Boom

A transportation system based solely on rivers and roads had one enormous gap—it did not provide an economical way to ship western farm produce directly east to the growing urban market of the seaboard states. The solution offered by the politicians and merchants of the Middle Atlantic and midwestern states was to build a system of canals to link seaboard cities directly to the Great Lakes, the Ohio, and ultimately the Mississippi.

The best natural location for a canal between a river flowing into the Atlantic and one of the Great Lakes was between Albany and Buffalo, a relatively flat stretch of more than 350 miles. When the New York legislature approved the bold project in 1817, no more than about 100 miles of canal existed in the entire United States. Credit for the enterprise belongs to New York's governor, De Witt Clinton, who

Illustration of a lock on the Erie Canal at Lockport, New York, 1838. The successful canal facilitated trade by linking the Great Lakes regions to the eastern seaports. ❖

convinced the state legislature that the project could be successfully financed by issuing bonds. In 1825, the completed canal was opened, to great public acclaim.

Some 364 miles long, 40 feet wide, and 4 feet deep, and containing 84 locks, the Erie Canal was the most spectacular engineering achievement of the young republic. Furthermore, it was a great economic success. It reduced the cost of moving goods from Buffalo to Albany to one-twelfth the previous rate. Easterners and Westerners could now buy each other's goods at sharply reduced prices. The canal also helped make New York City the unchallenged commercial capital of the nation.

The great success of the Erie Canal inspired other states to extend public credit for canal building. Between 1826 and 1834, Pennsylvania constructed an even longer and more elaborate canal, spanning the 395 miles from Philadelphia to Pittsburgh. But the Pennsylvania Main Line Canal did not do as well as the Erie, partly because of the bottleneck that developed at the crest of the Alleghenies, where canal boats had to be hauled over a high ridge on an inclined-plane railroad. Other states followed suit, and soon the nation's rivers and lakes were linked by an elaborate canal network.

The canal boom ended when it became apparent in the 1830s and 1840s that most of these waterways were unprofitable. State credit had been overextended, and the panic and depression of the late 1830s and early 1840s forced retrenchment. Moreover, by this time, railroads were beginning to compete successfully for the same traffic, and a new phase in the transportation revolution was beginning.

But canals should not be written off as economic failures that contributed little to the improvement of transportation. Some of them continued to be important arteries up to the time of the Civil War and even beyond. Furthermore, the failure of many of the canals was due solely to their inability to yield an adequate return on the money invested in them. The problem of financing tells little or nothing about their public usefulness. Had the canals been thought of as providing a service rather than yielding a profit—in the manner of modern interstate highways—they might have maintained a high reputation for serving the economic interests of the nation. As it was, they contributed enormously to creating vital economic ties between the agricultural West and the industrializing Northeast.

Emergence of a Market Economy

The desire to reduce the costs and increase the speed of shipping heavy freight over great distances laid the groundwork for a new economic system. With the advent of steamboats and canals, western farmers could inexpensively ship their crops both to the Northeast and New Orleans. This improved transport led to an increase in farm income and provided a stimulus for commercial agriculture.

The Beginning of Commercial Agriculture

At the beginning of the nineteenth century, the typical farming household consumed most of what it produced and sold only a small surplus in nearby markets. Most manufactured articles were produced at home. Easier and cheaper access to distant markets effected a decisive change in this pattern. Between 1800 and 1840, agricultural output increased remarkably. The rise in productivity was partly due to technological advances. Iron or steel plows proved better than wooden ones, the grain cradle replaced the scythe, and better varieties of crops, grasses, and livestock were introduced. But the availability of good land and a revolution in marketing were the most important spurs to profitable commercial farming. Transportation facilities made distant markets available and plugged farmers into a commercial network that provided credit and relieved them of the need to do their own selling.

The emerging exchange network encouraged movement away from diversified farming toward a regional concentration on staple crops. Wheat was the main cash crop in the North, and the center of its cultivation moved westward as soil depletion, pests, and plant disease lowered yields in older regions. On the rocky hillsides of New England, sheep raising was displacing the mixed farming of an earlier era. But the prime example of successful staple production in this era was the rise of the cotton kingdom in the South.

A number of factors made the South the world's greatest producer of cotton. First was the great demand generated by the rise of textile manufacturing in England and, to a lesser extent, in New England. Second was the effect of the cotton gin in processing. Invented by Eli Whitney in 1793, this simple device cut the labor costs involved in cleaning short-staple cotton. Third was the availability of good land in the Southeast. Similar to the movement of the center of wheat cultivation in the North, the center of cotton growing moved steadily westward from South Carolina and Georgia, primarily, toward the fertile plantation areas of Alabama, Mississippi, and Louisiana.

❖ A Look at the Past ❖

Merino Sheep

Increasing commercialism and industrialism affected both urban and rural dwellers during the early nineteenth century. Farmers could choose to participate in the changing economy in several ways. Supplying factories with raw materials and workers with food numbered among their options. Successful agriculture required farmers to alter their strategies. Some farmers intensified production, experimented with scientific methods, increased their herd sizes, and imported improved livestock breeds such as these very woolly merino sheep. Importing livestock, breeding improved varieties, and increasing production required money. What kind of a risk did a farmer take by enthusiastically producing for factories? What do the changes farmers made reveal about economic attitudes?

A fourth factor—the existence of slavery, which provided a flexible system of forced labor—permitted operations on a scale impossible for the family labor system of the agricultural North. Finally, the cotton economy benefited from the South's splendid natural transportation system, its great network of navigable rivers. The South had less need than other agricultural regions for artificial "internal improvements" such as canals and roads. Planters could simply establish themselves on or near a river and ship their crops to market via natural waterways.

Commerce and Banking

As regions specialized in the growing of commercial crops, a new system of marketing emerged. During an early or pioneer stage in many areas, farmers did their marketing personally. With the growth of country towns, local merchants took over the crop near the source, bartering clothing and other manufactured goods for produce. These intermediaries shipped the farmers' crops to larger local markets such as Pittsburgh, Cincinnati, and St. Louis. Cotton growers in the South were more likely to deal directly with factors (agents) in the port cities from which their crop was exported. But even in the South, intermediaries existed in inland towns such as Macon, Nashville, and Shreveport.

The extension of credit was a crucial element in the whole system. Farmers borrowed from local merchants, who received an advance of their own when they consigned the crop to a commission house or factor. The commission agents relied on credit from merchants or manufacturers at the ultimate destination, which might be Liverpool or New York City. The need for credit encouraged the growth of money and banking.

Before the revolutions in transportation and marketing, small-scale local economies could survive to a considerable extent on barter. But long-distance transactions involving credit and deferred payment required money and lots of it. Although the Constitution authorized only the federal government to issue money, in the early to mid-nineteenth century, the government printed no paper money and produced gold and silver coins in such inappreciable quantities that it utterly failed to meet the expanding economy's requirement for a circulating currency.

Private or state banking institutions filled the void by issuing banknotes, promises to redeem their paper in *specie*—gold or silver—at the bearer's request. The demand for money and credit during the economic boom after 1815 led to a vast increase in the number of state banks—from 88 to 208 in two years. The resulting flood of state banknotes caused this form of currency to depreciate well below its face value and threatened a runaway inflation. In an effort to stabilize the currency, Congress established a second Bank of the United States in 1816.

The Bank was expected to serve as a check on the state banks by forcing them to resume specie payments. But it did not perform this task well in its early years. In fact, its own free-lending policies contributed to an overextension of credit that led to financial panic and depression in 1819. As a result, hostility to banks became a prominent feature of American politics.

Early Industrialism

The growth of the market economy also created new opportunities for industrialists. In 1815, most manufacturing in the United States was still carried on in households, in the workshops of skilled artisans, or in small mills. The factory form of production, in which supervised workers operated or tended machines under one roof, was rare. Even in the American textile industry, most of the spinning of thread and weaving, cutting, and sewing of cloth was still done in the home.

Most of the clothing worn by Americans was made entirely by female family members. But a growing proportion was produced for market, rather than direct home consumption. Under the "putting-out system" of manufacturing, merchant capitalists provided raw material to people in their own homes, picked up the finished or semifinished products, paid the workers, and took charge of distribution. The putting-out system was centered in the Northeast, and besides textiles, such items as shoes and hats were made in this manner.

Articles that required greater skill were made primarily by artisans working in small shops in towns. But in the decades after 1815, the merchants who purchased from these workers gained greater control over production. Shops expanded in size, masters tended to become entrepreneurs rather than working artisans, and journeymen often became wage earners rather than aspiring masters. At the same time, the growing market for low-priced goods led to a stress on speed, quantity, and standardization of the methods of production.

Lowell, Massachusetts, became America's model industrial town in the first half of the nineteenth century. Textile mills sprang up throughout Lowell in the 1820s and 1830s, employing thousands of workers, mostly women. Workers are shown holding shuttles they used in their work at the looms. ❖

A fully developed factory system emerged first in textile manufacturing. The establishment of the first cotton mills that used the power loom as well as spinning machinery—thereby making it possible to turn fiber into cloth in a single factory—resulted from the efforts of a trio of Boston merchants, Francis Cabot Lowell, Nathan Appleton, and Patrick Tracy Jackson.

As the Boston Manufacturing Company, the associates began their operation in Waltham, Massachusetts, in 1813. Their phenomenal success led to the erection of larger and even more profitable mills. The mill at nearby Lowell became a great showplace for early American industrialization. Its large and seemingly contented workforce of unmarried women residing in supervised dormitories, its unprecedented scale of operation, its successful mechanization of almost every stage of production—all captured the American middle-class imagination in the 1820s and 1830s. But in the late 1830s and 1840s conditions in the mills changed for the worse as the owners began to require more work for lower pay, and some of the "mill girls" became militant labor activists. Other mills using similar methods sprang up throughout New England, and the region became the first important manufacturing area in the United States.

The shift away from the putting-out system to factory production changed the course of capitalistic activity in the region. Before the 1820s, New England merchants concentrated mainly on international trade. A major source of capital was the lucrative China trade carried on by fast, well-built New England vessels. When the success of Waltham and Lowell became clear, many merchants shifted their capital away from oceanic trade and into manufacturing. Politically, this change meant that representatives from New England no longer advocated a low tariff that favored exporters over importers. They now became leading proponents of a high duty rate designed to protect manufacturers from foreign competition.

The development of other "infant industries" in the wake of the War of 1812 was less dramatic and would not come to fruition until the 1840s and 1850s. But the first stirrings of an iron industry and a small arms industry were felt during this period. And although most manufacturing was centered in the Northeast, the West also made modest industrial progress as the number and size of facilities such as gristmills, slaughterhouses, and tanneries increased. Distilleries in Kentucky and Ohio were particularly active.

It should not be assumed, however, that America had already experienced an industrial revolution by 1840. Most of the nation's labor force was still employed in agriculture; fewer than one of every ten workers was directly involved in factory production. The revolution that did occur during these years was essentially one of distribution rather than production. The growth of a market economy of national scope was the principal economic development of this period. And it was one that had vast repercussions for all aspects of American life.

For those who benefited from it most directly, the market economy provided firm evidence of progress and improvement. But many of those who suffered from its periodic panics and depressions were receptive to politicians and reformers who attacked corporations and "the money power."

The Politics of Nation Building After the War of 1812

Geographic expansion, economic growth, and the changes in American life that accompanied them were bound in the long run to generate political controversy. Federal and state policies meant to encourage or control growth and expansion did not benefit farmers, merchants, manufacturers, and laborers equally. Conflicts inevitably arose. Northerners, Southerners, and Westerners were affected in different ways, too. But the temporary lack of a party system meant that politicians did not have to band together and offer the voters a choice of programs and ideologies. A myth of national harmony prevailed, culminating in the **Era of Good Feelings** during James Monroe's two terms as president.

Era of Good Feelings A descriptive term for the era of President James Monroe, who served two terms from 1817–1823. During Monroe's administration, partisan conflict abated and bold federal initiatives suggested increased nationalism.

Behind the facade, individuals and groups fought for advantage, as always, but without the public accountability and need for broad popular approval that a party system would have required. As a result, popular interest in national politics fell to a low ebb.

The absence of party discipline and programs did not completely immobilize the federal government. The president took important initiatives in foreign policy, Congress legislated on matters of national concern, and the Supreme Court made far-reaching decisions. The common theme of the public policies that emerged between the War of 1812 and the Age of Jackson was an awakening nationalism—a sense of American pride and purpose that reflected the events of the period.

The Republicans in Power

By the end of the War of 1812, the Federalist party was no longer a significant force in national politics, although the Republicans had adopted some of their rivals' policies. Retreating from their original philosophy of states' rights and limited government, Republican party leaders now openly embraced a national bank, a protective tariff for industry, and a program of federally financed internal improvements.

In Congress, Henry Clay of Kentucky took the lead in advocating that the government take action to promote economic development. The keystone of what Clay called the **American system** was a high protective tariff to stimulate industrial growth and provide a "home market" for the farmers of the West, making the nation economically self-sufficient and free from a dangerous dependence on Europe.

American system A national economic strategy championed by Kentucky Senator Henry Clay, the American system stressed high tariffs and internal improvements.

In 1816, Congress took the first step toward Clay's goal by passing a tariff that raised import duties an average of 20 percent. The tariff was passed to protect American industry from British competition and received patriotic support in all sections of the country. Americans viewed the act as a move toward economic independence, a necessity to protect political independence.

Later the same year, Congress voted to establish the second Bank of the United States. Organized much like the first Bank, it was a mixed public-private institution. The Bank served the government by providing a depository for its funds, an outlet for marketing its securities, and a source of redeemable banknotes that could be used for the payment of taxes or the purchase of public lands. State banking interests and strict constructionists opposed the bank bill, but the majority of Congress found it a necessary and proper means for promoting financial stability and meeting the federal government's constitutional responsibility to raise money from taxation and loans.

Legislation dealing with internal improvements made less headway. Except for the National Road, the federal government undertook no major transportation projects during the Madison and Monroe administrations. Both presidents believed that internal improvements were desirable but that a constitutional amendment was required before federal monies could legally be used for the building of roads and canals within individual states. Both men vetoed internal improvement bills. Consequently, public aid for the building of roads and canals continued to come almost exclusively from state and local governments.

Monroe as President

Like Jefferson before him, President Madison chose his own successor in 1816. James Monroe thus became the third successive Virginian to occupy the White House for two full terms. Experienced but stolid and unimaginative, he lacked the intellectual depth and agility of his predecessors, but he was reliable, dignified, and high-principled.

The keynote of Monroe's presidency was national harmony, which meant that he went out of his way to avoid controversy. Indeed, one newspaper writer announced that party strife was a thing of the past and that an "era of good feelings" had begun. The principal aim of Monroe's administrations was to see that the good feelings persisted. He wanted to end all sectional and economic differences and assert American power and influence on the world stage. His choice of a cabinet was well calculated to serve these purposes. His secretary of state, John Quincy Adams, was not only a diplomat of great experience and skill but also a New Englander. If recent precedent was to be followed, he would succeed Monroe as president and thus end the "Virginia dynasty." As secretary of war, Monroe chose John C. Calhoun, a leading Southerner who was at this time a fervent nationalist. To accommodate the old-line states' rights wing of the party, he appointed William C. Crawford of Georgia as secretary of the treasury.

The first challenge to Monroe's hopes for domestic peace and prosperity was the Panic of 1819, which ended the postwar boom. After a period of rampant inflation, easy credit, and massive land speculation, the Bank of the United States called in loans and demanded the immediate redemption in specie of the state banknotes in its possession. This retrenchment brought a drastic downturn in the economy, as prices fell sharply, businesses failed, and banks repossessed land bought on credit.

Congress responded slowly and weakly to the economic crisis. Monroe himself refused to exert strong leadership. He was able to remain above the fray and persuade the American public that he was in no way responsible for the state of the economy, nor was he in a position to do anything about it. Unlike a modern president, Monroe could retain his full popularity during hard times.

Monroe prized national harmony even more than economic prosperity. But during his first administration, a bitter controversy developed between the North and the South over the admission of Missouri to the Union. Once again, Monroe remained above the battle and suffered little damage to his own prestige. It was left entirely to Congress to deal with the nation's most serious domestic political crisis between the War of 1812 and the late 1840s.

The Missouri Compromise

In 1817, the Missouri territorial assembly applied for statehood. It was clear that Missouri expected to be admitted to the Union as a slave state. Since Missouri was the first state other than Louisiana to be carved out of the Louisiana Purchase, the resolution of the status of slaves there would have implications for the rest of the trans-Mississippi West.

When the question came before Congress in early 1819, submerged sectional fears and anxieties came bubbling to the surface. Many Northerners resented southern control of the presidency and the three-fifths clause of the Constitution. Southerners feared for the future of what they regarded as a necessary balance of power between the sections. Up until 1819, strict equality had been maintained by alternately admitting slave and free states. Because the North had a decisive majority in the House of Representatives, the South saw its equal vote in the Senate as essential to preserving the balance.

In February 1819, Congressman James Tallmadge of New York introduced an amendment to the statehood bill banning further introduction of slaves into Missouri and providing for the gradual emancipation of those already there. The amendment was approved by the House but voted down by the Senate. The issue remained unresolved until a new Congress convened in December 1819. In the meantime, the measure elicited hot debate. Southern senators saw the Tallmadge amendment as an attack on the principle of equality between the states—a northern ploy to upset the balance of power. They also were concerned about the future of African American slavery and the white racial privilege that went with it.

A separate statehood petition from the people of Maine suggested a way out of the impasse. In February 1820, the Senate passed the **Missouri Compromise,** voting to couple the admission of Missouri as a slave state with the admission of Maine as a free state. A further amendment was also passed prohibiting slavery in the rest of the Louisiana Purchase north of the southern border of Missouri, or above the latitude of 36°30'. The Senate's compromise then went back to the House where Henry Clay, who broke the proposal into three separate bills, adroitly maneuvered it through to narrow victory.

Missouri Compromise A sectional compromise in Congress in 1820 that admitted Missouri to the Union as a slave state and Maine as a free state. It also banned slavery in the remainder of the Louisiana Purchase territory above the latitude of 36°30'.

A major sectional crisis had been resolved. But the Missouri affair had ominous overtones for the future of North-South relations. Thomas Jefferson described the

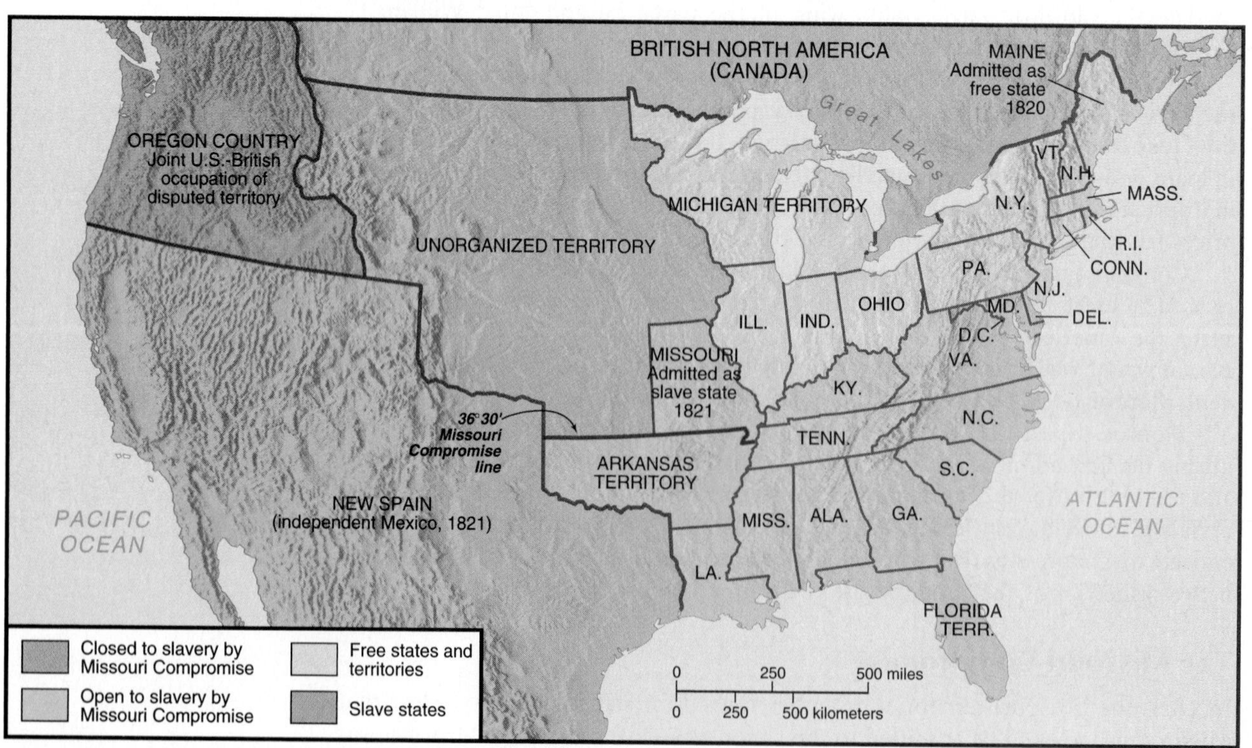

THE MISSOURI COMPROMISE, 1820–1821 *The Missouri Compromise kept the balance of power in the Senate by admitting Missouri as a slave state and Maine as a free state. The agreement temporarily settled the argument over slavery in the territories.*

controversy as "a fire bell in the night," threatening the peace of the Union. Clearly, the subject of slavery or its extension aroused deep sectional feeling. Emotional rhetoric about morality and fundamental rights issued from both sides. If the United States were to acquire any new territories in which the status of slavery had to be determined by Congress, renewed sectional strife would be inevitable.

Postwar Nationalism and the Supreme Court

While the Monroe administration was proclaiming national harmony and congressional leaders were struggling to reconcile sectional differences, the Supreme Court was making a more substantial and enduring contribution to the growth of nationalism and a strong federal government, thanks to Chief Justice John Marshall. A Virginian, a Federalist, and a devoted disciple of George Washington, Marshall served as chief justice from 1801 to 1835, and during that entire period, he dominated the Court as no other chief justice has ever done.

As the author of most of the major opinions issued by the Supreme Court during its formative period, Marshall gave shape to the Constitution and clarified the crucial role of the Court in the American system of government. He placed the protection of individual liberty, especially the right to acquire property, above the attainment of political, social, and economic equality. Ultimately he was a nationalist, believing that the strength, security, and happiness of the American people depended mainly on economic growth and the creation of new wealth. As he saw it, the Constitution existed to provide the political ground rules for a society of industrious and productive individuals who could enrich themselves while adding to the strength of the nation as a whole.

The role of the Supreme Court, in Marshall's view, was to interpret and enforce the ground rules, especially against the efforts of state legislatures to interfere with the constitutionally protected rights of individuals or combinations of individuals to acquire property through productive activity. The Court also permitted the federal government to assume broad powers so that it could fulfill its constitutional responsibility to promote the general welfare by encouraging economic development and national prosperity.

In a series of major decisions between 1819 and 1824, the Marshall Court enhanced the power of the judicial branch and used the contract clause of the Constitution (which prohibited a state from passing a law "impairing the obligations of contacts") to limit the power of state legislatures. It also strengthened the federal government by sanctioning a broad or loose construction of its constitutional powers and by clearly affirming its supremacy over the states.

In ***Dartmouth College* v. *Woodward*** (1819), the Marshall Court made the far-reaching determination that any charter granted by a state to a private corporation was fully protected by the contract clause. In practical terms, the Court's ruling in the Dartmouth case meant that the kinds of business enterprises then being incorporated by state governments—such as turnpike or canal companies and textile manufacturing firms—could hold on indefinitely to any privileges or favors that had been granted in their original charters. The decision therefore increased the power and independence of business corporations by weakening the ability of the states to regulate them or withdraw their privileges.

Dartmouth College v. *Woodward* Ruling in 1819, the Supreme Court decided that the Constitution protected charters given to corporations by states.

About a month after the Dartmouth ruling, in March 1819, the Marshall Court handed down its most important decision. In ***McCulloch* v. *Maryland,*** the Court ruled that a Maryland tax on the Bank of the United States was unconstitutional. The two main issues were whether Congress had the right to establish a national bank and whether a state had the power to tax or regulate an agency or institution created by Congress.

McCulloch v. *Maryland* Ruling on this banking case in 1819, the Supreme Court propped up the idea of "implied powers," meaning the Constitution could be broadly interpreted. This pivotal ruling also asserted the supremacy of federal power over state power.

In response to the first question, Marshall set forth his doctrine of "implied powers"—that the federal government could assume powers that helped it fulfill the "great object" for which it had been founded. Marshall thus struck a blow for "loose construction" of the Constitution. In answer to the second question, Marshall held that if a state had the power to tax a federal agency, it would also have the power to destroy it. Shot through the decision was the belief that the American people "did not design to make this government dependent on the states." In the continuing debate between states' righters and nationalists, the Marshall Court came down firmly on the side of the nationalists.

Gibbons v. *Ogden* In this 1824 case, the Supreme Court affirmed and expanded the power of the federal government to regulate interstate commerce.

In ***Gibbons* v. *Ogden*** (1824), a steamboat monopoly granted by the state of New York was challenged by a competing ferry service. The Supreme Court declared the New York grant unconstitutional in a move that further broadened the power of the federal government at the expense of the states by bolstering the right of Congress to regulate interstate commerce. At the same time, the Court encouraged the growth of a national market economy. The actions of the Supreme Court provide the clearest example of the main nationalistic trends of the postwar period—the acknowledgment of the federal government's major role in promoting the growth of a powerful and prosperous America and the rise of a nationwide capitalistic economy.

Nationalism in Foreign Policy: The Monroe Doctrine

The new spirit of nationalism was also reflected in foreign affairs. The main diplomatic challenge Monroe faced after his reelection in 1820 was how to respond to the successful revolt of most of Spain's Latin American colonies after the Napoleonic wars. Henry Clay and many other Americans favored immediate recognition of the new republics, believing that their neighbors to the south were simply following the example of the United States in its own struggle for independence.

Before 1822, the administration struck a policy of neutrality. But Congress clamored for recognition. Starting in 1822, Monroe reversed his position, and during the next four years, the United States officially recognized Mexico, Colombia, Chile, Argentina, Brazil, the Federation of Central American States, and Peru.

Recognizing the republics put the United States on a possible collision course with the major European powers. In 1822, Austria, Prussia, Russia, and France met in Verona and formed the Grand Alliance, a reactionary union committed to rolling back the tides of liberalism, self-government, and national self-determination that had arisen during the French Revolution and its Napoleonic aftermath. Although the Grand Alliance did not undertake direct intervention in Latin America, it did give France the green light to invade Spain and, if so disposed, to reconquer the empire. Both Great Britain and the United States were alarmed by this prospect.

American policy makers were particularly troubled by Czar Alexander I, who was attempting to extend Russian claims on the Pacific Coast of North America south to the 51st parallel—into the Oregon country that the United States wanted for itself. The Russian threat weighed heavily on the mind of Secretary of State Adams as he formulated foreign policy during Monroe's second term.

The threat from the Grand Alliance compelled America to move closer to Great Britain, which for trading reasons favored independent Latin American countries. In August 1823, the British foreign secretary, George Canning, suggested to the U.S. minister to Great Britain the possibility of joint Anglo-American action against the designs of the Alliance. Monroe, as well as former Presidents Jefferson and Madison, welcomed the suggestion and favored open cooperation with the British.

Secretary of State Adams, however, favored a different approach. He believed that the national interest would best be served by avoiding all entanglement in European politics while at the same time discouraging European intervention in the Americas. In addition, political ambition motivated Adams, and he did not want to be labeled pro-British. He therefore advocated unilateral action by the United States rather than some kind of joint declaration with the British.

In the end, Adams managed to swing Monroe around to his viewpoint. In his annual message to Congress on December 2, 1823, Monroe included a far-reaching statement on foreign policy that was actually written primarily by Adams. What came to be known as the **Monroe Doctrine** solemnly declared that the United States opposed any further colonization in the Americas or any effort by European nations to extend their political systems outside of their own hemisphere. In return, the United States pledged not to involve itself in the internal affairs of Europe or to take part in European wars.

Monroe Doctrine A key foreign policy made by President James Monroe in 1823, it declared the western hemisphere off-limits to new European colonization; in return, the United States promised not to meddle in European affairs.

Although the Monroe Doctrine made little impression on the great powers of Europe at the time it was proclaimed, it signified the rise of a new sense of independence and self-confidence in American attitudes toward the Old World. The Doctrine also reflected the inward-looking nationalism that had arisen after the War of 1812.

The Troubled Presidency of John Quincy Adams

Monroe endorsed John Quincy Adams to succeed him as president. An intelligent and high-minded New Englander and the son of the second president, Adams seemed remarkably well qualified for the highest office in the land. More than anyone else, except perhaps Monroe himself, he seemed to stand for a nonpartisan nationalism that put the public good above special interests. Early in his career, he had lost a seat in the Senate for supporting the foreign policies of Thomas Jefferson in defiance of the Federalist majority of his home state of Massachusetts. After becoming a National Republican, he served mainly in diplomatic posts, culminating in his tenure as secretary of state. In this office, he did more than negotiate treaties. Believing that the rising greatness of America should be reflected not only in economic development and territorial expansion but also in scientific and intellectual achievement, he single-handedly produced a monumental report prescribing a uniform system of weights and measures for the United States. For three years, he rose early every morning in order to put in several hours of research on this project before doing a full day's work conducting the nation's foreign policy. Uniformity of weights and measures, he argued, was essential to scientific and technological progress. Showing that his nationalism was not of a narrow and selfish kind, he called for an agreement with Great Britain and France to promote a single universal system.

Adams represented a type of leadership that could not survive the growth of the sectional and economic divisions foreshadowed by the Missouri controversy

CHRONOLOGY	
1813	Boston Manufacturing Company founds cotton mill at Waltham, Massachusetts
1815	War of 1812 ends
1816	James Monroe is elected president
1819	Supreme Court hands down far-reaching decisions in the Dartmouth College case and in *McCulloch* v. *Maryland* ❖ Adams-Onís Treaty cedes Spanish territory to the United States ❖ Financial panic is followed by a depression lasting until 1823
1820	Missouri Compromise resolves the nation's first sectional crisis ❖ Monroe is reelected president unanimously
1823	Monroe Doctrine is proclaimed
1824	Lafayette revisits the United States ❖ Supreme Court decides *Gibbons* v. *Ogden*
1825	Erie Canal is completed; Canal Era begins

and the fallout from the Panic of 1819. Adams did become president, but only after a hotly contested election that led to the revival of partisan political conflict. As the nation's chief executive, he tried to gain support for government-sponsored scientific research and higher education, only to find the nation was in no mood for public expenditures that offered nothing immediate and tangible to most voters. As a highly educated "gentleman," he projected an image that was out of harmony with a rising spirit of democracy and veneration of "the common man."

Conclusion: The End of the Era of Good Feelings

The Era of Good Feelings turned out to be a passing phase and something of an illusion. The idea that an elite group of nonpartisan statesmen could define common purposes and harmonize competing elements—the concept of leadership embodied in Monroe and Adams—would no longer be viable in the more contentious and democratic America of the Jacksonian era. Increasingly, the power of the "common man" and sectionalism would shape national debates and policy.

Key Terms

Adams-Onís Treaty, p. 166
Era of Good Feelings, p. 176
American system, p. 176
Missouri Compromise, p. 178
Dartmouth College v. *Woodward*, p. 179
McCulloch v. *Maryland*, p. 179
Gibbons v. *Ogden*, p. 180
Monroe Doctrine, p. 181

Recommended Reading

The standard surveys of the period between the War of 1812 and the age of Jackson are two works by George Dangerfield: *The Era of Good Feelings* (1952) and *Awakening of American Nationalism, 1815–1828* (1965); but see also the early chapters of Charles Sellers, *The Market Revolution: Jacksonian America, 1815–1846* (1991). For a positive account of the venturesome, entrepreneurial spirit of the age, see Joyce Appleby, *Inheriting the Revolution: The First Generations of Americans* (2000). On westward expansion, see Richard White, *It's Your Misfortune and None of My Own* (1992) and Malcolm J. Rohrbough, *The Trans-Appalachian Frontier* (1978).

Outstanding studies of economic transformation and the rise of a market economy are George R. Taylor, *The Transportation Revolution, 1815–1860* (1951); Paul W. Gates, *The Farmer's Age: Agriculture, 1815–1860* (1960); Stuart Bruchey, *Growth of the Modern American Economy* (1975); and Douglas C. North, *The Economic Growth of the United States, 1790–1860* (1961). Early manufacturing is described in David J. Jeremy, *Transatlantic Industrial Revolution* (1981) and Robert F. Dalzell, *The Boston Associates and the World They Made* (1987). On early mill workers, see Thomas Dublin, *Women at Work: The Transformation of Work and Community in Lowell, Massachusetts, 1826–1860* (1979).

On the Marshall Court's decisions see Robert K. Faulkner, *The Jurisprudence of John Marshall* (1968) and G. Edward White, *The Marshall Court and Cultural Change, 1815–1835* (1991). Samuel F. Bemis, *John Quincy Adams and the Foundations of American Policy* (1949) provides the classic account of the statesmanship that led to the Monroe Doctrine. But see also Ernest May, *The Making of the Monroe Doctrine* (1976), for a persuasive newer interpretation of how the doctrine originated.

For a list of additional titles related to this chapter's topics, please see http://www.ablongman.com/divine.

Suggested Web Sites

The Era of the Mountain Men

http://www.xmission.com/~drudy/amm.html
Private letters can speak volumes about the concerns and environment of the writers and recipients. Letters from early settlers west of the Mississippi River are offered on this site.

Prairietown, Indiana

http://www.connerprairie.org/explore/prairietown.html
This fictional model of a town and its inhabitants on the early frontier says much about America's movement westward and the everyday lives of Americans.

The Seminole Tribe of Florida

http://www.seminoletribe.com/
Before he was President, Andrew Jackson began a war against the Seminole Indians. This site presents information on their history and culture.

Erie Canal On-line

http://www.syracuse.com/features/eriecanal
This site, built around the diary of a fourteen-year-old girl who traveled from Amsterdam to Syracuse, New York, in the early nineteenth century, explores the construction and importance of the Erie Canal.

Whole Cloth: Discovering Science and Technology through American Textile History

http://www.si.edu/lemelson/centerpieces/wholecloth/
The Jerome and Dorothy Lemelson Center for the Study of Invention and Innovation/Society for the History of Technology put together this site which includes excellent activities and sources concerning early American manufacturing and industry.

Road Through the Wilderness: The Making of the National Road

http://www.connerprairie.org/historyonline/ntlroad.html
The National Road was a hot political topic in the Early Republic and was part of the beginning of the development of America's infrastructure. This on-line essay by historian Timothy Crumrin discusses the making of the National Road.

Chapter 10

The Triumph of White Men's Democracy

Democratic Space: The New Hotels

During the 1820s and 1830s the United States became a more democratic country for at least some of its population. The emerging spirit of popular democracy found expression in a new institution—the large hotel with several stories and hundreds of rooms. When he arrived in Washington to prepare for his administration, President-elect Andrew Jackson stayed in the recently opened National Hotel, only one of several large "first class" hotels that opened immediately before or during his presidency.

The hotel boom responded to the increasing tendency of Americans in the 1820s and 1830s to move about the country. It was to service the rising tides of travelers, transients, and new arrivals that entrepreneurs erected these large places of accommodation, which provided lodging, food, and drink on a large scale in the center of many cities. A prototype was the Boston Exchange Hotel, with its eight stories and three hundred rooms.

The "democratic" mingling of the social classes in these new hotels often caused foreigners to view them as "a true reflection of American society." Their very existence showed that people were on the move geographically and socially. Among their patrons were traveling salesmen, ambitious young men seeking to establish themselves in a new city, and restless pursuers of economic opportunities who were not yet ready to put down roots.

Hotel managers shocked European visitors by failing to enforce traditional social distinctions among their clientele. Under the "American plan," guests were required to pay for their meals, and everyone, regardless of class, ate at a common table. With two crucial exceptions—unescorted women and people of color—almost anyone who could pay enjoyed the kind of personal service previously available only to a privileged class.

THE HOTEL CULTURE REVEALED some of the limitations of the era's democratic ideals and aspirations. Blacks and women were excluded or discriminated against, just as they were denied suffrage at a time when it was being extended to all white males. The genuinely poor simply could not afford to patronize the hotels and were consigned to squalid rooming houses. If the social equality *within* the hotel reflected a decline in traditional rigid class lines, the broad gulf between potential patrons and those who could not pay the rates signaled the growth of inequality based squarely on wealth rather than inherited status.

Outline

Democracy in Theory and Practice

Jackson and the Politics of Democracy

The Bank War and the Second Party System

Heyday of the Second Party System

Conclusion: Tocqueville's Wisdom

The hotel life also reflected the emergence of democratic politics. Professional politicians of a new breed, pursuing the votes of a mass electorate, spent much of their time in hotels as they traveled about. Those elected to Congress or a state legislature often lodged and conducted political transactions in hotels.

The hotel can thus be seen as a fitting symbol for the democratic spirit of the age, one that shows its limitations as well as its strengths. The new democracy was first of all political, involving the extension of suffrage to virtually all white males and the rise of modern political parties appealing to a mass electorate. It was also social in that it undermined the habit of deferring to people because of their birth or ancestry and offered a greater expectation that individuals born in relatively humble circumstances could climb the ladder of success. But the ideals of equal citizenship and opportunity did not extend across the lines of race and gender, which actually hardened to some degree during this period.

Democracy in Theory and Practice

Historians have often viewed Andrew Jackson's coming to power—his election in 1828 and the boisterous "people's inauguration" that followed—as the critical moment when a democratic spirit took possession of American culture and public life. But that oversimplifies a very complex movement. The rise of Jackson took place in an atmosphere of ferment and a changing climate of opinion that turned America in a more democratic direction.

During the 1820s and 1830s, the term *democracy* first became generally accepted as a way of describing how American institutions were supposed to work. The Founders had defined democracy as direct rule by the masses of the people; most of them rejected that approach to government because it was at odds with their conception of a well-balanced republic led by a "natural aristocracy." For champions of popular government in the Jacksonian period, however, the people were truly sovereign and could do no wrong. "The voice of the people is the voice of God" was their clearest expression of principle.

Besides evoking this heightened sense of "popular sovereignty," the democratic impulse seemed to stimulate a process of social leveling. Early Americans had usually assumed that the rich and well-born should be treated with special respect and recognized as natural leaders of the community and guardians of its culture and values. By the 1830s, the disappearance of inherited social ranks and clearly defined aristocracies or privilege groups struck European visitors as the most radical feature of democracy in America. The spirit of deference was dying in America.

"Self-made men" of lowly origins could now rise more readily to positions of power and influence. Exclusiveness and aristocratic pretension were now likely to provoke popular hostility or scorn. But economic equality, in the sense of an equitable sharing of wealth, was not part of the agenda of mainstream Jacksonianism. The watchword was equality of *opportunity*, not equality of rewards. Historians now generally agree that economic inequality was actually increasing during this period of political and social democratization.

Democracy and Society

Although some inequalities persisted or even grew during the age of democracy, they did so in the face of a growing belief that equality was the governing principle of American society. What this meant in practice was that no one could expect special privileges because of family connections. The popular hero was the self-made man who had climbed the ladder of success through his own efforts without forgetting his origin.

Except for southern slaveholders, wealthy Americans could not depend on a distinctive social class for domestic service. Instead of keeping "servants," they hired "help"—household workers who sometimes insisted on sharing meals with their employers. No true American was willing to be considered a member of a servant class, and those engaged in domestic work considered it a temporary stopgap. Except as a euphemistic substitute for the word *slave*, the term *servant* virtually disappeared from the American vocabulary.

Another sign of equality was the decline of distinctive modes of dress for the upper and lower classes. The elaborate periwigs and knee breeches worn by eighteenth-century gentlemen gave way to short hair and pantaloons, a style that was adopted by men of all social classes. Those with a good eye for detail might detect subtle differences in taste or in the quality of materials, but the casual observer could easily conclude that all Americans belonged to a single social class.

Of course, Americans were not all of one social class. In fact, inequality based on control of productive resources was increasing during the Jacksonian period. The rise of industrialization was creating a permanent class of landless, low-paid wage earners in America's cities. In rural areas, there was a significant division between successful commercial farmers or planters and those who subsisted on marginal land. Nevertheless, European observers commented on the fact that all white males were equal before the law and at the polls.

Furthermore, traditional forms of privilege and elitism were indeed under strong attack, as evidenced by changes in the organization and status of the learned professions. State legislatures abolished the licensing requirements for physicians previously administered by local medical societies. As a result, practitioners of unorthodox modes of healing were permitted to compete freely with established medical doctors. The legal profession was similarly opened up to far more people. The result was not always beneficial.

For the clergy, "popular sovereignty" meant that they were increasingly under the thumb of the laity. Ministers had ceased to command respect merely because of their office, and to succeed in their calling, they were forced to develop a more popular and emotional style of preaching. Preachers, as much as politicians, prospered by pleasing the public.

In this atmosphere of democratic leveling, the popular press came to play an increasingly important role as a source of information and opinion. Written and read by common folk, hundreds of newspapers and magazines ushered the mass of white Americans into the political arena. New political views—which in a previous generation might have been silenced by those in power—could now find an audience. Reformers of all kinds could easily publicize their causes, and the press became the venue for the great national debates on issues such as the government's role in banking and the status of slavery in new states and territories. As a profession, journalism was open to anyone who was literate and believed they had something to say. The editors of newspapers with a large circulation were the most influential opinion makers of the age.

Democratic Culture

The democratic spirit also found expression in the rise of new forms of literature and art directed at a mass audience. The intentions of individual artists and writers varied considerably. Some sought success by pandering to popular taste in defiance of traditional standards of high culture. Others tried to capture the spirit of the age by portraying the everyday life of ordinary Americans rather than the traditional subjects of "aristocratic" art. A notable few hoped to use literature and art as a way of improving popular taste and instilling deeper moral and spiritual values. But all of them were aware that their audience was the broad citizenry of a democratic nation rather than a refined elite.

❖ A Look at the Past ❖

Portrait of Andrew Jackson

Andrew Jackson's presidency ushered in a more democratic era and his fashionable clothing reflects that spirit. By the early nineteenth century plain, dark fabrics had become common for men's suits. No longer did wealthy men flaunt their financial success by wearing sumptuous, richly colored fabrics trimmed with gold and lace. As decent-quality, manufactured textiles became more available and cheaper and ready-made clothing started to become available, fabric quality and fit became less likely to indicate expense. In short, distinctions in men's clothing lessened. The change from the elaborate and body-conscious fashions of the eighteenth century to the modest and somber styles of the nineteenth century suggests that other changes were underway in the culture as well. How do Jackson's clothes suggest an egalitarian society? Why did American men abandon elaborate, body-conscious fashions and adopt somber, concealing suits? In addition to becoming more democratic, in what other ways was the United States changing in the early nineteenth century and how did changes in men's fashion reflect those changes?

The romantic movement in literature, which came to the fore in the early nineteenth century in both Europe and America, valued strong feeling and mystical intuition over the calm rationality and appeal to common experience that had prevailed in the writing of the eighteenth century. Romanticism was not necessarily connected with democracy; in Europe, it sometimes went along with a reaffirmation of feudalism and the right of a superior few to rule over the masses. In the American setting, however, romanticism often appealed to the feelings and intuitions of ordinary people: the innate love of goodness, truth, and beauty that all people were thought to possess. Writers in search of popularity and economic success, however, often deserted the high plane of romantic art for crass sentimentalism—a willingness to pull out all emotional stops to thrill readers or bring tears to their eyes.

A mass market for popular literature was made possible by a rise in literacy and a revolution in the technology of printing. An increase in potential readers and a decrease in publishing costs led to a flood of lurid and sentimental novels, some of which became the first American best-sellers. Many of the new sentimental novels were written by and for women. Some female authors implicitly protested against their situation by portraying men in general as tyrannical, unreliable, or cruel and the women, whom these men made miserable, as resourceful individualists capable of making their own way. But the standard happy endings sustained the convention that a woman on her own was an unnatural thing, for a virtuous and protective man always turned up and saved the heroine from a truly independent life.

In the theater, melodrama became the dominant genre, involving the inevitable trio of beleaguered heroine, mustachioed villain, and a hero who arrives in the nick of time. Another favorite was the patriotic comedy in which the rustic Yankee foiled the foppish European aristocrat. Men and women of all classes went to the theater, and those in the cheap seats often openly voiced their displeasure with an actor or a play.

The spirit of popular sovereignty expressed itself less dramatically in the visual arts, but its influence was nonetheless felt. Beginning in the 1830s, painters turned from portraying great events and famous people to depicting scenes from everyday life. Democratic genre painting captured the lives of plain folk with both skill and understanding. Popular recreation and electioneering activity were common motifs.

Architecture and sculpture reflected the democratic spirit in another mode; they were viewed as civic art forms meant to extol the achievements of the republic. In the 1820s and 1830s, the classical Greek style, with its columned facades, was favored for banks, hotels, and private dwellings as well as for public buildings. Similarly, sculpture was intended strictly for public admiration or inspiration, and its principal subjects were the heroes of the republic.

Serious exponents of a higher culture and a more refined sensibility sought to reach the new public in the hope of elevating its taste or uplifting its morals. The "Brahmin poets" of New England—Henry Wadsworth Longfellow, James Russell Lowell, and Oliver Wendell Holmes—offered lofty sentiments to a receptive middle class; Ralph Waldo Emerson carried his philosophy of spiritual self-reliance to lyceums and lecture halls across the country; and great novelists such as Nathaniel Hawthorne and Herman Melville experimented with the popular romantic genres. But the ironic and pessimistic view of life that permeated the fiction of these two authors clashed with the optimism of the age, and their work failed to gain a large readership.

The ideal of art for art's sake was utterly alien to the instructional spirit of mid-nineteenth-century American culture. The responsibility of the artist in a democra-

William Sidney Mount, Rustic Dance After a Sleigh Ride, *1830. Mount's portrayals of country people folk dancing, gambling, playing music, or horse trading were pieces that appealed strongly to contemporaries. Art historians have found much to praise in his use of architecture, particularly that of the common barn, to achieve striking compositional effects.* ❖

tic society, it was generally assumed, was to contribute to the general welfare by encouraging virtue and proper sentiments. Only Edgar Allan Poe seemed to fit the European image of the romantic genius rebelling against middle-class pieties. The most original of the antebellum poets, Walt Whitman, sought to be a direct mouthpiece for the rising democratic spirit, but his abandonment of traditional verse forms and his freedom in dealing with the sexual side of human nature left him isolated and unappreciated during his most creative years.

The Democratic Ferment

The supremacy of democracy was most obvious in the new politics of universal white manhood suffrage and mass political parties. By the 1820s, most states had removed the last remaining barriers to voting participation by all white males. This change was not as radical or controversial as it would be later in nineteenth-century Europe; ownership of land was so common in the United States that a general suffrage did not mean men without property became a voting majority.

Accompanying this broadening of the electorate was a rise in the proportion of public officials who were elected rather than appointed. More and more judges, as well as legislative and executive officeholders, were chosen by the people. As a result, a new style of politicking developed, emphasizing dramatic speeches that played to the voters' fears and concerns.

Skillful and farsighted politicians such as Martin Van Buren in New York began in the 1820s to build stable statewide political organizations out of what had been loosely organized factions of the Jeffersonian party. Earlier politicians had regarded parties as a threat to republican virtue and had embraced them only as a temporary expedient. But in Van Buren's opinion, regular parties were an effective check on the temptation to abuse power, a tendency deeply planted in the human heart. The major breakthrough in American political thought during the 1820s and 1830s was the idea of a "loyal opposition," ready to capitalize politically on the mistakes or excesses of the "ins" without denying their right to act in the same way when the "ins" became the "outs."

Changes in the method of nominating and electing a president fostered the growth of a two-party system on the national level. By 1828, presidential electors were chosen by popular vote rather than by state legislatures in all but two of the twenty-four states. The need to mobilize grassroots support behind particular candidates required some form of national organization. When national nominating conventions made their appearance in 1831, the choice of candidates became a matter for representative party assemblies rather than congressional caucuses or ad hoc political alliances. These democratic practices generated far more widespread interest in politics. Between 1824 and 1840, the percentage of eligible voters who cast their ballot in presidential elections tripled.

Economic questions dominated the political controversies of the 1820s and 1830s. The Panic of 1819 and the subsequent depression heightened popular interest in government economic policy. Americans advanced several solutions for keeping the economy healthy. Some, especially small farmers, favored a return to a simpler and more "honest" economy without banks, paper money, and the easy credit that encouraged speculation. Others, particularly emerging entrepreneurs, saw salvation in government aid and protection for venture capital. Politicians and eventually political parties responded to these conflicting views.

The party disputes that arose over corporations, tariffs, banks, and internal improvements involved more than the direct economic concerns of particular interest groups. They were viewed in the context of republican fears of conspiracy against American liberty and equality. Charges of corruption and impending tyranny were common.

The notion that the American experiment was a fragile one, constantly threatened by power-hungry conspirators, eventually took two principal forms. For Jacksonians, it was "the money power" that endangered the survival of republicanism; for their opponents, it was men like Jackson himself, alleged "rabble-rousers" who duped the electorate into ratifying high-handed and tyrannical action contrary to the true interests of the nation.

An object of increasing concern for both sides was the role of the federal government. National Republicans and later the Whigs believed that government should take active steps to foster economic growth; Jacksonians only wanted to eliminate "special privileges." How best to guarantee equality of opportunity—whether by active governmental promotion of commerce and industry or by strict laissez-faire policies—was a hotly debated issue of the period.

For one group of dissenters, democracy took on a more radical meaning. Leaders of the workingmen's parties and trade unions condemned the growing gap between the rich and the poor resulting from early industrialization and the growth of the market economy. Society, in their view, was divided between "producers"—laborers, artisans, farmers, and small business owners who ran their own enterprises—and nonproducing "parasites"—bankers, speculators, and merchant capitalists. Their aim was to give the producers greater control over the fruits of their labor. They advocated such things as abolition of inheritance and a redistribution of land, as well as educational reforms, a ten-hour workday, abolition of imprisonment for debt, and a currency system based exclusively on hard money so that workers could no longer be paid in depreciated banknotes.

Northern abolitionists and early proponents of women's rights made another kind of effort to extend the meaning and scope of democracy. Radical men and women advocated immediate emancipation for slaves and equal rights for blacks and women. But Jacksonian America was too permeated with racism and male chauvinism to listen to such reformers. In some ways, the civil and political status of both blacks and women deteriorated during this "age of the common man" (see Chapter 12).

Jackson and the Politics of Democracy

The public figure who came to symbolize the triumph of democracy was Andrew Jackson, although he came out a loser in the presidential election of 1824. His victory four years later, his actions as president, and the great political party that formed around him refashioned national politics in a more democratic mold. No wonder historians have called the spirit of the age **Jacksonian Democracy.**

Jacksonian Democracy A historian's term for the political culture of white male citizens in the 1820s and 1830s. It celebrated the "self-made man" and rejected the idea that leaders should be drawn from the intellectual and economic elite. Andrew Jackson, the first "people's president," exemplified the spirit of the age.

The Election of 1824 and John Quincy Adams's Administration

The election of 1824 was one of the most complicated and controversial in American history. As Monroe's second term ended, the ruling Republican party was in disarray and could not agree on who should succeed to the presidency. The party's congressional caucus chose William Crawford of Georgia, an old-line Jeffersonian. But a majority of congressmen showed their disapproval of this outmoded method of nominating candidates by refusing to attend the caucus. Soon John Quincy Adams, Henry Clay, John C. Calhoun, and Andrew Jackson had their hats in the ring.

Initially Jackson was not given much of a chance. He was a military hero, not a national politician, and few party leaders believed that wartime victories were enough to catapult him into the White House. But after testing the waters, Calhoun withdrew and chose instead to run for vice president. Then Crawford suffered a debilitating stroke that weakened his chances. These events made Jackson the favorite in the South. He also found favor among those in the North and West who were disenchanted with the economic nationalism of Clay and Adams.

In the election, Jackson won a plurality of the electoral votes. But since he lacked the necessary majority, the contest was thrown into the House of Representatives, where the legislators were to choose from the three top candidates. Adams emerged victorious over Jackson and Crawford. Clay, who had just missed making the final three, provided the winning margin by persuading his supporters to vote for Adams. When Adams proceeded to appoint Clay as his secretary of state, the Jacksonians charged that a "corrupt bargain" had deprived their favorite of the presidency. Even though the charges were unproven, Adams assumed office under a cloud of suspicion.

Although he was a man of integrity and vision, Adams was an inept politician. He refused to bow to the public antipathy toward nationalistic programs and called for an expansion of governmental activity. Congress, however, had no intention of following Adams's lead.

The new Congress that was elected in 1826 was clearly under the control of men hostile to the administration and favorable to the presidential aspirations of Andrew Jackson. The main business before Congress was the tariff issue. Pressure for greater protection came not only from manufacturers but also from many farmers. The cotton-growing South—the only section where tariffs of all kinds were unpopular—was already safely in the general's camp. To gain popularity in the other sections, Jackson tacitly lent his support to the tariff of 1828. This **tariff of abominations** was a congressional grab bag that contained substantial across-the-board increases in duties—gifts for all sections save the South. It was not, however, simply a ploy to get Jackson elected; it was in fact an early example of how special interest groups can achieve their goals in democratic politics through the process of legislative bargaining known as logrolling.

tariff of abominations An 1828 protective tariff, or tax on imports, motivated by special interest groups. It resulted in a substantial increase in duties that angered many southern free traders.

Jackson Comes to Power

The campaign of 1828 actually began early in the Adams administration. Resurrecting the corrupt-bargain charge, Jackson's supporters began to organize on the state and local levels. So successful were their efforts that influential state and regional leaders who had supported other candidates in 1824 now rallied behind Jackson to create a formidable coalition.

The most significant of these leaders were Vice President Calhoun, who now spoke for the militant states' rights sentiment of the South; Senator Martin Van Buren, who dominated New York politics through the political machine known as the Albany Regency; and two Kentucky editors, Francis P. Blair and Amos Kendall, who worked to mobilize opposition to Henry Clay and his "American system" in the West. These men and their followers laid the foundation for the first modern American political party, the Democrats. And from this time on, national parties existed primarily to engage in a contest for the presidency. Without this great prize, there would have been little incentive to create national organizations out of the parties and factions developing in the states.

The election of 1828 saw the birth of a new era of mass democracy. Jackson's supporters made widespread use of such electioneering techniques as huge public rallies, torchlight parades, and lavish barbecues or picnics paid for by the candidate's organization. Personalities and mudslinging dominated the campaign, which reached its low point when Adams's supporters accused Jackson's wife, Rachel, of bigamy and adultery and Jackson's associates charged that Adams's wife was born out of wedlock.

What gave the Jacksonians the edge was their success in portraying their candidate as an authentic man of the people, despite his substantial fortune in land and slaves. They emphasized Jackson's backwoods upbringing, military record, and common sense unclouded by a fancy education. Adams, according to Democratic propagandists, was the exact opposite—an overeducated aristocrat, more at home in the salon and the study than among the plain people. Anti-intellectualism was a potent force, and Adams never really had a chance.

The result had the appearance of a landslide for Old Hickory. But the verdict of the people was not as decisive as the returns might suggest. Although Jackson had piled up massive majorities in some of the slave states, the voters elsewhere divided fairly evenly. Furthermore, it was not clear what kind of a mandate he had won. Most of the politicians in his camp favored states' rights and limited government as against the nationalism of Adams and Clay, but the general himself had never taken a clear public stand on such issues as banks, tariffs, and internal improvements. His victory was more a triumph of image and personality than the popular endorsement of a particular set of programs.

Jackson turned out to be one of the most forceful and domineering of American presidents. His most striking character traits were an indomitable will, an intolerance of opposition, and a prickly pride that would not permit him to forgive or forget an insult or a supposed act of betrayal. His violent temper had led him to fight a number of duels, and as a soldier his critics claimed he was guilty of using excessive force. His frontier background and military experiences had made him tough and resourceful but had also deprived him of the flexibility normally associated with successful politicians. Yet he generally got what he wanted.

Jackson's presidency began with his open endorsement of rotation of officeholders, or what his critics called the "spoils system." Although he did not actually depart radically from his predecessors in the degree to which he removed federal officeholders and replaced them with his supporters, he was the first president to defend the practice as a legitimate application of democratic doctrine. He contended that the duties of public officers were simple and that any man of intelligence could readily fill the positions.

Jackson also established a new kind of relationship with his cabinet. Cabinet members became less important than they had been in previous administrations. Old Hickory regarded himself as "the direct representative of the people" and his cabinet as an interchangeable set of administrators whose sole function was to carry out the will of the chief executive. He used his cabinet members more for consultation than for policymaking, and he diluted their influence even further by relying heavily on the advice of an unofficial and confidential set of advisers known as his Kitchen Cabinet.

Midway in his first administration, Jackson completely reorganized his cabinet. The apparent cause of this upheaval was the Peggy Eaton affair. Peggy O'Neale Eaton, the daughter of a Washington tavern owner, married Secretary of War John Eaton in 1829. Because of gossip about her moral character, the wives of other cabinet members refused to receive her socially. Jackson became her champion. Eventually all but one of his cabinet members resigned over the incident, and Jackson formed a fresh cabinet. Perhaps the most important consequence of the affair was that Martin Van Buren, although he resigned with the rest, also supported Peggy Eaton and therefore won Jackson's favor.

Indian Removal

The first major policy question before the Jackson administration concerned the fate of Native Americans. Jackson had long favored removing eastern Indians to lands beyond the Mississippi. His support of removal was no different from the policy of previous administrations. The only real issue was how rapidly and thoroughly the process should be carried out and by what means. At the time of Jackson's election, the states of Georgia, Alabama, and Mississippi were clamoring for quick action.

The greatest obstacle to voluntary relocation, however, was the Cherokee nation, which held land in Georgia, Alabama, North Carolina, and Tennessee. The Cherokees not only refused to move but also had instituted a republican form of government for themselves, achieved literacy in their own language, and made considerable progress toward adopting a settled agrarian way of life similar to that of southern whites. These were obviously not Indians in need of the "civilizing" benefits of the government's program, and missionaries and northeastern philanthropists argued that the Cherokees should be allowed to remain where they were.

Sequoyah's invention of the Cherokee alphabet enabled thousands of Cherokee to read and write primers and newspapers published in their own language. ❖

The southern states disagreed. Georgia, Alabama, and Mississippi extended their state laws over the Cherokee, moves that defied provisions of the Constitution giving the federal government exclusive jurisdiction over Indian affairs and also violated specific treaties. Jackson, however, endorsed the state actions. His own attitude was that Indians were children when they did the whites' bidding, and savage beasts when they resisted. In his December 1829 message to Congress, he advocated a new and more coercive removal policy. He denied Cherokee autonomy, asserted the primacy of states' rights over Indian rights, and called for the speedy and thorough removal of all eastern Indians to designated areas beyond the Mississippi.

Early in 1830, the president's congressional supporters introduced a bill to implement the policy. The ensuing debate was vigorous and heated, but senators and House members from the South and the western border states pushed the bill through. Jackson then moved quickly to conclude the necessary treaties, using the threat of unilateral government action to bludgeon the tribes into submission. In 1832, he condoned Georgia's defiance of a Supreme Court decision (*Worcester* v. *Georgia*) that denied the right of a state to extend its jurisdiction over tribal lands. The fate of the eastern Indians was sealed.

The members of a stubbornly resisting majority faction of the Cherokees held out until 1838 when military pressure forced them to march to Oklahoma. The trek, known as the **Trail of Tears,** was made under such harsh conditions that almost a quarter of the Indians died on the way. Nothing more than a ruthless land grab, the Cherokee removal exposed the prejudiced and greedy side of Jacksonian democracy.

Trail of Tears In the winter of 1838–1839, the Cherokee were forced to evacuate their lands in Georgia and travel under military guard to present-day Oklahoma. Due to exposure and disease, roughly one-quarter of the 16,000 forced migrants died en route.

The Nullification Crisis

During the 1820s, Southerners became increasingly fearful of federal encroachment on the rights of the states. Behind this concern, in South Carolina at least, was a strengthened commitment to the preservation of slavery and a resulting anxiety about possible uses of federal power to strike at that "peculiar institution." Hoping to keep the explosive slavery issue out of the political limelight, South Carolinians seized on another genuine grievance, the protective tariff, as the issue on which to take their stand in favor of state veto power over federal actions that they viewed as contrary to their interests. As a staple-producing and -exporting region, the South was hurt by any tariff that increased the prices for manufactured goods and threatened to undermine foreign markets by inciting counterprotection.

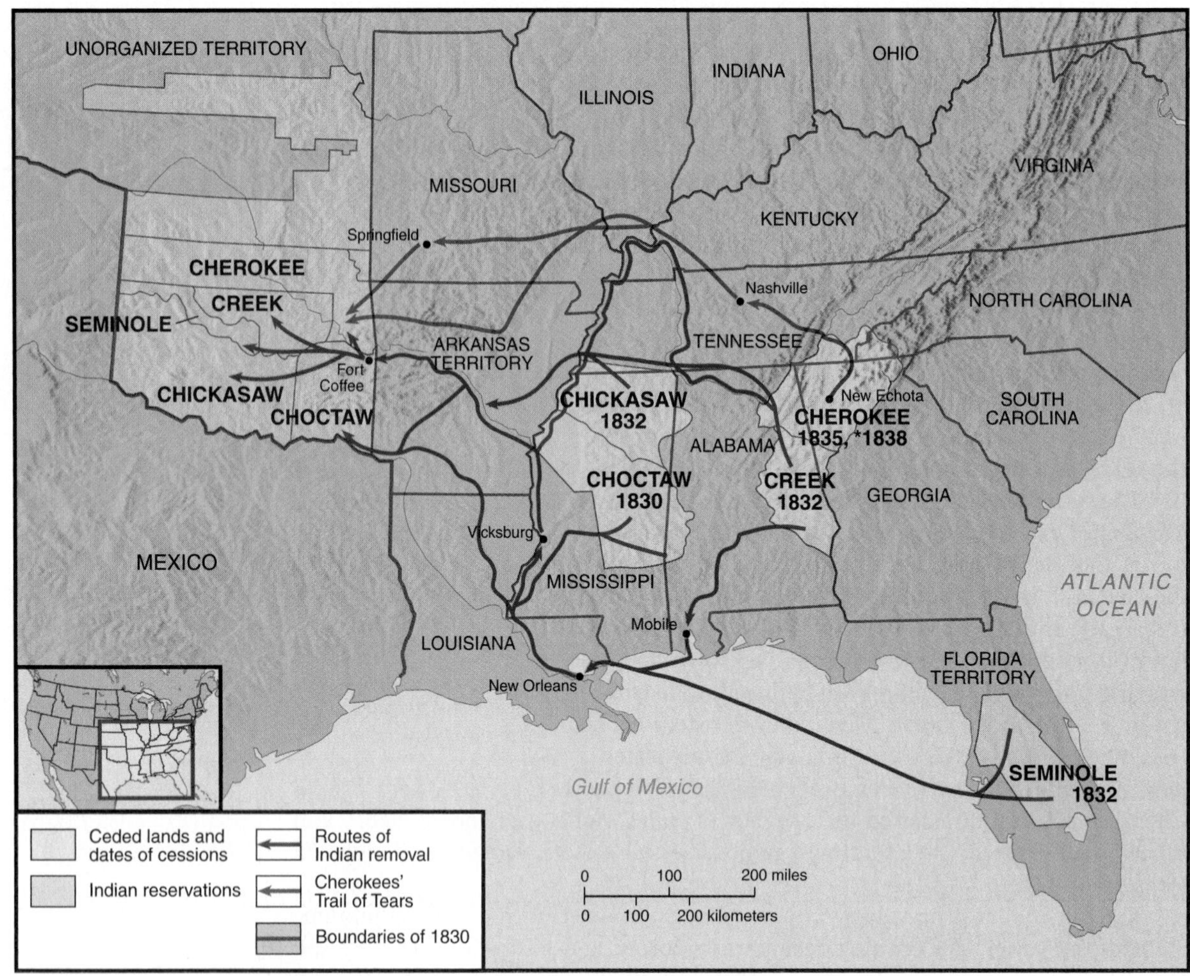

** Treaty signed in 1835 by minority factions forced removal in 1838.*

INDIAN REMOVAL *Because so many Native Americans, uprooted from their lands in the East, died on the forced march to Oklahoma, the route they followed became known as the Trail of Tears.* ❖

nullification The supposed right of any state to declare a federal law inoperative within its boundaries. In 1832, South Carolina created a firestorm when it attempted to nullify the federal tariff.

Vice President John C. Calhoun emerged as the leader of the states' rights insurgency in South Carolina. After the passage of the tariff of abominations in 1828, the state legislature declared the new duties unconstitutional and endorsed a lengthy disquisition—written anonymously by Calhoun—that affirmed **nullification,** or the right of an individual state to set aside federal law. Calhoun and South Carolina believed that Jackson would defend their position. They saw room for hope in the president's position on Georgia's de facto nullification of federal treaties upholding Indian tribal rights and his veto of a major internal improvement bill, the Maysville Road in Kentucky, based on a strict interpretation of the Constitution.

In the meantime, a bitter personal feud developed between Jackson and Calhoun. As Calhoun lost favor with Jackson because of his position on the Eaton affair, it became clear that Van Buren would be Jackson's designated successor. The personal breach between Jackson and Calhoun colored and intensified their confrontation over the nullification and tariff issues.

But there were also differences of principle. Although generally a defender of states' rights and strict construction of the Constitution, Jackson opposed the theory of nullification as a threat to the survival of the Union. The differences between Jackson and Calhoun came into the open at the Jefferson Day dinner in 1830, when Jackson offered the toast "Our Union: It must be preserved"—to which Calhoun responded: "The Union: next to Liberty most dear. May we always remember that it can only be preserved by distributing equally [its] benefits and the burdens."

In 1830 and 1831, the movement against the tariff gained strength in South Carolina. Calhoun resigned as vice president and openly took the lead. In 1832, Congress passed a new tariff that lowered the rates slightly but retained the principle of protection. Supporters of nullification then succeeded in persuading the South Carolina state legislature to call a special convention. When the convention met in November 1832, the members voted overwhelmingly to nullify the tariffs of 1828 and 1832 and to forbid the collection of customs duties within the state.

Jackson reacted with characteristic decisiveness. He asked Congress to vote him the authority to use the army to enforce the tariff. At the same time, he sought to pacify the nullifiers somewhat by recommending a lower tariff. Congress responded by enacting the Force Bill, which gave the president the military powers he sought, and the compromise tariff of 1833. Faced with the combination of force and compromise, South Carolina eventually rescinded the nullification ordinance. But to clearly demonstrate that they had not conceded their constitutional position, the convention delegates concluded their deliberations by nullifying the Force Bill.

The nullification crisis revealed that South Carolinians would not tolerate any federal action that seemed contrary to their interests or raised doubts about the institution of slavery. The nullifiers' principle of state sovereignty implied the right of secession as well as the right to declare laws of Congress null and void. Although in many ways Jackson was a pro-slavery president, some farsighted southern loyalists were alarmed by the Unionist doctrines the president propounded in his proclamation against nullification. More strongly than any previous president, he had asserted that the federal government was supreme over the states and that the Union was indivisible. What was more, he had justified the use of force against states that denied federal authority.

The Bank War and the Second Party System

Jackson's most important and controversial use of executive power was his successful attack on the Bank of the United States. The so-called **Bank War** revealed some of the deepest concerns of Jackson and his supporters and expressed their concept of democracy in a dramatic way. It also aroused intense opposition to the president and his policies, an opposition that crystallized in a new national party known as the Whigs. The destruction of the Bank and the economic disruption that followed brought to the forefront the issue of the government's relationship to the nation's financial system. Differences on this question helped sustain the new two-party system and provided the stuff of political controversy during the administration of Jackson's handpicked successor, Martin Van Buren.

Bank War Between 1832–1836, Andrew Jackson used his presidential power to fight and ultimately destroy the second Bank of the United States.

Biddle, the Bank Veto, and the Election of 1832

The Bank of the United States had long been embroiled in public controversy. The South and West openly blamed it for the Panic of 1819 and the depression that followed. But after Nicholas Biddle took over the Bank's presidency in 1823, it regained public confidence. Cultured and able, Biddle probably understood the mysteries of banking and currency better than any other American of his generation. But he was arrogant and vain, as sure of his own judgment as Jackson himself.

Old-line Jeffersonians had always opposed the Bank on the grounds that its establishment was unconstitutional and it placed too much power in the hands of a small, privileged group. Its influence on the national economy was tremendous, and because of this, it was a convenient scapegoat for anything that went wrong with the economy. In an era of rising democracy, the most obvious and telling objection to the Bank was simply that it possessed great power and privilege without being under popular control.

Jackson came into office with strong reservations about banking and paper money in general. He also harbored suspicions that branches of the Bank of the United States had illicitly used their influence on behalf of his opponent in the presidential election. In his annual messages in 1829 and 1830, he called on Congress to begin discussing ways of reducing the Bank's power.

Biddle began to worry about the fate of the Bank's charter when it came up for renewal in 1836. At the same time, Jackson's Kitchen Cabinet advised him that an attack on the Bank would provide a good party issue for the election of 1832. Biddle then made a fateful blunder. He determined to seek recharter by Congress in 1832, four years ahead of schedule. Senator Henry Clay, leader of the antiadministration forces on Capitol Hill, encouraged the move because he was convinced that Jackson had chosen the unpopular side of the issue. The bill to recharter, therefore, was introduced in the House and Senate in early 1832. It passed Congress with ease.

The next move was Jackson's, and he made the most of the opportunity. He vetoed the bill and defended his action with ringing statements of principle. The Bank was unconstitutional, he said, and even worse, because it was a monopoly, it violated the fundamental rights of the people in a democratic society. Jackson believed that the government should guarantee equality of opportunity, not grant privileges that provided special interests with exclusive advantages.

Jackson thus called on the common people to join him in fighting the "monster" corporation. His veto message was the first to go beyond strictly constitutional arguments to deal directly with social and economic issues. Congressional attempts to override the veto failed, and Jackson resolved to take the entire issue to the people in the upcoming presidential election, which he viewed as a referendum to decide whether he or the Bank would prevail.

The 1832 election pitted Jackson against Henry Clay, standard-bearer of the National Republicans. The Bank recharter was the major issue. In the end, Jackson

Aided by Van Buren (center), Jackson wields his veto rod against the Bank of the United States, whose heads represent the directors of the state branches. Bank president Nicholas Biddle is wearing the top hat. ❖

won a great personal triumph, garnering 219 electoral votes to 49 for Clay. As far as Old Hickory was concerned, he had his mandate.

Killing the Bank

Not content with preventing the Bank from getting a new charter, the victorious Jackson now resolved to attack it directly by removing federal deposits from Biddle's vaults. Jackson told Van Buren, "the bank . . . is trying to kill me, but I will kill it." Old Hickory regarded Biddle's opposition during the presidential race as a personal attack, part of a devious plot to destroy the president's reputation and deny him the popular approval that he deserved. As always, Jackson believed his opponents were not merely wrong but evil besides and deserved to be destroyed. Furthermore, he viewed the election result as his popular mandate to go after the Bank.

To remove the deposits from the Bank, Jackson had to overcome strong resistance in his own cabinet. When one secretary of the treasury refused to support the policy, he was shifted to another cabinet post. When a second balked at carrying out removal, he was replaced by Roger B. Taney, a Jackson loyalist and dedicated opponent of the Bank. Beginning in late September 1833, Taney ceased depositing government money in the Bank and began to withdraw the funds already there. The funds were then ill-advisedly placed in selected state banks. Opponents charged that the banks had been chosen for political rather than fiscal reasons and dubbed them Jackson's "pet banks." Since Congress refused to approve administration proposals to regulate the credit policies of these banks, Jackson's efforts to shift to a hard-money economy were quickly nullified by the use the state banks made of the new deposits. They extended credit more recklessly than before and increased the amount of paper money in circulation.

The Bank counterattacked by calling in outstanding loans and instituting a policy of credit contraction that helped bring on an economic recession. Biddle hoped to win support for recharter by demonstrating that weakening the Bank's position would be disastrous for the economy. But all he showed, at least to the president's supporters, was that they had been right all along about the Bank's excessive power. They blamed the economic distress on Biddle, and the Bank never did regain its charter.

Even more serious than the conflict over the Bank was the strong opposition to Jackson's fiscal policies that developed in Congress. Led by Henry Clay, the Senate approved a motion of censure against Jackson, charging him with exceeding his constitutional authority in removing the deposits. Jacksonians in the House were able to block such action, but the president was further humiliated when the Senate refused to confirm Taney as secretary of the treasury. Anti-Jacksonians were gaining strength.

The Emergence of the Whigs

The coalition that passed the censure resolution in the Senate provided the nucleus for a new national party, the **Whigs.** The leadership of the new party and a majority of its support came from National Republicans and ex-Federalists. But the Whigs also picked up critical backing from southern proponents of states' rights who had been upset by Jackson's stand on nullification and now saw an unconstitutional abuse of power in his withdrawal of federal deposits from the Bank of the United States. The Whig label was chosen because of its associations with both English and American Revolutionary opposition to royal power and prerogatives; its rallying cry was "executive usurpation" by the tyrannical designs of "King Andrew."

Whigs Members of the Whig party, which coalesced around opposition to Andrew Jackson. The name derived from the British Whigs, who opposed the king in the late seventeenth century. In general, the Whig party supported federal power and internal improvements but not territorial expansion. The party collapsed in the 1850s.

The Whigs also gradually absorbed the Anti-Masonic party, a surprisingly strong northeastern political movement that exploited traditional American fears of secret societies and conspiracies. They also appealed successfully to the moral concerns of the northern middle class under the sway of an emerging evangelical Protestantism. Anti-Masons detested Jacksonianism mainly because it stood for a toleration of diverse lifestyles. They believed that the government should restrict such "sinful" behavior as drinking, gambling, and breaking the Sabbath.

As the election of 1836 approached, the government's fiscal policies also provoked a localized rebellion among the urban, working-class elements of the Democratic coalition. This group favored a strict hard-money policy and condemned Jackson's transfer of federal deposits to the state banks as inflationary. Because they wanted working people to be paid in specie rather than inflated banknotes, the "Loco-Focos"—named for the matches they used for illumination when their opponents turned off the gaslights at a party meeting—went beyond opposition to the Bank of the United States and attacked state banks as well. Seeing no basis for cooperation with the Whigs, they established the independent Equal Rights party and nominated a separate state ticket in 1836.

Jackson himself had hard-money sentiments and probably regarded the "pet banks" solution as a temporary expedient. Nonetheless, in early 1836, he surrendered to congressional pressure and signed legislation allocating surplus federal revenues to the deposit banks, increasing their numbers and weakening federal controls over them. The result was runaway inflation, wild land speculation, and irresponsible printing of paper money. Reacting somewhat belatedly to the speculative mania he had helped create, Jackson pricked the bubble on July 11, 1836. He issued his **specie circular** stipulating that after August 15, only gold and silver would be accepted in payment for public lands. This action served to curb inflation and land speculation but did so in such a sudden and drastic way that it helped precipitate the financial panic of 1837.

specie circular In 1836, President Andrew Jackson issued this executive order that required purchasers of public land to pay in "specie," gold or silver coin, rather than paper money.

The Rise and Fall of Van Buren

As his successor, Jackson chose Martin Van Buren, a master of practical politics. The Democratic National Convention of 1835 unanimously confirmed Jackson's choice. Van Buren promised to "tread generally in the footsteps of General Jackson."

The newly created Whig party, reflecting the diversity of its constituency, was unable to decide on a single standard-bearer and chose instead to run three regional candidates—Daniel Webster in the East, William Henry Harrison in the Old Northwest, and Hugh Lawson White in the South. The Whigs hoped to deprive Van Buren of enough electoral votes to throw the election into the House of Representatives, where one of the Whigs might stand a chance.

The strategy proved unsuccessful. Van Buren won a clear victory. But the election foreshadowed future trouble for the Democrats, particularly in the South. There the Whigs ran virtually even. The emergence of a two-party system in the previously solid South resulted from two factors: opposition to some of Jackson's policies and the image of Van Buren as an unreliable Yankee politician.

The main business of Van Buren's administration was to straighten out the financial disorder resulting from the destruction of the Bank of the United States and the issuing of Jackson's specie circular. Van Buren took office in the face of a catastrophic depression. The **Panic of 1837** was not exclusively, or even primarily, the result of government policies. It was in fact international in scope and reflected some complex changes in the world economy that were beyond the control of American policymakers.

Panic of 1837 A financial depression that lasted until the 1840s.

But the Whigs were quick to blame the state of the economy on Jacksonian finance, and the administration had to make a politically effective response. Since Van Buren and his party were committed to a policy of laissez-faire on the federal level, there was little or nothing they could do to relieve economic distress through subsidies or relief measures. But the president could at least try to salvage the federal funds deposited in shaky state banks and devise a new system of public finance that would not contribute to future panics by fueling speculation and credit expansion.

Van Buren's solution was to establish a public depository for government funds with no connections whatsoever to commercial banking. His proposal for an "independent subtreasury" aroused intense opposition from the congressional Whigs, and it was not until 1840 that it was enacted into law. In the meantime, the economy had temporarily revived in 1838, only to sink again into a deeper depression the following year.

Van Buren's chances for reelection in 1840 were undoubtedly hurt by the state of the economy. But the principal reason for his defeat was that he lacked Jackson's charisma and was thus unable to overcome the extremely effective campaign mounted by the Whigs. The Whig party of 1840 was well organized on a grassroots level, and it found its own Jackson in William Henry Harrison, a military hero of advanced age, who was associated in the public mind with the battle of Tippecanoe and the winning of the West. To balance the ticket and increase its appeal in the South, they chose John Tyler of Virginia, a converted states' rights Democrat, to be Harrison's running mate.

Using the slogan "Tippecanoe and Tyler, Too," the Whigs pulled out all stops in their bid for the White House. Imitating the Jacksonian propaganda against Adams in 1828, they portrayed Van Buren as a luxury-loving aristocrat and compared him with their own homespun candidate. The Democrats tried but were unable to project Van Buren as a man of the people. Harrison won, and the Whigs gained control of both houses of Congress.

❖ A Look at the Past ❖

Columbian Star Dishes

The election of 1840 set a new standard for political campaigns: exuberant and energetic. Rallies and parades awakened interest while a vast array of campaign paraphernalia maintained that interest. Whigs used log cabins to suggest that wealthy William Henry Harrison actually possessed a humble origin. Fabric, bandannas, sheet music, and ceramics came decorated with Whig campaign emblems. Dishes in the Columbian Star pattern, made in England, were available for purchase as individual pieces, entire sets, and even in miniature sizes. Why would consumers willingly, and sometimes eagerly, set their tables with pro-Whig dishes? What does that willingness reveal about the political culture of the time?

Contrary to what most historians used to believe, personalities and hoopla did not decide the election of 1840. The economy was in dire straits, and the Whigs, unlike the Democrats, had a program that seemed to offer hope for a solution—the latest version of Henry Clay's American System. Whigs proposed to revive the Bank of the United States in order to restore fiscal stability, raise tariffs to protect manufacturers and manufacturing jobs, and distribute federal revenues to the states for internal improvements that would stimulate commerce and employment. Whig victories in the state and local elections of 1840, many of which preceded the presidential vote, strongly suggest that voters were responding to the party and its program, not merely to the man who headed the ticket and to the Whigs' newfound skill at entertaining the electorate.

Heyday of the Second Party System

second party system A historian's term for the national two-party rivalry between Democrats and Whigs. The second party system began in the 1830s and ended in the 1850s with the demise of the Whig party and the rise of the Republican party.

America's **second party system** came of age in the election of 1840. The rivalry of Democrats and Whigs made the two-party pattern an enduring feature of the electoral politics in the United States. During the 1840s, the two national parties competed on fairly equal terms for the support of the electorate. Allegiance to one party or the other became an important source of personal identity for many Americans and increased their interest and participation in politics.

In addition to drama and entertainment, the parties offered the voters a real choice of programs and ideologies. Whigs stood for a "positive liberal state," in which the government had the right and duty to subsidize or protect enterprises that could contribute to general prosperity and economic growth. Democrats advocated a "negative liberal state," in which the government would keep its hands off the economy.

Conflict over economic issues helped determine each party's base of support. In the Whig camp were many industrialists and merchants, plus a large proportion of farmers and planters who had adapted successfully to the market economy. Democrats appealed mainly to small farmers, workers, declining gentry, and emerging entrepreneurs who were excluded from the established commercial groups that stood to benefit most from Whig programs. But issues such as the tariff could further complicate this pattern; workers in protected industries often voted Whig, while importers normally voted for the Democrats and freer trade.

Economic interest was not the only factor behind the choice of parties. Lifestyles and ethnic or religious identities strongly affected party loyalties during this period. In the northern states, one way to tell the typical Whig from the typical Democrat was to see where each went on Sunday. Anyone at an evangelical Protestant church was likely to be a Whig. A person who belonged to a ritualized church—Catholic, Lutheran, or Episcopalian—or did not go to church at all was probably a Democrat.

The Democrats were the favored party of immigrants, Catholics, freethinkers, backwoods farmers, and persons of all classes who enjoyed traditional amusements condemned by the new breed of moral reformers. One thing that all the groups had in common was a desire to be left alone, with freedom to think and behave as they liked. The Whigs welcomed the market economy but wanted to restrain the individualism and disorder it created by enforcing cultural and moral values derived from the Puritan tradition. Most of those who sought to be "their brothers' keepers" were Whigs.

Nevertheless, party conflict in Congress continued to center on national economic policy. Whigs stood firm for a loose construction of the Constitution and for positive federal guidance and support for business and economic development. The Democrats persisted in their defense of strict construction, states' rights, and laissez-faire. Debates over tariffs, banking, and internal improvements remained vital and vigorous during the 1840s.

County Election *by George Caleb Bingham portrays the variety of activities that occurred on election day. Some men cast their ballots, while others exchange their views or enjoy refreshments. Note the absence of women in the scene.* ❖

True believers in both parties saw a deep ideological or moral meaning in the clash over economic issues. The Democrats were the party of individualism and personal liberty. For them, the role of government was to remove obstacles to individual rights, which could mean the right to rise economically, the right to drink hard liquor, or the right to be unorthodox in religion. Democrats were ambivalent about the rise of the market economy because of the ways it threatened individual independence. The Whigs, by contrast, were the party of orderly progress under the guidance of an enlightened elite. They believed that the propertied, the well-educated, and the pious were responsible for guiding the masses toward the common good. Believing that a market economy would benefit everyone in the long run, they had no qualms about the rise of commercial and industrial capitalism.

Each, in a sense, reflected one side of a broader democratic impulse. This Jacksonian legacy was a stress on individual freedom and ethnic or cultural tolerance (except for blacks). The Whigs perceived that in a republic, strong government could serve the general interest and further the spirit of national unity.

Conclusion: Tocqueville's Wisdom

The French traveler Alexis de Tocqueville, author of the most influential account ever written of the emergence of American democracy, visited the United States in 1831. He found much to praise in America, from the country's genius for local self-government to the participation of ordinary citizens in the affairs of their communities. But Tocqueville was also acutely aware of the limitations of American democracy. He knew that the kind of democracy white men were practicing in the

CHRONOLOGY

1824	House of Representatives elects John Quincy Adams president
1828	Congress passes the "Tariff of Abominations" ❖ Jackson is elected president over John Quincy Adams
1830	Jackson vetoes the Maysville Road bill ❖ Congress passes the Indian Removal Act
1831	Jackson reorganizes his cabinet ❖ First national nominating conventions meet
1832	Jackson vetoes the bill rechartering the Bank of the United States ❖ Jackson is reelected, defeating Henry Clay (National Republican candidate)
1832–1833	Crisis erupts over South Carolina's attempt to nullify the tariff of 1832
1833	Jackson removes federal deposits from the Bank of the United States
1834	Whig party comes into existence
1836	Jackson issues his "specie circular" ❖ Martin Van Buren is elected president
1837	Financial panic occurs, followed by depression lasting until 1843
1840	Congress passes the Independent Subtreasury Bill ❖ Harrison (Whig) defeats Van Buren (Democrat) for the presidency

Jacksonian era did not include women. He also believed that the nullification crisis foreshadowed the destruction of the Union and predicted that the problem of slavery would lead eventually to civil war and racial conflict. He noted the power of white supremacy, providing an unforgettable firsthand description of the sufferings of an Indian community in the course of forced migration to the West as well as a graphic account of the way free blacks were segregated and driven from the polls in northern cities. His belief that problems associated with slavery would endanger the Union was keenly prophetic.

Key Terms

Jacksonian Democracy, p. 190
tariff of abominations, p. 191
Trail of Tears, p. 193
nullification, p. 194
Bank War, p. 195
Whigs, p. 197
specie circular, p. 198
Panic of 1837, p. 198
second party system, p. 200

Recommended Reading

Arthur M. Schlesinger, Jr., *The Age of Jackson* (1945), sees Jacksonian democracy as a progressive protest against big business and stresses the participation of urban workers. Marvin Meyers, *The Jacksonian Persuasion: Politics and Belief* (1960), argues that Jacksonians appealed to nostalgia for an older America—"an idealized ancestral way" they believed was threatened by commercialization. Lee Benson, *The Concept of Jacksonian Democracy: New York as a Test Case* (1964), finds an ethnocultural basis for democratic allegiance. A sharply critical view of Jacksonian leadership—one that stresses opportunism, greed, and demagoguery—can be found in Edward Pessen, *Jacksonian America: Society, Personality, and Politics,* rev. ed. (1979). An excellent survey of Jacksonian politics is Harry L. Watson, *Liberty and Power* (1990), which stresses the crisis of "republicanism" at a time of "market revolution." Daniel Feller, *Jacksonian Promise: America, 1815–1840* (1995), focuses on the optimism that marked all sides of the political conflict and points to the similarities between the political parties. Development of the view that Jacksonianism was a negative reaction to the rise of market capitalism can be found in Charles Sellers, *The Market Revolution* (1991).

The classic study of the new party system is Richard P. McCormick, *The Second Party System: Party Formation in the Jacksonian Era* (1966). On who the anti-Jacksonians were, what they stood for, and what they accomplished, see Michael Holt's magisterial, *The Rise and Fall of the American Whig Party* (1999). James C. Curtis, *Andrew Jackson and the Search for Vindication* (1976), provides a good introduction to Jackson's career and personality. On Jackson's popular image, see John William Ward, *Andrew Jackson: Symbol for an Age* (1955). His Indian removal policy is the subject of Anthony F. C. Wallace, *The Long Bitter Trail: Andrew Jackson and the Indians* (1993). On the other towering political figures of the period, see Merrill D. Peterson, *The Great Triumvirate: Webster, Clay, and Calhoun* (1987). The culture of the period is well surveyed in Russel B. Nye, *Society and Culture in America, 1830–1860* (1960). Alexis de Tocqueville, *Democracy in America*, 2 vols. (1945), is a foreign visitor's wise and insightful analysis of American life in the 1830s.

On nullification, see William Freehling, *Prelude to Civil War: The Nullification Controversy in South Carolina, 1816–1836* (1966) and Richard B. Ellis, *The Union at Risk: Jacksonian Democracy, States' Rights, and the Nullification Crisis* (1987).

On the role of race in the formation of political parties and social divisions during this period, see David Roediger, *The Wages of Whiteness: Race and the Making of the American Working Class* (1991); Jean H. Baker, *Affairs of Party: The Political Culture of Northern Democrats in the Mid-Nineteenth Century* (1983); and Alexander Saxton, *The Rise and Fall of the White Republic: Class, Politics, and Mass Culture in Nineteenth-Century America* (1990).

For a list of additional titles related to this chapter's topics, please see http://www.ablongman.com/divine.

Suggested Web Sites

Indian Affairs: Laws and Treaties, compiled and edited by Charles J. Kappler (1904)

http://digital.library.okstate.edu/kappler

This digitized text at Oklahoma State University includes pre-removal treaties with the Five Civilized Tribes and other tribes.

Medicine of Jacksonian America

http://www.connerprairie.org/historyonline/jmed.html

Survival was far from certain in the Jacksonian Era. This site discusses some of the reasons and some of the possible cures of the times.

The University of Pennsylvania in 1830

http://www.archives.upenn.edu/histy/features/1830/

This "virtual tour" shows a fairly typical campus and what student life was like at one of the larger universities in the Antebellum Era.

Nineteenth-Century Scientific American On-Line

http://www.history.rochester.edu/ScientificAmerican/

Magazines and journals are windows through which we can view society. This site provides on-line editions of one of the more interesting nineteenth-century journals.

National Museum of the American Indian

http://www.si.edu/nmai

The Smithsonian Institution maintains this site, providing information about the museum, which is dedicated to the history and culture of Native Americans.

The Alexis de Tocqueville Tour: Exploring Democracy in America

http://www.tocqueville.org/

Text, images, and teaching suggestions are a part of this companion site to C-SPAN's programming on de Tocqueville.

Chapter 11

Slaves and Masters

Nat Turner's Rebellion: A Turning Point in the Slave South

On August 22, 1831, the worst nightmare of southern slaveholders became reality. A group of slaves in Southampton County, Virginia, rose in open and bloody rebellion. Their leader was Nat Turner, a preacher and prophet who believed God had given him a sign that the time was ripe to strike for freedom. When white forces dispersed the rampaging slaves forty-eight hours later, Turner's band had killed nearly sixty whites. The rebels were then rounded up and executed, along with dozens of other slaves who were vaguely suspected of complicity. Turner was the last to be captured, and he went to the gallows unrepentant, convinced he had acted in accordance with God's will.

Southern whites were determined to prevent another such uprising. Their anxiety and resolve were strengthened by the fact that 1831 also saw the emergence of a more militant northern abolitionism. Nat Turner and William Lloyd Garrison were viewed as two prongs of a revolutionary attack on the southern way of life. Afraid that abolitionist agitation might set about another revolt, southern whites launched a massive campaign to quarantine the slaves from possible exposure to antislavery ideas and attitudes.

A series of new laws severely restricted the rights of slaves to move about, assemble without white supervision, or learn to read and write. Other laws prevented white dissenters from publicly criticizing or even questioning the institution of slavery. The South rapidly became a closed society with a closed mind. Proslavery agitators sought to create a mood of crisis and danger requiring absolute unity and single-mindedness among the white population. This embattled attitude lay behind the growth of a more militant sectionalism and inspired threats to secede from the Union if security for slaveholding seemed to require it.

Outline

- The Divided Society of the Old South
- The World of Southern Blacks
- White Society in the Antebellum South
- Slavery and the Southern Economy
- Conclusion: Worlds in Conflict

We Americans

- Women of Southern Households

THE CAMPAIGN FOR REPRESSION after the Nat Turner rebellion apparently achieved its original aim. Turner's revolt was the last mass slave uprising. Slave resistance, however, did not end; it simply took less dangerous forms. Slaves sought or perfected other methods of asserting their humanity and maintaining their self-esteem. This heroic effort to endure slavery without surrendering to it gave rise to a resilient African American culture.

This culture combined unique family arrangements, religious ideas of liberation, and creative responses to the oppression of servitude. Among white Southerners, the need to police and control this huge population of enslaved people influenced every aspect of daily life and produced an increasingly isolated, divided, and insecure society. While long-standing racial prejudice contributed to the divided society, the determination of whites to preserve the institution of slavery derived in large part from the important role slavery played in the southern economy.

THE DIVIDED SOCIETY OF THE OLD SOUTH

Slavery would not have lasted as long as it did—and Southerners would not have reacted so strongly to real or imagined threats to its survival—if an influential class of whites had not had a vital and growing economic interest in this form of human exploitation. Since the early colonial period, forced labor had been considered essential to the South's plantation economy. In the period between the 1790s and the Civil War, plantation agriculture expanded enormously, and so did dependence on slave labor.

The fact that all whites were free and most blacks were slaves created a sharp cleavage between the races in Southern society. Yet the overwhelming importance of race gives an impression of a basic equality within the "master race" that some would say is an illusion. The truth may lie somewhere in between. In the language of sociologists, inequality in the **Old South** was determined in two ways: by class (differences in status resulting from unequal access to wealth and productive resources) and by caste (inherited advantages or disadvantages associated with racial ancestry). Awareness of both systems of social ranking is necessary for an understanding of southern society.

Old South The term refers to the slave-holding states between 1830 and 1860, when slave labor and cotton production dominated the economies of the southern states. This period is also known as the "antebellum era."

White society was divided by class and by region; both were important for determining a white Southerner's relationship to the institution of slavery. More than any other factor, the ownership of slaves determined gradations of social prestige and influence among whites. The large planters were the dominant class, and nonslaveholders were of lower social rank. Planters (defined as those who owned twenty or more slaves) tended to live in the plantation areas of the "Cotton Belt" stretching from Georgia across Alabama, Mississippi, Louisiana, and Texas, as well as lowcountry South Carolina. In upcountry and frontier areas lived yeoman farmers who owned no or just a few slaves.

In 1860, only one-quarter of all white Southerners belonged to families owning slaves. Even in the Cotton Belt, slaveholders were a minority of whites on the eve of the Civil War. Planters were the minority of a minority, just 4 percent of the total white population of the South in 1860. Three-fourths of all whites owned no slaves at all. Thus, Southern society was dominated by a planter class that was a numerical and geographically isolated minority; inequalities of class became divisions of region as well.

There were also divisions within black society. Most African Americans in the South were slaves, but a small number, about 6 percent, were free. Even free blacks faced increasing restrictions on their rights during the antebellum era. Among slaves, the great majority lived on plantations and worked in agriculture, but a small number worked either in industrial jobs or in a variety of tasks in urban settings. Even on plantations, there were some differences in status and experience between field hands and servants who worked in the house or in skilled jobs such as carpentry or blacksmithing. Yet because all blacks, even those who were free, suffered under the yoke of racial prejudice and legal inequality, these diverse experiences did not translate into the kind of class divisions that caused rifts within white Southern society. Rather, most blacks shared the goal of ending slavery.

THE WORLD OF SOUTHERN BLACKS

African Americans of the early to mid-nineteenth century experienced slavery on plantations; the majority of slaves lived on units owned by planters who had twenty or more slaves. The masters of these agrarian communities sought to ensure their personal safety and the profitability of their enterprises by using all the means—physical and psychological—at their command to make slaves docile and obedient. Through word and deed, they tried to convince the slaves that whites were superior and had a right to rule over blacks. As increasing numbers of slaves were converted to Christianity and attended white-supervised services, they were forced to hear, over and over again, that God had commanded slaves to serve and obey their masters.

Despite these pressures, most African Americans managed to retain an inner sense of their own worth and dignity. When conditions were right, they openly asserted their desire for freedom and equality and showed their disdain for white claims that slavery was a "positive good." Although slave culture did not normally provoke violent resistance to the slaveholders' regime, the inner world that slaves made for themselves gave them the spiritual strength to thwart the masters' efforts to take over their hearts and minds. After emancipation, this resilient cultural heritage would combine with the tradition of open protest created by rebellious slaves and free black abolitionists to inspire and sustain new struggles for equality.

Slaves' Daily Life and Labor

Slaves' daily life varied enormously depending on the region in which they lived and the type of plantation or farm on which they worked. On large plantations in the Cotton Belt, most slaves worked in "gangs" under an overseer. White overseers, sometimes helped by black "drivers," enforced a workday from sunup to sundown, six days a week. Cotton cultivation required year-round labor, so there was never a slack season under "King Cotton." Enslaved women and children were expected to work in the fields as well, often bringing babies and young children to the fields where they could be cared for by older children, and nursed by their mothers during brief breaks. Some older children worked in "trash gangs," doing lighter tasks such as weeding and yard cleaning.

Not all slaves in agriculture worked in gangs. In the low country of South Carolina and Georgia, slaves who cultivated rice worked under a task system that gave them more control over the pace of labor. With less supervision, many were able to complete their tasks within an eight-hour day. Likewise, slaves who lived on small farms often worked side by side with their masters rather than in large groups of slaves. Such intimacy, however, did not necessarily mean a leveling of power relationships, and despite masters' efforts to control the pace of work, even under the gang system, slaves resisted working on "clock" time, enforcing customary rights to take breaks and especially to take Sunday off completely.

While about three-quarters of slaves were field workers, slaves performed many other kinds of labor. They dug ditches, built houses, worked on boats and in mills (often hired out by their masters for a year at a time), and labored as house ser-

Although cotton cultivation required constant attention, many of the tasks involved were relatively simple. Thus on a plantation the majority of slaves, including women and children, were field hands who performed the same tasks. Here a slave family stands behind baskets of picked cotton in a Georgia cotton field. ❖

vants, cooking, cleaning, and gardening. Some slaves also worked within the slave community as preachers, caretakers of children, and healers, especially women. While white masters sometimes treated domestic workers or other personal servants as having a special status, it would be a mistake to assume that their ranking system was shared by slaves. What evidence we have suggests that those with highest status within slave communities were preachers and healers, people whose special skills and knowledge directly benefited their communities.

A small number of slaves, about 5 percent, worked in industry in the South, including mills, iron works, and railroad construction. Slaves in cities took on a wider range of jobs than plantation slaves—as porters, waiters, cooks, and skilled laborers in tradesmen's shops—and in general enjoyed more autonomy. Some urban slaves even lived apart from their masters and hired out their own time, returning a portion of their wages to their owners.

In addition to the work they did for their masters in the fields or in other jobs, most slaves kept gardens or small farm plots for themselves to supplement their daily food rations. They also fished, hunted and trapped animals. Many slaves also worked "overtime" for their own masters on Sundays or holidays in exchange for money or goods, or hired out their overtime hours to others. This underground economy suggests slaves' overpowering desire to provide for their families, sometimes even raising enough funds to purchase their freedom.

Slave Families, Kinship, and Community

More than any other, the African American family was the institution that prevented slavery from becoming utterly demoralizing. Contrary to what historians and sociologists used to believe, slaves had a strong and abiding sense of family and kinship. But the nature of the families or households that predominated on particular plantations or farms varied according to local circumstances. On large plantations with relatively stable slave populations, a substantial majority of slave children lived in two-parent households, and many marriages lasted for as long as twenty to thirty years. They were more often broken up by the death or sale of one of the partners than by voluntary dissolution of the union. Close bonds united mothers, fathers, and children, and parents shared child-rearing responsibilities (within the limits allowed by the masters). Marital fidelity was encouraged by masters who believed that stable unions produced more offspring and by Christian churches that viewed adultery and divorce as sinful.

But in areas where most slaves lived on farms or small plantations, and especially in areas of the upper South where the trading and hiring out of slaves was frequent, a different pattern seems to have prevailed. Under these circumstances, slaves frequently had spouses who resided on other plantations or farms, often some distance away, and ties between husbands and wives were looser and more fragile. The result was that female-headed families were the norm, and responsibility for child rearing was vested in mothers, assisted in most cases by female relatives and friends. Mother-centered families with weak conjugal ties were a natural response to the infrequent presence of fathers and to the prospect of their being moved or sold beyond visiting distance. Where the breakup of unions by sale or relocation could be expected at any time, it did not pay to invest all of one's emotions in a conjugal relationship. But whether the basic family form was nuclear or matrifocal (female-headed), the ties that it created were infinitely precious to its members. Masters acquired great leverage over the behavior of slaves by invoking the threat of family breakup through sale to enforce discipline.

The terrible anguish that usually accompanied the breakup of families through sale showed the depth of kinship feelings. After emancipation, thousands of freed slaves wandered about looking for spouses, children, or parents from whom they had been forcibly separated years before.

On large plantations, slave men and women formed stable monogamous unions that often lasted until the couple was broken up by the death or sale of one of the partners. This painting by Christian Mayr portrays a slave wedding celebrated in White Sulphur Springs, Virginia, in 1838. The wedding couple wears white attire. ❖

Feelings of kinship and mutual obligation extended beyond the nuclear family. Grandparents, uncles, aunts, and even cousins were often known to slaves through direct contact or family lore. Nor were kinship ties limited to blood relations. When families were broken up by sale, individual members who found themselves on plantations far from home were likely to be assimilated into new kinship networks. Orphans or children without responsible parents were quickly absorbed without prejudice into new families.

Studies of the slave family reveal that kinship provided a model for personal relationships and the basis for a sense of community. Elderly slaves were addressed as "uncle" and "aunty," and younger slaves commonly called each other "brother" or "sister." Slave culture was a family culture, and this was one of its greatest sources of strength and cohesion. The kinship network also provided a vehicle for the transmission of African American folk traditions from one generation to the next. Together with slave religion, kinship gave African Americans some sense that they were members of a community, not just a collection of individuals victimized by oppression.

African American Religion

From the realm of culture and fundamental beliefs, African Americans drew the strength to hold their heads high and look beyond their immediate condition. Religion was the cornerstone of this emerging African American culture. Black Christianity was far from a mere imitation of white religious forms and beliefs. This distinctive variant of evangelical Protestantism incorporated elements of African religion and stressed those portions of the Bible that spoke to the aspirations of an enslaved people thirsting for freedom.

Most slaves did not encounter Christianity in a church setting. There were a few independent black churches in the antebellum South, which mainly served free blacks and some urban slaves with indulgent masters. These included a variety of autonomous Baptist groups as well as Southern branches of the highly successful

African Methodist Episcopal (AME) Church, a national denomination founded in 1816 by the Reverend Richard Allen of Philadelphia. But the mass of blacks did not have access to the independent churches.

African Methodist Episcopal (AME) Church Richard Allen founded the African Methodist Episcopal Church in 1816 as the first independent black-run Protestant church in the United States. The AME Church was active in the promotion of abolition and the founding of educational institutions for free blacks.

Plantation slaves who were exposed to Christianity either attended the neighboring white churches or worshiped at home. On large estates, masters or white missionaries often conducted Sunday services. But white-sanctioned religious activity was only a superficial part of the slaves' spiritual life. The true slave religion was practiced at night, often secretly, and was led by black preachers.

This covert slave religion was a highly emotional affair that featured singing, shouting, and dancing. In some ways, the atmosphere resembled a backwoods revival meeting. But much of what went on was actually an adaptation of African religious beliefs and customs. The chanting mode of preaching—with the congregation responding at regular intervals—and the expression of religious feelings through rhythmic movements, especially the counterclockwise movement known as the ring shout, were clearly African in origin. The emphasis on sinfulness and fear of damnation that were core themes of white Evangelicalism played a lesser role among blacks. For them, religion was more an affirmation of the joy of life than a rejection of worldly pleasures and temptations.

Slave sermons and religious songs spoke directly to the plight of a people in bondage and implicitly asserted their right to be free. The most popular of all biblical subjects was the deliverance of the children of Israel from slavery in Egypt. Many sermons and songs refer to the crossing of Jordan and the arrival in the Promised Land. Other songs invoke the liberation theme in different ways. One recalls that Jesus had "set poor sinners free."

Most of the songs of freedom and deliverance can be interpreted as referring exclusively to religious salvation and the afterlife—and this was undoubtedly how slaves hoped their masters would understand them. But the slaves did not forget that God had once freed a people from slavery in this life and punished their masters. The Bible thus gave African Americans the hope that they, as a people, would repeat the experience of the Israelites and be delivered from bondage. During the Civil War, observers noted that freed slaves seemed to regard their emancipation as something that had been preordained, and some were inclined to view Lincoln as the reincarnation of Moses.

Besides being the basis for a deep-rooted hope for eventual freedom, religion also helped the slaves endure bondage without losing their sense of inner worth. Religious slaves sometimes regarded themselves as superior to their owners and believed that all whites were damned because of their unjust treatment of blacks.

More important, slave religion gave African Americans a chance to create and control a world of their own. Preachers, elders, and other leaders of slave congregations could acquire status within their own community that had not been conferred by whites. Although religion seldom inspired slaves to open rebellion, it must be regarded as a prime source of resistance to the dehumanizing effects of enslavement. It helped create a sense of community, solidarity, and self-esteem among slaves by giving them something of their own that they found infinitely precious.

Resistance and Rebellion

Open rebellion, the bearing of arms against the oppressors by organized groups of slaves, was the most dramatic and clear-cut form of slave resistance. In the period between 1800 and 1831, a number of slaves participated in revolts that showed their willingness to risk their lives in a desperate bid for liberation. In 1800, a Virginia slave named Gabriel Prosser mobilized a large band of his fellows to march on Richmond, but whites suppressed the uprising without any loss of white life. In 1811, another band of rebellious slaves was stopped as it moved on New Orleans brandishing guns, waving flags, and beating drums. In 1822, whites in Charleston,

South Carolina, uncovered an extensive and well-planned conspiracy, organized by a free black man named Denmark Vesey, to arm the slave population and take possession of the city.

As we have already seen, the bloodiest and most terrifying of all slave revolts was the Nat Turner insurrection of 1831. Although it was the last slave rebellion of this kind during the pre–Civil War period, armed resistance had not ended. In Florida, hundreds of black fugitives fought in the Second Seminole War (1835–1842) alongside the Indians who had given them a haven. Many of the blacks eventually accompanied their Indian allies to the trans-Mississippi West.

Only a tiny fraction of all slaves ever took part in organized acts of violent resistance against white power. Most realized that the odds against a successful revolt were very high, and bitter experience had shown them that the usual outcome was death to the rebels. As a consequence, therefore, they devised safer or more ingenious ways to resist white dominance.

Thousands of slaves showed their discontent and desire for freedom by running away. Although most fugitives never got beyond the neighborhood of the plantation, many escapees remained free for years by hiding in swamps or other remote areas, and a fraction made it to freedom in the North or Mexico. Some fugitives stowed away aboard ships; others traveled overland for hundreds of miles. One resourceful slave even had himself packed in a box and shipped to the North. Some escaped with the help of the **Underground Railroad,** an informal network of sympathetic free blacks (and a few whites) who helped fugitives make their way North. For the majority of slaves, however, flight was not a real option. Either they lived too deep in the South to have any chance of reaching free soil, or they were reluctant to leave family and friends behind. As a result the typical fugitive was a young, unmarried male from the upper South.

Underground Railroad A network of safe houses organized by abolitionists (usually free blacks) to aid slaves in their attempts to escape slavery in the North or Canada.

Slaves who did not revolt or run away often expressed discontent by engaging in indirect or passive resistance. Many slaves worked slowly and inefficiently, not because they were naturally lazy (as whites supposed) but as a gesture of protest. Others withheld labor by feigning illness or injury, stole provisions and committed acts of sabotage such as breaking tools, mistreating livestock, and setting barns on fire. The ultimate act of clandestine resistance was poisoning the master's food.

The basic attitude behind such actions was revealed in the folktales that slaves passed down from generation to generation. The famous Brer Rabbit stories showed how a small, apparently defenseless animal could overcome a bigger and stronger one through cunning and deceit. Such tales served as an allegory for the black view of the master-slave relationship. Other stories—which were not told in front of whites—openly portrayed the slave as a clever trickster outwitting the master.

Free Blacks in the Old South

Southern society was shaped by the need to protect slavery. The attacks of abolitionists and the constant fear of slave revolt hardened the line that divided free whites from enslaved blacks. This intensification of the South into an even more sharply defined "slave society" threatened the status of all blacks who tried to live freely in the South.

In the South, free blacks were subject to a set of direct controls that tended to make them semi-slaves. They were required to carry papers proving their free status, and their movements were strictly limited. Blacks were excluded from several occupations, prohibited from holding meetings or forming organizations, and often forced into a state of economic dependency barely distinguishable from slavery.

Although beset by special problems of their own, most free blacks identified with the suffering of the slaves. Many of them had once been slaves themselves or were the children of slaves. Often they had close relatives who were still in bondage.

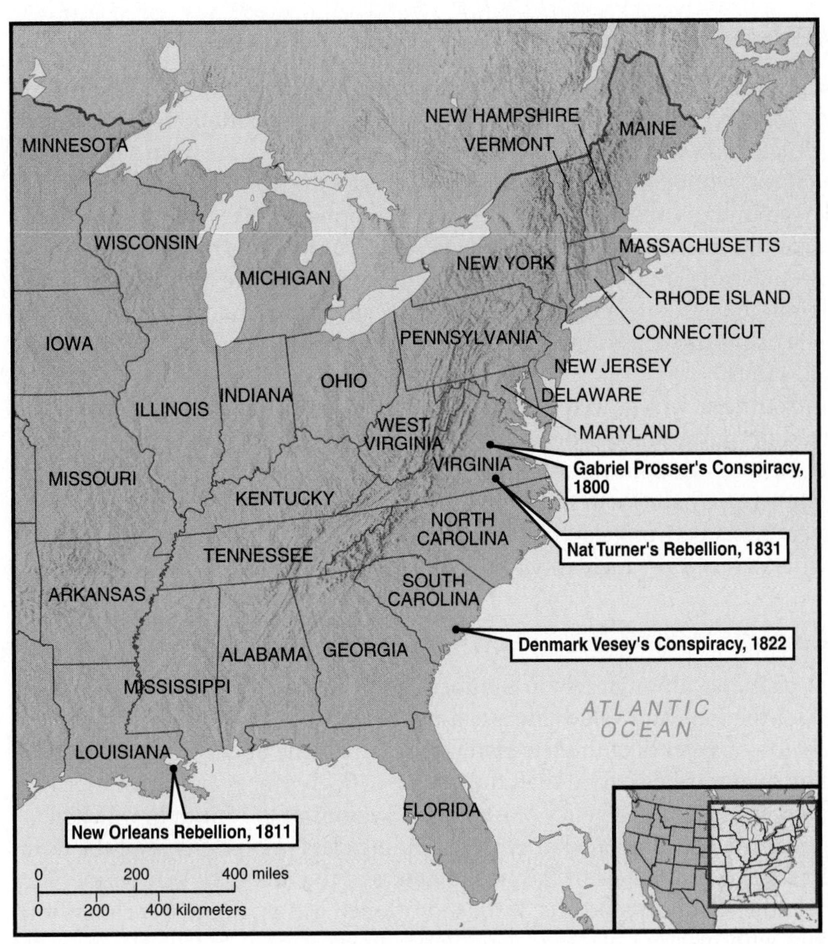

SLAVE REBELLIONS AND UPRISINGS, 1800–1831 *Although slave uprisings were infrequent, the fear that their slaves would rise up in rebellion was a constant worry for white slaveholders.*

Furthermore, they knew that as long as slavery existed, their own rights were likely to be denied, and even their freedom was at risk. Kidnapping or fraudulent seizure by slave-catchers was always a possibility.

Because of the elaborate system of control and surveillance, free blacks in the South were in a relatively weak position to work against slavery. Most free blacks found that survival depended on creating the impression of loyalty to the planter regime. In some parts of the lower South, groups of relatively privileged free Negroes, mostly of racially mixed origin, were sometimes persuaded that it was to their advantage to preserve the status quo. As skilled artisans and small-business owners dependent on white favors and patronage, they had little incentive to risk everything by taking the side of the slaves. In southern Louisiana, there was even a small group of mulatto planters who lived in luxury, supported by the labor of other African Americans.

However, although some free blacks were able to create niches of relative freedom, their position in southern society became increasingly precarious in the late antebellum period. Beginning in the 1830s, Southern whites sought to draw the line between free and unfree more firmly as a line between black and white. Free blacks were an anomaly in this system; increasingly, the Southern answer was to exclude, degrade, and even enslave those free people of color who remained within their borders. Just before the outbreak of the Civil War, a campaign developed in some southern states to carry the pattern of repression and discrimination to its logical conclusion: several state legislatures proposed laws giving free Negroes the choice of emigrating from the state or being enslaved.

White Society in the Antebellum South

Those who know the Old South only from modern novels, films, and television programs are likely to envision a land filled with majestic plantations, courtly gentlemen, elegant ladies, and faithful retainers. It is easy to conclude from such images that the typical white Southerner was an aristocrat who belonged to a family that owned large numbers of slaves. Certainly the great houses existed and some wealthy slaveholders did maintain an aristocratic lifestyle. But this was the world of only a small percentage of slaveowners and a minuscule portion of the total white population. The number of large planters who had the means to build great houses and entertain lavishly, those who owned at least fifty slaves, comprised less than 1 percent of all whites.

Most Southern whites were nonslaveholding yeoman farmers. Yet even those who owned no slaves grew to depend on slavery in other ways, whether economically, because they hired slaves, or psychologically, because having a degraded class of blacks below them made them feel better about their own place in society. However, the class divisions between slaveholders and nonslaveholders did contribute to the political rifts that became increasingly apparent on the eve of the Civil War.

The Planters' World

The great planters, although few in number, had a weighty influence on southern life. They set the tone and values for much of the rest of society. Although many of them were too busy tending to their plantations to become openly involved in politics, wealthy planters held more than their share of high offices and often exerted a decisive influence on public policy. Within those regions of the South in which plantation agriculture predominated, they were a ruling class in every sense of the term.

Contrary to legend, most of the great planters of the pre–Civil War period were self-made rather than descendants of the old colonial gentry. Some were ambitious young men who married planters' daughters. Others started as lawyers and used their fees and connections to acquire plantations.

As the Cotton Kingdom spread westward, the men who became the largest slaveholders were even less likely to have genteel backgrounds. A large proportion of them began as hard-driving businessmen who built up capital from commerce, land speculation, banking, and even slave trading. They then used their profits to buy plantations. The highly competitive, boom-or-bust economy of the Southwest put a greater premium on sharp dealing and business skills than on genealogy. To be successful, a planter had to be not only a good plantation manager, but also a shrewd entrepreneur who kept a careful eye on the market, the prices of slaves and land, and the extent of his indebtedness. Hence few planters could be men of leisure.

Likewise, the responsibility of running an extended household that produced much of its own food and clothing kept most plantation mistresses from being the idle ladies of legend—few Southern women fit the stereotype of the Southern belle sipping tea on the veranda. Not only were plantation mistresses a tiny minority of the women who lived and worked in the slave states before the Civil War, but even those who were part of the planter elite rarely led lives of leisure.

A small number of the richest and most secure plantation families did aspire to live in the manner of a traditional landed aristocracy, with big houses, elegant carriages, fancy-dress balls, and excessive numbers of house servants. Dueling, despite efforts to repress it, remained the standard way to settle "affairs of honor" among gentlemen. Another sign of gentility was the tendency of planters' sons to avoid "trade" as a primary or secondary career in favor of law or the military. Planters' daughters were trained from girlhood to play the piano, speak French, dress in the latest fashions, and sparkle in the drawing room or on the dance floor. The aristocratic style originated among the older gentry of the seaboard slave states, but by the 1840s and 1850s it had spread southwest as a second generation of wealthy planters began to displace the rough-hewn pioneers of the Cotton Kingdom.

Planters and Paternalism

No assessment of the planters' outlook or "worldview" can be made without considering their relations with their slaves. Planters owned more than half of all the slaves in the South and set standards for treatment and management. Most planters liked to think of themselves as benevolent masters and they often referred to their slavers as members of an extended patriarchal family. According to the ideology of paternalism, blacks were a race of perpetual children requiring care and supervision by superior whites. Paternalistic rhetoric increased greatly after abolitionists began to charge that most slaveholders were sadistic monsters.

There was, nevertheless, an element of truth in the planters' claim that their slaves were relatively well treated. Food, clothing, and shelter usually were sufficient to sustain life and labor at above the bare subsistence level; family life was encouraged and to some extent flourished; and average life expectancy, birthrate, and natural growth in population were only slightly below the average for southern whites. Certainly North American slaves of the pre–Civil War period enjoyed a higher standard of living than those in other New World slave societies, where slave populations usually failed to reproduce themselves.

But relatively good physical conditions for slaves does not demonstrate that planters put ethical considerations ahead of self-interest. The ban on the transatlantic slave trade in 1808 was effective enough to make the domestic reproduction of the slave force an economic necessity if the system was to be perpetuated. While some historians have argued that paternalism was part of a social system that was organized like a family hierarchy rather than a brutal, profit-making arrangement, there was no inconsistency between planters' paternalism and capitalism. Slaves were valuable property and the main tools of production for a booming economy, and it was in the interest of masters to see that their property remained in good enough condition to work hard and produce large numbers of children.

The testimony of slaves themselves and of some independent white observers suggests that masters of large plantations generally did not have close and intimate relationships with the mass of field slaves. The kind of affection and concern associated with a father figure appears to have been limited mainly to relationships with a few favored house servants or other elite slaves, such as drivers and highly skilled artisans. The field hands on large estates dealt mostly with overseers who were hired or fired because of their ability to meet production quotas.

When they were being most realistic, planters conceded that the ultimate basis of their authority was force and intimidation, rather than the natural obedience resulting due to a loving parent. Devices for inspiring fear included whipping—a common practice on most plantations—and the threat of sale away from family and friends. Planters and overseers maintained order by swift punishment for any infraction of the rules or even for a surly attitude.

❖ A Look at the Past ❖

Slave Clothing

Slaves typically received a yearly clothing allotment of one complete outfit and a pair of shoes. Slaves sometimes received cast-off clothing or lengths of decent fabric to make the year's new outfit, but generally they were given the cheapest fabric on the market, osnaburg, a coarse factory-woven cloth. While northern factories spun cotton and wove it into osnaburg for the southern market, men and women throughout New England earned extra money making brogans for slaves. Coarsely put together with soles pegged on rather than sewn, brogans were cheap and quick to make. How did slaves' clothing reinforce their position? What do northern fabric and shoes made especially for the slave market suggest about connections between slavery and the northern economy?

In spite of economic considerations, some masters inevitably yielded to the temptations of power or to their bad tempers and tortured or killed their slaves. Others raped slave women. Slaves had little legal protection against such abuse because their testimony was not accepted in court. Human nature being what it is, such a situation was bound to result in atrocities. As Harriet Beecher Stowe acknowledged in 1852 in *Uncle Tom's Cabin,* her celebrated antislavery novel, most slaveholders were not as sadistic and brutish as Simon Legree, but there was something terribly wrong with an institution that gave one human being nearly absolute power over another.

Small Slaveholders

As we have seen, 88 percent of all slaveholders in 1860 owned fewer than twenty slaves and thus were not planters in the usual sense of the term. Of these, the great majority had fewer than ten. Many were simply farmers who used one or two slave families to ease the burden of their own labor. Life on these small slaveholding farms was relatively spartan. Masters lived in log cabins or small frame cottages, and slaves lived in lofts or sheds that were not usually up to plantation housing standards.

For better or worse, relations between owners and their slaves were more intimate than on larger estates. Unlike planters, these farmers often worked in the fields alongside their slaves and sometimes ate at the same table or slept under the same roof. But such closeness did not necessarily result in better treatment. Both the best and the worst of slavery could be found on these farms, depending on the character and disposition of the master. Given a choice, most slaves preferred to live on plantations because they offered the sociability, culture, and kinship of the slave quarters, as well as better prospects for adequate food, clothing, and shelter.

Yeoman Farmers

yeoman Southern small landholders who owned no slaves and who lived primarily in the foothills of the Appalachian and Ozark mountains. These farmers were self-reliant and grew mixed crops, although they usually did not produce a substantial amount to be sold on the market.

Just below the small slaveholders on the social scale was a substantial class of **yeoman** farmers. Contrary to another myth about the Old South, most of these people did not fit the image of the degraded, shiftless, "poor white." The majority of the nonslaveholding rural population were proud, self-reliant farmers whose way of life did not differ markedly from that of family farmers in the Midwest during the early stages of settlement.

The yeomen were mostly concentrated in the backcountry where slaves and plantations were rarely seen. The foothills or interior valleys of the Appalachians and the Ozarks were unsuitable for plantation agriculture but offered reasonably good soils for mixed farming, and long stretches of "piney barrens" along the Gulf Coast were suitable for raising livestock. Slaveless farmers concentrated in these regions, giving rise to the "white counties" that complicated southern politics.

Yeoman women, much more than their wealthy plantation counterparts, participated in every dimension of household labor. They worked in the garden, made clothing and handicrafts, and even labored in the fields when it was necessary. Women in the most dire economic circumstances even worked for wages in small businesses or on nearby farms. They raised much larger families than their wealthier neighbors because having many children supplied a valuable labor pool for the family farm.

The lack of transportation facilities, more than some failure of energy or character, limited the prosperity of the yeomen. A large part of their effort was devoted to growing subsistence crops, mainly corn. Their principle source of cash was livestock, especially hogs. But since the livestock was generally allowed to forage in the woods rather than being fattened on grain, it was of poor quality and did not bring high prices or big profits to raisers.

Although they did not benefit directly from the peculiar institution, most yeomen and other nonslaveholders tolerated slavery and were fiercely opposed to abolitionism in any form. Many abolitionists could not understand the reasons for their position, for undoubtedly the yeoman were hurt economically by the existence of slavery and a planter class. Most yeomen were staunch Jacksonians who resented aristocratic pretensions and feared concentrations of power and wealth in the hands of the few. On issues involving representation, banking, and internal improvements, yeomen sometimes voted against the planters. Why, then, did they fail to respond to antislavery appeals that called on them to strike at the real source of planter power and privilege?

One reason was that some nonslaveholders hoped to get ahead in the world, and in the South this meant acquiring slaves of their own. Just enough of the more prosperous yeomen broke into the slaveholding classes to make this dream seem believable. Planters, anxious to ensure the loyalty of nonslaveholders, strenuously encouraged the notion that every white man was a potential master.

Even if they did not aspire to own slaves, white farmers often viewed black servitude as providing a guarantee of their own liberty and independence. Although they had no natural love of planters and slavery, they believed that abolition would lead to disaster. In part, their anxieties were economic; freed slaves would compete with them for land or jobs. But their racism went deeper than this. Emancipation was unthinkable because it would remove the pride and status that automatically went along with a white skin in this acutely race-conscious society. Slavery, despite its drawbacks, served to keep blacks "in their place" and to make all whites, however poor and uneducated they might be, feel that they were free and equal members of a master race.

A Closed Mind and a Closed Society

Despite the tacit assent of most nonslaveholders, the dominant class never lost its fear that lower-class whites would turn against slavery. They felt threatened from two sides: from the slave quarters where a new Nat Turner might be gathering his forces, and from the backcountry where yeomen and poor whites might heed the call of abolitionists and rise up against planter domination. Beginning in the 1830s, the ruling element tightened their grip on southern society and culture.

Before the 1830s, open discussion of the rights or wrongs of slavery had been possible in many parts of the South. Apologists commonly described the institution as "a necessary evil" and in the upper South there was significant support for the **American Colonization Society**'s program of gradual emancipation accompanied by deportation of the freedmen. By the end of 1832, however, all talk about emancipation had ended in the South. The argument that slavery was a positive good, rather than an evil slated for gradual elimination, won the day.

American Colonization Society Founded in 1817, this organization hoped to provide a mechanism by which slavery could be gradually eliminated. The Society advocated the relocation of free blacks (followed by freed slaves) to the African colony of Monrovia, present-day Liberia.

The positive good defense of slavery was an answer to the abolitionist charge that the institution was inherently sinful. The message was carried in a host of books, pamphlets, and newspaper editorials published between the 1830s and the Civil War. Who, historians have asked, was it meant to persuade? Partly, the argument was aimed at the North. But Southerners themselves were a prime target. In popularized forms, the message was used to arouse racial anxieties that tended to neutralize antislavery sentiment among the lower classes.

The proslavery argument was based on three main propositions. The first and foremost was that enslavement was the natural and proper status for people of African descent. Blacks, it was alleged, were innately inferior to whites and suited only for slavery. Biased scientific and historical evidence was presented to support this claim. Second, slavery was held to be sanctioned by the Bible and Christianity—a position made necessary by the abolitionist appeal to Christian ethics. Third, efforts were made to show that slavery was consistent with the humanitarian spirit of the nineteenth century. The plantation was seen as a sort of asylum providing guidance and care for a race that could not look after itself.

By the 1850s, the proslavery argument had gone beyond mere apology for the South and its peculiar institution and featured an ingenious attack on the free-labor system of the North. According to Virginian George Fitzhugh, the master-slave relationship was more humane than the one prevailing between employers and wage laborers in the North. Slaves had security against unemployment and a guarantee of care in old age, whereas free workers might face destitution and even starvation at any time. Fitzhugh believed that slave societies were more orderly, just, and peaceful than free societies.

In addition to arguing against the abolitionists, proslavery Southerners attempted to seal off their region from antislavery ideas and influences. Whites who were bold enough to criticize slavery publicly were mobbed or persecuted. One of the last and bravest of the southern abolitionists, Cassius M. Clay of Kentucky, armed himself with a brace of pistols when he gave speeches. Clergymen who questioned the morality of slavery were driven from their pulpits, and northern travelers suspected of being abolitionist agents were tarred and feathered. When abolitionists tried to send their literature through the mails during the 1830s, it was seized in southern post offices and publicly burned.

Such flagrant denials of free speech and civil liberties were inspired in part by fears that nonslaveholding whites and slaves would get subversive ideas. Hinton R. Helper's 1857 book *The Impending Crisis of the South,* an appeal to nonslaveholders to resist the planter regime, was suppressed with particular vigor. But the deepest fear was that slaves would hear the abolitionist talk or read antislavery literature and be inspired to rebel. Consequently, new laws were passed making it a crime to teach slaves to read and write. Free blacks, thought to be possible instigators of slave revolt, were denied basic civil liberties and were the object of growing surveillance and harassment.

All these efforts at thought control and internal security did not allay planters' fears of abolitionist subversion, lower-class white dissent, and, above all, slave revolt. The persistent barrage of proslavery propaganda and the course of national events in the 1850s created a mood of panic and desperation. By this time, an increasing number of Southerners had become convinced that safety from abolitionism and its associated terrors required a formal withdrawal from the Union—secession.

Slavery and the Southern Economy

Despite the internal divisions of Southern society, white Southerners from all regions and classes came to perceive their interests tied up with slavery. Southern society transformed itself according to the needs of the slave system because slavery was the cornerstone of the Southern economy. For the most part, the expansion of slavery—the number of slaves in the South more than tripled between 1810 and 1860 to nearly 4 million—can be attributed to the rise of King Cotton. The cotton-growing areas of the South were becoming more and more dependent on slavery, at the same time that agriculture in the upper South was actually moving away from the institution. Yet slavery continued to remain important to the economy of the upper South, through the slave trade. To understand Southern thought and behavior, it is necessary to bear in mind this major regional difference between a slave plantation society and a farming and slave trading region.

The Internal Slave Trade

Tobacco, the original plantation crop of the colonial period, continued to be the principal slave-cultivated commodity of the upper tier of southern states during the pre–Civil War era. But markets were often depressed, and profitable tobacco cultivation was hard to sustain for very long in one place because the crop rapidly depleted the soil. During the lengthy depression of the tobacco market that lasted from the 1820s to the 1850s, tobacco farmers in Virginia and Maryland experimented with fertilizer use, crop rotation, and diversified farming, all of which increased the need for capital but reduced the demand for labor.

As slave prices rose (because of high demand in the lower South) and demand for slaves in the upper South fell, the "internal" slave trade took off. Increasingly, the most profitable business for slaveholders in Virginia, Kentucky, Maryland, and the Carolinas was selling "surplus" slaves from the upper South to regions of the lower South, where staple crop production was more profitable. This interstate slave trade sent an estimated six to seven hundred thousand slaves in a southwesterly direction between 1815 and 1860. Historian Michael Tadman estimates that the chances of a slave child in the Upper South in the 1820s to be "sold South" by 1860 was as high as 30 percent. Such sales were wrenching, not only splitting families, but making it especially unlikely that the slaves sold would ever see friends or family again.

Some economic historians have concluded that the most important crop produced in the tobacco kingdom was not the "stinking weed" but human beings cultivated for the auction block. Respectable planters did not like to think of themselves as raising slaves for market, but few would refuse to sell some of their "people" if they needed money to get out of debt or make expensive improvements. For the region as a whole, the slave trade provided a crucial source of capital in a period of transition and innovation. Nevertheless, the fact that slave labor was declining in importance in the upper South meant the peculiar institution had a weaker hold on public loyalty there than in the cotton states. Diversification of agriculture was accompanied by a more rapid rate of urban and industrial development than was occurring elsewhere in the South. As a result, Virginians, Marylanders, and Kentuckians were seriously divided on whether their ultimate future lay with the Deep South's plantation economy or with the industrializing free-labor system that was flourishing just north of their borders.

The Rise of the Cotton Kingdom

The warmer climate and good soils of the lower tier of southern states made it possible to raise crops more naturally suited than tobacco or cereals to the plantation form of agriculture and the heavy use of slave labor, including rice and long-staple cotton along the coast of South Carolina and Georgia, and sugar in lower Louisiana. But cultivation of these crops was limited by natural conditions to peripheral, semitropical areas. It was the rise of short-staple cotton as the South's major crop that strengthened the hold of slavery and the plantation on the southern economy.

Short-staple cotton differed from the long-staple variety in two important ways: its bolls contained seeds that were much more difficult to extract by hand, and it could be grown almost anywhere south of Virginia and Kentucky—the main requirement was a guarantee of two hundred frost-free days. The invention of the **cotton gin** in 1793 ended the seed extraction problem and made short-staple cotton the South's major crop. Unlike rice and sugar, cotton could be grown on small farms as well as on plantations. But large planters enjoyed certain advantages that made them the main producers. Only relatively large operators could afford their own gins or possessed the capital to acquire the fertile bottomlands that brought the highest yields. They also had lower transportation costs because they were able to monopolize land along rivers and streams that were the South's natural arteries of transportation.

cotton gin Invented by Eli Whitney in 1793, this device for separating the seeds from the fibers of short-staple cotton enabled a slave to clean fifty times more cotton as by hand, which reduced production costs and gave new life to slavery in the South.

The first major cotton-producing regions were inland areas of Georgia and South Carolina but the center of production shifted rapidly westward during the

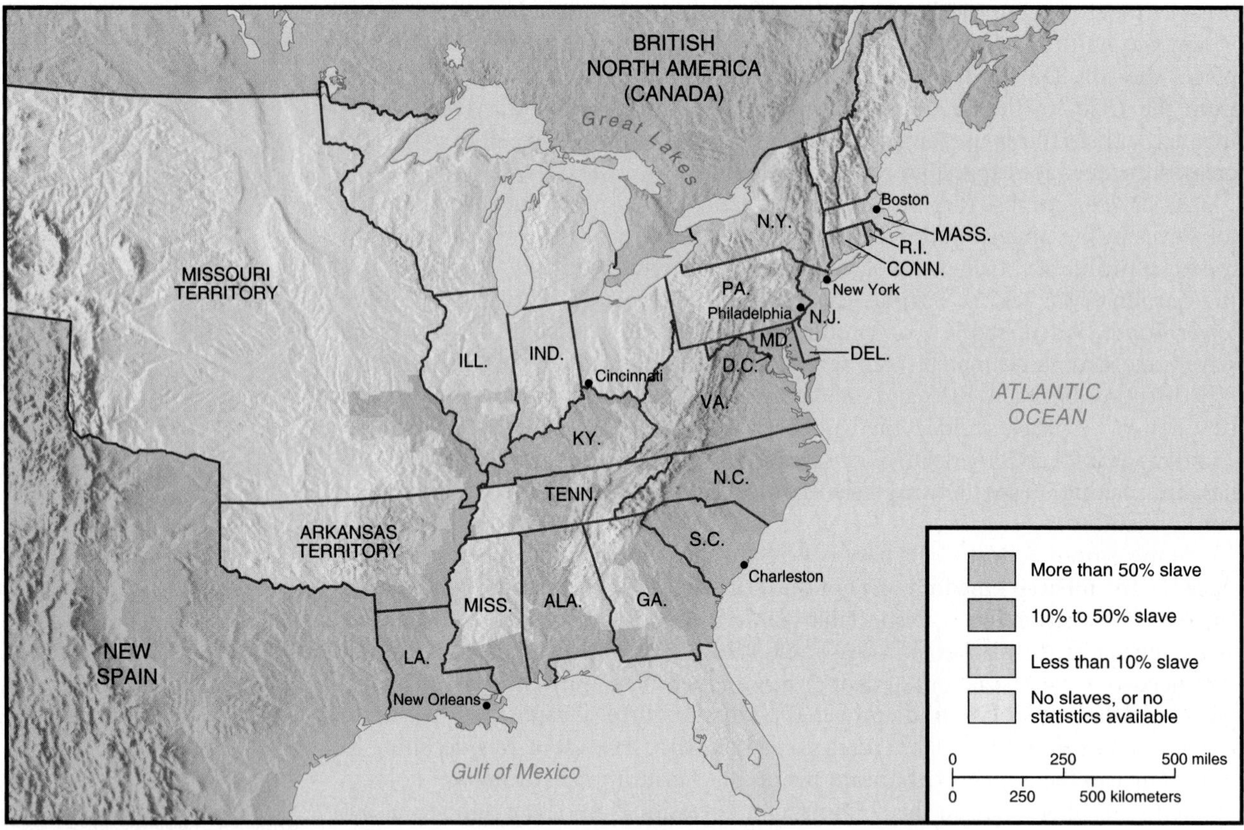

SLAVE CONCENTRATION, 1820 *In 1820, most slaves lived in the eastern seaboard states of Virginia and South Carolina and in Louisiana on the Gulf of Mexico.*

nineteenth century, first to Alabama and Mississippi and then to Arkansas, northwest Louisiana, and east Texas. The rise in total production that accompanied this geographic expansion was phenomenal. In 1792, the South's output of cotton was about 13,000 bales; in 1840, it was 1.35 million; and in 1860, production peaked at 4.8 million bales. Most of the cotton went to supply the booming textile industry of Great Britain.

"Cotton is king!" proclaimed a southern orator in the 1850s, and he was right. By that time, three-quarters of the world's supply of cotton came from the American South, and this single commodity accounted for more than half the total dollar value of American exports. Cotton growing and the network of commercial and industrial enterprises that marketed and processed the crop constituted the most important economic interest in the United States on the eve of the Civil War. Since slavery and cotton seemed inextricably linked, it appeared obvious to many Southerners that their peculiar institution was the keystone of national wealth and economic progress.

Despite its overall success, however, the rise of the Cotton Kingdom did not bring a uniform or steady prosperity to the lower South. Many planters worked the land until it was exhausted and then took their slaves westward to richer soils, leaving depressed and ravaged areas in their wake. Fluctuations in markets and prices also ruined many planters. Widespread depressions, including a wave of bankruptcies, followed the boom periods of 1815–1819, 1832–1837, and 1849–1860. But during the eleven years of rising output and high prices preceding the Civil War, the planters gradually forgot their earlier troubles and began to imagine they were immune to future economic disasters.

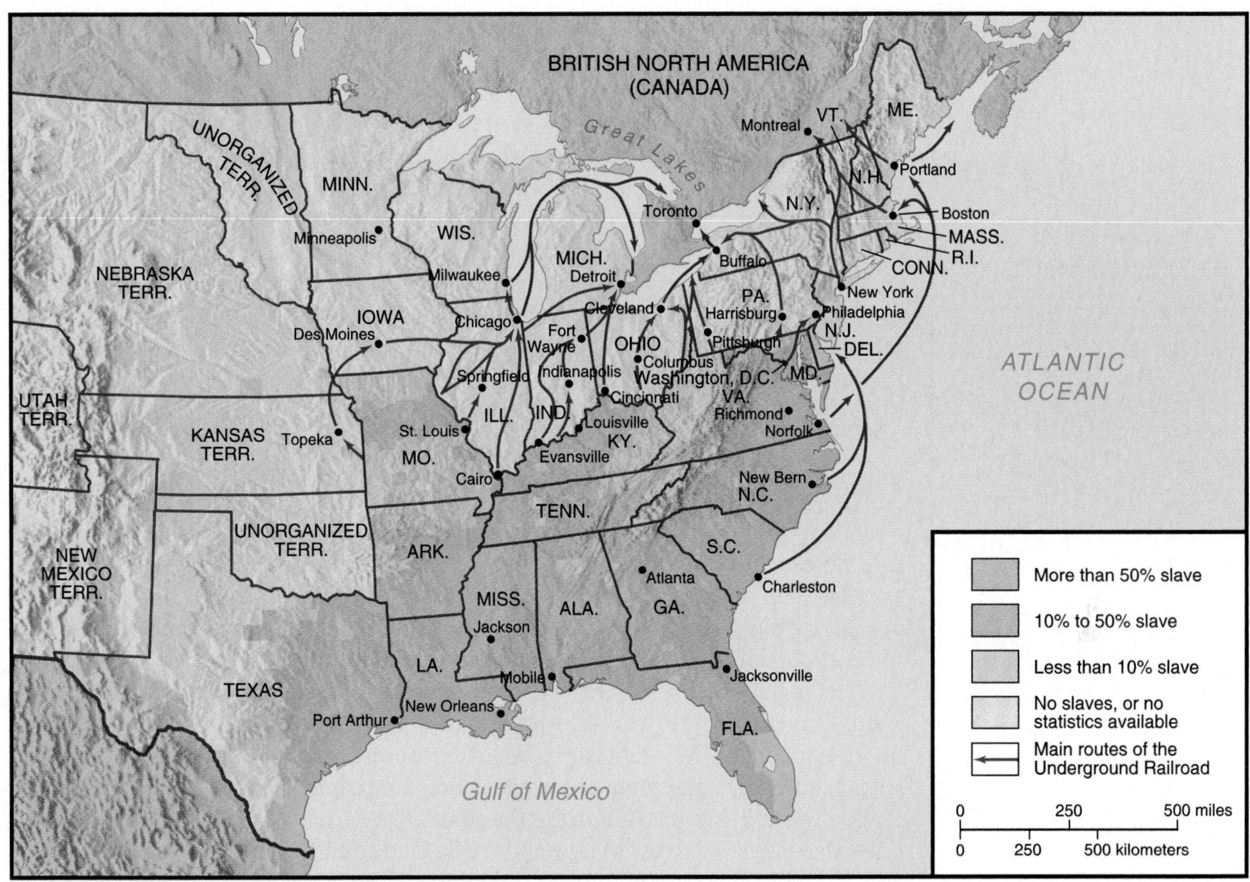

SLAVE CONCENTRATION, 1860 *In 1860, slavery had extended throughout the southern states, with the greatest concentrations of slaves in the states of the Deep South. There were also sizable slave populations in the new states of Missouri, Arkansas, Texas, and Florida.* ❖

Despite the insecurities associated with cotton production, most of the time the crop represented the Old South's best chance for profitable investment. Prudent planters who had not borrowed too heavily during flush times could survive periods of depression by cutting costs, making their plantations self-sufficient. For those with worn-out land, two options existed: they could sell their land and move west, or they could sell their slaves to raise capital for fertilization, crop rotation, and other improvements that could help them survive where they were. Hence planters had little incentive to seek alternatives to slavery, the plantation, and dependence on a single cash crop. From a purely economic point of view, they had every reason to defend slavery and to insist on their right to expand it.

Slavery and Industrialization

As the sectional quarrel with the North intensified, Southerners became increasingly alarmed by their region's lack of economic self-sufficiency. Dependence on the North for capital, marketing facilities, and manufactured goods was seen as evidence of a dangerous subservience to "external" economic interests. During the 1850s, Southern nationalists such as J. D. B. De Bow, editor of the influential *De Bow's Review,* called for the South to develop its own industries, commerce, and shipping. But such pleas for a diversified economy went unanswered. Men with capital were doing too well in plantation agriculture to risk their money in other ventures.

In the 1840s and 1850s, a debate raged among white capitalists over whether the South should use free whites or enslaved blacks as the labor supply for industry. Some leaders defended a white labor policy, arguing that factory work would provide new economic opportunities for a degraded class of poor whites. But other advocates of industrialization feared that the growth of a free working class would lead to social conflict among whites and preferred using slaves for all supervised manual labor. In practice, some factories employed slaves, others white workers, and a few even experimented with integrated workforces. As well as can be determined, mills that hired or purchased slave labor were just as profitable and efficient as those paying wages to whites. It is clear, however, that the union of slavery and cotton that was central to the South's prosperity impeded industrialization and left the region dependent on one-crop agriculture and on the North for capital and marketing.

The "Profitability" Issue

Some Southerners were making money, and a great deal of it, using slave labor to raise cotton. But did slavery yield a good return for the great majority of slaveholders who were not large planters? Did it provide the basis for general prosperity and a relatively high standard of living for the southern population in general, or at least for the two-thirds of it who were white and free? In short, was slavery profitable?

For many years historians believed that slave-based agriculture generally was not very lucrative. Planters' account books seemed to show at best a modest return on investment. In the 1850s, the price of slaves rose at a faster rate than the price of cotton, allegedly squeezing many operators. Some historians even concluded that slavery was a dying institution by the time of the Civil War. Profitability, they argued, depended on access to new and fertile land suitable for plantation agriculture, and virtually all such land within the limits of the United States had already been taken up by 1860. Hence slavery had allegedly reached its natural limits of expansion and was on the verge of becoming so unprofitable that it would fall of its own weight in the near future.

A more recent interpretation, based on modern economic theory, holds that slavery was in fact still an economically sound institution in 1860 and showed no signs of imminent decline. During the 1850s, planters usually could expect an annual return of 8 to 10 percent on capital invested. This yield was roughly equivalent

A row of steamboats in New Orleans await bales of cotton for shipment. By 1860 production of "king" cotton in the south peaked at 4.8 million bales. ❖

CHRONOLOGY

1793	Eli Whitney invents the cotton gin
1800	Gabriel Prosser leads abortive slave rebellion in Virginia
1811	Slaves revolt in Point Coupée section of Louisiana
1822	Denmark Vesey conspiracy uncovered in Charleston, South Carolina
1829	David Walker publishes *Appeal* calling for slave insurrection
1830	First National Negro Convention meets
1831	Slaves under Nat Turner rebel in Virginia, killing almost sixty whites
1832	Virginia legislature votes against gradual emancipation
1835–1842	Blacks fight alongside Indians in the Second Seminole War
1837	Panic of 1837 is followed by major depression of the cotton market
1849	Cotton prices rise, and a sustained boom commences
1852	Harriet Beecher Stowe's antislavery novel *Uncle Tom's Cabin* is published and becomes a best-seller
1857	Hinton R. Helper attacks slavery on economic grounds in *The Impending Crisis of the South;* the book is suppressed in the southern states
1860	Cotton prices and production reach all-time peak

to the best that could then be obtained from the most lucrative sectors of northern industry and commerce. Furthermore, it is no longer clear that plantation agriculture had reached its natural limits of expansion by 1860. Production in Texas had not yet peaked, and the construction of railroads and levees was opening up new areas for cotton growing elsewhere in the South. Those who argue that slavery was profitable and had an expansive future have made a strong and convincing case.

But the larger question remains: What sort of economic development did a slave plantation system foster? What portion of the southern population benefited from the system? Did it promote efficiency and progressive change? Economists Robert Fogel and Stanley Engerman have argued that the plantation was an internally efficient enterprise with good managers and industrious, well-motivated workers. Other economic historians have attributed the profitability almost exclusively to favorable market conditions.

Other evidence suggests that only the large plantations were profitable. Because of various factors—lack of credit, high transportation costs, and a greater vulnerability to market fluctuations—owners of smaller and nonslaveholding plantations had to devote a larger share of their acreage to subsistence crops. This kept their standard of living lower than that of most northern farmers. Slaves received sufficient food, clothing, and shelter for their subsistence and to make them strong enough to work, but their living standard was below that of the poorest free people in the United States.

The South's economic development was skewed in favor of a single route to wealth, open only to white men with access to capital. The concentration of capital and business energies on cotton production foreclosed the kind of diversified industrial and commercial growth that would have provided wider opportunities. Thus, in comparison to the industrializing North, the South was an underdeveloped region in which much of the population had little incentive to work hard. A lack of public education for whites and the denial of even minimal literacy to slaves represented a critical failure to develop human resources. The South's economy was probably condemned so long as it was based on slavery.

Conclusion: Worlds in Conflict

If slaves lived to some extent in a separate and distinctive world of their own, so did planters, less affluent whites, and even free blacks. The Old South was thus a deeply divided society—a kaleidoscope of groups divided by class, race, culture, and geography. What held it together and provided some measure of unity were a booming plantation economy and a web of customary relationships and loyalties that could obscure the underlying cleavages and antagonisms. The fractured and fragile nature of this society would soon become apparent when it was subjected to the pressures of civil war.

Key Terms

Old South, p. 205

African Methodist Episcopal (AME) Church, p. 209

Underground Railroad, p. 210

yeoman, p. 214

American Colonization Society, p. 215

cotton gin, p. 217

Recommended Reading

Major works that take a broad view of slavery are Kenneth M. Stampp, *The Peculiar Institution: Slavery in the Antebellum South* (1956), which stresses its coercive features; John W. Blassingame, *The Slave Community: Plantation Life in the Antebellum South* (1972), which focuses on slave culture and psychology; and Eugene D. Genovese, *Roll, Jordan, Roll: The World the Slaves Made* (1974), which probes the paternalistic character of the institution and the way in which slaves made a world for themselves within its bounds. An insightful interpretation of antebellum southern society is James Oakes, *Slavery and Freedom: An Interpretation of the Old South* (1990). For an overview of the history of slavery, see Peter Kolchin, *American Slavery, 1619–1877* (1993).

On the economics of slavery, see Gavin Wright, *The Political Economy of the Cotton South: Households, Markets, and Wealth in the Nineteenth Century* (1978). On women in the Old South, see Laura F. Edwards, *Scarlett Doesn't Live Here Anymore: Southern Women in the Civil War Era* (2000) and Deborah Gray White, *Ar'n't I a Woman: Female Slaves in the Plantation South* (1985). On the slave trade, see two excellent studies: Michael Tadman, *Speculators and Slaves: Masters, Traders, and Slaves in the Old South* (1989) and Walter Johnson, *Soul by Soul: Life Inside the Antebellum Slave Market* (1999). For the history of the slave family, see Herbert Gutman, *The Black Family in Slavery and Freedom, 1750–1925* (1976); Brenda Stevenson, *Life in Black and White: Family and Community in the Slave South* (1996); and Marie Jenkins Schwartz, *Born in Bondage: Growing Up Enslaved in the Antebellum South* (2000). For Southern law and slavery, see Thomas D. Morris, *Southern Slavery and the Law, 1619–1860* (1996) and Ariela J. Gross, *Double Character: Slavery and Mastery in the Antebellum Southern Courtroom* (2000).

Black resistance to slavery is described in Vincent Harding, *There Is a River: The Black Struggle for Freedom in America* (1981). Slave culture is examined in Albert J. Raboteau, *Slave Religion: The "Invisible Institution" in the Antebellum South* (1978); Lawrence W. Levine, *Black Culture and Consciousness: Afro-American Folk Thought from Slavery to Freedom* (1977); Sterling Stuckey, *Slave Culture: Nationalist Theory and the Foundations of Black America* (1987); and Sharla M. Fett, *Healing, Health, and Power on Southern Slave Plantations* (2002).

For a list of additional titles related to this chapter's topics, please see http://www.ablongman.com/divine.

SUGGESTED WEB SITES

"Been Here So Long": Selections from the WPA American Slave Narratives

http://newdeal.feri.org/asn/index.htm
Slave narratives are some of the more interesting primary sources about slavery.

Exploring Amistad

http://amistad.mysticseaport.org/main/welcome.html
Mystic Seaport runs this site that includes extensive collections of historical resources relating to the revolt and subsequent trial of enslaved Africans.

Africans in America: America's Journey Through Slavery

http://www.pbs.org/wgbh/aia/home.html
This PBS site contains images and documents recounting slavery in America.

Amistad Trials (1839–1840)

http://www.law.umkc.edu/faculty/projects/ftrials/amistad/AMISTD.HTM
Images, chronology, court and official documents comprise this site by Dr. Doug Linder at University of Missouri–Kansas City Law School.

Slave Narratives

http://docsouth.unc.edu/neh/neh.html
This site presents the telling narratives of several slaves housed at the Documents of the American South collection and the University of North Carolina.

The Settlement of African Americans in Liberia

http://www.loc.gov/exhibits/african/perstor.html
This site contains images and text relating to the colonization movement to return African Americans to Africa.

Images of African Americans from the Nineteenth Century

http://digital.nypl.org/schomburg/images_aa19/
The New York Public Library–Schomburg Center for Research in Black Culture site contains numerous visuals.

Images of African American Slavery and Freedom

http://lcweb.loc.gov/rr/print/082_slave.html
This site contains numerous photographs and other images of slaves and free blacks from the Library of Congress.

St. Louis Circuit Court Historical Records Project

http://stlcourtrecords.wustl.edu/resources.cfm
This site contains links to full-text reproductions of slaves' freedom suits in Missouri, including the Dred Scott case, and many other African American history links.

We Americans

Women of Southern Households

Harriet Jacobs, born enslaved in North Carolina in 1813, became a slave in James and Maria Norcom's household in 1825. James began to "whisper foul words" in Harriet's ears when she was a young teenager. Harriet had no one to whom she could turn, except for her free black grandmother, who lived in the town. Although her grandmother had been a slave, Harriet's master "dreaded her scorching rebukes" and furthermore "he did not wish to have his villainy made public." For a time, this wish to "keep up some outward show of decency" protected Harriet.

Harriet Jacobs's grandmother was an unusual woman, who had worked after hours for years to buy her children's freedom, only to be cheated out of her earnings at the end. Like most free black women, Harriet's grandmother was the unmarried head of her own household, separated long ago from the father of her children. Running their own households gave some free black women a measure of autonomy, but also left them with little support in the daily struggle against poverty and racism.

Maria Norcom, as the wife of a prominent doctor and large plantation owner, lived a life very different from Harriet's or her grandmother's. Yet it was not the life of carefree luxury sometimes portrayed in the magnolia-scented stereotypes of movies and books about the Old South. Compared to poorer women in the South, Maria had more access to education and periods of recreation and relaxation. But as a lady of the upper class, she was expected to master strict rules of womanhood that demanded moral purity and virtue. She also had to learn the personal and managerial skills necessary to oversee a household staffed by slaves.

Most southern white women worked hard to keep households and families together, and they all lived within a social system that denied them legal rights by placing them under the domination of husbands and fathers. James Norcom's behavior, while it certainly violated his vows of marriage, was not egregious enough to have won Maria a divorce under the laws of North Carolina.

Whether they were rich or poor, free or enslaved, women were, to a large degree, defined by their relationship to the head of the household, nearly always a white man. Although there were expectations that husbands would protect and care for their wives, women had little recourse against husbands who departed from those expectations. For example, Marion S. D. Converse, a woman from a prominent South Carolina family, dreaded her abusive second husband, Augustus. Through years of vicious beatings and jealous tirades, Marion was unable to escape the bonds of marriage because Augustus's deplorable conduct fell short of legal grounds for divorce in South Carolina (divorce was available only for abandonment or impotence). Yet Marion Converse was able to gain aid and protection from her prominent family, who shielded her from the worst consequences of an abusive marriage.

When Maria Norcom discovered her husband's overtures toward Harriet, she was distraught and took Harriet to sleep in her own room. Yet as Harriet later described it, Maria "pitied herself as a martyr; but she was incapable of feeling for the condition of shame and misery in which her unfortunate, helpless slave was placed." Harriet often woke to find Maria bending over her, and came to fear for her safety around this "jealous mistress." Harriet Jacobs's and Maria Norcom's stories illustrate that planters ruled their wives as well as their slaves. All southern women were embedded in a social system that gave authority over their lives and choices to men. Despite this commonality, few women were able to reach across the divides of race and class to recognize these similarities. Tormented by jealousy and humiliation, Maria came to blame the slave rather than her husband for their intimacy, imagining that Harriet herself had seduced him.

Harriet managed to elude her master's advances, in part due to Maria's vigilance. Yet faced with harsh choices, she bore two children by another white man in the hope that he would offer her some protection. This worked for a time, but in the end, only escape saved Harriet from James Norcom. Enslaved women such as Harriet Jacobs were the most vulnerable of Southern women. They were subject to a level of violence and sexual assault that was unknown to other women in the South; and when they were victims of violence they lacked even the limited legal defenses that were open to poor white women. Because black women were considered unable to give or withhold consent, it was not a crime to rape a black woman. And had Harriet fought back physically against her master's advances, she risked criminal prosecution and even death. For example, when the slave Celia killed the master who had been raping her for years, her court-appointed lawyer argued that she should not be criminally liable, based on a Georgia statute allowing women to use force to defend their "honor" against a rapist. The court, however, decreed that black women were not women within the meaning of the statute. Celia had no honor that the law recognized. She was thus convicted of murder, sentenced to death, and hanged.

Excluding black women from the laws of rape also reinforced common images of black women as either sexually aggressive Jezebels or sexless, nurturing mammies. The first stereotype justified the sexual exploitation of slave women and the second fed the slaveowners' fantasy that their slaves loved and cared for them. Harriet Jacobs found herself in such a difficult position because she wanted to be neither a Jezebel nor a mammy. Of course, neither of these images corresponded to the realities and hardships of slave life. Enslaved women were often assigned backbreaking labor that paid little attention to common distinctions about so-called women's work. They were expected to do all of the normal tasks assigned to women—sewing, washing, child care—as well as work a full day in the fields. Despite these brutal conditions, slave women organized communities and households, and tried to protect themselves against the worst excesses of the slave system. Harriet and her grandmother were involved in a complicated network of extended kin, and invested a great deal of energy in protecting brothers and sons from sale "up the river."

Harriet eventually escaped from the Norcoms in 1835, hiding in her grandmother's attic for seven years while she tried to induce Norcom to sell her children to their father, the attorney Samuel Tredwell Sawyer. Sawyer did eventually purchase the children, but did not emancipate them as he had promised; instead, he sent his daughter to Brooklyn, New York, to work as a house servant for his cousin, and kept his son as a slave at home. Although Harriet was eventually able to escape the bonds of slavery and join the battle to abolish it, it was a long time before she succeeded in being reunited with her children. Harriet's book, *Incidents in The Life of A Slave Girl, The Autobiography of Linda Brent*, was published in 1861, with the help of abolitionist novelist Lydia Maria Child. For many years, critics dismissed the narrative as either a work of fiction or the product of Child's own pen, but historians today have laid those charges to rest, recognizing Harriet Jacobs's important contribution to the struggle against slavery and to American literature.

We know much less about what happened to Maria Norcom, who neither kept a diary nor wrote her own story. All that we know is that she continued in her unhappy marriage to James Norcom. Her daughter Mary Matilda, when she came of age, pursued and attempted to reclaim Harriet as her slave under the Fugitive Slave Act. In order to thwart this effort, Harriet allowed an abolitionist friend to buy her and set her free.

In slaveholding households like that of the Norcoms, all the women, whether white or black, free or enslaved, were subject to the will of the master of the household. There were a few women, such as Harriet's grandmother, who lived outside of such male-dominated households, but most Southern women depended on white men legally and socially, giving them little recourse against men like James Norcom, who burst the bounds of decency. Yet even if Maria had had control over her own property, or equal say in the disposition of her daughter's property (for Harriet actually belonged to Mary Matilda), there is no evidence that she would have been any more likely than James to give Harriet her freedom, or allow her to be sold to the master she chose. Despite their shared submission to James, an impassable gulf separated Harriet and Maria, and its name was race. After the Civil War, Southern women, white and black, reorganized their households in a changed society, but it would still be another century before they began to bridge that gulf.

This 1836 engraving from an antislavery novel depicts a plantation mistress scolding a slave woman while the master looks on. Though white women were also subjugated to the authority of white men in southern society, the divide of race prevented plantation ladies and slaves from finding potential solidarity as women. ❖

Chapter 12

The Pursuit of Perfection

Redeeming the Middle Class

In the winter of 1830–1831, a wave of religious revival swept the northern states. For six months in Rochester, New York, Presbyterian evangelist Charles G. Finney preached almost daily, emphasizing that every man or woman had the power to choose Christ and a godly life. Finney broke with his church's traditional belief that it was God's inscrutable will that decided who would be saved when he preached that "sinners ought to be made to feel that they have something to do, and that something is to repent. That is something that no other being can do for them, neither God nor man, and something they can do and do now." He converted hundreds, and he urged them in turn to convert relatives, neighbors, and employees. If enough people enlisted in the evangelical crusade, Finney proclaimed, the millennium would be achieved within months.

Finney's call for religious and moral renewal fell on fertile ground in Rochester. The leading families in the bustling boomtown were divided into quarreling factions, and workingmen were breaking free from the control that their employers had previously exerted over their daily lives. More vigorous standards of proper behavior and religious conformity unified Rochester's elite and increased its ability to control the rest of the community. Evangelical Protestantism provided the middle class with a stronger sense of identity and purpose.

BUT THE WAR ON SIN was not always so unifying. Among those converted in Rochester and elsewhere were religious and moral reformers inspired to take the logical step from individual to societal reformation. They demanded that all social and political institutions measure up to the standards of Christian perfection. They proceeded to attack such collective "sins" as liquor traffic, war, slavery, and even government. Religiously inspired reformism cut two ways. It brought a measure of order and cultural unity to previously divided and troubled communities such as Rochester. But it also inspired a variety of more radical movements or experiments that threatened to undermine established institutions and principles. One of these—abolitionism—would trigger political upheaval and ultimately civil war.

OUTLINE

The Rise of Evangelicalism

Domesticity and Changes in the American Family

Institutional Reform

Reform Turns Radical

Conclusion: Counterpoint on Reform

The Rise of Evangelicalism

American Protestantism was in a state of constant ferment during the early nineteenth century. The separation of church and state was now complete. Dissenting groups, such as the Baptists and Methodists, welcomed full religious freedom because it offered a better chance to win new converts. But all pious Protestants were concerned about the spread of "infidelity"—a term they applied to Catholics, freethinkers, Unitarians, Mormons, and anyone else who was not an evangelical Christian. But they faced opposition to their effort to make the nation officially Protestant.

As deism—the belief in a God who expressed himself through natural laws accessible to human reason—declined in popularity in the early to mid-nineteenth century, Catholic immigration increased, and the spread of "Popery" became the main focus of evangelical concern. Both Catholics and Unitarians (who quietly carried forward the rationalistic traditions of the eighteenth century) resented and resisted the evangelicals' efforts to convert them to "the Christianity of the heart." Most of those who accepted Christ as their personal savior in revival meetings previously had been indifferent to religion rather than adhering to an alternative set of beliefs.

Revivalism provided the best way to extend religious values and build up church membership. The Great Awakening of the mid-eighteenth century had shown the wonders that evangelists could accomplish, and the new revivalists repeated this success by increasing the proportion of the population that belonged to Protestant churches, forming voluntary organizations, and mobilizing the faithful into associations to spread the gospel and reform American morals.

Although both the evangelical reformers and the new democratic politicians sought popular favor and assumed that individuals were free agents capable of self-direction and self-improvement, the leaders differed in important respects. Jacksonians idealized common folk pretty much as they found them and saw no danger to the community if individuals pursued their worldly interests. Evangelical reformers, by contrast, believed that the common people needed to be redeemed and uplifted. They did not trust a democracy of unbelievers and sinners. The republic would be safe, they insisted, only if a right-minded minority preached, taught, and agitated until the mass of ordinary citizens was reborn into a higher life.

The Second Great Awakening: The Frontier Phase

Second Great Awakening A series of evangelical Protestant revivals that swept over America in the early nineteenth century.

The **Second Great Awakening** began in earnest on the southern frontier around the turn of the century. Highly emotional camp meetings, organized usually by Methodists or Baptists, became a regular feature of religious life in the South and lower Midwest. On the frontier, the camp meeting met social as well as religious needs. In the sparsely settled southern backcountry, for many people the only way to get baptized, be married, or have a communal religious experience was to attend a camp meeting.

Rowdies and scoffers also attended. Mostly they drank whiskey, caroused, and fornicated on the fringes of the small city of tents and wagons. But sometimes they, too, fell into emotional fits and were converted. Evangelists loved to tell stories of such conversions or near conversions.

The camp meetings obviously provided an emotional outlet for rural people whose everyday lives were often lonely and tedious. But they could also promote a sense of community and social discipline. Conversion at a campaign meeting could be a rite of passage, signifying that a young man or woman had outgrown wild or antisocial behavior and was now ready to become a respectable member of the community. But for the most part, frontier revivalism remained highly individualistic. It strengthened personal piety and morality but did not stimulate organized benevolence or social reform.

Lithograph depicting a camp meeting. Religious revival meetings on the frontier attracted hundreds of people who camped for days to listen to the preacher and to share with their neighbors in a communal religious experience. Notice that the men and women are seated in separate sections. ❖

In the southern states, Baptists and Presbyterians eventually deemphasized camp meetings in favor of "protracted meetings" in local churches, which featured guest preachers holding forth day after day for up to two weeks. Southern evangelical churches grew rapidly in membership and influence during the first half of the nineteenth century and became the focus of community life in rural areas. Although they fostered societies to improve morals, they generally shied away from social reform. The conservatism of a slaveholding society discouraged radical efforts to change the world.

The Second Great Awakening in the North

Reformist tendencies were more evident in the distinctive kind of revivalism that originated in New England and western New York. The northern evangelists were mostly Congregationalists and Presbyterians, strongly influenced by the traditions of New England Puritanism. Their revivals, although somewhat less extravagant and emotional than those on the frontier, found fertile soil in small to medium-sized towns and cities. The northern brand of evangelism resulted in the formation of societies devoted to the redemption of the human race in general and American society in particular.

The reform movement began in New England as an effort to defend Calvinism against the liberal views of religion fostered by the Enlightenment. The Reverend Timothy Dwight, who became president of Yale College in 1795, and other like minds were alarmed by the growing tendency to view the Deity as the benevolent master architect of a rational universe rather than as an all-powerful and mysterious God. Some Congregationalist clergy reached the point of denying the doctrine of the Trinity, proclaiming themselves "Unitarians." Horrified when the Unitarians won control of the Harvard Divinity School, Dwight battled this liberal tendency by reaffirming the old Calvinist belief that man was sinful and depraved. But the harshness and pessimism of orthodox Calvinist doctrine, with its stress on original sin and predestination, had limited appeal in a republic committed to human freedom and progress.

Dwight himself made some concessions to the spirit of the age by agreeing that human beings had a limited control over their spiritual destiny. But a younger generation of Congregational ministers reshaped New England Puritanism to increase its appeal to people who shared the prevailing optimism about human capabilities.

The main theologian of early-nineteenth-century neo-Calvinism was Nathaniel Taylor, a disciple of Dwight. Taylor softened the doctrine of predestination and contended that every individual was a "free agent" who had the ability to overcome a natural inclination to sin. This reconciliation of original sin with "free agency" enabled the neo-Calvinists to compete with the revival denominations that preached that sinners had the ability to choose salvation.

The first great practitioner of the new evangelical Calvinism was Lyman Beecher, another of Dwight's pupils. In the period just before and after the War of 1812, Beecher helped promote a series of revivals in the Congregational churches of New England. Preaching his own homespun version of free agency, he induced thousands of churchgoers to acknowledge their sinfulness and surrender to God.

During the late 1820s, Beecher was forced to confront the new and more radical form of revivalism being practiced in western New York by Charles G. Finney. Upstate New York was a seedbed for religious enthusiasm. A majority of its population were transplanted New Englanders who had left behind their close-knit village communities and ancestral churches but not their Puritan consciences. Troubled by rapid economic changes and social dislocations, they were ripe for the assurances of a new faith and a sense of moral direction.

Although he worked within the Congregational and Presbyterian churches, Finney departed radically from traditional Calvinist doctrines. In his hands, the doctrine of free agency became unqualified free will. Indifferent to theological issues, Finney appealed strictly to emotion or the heart rather than to doctrine or reason. He eventually adopted the extreme view that it was possible for redeemed Christians to be totally free of sin—to be as perfect as their Father in Heaven.

Beginning in 1823, Finney conducted a series of highly successful revivals in the towns and cities of western New York. Even more controversial than his freewheeling approach to theology were the means he used to win converts. Finney sought instantaneous conversions through a variety of new methods including protracted meetings lasting all night or several days in a row. He achieved dramatic results. Sometimes listeners fell to the floor in fits of excitement and immediately sought God's grace.

Beecher and the eastern evangelicals were disturbed by Finney's new methods and by the hysteria that they produced. The preachers were also upset because he violated long-standing Christian tradition by allowing women to pray aloud in church. But it soon became clear that Finney was not merely stirring people to temporary peaks of excitement; he was also leaving strong and active churches behind him, and eastern opposition gradually weakened.

From Revivalism to Reform

Northern revivalists inspired a great movement for social reform. Converts were organized into voluntary associations that sought to stamp out sin and social evil and win the world for Christ. Most of the converts of northern revivalism were middle-class citizens already active in the lives of their communities. They were seeking to adjust to the bustling world of the market revolution in ways that would not violate their traditional moral and social values. Given the generally optimistic and forward-looking attitudes of such Americans, it is understandable that a wave of conversions would fuel hopes for the salvation of the nation and the world.

In New England, Beecher and his evangelical associates were behind the establishment of a great network of missionary and benevolent societies. Foreign missionaries spread the gospel to remote parts of the world, and organizations such as the American Bible Society distributed Bibles in areas of the West where there was a scarcity of churches and clergymen. Missionaries even reached out to the many poor people in American cities.

Evangelicals formed moral reform societies as well as missions. Some of these aimed at curbing irreligious activity on the Sabbath; others sought to stamp out dueling, gambling, and prostitution. Crusaders attempted to redeem the prostitutes as well as to curtail the activities of their patrons. Others believed that the cause of virtue would be better served by suppressing public discussion and investigation of sexual vices.

temperance movement
Temperance—moderation or abstention in the use of alcoholic beverages—attracted many advocates in the early nineteenth century. Their crusade against alcohol became a powerful social and political force.

Beecher was especially influential in the temperance crusade, the most successful of the reform movements. The **temperance movement** was directed at a real social evil, more serious in many ways than the drug problem of today. Since the Revolution, whiskey had become the most popular American beverage. It was cheaper than milk or beer and safer than water (which was often contaminated). Per capita annual consumption of distilled beverages in the 1820s was almost triple what it is today, and alcoholism had reached epidemic proportions.

The temperance reformers viewed indulgence in alcohol as a threat to public morality. Drunkenness was seen as a loss of self-control and moral responsibility

Temperance propaganda warned that the drinker who began with "a glass with a friend" would inevitably follow the direct path to poverty, despair, and death. ❖

that spawned crime, vice, and disorder. Above all, it threatened the family. The main target of temperance propaganda was the husband and father who abused, neglected, or abandoned his wife and children because he was a slave to the bottle. The drinking habits of the poor and laboring classes also aroused great concern, for the "respectable" and propertied elements lived in fear that lower-class mobs, crazed with drink, would attack private property.

Many of the evangelical reformers regarded intemperance as the greatest single obstacle to the achievement of a republic of God-fearing, self-disciplined citizens. In 1826, a group of clergymen organized the American Temperance Society to educate Americans about the evils of hard liquor. The society sent out lecturers, issued a flood of literature, and sponsored essay contests.

The campaign was enormously effective. Although it may be doubted whether large numbers of confirmed drunkards were actually cured, the movement did succeed in altering the drinking habits of middle-class Americans by making temperance a mark of respectability. Per capita consumption of hard liquor declined more than 50 percent during the 1830s.

Cooperating missionary and reform societies—collectively known as the "benevolent empire"—were a major force in American culture by the early 1830s. A new ethic of self-control and self-discipline was being instilled in the middle class that equipped individuals to confront a new world of economic growth and social mobility without losing their cultural and moral bearings.

Domesticity and Changes in the American Family

The evangelical culture of the 1820s and 1830s influenced the family as an institution and inspired new conceptions of its role in American society. For many parents, child rearing was viewed as essential preparation for the self-disciplined Christian life. Women—regarded as particularly susceptible to religious and moral influences—were increasingly confined to the domestic circle but assumed a greater importance within it.

Marriage for Love

The white middle-class American family underwent major changes in the decades between the Revolution and the mid-nineteenth century. One was the triumph of marriage for love. Parents now exercised even less control over their children's selection of mates than they had in the colonial period. The prompting of the heart, so important to religious conversion, was now seen as the primary factor in choosing a mate. It seems likely, too, that relations between husbands and wives were becoming more affectionate. In the main, eighteenth-century correspondence between spouses had been formal and distant in tone. The husband, for example, rarely confessed that he missed his wife or craved her company. By the early nineteenth century, first names, pet names, and terms of endearment like *honey* or *darling* were increasingly used by both sexes, and absent husbands frequently confessed that they felt lost without their mates. In return, wives assumed a more egalitarian tone and offered counsel on a wide range of subjects.

At its best, marriage had become more a matter of companionship and less an exertion of male dominance. But the change should not be exaggerated or romanticized. In law, and in cases of conflict between spouses, the husband remained the unchallenged head of the household. True independence or equality for women was impossible at a time when men held exclusive legal authority over a couple's property and children.

The Cult of Domesticity

Such power as women exerted within the home came from their ability to affect the decisions of men who had learned to respect their moral qualities and good sense. The evangelical movement encouraged this quiet expression of feminine influence. Revivals not only gave women a role in converting men but also made a feminized Christ the main object of worship. A nurturing, loving, merciful Savior, mediating between a stern father and his erring children, provided the model for woman's new role as spiritual head of the home. Membership in evangelical church-based associations inspired and prepared women for their new role as guardians of domestic culture and morality. Female reform societies taught them the strict ethical code they were to instill in other family members; organized mothers' groups gave instruction in how to build character and encourage piety in children.

Cult of Domesticity Term used by historians to describe the dominant gender role for white women in the antebellum period. The ideology of domesticity stressed the virtue of women as guardians of the home, which was considered their proper sphere.

Historians have described the new conception of woman's role as the **Cult of Domesticity** or the "Cult of True Womanhood." In the view of most men, woman's place was in the home and on a pedestal. The ideal wife was a model of piety and virtue who exerted a wholesome moral and religious influence over members of the coarser sex.

The sociological reality behind the cult of true womanhood was an increasing division between the working lives of men and women. In the eighteenth century and earlier, most economic activity had been centered in the home and nearby, and husbands and wives often worked together in a common enterprise. By early in the mid-nineteenth century, this way of life was limited mainly to rural areas. In towns and cities, the rise of factories and countinghouses severed the home from the workplace. Men went forth every morning to their places of labor, leaving their wives at home to tend the house and the children. The cult of domesticity made a virtue of the fact that men were solely responsible for running the affairs of the world and building up the economy.

A new concept of gender roles justified and glorified this pattern. The "doctrine of two spheres"—set forth in novels, advice literature, and the new ladies' magazines—sentimentalized the woman who kept a spotless house, nurtured her children, and offered her husband a refuge from the heartless world of commerce and industry. From a modern point of view, it is easy to condemn the cult of domesticity as a rationalization for male dominance. But most women of the time probably did not feel oppressed or degraded by the new arrangement. Women had never enjoyed equality, and the new norm of confinement to the home did not necessarily imply that women were inferior. By the standards of evangelical culture, women in the domestic sphere could be viewed as superior to men since women were in a good position to cultivate the "feminine" virtues of love and self-sacrifice and thus act as official guardians of religious and moral values.

The domestic ideology had real meaning only for relatively affluent women. Working-class wives were not usually employed outside the home during this period, but they labored long and hard within the household, often taking in washing or piecework to supplement a meager family income. Their endless domestic drudgery made a sham of the notion that women had the time and energy for the "higher things in life." Life was especially hard for African American women. Most of those who were "free Negroes" rather than slaves did not have husbands who made enough to support them, and they were obliged to serve in white households or work long hours at home doing other people's washing and sewing.

In urban areas, unmarried working-class women often lived on their own and toiled as household servants, in the sweatshops of the garment industry, or in factories. Barely able to support themselves and at the mercy of male sexual predators, they were in no position to identify with the middle-class ideal of elevated, protected womanhood. For some of them, the relatively well-paid life of the prostitute seemed to offer an attractive alternative to a life of loneliness and privation.

For middle-class women whose husbands earned a good income, however, freedom from industrial or farm labor offered tangible benefits. They now had the leisure to read extensively the new literature directed primarily at housewives, to participate in female-dominated charitable activities, and to cultivate deep and lasting friendships with other women. The result was a distinctively feminine subculture emphasizing sisterhood or "sorority." This growing sense of solidarity with other women often bridged economic and social gaps as demonstrated when upper- and middle-class women organized societies for the relief and rehabilitation of poor or "fallen" women.

For some women, the domestic ideal even sanctioned ladylike efforts to extend their sphere until it conquered the masculine world outside the home. This domestic feminism was reflected in women's involvement in crusades to stamp out such masculine sins as intemperance, gambling, and sexual vice. In the benevolent societies and reform movements of the Jacksonian era, women handled money, organized meetings and public appeals, made contracts, and sometimes even gave orders to male subordinates—activities they usually could not perform in their own households. The desire to extend the feminine sphere was also the motivating force behind the campaign to make schoolteaching a woman's occupation.

Women attempted to make the world a better place by properly rearing their children, who were captive pupils for the mother's instructions. Since women were considered particularly well qualified to transmit piety and morality to future citizens of the republic, the cult of domesticity exalted motherhood and encouraged a new concern with childhood as the time of life when "character" was formed.

❖ A Look at the Past ❖

Gothic Revival Cottage

Sentimentality and romanticism strengthened their hold on American culture after 1820. At the same time, a cult of domesticity arose, which promoted family life as critical to a person's moral regeneration. Evangelism and a wide variety of reform movements swept the nation as well. Middle-class Americans engaged enthusiastically in these social and cultural developments, spending money or hours buying or making materials that revealed their participation. New houses provided clean, neat spaces—and more of them—for families to pursue their interests together. Styles such as the Gothic Revival embodied the romantic and spiritual sentiments of the age. Gothic Revival presented home as more than a haven; home became a spiritual sanctuary. What does this house resemble? If homes became sanctuaries, what role did women play in creating and maintaining those sanctuaries?

The Discovery of Childhood

The nineteenth century has been called the "century of the child." More than before, childhood was seen as a distinct stage of life requiring the special and sustained attention of parents. The family now became "child-centered," which meant that the care, nurturing, and rearing of children was viewed as the family's prime function.

New customs and fashions heralded the "discovery" of childhood. Books aimed specifically at juveniles or providing expert advice to parents on child rearing began to roll off the presses. The ideal family described in the advice manuals and sentimental literature was bound together by affection rather than authority. Firm discipline remained at the core of "family government," but there was a change in the preferred method of enforcing good behavior. Corporal punishment declined, partially displaced by shaming or withholding of affection. The intended result of punishment was often described as "self-government," and to achieve it parents used guilt, rather than fear, as their main source of leverage.

❖ A Look at the Past ❖

Manufactured Toy

Manufactured toys, such as this pull toy, became common during the early nineteenth century and suggest dramatic changes in family life and consumer behavior. Before toys were manufactured in the United States, most parents or children themselves had to make toys or games from available materials, or if they were wealthy enough, they might purchase toys imported from Europe. The availability of cheap manufactured goods made of wood, cast iron, and tin gave mothers the opportunity to lavish attention on their children, without the toil. What does the emergence of a toy manufacturing industry reveal about attitudes towards children?

Child-centered families also meant smaller families. If nineteenth-century families had remained as large as those of earlier times, it would have been impossible to lavish so much care and attention on individual offspring. Between 1800 and 1850, the average family size declined about 25 percent, beginning a long-range trend lasting to the present day.

The practice of various forms of birth control undoubtedly contributed to this demographic revolution. Ancestors of the modern condom and diaphragm were openly advertised and sold during the pre–Civil War period, but it is likely that most couples controlled family size by practicing the withdrawal method or limiting the frequency of intercourse. Abortion was also surprisingly common and was on the rise.

Parents seemed to understand that having fewer children meant that they could provide their offspring with a better start in life. Such attitudes were appropriate to a society that was beginning to shift from agriculture to commerce and industry.

Institutional Reform

The family could not carry the whole burden of socializing and reforming individuals. Children needed schooling as well as parental nurture. Some adults, too, seemed to require special kinds of attention and treatment. Seeking to extend the advantages of "family government" beyond the domestic circle, reformers worked to establish or improve public institutions that were designed to shape individual character and instill a capacity for self-discipline.

The Extension of Education

The period from 1820 to 1850 saw an enormous expansion of free public schools. The new resolve to put more children in school for longer periods reflected many of the same values that exalted the child-centered family. It was believed that formal training at a character-building institution would prepare children to make a living and bear the burdens of republican citizenship when they became adults. Purely intellectual training at school was seen as less important than moral indoctrination.

Besides being an extension of the family, the school could also serve as a substitute for it. Educational reformers were alarmed at the masses of poor and immigrant children who allegedly lacked a proper home environment. The safety of the republic depended on schools to make up for this disadvantage.

Before the 1820s, schooling in the United States was a haphazard affair. The wealthy sent their children to private schools, and some of the poor sent their children to charity or "pauper" schools that were usually financed in part by state or local governments. Between the 1820s and the 1850s, the movement for publicly supported common schools made great headway in the North and had limited success in parts of the South. In theory, the common school was an egalitarian institution providing a free basic education for children of all backgrounds.

The agitation for expanded public education began in the 1820s and early 1830s as a central demand of the workingmen's movements in eastern cities. These artisans and tradespeople viewed free schools open to all as a way of countering the growing gap between rich and poor. Middle-class reformers soon seized the initiative, shaped educational reform toward the goal of social discipline, and provided the momentum needed for legislative success.

The most influential spokesman for the common school movement was Horace Mann of Massachusetts. As a lawyer and a member of the state legislature, Mann worked tirelessly for the establishment of a state board of education and adequate tax support for local schools. His philosophy of education was based on the premise that children were clay in the hands of teachers and school officials and could be molded to a state of perfection. Like the advocates of child rearing through moral influence rather than physical force, he discouraged corporal punishment except as a last resort.

Against those who argued that school taxes violated the rights of property, Mann countered that private property was actually held in trust for the good of the community. Education, he stressed, saved children from drifting into lives of poverty and vice and prepared them to become good, law-abiding citizens. Mann's conception of public education as a means of social discipline converted the middle and upper classes to his cause.

In practice, the new or improved public schools often alienated working-class pupils and their families rather than reforming them. Compulsory attendance laws deprived poor families of needed wage earners without guaranteeing new occupational opportunities for those with an elementary education. Furthermore, Catholic immigrants complained quite correctly that Mann and his disciples were trying to impose a uniform Protestant culture on the pupils.

In addition to the "three Rs" ("reading, 'riting, and 'rithmetic"), the essence of what was being taught in the public schools of the mid-nineteenth century was the "Protestant ethic"—industry, punctuality, sobriety, and frugality. These were the virtues stressed in the famous *McGuffey's Eclectic Readers,* which first appeared in 1836. Such moral indoctrination helped produce generations of Americans with personalities and beliefs adapted to the needs of an industrialized society. If the system did not encourage thinking for oneself, it did prepare people who could easily adjust to the regular routines of the factory or the office.

Fortunately, however, education was not limited to the schools or devoted exclusively to children. Every city and almost every town or village had a lyceum, debating society, or mechanic's institute where adults of all social classes could broaden their intellectual horizons. Young Abe Lincoln, for example, sharpened his intellect and honed his debating skills as a member of such an institute in New Salem, Illinois, in the early 1830s. Unlike the public schools, the lyceums and debating societies fostered independent thought and the spread of new ideas.

Discovering the Asylum

Some segments of the population were obviously beyond the reach of family government and character training provided in homes and schools. In the 1820s and 1830s, reformers became acutely aware of the dangers to society posed by an apparently increasing number of criminals, lunatics, and paupers. Their answer was to establish special institutions to provide a controlled environment in which the inmates could be reformed and rehabilitated.

In earlier times, the existence of paupers, lawbreakers, and insane persons was viewed as the consequence of divine judgment or original sin. For the most part, these people were dealt with in ways that did not isolate them from local communities. But dealing with deviants in a neighborly way broke down as economic development

Dorothea Dix (1802–1887). Her efforts on behalf of the mentally ill led to the building of more than thirty institutions in the United States and the reform and restaffing—with well-trained personnel—of existing hospitals. She died in Trenton, New Jersey, in 1887, in a hospital that she had founded. ❖

and urbanization made communities less cohesive. At the same time, reformers were concluding that all defects of mind and character were correctable—that the insane could be cured, criminals reformed, and paupers taught to pull themselves out of destitution. The result was the discovery of the asylum.

The 1820s and 1830s saw the emergence of state-supported prisons, insane asylums, and poorhouses. New York and Pennsylvania led the way in prison reform. In theory, prisons and asylums substituted for the family. The custodians were intended to act as parents by providing moral advice and training. In practice, these institutions were far different from the affectionate families idealized by the cult of domesticity. Their most prominent feature was the imposition of a rigid daily routine. The early superintendents and wardens believed that the enforcement of an inflexible and demanding set of rules and procedures would encourage self-discipline.

In retrospect, it is clear that the prisons, asylums, and poorhouses did not achieve the aims of their founders. A combination of naive theories and poor performance doomed these institutions to a custodial rather than a reformatory role. Public support was inadequate to meet the needs of the growing inmate population, and the personnel of these places of confinement lacked the training needed to help their charges. The result was overcrowding and the use of brutality to keep order.

But conditions would have been even worse without the efforts of a remarkable woman, Dorothea Dix, one of the most effective of all the pre–Civil War reformers. As a direct result of her skill in publicizing the inhumane treatment prevailing in prisons, almshouses, and insane asylums, fifteen states built new hospitals and improved supervision of penitentiaries and other institutional facilities.

Reform Turns Radical

During the 1830s, internal dissension split the great reform movement spawned by the Second Great Awakening. Efforts to promote evangelical piety, improve personal and public morality, and shape character through familial or institutional discipline continued and even flourished. But bolder spirits went beyond such goals and set their sights on the total liberation and perfection of the individual.

Divisions in the Benevolent Empire

Early-nineteenth-century reformers were generally committed to changing existing attitudes and practices gradually in ways that would not invite conflict or disrupt the fabric of society. But by the mid-1830s, a new mood of impatience and perfectionism surfaced within the benevolent societies. The Temperance Society, for example, split between radicals who insisted on a total commitment to "cold water" and moderates who were willing to overlook moderate wine and beer drinking. The same sort of division arose in the American Peace Society between those insisting on absolute pacifism and those willing to sanction "defensive wars."

The new perfectionism realized its most dramatic and important success within the antislavery movement. Before the 1830s, many of the people who expressed religious and moral concern over slavery were affiliated with the **American Colonization Society,** a benevolent organization founded in 1817. Most colonizationists admitted that slavery was an evil, but they believed it should be eliminated only gradually and with the cooperation of slaveholders. Reflecting the power of racial prejudice, they proposed to transport freed blacks to Africa as a way of relieving southern fears that a race war would erupt if slaves were simply released from bondage and allowed to remain in America. In 1821, the society established a colony in West Africa, named it Liberia, and settled several thousand American blacks there over the next decade.

American Colonization Society Founded in 1817, this organization hoped to provide a mechanism by which slavery could be gradually eliminated. The society advocated the relocation of free blacks (followed by freed slaves) to the African colony of Monrovia, present-day Liberia.

Colonization proved to be grossly inadequate as a step toward the elimination of slavery. Slaveholders rarely cooperated with the movement, and free blacks rejected the whole process. Black opposition to colonization helped persuade William Lloyd Garrison and other white abolitionists to repudiate the Colonization Society and support immediate emancipation without emigration.

Garrison launched a new and more radical antislavery movement in 1831 when he began to publish a journal called *The Liberator* in Boston. Garrison's rhetoric was as severe as his proposals were radical. As he wrote in the first issue of *The Liberator,* "I will be as harsh as the truth and as uncompromising as justice. . . . I will not retreat a single inch—AND I WILL BE HEARD."

The Abolitionist Enterprise

The abolitionist movement, like the temperance crusade, was a direct outgrowth of the Second Great Awakening. Many leading abolitionists had undergone conversion experiences in the 1820s and were already committed to a life of Christian activism before they dedicated themselves to freeing the slaves. Several were ministers or divinity students seeking a mission in life that would fulfill their spiritual and professional ambitions.

The career of Theodore Dwight Weld exemplified the connection between revivalism and abolitionism. Influenced strongly by Charles G. Finney, Weld underwent a conversion experience in 1826. He then became an itinerant lecturer for various reform causes. By the early 1830s, his attention was focused on the moral issue raised by the institution of slavery. After a brief flirtation with the colonization movement, he became a convert to abolitionism. Traveling throughout Ohio, where he and his associates founded Oberlin College as a center for abolitionist activity, he used the tried-and-true methods of the revival—fervent preaching, protracted meetings, the call for individuals to come forth and announce their redemption—in the cause of the antislavery movement. As a result of these efforts, northern Ohio and western New York became hotbeds of abolitionist sentiment.

Antislavery orators and organizers tended to have their greatest success in the smaller towns of the upper North. The typical convert came from an upwardly mobile family engaged in small business, the skilled trades, or market farming. In the cities, abolitionists were more likely to encounter fierce and effective opposition. Indeed, Garrison was once almost lynched in Boston.

Abolitionists who thought of taking their message to the fringes of the South had reason to pause, given the fate of the antislavery editor Elijah Lovejoy. In 1837, while attempting to defend himself and his printing press from a mob in Alton, Illinois, just across the Mississippi River from slaveholding Missouri, Lovejoy was shot and killed.

Racism was a major cause of antiabolitionist violence in the North. Rumors that abolitionists advocated or practiced interracial marriage could easily excite an urban crowd to destructive acts. Working-class whites tended to fear that economic and social competition with blacks would increase if abolitionists succeeded in freeing the slaves and making them citizens. But a striking feature of many of the mobs was that they were dominated by "gentlemen of property and standing." Upstanding citizens resorted to violence, it would appear, because abolitionism effectively threatened their conservative notions of social order and hierarchy.

By the end of the 1830s, the abolitionist movement was under great stress. Besides the burden of external repression, there was dissension within the movement. Becoming an abolitionist required an exacting conscience and unwillingness to compromise on matters of principle. These character traits also made it difficult for abolitionists to work together and maintain a united front against their opponents.

During the late 1830s, Garrison, the most visible spokesman for the cause, began to adopt positions that other abolitionists found extreme and divisive. He attacked government, clergy, and churches for refusing to take a strong antislavery stand, and he refused to work with any person or organization that did not fully support his crusade.

The positions alienated members of the Anti-Slavery Society who continued to hope that organized religion and the existing political system could be influenced or even taken over by abolitionists. But it was Garrison's stand on women's rights that led to an open break at the national convention of 1840. Many of his followers separated from Garrison and his organization when the Boston editor engineered the election of a female abolitionist to the executive committee of the Anti-Slavery Society.

The schism weakened Garrison's influence within the movement. When he later repudiated the U.S. Constitution as a proslavery document and called for northern secession from the Union, few antislavery people in the Middle Atlantic or midwestern states went along. Outside of New England, most abolitionists operated *within* churches and the political system. The **Liberty party,** organized in 1840, was their first attempt to enter the electoral arena under their own banner; it signaled a new effort to turn antislavery sentiment into political power.

Liberty party America's first antislavery political party, formed in 1840.

Black Abolitionists

From the beginning, the abolitionist movement depended heavily on the support of the northern free black community. Most of the early subscribers to Garrison's *Liberator* were African Americans. Black orators, especially escaped slaves such as Frederick Douglass, made northern audiences aware of the realities of bondage. But relations between white and black abolitionists were often tense and uneasy. Blacks protested that they did not have their fair share of leadership positions or influence over policy. Eventually a black antislavery movement emerged that was largely independent of the white-led crusade. The Negro Convention movement, which sponsored national meetings of black leaders beginning in 1830, provided an important forum for independent black expression.

Black newspapers, such as *Freedom's Journal,* first published in 1827, and the *North Star,* founded by Douglass in 1847, gave black writers a chance to preach their gospel of liberation to black readers. African American authors also produced a stream of books and pamphlets attacking slavery, refuting racism, and advocating various forms of resistance. One of the most influential publications was David Walker's *Appeal . . . to the Colored Citizens of the World,* which appeared in 1829. Walker denounced slavery in the most vigorous language possible and called for a black revolt against white tyranny.

Frederick Douglass, who escaped from slavery in 1838, became one of the most effective voices in the crusade against slavery. ❖

Free blacks in the North did more than make verbal protests against racial injustice. They were also the main conductors on the fabled Underground Railroad that opened a path for fugitives from slavery. Courageous ex-slaves such as Harriet Tubman and Josiah Henson made regular forays into the slave states to lead other blacks to freedom, and many of the "stations" along the way were run by free blacks. In northern towns and cities, free blacks organized "vigilance committees" to protect fugitives and thwart the slave-catchers. Groups of blacks even used force to rescue recaptured fugitives from the authorities.

Historians have debated the question of whether the abolitionist movement of the 1830s and early 1840s was a success or a failure. It failed to convert a majority of Americans to its position on the evil of slavery. And in the South, it provoked a more militant and uncompromising defense of slavery. The belief that peaceful agitation, or what abolitionists called "moral suasion," would convert slaveholders and their northern sympathizers to abolition was obviously unrealistic.

But in another sense the crusade was successful. It brought the slavery issue to the forefront of public consciousness and convinced a substantial and growing segment of the northern population that the South's peculiar institution was morally wrong and potentially dangerous to the American way of life. The politicians who later mobilized the North against the expansion of slavery into the territories drew their strength from the reservoir of antislavery attitudes and sentiment created by the abolitionists.

From Abolitionism to Women's Rights

Abolitionism also served as a catalyst for the women's rights movement. From the beginning, women were active participants in the abolitionist crusade. Some antislavery women defied conventional ideas of their proper sphere by becoming public speakers and demanding an equal role in the leadership of antislavery societies. The most famous of these were the Grimké sisters, Sarah and Angelina, who attracted enormous attention because they were the rebellious daughters of a South Carolina slaveholder.

The battle to participate equally in the antislavery crusade made a number of female abolitionists acutely aware of male dominance and oppression. For them, the same principles that justified the liberation of the slaves also applied to the emancipation of women from all restrictions on their rights as citizens. However, not all of the antislavery men agreed with the idea of equal rights for women.

Wounded by male reluctance to extend the cause of emancipation to include women, Lucretia Mott and Elizabeth Cady Stanton organized a new and independent movement for women's rights. The high point of their campaign was the famous 1848 **Seneca Falls Convention** in upstate New York. In a "declaration of sentiments," the delegates condemned the treatment of women by men and demanded the right to vote and to control their own property, person, and children. Rejecting the cult of domesticity and its doctrine of separate spheres, these women and their male supporters launched the modern movement for gender equality.

Seneca Falls Convention The first women's rights convention, held in 1848 in Seneca Falls, New York, and co-sponsored by women's rights reformers Elizabeth Cady Stanton and Lucretia Mott. Delegates at the convention drafted a "declaration of sentiments," patterned on the Declaration of Independence, but which declared that "all men and women are created equal."

Radical Ideas and Experiments

Hopes for individual or social perfection were not limited to reformers inspired by evangelicalism. Between the 1820s and 1850s, a great variety of schemes for human redemption came from persons who had rejected orthodox Protestantism. Some were freethinkers carrying on the traditions of the Enlightenment, but most were individuals seeking new paths to spiritual or religious fulfillment. A movement that achieved remarkable success or notoriety was spiritualism—the belief that one could communicate with the dead. These philosophical and religious radicals attacked established institutions, proscribed new modes of living, and founded utopian communities where they could put their ideas into practice.

A radical movement of foreign origin that gained a toehold in Jacksonian America was utopian socialism. In 1825–1826, the British manufacturer and reformer Robert Owen founded a community based on common and equal ownership of property at New Harmony, Indiana. About the same time, Owen's associate, Frances Wright, gathered a group of slaves at Nashoba, Tennessee, and set them to work earning their freedom in an atmosphere of "rational cooperation." The rapid demise of both model communities suggests that utopian socialism did not easily take root in American soil.

But the impulse survived. In the 1840s, a number of Americans became interested in the ideas of the French utopian theorist Charles Fourier, who called for cooperative communities in which everyone did a fair share of the work and tasks were assigned to natural abilities of the members. Between 1842 and 1852, about thirty Fourierist "phalanxes" were established in the northeastern and midwestern states. Like the Owenite communities, the Fourierist phalanxes were short-lived, surviving for an average of only two years.

utopianism Between the 1830s and 1850s, hopes for societal perfection—utopia—were widespread among evangelical Christians as well as secular humanists.

Shakers A religious group, formally known as the United Society of Believers, that advocated strict celibacy, gender equality, and communal ownership.

Oneida community Founded in 1848 in Oneida, New York, this Christian utopian community earned notoriety for institutionalizing a form of "free love."

Two of the most successful and long-lived manifestations of pre–Civil War **utopianism** were the Shakers and the Oneida community. The **Shakers**—officially known as the Millennial Church or the United Society of Believers—began as a religious movement in England. In 1774, a Shaker leader, Mother Ann Lee, brought the group's radical beliefs to the United States. Lee believed herself to be the feminine incarnation of Christ and advocated a new theology based squarely on the principle of sexual equality. The Shakers, named for their expressions of religious fervor through vigorous dancelike movements, believed in communal ownership and strict celibacy. They lived simply and minimized their contact with the outside world because they expected Christ's Second Coming to occur momentarily. The **Oneida community** was established in 1848 at Oneida, New York, and was inspired by an unorthodox brand of Christian perfectionism. Its founder, John Humphrey Noyes, believed the Second Coming of Christ had already occurred; hence human beings were no longer obliged to follow the moral rules that their previously fallen state had required. At Oneida, traditional marriage was outlawed, and a carefully regulated form of "free love" was put into practice.

transcendentalism An American version of the romantic and idealist thought that emerged in Europe in the early nineteenth century, this literary and philosophical movement held that individuals could rise above material reality and ordinary understanding.

It was a literary and philosophical movement known as **transcendentalism** that inspired the era's most memorable experiments in thinking and living on a higher plane. The main idea was that the individual could transcend material reality and ordinary understanding, attaining through a higher form of reason, or intuition, a oneness with the universe as a whole and with the spiritual forces that lay behind it. Transcendentalism was the major American version of the romantic and idealist thought that emerged in the early nineteenth century. Throughout the

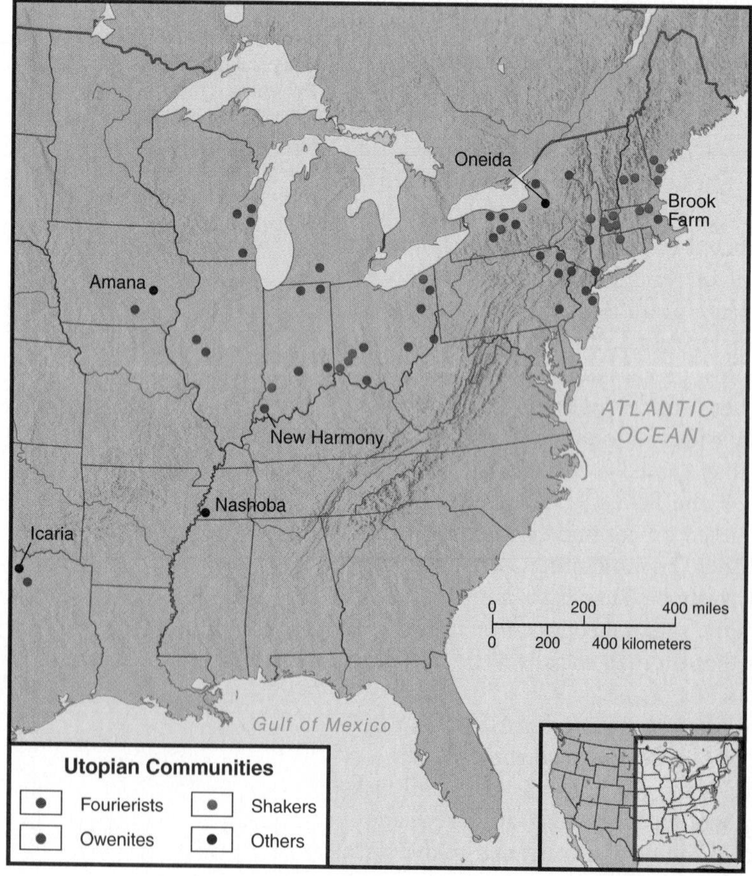

UTOPIAN COMMUNITIES BEFORE THE CIVIL WAR *The search for new paths to spiritual or religious fulfillment attracted many to utopian communitarian societies. By far the largest of these societies during the period before the Civil War was the Shakers, who by the 1830s had established twenty settlements in seven states with a combined membership of approximately six thousand. Their rule of celibacy meant that Shaker communities gained members through adoption and conversion, rather than by natural reproduction.* ❖

CHRONOLOGY

1801	Massive revival is held at Cane Ridge, Kentucky
1826	American Temperance Society is organized
1830–1831	Charles G. Finney evangelizes Rochester, New York
1831	William Lloyd Garrison publishes the first issue of *The Liberator*
1833	Abolitionists found the American Anti-Slavery Society
1836	American Temperance Society splits into factions
1836–1837	Theodore Weld advocates abolition in Ohio and upstate New York
1837	Massachusetts establishes a state board of education ❖ Abolitionist editor Elijah Lovejoy is killed by a proslavery mob
1840	American Anti-Slavery Society splits over women's rights and other issues
1841	Transcendentalists organize a model community at Brook Farm
1848	Feminists gather at Seneca Falls, New York, and found the women's rights movement
1854	Thoreau's *Walden* is published

Western world, romanticism was challenging the rationalism and materialism of the Enlightenment in the name of exalted feeling and cosmic spirituality. Most American transcendentalists were dissatisfied with rationalistic religions but were unable to embrace evangelical Christianity because of intellectual resistance to its doctrines. Instead they sought inspiration from a philosophical and literary idealism of German origin. Their prophet was Ralph Waldo Emerson, a brilliant essayist and lecturer who preached that each individual could commune directly with a benign spiritual force that animated nature and the universe—he called it the "oversoul."

Emerson was an advocate of self-reliance and avoided all involvement in organized movements or associations. But in the vicinity of Emerson's home in Concord, Massachusetts, a group of like-minded seekers of truth and spiritual fulfillment gathered during the 1830s and 1840s. One group of transcendentalists, led by the Reverend George Ripley, rejected Emerson's radical individualism and founded a cooperative community at **Brook Farm,** near Roxbury, Massachusetts, in 1841. For the next four years, they worked the land in common, conducted an excellent school on the principle that spontaneity rather than discipline was the key to education, and allowed ample time for conversation, meditation, communion with nature, and artistic activity of all kinds. The Brook Farm experiment ended in 1849.

Brook Farm This transcendentalist commune, founded in Massachusetts in 1841, attracted many leading creative figures during its brief existence.

Another experiment in transcendental living adhered more closely to the individualistic spirit of the movement. Between 1845 and 1847, Henry David Thoreau, a young disciple of Emerson, lived by himself in the woods along the shore of Walden Pond and carefully recorded his thoughts and impressions. In a sense, he pushed the ideal of "self-culture" to its logical outcome—a utopia of one. The result was *Walden* (published in 1854), one of the greatest achievements in American literature.

Conclusion: Counterpoint on Reform

One great American writer observed at close quarters the perfectionist ferment of the age but held himself aloof, suggesting in his novels and tales that pursuit of the ideal led to a distorted sense of human nature and possibilities. Nathaniel

Hawthorne's sense of human frailty and sinfulness made him skeptical about the lofty claims of transcendentalism and utopianism. He satirized transcendentalism as unworldly and overoptimistic and lampooned life in such cooperative communities as Brook Farm. His greatest novels, *The Scarlet Letter* (1850) and *The House of Seven Gables* (1851), imaginatively probed people's futile efforts to escape sin and evil. The world was imperfect, he suggested, and one simply had to accept that reality.

To be sure, the dreams of perfectionist reformers promised more than they could possibly deliver. Revivals could not make all men like Christ, temperance could not solve all social problems, abolitionist agitation could not bring a peaceful end to slavery, and transcendentalism could not fully emancipate people from the limitations and frustrations of daily life. But the reformers could argue that Hawthorne's skepticism and fatalism was a prescription for doing nothing in the face of intolerable evils. If the reform impulse was long on inspirational rhetoric but somewhat short on durable, practical achievements, it did challenge Americans to improve their country.

Key Terms

Second Great Awakening, p. 227
temperance movement, p. 230
Cult of Domesticity, p. 232
American Colonization Society, p. 236
Liberty party, p. 238
Seneca Falls Convention, p. 239
utopianism, p. 240
Shakers, p. 240
Oneida community, p. 240
transcendentalism, p. 240
Brook Farm, p. 241

Recommended Reading

Alice Felt Tyler, *Freedom's Ferment: Phases of American Social History from the Colonial Period to the Outbreak of the Civil War* (1944), gives a lively overview of the varieties of pre–Civil War reform activity. Ronald G. Walters, *American Reformers, 1815–1860,* rev. ed. (1997), provides a modern interpretation of these movements. Steven Mintz, *Moralists and Modernizers: America's Pre–Civil War Reformers* (1995), provides another good overview of the reform activities during this period. A particularly useful collection of documents on reform movements and other aspects of antebellum culture is David Brion Davis, *Antebellum American Culture: An Interpretive Anthology* (1979).

The best general work on the revivalism of the Second Great Awakening is William G. McLoughlin, *Modern Revivalism* (1959). A general survey of the religious ferment of this period is Nathan O. Hatch, *The Democratization of American Christianity* (1989). Paul E. Johnson, *A Shopkeeper's Millennium: Society and Revivals in Rochester, New York, 1815–1837* (1978), incisively describes the impact of the revival on a single community. The connection between religion and reform is described in Robert H. Abzug, *Cosmos Crumbling: American Reform and the Religious Imagination* (1994).

A good introduction to the changing roles of women and the family in nineteenth-century America is Carl N. Degler, *At Odds: Women and the Family in America from the Revolution to the Present* (1980). On the rise of the domestic ideology, see Nancy F. Cott, *The Bonds of Womanhood: "Woman's Sphere" in New England, 1780–1835* (1977). The condition of working-class women is incisively treated in Christine Stansell, *City of Women: Sex and Class in New York, 1789–1860* (1986). For an extended history of the *Cruger* case and an excellent legal history of marriage and divorce, see Hendrick Hartog, *Man and Wife in America: A History* (2000).

David J. Rothman, *The Discovery of the Asylum: Social Order and Disorder in the New Republic* (1971), provides a penetrating analysis of the movement for institutional reform. For good surveys of abolitionism, see James Brewer Stewart, *Holy Warriors: The Abolitionists and American Slavery* (1976) and Paul Goodman, *Of One Blood: Abolitionism and Racial Equality* (1998). On transcendentalism, see Charles Capper and Conrad E. Wright, *Transient and Permanent: The Transcendentalist Movement and Its Contexts* (1999).

For a list of additional titles related to this chapter's topics, please see http://www.ablongman.com/divine.

Suggested Web Sites

America's First Look into the Camera: Daguerreotype Portraits and Views, 1839–1862

http://memory.loc.gov/ammem/daghtml/daghome.html
The Library of Congress's daguerreotype collection consists of more than 650 photographs dating from 1839 to 1864. Portraits, architectural views, and some street scenes make up most of the collection.

1830s Clothing

http://www.connerprairie.org/historyonline/clothing.html
See how clothing worn in the Early Republic was quite different from what people wear today.

Votes for Women: Selections from the National American Woman Suffrage Association Collection, 1848–1921

http://memory.loc.gov/ammem/naw/nawshome.html
This Library of Congress site contains 167 books, pamphlets, and other artifacts documenting the suffrage campaign.

History of Women's Suffrage

http://www.rochester.edu/SBA/history.html
This site includes a chronology, important texts relating to woman suffrage, and biographical information about Susan B. Anthony and Elizabeth Cady Stanton.

By Popular Demand: "Votes for Women" Suffrage Pictures, 1850–1920

http://memory.loc.gov/ammem/vfwhtml/vfwhome.html
Portraits, suffrage parades, picketing suffragists, an antisuffrage display, and cartoons commenting on the movement make up this Library of Congress site.

Women in America, 1820 to 1842

http://xroads.virginia.edu/~HYPER/DETOC/FEM/home.htm
This University of Virginia site takes a look at women in antebellum America.

Godey's Lady's Book On-line

http://www.history.rochester.edu/godeys/
Here is on-line text of this interesting nineteenth-century journal.

Influence of Prominent Abolitionists

http://www.loc.gov/exhibits/african/afam006.html
An exhibit site from the Library of Congress, with pictures and text that discusses some of the key African American abolitionists and their efforts to end slavery.

Chapter 13

An Age of Expansionism

The Spirit of Young America

In the 1840s and early 1850s, politicians, writers, and entrepreneurs frequently proclaimed themselves champions of **Young America.** One of the first to use the phrase was Ralph Waldo Emerson, who told an audience of merchants and manufacturers in 1844 that the nation was entering a new era of commercial development, technological progress, and territorial expansion. Emerson suggested that a progressive new generation—the "Young Americans"—would lead this surge of physical development. More than a slogan and less than an organized movement, Young America stood for a positive attitude toward the market economy and industrial growth, a more aggressive and belligerent foreign policy, and a celebration of America's unique strengths and virtues.

Young Americans favored enlarging the national market by acquiring new territory. They called for the annexation of Texas, asserted an American claim to all of Oregon, and urged the appropriation of vast new territories from Mexico. They also celebrated the technological advances that would knit this new empire together, especially the telegraph and the railroad.

Young American attitudes found cultural and intellectual expression as well as economic and political beliefs. In 1845, a Washington journal hailed the election of the 49-year-old James K. Polk, at that time the youngest man to have been elected president, as a sign that youth would "dare to take antiquity by the beard, and tear the cloak from hoary-headed hypocrisy. Too young to be corrupt . . . it is Young America, awakened to a sense of her own intellectual greatness by her soaring spirit. It stands in strength, the voice of the majority." During the Polk administration, Young American writers and critics—mostly based in New York City—called for a new and distinctive national literature, free of subservience to European themes or models and expressive of the democratic spirit. Their organ was the *Literary World,* founded in 1847, and its ideals influenced two of the greatest writers that nation has produced: Walt Whitman and Herman Melville.

Whitman captured much of the exuberance, optimism, and expansion of Young America. He celebrated a nation whose limits were circumscribed only by the imagination. In *Moby-Dick,* Herman Melville produced a novel sufficiently original in form and conception to more than fulfill the demand of Young Americans for "a New Literature to fit the New Man in the New Age." But he was too deep a thinker not to see the perils that underlay the soaring ambition and aggressiveness of the new age. In the character of Ahab, the whaling captain who brings destruction of himself and his ship by his relentless pursuit of the white whale, Melville symbolized—among other things—the dangers facing a nation that was overreaching itself by indulging its pride and exalted sense of destiny with too little concern for the moral and practical consequences.

Outline

Movement to the Far West

Manifest Destiny and the Mexican-American War

Internal Expansionism

Conclusion: The Costs of Expansion

We Americans

The Irish in Boston, 1845–1865

The Young American ideal—the idea of a young country led by young men into new paths of prosperity and greatness—appealed to many people and found support across political party lines. But the attitude came to be identified primarily with young Democrats who wanted to move their party away from its traditional fear of the expansion of commerce and industry. Unlike old-line Jeffersonians and Jacksonians, Young Americans had no qualms about the market economy and the speculative, materialistic spirit it called forth.

Young America In the 1840s and early 1850s, many public figures, especially younger members of the Democratic party, used this term to describe a movement that advocated territorial expansion and industrial growth in the name of patriotism.

Before 1848, the Young American impulse focused mainly on the great expanse of western lands that lay just beyond the nation's borders. After the Mexican-American War, when territorial gains extended the nation's boundaries from the Atlantic to the Pacific, attention shifted to internal development. New discoveries of gold in the nation's western territories fostered economic growth, technological advances spurred industrialization, and increased immigration brought more people to populate the lands newly acquired—by agreement or by force.

Movement to the Far West

In the 1830s and 1840s, the westward movement of population left the valley of the Mississippi behind and penetrated the Far West all the way to the Pacific. Pioneers pursued fertile land and economic opportunities beyond the existing boundaries of the United States and thus helped set the stage for the annexations and international crises of the 1840s. Some went for material gain, others for adventure; a significant minority sought freedom from religious persecution. They carried American attitudes and loyalties with them into regions that were already occupied or at least claimed by Mexico or Great Britain. Whether they realized it or not, these pioneers were the vanguard of American expansionism.

Borderlands of the 1830s

Territorial ambition lured Americans northward as well as westward, and for a time it seemed that Canada might be a new frontier for expansionism. Conflicts over the border between America and British North America led periodically to calls for diplomatic or military action to wrest the northern half of the continent from the English. During the 1830s, tensions were particularly high as Americans and Canadians wrestled over the exact location of the border between Maine and New Brunswick. Finally, in 1842, Secretary of State Daniel Webster concluded an agreement with the British government, represented by Lord Ashburton. The **Webster-Ashburton Treaty** gave more than half of the disputed territory to the United States and established a definite northeastern boundary with Canada.

Webster-Ashburton Treaty This 1842 agreement with Britain resolved the boundary dispute between Maine and New Brunswick, Canada, setting the northeastern U.S. border.

On the other side of the continent, the United States and Britain both laid claim to Oregon, a vast area that lay between the Rockies and the Pacific from the 42nd parallel (the northern boundary of California) to the latitude of 54°40' (the southern boundary of Alaska). Although in 1818 the two nations had agreed to joint occupation, the Americans had strengthened their claim by acquiring Spain's rights to the Pacific Northwest in the Adams-Onís Treaty (see Chapter 9), and the British had gained effective control of the northern portion of the Oregon Country. Blocking an equitable division was the reluctance of both sides to surrender access to the Columbia River basin and the adjacent territory extending north to the 49th parallel (which later became the northern border of the state of Washington).

The Oregon Country was scarcely populated before 1840, but the same could not be said of the Mexican borderlands that lay directly west of Jacksonian America. By 1827, Mexican settlements in present-day New Mexico contained about 44,000

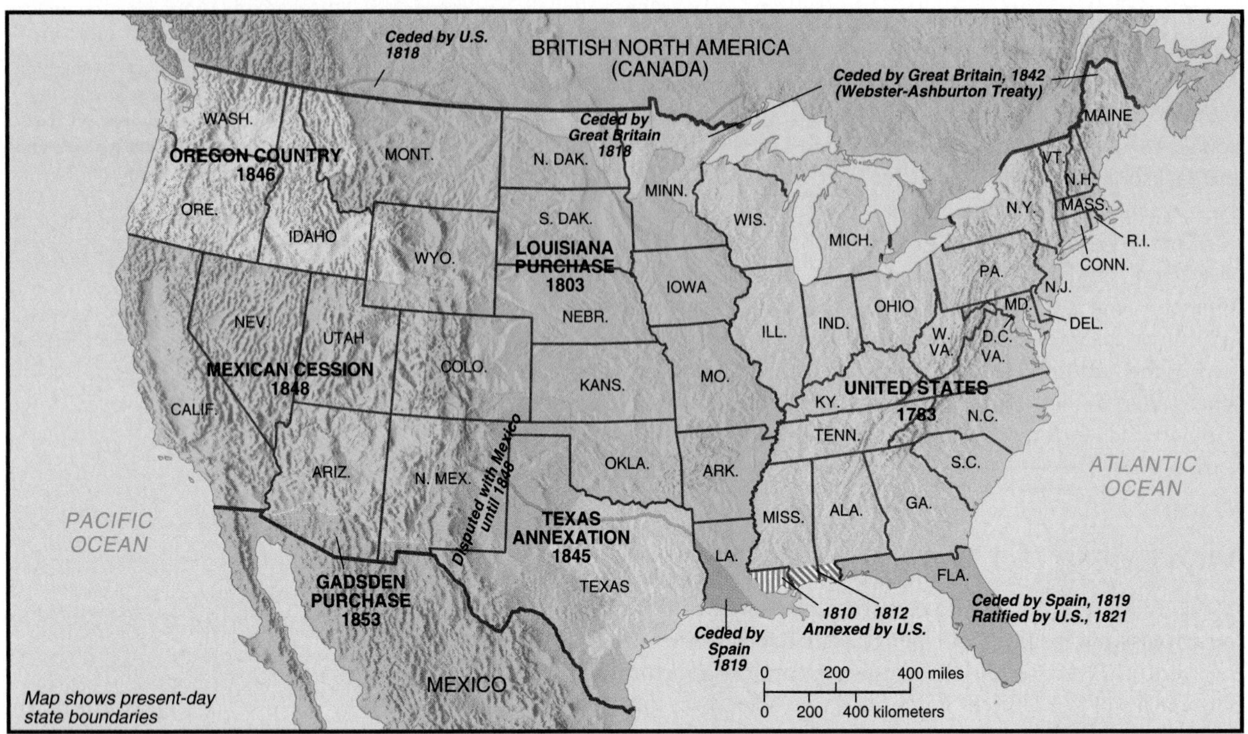

TERRITORIAL EXPANSION BY THE MID-NINETEENTH CENTURY *Fervent nationalists identified the growth of America through territorial expansion as the divinely ordained "Manifest Destiny" of a chosen people.* ❖

people. To save the province from economic stagnation, the Mexican authorities decided in 1822 to encourage trade between Santa Fe, the capital of New Mexico, and the United States. They succeeded in stimulating commercial prosperity, but they also whetted expansionist appetites on the Anglo side of the border.

California in the 1820s and 1830s was a more colorful, turbulent, and fragile northward expansion of Mexican civilization. Much less populous than New Mexico—there were only about four thousand Hispanic inhabitants in 1827—California was a land of huge estates and enormous herds of cattle. At the beginning of the 1830s, most of the land and the wealth of the province was controlled by the chain of twenty-one mission stations of the Catholic Church that stretched from San Diego to San Francisco.

In 1833, the Mexican government confiscated the church's lands and released the Indians from semislavery, but this in fact made their plight even worse. Rather than giving the land to the thirty thousand Christian Indians in California, the government awarded immense tracts to Mexican citizens. During the fifteen years that they held sway, the *rancheros,* as the large landowners were called, captured the fancy and aroused the envy of Anglo traders and visitors to California through their flamboyant lifestyle, superb horsemanship, and taste for violent and dangerous sports.

The Easterners who conveyed to the rest of the nation a romantic image of this sun-baked land of beautiful scenery and señoritas were mostly merchants and sailors involved in the oceanic trade between Boston and California ports. By the mid-1830s, several Yankee merchants had taken up permanent residence in towns such as Monterey and San Diego to conduct the California end of the business. The reports that they sent back about the Golden West sparked great interest in eastern business circles.

The Texas Revolution

At the same time as some Americans were trading with California, others were taking possession of Texas. In the early 1820s, Mexican officials encouraged settlers from the United States to settle in Texas. Newly independent Mexico granted Stephen F. Austin, son of a onetime Spanish citizen, a huge piece of land in hopes he would help attract and settle new colonists from the United States. Some fifteen other Anglo-American *empresarios* received land grants in the 1820s. In 1823, three hundred families from the United States were settled on the Austin grant, and within a year, the colony's population had swelled to 2021. The offer of fertile and inexpensive land attracted many American immigrants.

Friction soon developed between the Mexican government and the American colonists over such issues as the status of slavery and the Catholic Church. In 1829, Mexico formally freed all slaves under its jurisdiction, but the Texans simply ignored the decree. Mexican law also required that immigrants accept the Catholic faith, but this regulation also became a dead letter. The abuses of Mexican law grew, along with the size of the American population in Texas, and in 1830, the Mexican legislature prohibited further American immigration and importation of slaves to Texas.

But enforcement of the new law was feeble, and the flow of settlers, slaves, and smuggled goods continued virtually unabated. A long-standing complaint of the Texans was the failure of the Mexican constitution to grant them local self-government. In 1832, Texans showed their displeasure with Mexican rule by rioting in protest against the arrest of several Americans by the commander of the Galveston garrison.

Stephen Austin went to Mexico City in 1833 to present the Texans' grievances and seek concessions from the central government. He succeeded in having the ban against American immigration lifted but failed to win agreement for self-government. Then, as he was about to return to Texas, Austin was arrested and imprisoned for more than a year for writing a letter recommending that Texans set up a state government without Mexico City's consent.

In 1835, some Texans revolted against Mexico. The insurrectionists claimed that they were fighting for freedom against a long experience of oppression. Actually, Mexican rule had not been harsh, although it was inefficient and often corrupt. Furthermore, the Texans' devotion to "liberty" did not prevent them from defending slavery against Mexico's attempt to abolish it. Texans had done pretty much what they pleased, despite laws to the contrary and angry rumblings from south of the Rio Grande.

A more plausible justification for revolution was the Texans' fear of the future under the latest regime to be established in Mexico City. In 1834, General Antonio López de Santa Anna made himself dictator of Mexico and abolished the federal system of government. When news of these developments reached Texas late in the year, they were accompanied by rumors of the impending disfranchisement and even expulsion of American immigrants. Influenced by the rumors, the rebels tended to ascribe sinister motives to Santa Anna's new policy of enforcing tariff regulation by military force.

When he learned that the Texans were resisting customs collections, Santa Anna sent reinforcements. By October 1835, the two sides were engaged in a war. The first phase of the fighting ended when Stephen Austin laid siege to San Antonio with a force of five hundred men and after six weeks forced its surrender, thereby capturing most of the Mexican troops then in Texas.

The Republic of Texas

While early fighting was going on, delegates from the American communities met in convention and after some hesitation voted overwhelmingly to declare their independence on March 2, 1836. A constitution, based closely on that of the United

States, was adopted for the new Republic of Texas, and a temporary government was installed to carry on the military struggle.

Although the ensuing conflict was largely one of Americans against Mexicans, some Texas Mexicans, or *Tejanos*, joined the fray on the side of the Anglo rebels. They too wanted to be free from Santa Anna's heavy-handed rule, although after the rebellion many of them became victims of anti-Mexican prejudice.

Within days after Texas declared itself a republic, rebels and Mexican troops in San Antonio fought the famous battle of the **Alamo.** Myths about the battle have magnified the Anglo rebels' valor at the Mexicans' expense. It is true that 187 rebels fought off a far larger Mexican force, capitulating only after more than a week of battling. It is not true, however, that all of the rebels fought to the death—apparently eight men were captured and then executed. Moreover, the rebels fought from inside a strong fortress with superior weapons against march-weary Mexican conscripts. Nevertheless, their stand was brave, and their deaths gave the insurrection new inspiration.

Alamo In 1835, Americans living in the Mexican state of Texas fomented a revolution. Mexico lost the conflict, but not before its troops defeated and killed a group of American rebels at this fort in San Antonio.

A few days later, another Texas detachment was surrounded and captured in an open plain near the San Antonio River and was marched to the town of Goliad, where all 350 of its members were summarily executed. The "Goliad massacre" provoked the Texas rebels to even more desperate resistance.

The main Texas army, under General Sam Houston, moved quickly to avenge these early defeats. On April 21, 1836, Houston led his force of seven hundred men in a daring assault on Santa Anna's encampment near the San Jacinto River. Within fifteen minutes, the battle was over, the Mexican force defeated, and Santa Anna captured. The Mexican leader was marched to Velasco, where he was forced to sign treaties recognizing the independence of Texas and its claim to territory all the way to the Rio Grande.

Sam Houston, the hero of San Jacinto, became the first president of the Texas republic. He sought annexation to the United States, but Andrew Jackson and others believed that domestic politics, the sectional issue of the expansion of slavery, and the possibility of a war with Mexico made such an action untenable. Congress and the Jackson administration, however, did formally recognize Texas sovereignty, and during the following decade of independence, the population of the "Lone Star Republic" soared from 30,000 to 142,000.

Trails of Trade and Settlement

After New Mexico opened its trade to American merchants in 1822, a thriving commerce developed along the trail that ran from Independence, Missouri, to Santa Fe. To protect themselves from the hostile Indians whose territory they had to cross, the traders traveled in large caravans. The federal government assisted them by providing troops when necessary and by appropriating money to purchase rights of passage from various tribes. Even so, the trip across the Cimarron Desert and the southern Rockies was often hazardous. But profits from the exchange of textiles and other manufactured goods for furs, mules, and precious metals were substantial enough to make the risk worth taking.

Relations between the United States and Mexico soured following the Texas revolution, and this had a devastating effect on the Santa Fe trade. Much of the ill feeling was caused by the Texans' blundering efforts to get a piece of the Santa Fe action. After several clashes with the Texans, the Mexican government in 1842 passed a new tariff banning the importation of many of the goods sold by American merchants and prohibiting the export of gold and silver.

The famous Oregon Trail was the great overland route that brought the wagon trains of American migrants to the West Coast during the 1840s. The journey took about six months; most parties departed in May, hoping to arrive in November be-

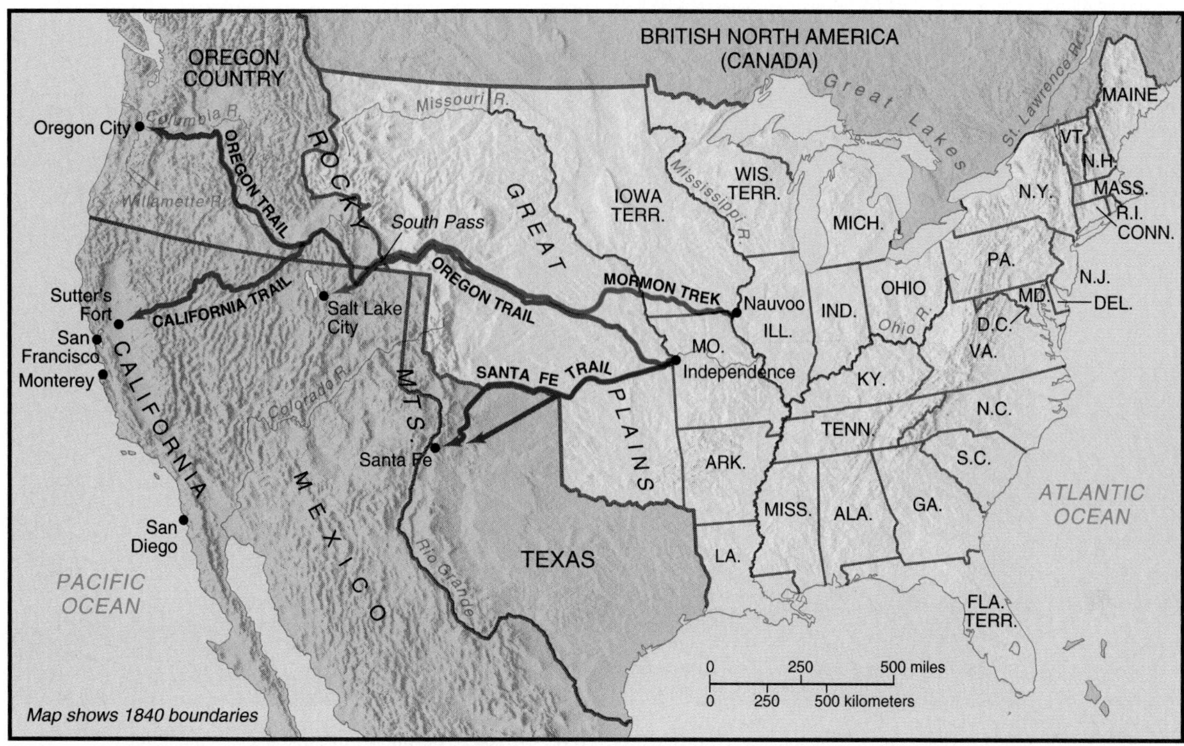

WESTERN TRAILS *Among the greatest hazards faced by those migrating to the West was the rough and unfamiliar terrain over which their wagon trains traveled.* ❖

fore the great snows hit the last mountain barriers. After small groups had made their way to both Oregon and California in 1841 and 1842, a mass migration—mostly to Oregon—began in 1843. These migrants were quick to demand the extension of full American sovereignty over the Oregon Country.

The Mormon Trek

Among the settlers moving west were members, known as Mormons, of the most successful religious denomination founded exclusively on American soil, the Church of Jesus Christ of Latter-day Saints. The background of the Mormon trek was a history of persecution in the eastern states. Joseph Smith of Palmyra, New York, the founder of Mormonism, revealed in 1830 that he had received over many years a series of revelations that called upon him to establish Christ's pure church on earth. As the prophet of this faith, he published the *Book of Mormon,* a new scripture that he claimed to have discovered and translated with the aid of an angel. It was the record of a community of pious Jews who left the Holy Land six centuries before the birth of Christ and sailed to the American continent. After his crucifixion and resurrection, Christ appeared to this community and proclaimed the Gospel. Four hundred years later, a fratricidal war annihilated the believing Christians but not all of the descendents of the original Jewish migrants. Mormons held that the survivors had contributed to the ancestry of the American Indians. This prophecy foretold the restoration of a purer Christianity that had once thrived on American soil. Smith and his followers were determined to establish a western Zion where they could practice their faith unmolested and carry out their special mission to convert the Native Americans.

Carl Christian Anton Christensen, Handcart, *ca. 1840. Instead of buying wagons and oxen, some groups of Mormon colonists made their trek to Deseret on foot, hauling their possessions in handcarts and working together as families to move their heavy loads.* ❖

In the 1830s, the Mormons established communities in Ohio and Missouri, but the former went bankrupt in the Panic of 1837 and the latter was the target of angry mobs and vigilante violence. In 1839, the Mormons found a temporary haven at Nauvoo, Illinois. But Smith soon reported new revelations that engendered dissension among his followers and hostility from neighboring "gentiles." Most controversial was his authorization of polygamy. In 1844, Smith was killed by a mob while being held in jail in Carthage, Illinois.

Smith's death confirmed the growing conviction of the Mormon leadership that they needed to move farther west to establish their Zion in the wilderness. In late 1845, Smith's successor, Brigham Young, decided to send a party of fifteen hundred men to assess the chances of maintaining a colony in the vicinity of the Great Salt Lake. In 1847, Young himself arrived in Utah and sent back word to the faithful that he had found the promised land.

The Mormon community that Young established in Utah is one of the great success stories of western settlement. In contrast to the extreme individualism and disorder that characterized the mining camps and other new communities, the state of Deseret (the name the Mormons originally applied to Utah) was a model of discipline and cooperation. Because of its communitarian form of social organization, its centralized government, and the religious dedication of its inhabitants, this frontier society was able to expand settlement in a planned and efficient way and develop a system of irrigation that "made the desert bloom."

After Utah came under American sovereignty in 1848, Deseret fought to maintain its autonomy and its custom of polygamy against the efforts of the federal government to extend American law and set up the usual type of territorial administration. In 1857, the Mormons and the federal government almost came to blows until President James Buchanan decided to use diplomacy rather than force.

Manifest Destiny and the Mexican-American War

The rush of settlers beyond the nation's borders in the 1830s and 1840s inspired politicians and propagandists to call for annexation of the areas that the migrants were occupying. Some went further and proclaimed that it was the **Manifest Destiny** of the United States to expand until it had absorbed all of North America, including Canada and Mexico. Such ambitions—and the policies they inspired—led to a major diplomatic confrontation with Great Britain and a war with Mexico.

Manifest Destiny Coined in 1845, this term referred to a doctrine in support of territorial expansion based on the beliefs that population growth demanded territorial expansion, that God supported American expansion, and that national expansion equaled the expansion of freedom.

Tyler and Texas

President John Tyler initiated the politics of Manifest Destiny. He was vice president when William Henry Harrison died in office in 1841 after serving scarcely a month. Tyler was a states' rights, proslavery Virginian who had been picked as Harrison's running mate to broaden the appeal of the Whig ticket. Profoundly out of sympathy with the mainstream of his own party, he soon broke with the Whigs in Congress, who had united behind the latest version of Henry Clay's American System. Despite the fact that he lacked a base in either of the major parties, Tyler hoped to be elected president in his own right in 1844. To accomplish this difficult feat, he needed a new issue around which he could build a following that would cut across established party lines.

In 1843, Tyler decided to put the full weight of his administration behind the annexation of Texas. He anticipated that this would be a popular move, especially in the slaveholding South, and would give him a solid base of support for the 1844 election.

To achieve his objective, Tyler enlisted the support of John C. Calhoun, the leading political defender of slavery and state sovereignty. Success or failure in the effort would constitute a decisive test of whether the North was willing to give the southern states a fair share of national power and adequate assurances for the future of their way of life. If antislavery sentiment succeeded in blocking the acquisition of Texas, the Southerners would at least know where they stood and begin to "calculate the value of the union."

To prepare the public for annexation, the Tyler administration launched a propaganda campaign in the summer of 1843. Rumors were circulated that the British were preparing to guarantee Texas independence and make a loan to that financially troubled republic in return for the abolition of slavery. Although the reports were groundless, the stories were believed and used to give urgency to the annexation cause.

The strategy of linking annexation explicitly to the interests of the South and slavery backfired politically. Northern antislavery Whigs charged that the whole scheme was a proslavery plot meant to advance the interest of one section of the nation against the other—an allegation that has more substance than most historians have been willing to acknowledge. Consequently, the Senate rejected the treaty of annexation by a decisive vote in June 1844.

The Triumph of Polk and Annexation

Tyler's initiative made the future of Texas the central issue in the 1844 campaign. But party lines held firm, and the president himself was unable to capitalize on it. Tyler tried to run as an independent, but his failure to gain significant support eventually forced him to withdraw from the race.

If the Democratic party convention had been held in 1843, as originally scheduled, ex-President Martin Van Buren would have won the nomination easily. But the convention was postponed until May 1844, and in the meantime the annexation question came to the fore. Van Buren persisted in the view he had held as president—that incorporation of Texas would arouse sectional strife and destroy the unity of the Democratic party. In an effort to keep the issue out of the campaign, Van Buren struck a gentleman's agreement with Henry Clay, the overwhelming favorite for the Whig nomination, that both of them would publicly oppose immediate annexation.

Van Buren's letter opposing annexation appeared just before the Democratic convention, and it cost him the nomination. Angry southern delegates invoked the rule requiring approval by a two-thirds vote. After several ballots, a dark horse candidate, James K. Polk of Tennessee, emerged triumphant. Polk, a protégé of Andrew Jackson, had been speaker of the House of Representatives and governor of Tennessee.

An avowed expansionist, Polk ran on a platform calling for the simultaneous annexation of Texas and assertion of American claims to all of Oregon. He identified himself and his party with the popular cause of turning the United States into a continental nation, an aspiration that attracted support in the North as well as in the South. The Whig nominee, Henry Clay, was basically antiexpansionist, but his sense of the growing popularity of Texas annexation among southern Whigs caused him to waffle on the issue during the campaign. This vacillation cost Clay the support of a small but crucial group of northern antislavery Whigs, who defected to the abolitionist Liberty party.

Polk won the fall election by a relatively narrow popular margin. His triumph in the electoral college was secured by victories in New York and Michigan, where the Liberty party candidate, James G. Birney, had taken away enough votes from Clay to affect the outcome. Although the election was hardly a clear mandate for expansionism, the Democrats claimed that the people were behind their aggressive campaign to extend the borders of the United States.

After the election, Congress reconvened to consider the annexation of Texas. The mood had changed as a result of Polk's victory, and leading Democratic senators were now willing to support Tyler's scheme for annexation by joint resolution of Congress. As a result, annexation was approved a few days before Polk took office.

The Doctrine of Manifest Destiny

The expansionist mood that accompanied Polk's election and the annexation of Texas was given a name and a rationale in the summer of 1845. John L. O'Sullivan, a proponent of the Young America movement and an influential editor, charged that foreign governments were conspiring to block the annexation of Texas in an effort to thwart "the fulfillment of our manifest destiny to overspread the continent allotted by providence for the free development of our yearly multiplying millions."

Besides coining the phrase "manifest destiny," O'Sullivan pointed to the three main ideas that lay behind it. One was that God was on the side of American expansionism. A second idea, implied in the phrase "free development," was that the spread of American rule meant the extension of democratic institutions. O'Sullivan's third premise was that population growth required the outlet that territorial acquisitions would provide. Behind this notion lurked the fear that growing numbers would lead to diminished opportunities and European-type socioeconomic class divisions if the restless and the ambitious were not given new lands to settle and exploit.

In its most extreme form, Manifest Destiny meant that the United States would someday occupy the entire North American continent; nothing less would appease its land-hungry population. The only question in the minds of fervent expansionists and Young Americans was whether the United States would acquire its vast new domain through a gradual, peaceful process of settler infiltration or through active diplomacy backed by force and the threat of war. The decision was up to President Polk.

Polk and the Oregon Question

In 1845 and 1846, the United States came closer to armed conflict with Great Britain than at any time since the War of 1812. The willingness of some Americans to go to war over Oregon was expressed in the Democratic rallying cry "Fifty-four forty or fight!" Polk fed this expansionist fever by laying claim in his inaugural address to all of the Oregon Country. Privately, however, he was willing to accept the 49th parallel. What made the situation so tense was that Polk was dedicated to an aggressive diplomacy of bluff and bluster.

In July 1845, Polk authorized Secretary of State James Buchanan to reply to the latest British request for terms by offering a boundary along the 49th parallel. The offer did not meet the British demand for all of Vancouver Island and free navigation of the Columbia River, and the British ambassador rejected the proposal out of hand. The rebuff infuriated Polk, who later called on Congress to terminate the agreement providing for joint occupation of the Pacific Northwest. Congress complied in April 1846.

Since abrogation of the joint agreement implied that the United States would attempt to extend its jurisdiction north to 54°40', the British government decided to take the diplomatic initiative in an effort to avert war while at the same time dispatching warships to the Western Hemisphere in case conciliation failed. Their new proposal accepted the 49th parallel as the border, gave Britain all of Vancouver Island, and provided for British navigation rights on the Columbia River. The Senate recommended that the treaty be accepted with the single change that British rights to navigate the Columbia be made temporary. It was ratified in that form on June 15.

Polk was prompted to settle the Oregon question because he now had a war with Mexico on his hands. His reckless diplomacy had brought the nation within an

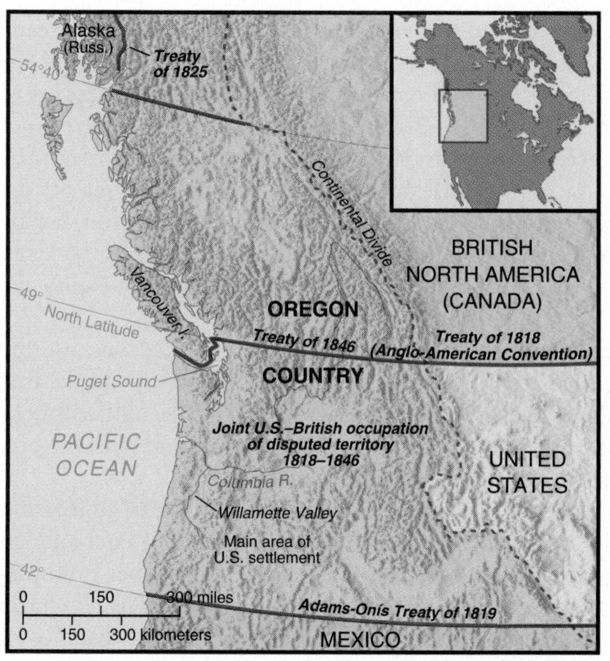

NORTHWEST BOUNDARY DISPUTE *President Polk's policy of bluff and bluster nearly involved the United States in a war with Great Britain over the disputed boundary in Oregon.* ❖

This 1846 cartoon titled "This Is the House That Polk Built" shows President Polk sitting forlornly in a house of cards representing the delicately balanced issues facing him. ❖

eyelash of being involved in two wars at the same time. American policymakers obtained what they wanted from the Oregon treaty, the splendid natural deep-water harbor of Puget Sound. However, by agreeing to a compromise on Oregon, Polk alienated expansionist advocates in the Old Northwest who had supported his earlier call for "all of Oregon."

For many Northerners, the promise of new acquisitions of the Pacific Northwest was the only thing that made annexation of Texas palatable. They hoped that new free states could be created to counterbalance the admission of slaveholding Texas to the Union. As this prospect receded, the charge of antislavery defenders that Texas annexation was a southern plot drew more support; to Northerners, Polk began to look more and more like a president concerned mainly with furthering the interests of his native region.

War with Mexico

While the United States was avoiding a war with Great Britain, it was getting into one with Mexico. Although they had recognized Texas independence in 1845, the Mexicans rejected the Lone Star Republic's unjustified claim to the unsettled territory between the Nueces River and the Rio Grande. When the United States annexed Texas and assumed its claim to the disputed area, Mexico broke off diplomatic relations and prepared for armed conflict.

Polk responded by placing troops in Louisiana on the alert and by dispatching emissary John Slidell to Mexico City. Polk hoped Slidell could resolve the boundary dispute and could persuade the Mexicans to sell New Mexico and California. Slidell's mission failed. In January 1846, Polk ordered General Zachary Taylor, commander of American forces in the Southwest, to advance well beyond the Nueces and proceed toward the Rio Grande, thus invading Mexican territory. By April, Taylor had taken up a position near Matamoros on the Rio Grande. On April 24, sixteen hundred Mexican troops crossed the river from the south and the following day attacked a small American detachment. After learning of the incident, Taylor sent word to the president: "Hostilities may now be considered as commenced."

This news was neither unexpected nor unwelcome. Polk was in fact already preparing his war message to Congress when he learned of the fighting on the Rio Grande. A short and decisive war, he had concluded, would force the cession of California and New Mexico to the United States. Thus shortly after Congress declared war on May 13, American forces under Colonel Stephen Kearny captured Santa Fe and took possession of New Mexico. Kearny's troops then set off for California, where Anglo settlers and so-called exploration expedition led by Captain John C. Frémont, aided by U.S. naval vessels, had revolted against Mexican rule. With the help of Kearny's forces, the Americans wrested control of California from Mexico.

Mexican-American War Conflict (1846–1848) between the United States and Mexico after the U.S. annexation of Texas, which Mexico still considered its own. As victor, the United States acquired vast new territories from Mexico.

The **Mexican-American War** lasted much longer than expected because the Mexicans refused to make peace despite a succession of military defeats. In the first major campaign of the conflict, Taylor followed up his victory in two battles fought north of the Rio Grande by crossing the river, taking Matamoros, and marching on Monterrey. In September, he captured the important northern city.

But Taylor's controversial decision to allow the Mexican garrison to go free and his unwillingness or inability to advance farther into Mexico angered Polk and led him to adopt a new strategy for winning the war and a new commander to implement it. General Winfield Scott was ordered to prepare an amphibious attack on Veracruz with the aim of placing an American army within striking distance of Mexico City itself. Taylor was left to hold his position in northern Mexico, where in

February 1847 he defeated a sizable Mexican army at Buena Vista. Taylor was hailed afterward as a national hero and conceivable presidential material.

The decisive Veracruz campaign was slow to develop because of the massive and careful preparations required. But in March 1847, the main American army, now under General Scott, finally landed near that crucial port city and laid siege to it. Veracruz fell after eighteen days, and then Scott began his advance on Mexico City. In the most important single battle of the war, Scott met forces under General Santa Anna at Cerro Gordo on April 17 and 18. In a well-commanded attack, Scott's forces defeated the Mexican army and opened the road to Mexico City. By August, American troops were drawn up in front of the Mexican capital. After a temporary armistice, Scott ordered the massive assault that captured the city on September 14.

Settlement of the Mexican-American War

Accompanying Scott's army was a diplomat, Nicholas P. Trist, who was authorized to negotiate a peace treaty whenever the Mexicans decided they had had enough. Despite a sequence of American victories, however, no Mexican leader was willing to invite the wrath of an intensely proud and nationalistic citizenry by agreeing to the kinds of terms Polk wanted to impose. By November, Polk was so irked by the delay that he ordered Trist to return to Washington.

Trist, to his credit, ignored Polk's instructions and continued to negotiate. On February 2, 1848, he signed a treaty that gained all the concessions he had been commissioned to obtain. The **Treaty of Guadalupe Hidalgo** ceded New Mexico and California to the United States for $15 million, established the Rio Grande as the border between Texas and Mexico, and promised that the United States government would assume the substantial claims of American citizens against Mexico. The Senate approved the treaty on March 10.

Treaty of Guadalupe Hidalgo Signed in 1848, this treaty ended the Mexican-American War. Mexico relinquished its claims to Texas and ceded an additional 500,000 square miles to the United States for $15 million.

As a result of the Mexican-American War, the United States gained half a million square miles of territory, including the present states of California, Utah, New Mexico, and Arizona and parts of Colorado and Wyoming. In 1853, a dispute over the southern boundary of the cession was resolved by the Gadsden Purchase, whereby the United States acquired the southernmost parts of present-day Arizona and New Mexico. But one intriguing question remains: Why, given the expansionist spirit of the age, did the United States not take *all* of Mexico, as many Americans desired?

Racism and anticolonialism help account for the decision. It was one thing to acquire thinly populated areas that could be settled by "Anglo-Saxon" pioneers; it was something else again to incorporate a large population that was mainly of mixed Spanish and Indian origin. These "mongrels," charged racist opponents of the "All Mexico" movement, could never be fit citizens of a self-governing republic. They would have to be ruled in the way that the British governed India, and the possession of colonial dependencies was contrary to American ideals and traditions.

The people actually making policy had more mundane and practical reasons for being satisfied with what was obtained at Guadalupe Hidalgo. What they had really wanted all along were the great California harbors of San Francisco and San Diego. From these ports, Americans could trade directly with the Orient and dominate the commerce of the Pacific. Once acquisition of California had been assured, policymakers had little incentive to press for more Mexican territory.

The war with Mexico divided the American public and provoked political dissension. A majority of the Whig party opposed the war in principle, arguing (correctly) that the United States had no valid claims to the area south of the Nueces. Whig congressmen voted for military appropriations while the conflict was going on, but they constantly criticized the president for starting it. More ominous was the charge from antislavery Northerners of both parties that the real purpose of the war was to spread the institution of slavery and increase the political power of the

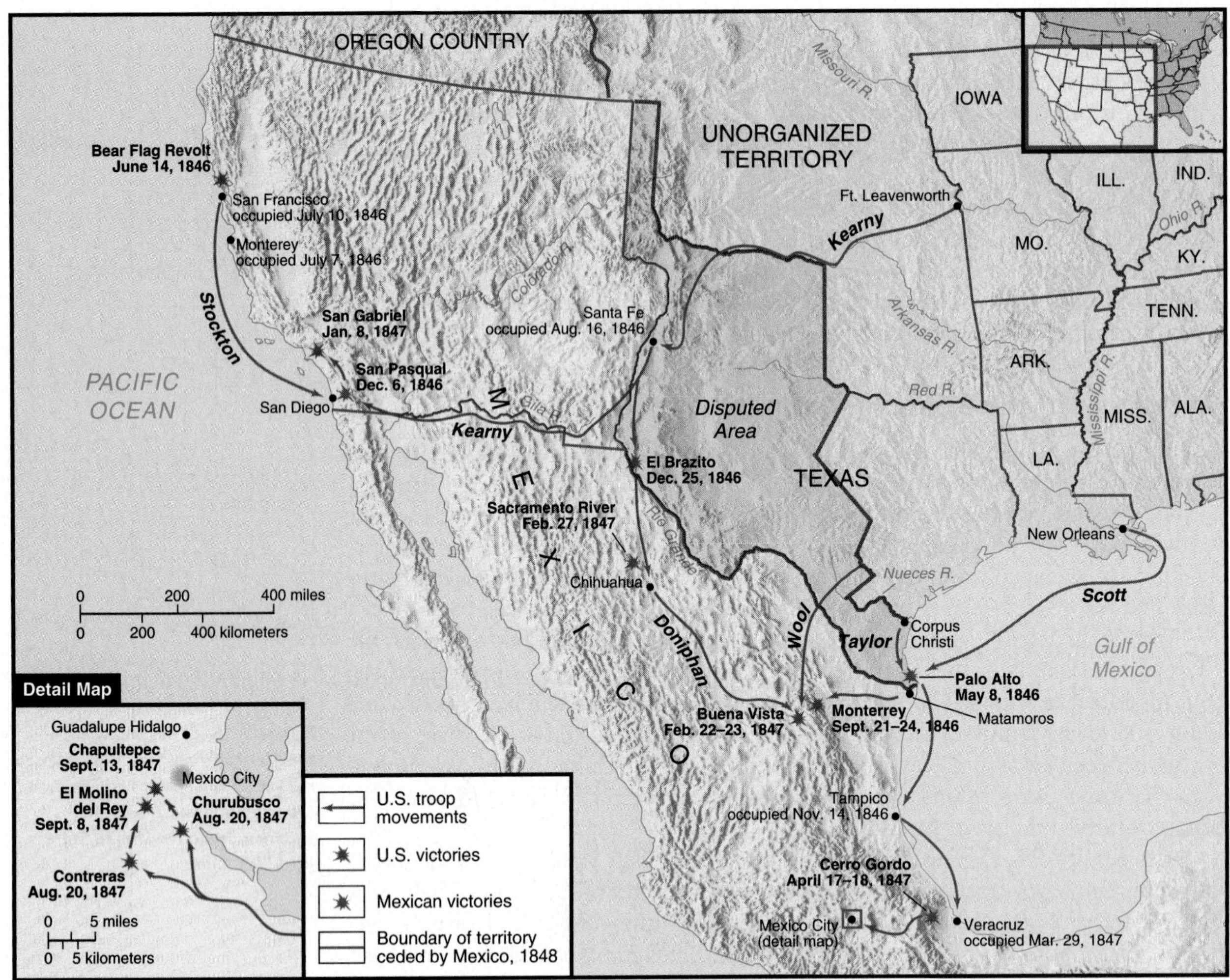

THE MEXICAN-AMERICAN WAR *The Mexican-American War added half a million square miles of territory to the United States, but the cost was high: $100 million and 13,000 lives.*

southern states. While battles were being fought in Mexico, Congress was debating a proposal to prohibit slavery in any territories that might be acquired from Mexico. A bitter sectional quarrel over the status of slavery in new areas was a major legacy of the Mexican-American War.

The domestic controversies aroused by the war and the propaganda of Manifest Destiny revealed the limits of mid-nineteenth-century American expansionism and put a damper on additional efforts to extend the nation's boundaries. Concerns about slavery and race blocked further southern expansion, and the desire to remain at peace with Great Britain prevented northern expansion. After 1848, Americans concentrated on populating and developing the vast territory already acquired.

Internal Expansionism

The expansionists of the 1840s saw a clear link between acquisition of new territory and other forms of material growth and development. In 1844, Samuel F. B. Morse perfected and demonstrated his electric telegraph. Simultaneously, the railroad was becoming increasingly important as a means of moving people and goods over great distances. Improvements in manufacturing and agricultural methods led to an upsurge in the volume and range of internal trade, and the beginnings of mass immigration were providing human resources for the exploitation of new areas and economic opportunities.

The discovery of gold in California in 1848 encouraged thousands of emigrants to move to the West Coast. The gold they unearthed spurred the national economy, and the rapid growth of population centers on the Pacific Coast inspired projects for transcontinental telegraph lines and railroad tracks.

When the spirit of Manifest Destiny and the thirst for acquiring new territory waned after the Mexican-American War, the expansionist impulse turned inward. The technological advances and population increase of the 1840s continued during the 1850s. The result was an acceleration of economic growth, a substantial increase in industrialization and urbanization, and the emergence of a new American working class.

The Triumph of the Railroad

More than anything else, the rise of the railroad transformed the American economy during the 1840s and 1850s. The technology for steam locomotives came from England, and in 1830 and 1831, two American railroads began commercial operation. Although the lines were practical and profitable, canals proved to be strong competitors, especially for the freight business. Passengers might prefer the speed of trains, but the lower unit cost of freight on the canal boats prevented most shippers from changing their habits. Furthermore, states such as New York and Pennsylvania that had invested heavily in canals resisted chartering a competitive form of transportation.

During the 1840s, rails extended beyond the northeastern and Middle Atlantic states, and mileage increased more than threefold, reaching a total of more than 9,000 miles by 1850. Expansion was even greater in the following decade, and by 1860, all the states east of the Mississippi had rail service. In addition, throughout the 1840s and 1850s, railroads cut deeply into the freight business of the canals and succeeded in driving many of them out of business.

The development of railroads had an enormous effect on the economy as a whole. Although the burgeoning demand for iron rails was initially met mainly by importation from England, that demand eventually spurred development of the domestic iron industry. Since railroads required an enormous outlay of capital, their promoters pioneered new methods for financing business enterprise. Railroad companies sold stock to the general public and helped set the pattern for the separation of ownership and control that characterizes the modern corporation.

But the gathering and control of private capital did not fully meet the needs of the early railroad barons. State and local governments, convinced that railroads were the key to their future prosperity, loaned the railroads money, bought their stock, and actively supported their development. Despite the dominant laissez-faire policy (which meant that the government should keep its hands off the economy), the federal government became involved by surveying the routes of projected lines and providing land grants. Thus a precedent was set for the massive land grants of the post–Civil War era.

The Industrial Revolution Takes Off

While railroads were initiating a revolution in transportation, American industry was entering a new phase of rapid and sustained growth. The factory mode of production, which had originated before 1840 in the cotton mills of New England (see Chapter 9), was extended to a variety of other products. Between 1830 and 1860,

The Age of Practical Invention

Year*	Inventor	Contribution	Importance/Description
1787	John Fitch	Steamboat	First successful American steamboat
1793	Eli Whitney	Cotton gin	Simplified process of separating fiber from seeds; helped make cotton a profitable staple of southern agriculture
1798	Eli Whitney	Jig for guiding tools	Facilitated manufacture of interchangeable parts
1802	Oliver Evans	Steam engine	First American steam engine; led to manufacture of high-pressure engines used throughout eastern United States
1813	Richard B. Chenaworth	Cast-iron plow	First iron plow to be made in three separate pieces, thus making possible replacement of parts
1830	Peter Cooper	Railroad locomotive	First steam locomotive built in America
1831	Cyrus McCormick	Reaper	Mechanized harvesting; early model could cut six acres of grain a day
1836	Samuel Colt	Revolver	First successful repeating pistol
1837	John Deere	Steel plow	Steel surface kept soil from sticking; farming thus made easier on rich prairies of Midwest
1839	Charles Goodyear	Vulcanization of rubber	Made rubber much more useful by preventing it from sticking and melting in hot weather
1842	Crawford W. Long	First administered ether in surgery	Reduced pain and risk of shock in surgery during operations
1844	Samuel F. B. Morse	Telegraph	Made long-distance communication almost instantaneous
1846	Elias Howe	Sewing machine	First practical machine for automatic sewing
1846	Norbert Rillieux	Vacuum evaporator	Improved method of removing water from sugar cane; revolutionized sugar industry and was later applied to many other products
1847	Richard M. Hoe	Rotary printing press	Printed an entire sheet in one motion; vastly speeded up printing process
1851	William Kelly	"Air-boiling process"	Improved method of converting iron into steel (usually known as Bessemer process because English inventor Bessemer had more advantageous patent and financial arrangements)
1853	Elisha G. Otis	Passenger elevator	Improved movement in buildings; when later electrified, stimulated development of skyscrapers
1859	Edwin L. Drake	First American oil well	Initiated oil industry in the United States
1859	George M. Pullman	Pullman passenger car	First railroad sleeping car suitable for long-distance travel

*Dates refer to patent or first successful use.

Source: From *Freedom and Crisis: An American History,* Third Edition, by Allen Weinstein and Frank Otto Gatell.

wool and iron production, shoemaking, and the firearms, clock, and sewing machine industries all moved toward the factory system.

The essential features of the factory mode of production were the gathering of a supervised workforce in a single place, the payment of cash wages to workers, the use of interchangeable parts, and manufacturing by "continuous process." Within a factory setting, standardized parts, manufactured separately and in bulk, could be efficiently and rapidly assembled into a final product by an ordered sequence of continuously repeated operations. Mass production, which involved the division of labor into a series of relatively simple and repetitive tasks, contrasted sharply with the traditional craft mode of production, in which a single worker produced the entire product out of raw materials.

New technology played an important role in the transition to mass production. Just as power looms and spinning machinery had made textile mills possible, the development of new and more reliable machines or industrial techniques revolutionized other industries. Elias Howe's invention of the sewing machine and Charles Goodyear's discovery of the process for vulcanizing rubber opened the way for the mass production of a wide range of consumer items.

Perhaps the greatest triumph of American technology during the mid-nineteenth century was the development of the world's most sophisticated and reliable machine tools. Such advances as the invention of the extraordinarily accurate measuring device known as the vernier caliper in 1851 and the first production of turret lathes in 1854 were signs of a special American aptitude for the kind of precision toolmaking that was essential to efficient industrialization.

Progress in industrial technology and organization did not mean that the United States had become an industrial society by 1860. Agriculture retained first place both as a source of livelihood for individuals and as a contributor to the gross national product. But farming itself, at least in the North, was undergoing a technological revolution of its own. John Deere's steel plow enabled midwestern farmers to cultivate the tough prairie soils that had resisted cast-iron implements, and Cyrus McCormick's mechanical reaper offered an enormous saving in the labor required for harvesting grain.

A dynamic interaction between advances in transportation, industry, and agriculture gave great strength and resiliency to the economy of the northern states during the 1850s. Railroads offered western farmers better access to eastern markets. After Chicago and New York were linked by rail in 1853, the flow of most midwestern farm commodities shifted from the north-south direction based on riverborne traffic that had still predominated in the 1830s and 1840s to an east-west pattern.

The mechanization of agriculture did more than lead to more efficient and profitable commercial farming; it also provided an additional impetus to industrialization, and its laborsaving features released manpower for other economic activities. The growth of industry and the modernization of agriculture can thus be seen as mutually reinforcing aspects of a single process of economic growth.

❖ A Look at the Past ❖

Steel Plow

In 1837, John Deere invented a plow with a smooth steel blade and successfully tested it on a farm in Illinois. Earlier plows had a blade made of cast iron. Deere's plow quickly became popular with pioneer farmers in the Midwest as an essential tool in cultivating the land. Why do you think Deere's new plow was necessary in the midwestern prairie? Why wouldn't a cast iron plow used in the East work equally well?

Mass Immigration Begins

The original incentive to mechanize northern industry and agriculture came in part from a shortage of cheap labor. Compared with the industrializing nations of Europe, the United States of the early nineteenth century was a labor-scarce economy. Since it was difficult to attract able-bodied men to work for low wages in factories or on farms, women and children were used extensively in the early textile mills, and commercial farmers had to rely heavily on the labor of their family members. Although laborsaving machinery eased the problem, by the 1840s and 1850s industrialization had reached a point where it needed far more unskilled workers. The growth of industrial work opportunities helped attract a multitude of European immigrants between 1840 and 1860.

Between 1820 and 1840, an estimated 700,000 immigrants arrived in the United States. During the 1840s, the substantial flow suddenly became a flood. No less than 4.2 million newcomers crossed the Atlantic between 1840 and 1860. This was the greatest influx in proportion to total population—then about 20 million—that the nation has ever experienced. The largest sources of the new mass immigration were Ireland and Germany.

The massive transatlantic movement had many causes; some people were "pushed" out of their homes, while others were "pulled" toward America. The great potato blight, which brought famine to a population that subsisted on this single crop, accounted for much of the emigration from Ireland. Escape to America was made possible by the low fares then prevailing on sailing ships bound from England to North America. Ships involved in the timber trade carried their bulky cargoes from Boston or Halifax to Liverpool. As an alternative to returning to America partly in ballast, they packed Irish immigrants into their holds.

The location of the ports involved in the lumber trade meant that most Irish arrived in Canada or New England. Immobilized by poverty and a lack of skills required for pioneering in the West, most of them remained in the Northeast. Forced to subsist as low-paid menial laborers and crowded into festering urban slums, they were looked down on by most native-born Americans.

The million or so Germans who also came in the late 1840s and early 1850s were somewhat more fortunate. Most of them were also peasants, but they fled hard times rather than outright catastrophe. Unlike the Irish, they often escaped with a small amount of capital with which to make a fresh start in the New World. Many German immigrants were artisans and sought to ply their trades in cities such as New York, St. Louis, Cincinnati, and Milwaukee. But a large portion of those with peasant backgrounds went back to the land. Many became successful midwestern farmers, and they generally encountered less prejudice and discrimination than the Irish.

What attracted most of the Irish, German, and other European immigrants to America was the promise of economic opportunity. Although a minority chose the United States because they admired its democratic political system, most immigrants were more interested in the chance to make a decent living than in voting or running for office. During times of prosperity and high demand for labor, America proved a powerful magnet to discontented Europeans.

Yet the arrival of large numbers of immigrants worsened the already serious problems of America's rapidly growing cities. The old "walking city" in which rich and poor lived in close proximity near the center of town was changing to a more segregated environment. The advent of railroads and horse-drawn streetcars enabled the affluent to move to the first American suburbs, while areas nearer commercial and industrial centers became the congested settlements of newcomers from Europe. Emerging slums, such as the notorious Five Points district in New York City, were characterized by overcrowding, poverty, disease, and crime. Recognizing that these conditions created potential dangers for the entire urban population, middle-class reformers worked for the professionalization of police forces, introduction of sanitary water and sewage disposal systems, and upgrading of housing standards. They made some progress in these endeavors in the period before the Civil War, but the lot of the urban poor, mainly immigrants, was not dramatically improved. For most of them, urban life remained unsafe, unhealthy, and unpleasant.

The New Working Class

A majority of the immigrants ended up as wage workers in factories, mines, and construction camps or as casual day laborers doing the many unskilled tasks required by urban and commercial growth. By providing a vast pool of cheap labor, they fueled and accelerated the Industrial Revolution.

CHRONOLOGY

1822	Santa Fe is opened to American traders
1823	Earliest American settlers arrive in Texas
1830	Mexico attempts to halt American migration to Texas
1831	American railroads begin commercial operation
1834	Cyrus McCormick patents the mechanical reaper
1835	Revolution breaks out in Texas
1836	Texas becomes an independent republic
1837	John Deere invents the steel plow
1841	President John Tyler is inaugurated
1842	Webster-Ashburton Treaty fixes the border between Maine and New Brunswick
1843	Mass migration to Oregon begins ◆ Mexico closes the Santa Fe trade to Americans
1844	Samuel F. B. Morse demonstrates the electric telegraph ◆ James K. Polk is elected president on platform of expansionism
1845	Mass immigration from Europe begins ◆ United States annexes Texas ◆ John L. O'Sullivan coins the slogan "manifest destiny"
1846	War with Mexico breaks out ◆ United States and Great Britain resolve the diplomatic crisis over Oregon
1847	American conquest of California is completed ◆ Mormons settle Utah ◆ American forces under Zachary Taylor defeat Mexicans at Buena Vista ◆ Winfield Scott's army captures Veracruz and defeats Mexicans at Cerro Gordo ◆ Mexico City falls to American invaders
1848	Treaty of Guadalupe Hidalgo consigns California and New Mexico to the United States ◆ Gold is discovered in California
1849	"Forty-niners" rush to California to dig for gold
1858	War is averted between Utah Mormons and United States forces

In the established industries and older mill towns of the Northeast, immigrants added to, or in some cases displaced, the native-born workers who had predominated in the 1830s and 1840s. In the textile mills especially, native female labor was replaced by foreign male workers. Irish males, employers found, were willing to perform tasks that native-born men had generally regarded as women's work.

The trend reveals much about the changing character of the American working class. In the 1830s, most male workers were artisans, while unskilled factory work was still largely the province of women and children. Both groups were predominantly of American stock. In the 1840s, the proportion of men engaged in factory work increased, although the workforce in the textile industry remained predominantly female. During that decade, working conditions in many mills deteriorated. Relations between management and labor became increasingly impersonal, and workers were pushed to increase their output. Workdays of twelve to fourteen hours were common.

The result was a new upsurge of labor militancy involving female as well as male factory workers. Workers' organizations petitioned state legislatures to pass laws limiting the workday to ten hours. Some such laws were actually passed, but they turned out to be ineffective because employers could still require a prospective worker to sign a special contract agreeing to longer hours as a condition of employment.

The employment of immigrants in increasing numbers between the mid-1840s and the late 1850s made it more difficult to organize industrial workers. Impoverished fugitives from the Irish potato famine tended to have lower economic expectations and little experience with labor organizations. Consequently, the Irish immigrants were willing to work for less and were not so prone to protest bad working conditions or organize into unions.

But the new working class of former rural folk did not make the transition to industrial wage labor easily or without protesting in subtle and indirect ways. Tardiness, absenteeism, drunkenness, loafing on the job, and other forms of resistance to factory discipline reflected deep hostility to the unaccustomed and seemingly unnatural routines of "continuous process" production. The adjustment to new styles and rhythms of work was painful and took time.

Conclusion: The Costs of Expansion

By 1860, industrial expansion and immigration had created a working class of men and women who seemed destined for a life of low-paid wage labor. This reality stood in contrast to America's self-image as a land of opportunity and upward mobility. The ideal still had some validity in rapidly developing regions of the western states, but it was mostly myth when applied to the increasingly foreign-born industrial workers of the Northeast.

Both internal and external expansion had come at a heavy cost. Tensions associated with class and ethnic rivalries were only one part of the price of rapid economic development. The acquisition of new territories became politically divisive and would soon lead to a catastrophic sectional controversy. From the late 1840s to the Civil War, the United States was a divided society in more senses than one, and the need to control or resolve these conflicts presented politicians and statesmen with a monumental challenge.

Key Terms

Young America, p. 245
Webster-Ashburton Treaty, p. 245
Alamo, p. 248
Manifest Destiny, p. 251
Mexican-American War, p. 254
Treaty of Guadalupe Hidalgo, p. 255

Recommended Reading

An overview of expansion to the Pacific is Ray A. Billington, *The Far Western Frontier, 1830–1860* (1956). The impulse behind Manifest Destiny has been variously interpreted. Albert K. Weinberg's classic *Manifest Destiny: A Study of National Expansionism in American History* (1935) describes and stresses the ideological rationale as does Anders Stephenson, *Manifest Destiny: American Expansion and the Empire of Right* (1995). Frederick Merk, *Manifest Destiny and Mission in American History* (1963), analyzes public opinion and shows how divided it was on the question of territorial acquisitions. Norman A. Graebner, *Empire on the Pacific: A Study in American Continental Expansionism* (1956), highlights the desire for Pacific harbors as a motive for adding new territory. The most complete and authoritative account of the diplomatic side of expansionism in this period is David M. Pletcher, *The Diplomacy of Annexation: Texas, Oregon, and the Mexican War* (1973). Charles G. Sellers, *James K. Polk: Continentalist, 1843–1846* (1966), is the definitive work on Polk's election and the expansionist policies of his administration. A very good account of the Mexican-American War is John S. D. Eisenhower, *So Far from God: The U.S. War with Mexico* (1989). On gold rushes, see Malcolm J. Rohrbough, *Days of Gold: The California Gold Rush and the American Nation* (1997) and Elliott West, *The Contested Plains: Indians, Goldseekers, and the Rush to Colorado* (1998).

Economic developments of the 1840s and 1850s are well covered in George R. Taylor, *The Transportation Revolution, 1815–1960* (1952) and Albert Fishlow, *American Railroads and the Transformation of the Ante-Bellum Economy* (1965). For an overview of immigration in this period, see the early chapters of Roger Daniels, *Coming to America: Immigration and Ethnicity in American Life* (1990). On the Irish, see Kerby A. Miller, *Emigrants and Exiles:*

Ireland and the Irish Exodus to America (1985). Oscar Handlin, *Boston Immigrants: A Study in Acculturation*, rev. ed. (1959), is a classic study of immigration to one city. A standard work on the antebellum working class is Sean Wilentz, *Chants Democratic: New York City and the Rise of the American Working Class, 1788–1850* (1984); for the new approach to labor history that emphasizes working-class culture, see Herbert G. Gutman, *Work, Culture, and Society in Industrializing America* (1976). For the rich public life of antebellum cities, see Mary P. Ryan, *Civic Wars: Democracy and Public Life in the American City During the Nineteenth Century* (1997). A pathbreaking and insightful study of workers in the textile industry is Thomas Dublin, *Women at Work: The Transformation of Work and Community in Lowell, Massachusetts, 1826–1860* (1979).

For a list of additional titles related to this chapter's topics, please see http://www.ablongman.com/divine.

Suggested Web Sites

Pioneering the Upper Midwest: Books from Michigan, Minnesota, and Wisconsin, ca. 1820–1910

http://memory.loc.gov/ammem/umhtml/umhome.html
This Library of Congress site looks at first-person accounts, biographies, promotional literature, local histories, ethnographic and antiquarian texts, colonial archival documents, and other works from the seventeenth to the early twentieth century. It covers many topics and issues that affected Americans in the settlement and development of the Upper Midwest.

The Mexican-American War Memorial Homepage

http://sunsite.dcaa.unam.mx/revistas/1847/
Images and text explain the causes, courses, and outcomes of the Mexican-American War.

On the Trail in Kansas

http://www.kancoll.org/galtrl.htm
This Kansas Collection site holds several good primary sources with images concerning the Oregon Trail and America's early movement westward.

Mountain Men and the Fur Trade

http://www.xmission.com/~drudy/amm.html
Private letters can speak volumes about the concerns and environment of the writers and recipients. Letters from early settlers west of the Mississippi River are offered on this site, along with other resources relating to explorers, trappers, and traders.

We Americans

THE IRISH IN BOSTON, 1845–1865

For the city of Boston, the period between 1845 and 1865 was an era of great change. Events half a world away rudely plucked more than fifty thousand Irish Catholic peasants from their homeland and transplanted them to a city that had hitherto been a homogeneous bastion of old-stock New England Puritanism. Some Bostonians viewed the mass of poor immigrants as an urban calamity. But the "invasion" was also a blessing, reinvigorating Boston with a substantial—and inimitable—Irish American contribution to its social, economic, and political life.

The Irish came to America because they had no other choice. By the early nineteenth century, large landowners on the "isle of wondrous beauty"—mainly of English descent—were masters over impoverished tenant farmers who had been forced by their wretched circumstances to live on a diet consisting mostly of potatoes. When a blight caused the potato crop to rot in the mid-1840s, Ireland entered a period known as the Great Hunger. During this "state of social decomposition" between 1845 and 1851, the only alternative to starvation for most Irish peasants was emigration. One million people emigrated and another million died of starvation or disease.

The immigrants disembarked at the large northeastern seaboard cities. Although the newcomers were of rural origins, they were too poor and sick to continue westward to America's rich agricultural regions; they settled where they were dropped. Boston's population nearly doubled, growing from 93,000 to 177,000 between 1840 and 1860. In part, the increase reflected the movement of a burgeoning native population from the country to the cities, but mainly it was the product of Ireland's Great Hunger.

Penniless and unskilled, the immigrants crowded into old buildings and warehouses that Boston's Yankees had abandoned—dark, unheated, unventilated, and unsanitary tenements. But as a social worker observed of the people living in Boston's Irish ghettos, "The Hibernian is first, last, and always a social being." In Ireland, poor tenant farmers had found comfort in lively conversation, sometimes made even more spirited by a convivial round of distilled refreshment, and nothing the immigrants found in Boston altered these customs. Talk came naturally to the Irish. They talked in the streets, in the shops, in the churches, in their homes—and in their saloons.

For men, by far the most popular locus of sociability was the corner saloon—where it was said a working man could not die of thirst. The Irish bar in Boston was devoid of frills. It featured wooden chairs, a long wooden bar with brass railings, card tables, sawdust-covered floors, and a philosophical bartender, who extended beer, whiskey, credit, and advice, in roughly equal doses. Irishmen sang, told stories, talked politics, or reminisced about the green fields and deep blue lakes of the Emerald Isle. In 1846, there were 850 liquor dealers in Boston, but by 1850 fully 1,500 saloons catered to the residents of the changing city.

Fortunately for Boston's capitalists and large-scale entrepreneurs, the most immediate need of the immigrants was employment—of any kind. At first the newcomers, who had been peasants in the "Ould Country," became street or yard laborers, but as it became apparent that the Irish were a potential pool of long-term proletarians—a large supply of workers who would remain in the least desirable jobs for low pay—capitalists responded by accelerating the Industrial Revolution in the Boston area. The number of industrial employees in Boston doubled in the decade of 1845–1855, and doubled again in the following decade. Moreover, Irish immigrants replaced much of the labor force from the early industrial era, especially in the textile mills of Boston's outlying suburbs. Irishmen were willing to work for lower wages than those paid to "mill girls," and were

Large numbers of Irish immigrants initially crowded into the disease-ridden slums and shanties of places such as Boston's Burgess Alley. This illustration of the deplorable living quarters of many of the city's immigrants is from the Report of the Committee on Internal Health on the Asiatic Cholera, issued in 1849. ❖

not so insistent on decent working conditions.

Although reluctant to work outside the home for wages, married Irish American women—who were usually raising a large family—often found themselves taking in lodgers, sewing at home for piece work rates on men's shirts and women's millinery, and doing other people's laundry. Their lot was frequently made more difficult by the long absences of their "railroading" husbands (Irishmen contracted out for months at a time to build and lay rails).

A large proportion of the Great Hunger immigrants from Ireland were unmarried women who, like their male counterparts, were desperate for employment. These Irishwomen relieved an acute shortage of domestics in New England. Few native-born American women would do household work for pay, not only because the job carried the stigma of servanthood, but also because New Englanders were not willing to pay good wages for what was sometimes a 24-hour responsibility. Many maids and cooks suffered from "shattered health." But for the single Irish American woman, the life of a domestic was often the best of a narrow range of alternatives. "Living in" removed her from much of the squalor and disease of tenement life. She usually had two afternoons a week for her own pursuits, and sometimes had the opportunity to take jaunts to seaside resorts on Cape Code with her employers.

Few of the first generation of Boston Irish escaped from the ranks of unskilled or semi-skilled labor. The discriminatory attitudes of Yankee employers contributed significantly to the relative lack of mobility. (Many good jobs were advertised with the qualification that "no Irish need apply.") But occupational mobility was also inhibited to some extent by the tendency of the Irish immigrants to place group security above individual advancement. They used strong communal activities and neighborhood organizations to their advantage in politics and union-building; success in local political clubs and the labor movement meant that Irish politicians and labor leaders in Boston channeled several generations of Irish Americans into secure but dead-end municipal and industrial jobs.

Although they were slow to rise out of the working class, the Irish energized the economy of Boston and soon won for themselves respect and power. They were the first large immigrant group to test the notion of America as a great melting pot. More than 150,000 Irish Americans served in the Civil War, eager to demonstrate their loyalty to their adopted country. But 1865 the Irish, through their persistent efforts, their skill at local organization, and their willingness to be Boston's reliable working class, had found a permanent place in America's most venerable Puritan stronghold.

Chapter 14

The Sectional Crisis

The Brooks–Sumner Brawl in Congress

On May 22, 1856, Representative Preston Brooks of South Carolina suddenly appeared on the floor of the Senate. He was looking for Charles Sumner, the antislavery senator from Massachusetts who had recently given a speech condemning the South for plotting to extend slavery to the Kansas Territory. When he found Sumner seated at his desk, Brooks proceeded to batter him over the head with a cane. Sumner made a desperate effort to rise, ripped his bolted desk from the floor, and then collapsed.

Sumner was so badly injured by the assault that he could not return to the Senate for three years. In parts of the North that were up in arms against the expansion of slavery, he was hailed as a martyr to the cause of "free soil." Brooks, denounced in the North as a bully, was lionized by his fellow Southerners and won reelection without opposition.

These contrasting reactions show how bitter sectional antagonism had become by 1856. Sumner spoke for the radical wing of the new Republican party, which was making a bid for national power by mobilizing the North against the alleged aggression of "the slave power." Southerners viewed the very existence of this party as an insult to their section of the country and a threat to its vital interests. Many Southerners believed that Sumner and his political friends were plotting against their way of life. By 1856, therefore, the sectional cleavage that would lead to the Civil War had already undermined the foundations of national unity.

Outline

The Compromise of 1850

Political Upheaval, 1852–1856

The House Divided, 1857–1860

Conclusion: Explaining the Crisis

We Americans

Hispanic America After 1848: A Case Study in Majority Rule

THE CRISIS OF THE MID-1850S came only a few years after the elaborate Compromise of 1850 had seemingly resolved the dispute over the future of slavery in the territories acquired as a result of the Mexican-American War. The renewed agitation over the extension of slavery was set in motion by the Kansas-Nebraska Act of 1854. This legislation revived the sectional conflict and led to the emergence of the Republican party. From that point on, a dramatic series of events heightened the mood of sectional confrontation and destroyed the prospects for a new compromise. The caning of Charles Sumner was one of these events, and violence on the Senate floor foreshadowed violence on the battlefield.

The Compromise of 1850

During the late 1840s, the leaders of the two major national parties, each with substantial followings in both the North and the South, had a vested interest in resolving the sectional crisis. Furthermore, the less tangible features of sectionalism—emotion and ideology—were not yet as divisive as they would later become. Hence a fragile compromise was achieved through a kind of give-and-take that would not be possible after the emergence of strong sectional parties in the mid-1850s.

The Problem of Slavery in the Mexican Cession

The Founders, who were generally opposed to slavery, had attempted to exclude the slavery issue from national politics as the price of uniting states committed to slavery and those in the process of abolishing it. The Constitution gave the federal government no definite authority to regulate or destroy the institution where it existed under state law. Thus it was easy to condemn slavery in principle but very difficult to develop a practical program to eliminate it without defying the Constitution.

Radical abolitionists viewed the problem clearly and resolved it by rejecting the law of the land in favor of a "higher law" prohibiting human bondage. But during the 1840s, the majority of Northerners showed that while they disliked slavery, they also detested abolitionism. They were inclined to view slavery as a backward institution and slaveholders as power-hungry aristocrats. But they regarded the Constitution as a binding contract between slave and free states and were likely to be prejudiced against blacks and reluctant to accept large numbers of them as free citizens. Consequently, they saw no legal or desirable way to bring about emancipation within the southern states.

However, the Constitution had not predetermined the status of slavery in *future* states. Congress had the right to require the abolition of slavery as the price of admission into the Union. An effort to use this power had led to the Missouri crisis of 1819–1820 (see Chapter 9). The resulting Missouri Compromise line was designed to decide future cases and maintain a rough parity between slave and free states. Slavery was thus allowed to expand with the westward movement of the cotton kingdom but was discouraged or prohibited above the line of 36°30'.

The tradition of providing both the free North and the slave South with opportunities for expansion and the creation of new states broke down when new territories were wrested from Mexico in the 1840s. Many Northerners were unwilling to see California and New Mexico as well as Texas admitted into the Union as slave states. Since it was generally assumed in the North that Congress had the power to prohibit slavery in new territories, a movement developed in Congress to do just that.

The Wilmot Proviso Launches the Free-Soil Movement

The Free-Soil crusade began in August 1846, only three months after the start of the Mexican War, when Congressman David Wilmot, a Pennsylvania Democrat, proposed an amendment to the military appropriations bill that would ban slavery in any territory that might be acquired from Mexico.

Wilmot spoke for a large number of northern Democrats who felt neglected and betrayed by the policies of the Polk administration. Reductions in tariff duties and Polk's veto of an internal improvement bill upset many Democrats. Still others felt betrayed because Polk had gone back on his pledge to obtain "all of Oregon" up to 54°40' and had then proceeded to wage war to win all of Texas. This twist in the course of Manifest Destiny convinced northern expansionists that the South and its interests were dominating the party and the administration.

Nevertheless, the pioneer Free-Soilers had a genuine interest in the issue actually at hand—the question of who would control and settle the new territories.

Combining an appeal to racial prejudice with opposition to slavery as an institution, Wilmot demanded that the new territories be opened only for white people. He wanted to give the common folk of the North a fair chance by excluding unfair competition with slavery and blacks from territory obtained in the Mexican cession.

Wilmot Proviso In 1846, shortly after the outbreak of the Mexican-American War, Congressman David Wilmot of Pennsylvania introduced this controversial amendment stating that any lands won from Mexico would be closed to slavery.

Northern Whigs backed the **Wilmot Proviso** because they shared the concern about the outcome of unregulated competition between slave and free labor in the territories. Many of the northern Whigs had opposed the annexation of Texas and the Mexican-American War. If expansion was inevitable, they were determined that it should not be used to increase the power of the slave states.

In the first House vote on the Wilmot Proviso, party lines crumbled and were replaced by a sharp sectional cleavage. After passing the House, the proviso was blocked in the Senate by a combination of southern influence and Democratic loyalty to the administration. When the appropriation bill went back to the House without the proviso, the administration's arm-twisting succeeded in changing enough northern Democratic votes to defeat the proviso.

Squatter Sovereignty and the Election of 1848

After a futile attempt was made to extend the Missouri Compromise line to the Pacific—a proposal that was unacceptable to Northerners because most of the Mexican cession lay south of the line—a new approach was devised that appealed especially to Democrats. Its main proponent was Senator Lewis Cass of Michigan, an aspirant for the party's presidential nomination. He wanted to leave the determination of the status of slavery in a territory to the actual settlers. From the beginning, this proposal contained an ambiguity that allowed it to be interpreted differently in the North and the South. For the northern Democrats, "squatter sovereignty"—or **popular sovereignty,** as it was later called—meant that settlers could vote slavery up or down at the first meeting of a territorial legislature. For the southern wing of the party, it meant that a decision would be made only at the time a convention drew up a constitution and applied for statehood. It was in the interest of national Democratic leaders to leave this ambiguity intact for as long as possible.

popular sovereignty The concept that the settlers of a newly organized territory have the right to decide (through voting) whether to accept slavery. Promoted as a solution to the slavery question, popular sovereignty became a fiasco in Kansas in the 1850s.

Congress failed to resolve the future of slavery in the Mexican cession in time for the election of 1848. The Democrats nominated Cass on a platform of squatter sovereignty. The Whigs evaded the question by running war hero General Zachary Taylor without a platform. Northern Whigs favoring restrictions on the expansion of slavery took heart from the general's promise not to veto any territorial legislation passed by Congress. Southern Whigs supported Taylor because the general was a southern slaveholder.

Free-Soil party Organized in 1848, this third party proposed to exclude slavery from federal territories and nominated former President Martin Van Buren in the presidential election of that year. Most Free Soilers eventually became Republicans.

Northerners who strongly supported the Wilmot Proviso were attracted by a third party movement. The **Free-Soil party** nominated former President Van Buren to carry their banner. Support for the Free-Soilers came mostly from Democrats and Whigs who opposed either the extension of slavery into the territories or the growing influence of the South in national policies. The founding of the Free-Soil party was the first significant effort to create a broadly based sectional party addressing itself to voters' concerns about the extension of slavery.

After a noisy and confusing campaign, Taylor came out on top, winning a majority of the electoral votes in both the North and the South. The Free-Soilers failed to carry a single state but were strong enough to run second behind Taylor in New York, Massachusetts, and Vermont.

Taylor Takes Charge

Once in office, Taylor devised a bold plan to decide the fate of slavery in the Mexican cession. He tried to engineer the immediate admission of California and

New Mexico to the Union as states, bypassing the territorial stage entirely and eliminating the whole question of the status of slavery in the federal domain. The proposal made practical sense in regard to California, which was filling up rapidly with settlers drawn there by the lust for gold. Under the administration's urging, Californians convened a constitutional convention and applied for admission to the Union as a free state. In underpopulated New Mexico, it proved impossible to get a statehood movement off the ground.

Instead of resolving the crisis, President Taylor's initiative only worsened it. Fearing that New Mexico as well as California would choose to be a free state, Southerners of both parties accused the president of trying to impose the Wilmot Proviso in a new form. The prospect that only free states would emerge from the entire Mexican cession inspired serious talk of secession.

In Congress, Senator John C. Calhoun of South Carolina saw a chance to achieve his long-standing goal of creating a southern voting bloc that would cut across regular party lines. He warmly greeted each new sign of southern discontent and sectional solidarity. In the fall and winter of 1849–1850, several southern states agreed to participate in a convention, to be held in Nashville in June, where grievances could be aired and demands made. For an increasing number of southern political leaders, the survival of the Union would depend on the North's response to southern demands.

Forging a Compromise

When it became clear that the president would not abandon or modify his plan to appease the South, independent efforts began in Congress to arrange a compromise. Hoping once again to play the role of "great pacificator," Senator Henry Clay of Kentucky offered a series of resolutions meant to restore sectional harmony. On the critical territorial question, his solution was to admit California as a free state and organize the rest of the Mexican cession with no explicit prohibition of slavery. He also sought to resolve a major boundary dispute between New Mexico and Texas by granting the disputed region to New Mexico while compensating Texas through federal assumption of its state debt. As a concession to the North on another issue—the existence of slavery in the District of Columbia—he recommended prohibiting the buying and selling of slaves in the nation's capital. Finally, he called for more vigorous enforcement of the Fugitive Slave Law.

Clay proposed the plan in February 1850, but it received a mixed reception. One obstacle was President Taylor's firm resistance to the proposal; another was the difficulty of getting congressmen to vote for it in the form of a single package or "omnibus bill." The logjam was broken in July by two crucial developments. President Taylor died and was succeeded by Millard Fillmore, who favored the compromise, and a decision was made to abandon the omnibus strategy for a series of measures that could be voted on separately. After the breakup of the omnibus bill, Democrats, led by Senator Stephen A. Douglas, replaced the original Whig sponsors as leaders of the compromise movement and maneuvered the separate provisions of the plan through Congress.

As finally approved, the **Compromise of 1850** differed somewhat from Clay's original proposals. The popular sovereignty principle was included in the bills organizing New Mexico and Utah as the price of Democratic support. In addition, half of the compensation to Texas for giving up its claims to New Mexico was paid directly to holders of Texas bonds.

Abolition of the slave trade in the District of Columbia and a new **Fugitive Slave Law** were also enacted. According to the provisions of the latter act, suspected fugitives were now denied a jury trial, the right to testify in their own behalf, and other minimal constitutional rights. As a result, there were no effective safeguards against false identification and the kidnaping of blacks who were legally free.

Compromise of 1850 This series of five congressional statutes temporarily calmed the sectional crisis. Among other things, the compromise made California a free state, ended the slave trade in the District of Columbia, and strengthened the Fugitive Slave Law.

Fugitive Slave Law Passed in 1850, this federal law made it easier for slaveowners to recapture runaway slaves; it also made it easier for kidnappers to take free blacks.

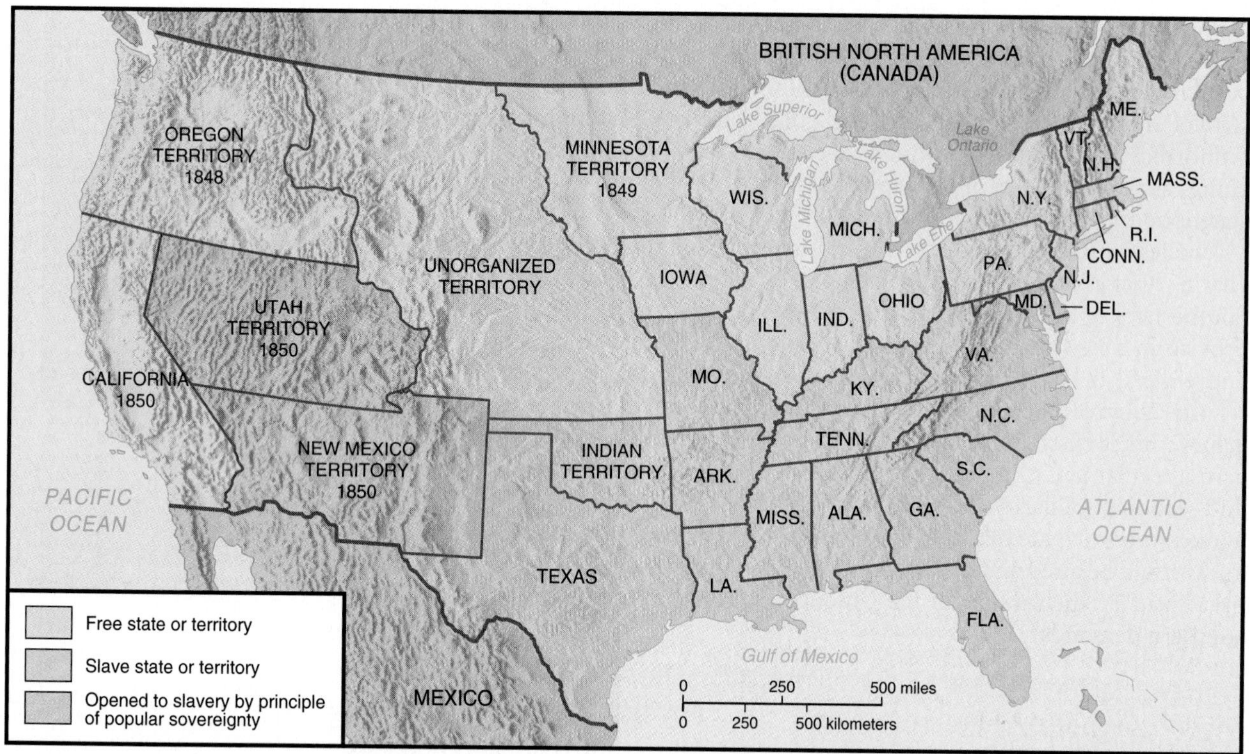

THE COMPROMISE OF 1850 *The "compromise" was actually a series of resolutions granting some concessions to abolitionists—admission of California as a free state, for example—and some to slaveholders, such as a stricter Fugitive Slave Law.*

The compromise passed because its key measures were supported by both northern Democrats and southern Whigs. No single bill was backed by a majority of the congressmen from both sections, and doubts persisted over the value or workability of a compromise that was really more like a cease-fire.

Yet the Compromise of 1850 did serve for a time as a basis for sectional peace. Southern moderates had carried the day, but southern nationalism remained strong. Southerners demanded strict northern adherence to the compromise, especially the Fugitive Slave Law, as the price for keeping threats of secession suppressed. In the North, the compromise received even greater support. The Fugitive Slave Law was unpopular in areas where abolitionism was particularly strong, and there were a few sensational rescues or attempted rescues of escaped slaves. But for the most part, the northern states adhered to the law during the next few years. When both the Democrats and the Whigs endorsed the compromise in their 1852 platforms, it appeared that sharp differences on the slavery issue had once again been banished from national politics.

Political Upheaval, 1852–1856

The second party system—Democrats versus Whigs—survived the crisis over slavery in the Mexican cession, but in the long run, the Compromise of 1850 may have weakened it. Although both national parties had been careful during the 1840s not to take stands on the slavery issue that would alienate their supporters in either section of the country, they had in fact offered voters alternative ways of dealing with the question. Democrats had endorsed headlong territorial expansion with the promise of a fair division of the spoils between slave and free states. Whigs had generally opposed annexation of acquisitions that were likely to bring the slavery question to the fore and threaten sectional harmony. Each strategy could be presented to southern voters as a good way to protect slavery and to Northerners as a good way to contain it.

The consensus of 1852 meant that the parties had to find other issues on which to base their distinctive appeals. Their failure to do so encouraged voter apathy and disenchantment with the major parties. When the Democrats sought to revive the Manifest Destiny issue in 1854, they inadvertently reopened the explosive issue of slavery in the territories. By this time, the Whigs were too weak and divided to respond with a policy of their own, and a purely sectional Free-Soil party, the Republicans, gained prominence. The collapse of the second party system released sectional agitation from the earlier constraints imposed by the competition of strong national parties.

The Party System in Crisis

The presidential campaign of 1852 was singularly devoid of major issues. Both parties ignored the slavery question. Some Whigs tried to revive interest in nationalistic economic policies; but with business thriving under the Democratic program which limited government involvement in the economy, such proposals sounded empty and unnecessary.

Another tempting issue was immigration. Many Whigs were upset by the massive influx from Europe, partly because most of the new arrivals were Catholics and the Whig following was largely evangelical Protestant. In addition, immigrants voted overwhelmingly Democratic. The Whig leadership was divided on whether to compete for the immigrant vote or to seek restrictions on immigrant voting rights.

The Whigs nominated General Winfield Scott, of Mexican-American War fame, who supported the faction that resisted nativism and sought to broaden the appeal of the party. However, Scott and his supporters were unable to break the Democratic grip on the immigrant vote, and some nativist Whigs apparently sat out the election to protest their party's disregard of their cultural prejudice.

But the main cause for Scott's crushing defeat was the support he lost in the South when he allied himself with the northern antislavery wing of the party, led by Senator William Seward of New York. The Democratic candidate, Franklin Pierce of New Hampshire, was a colorless nonentity compared to his rival, but he easily swept the Deep South and edged out Scott in most of the free states. The outcome revealed that the Whig party was in deep trouble because it lacked a program that would appeal to voters in both sections of the country.

Despite their overwhelming victory in 1852, the Democrats also had reasons for anxiety about the loyalty of their supporters. Voter apathy was strong, and Democratic leaders were placed in the uncomfortable position of having to appeal to both northern Free-Soilers and southern slaveholders.

The Kansas-Nebraska Act Raises a Storm

In January 1854, Senator Stephen A. Douglas proposed a bill to organize the territory west of Missouri and Iowa. Since this region fell within the area where slavery had been banned by the Missouri Compromise, Douglas hoped to head off southern opposition and keep the Democratic party united by disregarding the compromise line and setting up the territorial government in Kansas and Nebraska on the basis of popular sovereignty.

Douglas wanted to organize the region quickly because he was a strong supporter of the expansion of settlement and commerce. He hoped that a railroad would soon be built to the Pacific with Chicago or another midwestern city as its eastern terminus. A long controversy over the status of slavery in the Kansas-Nebraska area would delay the building of a railroad through the territory. Moreover, by trying to revive

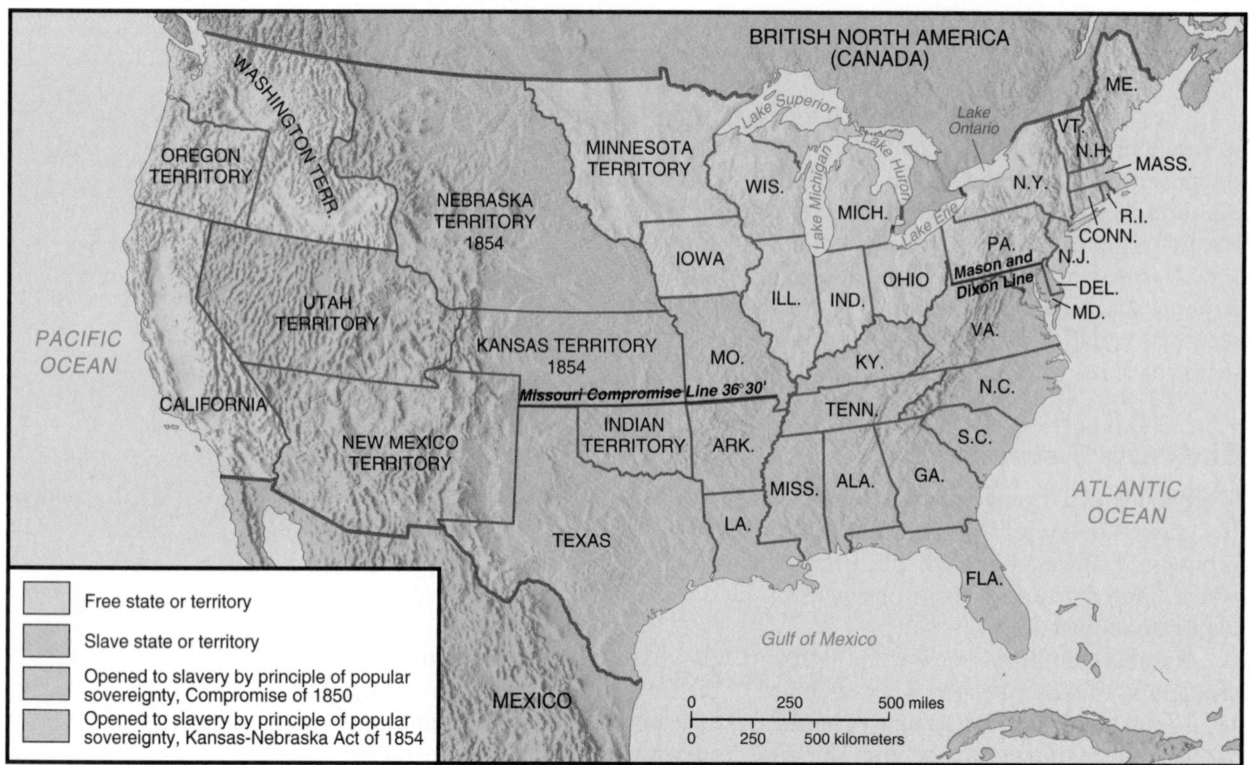

THE KANSAS-NEBRASKA ACT OF 1854 *The Kansas-Nebraska Act applied the principle of popular sovereignty to voters in the Kansas and Nebraska territories, allowing them to decide for themselves whether to permit slavery in their territories. The act repudiated the Missouri Compromise of 1820, which had prohibited slavery in the territory of the Louisiana Purchase north of 36°30' latitude.*

the spirit of Manifest Destiny, he hoped to strengthen the Democratic party and enhance his chances of becoming president.

The price of southern support, Douglas soon discovered, was the addition of an amendment explicitly repealing the Missouri Compromise. He reluctantly agreed. Although the bill then made its way through Congress, it split the Democratic party. A manifesto of "independent Democrats" denounced the bill as "a gross violation of a sacred pledge." For many Northerners, the **Kansas-Nebraska Act** was an abomination because it appeared to permit slavery in an area where it had previously been prohibited. More than ever, Northerners were receptive to the theme that there was a conspiracy to extend slavery.

Kansas-Nebraska Act This 1854 act repealed the Missouri Compromise, split the Louisiana Purchase into two territories, and allowed its settlers to accept or reject slavery by popular sovereignty. This act enflamed the slavery issue and led opponents to form the Republican party.

Douglas's bill had a catastrophic effect on the prospects for sectional harmony. It repudiated a compromise that many in the North regarded as binding. In defiance of the whole compromise tradition, it made a concession to the South on the issue of slavery extension without providing an equivalent concession to the North. From then on, northern sectionalists would be fighting to regain what they had lost, while Southerners would be battling just as furiously to maintain rights already conceded.

The act also destroyed what was left of the second party system. The already weakened Whig party disintegrated when its congressional representation split cleanly along sectional lines on the Kansas-Nebraska issue. The Democratic party survived, but northern desertions and southern gains resulting from recruitment of proslavery Whigs destroyed its sectional balance and placed the party under firm southern control.

Finally, the furor over Kansas-Nebraska doomed the efforts of the Pierce administration to revive an expansionist foreign policy. Pierce and Secretary of State William Marcy were committed to acquiring Cuba from Spain. But Northerners interpreted the administration's plan, made public in a memorandum known as the **Ostend Manifesto,** as an attempt to create a "Caribbean slave empire." The resulting storm of protest forced Pierce and his cohorts to abandon their scheme. The only tangible result of the southern expansionist dream of the 1850s was the purchase for $10 million of a 30,000-square-mile slice of Mexican territory south of the Gila River (the Gadsden Purchase, 1853). This acquisition completed the contiguous continental United States as it is known today.

Ostend Manifesto Written by American officials in 1854, this secret memo—later dubbed a "manifesto"—urged the acquisition of Cuba by any means necessary. When it became public, Northerners claimed it was a plot to extend slavery and the manifesto was disavowed.

An Appeal to Nativism: The Know-Nothing Episode

The collapse of the Whigs created the opening for a new political party. The anti-Nebraska sentiment of 1854 suggested that such a party might be organized on the basis of northern opposition to the extension of slavery to the territories. Before such a prospect could be realized, however, an alternative emerged in the form of a major political movement based on hostility to immigrants. For a time, it appeared that the Whigs would be replaced by a nativist party rather than an antislavery one.

Massive immigration of Irish and Germans (see Chapter 13), most of whom were Catholic, led to increasing tensions between ethnic groups during the 1840s and early 1850s. Protestants were suspicious and distrustful of the Catholics, whom they viewed as bearers of an alien culture. Nativist agitators charged that immigrants were agents of a foreign despotism, based in Rome, that was bent on overthrowing the American republic.

Political nativism first emerged during the 1840s in the form of local "American" parties protesting immigrant influence in cities such as New York and Philadelphia. The organizations were often secretive, and one group instructed its members to answer questions about their organization with the reply, "I know nothing." The political objective of the **Know-Nothing party** was to extend the period of naturalization in order to undercut immigrant voting strength and to keep aliens in their place.

Know-Nothing party After the collapse of the Whig party in the 1850s, this anti-immigrant and anti-Catholic party rose to national prominence. Though the party enjoyed some success in local and state elections, it failed to sustain its existence.

In 1854 and 1855, the nativist movement surfaced as a major political force, the American party. Most of the party's backing came from Whigs looking for a new home, but it also attracted some ex-Democrats. Know-Nothingism also appealed to native-born workers who feared competition from low-paid immigrants. Others supported the party simply as an alternative to the Democratic party. In the North,

Know-Nothings often charged that immigrant voters were stealing American elections. In the cartoon below, German and Irish immigrants, represented by German beer and Irish whiskey, steal a ballot box. An anti–Know-Nothing cartoon (right) portrays the Know-Nothings as gun-wielding ruffians.

the Know-Nothing candidates generally opposed the Kansas-Nebraska Act and gained some of their support from voters anxious about the expansion of slavery.

The success of the new party was so dramatic that it was compared to a hurricane. In 1854 and 1855, Know-Nothings won control of a number of state governments, ranging from Massachusetts to Maryland to Texas. By late 1855, the Know-Nothings showed every sign of displacing the Whigs as the nation's second party.

Yet almost as rapidly as it had arisen, the Know-Nothing movement collapsed. Its demise in 1856 is one of the great mysteries of American political history. Admittedly, as a national party, it was unable to mend the deep sectional divisions over the question of slavery in the territories. Less clear is why Know-Nothings failed to become the major opposition party to the Democrats in the North. The most persuasive explanation is that their Free-Soil Republican rivals, who were seeking to build a party committed to the containment of slavery, had an issue with wider appeal. The movement's peculiar "antipolitical" character also contributed to its rapid disintegration. Besides being a manifestation of real ethnic tensions, Know-Nothingism was a grassroots protest against the professional politicians who had led the Whig and Democratic parties. As a result, most of its spokesmen and elected officials were neither professional politicians nor established community leaders. With inexperienced leaders and a lack of cohesion, the Know-Nothings were unable to make effective use of power once they had it. When voters discovered that the Know-Nothings also *did* nothing, they looked for more competent and experienced leadership.

Kansas and the Rise of the Republicans

Republican party Political party established following the enactment of the Kansas-Nebraska Act in 1854. Republicans were opposed to the extension of slavery into the western territories.

The new **Republican party** was an outgrowth of the anti-Nebraska sentiment of 1854. The Republican name was first used in midwestern states to attract Free-Soil Democrats who refused to march under the Whig banner or support any candidate for high office who called himself a Whig.

When the Know-Nothing party split over the Kansas-Nebraska issue in 1856, most of the northern nativists went over to the Republicans. Although Republicans were more concerned with "the slave power conspiracy" than any alleged "popish plot," nativists did not have to abandon their religious prejudices; the party had the distinct flavor of evangelical Protestantism. On the local level, Republicans sometimes supported causes that reflected an anti-immigrant or anti-Catholic bias, such as defense of Protestant Bible reading in schools and opposition to state aid for parochial education.

Unlike the Know-Nothings, the Republican party was led by seasoned professional politicians, men who had earlier been prominent Whigs or Democrats. Good organizers, they built up an effective party apparatus in an amazingly short time. By early 1856, the new party was well established throughout the North and was preparing to make a serious bid for the presidency.

Underlying the rapid growth of the Republican party was the strong and growing appeal of its position on slavery in the territories. Republicans viewed the unsettled West as a land of opportunities, a place to which the ambitious and hardworking could migrate in the hope of improving their social and economic position. But if slavery were permitted to expand, the rights of "free labor" would be denied. Republicans emphasized that slave labor was unfair competition and retarded the commercial and industrial development of a region. They envisioned a West that was free and white.

Although passage of the Kansas-Nebraska Act raised the territorial issues and gave birth to the Republican party, it was the turmoil associated with attempts to implement popular sovereignty in Kansas that kept the issue alive and enabled the Republicans to increase their following throughout the North. In Kansas, a bitter and violent contest for control of the territorial government was waged between transplanted New Englanders and Midwesterners, who were militantly Free-Soil, and slaveholding settlers from Missouri. Joining the slaveholders were proslavery residents of Missouri who crossed over the border to vote illegally in territorial elections. In the first territorial election, slavery was wholeheartedly endorsed.

Settlers favoring free soil were already a majority of the actual residents of the territory when the fraudulently elected legislature denied them the right to agitate against slavery. To defend themselves and their convictions, they took up arms and established a rival territorial government under a constitution that outlawed slavery.

A small-scale civil war then broke out between the two regimes, culminating in May 1856 when proslavery adherents raided the free-state capital at Lawrence. Portrayed in Republican propaganda as the "sack of Lawrence," the incursion resulted in substantial property damage but no loss of life. In reprisal, antislavery zealot John Brown and several followers murdered five proslavery settlers in cold blood. During the next few months, a hit-and-run guerrilla war raged between free-state and slave-state factions.

The national Republican press had a field day with the events in Kansas, exaggerating the extent of the violence but correctly pointing out that the Pierce administration was favoring rule by a proslavery minority over a Free-Soil majority. Because the "sack of Lawrence" occurred at about the same time that Charles Sumner was assaulted on the Senate floor, the Republicans launched their 1856 campaign under the twin slogans, "Bleeding Kansas and Bleeding Sumner." The image of an evil and aggressive "slave power" South proved a potent device for arousing northern sympathies and winning votes.

Sectional Division in the Election of 1856

The Republican nominating convention displayed the strictly sectional nature of the new party. With no delegates from the Deep South in attendance, the Republicans called for a congressional prohibition of slavery in all territories. The nominee was John C. Frémont, the western explorer who had helped win California during the Mexican War.

The Democratic party nominated James Buchanan of Pennsylvania, who had a long career in public service. Their platform endorsed popular sovereignty. The American party, a Know-Nothing remnant that survived mainly as the rallying point for anti-Democratic conservatives in the border states and parts of the South, chose ex-President Millard Fillmore as its standard-bearer and received the backing of northern Whigs who hoped to revive the tradition of sectional compromise.

The election was really two separate races—one in the North between Frémont and Buchanan and the other in the South between Fillmore and Buchanan. With strong southern support and victories in four crucial northern states, Buchanan won. But the Republicans did remarkably well for a party that was scarcely a year old. Frémont swept the upper North with substantial majorities and won a larger proportion of the northern popular vote than either of his opponents. Since the free states had a substantial majority in the electoral college, a future Republican candidate could attain the presidency simply by overcoming a narrow Democratic margin in the lower North.

In the South, the results of the election brought a momentary sense of relief tinged with anxiety about the future. For Southerners, the very existence of a sectional party committed to restricting the expansion of slavery constituted an insult to their way of life. They felt threatened. Only the continued success of a unified Democratic party under southern influence or control could maintain sectional balance and "southern rights."

The House Divided, 1857–1860

The sectional quarrel deepened and became virtually irreconcilable in the years between the elections of 1856 and 1860. A series of incidents provoked one side or the other, heightened the tension, and ultimately brought the crisis to a head. Behind the panicky reaction to public events lay a growing sense that the North and South were so different in culture and so opposed in basic interests that they could no longer coexist in the same nation.

❖ A Look at the Past ❖

135,000 SETS, 270,000 VOLUMES SOLD.
UNCLE TOM'S CABIN
FOR SALE HERE.
AN EDITION FOR THE MILLION, COMPLETE IN 1 Vol., PRICE 37 1-2 CENTS.
" " IN GERMAN, IN 1 Vol., PRICE 50 CENTS.
" " IN 2 Vols., CLOTH, 6 PLATES, PRICE $1.50.
SUPERB ILLUSTRATED EDITION, IN 1 Vol., WITH 153 ENGRAVINGS,
PRICES FROM $2.50 TO $5.00.
The Greatest Book of the Age.

Poster for *Uncle Tom's Cabin*

Three hundred thousand Americans purchased *Uncle Tom's Cabin* in 1852, the year this poster appeared. While the poster might not have caused the sales, its design certainly appealed to middle-class readers. How does the scene depicted capture the ideal of domesticity? How does that ideal compare to the reality of slave life? Why would the scene appeal to middle-class Americans?

Cultural Sectionalism

Signs of cultural and intellectual cleavage had appeared well before the triumph of sectional politics. As early as the mid-1840s, the slavery issue split the Baptist and Methodist churches into northern and southern wings. Instead of unifying Americans around a common Protestant faith, the churches became nurseries of sectional discord. Increasingly, northern preachers and congregations denounced slaveholding as a sin, while most southern church leaders rallied to a biblical defense of the peculiar institution and became influential apologists for the southern way of life. In both the North and the South, ministers turned political questions into moral issues, reducing the prospects for compromise.

American literature also became sectionalized during the 1840s and 1850s. Southern men of letters such as William Gilmore Simms and Edgar Allan Poe wrote proslavery polemics, and lesser writers penned novels that seemed to glorify southern civilization at the expense of northern society. In the North, prominent men of letters, including Ralph Waldo Emerson and Henry David Thoreau, expressed strong antislavery sentiments in prose and poetry.

Literary abolitionism reached a climax in 1852 when Harriet Beecher Stowe published *Uncle Tom's Cabin,* a novel that sold more than 300,000 copies in a single year and fixed in the northern mind the image of the slaveholder as the brutal Simon Legree. Much of its emotional impact came from the book's portrayal of slavery as a threat to the family and the cult of domesticity. When the saintly Uncle Tom was sold away from his adoring wife and children, Northerners shuddered with horror and more than a few Southerners felt a painful twinge of conscience.

Southern defensiveness gradually hardened into cultural and economic nationalism. Southerners encouraged the use of proslavery textbooks, induced young men of the planter class to stay in the South for higher education, and sought to develop their own industry and commerce. Almost without exception, prominent southern educators and intellectuals of the late 1850s rallied behind the idea of a southern nation.

The Dred Scott Case

When James Buchanan was inaugurated on March 7, 1857, the dispute over the legal status of slavery in the territories was an open door through which sectional fears and hatreds could enter the political arena. Buchanan hoped to close that door by encouraging the Supreme Court to render a broad decision that would resolve the constitutional issue once and for all.

The Court was then about to render its decision in the case of *Dred Scott* v. *Sandford.* The case involved a Missouri slave who sued for his freedom on the grounds that he had lived for many years in an area where slavery had been outlawed by the Missouri Compromise. The Court, headed by Chief Justice Roger B. Taney, made several rulings in the case. First, it held that a slave was not a citizen and therefore had no right to sue in federal courts. Second, and more important for the general issue of slavery, the Court ruled that even if Scott had been a legitimate plaintiff, he would not have won his case. His residence in the Wisconsin Territory established no right to freedom because Congress had no power to prohibit slavery there. The Missouri Compromise was thus declared unconstitutional—and so, implicitly, was popular sovereignty, the main plank in the Republican platform.

In the North, especially among Republicans, the Court's verdict was viewed as the latest diabolical act of the "slave power conspiracy." Five of the six justices who voted in the majority, Northerners argued, were proslavery Southerners. Furthermore, the fact that Buchanan had played a role in the decision was widely known, and it was suspected that he had conspired with the justices in response to pressure from the prosouthern wing of the Democratic party.

Republicans denounced the decision as "a wicked and false judgment" and as "the greatest crime in the annals of the republic," but they stopped short of openly defying the Court's authority. Instead, they argued on narrow technical grounds that the decision as written was not binding on Congress and that a ban on slavery in the territories could still be enacted. The decision actually helped the Republicans build support because it lent credence to their claim that an aggressive slave power was dominating all branches of the federal government and attempting to use the Constitution to achieve its own ends.

The Lecompton Controversy

While the Dred Scott case was being decided, leaders of the proslavery faction in Kansas concluded that the time was ripe to draft a constitution and seek admission to the Union as a slave state. Since settlers with free-state views were now an overwhelming majority in the territory, the success of the plan required a rigged, gerrymandered election for convention delegates. When it became clear that the election was fixed, the free-staters boycotted it. The resulting constitution, drawn up at Lecompton, was certain to be rejected by Congress if a fairer election were not held.

To resolve the issue, supporters of the **Lecompton constitution** decided to permit a vote on the slavery provision alone, giving the electorate the narrow choice of allowing or forbidding the future importation of slaves. Since there was no way to vote for total abolition, the free-state majority again resorted to boycott, thus allowing ratification of a constitution that protected existing slave property and placed no restriction on importations. In a second referendum, proposed by the free-staters and boycotted by the proslavery forces, the Lecompton constitution was overwhelmingly rejected.

Lecompton constitution In 1857, a fraudulently elected group of pro-slavery delegates met in Lecompton, Kansas, and drafted a state constitution. After bitter debate, Congress narrowly denied Kansas' entry into the Union under this constitution.

The Lecompton constitution was such an obvious perversion of popular sovereignty that Stephen Douglas spoke out against it. But the Buchanan administration tried to push it through Congress in early 1858. The resulting debate was bitter and sometimes violent. The bill to admit Kansas into the Union as a slave state passed the Senate but was defeated in the House.

The Lecompton controversy seriously aggravated the sectional quarrel and made it truly irreconcilable. The issue strengthened Republicans' belief that the Democratic party was dominated by Southerners, and at the same time it split the Democratic party between the followers of Douglas and the backers of Buchanan.

For Douglas, the affair was a disaster; it destroyed his hopes of uniting the Democratic party and defusing the slavery issue through the application of popular sovereignty. In practice, popular sovereignty was an invitation to civil war. Furthermore, the Dred Scott decision protected Southerners' rights to own human property in federal territories. For his stand against Lecompton, Douglas was denounced as a traitor in the South, and his hopes of being elected president were greatly diminished.

Debating the Morality of Slavery

Douglas's more immediate problem was to win reelection to the Senate from Illinois in 1858. He faced surprisingly tough opposition from the Republican candidate, Abraham Lincoln, who set out to convince the voters that Douglas could not be relied on consistently to oppose the extension of slavery.

In the famous speech that opened his campaign, Lincoln tried to distance himself from his opponent by taking a more radical position. "'A house divided against itself cannot stand,'" he argued, paraphrasing a line from the Gospel of Mark. "I believe this government cannot endure, permanently half *slave* and half *free.*" He then described the chain of events between the Kansas-Nebraska Act and the Dred Scott decision as evidence of a plot to extend slavery, and he tried to link Douglas to that proslavery conspiracy by pointing to his rival's unwillingness to take a stand on the morality of slavery. Lincoln demanded that slavery be considered a moral, and not simply a political, issue.

In the subsequent series of debates that focused national attention on the Illinois senatorial contest, Lincoln hammered away at the theme that Douglas was a covert defender of slavery because he was not a principled opponent of it. Douglas responded by accusing Lincoln of endangering the Union by his talk of putting slavery on the path to extinction. Lincoln denied that he was an abolitionist but readily admitted that he, like the Founders, opposed any extension of slavery.

In the debate at Freeport, Illinois, Lincoln questioned Douglas on how he could reconcile popular sovereignty with the Dred Scott decision. Douglas responded that slavery could not exist without supportive legislation to sustain it and that territorial legislatures could simply refrain from passing a slave code if they wanted to keep it out. Coupled with his anti-Lecompton stand, Douglas's "Freeport Doctrine" hardened southern opposition to his presidential ambitions.

Douglas's most effective debating point was to charge that Lincoln's moral opposition to slavery implied a belief in racial equality. Lincoln, facing an intensely racist electorate, vigorously denied this charge and affirmed his commitment to white supremacy. He would grant blacks the right to the fruits of their own labor while denying them the "privileges" of citizenship. This was an inherently contradictory position, and Douglas made the most of it.

Although Republican candidates for the state legislature won a majority of the popular votes, the Democrats carried more counties and thus were able to send Douglas back to the Senate. Lincoln lost an office, but he won respect in Republican circles throughout the country. By stressing the moral dimension of the slavery question and undercutting any possibility of fusion between Republicans and Douglas Democrats, he had sharpened his party's ideological focus and had stiffened its backbone against any temptation to compromise the Free-Soil position.

The South's Crisis of Fear

After Kansas became a free territory instead of a slave state in August 1858, slavery in the territories became a symbolic issue rather than a practical and substantive one. The remaining unorganized areas in the Rockies and northern Great Plains were unlikely to attract slaveholding settlers. Nevertheless, Southerners continued to demand the "right" to take their slaves into territories, and Republicans persisted in denying it to them. Although they repeatedly promised not to interfere with slavery where it already existed, the Republicans did not gain the trust of the Southerners, who interpreted the Republicans' unyielding stand against the extension of slavery as a threat to southern rights and security.

A chain of events in late 1859 and early 1860 turned southern anxiety about northern attitudes and policies into a "crisis of fear." The first incident was John Brown's raid on Harpers Ferry, Virginia, in October 1859. Brown was a fervent abolitionist with the appearance of an Old Testament prophet. He believed he was God's chosen instrument "to purge this land with blood" and eradicate the sin of slaveholding. On October 16, he led a small band of men across the Potomac River from his base in Maryland and seized the federal arsenal and armory in Harpers Ferry.

Brown's aim was to commence a guerrilla war from havens in the Appalachians that would eventually extend to the plantation regions of the lower South. But the neighboring slaves did not rise up to join him, and his plan failed. In the fight with U.S. marines that followed, ten of Brown's men were killed or mortally wounded, along with seven of the townspeople and soldiers who opposed them.

The wounded Brown and his remaining followers were put on trial for treason against the state of Virginia. The subsequent investigation produced evidence that several prominent northern abolitionists had approved of Brown's plan and had raised money for his preparations. This revelation seemed to confirm southern fears that abolitionists were actively engaged in fomenting slave insurrection. Southerners were further stunned by the outpouring of sympathy and admiration for Brown in the North. His actual execution on December 2 completed Brown's elevation to the status of martyred saint of the antislavery cause.

Although Republican politicians were quick to denounce John Brown for his violent methods, Southerners interpreted the wave of northern sympathy as an expression of the majority opinion and the Republicans' "real" attitude. In the southern mind, abolitionists, Republicans, and Northerners were taking on one face.

John Brown, shown here barricaded at Harpers Ferry with his followers and hostages, looked on his fight against slavery as a holy campaign ordained by God. In his last speech to the court before his execution for conviction of murder, promoting slave insurrection, and treason, Brown proclaimed, "Now, if it is deemed necessary that I should forfeit my life for the furtherance of the ends of justice and mingle my blood further with the blood of my children and with the blood of millions in this slave country whose rights are disregarded by wicked, cruel, and unjust enactments—I say let it be done!" ❖

Within the South, the raid and its aftermath touched off a frenzy of fear. Southerners became increasingly vigilant for any sign of attack on their way of life, from without or from within.

Brown was scarcely in his grave when another set of events put southern nerves on edge. Next to abolitionist-abetted rebellions, the slaveholding South's greatest fear was that the nonslaveholding majority would turn against the master class and that the solidarity of southern whites would crumble. Hinton Rowan Helper's book *The Impending Crisis of the South,* which beseeched lower-class whites to resist planter dominance and abolish slavery in their own interest, was regarded by slaveholders as being even more seditious than *Uncle Tom's Cabin.* They feared the spread of "Helperism" among poor whites almost as much as the effect of "John Brownism" on the slaves.

The Republican candidate for speaker of the U.S. House of Representatives, John Sherman of Ohio, had endorsed Helper's book as a campaign document. Southern congressmen threatened secession if Sherman was elected, and feelings became so heated that some House members began to carry weapons on the floor of the chamber. A more moderate Republican was elected, and the impasse over the speakership was resolved, but the contest helped persuade Southerners that the Republicans were committed to stirring up class conflict among southern whites. The identification of Republicans with Helper's ideas may have been decisive in convincing many conservative planters that a Republican president in 1860 would be intolerable.

The Election of 1860

The Republicans, sniffing victory and generally unaware of the depth of southern feeling against them, met in Chicago on May 16 to nominate a presidential candidate. The initial front-runner, Senator William H. Seward of New York, proved unacceptable because of his reputation for radicalism and his long record of strong opposition to the nativist movement. Most delegates wanted a less controversial nominee who could win two or three of the northern states that had been in the Democratic column in 1856. Abraham Lincoln met their specifications: he was considered more moderate than Seward and had kept his personal distaste for Know-Nothingism to himself. In addition, his rise to prominence from humble beginnings embodied the Republican ideal of equal opportunity for all.

The platform, like the nominee, was meant to broaden the party's appeal in the North. Although a commitment to halt the expansion of slavery remained, economic matters received more attention than they had in 1856. The platform called for a high protective tariff, free homesteads, and federal aid for internal improvements. The platform was cleverly designed to bring most ex-Whigs into the Republican camp while also accommodating enough renegade Democrats to give the party a solid majority in the northern states.

The Democrats failed to present a united front against this formidable challenge. When the party first met in the sweltering heat of Charleston in late April, Douglas was unable to win the nomination because of southern opposition. He did succeed in getting the convention to endorse popular sovereignty as its slavery platform, but the price was a walkout by southern delegates who favored a federal slave code for the territories.

Unable to agree on a nominee, the convention adjourned to reconvene in Baltimore in June. When the pro-Douglas force won most of the contested seats, another and more massive southern walkout took place. The result was a fracture of the Democratic party. The delegates who remained nominated Douglas, reaffirming their commitment to popular sovereignty; the southern bolters convened elsewhere to nominate John Breckinridge of Kentucky on a platform pledging federal protection of slavery in the territories.

By the time the campaign got under way, four parties were running presidential candidates. In addition to the Republicans, the Douglas Democrats, and the "Southern Rights" Democrats, a remnant of conservative Whigs and Know-Nothings nominated John Bell of Tennessee under the banner of the Constitutional Union party. Taking no explicit stand on slavery in the territories, Bell and his backers tried to represent the spirit of sectional compromise. In effect, the race became separate two-party contests in each section: in the North, the real choice was between Lincoln and Douglas, and in the South, the only candidates with a fighting chance were Breckinridge and Bell.

In this cartoon from the 1860 election, candidates Lincoln and Douglas struggle for control of the country, while Breckinridge tears away the South. John Bell of the Constitutional Union party futilely attempts to repair the damage to the torn nation. ❖

When the results came in, the Republicans had achieved a stunning victory. By gaining the electoral votes of all the free states except a fraction of New Jersey's, Lincoln won a decisive majority. The Republican strategy of seeking power by trying to win the majority section was brilliantly successful. Fewer than 40 percent of Americans who went to the polls actually voted for Lincoln, but his support in the North was so solid that he would have won in the electoral college even if all three opposing parties had been unified behind a single candidate.

Most Southerners saw the results of the election as a catastrophe. A candidate and a party with no support in their own section had won the presidency on a platform viewed as insulting to southern honor and hostile to vital southern interests. For the first time in history, southern interests were in no way represented in the White House. Rather than accept permanent minority status in American politics and face the threat to black slavery and white "liberty" that was bound to follow, the political leaders of the lower South launched a movement for immediate secession from the Union.

Conclusion: Explaining the Crisis

Generations of historians have searched for the underlying causes of the crisis leading to the disruption of the Union but have failed to agree on an answer. Some have stressed the clash of economic interests between agrarian and industrializing nations. But this interpretation does not reflect the way people at the time expressed their concerns. The main issues in the sectional debates of the 1850s were whether slavery was right or wrong and whether it should be extended or contained. In the face of these issues, all economic considerations pale. Indeed, there was no necessity for the producers of raw materials to go to war with the people who marketed and processed them.

Another group of historians have blamed the crisis on "irresponsible" politicians and agitators on both sides of the debate. Public opinion, they argue, was whipped into a frenzy over issues that competent statesmen could have resolved. But this viewpoint has been sharply criticized for failing to acknowledge the depths of feeling that could be aroused by the slavery question and for underestimating the obstacles to a peaceful solution.

CHRONOLOGY

1846	David Wilmot introduces a proviso banning slavery in the Mexican cession
1848	Free-Soil party is founded ❖ Zachary Taylor (Whig) is elected president, defeating Lewis Cass (Democrat) and Martin Van Buren (Free-Soil)
1849	California seeks admission to the Union as a free state
1850	Congress debates sectional issues and enacts the Compromise of 1850
1852	Harriet Beecher Stowe publishes *Uncle Tom's Cabin* ❖ Franklin Pierce (Democrat) is elected president by a large majority over Winfield Scott (Whig)
1854	Congress passes Kansas-Nebraska Act, repealing the Missouri Compromise ❖ Republican party is founded in several northern states ❖ Anti-Nebraska coalitions score victories in congressional elections in the North
1854–1855	Know-Nothing party achieves stunning successes in state politics
1854–1856	Free-state and slave-state forces struggle for control of Kansas Territory
1856	Preston Brooks assaults Charles Sumner on the Senate floor ❖ James Buchanan (Democrat) wins the presidency despite a strong challenge in the North from John C. Frémont (Republican)
1857	Supreme Court decides the Dred Scott case legalizing slavery in all territories
1858	Congress refuses to admit Kansas to the Union under the proslavery Lecompton constitution ❖ Lincoln and Douglas debate
1859	John Brown raids Harpers Ferry, is captured and executed
1859–1860	Fierce struggle takes place over election of a Republican as speaker of the House
1860	Republicans nominate Abraham Lincoln for the presidency ❖ Democratic party splits into northern and southern factions with separate candidates and platforms ❖ Lincoln wins the presidency over Douglas (northern Democrat), Breckinridge (southern Democrat), and Bell (Constitutional Unionist)

The dominant modern view is that the crisis was rooted in profound ideological differences over the morality and utility of slavery as an institution. Most interpreters are now agreed that the conflict stemmed from the fact that the South was a slave society and was determined to stay that way, while the North was equally committed to a free-labor system. It is hard to imagine that secessionism would have developed if the South had followed the North's example and abolished slavery in the postrevolutionary period.

Nevertheless, the existence or nonexistence of slavery will not explain why the crisis came when it did and in the way that it did. Why did the conflict become "irreconcilable" in the 1850s and not earlier or later? Why did it take the form of a political struggle over the future of slavery in the territories? Adequate answers to both questions require an understanding of political developments that were not directly caused by tensions over slavery.

By the 1850s, the established Whig and Democratic parties were in trouble because they no longer offered the voters clear-cut alternatives on the economic issues that had been the bread and butter of politics during the heyday of the second party system. This situation created an opening for new parties and issues. The Republicans used the issue of slavery in the territories to build the first successful sectional party in American history. They called for "free soil" rather than freedom for blacks because abolitionism conflicted with the northern majority's commitment to white supremacy and its respect for the original constitutional compromise that established a hands-off policy toward slavery in the southern states.

If politicians seeking new ways to mobilize an apathetic electorate are seen as the main instigators of sectional crisis, the reason why certain appeals were more effective than others must still be explained. Why did the slavery extension issue arouse such strong feelings in the two sections during the 1850s? After all, the same issues had arisen earlier and had proved adjustable.

Ultimately, therefore, the crisis of the 1850s must be understood as social and cultural as well as political. Basic beliefs and values had diverged significantly in the North and the South between 1820 and the 1850s. In the free states, the rise of reform-minded evangelicalism had given a new sense of moral direction and purpose to a rising middle class adapting to the new market economy (see Chapter 12). At the same time, in much of the South, the slave plantation system prospered, and the notion that white liberty and equality depended on having enslaved blacks to do menial labor became more deeply entrenched.

When politicians appealed to sectionalism during the 1850s, therefore, they could evoke conflicting views of what constituted a good society. To most Northerners, the South—with its allegedly idle masters, degraded unfree workers, and shiftless poor whites—seemed in flagrant violation of the Protestant work ethic and the ideal of open competition. From the dominant southern point of view, the North was a land of hypocritical money-grubbers who denied the obvious fact that the dependent laboring classes—especially racially inferior ones—had to be kept under the kind of rigid control that only slavery could provide. Once these contrary views of the world had become the main themes of political discourse, sectional compromise was no longer possible.

Key Terms

Wilmot Proviso, p. 268
popular sovereignty, p. 268
Free-Soil party, p. 268
Compromise of 1850, p. 269
Fugitive Slave Law, p. 269
Kansas-Nebraska Act, p. 272
Ostend Manifesto, p. 273
Know-Nothing party, p. 273
Republican party, p. 274
Lecompton constitution, p. 277

Recommended Reading

The best general account of the politics of the section crisis is David M. Potter, *The Impending Crisis, 1848–1861* (1976). This well-written and authoritative work combines a vivid and detailed narrative of events with a shrewd and detailed interpretation of them. For a shorter overview, see Bruce C. Levine, *Half Slave and Half Free: The Roots of the Civil War* (1991). On the demise of the Whigs, see Michael F. Holt, *The Rise and Fall of the American Whig Party* (1999). The best treatment of the Know-Nothing movement is Tyler Anbinder, *Nativism and Slavery: The Northern Know-Nothings and the Politics of the 1850s* (1992). The most important studies of northern political sectionalism are Eric Foner, *Free Soil, Free Labor, Free Men: The Ideology of the Republican Party Before the Civil War* (1970), and William E. Gienapp, *The Origins of the Republican Party, 1852–1856* (1987), on the Republican party generally; and Don E. Fehrenbacher, *Prelude to Greatness: Lincoln in the 1850s* (1962) on Lincoln's rise to prominence. On the climactic events of 1857, see Don E. Fehrenbacher, *The Dred Scott Case: Its Significance in American Law and Politics* (1978), and Kenneth M. Stampp, *America in 1857: A Nation on the Brink* (1990). On the background of southern separatism, see William W. Freehling, *The Road to Disunion: Secessionists at Bay, 1776–1854* (1990), and William L. Barney, *The Road to Secession: A New Perspective on the Old South* (1972).

For a list of additional titles related to this chapter's topics, please see http://www.ablongman.com/divine.

SUGGESTED WEB SITES

Secession Era Editorials Project

http://history.furman.edu/~benson/docs/

Furman University is digitizing editorials about the secession crisis and already includes scores of them on this site.

John Brown Trial Links

http://www.law.umkc.edu/faculty/projects/ftrials/Brown.html

This site provides a list of excellent links to information about the trial of John Brown.

Abraham Lincoln and Slavery

http://odur.let.rug.nl/~usa/H/1990/ch5_p6.htm

This site discusses Lincoln's views and actions concerning slavery, especially the Lincoln-Douglas debates.

Bleeding Kansas

http://www.Kancoll.org/galbks.htm

Contemporary and later accounts of America's rehearsal for the Civil War comprise this Kansas Collection site.

The Compromise of 1850 and the Fugitive Slave Act

http://www.pbs.org/wgbh/aia/part4

From the series on Africans in America, an analysis of the Compromise of 1850 and of the effects of the Fugitive Slave Act on black Americans.

Words and Deeds in American History

http://lcweb2.loc.gov/ammem/mcchtml/corhome.html

A Library of Congress site containing links to Frederick Douglass, the Compromise of 1850, speeches by John C. Calhoun, Daniel Webster, and Henry Clay, and other topics from the Civil War era.

We Americans

Hispanic America After 1848

A Case Study in Majority Rule

With the discovery of gold in 1848, more than one thousand Californians of Mexican ancestry joined the frenetic rush to the Sierras. Among them was Don Antonio Franco Coronel, a Los Angeles school teacher, who lead a group of fellow *Californios* into the rich goldfields. Just months before the expedition, the United States and Mexico had concluded the Treaty of Guadalupe Hidalgo, which transformed Coronel and his companions from Mexicans to Americans. At the insistence of the Mexican government, the treaty stipulated that Mexicans living in the newly acquired territories would be granted "all the rights of citizens of the United States . . . according to the principles of the Constitution." Coronel's gold-seeking enterprise would put that promise to the test. While panning rivers and staking claims, Coronel's company came into competitive contact with large numbers of Yankee miners. The interactions between the two ethnic communities suggested that a rough road lay ahead for Hispanic Americans.

Upon arriving in gold country, Coronel and his men immediately hit pay dirt. In the first day alone, Coronel pulled 45 ounces of gold from the ground; within eight days, one of his associates had amassed a pile of gold weighing a staggering 52 pounds. The *Californios* seemed to have a head start in the race for gold. They understood the terrain, cooperated among themselves, and were familiar with the best mining techniques. Not surprisingly, their dramatic successes stirred the envy of their Anglo-American competitors. Although the Mexican-American War technically had made the Yankee and Hispanic miners compatriots, the tensions of gold fever exposed the shallowness of that new relationship.

After a year of relatively peaceful competition, Anglo miners began to express their resentments. Lumping *Californios* with all other "foreigners," they unleashed a barrage of physical and political attacks against their competitors. Lynch mobs, camp riots, and legal harassment were common forms of Yankee intimidation. Despite their entitlements to the rights of citizenship, the *Californios* were badgered and bullied into retreat. Fearing for his life, Coronel returned to Southern California, where Hispanics still outnumbered the newcomers. Earning prestige and prosperity in Los Angeles, Coronel went on to become mayor and state treasurer. But to the end of his life, he still painfully remembered his experience in Northern California, where his rights as a U.S. citizen were so easily disregarded by his fellow Americans.

Coronel's experiences exemplify two truths about the effect of U.S. expansion on the lives of Mexicans who suddenly found themselves in American territory. First, in areas where Anglo-American settlement grew rapidly—such as Northern California—the Hispanic community typically faced discrimination, intimidation, and a denial of the very civil rights that Guadalupe Hidalgo had

Blessing of the Enrequita Mine, 1860, by Alexander Edouart. Spaniards and Mexicans, men and women, surround the makeshift altar where the priest is saying the blessing to dedicate the Enrequita Mine in northern California. The idyllic scene does not hint at the violent and rough treatment Hispanic miners experienced during the California gold rush days. ❖

supposedly guaranteed. Second, in areas where the Hispanic population remained a majority—such as Southern California—Spanish-speaking Americans were able to exercise the rights of republican citizenship, often wielding considerable political influence. Coronel had a taste of both experiences, going from intimidated miner to powerful politician. However, as Anglo settlers began to stream into Southern California, even that region ceased to be a safe haven for Hispanic rights.

By the mid-1840s Hispanics living in Texas, known as *Tejanos,* were outnumbered by Anglos at a ratio of twenty to one. True to the pattern described above, this decided minority faced intense prejudice. Among the most notable victims of this prejudice was Juan Sequin, a hero of the Texas War for Independence. Perhaps no *Tejano* family fell further or faster than that of Don Martin de Leon. The scion of an aristocratic family, de Leon had spearheaded Spanish efforts to colonize Texas and continued to organize settlements after Mexican independence. Establishing extensive cattle ranches, the de Leons enjoyed prominence and wealth on their holdings. As with most *Tejanos,* they fervently supported the struggle for Texan independence, fighting shoulder to shoulder with their Anglo neighbors. But when the war ended, the de Leon estate fell under siege from the surging wave of new settlers. Relying on the intricacies of Anglo-American law and the power of an electoral majority, the newcomers quickly encroached on de Leon's lands. With frightening rapidity, the family was reduced from its preeminent position to abject poverty.

The de Leons were not alone. A contemporary observed that many Anglo settlers worked "dark intrigues against the native families, whose only crime was that they owned large tracts of land and desirable property." Even after U.S. annexation of the Lone Star Republic, Hispanics continued to be pushed off their land. In 1856, a Texas newspaper reported, "The people of Matagorda county have held a meeting and ordered every Mexican to leave the county. To strangers this may seem wrong, but we hold it to be perfectly right and highly necessary." For many Mexican Americans, life on U.S. soil taught the cruelest lesson in white man's democracy.

Yet majority rule actually worked to the favor of Hispanics living in New Mexico, where they enjoyed numerical dominance. When U.S. troops entered Santa Fe in 1846, Albino Chacón, a prominent city judge, controlled his own future. Although he had been loyal to the Mexican government throughout the war, the U.S. Army offered him the opportunity to retain his judgeship. Given similar offers, other New Mexicans who had initially opposed the U.S. invasion accepted positions of prominence, such as Donanciano Vigil, who served as interim governor of the territory. But Chacón lived by a strict code of honor and could not switch loyalties so easily. Opting for exile, Chacón moved out of Santa Fe, left the practice of law, and took up farming. Aside from such self-imposed changes, however, American rule actually had little impact on most New Mexicans' lives. Hispanics still formed the demographic and political backbone of the territory and often served their new nation with distinction. Chacón's own son, Rafael, served as a Union officer during the Civil War, winning acclaim in defending New Mexico against a Confederate invasion from Texas, and was eventually elected as territorial senator. Rafael's son studied law at Notre Dame and held several important positions in the Department of Justice. Majority status afforded New Mexican Hispanics opportunities in the American system that were denied their compatriots living in Anglo-dominated regions.

As settlement increased throughout the century, such Hispanic-controlled communities dwindled. The rise of the railroad acted as a funnel through which Anglo-Americans poured into western territories, and remaining pockets of Hispanic dominance rapidly disappeared. Majoritarianism and racism combined to place Hispanics in a position subordinate to the Anglo newcomers. Throughout the region the story was sadly similar; as Hispanic Americans lost their majority status, they also lost many of their basic rights.

Chapter 15

Secession and the Civil War

The Emergence of Lincoln

President Abraham Lincoln was striking in appearance—at 6 feet 4 inches in height, he seemed even taller because of his disproportionately long legs and his habit of wearing a high silk "stovepipe" hat. His career prior to taking up residence in the White House in 1860 was less remarkable than his person, however. A look at his previous experience certainly provided no guarantee that he would one day tower over most of our other presidents in more than physical height.

Born to poor and illiterate parents on the Kentucky frontier in 1809, Lincoln received a few months of formal schooling in Indiana after the family moved there in 1816. But mostly he educated himself, reading and rereading a few treasured books by firelight. In 1831, when the family migrated to Illinois, he left home to make a living for himself. After failing as a merchant, he found a path to success in law and politics. Lincoln combined exceptional political and legal skills with a down-to-earth, humorous way of addressing jurors and voters. He became a leader of the Whig party in Illinois and one of the most sought-after of the lawyers who rode the central Illinois judicial circuit.

The high point of his political career as a Whig was one term in Congress (1847–1849), but he alienated much of his constituency by opposing the Mexican-American War and wisely chose not to run for reelection. In 1848, he campaigned vigorously and effectively for Zachary Taylor, but the new president failed to appoint Lincoln to a patronage job he coveted. Disappointed by his political fortunes, Lincoln concentrated on building his law practice.

The Kansas-Nebraska Act of 1854, with its advocacy of popular sovereignty, provided Lincoln with an opportunity to reconcile his driving ambition for political success with his personal convictions. Lincoln had long believed that slavery was an unjust institution that should be tolerated only to the extent that the Constitution and the tradition of sectional compromise required. Attacking Stephen Douglas's plan on popular sovereignty, Lincoln threw in his lot with the Republicans and assumed leadership of the new party in Illinois. He attracted national attention in his bid for Douglas's Senate seat in 1858 and happened to have the right qualifications when the Republicans chose a presidential nominee in 1860.

After Lincoln's election provoked southern secession and plunged the nation into the greatest crisis in its history, there was understandable skepticism about him in many quarters. After all, the onetime rail-splitter from Illinois had never been a governor, senator, cabinet officer, or high-ranking military officer. But some of his training as a prairie politician would prove extremely useful in the years ahead.

Outline

The Storm Gathers

Adjusting to Total War

Fight to the Finish

Conclusion: An Organizational Revolution

Another reason for Lincoln's effectiveness as a war leader was that he identified wholeheartedly with the northern cause and could inspire others to make sacrifices for it. In his view, the issue in the conflict was nothing less than the survival of the kind of political system that gave men like himself a chance for high office. For Lincoln, a government had to be strong enough to maintain its own existence and guarantee equality of opportunity.

THE CIVIL WAR TESTED AMERICA'S ABILITY to preserve its democratic form of government in the face of domestic foes. It put on trial the very principle of democracy at a time when most European nations had rejected political liberalism and accepted the view that popular government would inevitably collapse into anarchy. As Lincoln put it in the Gettysburg Address, the only cause great enough to justify the enormous sacrifice of life on the battlefields was the struggle to preserve the democratic ideal, to ensure that "government of the people, by the people, and for the people, shall not perish from the earth."

As he prepared to take office in 1861, Abraham Lincoln could scarcely anticipate the challenges he would face. The immediate problem was how to respond to the secession of the Deep South. But secession was just an expression of the larger question: Did the authority of the federal government outweigh the power of the individual states? No less important were questions about slavery: Was it morally acceptable for one person to "own" another? Could the Union continue to exist half-slave and half-free?

The sectionalism that had already led to a number of violent incidents—bloody fighting in Kansas, John Brown's raid on Harpers Ferry, his conviction on charges of treason against Virginia, and his eventual execution—continued to mount. Finally irreconcilable differences erupted into total war that left no part of society—North or South—untouched.

THE STORM GATHERS

Lincoln's election provoked the secession of seven states of the Deep South but did not lead immediately to armed conflict. Before the sectional quarrel turned from a cold war into a hot one, two things had to happen. A final effort to defuse the conflict by compromise and conciliation had to fail, and the North needed to develop a firm resolve to maintain the Union by military action. Both of these developments may seem inevitable today, but for most Americans living at the time, it was not clear until the guns blazed at Fort Sumter that the sectional crisis would have to be resolved on the battlefield.

The Deep South Secedes

South Carolina, which had long been in the forefront of southern rights and proslavery agitation, was the first state to leave the Union, on December 20, 1860. The constitutional theory behind secession was that the Union was a "compact" among sovereign states, each of which could withdraw from the Union by a vote of a convention similar to the one that had ratified the Constitution in the first place. The South Carolinians justified seceding at this time by charging that "a sectional party" had elected a president hostile to slavery.

In other states of the cotton kingdom, there was similar outrage at Lincoln's election but less certainty about how to respond to it. Some Southerners, labeled **cooperationists,** believed that the South should respond as a unit, after holding a southern convention. South Carolina's unilateral action, however, set a precedent.

cooperationists In late 1860, southern secessionists debated two strategies: unilateral secession by each state or "cooperative" secession by the South as a whole. The cooperationists lost the debate.

When conventions in six other states of the Deep South met during January 1861, delegates favoring immediate secession were everywhere in the majority. By February 1, seven states had removed themselves from the Union: South Carolina,

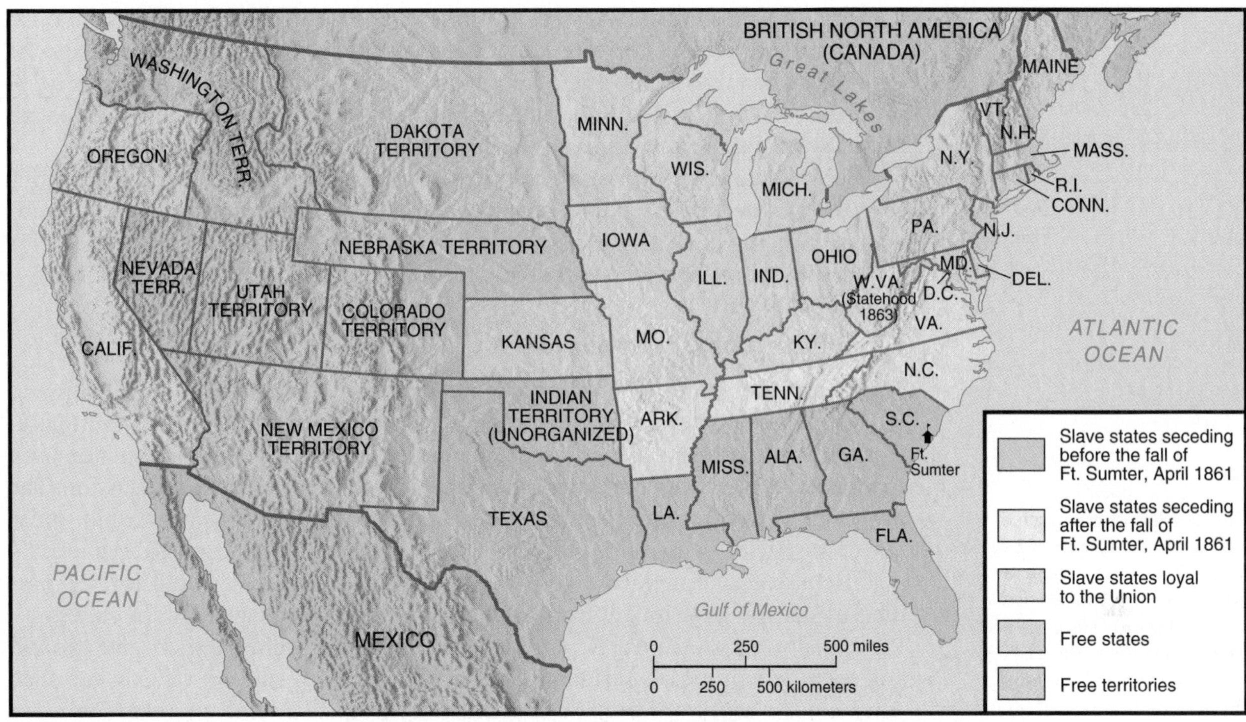

SECESSION *The fall of Fort Sumter was a watershed for the secessionist movement. With no room left for compromise, slave states of the Upper South chose to join the Confederacy.* ❖

Alabama, Mississippi, Florida, Georgia, Louisiana, and Texas. In the upper South, however, calls for immediate secession were unsuccessful; majority opinion in Virginia, North Carolina, Tennessee, and Arkansas did not subscribe to the view that Lincoln's election was a sufficient reason for breaking up the Union.

Delegates from the Deep South met in Montgomery, Alabama, on February 4 to establish the Confederate States of America. Relatively moderate leaders dominated the proceedings and defeated or modified some of the pet schemes of a radical faction composed of extreme southern nationalists. Voted down were proposals to reopen the Atlantic slave trade, to count *all* slaves in determining congressional representation instead of three-fifths, and to prohibit the admission of free states to the new Confederacy.

The resulting provisional constitution was surprisingly similar to that of the United States. Most of the differences merely spelled out traditional southern interpretations of the federal charter. The central government was denied the authority to impose protective tariffs, subsidize internal improvements, or interfere with slavery in the states and was required to pass laws protecting slavery in the territories. As provisional president and vice president, the convention chose Jefferson Davis of Mississippi and Alexander Stephens of Georgia, men who had previously resisted secessionist agitation.

The moderation shown in Montgomery resulted in part from a desire to win support for the cause of secessionism in the reluctant states of the upper South. But it also revealed that proslavery reactionaries had never succeeded in getting a majority behind them. Most Southerners were staunchly proslavery but had been opposed to dissolving the Union and repudiating their traditional patriotic loyalties so long as there had been good reasons to believe that slavery was protected from northern interference.

The panic following Lincoln's election destroyed that sense of security. But it was clear from the actions of the Montgomery convention that the goal of the new converts to secessionism was not to establish a slaveholders' reactionary utopia. They only wished to recreate the Union that existed before the rise of the Republican party, and they opted for secession only when it seemed clear that separation was the only way to achieve their aim. Some optimists even predicted that all of the North except New England would eventually join the Confederacy.

Secession and the formation of the Confederacy thus amounted to a very conservative and defensive kind of "revolution." The only justification for southern independence on which a majority could agree was the need for greater security for slavery and the social relations that institution entailed.

The Failure of Compromise

While the Deep South was opting for independence, moderates in the North and the border slave states were trying to devise a compromise that would stem the secessionist tide before it could engulf the entire South. In Congress, Senator John Crittenden of Kentucky presented a plan that served as the focus for discussion. The proposed **Crittenden compromise** advocated extending the Missouri Compromise line to the Pacific to guarantee the protection of slavery in the southwestern territories. He also recommended a constitutional amendment that would forever prohibit the federal government from abolishing or regulating slavery in the states.

Crittenden compromise
Faced with the specter of secession and war, Congress tried and failed to resolve the sectional crisis in the months between Lincoln's election and inauguration. The leading proposal, introduced by Kentucky Senator John Crittenden, would have extended the Missouri Compromise line west to the Pacific.

Initially, congressional Republicans showed some willingness to give ground and take these proposals seriously. However, Republican support quickly vanished when Lincoln sent word from Springfield that he was adamantly opposed to the extension of the compromise line. With Lincoln opposing the plan, Republicans voted against it in committee. When the senators and congressmen of the seceding states also voted against the plan, it was doomed to defeat.

Some historians have blamed Lincoln and the Republicans for causing unnecessary war by rejecting a compromise that would have appeased southern pride without providing any practical opportunity for the expansion of slavery. But it is quite possible that the secessionists, who wanted slavery protected in *all* territories, would not have been satisfied even if the Republicans had approved the plan.

Furthermore, Lincoln and his followers had what they considered very good reasons for not making territorial concessions. They mistakenly believed that secessionism reflected a minority opinion in the South and that a strong stand would win the support of southern Unionists and moderates. In addition, Lincoln took his stand on free soil seriously. He did not want to give slaveholders any chance to enlarge their domain.

Lincoln was also convinced that backing down in the face of secessionist threats would fatally undermine the democratic principle of majority rule. In his inaugural address of March 4, 1861, he recalled that during the winter, many "patriotic men" had urged him to accept a compromise that would "shift the ground" on which he had been elected. But to do so would have signified that a victorious presidential candidate "cannot be inaugurated till he betrays those who elected him by breaking his pledges, and surrendering to those who tried and failed to defeat him at the polls." Making such a concession would mean that "this government and all popular government is already at an end."

And the War Came

By the time of Lincoln's inauguration, seven states had seceded, formed an independent republic, and seized most federal forts and other installations in the Deep South without firing a shot. Lincoln's predecessor, James Buchanan, rejected the right of secession but refused to use coercion to maintain federal authority. Many Northerners agreed with his stand.

The collapse of compromise efforts narrowed the choice to peaceful separation or war. By early March, the tide of public opinion was beginning to shift in favor of strong action to preserve the Union. Even in the business community, sentiment mounted in favor of a coercive policy.

In his inaugural address, Lincoln called for a cautious and limited use of force. He would defend federal forts and installations not yet in Confederate hands but would not attempt to recapture the ones already taken. He thus tried to shift the burden for beginning hostilities to the Confederacy. As Lincoln spoke, only four military installations within the seceded states were still held by United States forces. The most important and vulnerable of these installations was Fort Sumter, inside Charleston harbor. The Confederacy demanded the surrender of the garrison, and shortly after taking office, Lincoln was informed that Sumter could not hold out much longer without reinforcements and supplies.

After some initial indecision and opposition from his cabinet, Lincoln decided to reinforce the fort, and he so informed the governor of South Carolina on April 4. The Confederacy regarded the sending of provisions as a hostile act and began shelling the fort near dawn on April 12. After forty hours of bombardment, the commander of the Union forces surrendered, and the Confederate flag was raised over Fort Sumter. The South had won a victory but had also assumed responsibility for firing the first shot.

On April 15, Lincoln proclaimed that an insurrection existed in the Deep South and called on the militia of the loyal states to provide 75,000 troops for short-term service to put it down. Two days later, a Virginia convention voted to join the Confederacy. Within the next five weeks, Arkansas, Tennessee, and North Carolina followed suit. Lincoln's policy of coercion forced them to choose sides, and they opted to join the other slave states in the Confederacy.

In the North, the firing on Fort Sumter evoked strong feelings of patriotism and dedication to the Union. Like many other Northerners, Stephen Douglas, Lincoln's former political rival, pledged his full support for the crusade against secession and literally worked himself to death rallying midwestern Democrats

This contemporary Currier and Ives lithograph depicts the bombardment of Fort Sumter on April 12–13, 1861. The soldiers are firing from Fort Moultrie in Charleston Harbor, which the Union garrison had evacuated the previous December in order to strengthen Fort Sumter. ❖

behind the government. Everyone assumed that the war would be short and not very bloody. It remained to be seen whether Unionist fervor could be sustained through a long and costly struggle.

The entire Confederacy comprised only eleven of the fifteen states in which slavery was lawful. In the border slave states of Maryland, Delaware, Kentucky, and Missouri, a combination of local Unionism and federal intervention thwarted secession. By taking care to respect Kentucky's neutrality, using martial law ruthlessly in Maryland, and stationing regular troops in Missouri, Lincoln kept these crucial border states in the Union.

Hence the Civil War was not, strictly speaking, a struggle between slave and free states. More than anything else, conflicting views on the right of secession determined the ultimate division of states and the choices of individuals in areas where sentiment was divided. General Robert E. Lee, for example, was neither a defender of slavery nor a southern nationalist. But he followed Virginia out of the Union because he was the loyal son of a "sovereign state." Although concern about the future of slavery had driven the Deep South to secede in the first place, the war was seen less as a struggle over slavery than as a contest to determine whether the Union was indivisible.

Adjusting to Total War

The Civil War was a "total war" because the North could achieve its aim of restoring the Union only if the South was so thoroughly defeated that its separatist government was overthrown. It was a long war because the Confederacy put up "a hell of a fight" before it would agree to be put to death. A total war is a test of societies, economies, and political systems as well as a battle of wits between generals and military strategists.

Prospects, Plans, and Expectations

If the war was to be decided by sheer physical strength, the North had an enormous edge in population, industrial capacity, and railroad mileage. Nevertheless, the South also had some advantages. To achieve its aim of independence, the Confederacy needed only to defend its own territory successfully. The North, by contrast, had to invade and conquer the South. Consequently, the Confederacy faced a less serious supply problem, had a greater capacity to choose the time and place of combat, and could take advantage of familiar terrain and a friendly civilian population.

The nature of the war meant that southern leaders could define their cause as defense of their homeland against a Yankee invasion. It seemed doubtful in 1861 that Northerners would be willing to make an equal sacrifice for the relatively abstract principle that the Union was sacred and perpetual.

Confederate optimism on the eve of the war was also fed by more dubious calculations. It was widely assumed that Southerners, who were accustomed to riding and shooting, would make better soldiers than Yankees. When most of the large proportion of high-ranking officers in the U.S. Army who were of southern origin resigned to accept Confederate commands, Southerners confidently anticipated that their armies would be better led. Finally, Southerners assumed that if external help was needed, England and France would come to their aid because those nations depended on southern cotton.

Both sides based their strategies on their advantages. The choice before President Davis, who assumed personal direction of the Confederate military effort, was whether to stay on the defensive or seek a sudden and dramatic victory by invading the North. He chose to wage an essentially defensive war in the hope that the North would soon tire of the blood and sacrifice and allow the Confederacy to go its own way.

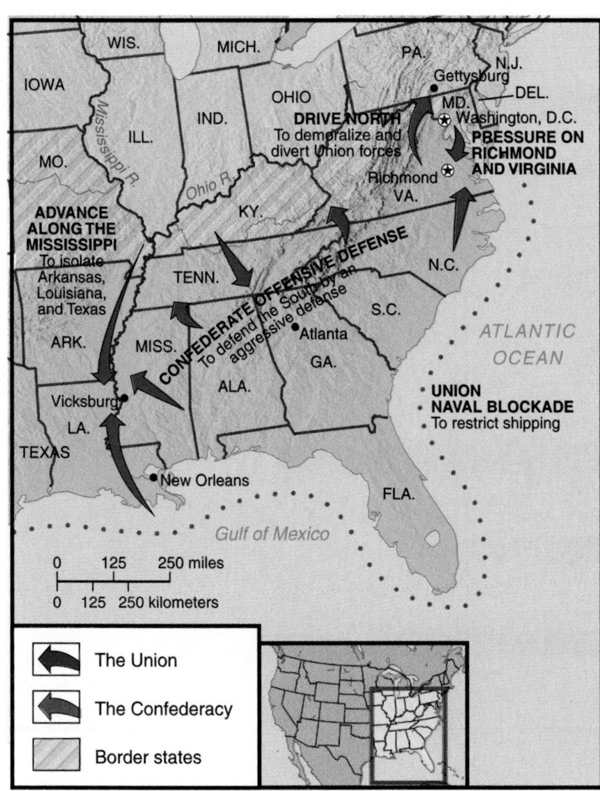

OVERVIEW OF CIVIL WAR STRATEGY *Confederate military leaders were convinced that the South could not be defended unless they took the initiative to determine where critical battles would be fought.* ❖

Northern military planners had greater difficulty in working out a basic strategy, and it took a great deal of trial and error before there was a clear sense of what had to be done. Some optimists believed that the war could be won quickly and easily by sending an army to capture the Confederate capital of Richmond, scarcely 100 miles from Washington. The early battles in Virginia ended the casual optimism. Other Northerners favored a plan called the **anaconda policy.** Like a great boa constrictor, the North would squeeze the South into submission by blockading the southern coasts, seizing control of the Mississippi, and cutting off supplies of food and other essential commodities. This plan pointed to the West as the main focus of military operations.

anaconda policy A key point in the Union's war strategy was encircling the South as an anaconda squeezes its prey. This plan entailed a naval blockade and the capture of the Mississippi River corridor.

Eventually, Lincoln decided on a two-front war. He would keep the pressure on Virginia while at the same time authorizing an advance down the Mississippi Valley. He also attached great importance to the coastal blockade and expected naval operations to seize the ports through which goods entered and left the Confederacy. His basic plan of applying pressure and probing for weaknesses at several points simultaneously was a good one because it took maximum advantage of the northern superiority in manpower and material. But it required better military leadership than the North possessed at the beginning of the war and took a painfully long time to put into effect.

Mobilizing the Home Fronts

The North and the South faced similar problems in trying to create the vast support systems needed by armies in the field. At the beginning of the conflict, both sides had more volunteers than could be armed and outfitted. But as hopes for a short and easy war faded, the pool of volunteers began to dry up. To resolve the problem, the Confederacy passed a conscription law in April 1862, and the Union edged toward a draft in July when Congress gave Lincoln the right to assign manpower quotas to each state and resort to conscription if they were not met.

RESOURCES OF THE UNION AND THE CONFEDERACY, 1861

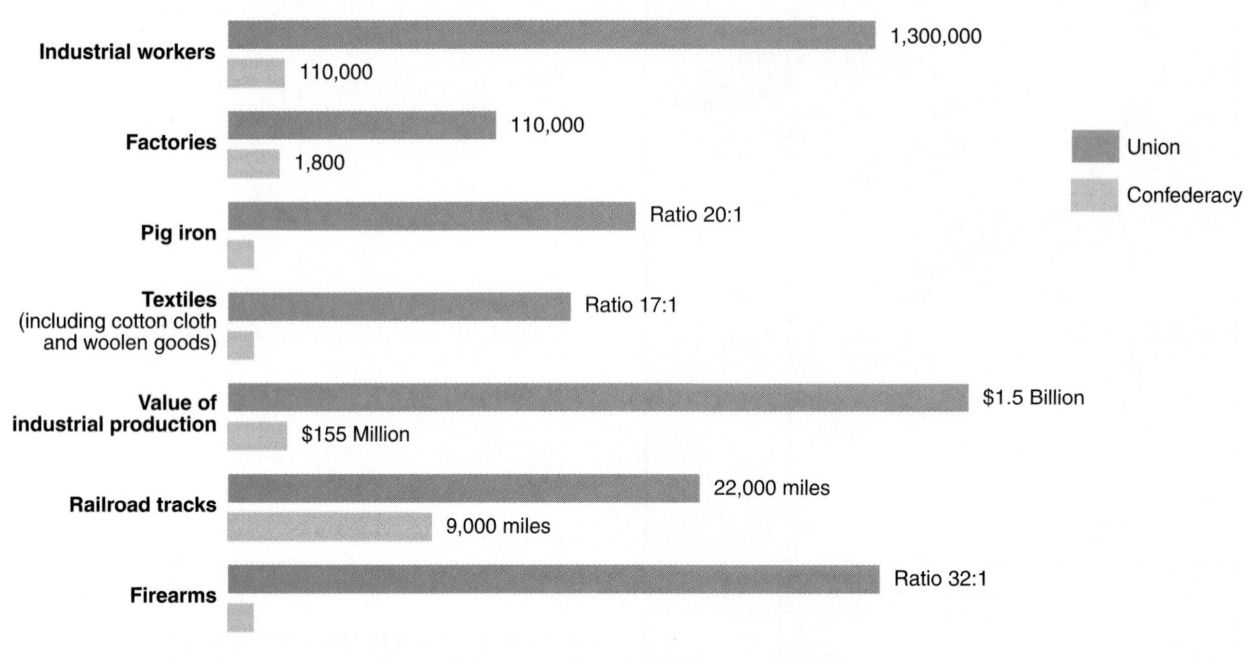

To produce the materials of war, both governments relied mainly on private industry. In the North, especially, the system of contracting with private firms and individuals to support the army often resulted in corruption, inefficiency, and shoddy goods. But the North's economy was strong at the core, and by 1863, its factories and farms were producing more than enough to provision the troops without significantly lowering the living standards of the civilian population.

The southern economy was much less adaptable to the needs of total war. Dependent on the outside world for most of its manufactured goods before the war, the Union blockade forced the southern government to sponsor a crash program to produce its own war materials and to encourage private enterprise. Astonishingly, the Confederate Ordnance Bureau succeeded in producing or procuring sufficient armaments to keep southern armies well supplied throughout the conflict.

Southern agriculture, however, failed to meet the challenge. Planters were reluctant to switch from cotton to foodstuffs, and the South's internal transportation system was inadequate. Its limited rail network was designed to link plantation regions to port cities rather than connect food-producing areas with centers of population. And when northern forces penetrated parts of the South, they created new gaps in the system. To supply the troops, the Confederate commissary resorted to impressment of agricultural produce, a policy so fiercely resisted by farmers and local politicians that it eventually had to be abandoned. By 1863, civilians in urban areas were rioting to protest food shortages.

Another challenge faced by both sides was how to finance an enormously costly struggle. Neither side was willing to resort to the heavy taxation that was needed to maintain fiscal integrity. Americans, it seems, were more willing to die for their government than to pay for it. Besides floating loans and selling bonds, both treasuries deliberately inflated the currency by printing large quantities of paper money that could not be redeemed in gold and silver. Runaway inflation was the inevitable result. But the problem was much less severe in the North because of the overall strength of its economy and the willingness of its citizens to buy bonds and pay taxes.

The Confederacy was hampered from the outset by a severe shortage of readily disposable wealth that could be tapped for public purposes. Land and cotton could not easily be turned into rifles and cannons, and the southern treasury had to accept payments "in kind." As a result, Confederate "assets" eventually consisted mainly of bales of cotton that were unexportable because of the blockade. As the Confederate government fell deeper and deeper into debt and printed more and more paper money, its rate of inflation soared out of sight.

❖ A Look at the Past ❖

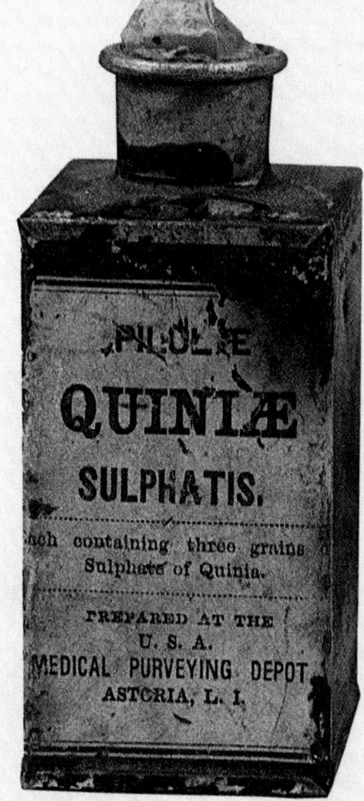

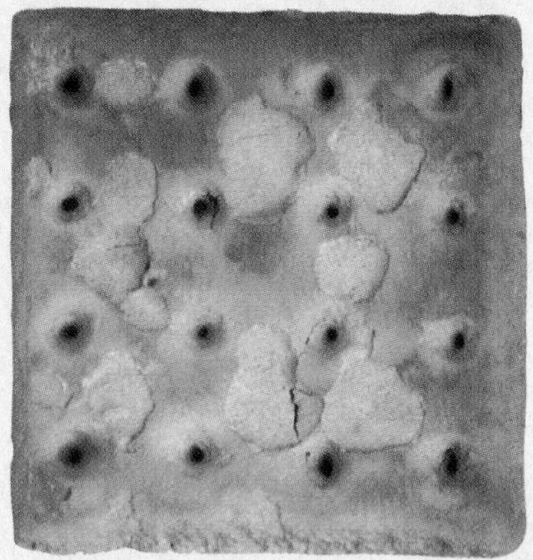

Civil War Rations

Civil War soldiers depended on hardtack, a saltless hard biscuit, as a food staple. Quinine, a remedy for malaria, also represented an essential supply for soldiers. Together, these items testify to the hardships soldiers endured. If these were essential supplies, how common do you suppose were disease, hunger, and malnutrition?

Political Leadership: Northern Success and Southern Failure

Total war also forced political adjustment, and both the Union and the Confederacy had to face the question of how much democracy and individual freedom could be permitted when military success required an unprecedented exercise of governmental authority. Since both constitutions made the president commander in chief of the army and navy, Lincoln and Davis took actions that would have been regarded as arbitrary or even tyrannical in peacetime.

Lincoln was especially bold in assuming new executive powers. After the fighting started at Fort Sumter, he expanded the regular army and advanced public money to private individuals without authorization by Congress. On April 27, 1861, he declared martial law, which enabled the military to arrest and detain without trial civilians suspected of aiding the enemy, and he suspended the writ of habeas corpus in the area between Philadelphia and Washington. This latter action was deemed necessary because of mob attacks on Union troops passing through Baltimore. In September 1862, Lincoln extended this authority to all parts of the United States where "disloyal" elements were active. He argued that preservation of the Union justified such actions. In fact, most of the thousands of civilians arrested by military authorities were suspected deserters and draft dodgers, refugees, smugglers, or people who were simply found wandering in areas under military control.

For the most part, however, the Lincoln administration showed restraint and tolerated a broad spectrum of political dissent. "Politics as usual" persisted to a surprising degree. Anti-administration newspapers were allowed to criticize the president and his party almost at will, and opposition to Lincoln's programs was freely voiced in Congress.

Jefferson Davis proved a less effective war leader than Lincoln. He defined his powers as commander in chief narrowly and literally, which meant that he assumed personal direction of the armed forces but left policymaking for the mobilization and control of the civilian population primarily to the Confederate Congress. Unfortunately, Davis overestimated his capacities as a strategist and lacked the tact to handle field commanders who were as proud and testy as he was.

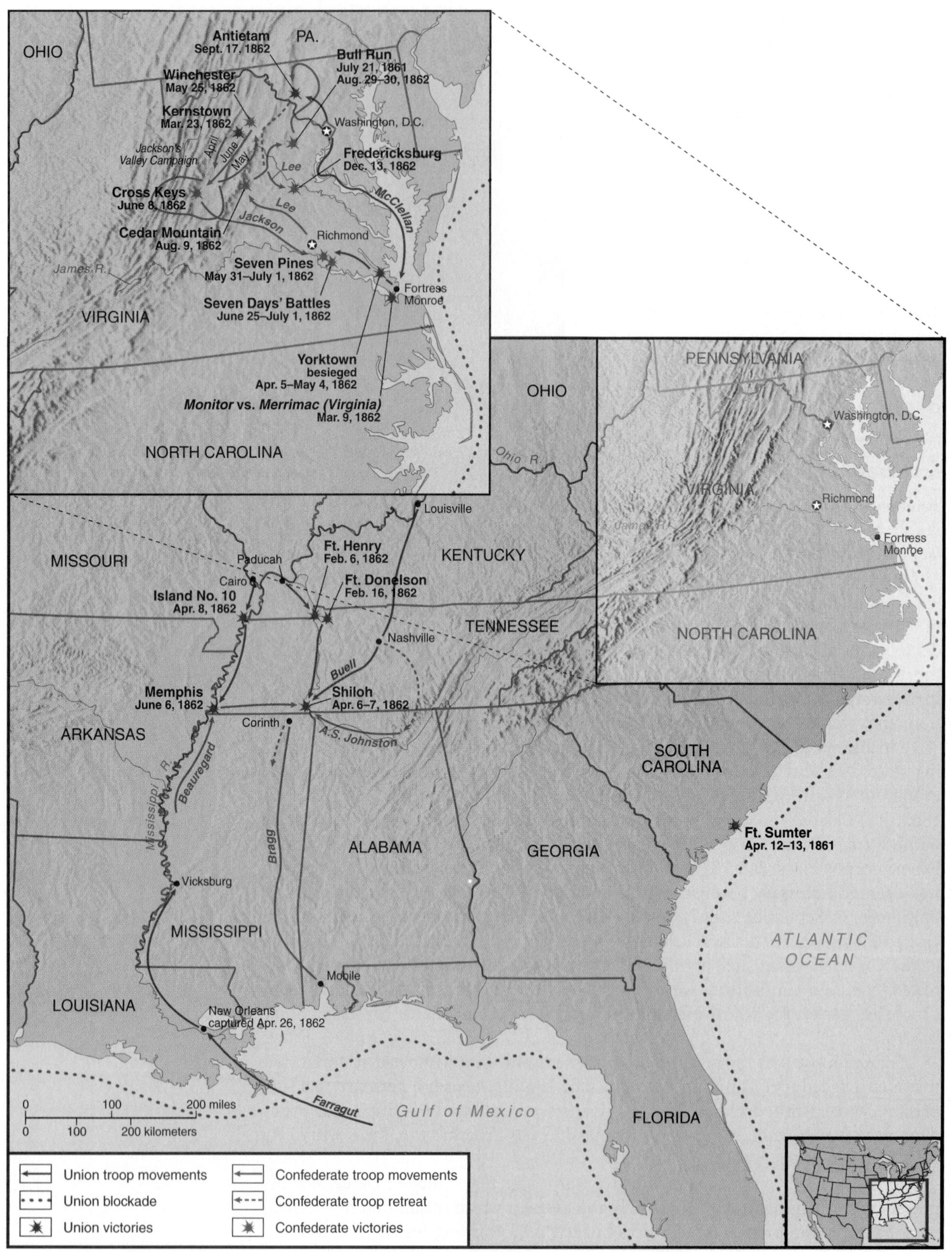

CIVIL WAR, 1861–1862 *Defeats on the battlefield forced a change in the Union's initial military campaign of capturing Richmond, the Confederate capital. The Union's targets in the West were the key cities of Vicksburg and New Orleans.*

Davis's greatest failing, however, was his lack of initiative and leadership in dealing with the problems of the home front. He devoted little attention to a deteriorating economic situation that caused great hardship and sapped Confederate morale. In addition, although the South had a much more serious problem of internal division and disloyalty than the North, he chose to be extremely cautious in his use of martial law.

As the war dragged on, Davis's political and popular support eroded. He was opposed and obstructed by state governors who resisted conscription and other Confederate policies that violated the tradition of states' rights. The Confederate Congress and southern newspapers similarly criticized Davis's policies. His authority was further undermined because he did not even have an organized party behind him. As a result, it was difficult to mobilize the support required for hard decisions and controversial policies.

Early Campaigns and Battles

The war's first major battle was a disaster for northern arms. Against his better judgment, General Winfield Scott responded to the "On to Richmond" clamor and ordered poorly trained Union troops under General Irvin McDowell to advance against the Confederate forces gathered at Manassas Junction, Virginia. They attacked the enemy position near Bull Run Creek on July 21. Confederate forces held the line against the northern assault until reinforcements arrived and then counterattacked. The routed northern forces quickly broke ranks and fled toward Washington and safety. The humiliating defeat at Bull Run led to a shake-up of the northern high command. The man of the hour was George McClellan, who first replaced McDowell and then became general in chief when Scott was eased into retirement. A cautious disciplinarian, McClellan spent the fall and winter drilling his troops and whipping them into shape, much to the anxiety of a more and more impatient Lincoln.

Before McClellan moved, Union forces in the West won some important victories. In February 1862, a joint military-naval operation, commanded by General Ulysses S. Grant, captured Fort Henry on the Tennessee River and Fort Donelson on the Cumberland. The Confederate Army was forced to withdraw from Kentucky and middle Tennessee, amassing its western forces at Corinth, Mississippi. The Union Army slowly followed, but on April 6, the South launched a surprise attack. In the battle of Shiloh, one of the bloodiest of the war, only the timely arrival of reinforcements prevented the annihilation of Union troops backed up against the Tennessee River. After a second day of fierce fighting, the Confederates retreated to Corinth, leaving the enemy forces battered and exhausted.

Although the military effort to seize control of the Mississippi Valley was temporarily halted at Shiloh, the Union Navy soon contributed dramatically to the pursuit of that objective. On April 26, a fleet coming up from the Gulf captured the port of New Orleans. Besides securing the mouth of the Mississippi, the occupation of New Orleans climaxed a series of naval and amphibious operations around the edges of the Confederacy that provided strategically located bases for the northern blockade. The last serious challenge to the North's naval supremacy ended on March 9, 1862, when the Confederate ironclad vessel *Virginia* (originally the USS *Merrimack*) was driven back by the *Monitor,* an armored and turreted Union gunship.

Successes around the edges of the Confederacy did not relieve northern frustration at the inactivity or failure of Union forces on the eastern front. Finally, at Lincoln's insistence, McClellan started toward Richmond. He advanced his forces by water to the peninsula southeast of the Confederate capital and began his march toward Richmond in early April 1862. By late May, his forces had pushed to within

20 miles of the city. There he stopped, awaiting the additional troops that he expected Lincoln to send.

The reinforcements were not forthcoming because the president believed that they were needed to defend Washington. While McClellan was inching his way up the peninsula, a relatively small southern force under General Thomas J. "Stonewall" Jackson was on the rampage in the Shenandoah Valley. When it appeared by late May that Jackson might be poised to march east and attack the Union capital, Lincoln decided to withhold troops from McClellan.

If McClellan had moved more boldly and decisively, he probably could have captured Richmond with the forces he had. But a combination of faulty intelligence reports and his own natural caution led him to falter in the face of what he wrongly believed to be superior numbers. At the end of May, the Confederates under Joseph E. Johnston took the offensive when they discovered that McClellan's army was divided on either side of the Chickahominy River. In the battle of Seven Pines, McClellan was barely able to withstand the assault. During the battle, General Johnston was severely wounded; succeeding him in command of the Confederate Army of Northern Virginia was native Virginian and West Point graduate Robert E. Lee.

Toward the end of June, Lee began an all-out effort to expel McClellan from the outskirts of Richmond. In a series of battles that lasted seven days, the two armies clawed at each other indecisively. Nevertheless, McClellan decided to retreat down the peninsula to a more secure base. This backward step convinced Lincoln that the peninsula campaign was an exercise in futility.

On July 11, Lincoln appointed General Henry W. Halleck general in chief and through Halleck ordered McClellan to withdraw his army from the peninsula to join a force under General John Pope that was preparing to move on Richmond by an overland route. Before the ever-cautious McClellan could reach Pope, however, the Confederates attacked the overland army near Bull Run. In a battle superbly commanded by Lee, Pope was forced to retreat to Washington, where he was stripped of his command.

Lee proceeded to lead his exuberant troops on an invasion of Maryland, in the hope of isolating Washington from the rest of the North. McClellan caught up with him at Antietam, near Sharpsburg, and the bloodiest one-day battle of the war ensued. The result was a draw, but Lee was forced to fall back south of the Potomac. McClellan was slow in pursuit, and Lincoln blamed him for letting the enemy escape.

Convinced that McClellan was fatally infected with "the slows," Lincoln once again sought a more aggressive general and put Ambrose E. Burnside in command of the Army of the Potomac. Aggressive but rather dense, Burnside's limitations were disastrously revealed at the battle of Fredericksburg, Virginia, on December 13, 1862, when he launched a deadly charge against a Confederate uphill position.

After Antietam, Lincoln visited McClellan's headquarters to urge the general to take action. McClellan is on the left facing the president. ❖

The range and accuracy of small arms fire made such a charge utter folly. Thus ended a year of bitter failure for the North on the eastern front.

The Diplomatic Struggle

The critical period of Civil War diplomacy was 1861–1862, when the South was making every effort to induce major foreign powers to recognize its independence and break the Union blockade. The hope that England and France could be persuaded to involve themselves in the war on the Confederate side stemmed from the fact that these nations depended on the South for three-quarters of their cotton supply.

The Confederate commissioners sent to England and France in May 1861 succeeded in gaining recognition of southern "belligerency," which meant that the new government could claim some of the international rights of a nation at war, such as purchasing and outfitting privateers in neutral ports. As a result, Confederate raiders, built and armed in British shipyards, devastated northern shipping to such an extent that insurance costs eventually forced most of the American merchant marines off the high seas for the duration of the war.

In the fall of 1861, the Confederate government dispatched James M. Mason and John Slidell to be its permanent envoys to England and France, respectively, and instructed them to push for full recognition of the Confederacy. They took passage on the British steamer *Trent,* which was stopped and boarded in international waters by a United States warship. Mason and Slidell were taken into custody by the Union captain, causing a diplomatic crisis that nearly led to war between England and the United States. After several weeks of international tension, Lincoln and Secretary of State William H. Seward made the prudent decision to allow the Confederates to proceed to their destinations.

The envoys might as well have stayed home; they failed in their mission to obtain full recognition of the Confederacy from either England or France. The anticipated cotton shortage was slow to develop, for the bumper crop of 1860 had created a large surplus in British and French warehouses. For a time in the fall of 1862, the French ruler, Napoleon III, toyed with the idea of recognition, but he refused to act without British support. British leaders feared that recognition would lead to a war with the United States; the U.S. minister to Great Britain, Charles Francis Adams, knew well how to play on those fears. Only if the South won decisively on the battlefield would Britain be willing to risk the dangers of recognition and intervention.

The cotton famine finally hit in late 1862, causing massive unemployment in the British textile industry. But contrary to southern hopes, public opinion did not compel the government to abandon its neutrality and use force to break the Union blockade. Influential interest groups, which actually benefited from the famine, provided the crucial support for continuing a policy of nonintervention. Among these groups were owners of large cotton mills who had made bonanza profits on their existing stocks and were happy to see weaker competitors go under while they awaited new sources of supply. By early 1863, cotton from Egypt and India put the industry back on the track toward full production. Other obvious beneficiaries of nonintervention were manufacturers of wool and linen textiles, munitions makers who supplied both sides, and shipping interests that profited from the decline of American competition on the world's sea lanes. Since the British economy as a whole gained more than it lost from neutrality, it is not surprising that there was little effective pressure for a change in policy.

By early 1863, when it was clear that "King Cotton diplomacy" had failed, the Confederacy broke off formal relations with Great Britain. For the European powers, the advantages of getting involved in the conflict were not worth the risk of a war with the United States. Independence for the South would have to be won on the battlefield.

Fight to the Finish

The last two and one-half years of the struggle saw the implementation of more radical war measures. The most dramatic and important of these was the North's effort to follow through on Lincoln's decision to free the slaves and bring the black population into the war on the Union side. The tide of battle turned in the summer of 1863, but the South continued to resist valiantly for two more years until finally overcome by the sheer weight of the North's advantages in manpower and resources.

The Coming of Emancipation

At the beginning of the war, when the North still hoped for a quick and easy victory, only dedicated abolitionists favored turning the struggle for the Union into a crusade against slavery. But as it became clear how difficult it was going to be to suppress the "rebels," congressional and public sentiment developed for striking a fatal blow at the South's economic and social system by pressing for the freedom of its slaves. By this time, slaves were deserting their plantations in areas where the Union forces were close enough to offer a haven. In this way, they put pressure on the government to determine their status and, in effect, offered themselves as a source of manpower to the Union on the condition that they be made free.

Although Lincoln favored freedom for blacks as an ultimate goal, he was reluctant to commit his administration to a policy of immediate emancipation. In the fall of 1861 and again in the spring of 1862, he disallowed the orders of field commanders who sought to free slaves in areas occupied by their forces, thus angering the strongly antislavery Republicans known as "Radicals." Lincoln's caution stemmed from an effort to avoid alienating Unionist elements in the border slave states and from his own preference for a gradual, compensated form of emancipation.

Lincoln was also aware that one of the major obstacles to any program leading to emancipation was the strong racial prejudice of most whites in the North and the South. Pessimistic about the prospects of equality for blacks in the United States, Lincoln coupled his moderate proposals with a plea for government subsidies to support the voluntary "colonization" of free blacks outside the United States, and he actively sought places that would accept them.

But the slaveholding states that remained loyal to the Union refused to endorse Lincoln's gradual plan, and the failure of Union arms in the spring and summer of 1862 increased the public clamor for striking directly at the South's peculiar institution. Responding to political pressure, on September 22, 1862, Lincoln issued his preliminary **Emancipation Proclamation.** Had he failed to act, he would have split the Republican party, most of whose members favored emancipation. The proclamation gave the Confederate states one hundred days to give up the struggle without losing their slaves.

Emancipation Proclamation On January 1, 1863, President Lincoln proclaimed that the slaves of the Confederacy were free. Since the South had not yet been defeated, the proclamation did not immediately free anyone, but it made emancipation an explicit war aim of the North.

When there was no response from the South and no enthusiasm in Congress for Lincoln's gradual, compensated plan, the president on January 1, 1863, declared that all slaves in those areas under Confederate control "shall be . . . thenceforward, and forever free." He justified the final proclamation as an act of "military necessity" sanctioned by the war powers of the president and authorized the enlistment of freed slaves in the Union army. The language and tone of the document had "all the grandeur of a bill of lading," and made it clear that blacks were being freed for reasons of state and not out of humanitarian conviction.

Despite its uninspiring origin and limited application—it did not extend to loyal slave states or occupied areas—the proclamation did enunciate the abolition of slavery as a war aim. It also accelerated the breakdown of slavery as a labor system. As word spread among the slaves that emancipation was now official policy, larger numbers of them were inspired to run off and seek the protection of approaching northern armies. Approximately one-quarter of the slave population gained freedom during the war under the terms of the Emancipation Proclamation and thus deprived the South of an important part of its agricultural workforce.

African Americans and the War

Almost 200,000 African Americans, most of them newly freed slaves, eventually served in the Union armed forces and made a vital contribution to the North's victory. Although they were enrolled in segregated units under white officers, initially paid less than their white counterparts, and used disproportionately for garrison duty or heavy labor behind the lines, "blacks in blue" fought heroically in several major battles during the last two years of the war.

Those freed during the war who did not serve in the military were often conscripted to serve as contract wage laborers on cotton plantations owned or leased by "loyal" white planters within the occupied areas of the Deep South. Abolitionists protested that the coercion used by military authorities to get blacks back into the cotton fields amounted to slavery in a new form, but those in power argued that the necessities of war and the northern economy required such "temporary" arrangements. To some extent, regimentation of the freedmen within the South was a way of assuring racially prejudiced Northerners that emancipation would not result in an influx of black refugees to their region of the country.

The heroic performance of African American troops and the easing of northern anxieties about massive black migration led to a deepening commitment to emancipation as a permanent and comprehensive policy. Realizing that his proclamation had a shaky constitutional foundation, Lincoln pressed for an amendment outlawing involuntary servitude. After supporting its inclusion as a central plank in the Republican platform of 1864, Lincoln used all his influence to win congressional approval for the new Thirteenth Amendment. The cause of freedom for blacks and the cause of the Union had at last become one and the same. Lincoln, despite his earlier hesitations and misgivings, had earned the right to go down in history as "the great emancipator."

The Tide Turns

By early 1863, the Confederate economy was in shambles, and its diplomacy had collapsed. The social order of the South was also showing signs of severe strain. Masters were losing control of their slaves, and nonslaveholding whites were becoming disillusioned with the hardships of a war that some of them described as a "rich man's war and a poor man's fight." Yet the North was slow to capitalize on the South's internal weaknesses; it had its own serious morale problems. The long series of defeats on the eastern front had engendered war weariness, and the new policies that "military necessity" forced the government to adopt encountered fierce opposition.

Although popular with Republicans, emancipation was viewed by most Democrats as a betrayal of northern war aims. Racism was a main ingredient in their opposition to freeing blacks. Especially in the Midwest, Democrats used the backlash against the proclamation to win political support. The Enrollment Act of March 1863, which provided for outright conscription, provoked a violent response from those unwilling to fight for the rights of blacks and too poor to buy exemption from the draft. A series of antidraft riots culminated in the bloodiest domestic disorder in American history, the New York riot of July 1863. A New York mob, composed mainly of Irish American laborers, burned the draft offices, the homes of leading Republicans, and an orphanage for black children. At least 120 people died before federal troops restored order. Besides racial prejudice, the draft riots also reflected working-class anger at the wartime privileges and prosperity of the middle and upper classes.

This 1890 lithograph by Kurz and Allison commemorates the 54th Massachusetts Colored Regiment charging Fort Wagner, South Carolina, in July 1863. The 54th was the first African American unit recruited during the war. Charles and Lewis Douglass, sons of Frederick Douglass, served with this regiment. ❖

Copperheads Northern Democrats suspected of being indifferent or hostile to the Union cause in the Civil War.

To fight dissension and "disloyalty," the government used its martial law authority to arrest the alleged ringleaders. Patriotic private organizations also issued a barrage of propaganda aimed at what they believed was a vast secret conspiracy to undermine the northern war effort. Historians disagree about the real extent of covert and illegal antiwar activity, but militant advocates of "peace at any price"—popularly known as **Copperheads**—were active in some areas, especially among the immigrant working classes of large cities and in southern Ohio, Indiana, and Illinois.

The only effective way to overcome the disillusionment that fed the peace movement was to start winning battles and thus convince the northern public that victory was assured. But before this could happen, the North suffered one more humiliating defeat on the eastern front. In early May 1863, Union forces under General Joseph Hooker were routed at Chancellorsville, Virginia, by a much smaller Confederate army masterfully led by Robert E. Lee.

In the West, however, a major Union triumph was taking shape. For more than a year, General Grant had been trying to put his forces in position to capture Vicksburg, Mississippi, the almost inaccessible Confederate bastion that kept the North from controlling the Mississippi River. Finally, in late March 1863, he crossed the river north of the city and moved his forces to a point south of it, where he joined up with naval forces that had run the Confederate batteries mounted on Vicksburg's high bluffs. In one of the boldest campaigns of the war, Grant crossed the river, deliberately cutting himself off from his sources of supply, and marched into the interior of Mississippi. Living off the land and out of communication with an anxious and perplexed Lincoln, his troops won a series of victories and advanced on Vicksburg from the east. After unsuccessfully assaulting the city's defenses, Grant settled down for a siege on May 22.

In an effort to turn the tide of the war, President Davis approved Lee's plan for an all-out invasion of the Northeast. Although this plan provided no hope for relieving Vicksburg, it might lead to a dramatic victory that would more than compensate for the probable loss of the Mississippi stronghold. Lee's army crossed the Potomac in June and kept going until it reached Gettysburg, Pennsylvania. There Lee confronted a Union army that had taken up strong defensive positions on Cemetery Ridge and Culp's Hill.

On July 2, a series of Confederate attacks failed to dislodge General George Meade's troops from the high ground they occupied. The following day, Lee faced the choice of retreating to protect his lines of communication or launching a final, desperate assault. With more boldness than wisdom, he chose to make a direct attack on the strongest part of the Union line. The resulting charge on Cemetery Ridge was disastrous; advancing Confederate soldiers dropped like flies under the barrage of Union artillery and rifle fire.

Retreat was now inevitable, and Lee withdrew his battered troops to the Potomac, only to find that the river was at flood stage and could not be crossed for several days. For some reason, Meade failed to follow up his victory with a vigorous pursuit, and Lee was allowed to escape a trap that could have resulted in his annihilation. Vicksburg fell to Grant on July 4, the same day that Lee began his withdrawal, and Northerners rejoiced at the twin Independence Day victories. The Union had secured control of the Mississippi and had at last won a major battle in the East. But Lincoln's joy turned to frustration when he learned that his generals had missed the chance to capture Lee's army and bring a quick end to the war.

Last Stages of the Conflict

Later in 1863, the North finally gained control of the middle South, an area where indecisive fighting had been going on since the beginning of the conflict. The main Union target was Chattanooga, "gateway to the Southeast." In September, Union forces maneuvered the Confederates out of the city but were in turn eventually surrounded and besieged there by southern forces. After Grant arrived from Vicksburg to take command, the encirclement was broken by daring assaults on the Confederate positions on Lookout Mountain and Missionary Ridge. As a result of its success in the battle of Chattanooga, the North was poised for an invasion of Georgia.

Grant's victories in the West earned him promotion to general in chief of all the Union armies. After assuming that position in March 1864, he ordered a multipronged offensive to finish off the Confederacy. The main movements were a march on Richmond under his personal command and a thrust by the western armies, now led by General William T. Sherman, in the direction of Atlanta and the heart of Georgia.

In May and early June, Grant and Lee fought a series of bloody battles in northern Virginia that tended to follow a set pattern. Lee would take up an entrenched position in the path of the invading force, and Grant would attack it, sustaining heavy losses but also inflicting casualties that the shrinking Confederate Army could ill afford. When his direct assault had failed, Grant would move to his left, hoping in vain to maneuver Lee into a less defensible position. After losing about sixty thousand men, Grant decided to change his tactics and moved his army to the south of Richmond. There he drew up before Petersburg, a rail center that linked Richmond to the rest of the Confederacy; after failing to take it by assault, he settled down for a siege.

The siege of Petersburg was a long, drawn-out affair, and the resulting stalemate caused northern morale to plummet during the summer of 1864. Lincoln was facing reelection, and his failure to end the war dimmed his prospects. Although nominated with ease in June, Lincoln confronted growing opposition within his

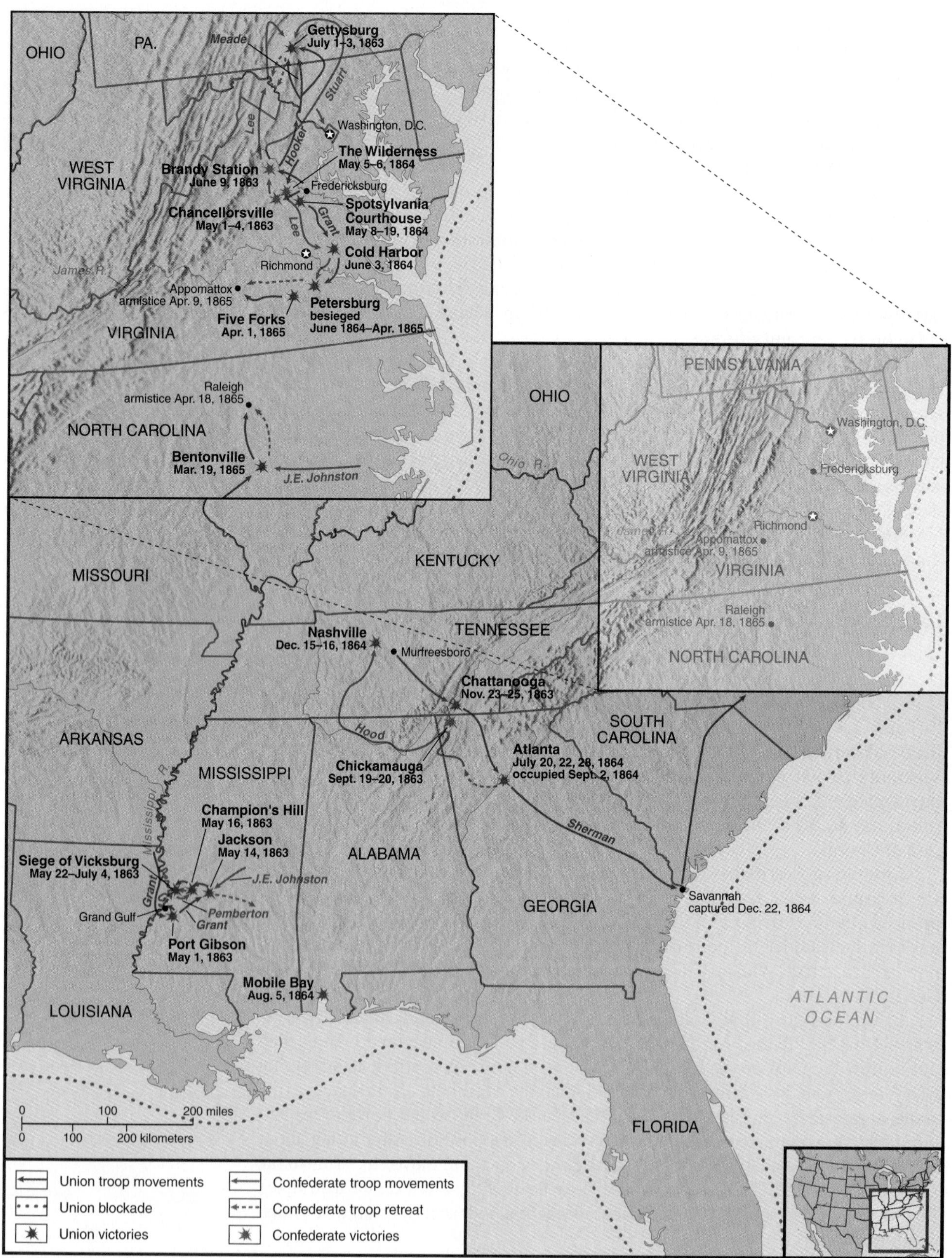

CIVIL WAR, 1863–1865 *In the western theater of the war, Grant's victories at Port Gibson, Jackson, and Champion's Hill cleared the way for his siege of Vicksburg. In the east, after the hard-won Union victory at Gettysburg, the South never again invaded the north. In 1864 and 1865 Union armies gradually closed in on Lee's confederate forces in Virginia. Leaving Atlanta in flames, Sherman marched to the Georgia coast, took Savannah, then moved his troops north through the Carolinas. Grant's army, though suffering enormous losses, moved on toward Richmond, marching into the Confederate capital on April 3, 1865, and forcing surrender.* ❖

own party, especially from Radicals who disagreed with his apparently lenient approach to the future restoration of seceded states to the Union.

The Democrats seemed in a good position to capitalize on Republican divisions and make a strong bid for the White House. Their platform appealed to war weariness by calling for a cease-fire followed by negotiations to reestablish the Union. The party's nominee, General George McClellan, announced that he would not be bound by the peace plank and would pursue the war. But he promised to end the conflict soon because he would not insist on emancipation as a condition for reconstruction. By late summer, Lincoln believed he would probably be defeated.

Northern military successes changed the political outlook. Sherman's invasion of Georgia went well. On September 2, Atlanta fell, and northern forces occupied the hub of the Deep South. The news unified the Republican party behind Lincoln. The election in November was almost an anticlimax; Lincoln won 212 of a possible 233 electoral votes and 55 percent of the popular vote. The Republican cause of "liberty and Union" was secure.

The concluding military operations revealed the futility of further southern resistance. Sherman marched almost unopposed through Georgia to the sea, destroying nearly everything of possible military or economic value in a corridor 300 miles long and 60 miles wide. The Confederate army that had opposed him at Atlanta moved northward into Tennessee, where it was defeated and almost destroyed by Union forces at Nashville in mid-December. Sherman captured Savannah on December 22. He then turned north and marched through the Carolinas, intending to join up with Grant at Petersburg.

While Sherman was bringing the war to the Carolinas, Grant finally ended the stalemate at Petersburg. When Lee's starving and exhausted army tried to break through the Union lines, Grant renewed his attack and forced the Confederates to abandon Petersburg and Richmond on April 2, 1865. A week later, Lee recognized that future fighting was pointless and surrendered his army at Appomattox Courthouse on April 9.

But the joy of the victorious North turned to sorrow and anger when actor John Wilkes Booth assassinated Abraham Lincoln at Ford's Theater in Washington on April 14. Although Booth had a few accomplices, popular theories that the assassination was the result of a vast conspiracy involving Confederate leaders or, according to another version, Radical Republicans, have never been substantiated and are extremely implausible. The man who had spoken at Gettysburg of the need to sacrifice for the Union cause had himself given "the last full measure of devotion." Four days after Lincoln's death, the only remaining Confederate force of any significance, the troops under Joseph E. Johnston, who had been opposing Sherman in North Carolina, laid down their arms. The Union was saved.

Effects of the War

The nation that emerged from four years of total war was not the same America that had split apart in 1861. More than 618,000 young men were in their graves, and the widows and sweethearts they left behind temporarily increased the proportion of unmarried women in the population. Some members of this generation of involuntary spinsters sought new opportunities for making a living or serving the community that went beyond the purely domestic roles previously prescribed for women. Some of the northern women who were prominent in wartime service organizations became leaders of postwar philanthropic and reform movements.

At enormous human and economic cost, the nation had emancipated four million African Americans from slavery, but it had not yet resolved that they should be equal citizens. At the time of Lincoln's assassination, most northern states still denied blacks equality under the law and the right to vote. Whether the North would

During the war, many women replaced skilled male workers in the manufacturing labor force. These women are filling cartridges in the U.S. Arsenal at Watertown, New York. ❖

extend more rights to southern freedmen than it had granted to "free Negroes" was an open question.

The impact of the war on white working people was also unclear. Those in the industrializing parts of the North had suffered and lost ground economically because prices had risen much faster than wages during the conflict. But Republican rhetoric stressing "equal opportunity" and the "dignity of labor" raised hopes that the crusade against slavery could be broadened into a movement to improve the lot of working people in general. Foreign-born workers had an additional reason to be optimistic: the fact that so many immigrants had fought and died for the Union cause had—for the moment—weakened nativist sentiment and encouraged ethnic tolerance.

What the war definitely decided was that the federal government was supreme over the states and had broad constitutional authority to act on matters affecting the "general welfare." The southern principle of state sovereignty and strict construction died at Appomattox; the United States was on its way to becoming a true nation-state with an effective central government. Although the states retained many powers and the Constitution placed limits on what the national government could do, the war ended all question about where ultimate authority rested.

A broadened definition of federal powers had its greatest impact in the realm of economic policy. During the war, Republican-dominated Congresses passed a rash of legislation designed to give stimulus and direction to the nation's economic development. Taking advantage of the absence of southern opposition, Republicans rejected the pre–Civil War tradition of laissez-faire and enacted a Whiggish program of active support for business and agriculture. In 1862, Congress passed a high protective tariff, approved a homestead act intended to encourage settlement of the West by providing free land to settlers, granted huge tracts of public land to railroad companies to support the building of a transcontinental railroad, and gave the states land for the establishment of agricultural colleges. The following year,

CASUALTIES OF WAR

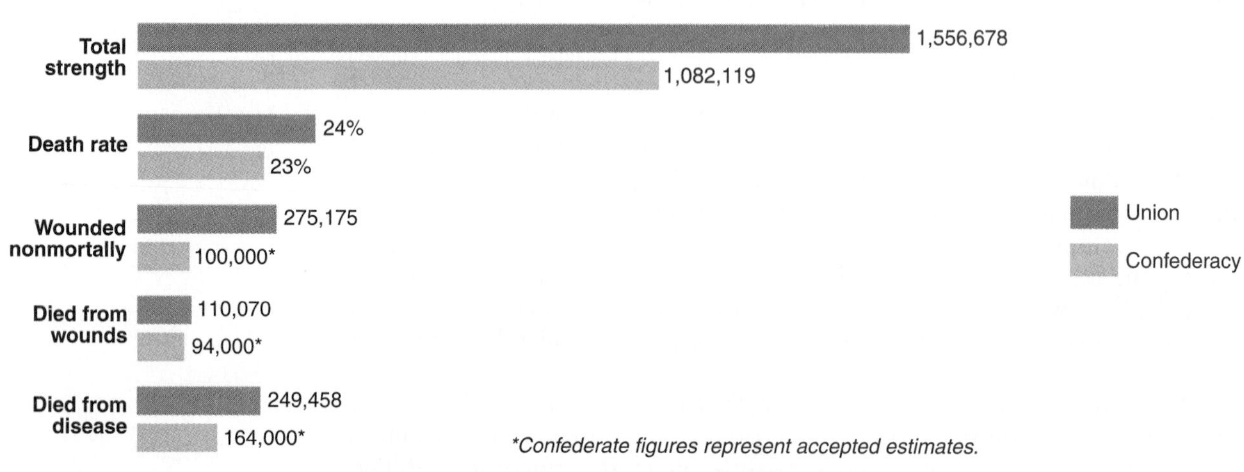

CHRONOLOGY	
1860	South Carolina secedes from the Union (December)
1861	Rest of Deep South secedes: Confederacy is founded (January–February) ❖ Fort Sumter is fired on and surrenders to Confederate forces (April) ❖ Upper South secedes (April–May) ❖ South wins the first battle of Bull Run (July)
1862	Grant captures Forts Henry and Donelson (February) ❖ Farragut captures New Orleans for the Union (April) ❖ McClellan leads an unsuccessful campaign on the peninsula southeast of Richmond (March–July) ❖ South wins the second battle of Bull Run (August) ❖ McClellan stops Lee at Antietam (September) ❖ Lincoln issues a preliminary Emancipation Proclamation (September) ❖ Lee defeats a Union army at Fredericksburg (December)
1863	Lincoln issues the final Emancipation Proclamation (January) ❖ Lee is victorious at Chancellorsville (May) ❖ North gains major victories at Gettysburg and Vicksburg (July) ❖ Grant defeats Confederate forces at Chattanooga (November)
1864	Grant and Lee battle in northern Virginia (May–June) ❖ Atlanta falls to Sherman (September) ❖ Lincoln is reelected president, defeating McClellan (November) ❖ Sherman marches through Georgia (November–December)
1865	Congress passes Thirteenth Amendment, abolishing slavery (January) ❖ Grant captures Petersburg and Richmond ❖ Lee surrenders at Appomattox (April) ❖ Lincoln is assassinated by John Wilkes Booth (April) ❖ Remaining Confederate forces surrender (April–May)

Congress set up a national banking system. The notes that the national banks issued became the country's first standardized and reliable circulating currency.

The wartime achievements added up to a decisive shift in the relationship between the federal government and private enterprise. The Republicans took a limited government that did little more than seek to protect the marketplace from the threat of monopoly and changed it into an activist state that promoted and subsidized the efforts of the economically industrious and ambitious.

Conclusion: An Organizational Revolution

The most pervasive effect of the war on northern society was to encourage an "organizational revolution." Aided by government policies, venturesome businessmen took advantage of the new national market created by military procurement to build larger firms that could operate across state lines; some of the huge corporate enterprises of the postwar era began to take shape. Philanthropists also developed more effective national associations. Both the men who served in the army and the men and women who supported them on the home front became accustomed to working in large, bureaucratic organizations of a kind that had scarcely existed before the war.

Ralph Waldo Emerson, the era's most prominent man of letters, noted that the conflict encouraged a dramatic shift in American thought about the relationship between the individual and society. Before the war, Emerson championed the individual who stood apart from institutions and organizations and sought fulfillment in an inner world of imagination and cosmic intuition. During the conflict, he began to exalt the claims of organization, government, and "civilization" over the endeavors of "the private man." In purging his philosophy of extreme individualism and hailing the need to accept social discipline and participate in organized, cooperative activity, Emerson epitomized the way the war affected American thought and patterns of behavior.

The North won the war mainly because it had shown a greater capacity than the South to organize, innovate, and modernize. Its victory meant that the nation as a whole would now be ready to embrace the conception of progress that the North had affirmed in its war effort—not only pursuing advances in science and technology but also bringing together and managing large numbers of men and women for economic and social goals. The Civil War was thus a catalyst for the great transformation of American society from an individualistic society of small producers into the more highly organized and "incorporated" America of the late nineteenth century.

Key Terms

cooperationists, p. 288
Crittenden compromise, p. 290
anaconda policy, p. 293
Emancipation Proclamation, p. 300
Copperheads, p. 302

Recommended Reading

The best one-volume history of the Civil War is James M. McPherson, *Battle Cry of Freedom: The Civil War Era* (1988). Other valuable surveys of the war and its aftermath are J. G. Randall and David Herbert Donald, *The Civil War and Reconstruction,* 2nd ed. (1969), and James M. McPherson, *Ordeal by Fire: The Civil War and Reconstruction* (1981). An excellent shorter account is David Herbert Donald, *Liberty and Union* (1978). The Confederate experience is covered in Clement Eaton, *A History of the Southern Confederacy* (1954), and Emory M. Thomas, *The Confederate Nation, 1861–1865* (1979). Eaton stresses internal problems and weaknesses; Thomas highlights achievements under adversity. Gary W. Gallagher, *The Confederate War* (1997) argues, contrary to a common view, that the South lost the war simply because it was overpowered and not because of low morale or lack of a will to win. On the North's war effort, see Phillip Paludan, *A People's Contest: The Union and the Civil War, 1861–1865* (1988). The best one-volume introduction to the military side of the conflict is still Bruce Catton, *This Hallowed Ground: The Story of the Union Side of the Civil War* (1956).

Lincoln's career and wartime leadership are well treated in David Herbert Donald, *Lincoln* (1995). Another competent biography is Stephen B. Oates, *With Malice Toward None: The Life of Abraham Lincoln* (1977). A penetrating analysis of events immediately preceding the fighting is Kenneth M. Stampp, *And the War Came: The North and the Sectional Crisis* (1950). John Hope Franklin, *The Emancipation Proclamation* (1963), is a good short account of the North's decision to free the slaves. An incisive account of the transition from slavery to freedom is Barbara Jeanne Fields, *Slavery and Freedom on the Middle Ground: Maryland in the Nineteenth Century* (1985). The circumstances and activities of southern women during the war are covered in Drew Faust, *Mothers of Invention: Women of the Slaveholding States in the American Civil War* (1996) and in Laura F. Edwards, *Scarlett Doesn't Live Here Anymore: Southern Women in the Civil War Era* (2002). The experiences of northern women are described in Elizabeth D. Leonard, *Yankee Women: Gender Battles in the Civil War* (1994). Five leading historians offer conflicting interpretations in their attempts to explain the South's defeat in *Why the North Won the Civil War,* edited by David Donald (1960). A brilliant study of the writings of those who experienced the war is Edmund Wilson, *Patriotic Gore: Studies in the Literature of the American Civil War* (1962). On the intellectual impact of the war, see George M. Fredrickson, *The Inner Civil War: Northern Intellectuals and the Crisis of the Union,* 2nd ed. (1993).

For a list of additional titles related to this chapter's topics, please see http://www.ablongman.com/divine.

Suggested Web Sites

The American Civil War Homepage

http://sunsite.utk.edu/civil-war/warweb.html
This site has a great collection of hypertext links to the most useful identified electronic files about the American Civil War.

The Valley of the Shadow: Living the Civil War in Pennsylvania and Virginia

http://jefferson.village.virginia.edu/vshadow/vshadow.html
This project tells the histories of two communities on either side of the Mason-Dixon line during the Civil War. It includes narrative and an electronic archive of sources.

Civil War @ Charleston

http://www.awod.com/gallery/probono/cwchas/cwlayout.html
This site covers the history of the Civil War in and around Charleston, South Carolina.

Abraham Lincoln Association

http://www.alincolnassoc.com/
This site allows you to search digital versions of Lincoln's papers.

Crisis at Fort Sumter

http://www.tulane.edu/~latner/CrisisMain.html
This well-crafted use of hypermedia with assignments or problems explains and explores the events in and around the start of the Civil War.

U.S. Civil War Center

http://www.cwc.lsu.edu/
This is a site whose mission is to "locate, index, and/or make available all appropriate private and public data regarding the Civil War and to promote the study of the Civil War from the perspectives of all professions, occupations, and academic disciplines."

The Papers of Jefferson Davis Home Page

http://jeffersondavis.rice.edu
This site tells about the collection of Jefferson Davis Papers and includes a chronology of his life, a family genealogy, some key Davis documents on-line, and a collection of related links.

History of African Americans in the Civil War

http://www.itd.nps.gov/cwss/history/aa_history.htm
This National Park Service site explores the history of the United States Colored Troops.

Civil War Women

http://scriptorium.lib.duke.edu/collections/civil-war-women.html
This site includes original documents, links, and biographical information about several women and their lives during the Civil War.

Assassination of President Abraham Lincoln

http://memory.loc.gov/ammem/alhtml/alrintr.html
Part of the American Memory series with introduction, timeline, and gallery.

Selected Civil War Photographs

http://memory.loc.gov/ammem/cwphtml/cwphome.html
Library of Congress site with more than 1,000 photographs, many from Matthew Brady.

A Timeline of the Civil War

http://www.historyplace.com/civilwar/index.html
A complete timeline of the Civil War, well illustrated with photographs.

National Civil War Association

http://www.ncwa.org/info.html
One of the many Civil War Reenactment organizations in the United States.

Chapter 16

The Agony of Reconstruction

Robert Smalls and Black Politicians During Reconstruction

During the Reconstruction period immediately following the Civil War, African Americans struggled to become equal citizens of a democratic republic. They produced a number of remarkable leaders who showed that blacks were as capable as other Americans of voting, holding office, and legislating for a complex and rapidly changing society. Among these leaders was Robert Smalls of South Carolina. Although virtually forgotten by the time of his death in 1915, Smalls was perhaps the most famous and most widely respected southern black leader of the Civil War and Reconstruction era. His career reveals some of the main features of the African American experience during that crucial period.

Born a slave in 1839, Smalls had a white father whose identity has never been clearly established. But his white ancestry apparently gained him some advantages, and as a young man he was allowed to live and work independently, hiring his own time from a master who may have been his half-brother. Smalls worked as a sailor and trained himself to be a pilot in Charleston harbor. When the Union Navy blockaded Charleston in 1862, Smalls, who was then working in a Confederate steamship called the *Planter,* saw a chance to win his freedom in a particularly dramatic way. At three o'clock in the morning on May 13, 1862, when the white officers of the *Planter* were ashore, he took command of the vessel and its slave crew, sailed it out of the heavily fortified harbor, and surrendered it to the Union Navy. Smalls immediately became a hero to those antislavery Northerners who were seeking evidence that the slaves were willing and able to serve the Union. The *Planter* was turned into a Union transport, and Smalls was made its captain after being commissioned as an officer in the armed forces of the United States. During the remainder of the war, he rendered conspicuous and gallant service as captain and pilot of Union vessels off the coast of South Carolina.

Like a number of other African Americans who had fought valiantly for the Union, Smalls went on to a distinguished political career during Reconstruction, serving in the South Carolina constitutional convention, the state legislature, and several terms in the U.S. Congress. He was also a shrewd businessman and became the owner of extensive properties in Beaufort, South Carolina, and its vicinity. (His first purchase was the house of his former master, where he had spent his early years as a slave.) As the leading citizen of Beaufort during Reconstruction and for some years thereafter, he acted like many successful white Americans, acquiring both wealth and political power. The electoral organization he established resembled in some ways the well-oiled political machines being established in northern towns

Outline

The President versus Congress

Reconstructing Southern Society

Retreat from Reconstruction

Reunion and the New South

Conclusion: The "Unfinished Revolution"

and cities. His was so effective that Smalls was able to control local government and get himself elected to Congress even after the election of 1876 had placed the state under the control of white conservatives bent on depriving blacks of political power. Organized mob violence defeated him in 1878, but he bounced back to win a contested congressional election in 1880 by decision of Congress. He did not leave the House of Representatives for good until 1886, when he lost another contested election that had to be decided by Congress. It revealed the changing mood of the country that his white challenger was seated despite evidence of violence and intimidation against black voters.

In their efforts to defeat him, Smalls's white opponents frequently charged that he had a hand in the corruption that was allegedly rampant in South Carolina during Reconstruction. But careful historical investigation shows that he was, by the standards of the time, an honest and responsible public servant. In the South Carolina convention of 1868 and later in the state legislature, he was a conspicuous champion of free and compulsory public education. In Congress, he fought for the enactment and enforcement of federal civil rights laws. Not especially radical on social questions, he sometimes bent over backward to accommodate what he regarded as the legitimate interests and sensibilities of South Carolina whites. Like other middle-class black political leaders in Reconstruction-era South Carolina, he can perhaps be faulted in hindsight for not doing more to help poor blacks gain access to land of their own. But in 1875, he sponsored congressional legislation that opened for purchase at low prices the land in his own district that had been confiscated by the federal government during the war. As a result, blacks were able to buy most of it, and they soon owned three-fourths of the land in Beaufort and its vicinity.

Smalls spent the later years of his life as U.S. collector of customs for the port of Beaufort, a beneficiary of the patronage that the Republican party continued to provide for a few loyal southern blacks. But the loss of real political clout for Smalls and men like him was one of the tragic consequences of the failure of Reconstruction.

FOR A BRIEF PERIOD OF YEARS, black politicians such as Robert Smalls exercised more power in the South than they would for another century. A series of political developments on the national and regional stage made Reconstruction "an unfinished revolution," promising but not delivering true equality for newly freed African Americans. National party politics, shifting priorities among Northern Republicans, and white Southerners' commitment to white supremacy, which was backed by legal restrictions as well as massive extra-legal violence against blacks, all combined to stifle the promise of Reconstruction. Yet the Reconstruction era also saw major transformations in American society in the wake of the Civil War—new ways of organizing labor and family life, new institutions within and outside of the government, and new ideologies regarding the role of institutions and government in social and economic life. Many of the changes begun during Reconstruction laid the groundwork for later revolutions in American life.

THE PRESIDENT VERSUS CONGRESS

The problem of how to reconstruct the Union in the wake of the South's military defeat was one of the most difficult challenges ever faced by American policymakers. The Constitution provided no firm guidelines, and once emancipation became a northern war aim, the problem was compounded by a new issue: How far should the federal government go to secure freedom and civil rights for four million former slaves?

The debate that evolved led to a major political crisis. Advocates of a minimal Reconstruction policy favored quick restoration of the Union with no protection for the freed slaves beyond the prohibition of slavery. Proponents of a more radical policy wanted readmission of the southern states to be dependent on guarantees that "loyal" men would replace the Confederate elite and that blacks would acquire some of the basic rights of American citizenship. The White House favored the minimal approach, while Congress came to endorse the more radical policy. The resulting struggle between Congress and the chief executive was the most serious clash between two branches of government in the nation's history.

Wartime Reconstruction

Tension between the president and Congress over how to reconstruct the Union began during the war. Although Lincoln did not set forth a final and comprehensive plan, he did indicate that he favored a lenient and conciliatory policy toward Southerners who would give up the struggle and repudiate slavery. In December 1863, he offered a full pardon to all Southerners (with the exception of certain classes of Confederate leaders) who would take an oath of allegiance to the Union and acknowledge the legality of emancipation. This **Ten Percent Plan** provided that once 10 percent or more of the voting population of any occupied state had taken the oath, they were authorized to set up a loyal government. By 1864, Louisiana and Arkansas had established fully functioning Unionist governments.

Ten Percent Plan Reconstruction plan proposed by President Lincoln as a quick way to readmit the former Confederate states. It called for full pardon of all Southerners except Confederate leaders and readmission to the Union for any state after 10 percent of its voters in the 1860 election signed a loyalty oath and the state abolished slavery.

Lincoln's policy was meant to shorten the war by offering a moderate peace plan. It was also intended to further his emancipation policy by insisting that the new governments abolish slavery. When constitutional conventions operating under the 10 percent plan in Louisiana and Arkansas dutifully abolished slavery in 1864, emancipation came closer to being irreversible.

But Congress was unhappy with the president's reconstruction experiments and in 1864 refused to seat the Unionists elected to the House and Senate from Louisiana and Arkansas. A minority of congressional Republicans—the fiercely antislavery **Radical Republicans**—favored strong protection for black civil rights and provision for their franchisement as a precondition for the readmission of southern states. A larger group of moderates also opposed Lincoln's plan, but they did so primarily because they did not trust the repentant Confederates who would play a major role in the new governments.

Radical Republicans The Radical Republicans in Congress, headed by Thaddeus Stevens and Charles Sumner, insisted on black suffrage and federal protection of civil rights of African Americans. They gained control of Reconstruction in 1867 and required the ratification of the Fourteenth Amendment as a condition of readmission for former Confederate states.

Also disturbing Congress was a sense that the president was exceeding his authority by using executive powers to restore the Union. Lincoln operated on the theory that secession, being illegal, did not place the Confederate states outside the Union in a constitutional sense. Since individuals and not states had defied federal authority, the president could use his pardoning power to certify a loyal electorate, which could then function as the legitimate state government. The dominant view in Congress, however, was that the southern states had forfeited their place in the Union and that it was up to Congress to decide when and how they would be readmitted.

After refusing to recognize Lincoln's 10 percent governments, Congress passed a Reconstruction bill of its own in July 1864. Known as the **Wade-Davis Bill,** the legislation required that 50 percent of the voters take an oath of future loyalty before the restoration process could begin. Once this had occurred, those who could swear that they had never willingly supported the Confederacy could vote in an election for delegates to a constitutional convention. Lincoln exercised a pocket veto by refusing to sign the bill before Congress adjourned, angering many congressmen.

Wade-Davis Bill In 1864, Congress passed the Wade-Davis bill to counter Lincoln's Ten Percent Plan for Reconstruction. The bill required that a majority of a former Confederate state's white male population take a loyalty oath and guarantee equality for African Americans. President Lincoln pocket-vetoed the bill.

Congress and the president remained stalemated on the Reconstruction issue for the rest of the war. During his last months in office, however, Lincoln showed a willingness to compromise. But he died without clarifying his intentions, leaving historians to speculate on whether his quarrel with Congress would have escalated or been resolved. Given Lincoln's record of political flexibility, the best bet is that he would have come to terms with the majority of his party.

Andrew Johnson at the Helm

Andrew Johnson, the man suddenly made president by an assassin's bullet, attempted to put the Union back together on his own authority in 1865. But his policies eventually put him at odds with Congress and the Republican party and provoked a serious crisis in the system of checks and balances among the branches of the federal government.

Johnson's approach to Reconstruction was shaped by his background. Born in dire poverty in North Carolina, he migrated as a young man to eastern Tennessee, where he made his living as a tailor. Although poorly educated (he did not learn to write until adulthood), Johnson was an effective stump speaker who railed against the planter aristocracy. Entering politics as a Jacksonian Democrat, he became the political spokesman for Tennessee's nonslaveholding whites. He advanced from state legislator to congressman to governor and in 1857 was elected to the U.S. Senate.

When Tennessee seceded in 1861, Johnson was the only senator from a Confederate state who remained loyal to the Union and continued to serve in Washington. But his Unionism did not include antislavery sentiments or friendship for blacks. He wished that "every head of family in the United States had one slave to take the drudgery and menial service off his family."

During the war, while acting as military governor of Tennessee, Johnson implemented Lincoln's emancipation policy as a means of destroying the power of the hated planter class rather than as a recognition of black humanity. He was chosen as Lincoln's running mate in 1864 in order to strengthen the ticket. No one expected that this southern Democrat and fervent white supremacist would ever become president.

Some Radical Republicans initially welcomed Johnson's ascent to the nation's highest office. Like the Radicals themselves, he was loyal to the Union and believed that ex-Confederates should be treated severely. He seemed more likely than Lincoln to punish southern "traitors" and prevent them from regaining political influence. Only gradually did Johnson and the Republican majority in Congress drift apart.

The Reconstruction policy that Johnson initiated on May 29, 1865, created some uneasiness among the Radicals, but most other Republicans were willing to give it a chance. Johnson placed North Carolina and eventually other states under appointed provisional governors mainly chosen from among prominent southern politicians who had opposed the secession movement and had rendered no conspicuous service to the Confederacy. They were then responsible for calling constitutional conventions to elect "loyal" officeholders. Johnson's plan was specially designed to prevent his longtime adversaries, the planter class, from participating in the reconstruction of southern state governments.

Johnson urged the conventions to declare the ordinances of secession illegal, repudiate the Confederate debt, and ratify the **Thirteenth Amendment** abolishing slavery. After governments had been reestablished under constitutions meeting these conditions, the president assumed that the process of Reconstruction would be complete and that the ex-Confederate states would regain their full rights under the Constitution.

Thirteenth Amendment Ratified in 1865, this amendment to the U.S. Constitution prohibited slavery and involuntary servitude.

Many congressional Republicans were troubled by the work of the southern conventions, which balked at fully implementing Johnson's recommendations. Furthermore, in no state was even limited black suffrage approved. Johnson, however, seemed eager to give southern white majorities a free hand in determining the civil and political status of freed slaves.

Republican uneasiness turned to disillusionment and anger when the state legislatures elected under the new constitutions proceeded to pass **Black Codes** subjecting the former slaves to a variety of special regulations and restrictions on their freedom. Especially troubling were vagrancy and apprenticeship laws that forced

Black Codes Laws passed by Southern states immediately after the Civil War in an effort to maintain the pre-war social order. The codes attempted to tie freedmen to field work and prevent them from becoming equal to white Southerners.

In this cartoon, President Andrew Johnson (left) and Thaddeus Stevens, the Radical Republican Congressman from Pennsylvania, are depicted as train engineers in a deadlock on the tracks. Indeed, neither Johnson nor Stevens would give way on his plans for Reconstruction. ❖

blacks to work and denied them a choice of employers. To Radicals, the Black Codes looked suspiciously like slavery under a new guise.

The growing rift between the president and Congress came into the open in December when the House and Senate refused to seat the recently elected southern delegation. Instead of endorsing Johnson's work and recognizing the state governments he had called into being, Congress established a joint committee, chaired by William Pitt Fessenden of Maine, to review Reconstruction policy and set further conditions for readmission of the seceded states.

Congress Takes the Initiative

The struggle over how to reconstruct the Union ended with Congress doing the job all over again. The clash between Johnson and Congress was a matter of principle and could not be reconciled. Johnson's stubborn and prideful nature did not help his political cause. But the root of the problem was that he disagreed with the majority of Congress on what Reconstruction was supposed to accomplish. An heir of the Democratic states' rights tradition, he wanted to restore the prewar federal system as quickly as possible, except for the prohibition on slavery and secession.

Most Republicans wanted firm guarantees that the old southern ruling class would not regain regional power and national influence by devising new ways to subjugate blacks. They favored a Reconstruction policy that would give the federal government authority to limit the political role of ex-Confederates and provide some protection for black citizenship.

Except for a few extreme Radicals, Republican leaders were not convinced that blacks were inherently equal to whites. They were certain, however, that all citizens should have the same basic rights and opportunities. Principle coincided easily with political expediency; southern blacks were likely to be loyal to the Republican party that had emancipated them and thus increase that party's political power in the South.

The disagreement between the president and Congress became irreconcilable in early 1866 when Johnson vetoed two bills that had passed with overwhelming Republican support. The first bill extended the life of the **Freedmen's Bureau**—a temporary agency charged with providing former slaves with relief, legal help, and educational and employment assistance. The second, a civil rights bill, was intended to nullify the detested Black Codes and guarantee "equal benefit of all laws."

Freedman's Bureau Agency established by Congress in March 1865 to provide freedmen with shelter, food, and medical aid and to help them establish schools and find employment.

The vetoes shocked moderate Republicans, who had expected Johnson to accept the relatively modest measures. Congress promptly passed the Civil Rights Act over Johnson's veto, signifying that the president was now hopelessly at odds with most of the congressmen from what was supposed to be his own party.

Johnson soon revealed that he intended to abandon the Republicans and place himself at the head of a new conservative party uniting the small minority of Republicans who supported him with a reviving Democratic party that was rallying behind his Reconstruction policy. As the elections of 1866 neared, Johnson stepped up his criticism of Congress.

Fourteenth Amendment Ratified in 1868, this amendment provided citizenship to the ex-slaves after the Civil War and constitutionally protected equal rights under the law for all citizens. Its provisions were used by Radical Republicans to enact a congressionally controlled Reconstruction policy in the former Confederate states.

Meanwhile, the Republican majority on Capitol Hill passed the **Fourteenth Amendment.** This, the most important of the constitutional amendments, gave the federal government responsibility for guaranteeing equal rights under the law to all Americans. The major section defined national citizenship for the first time as extending to "all persons born or naturalized in the United States." The states were prohibited from abridging the rights of American citizens and could neither "deprive any person of life, liberty, or property, without due process of law; nor deny to any person . . . equal protection of the laws." The amendment was sent to the states with an implied understanding that Southerners would be readmitted to Congress only if their states ratified it.

The congressional elections of 1866 served as a referendum on the Fourteenth Amendment. With the support of Johnson, all the southern states except Tennessee rejected the amendment. But bloody race riots in Memphis and New Orleans and maltreatment of blacks throughout the South made it painfully clear that southern state governments were failing abysmally to protect the "life, liberty, or property" of the ex-slaves.

Johnson further weakened his cause by taking the stump on behalf of candidates who supported his policies. His undignified speeches and his inflexibility enraged northern voters. The Republican majority in Congress increased to a solid two-thirds in both houses, and the radical wing of the party gained strength at the expense of moderates and conservatives.

Congressional Reconstruction Plan Enacted

Congress was now in a position to implement its own plan for Reconstruction. In 1867 and 1868, it passed a series of acts that reorganized the South on a new basis. Generally referred to as **Radical Reconstruction,** these measures actually represented a compromise between genuine Radicals and the more moderate elements within the party.

Radical Reconstruction The Reconstruction Acts of 1867 divided the South into five military districts. They required the states to guarantee black male suffrage and to ratify the Fourteenth Amendment as a condition of their readmission to the Union.

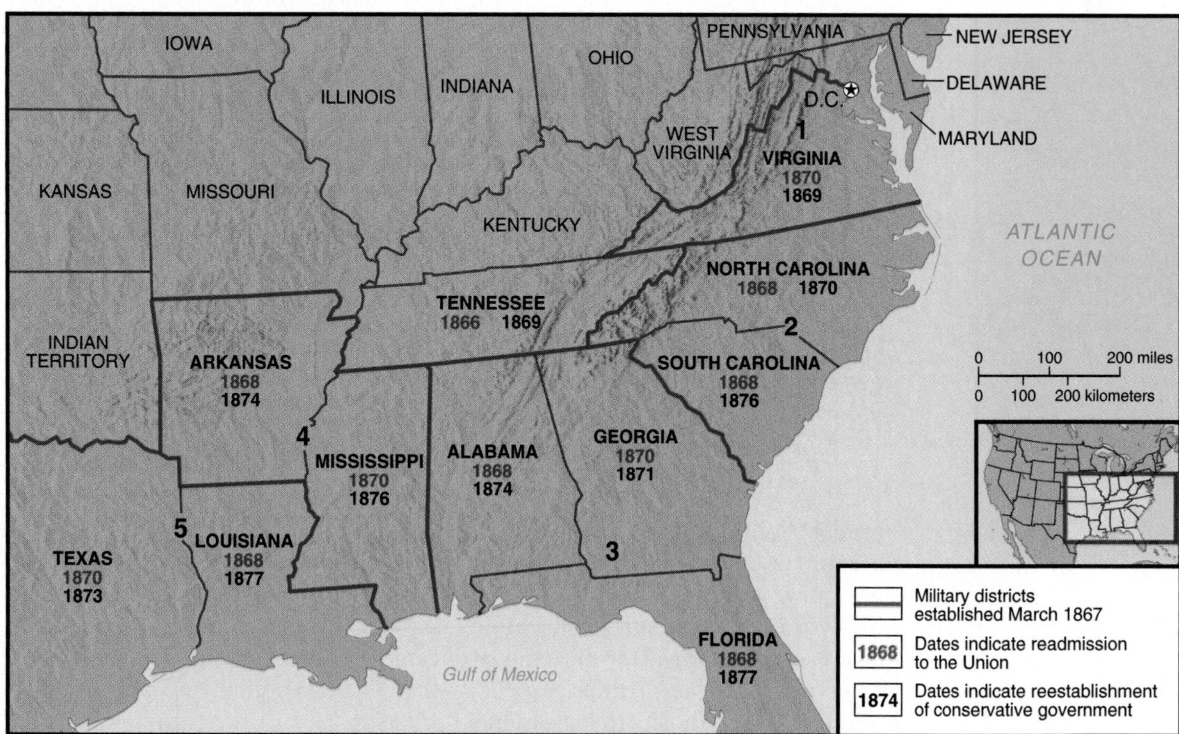

RECONSTRUCTION *During the Reconstruction era, the southern state governments passed through three phases: control by white ex-Confederates; domination by Republican legislators, both black and white; and, finally, the regain of control by conservative white Democrats.*

Reconstruction Amendments, 1865–1870

Amendment	Main Provisions	Congressional Passage (2/3 majority in each house required)	Ratification Process (3/4 of all states required, including ex-Confederate states)
13	Slavery prohibited in United States	January 1865	December 1865 (27 states, including 8 southern states)
14	National citizenship; State representation in Congress reduced proportionally to number of voters disfranchised; Former Confederates denied right to hold office; Confederate debt repudiated	June 1866	Rejected by 12 southern and border states, February 1867; Radicals make readmission of southern states hinge on ratification; ratified July 1868
15	Denial of franchise because of race, color, or past servitude explicitly prohibited	February 1869	Ratification required for readmission of Virginia, Texas, Mississippi, Georgia; ratified March 1870

Consistent Radicals, such as Charles Sumner of Massachusetts and Thaddeus Stevens of Pennsylvania, wanted to reshape southern society before readmitting ex-Confederates to the Union. Their program required an extended period of military rule, confiscation and redistribution of large landholdings among freedmen, and federal aid for schools that would educate blacks for citizenship. But the majority of Republican congressmen found such a program unacceptable because it broke with American traditions of federalism and regard for property rights.

The First Reconstruction Act, passed over Johnson's veto on March 2, 1867, did place the South under military rule—but only for a short period. The act opened the way for the readmission of any state that framed and ratified a new constitution providing for black suffrage. Since blacks (but not ex-Confederates) were allowed to participate in this process, Republicans thought they had found a way to ensure that "loyal men" would dominate the new governments.

Radical Reconstruction was based on the dubious assumption that once blacks had the vote, they would have the power to protect themselves against the efforts of white supremacists to deny them their rights. The Reconstruction Acts thus signaled a retreat from the true Radical position that a sustained use of federal authority was needed to complete the transition from slavery to freedom and prevent the resurgence of the South's old ruling class.

Even so, congressional Reconstruction did have a radical aspect. It strongly endorsed black suffrage. The principle that even the poorest and most underprivileged should have access to the ballot box was bold and innovative. The problem was how to enforce it under conditions then existing in the postwar South.

The Impeachment Crisis

President Johnson was unalterably opposed to the congressional Reconstruction program, and he did everything within his power to prevent its full implementation. Congress responded by passing laws designed to limit presidential authority over Reconstruction matters. One of the measures was the Tenure of Office Act, requiring Senate approval for the removal of cabinet officers and other officials whose appointment had needed the consent of the Senate. Another measure sought to limit Johnson's authority to issue military orders.

Johnson objected vigorously to the restrictions on the grounds that they violated the constitutional doctrine of the separation of powers. Faced with Johnson's opposition, some congressmen began to call for his impeachment. When Johnson tried to discharge Secretary of War Edwin Stanton—the only Radical in his cabinet—the proimpeachment forces grew.

In January 1868, Johnson ordered General Grant to take over Stanton's job as head of the War Department. But Grant had his eye on the Republican presidential nomination and refused to defy Congress. Johnson then appointed General Lorenzo Thomas. Vexed by this apparent violation of the Tenure of Office Act, the House of Representatives voted overwhelmingly to impeach the president, and he was placed on trial before the Senate.

Johnson narrowly avoided conviction and removal from office when the impeachment effort fell one vote short of the necessary two-thirds. This outcome resulted in part from a skillful defense. Responding to the charge that Johnson had deliberately violated the Tenure of Office Act, the defense contended that the law did not apply to the removal of Stanton because he had been appointed by Lincoln.

The prosecution was more concerned that Johnson had abused the powers of his office in an effort to sabotage the congressional Reconstruction policy. Obstructing the will of the legislative branch, they claimed, was sufficient grounds for conviction. The Republicans who broke ranks to vote for acquittal feared that removal of a president for essentially political reasons would threaten the constitutional balance of powers and open the way to legislative supremacy over the executive. In addition, more conservative Republicans opposed the man who, as president pro tem of the Senate, would have succeeded Johnson, Ohio Senator Benjamin Wade.

The impeachment episode helped create an impression in the public mind that the Radicals were ready to turn the Constitution to their own use to gain their objectives. But the evidence of congressional ruthlessness and illegality is not as strong as most historians used to think. Modern legal scholars have found merit in the Radicals' claim that their actions did not violate the Constitution.

The failed conviction effort was an embarrassment to congressional Republicans, but the episode did ensure that Reconstruction in the South would proceed as the majority in Congress intended. During the trial, Johnson helped influence the verdict by pledging to enforce the Reconstruction Acts, and he held to this promise during his remaining months in office.

Reconstructing Southern Society

The Civil War left the South devastated, demoralized, and destitute. Slavery was dead, but what this meant for future relationships between whites and blacks was still in doubt. Most whites were determined to restrict the freedmen's rights, and many blacks were just as set on achieving real independence. For blacks, the acquisition of land, education, and the vote seemed the best means of achieving their goal. The thousands of Northerners who went south after the war for economic or humanitarian reasons hoped to extend Yankee "civilization" to what they viewed as a barbarous region. For most of them, this reformation required the aid of the freedmen.

The struggle of these groups to achieve their conflicting goals bred chaos, violence, and instability. It was not the ideal setting for an experiment in interracial democracy. When the federal government's support of reform faltered, the forces of reaction and white supremacy were unleashed.

Reorganizing Land and Labor

The Civil War scarred the southern landscape and wrecked its economy. Many plantations were ruined, and several major cities, including Atlanta and Richmond, were gutted by fire. Most factories were dismantled or destroyed, and long stretches of railroad were torn up.

Nor was there adequate investment capital for rebuilding. The substantial wealth represented by Confederate currency and bonds had melted away, and emancipation of the slaves had divested the propertied classes of their most valuable and productive assets. According to some estimates, the South's per capita wealth in 1865 was only about half what it had been in 1860.

Recovery could not even begin until a new labor system replaced slavery. The lack of capital hindered the rebuilding of plantations, and most Americans assumed that southern prosperity would depend on plantation-grown cotton. In addition, southern whites believed that blacks would work only under compulsion, and freedmen resisted labor conditions that recalled slavery.

Blacks strongly preferred to be small independent farmers rather than plantation laborers. For a time, they had reason to hope that the federal government would support their ambitions. Some 40-acre land grants were given by federal authorities to freedmen. By July 1865, forty thousand black farmers were at work on 300,000 acres of what they thought would be their own land.

But for most of them, the dream of "40 acres and a mule" was not to be realized. Neither President Johnson nor most congressmen favored a program of land confiscation and redistribution. Consequently, the vast majority of blacks in physical possession of small farms failed to acquire title and were left with little or no prospect of becoming landowners.

Despite their poverty and landlessness, ex-slaves were reluctant to settle down and commit themselves to wage labor for their former masters. Many took to the road, hoping to find something better. Some were still expecting grants of land, but others were simply trying to increase their bargaining power. As the end of 1865 drew nearer, many freedmen had still not signed up for the coming season; anxious planters feared that they were plotting to seize the land by force. Within a few weeks, however, most of the holdouts signed for the best terms they could get. The most common form of agricultural employment in 1866 was contract labor. Under this system, workers committed themselves for a year in return for fixed wages. Although blacks occasionally received help from the Freedmen's Bureau, more often than not they were worked hard and paid little, and the contracts normally protected the employers more than the employees.

sharecropping After the Civil War, the southern states adopted a sharecropping system as a compromise between former slaves, who wanted land of their own, and former slave owners, who needed labor. The landowners provided land, tools, and seed to a farming family, who in turn provided labor. The resulting crop was divided between them, with the farmers receiving a "share" of one-third to one-half of the crop.

Growing up alongside the contract system and eventually displacing it was the alternative capital-labor relationship of **sharecropping**—the right to work a small piece of land independently in return for a fixed share of the crop produced on it, usually one-half. A shortage of labor gave the freedmen enough leverage to force this arrangement on planters who were unwilling, but many landowners found it advantageous because it did not require much capital and forced the tenant to share the risks of crop failure or a fall in cotton prices.

Blacks initially viewed sharecropping as a step up from wage labor in the direction of landownership. But during the 1870s, this form of tenancy evolved into a new kind of servitude. Croppers had to live on credit until their cotton was sold, and planters or merchants seized the chance to "provision" them at high prices and exorbitant rates of interest. Soon croppers discovered that debts multiplied faster than profits. Furthermore, various methods were eventually devised to bind indebted tenants to a single landlord for extended periods, although some economic historians argue that considerable movement was still possible.

Black Codes: A New Name for Slavery?

While landless African Americans in the countryside were being reduced to economic dependence, those in towns and cities found themselves living in an increasingly segregated society. The Black Codes of 1865 attempted to require separation of the races in public places and facilities; when most of the codes were overturned by federal authorities as violations of the Civil Rights Act of 1866, the same end was often achieved through private initiative and community pressure. Blacks found it almost impossible to gain admittance to most hotels, restaurants, and other privately owned establishments catering to whites. Although separate black, or "Jim Crow," cars were not yet the rule on railroads, African Americans were often denied first-class accommodations. After 1868, black-supported Republican governments passed civil rights acts requiring equal access to public facilities, but little effort was made to enforce the legislation.

The Civil War brought emancipation to slaves, but the sharecropping system kept many of them economically bound to their employers. At the end of a year the sharecropper tenants might owe most—or all—of what they had made to their landlord. Here a sharecropping family poses in front of their cabin. Ex-slaves often built their living quarters near woods in order to have a ready supply of fuel for heating and cooking. The cabin's chimney lists away from the house so that it can be easily pushed away from the living quarters should it catch fire. ❖

The Black Codes had other onerous provisions meant to control African Americans and return them to quasi-slavery. Most codes even made black unemployment a crime, which meant blacks had to make long-term contracts with white employers or be arrested for vagrancy. Others limited the rights of African Americans to own property or engage in occupations other than those of servant or laborer. The codes were set aside by the actions of Congress, the military, and the Freedmen's Bureau, but vagrancy laws remained in force across the South.

Furthermore, private violence and discrimination against blacks continued on a massive scale unchecked by state authorities. Hundreds, perhaps thousands, of blacks were murdered by whites in 1865–1866, and few of the perpetrators were brought to justice. The imposition of military rule in 1867 was designed in part to protect former slaves from such violence and intimidation, but the task was beyond the capacity of the few thousand troops stationed in the South. When new constitutions were approved and states readmitted to the Union under the congressional plan in 1868, the problem became more severe. White opponents of Radical Reconstruction adopted systematic terrorism and organized mob violence to keep blacks away from the polls.

The freed slaves tried to defend themselves by organizing their own militia groups for protection and to assert their political rights. However, the militia groups were not powerful enough to overcome the growing power of the anti-Republican forces. As the military presence was progressively reduced, the new Republican regimes were left to fight a losing battle against armed white supremacists.

Republican Rule in the South

Hastily organized in 1867, the southern Republican party dominated the constitution-making of 1868 and the regimes that came out of it. The party was an attempted coalition of three social groups: businessmen seeking aid for economic development, poor white farmers, and blacks. Although all three groups had different goals, their opposition to the old planter ruling class appeared to give them a basis for unity.

To be sure, the coalition faced difficulties even within its own ranks. Small farmers of the yeoman class had a bred-in-the-bone resistance to black equality. Conservative businessmen questioned costly measures for the elevation or relief of the lower classes of either race. In some states, astute Democratic politicians exploited the divisions by appealing to disaffected white Republicans.

But during the relatively brief period when they were in power in the South, the Republicans chalked up some notable achievements. They established (on paper at least) the South's first adequate system of public education, democratized state and local government, and appropriated funds for an enormous expansion of public services and welfare responsibilities.

Important though it was, social and political reform took second place to the major effort that Republicans made to foster economic development and restore southern prosperity by subsidizing the construction of railroads and other internal improvements. Although it addressed the region's real economic needs and was initially very popular, the policy of aiding railroads turned out disastrously. Extravagance, corruption, and the determination of routes based on political rather than sound economic considerations meant an increasing burden of public debt and taxation; the policy did not produce the promised payoff of reliable, cheap transportation. Subsidized railroads frequently went bankrupt, leaving the taxpayers holding the bag. When the Panic of 1873 brought many southern state governments to the verge of bankruptcy and railroad building came to an end, it was clear that the Republicans' "gospel of prosperity" through state aid to private enterprise had failed miserably. Their political opponents, most of whom had originally favored these policies, now saw an opportunity to make gains by charging that Republicans had ruined the southern economy.

These activities were often accompanied by inefficiency, waste, and corruption. State debts and tax burdens rose enormously, mainly because governments had undertaken heavy new responsibilities but partly as a result of waste and graft. In short, the Radical regimes brought needed reforms to the South, but they were not always model governments.

Southern corruption, however, was not exceptional, nor was it a special result of the extension of suffrage to uneducated blacks, as critics of Radical Reconstruction have claimed. It was part of a national pattern during an era when private interests considered buying government favors a part of the cost of doing business, and many politicians expected to profit by obliging them.

Blacks bore only a limited responsibility for the dishonesty of the Radical governments because they never controlled a state government and held few major offices. The biggest grafters were opportunistic whites; some of the most notorious were **carpetbaggers**—recent arrivals from the North—but others were native Southerners. Some black legislators went with the tide and accepted "loans" from those railroad lobbyists who would pay most for their votes, but the same men could usually be depended on to vote the will of their constituents on civil rights or educational issues. Although blacks who served or supported corrupt and wasteful regimes did so because they had no alternative, opponents of Radical Reconstruction were able to capitalize on racial prejudice and persuade many Americans that "good government" was synonymous with white supremacy. Contrary to myth, the small number of blacks elected to state or national office during Reconstruction demonstrated on the average more integrity and competence than their white counterparts. Most were fairly well educated, having been free Negroes or unusually privileged slaves before the war. Many battled tirelessly to promote the interests of their race.

carpetbaggers This term was applied to Northerners who moved to the South after the Civil War in order to aid in the reconstruction of the South or to invest in the southern economy. It derives from the claim that these Northerners carried everything they owned in one bag.

Claiming Public and Private Rights

As important as party politics to the changing political culture of the Reconstruction South were the ways that freed slaves claimed rights for themselves. They did so not only in negotiations with employers and in public meetings and convention halls, but also through the institutions they created, and perhaps most important, the households they formed.

On either side of Frederick Douglass on this poster are two African American heroes of the Reconstruction era. Senator Blanche K. Bruce of Mississippi, on the left, was the first African American to be elected to a full term in the U.S. Senate. Senator Hiram R. Revels, also representing Mississippi, was elected to the Senate in 1870 to fill the seat previously occupied by Confederate President Jefferson Davis. ❖

As one black corporal in the Union Army told an audience of ex-slaves, "The Marriage covenant is at the foundation of all our rights. In slavery we could not have *legalized* marriage: *now* we have it . . . and we shall be established as a people." Through marriage, African Americans claimed citizenship. Freedmen hoped that marriage would allow them to take on not only political rights, but the right to control the labor of wives and children.

Many states' Black Codes included apprenticeship provisions, providing for freed children to be apprenticed by courts to some white person (with preference given to former masters) if their parents were paupers, unemployed, of "bad character," or even simply if it were found to be "better for the habits and comfort of a child." Ex-slaves struggled to win their children back from what often amounted to re-enslavement for arbitrary reasons. Freed people challenged the apprenticeship system in county courts, and through the Freedmen's Bureau.

While many former slaves lined up eagerly to formalize their marriages, many also retained their own definitions of marriage. Perhaps as many as 50 percent of ex-slaves chose not to marry legally, and whites criticized them heavily for it. African American leaders worried about this refusal to follow white norms. Yet many poor blacks continued to recognize as husband and wife people who cared for and supported one another without benefit of legal sanction. The new legal system punished couples who deviated from the legal norm through laws against bastardy, adultery, and fornication. Furthermore, the Freedmen's Bureau made the marriage of freedpeople a priority so that husbands, rather than the federal government, would be legally responsible for families' support.

Some ex-slaves used the courts to assert rights against white people as well as other blacks, suing over domestic violence, child support, assault, and debt. Freedwomen sued their husbands for desertion and alimony, in order to enlist the

Freedman's Bureau to help them claim property from men. Other ex-slaves mobilized kin networks and other community resources to make claims on property and family.

Immediately after the war, freed people flocked to create institutions that had been denied to them under slavery: churches, fraternal and benevolent associations, political organizations, and schools. Many joined all-black denominations such as the African Methodist Episcopal church, which provided freedom from white dominance and a more congenial style of worship. Black women formed all-black chapters of organizations such as the Women's Christian Temperance Union, and their own women's clubs to oppose lynching and work for "uplift" in the black community.

A top priority for most ex-slaves was the opportunity to educate their children; the first schools for freed people were all-black institutions established by the Freedmen's Bureau and various northern missionary societies. At the time, having been denied all education during the antebellum period, most blacks viewed separate schooling as an opportunity rather than as a form of discrimination. However, these schools were precursors to the segregated public school systems first instituted by Republican governments. Only in city schools of New Orleans and at the University of South Carolina were there serious attempts during Reconstruction to bring white and black students together in the same classrooms.

In a variety of ways, African American men and women during Reconstruction claimed freedom in the "private" realm as well as the public sphere, by claiming rights to their own families and building their own institutions. They did so in the face of the vigorous efforts of their former masters as well as the new government agencies to control their private lives and shape their new identities as husbands, wives, and citizens.

Retreat from Reconstruction

The era of Reconstruction began coming to an end almost before it started. Although it was only a scant three years from the end of the Civil War, the impeachment crisis of 1868 represented the high point of popular interest in Reconstruction issues. That year, Ulysses S. Grant was elected president. Many historians blame Grant for the corruption of his administration and for the inconsistency and failure of his southern policy. He had neither the vision nor the sense of duty to tackle the difficult challenges the nation faced. From 1868 on, political issues other than southern Reconstruction moved to the forefront of national politics, and the plight of African Americans in the South receded in white consciousness.

Rise of the Money Question

In the years immediately following the Civil War, the question of how to manage the nation's currency and, more specifically, what to do about "greenbacks"—paper money issued during the war—competed with Reconstruction and corruption issues for public attention. Defenders of "sound" money, mostly financial interests in the East, wanted the greenbacks withdrawn from circulation and Civil War debts redeemed in specie payments (silver and gold). Opponents of this hard-money policy and the resulting deflation of the currency were mainly credit-hungry Westerners and expansionist-minded manufacturers, known as **greenbackers,** who wanted to keep greenbacks in circulation. Both political parties had hard- and easy-money factions, preventing the money question from becoming a heated presidential election issue in 1868 and 1872.

greenbackers Members of the National Greenback Party, founded in 1874, who wanted to keep wartime paper money (greenbacks) in circulation. They believed that a floating currency, not tied to either gold or silver, would provide relief to debtors and impoverished farmers by increasing the money supply.

But the Panic of 1873, which brought much of the economy to its knees, led to agitation to inflate the currency by issuing more paper money. Debt-ridden farmers, who would be the backbone of the greenback movement for years to come, now joined the easy-money clamor for the first time. Responding to the money and credit crunch, Congress moved in 1874 to authorize a modest issue of new greenbacks, but Grant vetoed the bill. In 1875, Congress enacted the Specie Resumption Act, which provided for a gradual reduction of greenbacks leading to full resumption of specie payment by 1879. The act was interpreted as deflationary, and farmers and workers, who were already suffering from deflation, reacted with dismay and anger.

The Democratic party could not capitalize adequately on these sentiments because of the influence of its own hard-money faction, and in 1876, an independent Greenback party entered the national political arena. Greenbackers kept the money issue alive through the next decade.

Final Efforts of Reconstruction

The Republican effort to make equal rights for blacks the law of the land culminated in the **Fifteenth Amendment,** ratified in 1870, which prohibited any state from denying a male citizen the right to vote because of race, color, or previous condition of servitude. Much to the displeasure of advocates of women's rights, however, the amendment made no provision for female suffrage. And states could still limit male suffrage by imposing literacy tests, property qualifications, or poll taxes allegedly applying to all racial groups; such devices would eventually be used to strip southern blacks of the right to vote. But the makers of the amendment did not foresee this result.

Fifteenth Amendment Ratified in 1870, this amendment prohibited the denial or abridgment of the right to vote by the federal government or state governments on the basis of race, color, or prior condition as a slave. It was intended to guarantee African Americans the right to vote in the South.

The Grant administration was charged with enforcing the amendment and protecting black voting rights in the reconstructed states. Since survival of the Republican regimes depended on black support, political partisanship dictated federal action, even though the North's emotional and ideological commitment to black citizenship was waning.

Between 1868 and 1872, the main threat to southern Republican regimes came from the **Ku Klux Klan** and other secret societies bent on restoring white supremacy by intimidating blacks who sought to exercise their political rights. A grassroots vigilante movement rather than a centralized conspiracy, the Klan thrived on local initiative and gained support from whites of all social classes. Its secrecy, decentralization, popular support, and utter ruthlessness made it very difficult to suppress. Blacks who voted ran the risk of being verbally intimidated, whipped, or even murdered.

Ku Klux Klan A secret terrorist society first organized in Tennessee in 1866. The original Klan's goals were to disenfranchise African Americans, stop Reconstruction, and restore the prewar social order of the South. The Ku Klux Klan reformed after World War II to promote white supremacy in the wake of the "Second Reconstruction."

The methods were first used effectively in the presidential election of 1868. Terrorism by white supremacists cost Grant the electoral votes of Louisiana and Georgia. In Louisiana, political violence claimed hundreds of lives, and in Arkansas, more than two hundred Republicans were assassinated. Thereafter, Klan terrorism was directed mainly at Republican state governments. Insurrections broke out in Arkansas, Tennessee, North Carolina, and parts of South Carolina. In Tennessee, North Carolina, and Georgia, Klan activities helped undermine Republican control, thus allowing the Democrats to come to power in all those states by 1870.

Faced with the violent overthrow of the southern Republican party, Congress and the Grant administration were forced to act. A series of laws passed in 1870 and 1871 sought to enforce the Fifteenth Amendment by providing federal protection for black suffrage and authorizing use of the army against the Klan. Although the **Force Acts,** also known as the Ku Klux Klan Acts, did not totally destroy the Klan, the enforcement effort was vigorous enough to put a damper on hooded terrorism and ensure relatively fair and peaceful elections in 1872.

Force Acts Congress attacked the Ku Klux Klan with three Enforcement or "Force" Acts in 1870–71. Designed to protect black voters in the South, these laws placed state elections under federal jurisdiction and imposed fines and imprisonment on those guilty of interfering with any citizen exercising his right to vote.

A heavy black turnout in the elections enabled the Republicans to hold on to power in most states of the Deep South, despite efforts of the Democratic-Conservative opposition to woo Republicans by taking moderate positions on racial and economic issues. This setback prompted the Democratic-Conservatives

❖ A Look at the Past ❖

Cartoon "Worse Than Slavery"

Political cartoonist Thomas Nast offered his commentary on and critique of contemporary events through his cartoons in *Harper's Weekly*, a popular magazine that had a circulation of more than 100,000 readers. This Nast cartoon, "Worse Than Slavery," appeared in the magazine on October 24, 1874. Carefully examine the individuals and items depicted in the cartoon. Note that the phrase near the top of the drawing, "This is a white man's government," is a quotation from the 1868 Democratic Party platform. According to the cartoon, what conditions or events are "worse than slavery"? What view of Reconstruction policy does the cartoonist appear to be expressing?

to make a significant change in their strategy and ideology. No longer did they try to take votes away from the Republicans by proclaiming support for black suffrage and government aid to business. Instead, they began to appeal openly to white supremacy and to the traditional Democratic agrarian hostility to governmental promotion of economic development. Consequently, they were able to bring back to the polls a portion of the white electorate, mostly small farmers, who had not been turning out because they were alienated by the leadership's apparent concessions to Yankee ideas.

The new and more effective electoral strategy dovetailed with a resurgence of violence meant to reduce Republican—especially black Republican—voting. The new reign of terror differed from the previous Klan episode; its agents no longer wore masks but acted quite openly. They were effective because the northern public was increasingly disenchanted with federal intervention on behalf of what were widely viewed as corrupt and tottering Republican regimes. Grant used force in the South for the last time in 1874. When an unofficial militia in Mississippi instigated a series of bloody race riots prior to the state elections in 1875, Grant refused the governor's request for federal troops. As a result, intimidation kept black voters away from the polls.

By 1876, Republicans held on to only three southern states—South Carolina, Louisiana, and Florida. Partly because of Grant's hesitant and inconsistent use of presidential power but mainly because the northern electorate would no longer tolerate military action to sustain Republican governments and black voting rights, Radical Reconstruction was falling into total eclipse.

Spoilsmen versus Reformers

One reason Grant found it increasingly difficult to take strong action to protect southern Republicans was the charge by reformers that his administration was propping up bad governments in the South for personal and partisan advantage. In some cases, the charges held a measure of truth.

The Republican party in the Grant era was rapidly losing the idealism and high purpose associated with the crusade against slavery. By the beginning of the 1870s, men who had been the conscience of the party had been replaced by a new breed of Republicans, such as Senator Roscoe Conkling of New York, whom historians have dubbed "spoilsmen" or "politicos." More often than not, Grant sided with the spoilsmen of his party.

During Grant's first administration, an aura of scandal surrounded the White House but did not directly implicate the president. In 1869, the financial buccaneer Jay Gould enlisted the aid of a brother-in-law of Grant's to further a fantastic scheme to corner the gold market. Gould failed in the attempt, but he did manage to come away with a huge profit.

Grant's first-term vice president, Schuyler Colfax of Indiana, was directly involved in the notorious Crédit Mobilier scandal. Crédit Mobilier was a construction company that actually served as a fraudulent device for siphoning off profits that should have gone to the stockholders of the Union Pacific Railroad, which was the beneficiary of massive federal land grants. To forestall government inquiry into this arrangement, Crédit Mobilier stock was distributed to influential congressmen. The whole business came to light just before the campaign of 1872.

Republicans who could not tolerate such corruption or had other grievances against the administration broke with Grant in 1872 and formed a third party committed to "honest government" and "reconciliation" between the North and the South. The Liberal Republicans, led initially by such high-minded reformers as Senator Carl Schurz of Missouri, endorsed reform of the civil service to curb the corruption-breeding patronage system and advocated strict laissez-faire economic policies, which meant low tariffs, an end to government subsidies for railroads, and hard money.

The Liberal Republicans' national convention nominated Horace Greeley, editor of the respected *New York Tribune* newspaper. This was a curious and divisive choice, seeing that Greeley was at odds with the founder of the movement on the tariff question and indifferent to civil service reform. The Democrats also endorsed Greeley, mainly because he vowed to end Radical Reconstruction. Greeley, however, did not attract support and was soundly defeated by Grant.

Grant's second administration bore out the reformers' worst suspicions about corruption in high places. In 1875, the public learned that federal revenue officials had conspired with distillers to defraud the government of millions of dollars in liquor taxes. Grant's private secretary, Orville E. Babcock, was indicted as a member of the "Whiskey Ring" and was saved from conviction only by the president's personal intercession. The next year, Grant's secretary of war, William E. Belknap, was impeached by the House after an investigation revealed that he had taken bribes for the sale of Indian trading posts. He avoided a Senate conviction by leaving office before the trial.

There is no evidence that Grant profited personally from any of the misdeeds of his subordinates. Yet he is not entirely without blame for the corruption of his administration. He failed to take action against the malefactors, and even after their guilt had been clearly established, he tried to shield them from justice. Ulysses S. Grant was the only president between Jackson and Wilson to serve two full and consecutive terms. But unlike other chief executives so favored by the electorate, Grant is commonly regarded as a failure. Although the problems he faced would have challenged any president, the shame of Grant's administration was that he made loyalty to old friends a higher priority than civil rights or sound economic principles.

Reunion and the New South

The end of Radical Reconstruction in 1877 opened the way to a reconciliation of North and South. But the costs of reunion were high for less privileged groups in the South. The civil and political rights of blacks, left unprotected, were stripped away by white supremacist regimes. Lower-class whites saw their interests sacrificed to those of capitalists and landlords. Despite the rhetoric hailing a prosperous "New South," the region remained poor and open to exploitation by northern business interests.

The Compromise of 1877

The election of 1876 pitted Rutherford B. Hayes of Ohio, an honest Republican governor, against Governor Samuel J. Tilden of New York, a Democratic reformer. Honest government was apparently the electorate's highest priority. When the returns came in, Tilden had clearly won the popular vote and seemed likely to win a narrow victory in the electoral college. But the result was placed in doubt when the returns from the three southern states still controlled by the Republicans were contested. If Hayes were to be awarded these three states, plus one contested electoral vote in Oregon, Republican strategists realized, he would triumph in the electoral college by a single vote.

The outcome of the election remained undecided for months. To resolve the impasse, Congress appointed a special electoral commission of fifteen members to determine who would receive the votes of the disputed states. The commission split along party lines and voted 8 to 7 to award Hayes the disputed states. But this decision still had to be ratified, and in the House there was strong Democratic opposition.

To ensure Hayes's election, Republican leaders negotiated secretly with conservative southern Democrats, some of whom seemed willing to abandon their opposition if the last troops were withdrawn and "home rule" was restored to the South. Vague pledges of federal support for southern railroads and internal improvements were made, and Hayes assured southern negotiators that he had every intention of ending Reconstruction. Eventually, an informal bargain, dubbed the **Compromise of 1877,** was struck. Precisely what was agreed to and by whom remains a matter of dispute, but one thing at least was understood by both sides: Hayes would be president, and southern Republicans would be abandoned to their fate.

Compromise of 1877 The Compromise of 1877 was struck during the contested presidential election of 1876. In the compromise, Democrats accepted the election of Rutherford B. Hayes (Republican) in exchange for the withdrawal of federal troops from the South and the ending of Reconstruction.

With southern Democratic acquiescence, the main opposition was overcome, and Hayes took the oath of office. He immediately ordered the army not to resist a Democratic takeover in South Carolina and Louisiana. Thus fell the last of the Radical governments.

"Redeeming" a New South

The men who came to power after the ending of Radical Reconstruction in one southern state after another are usually referred to as the **Redeemers.** They had differing backgrounds and previous loyalties. Some were members of the Old South's ruling planter class who had warmly supported secession and now sought to reestablish the old order with as few changes as possible. Others, of middle-class origin or outlook, favored commercial and industrial interests over agrarian groups and called for a New South, committed to diversified economic development. A third group consisted of professional politicians bending with the prevailing winds.

Redeemers Redeemers were a loose coalition of prewar Democrats, Confederate Army veterans, and Southern Whigs who took over southern state governments in the 1870s, supposedly "redeeming" them from the corruption of Reconstruction. They shared a commitment to white supremacy and laissez-faire economics.

Rather than supporters of any single ideology or program, these leaders can perhaps best be understood as power brokers mediating among the dominant interest groups of the South in ways that served their own political advantage. In many ways, the "rings" that they established on the state and county levels were analogous to the political machines developing at the same time in northern cities.

They did, however, agree on and endorse two basic principles: laissez-faire and white supremacy. Laissez-faire, the notion that government should be limited and neutral in its economic activities, could unite planters, frustrated at seeing direct state support going to businessmen, and capitalist promoters, who had come to realize that low taxes and freedom from government regulation were even more advantageous than state subsidies. It soon became clear that the Redeemers responded only to privileged and entrenched interest groups, especially landlords, merchants, and industrialists, and offered little or nothing to tenants, small farmers, and working people. As industrialization began to gather steam in the 1880s, Democratic regimes became increasingly accommodating to manufacturing interests and hospitable to agents of northern capital who were gaining control of the South's transportation system and its extractive industries.

White supremacy was the principal rallying cry that brought the Redeemers to power in the first place. Once in office, they found that they could stay there by charging that opponents of ruling Democratic cliques were trying to divide the "white man's party" and open the way for a return to "black domination." Appeals to racism could also deflect attention away from the economic grievances of groups without political clout.

The new governments were more economical than those of Reconstruction, mainly because they cut back drastically on appropriations for schools and other needed public services. But they were scarcely more honest. Embezzlement of public funds and bribery of public officials continued to an alarming extent.

The Redeemer regimes of the late 1870s and 1880s badly neglected the interests of small white farmers. Whites, as well as blacks, were suffering from the notorious crop lien system, which gave the local merchants who advanced credit at high rates of interest during the growing season the right to take possession of the harvested

Perhaps no event better expresses the cruel and barbaric nature of the racism and white supremacy that swept the South after Reconstruction than lynching. Although lynchings were not confined to the South, most occurred there, and African American men were the most frequent victims. Here two men lean out of a barn window above a black man who is about to be hanged. Others below prepare to set on fire the pile of hay at the victim's feet. Lynchings were often public events, drawing huge crowds to watch the victim's agonizing death. ❖

Supreme Court Decisions Affecting Black Civil Rights, 1875–1900

Case	Effects of Court's Decisions
Hall v. *DeCuir* (1878)	Struck down Louisiana law prohibiting racial discrimination by "common carriers" (railroads, steamboats, buses). Declared the law a "burden" on interstate commerce, over which states had no authority.
United States v. *Harris* (1882)	Declared federal laws to punish crimes such as murder and assault unconstitutional. Declared such crimes to be the sole concern of local government. Ignored the frequent racial motivation behind such crimes in the South.
Civil Rights Cases (1883)	Struck down Civil Rights Act of 1875. Declared that Congress may not legislate on civil rights unless a state passes a discriminatory law. Declared the Fourteenth Amendment silent on racial discrimination by private citizens.
Plessy v. *Ferguson* (1896)	Upheld Louisiana statute requiring "separate but equal" accommodations on railroads. Declared that segregation is *not* necessarily discrimination.
Williams v. *Mississippi* (1898)	Upheld state law requiring a literacy test to qualify for voting. Refused to find any implication of racial discrimination in the law, although it permitted illiterate whites to vote if they "understood" the Constitution. Using such laws, southern states rapidly disfranchised blacks.

crop on terms that buried farmers deeper and deeper in debt. As a result, increasing numbers of whites lost title to their homesteads and were reduced to tenancy.

The Rise of Jim Crow

Jim Crow laws Laws enacted by states to segregate the population. They became widespread in the South after Reconstruction.

African Americans bore the greatest hardships imposed by the new order. From 1876 through the first decade of the twentieth century, Southern states imposed a series of restrictions on black civil rights known as **Jim Crow laws.** While segregation and disfranchisement began as informal arrangements, they culminated in a legal regime of separation and exclusion that took firm hold in the 1890s.

The rise of Jim Crow in the political arena was especially bitter for Southern blacks who realized that only political power could ensure other rights. The Redeemers had promised, as part of the understanding that led to the end of federal intervention in 1877, to respect the rights of blacks as set forth in the Fourteenth and Fifteenth Amendments. But when blacks tried to vote Republican in the "redeemed" states, they encountered renewed violence and intimidation. Blacks who withstood the threat of losing their jobs or being evicted from tenant farms if they voted for Republicans were visited at night and literally whipped into line. The message was clear: Vote Democratic, or vote not at all.

Furthermore, white Democrats now controlled the electoral machinery and were able to manipulate the black vote by stuffing ballot boxes, discarding unwanted votes, or reporting fraudulent totals. Some states also imposed complicated new voting requirements to discourage black participation. Full-scale disfranchisement did not occur until literacy tests and other legalized obstacles to voting were imposed in the period from 1890 to 1910, but by that time, less formal and comprehensive methods had already made a mockery of the Fifteenth Amendment.

Nevertheless, blacks continued to vote freely in some localities until the 1890s; a few districts, like the one Robert Smalls represented, even elected black Republicans to Congress during the immediate post-Reconstruction period. The last of these, Representative George H. White of North Carolina, served until 1901.

The dark night of racism that fell on the South after Reconstruction seemed to unleash all the baser impulses of human nature. Between 1889 and 1899, an average of 187 blacks were lynched every year for alleged offenses against white supremacy. Those convicted of petty crimes against property were often little better off; many were condemned to be leased out to private contractors whose brutality rivaled that of the most sadistic slaveholders. The convict-lease system enabled entrepreneurs, such as mine owners and extractors of forest products, to rent prisoners from the state and treat them as they saw fit. Unlike slaveowners, they suffered no loss when a forced laborer died from overwork. Finally, the dignity of blacks was cruelly affronted by the wave of segregation laws passed around the turn of the century, to some extent a white reaction to the refusal of many blacks to submit to voluntary segregation of railroads, streetcars, and other public facilities.

The North and the federal government did little or nothing to stem the tide of racial oppression in the South. A series of Supreme Court decisions between 1878 and 1898 gutted the Reconstruction amendments and the legislation passed to enforce them, leaving blacks virtually defenseless against political and social discrimination.

Conclusion: The "Unfinished Revolution"

By the late 1880s, the wounds of the Civil War were healing, and white Americans were seized by the spirit of sectional reconciliation. "Reunion" was becoming a cultural as well as political reality. But whites could come back together only because Northerners had tacitly agreed to give Southerners a free hand in their efforts to reduce blacks to a new form of servitude. The "outraged, heart-broken, bruised, and bleeding" African Americans of the South paid the heaviest price for sectional reunion. Reconstruction remained, in the words of historian Eric Foner, an "unfinished revolution." It would be another century before African Americans rose up once more to demand full civil and political rights.

Chronology

1863	Lincoln sets forth his 10 percent Reconstruction plan
1864	Wade-Davis Bill passes Congress, is pocket-vetoed by Lincoln
1865	Johnson moves to reconstruct the South on his own initiative ❖ Congress refuses to seat representatives and senators elected from states reestablished under the presidential plan
1866	Congress passes the Fourteenth Amendment ❖ Republicans increase their congressional majority in the fall elections
1867	First Reconstruction Act is passed over Johnson's veto
1868	Johnson is impeached, avoids conviction by one vote ❖ Grant wins the presidential election, defeating Horatio Seymour
1869	Congress passes the Fifteenth Amendment, granting blacks the right to vote
1870–1871	Congress passes the Force Acts to protect black voting rights in the South
1872	Grant is reelected president, defeating Horace Greeley, candidate of the Liberal Republicans and Democrats
1873	Financial panic plunges the nation into a depression
1875	Congress passes the Specie Resumption Act ❖ "Whiskey Ring" scandal is exposed
1876–1877	Disputed presidential election is resolved in favor of Republican Hayes over Democrat Tilden
1877	"Compromise of 1877" results in an end to military intervention in the South and the fall of the last Radical governments

Key Terms

Ten Percent Plan, p. 312
Radical Republicans, p. 312
Wade-Davis Bill, p. 312
Thirteenth Amendment, p. 313
Black Codes, p. 313
Freedman's Bureau, p. 314
Fourteenth Amendment, p. 314
Radical Reconstruction, p. 315
sharecropping, p. 318
carpetbaggers, p. 320
greenbackers, p. 322
Fifteenth Amendment, p. 323
Ku Klux Klan, p. 323
Force Acts, p. 323
Compromise of 1877, p. 326
Redeemers, p. 327
Jim Crow laws, p. 328

Recommended Reading

The best one-volume account of Reconstruction is Eric Foner, *Reconstruction: America's Unfinished Revolution* (1988). Two excellent short surveys are Kenneth M. Stampp, *The Era of Reconstruction, 1865–1877* (1965), and John Hope Franklin, *Reconstruction: After the Civil War* (1961). Both were early efforts to synthesize modern "revisionist" interpretations. W. E. B. DuBois, *Black Reconstruction in America, 1860–1880* (1935), remains brilliant and provocative. On the politics of Reconstruction, see Stephen David Kantrowitz, *Ben Tillman and the Reconstruction of White Supremacy* (2001), Laura F. Edwards, *Gendered Strife and Confusion: The Political Culture of Reconstruction* (1997), J. Morgan Kousser and James M. McPherson, eds., *Region, Race, and Reconstruction: Essays in Honor of C. Vann Woodward* (1982), and Eric Foner, *Nothing But Freedom: Emancipation and Its Legacy* (1983).

Leon F. Litwack, *Been in the Storm So Long: The Aftermath of Slavery* (1979), provides a moving portrayal of the black experience of emancipation. On changing society and family life during Reconstruction, see Noralee Frankel, *Freedom's Women: Black Women and Families in Reconstruction Era Mississippi* (1999), Dylan Penningroth, *Claiming Kin and Property: African American Life Before and After Emancipation* (2003), and Amy Dru Stanley, *From Bondage to Contract: Wage Labor, Marriage, and the Market in the Age of Slave Emancipation* (1998). On what freedom meant in economic terms, see Gerald David Jaynes, *Branches Without Roots: Genesis of the Black Working Class in the American South, 1862–1882* (1986). A work that focuses on ex-slaves' attempts to create their own economic order is Julie Saville, *The Work of Reconstruction: Free Slave to Wage Laborer in South Carolina, 1860–1870* (1994). The best overview of the postwar southern economy is Gavin Wright, *Old South, New South* (1986). On the end of Reconstruction, see David W. Blight, *Race and Reunion: The Civil War in American Memory* (2000). On the character of the post-Reconstruction South, see the classic work by C. Vann Woodward, *Origins of the New South, 1877–1913* (1951) and Edward Ayers, *The Promise of the New South* (1992).

For a list of additional titles related to this chapter's topics, please see http://www.ablongman.com/divine.

Suggested Web Sites

Diary and Letters of Rutherford B. Hayes

http://www.ohiohistory.org/onlinedoc/hayes/index.cfm
The Rutherford B. Hayes Presidential Center in Fremont, Ohio, maintains this searchable database of Hayes's writings.

Images of African Americans from the Nineteenth Century

http://digital.nypl.org/schomburg/images_aa19/
The New York Public Library–Schomburg Center for Research in Black Culture site contains numerous visuals.

Freedmen and Southern Society Project (University of Maryland, College Park)

http://www.inform.umd.edu/ARHU/Depts/History/Freedman/home.html
This site contains a chronology and sample documents from several print collections or primary sources about emancipation and freedom in the 1860s.

Andrew Johnson

http://www.whitehouse.gov/WH/glimpse/presidents/html/aj17.html
White House history of Johnson.

Ulysses S. Grant

http://www.whitehouse.gov/WH/glimpse/presidents/html/ug18.html
White House history of Grant.

History of the Suffrage Movement

http://www.rochester.edu/SBA
This site includes a chronology, important texts relating to woman suffrage, and biographical information about Susan B. Anthony and Elizabeth Cady Stanton.

Chapter 17

The West: Exploiting an Empire

Lean Bear's Changing West

In 1863, federal Indian agents took a delegation of Cheyenne, Arapaho, Comanche, Kiowa, and Plains Apache to visit the eastern United States, hoping to impress them with the power of the white man. The visitors were, in fact, impressed. In New York City, they stared at the tall buildings and crowded streets, so different from the wide-open plains with which they were accustomed. They visited the museum of the great showman Phineas T. Barnum, who in turn put them on display; they even saw a hippopotamus.

In Washington, they met with President Abraham Lincoln. Lean Bear, a Cheyenne chief, assured Lincoln that Indians wanted peace but worried about the numbers of white people who were pouring into their country. Lincoln swore friendship, said the Indians would be better off if they began to farm, and promised he would do his best to keep the peace. But, he said, smiling at Lean Bear, "You know it is not always possible for any father to have his children do precisely as he wishes them to do."

Lean Bear, who had children of his own, had understood what Lincoln had said in Washington, at least in a way. Just a year later, back on his own lands, he watched as federal troops, Lincoln's "children," approached his camp. Wearing a peace medal that Lincoln had given him, Lean Bear rode slowly toward the troops to once again offer his friendship. When he was twenty yards away, they opened fire, then rode closer, and fired again and again into his fallen body.

AS LEAN BEAR HAD FEARED, in the last decades of the nineteenth century, a flood of settlers ventured into America's newest and last West. Prospectors searched for "pay dirt," railroads crisscrossed the continent, eastern and foreign capitalists invested in cattle and land bonanzas, and farmers took up the promise of free western lands. In the rhetoric of the day, the West was a land of hope and abundance.

With the end of the Civil War, white Americans again claimed a special destiny to expand across the continent. In the process, they crushed the culture of the American Indians and ignored the special contributions of other nationalities, such as the Chinese miners and laborers and the Mexican herdsmen. As millions moved west, new states were carved out of the vast lands beyond the Mississippi. By 1900, there were forty-five states in the Union; only Arizona, New Mexico, and Oklahoma remained territories.

Outline

Beyond the Frontier

Crushing the Native Americans

Settlement of the West

The Bonanza West

Conclusion: The Meaning of the West

We Americans

Blacks in Blue: The Buffalo Soldiers in the West

The West became a great colonial empire, harnessed to eastern capital and tied increasingly to national and international markets. Western economies depended to an unusual degree on the federal government, which subsidized their railroads, distributed their land, and spent millions of dollars for the upkeep of soldiers and Indians.

By the 1890s, the West of the buffalo and Indian was gone, replaced by cities, health resorts, and the latest magazines. The beginnings of irrigated agriculture pointed toward the future of the West. Ghost towns, abandoned farms, and scarred earth left behind by miners and farmers reflected the less favorable side of settlement. The West, the mythic land of cowboys and quick fortunes, was also a place of conquest and exploitation.

Beyond the Frontier

The line of white settlement had reached the edge of the timber country of Missouri by 1840. Beyond lay an enormous land of rolling prairies, parched deserts, and rugged, majestic mountains. Emerging from the timber country, travelers first encountered the Great Plains. The Prairie Plains, the eastern part of the region, enjoyed rich soil and good rainfall. To the west were the High Plains, rough and semiarid, rising gently to the foothills of the Rocky Mountains.

Running from Alaska to central New Mexico, the Rockies presented a formidable barrier. Although the passes were rich in beaver and gold, most travelers hurried through them, emerging in the desolate basin of present-day southern Idaho and Utah. Indians lived there, scrabbling out a bare subsistence by digging for roots, seeds, and berries. To the west, the lofty Coast ranges—the Cascades and the Sierra Nevada—held back rainfall; beyond were the temperate lands of the Pacific Coast.

Early explorers and mapmakers thought the country beyond the Mississippi uninhabitable. Between 1815 and 1860, American maps showed this land as the "Great American Desert." Settlement paused on the edge of the Plains, which daunted settlers dashing across them for California and Oregon.

Few rivers cut through the Plains. Those that did flooded in spring and trickled in summer. The land lacked rainfall for crops and lumber for homes and fences; the cast-iron plow and ax—the tools of eastern settlement—were virtually useless on the tough and treeless Plains soil.

Hot winds seared the Plains in summer, and blizzards and hailstorms froze them in winter. Despite these extremes, wildlife roamed in profusion—antelope, wolves, coyote, jackrabbits, and prairie dogs. The American bison, better known as the buffalo, grazed in enormous herds from Mexico to Canada. In 1865, perhaps 15 million buffalo lived on the Plains.

Crushing the Native Americans

In 1867, when Horace Greeley, editor of the *New York Tribune,* urged New York City's unemployed to head West, where "you will crowd nobody, starve nobody," he, like most of his countrymen, ignored the fact that large numbers of people already lived there. In 1865, nearly a quarter of a million Indians lived in the western half of the country. The Cherokee and other tribes were resettled there after being forced out of their eastern lands by advancing white settlement. Other tribes, such as the Hopi, Zuni, Navajo, Apache, Chinook, and Shasta, were native to the region. By the 1870s, most of these tribes had been destroyed or beaten into submission. The powerful Ute, crushed in 1855, ceded most of their Utah lands to the United States and settled on a small reservation near the Great Salt Lake. The Navajo and Apache fought back desperately, but between 1865 and 1873, they too were confined to reservations. California Indians succumbed to the contagious diseases carried by whites during the Gold Rush of 1849. By 1880, fewer than twenty thousand Indians remained in all of California.

Life of the Plains Indians

Nearly two-thirds of the Indians west of the Mississippi lived on the Great Plains. The Plains tribes included the Sioux, Blackfoot, Cheyenne, Crow, Arapaho, Pawnee, Kiowa, Apache, and Comanche. Nomadic and warlike, the Plains Indians depended on the buffalo—and later the horse as well—for their existence. Skilled horsemen and warriors, the Plains Indians were the superior adversaries in conflicts with white settlers and cavalry. Even the introduction of the new Colt six-shooters during the 1850s did not entirely offset the Indians' advantage.

Migratory by culture, the Plains Indians formed tribes of several thousand people but lived in smaller "bands" of three hundred to five hundred. Each band was governed by a chief and a council, and each acted independently, which caused difficulties for the United States government. The bands followed and lived off the buffalo, using every part of the animal to provide food, clothing, shelter, and even fuel.

Warfare between tribes usually took the form of brief raids and skirmishes. Plains Indians fought few prolonged wars and rarely coveted territory. Most conflicts involved only a few warriors intent on stealing horses or "counting coups"—touching an enemy's body with the hand or a special stick. Certain tribes did, however, develop a fierce warrior class.

The Plains tribes divided labor by gender. Men hunted, traded, supervised ceremonial activities, and cleared ground for planting. Women were responsible for child rearing and artistic creativity. They also performed the camp work, grew vegetables, prepared buffalo meat and hides, and gathered roots and berries. Men were respected for their prowess in hunting and war, women for their skill with quill and paint.

"As Long as Waters Run": Searching for an Indian Policy

Before the mid-nineteenth century, Americans used the land west of the Mississippi as "one big reservation." The government named the area Indian Country, moved eastern tribes there with firm treaty guarantees, and in 1834 passed the Indian Intercourse Act, which prohibited any white person from entering Indian Country without a license.

The situation changed in the 1850s. Americans pushed toward the goldfields and the rich farmland of the West Coast. To clear the way for settlement, the federal government in 1851 abandoned "one big reservation" in favor of a new policy of "concentration." For the first time, it assigned boundaries to each tribe. The land was given to the tribes for "as long as waters run and the grass shall grow."

The concentration policy lasted only a few years. Accustomed to hunting widely for buffalo, many Indians refused to stay within their assigned areas. White settlers poured into Indian lands, then called on the government to protect them. In the 1850s, Indians were pushed out of Kansas and Nebraska; in 1859, gold miners moved into the Pikes Peak country, touching off warfare with the Cheyenne and Arapaho. Although the two tribes fought hard, they were no match for the federal government. In 1864, they asked for peace. Certain that the war was over, Chief Black Kettle led his seven hundred followers to camp on Sand Creek in southeastern Colorado. Early on the morning of November 29, 1864, a Colorado militia led by Colonel John M. Chivington attacked the sleeping Indians, clubbing, stabbing, and scalping Indian men, women, and children. The Chivington massacre set off angry protests in Colorado and the East. The government condemned the "gross and

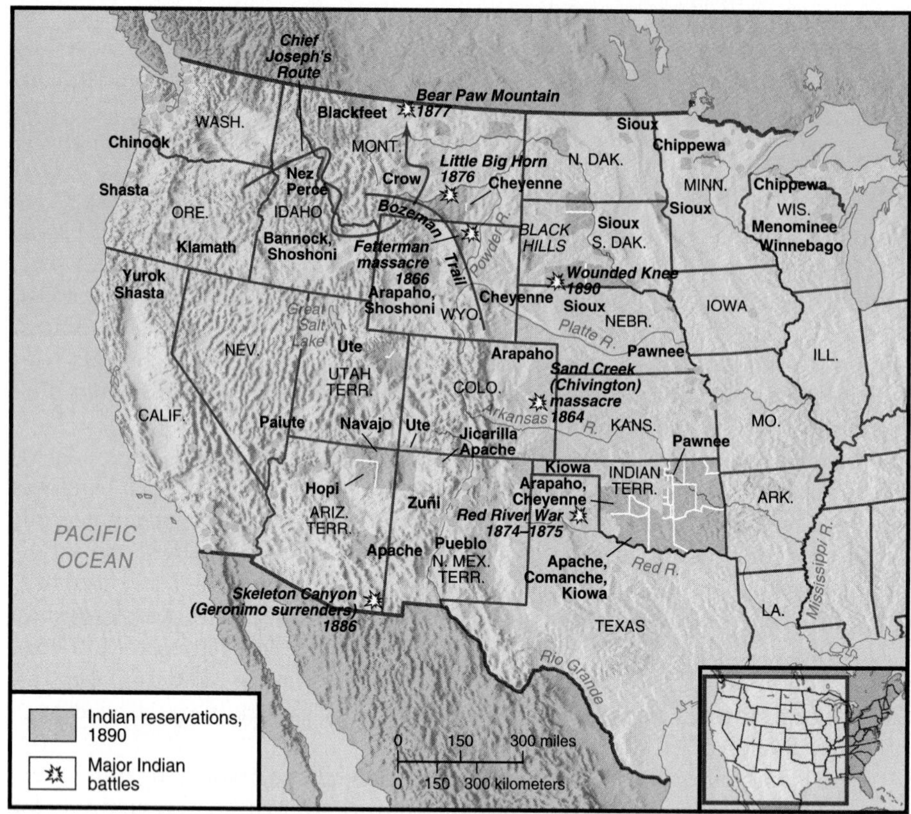

NATIVE AMERICANS IN THE WEST: MAJOR BATTLES AND RESERVATIONS
"They made us many promises, more than I remember, but they never kept but one; they promised to take our land, and they took it." So said Red Cloud of the Oglala Sioux, summarizing Native American–white relations in the 1870s. ❖

wanton outrages." Still, the two tribes were forced to surrender their Sand Creek reservation in exchange for lands elsewhere.

Before long, the powerful Sioux were on the warpath in the great Sioux War of 1865–1867. An invasion of gold miners in Montana touched off the war, which flared even more intensely when the federal government announced plans to connect the various mining towns by building the Bozeman Trail through the heart of the Sioux hunting grounds. Red Cloud, the Sioux chief, was determined to stop the trail. In December 1866, pursued by a U.S. army column under Captain William J. Fetterman, he lured the incautious Fetterman deep into the wilderness, ambushed him, and wiped out all eighty-two soldiers in his command.

The Fetterman massacre, coming so soon after the Chivington massacre, sparked a public debate over the nation's Indian policy. The debate reflected differing white views of the Indians. In the East, some humanitarian and church groups wanted a humane peace policy, directed toward educating and "civilizing" the tribes. Many people, in the East and the West, questioned this approach, convinced that Indians were savages unfit for civilization. Westerners in general favored firm control over the Indians, including swift punishment of any who rebelled.

In 1867, the peace advocates won the debate. Halting construction on the Bozeman Trail, Congress created a peace commission to end the Sioux War. After studying the situation, the peace commission agreed that only one policy offered a permanent solution: a policy of "small reservations" to isolate the Indians on distant lands, teach them to farm, and gradually "civilize" them.

The commission chose two areas to hold all the Plains Indians. The 54,000 Indians on the northern Plains would be moved north of the Black Hills in Dakota

Territory. On the southern Plains, the 86,000 Indians would be moved into present-day Oklahoma. Both regions were considered unattractive to whites. In both areas, tribes would be assigned to specific reservations where government agents could supervise them.

Final Battles on the Plains

Few Indians settled peacefully into life on the new reservations. Young warriors and minor chiefs denounced the treaties and drifted back to the open countryside. In the Southwest, the Kiowa and Comanche rampaged through the Texas Panhandle until the army crushed them into submission in the Red River War of 1874–1875.

On the northern Plains, fighting resulted from the Black Hills Gold Rush of 1875. As prospectors tramped across Indian hunting grounds, the Sioux—led by Rain-in-the-Face, the great war chief Crazy Horse, and the famous medicine man Sitting Bull—gathered to stop them. One army column, under flamboyant Lieutenant Colonel George A. Custer, pushed recklessly ahead in pursuit of the Indians, eager to claim the victory. On the morning of June 25, 1876, thinking he had a small band of Indians surrounded on the banks of the Little Bighorn River in Montana, Custer divided his column and took 265 men toward the Indian village. Instead of fighting a small band, he discovered that he had stumbled on the main Sioux camp of 2,500 warriors. By midafternoon, it was over: Custer and his men were dead. Custer was largely responsible for the loss, but "Custer's Last Stand," set in blazing headlines across the country, signaled a nationwide demand for revenge. Within a few months, the Sioux were surrounded and subdued.

The Sioux War ended the major Indian warfare in the West, but occasional outbreaks occurred for several years thereafter. In 1877, the Nez Percé tribe of Oregon, a people who had warmly welcomed Lewis and Clark in 1805, rebelled under Chief Joseph but were defeated and sent to barren lands in the Indian Country of Oklahoma, where most of them died from disease. In 1890, the Teton Sioux of South Dakota, bitter and starving, became restless. Many of them turned to the **Ghost Dances,** a set of dances and rites designed to bring back Indian lands and cause the whites to disappear.

Ghost Dances A religious movement that arose in the late nineteenth century under the prophet Wavoka, a Paiute Indian. It involved a set of dances and rites that its followers believed would cause white men to disappear and restore lands to the Native Americans.

The army intervened to stop the dancing, touching off violence that killed Sitting Bull and a number of other warriors. Frightened Indians fled southwest to join other Ghost Dancers under the aging chief Big Foot. Moving quickly, troops caught up with Big Foot's band, who agreed to come to the army camp on Wounded Knee Creek in South Dakota. An Indian, it is thought, fired the first shot, which was returned by the army's new machine guns. Firing a shell a second, they shredded tepees and people. In the infamous **Wounded Knee Massacre,** about two hundred men, women, and children were killed in the snow.

Wounded Knee Massacre In December 1890, troopers of the Seventh Cavalry, under orders to stop the Ghost Dance religion among the Sioux, took Chief Big Foot and his followers to a camp on Wounded Knee Creek in South Dakota. Violence ensued and about two hundred Native Americans were killed.

The End of Tribal Life

The final step in Indian policy came in the 1870s and 1880s. Some reformers had long argued against segregating the Indians on reservations, urging instead that the nation assimilate them individually into white culture. These "assimilationists" wanted to use education, land policy, and federal law to eradicate tribal society.

Congress began to adopt the policy in 1871 when it ended the practice of treaty making with Indian tribes. Because tribes were no longer separate nations, they lost many of their political and judicial functions, and the power of the chiefs was weakened. Increasingly, Indians became answerable in regular courts for certain crimes.

While Congress worked to break down the tribes, educators trained young Indians to adjust to white culture. Schools such as the Carlisle Indian School in Carlisle, Pennsylvania, taught students to fix machines and farm. They also forced

This pictogram by Oglala Sioux Amos Bad Heart Bull is a Native American version of the Battle of Little Bighorn, also known as Custer's Last Stand. ❖

them to trim their long hair, speak English, dress like "civilized" whites, and discontinue tribal ceremonies and dances. "Kill the Indian and save the man," said the founder of the Carlisle School.

Land ownership was the final and most important link in the new policy. Indians who owned land, it was thought, would become responsible, self-reliant citizens. Deciding to give each Indian a farm, Congress in 1887 passed the **Dawes Severalty Act,** the most important legal development in Indian-white relations in more than three centuries.

Dawes Severalty Act Legislation passed by Congress in 1887 that aimed at breaking up traditional Indian life by promoting individual land ownership. It divided tribal lands into small plots that were distributed among members of each tribe, with provisions for Indian education and eventual citizenship.

Aiming to end tribal life, the Dawes Act divided tribal lands into small plots for distribution among members of the tribe. Each family head received 160 acres, single adults 80 acres, and children 40 acres. To keep the Indians' land from falling into the hands of speculators, the federal government held it in trust for twenty-five years. In addition, American citizenship was granted to Indians who accepted their land, lived apart from the tribe, and "adopted the habits of civilized life."

Through the Dawes Act, 47 million acres of land were distributed to Indians and their families. There were another 90 million acres in the reservations, and these lands, often the most fertile, were sold to white settlers. To evade the twenty-five year rule, speculators leased rather than purchased the land from the Indians. Many Indians knew little about farming. Their tools were rudimentary, and in the culture of the Plains Indians, farming was women's work. In 1934, the government returned to the idea of tribal land ownership, but by then, 138 million acres of Indian land had shrunk to 48 million acres, half of which was barren.

The final blow to tribal life came with the virtual extermination of the buffalo, the Plains Indians' chief resource and the basis for their unique way of life. The slaughter began in the 1860s as the transcontinental railroads pushed west and accelerated after 1871 when a Pennsylvania tannery discovered that buffalo hides made valuable leather. Professional hunters such as William F. "Buffalo Bill" Cody swarmed across the Plains, killing millions of the helpless beasts—three million a year between 1872 and 1874. A good hunter killed a hundred buffalo a day; skinners took off the hides, removed the tongue, hump, and tallow, and left the rest. The waste was incredible, and by 1883, the buffalo were almost gone. When the government later set out to produce the famous "Buffalo nickel," the designer had to go to the Bronx Zoo in New York City to find a living specimen.

By 1900, there were only 200,000 Indians in the country, most of them on reservations. Poverty, alcoholism, and unemployment were growing problems. Indians, no longer able to live off the buffalo, became wards of the state. Once possessors of the entire continent, they had been crowded into smaller and smaller areas, overwhelmed by the demand to become settled, literate, and English-speaking, like the white man.

Even as the Indians lost their identity, they entered the romantic folklore of the West. Dime novels told exciting tales of Indians fighting on the Plains. Buffalo Bill Cody turned it all into a profitable business. Beginning in 1883, Cody's Wild West Show ran for more than three decades, playing to viewers in the United States and Europe. Perhaps the end of an era was most fittingly symbolized in 1885 when Sitting Bull himself, victor over Custer at the battle of Little Big Horn, performed in the show.

Settlement of the West

Between 1870 and 1900, white—and some black—Americans settled the enormous total of 430 million acres west of the Mississippi; they occupied more land than in all the years before 1870. People moved west for many reasons. Some sought adventure; others wanted to escape the drab routine of the factory or city life. Many moved to California for their health. The Mormons settled Utah to escape religious persecution.

Whatever the specific reason, most people moved west to better their lot. On the whole, their timing was good, for as the nation's population grew, so did demand for the livestock and the agricultural, mineral, and lumber products of the expanding West. Contrary to older historical views, the West did not act as a major "safety valve," an outlet for social and economic tensions. The poor and unemployed did not have the means to move there and establish farms; most people moved west in periods of expanding demand, when the prospects for making money from this new land looked brightest.

Men and Women on the Overland Trail

The first movement west aimed not for the nearby Plains but for California and Oregon. Between 1848 and 1878, perhaps half a million individuals made the long journey over the **Overland Trail** leading west. Some walked; others rode horses alone or in small groups. About half joined great caravans that inched across the 2,000 miles between the Missouri River and the Pacific Coast.

Overland Trail The route taken by thousands of travelers from the Mississippi Valley to the Pacific Coast in the last half of the nineteenth century. It was extremely difficult, often taking six months or more to complete.

More often than not, men made the decision to make the crossing; wives either went along or faced being left behind. Four out of five men on the Overland Trail had moved before. Most had little cash, but they needed only strong legs, a few staples, and a willingness to tighten the belt when game was scarce. The majority of people traveled in family groups, including in-laws, grandchildren, aunts, and uncles, meaning that their "quest for something new would take place in the context of the very familiar."

Individuals and wagon trains set out from various points along the Missouri River. Leaving in the spring and traveling through the summer, they hoped to reach their destination before the first snowfall. During April, travelers gradually assembled in spring camp. There they carefully packed their wagons, elected the train's leaders, and decided on the rules that they would observe during their trip west.

Setting out in early May, travelers divided the enormous route into manageable portions. From a distance, the white-topped wagons seemed driven by a common force, but in fact, internal discipline was a constant problem. Arguments erupted over the pace of the march, the choice of campsites, whether to rest or push on. Elected leaders quit; new ones were chosen.

Men, women, and children had different tasks on the trail. Men concerned themselves almost entirely with hunting, guard duty, and transportation. The women prepared the food, and the children kindled the fire, brought water to camp, and searched for wood and other fuel. Rising before the sun and walking 15 miles a day, in searing heat and mountain cold, travelers were weary by late afternoon.

For women, the trail was lonely, and they worked to exhaustion. Before long, they adjusted their clothing to the harsh conditions, adopting the new bloomer pants or shortening their skirts. Like men, they carried firearms in case of Indian attacks. Most emigrants, however, saw few Indians en route.

What they did often see was trash, miles of it, for the overland travelers dumped garbage, tin cans, furniture, tools, and clothing willy-nilly on their way west. They abandoned wagons, deserted dying animals, and stirred up dust to such an extent that drivers wore goggles to see.

The first stage of the journey was deceptively easy, and travelers usually reached Fort Kearney, in the Nebraska Territory, by late May. From there the trip became more demanding. Summer heat baked the route to Fort Laramie, on the eastern edge of the Wyoming Territory. Anxious to beat the early snowfalls, travelers rested a day or two at the fort, then hurried on to South Pass, the best route through the forbidding Rockies. Although still summer, the mountain nights were so cold that ice formed atop the water buckets.

Beyond South Pass, migrants went in different directions; some headed south through Utah, others toward Fort Hall in Idaho and then on to California. Months of hard traveling were still before them. They had to cross deserts and the towering Sierra Nevada. Not until September or October would they reach the verdant Sacramento Valley.

Under the best of conditions, the trip took almost six months—hard, grueling labor, sixteen hours a day, dawn to dusk. Journeying halfway across the continent was a never-to-be-forgotten experience for those who did it. The wagon trains, carrying the dreams of thousands of individuals, reproduced society in small focus: individualistic, hopeful, mobile, divided by age and gender roles, apprehensive, yet willing to strike out for the distant and the new.

Land for the Taking

As railroads pushed west in the 1870s and 1880s, locomotive trains replaced wagon trains, but the shift was gradual. Like many Americans, thousands of Europeans traveled by rail to designated outfitting places and then continued their trek in wagons drawn by oxen. Traffic flowed in both directions; eager settlers heading west passed defeated ones returning east. Immigrants from Asia and Mexico joined the flow by moving to the American West from the east and south.

Why did they come? In a word, land. The federal government had promised to give land to the head of each family that settled in the new territories. A popular camp song reflected this motive:

> Come along, come along—don't be alarmed.
>
> Uncle Sam is rich enough to give us all a farm.

Uncle Sam owned about 1 billion acres of land in the 1860s, much of it mountain and desert land unsuited for agriculture. By 1890, the government had distributed 48 million acres under the **Homestead Act of 1862.** But far more acres were sold—to private citizens, to corporations, and to the states. Huge tracts were granted to railroad companies to tempt them to build across the unsettled West.

Homestead Act of 1862 Legislation granting 160 acres of land to anyone who paid a $10 fee and pledged to live on and cultivate the land for five years. The act encouraged a large migration to the West.

The Homestead Act of 1862, a law of great significance, gave 160 acres of land to anyone who would pay a $10 registration and pledge to live on it and cultivate it for five years. The offer set off a mass migration of land-hungry Europeans dazzled by a country that gave its land away. Americans also seized on the act's provisions, and between 1862 and 1900, nearly 600,000 families claimed free homesteads under it.

Yet the Homestead Act did not work as Congress had hoped. Tailored to the timber and water conditions of the East, the act was not suited to the semiarid West. Without irrigation, a 160-acre farm was simply not large enough to be self-supporting on the Great Plains.

The Timber Culture Act of 1873 attempted to adjust the Homestead Act to western conditions. It allowed homesteaders to claim an additional 160 acres if they planted trees on a quarter of it within four years. A successful act, it encouraged forestation and expanded farms to a workable size. By contrast, the Desert Land Act of 1877, which allowed individuals to obtain 640 acres in the arid states for $1.25 an acre, provided that they irrigated part of it within three years, invited wholesale fraud; irrigation was sometimes interpreted by ranchers as a bucket of water dumped on the ground.

The Timber and Stone Act of 1878 permitted anyone in California, Nevada, Oregon, and Washington to buy up to 160 acres of forestland, deemed "unfit for cultivation," for $2.50 an acre. As the ranchers had, timber companies used employees to file false claims and other fraudulent practices to acquire more land than the law allowed.

Speculators made ingenious use of the land laws. Sending agents in advance of settlement, they moved along choice river bottoms or irrigable areas, accumulating large holdings to be held for high prices. In the arid West, where control of water meant control of the surrounding land, shrewd ranchers plotted their holdings accordingly. In Colorado, one cattleman, John F. Iliff, owned only 105 small parcels of land, but by placing them around the few waterholes, he effectively dominated an empire stretching over 6,000 square miles.

Half a billion acres of western land were given or sold to speculators and corporations. At the same time, only 600,000 homestead patents were issued, covering 80 million acres. Thus only one acre in every nine initially went to individual pioneers, the intended beneficiaries of the nation's largesse.

Water, in fact, became the dominant western issue, since much of the trans-Mississippi West was arid, receiving less than 20 inches of rainfall annually. People speculated in water as if it were gold and planned great irrigation systems to "make the desert bloom." The federal government helped fuel their dreams. The 1902 **National Reclamation Act (Newlands Act)** set aside most of the proceeds from the sale of public lands in sixteen western states to finance irrigation projects. Over the next decades, dams, canals, and irrigation systems channeled water into dry areas, creating a "hydraulic" society where control of water often brought enormous power.

National Reclamation Act (Newlands Act) Passed in 1902, legislation that set aside the majority of the proceeds from the sale of public land in sixteen Western states to fund irrigation projects in the arid states.

As beneficiaries of the government's policy of land grants for railway construction, the railroad companies were the West's largest landowners. Eager to have immigrants settle on the land they owned and also to boost their freight and passenger business, the companies sent attractive sales brochures to the East and Europe, touting life in the West. Union Pacific's advertisement described the rocky Platte Valley in Nebraska as "a flowery meadow clothed in nutritious grasses."

As new areas of the West opened, they were organized as territories under the control of Congress and the president. The president appointed the governor and

Railroad companies distributed elaborately illustrated brochures and broadsides to lure people to the West, where they could settle on land owned by the railroads, such as the 3 million acres in Nebraska advertised in this Union Pacific poster. ❖

judges in each territory; Congress detailed their duties, set their budgets, and oversaw their activities. Territorial officials had almost absolute power over the territories.

The Spanish-Speaking Southwest

In the nineteenth century, almost all Spanish-speaking people in the United States lived in California, Arizona, New Mexico, Texas, and Colorado. Their numbers were small, but the influence of their culture and institutions was large. In some respects, the southwestern frontier was more Hispanic American than Anglo-American.

Pushing northward from Mexico, the Spanish brought to the Southwest irrigation, stock raising, weaving, and mining. Both the Spanish and, later, the Mexicans created the legal framework for distributing land and water. They gave large grants of land to communities for grazing, to individuals as rewards for service, and to the various Indian pueblos (villages).

The Californios, descendants of the original colonizers of California, began to lose their once vast landholdings to drought and mortgages after the 1860s. Some turned to banditry; others lived in poverty and remembered better days. But as the Californios died out, Mexican Americans continued the Spanish-Mexican influence. In 1880, one-quarter of the residents of Los Angeles County were Spanish-speaking.

In New Mexico, Hispanic culture dominated the territory. The movement of Anglo ranchers onto contested Spanish land grants met with resistance by hooded nightriders in the 1880s. Spanish-speaking citizens remained the majority ethnic group in New Mexico until the 1940s.

Throughout the Southwest, the Spanish-Mexican heritage gave a distinctive shape to society. Men headed the family and dominated economic life. Women had substantial economic rights (though few political ones), and they enjoyed a status their English-American counterparts did not have. Wives kept full control of property acquired before marriage; they also held half-title to all property in a marriage, which later caused many southwestern states to pass community property laws.

In addition, the Spanish-Mexican heritage fostered a modified economic caste system, a strong Roman Catholic influence, and the primary use of the Spanish language. Continuous immigration from Mexico kept language and cultural ties strong. Spanish names and customs spread, even among Anglos. Confronted by Sheriff Pat Garrett in a darkened room, New Mexico's famous outlaw, Billy the Kid, died asking, *"Quién es? Quién es?"* ("Who is it? Who is it?")

The Bonanza West

Between 1850 and 1900, wave after wave of newcomers swept over the trans-Mississippi West. There were riches for the taking, hidden in gold-washed streams, spread lushly over grass-covered prairies, or available in the gullible minds of greedy newcomers. The nineteenth-century West took shape in the search for mining, cattle, and land bonanzas that drew eager settlers from the East and around the world.

As with all bonanzas, the consequences in the West were uneven growth, boom-and-bust economic cycles, and wasted resources. As a society, it seemed constantly in the making. People moved here and there, following river bottoms, gold strikes, railroad tracks, and other opportunities. "Instant cities" such as San Francisco, Salt Lake City, and Denver arose, and cow towns and mining camps sprang up seemingly overnight. San Francisco grew to a third of a million people in a little more than two decades; Boston took more than two centuries to do the same.

The Mining Bonanza

Mining was the first important magnet to attract people to the West. Many came to "strike it rich" in gold and silver, but at least half the newcomers had no intention of working in the mines. Instead, they provided food, clothing, and services to the thousands of miners. For example, Leland Stanford and Collis P. Huntington, who later built the Central Pacific Railroad, set up a general store in Sacramento where they sold shovels and supplies.

The California **Gold Rush of 1849** began the mining boom and set the pattern for subsequent experience. Individual prospectors made the first strikes, discovering pockets of gold along streams flowing westward from the Sierra Nevada. Practicing a simple process called **placer mining,** they needed only a shovel, a washing pan, and a good claim. As the placers gave out, a great deal of gold remained, but it was locked in quartz or buried deep in the earth. Mining became an expensive business, far beyond the reach of the average miner.

Gold Rush of 1849 Individual prospectors made the first gold strikes along the Sierra Nevada Mountains in 1849, touching off the mining boom that helped shape the development of the West and set the pattern for subsequent strikes in other regions.

placer mining A form of mining that required little technology or skill, placer mining techniques included using a shovel and a washing pan to separate gold from the ore in streams and riverbeds.

Large corporations moved in to dig the deep shafts and finance costly equipment. Eastern and European financiers assumed control, labor became unionized, and mining towns took on some of the characteristics of industrial cities. Individual prospectors, meanwhile, dashed on to the next find. Unlike other frontiers, the mining frontier moved from west to east as the original California miners hurried eastward in search of the big strike.

In 1859, fresh strikes were made near Pikes Peak in Colorado and in the Carson River Valley of Nevada. News of both discoveries set off wild migrations, and the gold near Pikes Peak quickly played out. But the Nevada find uncovered a thick, bluish black ore that was almost pure silver and gold. A quick-witted drifter named Henry T. P. Comstock talked his way into partnership in the claim, and word of the **Comstock Lode** flashed over the mountains.

Comstock Lode Discovered in 1859 near Virginia City, Nevada, this ore deposit was the richest discovery in the history of mining. Between 1859 and 1879 it produced silver and gold worth more than $306 million.

Thousands of miners climbed the Sierra Nevada that summer of 1859. But the biggest strike was yet to come. In 1873, John W. Mackay and three partners formed a company to dig deep into the mountain, and at 1,167 feet they hit the Big Bonanza, a seam of gold and silver more than 54 feet wide. It was the richest discovery in the history of mining. Although most of the profits went to financiers and corporations, Mackay himself became the richest person in the world.

In the 1860s and 1870s, important strikes were made in Washington, Idaho, Nevada, Colorado, Montana, Arizona, and the Dakota Territory. Miners flocked from strike to strike, and new camps and mining towns sprang up overnight. The miners were extremely mobile, usually moving on when the pay dirt played out.

The final fling came in the Black Hills rush of 1874–1876. The army had tried to keep miners out of the area, the heart of the Sioux hunting grounds, and even sent a scientific party under Colonel George A. Custer to disprove the rumors of gold. Instead, Custer found gold all over the hills, and the rush was on. Miners, gamblers, desperadoes, and prostitutes flocked to Deadwood, the most lawless of all the mining camps.

Towns such as Deadwood, in the Dakota Territory; Virginia City, Nevada; Leadville, Colorado; and Tombstone, Arizona, began a new process in the frontier experience. Unlike the rural setting of the farming frontier, the mining camp became the germ of a city, and theaters, the latest fashions, schools, and lending libraries

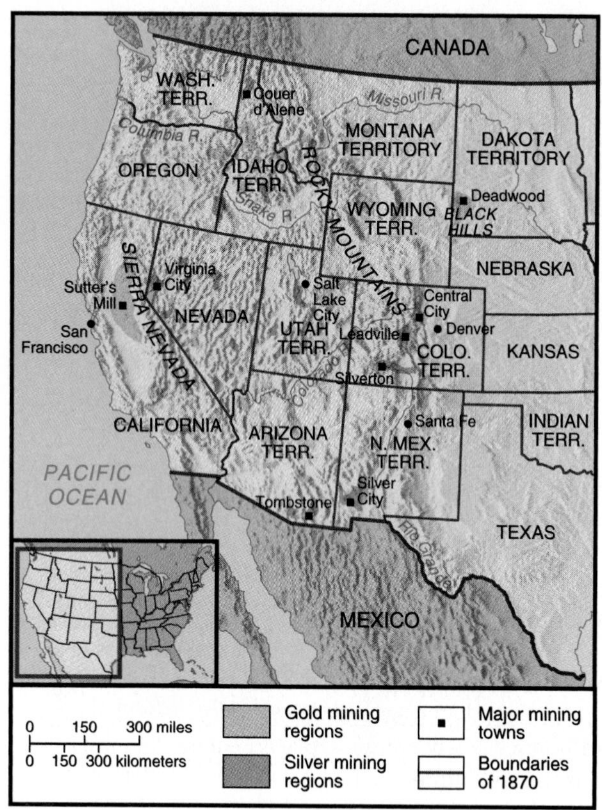

MINING REGIONS OF THE WEST *Gold and silver mines dotted the West, drawing settlers and encouraging political organization in many areas.* ❖

came quickly to them, providing civilized refinements not available on other frontiers. But urbanization also created the need for municipal government, sanitation, and law enforcement.

Mining camps were governed by a simple democracy. Soon after a strike, the miners in the area met to organize a mining "district" and adopted rules governing behavior in it. Rules regulated the size and boundaries of claims, established procedures for settling disputes, and set penalties for crimes. Petty criminals were banished from the district; serious offenders were hanged. Early visitors to the mining country were struck by the way miners, solitary and competitive, joined together, founded a camp, and created a society.

The camps were mostly male, made up of "men who can rough it" and a few women of "spirit and energy." Prostitutes followed the camps around the West, and "respectable" women were objects of curiosity. Some women worked claims, but more often they took jobs as cooks, housekeepers, and seamstresses—for wages considerably higher than in the East.

The lure of gold drew large numbers of Chinese, Chileans, Peruvians, Mexicans, English, French, and Germans to the mining camps. The Latin Americans brought valuable mining techniques, and the painstaking Chinese profitably worked claims others had abandoned. In the 1860s, almost one-third of the miners in the West were Chinese.

Hostility often surfaced against foreign miners, particularly the French, Latin Americans, and Chinese. In California, special taxes were levied to drive away foreign competition. Finally, after several riots and intense political pressure, Congress passed the Chinese Exclusion Act of 1882, which suspended immigration of Chinese laborers for ten years.

By the 1890s, the early mining bonanza was over. All told, the western mines contributed billions of dollars to the economy. They helped finance the Civil War and provided needed capital for industrialization. The vast boost in silver production thanks to the Comstock Lode changed the relative value of gold and silver, the bases of American currency. Bitter disputes over the currency affected politics and led to the famous "battle of the standards" during the presidential election of 1896 (see Chapter 20).

The mining frontier populated portions of the West and sped its political organization. Nevada, Idaho, and Montana were granted early statehood because of mining. Merchants, editors, lawyers, and ministers flocked to the frontier and established permanent settlements. But the industry also left behind painful scars in the form of ravaged Indian reservations, pitted hills, and lonely ghost towns.

Gold from the Roots Up: The Cattle Bonanza

"There's gold from the grass roots down," said California Joe, a guide in the gold districts of the Dakota Territory in the 1870s, "but there's more gold from the grass roots up." Ranchers began to recognize the potential of the vast grasslands of the West. The Plains were covered with buffalo or grama grass, a wiry variety with short, hard stems. Cattle thrived on it.

For twenty years after 1865, cattle ranching dominated the "open range," a vast, fenceless area extending from the Texas Panhandle north into Canada. Such techniques of the business as branding, roundups, and roping came from Mexico. The cattle themselves, the famous Texas longhorns, also came from Mexico. Although their meat was coarse and stringy, they fed a nation hungry for beef at the end of the Civil War.

The problem was to get the beef to eastern markets, and Joseph G. McCoy, a livestock shipper from Illinois, solved it. Looking for a way to market Texas beef, McCoy conceived the idea of taking the cattle on "long drives" to railheads in Kansas. After several rebuffs, the persistent McCoy signed a contract in 1867 with the Hannibal and St. Joseph Railroad. Searching for an appropriate rail junction, he settled on the sleepy Kansas town of Abilene.

In September 1867, McCoy shipped the first train of twenty cars of longhorn cattle. By the end of the year, a thousand carloads had followed, all headed for Chicago markets. In 1871, some 700,000 head of Texas cattle reached Abilene. The profits were enormous; drivers bought cheap Texas steers for $7 a head and sold them for $60 or $70 each at a northern railhead.

Cowboys pushed steers northward on the Chisholm and other trails in herds of two to three thousand. Novels and films have portrayed the mounted herdsmen as white, but at least one-quarter of them were black and possibly another quarter were Mexicans. A typical crew on the trail north might have eight men, half of

❖ A Look at the Past ❖

Cowboy Clothing

Cowboys hold a special place in American mythology, representing rugged individuals able to survive in the wilderness. They symbolize another element of our nation's history: the variety of people who formed the country. African Americans, Mexican Americans, Anglo-Americans, and others rode the plains. The clothes cowboys wore during the mid-nineteenth century, such as these wool caballeros pants trimmed with gold braid and with flared legs that button down the sides, show the cultural mixing that took place in the West and how people adapted to the demands of the environment. By the end of the nineteenth century, cowboy heroes, such as those in Buffalo Bill's Wild West Show, no longer wore serapes, sashes, short jackets, or pants such as these that shared Spanish and Mexican origins. What does the change in cowboy fashion suggest about attitudes toward Mexicans? Why would it matter that cowboy heroes wore clothes that reflected Anglo origins, rather than Mexican?

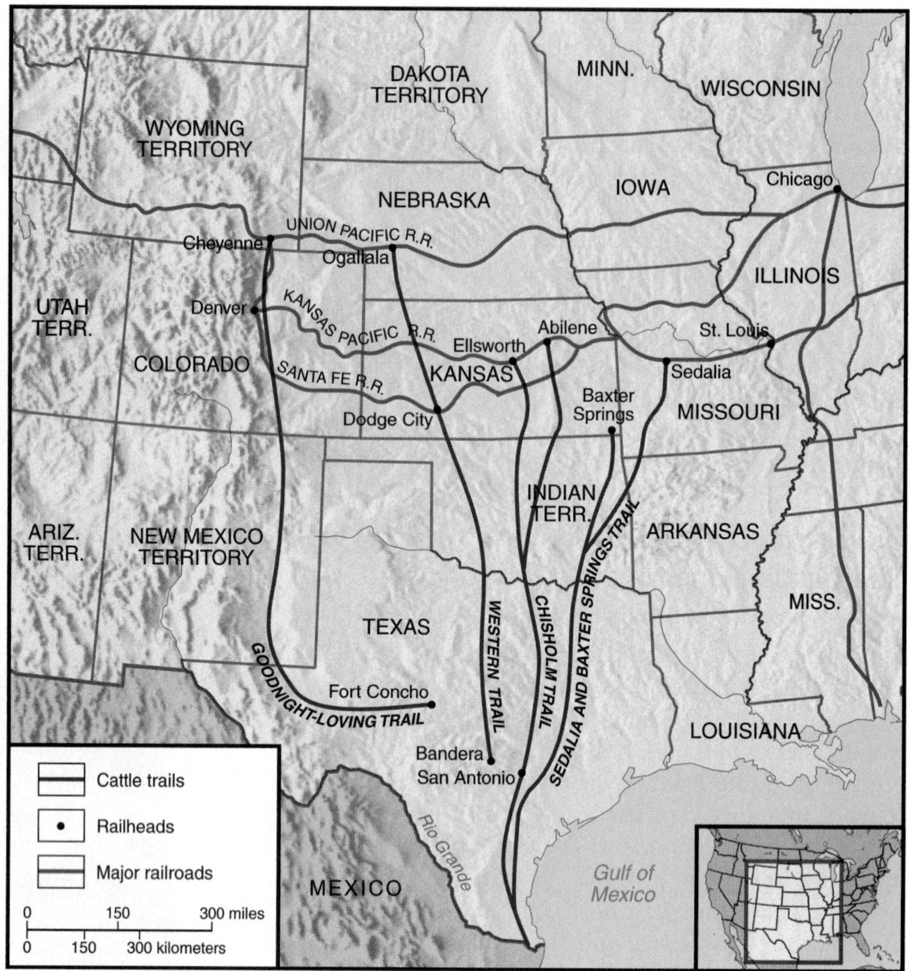

CATTLE TRAILS *Cattle raised in Texas were driven along the cattle trails to the northern railheads, and trains carried them to market.* ❖

them black or Mexican. Most of the trail bosses were white; they earned about $125 a month.

Like miners, cattlemen lived beyond the formal reach of the law and so established their own. A cowboy who shot another was hanged on the spot. Ranchers adopted rules for cattle ownership, branding, roundups, and drives, and they formed associations to enforce them. The Wyoming Stock Growers' Association, the largest and most formidable, was often "the law" in Wyoming and extended its reach well into Colorado, Nebraska, Montana, and the Dakota Territory.

Hollywood to the contrary, there was little violence in the booming cow towns. Doc Holliday and William B. (Bat) Masterson never killed anyone, and the number of homicides in a year never topped five in any cattle town. In fact, famous western sheriffs such as Wild Bill Hickok and Wyatt Earp repaired streets and sidewalks far more frequently than they used their guns.

By 1880, more than six million head of cattle had been driven to northern markets. But the era of the great cattle drive was ending. Farmers were planting wheat on the old buffalo ranges; barbed wire, a recent invention, cut across the trails and divided up the big ranches. Mechanical improvements in slaughtering, refrigerated transportation, and cold storage modernized the industry. Ranchers bred the Texas longhorns with heavier Hereford and Angus bulls, and as the new breeds proved profitable, more and more ranches opened on the northern ranges. By the mid-

1880s, large investments had transformed ranching into big business, often controlled by absentee owners.

By 1885, the northern ranges were becoming dangerously overcrowded. To make matters worse, the winter of 1885–1886 was cold, and the following summer was one of the hottest on record. Waterholes dried up; the grass turned brown. Beef prices fell. The winter of 1886–1887 was one of the worst in western history. Temperatures dropped to 45 degrees below zero, and cattle that once would have saved themselves by drifting ahead of the storms perished when they came up against the new barbed wire fences. When the snows thawed, ranchers found tens of thousands of carcasses stacked up against fences.

The cattle business recovered, but it took different directions. Outside capital, so plentiful in the boom years, dried up. Ranchers began fencing their lands, reducing the size of their herds, and growing hay for winter food. To the dismay of cowboys, mowing machines and hay rakes became as important as chuck wagons and branding irons. The last roundup on the northern ranges took place in 1905. Ranches grew smaller, and some ranchers switched to raising sheep. Homesteaders, armed with barbed wire and new strains of wheat, pushed onto the Plains, and the day of the open range was over.

Sodbusters on the Plains: The Farming Bonanza

Like miners and cattlemen, millions of farmers moved west in the decades after 1870 to seek crop bonanzas and new ways of life. Some realized their dreams; many fought just to survive.

Between 1870 and 1900, farmers cultivated more land than ever before in American history. They peopled the Plains from the Dakota Territory to Texas, pushed the Indians out of their last sanctuary in Oklahoma, and poured into the basins and foothills of the Rockies. By 1900, the western half of the nation contained almost 30 percent of the population, compared to less than 1 percent just a half-century earlier.

Unlike mining, farm settlement often followed predictable patterns, taking population from states east of the frontier line and moving gradually westward. The movement slumped during the depression of the 1870s, but after several years of above-average rainfall on the Great Plains, a new wave of optimism carried thousands more west. Between 1870 and 1900, the population on the Plains tripled.

In some areas, the newcomers were blacks who had fled the South, fed up with beatings and murders, crop liens, and the Black Codes that institutionalized their subordinate status. In 1879, about six thousand African Americans known as the **Exodusters** left their homes in Louisiana, Mississippi, and Texas to establish new and freer lives in Kansas, the home of John Brown and the Free-Soil campaigns of the 1850s. Once there, they farmed or worked as laborers; women worked in the fields alongside the men or cleaned houses and took in washing to make ends meet. All told, the Exodusters homesteaded 20,000 acres of land, and though they met prejudice, it was not as extreme as they had known at home.

Exodusters A group of about six thousand African Americans who left their homes in Louisiana, Mississippi, and Texas in 1879, seeking freer lives in Kansas, where they worked as farmers or laborers.

Other African Americans moved to Oklahoma, thinking they might establish the first African American state. Whether headed for Oklahoma or Kansas, they picked up and moved in sizable groups that were based on family units; they took with them the customs they had known, and in their new homes they were able, for the first time, to have some measure of self-government.

For blacks and whites alike, farming on the Plains presented new problems. There was little surface water, and wells ranged between 50 and 500 feet deep. Lumber for homes and fences was also scarce. Water could be brought to the surface by windmills and lumber could be imported, but both solutions required more money than most farmers had.

Unable to afford wood, farmers often started out in dreary sod houses. Cut into 3-foot sections, the thick prairie sod was laid like brick. Since glass was scarce, cloth hung over the windows; a blanket was hung from the ceiling to make two rooms. A sod house provided little light or air but cost only $2.78 to build.

Outside, the Plains environment sorely tested the men and women who moved there. Neighbors were distant; the land stretched on as far as the eye could see. Always the wind blew. A sense of loneliness and desolation pervaded prairie life.

In winter, savage storms swept the open grasslands. Summertime temperatures stayed near 110 degrees for weeks at a time. Fearsome rainstorms, building in the summer's heat, beat down the young corn and wheat. The summers also brought grasshoppers, flying in swarms so huge they shut out the sun. The grasshoppers ate everything in sight: crops, clothing, mosquito netting, tree bark, even plow handles.

❖ A Look at the Past ❖

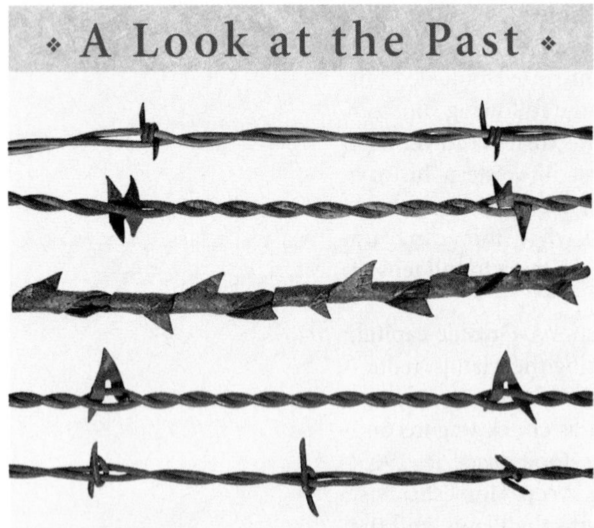

Barbed Wire

Barbed wire forever altered land use in the West. Perfected in 1874, barbed wire made effective, economical fencing. Reflecting its importance to western farmers, barbed wire soon came in hundreds of varieties, including decorative versions. Most variations performed equally well, however, making so many designs unnecessary. Why do you think so many types existed?

New Farming Methods

Farmers embraced new technology to meet conditions on the Plains. Cheap and effective fencing material became available with the invention of barbed wire by an Illinois farmer, Joseph Glidden, in 1874. Other inventions, similarly designed to meet the new conditions, included James Oliver's patented chilled-iron plow with a smooth-surface mold board that did not clog in the thick prairie soils.

Farming techniques also adapted to the new environment. **Dry farming** helped compensate for the lack of rainfall. By plowing furrows 12 to 14 inches deep and creating a dust mulch to fill the furrows, farmers loosened the soil and slowed evaporation. New milling methods were developed in the 1870s to process the hard-kerneled imported varieties of wheat. Scientific agriculture advanced with new discoveries linking soil minerals and plant growth. The Hatch Act, passed in 1887, established a network of agricultural experiment stations that provided information about the new discoveries to farmers.

dry farming A farming technique developed to allow farming in the more arid parts of the West. Furrows were plowed a foot or so deep and filled with a dust mulch to loosen soil and slow evaporation.

In the late 1870s, huge **bonanza farms** arose, run by the new machinery and financed with outside capital. Oliver Dalrymple, the most famous of the bonanza farmers, hired armies of workers, bought machinery by the carload, and planted on a scale that dazzled the West. Using 200 pairs of harrows, 155 binders, and 16 threshers, Dalrymple produced 600,000 bushels of wheat in 1881. He and other bonanza managers profited from the economics of scale, buying materials at wholesale prices and receiving rebates from the railroads.

bonanza farms Huge farms covering thousands of acres on the Great Plains. In relying on large size and new machinery, they represented a development in agriculture similar to that taking place in industry

Then a period of drought began. Rainfall dropped between 1885 and 1890, and the large-scale growers found it hard to compete with smaller farmers who diversified their crops and cultivated more intensively. Many of the large bonanzas slowly disintegrated, and Dalrymple himself went bankrupt in 1896.

Discontent on the Farm

Struck by the drabness of rural life, Oliver H. Kelley, a clerk in the Department of Agriculture, in 1867 founded the **National Grange of the Patrons of Husbandry,** known simply as the Grange. The Grange provided social, cultural, and educational activities for its members. Its constitution banned involvement in politics, but Grangers often ignored it and supported railroad regulation and other measures.

National Grange of the Patrons of Husbandry Founded by Oliver H. Kelly in 1867, the Grange sought to relieve the drabness of farm life by providing a social, educational, and cultural outlet for its members. It also set up grain elevators, cooperative stores, warehouses, insurance companies, and farm machinery factories.

The Grange grew rapidly during the depression of the 1870s, and by 1875, it had more than 800,000 members. Local Granges set up cooperative stores, grain elevators, warehouses, insurance companies, and farm machinery factories. Many failed, but in the meantime the organization made its mark. Discontent grew, spilling over into the turbulent Populist movement of the 1890s. (See Chapter 20 for a more detailed discussion.)

Like the cattle boom, the farming boom ended sharply after 1887. A severe drought that year cut harvests, and other droughts followed in 1889 and 1894. Thousands of new farmers were wiped out on the western Plains. Between 1888 and 1892, more than half the population of western Kansas left.

Farmers grew angry and restless. They complained about declining crop prices, rising railroad rates, and heavy mortgages. In the wheat-growing Plains, the economic problems were persistent. Returning home to Iowa in 1889, the author Hamlin Garland found his farming friends caught up "in a sullen rebellion against government and against God."

Although many farmers were unhappy, the peopling of the West in those years transformed American agriculture. The states beyond the Mississippi became the garden land of the nation. California sent fruit, wine, and wheat to eastern markets. Under the Mormons, Utah flourished with irrigation. Texas beef stocked the country's tables, and vast wheat fields, stretching to the horizon, covered Minnesota, the Dakotas, Montana, and eastern Colorado. All produced more than Americans could consume. By 1890, American farmers were exporting large amounts of wheat and other crops.

Farmers became more commercial and scientific. They needed to know more and work harder. Mail-order houses and rural free delivery diminished their isolation and tied them ever closer to the national future. "This is a new age to the farmer," said a statistician in the Department of Agriculture in 1889. "He is now, more than ever before, a citizen of the world."

The Final Fling

As the West filled in with people, pressure mounted on the federal government to open the last Indian territory, Oklahoma, to settlers. Congress and the president responded, forcing the Creek and Seminole to surrender their rights. President Benjamin Harrison announced the opening of the Oklahoma District as of noon, April 22, 1889.

Preparation was feverish all along the frontier. On the morning of April 22, nearly 100,000 people lined the Oklahoma borders. At noon, the starting flag dropped, and horses and wagons loaded with people and hopes moved into the "last" territory. By sunset that day, settlers had claimed twelve thousand homesteads, and the 1,920,000 acres of the Oklahoma District were officially settled. Reflecting the speed of western settlement, a character in Edna Ferber's novel *Cimarron* declared: "Creation! Hell! That took six days. This was done in one."

Conclusion: The Meaning of the West

Between the Civil War and 1900, the West witnessed one of the greatest migrations in history. With the Indians driven into smaller and smaller areas, farms, ranches, mines, and cities rose up on the vast lands from the Mississippi to the Pacific. The 1890 census noted that for the first time in the country's history, "there can hardly be said to be a frontier line."

Picking up the theme, historian Frederick Jackson Turner, in an influential 1893 paper, claimed that the existence of the frontier and of free land explained American development. It shaped customs and character; gave rise to independence, self-confidence, and individualism; and fostered invention and adaptation. Historians have substantially modified **Turner's thesis** by pointing to frontier

Turner's thesis Put forth by historian Frederick Jackson Turner in an 1893 paper, this thesis asserted that the existence of a frontier and its settlement had shaped American character; given rise to individualism, independence, and self-confidence; and fostered the American spirit of invention and adaptation.

CHRONOLOGY

1849	Gold draws prospectors to California
1859	More gold discoveries are made in Colorado and Nevada
1862	Congress passes the Homestead Act, encouraging western settlement
1864	Nevada is admitted to the Union ❖ Colonel John Chivington leads a massacre of Indians at Sand Creek, Colorado
1865–1867	Sioux fight white miners and the U.S. Army in the Great Sioux War
1866	"Long drive" of cattle touches off cattle bonanzas
1867	Horace Greeley urges Easterners to go west ❖ National Grange of the Patrons of Husbandry is founded to enrich farmers' lives
1867–1868	Policy of "small reservations" for Indians is adopted
1873	Congress passes the Timber Culture Act ❖ Big Bonanza is discovered on the Comstock Lode in Nevada
1874	Joseph F. Glidden invents barbed wire ❖ Discovery of gold in Dakota Territory sets off Black Hills Gold Rush
1876	Colorado is admitted to the Union ❖ Custer and his men are defeated and killed by the Sioux at Little Bighorn
1883	Museum expedition discovers fewer than two hundred buffalo in the West ❖ Buffalo Bill Cody organizes and begins touring with his Wild West Show
1886–1887	Severe drought and winter damage cattle and farming bonanzas
1887	Congress passes the Dawes Severalty Act, making Indians individual landowners ❖ Hatch Act provides funds for the establishment of agricultural experiment stations
1889	Washington, Montana, and the Dakotas are admitted to the Union ❖ Oklahoma Territory is opened to settlement
1890	Idaho and Wyoming are admitted to Union ❖ Teton Sioux are massacred at Wounded Knee, South Dakota
1893	Young historian Frederick Jackson Turner analyzes the closing of the frontier

conservatism and imitativeness, the influence of various ethnic groups, and the persistence of European ideas and institutions. Most recently, they have shown that family and community loomed just as large as individualism on the frontier.

Rejecting Turner almost completely, a group of "new Western historians" has advanced a different and complex view of the West. They emphasize the region's racial and ethnic diversity, show a concern for the environmental consequences of the westward migration, detail the role of women, and trace the struggles between economic interests. White English-speaking Americans, they suggest, could be said to have conquered the West rather than settled it.

The West, in this view, was not settled by a wave of white migrants moving across the continent but by a set of waves—Anglo, Mexican American, African American, Asian American, and others—moving from different directions and interacting with one another and with Native Americans. These movements and clashes created the modern West, a process that continues today.

But of one thing there can be no doubt: the West as an image and an economic reality exerted a powerful influence in the nineteenth and twentieth centuries. Immigrants were drawn there, and natural resources were hauled from there. The West was the first American empire, and it had a profound impact on the American mind and imagination.

Key Terms

Ghost Dances, p. 335
Wounded Knee Massacre, p. 335
Dawes Severalty Act, p. 336
Overland Trail, p. 337
Homestead Act of 1862, p. 339
National Reclamation Act (Newlands Act), p. 339
Gold Rush of 1849, p. 341
placer mining, p. 341
Comstock Lode, p. 341
Exodusters, p. 345
dry farming, p. 346
bonanza farms, p. 346
National Grange of the Patrons of Husbandry, p. 346
Turner's thesis, p. 347

Recommended Reading

The best traditional account of the movement west is Ray Allen Billington, *Westward Expansion* (1967), which also has a first-rate bibliography. Walter Prescott Webb, *The Great Plains* (1931) offers a fascinating analysis of development on the Plains.

For examples of the work of "new Western historians," see Donald Worster, *Rivers of Empire* (1985), a powerful study of the "hydraulic" society, and his *Under Western Skies: Nature and History in the American West* (1992); William Cronon, *Nature's Metropolis: Chicago and the Great West* (1991), a provocative analysis of the relationship of Chicago and the West; Patricia Nelson Limerick, *The Legacy of Conquest* (1987); and Richard White, *"It's Your Misfortune and None of My Own": A History of the American West* (1991).

More recent authors have taken fresh and stimulating looks at older or ignored questions. Robert R. Dykstra, *The Cattle Towns* (1968), examines five Kansas cattle towns, with interesting results. Elliott West discusses the Plains in *The Contested Plains: Indians, Goldseekers, and the Rush to Colorado* (1998). Gregory Nobles, *American Frontiers: Cultural Encounters and Continental Conquest* (1997), is an engaging synthesis of frontier history.

There are a number of insightful recent studies of the environment, including Andrew C. Isenberg, *The Destruction of the Bison: An Environmental History, 1750–1920* (2000), Shepard Krech III, *The Ecological Indian: Myth and History* (1999), Karl Jacoby, *Crimes Against Nature: Squatters, Poachers, Thieves, and the Hidden History of American Conservation* (2001), and Dan L. Flores, *The Natural West: Environmental History in the Great Plains and Rocky Mountains* (2001). Susan Lee Johnson, *Roaring Camp: The Social World of the California Gold Rush* (2000), is a fascinating examination of the gold camps.

On the Native Americans, there are a number of valuable works, including R. Douglas Hurt's excellent *Indian Agriculture in America* (1987), Janet A. McDonnell, *The Dispossession of the American Indian, 1887–1934* (1991), Robert A. Trennert, Jr., *The Phoenix Indian School* (1988), Scott Riney, *The Rapid City Indian School, 1898–1933* (1999), Paul H. Carlson, *The Plains Indians* (1998), and John William Sayer, *Ghost Dancing the Law: The Wounded Knee Trials* (1997).

Nell Irvin Painter, *Exodusters: Black Migration to Kansas After Reconstruction* (1976), tells the story of the Exodusters, as Monroe Lee Billington does for New Mexico's *Buffalo Soldiers, 1866–1900* (1991). Also see Frank N. Schubert, *Buffalo Soldiers, Braves, and the Brass* (1993).

Julie Roy Jeffrey, *Frontier Women: The Trans-Mississippi West* (1979), Joanna L. Stratton, *Pioneer Women: Voices from the Kansas Frontier* (1981), and Deena J. González, *Refusing the Favor: The Spanish-Mexican Women of Santa Fe, 1820–1880* (1999), are perceptive works on a neglected topic. John Mack Faragher, *Women and Men on the Overland Trail* (1979), and John Phillip Reid, *Law for the Elephant* (1980), examine relationships on the trails west.

For a list of additional titles related to this chapter's topics, please see http://www.ablongman.com/divine.

Suggested Web Sites

Indian Affairs: Laws and Treaties, compiled and edited by Charles J. Kappler (1904)

http://digital.library.okstate.edu/kappler
This digitized text at Oklahoma State University includes pre-removal treaties with the Five Civilized Tribes and other tribes.

Native American Documents Project

http://www.csusm.edu/projects/nadp/nadp.htm
California State University at San Marcos has several digital documents relating to Native Americans on this site.

Geronimo

http://odur.let.rug.nl/~usa/B/geronimo/geronixx.htm
This site contains biographical and autobiographical information about this famous Native American who resisted European American domination.

National Museum of the American Indian

http://www.si.edu/nmai
The Smithsonian Institution maintains this site, providing information about the museum. The museum is dedicated to everything about Native Americans.

The Northern Great Plains, 1880–1920: Photographs from the Fred Hultstrand and F. A. Pazandak Photograph Collections

http://memory.loc.gov/ammem/award97/ndfahtml/ngphome.html

This American Memory site from the Library of Congress contains "two collections from the Institute for Regional Studies at North Dakota State University" with "900 photographs of rural and small town life at the turn of the century." Included are "images of sod homes and the people who built them; images of farms and the machinery that made them prosper; and images of one-room schools and the children that were educated in them."

On the Trail in Kansas

http://www.Kancoll.org/galtrl.htm

This Kansas Collection site holds several good primary sources with images concerning the Oregon Trail and America's early movement westward.

"California as I Saw It": First-Person Narratives of California's Early Years, 1849–1900

http://memory.loc.gov/ammem/cbhtml/cbhome.html

This site is a part of the American Memory series and contains "full texts and illustrations of 190 works documenting the formative era of California's history through eyewitness accounts." It covers the Gold Rush, the interaction of various groups, and the settling of the region.

Home on the Range/Cowboy Heritage

http://history.cc.ukans.edu/heritage/old_west/cowboy.html

This site tells this history of the cattle trails and towns such as Dodge City with useful text, links, documents, and maps.

The Evolution of the Conservation Movement, 1850–1920

http://memory.loc.gov/ammem/amrvhtml/conshome.html

This American Memory site brings together scores of primary sources and photographs about "the historical formation and cultural foundations of the movement to conserve and protect America's natural heritage."

Heroes and Villains in Kansas

http://www.Kancoll.org/galhero.htm

The Kansas Collection Gallery of both famous and little known people who made up the history of the state.

Blacks in Blue

The Buffalo Soldiers in the West

On Saturday afternoons, youngsters used to sit in darkened movie theaters and cheer the victories of the U.S. Cavalry over the Indians. Typically, the Indians were about to capture a wagon train when army bugles suddenly sounded. Then the blue-coated cavalry charged over the hill. Few in the theaters cheered for the Indians; fewer still noticed the absence of black faces among the on-charging cavalry. But, in fact, more than two thousand African American cavalrymen served on the western frontier between 1867 and 1890. Known as the "buffalo soldiers," they made up one-fifth of the U.S. Cavalry.

Black troops were first used on a large scale during the Civil War. Organized in segregated units, with white officers, they fought with distinction. Nearly 180,000 blacks served in the Union army; 34,000 of them died. When the war ended in 1865, Congress for the first time authorized black troops to serve in the regular peacetime army. In addition to infantry, it created two cavalry regiments—the Ninth and Tenth, which became known as the famous buffalo soldiers.

Like other black regiments, the Ninth and Tenth Cavalry had white officers who took special examinations before they could serve. The chaplains were assigned not only to preach but to teach reading, writing, and arithmetic. The food was poor; racism was widespread. The army stocked the first black units with worn-out horses, a serious matter to men whose lives depended on the speed and stamina of their mounts. "Since our first mount in 1867 this regiment has received nothing but broken down horses and repaired equipment," an officer said in 1870.

Many white officers refused to serve with black troops. George A. Custer, the handsome "boy general," turned down a position in the Ninth and joined the new Seventh Cavalry, headed for disaster at Little Bighorn. The *Army and Navy Journal* carried ads that told a similar story:

> **A FIRST LIEUTENANT**
> **OF INFANTRY**
> (white)
> Stationed at a
> **very desirable post**
> in the Department of the South
> desires a transfer with
> an officer of the same grade
> **on equal terms**
> if in a white regiment
> but if in a colored regiment
> **a reasonable bonus**
> would be expected.

There was no shortage of black troops for the officers to lead. Blacks enlisted because the army offered some advancement in a closed society. It also paid $13 a month, plus room and board.

In 1867, the Ninth and Tenth Cavalry were posted to the West, where they remained for two decades. Under Colonel Benjamin H. Grierson, a Civil War hero, the Tenth went to Fort Riley, Kansas; the regiment arrived in the midst of a great Indian war. The Kiowa, Comanche, Cheyenne, Arapaho, and Sioux were on the warpath. Troopers of the Tenth defended farms, stages, trains, and work crews building railroad tracks to the West. Cornered by a band of Cheyenne, they beat back the attack and won a new name. They had been known as the "brunettes" or "Africans," but the Cheyenne now called them the buffalo soldiers, a name that soon applied to all African American soldiers in the West.

From 1868 to 1874, the Tenth served on the Kansas frontier. The dull winter days were filled with drills and scouting parties outside the post. In spring and summer, the good weather brought forth new forays. Indian bands raided farms and ranches and stampeded cattle herds on the way north from Texas. They struck and then melted back into the reservations.

The Ninth Cavalry also had a difficult job. Commanded by Colonel Edward Hatch, who had served with Grierson in the Civil War, it was stationed in West Texas and along the Rio Grande. The summers were so hot that men collapsed with sunstroke, the winters so cold that water froze in canteens. Native Americans from outside the area frequently raided it. From the north, Kiowa and Comanche warriors rode down the Great Comanche War Trail; Kickapoo crossed the Rio Grande from Mexico. Gangs of Mexican bandits and restless Civil War veterans roamed and plundered at will.

In 1874–1875, the Ninth fought in the great Red River War, in which the Kiowa and Comanche, fed up with conditions on the reservations, revolted against Grant's peace policy.

Although they were not, in fact, treated as well as the white soldiers in their regiments, many African American cavalrymen such as those pictured here were probably drawn into service by hard-sell recruitment posters promising them equal pay and rations and entitlement to any horses or goods taken from the Indians. ❖

Marching, fighting, then marching again, the soldiers harried and wore out the Indians, who finally surrendered in the spring of 1875. Herded into a new and desolate reservation, the Mescalero Apache of New Mexico took to the warpath in 1877 and again in 1879. Each time, it took a year of grueling warfare to effect their surrender. In 1886, black cavalrymen surrounded and captured the famous Apache chief Geronimo. In that and other campaigns, several buffalo soldiers won the Congressional Medal of Honor.

Black troops hunted Big Foot and his band before the slaughter at Wounded Knee in 1890, and they served in many of the West's most famous Indian battles. While one-third of all army recruits deserted between 1865 and 1890, the Ninth and Tenth Cavalry had few desertions. In 1880, the Tenth had the fewest desertions of any regiment in the country.

It was ironic that in the West, black men fought red men to benefit white men. Once the Indian wars ended, the buffalo soldiers worked to keep illegal settlers out of Indian or government land; much of this land was later opened to settlement. Both regiments saw action in the Spanish-American War, the Ninth at San Juan Hill, the Tenth in the fighting around Santiago. Unlike white veterans of the same campaigns, the old buffalo soldiers were forgotten in retirement, although some of them had the satisfaction of settling on the western lands they had done so much to pacify.

Chapter 18

The Industrial Society

A Machine Culture

In 1876, Americans celebrated a century of independence. Survivors of a recent civil war, they observed the centenary proudly and rather self-consciously in song and speech and in a grand Centennial Exposition, held in Philadelphia, Pennsylvania.

Spread over 13 acres, the exposition focused more on the present than the past, featuring machines, inventions, and new products. Fairgoers saw linoleum, a new, easy-to-clean floor covering. For the first time, they tasted root beer and the exotic banana, wrapped in foil and selling for a dime. They saw their first bicycle, an awkward, high-wheeled contraption with solid tires.

Machinery was the focus of the exposition, and Machinery Hall was the most popular building. Here were the products of an ever-improving civilization. Long lines of the curious waited to see Alexander Graham Bell's new device, the telephone. Thomas A. Edison displayed several recent inventions. The typewriter, the elevator, and the Westinghouse railroad air brake similarly amazed the fairgoers.

But the exhibit drawing the largest crowds was the mighty Corliss engine, the focal point of the exposition. A giant steam engine, it dwarfed everything in Machinery Hall. Alone it supplied power for the eight thousand other machines on the exposition grounds. The Corliss captured the nation's imagination, symbolizing America's swift movement toward an industrial and urban society.

AT THE START OF THE CIVIL WAR, the United States lagged well behind industrializing nations such as Great Britain, France, and Germany. By 1900, it had vaulted far into the lead, with a manufacturing output that exceeded the *combined* output of its three European rivals. During the same years, cities grew, technology advanced, and farm production rose. Developments in manufacturing, mining, agriculture, transportation, and communication transformed American society.

Outline

Industrial Development

An Empire on Rails

An Industrial Empire

The Sellers

The Wage Earners

Conclusion: Industrialization's Benefits and Costs

The Corliss engine, a "mechanical marvel" at the Centennial Exposition, was a prime example of the giantism so admired by the public. ❖

Industrial Development

American industry owed its remarkable growth to several considerations. It fed on an abundance of natural resources: coal, iron, timber, petroleum, waterpower. Labor was also abundant, drawn from established farm families and the hosts of European immigrants who flocked to America. Nearly eight million immigrants arrived in the 1870s and 1880s; another fifteen million came between 1890 and 1914.

The burgeoning population led to expanded markets, which new devices such as the telegraph and telephone helped exploit. Swiftly growing urban populations devoured goods, and the railroads linked cities and opened a national market. Within its boundaries, the United States had the largest free trade market in the world, while tariff barriers partially protected its producers from outside competition.

Expansive market and labor conditions buoyed the confidence of European and American investors who provided large amounts of capital. Technological progress and invention increased productivity in many important industries and also helped foster a firm agricultural base, on which industrialization depended.

Eager to promote economic growth, government at all levels—federal, state, and local—gave manufacturers money, land, and other resources. The American system of government itself was a boon to industry, thanks to its stability, its commitment to the concept of private property, and its reluctance to regulate industrial activity.

In this atmosphere, entrepreneurs flourished. Taking steps crucial for industrialization, they organized, managed, and assumed the financial risks of the new enterprises. Admirers called them "captains of industry"; foes labeled them "robber barons." To some degree, they were both—creative *and* acquisitive. If sometimes they seemed larger than life, it was because they dealt in concepts, distances, and quantities often unknown to earlier generations.

Industrial growth, it must be remembered, was neither steady nor inevitable. Growth varied from industry to industry and from year to year. It was concentrated in the North and East. The more sparsely settled West provided raw materials, while the South had to rebuild after wartime devastation.

Still, industrial development proceeded at an extraordinary pace. Between 1865 and 1914, the real gross national product (GNP)—the total monetary value of all goods and services produced in a year, with prices held stable—grew at an average rate of more than 4 percent a year. As one economic historian noted, "Never before had such rapid growth continued for so long."

An Empire on Rails

A revolution in transportation and communication occurred in the nineteenth century. The steamship sliced in half the time it took to cross the Atlantic. The telegraph, flashing messages almost instantaneously along miles of wire, transformed communications, as did the telephone a little later. But the railroad wrought the largest changes of all. Along with Bessemer steel, it was the most significant technical innovation of the century.

More than most innovations, the railroad dramatically affected economic and social life. It contributed advantages that canals and other inland waterways could not match. Those advantages included more direct routes, greater speed, greater safety and comfort than other modes of land travel, more dependable schedules, a larger volume of traffic, and year-round service. A day's land travel on stagecoach or horseback might cover 50 miles. The railroad covered 50 miles in little more than an hour. It went where canals and rivers did not go—directly to the loading platforms of great factories or across the arid West.

Linking widely separated cities and villages, the railroad ended the relative isolation and self-sufficiency of the country's "island communities." It tied people together, brought in outside products, fostered greater interdependence, and encouraged economic specialization. The railroad forged a national market and in so doing pointed the way toward mass production and mass consumption, two of the hallmarks of twentieth-century society.

It also pointed the way toward a new kind of business development. Railroads were America's first big business, stretching over thousands of miles, employing thousands of people, dealing with countless consumers, and requiring a scale of organization and decision making unknown in earlier business. Year by year, railroad companies consumed great quantities of iron, steel, coal, lumber, and glass; such purchases stimulated growth and employment in numerous industries.

No wonder, then, that the railroad captured the country's imagination so completely. Walt Whitman, the poet, chanted the locomotive's praises: "Emblem of motion and power—pulse of the continent . . . Fierce-throated beauty!" For nearly a hundred years, children gathered at depots, paused in fields to wave as the express flashed by, listened at night to far-off whistles, and wondered what lay down the tracks. They lived in a world grown smaller.

Building the Empire

When the Civil War ended, the country already had 35,000 miles of track, and much of the railroad system east of the Mississippi River was in place. Farther west, the rail network stood poised on the edge of settlement. Although America already had nearly as much railroad track as the rest of the world, rail construction increased spectacularly after 1865. Trackage peaked at 254,037 miles in 1916, just before the industry began its long decline into the mid-twentieth century.

To build such an empire took vast amounts of capital. American and European investors provided some of the money; government supplied the rest. Altogether local and state governments gave railroad companies about $525 million. In addition, the federal government donated millions of acres of public land to the railroad companies. Federal land grants helped build 18,738 miles of track, less than 8 percent of the rail system. The companies sometimes sold the land to raise cash but more often used it as security for bonds or loans.

Beyond doubt, the grants of cash and land promoted waste and corruption. The companies built fast and wastefully, eager to collect the subsidies that went with each mile of track. The corruption involved in the Crédit Mobilier is but one example of the excesses of the railroad companies.

Yet on balance, the grants probably worked more benefits than evils. As Congress had hoped, the grants were the lure for railroad building across the rugged, unsettled West, where it would be years before the revenues would repay construction. The grants seemed necessary in a nation that, unlike Europe, expected private enterprise to build the railroads. In return for aid, Congress required the railroads to carry government freight, troops, and mail at substantially reduced rates.

Linking the Nation via Trunk Lines

The early railroads may seem to have linked different regions, but in fact they did not. Built with little regard for through traffic, they were designed more to protect local interests than to tap outside markets. To avoid cooperating with other lines, they adopted conflicting schedules, built separate depots, and used tracks of varying widths.

The Civil War showed the value of fast, long-distance transportation, and after 1865, railroad managers worked to provide it. In a burst of consolidation, the large swallowed the small; integrated rail networks became a reality. Railroads also adopted standard schedules, signals, equipment, and finally, in 1866, the standard track width (or gauge) of 4 feet, 8½ inches.

trunk lines Four major railroad networks designed to connect the eastern seaports to the Great Lakes and western rivers emerged after the Civil War. They reflected the growing integration of transportation across the country that helped spur large-scale industrialization.

In the Northeast, four great **trunk lines** took shape, all intended to link eastern seaports with the rich traffic of the Great Lakes and western rivers. Like a massive river system, trunk lines drew traffic from dozens of tributaries (feeder lines) and carried it to major markets. The Baltimore and Ohio Railroad was one. The Erie Railroad, running from New York City to Chicago, ran parallel to the New York Central Railroad built by Cornelius Vanderbilt. The fourth line, the Pennsylvania Railroad, initially ran from Philadelphia to Pittsburgh, but it was expanded to unite Cincinnati, Indianapolis, St. Louis, Chicago, New York City, Baltimore, and Washington. In the war-damaged South, consolidation took longer. But by 1900, just four decades after secession, the South had five major systems that tied into a national transportation network.

Over the rail system, passengers and freight moved in relative speed, comfort, and safety. Automatic couplers (1868), air brakes (1869), refrigerated cars (1867), dining cars, heated cars, Pullman sleeping cars, and stronger locomotives transformed railroad service. Passenger miles per year increased from 5 billion in 1870 to 16 billion in 1900. The railroads even changed time, establishing a standard system of time zones for the country.

Rails Across the Continent

The dream of a transcontinental railroad stretched back many years but had always succumbed to sectional quarrels over the route. In 1862 and 1864, with the South out of the picture, Congress passed legislation to build the first transcontinental line. The act incorporated the Union Pacific Railroad Company to build westward from Nebraska to meet the Central Pacific Railroad Company, building eastward from the Pacific Coast. The federal government directly subsidized construction with grants of land and cash loans.

Construction began simultaneously at Omaha and Sacramento in 1863, lagged during the war, and moved vigorously ahead in 1865. It became a race, each company vying for land, loans, and potential markets. Along the way, construction crews for both companies confronted dangerous and difficult obstacles. Workers of the Union Pacific encountered frequent Indian attacks but had the advantage of building over flat prairie. Central Pacific crews faced more trying conditions in the high Sierra Nevada along California's eastern border. Under the most difficult conditions, Central Pacific workers, most of them Chinese, dug, blasted, and pushed their way slowly east.

On May 10, 1869, the two lines met at Promontory, Utah, near the northern tip of the Great Salt Lake. The Union Pacific and Central Pacific presidents hammered in a golden spike (both missed it on the first try), and the dreamed-of connection was made.

The transcontinental railroad symbolized American unity and progress. Along with the Suez Canal, completed the same year, it helped knit the world together. Bret Harte, the exuberant poet of the West, wrote of the coupling at Promontory:

> What was it the Engines said,
>
> Pilots touching,—head to head
>
> Facing on the single track,
>
> Half a world behind each back?

Cornelius, the "Commodore" Vanderbilt, in this cartoon of the "Modern Colossus of (Rail) Roads," is shown towering over his rail empire and pulling the strings to control its operations. In addition to the New York Central, Vanderbilt gained control of the Hudson River Railroad, the Lake Shore and Michigan Southern Railway, and the Canadian Southern Railway. ❖

In the next twenty-five years, four more railroads reached the coast. By the 1890s, business leaders talked comfortably of railroad systems stretching deep into South America and across the Bering Strait to Asia, Europe, and Africa. In an age of progress, anything seemed possible.

Problems of Growth

Overbuilding during the 1870s and 1880s caused serious problems for the railroads. Lines paralleled each other, and where they did not, speculators such as Jay Gould often laid one down to force a rival line to buy the new one out at inflated prices. Speculators like Gould bought and sold railroads like toys and watered their stock—distributed it in excess of the real value of the assets—in the process.

Competition was severe, and managers fought desperately for traffic. They offered special rates and favors: free passes for large shippers; low rates on bulk freight, carload lots, and long hauls; and rebates—secret, privately negotiated reductions below published rates. Soon fierce rate wars convinced managers that ruthless competition helped no one.

At first, managers tried to control competition by sharing traffic, but intense competitive pressures killed every agreement. Customers grew adept at bargaining for rebates and other privileges, and railroads rarely felt able to refuse them.

Failing to cooperate, railroad owners next tried to consolidate. Through purchase, lease, and merger, they gobbled up competitors and built "self-sustaining systems" that dominated entire regions. But many of these systems, expensive and unwieldy, collapsed in the Panic of 1893.

Needing money, railroads turned naturally to bankers, who finally imposed order on the industry. J. Pierpont Morgan, head of the New York investment house of J. P. Morgan and Company, took the lead. The most powerful figure in American finance, Morgan liked efficiency, combination, and order. He disliked "wasteful" competition. In 1885, during a bruising rate war between the New York Central and the Pennsylvania, Morgan invited the combatants to a conference aboard his palatial steam yacht. There he arranged a traffic-sharing agreement and collected a $1 million fee. Bringing peace to an industry could be profitable. It also satisfied Morgan's passion for stability.

After 1893, Morgan and a few other bankers refinanced ailing railroads and in so doing took control of the industry. Their methods were direct: fixed costs and debt were ruthlessly cut, new stock was issued to provide capital, rates were stabilized, rebates and competition were eliminated, and control was vested in a "voting trust" of handpicked trustees. By 1900, Morgan and his methods dominated American railroading.

As the new century began, the railroads had pioneered the pattern followed by most other industries. Seven giant systems controlled nearly two-thirds of the mileage, and they in turn answered to a few investment banking firms like the house of Morgan. For good and ill, a national transportation network, centralized and relatively efficient, was now in place.

An Industrial Empire

Along with railroads, the new industrial empire was based on a number of dramatic innovations, including steel, oil, and inventions of all kinds that transformed ordinary life. Harder and more durable than other kinds of iron, steel wrought changes in manufacturing, agriculture, transportation, and architecture. It permitted longer bridges, taller buildings, stronger railroad track, better plows, heavier machinery, and faster ships. From the 1870s onward, steel output became the worldwide accepted measure of industrial progress.

The Bessemer process, developed in the 1850s by Henry Bessemer in England and independently by William Kelly in the United States, made it possible. Both men discovered that a blast of air through molten iron burned off carbon and other impurities, resulting in steel of a more uniform and durable quality. The discovery transformed the industry. Earlier methods had produced amounts a person could lift; a Bessemer converter dealt with 5 tons of molten metal at a time. The mass production of steel was now possible.

Carnegie and Steel

Bessemer plants demanded extensive capital investment, abundant raw material, sophisticated production techniques, and modern research departments. Costly to build, they limited entry into the industry to the handful who could afford them.

Great steel districts arose in Ohio, Alabama, and Pennsylvania—especially near Pittsburgh, which became the center of the industry. Output shot up; by 1890, the United States took the world lead in production.

Iron ore abounded in the fabulous deposits near Lake Superior, the greatest deposits in the world. Through a series of intricate steps involving large and complex machines, such as giant steam shovels, the raw ore was transported to the steel mills.

Like the railroads, steel companies grew larger and larger. As operations expanded, managers needed greater skills. Product development, marketing, and consumer preferences became important. Competition was fierce, and steel companies, like the railroads, tried secret agreements, pools, and consolidation. During the 1880s and 1890s, they moved toward **vertical integration,** a type of organization in which a single company owns and controls the entire process, from unearthing of the raw materials to the manufacture and sale of the finished product.

vertical integration A form of business organization in which a single firm owns and controls the entire process of production, from the procurement of raw materials to the manufacture and sale of the finished product.

Andrew Carnegie emerged as the undisputed master of the industry. Born in Scotland, he came to the United States in 1848 at the age of 12. Settling near Pittsburgh, he went to work as a bobbin boy in a cotton mill, earning $1.20 a week. In 1852, his hard work and skill in a telegraph office caught the eye of Thomas A. Scott of the Pennsylvania Railroad. By 1859, Carnegie had become a divisional superintendent with the company. He was 24.

Soon rich from shrewd investments, Carnegie plunged into the steel industry in 1872. On the Monongahela River south of Pittsburgh he built the giant J. Edgar Thomson Steel Works. With his warmth and salesmanship, he attracted able subordinates whom he drove hard and paid well. Carnegie kept the wages of the laborers in his mills low, disliked unions, and crushed a violent strike at his Homestead works near Pittsburgh in 1892.

In 1878, Carnegie won the steel contract for the Brooklyn Bridge. As city building boomed during the 1880s, he converted the huge Homestead works to the manufacture of structural beams and angles, which went into the first skyscrapers. Carnegie profits mounted: from $2 million in 1888 to $40 million in 1900. Employing twenty thousand people, it was the largest industrial company in the world.

In 1901, Carnegie sold out. Believing that wealth brought social obligations, he wanted to devote his full time to philanthropy. J. Pierpont Morgan, who in the late 1890s had put together several rival steel companies, paid Carnegie almost half a billion dollars for Carnegie Steel.

Drawing other companies into the combination, Morgan on March 3, 1901, announced the creation of the United States Steel Corporation. The first billion-dollar company, it employed 168,000 people, produced 9 million tons of iron and steel a year, and controlled three-fifths of the country's steel business. Soon there were other giants, and as the nineteenth century ended, steel products—rare just thirty years before—had altered the landscape. Huge firms, investment bankers, and professional managers dominated the industry.

The machinery dwarfs the workers in this colored engraving of steel making using the Bessemer process at Andrew Carnegie's Pittsburgh steel works. Men worked twelve hours a day in the blazing heat and deafening roar of the machines. ❖

Rockefeller and Oil

Petroleum worked comparable changes in the economic and social landscape, although mostly after 1900.

John D. Rockefeller, satirized in a 1901 Puck *cartoon, is enthroned on oil, the base of his empire; his crown is girded by other holdings.* ❖

Distilled into oil, it lubricated the machinery of the industrial age. Kerosene, another major distillate of petroleum, brought inexpensive illumination into almost every home. Since tallow candles and whale oil were expensive to burn, many people went to bed at nightfall. Kerosene lamps opened the evenings to activity, which altered the patterns of life.

Like other changes in these years, the oil boom happened with surprising speed. In the mid-1850s, petroleum was a bothersome, smelly fluid that occasionally rose to the surface of springs and streams. But in 1859, Edwin L. Drake drilled the first oil well near Titusville in northwest Pennsylvania, and "black gold" fever struck. Chemists soon discovered ways to turn petroleum into lubricating oil, grease, paint, wax, varnish, naphtha, and paraffin. In just a few years, there was a world market for oil.

At first, growth of the oil industry was chaotic. Early drillers and refiners produced for local markets, and since drilling wells and even erecting refineries cost little, competition flourished. Output fluctuated dramatically; prices rose and fell with devastating effect.

A young merchant from Cleveland named John D. Rockefeller imposed order on the industry. Beginning in 1863, at the age of 24, he built a titan of corporate business, the Standard Oil Company. Like Morgan, Rockefeller considered competition wasteful, small-scale enterprise inefficient, and consolidation the path of the future. Methodically, Rockefeller absorbed or destroyed competitors in Cleveland and elsewhere. As ruthless in his methods as Carnegie, he lacked the steel master's spontaneous charm. Like Carnegie, he demanded efficiency, relentless cost cutting, and the latest technology. He was a man of great vision, and he attracted exceptional lieutenants.

Paying careful attention to detail, Rockefeller realized that in large-scale production, even small reductions meant huge savings. In one famous incident, he reduced the number of drops of solder on kerosene cans from forty to thirty-nine. In the end, Rockefeller triumphed over his competitors by marketing products of high quality at the lowest unit cost. But he employed other, less savory methods as well. He threatened rivals and bribed politicians, exploited railroad rebates, and employed spies to harass the customers of competing refiners. By 1879, he controlled 90 percent of the country's oil-refining capacity.

Vertically integrated, Standard Oil owned wells, timberlands, barrel and chemical plants, refineries, warehouses, pipelines, and fleets of tankers and oil cars. Its marketing organization served as a model for the industry, and it exported oil throughout the world.

trust A business-management device designed to centralize and make more efficient the management of diverse and far-flung business operations. It allowed stockholders to exchange their stock certificates for trust certificates, on which dividends were paid.

To manage it all, the company developed a new plan of business organization, the **trust,** which had profound significance for American business. In 1882, Samuel T. C. Dodd, Standard's attorney, set up the Standard Oil Trust, with a board of nine trustees empowered "to hold, control, and manage" all of Standard's properties. As Dodd intended, the trust immediately centralized control of Standard's far-flung empire.

Competition almost disappeared; profits soared. A trust movement swept the country, as industries with similar problems—whiskey, lead, and sugar, among others—followed Standard's example. The word *trust* became synonymous with monopoly, amid vehement public protests. *Antitrust* became a watchword for a generation of reformers from the 1880s through 1920. But Rockefeller's purpose had been *management* of a monopoly, not monopoly itself, which he had already achieved.

During the 1890s, Rockefeller helped pioneer another form of industrial consolidation, the holding company. Taking advantage of an 1889 New Jersey law that allowed one company to purchase another, he moved Standard Oil to New Jersey and bought up his own subsidiaries to form a holding company. The trust, he had learned, was cumbersome, and it was under attack in Congress and the courts. Holding companies offered the next step in industrial development. They were simply large-scale mergers in which a central corporate organization purchased the stock of the member companies and established direct, formal control. Soon other companies followed Rockefeller's example, and by 1900, a mere 1 percent of the nation's companies controlled more than one-third of its industrial production.

Rockefeller retired in 1897 with a fortune of nearly $900 million, but for Standard Oil and petroleum in general, the most expansive period was yet to come. The great oil pools of Texas and Oklahoma had not yet been discovered. There were only four usable automobiles in the country, and the day of the gasoline engine lay just ahead.

The Business of Invention

During the last third of the nineteenth century, an extraordinary group of American inventors added to the world's knowledge. Some inventions gave rise to new industries; a few actually changed the quality of life. The number of patents issued to inventors reflected the trend. Between 1790 and 1860, the U.S. Patent Office issued just 36,000 patents; in the decade of the 1890s alone, it issued more than 200,000.

Some of the inventions transformed communications. In 1866, Cyrus W. Field improved the transatlantic cable linking the telegraph networks of Europe and the United States. By 1900, land and submarine cables reached around the world. Diplomats and business leaders could now "talk" to their counterparts in Berlin or Hong Kong. Even before the telephone, the cables quickened the pace of diplomacy, revolutionized journalism, and allowed businesses to expand and centralize.

The typewriter (1867), stock ticker (1867), cash register (1879), and adding machine (1888) helped business transactions. High-speed looms and sewing machines transformed the clothing industry, which for the first time in history turned out ready-made clothes for the masses.

Other innovations improved the diet. There were new processes for flour, canned meat, vegetables, condensed milk, and even beer. Refrigerated railroad cars, ice-cooled, brought fresh fruit from Florida and California to all parts of the country. In the 1870s, Gustavus F. Swift, a Chicago meatpacker, hit on the idea of using the cars to distribute meat nationwide. Setting up "dissembly" factories to butcher meat (Henry Ford later copied them for his famous "assembly" lines), he started what a newspaper called an "era for cheap beef."

No innovation, however, rivaled in importance the telephone and the use of electricity for light and power. The telephone was the work of Alexander Graham Bell, a teacher of the deaf. Bell experimented with ways to transmit speech electrically, and he developed electrified metal disks that converted sound waves to electrical impulses and back again. On March 10, 1876, he transmitted the first sentence over a telephone: "Mr. Watson, come here; I want you." By 1905, there were ten million telephones in the country—one for almost every ten people.

Thomas Alva Edison invented an array of processes and products of incalculable significance. Born in 1847, Edison had little formal education, although he was an avid reader. After earning a reputation for his work in telegraphy, Edison built and organized the first modern research laboratory at Menlo Park, New Jersey.

In 1877, Edison invented a "telephone repeater," which became the phonograph. Those unable to afford a phone, he thought, could record their voices for replay from a central telephone station. Using tin foil wrapped around a grooved, rotating cylinder, he shouted the verses of "Mary Had a Little Lamb" and then listened in awe as the machine played them back. Within a generation, Edison's invention had evolved into the phonograph record. For the first time in history, people could listen again and again to a favorite piece of music. The phonograph made human experiences repeatable in a way never before possible.

In 1879 came an even larger triumph, the incandescent lamp. In tackling this idea, Edison set out to do nothing less than change light. A trial-and-error inventor, he tested sixteen hundred materials before producing the carbon filament he wanted. With the financial backing of J. Pierpont Morgan, he organized the Edison Illuminating Company and built the Pearl Street power station in New York City. Power stations soon opened in Boston, Philadelphia, and Chicago. In a nation alive with light, the habits of centuries changed. A flick of the switch lit homes and factories at any hour of the day or night.

In a rare blunder, Edison based his system on low-voltage direct current, which could be transmitted only about 2 miles. George Westinghouse demonstrated the advantages of high-voltage alternating current, transmitted over great distances. With the inventor Nikola Tesla, Westinghouse developed an alternating-current motor that could convert electricity into mechanical power. Electricity could light a lamp or illuminate a skyscraper, pull a streetcar or drive an entire railroad, run a sewing machine or power a mammoth assembly line. Buried under pavement or strung from pole to pole, wires of every description—trolley, telephone, and power—soon distinguished the modern city.

The Sellers

The increased output of the industrial age was one thing, but the products still had to be sold, and that gave rise to the new "science" of marketing. Some business leaders built extensive marketing organizations of their own. Others relied on retailers, merchandising techniques, and advertising, developing a host of methods to convince consumers to buy.

In 1867, businesses spent about $50 million on advertising; in 1900, they spent more than $500 million, and the figure was increasing rapidly. The rotary press (1875) churned out newspapers and, with rotogravure illustrations, began a new era in newspaper advertising. Brand names became popular; already Kellogg was promising cornflake eaters "Genuine Joy, Genuine Appetite, Genuine Health and therefore Genuine Complexion."

Bringing producer and consumer together, nationwide advertising was the final link in the national market. From roadside signs to newspaper ads, it pervaded American life. In a candid address, the owner of the *Ladies' Home Journal* told an audience of manufacturers that he published his magazine not for the benefit of American women but for them, the people who manufactured products, to sell to American women.

R. H. Macy in New York, John Wanamaker in Philadelphia, and Marshall Field in Chicago turned the department store into a national institution. There people could browse (a relatively new concept) and buy. Innovations in pricing, display, and advertising helped customers develop wants they did not know they had. In 1870, Wanamaker took out the first full-page newspaper ad.

The "chain store"—an American term—spread across the country. The Atlantic & Pacific Tea Company opened its first grocery store in 1859, and by 1915, there were a thousand A&Ps. In 1880, F. W. Woolworth opened the first "five and ten cent store"; twenty years later, he had fifty-nine of them. Sears, Roebuck and Company and Montgomery Ward sold to rural customers through mail-order catalogs—a means of selling that depended on effective transportation and a high level of customer literacy. By the early 1900s, Sears was distributing six million catalogs annually.

❖ A Look at the Past ❖

Cash Register

Mass-produced goods of every kind flooded markets in the late 1800s. Industrial productivity made the flood possible and consumer spending fueled production. Railroads and free mail delivery after 1896 brought factory-made goods even to consumers who lived in remote, rural locations. In cities, department stores transformed shopping into a pleasurable experience. By the 1880s retailers were investing in cash registers that tallied sales. Previously, merchants recorded sales by hand into daybooks and later, when closed for business, transcribed the sales into a ledger. This wooden model from 1890 registered sales with ceramic balls, which dropped into a labyrinth of tracks to mark daily totals. How did the cash register transform the act of selling goods? Why did merchants invest in them?

Advertising, brand names, chain stores, and mail-order houses brought Americans of all varieties into a national market. Even as the country grew, a certain homogeneity of goods bound it together. There was a common language of consumption. The market, some contemporaries thought, bridged regional, class, and even ethnic differences.

The theory had limits; ethnic and racial differences remained deep in the society. But Americans *had* become a community of consumers, surrounded by goods unavailable just a few decades before and able to purchase them. They had learned to make, want, and buy. As Arthur Miller, a twentieth-century playwright, said in *The Price:* "Years ago a person, he was unhappy, didn't know what to do with himself—he'd go to church, start a revolution—*something.* Today you're unhappy? Can't figure it out? What is the salvation? Go shopping."

The Wage Earners

Although entrepreneurs were important, it was the labor of millions of men and women that built the new industrial society. Their individual stories, nearly all unrecorded, reflected the achievement, drama, and pain of these years. In a number of respects, their lot improved during the last quarter of the nineteenth century. Real wages rose, working conditions got better, and the workers' influence in national affairs increased. Like others, workers also benefited from expanding health and educational services.

Working Men, Working Women, Working Children

Still, life for workers was not easy. Before 1900, most wage earners worked ten hours a day, six days a week. If skilled, they earned around 20 cents an hour; if unskilled, about half that. Most earned between $400 and $500 a year, at a time when it took about $600 to live decently. Construction workers, machinists, government employees, printers, clerical workers, and western miners made more than the average.

Eastern coal miners, agricultural workers, garment workers, and unskilled factory hands made considerably less.

There were few holidays or vacations and little respite from the grueling routine. Work was not only exhausting but also often dangerous. Safety standards were low, and accidents were common. On the railroads, one in every 26 workers was injured and one in every 399 killed each year. Thousands suffered from chronic illness, unknowing victims of dust, chemicals, and other pollutants.

The breadwinner might be a woman or a child; both worked in increasing numbers. Between 1870 and 1900, the number of working children rose nearly 130 percent, and the percentage of women who worked rose from 15 to 20 percent. Most working women were young and single. Many began work at age 16 or 17, worked five or six years, married, and quit. As clerical work expanded, women learned new skills such as typing and stenography. Moving into formerly male occupations, they became secretaries, bookkeepers, typists, telephone operators, and clerks in the new department stores. The number of women gainfully employed rose from 2.6 million in 1880 to 5.3 million in 1900.

A very few women became ministers, lawyers, and doctors, but change was slow, and in the 1880s, some law schools were still refusing to admit women because they "had not the mentality to study law." Among women entering the professions, the overwhelming majority became nurses, schoolteachers, and librarians. Consequently, those fields underwent a process of *feminization:* as women became the majority of the workers, a small number of men took the management roles, and most men left for other jobs, lowering the profession's status.

In most jobs, status and pay were allotted unequally between men and women. Many people of both sexes thought a woman's place was in the home. When employed in factories, women tended to occupy jobs that were viewed as natural extensions of household activities. They made clothes and textiles, processed food, and made cigars, tobacco, and shoes.

In general, adults earned more than children, the skilled more than the unskilled, native-born more than foreign-born, Protestants more than Catholics or Jews, and whites more than blacks or Asians. On average, women made a little more than half as much as men. These economic realities reflected bias based on race, creed, and gender. In the industrial society white, native-born Protestants—the bulk of the population, though by 1900 no longer the bulk of the workforce—reaped the greatest rewards.

Blacks labored on the fringes, usually in menial occupations. They earned less than other workers at almost every level of skill. On the Pacific Coast, the Chinese—and later the Japanese—lived in enclaves and suffered periodic attacks of discrimination. At times, immigration of both Chinese and Japanese was prohibited through legislation such as the **Chinese Exclusion Act.** Passed by Congress in 1882, the act banned the entry of Chinese workers for ten years.

Chinese Exclusion Act
Legislation passed in 1882 that excluded Chinese immigrant workers for ten years and denied U.S. citizenship to Chinese nationals living in the United States. It was the first U.S. exclusionary law that was aimed at a specific racial group.

Culture of Work

Among almost all groups, industrialization shattered age-old patterns, including work habits and the culture of work. It made people adapt "older work routines to new necessities and strained those wedded to premodern patterns of labor." Men and women fresh from farms were not accustomed to the factory's discipline. Now they worked indoors rather than out, paced themselves to the clock rather than the movements of the sun, and followed the needs of the market rather than the natural rhythms of the seasons. They had foremen and hierarchies and strict rules. Piecework determined wages, and always there was the relentless clock.

As industries grew larger, work became more impersonal. Machines displaced skilled artisans, and the unskilled tended them for employers they never saw. Workers picked up and left their jobs with startling frequency, and factories drew on a churning, highly mobile labor supply. Many workers were seemingly rootless, moving wherever new opportunities beckoned.

Substantial economic and social mobility accompanied the geographic mobility. The rags-to-riches stories of Horatio Alger had always said so, and careers such as Andrew Carnegie's seemed to confirm it. The actual record was considerably more limited. Most business leaders in the period came from well-to-do or middle-class families of old American stock. Still, many workers made major progress during their lifetimes. Movement from the working class to the middle class was not an uncommon occurrence.

The chance for advancement played a vital role in American industrial development. It gave workers hope, wedded them to the system, and tempered their response to the appeal of labor unions and working-class agitation. Very few workers rose from rags to riches, but a great many rose to better jobs and higher status.

❖ A Look at the Past ❖

Typewriter

By the end of the nineteenth century, typewriters became increasingly common in offices. The earliest typewriters worked in a variety of ways and did not even have similar keyboards. By the 1890s, however, the keyboard known today had become standard. The standardized keyboard made it easier for people to learn to type, and also made it possible to type more quickly. The awkward arrangement on the keyboard intentionally slowed typists to prevent keys from jamming as a result of rapid typing. Even though typewriters did not work as quickly as typists could, they offered numerous advantages over pen and ink. What do typewriters suggest about business practices? How did they affect the amount of paper used in offices? How could typed and printed forms alter the pace of business?

Labor Unions

Weak throughout the nineteenth century, labor unions never attracted more than 2 percent of the total labor force or more than 10 percent of industrial workers. To many workers, unions seemed "foreign," radical, out of step with the American tradition of individual advancement. Craft, ethnic, and other differences fragmented the labor force, and its extraordinary mobility made organization difficult. Employers strongly opposed unions. Said one U.S. Steel executive, "If a worker sticks up his head, hit it." As the national economy emerged, however, national labor unions gradually took shape. The early unions often represented skilled workers in local areas, but in 1866, William H. Sylvis united several unions into a single national organization, the National Labor Union. Sylvis sought long-range humanitarian reforms rather than specific, bread-and-butter goals. A talented propagandist, he won over many members, but when he died in 1869, the organization did not long survive him.

The year Sylvis died, Uriah S. Stephens and a group of Philadelphia garment workers formed a far more successful organization, the Noble and Holy Order of the Knights of Labor, known simply as the **Knights of Labor.** A secret fraternal order, it grew slowly through the 1870s until Terence V. Powderly ended the secrecy and embarked on an aggressive program. The Knights welcomed all laborers, regardless of skill, creed, gender, or color.

Harking back to the Jacksonians, the Knights set the "producers" against monopoly and special privilege. As members they excluded only "nonproducers"—bankers, lawyers, liquor dealers, and gamblers. Since employers were "producers," they could join; and since workers and employers had common interests, workers should not strike. The order's program included the eight-hour workday and the

Knights of Labor Also known as the Noble and Holy Order of the Knights of Labor. Founded in 1869, this labor organization pursued broad-gauged reforms as much as practical issues such as wages and hours.

abolition of child labor, but more often it focused on uplifting, utopian reform, such as ending drunkenness and establishing worker-run factories, railroads, and mines.

Membership grew steadily—from 42,000 in 1882 to a peak of 725,000 in 1886. But neither Powderly nor the union's loose structure could handle the growth, and when Jay Gould crushed their strike on the Texas and Pacific Railroad, the Knights crumbled. In 1886, the Haymarket Riot (to be discussed shortly) turned public sympathy against unions such as the Knights. By 1890, the order had shrunk to 100,000 members. A few years later, it was virtually defunct.

American Federation of Labor (AFL) Founded by Samuel Gompers in 1886, the AFL was a loose alliance of national craft unions that organized skilled workers by craft and worked for specific practical objectives such as higher wages, shorter hours, and better working conditions.

As the Knights waxed and waned, another organization emerged that was to endure. Founded in 1886, the **American Federation of Labor (AFL)** was a loose alliance of national craft unions. Unlike the Knights, it organized only skilled workers along craft lines, avoided politics, and worked for specific practical objectives. Samuel Gompers, the founder and longtime president, was determined to better the material lives of the workers. He accepted capitalism, and for labor he wanted simply a recognized place within the system and a greater share of the rewards.

Unlike Powderly, Gompers and the AFL assumed that most workers would remain workers throughout their lives. The task, then, lay in improving lives in "practical" ways: higher wages, shorter hours, and better working conditions. The AFL offered some attractive assurances to employers. As trade unionists, they would use the strike and boycott, but only to achieve limited gains, and if treated fairly, they would provide a stable labor force.

By the 1890s, the AFL was the most important labor group in the country. By 1901, the organization had more than a million members, or almost one-third of the country's skilled workers, and by 1914, it had more than two million. The great majority of workers, skilled and unskilled, remained unorganized, but Gompers and the AFL had become a significant force in national life.

Although two of the AFL's national affiliates accepted women as members, others prohibited them outright, and Gompers himself often complained that women workers undercut the pay scales for men. Conditions improved after 1900, but unions remained largely a man's world. The AFL did not expressly forbid black workers from joining, but member unions used high initiation fees, technical examinations, and other means to discourage black membership.

Labor Unrest

Workers used various means to adjust to the factory age. To the dismay of managers and "efficiency" experts, they often dictated the pace and quality of their work, and they set the tone of the workplace. Friends and relatives of newly arrived immigrants obtained jobs for them, taught them how to deal with factory conditions, and humanized the workplace.

Many employers believed in an "iron law of wages" in which supply and demand, not the welfare of their workers, dictated pay. Wanting a docile labor force, employers fired workers who joined unions, hired scabs to replace strikers, and used a powerful new weapon, the court injunction, to quell strikes. The injunction, which forbade workers to interfere with their employers' business, was used to break the great Pullman strike of 1894, and the Supreme Court upheld use of the injunction in *In re Debs* (1895).

As employers' attitudes hardened, strikes and violence broke out. Between 1880 and 1900, there were more than 23,000 strikes involving 6.6 million workers. The railroad strike of 1877 paralyzed railroads from West Virginia to California, resulting in the deaths of more than one hundred workers, and required federal troops to suppress it. In another year, 1886, more than 600,000 workers were off the job because of strikes and lockouts.

The worst incident took place in Chicago. In early May 1886, police, intervening in a strike at the McCormick harvester works, shot and killed two workers. The

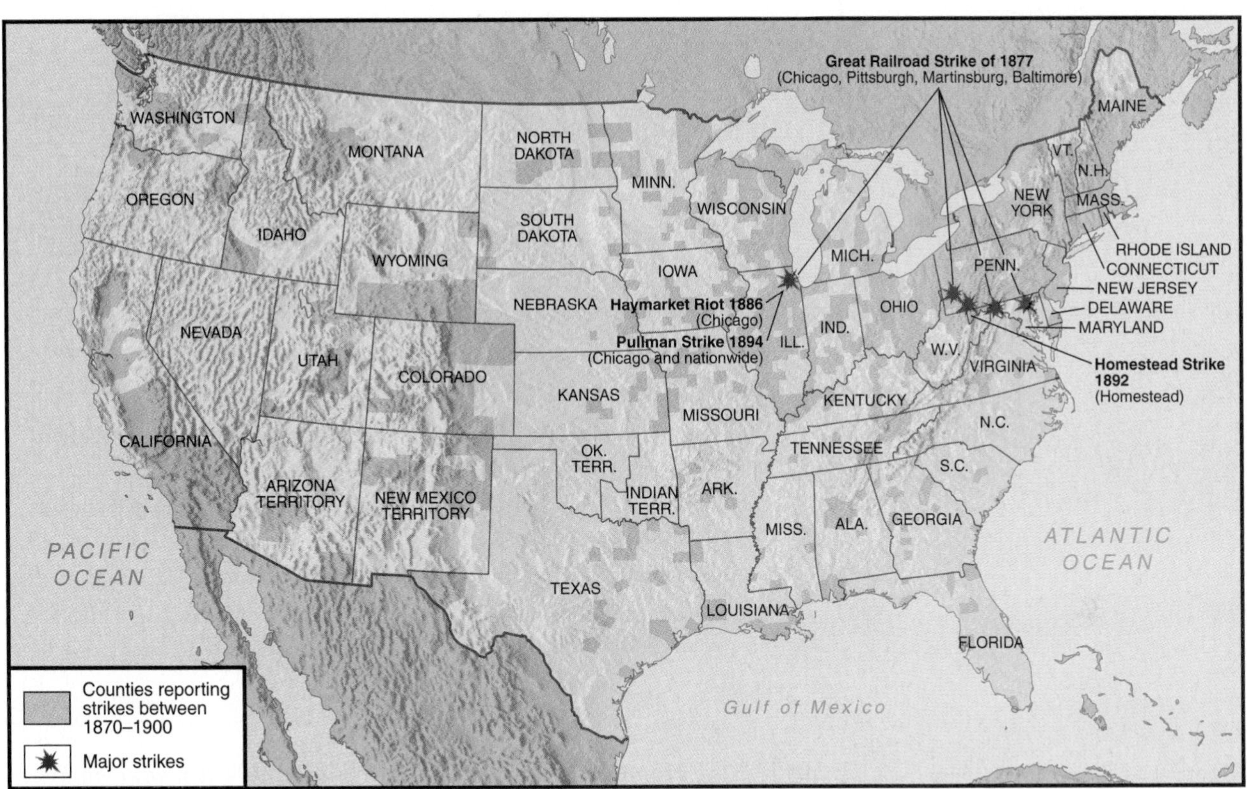

LABOR STRIKES, 1870–1890 *More than 14,000 strikes occurred in the 1880s and early 1890s, involving millions of workers. Labor violence brought public clamor against labor unions. Four violent strikes in particular weakened the labor movement—the Great Railroad strike of 1877, the Haymarket Riot of 1886, the Homestead Strike of 1892, and the Pullman Strike of 1894.* ✧

next evening, May 4, labor leaders called a protest meeting at Haymarket Square, near downtown Chicago. The meeting was peaceful, but police ordered the crowd to disperse. Someone threw a dynamite bomb, instantly killing one policeman and fatally wounding six others. Police fired into the crowd, killing four.

No one ever discovered who threw the bomb, but many Americans immediately labeled the incident the **Haymarket Riot** and demanded action against labor "radicalism." Cities strengthened their police forces and armories. Chicago police rounded up eight anarchists who were found guilty of murder on the basis of incendiary opinions. Although there was no evidence of their complicity in the bomb-throwing incident, four were hanged, one committed suicide, and three were jailed.

Haymarket Riot On May 4, 1886, a demonstration in Chicago's Haymarket Square to protest the slayings of two workers during a strike turned into a violent riot after a bomb explosion killed seven policemen.

Violence again broke out in the unsettled conditions of the 1890s. In 1892, Carnegie and Henry Clay Frick, his partner and manager, lowered wages nearly 20 percent at the Homestead steel plant. The Amalgamated Iron and Steel Workers, an AFL affiliate, struck, and Frick responded by locking the workers out of the plants. The workers surrounded it, and Frick, furious, hired a small private army of Pinkerton detectives to drive them off. Before the battle ended, the detectives were forced to surrender, and thirteen people were killed.

A few days later, the Pennsylvania governor ordered the state militia to impose peace at Homestead. On July 23, an anarchist named Alexander Berkman, who was not one of the strikers, walked into Frick's office and shot and stabbed him. Incredibly, Frick survived, watched the police take Berkman away, called in a doctor to bandage his wounds, and stayed in the office until closing time. The Homestead works reopened under military guard in late July; in November, the strikers gave up.

CHRONOLOGY

1859	First oil well is drilled near Titusville, Pennsylvania
1866	William Sylvis establishes the National Labor Union
1869	Transcontinental railroad is completed at Promontory, Utah ❖ Knights of Labor is organized
1876	Alexander Graham Bell invents the telephone ❖ Centennial Exposition is held in Philadelphia
1877	Railroads cut workers' wages, provoking a bloody and violent strike
1879	Thomas A. Edison invents the incandescent lamp
1881	Samuel Gompers founds the American Federation of Labor (AFL)
1882	Rockefeller's Standard Oil Company becomes the nation's first trust ❖ Edison opens the first electricity generating station in New York
1886	Labor protest erupts in violence in the Haymarket Riot in Chicago ❖ Railroads adopt a standard gauge
1892	Workers strike at the Homestead steel plant in Pennsylvania
1901	J. P. Morgan announces the formation of U.S. Steel Corporation, the nation's first billion-dollar company

Homestead Strike In July 1892, wage-cutting at Andrew Carnegie's Homestead Steel plant in Pittsburgh provoked this violent strike. Using ruthless force and strikebreakers, company officials effectively broke the strike and destroyed the union.

Events like the **Homestead Strike** troubled many Americans, who wondered whether industrialization, for all its benefits, might carry a heavy price in social upheaval, class tensions, and even outright warfare. Most workers did not share in the immense profits of the industrial age, and as the nineteenth century came to a close, some felt the need to rebel against the inequity.

Conclusion: Industrialization's Benefits and Costs

In the half century after the Civil War, the United States became the leading industrial nation in the world. On the one hand, industrialization meant "progress," growth, world power, and fulfillment of the American promise of abundance. For the bulk of the population, the standard of living—a particularly American concept—rose. But on the other hand, industrialization also meant rapid change, social instability, exploitation of labor, and growing disparity in income between rich and poor. Industry flourished, but control rested in fewer and fewer hands. Maturing quickly, the young system embarked on a new corporate capitalism: giant businesses, interlocking in ownership, managed by a new professional class, and selling an expanding variety of goods in an increasingly controlled market. As goods spread through American society, so did a sharpened and aggressive materialism. Workers felt the strains of the shift to a new social order.

In 1902, a well-to-do New Yorker named Bessie Van Vorst decided to see what it was like to work for a living in a factory. Disguising herself in worn, inexpensive clothes, she went to Pittsburgh and got a job in a canning factory. She worked ten hours a day, six days a week, including four hours on Saturday afternoons when she and the other women, on hands and knees, scrubbed the tables, the stands, and the entire factory floor. She worked until her body ached and her hands blistered, until the noise of the machines and monotony of the labor made her dazed and weary. She earned $4.20 a week, $3 of which went for food alone. Van Vorst was lucky; she could return to her comfortable life in New York. The working men and women around her were not so fortunate. They stayed on the factory floor and, by the dint of their labor, created a new industrial society.

Key Terms

trunk lines, p. 356
vertical integration, p. 359
trust, p. 360
Chinese Exclusion Act, p. 364
Knights of Labor, p. 365
American Federation of Labor (AFL), p. 366
Haymarket Riot, p. 367
Homestead Strike, p. 368

Recommended Reading

Samuel P. Hays, *The Response to Industrialism: 1885–1914* (1957), is an influential interpretation of the period. Douglass C. North, *Growth and Welfare in the American Past: A New Economic History* (1966), is stimulating. David Montgomery, *The Fall of the House of Labor* (1987), is an outstanding study of labor in the period. Richard Franklin Bensel, *The Political Economy of American Industrialization, 1877–1900* (2000), and Charles Perrow, *Organizing America: Wealth, Power, and the Origins of Corporate Capitalism* (2002), trace the underlying ideas of the new industrialization.

Alfred D. Chandler, *The Visible Hand: The Managerial Revolution in American Business* (1978), Olivier Zunz, *Making America Corporate, 1870–1920* (1990), and JoAnne Yates, *Control Through Communication: The Rise of System in American Management* (1989), are perceptive. The railroad empire is treated in John R. Stilgoe, *Metropolitan Corridor: Railroads and the American Scene* (1983), John Hoyt Williams, *A Great and Shining Road: The Epic Story of the Transcontinental Railroad* (1988), and John F. Stover, *American Railroads* (1961); its legal implications in, James W. Ely, Jr., *Railroads and American Law* (2001), and Barbara Young Welke, *Recasting American Liberty: Gender, Race, Law, and the Railroad Revolution, 1865–1920* (2001). On the steel industry, see Peter Temin, *Iron and Steel in Nineteenth-Century America* (1964).

Two superb books by Sam Bass Warner, Jr., *Streetcar Suburbs: The Process of Growth in Boston, 1870–1900* (1962), and *The Urban Wilderness: A History of the American City* (1973), examine technology and city development. The wage earner is examined in Herbert G. Gutman, *Work, Culture, and Society in Industrializing America* (1976), and Joshua L. Rosenbloom, *Looking for Work, Searching for Workers: American Labor Markets during Industrialization* (2002). Two books by Stephan Thernstrom, *Poverty and Progress: Social Mobility in the Nineteenth-Century City* (1964) and *The Other Bostonians: Poverty and Progress in the American Metropolis, 1880–1970* (1973), examine mobility. Philip S. Foner, *Women and the American Labor Movement*, 2 vols. (1979), Susan E. Kennedy, *If All We Did Was to Weep at Home* (1979), Barbara Mayer Wertheimer, *We Were There: The Story of Working Women in America* (1977), and Alice Kessler-Harris, *Out to Work: A History of Wage-Earning Women in the United States* (1982), are excellent on the subject of women in the workplace.

For a list of additional titles related to this chapter's topics, please see http://www.ablongman.com/divine.

Suggested Web Sites

Alexander Graham Bell Family Papers at the Library of Congress

http://memory.loc.gov/ammem/bellhtml/bellhome.html
This site contains papers from 1862 to 1939, but includes a chronology, images, selected documents, and interpretive essays about Bell.

The Richest Man in the World: Andrew Carnegie

http://www.pbs.org/wgbh/amex/carnegie/
This American Experience/PBS site provides images and text about Carnegie's life and activities.

The Anarchy Archives at Pitzer University

http://dwardmac.pitzer.edu/Anarchist_Archives/archivehome.html
This archive includes classic anarchist texts, especially information and graphics about the Haymarket Riot.

John D. Rockefeller and the Standard Oil Company

http://www.micheloud.com/FXM/SO/
This study with accompanying images by François Micheloud tells of the rise of Rockefeller and his mammoth company.

National Refinery Company

http://www.enarco.com/
This positive history of the company reflects the industrial changes of late-nineteenth-century America.

American Labor History

http://www.geocities.com/CollegePark/Quad/6460/AmLabHist/index.html
This site takes a general look at the history of labor in America.

Labor-Management Conflict in American History

http://www.history.ohio-state.edu/projects/laborconflict/
This site at Ohio State University includes primary accounts of some of the major events in the history of labor-management conflict in the late nineteenth and early twentieth centuries.

Samuel Gompers Papers at the University of Maryland

http://www.inform.umd.edu/HIST/Gompers/web1.html
This site includes information about the papers project but also has a photo gallery, selected documents, and a brief history of the first president of the American Federation of Labor.

Chapter 19

Toward an Urban Society, 1877–1900

The Overcrowded City

One day around 1900, Harriet Vittum, a settlement house worker in Chicago, went to the aid of a young Polish girl who lived in a nearby slum. The girl, aged 15, had discovered she was pregnant and had taken poison. An ambulance was on the way, and Vittum, told of the poisoning, rushed over to do what she could.

When Vittum arrived at the girl's squalid three-room apartment, she found the rooms crammed with at least fourteen boarders and young children, some sleeping on the floor. Glancing out the window, Vittum saw the wall of another building so close she could reach out and touch it. She was struck by the girl's life in the crowded tenement, with its lack of light and air. Did she have the right, Vittum asked herself, to bring the girl back "to the misery and hopelessness of the life she was living in that awful place?"

The young girl died, and in later years, Vittum often told her story. It was easy to see why. The girl's life in the slum reflected the experience of millions of other people in the late nineteenth century. The glitter and excitement of the cities attracted people from rural America, Europe, South America, and Asia. Between 1860 and 1910, the number of people living in American cities increased sevenfold. They were lured by the prospects of greater economic opportunities, but their lives were often bleak and painful.

TWO MAJOR FORCES RESHAPED AMERICAN SOCIETY between 1870 and 1920: industrialization and urbanization. In these years, cities grew upward and outward, attracting millions of newcomers and influencing politics, education, entertainment, and family life. By 1920, they had become the center of American economic, social, and cultural life.

Outline

The Lure of the City

Social and Cultural Change, 1877–1900

The Stirrings of Reform

Conclusion: The Pluralistic Society

We Americans

Ellis Island: Isle of Hope, Isle of Tears

THE LURE OF THE CITY

Between 1870 and 1900, the city—like the factory—became a symbol of a new America. Drawn from farms, small towns, and foreign lands, newcomers swelled the population of older cities and created new ones almost overnight. At the beginning of the Civil War, only one-sixth of the American people lived in communities of eight thousand people or more. By 1900, one-third did; by 1920, one-half.

The movement to urban life brought explosive growth. Thousands of years of history had produced only a handful of cities in which more than half a million people lived. In 1900, the United States had six such cities, including three—New York, Chicago, and Philadelphia—with populations more than a million.

Skyscrapers and Suburbs

Beginning in the 1800s, a revolution in technology transformed American cities. The age of steel and glass produced the skyscraper; the streetcar produced the suburbs and new residential patterns.

On the eve of the change, American cities were a crowded jumble of small buildings. Buildings were usually made of masonry, and since the massive walls had to support their own weight, they could be no taller than a dozen or so stories. Steel frames and girders ended that limitation and allowed buildings to soar higher and higher. "Curtain walls," which concealed the steel framework, were no longer load-bearing; they were pierced by many windows that let in fresh air and light.

To a group of talented Chicago architects, the new trends served as a springboard for innovative forms. The leaders of the movement were John Root and Louis H. Sullivan, both of whom were attracted by the chance to rebuild Chicago after the great fire of 1871. Root noted that the fire had fed on fancy exterior ornamentation, and he developed a plain stripped-down style, bold in mass and form—the keynotes of modern architecture. He also expounded on his belief that in an age of business, the office tower, more than the church or the government building, symbolized society, and he designed buildings that followed his code of simplicity, stability, breadth, and dignity. Sullivan, who had studied at MIT and in Paris before settling in Chicago, had his great inspiration in 1866, at the age of 30, when he conceived of the skyscraper. Sullivan's skyscrapers changed the urban skyline.

Architects must discard "books, rules, precedents," Sullivan announced; responding to the new, they should design for a building's function. "Form follows function," Sullivan believed, and he passed the idea on to a talented disciple, Frank Lloyd Wright. The modern city should stretch to the sky, "rising in sheer exaltation."

Electric elevators carried passengers upward in the new skyscrapers. During the same years, streetcars carried them outward to expanded boundaries that transformed urban life. Urban centers were no longer "walking cities," confined to a radius of 2 or 3 miles, a distance an individual might walk. Streetcar systems extended the radius and changed the urban map. Cable lines, electric surface lines, and elevated rapid transit brought shoppers and workers into central business districts and sped them home again. Cheap to ride, the mass transit systems fostered commuting; widely separated business and residential districts sprang up. The middle class moved farther and farther out to the leafy greenness of the suburbs.

As the middle class moved out of the cities, the immigrants and working class poured in. They took over the older brownstones, row houses, and workers' cottages, turning them under the sheer weight of numbers into the slums of the central city. In the cities of the past, classes and occupations had been thrown together. The streetcar city, sprawling and specialized, became a more fragmented and stratified society with middle-class residential rings surrounding a business and working-class core.

Tenements and the Problems of Overcrowding

In the shadows of the skyscrapers, grimy rows of tenements filled the central city. As Jacob Riis illustrated in words and pictures in *How the Other Half Lives* (1890), it was a world of dark halls, poor ventilation, and squalid conditions.

Tenement houses on small city lots crowded people into cramped apartments. In 1890, nearly half the dwellings in New York City were tenements. That year, more than 1.4 million people lived on Manhattan Island, one ward of which had a population density of 334,000 people per square mile. Many people lived in alleys and basements so dark they could not be photographed until flashlight photography was invented in 1887.

Everywhere was the smell of poverty and neglect. In the 1870s and 1880s, cities stank. One problem was horse manure, hundreds of tons of it a day in every city. Another was the privy, "a single one of which," said a leading authority on public health, "may render life in a whole neighborhood almost unendurable in the summer."

Cities dumped their wastes into the nearest body of water, then drew drinking water from the same site. Many built modern, purified waterworks but could not keep pace with spiraling growth. Factories, the pride of the era, polluted the urban air. At night, Pittsburgh looked and sounded like "Hell with the lid off," according to contemporary observers. Smoke poured from hundreds of glass factories, iron and steel mills, and oil refineries.

Crime was another growing problem. The nation's homicide rate nearly tripled in the 1880s, much of the increase coming in the cities. Slum youths formed street gangs and committed crimes. In San Francisco, the gangs gave rise to the new word *hoodlums,* described by a disgusted English traveler as "young embryo criminals" who robbed and murdered at night.

After remaining constant for many decades, the suicide rate rose steadily between 1870 and 1900. Alcoholism was also on the rise, especially among men. A 1905 survey of Chicago counted as many drinking establishments as grocery stores, meat markets, and dry goods stores combined.

Strangers in a New Land

Some of the new city dwellers had moved from farms and small towns; many others arrived from abroad. Most of those came from Europe, where unemployment, food shortages, and increasing threats of war sent millions fleeing across the Atlantic to make a fresh start in the United States. Italians first came in large numbers to escape an 1887 cholera epidemic in southern Italy; tens of thousands of Jews sought refuge from the pogroms (anti-Jewish massacres) that swept Russia and Poland after 1880. The immigration was so great that by 1890, about 15 percent of the U.S. population was foreign-born.

Most newcomers were job seekers. Nearly two-thirds were men; most were between the ages of 15 and 40 and unskilled. They tended to crowd into northern seaboard cities, settling in areas where others of their nationality or region had settled.

They were often dazzled by what they saw. They stared at electric lights, indoor plumbing, streetcars, ice cream, lemons, and bananas. America's teeming markets, department stores, and Woolworth's new five-and-dime stores offered goods unknown in the homeland.

Cities had increasingly large foreign-born populations. In 1900, three-fourths of Chicago's population was foreign-born or of foreign-born parentage, two-thirds of Boston's, and one-half of Philadelphia's. In New York City, where most immigrants entered the country and many stayed, four out of five residents in 1890 were of foreign birth or foreign parentage.

Beginning in the 1880s, the sources of immigration shifted dramatically away from northern and western Europe, the chief source of immigration for more than

In a Puck *cartoon titled "Looking Backward," the shadows of their immigrant origins loom over the rich and powerful who want to deny the "new" immigrants from central and southern Europe admission to the United States. The caption on the cartoon reads, "They would close to the newcomer the bridge that had carried them and their fathers over."* ◆

two centuries. More and more immigrants came from southern and eastern Europe: Italy, Greece, Austria-Hungary, Poland, and Russia. The **new immigrants** tended to be Catholics or Jews rather than Protestants, and they often spoke "strange" languages. Most were poor and uneducated; sticking together in communities, they clung to their native tongues, customs, and religions.

new immigrants Starting in the 1880s, immigration into the United States began to shift from northern and western Europe, its source for most of the nation's history, to southern and eastern Europe. These "new" immigrants tended to be poor, non-Protestant, and unskilled; they tended to stay in close-knit communities and retain their languages, customs, and religions.

More than any previous group, the new immigrants troubled the mainstream society. Could they be assimilated? Did they share "American" values? Sneering epithets became part of the national vocabulary: *wop* and *dago* for Italians; *bohunk* for Bohemians, Hungarians, and other Slavs; *grease-ball* for Greeks; and *kike* for Jews. Anti-Catholicism and anti-Semitism led to shameful treatment of the immigrants. In 1889, the head of the Fresh Air Fund, a program that sent New York City children on vacations to the suburbs, noted that "no one asked for Italian children." By the end of the 1890s, a number of organizations worked to restrict or end immigration.

Immigrants and the City

Industrial capitalism—the world of factories and machines—tested the immigrants and placed an enormous strain on their families. Many immigrants came from peasant societies where life proceeded according to outdoor routine and age-old tradition. In their new city homes, they found both new freedoms and a novel set of customs and expectations. Historians have only recently begun to discover the remarkable ways in which they learned to adjust.

Like native-born families, most immigrant families were nuclear in structure, consisting of two parents and their children. Generally, the men were wage earners; the women, household managers and mothers. The father normally played a minor role in child rearing or managing the family finances. "His to earn and hers to spend" was the standard of domestic virtue.

Although patterns varied between ethnic groups and between economic classes within ethnic groups, immigrants tended to marry within the group more than did the native-born. Immigrants also tended to marry at a later age than natives, and they tended to have more children, a fact that worried nativists opposed to immigration.

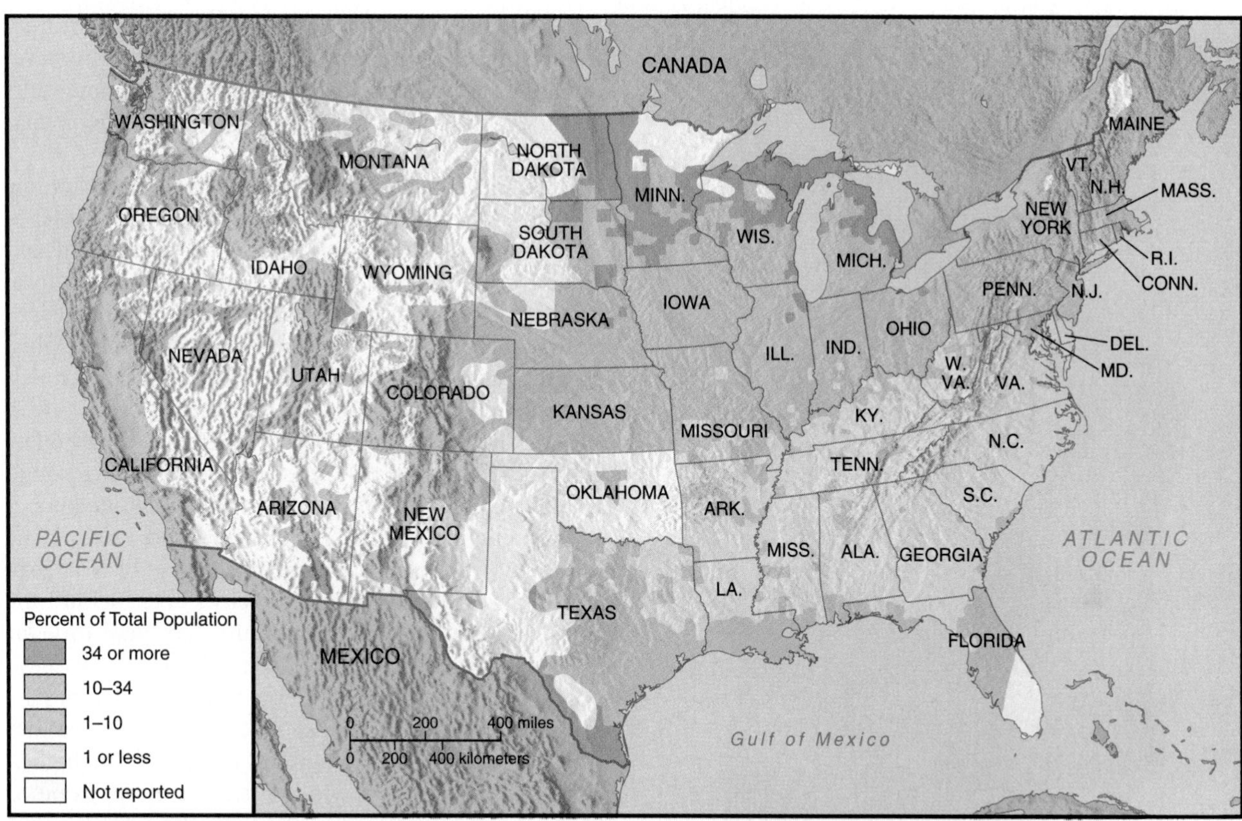

FOREIGN-BORN POPULATION, 1890 *Many immigrants settled in the rapidly growing cities of the northeast, where factory jobs were more plentiful than in the South. Immigrants looking for land to farm made their way west to the grain belt of the Midwest.* ❖

Most immigrants tried to retain their traditional culture for themselves and their children while at the same time adapting to life in their new country. To do this, they spoke their native language, practiced their religious faith, read their own newspapers, established their own schools, and formed a myriad of social organizations to maintain ties between members of the group.

Immigrant associations offered fellowship in a strange land. They helped newcomers find jobs and homes; they provided important services such as unemployment and health insurance. Some groups were no larger than a neighborhood; others spread nationwide. Many women belonged to and participated in the work of the immigrant associations; in addition, there were groups exclusively for women. Such associations as the Polish National Alliance served to maintain Old World traditions while helping members become accustomed to American life.

Church, school, and fraternal societies shaped the way in which immigrants adjusted to life in America. Eastern European Jews established synagogues and religious schools wherever they settled to preserve their ancient heritage. Among groups such as the Irish and the Poles, the Roman Catholic Church provided spiritual and educational guidance. In the parish schools, Polish priests and nuns taught Polish American children in the Polish language about Polish as well as American culture. By preserving language, religion, and heritage, they shaped the city—and the country—as much as it shaped them.

The House that Tweed Built

Closely connected with explosive urban growth was the emergence of the powerful city political machine. As cities grew, lines of responsibility in city governments became hopelessly confused, increasing the opportunity for corruption and greed. Burgeoning populations required streets, buildings, and public services; immigrants needed even more services. In this situation, party machines played an important role.

The machines traded services for votes. Loosely knit, they were headed by a strong, influential leader—the "boss"—who tied together a network of ward and precinct captains, each of whom looked after his local constituents. During the second half of the nineteenth century, such cities as New York, Chicago, Philadelphia, and San Francisco developed powerful political machines.

William M. Tweed, head of the famed Tweed Ring in New York, provided the model for them all. Nearly 6 feet tall, weighing almost 300 pounds, Tweed rose through the ranks of the New York Democratic machine known as Tammany Hall. A man of culture and warmth, he moved easily between the rough back alleys of New York and the parlors and clubs of the city's elite. Behind the scenes, he headed a ring that plundered New York for tens of millions of dollars.

The New York County Courthouse was his masterpiece. The three-story "House that Tweed Built" was designed to cost $250,000, but the bill ran a bit higher. Furniture, carpets, and window shades alone came to more than $5.5 million. In the end, the building cost more than $13 million—and in 1872, when Tweed fell, it was still not finished.

Some bosses were plainly corrupt; others believed in "honest graft," a term Tammany's George Washington Plunkitt coined to describe "legitimate" profits made from advance knowledge of city projects. Why did voters keep them in power? The answers are complex, but for the most part, the bosses stayed in power because they paid attention to the needs of the least privileged city voters. They offered valued services in an era when neither government nor business lent a hand.

If an immigrant, tired and bewildered after the long crossing, came looking for a job, bosses like Tweed found him one in city offices or local business. If a family's breadwinner died or was injured, the bosses donated food and clothing and saw to it that the family made it through the crisis. They contributed to hospitals, orphanages, and dozens of worthy neighborhood causes.

Most bosses became wealthy; they looked after their own needs first. Reformers occasionally ousted them. But reformers rarely stayed in power long. Drawn mainly from the middle and upper classes, they had little understanding of the needs of the poor. Before long, they returned to private concerns, and the bosses cheerily took power again.

❖ A Look at the Past ❖

Toy Bank

Political boss William Tweed of Tammany Hall pockets money as a mechanical bank. This bank was first patented in the 1870s, after Tweed's fall from power in 1872, and it became a very popular model. While charming children with his moving hand and head that nodded thanks upon the deposit of a coin, the bank also satirized the political machines, graft, and corruption. What does such a satirical toy suggest about attitudes toward politicians and political corruption at the time? Why do you think the bank was so popular?

Social and Cultural Change, 1877–1900

From 1877 to the 1890s, the nation underwent sweeping changes that affected economic, political, and social life. Technology changed mores; bright lights and new careers drew young men and women to the cities; family ties loosened. Cities, suburbs, and factories took new forms. While many people worked harder and harder, others had increased leisure time. Thanks to advancing technology, news flashed quickly across the oceans, and for the first time in history, people shook open their evening newspapers to read of that day's events in distant lands.

Old issues—questions of racial, social, and economic justice and of federal-state relations—were not settled, but people wanted new directions. Politics lost the sharp focus of the Civil War and its aftermath. With the end of Reconstruction, concern over the Union and slavery faded into the past.

In 1877, the country had 47 million people; a little more than a decade later, there were nearly 63 million. Nine-tenths of the population was white; just under one-tenth was black. The bulk of the white population, most of whom were Protestant, came from the so-called Anglo-Saxon countries of northern Europe. WASPS—white Anglo-Saxon Protestants—dominated American society.

Most people still lived on farms or in small towns. Their lives revolved around the farm, the church, and the general store. In 1880, nearly 75 percent of the population lived in communities of fewer than 2500 people. In 1900, in the midst of city growth, 60 percent still did. The average family in 1880 had three children, and life expectancy was about forty-three years. By 1900, it had risen to forty-seven years, the result of improved health care. For blacks and other minorities, often living in unsanitary rural areas, life expectancy was substantially lower: thirty-three years in 1900.

Meals tended to be heavy, and so did people. Even breakfast had several courses and could include steak, eggs, fish, potatoes, toast, and coffee. Food prices were low. Toward the end of the century, eating habits changed. New packaged breakfast cereals became popular, fresh fruit and vegetables came in on fast trains from Florida and California, and commercially canned food processing became safer and cheaper. The newfangled ice box, cooled by blocks of ice, kept food fresher.

Medical science was in the midst of a major revolution. Louis Pasteur's recent discovery that germs cause infection and disease created the new science of microbiology and led the way to the development of vaccines and other preventive measures. But tuberculosis, typhoid, diphtheria, and pneumonia—all then curable—were still the leading causes of death. Many families knew the wrenching pain of a child's death. Infant mortality declined between 1877 and 1900, but the great drop did not come until after 1920.

There were few hospitals and no hospital insurance. Most patients stayed at home, although medical practice expanded rapidly. In the field of surgery, anesthetics—ether and chloroform—eliminated pain, and antiseptic practices helped prevent postoperative infections. An earlier discovery—nitrous oxide, called laughing gas—eased the discomfort of dentistry. The new science of psychology began to explore the mind, hitherto uncharted. William James, a leading American psychologist and philosopher, stressed the importance of the environment on human development.

Manners and Mores

The code of Victorian morality set the tone for the era. The code prescribed stern standards of dress, manners, and sexual behavior. It was both obeyed and disobeyed, and it reflected the tensions of a generation that was undergoing a change in moral standards.

In 1877, children were to be seen and not heard. They spoke when spoken to, listened rather than chattered—at least that was the ideal. Older boys and girls were often chaperoned, although they could always find moments alone. They played kissing games such as post office and spin the bottle; they puffed cigarettes behind the barn. Counterbalancing such youthful exuberance was strong pride in virtue and self-control. "Thank heaven I am absolutely pure," Theodore Roosevelt wrote in 1880 after proposing to Alice Lee. "I can tell Alice everything I have ever done."

Gentlemen of the middle class dressed in heavy black suits, derby hats, and white shirts with paper collars. Women wore tight corsets, long dark dresses, and black shoes reaching well above the ankles. As with so many things, styles changed dramatically toward the end of the century, spurred in part by new sporting fads such as golf, tennis, and bicycling, which required looser clothing. Middle-class women adopted tailored suits and "shirtwaist" blouses modeled after men's shirts.

Religious and patriotic values were strong. A center of community life, the church often set the tenor for family and social relationships. In the 1880s, eight out of ten church members were Protestants; most of the rest were Roman Catholics. Evangelists such as Dwight L. Moody conducted successful mass revival meetings across the country.

Mugwumps Drawing their members mainly from the educated and upper class, these reformers crusaded for lower tariffs, limited federal government, and civil service reform to end political corruption.

Women's Christian Temperance Union (WCTU) Founded by Francis E. Willard, this organization campaigned to end drunkenness and the social ills that accompanied it.

With slavery abolished, reformers turned their attention to new moral and political issues. One group, known as the **Mugwumps,** worked to end corruption in politics. Drawn mostly from the educated and upper class, they included important newspaper and magazine editors. Other zealous reformers campaigned for prohibition of the sale of intoxicating liquors, hoping to end the social evils that stemmed from drunkenness. In 1874, the **Women's Christian Temperance Union (WCTU)** was formed to combat the consumption of alcohol. By 1898, the WCTU had ten thousand branches and half a million members.

In New York City, Anthony Comstock formed the Society for the Suppression of Vice, which supervised public morality. At his behest, Congress passed the Comstock Law (1873) prohibiting the mailing or transporting of "obscene, lewd or lascivious" articles. The law was not successful, and Comstock reported frequent violations of the act.

Leisure and Entertainment

In the 1870s, people tended to rise early. After dressing and eating, they went off to work and school; housewives marketed daily. In the evenings, families gathered in the "second parlor" or living room, where the children did their lessons, played games, sang around the piano, and listened to the day's verse from the Bible.

Indoor popular games included cards, dominoes, backgammon, chess, and checkers. Many of them were instructional as well as entertaining. The newest outdoor game was croquet, so popular that candles were mounted on the wickets to allow play at night. It was the first outdoor game designed for play by both sexes, and it frequently served as a setting for courtship.

New York's Broadway was the center of the theater, but road shows took popular plays to many cities and towns. American taste in the theater ran to intrigue, swordplay, melodrama, and grandiloquent language. Most plays were imported from Europe; the United States had few serious playwrights.

Sentimental ballads remained the most popular musical form, but the insistent syncopated rhythms of ragtime were being heard. By the time the strains of Scott Joplin's "Maple Leaf Rag" (1899) popularized ragtime, critics complained that "a wave of vulgar, filthy and suggestive music has inundated the land." Critics of ragtime took more comfort from the growth of classical music, which flourished during these years.

In the hamlets and small towns of America, traveling circuses were enormously popular. The larger circuses, run by entrepreneurs such as P. T. Barnum and James A. Bailey, played the cities, but every town attracted its own smaller versions. When the circus left town, Buffalo Bill's Wild West Show arrived, reenacting Indian field battles and displaying frontier marksmanship.

Football and baseball contests attracted avid fans. The years between 1870 and 1900 saw the rise of organized spectator sports, a trend reflecting the new uses of leisure. Baseball's first professional team, the Cincinnati Red Stockings, appeared in 1869, and baseball soon became the preeminent national sport. In 1869, Princeton and Rutgers played the first intercollegiate football game. Soon other schools picked up the sport, and by the early 1890s, crowds of fifty thousand or more attended the most popular contests. Boxing, though outlawed in most states, also gained a large following. John L. Sullivan, the era's most popular champion, won the last bare-knuckle heavyweight championship fight when he defeated Jake Kilrain in 1889 in a brutal seventy-five-round contest.

As gas and electric lights brightened the night and streetcars crisscrossed city streets, leisure habits changed. With so many things to do, people stayed home less often. New York City's first electric sign appeared in 1881, and people filled the streets on their way to the theater, vaudeville shows, or dance halls or just out for an evening stroll.

Victorian fashion ideals for women emphasized elaborate, confining dress styles with tiny waistlines and full skirts that reached to the floor. Throughout the 1890s, as women began to participate in some of the new sports or go to work in factories, stores, or business offices, styles gradually became less restrictive. This 1900 cover of Ladies' Home Journal *shows women wearing tailored jackets and simple pleated skirts hemmed above the ankle playing golf with men.* ✦

Changes in Family Life

Industrialization and urbanization changed family relationships. On the farm, parents and children worked more or less together, and the family was a producing unit. In factories, family members rarely worked together. In working-class families, mothers, fathers, and children separated at dawn and returned, ready for sleep, at dark. Middle-class fathers began to move their families out of the city to the suburbs; they commuted to work on the new streetcars, leaving wives and children at home and school.

Increasingly, middle-class wives and children became isolated from the world of work. Unlike the rural or urban working class—where mothers and children as well as fathers labored to support the family economy—middle-class families turned inward. Older children spent more time in adolescence, and periods of formal schooling were lengthier. Fewer wives participated directly in their husbands' work. As a result, they and their children occupied what contemporaries called a "separate sphere of domesticity," a place apart from the crass materialism of the outside world.

As the middle-class family's economic function declined, it took on increased emotional significance. "In the old days," said a woman in 1907, "a married woman was supposed to be a frump and a bore and a physical wreck. Now you are supposed to keep up intellectually, to look young and well and be fresh and bright and entertaining." Nonetheless, while society's leaders spoke fondly of the value of homemaking, the status of housewives declined under the factory system, which emphasized money rewards and devalued household labor.

Underlying all the changes was one of the modern world's most important trends, a major decline in fertility rates that lasted from 1800 to 1939. Although blacks, immigrants, and rural dwellers continued to have more children than white U.S.-born city dwellers, the trend affected all races and classes. Late marriages accounted for part of the decline, but a more important factor was the conscious decision by women and men to postpone or limit families. Women decided in some cases to devote greater attention to a smaller number of children and in other cases to pursue their own careers. In large part, the decline in fertility stemmed from people's responses to the social and economic forces around them, the rise of cities and industry. As a result, they reshaped some of the fundamental attitudes and institutions of American society.

Changing Views: A Growing Assertiveness Among Women

In and out of the family, there was a growing recognition of the self-sufficient working women who were entering the workforce in increasing numbers. Most were single and worked because of economic necessity. For many Americans, this "new woman" was regarded as a threat, a corruption of the ideal woman of men's imaginations, innocent, helpless, and good.

Views changed, albeit slowly. One important change occurred in the legal codes pertaining to women, particularly in the common-law doctrine of *femme couverte.* Under that doctrine, wives were chattel of their husbands; they could not legally control their own earnings, property, or children unless they had drawn up a specific contract before marriage. By 1890, many states had substantially revised the doctrine to allow wives control of their own earnings and inherited property. In cases of divorce, which rose sharply in the last third of the century, the new laws also recognized women's rights to custody or joint custody of their children.

In the 1870s and 1880s, a growing number of women were asserting their humanness and seeking self-fulfillment. Increasing interest in medical and psychological studies led women such as Charlotte Perkins Gilman, author of *Women and Economics* (1898), to argue that what men called womanly "innocence" was really ignorance; they began approaching old taboos—menstruation, sexual intercourse, childbirth—as natural functions and appropriate subjects of open inquiry.

More and more women were willing to voice their opinions about public policy, too, espousing causes with new fervor. They fought for the vote, lobbied for equal pay, and protested against price gouging by merchants, sometimes taking to the streets in organized demonstrations. Susan B. Anthony, fined $100 (which she refused to pay) when she tried to vote in the presidential election of 1872, helped form the **National American Woman Suffrage Association** in 1890 to work for female franchisement.

National American Woman Suffrage Association Founded by Susan B. Anthony in 1890, this organization worked to secure women the right to vote through careful organization and peaceful lobbying.

Educating the Masses

Continuing a trend that stretched back a hundred years, childhood was becoming a distinct time of life. There was still only a vague concept of adolescence, but the role of children was changing. Children were no longer perceived as "little adults," valued for the additional financial gain they might bring into the family. Now children were to grow and learn and be nurtured rather than rushed into adulthood.

As a result, schooling became more important, and American educators came closer than ever before to universal education. More states and territories made school attendance compulsory, more public schools were constructed, and more money was spent on education. Between 1870 and 1900, illiteracy declined from 20 percent to just over 10 percent of the population. Still, even as late as 1900, the average adult had only five years of schooling.

Most schools stressed a highly structured curriculum, focused on discipline and routine in a rigid environment. School began early; boys attended all day, but girls often stayed home after lunch, since it was thought they needed less in the way of learning. On the teacher's command, students stood and recited from *Webster's Spellers* and *McGuffey's Eclectic Readers,* the period's two most popular textbooks, which taught ethics, values, and religion as well as reading. In the *Readers,* boys grew up to be heroes, girls grew up to be mothers, and hard work always meant success.

The South lagged far behind in education. Family size was about twice as large as in the North, and a greater proportion of the population lived in isolated rural areas. Many southern states refused to adopt compulsory education laws. Most important, Southerners insisted on maintaining separate school systems to segregate the races. Supported by the 1896 U.S. Supreme Court decision in ***Plessy* v. *Ferguson,*** which upheld the constitutionality of "separate but equal" facilities, segregated schooling added a devastating financial burden to education in the South.

Plessy v. *Ferguson* A Supreme Court case in 1896 that established the doctrine of "separate but equal" and upheld a Louisiana law requiring that blacks and whites occupy separate rail cars.

North Carolina and Alabama mandated segregated schools in 1876, South Carolina and Louisiana in 1877, Mississippi in 1878, and Virginia in 1882. The laws often implied that the schools would be "separate but equal," but they rarely were. In 1890, only 35 percent of black children attended school in the South; 55 percent of white children did. At that time, nearly two-thirds of the country's black population was illiterate.

Educational techniques changed after the 1870s. Educators paid more attention to early elementary education. The kindergarten movement, started in St. Louis in 1873, spread across the country. In kindergartens, 4- to 6-year-olds learned by playing, not by rigid discipline. For older children, social reformers advocated "practical" courses in manual training and homemaking. For the first time, education became a field of university study. Teacher training became increasingly professional. By 1900, there were 345 normal schools (teacher-training institutions) throughout the United States.

Higher Education

Nearly 150 new colleges and universities opened in the twenty years between 1880 and 1900. The Morrill Land Grant Act of 1862 gave large grants of land to the states for the establishment of colleges to teach "agriculture and the mechanical arts." The act fostered sixty-nine "land-grant" institutions. Private philanthropy, born of the large fortunes of the industrial age, also spurred growth in higher education. Leland Stanford gave $24 million to endow Stanford University, and John D. Rockefeller gave $34 million to found the University of Chicago.

As universities increased, their function changed, and their curriculum broadened. No longer did they exist primarily to train young men for the ministry. They moved away from the classical curriculum of rhetoric, mathematics, Latin, and Greek toward "reality and practicality." The Massachusetts Institute of Technology (MIT), founded in 1861, focused on science and engineering.

Influenced by the new German universities, which emphasized specialized research, Johns Hopkins University in Baltimore opened the nation's first separate graduate school in 1876. By 1900, more than nine thousand Americans had studied in Germany, and some of them returned home to become presidents of institutions such as Harvard, Yale, Columbia, the University of Chicago, and Johns Hopkins.

One of them, Charles W. Eliot, who became president of Harvard in 1869 at the age of 35, set up an elective system in which students chose their own courses rather than following a rigidly prescribed curriculum. Lectures and discussions replaced rote recitation, and courses in the natural and social sciences, fine arts, and modern languages multiplied.

Educational opportunities also increased for women. A number of women's colleges opened, including Vassar (1865), Wellesley (1875), Smith (1875), and Radcliffe (1893). The land-grant colleges of the Midwest, open to women from the outset, spurred a nationwide trend toward coeducation. By 1900, women made up about 40 percent of college students.

Fewer opportunities existed for African Americans and other minorities. Most colleges did not accept minorities, and few applied. W. E. B. Du Bois, the brilliant black sociologist and civil rights leader, attended Harvard in the late 1880s but found the society of Harvard Yard closed against him. Black students turned to black colleges such as Hampton Normal and Industrial Institute in Virginia, which were often supported by whites who favored manual training for blacks. At the Tuskegee Institute in Alabama, which opened in 1881, Booker T. Washington, an ex-slave, put his educational ideals into practice. By 1900, Tuskegee was a model industrial and agricultural training school. It offered instruction in thirty trades to fourteen hundred students.

Washington stressed patience, manual training, and hard work. Rather than fighting for equal rights, blacks should acquire property and show they were worthy

A physics lecture at the University of Michigan in the late 1880s or early 1890s. The land-grant university admitted women, but seating in the lecture hall was segregated by gender—although not by race. Notice that both whites and African Americans are seated in the back rows of the men's section. ❖

of their rights. Outlined most forcefully in Washington's speech in Atlanta, the philosophy became known as the Atlanta Compromise; many whites and some blacks welcomed it. Acknowledging white domination, it called for slow progress through self-improvement, not through lawsuits or agitation. But Washington did believe in black equality. Often secretive in his methods, he worked behind the scenes to organize black voters and lobby against harmful laws. In his own way, he bespoke a racial pride that contributed to the rise of black nationalism in the twentieth century.

Du Bois wanted a more aggressive strategy. Born in 1868, the son of poor parents, he studied at Fisk University in Tennessee and the University of Berlin before he went to Harvard. Unable to find a teaching job in a white college, he took a low-paying research position at the University of Pennsylvania. He had no office but did not need one. Du Bois used the new discipline of sociology, which emphasized factual observation in the field, to study the condition of blacks.

Notebook in hand, he set out to examine crime in Philadelphia's black Seventh Ward. He interviewed five thousand people, mapped and classified neighborhoods, and produced *The Philadelphia Negro* (1898), a book of nearly a thousand pages. The first study of the effect of urban life on blacks, it cited a wealth of statistics, all suggesting that crime in the ward stemmed not from inborn degeneracy but from the environment in which blacks lived. Change the environment, and people would change, too; education was a good way to go about it. Calling for integrated schools with equal opportunity for all, Du Bois also urged blacks to educate their "talented tenth," a highly trained intellectual elite, to lead them.

Throughout higher education, there was increased emphasis on professional training, particularly in medicine, dentistry, and law. Enrollments swelled, even as standards of admissions of the early twentieth century tightened. Doctors, lawyers, and others became part of a growing middle class that shaped the concerns of the Progressive Era.

Although fewer than 5 percent of the college-age population attended college between 1877 and 1890, the new trends had great impact. A generation of men and women encountered new ideas that changed their views of themselves and society. Many students emerged from American colleges with a heightened sense of the social problems facing the nation and the belief that they could help cure society's ills.

The Stirrings of Reform

Intellectual beliefs of the period emphasized the slow process of evolution rather than radical reform. This stress on the slow pace of change reflected the doctrine of **social Darwinism,** based on the evolutionary theories of Charles Darwin and the writings of English social philosopher Herbert Spencer. In several influential books, Spencer applied Darwinian principles of natural selection to society, combining biology and sociology in a theory of "social selection" that explained human progress. Like animals, society evolved, slowly, by adapting to the environment. The "survival of the fittest"—an expression that Spencer, not Darwin, invented—preserved the strong and weeded out the weak.

social Darwinism Adaptation of Charles Darwin's theory of evolution, this theory held that the "laws" of evolution applied to human life, that change or reform therefore took centuries, and that the "fittest" would succeed in business and social relationships. It promoted the ideas of competition and individualism; it saw as futile any intervention of government into human affairs; and it was used by influential members of the economic and social elite to oppose reform.

Social Darwinism had a number of influential followers in the United States, including William Graham Sumner, a prominent professor at Yale University who was also a forceful writer. He argued that government action on behalf of the poor or weak interfered with evolution and sapped the species. Reform tampered with the laws of nature and was ultimately harmful to society as a whole.

The influence of social Darwinism on American thinking has been exaggerated, but in the powerful hands of Sumner and others, it did influence some journalists, ministers, and policymakers. Between 1877 and the 1890s, however, it came under increasing attack. In fields such as religion, economics, politics, literature, and law, thoughtful people raised questions about established conditions and suggested the need for reform.

New Currents in Social Thought

Henry George's nationwide best-seller *Progress and Poverty* (1879) led the way to a more critical appraisal of American society in the 1880s and beyond. The book jolted traditional thought by questioning the assumptions of social Darwinism.

"The present century," George wrote, "has been marked by a prodigious increase in wealth-producing power. . . . It was natural to expect, and it was expected, that . . . real poverty [would become] a thing of the past." Such, however, was not the case. Instead, he argued, "the wealthy class is becoming more wealthy; but the poorer class is becoming more dependent."

George proposed a simple solution. Land formed the basis for wealth; a "single tax" on it, replacing all other taxes, would equalize wealth and raise revenue to help the poor. "Single-tax" clubs sprang up around the country, but George's solution, simplistic and unappealing, had much less impact than his analysis of the problem itself. He raised questions a generation of readers set out to answer.

George's emphasis on deprivation in the environment excited a young country lawyer in Ashtabula, Ohio, named Clarence Darrow. Unlike the social Darwinists, Darrow was sure that criminals were made and not born. They grew out of "the unjust condition of human life." In the mid-1880s, he left for Chicago and a forty-year career working to convince people that poverty lay at the root of crime.

As Darrow rejected the implications of social Darwinism, in similar fashion did Richard T. Ely and a group of young economists poke holes in traditional economic thought. Ely attacked classical economics for its dogmatism, simple faith in laissez-faire, and reliance on self-interest as a guide for human conduct. He refused to "acknowledge laissez-faire as an excuse for doing nothing while people starve."

In 1885, Ely led a small band of rebels in founding the American Economic Association, which linked economics to social problems and urged government intervention in economic affairs. Social critic Thorstein Veblen saw economic laws as a mask for human greed. In *The Theory of the Leisure Class* (1899), Veblen analyzed the "predatory wealth" and "conspicuous consumption" of the business class.

Lawyer Edward Bellamy dreamed of a cooperative society where poverty, greed, and crime no longer existed. Bellamy published *Looking Backward, 2000–1887* in 1887 and became a national reform figure virtually overnight. The novel's protagonist, Julian West, falls asleep in 1887 and awakes in the year 2000. He finds himself in a socialist utopia where cooperation, rather than competition, is the watchword. The vision captured the imagination of many Americans, who responded by calling for the nationalization of public utilities and a wider distribution of wealth.

Walter Rauschenbusch, a young Baptist minister, read widely from the writings of Bellamy, George, and other social reformers. When he took his first church post in Hell's Kitchen, a blighted area of New York City, he soon discovered the weight of the slum environment. In the 1890s, Rauschenbusch became a professor at the Rochester Theological Seminary, and he began to expound on the responsibility of organized religion to advance social justice.

Some Protestant sects stressed individual salvation and a better life in the next world, not in this one. Poverty was evidence of sinfulness; the poor had only themselves to blame. Wealth and destitution, suburbs and slums—all formed part of God's plan.

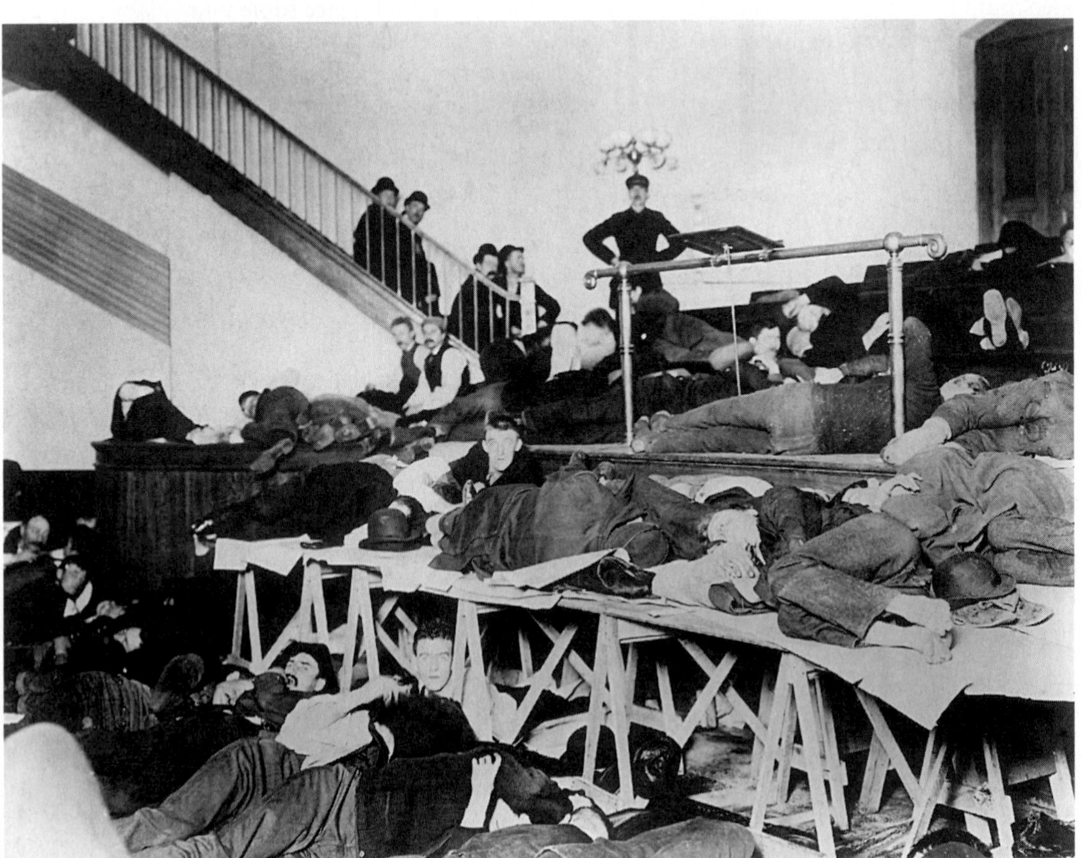

Men sleeping in crowded conditions at the Salvation Army headquarters in New York City, 1897. The Salvation Army's missions for the homeless tended to the material and spiritual needs of the poor, unemployed, and outcast in the city's slums. ◆

Challenging those traditional doctrines, a number of churches in the 1880s began establishing missions in the city slums. Living among the poor and the homeless, the urban missionaries grew impatient with religious doctrines that endorsed the status quo. Instead, many of them supported the emerging religious philosophy known as the **Social Gospel,** which focused on improving living conditions as well as saving souls. Churches became centers for social uplift as well as religious activity.

Social Gospel Preached by a number of urban Protestant ministers, this doctrine focused as much on improving the conditions of life on earth as on saving souls for the hereafter. Its adherents worked for child-labor laws and measures to alleviate poverty.

The most active Social Gospel leader was Washington Gladden, a Congregational minister and prolific writer. Linking Christianity to the social and economic environment, Gladden spent a lifetime working for "social salvation." Emphasizing a fellowship of love, he denounced competition, urged an "industrial partnership" between employers and employees, and called for efforts to help the poor.

The Settlement Houses

A growing number of social workers, living in the urban slums, shared Gladden's concern. Like Tweed and Plunkitt, they appreciated the dependence of the poor; unlike them, they wanted to eradicate the conditions that underlay it.

Youthful, idealistic, and mostly middle-class, these social workers established **settlement houses** to help the poor. The first such house was opened in New York City in 1886; by 1910, there were more than four hundred of them. Reformers such as Jane Addams, who established the famous Hull House in Chicago (1889), wanted to bridge the socioeconomic gap between rich and poor and to bring education, culture, and hope to the slums. They sought to create in the heart of the city the values and sense of community of small-town America.

settlement houses Located in poor districts of major cities, these were community centers that tried to soften the impact of urban life for immigrant and other families. Often run by young, educated women, they provided social services and a political voice for their neighborhoods.

Many of the settlement workers were women, some of them college graduates who found that society had little use for their talents and energy. When Jane Addams opened Hull House, she was 29 years old. Endowed with a forceful and winning personality, she intended "to share the lives of the poor" and humanize the industrial city. Her staff stressed education, offering classes in elementary English and Shakespeare, lectures on ethics and the history of art, and courses in cooking, sewing, and manual skills.

Like settlement workers in other cities, Addams and her colleagues studied the immigrants in nearby tenements. Finding people of eighteen different nationalities living within one square mile of Hull House, they taught them American history and the English language yet also encouraged them, through folk festivals and arts, to preserve their heritage. Other settlement workers—among them Robert Woods in Boston and Lillian Wald in New York City—concentrated on such social and human problems as hunger, school dropouts, exploitive child labor, and health care for the poor.

A Crisis in Social Welfare

When the depression of 1893 struck, it jarred the young settlement workers, many of whom had just begun their work. In cities and towns across the country, traditional methods of helping the needy foundered in the crisis. Gradually, a new class of professional social workers arose to fill the need. Unlike the church and charity volunteers, these social workers wanted not only to feed the poor but also to study their condition and alleviate it. Revealingly, they called themselves "case workers" and daily collected data on the income, housing, jobs, health, and habits of the poor. Prowling tenement districts, they gathered information about the number of rooms, number of occupants, ventilation, and sanitation, putting together a fund of useful data.

Studies of the poor popped up everywhere. Walter Wyckoff embarked in 1891 on what he called "an experiment in reality." For eighteen months, he worked as an unskilled laborer in jobs from Connecticut to California. Wyckoff summarized his

CHRONOLOGY

1862	Morrill Land Grant gives land to states for establishment of colleges
1869	Rutgers and Princeton play in the nation's first intercollegiate football game ❖ Cincinnati Red Stockings, baseball's first professional team, is organized
1873	Comstock Law bans obscene articles from the U.S. mail ❖ Nation's first kindergarten opens in St. Louis, Missouri
1874	Women's Christian Temperance Union formed to crusade against evils of liquor
1876	Johns Hopkins University opens the first separate graduate school
1879	Henry George analyzes problems of urbanizing in *Progress and Poverty* ❖ Salvation Army arrives in the United States
1881	Booker T. Washington opens the Tuskegee Institute in Alabama
1883	Metropolitan Opera opens in New York
1885	Home Insurance Building, the country's first metal-frame structure, is erected in Chicago
1887	Edward Bellamy promotes the idea of a socialist utopia in *Looking Backward, 2000–1887*
1889	Jane Addams opens Hull House in Chicago
1890	National American Woman Suffrage Association is formed to work for women's right to vote
1894	Immigration Restriction League is formed to limit immigration from southern and eastern Europe
1896	Supreme Court decision in *Plessy* v. *Ferguson* establishes the constitutionality of "separate but equal" facilities for blacks and whites ❖ John Dewey's Laboratory School for testing and practice of new educational theory opens at the University of Chicago

findings in *The Workers* (1897), a book immediately hailed as a major contribution to sociology. Following Wyckoff's lead, other investigators examined the lives of domestic servants, miners, lumberjacks, and factory laborers. Calls for reform of urban life grew louder, spawning numerous task forces and civic organizations committed to that purpose.

Conclusion: The Pluralistic Society

"The United States was born in the country and moved to the city," historian Richard Hofstadter said. Much of that movement occurred during the nineteenth century when the United States was the most rapidly urbanizing nation in the Western world. American cities bustled with energy; they absorbed millions of migrants from Europe and other parts of the world. The migration, and the urban growth that accompanied it, reshaped American politics and culture.

The 1920 census showed that, for the first time, most Americans lived in cities. It also revealed that about half the population was descended from people who arrived after the American Revolution. As European, African, and Asian cultures met in the American city, a culturally pluralistic society emerged. The residents of the United States proudly declared their hybrid cultural identities as Polish Americans, African Americans, Irish Americans, and so on. The metaphor of the melting pot reflected a new national image as, in the decades after the 1870s, a jumble of ethnic and racial groups responded to the challenges of industrialization and urbanization.

Key Terms

new immigrants, p. 374

Mugwumps, p. 378

Women's Christian Temperance Union (WCTU), p. 378

National American Woman Suffrage Association, p. 380

Plessy v. *Ferguson*, p. 380

social Darwinism, p. 383

Social Gospel, p. 383

settlement houses, p. 385

Recommended Reading

On urban America, see Sam Bass Warner, Jr., *Streetcar Suburbs* (1962) and *The Urban Wilderness* (1972). William R. Taylor, *In Pursuit of Gotham: Culture and Commerce in New York* (1992), Eric H. Monkkonen, *America Becomes Urban* (1988), Sven Beckert, *The Monied Metropolis: New York City and the Consolidation of the American Bourgeoisie, 1850-1896* (2001), and David Schuyler, *The New Urban Landscape* (1986), are also valuable. See also two books by Jon C. Teaford: *The Unheralded Triumph: City Government in America, 1870–1900* (1984) and *City and Suburb: The Political Fragmentation of Metropolitan America, 1850–1970* (1979).

For family life, see Joseph Kett, *Rites of Passage: Adolescence in America* (1977), Elaine Tyler May, *Great Expectations: Marriage and Divorce in Post-Victorian America* (1980), Steven Mintz, *A Prison of Expectations: The Family in Victorian Culture* (1983), Stephen M. Frank, *Life With Father: Parenthood and Masculinity in the Nineteenth-Century American North* (1998), and Norma Basch, *In the Eyes of the Law: Women, Marriage, and Property in Nineteenth-Century New York* (1982). Karen Lystra, *Searching the Heart: Women, Men, and Romantic Love in Nineteenth-Century America* (1989), is valuable.

Urban reform is examined in Judith Ann Trolander, *Professionalism and Social Change: From the Settlement House Movement to Neighborhood Centers, 1886 to the Present* (1987), Shannon Jackson, *Lines of Activity: Performance, Historiography, Hull-House Domesticity* (2001), Allen F. Davis, *Spearheads for Reform: The Social Settlements and the Progressive Movement, 1890–1914* (1967), and *American Heroine: The Life and Legend of Jane Addams* (1973).

For a list of additional titles related to this chapter's topics, please see http://www.ablongman.com/divine.

Suggested Web Sites

The American Experience: America 1900

http://www.pbs.org/wgbh/amex/1900/

This site is the companion site to the PBS documentary. It includes audio clips of respected historians on the economics, politics, and culture of 1900, a primary source database, a timeline of the year, downloadable software to compile a personal family tree, and other materials.

Touring Turn-of-the-Century America: Photographs from the Detroit Publishing Company, 1880–1920

http://memory.loc.gov/ammem/detroit/dethome.html

This Library of Congress collection has thousands of photographs from turn-of-the-century America.

World's Columbian Exposition: Idea, Experience, Aftermath

http://xroads.virginia.edu/~MA96/WCE/title.html

This site has a virtual tour of the fair, along with contemporary reactions and modern analysis.

United States History: The Gilded Age (1890) to World War I

http://www.emayzine.com/lectures/Gilded~1.htm

This site consists of a good overview essay of the era.

Chapter Three: American Socialists and Reformers

http://www.vineyard.net/vineyard/history/pdgech3.htm

This site includes a fine essay about Edward Bellamy and some of the movements and ideas he inspired.

Jan Addams Hull-House Museum

http://www.uic.edu/jaddams/hull/hull_house.html

This site offers information on Addams, her settlement house programs, and the neighborhoods they served.

African American Perspectives: Pamphlets from the Daniel A. P. Murray Collection, 1818–1907

http://memory.loc.gov/ammem/aap/aaphome.html

This collection includes writings of famous African Americans including Frederick Douglass, Booker T. Washington, Ida B. Wells-Barnett, Benjamin W. Arnett, Alexander Crummel, and Emanuel Love.

We Americans

Ellis Island

Isle of Hope, Isle of Tears

Ten years after he left Selo, his small Bulgarian village, for the United States, Michael Gurkin returned to tell of the wonders he had seen, including "buildings that scratched the sky," rooms in them that moved up and down, buttons that, when pushed, lit a house or a street. Stoyan Christowe, 13, listened intently, caught up in the "Americamania," as he called it, that swept through his village. Soon he was on his way to the new land, his pockets stuffed with walnuts, because he was too young to drink the farewell toast.

Unknowingly, he had joined a flood of people who were making their way to the United States. Between 1880 and 1920, a period of just forty years, a remarkable total of 23.5 million immigrants arrived in the country. They came from around the world, though mostly from Europe, driven from their homelands by economic, religious, or other troubles, lured across the ocean by the chance for a better life. They entered the country through several ports, but by far the most—about seven out of every ten—landed in the city of New York.

Until 1892, they landed at a depot known as Castle Garden, a sprawling building on the tip of Manhattan Island. When it could no longer handle the flow, the entry site was moved to Ellis Island, a bank of sand and shells, close to the Statue of Liberty. Contractors erected a wooden structure, which opened in 1892 and burned down five years later. They then put up the current edifice, an imposing red brick building with triple-arch entrances and corner steeples. A small city, it had dormitories, a hospital, a post office, and showers that could bathe eight thousand people a day. It opened in 1900.

The change to Ellis Island represented more than just a shift in site. Entrance at Castle Garden had been fairly informal, since control over immigration still rested largely in the hands of the states. Officials merely registered newcomers, a process that took about thirty seconds.

In 1891, worried about the growing numbers of people who wanted in, Congress acted to bring immigration under federal control. Ellis Island was given tasks Castle Garden had never had, including mandates to keep out people some Americans considered undesirable. It became, one observer said, "the nearest earthly likeness to the Final Day of Judgement, when we have to prove our fitness to enter Heaven."

Many of those who sailed into the harbor, it should be remembered, never passed through the island at all. Arriving in first or second class, they had a fast on-board examination and went ashore, monied enough, it was assumed, not to become wards of the state. But those in third class—"steerage" as it was known—had a very different experience, and they faced it full of fear that they would fail some test and be sent back home.

The day they docked, Christowe and others washed thoroughly, hoping to look clean enough to pass inspection. Crowding the ship's rails, they gazed in wonder at the statue in the harbor, its arm lifted in the air. It was a saint, some guessed; Christopher Columbus, others said. It was a monument to freedom, Christowe was told, with Emma Lazarus's inviting poem at its base, "Give me your tired, your poor, Your huddled masses yearning to breathe free."

Once on the island, those huddled masses were under scrutiny from the moment they landed. Officials watched them climb the stairs, looking for heart problems or lameness. Physicians administered the "six-second exam," checking quickly for disabilities or contagious diseases. If anything seemed out of sort, they put a chalk mark on the immigrant's coat calling for closer examination.

The next exam was the most feared of all: a doctor using a tailor's buttonhook to pull back eyelids to look for signs of diseases such as trachoma, a highly contagious bacterial eye infection that could lead to blindness. Most immigrants had never heard of trachoma, nor even knew they had the disease, but it alone could strand them in the island's hospital or put them on a boat back home.

No one who went through the exam ever forgot it, as an immigrant poet wrote:

> A stranger receives us
>
> Harshly and asks: "And your health?"
>
> He examines us. His look
>
> Assesses us like dogs.

A view of the landing station at Ellis Island in 1905, where millions of immigrants entered the country. ❖

He studies in depth
Eyes and mouth. No doubt
That if he'd probed our hearts
He would have seen the wound.

Immigrants with chalk marks were herded to the left, while most went to the right, filing by a matron who searched the faces of women for evidence of "loose character." With so many languages among the arrivals, there were few written signs, and officials used metal barricades to guide people along, "like puppets on conveyor-belts," Christowe later recalled.

Last there were the inspectors, seated behind desks, asking name, age, occupation, among dozens of other questions. On a busy day, the inspectors had two minutes to decide the fate of a newcomer. Those who "failed" went before a feared Board of Special Inquiry for final decision. For most immigrants the whole process took less than five hours; many others, held for proof of funds or further examination, spent days in the dormitories or hospital. Despite the harsh rumors, no more than 3 percent in a given year were turned away.

Still, it was becoming harder and harder to get in. People who feared the effect of immigrants on the nation clamored to keep them out. Some worried about the numbers of people who were arriving; others about disease or "radical" political views. Some did not like the shift in immigration after 1890 from largely Protestant northern and western Europe to Catholics, Jews, and others from southern and eastern Europe.

Reflecting such concerns, Congress passed laws to keep certain types of people out. In 1875, it prohibited the entrance of criminals and prostitutes. In 1882, it barred convicts and lunatics and excluded laborers from China, the first measure aimed directly at a racial group. In 1885, it banned the entry of laborers under contract, imported by industries to work at low wages; in 1891, polygamists and people with "loathsome" diseases; in 1903, anarchists. In 1917, it passed, over Woodrow Wilson's veto, a literacy test that required immigrants to read a passage in their native tongue.

The great burst of immigration, halted during World War I, ended with the adoption of restrictive legislation in the 1920s. Ellis Island became more and more a detention center for "radicals" and other people awaiting deportation. Once the gateway to the United States, the famous island had become an exit.

Ellis Island closed in 1954; in 1965, recognizing its historic importance, the government made it a national monument. It reopened in 1990 as a museum of American immigration, and is so popular it attracts more than two million tourists a year; many retrace the footsteps of their own ancestors who had landed there. Stoyan Christowe's name is in the records there. Starting with a miserable job in a railroad yard in St. Louis, he went to college, served in military intelligence during World War II, wrote several books, and became a member of the Vermont legislature.

His experience on Ellis Island blended into the nation's experience. More than 100 million Americans—about four in every ten—trace their ancestry to those who found a new home through its gates.

Chapter 20

Political Realignments in the 1890s

Hardship and Heartache

In June 1894, Susan Orcutt, a young farm woman from western Kansas, wrote the governor of her state a letter. She was desperate. The nation was in the midst of a devastating economic depression, and like thousands of other people, she had no money and nothing to eat. "I take my pen in hand to let you know that we are starving to death," she wrote. There appeared to be no hope. Her husband had been to ten counties and could not find work, and her family had run out of food.

As bad as conditions were on the farms, they were no better in the cities. Thousands of homeless, starving men wandered in the streets, and charity societies and churches could not help the huge numbers of people who were in need. The records of the Massachusetts state medical examiner told a grim story of despondency and suicide. Rather than face more hunger and humiliation, men and women took their own lives.

Lasting until 1897, the depression was the decisive event of the decade. At its height, three million people were unemployed—20 percent of the workforce. The human costs were enormous, even among the well-to-do. "They were for me years of simple Hell," shattering "my whole scheme of life," said Charles Francis Adams, descendant of two American presidents.

THE DEPRESSION OF THE 1890S had profound and lasting effects. Bringing to a head many of the tensions that had been building in society, it increased rural hostility toward the cities, brought about a bitter fight over the currency, and changed people's thinking about government, unemployment, and reform. There were outbreaks of warfare between capital and labor, farmers demanded a fairer share of economic and social benefits, and the "new" immigrants came under fresh attack.

Under the cruel impact of the depression, ideas changed in many areas, including a stronger impulse toward reform, a larger role for the presidency, and a call for help from many farmers and laborers. One of the most important of these areas was politics. A realignment of the American political system, in process since the end of Reconstruction, finally reached fruition in the 1890s, establishing new patterns that gave rise to the Progressive Era and lasted well into the twentieth century.

OUTLINE

Politics of Stalemate

Republicans in Power: The Billion-Dollar Congress

The Rise of the Populist Movement

The Crisis of the Depression

Changing Attitudes

The Presidential Election of 1896

The McKinley Administration

Conclusion: A Decade's Dramatic Changes

Politics of Stalemate

Politics was a major fascination of the Gilded Age, as both mass entertainment and sport. Millions of Americans read party newspapers, listened to three-hour speeches by party leaders, and turned out in enormous numbers to vote. In the six presidential elections between 1876 and 1896, an average of almost 80 percent of the electorate voted.

White males made up the bulk of the electorate; until after the turn of the century, women could vote in national elections in only four western states. In 1875, the Supreme Court, in *Minor* v. *Happersett,* upheld the power of the states to deny the right to women, and Congress continued to refuse to pass a constitutional amendment for woman suffrage. In addition, black men were increasingly kept from the polls by various methods. In 1877, Georgia adopted the poll tax, which forced voters to pay an annual tax for the right to vote. It was a tax few blacks could afford to pay. In 1898, Louisiana adopted the famous "grandfather clause," demanding a literacy test for all voters except the sons and grandsons of those who had voted in the state before 1867—a time, of course, when no blacks could vote. The number of registered black voters in Louisiana decreased from 130,334 in 1896 to 1,342 in 1904.

The Party Deadlock

The 1870s and 1880s were still dominated by the Civil War generation, the unusual group of people who rose to power in the turbulent 1850s. Five of the six presidents elected between 1865 and 1900 had served in the war, as had many civic, business, and religious leaders.

Party loyalties—rooted in Civil War traditions, ethnic and religious differences, and perhaps class distinctions—were remarkably strong. Although linked to the defeated Confederacy, the Democrats revived quickly after the war. In 1874, they gained control of the House of Representatives, which they maintained for all but four of the next twenty years. While identification with civil rights and military rule cut Republican strength in the South, the Democratic party's principles of states' rights, decentralization, and limited government won supporters everywhere.

The Republicans pursued policies in which local interests merged into nationwide patterns, and government became an instrument to promote moral well-being and material wealth. The Republicans passed the Homestead Act (1862), granted subsidies to the transcontinental railroads, and pushed other measures to encourage economic growth. They also enacted legislation to protect civil rights and advocated a high protective tariff as a tool of economic policy.

In national elections, sixteen states, mostly in New England and the North, consistently voted Republican; fourteen states, mostly in the South,

❖ A Look at the Past ❖

Ballot Box

Until the 1890s, political parties printed their own ballots, which voters requested in order to cast a ballot. Voters revealed their political decisions simply by obtaining a ballot. Glass ballot boxes such as this one made it possible for others to witness that the voter actually cast the ballot. While today voters make their decisions and cast their votes privately, before 1890 voting was a visible, public act, and political intimidation could and did occur. Why would Americans use such a system? Why did they change to secret balloting at the end of the nineteenth century?

consistently voted Democratic. Elections therefore depended on a handful of "doubtful" states—New York, New Jersey, Connecticut, Ohio, Indiana, and Illinois—which received special attention at election time. Presidential candidates usually came from these states. From 1868 to 1912, eight of the nine Republican presidential candidates and six of the seven Democratic candidates came from these states, especially New York and Ohio.

The two parties were evenly matched, and elections were closely fought. In three of the five presidential elections between 1876 and 1892, the victor won by less than 1 percent of the vote; in 1876 and 1888, the losing candidates actually received more popular votes than the winners but lost in the electoral college. Knowing that small mistakes could lose elections, politicians became extremely cautious. It was difficult to govern. Only twice during these years did one party control both the presidency and the two houses of Congress.

Historians once believed that politicians accomplished little between 1877 and 1900, but they were wrong. After the impeachment of Andrew Johnson, the authority of the presidency dwindled in relation to congressional strength. For the first time in many years, power rested in Congress and, even more significant, in state and local governments.

Experiments in the States

Across the country, state bureaus and commissions were established to regulate the new industrial society. Commodities shippers, especially farmers and merchants, in protest against the railroads' policies of rate discrimination and other corrupt practices, turned to the states for government action. By 1900, twenty-eight states had established commissions to oversee the railroads. These early commissions served as models for later policy at the federal level.

Illinois had one of the most thoroughgoing provisions. Responding to local merchants who were upset with existing railroad rate policies, the Illinois state constitution of 1870 declared railroads to be public highways and authorized the state legislature to pass laws establishing maximum rates and preventing rate discrimination. In the important case of *Munn* v. *Illinois* (1877), the Supreme Court upheld the Illinois legislation.

But the Court soon weakened that judgment. In the *Wabash* case of 1886 (*Wabash, St. Louis & Pacific Railway Co.* v. *Illinois*), it narrowed the *Munn* rule and held that states could not regulate commerce extending beyond their borders. Only Congress could do that. The *Wabash* decision spurred Congress to pass the Interstate Commerce Act (1887), which created the **Interstate Commerce Commission (ICC)** to investigate and oversee railroad activities and outlawed rebates and pooling agreements. The ICC became the prototype of the federal commissions that today regulate many parts of the economy.

Interstate Commerce Commission (ICC) The first federal regulatory agency, created by Congress in 1887 to investigate and oversee railroad activities.

Reestablishing Presidential Power

Johnson's impeachment, the scandals of the Grant years, and the controversy surrounding the 1876 election (see Chapter 16) weakened the presidency. During the last two decades of the nineteenth century, presidents fought to reassert their authority, and by 1900, they had largely succeeded. The late 1890s, in fact, mark the birth of the modern powerful presidency.

Rutherford B. Hayes entered the White House with his title clouded by the disputed election of 1876. Although opponents called him "His Fraudulency," he worked to reassert the authority of the presidency. Hayes worked for reform in the civil service, placed well-known reformers in high offices, and by ordering the last troops out of South Carolina and Louisiana, ended military Reconstruction. Committed to the gold standard, in 1878 he vetoed a bill that called for the partial coinage of silver, but Congress passed this **Bland-Allison Silver Purchase Act** over his veto.

Bland-Allison Silver Purchase Act This 1878 act, a compromise between groups favoring the coinage of silver and those opposed to it, called for the partial coinage of silver.

James A. Garfield, a Union army hero and longtime member of Congress, succeeded Hayes. Ambitious and eloquent, Garfield planned to reunite the Republican party, lower the tariff to reduce surplus revenues, and assert American economic and strategic interests in Latin America. But he was soon besieged by office seekers. Each one wanted a government job, and each one thought nothing of cornering the president on every occasion. On July 2, 1881, Charles J. Guiteau, a deranged lawyer and disappointed office seeker, shot Garfield. Suffering through the summer, Garfield died on September 19, and Vice President Chester A. Arthur became president.

Arthur was a better president than many had expected. He modernized the navy and worked to lower the tariff; in 1883, with his backing, Congress passed the **Pendleton Act** to reform the civil service. In part a reaction against Garfield's assassination, the act created a bipartisan Civil Service Commission to administer competitive examinations and appoint officeholders on the basis of merit.

Pendleton Act Passed by Congress in 1883, this act sought to lessen the involvement of politicians in the running of the government. It created a bipartisan commission to administer competitive exams to candidates for civil service jobs and to appoint officeholders based on merit. It also outlawed forcing political contributions from appointed officials.

In the election of 1884, Grover Cleveland, the Democratic governor of New York, narrowly defeated Republican nominee James G. Blaine. The first Democratic president since the outbreak of the Civil War, Cleveland was known for his honesty, stubbornness, and hard work. His first term in the White House (1885–1889) reflected the Democratic party's desire to curtail federal activities. Cleveland vetoed more bills than all his predecessors combined. Late in 1887, he committed himself and the Democratic party to lower the tariff. The Republicans accused him of undermining American industries, and in 1888, they nominated for the presidency Benjamin Harrison, a defender of the tariff. Although Cleveland garnered ninety thousand more popular votes, Harrison won in the electoral college.

Republicans in Power: The Billion-Dollar Congress

Despite Harrison's narrow margin, the election of 1888 was the most sweeping victory for either party in almost twenty years; it gave the Republicans the presidency and control of both houses of Congress. Eager to block Republican-sponsored laws, the Democrats in Congress used minority tactics, especially the "disappearing quorum" rule, which let members of the House of Representatives join in debate but then refuse to answer the roll call to determine if a quorum was present.

After two months of such tactics, the Republicans had had enough. On January 29, 1890, they fell two votes short of a quorum, and Speaker of the House Thomas B. Reed made congressional history. "The Chair," he said, "directs the Clerk to record the following names of members present and refusing to vote." Tumult continued for days, but in mid-February, the Republicans adopted the Reed rules and proceeded to enact the party's program.

Law after law poured out of the 1890 Republican Congress; Democrats labeled it the "Billion-Dollar Congress" for spending that much in appropriations and grants. The Republicans passed the McKinley Tariff Act, which raised tariff duties about 4 percent, higher than ever before. In addition, the act used duties to promote new industries.

A toy scale pitting the presidential candidates of 1888 (Harrison and Cleveland) against each other invites participation in determining the election outcome. More than a plaything, the scale symbolized the high level of voter participation during the late nineteenth century when elections hung in balance until the last vote was counted. ❖

Sherman Antitrust Act Passed by Congress in 1890, this act was the first federal antitrust legislation. Penalties for violations were strict, ranging from fines to imprisonment and even the dissolution of guilty trusts.

The Republicans also passed the **Sherman Antitrust Act,** the first federal attempt to regulate big business. As the initial attempt to deal with the problem of trusts and industrial growth, the act shaped all later antitrust policy. It declared illegal "every contract, combination in the form of trust or otherwise, or conspiracy, in restraint of trade or commerce." Penalties for violation were stiff, including fines and imprisonment and the dissolution of guilty trusts.

One of the most important laws Congress has enacted, the Sherman Antitrust Act made the United States virtually the only industrial nation to regulate business combinations. It tried to restore competition in the marketplace to appease small businessmen. But the Supreme Court crippled the act in *United States* v. *E. C. Knight Co.* (1895) by ruling that it applied only to commerce and not to manufacturing. Not until after the turn of the century did the antitrust law gain fresh power.

Sherman Silver Purchase Act An 1890 act that attempted to resolve the controversy over silver coinage. Under it, the U.S. Treasury would purchase 4.5 million ounces of silver each month and issue legal tender (in the form of Treasury notes) for it.

Another measure, the **Sherman Silver Purchase Act,** was intended to end the troublesome problem of silver as part of the nation's currency. Support for silver coinage was especially strong in the South and West, where people thought it might inflate the currency, raise wages and crop prices, and challenge the hated power of the gold-oriented Northeast. Eager to avert the free coinage of silver, which would require the coinage of all silver presented at U.S. mints, President Harrison and other Republican leaders pressed for a compromise that took shape in the Sherman Silver Purchase Act of 1890.

The act directed the Treasury to purchase 4.5 million ounces of silver a month and to issue legal tender in the form of Treasury notes in payment for it. The act was a compromise; it satisfied both sides. Opponents of silver were pleased that it did not include free coinage. Silverites were delighted that the monthly purchases would buy up most of the country's silver production and move the country toward a bimetallic system based on silver and gold.

As a final measure, Republicans in the House passed a federal elections bill to protect the voting rights of blacks in the South. It set off a storm of denunciation among the Democrats, who called it a "force bill" that would station army troops in the South. Defeated in the Senate, it was the last major effort until the 1950s to enforce the Fifteenth Amendment to the Constitution.

The 1890 elections crushed the Republicans, who lost seventy-eight seats in the House, an extraordinary reversal. Political veterans went down to defeat, and new leaders vaulted to sudden prominence. In the Midwest state elections, as well as the national elections, Democrats made substantial gains.

The Rise of the Populist Movement

The elections of 1890 drew attention to a fast-growing movement among farmers that soon came to be known as populism. The movement had begun rather quietly, and for a time it went almost unnoticed in the press. But during the summer of 1890, thousands of hard-pressed farmers from the South and West made their problems known. At campgrounds, they picnicked, talked, and listened to recruiters from an organization called the **National Farmers' Alliance and Industrial Union,** which promised unified action to solve agricultural problems.

National Farmers' Alliance and Industrial Union One of the largest reform movements in American history, the Farmer's Alliance sought to organize farmers in the South and West to fight for reforms, including measures to overcome low crop prices, burdensome mortgages, and high railroad rates. The alliance ultimately organized a political party, the People's (Populist) party.

The Farm Problem

Farm discontent was a worldwide phenomenon between 1870 and 1900. With the new means of transportation and communication, farmers everywhere were caught up in a complex international market that they neither controlled nor entirely understood.

American farmers complained bitterly about declining prices for their products, rising railroad rates for shipping them, and burdensome mortgages. Some of the grievances were valid. Farm profits were certainly low, and the prices of farm commodities fell between 1865 and 1890. But they did not fall as low as other commodity prices. Farmers received less for their crops, but their purchasing power in fact increased.

Neither was the farmers' griping about rising railroad rates entirely justified. Rates actually fell during these years, benefiting shippers of all products. Farm mortgages, while certainly burdensome, were common because many farmers mortgaged their property to expand their holdings or buy new farm machinery. Most mortgages were short, and the new machinery enabled farmers to triple their output and increase their income.

The actual situation varied from area to area and year to year. Still, many farmers were convinced that their condition had declined, and this perception sparked growing anger. In an age excited about factories, farmers were seen as "hayseeds," to use a word that first appeared in 1889. A literature of rural disillusionment emerged, most notably Hamlin Garland's writings, which described the grimness of farm life.

Populist Mary E. Lease advised farmers to "raise less corn and more hell." She also said, "If one man has not enough to eat three times a day and another man has $25 million, that last man has something that belongs to the first." ❖

The Fast-Growing Farmers' Alliance

By the end of the 1880s, farmers had formed two major organizations: the National Farmers' Alliance, located on the Plains west of the Mississippi and known as the Northwestern Alliance, and the Farmers' Alliance and Industrial Union, based in the South and known as the Southern Alliance.

The Southern Alliance began in Texas in 1875 but did not assume major proportions until Dr. Charles W. Macune took over the leadership in 1886. Its agents spread across the South, where farmers were fed up with crop liens, depleted lands, and sharecropping. By 1890, the Southern Alliance claimed more than a million members. Like the Grange, the Alliance distributed educational materials, and it also established cooperative grain elevators, marketing associations, and retail stores.

Loosely affiliated with the Southern Alliance, the separate Colored Farmers' National Alliance and Cooperative Union enlisted black farmers in the South. Claiming more than a million members, it probably had closer to 250,000. Blacks organized at considerable peril. In 1891, when black cotton pickers struck for higher wages near Memphis, the strike was violently put down; fifteen strikers were lynched. The abortive strike ended the Colored Farmers' Alliance.

On the Plains, the Northwestern Alliance, a smaller organization, was formed in 1880. But it lacked the centralized organization of the Southern Alliance. In 1889, the Southern Alliance changed its name to the National Farmers' Alliance and Industrial Union and persuaded the three strongest state alliances on the Plains to join. Thereafter, the new organization dominated the Alliance movement.

The Alliance turned early to politics. In the West, its leaders rejected both the Republicans and the Democrats and organized their own party. The Southern Alliance resisted the idea of a new party for fear it might divide the white vote, thus undercutting white supremacy. Instead, the Southerners wanted to capture control of the dominant Democratic party. But regardless of their political positions, such figures as Leonidas Polk, president of the National Farmers' Alliance; Jeremiah Simpson of Kansas; and Mary E. Lease provided the movement with forceful leadership.

Meeting in Ocala, Florida, in 1890, the Alliance adopted the **Ocala Demands,** the platform it pushed for as long as it existed. First and foremost, the demands called for the creation of a "subtreasury system," which would allow farmers to store their crops in government warehouses. In return, they could claim Treasury notes for up to 80 percent of the local market value of the crop, a loan to be repaid when the crops were sold. Farmers could thus hold their crops for the best price. The Ocala Demands also urged the free coinage of silver, an end to protective tariffs and national banks, a federal income tax, the direct election of senators, and stricter regulation of the railroad companies.

Ocala Demands Adopted by the Farmers' Alliance at an 1890 meeting in Ocala, Florida, these demands became the organization's main platform. They called for the creation of a system to allow farmers to store their crops until they could get the best price, the free coinage of silver, an end to protective tariffs and national banks, a federal income tax, the direct election of senators by voters, and tighter regulation of railroads.

The Alliance strategy worked well in the elections of 1890. Alliance leaders claimed thirty-eight Alliance supporters elected to Congress, with at least a dozen more pledged to Alliance principles.

The People's Party

People's (or Populist) party This political party was organized in 1892 by farm, labor, and reform leaders, mainly from the Farmers' Alliance. It offered a broad-based reform platform reflecting the Ocala Demands. After 1896, it became identified as a one-issue party focused on free silver and gradually died away.

After the 1890 elections, Northern Alliance leaders urged the formation of a national third party to promote reform. In July 1892, a convention in Omaha, Nebraska, established the new **People's (or Populist) party.** Disillusioned with the response of the Democrats to agrarian difficulties, Southern Alliance leaders joined the new party. In the South, party members, known as Populists, worked with some success to unite black and white farmers under the same party banner.

The delegates at the Omaha convention nominated James B. Weaver of Iowa to run for president in 1892. As its platform, the People's party adopted many of the Ocala Demands. Weaver won 1,039,000 votes, the first third-party presidential candidate ever to attract more than a million votes, and he carried several western states for a total of twenty-two electoral votes. The Populists elected governors in Kansas and North Dakota, ten congressmen, five senators, and about fifteen hundred members of state legislatures.

Despite the Populists' victories, the election brought disappointment. Using fraud and manipulation, Southern Democrats deflected the Populists' efforts; Weaver was held to less than a quarter of the vote in almost every Southern state. He lost heavily in most urban areas and failed to win over most farmers in the settled Midwest. In no midwestern state except Kansas and North Dakota did he win as much as 5 percent of the vote. Although the Populists did run candidates in the next three presidential elections, their heyday was over.

While it lived, the People's party was one of the most powerful protest movements in American history. Catalyzing the feelings of hundreds of thousands of farmers, it attempted to solve specific economic problems while advancing a larger vision of harmony and community, in which people who cared about one another were rewarded for what they produced.

The Crisis of the Depression

Building on the Democratic party's sweeping triumph in the midterm elections of 1890, Grover Cleveland decisively defeated incumbent President Benjamin Harrison in 1892. For the first time since the 1850s, the Democrats controlled the White House and both branches of Congress.

Unfortunately for Cleveland, the Panic of 1893 struck almost as he took office. The economy had expanded too rapidly in the 1870s and 1880s. The mood changed early in 1893. Business confidence sagged, and investors became timid and uneasy. Panic hit the stock market. During 1893, fifteen thousand businesses and more than six hundred banks closed.

The year 1894 was even worse. By midyear, the number of unemployed stood at three million. One out of every five workers was unemployed, and unprecedented numbers of needy people taxed the ability of churches and charities to help. In the summer, a heat wave and drought struck the farm belt west of the Mississippi River. Corn withered in the fields. In the South, the price of cotton fell below 5 cents a pound, far under the break-even point.

People became restless and angry. There was even talk of revolution and bloodshed. "Everyone scolds," Henry Adams, the historian, wrote a British friend. "Everyone also knows what ought to be done. Everyone reviles everyone who does not agree with him, and everyone differs, or agrees only in contempt for everyone else. As far as I can see, everyone is right."

Coxey's Army and the Pullman Strike

Some of the unemployed wandered across the country—singly, in small groups, and in small armies. During 1894, there were some fourteen hundred strikes involving more than a half million workers. On Easter Sunday 1894, an unusual "army" of perhaps three hundred people left Massillon, Ohio. At its head rode "General" Jacob S. Coxey, a middle-aged businessman who wanted Congress to print $500 million to finance a massive road-building program that would put the nation's jobless to work.

Other armies sprang up around the country, and all headed for Washington armed with other demands and hopes. Coxey himself reached Washington on May 1, 1894, after a difficult, tiring march. Police were everywhere. Coxey made it to the foot of the Capitol steps, but before he could do anything, the police were on him. He was clubbed, arrested for trespassing, and sentenced to twenty days in jail.

The armies melted away, but discontent did not. The great **Pullman Strike**—one of the largest strikes in the country's history—began just a few days after Coxey's arrest when the employees of the Pullman Palace Car Company struck to protest wage cuts, continuing high rents for company-owned housing, and layoffs. On July 26, 1894, the American Railway Union (ARU) under Eugene V. Debs joined the strike by refusing to handle trains that carried Pullman sleeping cars.

Pullman Strike Beginning in May 1894, this strike of employees at the Pullman Palace Car Company near Chicago was one of the largest strikes in American history. Extending into twenty-seven states and territories, it effectively paralyzed the western half of the nation. President Grover Cleveland secured an injunction to break the strike on the grounds that it obstructed the mail and sent federal troops to enforce it.

Within hours, the strike paralyzed the western half of the nation. Grain and livestock could not reach markets. Factories shut down for lack of coal. The strike renewed talk of class warfare. In Washington, President Cleveland decided to break it because it obstructed delivery of the mail.

On July 2, he secured a court injunction against the ARU and ordered troops to Chicago. When they arrived on Independence Day, violence broke out, and mobs composed mostly of nonstrikers overturned freight cars, looted, and burned. Restoring order, the army occupied railroad yards in Illinois, California, and other points. By late July, the strike was over; Debs was jailed for violating the injunction.

The Pullman strike had far-reaching consequences for the development of the labor movement. Upholding Debs's sentence in *In re Debs* (1895), the Supreme Court endorsed the use of the injunction in labor disputes, thus giving business and government an effective antilabor weapon that hindered union growth in the 1890s. The strike also catapulted Debs into prominence. Working people resented Cleveland's actions in the strike.

The Miners of the Midwest

The plight of miners in the Illinois, Indiana, and Ohio coalfields illustrated the personal and social impact of the depression. Even in the best of times, mining was a dirty and dangerous business. Mines often closed for as long as six months, and wages fell with the depression.

Mining was often a family occupation, passed down from father to son. It demanded delicate judgments about when to blast, where to follow a seam, and how to avoid rockfalls. Until 1890, English and Irish immigrants dominated the business, moving from mine to mine. They were poorly paid and usually lived in flimsy shacks that were owned by the mining company. After 1890, immigrants from southern and eastern Europe came to the mines to find work.

As the depression deepened, tensions grew between miners and their employers and between the "old" miners and the "new." The new miners, who usually spoke no English and lacked many skills, were often blamed for accidents, but they were willing to work longer hours for less pay.

In April 1894, a wave of wage reductions sparked an explosion of labor unrest in the mines. The United Mine Workers, a struggling union formed just four years earlier, called for a strike of bituminous coal miners, and on April 21, virtually all midwestern and Pennsylvania miners quit working. The flow of coal slackened; cities faced blackouts; factories closed.

The violence that soon broke out followed a significant pattern. The new miners were much more prone than the old miners to violent action to win a strike. The depression hit them especially hard. In many areas, anger and frustration turned the 1894 strikes into outright war.

For nearly two weeks in June 1894, fighting rocked the coalfields. Mobs ignited mine shafts, dynamited coal trains, and defied the state militias. Although miners of all backgrounds participated in the violence, the new miners led the most radical and destructive assaults.

Shocked by the violence, public opinion shifted against the strikers. The strike ended in a matter of weeks, but its effects lingered. English and Irish miners moved out into other jobs or up into supervisory positions. Jokes and songs poked cruel fun at the new immigrants. The United Mine Workers, dominated by the older miners, began in 1896 to persuade Congress to stop the "demoralizing effects" of immigration.

The Pullman strike, which occurred at the same time, pulled attention away from the crisis in the coalfields, even though the miners' strike involved three times as many workers and provided a revealing glimpse of the tensions within American society. The miners of the Midwest were the first large group of skilled workers seriously affected by the flood of immigrants from southern and eastern Europe. Buffeted by depression, they reflected the social and economic discord that permeated every industry.

A United Mine Workers certificate of membership illustrates some of the work undertaken by the brother members. The United Mine Workers of America was formed in 1890 in Columbus, Ohio, and sought to provide its members with a safe workplace and fair wages and benefits. Although the union pledged to seek ways to maintain peace between miners and their employers and to make strikes unnecessary, such means as arbitration and conciliation often failed and strikes did occur, many of them violent and destructive. ❖

A Beleaguered President

President Cleveland was sure that he knew the cause of the depression. The Sherman Silver Purchase Act of 1890, he believed, had damaged business confidence, exhausted the Treasury's gold reserve, and caused the panic. The solution to the depression was equally simple: repeal the act.

In June 1893, Cleveland summoned Congress into special session. Rejecting the silverites' pleas for a compromise, Cleveland pushed the repeal bill through Congress, and on November 1, 1893, he signed it into law. Ever sure of himself, he had staked everything on a single measure.

Repeal of the Sherman Silver Purchase Act was probably a necessary action. It responded to the realities of international finance, reduced the flight of gold out of the country, and over the long run boosted business confidence. Unfortunately, it contracted the currency at a time when inflation might have helped. It also failed to bring economic revival. The stock market remained listless, businesses continued to close, unemployment spread, and farm prices dropped.

The repeal battle of 1893 discredited the conservative Democrats who had dominated the party since the 1860s. Reshaping the politics of the country, it confined the Democratic party largely to the South, helped the Republicans become the majority party in 1894, and strengthened the position of the silver Democrats in their bid for the presidency in 1896. By 1896, most Americans believed that Cleveland's economic policies had not benefited the country.

Breaking the Party Deadlock

In 1894, Cleveland and the Democrats tried to fulfill their long-standing promise to reduce the tariff. The Wilson-Gorman Tariff Act, passed by Congress that year, contained only modest reductions in duties. It also imposed a small income tax, a provision the Supreme Court overturned in 1895. Discouraged, Cleveland let the bill become law without his signature.

The Democrats were buried in the elections of 1894, suffering the greatest defeat in congressional history. Wooing labor and the unemployed, the Populists made striking inroads in parts of the South and West, yet these didn't go quite far enough. Across the country, the discontented tended to vote for the Republicans, not the Populists.

For millions of people, Grover Cleveland became a scapegoat for the country's economic ills. The Democratic party split, and southern and western Democrats deserted him in droves. At Democratic conventions, Cleveland's name evoked jeers.

The elections of 1894 marked the end of the party deadlock that had existed since the 1870s. The Democrats lost, the Populists gained somewhat, and the Republicans became the majority party in the country. The Republican doctrines of activism and national authority, repudiated in the elections of 1890, became more attractive in the midst of depression.

CHANGING ATTITUDES

Across the country, people were rethinking older ideas about government, the economy, and society. The depression, brutal and far-reaching, undermined traditional views. As men and women concluded that established ideas had failed to deal with the depression, they looked for new ones.

In prosperous times, Americans had thought of unemployment as the result of personal failure, affecting primarily the lazy and the immoral. Now, in the midst of depression, everyone knew people who were both worthy *and* unemployed. People began to debate issues they had long taken for granted. New discussion clubs, women's clubs, reform societies, university extension centers, church groups, and farmers' societies all gave people a place to discuss alternatives to the existing order. Pressures for reform increased, and demand grew for government intervention to help the poor and the unemployed.

"Everybody Works But Father"

As husbands and fathers lost their jobs, more and more women and children went to work. Even as late as 1901, well after the depression had ended, a study of working-class families showed that more than half the principal breadwinners were out of work. So many women and children worked that in 1905 the song "Everybody Works but Father" became a popular hit.

During the 1890s, the number of working women rose from 4 million to 5.3 million. Trying to make ends meet, they took in boarders and found jobs as laundresses, cleaners, or domestics. Where possible, they worked in offices and factories. Far more black urban women than white worked to supplement their husbands' meager earnings. Women worked as telegraph and telephone operators, as clerks in the new five-and-tens and department stores, and as nurses, typists, and teachers.

The depression also caused an increasing number of children to work. During the 1890s, boys and girls under 16 years of age made up nearly a third of the labor force of the southern textile mills. In most cases, children worked not in factories but in farming and city street trades such as peddling and shoe shining. In 1900, the South had more than half the child laborers in the nation.

Concerned about child labor, middle-class women in 1896 formed the League for Protection of the Family, which called for compulsory education to get children out of factories and into classrooms. Soon other organizations were started to fight for reforms in the fields of child welfare, education, and sanitation.

Changing Themes in Literature

The depression also gave impetus to a growing movement in literature toward realism and naturalism. In the years after the Civil War, literature often reflected the mood of romanticism—sentimental and unrealistic. But after the 1870s, a number of talented authors rejected romanticism in favor of realism. Determined to portray life as it was, they studied local dialects, wrote regional stories, and emphasized the "true" relationships between people. In doing so, they reflected broader trends in the society: industrialism; evolutionary theory, which emphasized the effects of environment on humans; and the new philosophy of pragmatism, which stressed the relativity of values. (See Chapter 22 for a more detailed discussion of pragmatism.)

A regionalist author who soon outgrew that genre, Mark Twain went on to become the country's most outstanding realist writer. Growing up along the Mississippi River in Hannibal County, Missouri, the young Samuel Langhorne Clemens observed life around him with a humorous and skeptical eye. Adopting a pen name from the river term *mark twain* ("two fathoms"), he drew on his own experiences. In such books as *The Adventures of Huckleberry Finn* (1884), Twain used dialect and common speech instead of literary language, touching off a major change in American prose style.

William Dean Howells came more slowly to the realistic approach. Writing initially about the happier side of life, he grew worried about the impact of industrialization. In his more powerful works, he portrayed an urban society that produced great riches—at a terrible price. In the poem "Society" (1895), he compared society to a splendid ball at which men and women danced on flowers covering the bodies of the poor.

Other writers became impatient even with realism. Pushing Darwinian theory to its limits, they wrote of a world in which a cruel and merciless environment determined human fate. Often focusing on economic hardship, naturalist writers scrutinized the poor, the lower classes, and the criminal mind; they brought to their writing the social worker's passion for direct and honest experience.

Stephen Crane spent a night in a 7-cent lodging house on the Bowery and in "An Experiment in Misery" captured the smells and sounds of the poor. He also depicted the carnage of war in *The Red Badge of Courage* (1895). Frank Norris assailed the power of big business in two dramatic novels, *The Octopus* (1901) and *The Pit* (1903), both emphasizing individual futility in the face of the heartless corporations. Jack London traced the power of nature over civilized society in novels such as *The Call of the Wild* (1903) and *The Sea Wolf* (1904).

Theodore Dreiser, the foremost naturalist writer, grimly portrayed a dark world in which human beings were tossed about by forces beyond their understanding or control. In his great novel *Sister Carrie* (1901), he followed a young farm girl who took a job in a Chicago shoe factory. Like other naturalists, Dreiser focused on environment and character. He thought writers should tell the truth about human affairs, not fabricate romance.

The Presidential Election of 1896

The election of 1896 was known as the "battle of the standards" because it involved the gold and silver standards of value in the monetary system of the nation. New voting patterns replaced old, the new majority party confirmed its control of the country, and national policy shifted to suit the new realities.

The Mystique of Silver

People wanted quick solutions to the economic crisis. During 1896, unemployment shot up, and farm income and prices fell to their lowest point of the decade. The silverites offered a solution, simple but compelling: the free and independent coinage of silver at the ratio of sixteen to one. Free coinage meant that the U.S. mints would coin all the silver offered to them. Independent coinage meant that the country would coin silver regardless of the policies of other nations, nearly all of which were on the gold standard.

Above all, the silverites believed in a quantity theory of money: The amount of money in circulation determined the level of activity in the economy. A shortage of money meant declining activity and depression. Silver meant more money and thus prosperity. Added to the currency, it would increase the money supply and stir new economic activity.

By 1896, silver was a symbol. It had moral and patriotic dimensions and stood for a wide range of popular grievances. For many Americans, it reflected rural values rather than urban ones, suggested a shift of power away from the Northeast, and spoke for the downtrodden instead of the well-to-do.

Silver was a social movement, one of the largest in American history, but its life span turned out to be brief. As a mass phenomenon, it flourished between 1894 and 1896, then succumbed to electoral defeat, the return to prosperity, and the onset of fresh concerns. But in its time, it bespoke a national mood and won millions of followers.

The Campaign and Election

Scenting victory over the discredited Democrats, numerous Republicans fought for the party's presidential nomination. In the end, William McKinley, an able, calm Civil War veteran, won the nomination. As a congressman, he had been the chief sponsor of the tariff act named for him. In the months before the 1896 national convention, Marcus A. Hanna, his campaign manager and trusted friend, raised

$16 million and built up a powerful national organization that proved successful. McKinley's platform favored the gold standard.

Despite President Cleveland's opposition, more than twenty Democratic states' platforms came out for free silver in 1894. Power in the party shifted to the South, where it remained for decades. The party's base narrowed; its outlook increasingly reflected southern views on silver, race, and other issues. In effect, the Democrats became a sectional—no longer a national—party.

The anti-Cleveland Democrats had their issue, but they lacked a leader. Out in Nebraska, William Jennings Bryan saw the opportunity. He was barely 36 years old and had relatively little political experience. But he had spent months wooing support, and he was a captivating public speaker.

From the outset of the 1896 Democratic convention, the silver Democrats were in charge, and they put together a platform that stunned the Cleveland wing of the party. It demanded the free coinage of silver, attacked Cleveland's actions in the Pullman strike, and censured his 1895 and 1896 gold bond sales. On July 9, as delegates debated the platform, Bryan's moment came. Striding to the stage, he stood for an instant, a hand raised for silence, waiting for the applause to die down.

He spoke with confidence, captivating the delegates. The country, he said, praised businessmen but forgot that laborers, miners, and farmers were businessmen, too. He defended silver and in his famous closing said, "Having behind us the producing masses of this nation and the world . . . we will answer their demand for a gold standard by saying to them: 'You shall not press down upon the brow of labor this crown of thorns, you shall not crucify mankind upon a cross of gold.'" He ended with his arms outstretched as on a cross. Suddenly there was pandemonium. When the tumult subsided, the delegates adopted the anti-Cleveland platform, and the next day, Bryan won the presidential nomination.

The religious symbolism in Bryan's "Cross of Gold" speech is satirized in this cartoon, but his stirring rhetoric captivated his audience and won him the Democratic presidential nomination for the election of 1896. ❖

The Democratic convention presented the Populists with a dilemma. The People's party had staked everything on the assumption that neither major party would endorse silver. Now it faced a painful choice: nominate an independent ticket and risk splitting the silverite forces, or nominate Bryan and give up its separate identity as a party.

The choice was unpleasant, and it shattered the People's party. Meeting late in July, the party's national convention nominated Bryan, but the Populists' endorsement probably hurt Bryan as much as it helped. It won him relatively few votes, since many Populists would have voted for him anyway. It identified him as a Populist, which he was not, and allowed the Republicans to accuse him of heading a ragtag army of malcontents.

In August 1896, Bryan set off on a campaign that became an American legend. Much of the conservative eastern press had deserted him, and he took his campaign directly to the voters, the first presidential candidate to do so in a systematic way. By his own count, Bryan traveled 18,009 miles, visited twenty-seven states, and spoke six hundred times to a total of three million people. He built skillfully on a new "merchandising" style of campaign in which he worked to educate and persuade voters.

Bryan summoned voters to an older America, a land where farms were as important as factories, where the virtues of rural and religious life outweighed the doubtful lure of the city, where common people still ruled and opportunity existed. He drew on the Jeffersonian tradition of rural virtue, distrust of central authority, and abiding faith in the powers of human reason.

McKinley let voters come to him. Railroads brought them by the thousands into his hometown of Canton, Ohio, and he spoke to them from his front porch. Never had a party spent so much money on a campaign. Through use of the press, he reached fully as many people as Bryan's more strenuous effort. Appealing to labor, immigrants, wealthy farmers, businessmen, and the middle class, McKinley defended economic nationalism and the advancing urban-industrial society.

On election day, voter turnout was extraordinarily high, a measure of the intense interest, but McKinley won a clear victory, capturing 50 percent of the vote to Bryan's 46 percent. The election struck down the Populists, whose totals sagged nearly everywhere. Although many Populist proposals were later adopted—the graduated income tax, crop loans to farmers, and the secret ballot, for example—the party never again could win a majority of the voters. It vanished after 1896.

The McKinley Administration

The election of 1896 cemented the voter realignment of 1894 and initiated a generation of Republican rule. For more than three decades after 1896, with only a brief Democratic resurgence under Woodrow Wilson, the Republicans remained the country's majority party.

McKinley took office in 1897 under favorable circumstances. To everyone's relief, the economy had begun to revive. The stock market rose, factories once again churned out goods, and farmers prospered. Discoveries of gold in Australia and Alaska and new extraction techniques enlarged the world's gold supply, decreased its price, and inflated the currency as the silverites had hoped.

McKinley and the Republicans basked in the glow. They became the party of progress and prosperity, an image that helped them win victories until the 1930s. McKinley's popularity soared. An activist president, he set the policies of the administration. He maintained close ties with Congress and worked hard to educate the public on national choices and priorities. McKinley struck new relations with the press and traveled far more than previous presidents. In some ways, he began the modern presidency.

In July 1897, with his support, Congress passed the Dingley Tariff, which raised average tariff duties to a record level. As the final burst of nineteenth-century protectionism, it caused trouble for the Republican party. By the end of the 1890s, however, even some Republicans themselves had begun to conclude that the tariff had outlived its usefulness in the maturing American economy.

From the 1860s to the 1890s, the Republicans had built their party on a pledge to *promote* economic growth through the use of state and national power. By 1900, with the industrial system firmly in place, the focus had shifted. The need to *regulate,* to control the effects of industrialism, became a central public concern of the new century.

McKinley prodded his party to move toward regulation, but he died before his plans matured. One problem was the government's need for revenue. Tariff duties

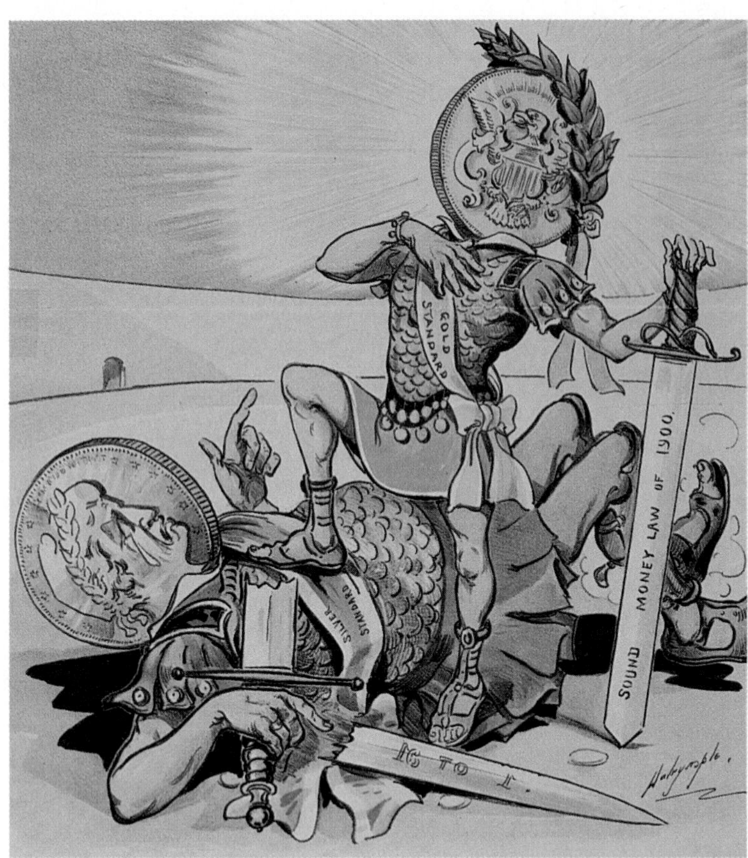

Gold triumphs over silver in this Puck *cartoon referring to the Gold Standard Act of 1900.* ❖

were one of the few taxes the public would support. The Spanish-American War of 1898 persuaded people to accept greater federal power and, with it, new forms of taxation. By the end of the nineteenth century, McKinley realized that economic nationalism, the creed on which he was raised, was a dying concept.

In 1898 and 1899, the McKinley administration focused on the war with Spain, the peace treaty that followed, and the dawning realization that the war had thrust the United States into a position of world power. In March 1900, Congress passed the **Gold Standard Act,** which declared gold the standard of currency and ended the silver controversy that had dominated the 1890s.

Gold Standard Act Passed by Congress in 1900, this law declared gold the nation's standard of currency—meaning that all currency in circulation had to be redeemable in gold. The United States remained on the gold standard until 1933.

The presidential campaign of 1900 was a replay of the McKinley-Bryan fight of 1896. McKinley's running mate was Theodore Roosevelt, hero of the Spanish-American War (see Chapter 21) and former governor of New York, who was nominated for vice president to capitalize on his popularity and, his enemies hoped, to sidetrack his political career into oblivion. McKinley won in a landslide. But on September 6, 1901, mere months after his second inauguration, McKinley was shot while standing in a receiving line at the Pan-American Exposition in Buffalo, New York. His assailant was Leon Czolgosz, a 28-year-old unemployed laborer and anarchist. On September 14, McKinley died, and Vice President Theodore Roosevelt became president. The new century had begun in earnest.

Conclusion: A Decade's Dramatic Changes

As the funeral train carried McKinley's body back to Ohio, Mark Hanna, McKinley's old friend and ally, sat slumped in his parlor car. "I told William McKinley it was a mistake to nominate that wild man at Philadelphia," he mourned. "I asked him if he

CHRONOLOGY

1876	Mark Twain publishes *The Adventures of Tom Sawyer,* setting off a major change in American literary style
1877	Disputed election of 1876 results in the awarding of the presidency to Republican Rutherford B. Hayes
1880	Republican James A. Garfield is elected president
1881	Garfield is assassinated; Vice President Chester A. Arthur becomes president
1884	Democrat Grover Cleveland is elected president, defeating Republican James G. Blaine
1887	Cleveland calls for a lowering of tariff duties
1888	Republican Benjamin Harrison wins the presidential election
1889	National Farmers' Alliance and Industrial Union is formed to address the problems of farmers
1890	Republican-dominated Congress enacts the McKinley Tariff Act, the Sherman Antitrust Act, and the Sherman Silver Purchase Act ❖ Farmers' Alliance adopts the Ocala Demands
1892	Democrat Cleveland defeats Republican Harrison for the presidency ❖ People's party is formed
1893	Financial panic touches off a depression that lasts until 1897 ❖ Sherman Silver Purchase Act is repealed
1894	Coxey's Army marches on Washington ❖ Employees of Pullman Palace Car Company strike
1896	Republican McKinley defeats William Jennings Bryan, Democratic and Populist candidate
1897	Gold is discovered in Alaska ❖ Dingley Tariff Act raises tariff duties
1900	McKinley is reelected, again defeating Bryan ❖ Gold Standard Act establishes gold as the standard of currency
1901	McKinley is assassinated; Vice President Theodore Roosevelt assumes the presidency ❖ Naturalist writer Theodore Dreiser publishes *Sister Carrie*

realized what would happen if he should die. Now look, that damned cowboy is president of the United States!"

The nation had changed—not so much because "that damned cowboy" was suddenly president, but because events of the 1890s had had powerful effects. In the course of that decade, political patterns shifted, the presidency acquired fresh power, and massive unrest prompted social change. The war with Spain brought a new empire and worldwide responsibilities. Economic hardship posed difficult questions about industrialization, urbanization, and the quality of American life. Worried, people embraced new ideas and causes. Reform movements begun in the 1890s flowered in the Progressive Era after 1900.

Technology continued to alter the way Americans lived. In 1896, Henry Ford produced a two-cylinder, four-horsepower car. At Kitty Hawk, North Carolina, Wilbur and Orville Wright, two bicycle manufacturers, neared the birth of powered flight. The pace of the world was quickening.

The realignments that reached their peak in the 1890s shaped nearly everything that came after them. In character and influence, the 1890s were as much a part of the twentieth century as of the nineteenth and continue to have repercussions into the twenty-first century.

Key Terms

Interstate Commerce Commission (ICC), p. 392
Bland-Allison Silver Purchase Act, p. 393
Pendleton Act, p. 393
Sherman Antitrust Act, p. 394
Sherman Silver Purchase Act, p. 394
National Farmers' Alliance and Industrial Union, p. 394
Ocala Demands, p. 395
People's (or Populist) Party, p. 396
Pullman Strike, p. 397
Gold Standard Act, p. 404

Recommended Reading

The best study of the 1890s depression is Charles Hoffman, *The Depression of the Nineties: An Economic History* (1970). H. Wayne Morgan, *From Hayes to McKinley: National Party Politics, 1877–1896* (1969), Michael E. McGerr, *The Decline of Popular Politics: The American North, 1865–1928* (1986), Mark Lawrence Kornbluh, *Why America Stopped Voting: The Decline of Participatory Democracy and the Emergence of Modern American Politics* (2000), and Richard J. Jensen, *The Winning of the Midwest* (1971) are good on politics. David P. Thelen, *The New Citizenship: Origins of Progressivism in Wisconsin, 1885–1900* (1972), Carl Smith, *Urban Disorder and the Shape of Belief: The Great Chicago Fire, the Haymarket Bomb, and the Model Town of Pullman* (1995), and Douglas W. Steeples and David O. Whitten, *Democracy in Desperation: The Depression of 1893* (1998), stress the impact of the depression on ideas and attitudes. C. Vann Woodward examines the South in *Origins of the New South, 1877–1913* (1951). Also, Michael Perman, *Struggle for Mastery: Disfranchisement in the South, 1888–1908* (2001).

On Populism, see John D. Hicks, *The Populist Revolt* (1931), Lawrence Goodwyn, *Democratic Promise: The Populist Moment in America* (1976), Steven Hahn, *The Roots of Southern Populism* (1983), and Elizabeth Sanders, *Roots of Reform: Farmers, Workers, and the American State, 1877–1917* (1999). Steven W. Usselman, *Regulating Railroad Innovation: Business, Technology, and Politics in America, 1840–1920* (2002), looks at regulatory reform.

For a list of additional titles related to this chapter's topics, please see http://www.ablongman.com/divine.

Suggested Web Sites

World's Columbian Exposition: Idea, Experience, Aftermath

http://xroads.virginia.edu/~MA96/WCE/title.html
This site has a virtual tour of the fair, along with contemporary reactions and modern analysis.

Pullman Links on the Web—Historic Pullman Foundation

http://www.pullmanil.org/links.htm
This page offers several links to sites with Pullman-related information, including a section of sites on the Pullman strike and labor history.

Election of 1896

http://jefferson.village.virginia.edu/seminar/unit8/home.htm
This University of Virginia site contains biographical information, images, cartoons, and related links about the pivotal 1896 election.

The Era of William McKinley

http://www.history.ohio-state.edu/projects/mckinley/default.htm
This site contains numerous images from various stages of William McKinley's career along with a brief biographical essay. This Ohio State University site also has a section with an excellent collection of cartoons from the era.

Chapter 21

Toward Empire

Roosevelt and the Rough Riders

When war with Spain began in April 1898, many Americans regretted it, but others welcomed it. Many people believed that nations must fight every now and then to prove their power and test the national spirit.

Theodore Roosevelt, the 39-year-old assistant secretary of the navy, was one of them. For months, Roosevelt had argued strenuously for war with Spain, first on grounds of freeing Cuba and expelling Spain from the hemisphere; second, to take Americans' minds off material gain; and third, because the army and navy needed the practice.

When the war finally came, Roosevelt resigned his navy post and joined the army. In those days, officers supplied their own uniforms, and Roosevelt, the son of well-to-do parents, wanted his to be stylish. He ordered it from Brooks Brothers, the expensive New York clothier. He also chose to enlist his own regiment, and after a few telephone calls to friends and telegrams to several western governors asking for "good shots and good riders," he had more than enough men. The First United States Volunteer Cavalry was an intriguing mix of Ivy League athletes and western frontiersmen that became known as the Rough Riders.

Eager for war, the men trained hard and played harder. Discipline was lax, and officers and enlisted men got along well together. Everyone howled with joy when orders came to join the invasion army for Cuba, and the Rough Riders set sail on June 14, 1898. Lieutenant Colonel Roosevelt performed a war dance for the troops the night before.

ROOSEVELT BELIEVED THE WAR would establish the United States as a world power, whose commerce and influence would extend around the globe, particularly in Latin America and Asia. As he hoped, the nation in the 1890s underwent dramatic expansion, building on the foreign policy approaches of administrations from Abraham Lincoln to William McKinley. Policymakers fostered business interests abroad, strengthened the navy, and extended American influence into Latin America and the Pacific. Differences over Cuba resulted in a war with Spain that brought new colonies and colonial subjects, establishing for the first time an American overseas empire.

OUTLINE

America Looks Outward

War with Spain

Acquisition of Empire

Conclusion: Outcome of the War with Spain

America Looks Outward

The overseas expansion of the 1890s differed in several important respects from earlier expansionist moves of the United States. The American republic had always pursued growth, but as settlers pushed westward, most of the lands they moved into were contiguous to existing territories of the United States and were earmarked for settlement.

The expansion of the 1890s involved the acquisition of island possessions, most of them already thickly populated. The new territories were intended less for settlement than for their usefulness as naval bases, trading outposts, or commercial centers on major trade routes. They were viewed primarily as colonies, not as states in the making—a natural outgrowth of a century of expansionist tendencies in thought and foreign policy.

Catching the Spirit of Empire

Most people in most times in history tend to look at domestic concerns, and Americans in the years following the Civil War were no exception. They focused on Reconstruction, the movement westward, and the growing industrial system. Throughout the nineteenth century, Americans enjoyed "free security" without fully appreciating it. Sheltered by two oceans and the British navy, they could enunciate bold policies such as the Monroe Doctrine while remaining virtually impervious to foreign attack.

isolationism A belief that the United States should stay out of entanglements with other nations. It was widespread after the Spanish-American War in the late 1890s and influenced later U.S. foreign policy.

imperialism The policy of extending a nation's power through military conquest, economic domination, or annexation.

In those circumstances, a sense of **isolationism** spread, a desire to stay out of foreign entanglements. Some people even urged the abolition of the foreign service, considering it an unnecessary expenditure, a dangerous profession that might lead to involvement in the struggles of the world's great powers. But such voices lost much of their force by the 1870s, when Americans began taking an increased interest in events abroad. The growing sense of internationalism stemmed in part from the telegraphs, telephones, and undersea cables that kept people better informed about political and economic developments in distant lands. And despite minimal interest in American **imperialism,** most Americans continued to be enthusiastic about the expansion of the country's borders.

Several developments combined to shift attention outward across the seas. The end of the frontier, announced officially in the census report of 1890, sparked fears about diminishing opportunities at home. Further growth, it seemed, must take place abroad.

Factories and farms multiplied, producing more goods than the domestic market could consume. Both farmers and industrialists looked for new overseas markets, and the growing volume of exports changed the nature of U.S. trade relations. American exports of merchandise amounted to $393 million in 1870, $858 million in 1890, and $1.4 billion in 1900.

Political leaders began to argue for the vital importance of foreign markets to continue economic growth. Some of them—James G. Blaine, secretary of state under Garfield and Harrison, for one—were caught up in the exhilaration of a worldwide scramble for empire. Like the European powers, they coveted the markets of Latin America, Asia, and Africa. The idea of imperialistic expansion was in the air, and great powers measured their greatness by the colonies they acquired. Inevitably, some Americans succumbed to the spirit and wanted to enter the international hunt for territory.

Intellectual currents that supported expansion drew on Charles Darwin's theories of evolution. Applied to human and social development, Darwin's biological concepts seemed to call for the triumph of the fit and the elimination of the unfit. Theodore Roosevelt, and many like-minded people, lauded virile and adventurous qualities and regarded them as a sign of America's greatness.

The "biogenetic law," formulated by German biologist Ernst Haeckel, suggested that the development of the race paralleled the development of the individual. Primitive peoples were thus in the arrested stages of childhood or adolescence; they needed supervision and protective treatment. In a similar vein, John Fiske, a popular writer and lecturer, argued for Anglo-Saxon racial superiority, a result of the process of natural selection. The English and Americans, Fiske said, would occupy every land on the globe that was not already "civilized," bringing the advances of commerce and democratic institutions.

Such views were widespread among the lettered and unlettered alike. The career of Josiah Strong, a Congregational minister and fervent expansionist, suggested the strength of the developing ideas. A champion of overseas missionary work, in 1885 he published a book titled *Our Country: Its Possible Future and Its Present Crisis.* An immediate best-seller, the book called on foreign missions to civilize the world under the Anglo-Saxon races. Strong also believed that American commerce should follow the missionary. The result, he maintained, would be good for everyone involved.

Taken together, these developments in social, political, and economic thought prepared Americans for a larger role in the world. The change was gradual, but by the 1890s, Americans found themselves ready to reach out into the world in a more determined and deliberate fashion than ever before. For almost the first time, they felt the need for an outward direction in foreign policy.

❖ A Look at the Past ❖

Trade Card

Trade cards—postcard-sized advertisements—provided manufacturers with attractive, richly colored attention-grabbers. As firms entered national and even international markets, advertising became increasingly important as a way to promote brand identification and loyalty. The Singer Sewing Machine Company commissioned a set of trade cards in the 1890s, including the one shown here, that showed its products being used around the world. This card, made in 1892, reveals U.S. interest in the Philippines before the Spanish-American War. Why would Singer depict sewing machines used in foreign lands as a way to attract U.S. consumers? How are Filipinos depicted on this card? How does it seem Americans viewed Filipinos and other Asians?

Foreign Policy Approaches, 1867–1900

Rarely consistent, American foreign policy in the last third of the nineteenth century took different approaches to different areas of the world. In relation to Europe, where the dominant world powers were, policymakers promoted trade and tried to avoid diplomatic entanglements. In North and South America, they based policy on the Monroe Doctrine, a recurrent dream of annexing Canada or Mexico, a hope for extensive trade, and pan-American unity against the nations of the Old World. In the Pacific, they coveted Hawaii and other outposts on the sea lanes to China.

Secretary of State William Henry Seward, who served from 1861 to 1869, aggressively pushed an expansive foreign policy. He developed a vision of an American empire stretching south into Latin America and west to the shores of Asia. His vision included Canada and Mexico, islands in the Caribbean as strategic bases to protect a canal across Central America, and Hawaii and other islands as stepping-stones to Asia.

Seward tried unsuccessfully to negotiate a commercial treaty with the kingdom of Hawaii in 1867, the same year he annexed the Midway Islands. Also in 1867, he concluded a treaty with Russia for the purchase of Alaska (promptly labeled "Seward's Folly"), part of a plan to sandwich western Canada between American territory as a prelude to its annexation. In all this, Seward's target remained the Asian market, which he and many others considered a virtually bottomless outlet for farm and manufactured goods. As the American empire spread, he thought, Mexico City would become its capital.

Hamilton Fish followed Seward as secretary of state, serving under President Ulysses S. Grant. An avid expansionist, Grant wanted to extend American influence in the Caribbean and the Pacific; Fish often had to restrain him. They moved first to repair relations with Great Britain, which had become strained during the Civil War. Negotiating patiently, Fish signed the Treaty of Washington in 1871, providing for arbitration of the *Alabama* claims issue—U.S. demands that Britain pay for damages caused by the Confederate vessel *Alabama*, which had been built and outfitted in British shipyards—and other nettlesome controversies. The treaty, one of the landmarks in the peaceful settlement of international disputes, marked a significant step in cementing Anglo-American relations.

Grant and Fish looked most eagerly to Latin America. In 1870, Grant became the first president to proclaim the nontransfer principle—"hereafter no territory on this continent shall be regarded as subject to transfer to a European power." Fish also promoted the independence of Cuba, restive under Spanish rule.

James G. Blaine's first stint as secretary of state lasted only six months, until Garfield's assassination, but he laid extensive plans to establish closer commercial relations with Latin America. When he returned to the State Department in 1889 under President Benjamin Harrison, he moved to expand markets in Latin America. He envisaged a hemisphere system of peaceful intercourse, arbitration of disputes, and expanded trade. He also wanted to annex Hawaii.

In general, Harrison and Blaine focused on pan-Americanism and tariff reciprocity. Blaine presided over the first Inter-American Conference in Washington on October 2, 1889, which Blaine hoped would unite Latin America and the United States in a customs union and create a way to settle conflicts. Although the nineteen countries that were represented refused to accept Blaine's full program, the conference was a major step in hemisphere relations and led to later meetings promoting trade and other agreements. It created an international bureau that later became the Pan-American Union for the exchange of political, scientific, and cultural information.

Reciprocity, Harrison and Blaine hoped, would divert Latin American trade from Europe to the United States. Working hard to sell the idea in Congress, Blaine lobbied for a reciprocity provision in the McKinley Tariff Act of 1890 (see Chapter 20). Once that was enacted, he negotiated important reciprocity treaties with most Latin American nations, resulting in greater American exports of flour, grain, meat, iron, and machinery. But the Wilson-Gorman Tariff Act (1894) ended reciprocity.

Grover Cleveland, Harrison's successor, pursued an aggressive policy toward Latin America. In 1895, he brought the United States precariously close to war with Great Britain over a boundary dispute between Venezuela and British Guiana. Cleveland sympathized with Venezuela, and he and Secretary of State Richard Olney urged Britain to arbitrate the dispute. When Britain failed to act, Olney drafted a stiff diplomatic note affirming the Monroe Doctrine and denying European nations the right to meddle in Western Hemisphere affairs.

Lord Salisbury, the British foreign secretary, rejected Olney's arguments, whereupon Cleveland asked Congress for authority to appoint a commission to decide the boundary and enforce its decision. This veiled threat of war, coupled with British diplomatic problems in Africa and Europe, forced Britain to change its position, and the dispute was peacefully arbitrated.

The Venezuelan incident demonstrated growing American power of persuasion in the Western Hemisphere. Cleveland and Olney had forced Great Britain to recognize United States dominance, and they had sharpened American influence in Latin America. The Monroe Doctrine assumed new importance.

The Lure of Hawaii and Samoa

The islands of Hawaii offered a tempting way station to Asian markets. In the early 1800s, they were already called the "Crossroads of the Pacific," and trading ships of many nations stopped there. In 1820, the first American missionaries arrived to convert the islanders to Christianity. Like missionaries elsewhere, they advertised Hawaii's economic and other benefits and attracted new settlers, whose children later came to dominate Hawaiian political life and play an important role in annexation.

After the Civil War, the United States tightened its connections with the islands. The reciprocity treaty of 1875 allowed Hawaiian sugar to enter the United States free of duty and increased Hawaiian economic dependence on the United States. In addition, its political clauses effectively made Hawaii an American protectorate.

Following the 1875 treaty, white Hawaiians became more and more influential in the islands' political life. The McKinley Tariff Act of 1890 ended the special status given Hawaiian sugar and in addition awarded American producers a bounty of 2 cents a pound. Hawaiian sugar production dropped dramatically, unemployment rose, and property values fell. Soon thereafter, Queen Liliuokalani, a strong-willed nationalist, retaliated by decreeing a new constitution that gave greater power to native Hawaiians.

Unhappy, the American residents revolted in early 1893 and called on the United States for help. John L. Stevens, the American minister in Honolulu, sent 150 marines ashore, and within three days, the bloodless revolution was over. On February 14, 1893, Harrison's secretary of state, John W. Foster, and delegates of the new government signed a treaty annexing Hawaii to the United States. But only two weeks remained in Harrison's term, and the Senate refused to ratify the treaty. The new president, Cleveland, who disapproved of the American-instigated rebellion, withdrew the treaty and demanded that the queen be restored to her throne. However, the provisional government in Hawaii politely refused and instead proclaimed Hawaii a republic.

The debate over Hawaiian annexation continued through the 1890s. Those in favor of annexation pointed to Hawaii's strategic location, argued that Japan or other powers might seize the islands if the United States did not do so, and suggested that Americans had a responsibility to civilize and Christianize the native Hawaiians. Opponents warned that annexation might lead to a colonial army and colonial problems, the inclusion of a "mongrel" population in the United States, and rule over an area not destined for statehood.

Annexation came swiftly in July 1898 in the midst of excitement over victories in the Spanish-American War. Even before the war, President William McKinley had called for annexation, but opposition was still strong. The outbreak of war caused annexationists to redouble their efforts. McKinley and congressional leaders sought a joint resolution for annexation, which required only a majority of both houses. The annexation measure moved quickly through Congress, and McKinley signed it on July 7, 1898. His signature, giving the United States a naval and commercial base in the mid-Pacific, realized a goal of policymakers since the 1860s.

Hawaii represented a step toward China; the Samoan Islands, 3,000 miles to the south, sat astride the sea lanes of the South Pacific. In 1878, the United States acquired the use of Pago Pago, a harbor on the island of Tutuila. Great Britain and Germany also secured treaty rights in Samoa, and thereafter the three nations jockeyed for position.

The situation grew tense in 1889 when warships from all three countries gathered in a Samoan harbor. But a sudden typhoon destroyed the fleets, and tensions eased. A month later, delegates from the three countries met in Berlin to negotiate the problem. For a time, the indigenous population was granted some degree of authority, but in 1899, the United States and Germany divided Samoa and compensated Britain with lands elsewhere in the Pacific.

The New Navy

Large navies were vital in the scramble for colonies, but in the 1870s, the United States had almost no navy. One of the most powerful fleets in the world during the Civil War, the American navy had fallen into rapid decline. Ships rotted, and many officers left the service.

Conditions changed during the 1880s. A group of rising young officers, steeped in a new naval philosophy, argued for an expanded navy equipped with fast, aggressive ships capable of fighting battles across the seas. Big-navy proponents pointed to the growing navies of Great Britain, France, and Germany, arguing that the United States needed greater fleet strength to protect its interests in the Caribbean and the Pacific.

In 1883, Congress authorized construction of four steel ships, marking the beginning of the new navy. The initial building program focused on lightly armored, fast cruisers for raiding enemy merchant ships and protecting American shores, but after 1890, the program shifted to the construction of a seagoing, offensive battleship navy capable of challenging the strongest fleets of Europe.

Alfred Thayer Mahan and Benjamin F. Tracy were major influences behind the new navy. Austere and scholarly, Mahan was the era's most influential naval strategist. He devoted a lifetime to studying the role of sea power in history, summarizing his beliefs in major books: *The Influence of Sea Power upon History, 1660–1783* (1890) and *The Interest of America in Sea Power* (1897).

Mahan's reasoning was simple and persuasive. Industrialism, he argued, produced vast surpluses of agricultural and manufactured goods, for which markets had to be found. Markets involved distant ports; reaching them required a large merchant marine and a powerful navy to protect it. Navies, in turn, needed coaling stations and repair yards. Coaling stations meant colonies, and colonies became strategic bases, the foundation of a nation's wealth and power. The bases might serve as markets themselves, but they were more important as stepping-stones to other objectives, the markets of Latin America and Asia.

Mahan called attention to the worldwide race for power, a race, he warned, the United States could not afford to lose. To compete in the struggle, the United States needed strategic bases; a powerful, oceangoing navy; a canal across the isthmus connecting North and South America, to link the East Coast with the Pacific; and Hawaii as a way station on the route to Asia.

One of the many men Mahan impressed was Benjamin F. Tracy, who became Harrison's secretary of the navy in 1889. Tracy joined with big-navy advocates in Congress to push for a far-ranging battleship fleet that would be capable of attacking distant enemies. He actually wanted two fleets: eight battleships in the Pacific and twelve in the Atlantic. He got four first-class battleships.

In 1889, when Tracy entered office, the United States ranked twelfth among world navies; in 1893, when he left, it ranked seventh and was climbing rapidly. By the end of the decade, the navy had seventeen steel battleships and six armored cruisers, and it ranked third in the world.

War with Spain

The war with Spain in 1898 built a mood of national confidence; altered older, more insular patterns of thought; and reshaped the way Americans saw themselves and the world. When the war ended, American possessions stretched into the Caribbean and deep into the Pacific.

The Spanish-American War established the United States as a world power for the twentieth century. It brought colonies and millions of colonial subjects and confirmed the long-standing belief in the superiority of the New World over the Old. Americans felt more certain than ever that they were touched with a special destiny.

A War for Principle

By the 1890s, Cuba and the nearby island of Puerto Rico comprised nearly all that remained of Spain's once vast empire in the New World. Cuban insurgents had rebelled against Spanish rule several times, but they had failed to free their country. The depression of 1893 damaged the Cuban economy, and the Wilson-Gorman Tariff of 1894 prostrated it. Duties on sugar, Cuba's lifeblood, were raised 40 percent. With the island's sugar market in ruins, discontent with Spanish rule heightened, and in late February 1895, revolt again broke out.

Cuban insurgents established a junta in New York City to raise money, purchase weapons, and wage a propaganda war to sway American public opinion. Conditions in Cuba were grim. The insurgents engaged in a hit-and-run, scorched-earth policy to force the Spanish to leave while the Spanish commander tried to corner the rebels in the eastern end of the island and destroy them.

After initial failures, Spain in January 1896 sent General Valeriano Weyler y Nicolau to Cuba. Relentless and brutal, Weyler gave the rebels ten days to lay down their arms. He then put into effect a "reconcentration" policy designed to move the native population into camps and liquidate the rebels' popular base. Herded into fortified areas, Cubans died by the thousands, victims of unsanitary conditions, overcrowding, and disease.

There ensued a wave of compassion for the insurgents, stimulated by the newspapers. The so-called yellow press, a group of circulation-hungry New York City newspapers led by Joseph Pulitzer's *New York World* and William Randolph Hearst's *New York Journal,* printed lurid stories of Spanish atrocities.

But **yellow journalism** did not cause the war. It stemmed from larger conflicts in policies and perceptions between Spain and the United States. Throughout his presidency, Grover Cleveland counseled neutrality, and initially President McKinley, who came into office in March 1897, did the same. But McKinley tilted more toward the insurgents. Before the end of 1897, the new president was criticizing Spain's "uncivilized and inhuman" conduct. The United States, he made clear, did not contest Spain's right to fight the rebellion but insisted it be done within humane limits.

yellow journalism In order to sell newspapers to the public before and during the Spanish-American War, publishers William Randolph Hearst and Joseph Pulitzer engaged in blatant sensationalizing of the news, which became known as "yellow journalism." It helped turn U.S. public opinion against Spain's actions in Cuba.

Late in 1897, a change in government in Madrid brought a temporary lull in the crisis. The new government recalled Weyler and agreed to offer the Cubans some form of autonomy. The new initiatives pleased McKinley, though he again warned Spain that it must find a humane end to the rebellion. Then, in January 1898, Spanish army officers led riots in Havana against the new autonomy policy and shook the president's confidence in Madrid's control over conditions in Cuba.

McKinley ordered the battleship *Maine* to Havana to "show the flag" and to evacuate American citizens if necessary. On February 9, 1898, the *New York Journal* published a private letter stolen from Enrique Dupuy de Lôme, the Spanish ambassador in Washington. In the letter, de Lôme called McKinley "weak" and "a would-be politician." Many Americans were angered by the insult; McKinley himself was more worried about other sections of the letter, which revealed Spanish insincerity

Lithograph commemorating the sinking of the Maine *in Havana harbor on February 15, 1898, killing 266 men. Coverage of the incident in the "yellow" press encouraged readers to believe that Spanish bombs or torpedoes had sunk the ship.* ❖

in the negotiations. De Lôme immediately resigned and went home, but the damage was done.

A few days later, on February 15, an explosion tore through the hull of the *Maine,* sinking the ship and killing 266 sailors. McKinley cautioned patience, but Americans cried out for war. Soon they were chanting a new slogan: "Remember the *Maine* and to Hell with Spain!"

Recent studies of the *Maine* incident blame the sinking on an accidental internal explosion, but in 1898, Americans suspected Spain, especially after the report of an investigating board attributed the sinking to an external (and thus presumably Spanish) explosion.

In early March 1898, McKinley asked Congress for $50 million in emergency defense appropriations, a request Congress promptly approved. On March 27, McKinley cabled Spain his final terms. He asked Spain to declare an armistice, end the reconcentration policy, and—implicitly—move toward Cuban independence. The Spanish answer conceded some things, but not, in McKinley's judgment, the important ones. It made no mention of a true armistice, McKinley's offer to mediate, or Cuba's independence.

Reluctantly, McKinley prepared his war message, which Congress heard on April 11, 1898. Eight days later, Congress passed a joint resolution declaring Cuba independent and authorizing the president to use the army and navy to expel the Spanish from the island. The **Teller Amendment,** offered by Colorado Senator Henry M. Teller, pledged that the United States had no intention of annexing Cuba. On April 25, Congress passed a declaration of war, and late that afternoon McKinley signed it.

Teller Amendment In this amendment, sponsored by Senator Henry M. Teller of Colorado, the United States pledged that it did not intend to annex Cuba and that it would recognize Cuban independence from Spain after the Spanish-American War.

Some historians have suggested that McKinley was weak and indecisive in confronting the war hysteria in the country; others have called him a wily manipulator for war and imperial gains. In truth he was neither. Throughout the Spanish crisis, McKinley pursued a moderate middle course that sought to protect American interests, promote Cuba's independence, and allow Spain time to adjust to the loss of the remnant of empire. He also wanted peace, but in the end, the conflicting national interests of the two countries brought them to war.

"A Splendid Little War"

Ten weeks after the declaration of war, the fighting was over. For Americans, they were ten glorious, dizzying weeks, with victories to fill every headline and slogans to suit every taste. Relatively few Americans died, and the quick victory seemed to verify burgeoning American power. John Hay, soon to be McKinley's secretary of state, called it "a splendid little war."

At the outset, the United States was militarily unprepared. Like the navy, the army had shrunk drastically since the end of the Civil War. In 1898, the regular army consisted of only 28,000 officers and men, most of them more experienced in quelling Indian uprisings than fighting large-scale battles.

When McKinley called for 125,000 volunteers, as many as one million young Americans responded. Men clamored to join the newly formed National Guard units. The secretary of war feared "there is going to be more trouble to satisfy those who are not going than to find those who are willing to go."

Problems of equipment and supply quickly appeared. Some units went into battle carrying Civil War Springfield rifles whose cartridges gave off a puff of smoke when fired, neatly marking the troops' position. Food was also a problem, as was sickness. Tainted food and tropical diseases felled more American troops than enemy bullets.

Americans then believed that "a foreign war should be fought by the hometown military unit acting as an extension of their community." Soldiers identified with their hometowns and thought of themselves as members of a town unit in a national army. Not surprisingly, then, National Guard units mirrored the social patterns of their communities. Since everyone knew each other, there was an easygoing familiarity. Enlisted men resented officers who grabbed too much authority and expected officers and men to call each other by their first names.

Each community thought of the hometown unit as *its* unit, an extension of itself. There was little government-imposed censorship in the war with Spain, and fresh news arrived with each letter home. Small-town newspapers printed news of the men, and towns sent food, clothing, and occasionally even local doctors to the front.

"Smoked Yankees"

When the invasion force sailed for Cuba, nearly one-fourth of it was black. In 1898, the regular army included four regiments of black soldiers, the Twenty-Fourth and Twenty-Fifth Infantry and the Ninth and Tenth Cavalry. Black regiments had served with distinction in campaigns against the Indians in the West. Most black troops were posted in the West; no eastern community would accept them. When McKinley called for volunteers, more than ten thousand black troops volunteered for the National Guard.

Orders quickly went out to the four black regular-army regiments in the West to move to camps in the South to prepare for the invasion of Cuba. Crowds and cheers followed the troop trains across the Plains, but as they crossed into Kentucky and Tennessee, the cheering stopped. Station restaurants refused to serve the troops; all waiting rooms were segregated.

Many soldiers were not prepared to put up with the shameful treatment. Those stationed near Chickamauga Park, Tennessee, shot at some whites who insulted them and desegregated the railroad cars on the line in Chattanooga. Similar incidents broke out elsewhere in the South. Just before the army's departure for Cuba, the tensions in Tampa, Florida, erupted in a night of rioting during which three white and twenty-seven black soldiers were wounded. Such events demonstrated the irony of black American soldiers committed to fight for Cuban independence. As one black wondered, "Is America any better than Spain?"

Segregation continued on some of the troop ships. But the confusion of war often ended the problem, if only temporarily. Blacks took command as white officers died, and Spanish troops soon came to fear the "smoked Yankees," as they called them. Black soldiers played a major role in the Cuban campaign and probably staved off defeat for the Rough Riders at San Juan Hill. In Cuba, they won twenty-six Certificates of Merit and five Congressional Medals of Honor.

The Course of the War

Mahan's Naval War College had begun studying strategy for a war with Spain in 1895. By 1898, it had a detailed plan for operations in the Caribbean and the Pacific. Naval strategy was simple: destroy the Spanish fleet, damage Spain's merchant marine, and harry the colonies or the coast of Spain. The army's task was more difficult. It must defend the United States, invade Cuba and probably Puerto Rico, and undertake possible action in far-flung places such as the Philippines or Spain.

At first, McKinley moved cautiously. On the afternoon of April 20, 1898, he summoned the strategists to the White House and, to the dismay of those who wanted a more aggressive policy, decided on the limited strategy of blockading Cuba, sending arms to the insurgents, and annoying the Spanish with small thrusts by the army.

Victories soon changed the strategy. In the case of war, long-standing naval plans had called for a holding action against the Spanish base in the Philippines. On May 1, 1898, with the war barely a week old, Commodore George Dewey, commander of the Asiatic Squadron located at Hong Kong, crushed the Spanish fleet in Manila Bay. Suddenly, Manila and the Philippines lay within American grasp. Dewey had no troops to attack the Spanish army in Manila, but the War Department, stunned by the speed and size of the victory, quickly raised an expeditionary force.

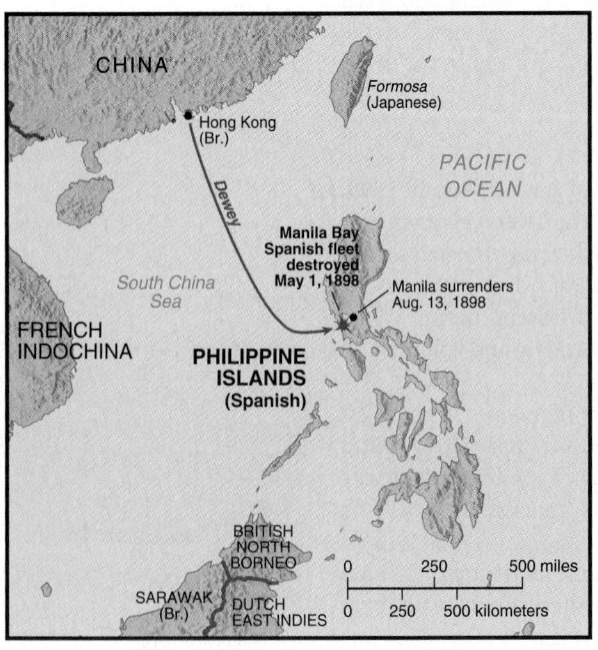

SPANISH-AMERICAN WAR: PACIFIC THEATER
Commodore Dewey, promoted to admiral immediately after the naval victory at Manila Bay, was the first hero of the war.

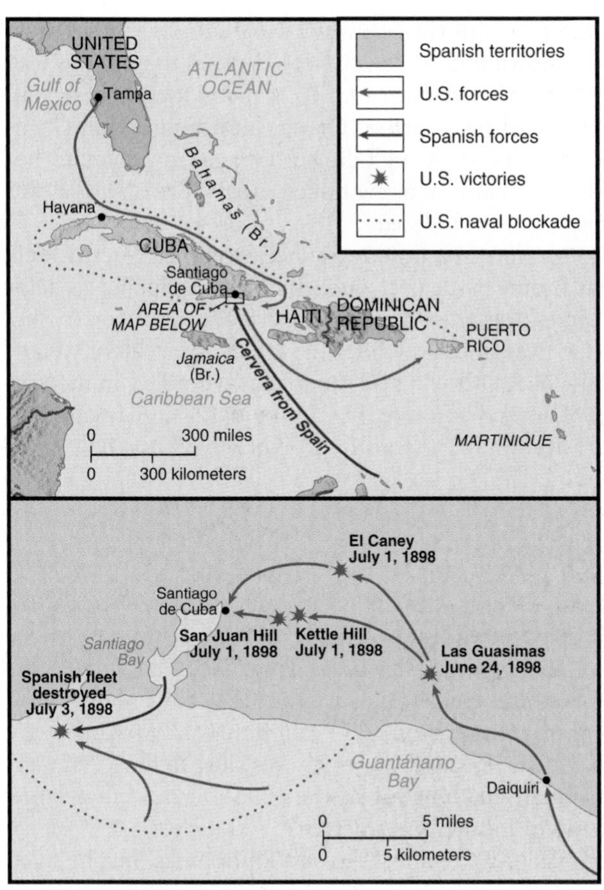

SPANISH-AMERICAN WAR: CARIBBEAN THEATER
President McKinley set up a "war room" in the White House, following the action on giant war maps with red and white marking pins.

On August 13, 1898, the troops accepted the surrender of Manila and with it the Philippines.

McKinley and his aides were worried about Admiral Pascual Cervera's main Spanish fleet, thought to be headed across the Atlantic for an attack on Florida. In mid-May, Cervera slipped secretly into the harbor of Santiago de Cuba, a city on the island's southern coast. But a spy in the Havana telegraph office alerted the Americans, and on May 28 a superior American force under Admiral William T. Sampson bottled Cervera up.

On June 14, an invasion force of about seventeen thousand men set sail from Tampa. Seven days later, they landed at Daiquiri on Cuba's southeastern coast. All was confusion, but the Spanish offered no resistance. Immediately, the Americans pushed west toward Santiago, which they hoped to surround and capture. At first, the advance was peaceful through the lush tropical countryside.

The first battle broke out at Las Guasimas, a crossroads on the Santiago road. After a sharp fight, the Spanish fell back. On July 1, the Rough Riders, troops from the four black regiments, and the other regulars reached the strong fortifications at El Caney and San Juan Hill. Black soldiers of the Twenty-Fifth Infantry charged the El Caney blockhouses. For the better part of a day, the defenders fought stubbornly and held back the army's elite corps. In the confusion of battle, Roosevelt rallied an assortment of infantry and cavalry to take Kettle Hill, adjacent to San Juan Hill.

They charged directly into the Spanish guns, Roosevelt at their head. Losses were heavy. Dense foliage concealed the enemy; smokeless powder gave no clue to their position. At nightfall, the surviving Spanish defenders withdrew, and the Americans prepared for the counterattack. The worst, many soldiers feared, was yet to come.

American troops now occupied the ridges overlooking Santiago. They were weakened by sickness, a fact unknown to the Spanish, who decided the city was lost. The Spanish command in Havana ordered Cervera to run for the open sea, although he knew the attempt would be hopeless. On the morning of July 3, his squadron steamed down the bay and out through the harbor's narrow channel, but the waiting American fleet closed in, and in a few hours, every Spanish vessel was destroyed. Two weeks later, Santiago surrendered.

Soon thereafter, army troops, meeting little resistance, occupied Puerto Rico. Cervera had commanded Spain's only battle fleet, and when it sank, Spain was helpless against attacks on the colonies or even its own shores. The war was over. Lasting 113 days, it took relatively few lives, most of them the result of accident, yellow fever, malaria, and typhoid in Cuba. Of the 5,500 Americans who died in the war, only 379 were killed in battle. The navy lost one man in the battle at Santiago Bay, and one sailor died of heat prostration in the stunning victory in Manila Bay.

Acquisition of Empire

The United States emerged from the war with an expansion of its territory and an even larger expansion of its responsibilities. According to the preliminary peace agreement, Spain granted independence to Cuba, ceded Puerto Rico and the Pacific island of Guam to the United States, and allowed Americans to occupy Manila until the two countries reached final agreement on the Philippines. To McKinley, the Philippines were the problem. Unlike Puerto Rico, which was close to the U.S. mainland, and Guam, which was small and unknown, the Philippines were a large, sprawling archipelago thousands of miles from America.

McKinley weighed a number of alternatives for the Philippines, but he liked none of them. He did not want to give the islands back to Spain; public opinion would not allow it. Nor did he want to turn them over to another world power. Germany, Japan, Great Britain, and Russia had all expressed interest in them. He considered independence for the islands but was soon talked out of it. Nearly everyone who had been there believed that the people were not ready for independence. Sifting the choices, McKinley decided that there was only one practical policy: annex the Philippines, with an eye to future independence after a period of tutelage.

At first hesitant, American opinion was swinging to the same conclusion. Religious and missionary organizations appealed to McKinley to hold on to the Philippines in order to "Christianize them." Some merchants and industrialists saw them as the key to the China market and the wealth of Asia. Many Americans simply regarded them as the legitimate fruits of war.

In October 1898, representatives of the United States and Spain met in Paris to discuss a peace treaty. Spain agreed to recognize Cuba's independence, to assume the Cuban debt, and to cede Puerto Rico and Guam to the United States. Acting on instructions from McKinley, the American representatives demanded the cession of the Philippines. In return, the United States offered a payment of $20 million. Spain resisted but had little choice, and on December 10, 1898, the American and Spanish representatives signed the **Treaty of Paris.**

Treaty of Paris Signed by the United States and Spain in December 1898, this treaty ended the Spanish-American War. Under its terms, Spain recognized Cuba's independence and assumed the Cuban debt; it also ceded Puerto Rico, Guam, and the Philippines to the United States.

Submitted to the Senate for ratification, the treaty set off a storm of debate throughout the country. Such prominent Americans as Andrew Carnegie, Jane Addams, William Jennings Bryan, and Mark Twain argued forcefully against annexation of the Philippines. While some anti-imperialists feared the importation of cheap labor from new Pacific colonies and others argued against assimilation of different races, most anti-imperialists focused on a different argument: the exercise of tyranny abroad, they argued, would result in tyranny at home; the very principles of independence and self-determination on which the country was founded would be violated by annexation.

In November 1898, opponents of expansion formed the **Anti-Imperialist League** to fight against the peace treaty. Membership centered in New England; the cause was less popular in the West and South. It enlisted more Democrats than Republicans, though never a majority of either. The anti-imperialists lacked a coherent program. Most simply wished that Dewey had sailed away after beating the Spanish at Manila Bay.

Anti-Imperialist League This organization formed in November 1898 to fight against the Treaty of Paris, which ended the Spanish-American War. Members opposed the acquisition of overseas colonies by the United States, believing it would subvert American ideals and institutions.

The debate in the Senate lasted a month. McKinley pressed hard for ratification, and Bryan, though opposed to annexation, supported ratification simply to end the war. Still, on the final weekend before the vote, the treaty was two votes short. That Saturday night, news reached Washington that fighting had broken out between American troops and Filipino insurgents who demanded immediate independence. The news increased pressure to ratify the treaty, which the Senate did on February 6, 1899. The United States had a colonial empire.

Guerrilla Warfare in the Philippines

Historians rarely write of the **Philippine-American War,** but it was an important event in American history. The war with Spain was over in a few months; war with the Filipinos lasted more than three years. For the first time, Americans fought men of a different color in an Asian guerrilla war. The Philippine-American War of

Philippine-American War A war fought from 1899 to 1903 to quell Filipino resistance to U.S. control of the Philippine Islands. Although often forgotten, it lasted longer than the Spanish-American War itself and resulted in more casualties.

A Look at the Past

Cartoon "School Begins"

Uncle Sam teaches a diverse group of students about civilization in this *Puck* cartoon. In the first row, receiving special attention are recent U.S. acquisitions: Cuba, Puerto Rico, Hawaii, and the Philippines. Carefully examine all the individuals in the cartoon. Who stands outside the classroom and why? How do the students in the first row compare to others in the classroom? Read the message on the chalkboard and consider its meaning. According to this cartoon, how do Americans regard other races and ethnicities? How would Americans define civilization?

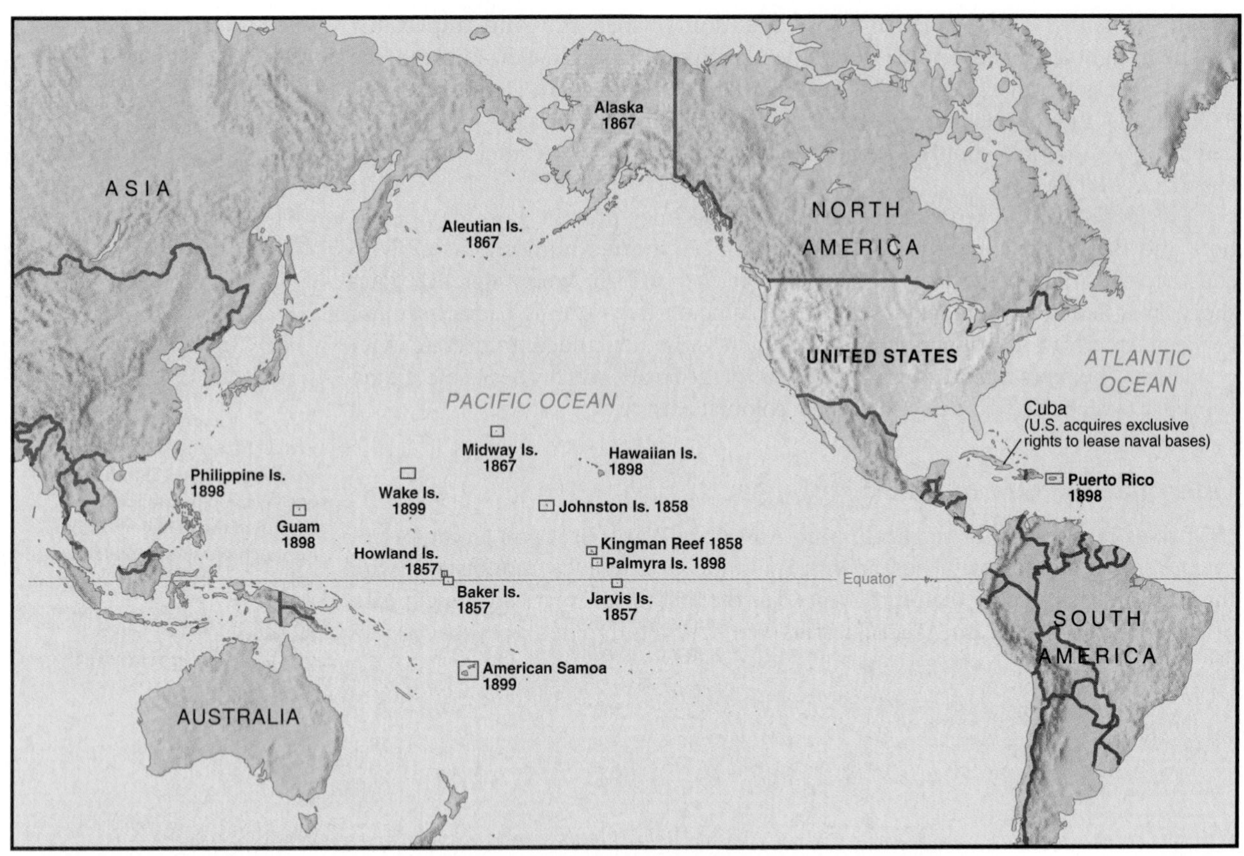

AMERICAN EMPIRE, 1900 *With the Treaty of Paris, the United States gained an expanded colonial empire stretching from the Caribbean to the far Pacific. It embraced Puerto Rico, Alaska, Hawaii, part of Samoa, Guam, the Philippines, and a chain of Pacific islands. The dates on the map refer to the date of U.S. acquisition.* ❖

1899–1902 took a heavy toll: 4,300 Americans and perhaps as many as 57,000 Filipinos.

Emilio Aguinaldo, the Filipino leader, had welcomed the Spanish-American War. Certain that the United States would grant independence, he had worked for an American victory. On June 12, 1898, the insurgents proclaimed their independence from Spain. Then, cooperating with the Americans, they drove the Spanish out of many areas of the islands. In the liberated regions, Aguinaldo established local governments. He waited impatiently for American recognition, but McKinley and others doubted that the Filipinos were ready. Shortly thereafter, fighting broke out between Filipinos and Americans.

Although by late 1899 the American army had defeated and dispersed the organized Filipino army, Aguinaldo and his followers continued to wage a guerrilla war. The Americans used Weyler-like tactics. After any attack on an American patrol, they burned all the houses in the nearest district. They established protected "zones" and herded Filipinos into them. Seizing or destroying all food outside the zones, they starved many guerrillas into submission.

Bryan tried to turn the election of 1900 into a debate over imperialism, but his attempt failed. For one thing, he himself refused to give up the silver issue, which cost him support among anti-imperialists in the Northeast, who were for gold. McKinley, moreover, was able to take advantage of the surging economy, and he could defend expansion as an accomplished fact. Riding a wave of patriotism and prosperity, McKinley won the election handily.

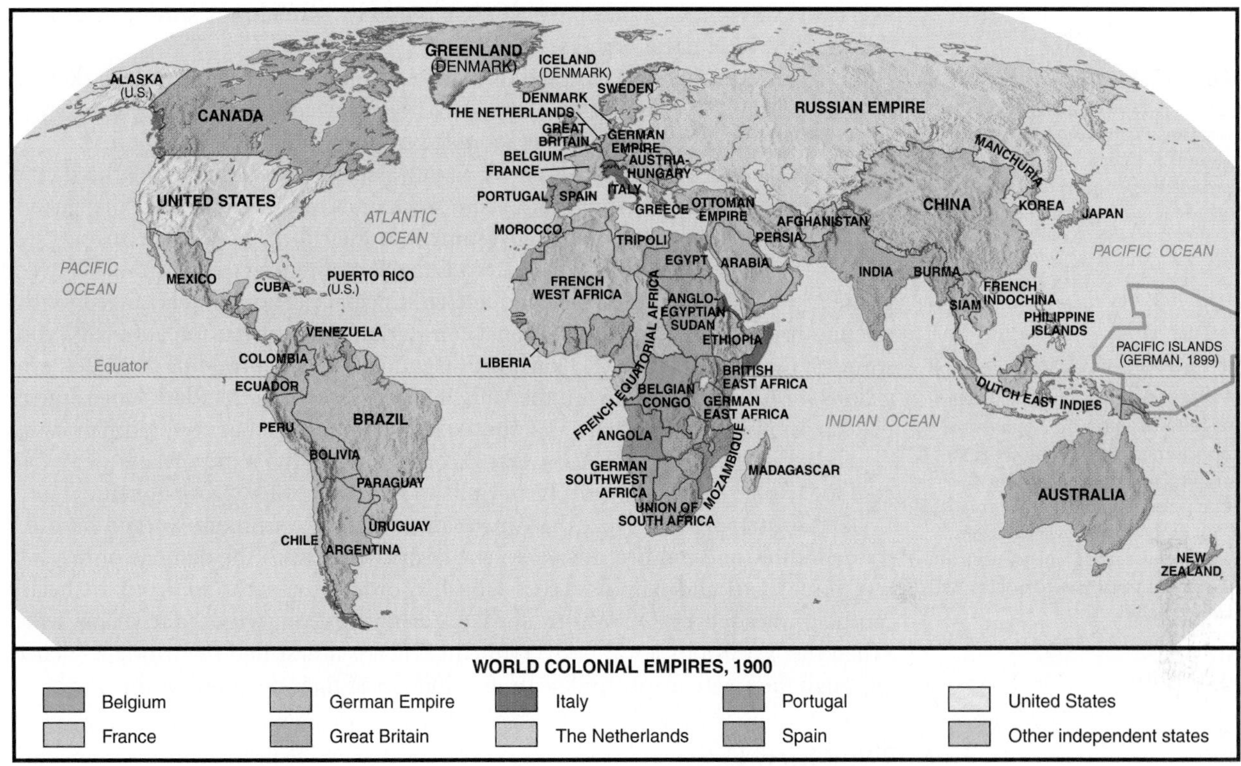

WORLD COLONIAL EMPIRES, 1900 *Events of the nineteenth century increased European hegemony over the world. By 1900, most independent African nations had disappeared, and the major European nations had divided the continent among themselves. In the East, the European powers and Japan took advantage of China's internal weakness to gain both trading ports and economic concessions.* ❖

In 1900, McKinley sent a special Philippine commission under William Howard Taft to establish a civil government. The following year, Aguinaldo was captured. Back in Manila, he signed a proclamation urging his people to end the fighting. On July 4, 1901, authority was transferred from the army to Taft, who was named the civilian governor of the islands, and his civil commission.

Given broad powers, the Taft Commission introduced many changes. The Americans built new schools, roads, and bridges. They reformed the judiciary, reconstructed the tax system, and introduced sanitation and vaccination programs. Taft also encouraged Filipino participation in government. Slowly, the Filipinos moved toward independence, which came on July 4, 1946, nearly fifty years after Aguinaldo proclaimed it.

Governing the Empire

Ruling the colonies raised new and perplexing questions. How could—and how should—the distant dependencies be governed? Did their inhabitants have the rights of American citizens? Did "the Constitution follow the flag"?

In a series of cases between 1901 and 1904, the Supreme Court asserted the principle that the Constitution did not automatically and immediately apply to the people of an annexed territory and did not confer on them all the privileges of United States citizenship. Instead, Congress could specifically extend such constitutional provisions as it saw fit.

Four dependencies—Hawaii, Alaska, Guam, and Puerto Rico—were organized quickly. In 1900, Congress granted territorial status to Hawaii and gave American citizenship to all citizens of the Hawaiian republic. A similar maneuver made Alaska a territory in 1912. Guam and the Samoan island of Tutuila were simply placed under the control of naval officers.

Foraker Act This act established Puerto Rico as an unorganized U.S. territory. Puerto Ricans were not given U.S. citizenship, but the U.S. president appointed the island's governor and governing council.

Puerto Ricans readily accepted the war's outcome, and in 1900, the **Foraker Act** established civil government in Puerto Rico. It organized the island as a territory. In 1917, United States citizenship was extended to the residents of the island.

Cuba proved a trickier matter. McKinley asserted the authority of the United States over conquered territory and promised to govern the island until the Cubans had established a firm and stable government of their own. To oversee this process, McKinley sent General Leonard Wood to Cuba. Wood moved quickly to bring order to the country. Early in 1900, he conducted municipal elections and arranged for the election of delegates to a constitutional convention. The convention adopted a constitution modeled on the U.S. Constitution and, at Woods's prodding, included provisions for future relations with the United States. Known as the **Platt Amendment,** the provisions stipulated that Cuba should make no treaties that might impair its independence and acquire no debts that it could not pay; most important, it empowered the United States to intervene in Cuba to maintain orderly government.

Platt Amendment This amendment to the new Cuban constitution authorized U.S. intervention in Cuba to protect its interests. Cuba pledged not to make treaties with other countries that might compromise its independence, and it granted naval bases to the United States.

Between 1898 and 1902, the American military government worked hard for the economic and political revival of the island. It repaired the damage of the civil war, built roads and schools, and established order in rural areas. A public health campaign headed by Dr. Walter Reed, an army surgeon, wiped out yellow fever. When the last troops left in May 1902, the Cubans at last had their independence, although they were firmly under the domination of their neighbor to the north.

The Open Door

Poised in the Philippines, the United States had become an Asian power on the doorstep of China. Weakened by years of warfare, China in 1898 and 1899 was unable to resist foreign influence. Japan, England, France, Germany, and Russia eyed it covetously, dividing the country into "spheres of influence." They forced China to grant "concessions" that allowed them exclusive rights to develop particular areas and threatened American hopes for extensive trade with the country.

In this 1899 cartoon, "Putting His Foot Down" from Puck, *the nations of Europe are getting ready to cut up China to expand their spheres of influence, but Uncle Sam stands firm on American commitments to preserve China's sovereignty.* ❖

CHRONOLOGY

1867	United States purchases Alaska from Russia ❖ Midway Islands are annexed
1871	Treaty of Washington between the United States and Great Britain sets a precedent for the peaceful settlement of international disputes
1875	Reciprocity treaty with Hawaii binds Hawaii economically and politically to the United States
1878	United States acquires a naval base in Samoa
1883	Congress approves funds for construction of the first modern steel ships; beginning of the modern navy
1887	New treaty with Hawaii gives United States exclusive use of Pearl Harbor
1889	First Inter-American Conference meets in Washington, D.C.
1893	American settlers in Hawaii overthrow Queen Liliuokalani; provisional government is established
1895	Cuban insurgents rebel against Spanish rule
1898	Battleship *Maine* explodes in Havana harbor (February) ❖ Congress declares war against Spain (April) ❖ Commodore Dewey defeats the Spanish fleet at Manila Bay (May) ❖ United States annexes Hawaii (July) ❖ Americans defeat the Spanish at El Caney, San Juan Hill (actually Kettle Hill), and Santiago (July) ❖ Spain sues for peace (August) ❖ Treaty of Paris ends the Spanish-American War (December)
1899	Congress ratifies the Treaty of Paris ❖ United States sends Open Door notes to Britain, Germany, France, Russia, Japan, and Italy ❖ Philippine-American War erupts
1900	Foraker Act establishes civil government in Puerto Rico ❖ Boxer Rebellion in China occurs
1901	Platt Amendment authorizes American intervention in Cuba
1902	Philippine-American War ends with an American victory

McKinley first outlined a new China policy in September 1898. He wanted Asian trade to be conducted on the analogy of an "open door," meaning that all countries would have an equal opportunity to compete for the Asian markets. In September 1899, Secretary of State Hay addressed identical diplomatic notes to England, Germany, and Russia, and later to France, Japan, and Italy, asking them to join the United States in establishing the **Open Door policy.** This policy urged three agreements: nations possessing a sphere of influence would respect the rights and privileges of other nations in that sphere, the Chinese government would continue to collect tariff duties in all spheres, and nations would not discriminate against other nations in levying port dues and railroad rates within their respective spheres of influence.

Open Door policy Established in a series of notes by Secretary of State John Hay in 1900, this policy established free trade between the United States and China and attempted to enlist major European and Asian nations in recognizing the territorial integrity of China. It marked a departure from the American tradition of isolationism and signaled the country's growing involvement in the world.

Under the Open Door policy, the United States could retain many commercial advantages that were endangered by the partition of China into spheres of influence. McKinley and Hay also attempted to preserve for the Chinese some semblance of national authority. None of the countries fully accepted the Open Door policy, but Hay turned the situation to American advantage by boldly announcing in March 1900 that all the powers had agreed to it.

The policy's first test came just three months later with the outbreak of the Boxer Rebellion in Peking (Beijing). In June 1900, a secret and intensely nationalistic Chinese society called the Boxers tried to oust all foreigners from the country. Overrunning Peking, they drove foreigners into their legations and penned them up for nearly two months. In the end, the United States joined Britain, Germany, and other powers in sending troops to lift the siege.

Fearing that the rebellion gave some nations, especially Germany and Russia, an excuse to expand their spheres of influence, Hay took quick action to emphasize American policy. In July, he sent off another round of Open Door notes affirming the U.S. commitment to equal commercial opportunity and respect for China's independence. Whereas the first Open Door notes had implied recognition of China's continued independence, the second notes explicitly stated the need to preserve it. The two notes set the policy that would guide American diplomacy in the Far East.

Conclusion: Outcome of the War with Spain

The war was over. Roosevelt, now famous, was elected governor of New York. He would soon become McKinley's vice president and then president of the United States. For other Americans, heroism was not so profitable. Bravery in Cuba and the Philippines won some recognition for black soldiers, but the war itself set back the cause of civil rights. It spurred talk about "inferior" races, at home and abroad, and forged new bonds between whites in the North and South. A fresh outburst of segregation and lynching occurred during the decade after the war.

In a little more than a century, the United States had grown from thirteen small states strung along a thin strip of Atlantic coastline into a world power that stretched from the Atlantic and the Caribbean to the far side of the Pacific. As Seward and others had hoped, the nation now dominated its own hemisphere, dealt with European powers on equal terms, and exerted great influence in Asia.

Key Terms

isolationism, p. 408
imperialism, p. 408
yellow journalism, p. 413
Teller Amendment, p. 414
Treaty of Paris, p. 418
Anti-Imperialist League, p. 419
Philippine-American War, p. 419
Foraker Act, p. 422
Platt Amendment, p. 422
Open Door policy, p. 423

Recommended Reading

The best general account of the development of American foreign policy during the last part of the nineteenth century is Walter LaFeber, *The New Empire: An Interpretation of American Expansion, 1860–1898* (1963). William Appleman Williams, *The Tragedy of American Diplomacy* (1959), examines the economic motives for expansion. See also Paul Wolman, *Most Favored Nation: The Republican Revisionists and U.S. Tariff Policy, 1897–1912* (1992) and Laura Wexler, *Tender Violence: Domestic Visions in an Age of U.S. Imperialism* (2000). Lewis L. Gould persuasively reassesses McKinley's diplomacy and wartime leadership in *The Presidency of William McKinley* (1980).

Also helpful are Michael H. Hunt, *Ideology and Foreign Policy* (1987), Tom E. Terrill, *The Tariff, Politics, and American Foreign Policy, 1874–1901* (1973), and Matthew Frye Jacobson, *Barbarian Virtues: The United States Encounters Foreign Peoples at Home and Abroad, 1876–1917* (2000).

Graham A. Cosmas presents a detailed account of military organization and strategy in *An Army for Empire: The United States Army in the Spanish-American War* (1971); Willard B. Gatewood, Jr., offers a fascinating glimpse of the thoughts of some black soldiers in the war in *"Smoked Yankees" and the Struggle for Empire: Letters from Negro Soldiers, 1898–1902* (1971). Ivan Musicant, *Empire by Default: The Spanish-American War and the Dawn of the American Century* (1998), Kristin L. Hoganson, *Fighting for American Manhood: How Gender Politics Provoked the Spanish-American and Philippine-American Wars* (1998), and John L. Offner, *An Unwanted War: The Diplomacy of the United States and Spain over Cuba, 1895–1898* (1992), trace the background to the war with Spain. Brian McAllister Linn, *The Philippine War, 1899–1902* (2000), examines the often forgotten war against the Filipinos. Gerald F. Linderman relates the war to the home front in *The Mirror of War: American Society and the Spanish-American War* (1974).

For a list of additional titles related to this chapter's topics, please see http://www.ablongman.com/divine.

SUGGESTED WEB SITES

William McKinley and the Spanish-American War

http://www.history.ohio-state.edu/projects/mckinley/SpanAmWar.htm
Part of Ohio State University's site about William McKinley, this part highlights the Spanish-American War with an essay and photos.

The Spanish-American War in Motion Pictures

http://memory.loc.gov/ammem/sawhtml/sawhome.html
This Library of Congress Web presentation features sixty-eight films of the Spanish-American War, the first war to be documented in motion pictures.

The World of 1898: The Spanish-American War

http://www.loc.gov/rr/hispanic/1898/
This Library of Congress site offers resources and documents about the Spanish-American War and the people who participated in or commented about it.

Sentenaryo/Centennial: The Philippine Revolution and Philippine-American War

http://www.boondocksnet.com/centennial/index.html
Jim Zwick organizes primary documents, images, and essays focusing on the Philippines and American involvement.

Anti-Imperialism in the United States, 1898–1935

http://www.boondocksnet.com/ail98-35.html
Jim Zwick edits this extensive site, collating a large number of primary documents about anti-imperialism in America.

The Age of Imperialism

http://www.smplanet.com/imperialism/toc.html
Focusing on the period around the turn of the century, this site puts much information about American imperialism in one place.

Images from the Philippine-United States War

http://historicaltextarchive.com/USA/twenty/filipino.html
This site includes several images from the Philippihe-American War, one of the least discussed military engagements in American history.

Theodore Roosevelt Association

http://www.theodoreroosevelt.org/
This site contains much biographical and research information about this famous American.

Chapter 22

The Progressive Era

Muckrakers Call for Reform

In 1902, Samuel S. McClure, the shrewd owner of *McClure's Magazine,* sensed something astir in the country that his reporters were not covering. Like *Life,* the *Ladies' Home Journal,* and *Cosmopolitan, McClure's* was reaching more and more people—more than a quarter of a million readers a month. Americans were snapping up the new popular magazines filled with eye-catching illustrations and up-to-date fiction.

McClure was always chasing new ideas and readers, and in 1902, certain that something was happening in the public mood, he told one of his staff editors, 36-year-old Lincoln Steffens, "Get out of here, travel, go—somewhere. . . ." Following McClure's suggestion, Steffens boarded a train and headed west, determined to understand the temper of the nation. In St. Louis, he came across a young district attorney named Joseph W. Folk who had found a trail of corruption linking politics and some of the city's respected business leaders. "It is good business men," Folk stressed, "that are corrupting our bad politicians." Steffens's story, "Tweed Days in St. Louis," appeared in the October 1902 issue of *McClure's.*

The November *McClure's* carried the first installment of Ida Tarbell's scathing "History of the Standard Oil Company," and in January 1903, Steffens was back with "The Shame of Minneapolis," another tale of corrupt partnership between business and politics. McClure had what he wanted. In an editorial in the January issue, he deplored the corruption in American life, "capitalists, working men, politicians, citizens—all breaking the law, or letting it be broken."

Readers were enthralled, and articles and books by other **muckrakers**—Theodore Roosevelt coined the unflattering term in 1906 to describe the practice of exposing the corruption of public and prominent figures—spread swiftly. Muckraking flourished from 1903 to 1909, and while it did, good writers and bad investigated almost every corner of American life: government, labor unions, big business, Wall Street, health care, the food industry, child labor, women's rights, prostitution, ghetto living, and life insurance.

Outline

The Changing Face of Industrialism

Society's Masses

Conflict in the Workplace

A New Urban Culture

Conclusion: A Ferment of Discovery and Reform

AS MCCLURE HAD HOPED, Steffens *had* found something astir in the country, something so important and pervasive that it altered the course of American history. The muckrakers were a journalistic voice of this larger movement in American society. Called **progressivism,** it lasted from the mid-1890s through World War I. Like muckraking itself, it reflected concern with the state of society and a conviction that human compassion and scientific investigation could bring problems to light and solve them. Progressivism took on the character of Theodore Roosevelt and

Woodrow Wilson, two important national spokesmen, but it affected large numbers of people and expressed at many levels the excitement of progress and change.

The Changing Face of Industrialism

Significant changes occurred in the industrial system during the years between the 1890s and World War I. The rapid growth of businesses gave rise to the widely feared trust-forming movement and the progressives' desire to regulate it. Both progressives and business leaders drew on similar visions of the country: complex, expansive, hopeful, managerially minded, and oriented toward results and efficiency. In working for reform, the progressives drew on the managerial methods of a business world they sought to regulate.

Businesses got large in the three decades after the Civil War, but in the years between 1895 and 1915 they became mammoth, employing thousands of workers and equipped with assembly lines to turn out huge numbers of the company's product. Inevitably, management attitudes changed, as did business organization and worker roles.

McCLURE'S MAGAZINE
APRIL, 1904
Enemies of the Republic
By LINCOLN STEFFENS
The Breaking Up of the Standard Oil Trust
By IDA M. TARBELL
The Negro—Part Two
By THOMAS NELSON PAGE
SEVEN SHORT STORIES
Illustrations in Color
S. S. McCLURE CO. NEW YORK AND LONDON

At the beginning of the twentieth century, McClure's Magazine *was at the forefront of the journalistic crusade for reform, which took the form of muckraking articles by such writers as Ida Tarbell. The cover of* McClure's *April 1904 edition draws readers not with lively illustrations, but with the best in investigative journalism, and reveals American interest in corruption.* ❖

The Innovative Model T

Mass production of automobiles began in the first years of the century. Using an assembly-line system that foreshadowed later techniques, Ransom E. Olds turned out five thousand Olds runabouts in 1904. And just a year earlier, Henry Ford and a small group of associates had founded the Ford Motor Company, the firm that transformed the business.

Ford was 40 years old. At first, like many others in the newborn automobile industry, he concentrated on building luxury and racing cars. He even raced his own cars; in 1904, he set the world's land speed record—more than 90 miles per hour. However, his expensive cars found few buyers.

In 1907, he lowered the price, and sales picked up. Ford learned an important lesson of the modern economy: a smaller unit profit on a large number of sales could generate enormous revenues. Early in 1908, he introduced the Model T, a stripped-down, four-cylinder, 20-horsepower "Tin Lizzie," costing $850 and available only in black. Eleven thousand were sold the first year.

muckrakers Unflattering term coined by Theodore Roosevelt to describe the writers who made a practice of exposing the wrongdoings of public figures. Muckraking flourished from 1903 to 1909 in magazines such as *McClure's* and *Collier's,* exposing social and political problems and sparking reform.

progressivism Movement for social change between the late 1890s and World War I. Its origins lay in a fear of big business and corrupt government and a desire to improve the lives of countless Americans. Progressives set out to cure the social ills brought about by industrialization and urbanization, social disorder, and political corruption.

"I am going to democratize the automobile," Ford proclaimed. The key was mass production, and after many experiments, Ford copied the techniques of meatpackers, who moved animal carcasses along overhead trolleys from station to station. Adapting the process to automobile assembly, Ford in 1913 set up moving assembly lines in his plant in Highland Park, Michigan, that dramatically reduced the time and cost of producing cars. In 1914, he sold 248,000 Model Ts. That year it took ninety-three minutes to assemble a car. By 1925, the Ford plant was turning out a new car every ten seconds of the working day.

While Ford was putting more and more cars on the road, the 1916 Federal Aid Roads Act set the framework for road building in the twentieth century. Removing control from county governments, it required every state desiring federal funds to establish a highway department to plan routes, oversee construction, and maintain roads. Providing for a planned highway system, the act produced a national network of two-lane, all-weather intercity roads.

The Burgeoning Trusts

As businesses like Ford's grew, capital and organization became increasingly important, and the result was the formation of a growing number of trusts. Standard Oil started the trend in 1882, but the greatest momentum came between 1898 and 1903. A series of mergers and consolidations swept the economy. Many smaller firms disappeared, swallowed up by giant commercial enterprises. By 1904, large corporations of one form or another controlled nearly two-fifths of the capital in U.S. manufacturing.

The result was not monopoly but *oligopoly*—control of a commodity or service by a small number of large, powerful companies. Six great financial groups dominated the railroad industry; a handful of holding companies controlled utilities and steel. Rockefeller's Standard Oil owned about 85 percent of the oil business. Copper, tobacco, rubber, and other products were likewise held by only a few producers.

By 1909, just 1 percent of the industrial firms were producing nearly half of the manufactured goods. Giant businesses reached abroad for raw materials and new markets. United Fruit, an empire of plantations and steamships in the Caribbean, exploited opportunities created by victory in the war with Spain. U.S. Steel worked with overseas companies to fix the price of steel rails, an unattainable dream just a few years before.

Though the trend has been overstated, finance capitalists such as J. P. Morgan tended to replace the industrial capitalists of an earlier era. Able to finance the mergers and reorganizations, investment bankers played a greater and greater role in the economy. A multibillion-dollar financial house, J. P. Morgan and Company operated a network of control that ran from New York to every industrial and financial center in the nation. Like other investment firms, it held directorships in many corporations, creating "interlocking directorates" that allowed it to control many businesses.

Massive business growth set off a decadelong debate over what government should do about the trusts. Some critics wanted simply to break them up. Others argued that large-scale business was a mark of the times; it produced more goods and better lives. The debate over the trusts influenced politics throughout the Progressive Era.

As early as 1886, cartoonist Thomas Nast attacked trusts. Here the people's welfare is sinking as the Statue of Liberty is defaced. ❖

Managing the Machines

Mass production changed the direction of American industry. Size, system, organization, and marketing became increasingly important. Management focused on speed and product, not on workers. Assembly-line technology changed tasks and, to some extent, values. The goal was no longer to make a unique product that would be better than the one before. The goal now was to make each product come off the line exactly alike.

In a development that rivaled assembly lines in importance, businesses established industrial research laboratories where scientists and engineers developed new products. General Electric founded the first one in 1900 in a barn. It proved so successful that Du Pont, Eastman Kodak, and Standard Oil soon established research laboratories of their own. As the source of new ideas and technology, the labs altered life in the twentieth century.

Through all this, business operations became large-scale, mechanized, and managed. By 1920, close to one-half of all industrial workers labored in factories employing more than 250 people. More than a third worked in factories that were part of multiplant companies.

Industries that processed materials—iron and steel, paper, cement, and chemicals—were increasingly automated and operated continuously. In the glass industry, new machines ended the domination of highly skilled and well-paid craft workers. The machines turned out plate glass and ribbons of automobile window glass, and workers tending them could not fall behind. Foremen still managed the laborers on the factory floor, but more and more the rules came down from a central office where trained, professional managers supervised production flow. Workers lost control of the work pace. Employers sped up the conveyor belt to heighten production. In the automobile industry, output per worker-hour multiplied an extraordinary four times between 1909 and 1919.

Folkways of the workplace—workers passing job-related knowledge to each other, setting their own pace, and in effect running the shop—gave way to "scientific" labor management. More than anyone else, Frederick Winslow Taylor, an inventive mechanical engineer, strove to extract maximum efficiency from each worker. Taylor proposed two major reforms. First, management must take responsibility for job-related knowledge and classify it into "rules, laws, and formulae." Second, management should control the workplace "through *enforced* standardization of methods, *enforced* adoption of the best implements and working conditions, and *enforced* cooperation."

Taylor's methods included training workers for particular tasks, time-and-motion studies, and differential pay rates that rewarded those who worked fastest. Armed with stopwatches, his disciples reduced a factory's operations to the simplest tasks, then devised the most efficient way to perform them. The doctrine of scientific management spread throughout American industry.

Workers caught up in the changing industrial system experienced the benefits of efficiency and productivity; in some industries, they earned more. But they suffered important losses as well. Performing repetitive tasks, they seemed part of the machinery, to whose pace and needs they moved. Bored, they might easily have lost pride of workmanship, though many workers, it is clear, did not. Jobs became not only monotonous but also dangerous. Under pressure of speed, boredom or miscalculation could bring disaster. Meat cutters sliced fingers and hands. Forty-six steel workers were killed on the job in just one mill in 1906. Injuries were part of many jobs.

In March 1911, a fire at the Triangle Shirtwaist Company in New York focused attention on unsafe working conditions. Seamstresses were trapped in the building because exit doors had been closed and locked by the company to prevent theft and to shut out union organizers. Many died in the stampede down the narrow stairways or the single fire escape. Others leaped from the building's top floors to escape the flames. One hundred and forty-six people died.

A few days later, eighty thousand people marched silently in the rain in a funeral procession up Fifth Avenue. The protests impelled New York's governor to appoint a state factory investigating commission that recommended laws to shorten the workweek and improve safety conditions in factories and stores.

Society's Masses

National networks of products and consumers helped fuel the mass society, which depended on an enormous increase in the labor force to work in the factories, mines, and forests. Immigration soared, and women, blacks, and Mexican Americans played larger roles.

For many of these people, life was harsh, spent in crowded slums and long hours on the job. Fortunately, the massive unemployment of the 1890s was over, and there was great demand for skilled labor. But the less skilled continued to be the less fortunate. They fought to make a living, and many, too, fought to improve their lot. Their efforts, along with the efforts of the reform-minded people who came to their aid, became another important hallmark of the Progressive Era.

Better Times on the Farm

While people continued to flee the farms—by 1920, fewer than one-third of all Americans lived on farms, and fewer than half lived in rural areas—farmers themselves prospered, the beneficiaries of greater production and expanding urban markets. Rural free delivery (RFD)—delivery of mail to the farmhouse door, begun in 1893—helped diminish the farmers' sense of isolation, opening their lives to urban thinking, national advertising, and political events. In 1911, more than one billion newspapers and magazines were delivered over RFD routes.

Parcel post (1913) permitted the sending of packages through the U.S. mail. Mail-order houses flourished; rural merchants suffered. Within a year, 300 million packages were being mailed annually. Although telephones and electricity did not reach most rural areas for decades, better roads, mail-order catalogs, and other innovations knit farmers into the larger society. Early in the new century, Mary E. Lease—who in her Populist days had urged Kansas farmers to raise less taxes and more hell—moved to Brooklyn.

Farmers still had problems. Land prices rose with crop prices, and farm tenancy increased, especially in the South. In South Carolina, Georgia, Alabama, and

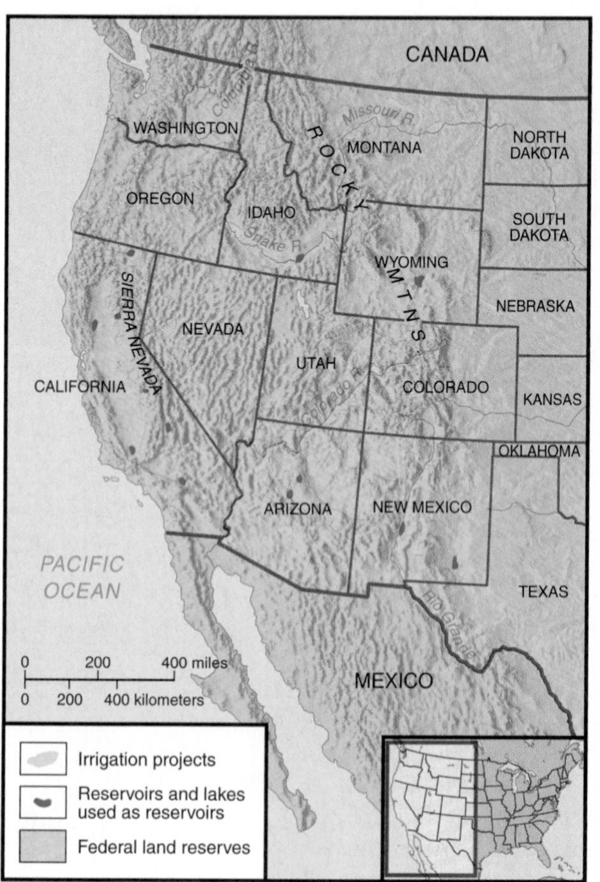

IRRIGATION AND CONSERVATION IN THE WEST TO 1917 *To make the arid lands of the western states productive, the state and federal governments regulated the water supply through irrigation projects and the creation of water reservoirs. The federal government also created land reserves.*

Mississippi, nearly two-thirds of the farms were run by tenant farmers. Many southern tenant farmers were African Americans, and they suffered from farm-bred diseases. In 1909, the Rockefeller Sanitary Commission began a sanitation campaign that eventually wiped out the hookworm disease, and in 1912, the U.S. Public Health Service began work on rural malaria.

In the arid West, irrigation transformed the land as the federal government and private landholders joined to import water from mountain watersheds. Dams and canals channeled water into places such as California's Imperial Valley, and as the water streamed in, cotton, cantaloupes, oranges, tomatoes, lettuce, and other crops streamed out to national markets. But as the land blossomed, the division between owners and workers sharpened, and migrant workers and immigrants from Mexico, China, and Japan worked long, backbreaking hours for meager rewards.

Women and Children at Work

Women worked in larger and larger numbers. In 1900, more than five million worked. Of those employed, single women outnumbered married women by seven to one. Most women held service jobs. Only a small number held higher-paying jobs as professionals or managers.

In the 1890s, women made up more than a quarter of medical school graduates. Adopting rigid standards, men gradually squeezed them out. Few women taught in colleges and universities, and those that did were expected to resign if they married. Men believed that once a woman became a "homemaker," she should have no other job.

More women than men graduated from high school, and with professions such as medicine and science largely closed to them, they often turned to the new "business schools" that offered training in stenography, typing, and bookkeeping. In 1920, more than a quarter of all employed women held clerical jobs. Many others taught school.

In 1907 and 1908, investigators studied 22,000 women workers in Pittsburgh; 60 percent of them earned less than $7 a week, the minimum for "decent living." Fewer than 1 percent held skilled jobs; most tended machines, wrapped and labeled, or did handwork that required no particular skill. Black women had always worked, and in far larger numbers than their white counterparts. The reason was usually economic; an African American man or woman alone could rarely earn enough to support a family. Unlike many white women, black women tended to remain in the labor force after marriage or the start of a family. They also had less opportunity for job advancement, and in 1920, between one-third and one-half of all African American women who were working were restricted to personal and domestic service jobs.

Critics charged that women's employment endangered the home, threatened reproductive functions, and even robbed them of their "special charm." Adding to the fears, the birthrate continued to drop between 1900 and 1920, and the divorce rate soared. By 1916, there was one divorce for every nine marriages, compared to one for every twenty-one in 1880.

Many children also worked. In 1900, about three million children—nearly 20 percent of those between the ages of 5 and 15—held full- or almost full-time jobs. Thousands of children worked in mines and southern cotton mills. The use of child labor shrank as states passed compulsory education and minimum age laws. Families focused greater and greater attention on the children, and child rearing became a central concern of family life.

As the middle-class family changed from an economic to an emotional unit, middle-class women claimed increasing pride in homemaking and motherhood. Mother's Day, as a national holiday, was formally established in 1913. Women who preferred fewer children turned increasingly to birth control, which became a more acceptable practice. Margaret Sanger, a nurse and an outspoken social reformer, led a campaign to give physicians broad discretion in prescribing contraceptives. Her efforts were resisted by the imposition of a ban on interstate transportation of contraceptive devices and information under the federal Comstock Law.

The Niagara Movement and the NAACP

At the turn of the twentieth century, eight of every ten blacks lived in rural areas, mainly in the South. Most were poor sharecroppers. Jim Crow laws segregated many schools, railroad cars, hotels, and hospitals. Poll taxes and other devices disfranchised blacks and many poor whites. Violence was common; between 1900 and 1914, white mobs murdered more than a thousand black people, often mutilating them and burning them alive.

Many blacks labored in the cotton farms, railroad camps, sawmills, and mines of the South under conditions of peonage—trading their lives and labor for food and shelter. Often illiterate, they were forced to sign contracts that tied them to their jobs. Armed guards patrolled the camps and whipped anyone caught trying to escape. Few unions admitted blacks to their ranks, and almost always blacks earned less than whites in the same job. The illiteracy rate among blacks dropped from 45 percent in 1900 to 30 percent in 1910, but nowhere were they given equal school facilities, teachers' salaries, or educational materials.

In 1905, a group of black leaders met near Niagara Falls, New York, and pledged action on behalf of voting, equal access to economic opportunity, integration, and equality before the law. At their head was sociologist W. E. B. Du Bois, professor of history and economics at Atlanta University. Rejecting Booker T. Washington's gradualist approach, the **Niagara Movement** claimed for blacks "every single right that belongs to a freeborn American, political, civil, and social; and until we get these rights we will never cease to protest." It kept alive a program of militant action focusing on equal rights and the education of black youth, and it spawned later civil rights movements. In *The Souls of Black Folk* (1903) and other works, Du Bois eloquently called for justice and equality.

Niagara Movement A movement, led by W. E. B. Du Bois, that focused on equal rights and the education of African American youth. Rejecting the gradualist approach of Booker T. Washington, members kept alive a program of militant action and claimed for African Americans all the rights afforded to other Americans.

Race riots broke out in Atlanta, Georgia, in 1906 and in Springfield, Illinois, in 1908. White mobs invaded black neighborhoods, burning, looting, and killing. William E. Walling, a wealthy southerner and settlement house worker; Mary Ovington, a white anthropology student; and Oswald Garrison Villard, grandson of the famous abolitionist William Lloyd Garrison, were outraged. Along with other reformers, white and black, they issued a call for the conference that organized the **National Association for the Advancement of Colored People (NAACP),** which swiftly became the most important civil rights organization in the country. Created in 1909, within five years the NAACP grew to more than six thousand members. The eight top officers included one black—W. E. B. Du Bois, director of publicity and research.

National Association for the Advancement of Colored People (NAACP) Created in 1909, this organization quickly became one of the most important civil rights organizations in the country. It pressured employers, labor unions, and the government on behalf of African Americans.

Joined by the National Urban League, founded in 1911, the NAACP pressured employers, labor unions, and the government on behalf of African Americans. It won some victories, but blacks continued to experience disfranchisement, poor job opportunities, and segregation. Little of progressivism's progress came their way.

"I Hear the Whistle": Immigrants in the Labor Force

Between 1901 and 1920, an extraordinarily high total of 14.5 million immigrants entered the country, more than in any previous twenty-year period. Continuing the trend begun in the 1880s, many came from southern and eastern Europe. Still called the "new" immigrants, they met hostility from older immigrants of northern European stock, who questioned their values and appearance.

Labor agents—called *padroni* among the Italians, Greeks, and Syrians—recruited immigrant workers, found them jobs, and deducted a fee from their wages. Headquartered in Salt Lake City, Leonidas G. Skliris, the "Czar of the Greeks," provided workers for the Utah Copper Company and the Western Pacific Railroad. Agents similarly distributed immigrant workers to major eastern and midwestern cities.

Immigration moved both ways. Fifty percent or more of some groups returned to the "old country." Some migrants—Italian men, in particular—virtually commuted, returning home every slack season. These temporary migrants became known as **birds of passage.** The outbreak of World War I interrupted the practice and "trapped" in the United States hundreds of thousands of Italians and others who had planned to return to Europe.

birds of passage Temporary migrants who came to the United States to work and save money and then returned home to their native countries during the slack season.

Older residents lumped the newcomers together, ignoring geographic, religious, and other differences. Preserving important regional distinctions, Italians tended to settle as Calabreses, Venetians, Abruzzis, and Sicilians. Native-born Americans viewed them all simply as Italians. Henry Ford and other employers tried to erase the differences through English classes and deliberate "Americanization" programs. In similar fashion, the International Harvester Corporation taught Polish laborers to speak English, but it had other lessons to impart as well. Factory Americanization programs were designed to produce good factory workers as well as good American citizens.

Fewer people immigrated from China in these years, deterred in part by anti-Chinese laws and hostility. In the early 1880s, there were about 125,000 Chinese in America, but by 1920, that figure had declined to just over 60,000. And those Chinese who were in America often wanted only to make money and return home. While in America, most lived in communities, dominated by the elderly, where men outnumbered women ten to one. Hard work and communal ties marked their time in the United States.

As the Chinese immigration slowed to a trickle, Japanese and Mexican immigration increased. In 1920, more than 110,000 Japanese immigrants were living in America. At the beginning of the twentieth century, Mexicans for the first time immigrated in large numbers, especially after a revolution in Mexico in 1910 forced many to flee across the border. (The exact number is unknown.) Almost all came from the Mexican lower class, eager to escape peonage and violence in their native land. Labor agents, usually in the employ of either large corporations or ranchers, recruited Mexican workers. After the turn of the century, almost 10 percent of the entire population of Mexico moved to the American Southwest.

The Mexican immigrants helped transform the Southwest. They built highways, dug irrigation ditches, laid railroad track, and picked cotton and vegetables. Yet American society imposed harsh rules on these people. Segregation laws and practices often kept them out of hotels or other public accommodations. Schools either barred them or, ironically, tried to anglicize them in segregated facilities. Yet again, Mexican Americans clung to their culture.

Nativist sentiment, which had accompanied earlier waves of immigration, intensified. Old-stock Americans sneered at the newcomers' dress and language. Racial theories emphasized the superiority of northern Europeans, and the new "science" of eugenics suggested controls over the population growth of "inferior" peoples. Hostility against Catholics and Jews was common but touched other groups as well. In 1902, immigration from China—suspended since 1882—was entirely prohibited.

Congress passed statutes requiring literacy tests designed to curtail immigration from southern and eastern Europe, but they were vetoed by Presidents Taft and Wilson. In 1917, Congress passed such a measure over Wilson's veto. Other bills tried to limit immigration from Mexico and Japan.

Conflict in the Workplace

Assembly lines, speed-ups, long hours, and low wages produced a dramatic increase in American industrial output and profits after 1900; they also gave rise to numerous strikes and other kinds of labor unrest. Sometimes strikes took place through actions of unions; sometimes workers just decided that they had had enough and walked off the job. Whatever the cause, strikes were frequent.

Strikes and absenteeism increased after 1910; labor productivity dropped 10 percent between 1915 and 1918, the first such decline in memory. Workers changed jobs in droves. Union membership grew. In 1900, only about one million workers belonged to unions; by 1920, five million belonged, about 13 percent of the workforce. But only 1.5 percent of female workers belonged to unions in 1910 due to gender discrimination.

As tensions grew between capital and labor, some middle-class Americans became fearful that unless something was done to improve the workers' situation, there might be violence or even revolution. This fear, along with some genuine desire to improve labor's lot, motivated some of the labor-oriented reforms of the Progressive Era.

Samuel Gompers's American Federation of Labor (AFL), by far the largest union organization, remained devoted to the interests of skilled craftsmen. While striving for better wages and working conditions, it also sought to limit entry into the craft and protect worker prerogatives. Within limits, the AFL found acceptance among giant business corporations eager for conservative policies and labor stability.

Of the 8 million female workers in 1910, only 125,000 belonged to unions. Gompers continued to resist organizing them, saying they were too emotional and, as union organizers, "had a way of making serious mistakes." Margaret Dreier Robins, an organizer of proven skill, scoffed at that.

Women's Trade Union League (WTUL) Founded in 1903, this organization worked to organize women into trade unions. It also lobbied for laws to safeguard female workers and backed several successful strikes, especially in the garment industry.

Robins helped found the **Women's Trade Union League (WTUL)** in 1903. The WTUL led the effort to organize women into trade unions, to lobby for legislation protecting female workers, and to educate the public on the problems and needs of working women. It took in all working women who would join, regardless of skill (though not, at first, African American women), and it won crucial financial support from well-to-do women. Robins's close friend Jane Addams belonged, as did Mary McDowell, the "Angel of the Stockyards," who worked with slaughterhouse workers in Chicago; Julia Lathrop, who tried to improve the lot of wage-earning children; and Dr. Alice Hamilton, a pioneer in American research on the causes of industrial disease. The WTUL never had many members—a few thousand at most—but its influence extended far beyond its membership.

Industrial Workers of the World (IWW) Founded in 1905, this radical union, also known as the Wobblies, aimed to unite the American working class into one union to promote labor's interests. It worked to organize unskilled and foreign-born laborers, advocated social revolution, and led several major strikes.

Unlike the AFL, the **Industrial Workers of the World (IWW)** tried to organize the unskilled and foreign-born laborers working in the mass production industries. Founded in Chicago in 1905, it aimed to unite the American working class into a mammoth union to promote labor's interests. The IWW—or Wobblies, as they were known—urged social revolution to create a workers' world.

The IWW led a number of major strikes; two in 1912, in Lawrence, Massachusetts, and Paterson, New Jersey, attracted national attention. Lawrence seized the limelight when the strikers sent their ill-clad and hungry children out of the city to stay with sympathetic families; Paterson did so when they rented New York's Madison Square Garden for a massive labor pageant. They believed that a series of local strikes would intensify capitalists' repression, then bring about a general strike, and eventually usher in a workers' commonwealth.

The IWW fell short of these objectives, but during its lifetime—from 1905 to the mid-1920s—it made major gains among immigrant workers in the Northeast, migrant farm labor on the Plains, and loggers and miners in the South and Far West. In factories such as Ford's, it recruited workers resentful of the speed-ups on the assembly lines.

Holding signs and banners that proudly display their union allegiance, including a sign with the slogan "An injury to one is an injury to all," women of the Industrial Workers of the World participate in a strike at the Oliver Iron and Steel Company in Pittsburgh, Pennsylvania, in 1913. The Clayton Act, passed by Congress in 1914, legalized picketing and other union activity. ❖

Concerned about labor unrest, business leaders turned to the new fields of applied psychology and personnel management. A school of industrial psychology emerged. A few businesses established industrial relations departments, hired public relations firms to improve their corporate image, and linked productivity to job safety and happiness. Ivy L. Lee, a pioneer in the field of corporate public relations, advised such corporate clients as Standard Oil and the Pennsylvania Railroad on how to improve relations with labor and the public.

On January 5, 1914, Henry Ford took another significant step: he announced the $5 day. With a single stroke, he doubled the wage rate for common labor, reduced the working day from nine hours to eight, and established a personnel department to place workers in appropriate jobs. As a result, Ford had the pick of the labor force. Turnover declined; absenteeism fell to 0.3 percent; output increased; the IWW at Ford collapsed. At first scornful of the "utopian" plan, business leaders across the country soon copied it.

A New Urban Culture

For many Americans, the quality of life improved significantly between 1900 and 1920. Jobs were relatively plentiful, and in a development of great importance, more and more people were entering the professions as doctors, lawyers, teachers, and engineers. With comfortable incomes, a growing middle class could take advantage of new lifestyles, inventions, and forms of entertainment. Mass consumption, promoted by a mushrooming advertising industry, fueled industry's mass production. Advertisers used sampling techniques, market testing, and research in their effort to sell products.

Mass production swept the clothing industry and dressed more Americans better than any people ever before. Manufacturers developed standard clothing and shoe sizes that fit most bodies. These "off the rack" items resulted in less expensive clothes and blurred the distinctions between rich and poor. By 1900, fully 90 percent of men and boys wore the new ready-to-wear clothes.

❖ A Look at the Past ❖

Sears Catalog

Rural Americans gained access to the same array of consumer goods that urban dwellers had when mail-order companies, such as Sears, Roebuck and Company, offered goods through the mail. Rural Free Delivery, begun in 1893, made shopping by mail easier than visiting the local general store. Sears targeted rural consumers and designed the catalog to appeal to those consumers. Notice the cover decoration depicting goods spilling out in front of the farmstead. Why do you think the cover includes information about the firm's incorporation and capital? Why are there references from banks? Does the cover suggest that rural Americans were completely comfortable about mail order or that they needed reassurance? Why might some consumers have been nervous about mail order?

The income of people who worked in manufacturing more than tripled from an average of $418 a year in 1900 to $1,342 a year in 1920. While the middle class expanded, the rich also grew richer. By 1920, a mere 5 percent of the population received almost one-fourth of all income.

In 1920, the median age of the population was only 25. (It is now 38.) Immigration accounted for part of the youthfulness, as most immigrants were young, and so did death rates. Thanks to medical advances and better living conditions, death rates dropped in the early years of the century, and the average life span increased. Between 1900 and 1920, life expectancy rose dramatically: for white women, from 49 to 56 years; for white men, from 47 to 54 years; for blacks and other minorities, from 33 to 45 years.

Infant mortality remained high. In comparison to today, fewer babies on average survived to adolescence, and fewer people survived beyond middle age. As a result, there were relatively fewer older people—in 1900, only 4 percent of the population was older than 65, compared to 13 percent today. Still, improvements in health care helped people live longer, and as a result, the incidence of cancer and heart disease increased.

Cities grew, and by any earlier standards, they grew on a colossal scale. Downtowns became a central hive of skyscrapers, department stores, warehouses, and hotels. Strips of factories radiated from the center. As street railways spread, cities took on a systematic pattern of socioeconomic segregation, usually in rings. Immigrants lived in the innermost ring, and wealthy suburbs occupied the outermost rings.

The giants were New York, Chicago, and Philadelphia, industrial cities that turned out every kind of product. Smaller cities such as Rochester, New York, or Cleveland, Ohio, specialized in manufacturing a specific line of goods or processing regional products for the national market. Railroads tied things together.

Step by step, cities took their twentieth-century form. Between 1909 and 1915, Los Angeles passed a series of ordinances that gave rise to modern urban zoning. For the first time, ordinances divided a city into three districts of specified use: a residential area, an industrial area, and a mixed area open to residences and a limited list of industries. Other cities followed suit. New York's zoning law of 1916 was copied across the nation.

Zoning gave order to city development, keeping skyscrapers out of factory districts and factories out of the suburbs. It also had powerful social repercussions. In the South, zoning became a tool to extend racial segregation; in northern cities, it acted against ethnic minorities. Jews in New York, Italians in Boston, Poles in Detroit, blacks in Chicago—zoning laws kept them all at arm's length.

Popular Pastimes

Thanks to changing work rules and mechanization, many Americans benefited from more leisure time. The average workweek for manufacturing laborers fell from sixty hours in 1890 to fifty-one in 1920. White-collar workers often spent even less time at the office. The new leisure time gave more people more opportunity for pleasurable diversions.

People flocked to places of entertainment. Baseball entrenched itself as the national pastime. Attendance at major league games doubled between 1903 and 1910. Football also drew fans, although critics attacked the sport's violence and the use of "tramp athletes," nonstudents whom colleges paid to play. In 1905, the worst year, 18 players were killed and 150 seriously injured. Prodded by Theodore Roosevelt, representatives of the major colleges formed the Intercollegiate Athletic Association to clean up the sport; in 1910, that organization was renamed the National Collegiate Athletic Association.

Movie theaters opened everywhere. By 1910, there were ten thousand of them, drawing a weekly audience of ten million people. Admission was usually 5 cents, and movies stressing laughter and pathos—soundless but accompanied by piano or organ—appealed to a mass market. In 1915, D. W. Griffith, a talented and creative—as well as racist—director, produced the first movie spectacular, *The Birth of a Nation.*

Before 1910, band concerts were the country's most popular entertainment. As many as twenty thousand amateur bands played in parks on summer Sunday afternoons. John Philip Sousa, the famous "March King," led a touring band that profited from the self-confident nationalism that followed the Spanish-American War. Robust, patriotic marches such as "The Stars and Stripes Forever" (1896) earned him wealth and popularity.

Soon automobiles and phonographs began to lure audiences away from the concerts. Early phonograph records were usually of vaudeville skits; orchestral recordings began in 1906. In 1919, some 2.25 million phonographs were produced; two years later, more than 100 million records were sold. People sang less and listened more.

The faster rhythms of syncopated ragtime became the rage, especially after Irving Berlin, a Russian immigrant, wrote "Alexander's Ragtime Band" in 1911. Ragtime set off a nationwide dance craze. European waltzes and polkas gave way to a host of new American dances, many with animal names: the fox trot, bunny hop, turkey trot, snake, and kangaroo dip. Partners were not allowed to dance too close; bouncers tapped them on the shoulder if they got closer than 9 inches.

Vaudeville, increasingly popular after 1900, reached maturity around 1915. Drawing on the immigrant experience and the rich variety of city life, it included skits, songs, comics, acrobats, and magicians. Dances and jokes expressed an earthiness new to mass audiences. By 1914, stage runways extended into the crowd; female performers had bared their legs, and costumes revealed the midriff as well.

In songs such as "St. Louis Blues" (1914), W. C. Handy took the black southern folk music of the blues to northern cities. Gertrude "Ma" Rainey sang in black vaudeville for nearly thirty-five years, and she discovered the 12-year-old Bessie Smith, who became the "Empress of the Blues." Another musical innovation came from New Orleans. Charles "Buddy" Bolden, Ferdinand "Jelly Roll" Morton, and Louis "Satchmo" Armstrong played an improvisational music that had no formal name. Reaching Chicago, it was finally named "jazz." Jazz jumped, and jazz musicians relied on feeling and mood.

Popular fiction reflected changing interests. Kate Douglas Wiggins's *Rebecca of Sunnybrook Farm* (1903) showed the continuing popularity of rural themes. Westerns also sold well, but readers turned more and more to detective thrillers with hard-bitten city detectives and science fiction tales featuring the latest dream in technology. The Tom Swift series, begun in 1910, looked ahead to spaceships, ray guns, and gravity nullifiers. Edward L. Stratemeyer, the mind behind Tom Swift, brought the techniques of mass production to book writing. He employed a stable of writers to turn out hundreds of Tom Swift, Rover Boys, and Bobbsey Twins stories for young readers.

Experimentation in the Arts

"There is a state of unrest all over the world in art as in all other things," the director of New York's Metropolitan Museum said in 1908. "It is the same in literature, as in music, in painting, and in sculpture." Isadora Duncan and Ruth St. Denis transformed the dance. Departing from traditional ballet steps, both women stressed improvisation, emotion, and the human form. Draped in flowing robes, Duncan told her students to "listen to the music with your soul. . . . Unless your dancing springs from an inner emotion and expresses an idea, it will be meaningless." After a triumphant performance with the New York Symphony in 1908, her ideas and techniques swept the country.

The lofts and apartments of New York's Greenwich Village attracted artists, writers, and poets interested in experimentation and change. To these artists, the

George Bellows, Cliff Dwellers *(1913). Bellows was part of the Ashcan School of painters, so named for their preference for depicting the realities of modern urban life, including its streets and slums, backyards and bars.* ❖

CHRONOLOGY

1898	Mergers and consolidations begin to sweep the business world, leading to fear of trusts
1900	General Electric founds the first industrial research laboratory
1903	Ford Motor Company is formed ❖ W. E. B. Du Bois calls for justice and equality for African Americans in *The Souls of Black Folk* ❖ Women's Trade Union League is formed to organize women workers
1905	Industrial Workers of the World (IWW) is established ❖ African American leaders inaugurate the Niagara Movement, advocating integration and equal opportunity for African Americans
1909	Campaign by Rockefeller Sanitary Commission wipes out hookworm disease
1910	NAACP is founded ❖ National Collegiate Athletic Association is formed
1911	Frederick Winslow Taylor publishes *The Principles of Scientific Management* ❖ Fire at the Triangle Shirtwaist Company kills 146 people v Irving Berlin popularizes the rhythm of ragtime with "Alexander's Ragtime Band" ❖ National Urban League is created
1912	IWW leads strikes in Massachusetts and New Jersey ❖ Harriet Monroe begins publishing *Poetry* magazine
1913	Ford introduces the moving assembly line at its Highland Park, Michigan, plant ❖ Mother's Day becomes a national holiday ❖ Show at the New York Armory presents modernist paintings, prints, and sculptures
1915	D. W. Griffith produces the first movie spectacular, *The Birth of a Nation* ❖ T. S. Eliot publishes "The Love Song of J. Alfred Prufrock"
1916	Federal Aid Roads Act creates a national road network ❖ Margaret Sanger forms the New York Birth Control League
1917	Congress passes a law requiring a literacy test for all immigrants

city was the focus of national life and the sign of a new culture. Robert Henri and the realist painters—known to their critics as the **Ashcan School**—relished the city's excitement. They wanted "to paint truth and to paint it with strength and fearlessness and individuality." Their paintings depicted street scenes, colorful crowds, and slum children swimming in the river.

Ashcan School This school of early twentieth-century realist painters took as their subjects the slums and streets of the nation's cities and the lives of ordinary urban dwellers. They often celebrated life in the city but also advocated political and social reform.

In 1913, a show at the New York Armory presented sixteen hundred modernist paintings, prints, and sculptures. The work of Picasso, Cézanne, Matisse, Brancusi, Van Gogh, and Gauguin dazed and dazzled American observers. Critics attacked the show as worthless and depraved, but it was a clear glimpse of the future of art. The Postimpressionists changed the direction of twentieth-century art and influenced adventuresome American painters. John Marin, Max Weber, Georgia O'Keeffe, Arthur Dove, and other modernists experimented in ways foreign to Henri's realists. Using bold colors and abstract patterns, they defied convention and worked to capture the energy of urban life.

Poetry experienced an extraordinary outburst. In 1912, Harriet Monroe started the magazine *Poetry* in Chicago; Ezra Pound and Vachel Lindsay, both daring experimenters with ideas and verse, were featured in the first issue. T. S. Eliot published the classic "Love Song of J. Alfred Prufrock" in *Poetry* in 1915. Attacked bitterly by conservative critics, the poem established Eliot's leadership among a group of poets who rejected traditional meter and rhyme as artificial constraints. Eliot, Pound, and Amy Lowell, among others, believed that the poet's task was to capture fleeting images in verse. Others experimenting with new techniques in poetry included Robert Frost, Edgar Lee Masters, and Carl Sandburg. True to the increasingly urban vision of America, Sandburg's poem "Chicago" celebrated the vitality of the city.

Conclusion: A Ferment of Discovery and Reform

Manners and morals change slowly, yet in the first two decades of the century, sweeping change was under way: anyone who doubted it could visit a gallery, see a film, listen to music, or read one of the new literary magazines. Garrets and galleries were filled with a breathtaking sense of excitement about new forms of expression.

The ferment of progressivism in the city, state, and nation reshaped the country. In a burst of reform, people built playgrounds, restructured taxes, regulated business, won the vote for women, shortened working hours, altered political systems, opened kindergartens, and improved factory safety. They tried to fulfill the national promise of dignity and liberty.

Across America, there was a mood of excitement, a feeling expressed in the best efforts of artists and politicians. Racism, repression, and labor conflict were present, but there was also talk of hope, progress, and change. In politics, science, journalism, education, and a host of other fields, people believed for a time that they could make a difference, and in trying to do so, they became part of the progressive generation.

Key Terms

muckrakers, p. 427
progressivism, p. 427
Niagara Movement, p. 432
National Association for the Advancement of Colored People (NAACP), p. 432
birds of passage, p. 433
Women's Trade Union League (WTUL), p. 434
Industrial Workers of the World (IWW), p. 434
Ashcan School, p. 439

Recommended Reading

There are several important analyses of the Progressive Era, including Robert H. Wiebe, *The Search for Order, 1877–1920* (1967); Richard Hofstadter, *The Age of Reform* (1955); Samuel P. Hays, *The Response to Industrialism* (1957); and Gabriel Kolko, *The Triumph of Conservatism* (1963). C. Vann Woodward, *Origins of the New South 1877–1913* (1951), is a superb account of developments in the South, along with William A. Link, *The Paradox of Southern Progressivism, 1880–1930* (1992).

George William Shea, *Spoiled Silk: The Red Mayor and the Great Paterson Textile Strike* (2001), and Elliot J. Gorn, *Mother Jones: The Most Dangerous Woman in America* (2001), look at radical labor movements; David I. Macleod, *The Age of the Child: Children in America, 1890–1920* (1998), at children; Nancy C. Unger, *Fighting Bob LaFollette: The Righteous Reformer* (2000), and Patricia A. Schechter, *Ida B. Wells-Barnett and American Reform, 1880–1930* (2001), at specific reformers. Gary Scott Smith, *The Search for Social Salvation: Social Christianity and America, 1880–1925* (2000), and Thomas Winter, *Making Men, Making Class: The YMCA and Workingmen, 1877–1920* (2002), examine the role of religion.

James T. Kloppenberg, *Uncertain Victory: Social Democracy and Progressivism in European and American Thought, 1870–1920* (1986), examines progressivism at home and abroad. C. Vann Woodward, *The Strange Career of Jim Crow* (1955), traces the civil rights setbacks of the Progressive Era.

For a list of additional titles related to this chapter's topics, please see http://www.ablongman.com/divine.

Suggested Web Sites

NAACP Online

http://www.naacp.org/
The National Association for the Advancement of Colored People official Web site explains its mission and includes a primary document explaining the start of the NAACP.

The Evolution of the Conservation Movement, 1850–1920

http://memory.loc.gov/ammem/amrvhtml/conshome.html
This American Memory site brings together scores of primary sources and photographs about "the historical formation and cultural foundations of the movement to conserve and protect America's natural heritage."

The Triangle Shirtwaist Factory Fire, March 25, 1911

http://www.ilr.cornell.edu/trianglefire/
The Kheel Center for Labor-Management Documentation and Archives at Cornell University put together this excellent site composed of oral histories, cartoons, images, and essays.

Labor-Management Conflict in American History

http://www.history.ohio-state.edu/projects/laborconflict/
This site at Ohio State University includes primary accounts of some of the major events in the history of labor-management conflict in the late nineteenth and early twentieth centuries.

Inside an American Factory: The Westinghouse Works, 1904

http://lcweb2.loc.gov/ammem/papr/west/westhome.html
Part of the American Memory Project at the Library of Congress, this site provides a glimpse inside a turn-of-the-century factory.

African American Women Writers of the Nineteenth Century

http://digital.nypl.org/schomburg/writers_aa19/
The New York Public Library's Schomburg Center for Research in Black Culture maintains this site that contains a large number of digital texts by African American women of the nineteenth century.

Touring Turn-of-the-Century America: Photographs from the Detroit Publishing Company, 1880–1920

http://memory.loc.gov/ammem/detroit/dethome.html
This Library of Congress collection has thousands of photographs from turn-of-the-century America.

Bill Haywood Trial (1907)

http://www.law.umkc.edu/faculty/projects/ftrials/haywood/haywood.htm
This site contains images, chronology, court, and official documents maintained by Dr. Doug Linder at University of Missouri-Kansas City Law School.

Margaret Sanger Papers Project

http://www.nyu.edu/projects/sanger/
This site at New York University contains information about Margaret Sanger and digital versions of several of her works.

Scott Joplin, 1868-1917

http://www.lsjunction.com/people/joplin.htm
This site offers information on Joplin and ragtime music.

National Arts and Crafts Archives

http://arts-crafts.com/index.html
This site serves as a guide to materials on the Arts and Crafts movement, which lasted roughly from 1890 to 1929.

Chapter 23

From Roosevelt to Wilson in the Age of Progressivism

The Republicans Split

On a sunny spring morning in 1909, Theodore Roosevelt left New York for an African safari. An ex-president at the age of 50, he had turned over the White House to his chosen successor, William Howard Taft, and now he was off to hunt wild game. Some hoped he would not return. "I trust some lion will do its duty," Wall Street magnate J. P. Morgan said. Though he had built a reputation as an ardent conservationist, Roosevelt shot lions, elephants, hippos, rhinoceroses, and other animals, acquiring nearly three hundred trophies in all.

Afterward, Roosevelt set off on a tour of Europe. He argued with the pope, dined with the king and queen of Italy, and happily spent five hours reviewing troops of the German empire. He also followed events back home, where, in the judgment of many friends, Taft was not working out as president.

Taft was puzzled by his lack of success. Honest and warmhearted, he had intended to continue Roosevelt's policies. But events turned out differently. The conservative and progressive wings of the Republican party split, and Taft often sided with the conservatives. Progressive Republicans urged Roosevelt to take control again of the party and the country.

Roosevelt returned to New York harbor on June 18, 1910, to the sound of naval guns and loud cheers. Greeting Gifford Pinchot, a close friend and one of Taft's leading opponents, with a hearty "Hello, Gifford," Roosevelt slipped away to his home in Oyster Bay, New York, where other friends awaited him.

Taft, who still viewed himself as a disciple of Roosevelt's, invited Teddy to spend a night or two at the White House, but the ex-president declined. Relations between the two friends cooled. "It is hard, very hard," Taft said in 1911, "to see a devoted friendship going to pieces like a rope of sand."

A YEAR LATER, NO HINT OF FRIENDSHIP remained as Taft and Roosevelt engaged in a desperate fight for the Republican presidential nomination. Taft won the nomination, but Roosevelt, angry and ambitious, bolted and helped form a new party, the Progressive (or "Bull Moose") party, to unseat Taft and capture the White House. With Taft, Roosevelt, Woodrow Wilson (the Democratic party's candidate), and Socialist party candidate Eugene V. Debs all in the race, the election of 1912 became one of the most exciting in American history.

OUTLINE

The Spirit of Progressivism

Reform in the Cities and States

The Republican Roosevelt

Roosevelt Progressivism at Its Height

The Ordeal of William Howard Taft

Woodrow Wilson's New Freedom

Conclusion: The Fruits of Progressivism

It was also one of the most important. The election of 1912 became a forum for Americans' concerns about the social and economic effects of urban-industrial growth. Each candidate offered a different vision for the future, and each expressed an aspect of progressive reform.

Those currents built on a number of important developments, including the rise of a new professional class, reform movements designed to cure problems in the cities and states, and the activist, achievement-oriented administrations of Roosevelt and Wilson. Together they produced the age of Progressivism.

The Spirit of Progressivism

For more than two decades, progressivism dominated American life, and in one way or another, it influenced almost everything that came after it. Politically, it fostered a reform movement that sought solutions for the problems of city, state, and nation. Intellectually, it drew on the expertise of the new social sciences and reflected a shift from older absolutes such as religion to newer schools of thought that emphasized relativism and physiological explanations for behavior and the role of the environment in human development. Culturally, it inspired fresh modes of expression in dance, film, painting, literature, and architecture. Touching individuals in different ways, progressivism became a set of attitudes as well as a definable movement.

Unlike populism, which grew mostly in the rural South and West, progressivism drew support across society. Progressivism appealed to the expanding middle class, prosperous farmers, and skilled laborers; it also attracted significant support in the business community. Leadership came mainly from young, educated men and women. Many of them belonged to the professions—law, medicine, religion, business, teaching, and social work—and they thought they could use their expertise to improve society. They believed in progress and disliked waste. No single issue or concern united them all, but they shared a desire for change. Some wanted to purify municipal politics, others to clean up city streets or to eradicate prostitution. They were Democrats, Republicans, socialists, and independents.

Progressives believed that if people knew the truth, they would act on it. Progress depended on knowledge. The progressives stressed individual morality and collective action, the scientific method, and the value of expert opinion. Like contemporary business leaders, they valued system, planning, management, and predictability. They wanted not only reform but also efficiency.

Historians once viewed progressivism as the triumph of one group in society over another: urban reformers challenged city bosses; farmers took on powerful railroads. Now they stress the way progressivism brought people together rather than driving them apart. Disparate groups united in an effort to improve the well-being of many groups in society.

The Rise of the Professions

Progressivism fed on an organizational impulse that encouraged people to join forces, share information, and solve problems. Between 1890 and 1920, a host of national societies and associations took shape—nearly four hundred of them in just three decades. Groups such as the National Child Labor Committee, which lobbied for legislation to regulate the employment and working conditions of children, were formed to attack specific issues. Other groups reflected one of the most significant developments in American society at the turn of the century—the rise of the professions.

Growing rapidly in these years, the professions—law, medicine, religion, business, teaching, and social work—were the source of much of the leadership of the progressive movement. The professions attracted young, educated men and women, who in turn were part of a larger trend: a dramatic increase in the number of individuals working in administrative and professional jobs. In businesses, these people were managers, architects, technicians, and accountants. In city governments, they were experts in everything from education to sanitation. They organized and ran the urban-industrial society.

Together these professionals formed part of a new middle class whose members did not derive their status from birth or inherited wealth, as had many members of the older middle class. Instead, they moved ahead through education and personal accomplishment. They had worked to become doctors, lawyers, ministers, and teachers. Proud of their skills, they were ambitious and self-confident, and they thought of themselves as experts who could use their knowledge for the benefit of society.

As a way of asserting their status, they formed professional societies to look after their interests and govern entry into their professions. Just a few years before, for example, a doctor had become a doctor simply by stocking up on patent medicines and hanging out a sign. Now, doctors began to insist they were part of a medical profession, and they wanted to set educational requirements and minimum standards for practice. In 1901, they reorganized the American Medical Association (AMA) and made it into a modern national professional society.

Other groups and professions showed the same pattern. Lawyers formed bar associations, created examining boards, and lobbied for regulations restricting entry into the profession. Teachers organized the National Education Association (1905) and pressed for teacher certification and compulsory education laws. Social workers formed the National Federation of Settlements (1911); business leaders created the National Association of Manufacturers (1895) and the U.S. Chamber of Commerce (1912); and farmers joined the National Farm Bureau Federation to spread information about farming and to try to improve their lot.

The Social-Justice Movement

Progressivism began in the cities during the 1890s. It first took hold among settlement workers and others interested in freeing individuals from the crushing impact of the slum and the factory. Ministers, intellectuals, social workers, and lawyers joined in a **social-justice movement** that focused national attention on the need for tenement house laws, more stringent child-labor legislation, and better working conditions for women. They brought pressure on municipal agencies for more and better parks, playgrounds, day nurseries, schools, and community services. Blending private and public action, settlement leaders turned increasingly to government aid.

social-justice movement During the 1890s and after, this important movement attracted followers who sought to free people from the often devastating impact of urban life. It focused on the need for tenement house laws, more stringent child-labor regulations, and better working conditions for women. Social-justice reformers also put pressure on municipal agencies for better community services and facilities.

Social-justice reformers were more interested in societal cures than individual charity. Unlike earlier reformers, they saw problems as endless and interrelated; individuals became part of a city's larger patterns. With that insight, social service casework shifted from a focus on an individual's well-being to a scientific analysis of whole neighborhoods, occupations, and classes.

In 1900, Lawrence Veiller, a young social worker, put together a tenement house exhibition that included more than a thousand photographs, detailed maps of slum districts, statistical tables and charts, and graphic cardboard depictions of tenement blocks. Veiller correlated data on poverty and disease with housing conditions. Stirred by the public outcry, Governor Theodore Roosevelt appointed the New York State Tenement House Commission to do something about the problem.

With Veiller's success as a model, study after study analyzed the condition of the poor. Seeing their common problems, social-justice reformers formed the National Conference of Charities and Corrections, which in 1915 became the National Conference of Social Work. Through it, social workers discovered one another's efforts, shared methodology, and tried to establish themselves as a separate field within the social sciences. They formed professional schools at Harvard, the University of Chicago, and other major universities, and in 1909 they published their own magazine, *The Survey.* Instead of piecemeal reforms, they aimed at a comprehensive program of minimum wages, maximum hours, workers' compensation, and widows' pensions.

The Purity Crusade

Working in city neighborhoods, social-justice reformers were often struck by the degree to which alcohol affected the lives of the people they were trying to help. Workers drank away their wages; some men spent more time at the saloon than at home. Drunkenness caused violence, and it angered employers, who did not want intoxicated workers on the job. In countless ways, alcohol wasted human resources, the reformers believed, and along with business leaders, ministers, and others, they launched a crusade to remove the evils of drink from American life.

At the head of the crusade was the Women's Christian Temperance Union (WCTU), which had grown steadily since its founding in the 1870s. By 1911, the WCTU had nearly a quarter of a million members, the largest organization of women in American history to that time. In 1893, it was joined by the Anti-Saloon League, and together the groups pressed to abolish alcohol and the places where it was consumed. In the midst of the moral fervor of World War I, they succeeded, and the Eighteenth Amendment to the Constitution, prohibiting the manufacture, sale, and transportation of intoxicating liquors, took effect in January 1920.

The amendment encountered troubles later in the 1920s as the social atmosphere changed, but at the time it passed, progressives thought prohibition was a major step toward eliminating social instability and moral wrong. In a similar fashion, some progressive reformers also worked to get rid of prostitution, convinced that poverty and ignorance drove women to the trade. By 1915, nearly every state had banned brothels, and in 1910, Congress passed the Mann Act, which prohibited the interstate transportation of women for immoral purposes. Like the campaign against liquor, the campaign against prostitution reflected the era's desire to purify and elevate, often through the instrument of government action.

Woman Suffrage, Women's Rights

Women played an essential role in the social-justice movement. Feminists were particularly active, especially in the political sphere, between 1890 and 1914. Working-class as well as college-educated women pushed for reforms. From 1890 to 1910, the work of a number of national women's organizations, including the National Council of Mothers and the Women's Trade Union League, furthered the aims of the progressive movement. The National Association of Colored Women, the first black-sponsored social service agency in the nation, was founded in 1895.

Organizations such as the General Federation of Women's Clubs transformed literary meetings into social-action gatherings. Drawing attention to women's concern for social reform, Sarah P. Decker, who became president of the federation in 1904, told the members of her organization, "Dante is dead. . . . I think it is time that we dropped the study of his *Inferno* and turned our attention to our own."

Reluctant at first, the federation eventually lent support to woman suffrage, a cause that dated back to 1848. The suffrage movement suffered from disunity, male opposition, disagreement over whether to seek action at the state or national level, resistance from the Catholic Church, and opposition from liquor interests, who linked the cause to prohibition.

Women in the social-justice movement needed to influence elected officials—most of them men—whom women could not reach through the vote. Because politics was an avenue for reform, women activists became involved in the suffrage

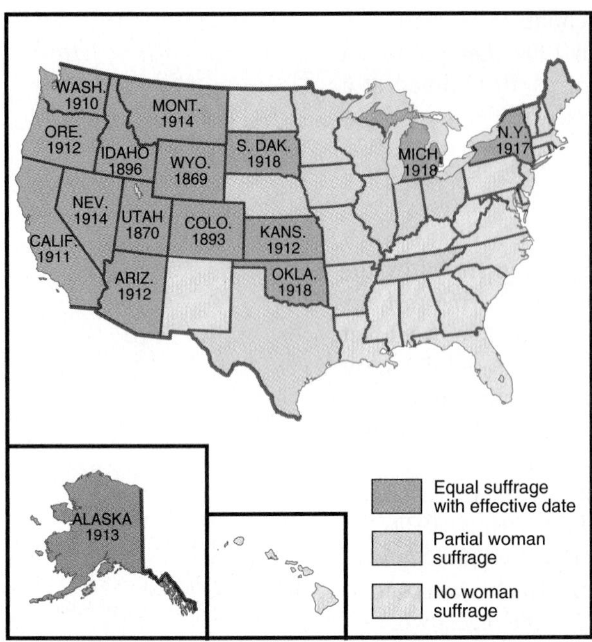

WOMAN SUFFRAGE BEFORE 1920 *State-by-state gains in woman suffrage were limited to the Far West and were agonizingly slow in the early years of the twentieth century.* ❖

movement in growing numbers. After years of disagreement, the two major suffrage organizations, the National Woman Suffrage Association and the American Woman Suffrage Association, merged in 1890 to form the National American Woman Suffrage Association. The merger opened a new phase of the suffrage movement, characterized by unity and a tightly controlled national organization.

In 1900, Carrie Chapman Catt became president of the National American Woman Suffrage Association, which by 1920 had nearly two million members. The association believed in peaceful lobbying to win the vote. Members of the Congressional Union, such as Alice Paul, were more militant. They interrupted public meetings, focused on Congress rather than the states, and in 1917 picketed the White House. The issue attracted many progressives, who believed woman suffrage would purify politics. In 1918, the House passed a constitutional amendment stating simply that the right to vote shall not be denied "on account of sex." The Senate and enough states followed, and after three generations of suffragist efforts, the Nineteenth Amendment took effect in 1920.

The social-justice movement had the most success in passing state laws limiting the working hours of women. By 1913, thirty-nine states had set maximum working hours for women or banned the employment of women at night. As early as 1900, twenty-eight states had laws regulating child labor. But the courts often ruled against such laws, and families, needing extra income, sometimes ignored them.

In 1916, President Woodrow Wilson backed a law to limit child labor, the Keating-Owen Act, but the Supreme Court, in *Hammer* v. *Dagenhart* (1918), overturned it as an improper regulation of local labor conditions. In 1919, Congress tried again in the Second Child Labor Act, also struck down by the Court in *Baily* v. *Drexel Furniture Company* (1922). Not until the 1930s did Congress succeed in passing a national child labor law that the Supreme Court allowed to stand.

A Ferment of Ideas: Challenging the Status Quo

A dramatic shift in ideas became one of the most important forces behind progressive reform. Most of the ideas focused on the role of the environment in shaping human behavior. Progressive reformers accepted society's growing complexity and called for a more scientific approach to social problems, allowed room for new the-

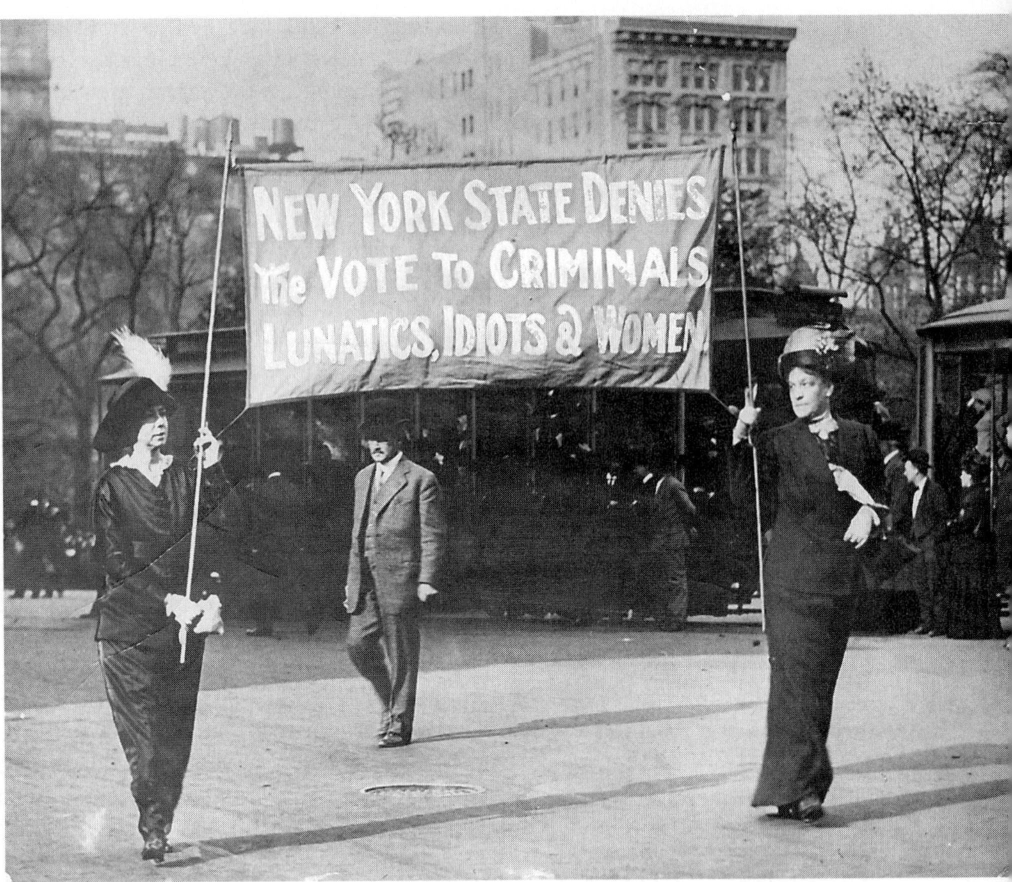

Woman suffrage was a key element in the social-justice movement. Without the right to vote, women working actively for reform had little real power to influence elected officials to support their endeavors. ❖

ories, and rejected age-encrusted divine or natural "laws" in favor of ideas and actions that worked.

A new doctrine, called **pragmatism,** emerged in this ferment of ideas. It came from William James, the Harvard psychologist who was the key figure in American thought from the 1890s to World War I. A warm, tolerant person, James believed that truth should work for the individual, and it should work best not in abstraction but in action. "True ideas are those we can assimilate, validate, corroborate, and verify. False ideas are those we cannot."

pragmatism A doctrine that emerged in the early twentieth century, built largely on the ideas of psychologist and philosopher William James. Pragmatists were impatient with theories that held truth to be abstract; they believed that truth should work for the individual. They also believed that people were not only shaped by their environment but also helped to shape it. Ideas that worked, according to pragmatists, became truth.

People, James thought, were not only shaped by their environment but gave it shape. In *Pragmatism* (1907), he praised "tough-minded" individuals who could live effectively in a world with no easy answers. The tough-minded accepted change; they knew how to pick manageable problems, gather facts, discard ideas that did not work, and act on those that did. Ideas that worked became truth. "What is the 'cash value' of a thought, idea or belief?" James asked. Does it work? Does it make a difference to the individual who experiences it? "The ultimate test for us of what a truth means," said James, "is the conduct it dictates."

The most influential educator of the Progressive Era, John Dewey, applied pragmatism to educational reform. He introduced an educational revolution, stressing children's needs and capabilities. Dewey argued that thought evolves in relation to the environment and that education is directly related to experience. New ideas in education, he said, are "as much a product of the changed social situation, and as much an effort to meet the needs of the society that is forming, as are changes in modes of industry and commerce." He opposed memorization and dogmatic, authoritarian teaching methods; he emphasized personal growth, free inquiry, creativity, and cooperative learning.

Rejecting the older view of the law as universal and unchanging, lawyers and legal theorists instead interpreted it as a reflection of the environment—an instrument for social change. A movement grew among judges for "sociological jurisprudence" that related the law to social reform. Increasingly, judges and lawyers began to consider crime as much the result of problems in society as a reflection of individual weakness.

Louis D. Brandeis's career illustrated the change. A rich corporate lawyer, he changed his mind about social issues during the depression of the 1890s, and as the "people's attorney," he fought corporate abuses and political corruption. In 1908, he accepted an invitation from the National Consumers' League to defend an Oregon law limiting working hours for women to ten hours a day.

Brandeis decided on a new kind of argument. With the help of health-care reformer Lillian Wald, he compiled masses of medical and sociological data, and in the 104-page brief he submitted to the Court, only two pages were devoted to traditional legal precedents. The rest consisted of reports from factory inspectors, health and hygiene commissioners, and expert commissions, all showing that the ten-hour law was necessary to protect the health, safety, and morals of women in Oregon.

Muller v. *Oregon* This 1908 Supreme Court decision established special protections for working women, upholding an Oregon law that limited women working in factories and laundries to a ten-hour work day.

Brandeis brief Filed by attorney Louis D. Brandeis in the 1908 Supreme Court case of *Muller* v. *Oregon,* this brief presented only two pages of legal precedents, but 115 pages of sociological evidence on the negative effects of long workdays on women's health and thus on women as mothers. The brief expanded the definition of legal evidence.

Agreeing, the Supreme Court in ***Muller* v. *Oregon*** (1908) upheld the Oregon statute, and the famous **Brandeis brief,** based on environmental data rather than legal precedent, influenced lawyers and courts across the country. Like so many other reform efforts during these years, it assumed that changes in the environment could improve the lives of people and produce a better society.

Socialism, a reformist political philosophy, grew dramatically before the First World War. Organized in 1901, the Socialist party of America doubled in membership between 1904 and 1908, then tripled in the four years after that. By 1911, there were Socialist mayors in thirty-two cities. Although its doctrines were aimed at an urban proletariat, the Socialist party also drew support in parts of the rural South and West.

Eugene V. Debs, five times the party's presidential candidate, offset the popular image of the wild-eyed radical. A gentle and reflective man, Debs never developed a cohesive platform, but he was an eloquent, passionate, and visionary leader. He led the American Railway Union into the Pullman strike. Running for president, he garnered 100,000 votes in 1900; 400,000 in 1904; and 900,000 in 1912, the party's peak year.

Reform in the Cities and States

Believing in government as an agent of change, the progressives wanted to curb the influence of "special interests" and make government follow the public will. Once this goal had been achieved, they welcomed government action at whatever level was appropriate. The use of federal power increased, along with the power and prestige of the presidency. Most important, the progressives believed in the ability of experts to solve problems. At every level, thousands of commissions and agencies took form. Staffed by trained experts, they oversaw a multitude of matters, from railroad rates to public health.

Interest Groups and the Decline of Popular Politics

Placing government in the hands of experts was one way to get it out of the clutches of politicians and political parties. The direct primary, which allowed voters rather than parties to choose candidates for office, was another way. Such initiatives were part of a fundamental change in the way Americans viewed their political systems.

One sign of the change was that fewer and fewer people were going to the polls. Voter turnout dropped dramatically after 1900, when the intense partisanship of the decades after the Civil War gave way to media-oriented political campaigns based largely on the personalities of the candidates. From 1876 to 1900, the average turnout in presidential elections was 77 percent. From 1900 to 1916, it was 65 percent, and in the 1920s, it dropped to 52 percent, close to the average today. Turnout was lowest among young people, immigrants, the poor, and, ironically, the newly franchised women.

It was particularly low in the South, where conservative whites used restrictive election laws to keep blacks and others from the polls. Although the decline in the North was less sharp, the reasons for it were more complex. By the 1920s, as many as one-quarter of all eligible northern voters never cast a ballot.

There were numerous causes for the fall-off, but among the most important was the fact that people had found another way to achieve some of the objectives they had once assigned to political parties. They had found the "interest group," a means of action that assumed importance in this era and has been a major feature of politics ever since. Professional societies, trade associations, labor organizations, farm lobbies, and scores of other interest groups worked outside the party system to pressure government for things their members wanted. Social workers, women's clubs, reform groups, and others learned to apply pressure in similar ways, and the result was much of the significant legislation of the Progressive Era.

Reform in the Cities

In the early years of the twentieth century, urban reform movements spread across the nation. In 1894, the National Municipal League was organized, and it became the forum for debate over civic reform, changes in the tax laws, and municipal ownership of public utilities. Within a few years, nearly every city had a variety of clubs and organizations directed at improving the quality of city life.

In the 1880s, reformers would call an evening conference, pass resolutions, and then go home; after 1900, they formed associations, adopted long-range policies, and hired employees to achieve them. In the mid-1890s, only Chicago had an urban reform league with a full-time paid executive; within a decade, there were such leagues in every major city.

In one locale after another, reformers reordered municipal government. They broadened the scope of utility regulation, restricted city franchises, updated tax assessments, and tried to clean up the electoral machinery. Committed to efficiency and, above all, results, they developed a trained civil service to oversee planning and day-to-day operations.

In constructing their model governments, urban reformers often turned to recent advances in business management and organization. They stressed continuity and expertise, a system in which professional experts staffed a government overseen by elected officials. They hired engineers to manage utility and water systems, physicians and nurses to improve public health, and city planners to supervise park and highway development. The growing number of experts and commissions widened the gap between voters and decision makers but dramatically improved the efficiency of government.

As cities exploded in size, they freed themselves from the tight controls of state legislatures and began to experiment with their governments. Galveston, Texas, struggling to recover from a devastating hurricane in 1900, pioneered the commission form of government, with commissions of appointed experts, rather than elected officials, running the city. Other cities simply hired a city manager.

In the race for reform, a number of city mayors won national reputations working to modernize taxes, clean up politics, lower utility rates, and control the awarding of valuable city franchises. In Toledo, Ohio, Mayor Samuel M. ("Golden Rule") Jones labored to improve the quality of life for the people in his city. In Cleveland, Ohio, Mayor Tom L. Johnson also fought to improve city life. He cut down on corruption, cut off special privileges, updated taxes, and gained Cleveland a reputation as the country's best-governed city.

Finding it difficult to regulate powerful city utilities and keep their costs down, Johnson and mayors in other cities turned more and more to public ownership of gas, electricity, water, and transportation. Called "gas and water socialism"—in which cities owned their own gas, electricity, water, and other utilities—the idea spread swiftly. In 1896, fewer than half of American cities owned their own waterworks; by 1915, almost two-thirds did.

Action in the States

Reformers soon discovered, however, that many problems lay beyond a city's boundaries, and they turned for action to the state government. From the 1890s to 1920, they worked to stiffen state laws governing the labor of women and children, create and strengthen commissions to regulate railroads and utilities, impose corporate and inheritance taxes, improve mental and penal institutions, and allocate more funds for state universities, the training ground for the experts and educated citizenry needed for the new society.

Maryland passed the first workers' compensation law in 1902; soon most industrial states had such legislation. Between 1900 and 1920, states also increasingly adopted factory inspection laws, mandated insurance for the victims of factory accidents, and enacted employers' liability laws.

New York was one of the states that led the way. Around 1905, a series of dramatic investigations revealed a systematic and corrupt alliance between politicians and business leaders in the gas, electricity, and insurance industries. Responding immediately, an angry public supported greater state regulation and management by independent expert commissions. In 1905 and 1906, the state established regulatory boards to oversee utilities and insurance; it also outlawed corporate contributions to political campaigns and restricted business lobbying in the state legislature.

To regulate business, virtually every state created regulatory commissions, empowered to examine corporate books and hold public hearings. Building on earlier experience, after 1900 they were given new power to initiate actions, rather than await complaints, and in some cases to set maximum prices and rates. State regulatory commissions pioneered methods later adopted in federal legislation of 1906 and 1910. Some business leaders supported the federal laws, preferring one regulatory agency to dozens of separate state commissions.

Historians have long praised the regulation movement, but the commissions did not always act wisely or even in the public interest. Elective commissions often produced commissioners who had little knowledge of corporate affairs. Appointive commissions sometimes fared better, but they, too, had to oversee extraordinarily complex businesses such as the railroads, shaping everything from wages to train schedules.

Emphasizing people's involvement in politics, progressives, like the populists, backed three measures to make officeholders responsive to popular will: the initiative, which allowed voters to propose new laws; the referendum, which allowed them to accept or reject a law at the ballot box; and the recall, which gave them a way to remove an elected official from office. They also backed the direct election of senators and direct primaries as instruments to expand the role of the electorate.

As attention shifted from the cities to the states, reform governors throughout the country won growing reputations. Robert M. La Follette of Wisconsin—talented, aggressive, and a superb stump speaker—became the most famous of a group that included Hiram Johnson in California, Woodrow Wilson in New Jersey, and Charles Evans Hughes in New York. In 1901, La Follette became governor of Wisconsin. In the following six years, he put together the "Wisconsin Idea," one of the most important reform programs in the history of state government. He established an industrial commission to regulate factory safety and sanitation; improved education, workers' compensation, public utility controls, and resource conservation; and lowered railroad rates. In addition, under La Follette, Wisconsin also became the first to adopt a state income tax.

Like other progressives, La Follette drew on expert advice and relied on academic figures such as Richard Ely at the University of Wisconsin to provide facts and figures to support the measures he favored. Theodore Roosevelt called La Follette's Wisconsin "the laboratory of democracy," and the Wisconsin Idea soon spread to many other states.

After 1905, the progressives looked more and more to Washington. For one thing, Theodore Roosevelt was there. But progressives also had a growing sense that many concerns—corporations and conservation, factory safety, child labor—crossed state lines. Federal action seemed desirable; specific reforms fit into a larger plan perhaps best seen from the nation's center. Within a few years, La Follette and Hiram Johnson became senators, and while reform went on back home, the focus of progressivism shifted to Washington.

The Republican Roosevelt

When President William McKinley died of gunshot wounds in September 1901 (see Chapter 20), Vice President Theodore Roosevelt succeeded him in the White House. Roosevelt continued some of McKinley's policies, developed others of his own, and brought to them all the particular exuberance of his own personality.

Only 42, Roosevelt was then the youngest president in American history. Open, aggressive, and high-spirited, he worked long hours; a steady procession of politicians, labor leaders, industrialists, poets, artists, and writers paraded through the White House. Most of the people who met Roosevelt were captivated by his charming manner and impressed by the breadth of his knowledge.

If McKinley cut down on presidential isolation, Roosevelt virtually ended it. The presidency, he thought, was the "bully pulpit," a forum of ideas and leadership for the nation. The president was a "steward of the people," and the self-confident Roosevelt enlisted talented associates to help him steer the ship of state.

In 1901, Roosevelt invited Booker T. Washington, the prominent black educator, to lunch at the White House. Many Southerners protested, and they protested again when Roosevelt appointed several blacks to important federal offices in South Carolina and Mississippi. At first, Roosevelt tried to build a biracial, "black and tan" southern Republican party. He also denounced lynching and ordered the Justice Department to act against peonage.

But the president soon retreated to a position consistent with his own belief in black inferiority. He joined others in blaming black soldiers stationed near Brownsville, Texas, after a night of violence there in August 1906. Acting quickly and on little evidence, he discharged "without honor" three companies of black troops. Six of the soldiers who were discharged held the Congressional Medal of Honor.

Busting the Trusts

Like most people, Roosevelt wavered on the trusts. Large-scale production and industrial growth, he believed, were natural and beneficial; they needed only to be controlled. Still, he questioned the trusts' impact on local enterprise and individual opportunity. Distinguishing between "good" and "bad" trusts, he pledged to protect the former while controlling the latter.

At first, Roosevelt hoped the glare of publicity would be enough to uncover and correct business evils, and in public, he both praised and attacked the trusts. To aid him in this task, he asked Congress in 1903 to create the Department of Commerce and Labor, with a Bureau of Corporations empowered to investigate businesses engaged in interstate commerce. When Congress hesitated, Roosevelt mustered public opinion behind the legislation, which then easily passed.

A 1909 cartoon illustrates Theodore Roosevelt's promise to break up only those "bad trusts" that were hurtful to the general welfare. Despite his reputation as a trust buster, Roosevelt dissolved relatively few trusts. ❖

Roosevelt also undertook more direct legal action. On February 14, 1902, he instructed the Justice Department to bring suit against the Northern Securities Company for violation of the Sherman Antitrust Act. It was a shrewd move. A mammoth holding company, Northern Securities controlled the massive rail networks of the Northern Pacific, the Great Northern, and the Chicago, Burlington and Quincy railroads. Some of the most prominent names in business were behind the giant company, including J. P. Morgan and Company and the Rockefeller interests. Morgan was shocked; he complained that the president had not acted like a "gentleman."

In 1904, the Supreme Court, in a five-to-four decision, upheld the suit against Northern Securities and ordered the company dissolved. Roosevelt was jubilant, and he followed up the victory with several other antitrust suits. Between 1902 and 1907, he moved against the beef trust, the American Tobacco Company, the Du Pont Corporation, and Standard Oil.

But Roosevelt's policies were not always clear, nor were his actions always consistent. He frequently took the advice of important business leaders, and he asked for (and received) business support in his bid for reelection in 1904 (including $150,000 from Morgan). In 1907, he even permitted Morgan's U.S. Steel to absorb the Tennessee Coal and Iron Company, an important competitor.

Roosevelt, in truth, was not a "trust buster," although he was frequently called that. William Howard Taft, his successor in the White House, initiated forty-three antitrust indictments in four years—nearly twice as many as the twenty-five Roosevelt initiated in the seven years of his presidency.

"Square Deal" in the Coalfields

A few months after announcing the Northern Securities suit, Roosevelt intervened in a major labor dispute involving the anthracite coal miners of northeastern Pennsylvania. Led by John Mitchell, a moderate labor leader, the United Mine Workers demanded wage increases, an eight-hour workday, and company recognition of the union. The coal companies refused, and in May 1902, some 140,000 miners walked off the job. The mines closed.

As months passed and the strike continued, coal prices rose. As winter approached, schools, hospitals, and factories ran short of coal. Public opinion turned against the companies. Morgan and other industrial leaders privately urged them to settle, but George F. Baer, head of one of the largest companies, refused: "The rights and interests of the laboring man," Baer said, "will be protected and cared for—not by the labor agitators, but by the Christian men to whom God in his infinite wisdom has given the control of the property interests of this country."

Roosevelt was furious. Complaining of the companies' arrogance, he invited both sides in the dispute to an October 1902 conference at the White House. There Mitchell took a moderate tone and offered to submit the issues to arbitration, but the companies refused to budge. Roosevelt ordered the army to prepare to seize the mines and then leaked word of his intent to Wall Street leaders.

Alarmed, Morgan and others again urged a settlement, and at last the companies agreed to accept the recommendations of an independent commission to be appointed by the president. In late October, the strikers returned to work, and in March 1903, the commission awarded them a 10 percent wage increase and a cut in working hours. It recommended, however, against union recognition. The coal companies, in turn, were encouraged to raise prices to offset the wage increase.

Roosevelt came increasingly to see the federal government as an honest and impartial broker between powerful elements in society. Rather than leaning toward labor, he pursued a middle path to curb corporate or labor abuses, abolish privilege, and enlarge individual opportunity. Often he backed reforms in part to head off more radical measures.

During the 1904 campaign, Roosevelt called his actions in the coal miners' strike a "square deal" for both labor and capital, a term that stuck to his administration. Roosevelt was not the first president to take a stand for labor, but he was the first to bring opposing sides in a labor dispute to the White House to settle it. He was the first to threaten to seize a major industry, and he was the first to appoint a commission whose decision both sides agreed to accept.

Roosevelt Progressivism at Its Height

In the election of 1904, the popular Roosevelt soundly drubbed his Democratic opponent, Alton B. Parker of New York, and the Socialist party candidate, Eugene V. Debs of Indiana. In a landslide victory, he received 57 percent of the vote to Parker's 38 percent. Overjoyed, he pledged that "under no circumstances will I be a candidate for or accept another nomination," a statement he later regretted.

Following his election, Roosevelt laid out a reform program that included railroad regulation, employers' liability for federal employees, greater federal control over corporations, and laws regulating child labor, factory inspection, and slum clearance in the District of Columbia. He turned first to railroad regulation. In 1903, he had worked with Congress to pass the moderate Elkins Act to prohibit railroad rebates and increase the powers of the Interstate Commerce Commission (ICC). In 1904 and 1905, he wanted much more, and he urged Congress to empower the ICC to set reasonable and nondiscriminatory rates and prevent inequitable practices.

Widespread demand for railroad regulation strengthened Roosevelt's hand. He maneuvered cannily, skillfully trading congressional support for a strong railroad measure in return for his promise to postpone a reduction of the tariff. The result was the passage of the **Hepburn Act** of 1906, strengthening the rate-making power of the ICC. It made ICC orders binding, pending any court appeals, thus placing the burden of proof on the companies. Delighted, Roosevelt viewed the Hepburn Act as a major step in his plan for continuous, expert federal control over industry.

Hepburn Act A law that strengthened the rate-making power of the Interstate Commerce Commission, reflecting the era's desire to control the power of the railroads. It increased the ICC's membership from five to seven, empowered it to fix reasonable railroad rates, and broadened its jurisdiction. It also made ICC rulings binding pending court appeals.

President Roosevelt signed two important laws to regulate the food and drug industries. Both laws reflected public outcry over adulterated and poisonous food and drugs. Muckraking articles had touched frequently on filthy conditions in meatpacking houses, and Upton Sinclair's book *The Jungle* (1906) described them in terms graphic enough to send people reeling from the dinner table.

After reading *The Jungle,* Roosevelt ordered an investigation. The result, he said, was "hideous." Meat sales plummeted in the United States and Europe. Alarmed, the meatpackers themselves supported a reform law. The Meat Inspection Act of 1906, stiffer than the packers had wanted, set rules for sanitary meatpacking and government inspection of meat products.

A second measure, the Pure Food and Drug Act, passed more easily. Samuel Hopkins Adams, a reporter for *Collier's* magazine who had once considered a medical career, exposed the dangers of patent medicines. He sent medicine samples to Dr. Harvey W. Wiley, the chief chemist in the Department of Agriculture, for analysis. Wiley and his "poison squad" had previously tested various food preservatives, determined to put an end to adulterated foods. The evidence in hand, Wiley pushed for regulation, Roosevelt joined the fight, and the act passed on June 30, 1906, helped along by the appearance in February of Sinclair's *Jungle.* It represented a pioneering effort, through required labeling information, to ban the manufacture and sale of adulterated, misbranded, or unsanitary food or drugs.

An expert on birds, Roosevelt loved nature and the wilderness, and some of his most enduring accomplishments came in the field of **conservation.** Working closely with Gifford Pinchot, chief of the Forest Service, he established the first comprehensive national conservation policy. He undertook a major reclamation program and strengthened the forest preserve program. Broadening the concept of conservation, he placed power sites, coal lands, and oil reserves as well as national forests in the public domain. To Roosevelt, conservation meant the wise use of natural resources, not locking them away, so those who thought the wilderness should be preserved rather than developed generally opposed his policies.

As 1908 approached, Roosevelt became increasingly strident in his demand for sweeping reforms. He attacked "malefactors of great wealth," urged greater federal regulatory powers, criticized the conservatism of the federal courts, and called for laws protecting factory workers. Many business leaders blamed him for a severe financial panic in the autumn of 1907, and conservatives in Congress stiffened their opposition. Divisions between Republican conservatives and progressives grew.

Immensely popular, Roosevelt prepared in 1908 to turn over the White House to William Howard Taft, his close friend and colleague. He assured Americans that Taft would carry on his policies. As expected, Taft soundly defeated the Democratic standard-bearer, William Jennings Bryan. The Republicans retained control of Congress. Taft prepared to move into the White House, ready and willing to carry on the Roosevelt legacy.

❖ A Look at the Past ❖

Patent Medicine

Patent medicines such as this cough and kidney remedy had long been popular. Note the many ailments it claimed to relieve, the ingredients, and the statement of compliance with the Pure Food and Drug Act. Based on this information, do you think Reid's Cough and Kidney Remedy was effective? If not, why do you suppose people continued to buy it? What questions does this medicine raise about health, medical care, and the effectiveness of government regulations at the time?

The Ordeal of William Howard Taft

conservation As president, Theodore Roosevelt made this principle one of his administration's top goals. Conservation in his view aimed at protecting the nation's natural resources, but called for the wise use of them rather than locking them away.

The Republican national convention that nominated Taft satisfied neither Roosevelt nor Taft. The conservative Republicans controlled the convention, and the platform reflected conservative views on labor, the courts, and other issues. La Follette and other progressive Republicans were openly disappointed.

Taking office in 1909, Taft felt "just a bit like a fish out of water." A graduate of Yale Law School and a distinguished judge, Taft's public service record was impressive. As the head of the Philippine Commission and later as the first governor general of the Philippines, he had shown a talent for organization. In 1904, Roosevelt appointed him secretary of war, a post that again highlighted Taft's administrative

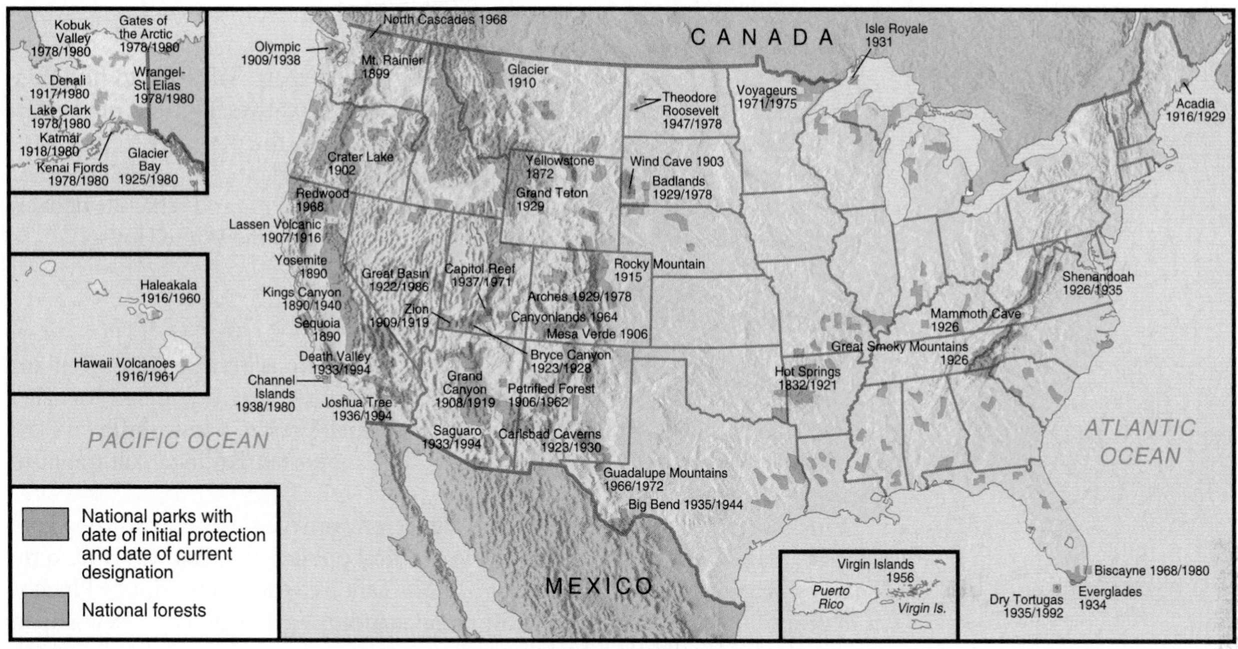

NATIONAL PARKS AND FORESTS *During the presidency of Theodore Roosevelt, who considered conservation his most important domestic achievement, millions of acres of land were set aside for national parks and forests.* ❖

skill. A good-natured man, Taft preferred diplomacy to warfare, and he liked to work behind the scenes rather than in the spotlight.

Weighing close to 300 pounds, Taft enjoyed conversation, golf and bridge, good food, and plenty of rest. He was also honest, kindly, and amiable, and in his own way he knew how to get things done. Next to Roosevelt, however, he seemed lazy and spiritless.

Taft's years as president were not happy. He presided over a Republican party torn with tensions that Roosevelt had either brushed aside or concealed. The tariff, business regulation, and other issues split conservatives and progressives, and Taft often wavered or sided with the conservatives. He never had Roosevelt's faith in the ability of government to impose reform and alter individual behavior, and his ear was attuned more toward business than labor and the unions.

Party Insurgency

Taft started his term with an attempt to curb the powerful Republican speaker of the House, crusty Joseph "Uncle Joe" Cannon of Illinois. Using the powers of his position, Cannon set House procedures, appointed committees, and virtually dictated legislation. He often opposed reform. In March 1909, thirty Republican congressmen joined Taft's efforts to curb Cannon's power, but Cannon retaliated and, threatening to block all tariff bills, forced a compromise. Taft stopped the anti-Cannon campaign for Cannon's pledge to help with tariff cuts.

The House quickly passed a bill providing for lower rates, but in the Senate, protectionists raised them. Senate leader Nelson A. Aldrich of Rhode Island introduced a revised bill that added more than eight hundred amendments to the House rates. Angry, La Follette and other Republicans attacked the bill as the child of special interests and urged Taft to defeat the high-tariff proposal. Taft wavered but in the end backed Aldrich. The Payne-Aldrich Act, passed in November 1909, called for higher rates than the original House bill, though it lowered them from the

Dingley Tariff of 1897. An unpopular law, it helped discredit Taft and revealed the tensions in the Republican party.

Republican progressives and conservatives drifted apart. Taft tried to find middle ground but leaned more and more toward the conservatives. By 1910, progressive Republicans no longer looked to Taft for leadership. To the president's embarrassment, progressive congressmen were able, without presidential support, to curtail Speaker Cannon's authority to dictate committee assignments and schedule debates. In progressive circles, hopes grew of returning Roosevelt to the White House.

The Ballinger-Pinchot Affair

The conservation issue dealt another blow to the relations between Roosevelt and Taft. In 1909, Richard A. Ballinger, Taft's secretary of the interior, offered for sale a million acres of public land that Pinchot, Taft's chief forester, had withdrawn from sale. Pinchot protested. After investigating, Taft supported Ballinger, although he asked Pinchot to remain in office.

Pinchot refused to drop the matter. He secretly provided material for two anti-Ballinger magazine articles, and he wrote a critical public letter that was read to the Senate by Senator Jonathan P. Dolliver of Iowa. Taft fired the insubordinate Pinchot, an appropriate action, but again lost some standing in the process. Newspapers wrongly portrayed the president as an opponent of conservation.

The Ballinger-Pinchot controversy obscured Taft's important contributions to conservation. He won from Congress the power to remove lands from sale, and he used it to conserve more land than Roosevelt did. Still, the controversy tarred Taft; it also upset Roosevelt and widened the gulf between the two men.

Taft Alienates the Progressives

Interested in railroad regulation, Taft backed a bill in 1910 to empower the ICC to fix maximum railroad rates. Although it was hotly debated, the Mann-Elkins Act of 1910 gave something to everyone. It gave the ICC power to set rates, stiffened long- and short-haul regulations, and placed telephone and telegraph companies under ICC jurisdiction. These provisions delighted progressives. The act also created a Commerce Court to hear appeals from ICC decisions, an addition that pleased conservatives. Progressive Republicans wanted to amend the bill to strengthen it, but Taft raised the issue of party loyalty and further alienated the progressives.

Taft attempted to defeat the progressive Republicans in the 1910 elections. He assisted in the establishment of antiprogressive organizations, and he opposed progressive Republican candidates for the Senate, including Hiram Johnson of California. Progressive Republicans retaliated by organizing a nationwide network of anti-Taft Progressive Republican Clubs.

The 1910 election results were a major setback for Taft and the Republicans, both conservatives and progressives. In party primaries, progressive Republicans overwhelmed most Taft candidates, and in November, the Democrats beat virtually everyone. For the first time since 1894, Republicans lost control of both the House and the Senate.

Despite the defeat, Taft pushed through several important progressive measures before his term ended. With the help of the new Democratic House, he backed laws to regulate safety in mines and on railroads, create a Children's Bureau in the federal government, establish employers' liability for all work done on government contracts, and mandate an eight-hour workday for government workers.

In 1909, Congress initiated a constitutional amendment authorizing an income tax, perhaps the most significant legislative measure of the twentieth century. The Sixteenth Amendment took effect early in 1913. A few months later, another important progressive goal was realized when the direct election of senators was ratified as the Seventeenth Amendment to the Constitution.

An ardent supporter of competition, Taft relentlessly pressed a campaign against trusts. In 1911, the Supreme Court, in cases against Standard Oil and American Tobacco, established the "rule of reason," which allowed the Court to determine whether a business exerted a "reasonable" restraint on trade. Taft thought the decisions gave the Court too much discretion, and he pushed ahead with the antitrust effort.

In October 1911, he sued U.S. Steel for its acquisition of the Tennessee Coal and Iron Company in 1907. Roosevelt had approved the acquisition, and the suit seemed designed to impugn that action. Furious, Roosevelt listened more and more to anti-Taft Republicans who urged him to run for president. In February 1912, he announced: "My hat is in the ring."

"I'm feeling like a bull moose!" declared Teddy Roosevelt while campaigning in 1912 as a Progressive and inadvertently renaming the new political party. The patch depicts a strong, independent animal, much like TR himself. In 1904 Roosevelt had won reelection by promising to give Americans a "square deal." ❖

Differing Philosophies in the Election of 1912

Delighted Democrats looked on as Taft and Roosevelt fought for the Republican nomination. As the incumbent president, Taft controlled the party machinery, and when the Republican convention met in June 1912, he took the nomination. In early July, the Democrats met in Baltimore and, after a forty-six-ballot struggle, nominated Woodrow Wilson, the reform-minded governor of New Jersey.

A month later, the anti-Taft and progressive Republicans—now calling themselves the **Progressive party**—whooped it up in Chicago. Nominating Roosevelt for president, the Progressive—soon known as the "Bull Moose"—party convention set the stage for a lively three-cornered presidential contest.

Taft was out of the running before the campaign even began. He stayed at home and made no speeches before the election. Roosevelt campaigned strenuously for his Bull Moose platform, a program he called **New Nationalism.** It demanded a national approach to the country's affairs and a strong president to deal with them. New Nationalism exalted the execution and the expert; urged social-justice reforms to protect workers, women, and children; and accepted "good" trusts. New Nationalism encouraged large concentrations of labor and capital, serving the nation's interests under a forceful federal executive. For the first time in the history of a political party, the Progressive campaign enlisted women in its organization, and New Nationalism gained their widespread support. Some labor and business leaders, seeking relief from destructive competition and labor strife, also got behind the new party.

Wilson, in contrast, set forth a program called the **New Freedom** that emphasized business competition and small government. A states' rights Democrat, he wanted to rein in federal authority, using it only to sweep away special privilege, release individual energies, and restore competition. He echoed the Progressive party's social-justice objectives while continuing to attack Roosevelt's planned state. For Wilson, the vital issue was not a planned economy but a free one.

In New Nationalism and the New Freedom, the election of 1912 offered competing philosophies of government. Both Roosevelt and Wilson saw the central problem of the American nation as the effect of economic growth on individuals

Progressive party Also known as the "Bull Moose" party, this political party was formed by Theodore Roosevelt in an attempt to advance progressive ideas and unseat President William Howard Taft in 1912.

New Nationalism Theodore Roosevelt's program in his campaign for the presidency in 1912, the New Nationalism called for a national approach to the country's affairs and a strong president to deal with them. It also called for efficiency in government and society; urged protection of children, women, and workers; accepted "good" trusts; and exalted the expert and the executive. Additionally, it encouraged large concentrations of capital and labor.

New Freedom Woodrow Wilson's program in his campaign for the presidency in 1912, the New Freedom emphasized business competition and small government. It sought to rein in federal authority, release individual energy, and restore competition. It echoed many of the progressive social-justice objectives while pushing for a free economy rather than a planned one.

and society. Both focused on the government's relation to business, both believed in bureaucratic reform, and both wanted to use government to protect the ordinary citizen. But Roosevelt welcomed federal power, national planning, and business growth; Wilson distrusted them all.

On election day, Wilson won 6.3 million votes to 4.1 million for Roosevelt, 3.5 million for Taft, and 900,000 for Eugene V. Debs, the Socialist party candidate. In the worst defeat ever suffered by an incumbent, Taft garnered only eight electoral votes. The Democrats also won outright control of both houses of Congress.

Woodrow Wilson's New Freedom

If under Roosevelt social reform took on the excitement of a circus, under Wilson, one historian said, "it acquired the dedication of a sunrise service." Born in Virginia in 1856, the son of a Presbyterian minister, Wilson was a moralist; he reached judgments easily that, once reached, were rarely discarded.

After graduating from Princeton University and the University of Virginia Law School, Wilson found that practicing law bored him. Shifting to history and political science, he taught at Princeton from 1890 to 1902, when he became president of the university. Eight years later, he was governor of New Jersey, where he compiled a strong record as a reformer. Although Wilson's rise was rapid and he knew relatively little about national issues and personalities, he learned fast. In some ways, the lack of experience served him well. He had few political debts to repay, and he brought fresh perspectives to older issues.

Wilson loved ideas but was sensitive to criticism and prone to self-righteousness. He often turned differences of opinion into bitter personal quarrels. Like Roosevelt, he believed in strong presidential leadership. He cooperated closely with Democrats in Congress, and his legislative record places him among the most effective presidents. Cold and aloof in individual conversation, Wilson could move crowds with graceful oratory. Unlike Taft, and even more than Roosevelt, he could inspire.

The New Freedom in Action

On the day of his inauguration, Wilson called Congress into special session to lower the tariff. When the session opened on April 8, 1913, Wilson himself was there, the first president since John Adams in 1801 to appear personally before Congress. In forceful language, he urged Congress to reduce tariff rates.

Wilson worked hard and skillfully to get the bill through Congress. The result was a triumph for Wilson and the Democratic party. The **Underwood Tariff Act** passed in 1913. The first tariff cut in nineteen years, it lowered rates about 15 percent and removed duties from sugar, wool, and several other consumer goods. To make up for lost revenue, the act also levied a modest, graduated income tax, authorized under the just-ratified Sixteenth Amendment. Marking a significant shift in the American tax structure, it imposed a 1 percent tax on individuals and corporations earning more than $4,000 annually and an additional 1 percent tax on incomes greater than $20,000.

Underwood Tariff Act An early accomplishment of the Wilson administration, this law reduced the tariff rates of the Payne-Aldrich law of 1909 by about 15 percent. It also levied a graduated income tax to make up for the lost revenue.

The act reflected the new unity of the Democratic party and the ability of Wilson as a leader. Encouraged by his success, Wilson decided to keep Congress in session through the hot Washington summer. Now he focused on banking reform, and the result in December 1913 was the **Federal Reserve Act,** the most important domestic law of his administration.

Federal Reserve Act One of the most important laws in the history of the country, this 1913 act created a central banking system, consisting of twelve regional banks governed by the Federal Reserve Board.

Meant to provide the United States with a sound yet flexible currency, the act established the country's first efficient banking system since Andrew Jackson killed the Second Bank of the United States in 1832. It created twelve regional banks, each to serve a district. These banks answered to the Federal Reserve Board, appointed by the president, which governed the nationwide system.

A compromise law, the act blended public and private control of the banking system. Private bankers owned the Federal Reserve banks but answered to the presidentially appointed Federal Reserve Board. The Reserve banks were authorized to issue currency and through the discount rate—the interest rate at which they loaned money to member banks—could raise or lower the amount of money in circulation. Monetary affairs no longer depended solely on the price of gold. Within a year, nearly half the nation's banking resources were in the Federal Reserve System.

The **Clayton Antitrust Act** (1914) completed Wilson's initial legislative program. Motivated in part by the revelations of a congressional committee about the power of interlocking directorates—management and control of competing companies by executives from an interrelated business group—the Clayton Act outlawed such directorates and prohibited unfair trade practices. It forbade pricing policies that created monopoly, and it made corporate officers personally responsible for antitrust violations. Delighting Samuel Gompers and the labor movement, the act declared that unions were not conspiracies in restraint of trade, outlawed the use of injunctions in labor disputes unless necessary to protect property, and approved lawful strikes and picketing.

Clayton Antitrust Act An attempt to improve the Sherman Anti-Trust Act of 1890, this law outlawed interlocking directorates (companies in which the same people served as directors), forbade policies that created monopolies, and made corporate officers responsible for anti-trust violations. Benefiting labor, it declared that unions were not conspiracies in restraint of trade and outlawed the use of injunctions in labor disputes unless they were necessary to protect property.

A related law established the powerful Federal Trade Commission to oversee business methods. The commission could demand special and annual reports, investigate complaints, and order corporate compliance, subject to court review. Although Wilson initially opposed the commission concept, he soon came to see it as the cornerstone of his antitrust plan. To reassure business leaders, he appointed a number of conservatives to the new commission and to the Federal Reserve Board.

In November 1914, Wilson proudly announced the completion of his New Freedom program. Tariff, banking, and antitrust laws promised a brighter future, he said. Many progressives, however, believed the process of reform had only begun.

Wilson Moves Toward the New Nationalism

Distracted by the start of war in Europe, Wilson gave less attention to domestic issues for more than a year. When he returned to concern with reform, he adopted more and more of Roosevelt's New Nationalism and blended it with the New Freedom in ways that set it off from his earlier policies.

One of Wilson's problems was Congress. To his dismay, the Republicans gained substantially in the 1914 elections. At the same time, a recession struck the economy, which had been hurt by the outbreak of the European war in August 1914. Some business leaders blamed the tariff and other New Freedom enactments. On the defensive, Wilson began to cooperate more with bankers and industrialists. He refused to support a bill providing minimum wages for women workers, sidetracked a child labor bill on the ground that it was unconstitutional, and opposed a bill to establish long-term credits for farmers. He also refused to endorse woman suffrage, arguing that it was a matter for the states to decide.

Wilson's record on race disappointed blacks and many progressives. He had appealed to black voters during the 1912 election but did little to justify their support once in office. A Virginian himself, he appointed many Southerners to high office, and for the first time since the Civil War, southern segregationist views on race dominated the nation's capital.

As the year 1916 began, Wilson again pushed for reform, and the result—a virtual river of reform laws—began the second, national-minded phase of the New Freedom. In part, Wilson was motivated by the approaching presidential election; he was, after all, a minority president. Moreover, many progressives were voicing disappointment with Wilson's limited reforms and his failure to support more advanced reform legislation such as farm credits, child labor, and woman suffrage.

Moving quickly to patch up the problem, Wilson named Louis D. Brandeis to the Supreme Court in January 1916. Popular among progressives, Brandeis was also the first Jew to serve on the Court. In May, Wilson reversed his stand on federally backed farm loans. The Federal Farm Loan Act of 1916 created the Federal Farm Loan Board to give farmers credit in a manner similar to the Federal Reserve's benefits for trade and industry.

Wilson was already popular within the labor movement. He had defended union recognition and collective bargaining. In 1913, he appointed William B. Wilson, a respected leader of the United Mine Workers, as the first head of the Labor Department. In 1914, in Ludlow, Colorado, state militia and mine guards fired machine guns into a tent colony of coal strikers, killing twenty-one men, women, and children. Outraged, Wilson stepped in and used federal troops to end the violence while negotiations to end the strike went on.

In August 1916, a threatened railroad strike again revealed Wilson's sympathies with labor. Like Roosevelt, he invited the two sides to the White House, where he urged the railroad companies to grant an eight-hour workday while asking labor

Miners in Ludlow, Colorado, went on strike in September 1913 for better working conditions and union recognition. Expecting eviction from company housing, they built a tent colony near the company town. The company, John D. Rockefeller's Colorado Fuel and Iron Company, hired guards to break the strike. On Easter Sunday evening, April 20, 1914, state troops and guards sprayed the tents with gunfire, then soaked the tents with kerosene and set the colony afire. Twenty-one of the colonists died, including eleven children. ❖

leaders to abandon the demand for overtime pay. Labor leaders accepted the proposal; railroad leaders did not. Soon Wilson signed the Adamson Act (1916), which imposed the eight-hour workday on interstate railways. The act ended the threat of a strike and expanded the federal government's authority to regulate industry.

With Wilson leading the way, the flow of reform legislation continued until the election. The Federal Workmen's Compensation Act established workers' compensation for government employees. The Keating-Owen Act, the first federal child labor law, prohibited the shipment in interstate commerce of products manufactured by children under the age of 14. The Warehouse Act authorized licensed warehouses to issue negotiable receipts for farm products deposited with them. During the campaign, Wilson endorsed the eight-hour workday for all the nation's workers and came out in support of woman suffrage.

The 1916 presidential election was close, but Wilson won it on the issues of peace and progressivism. By the end of 1916, he and the Democratic party had enacted most of the important parts of Roosevelt's Progressive party platform of 1912. To do it, Wilson abandoned portions of the New Freedom and accepted much of New Nationalism, including greater federal power and commissions governing trade and tariffs. In mixing the two programs, he blended some of the competing doctrines of the Progressive Era, established the primacy of the federal government, and foreshadowed the pragmatic outlook of Franklin D. Roosevelt's New Deal of the 1930s.

Conclusion: The Fruits of Progressivism

The election of 1916 showed how deeply progressivism had reached into American society. Candidates were vying for the reform-minded vote, and the future seemed to belong to reform. In retrospect, however, 1916 marked the beginning of progressivism's decline. Many of the problems the progressives addressed they did not solve, and some important ones, like race, they did not even tackle. Yet their regulatory commissions, direct primaries, city improvements, and child labor laws marked an era of important and measured reform.

In 1909, Taft rode to his inauguration in a horse-drawn carriage; in 1913, Wilson rode in an automobile, and change was evident throughout the country. The institution of the presidency expanded. Independent commissions, operating within flexible laws, supplemented executive authority.

These developments owed a great deal to both Roosevelt and Wilson. Wanting to manage a complex society, Roosevelt developed a simple formula: expert advice; growth-minded policies; a balancing of business, labor, and other interests; the use of publicity to gather support; and stern but often permissive oversight of the economy. He strengthened the executive office and called on young professional, well-educated, public-minded citizens to help him. "I believe in a strong executive," he said. "I believe in power."

Wilson came to office with different ideas, wanting to dismantle much of Roosevelt's governing apparatus. But driven by outside forces and changes in his own thinking, Wilson soon moved in directions similar to those Roosevelt had championed. Starting out to disperse power, he consolidated it, creating governmental agencies to regulate economic forces and correct abuses.

Through such movements, government at all levels accepted responsibility for the welfare of various elements in the social order. A reform-minded and bureaucratic society took shape, one in which men and women, labor and capital, political parties and social classes competed for shares in the expansive framework of twentieth-century life. But there were limits to reform. As both Roosevelt and Wilson found, the new government agencies, understaffed and underfinanced, depended in the end on the responsiveness of the sectors they sought to regulate.

CHRONOLOGY

1894	National Municipal League is formed to work for reform in cities
1900	Galveston, Texas, is the first city to try the commission form of government
1901	Theodore Roosevelt becomes president ❖ Robert M. La Follette is elected reform governor of Wisconsin ❖ Doctors reorganize the American Medical Association ❖ Socialist party of America is organized
1902	Roosevelt sues the Northern Securities Company for violation of the Sherman Antitrust Act ❖ Coal miners in northeastern Pennsylvania strike ❖ Maryland is the first state to pass a workers' compensation law
1903	Department of Commerce and Labor is created
1904	Roosevelt is elected to second term
1906	Hepburn Act strengthens the ICC ❖ Upton Sinclair attacks the meatpacking industry in *The Jungle* ❖ Congress passes the Meat Inspection Act and the Pure Food and Drug Act
1908	Taft is elected president ❖ Supreme Court upholds an Oregon law limiting working hours for women in *Muller* v. *Oregon*
1909	Payne-Aldrich Tariff Act divides the Republican party
1910	Mann-Elkins Act is passed to regulate the railroads ❖ Taft fires Gifford Pinchot, head of U.S. Forest Service ❖ Democrats sweep midterm elections
1912	Progressive party is formed, nominates Roosevelt for president ❖ Woodrow Wilson is elected president
1913	Underwood Tariff Act lowers rates ❖ Federal Reserve Act reforms the U.S. banking system ❖ Sixteenth Amendment authorizes Congress to collect taxes on incomes
1914	Clayton Antitrust Act strengthens antitrust legislation
1916	Wilson wins reelection
1918	Supreme Court strikes down a federal law limiting child labor in *Hammer* v. *Dagenhart*
1920	Nineteenth Amendment gives women the right to vote

Soon there was a far darker cloud on the horizon. The spirit of progressivism rested on a belief in human potential, peace, and progress. After Napoleon's defeat in 1815, a century of peace began in western Europe, and as the decades passed, war seemed a dying institution. It was not to be. In 1914, the most devastating of wars broke out in Europe, and within three years, Americans were fighting and dying on the battlefields of France.

KEY TERMS

social-justice movement, p. 444
pragmatism, p. 447
Muller v. *Oregon*, p. 448
Brandeis brief, p. 448
Hepburn Act, p. 453
conservation, p. 454
Progressive party, p. 457
New Nationalism, p. 457
New Freedom, p. 457
Underwood Tariff Act, p. 458
Federal Reserve Act, p. 458
Clayton Antitrust Act, p. 459

Recommended Reading

George Mowry, *The Era of Theodore Roosevelt* (1958), and Arthur S. Link, *Woodrow Wilson and the Progressive Era* (1954), trace the social and economic conditions of the period. See also John M. Blum's perceptive and brief *The Republican Roosevelt* (1954) and Kathleen Dalton, *Theodore Roosevelt: A Strenuous Life* (2002). The definitive biography of Wilson is Arthur S. Link, *Wilson,* 5 vols. (1947–1965).

Samuel P. Hays offers an influential interpretation of progressivism in *Conservation and the Gospel of Efficiency* (1959) as does Nancy Cohen, *The Reconstruction of American Liberalism, 1865–1914* (2002), for the broader period. Albro Martin, *Enterprise Denied: Origins of the Decline of American Railroads, 1897–1917* (1971), argues persuasively that reformers damaged as well as regulated. Samuel Haber, *The Quest for Authority and Honor in the American Professions, 1750–1900* (1991), examines the changing nature of the professions.

For a list of additional titles related to this chapter's topics, please see http://www.ablongman.com/divine.

Suggested Web Sites

Theodore Roosevelt Association

http://www.theodoreroosevelt.org/
This site contains much biographical and research information about this famous American.

Woodrow Wilson

http://www.ipl.org/ref/POTUS/wwilson.html
This page contains basic factual data about his election and presidency, speeches, and on-line biographies.

History of the Suffrage Movement

http://www.rochester.edu/SBA
This site includes a chronology, important texts relating to woman suffrage, and biographical information about Susan B. Anthony and Elizabeth Cady Stanton.

Women and Social Movements in the United States, 1775–2000

http://womhist.binghamton.edu/
This site offers essays and primary documents on women in social movements.

Chapter 24

The Nation at War

The Sinking of the Lusitania

On the morning of May 1, 1915, the German government printed an important advertisement in the *New York World.* It warned American travelers that a state of war existed in Europe and that waters adjacent to Great Britain were part of the war zone. It emphasized that "travelers sailing in the war zone on ships of Great Britain or her allies do so at their own risk." At 12:30 that afternoon, the British steamship *Lusitania* set sail from New York to Liverpool. The passenger list of 1,257 was the largest since the outbreak of war in Europe. Alfred G. Vanderbilt, the millionaire sportsman, was aboard; so were several other famous Americans. Some passengers chose the *Lusitania* for speed; others liked the unmatched comfort of its modern staterooms.

Six days later, the *Lusitania* reached the coast of Ireland. German submarines, known as "U-boats," patrolled these dangerous waters. When the war began in 1914, Great Britain imposed a naval blockade of Germany. In return, Germany in February 1915 declared the area around the British Isles a war zone; all enemy vessels, armed or unarmed, were at risk. Germany had only a handful of U-boats, but submarine warfare was new and frightening. On behalf of the United States, President Woodrow Wilson protested the German action, and on February 10, he warned Germany of its "strict accountability" for any American losses resulting from U-boat attacks.

As in peacetime, the *Lusitania* sailed straight ahead, with no zigzag maneuvers to throw off pursuit. But the submarine U-20 was there, and the commander, seeing a large ship, fired a single torpedo. Seconds after it hit, a boiler exploded and blew a hole in the *Lusitania's* side. In eighteen minutes it sank. Nearly 1,200 people died, including 128 Americans.

The sinking, the worst since the loss of the *Titanic,* horrified Americans. Most Americans, however, wanted to stay out of war; like Wilson, they hoped negotiations could solve the problem.

In a series of diplomatic notes, Wilson demanded a change in German policy. The first *Lusitania* note (May 13, 1915) called on Germany to abandon unrestricted submarine warfare, disavow the sinking, and compensate for lost American lives. Germany sent an evasive reply, and Wilson drafted a second *Lusitania* note (June 9) insisting on specific pledges. A third note (July 21)—almost an ultimatum—warned Germany that the United States would consider similar sinkings "deliberately unfriendly" acts.

Wilson was unaware that Germany had already ordered U-boat commanders not to sink passenger liners without warning. In August 1915, a U-boat mistakenly torpedoed the British liner *Arabic,* killing two Americans. Wilson protested, and Germany, eager to keep the United States out of war, backed down. In the *Arabic*

Outline

A New World Power

Foreign Policy Under Wilson

Toward War

Over There

Over Here

The Treaty of Versailles

Conclusion: Postwar Disillusionment

pledge (September 1), Germany promised to stop and warn liners unless they tried to resist or escape.

ALTHOUGH WILSON'S DIPLOMACY had achieved his immediate goal, the *Lusitania* and *Arabic* crises highlighted the elements that led to war. Trade and travel tied the world together, and Americans no longer hid behind safe ocean barriers. New weapons, such as the submarine, strained old rules of international law. But while Americans sifted the conflicting claims of Great Britain and Germany, they hoped for peace. A generation of progressives, inspired with confidence in human progress, did not easily accept war.

Wilson also hated war, but he found himself caught up in a worldwide crisis that demanded the best in American will and diplomacy. In the end, diplomacy failed, and in April 1917, the United States entered a war that changed the nation's history. Building on several major trends in American foreign policy since the 1890s, the years around World War I firmly established the United States as a world power, confirmed the country's dominance in Latin America, and ended with a war with Germany and her allies that had far-reaching results, including establishing the United States as one of the world's foremost economic powers.

A New World Power

As in the late nineteenth century, Americans after 1900 paid little attention to foreign affairs. People focused on what was going on at home. Foreign affairs, they reasoned, was the job of the president, an attitude that suited the interests of Roosevelt, Taft, and Wilson.

American foreign policy from 1901 to 1920 was aggressive and nationalistic. During these years, the United States dominated the Caribbean and intervened in Europe, the Far East, and Latin America.

In 1898, the United States left the peace table possessing the Philippines, Puerto Rico, and Guam. Administering distant lands required a colonial policy and a more outward approach in foreign policy. From the Caribbean to the Pacific, policymakers paid attention to issues and countries they had earlier ignored. Like other nations in these years, the United States built a large navy, protected its colonial empire, and became increasingly involved in international affairs.

The nation also became more and more involved in economic ventures abroad. Turning out goods from textiles to steel, mass production industries sold products overseas, and financiers invested in Asia, Africa, Latin America, and Europe. Though investments and trade never wholly dictated American foreign policy, they fostered greater involvement in foreign lands.

"I Took the Canal Zone"

Convinced the United States should take a more active international role, Theodore Roosevelt spent his presidency preparing the nation for world power. Along with Secretary of War Elihu Root, he modernized the army, established the Army War College, imposed stiff tests for the promotion of officers, and created a general staff to oversee military planning and mobilization. Determined to end dependence on the British fleet, Roosevelt doubled the navy's strength during his term in office.

Stretching his authority to the limit, Roosevelt took steps to consolidate the country's new position in the Caribbean and Central America. European powers, which had long resisted American initiatives there, now accepted American supremacy. Preoccupied with problems elsewhere, Great Britain agreed to U.S. plans for a canal across the isthmus of Central America, withdrawing military forces from the area. Secretary of State John Hay negotiated with Britain the Hay-Pauncefote

Treaty of 1901, which permitted the United States to construct and control an isthmian canal, providing it would be free and open to ships of all nations.

Delighted, Roosevelt set to selecting the course. One route, 50 miles long, wandered through the rough, swampy terrain of the Panama region of Colombia. A French company had recently tried and failed to dig a canal there. Another possible route, through mountainous Nicaragua, was four times as long but followed natural waterways, which would make construction easier. The Isthmian Canal Commission decided in 1899 that the shorter route through Panama was preferable.

Roosevelt backed the idea, and he authorized Hay to negotiate an agreement with the Colombian chargé d'affaires, Thomas Herrán. The Hay-Herrán Convention (1903) gave the United States a ninety-nine-year lease, with option for renewal, on a canal zone 6 miles wide. In exchange, the United States agreed to pay Colombia a onetime fee of $10 million and an annual rental of $250,000.

To Roosevelt's dismay, the Colombian Senate rejected the treaty. Calling the Colombians "contemptible little creatures," Roosevelt considered seizing Panama, then hinted that he would welcome a Panamanian revolt for independence. In November 1903, the Panamanians took the hint, and Roosevelt moved quickly to support them. Sending the cruiser *Nashville* to prevent Colombian troops from putting down the revolt, he promptly recognized the new republic of Panama.

Hay-Bunau-Varilla Treaty A 1903 treaty granting the United States control over a canal zone 10 miles wide across the Isthmus of Panama. In return, the United States guaranteed the independence of Panama and agreed to pay Colombia a onetime fee of $10 million and an annual rental of $250,000.

Two weeks later, the **Hay-Bunau-Varilla Treaty** with Panama granted the United States control of a canal zone 10 miles wide across the Isthmus of Panama. In return, the United States guaranteed the independence of Panama and agreed to pay the same fees offered Colombia. On August 15, 1914, the first ocean steamer sailed through the completed canal, which cost $375 million to build.

Roosevelt's actions angered many Latin Americans. Colombian-American relations remained strained until 1921, when the United States agreed to pay Colombia $25 million in cash and give it preferential treatment in using the canal. For his part, however, Roosevelt stoutly defended his actions. "I took the Canal Zone," he said, "and let Congress debate; and while the debate goes on, the Canal does also."

The Roosevelt Corollary

With interests in Puerto Rico, Cuba, and the Canal Zone, the United States developed a Caribbean policy to ensure its dominance in the region. It established protectorates over some countries and subsidized others to keep them dependent. When necessary, it even purchased territories to keep them out of the hands of other powers, as in the case of the Virgin Islands, bought from Denmark in 1917 to prevent Germany from acquiring them.

From 1903 to 1920, the United States intervened often in Latin America to protect the canal, promote regional stability, and exclude foreign influence. One problem worrisome to American policymakers was the scale of Latin American debts to European powers. Many countries in the Western Hemisphere owed money to European governments and banks, yet these same nations were poor, prone to revolution, and unable to pay. The situation invited European intervention. In 1902, Venezuela defaulted on debts; England, Germany, and Italy sent Venezuela an ultimatum and blockaded its ports. American pressure forced a settlement of the issue, but the general problem remained.

Roosevelt Corollary President Theodore Roosevelt's 1904 foreign policy statement, a corollary to the Monroe Doctrine, asserting that the United States would intervene in Latin American affairs if the countries themselves could not keep their affairs in order. It effectively made the United States the policeman of the Western Hemisphere.

In 1904, when the Dominican Republic defaulted on its debts, Roosevelt was ready with a major announcement. Known as the **Roosevelt Corollary** to the Monroe Doctrine, the policy warned Latin American nations to keep their affairs in order or face American intervention. Applying the new policy immediately, the president took charge of the Dominican Republic's revenue system, and within two years, he had also established protectorates in Panama and Cuba. In Cuba, Roosevelt tied the action to the Platt Amendment to the Cuban constitution. Continued by Taft, Wilson, and other presidents, the Roosevelt Corollary guided

A cartoon from Judge *titled "The World's Constable." The Roosevelt Corollary claimed the right of the United States to exercise "an international police power," enforced by what many referred to as a "big stick" diplomacy.* ❖

American policy in Latin America until the 1930s, when Franklin D. Roosevelt's Good Neighbor policy replaced it.

Ventures in the Far East

The Open Door policy toward China and possession of the Philippine Islands shaped American actions in the Far East. Roosevelt wanted to balance Russian and Japanese power in the area, and he was not unhappy at first when war broke out between them in 1904. As Japan won victory after victory, however, Roosevelt became concerned. He accepted Japan's request to mediate the conflict and in August 1905 convened a peace conference at Portsmouth, New Hampshire. The conference ended the war, but Japan emerged as the dominant force in the Far East. Adjusting policy, Roosevelt sent Secretary of War Taft to Tokyo to negotiate the Taft-Katsura Agreement (1905), which recognized Japan's dominance over Korea in return for its promise not to invade the Philippines. Giving Japan a free hand in Korea violated the Open Door policy, but Roosevelt argued that he had little choice.

In a show of strength, he sent the American fleet around the world, including a safe stop in Tokyo in October 1908. For the moment, Japanese-American relations improved, despite Japan's resentment over the segregation of Asian children in San Francisco's public schools in 1906. In 1908, the two nations signed the comprehensive Root-Takahira Agreement in which they promised to maintain the status quo in the Pacific, uphold the Open Door, and support Chinese independence.

In later years, tensions grew in the Far East. Japan's anger mounted in 1913 when the California legislature prohibited Japanese residents from owning property in the state. By the start of the First World War, Japan longed for an Asian empire and eyed American possessions in the Pacific.

In foreign as well as domestic affairs, President Taft tried to continue Roosevelt's policies. As secretary of state he chose Philander C. Knox, and together

"dollar diplomacy" This policy, adopted by President William Howard Taft and Secretary of State Philander C. Knox, sought to promote U.S. financial and business interests abroad and to replace military alliances with economic ties, with the idea of increasing American influence and securing lasting peace.

they pursued a policy of **"dollar diplomacy"** to promote American financial and business interests abroad. The policy had profit-seeking motives, but it also aimed to substitute economic ties for military alliances and bring lasting peace.

In the Far East, Knox worked closely with Willard Straight, an agent of American bankers, who argued that dollar diplomacy was the financial arm of the Open Door. However, Knox's attempt to convince England, Japan, and Russia to join the United States in an international syndicate to loan China money to purchase the Manchurian railroads failed. The outcome was a blow to American policy and prestige in Asia. Instead of cultivating friendship, as Roosevelt had envisioned, Taft started an intense rivalry with Japan for commercial advantage in China.

Foreign Policy Under Wilson

When he took office in 1913, Woodrow Wilson knew little about foreign policy. "It would be the irony of fate if my administration had to deal chiefly with foreign affairs," he told a friend. And so it was. During his two terms, Wilson faced crisis after crisis in this area, including the outbreak of World War I.

A supremely self-confident man, Wilson conducted his own diplomacy. He had little respect for the party regulars who received diplomatic posts as patronage plums. He composed important diplomatic notes on his own typewriter, sent personal emissaries abroad, and carried on major negotiations without the knowledge of his secretary of state. The idealistic Wilson believed in a principled, ethical world in which militarism, colonialism, and war were brought under control. Rejecting the policy of dollar diplomacy, Wilson initially chose a course of **moral diplomacy,** designed to bring right to the world, preserve peace, and extend to other people the blessings of democracy.

moral diplomacy Policy adopted by President Woodrow Wilson that rejected the approach of "dollar diplomacy." Rather than focusing mainly on economic ties with other nations, Wilson's policy was designed to bring right principles to the world, preserve peace, and extend to other peoples the blessings of democracy.

Conducting Moral Diplomacy

William Jennings Bryan, whom Wilson appointed as secretary of state, was also an amateur in foreign relations. A populist who put his trust in the common people, he was skeptical of experts in the State Department. Bryan was a fervent pacifist, and like Wilson, he believed in the American duty to "help" less favored nations.

In 1913 and 1914, he embarked on an idealistic campaign to negotiate treaties of arbitration throughout the world. Known as "cooling-off" treaties, they provided for submitting all international disputes to permanent commissions of investigation. Neither party could declare war or increase armaments until the investigation ended. The idea drew on the popularity of commissions and a sense that reasonable people could settle disputes without resorting to war. Bryan negotiated cooling-off treaties with thirty nations, but none was ever used.

Wilson and Bryan promised a dramatic new approach in Latin America, concerned not with the "pursuit of material interest" but with "human rights" and "national integrity." Their promise, however, went unfulfilled, and in the end, they continued the Roosevelt-Taft policies. Wilson defended the Monroe Doctrine, gave unspoken support to the Roosevelt Corollary, and intervened in Latin America more than either Roosevelt or Taft had. By 1917, American troops "protected" Nicaragua, Haiti, the Dominican Republic, and Cuba.

Troubles Across the Border

Porfirio Díaz, president of Mexico for thirty-seven years, was overthrown in 1911. Díaz had encouraged foreign investments in Mexican mines, railroads, oil, and land; by 1913, Americans had invested more than $1 billion. His overthrow led to a decade of violence that tested Wilson's policies and brought the United States close to war with Mexico.

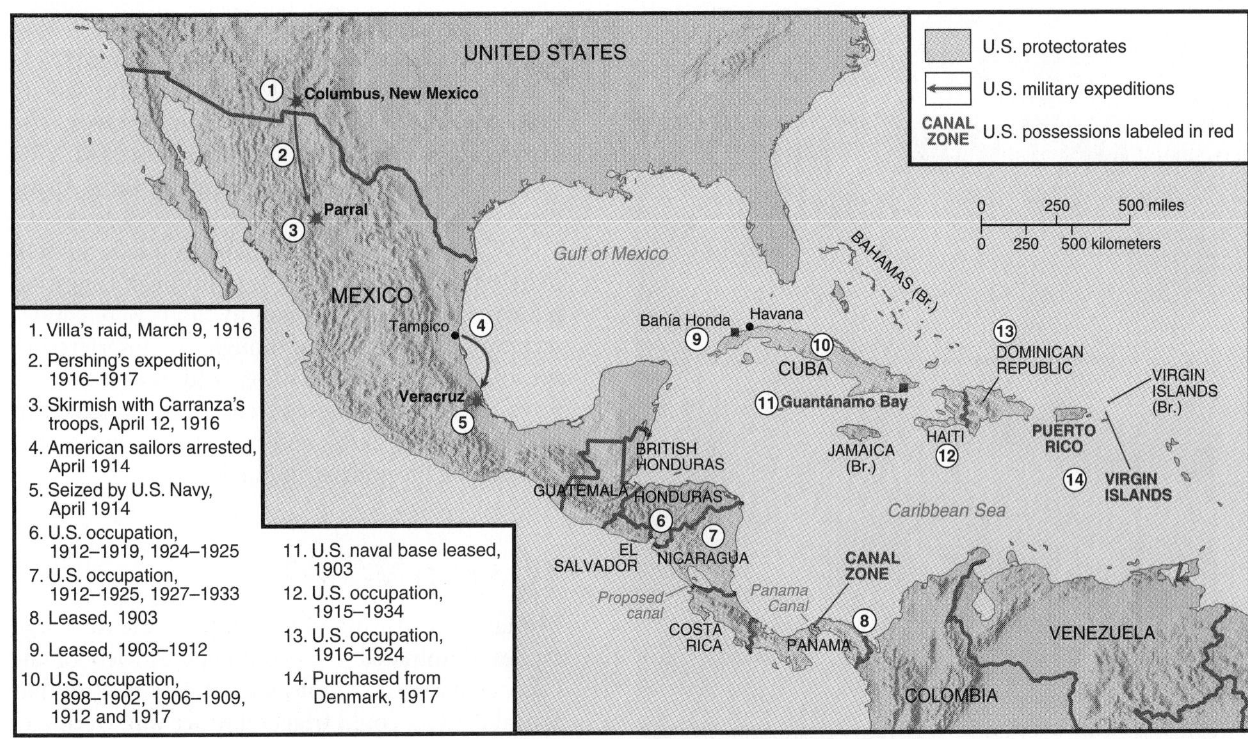

ACTIVITIES OF THE UNITED STATES IN THE CARIBBEAN, 1898–1930s *During the first three decades of the twentieth century, the United States policed the Caribbean, claiming the right to take action when it judged Latin American countries were doing a bad job of running their affairs.* ❖

A liberal reformer, Francisco I. Madero, followed Díaz as president. But Madero soon lost control of the troubled country. With support from wealthy landowners, the army, and the Catholic Church, General Victoriano Huerta ousted Madero in 1913, threw him in jail, and arranged his murder. Most European nations immediately recognized Huerta, but Wilson refused to do so. Instead, he announced a new policy toward revolutionary regimes in Latin America. To win American recognition, they must not only exercise power but also reflect "a just government based upon law, not upon arbitrary or irregular force."

On that basis, Wilson withheld recognition from Huerta and maneuvered to oust him. Early in 1914, Wilson stationed naval units off Mexico's ports to cut off arms shipments to the Huerta regime. On April 9, 1914, several American sailors, ashore in Tampico to purchase supplies, were arrested. They were promptly released, but the American admiral demanded an apology and a twenty-one-gun salute to the American flag. Huerta agreed—if the Americans also saluted the Mexican flag.

Shortly after Wilson asked Congress for authority to use military force if needed, he learned that a German ship was landing arms at Veracruz on Mexico's eastern coast. With Wilson's approval, American warships shelled the harbor, and marines took the city. Outraged, Mexicans of all factions denounced the invasion, and for a time, the two countries hovered on the edge of war. Only a hasty diplomatic retreat by Wilson avoided more serious hostilities.

In July 1914, cut off from funds, Huerta resigned. Wilson recognized the new government, headed by Venustiano Carranza. Early in 1916, Francisco ("Pancho") Villa, one of Carranza's generals, revolted. Hoping to goad the United States into an action that would help him seize power, he raided border towns, injuring American civilians. Stepping up his assault, Villa murdered thirty-three Americans in Mexico and the United States.

Stationing militia along the border, Wilson ordered General John J. Pershing on a punitive expedition to seize Villa in Mexico. Pershing led six thousand troops deep into Mexican territory. The expedition was a failure. Carranza protested, Villa eluded Pershing, and Wilson finally ordered his general home.

Wilson's policy had laudable goals: he wanted to help the Mexicans achieve political and agrarian reform. But his motives and methods were condescending. With little forethought, he interfered in the affairs of another country, and in doing so, he revealed the themes—moralism combined with pragmatic self-interest and a desire for peace—that also shaped his policies in Europe.

❖ A Look at the Past ❖

Sheet Music Cover

In 1915, the song "I Didn't Raise My Boy to Be a Soldier," written by Alfred Bryan and Al Piantadosi and performed by many different singers, was very popular in the Unites States. This cover of the song's sheet music includes a photograph of one of the song's performers and an illustration of a mother embracing her son with scenes of battle in their thoughts. What emotions do you think this image stirred in its audience? What do the song title and cover art suggest about the role women played in the peace movement during World War I? Do the sentiments expressed by this cover help explain why it took years before the United States entered the war?

Toward War

By May 1914, the mood in Europe was tense. Large armies dominated the Continent. A web of alliances entangled nations, maximizing the risk that a local conflict could trigger a wider war. Germany and its allies Austria-Hungary and Turkey dominated central Europe. Linked in their own alliance, England, France, and Russia agreed to aid each other in case of attack.

On June 28, 1914, a Balkan assassin in the service of Serbia murdered Archduke Franz Ferdinand, heir to the Austro-Hungarian throne. Within weeks, Germany, Turkey, and Austria-Hungary (the Central Powers) were at war with England, France, and Russia (the Allied Powers). Americans were shocked at the events. Wilson immediately proclaimed neutrality and asked Americans to remain "impartial in thought as well as in action." Privately, Wilson was stunned. A lifelong admirer of the British and their government, he said, "Everything I love most in the world is at stake."

The Neutrality Policy

In general, Americans accepted neutrality. They saw no need to enter the conflict, especially after the Allies in September 1914 halted the first German drive toward Paris. Many progressives saw added reason to resist. War violated the very spirit of progressive reform. Why demand safer factories and then kill men by the millions in war? Progressives and others tended to put the blame for war on the greed of "munition manufacturers, stockbrokers, and bond dealers" eager for wartime profits. Above all, progressives were sure that war would end reform. It consumed money and attention; it inflamed emotions. As a result, many progressives—including Jane Addams, Frederick C. Howe, and Lillian Wald—fought to keep the United States out of war.

The war's outbreak also tugged at the emotions of millions of immigrant Americans. Those who came from the British Isles tended to support the Allies; those from Ireland tended to support Germany, hoping that Britain's wartime troubles might free their homeland from British domination. The large population of German Americans often sympathized with the Central Powers.

At the deepest level, a majority in the country, bound by common language and institutions, sympathized with the Allies and blamed Germany for the war. When the war began, Germany invaded Belgium to strike at France, in violation of a treaty, which the German chancellor called "just a scrap of paper." Many Americans resented this arrogance and were even more aghast when German troops executed Belgian civilians who resisted. Both sides sought to sway American opinion, and fierce propaganda campaigns flourished. But in the end, the propaganda probably made little difference. Ties of heritage and the course of the war decided the American position. But whichever side they cheered for, Americans preferred simply to remain at peace.

Freedom of the Seas

The demands of trade tested American neutrality and confronted Wilson with difficult choices. Under international law, neutral countries were permitted to trade in nonmilitary goods with all belligerent countries. But Great Britain controlled the seas, and it intended to cut off shipments of war materials to the Central Powers.

As soon as war broke out, Britain blockaded German ports and limited the goods Americans could sell to Germany. As time passed, Britain stepped up the economic sanctions by forbidding the shipment to Germany of all foodstuffs and most raw materials. British ships often stopped U.S. ships and confiscated cargoes.

Again and again, Wilson protested such infringements of neutral rights. Sometimes Britain complied, sometimes not, and Wilson often grew angry. But needing American support and supplies, Britain pursued a careful strategy to disrupt German-American trade without disrupting Anglo-American relations. When necessary, it paid (or promised to pay) American businesses for lost trade with Germany.

Other than the German U-boats, there were no constraints on trade with the Allies, and a flood of Allied war orders fueled the American economy. To finance the purchases, the Allies turned to American bankers for loans. By 1917, loans to Allied governments exceeded $2 billion, while loans to Germany came to only $27 million.

Loans and trade drew the United States ever closer to the Allied cause. And even though Wilson often protested British maritime policy, the protests involved American goods and money, whereas Germany's submarine policy threatened American lives.

The U-Boat Threat

A relatively new weapon, the submarine strained the guidelines of international law. Traditional law required a submarine to surface, warn the target to stop, send a boarding party to check papers and cargo, and then allow time for passengers and crew to board lifeboats before sinking the vessel. Flimsy and slow, submarines could ill afford to surface while the prey radioed for help. If they did surface, they might be rammed or blown up by deck guns.

When Germany announced its submarine campaign in February 1915, Wilson protested sharply. The Germans promised not to sink American ships, and thereafter the issue became the right of Americans to sail on the ships of belligerent nations. Bryan urged Wilson to forbid Americans to travel in the war zones, but the president, determined to stand by the principles of international law, refused.

Wilson reacted more harshly in May 1915 when U-boats sank the *Lusitania* and again in August when they attacked the *Arabic.* He demanded that the Germans protect passenger vessels and pay for American losses. Fearing war, Bryan resigned as secretary of state and was replaced by Robert Lansing, a State Department counselor who favored the Allies. He urged strong stands against German violations of American neutrality.

In February 1916, Germany declared unrestricted submarine warfare against all *armed* ships. A month later, a U-boat torpedoed the unarmed French channel steamer *Sussex,* without warning, injuring several Americans. Lansing urged Wilson to break relations with Germany. On April 18, Wilson sent an ultimatum to Germany that unless it immediately called off attacks on cargo and passenger ships, the United States would sever relations. Germany's kaiser, convinced he did not yet have enough submarines to risk war, yielded. In the *Sussex* pledge of May 4, 1916, he agreed to Wilson's demands and promised to shoot on sight only ships of the enemy's navy. He tried to impose the condition that the United States compel the Allies to end their blockade.

The *Sussex* pledge marked the beginning of a short period of friendly relations between Germany and the United States. The agreement applied not just to passenger liners but to *all* merchant ships, belligerent or not. There was one problem: Wilson had taken such a strong position that if Germany renewed submarine warfare on merchant shipping, war with the United States was likely. Nevertheless, most Americans viewed the agreement as a diplomatic stroke for peace by Wilson, and the issues of peace and preparedness dominated the presidential election of 1916.

"He Kept Us Out of War"

The preparedness issue pitted antiwar groups against those who wanted to ready themselves for war. The American Rights Committee and other groups urged stepped-up military measures. In the summer of 1915, they persuaded the War Department to hold a training camp in Plattsburg, New York, in which regular army officers trained civilian volunteers in modern warfare.

Bellicose as always, Teddy Roosevelt led the preparedness campaign. He called Wilson "yellow" for not pressing Germany harder. Defending the military's state of readiness, Wilson refused to be stampeded just because "some amongst us are nervous and excited."

Wilson's position was attacked from both sides: preparedness advocates charged cowardice, while pacifists denounced any attempt at military readiness. The difficulty of his position, plus the growing U-boat crisis, soon changed Wilson's mind. In mid-1915, he asked the War Department to increase military planning, and he quietly notified congressional leaders of a switch in policy. Later that year, Wilson approved large increases in expenditures for the army and navy, a move that upset many peace-minded progressives.

As their standard-bearer in the presidential election of 1916, the Republicans nominated Charles Evans Hughes, a moderate justice of the Supreme Court. Hughes, a dull campaigner, called for a tougher line against Germany. The Democrats nominated Wilson in a convention marked by spontaneous demonstrations for peace. Picking up the antiwar theme, perhaps with reservation, Wilson said in October: "I am not expecting this country to get into war." The campaign slogan, "He kept us out of war," was repeated again and again.

On election night, Hughes had swept most of the East, and Wilson retired at 10 P.M., thinking he had lost. During the night, the results came in from California, New Mexico, and North Dakota; all supported Wilson. Holding the Democratic South, Wilson carried key states in the Midwest and West and won reelection. He took large portions of the labor and progressive vote, and women—who could vote in presidential elections in twelve states—voted heavily for him.

The Final Months of Peace

Just before election day, Great Britain further limited neutral trade, and there were reports from Germany of a renewal of unrestricted submarine warfare. Fresh from his election victory, Wilson redoubled his efforts for peace.

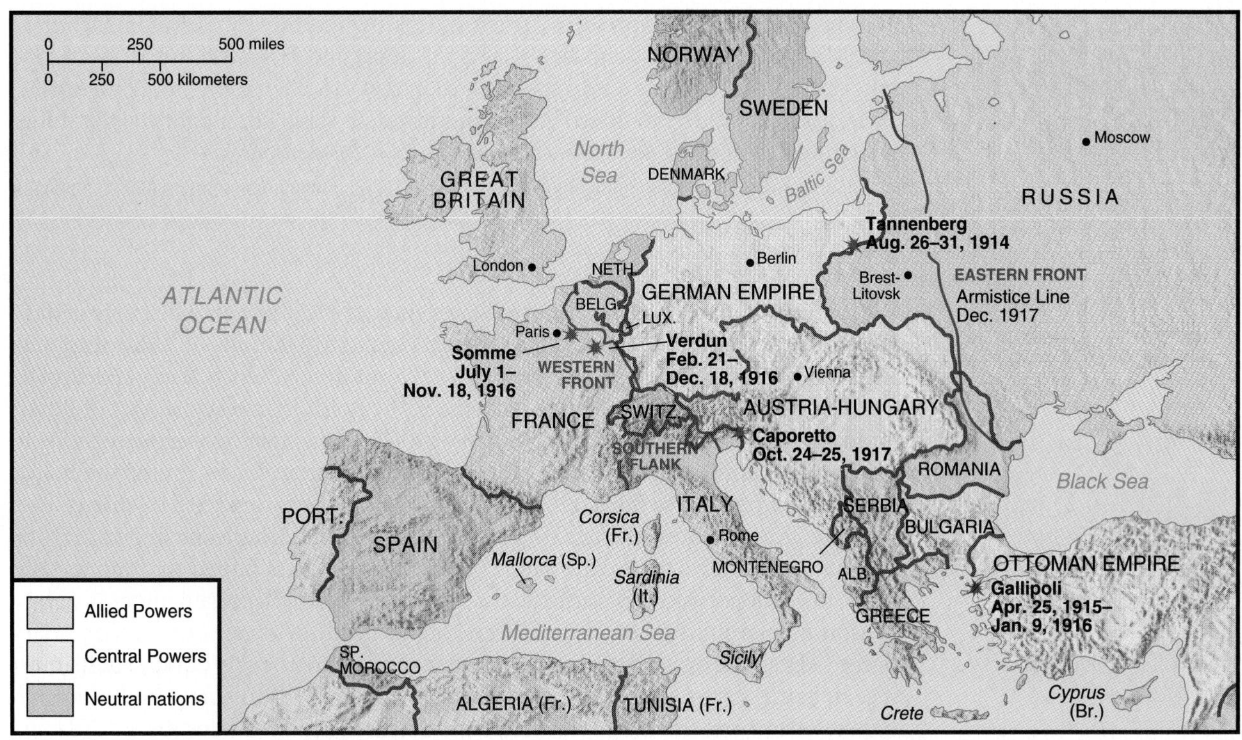

EUROPEAN ALLIANCES AND BATTLEFRONTS, 1914–1917 *Allied forces suffered early defeats on the eastern front (Tannenberg) and in the Dardanelles (Gallipoli). In 1917, the Allies were routed on the southern flank (Caporetto); the western theater then became the critical arena of the war.* ❖

In December 1916, he sent messages to both sides asking them to state their war aims. The Allies refused, although they promised privately to negotiate if the German terms were reasonable. The Germans replied evasively but in January 1917 revealed their real objectives. Close to forcing Russia out of the war, Germany sensed victory and craved territory—in eastern Europe, Africa, Belgium, and France.

On January 22, in an eloquent speech before the Senate, Wilson called for a "peace without victory." Outlining his own aims, he urged respect for all nations, freedom of the seas, arms limitations, and a league of nations to keep the peace. The speech made a great impression on many Europeans, but it was too late. The Germans had decided a few weeks before to unleash the submarines and gamble on a quick end to the war.

On January 31, the German ambassador in Washington informed Lansing that beginning February 1, U-boats would sink on sight all ships—passenger or merchant, neutral or belligerent, armed or unarmed—in the waters around England and France. German leaders estimated that if their submarine campaign were successful, they could win the war in six months. As he had pledged in 1916, Wilson broke off relations with Germany, although he still hoped for peace.

On February 25, the British government privately gave Wilson a telegram intercepted from Arthur Zimmermann, the German foreign minister, to the German ambassador in Mexico. A day later, Wilson asked Congress for authority to arm merchant ships to deter U-boat attacks. To prevent a filibuster, Wilson divulged the contents of the Zimmermann telegram: it proposed an alliance with Mexico in case of war with the United States, offering financial support and recovery of Mexico's "lost territory" in Texas, New Mexico, and Arizona.

Spurred by a wave of public indignation, the House passed Wilson's measure, but La Follette and others still blocked action in the Senate. On March 9, 1917,

Wilson ordered merchant ships armed on his own authority. Between March 12 and March 21, U-boats sank five American ships, and Wilson decided to wait no longer. He called Congress into special session and at 8:30 in the evening on April 2, 1917, asked for a declaration of war. Americans, he said, "shall fight for the things which we have always carried nearest our hearts—for democracy."

Over There

With a burst of patriotism, the United States entered a war its new allies were in danger of losing. That same month, the Germans sank 881,000 tons of Allied shipping, the greatest amount of the war. Mutinies broke out in the French army, and a costly British drive in Flanders stalled. In November, the Bolsheviks seized power in Russia and soon signed a separate peace treaty with Germany, freeing German troops to concentrate on the fight in the west. German and Austrian forces routed the Italian army on their southern flank, and the Allies braced for a spring 1918 offensive.

The United States was not prepared for war. Some Americans hoped that the declaration of war itself might daunt the Germans; others hoped that money and arms, not troops, would be sufficient to produce victory. Bypassing older generals, Wilson named John J. "Black Jack" Pershing to head the American Expeditionary Force (AEF). The army Pershing inherited was small and poorly equipped. Its most recent battle experience had been chasing Pancho Villa unsuccessfully around northern Mexico. And it had no war plans to fight Germany in Europe.

Mobilization

Although some members of Congress preferred a voluntary army of the kind that had fought in the Spanish-American War, Wilson turned to conscription, which he believed was both efficient and democratic. In May 1917, Congress passed the **Selective Service Act,** providing for the registration of all men between the ages of 21 and 30. The act eventually accounted for the induction of about 2.8 million men into the army.

Selective Service Act This 1917 law provided for the registration of all American men between the ages of 21 and 30 for a military draft. The age limits were later changed to 18 and 45.

The draft included black men as well as white, and four African American regiments were among the first sent into action. Despite their contributions, however, no black soldiers were allowed to march in the victory celebration that eventually took place in Paris.

War in the Trenches

The Great War, later referred to as World War I, may have been the most terrible war of all time. After the early offensive, the European armies dug themselves into trenches, in places only hundreds of yards apart. Artillery, poison gas, hand grenades, and a new weapon—rapid-fire machine guns—kept them pinned down. Even in moments of respite, the mud, rats, cold, fear, and disease took a heavy toll. Deafening bombardments shook the earth, and there was a high incidence of the psychological disorder known as "shell shock." From time to time troops went "over the top" of the embankments in an effort to break through, but the costs were enormous and the gains slight.

The first American soldiers reached France in June 1917. By the war's end, two million men had crossed the Atlantic. No troop ships were sunk, a credit to the British and American navies. After the summer of 1917, a convoy system developed by Admiral William S. Sims that used Allied destroyers to escort merchant vessels across the ocean cut shipping losses in half.

As expected, on March 21, 1918, the Germans launched a massive assault in western Europe. By May, they had driven Allied forces back to the Marne River, just

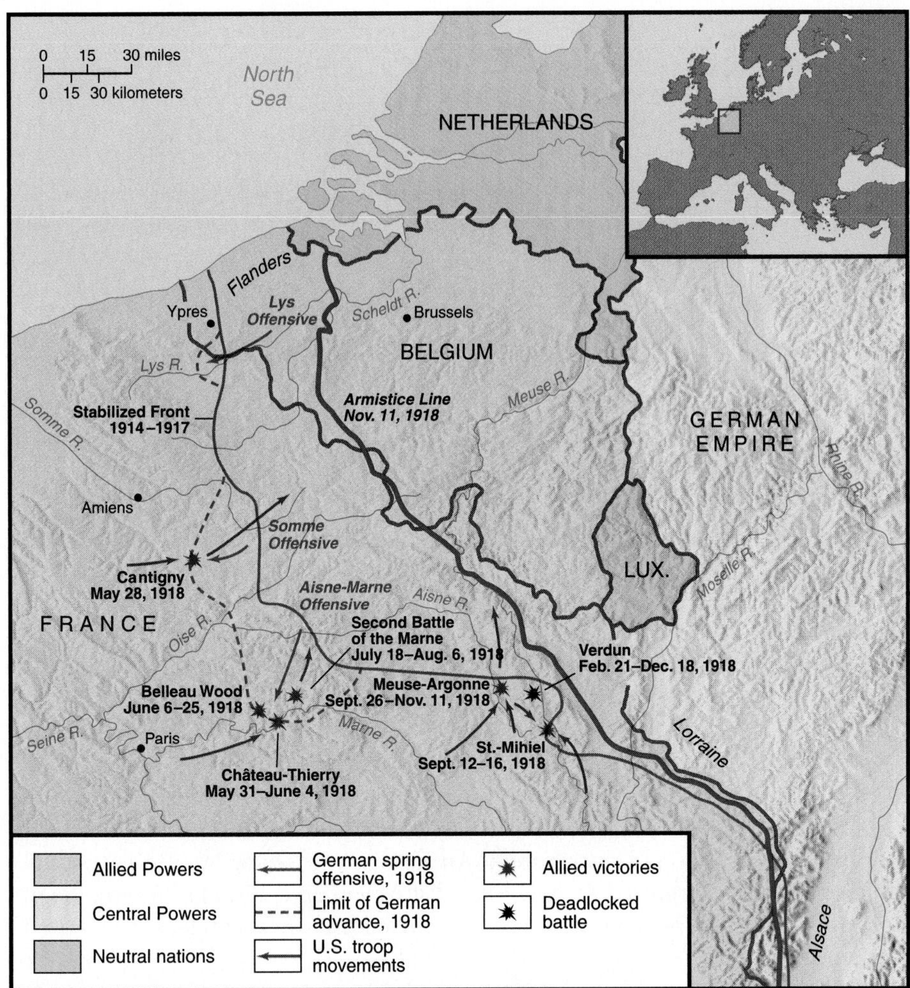

THE WESTERN FRONT: U.S. PARTICIPATION, 1918 *The turning point of the war came in July, when the German advance was halted at the Marne. The "Yanks," now a fighting force, were thrown into the breach. They played a dramatic role in stemming the tide and mounting the counteroffensives that ended the war.* ❖

50 miles from Paris. More than 27,000 Americans saw their first action. They blocked the Germans at the town of Château-Thierry and four weeks later forced them out of Belleau Wood, a crucial strongpoint. On July 15, the Germans threw everything into a last drive for Paris, but in three days they were finished.

With the German drive stalled, the Allies counterattacked along the entire front. On September 12, 1918, half a million Americans and a smaller contingent of French drove the Germans from the St.-Mihiel salient. Two weeks later, 896,000 Americans attacked between the Meuse River and the Argonne Forest. Focusing on the main railroad supply line for the German army in the West, they broke through in early November, cut the line, and drove the Germans back along the whole front.

The German high command knew that the war was lost. At 4 A.M. on November 11, Germany signed the armistice. The AEF lost 48,909 soldiers, and 230,000 were wounded; losses to disease brought the total dead to more than 112,000. The American contribution was vital, although small in comparison to the enormous costs to European nations, which lost more than three million soldiers. Fresh, enthusiastic American troops raised Allied morale; they helped turn the tide at a crucial point in the war. American soldiers, white and black, distinguished themselves during the last months of the terrible war.

German prisoners and American wounded returning from the front lines of the Meuse-Argonne. More Americans died in that campaign than in the rest of the war. The painting is by Harvey Dunn, one of eight official artists with the American Expeditionary Force. ❖

Over Here

Victory at the front depended on economic and emotional mobilization at home. Consolidating federal authority, Wilson moved quickly in 1917 and 1918 to organize war production and distribution. An idealist who knew how to sway public opinion, he also recognized the need to enlist American emotions. To him, the war for people's minds, the "conquest of their convictions," was as vital as events on the battlefield.

The Conquest of Convictions

Committee on Public Information (CPI) Created in 1917 by President Wilson and headed by progressive journalist George Creel, this organization rallied support for American involvement in World War I through art, advertising, and film.

A week after war was declared, Wilson formed the **Committee on Public Information (CPI)** and asked George Creel, an outspoken progressive journalist, to head it. Creel recruited thousands of people in the arts, advertising, and the film industry to publicize the war. He worked out a system of voluntary censorship with the press, plastered walls with colorful posters, and issued more than 75 million pamphlets.

Creel also enlisted 75,000 "four-minute men" to give quick speeches at public gatherings and places of entertainment on the themes "Why We Are Fighting" and "The Meaning of America." By 1918, they were portraying the Germans as bloodthirsty Huns bent on world conquest. Exploiting a new medium, the CPI promoted films such as *The Kaiser: The Beast of Berlin.* Creel secretly subsidized several prowar groups and formed the CPI's Division of Industrial Relations to rally labor to the war.

Helped along by the propaganda campaign, anti-German sentiment spread rapidly. Many schools stopped offering instruction in the German language, sauerkraut was renamed "liberty cabbage," and orchestral works by Bach, Beethoven, and Brahms vanished from some symphonic programs. German Americans and antiwar figures were badgered, beaten, and in some cases killed.

Vigilantism, sparked often by superpatriotism of a ruthless sort, flourished. Frequently, it focused on radical antiwar figures such as Frank Little, an IWW official in Butte, Montana, who was taken from his boardinghouse in August 1917, tied to the rear of an automobile, and dragged through the street until his kneecaps were scraped off. He was then hanged.

Rather than curbing the repression, Wilson encouraged it. At his request, Congress passed the **Espionage Act** of 1917, which authorized sentences of up to twenty years in prison for persons found guilty of aiding the enemy, obstructing the recruitment of soldiers, or encouraging disloyalty. It allowed the postmaster general to remove from the mails materials that incited treason or insurrection.

Espionage Act This law, passed after the United States entered World War I, imposed sentences of up to twenty years on anyone found guilty of aiding the enemy, obstructing recruitment of soldiers, or encouraging disloyalty. It allowed the postmaster general to remove from the mail any materials that incited treason or insurrection.

In 1918, Congress passed the **Sedition Act,** imposing harsh penalties on anyone using "disloyal, profane, scurrilous, or abusive language" about the U.S. government, flag, or uniform. In all, more than fifteen hundred persons were arrested under the new laws, some for such trivial offenses as laughing at rookies drilling at an army camp.

Sedition Act A wartime law that imposed harsh penalties on anyone using "disloyal, profane, scurrilous, or abusive language" about the U.S. government, flag, or armed forces.

The sedition laws clearly went beyond any clear or present danger. There were German spies in the country, to be sure, but the threat did not warrant a nationwide program of repression. Conservatives seized on the laws to stamp out socialists. In 1918, Eugene V. Debs, the Socialist party leader, delivered a speech denouncing capitalism and the war. He was convicted for violation of the Espionage Act and spent the war in a penitentiary in Atlanta. Nominated as the Socialist party candidate in the presidential election of 1920, Debs—prisoner 9653—won nearly a million votes, but the socialist movement never fully recovered from the repression of the war.

In fostering hostility toward anything that smacked of dissent, the war also gave rise to the great Red Scare that began in 1919. Pleased at first with the Russian Revolution, Americans turned quickly against it after Lenin and the Bolsheviks seized control late in 1917. The Americans feared Lenin's anticapitalist program, and they denounced his decision in early 1918 to make peace with Germany because it freed German troops to fight in France. In the summer of 1918, Wilson even cooperated with the Allied leaders and sent American troops into Russia in an attempt to bring down the fledgling Bolshevik government. Although the plan failed to achieve its goals, Wilson joined in an economic blockade of Russia, sent weapons to anti-Bolshevik insurgents, and refused to recognize Lenin's government. His actions soured Russian-American relations for decades.

A Bureaucratic War

Quick, effective action was needed to win the war. To meet the need, Wilson and Congress set up an array of new federal agencies, nearly five thousand in all. Staffed largely by businessmen, the agencies drew on funds and powers of hitherto unknown scope.

The **War Industries Board (WIB),** one of the most powerful of the agencies, oversaw the production of all American factories. Headed by millionaire Bernard M. Baruch, it determined priorities, allocated raw materials, and fixed prices. It told manufacturers what they could and could not make. Working closely with business, Baruch for a time acted as the dictator of the American economy.

War Industries Board (WIB) A wartime government agency that determined priorities, allocated raw materials, and fixed prices; it told manufacturers what they could and could not produce.

Herbert Hoover, the hero of a campaign to feed starving Belgians, headed a new **Food Administration,** and he set out with customary energy to supply food to the armies overseas. Appealing to the "spirit of self-sacrifice," Hoover convinced people to save food by observing "meatless" and "wheatless" days. He fixed prices to boost production, bought and distributed wheat, and encouraged people to plant "victory gardens" at their homes, churches, and schools.

Food Administration A wartime government agency that encouraged Americans to save food in order to supply the armies overseas. It fixed prices to boost production, asked people to observe "meatless" and "wheatless" days to conserve food, and promoted the planting of "victory gardens" behind homes, schools, and churches.

Other agencies rationed fuel and regulated railroads, shipping, and foreign trade. The government intervened in American life as never before: when strikes threatened the telephone and telegraph companies, it simply seized and ran them. The partnership between government and business grew closer. As government expanded, business expanded as well, responding to wartime contracts. Industries such as steel, aluminum, and cigarettes boomed in a war that displayed the triumph of large-scale industrial organization.

FOOD WILL WIN THE WAR
You came here seeking Freedom
You must now help to preserve it
WHEAT is needed for the allies
Waste nothing
204
UNITED STATES FOOD ADMINISTRATION

The U.S. Food Administration urged immigrants and newcomers to America to make sacrifices in the cause of freedom. ❖

Labor in the War

The war also brought organized labor into the partnership with government, although the results were more limited than in the business-government alliance. Samuel Gompers, president of the AFL, served on Wilson's Council of National Defense, an advisory group formed to unify business, labor, and government. Gompers hoped to trade labor peace for labor advances, and he formed the War Committee on Labor to enlist workers' support for the war. With the blessing of the Wilson administration, union membership grew rapidly during the war.

Hoping to encourage production and avoid strikes, Wilson adopted many of the objectives of the social-justice reformers. He supported an eight-hour workday in war-related industries and improved wages and working conditions. The War Labor Board (WLB), headed by Felix Frankfurter, standardized wages and hours, and at Wilson's direction, it protected the right of labor to organize and bargain collectively. Although it did not forbid strikes, it used various tactics to discourage them.

The WLB also ordered that women be paid equal wages for equal work in war industries. Women, blacks, and Mexican Americans filled the labor shortage caused by the draft and the end of large-scale European immigration to America. A million women worked in war industries. Although most held "women's jobs," some were given new opportunities and in some cases higher pay. Working women shared a new sense of confidence and increased expectations.

Looking for more people to fill wartime jobs, corporations found another major source among southern blacks. Beginning in 1916, northern labor agents traveled across the South, promising jobs, high wages, and free transportation. The movement northward became a flood. Between 1916 and 1918, nearly half a million blacks left the Old South for the booming industrial cities of St. Louis, Chicago, Detroit, and Cleveland.

Most of the newcomers were young, unmarried, and semiskilled. The men found jobs in factories, railroad yards, steel mills, packing houses, and coal mines; the women worked in textile factories, department stores, and restaurants. In their new homes, blacks found greater racial freedom but also different living conditions. Northern industrial society struck many blacks as impersonal and lonely, a society ruled by clocks and shop supervisors.

Racial tensions increased, resulting in part from growing competition for housing and jobs. In 1917, a race war in East St. Louis, Illinois, killed nine whites and about forty blacks. In 1919, race riots occurred in Washington, Chicago, New York City, and Omaha. Lynch mobs killed forty-eight blacks in 1917, sixty-three in 1918, and seventy-eight in 1919. Ten of the victims in 1919 were war veterans, several still in uniform.

Blacks were more and more inclined to fight back. Two hundred thousand black soldiers had served in France—42,000 as combat troops. Returning home, they expected better treatment. W. E. B. Du Bois spoke of a "New Negro," proud and more militant: "We return. We return from fighting. We return fighting."

Eager for cheap labor, farmers and ranchers in the Southwest persuaded the federal government to relax immigration restrictions, and between 1917 and 1920,

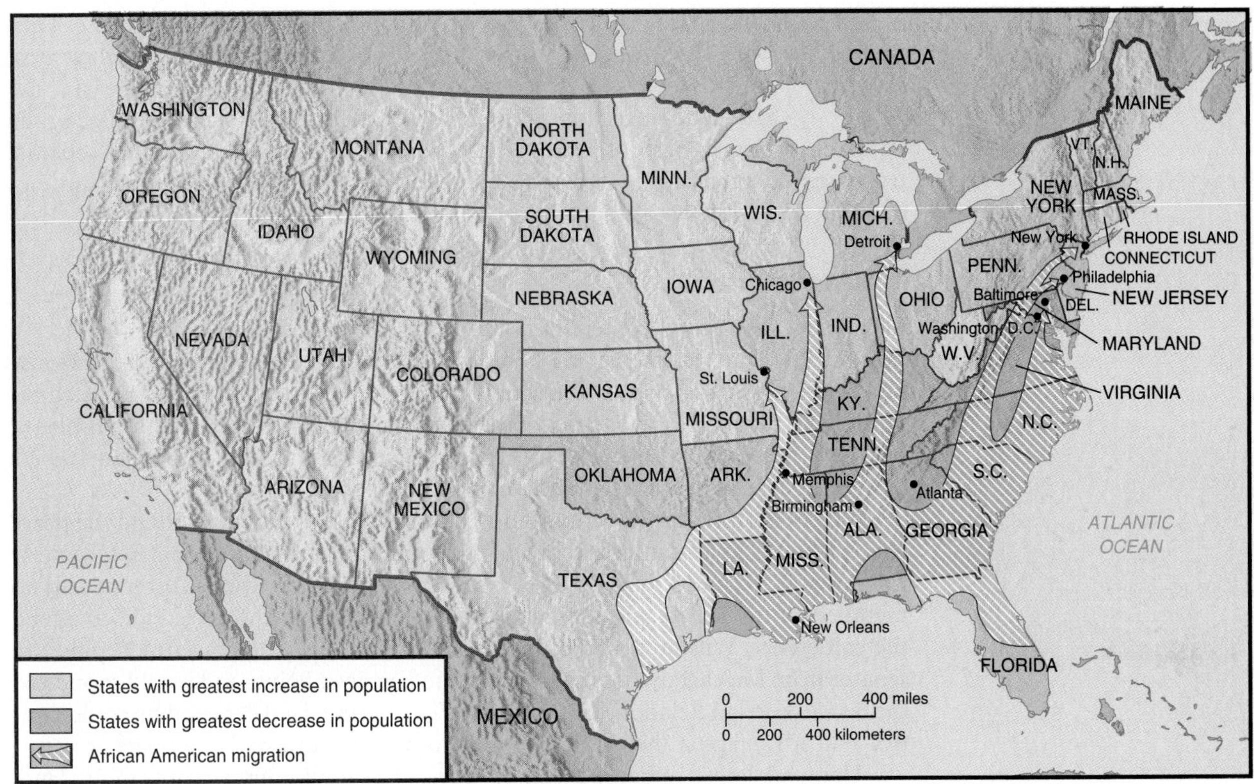

AFRICAN AMERICAN MIGRATION NORTHWARD, 1910–1920 *The massive migration of African Americans from the South to the North during World War I changed the dynamics of race relations in the United States.* ❖

more than 100,000 Mexicans migrated into Texas, New Mexico, Arizona, and California. Tens of thousands of Mexican Americans moved to Chicago, St. Louis, Omaha, and other northern cities to take wartime jobs. Often scorned and insecure, they created urban *barrios,* similar to the Chinatowns and Little Italys around them.

Like most wars, World War I affected patterns at home as much as abroad. Business profits grew, factories expanded, and industries turned out huge amounts of war goods. Government authority swelled, and people came to expect different things of their government. Labor made some gains, as did women and blacks. Society assimilated some of the shifts, but social and economic tensions continued to grow, and when the war ended, they spilled over in the strikes and violence of the Red Scare of 1919 (see Chapter 25).

The United States emerged from the war the strongest economic power in the world. In 1914, it was a debtor nation: American citizens owed foreign investors about $3 billion. Five years later, the United States had become a creditor nation. Foreign governments owed more than $10 billion, and foreign citizens owed American investors nearly $3 billion. The war marked a drastic shift in economic power between Europe and America.

The Treaty of Versailles

Long before the fighting ended, Wilson began to formulate plans for the peace. On January 8, 1918, appearing before Congress to rebut Bolshevik arguments that the war was merely a struggle among imperialists, the president outlined terms for a far-reaching, nonpunitive settlement. Wilson's **Fourteen Points** were generous and farsighted, but they failed to satisfy wartime emotions.

Fourteen Points In January 1918, President Wilson presented these terms for a far-reaching, nonpunitive settlement of World War I. He called, among other things, for removal of barriers to trade, open peace accords, reduction of armaments, and the establishment of a League of Nations. The Points were largely rejected by European nations.

England and France distrusted Wilsonian idealism as the basis for peace. They wanted Germany disarmed and crippled; they wanted its colonies; and they were skeptical of the principle of self-determination. As the end of the war neared, the Allies, who had made secret commitments with one another, balked at making the Fourteen Points the basis of peace. When Wilson threatened to negotiate a separate treaty with Germany, however, they accepted. Wilson had won an important victory, but difficulties lay ahead.

A Peace at Paris

Just before the peace conference began, Wilson appealed to voters to elect a Democratic Congress in the 1918 elections. The Democrats lost both the House and Senate, enabling Wilson's opponents to announce that voters had rejected his policies. In fact, the Democratic losses stemmed largely from domestic problems, but they hurt Wilson, who would soon be negotiating with European leaders buoyed by rousing victories at their own polls.

Two weeks after the election, Wilson announced that he would attend the peace conference. This was a dramatic break from tradition, and his personal involvement drew attacks from Republicans. They renewed the criticism when Wilson named no members of the Senate and no prominent Republicans to the delegation to attend the conference. Wilson passed over Henry Cabot Lodge, the powerful Republican senator from Massachusetts who opposed the Fourteen Points and would soon head the Senate Foreign Relations Committee. Wilson wanted a delegation he could control—an advantage at the peace table but not in any battle over the treaty at home.

Upon his arrival in Europe, Wilson received a tumultuous welcome in England, France, and Italy. Overwhelmed, Wilson was sure that people shared his goals, but he was wrong: like their leaders, they hated Germany and wanted victory unmistakably reflected in the peace plan.

Woodrow Wilson's Fourteen Points, 1918: Success and Failure in Implementation

	Point	Result
1.	Open covenants of peace openly arrived at	Not fulfilled
2.	Absolute freedom of navigation on the seas in peace and war	Not fulfilled
3.	Removal of all economic barriers to the equality of trade among nations	Not fulfilled
4.	Reduction of armaments to the level needed only for domestic safety	Not fulfilled
5.	Impartial adjustments of colonial claims	Not fulfilled
6.	Evacuation of all Russian territory; Russia to be welcomed into the society of free nations	Not fulfilled
7.	Evacuation and restoration of Belgium	**Fulfilled**
8.	Evacuation and restoration of all French lands; return of Alsace-Lorraine to France	**Fulfilled**
9.	Readjustment of Italy's frontiers along lines of Italian nationality	Compromised
10.	Self-determination for the former subjects of the Austro-Hungarian Empire	Compromised
11.	Evacuation of Rumania, Serbia, and Montenegro; free access to the sea for Serbia	Compromised
12.	Self-determination for the former subjects of the Ottoman Empire; secure sovereignty for Turkish portion	Compromised
13.	Establishment of an independent Poland, with free and secure access to the sea	**Fulfilled**
14.	Establishment of a League of Nations affording mutual guarantees of independence and territorial integrity	Not fulfilled

Sources: Data from G. M. Gathorne-Hardy, *The Fourteen Points and the Treaty of Versailles* (Oxford Pamphlets on World Affairs, no. 6, 1939), pp. 8–34; Thomas G. Paterson et al., *American Foreign Policy: A History Since 1900*, 2nd ed., vol. 2, pp. 282–293.

EUROPE AFTER THE TREATY OF VERSAILLES, 1919 *The treaty changed the map of Europe, creating a number of new and reconstituted nations.* ❖

Opening in January 1919, the Peace Conference at Paris continued until May. Although twenty-seven nations were represented, the "Big Four" dominated it: Wilson; Georges Clemenceau, the stubborn French premier who was determined to end the German threat forever; David Lloyd George, the crafty British prime minister who had pledged to squeeze Germany "until the pips squeak"; and the Italian prime minister, Vittorio Orlando. A clever negotiator, Wilson traded various "small" concessions for his major goals—national self-determination, a reduction in tensions, and a league of nations to enforce the peace.

Wilson had to surrender some important principles. Instead of peace without victory, the treaty made Germany accept responsibility for the war and demanded enormous reparations. It made no mention of disarmament, free trade, or freedom of the seas, and it violated the goal of self-determination. Instead of an open covenant openly arrived at, the treaty was drafted behind closed doors.

But Wilson deflected some of the most extreme Allied demands, and he won his coveted Point 14, the League of Nations, designed "to achieve international peace and security." The League included a general assembly; a smaller council composed of the United States, Great Britain, France, Italy, Japan, and four nations to be elected by the assembly; and a court of international justice. League members pledged to submit every dispute that threatened peace for arbitration and to enjoin military and economic sanctions against nations resorting to war. Article X, for Wilson the heart of the League, obligated members to protect each other's independence and territorial integrity.

Draft treaty in hand, Wilson returned home in February 1919 to discuss it with Congress and the people. Public opinion polls showed that most Americans favored the League, but there was strong congressional opposition to it. Thirty-seven senators, including Lodge, said they would not vote for the treaty without amendment. Should those numbers hold up, Lodge had enough votes to defeat it.

Returning to Paris, Wilson attacked his critics while privately working for changes to improve the chances of Senate approval. The Allies won major concessions in return, but they amended the League draft treaty, agreeing that domestic affairs remained outside the League's jurisdiction, exempting the Monroe Doctrine, and allowing nations to withdraw after two years' notice. On June 28, 1919, they signed the treaty in the Hall of Mirrors at Versailles, and Wilson started home for his most difficult fight.

Rejection in the Senate

There were ninety-six senators in 1919, forty-nine of them Republicans. Fourteen Republicans, led by William E. Borah of Idaho, were the "irreconcilables" who opposed the League on any grounds. Frank B. Kellogg of Minnesota led a group of twelve "mild reservationists" who accepted the treaty but wanted to insert several conditions that would not greatly weaken it. Finally, there were the Lodge-led "strong reservationists," twenty-three in all, who wanted major changes that the Allies would have to approve.

With only four Democratic senators opposed to the treaty, the Democrats and compromise-minded Republicans had enough votes to ratify it, once a few reservations were inserted. Playing for time to allow public opposition to grow, Lodge scheduled lengthy hearings on the treaty. Democratic leaders urged Wilson to appeal to the Republican "mild reservationists," but he angrily refused.

Fed up with Lodge's tactics, Wilson set out in early September to take the case directly to the people. In Pueblo, Colorado, toward the end of his tour, he delivered one of the most eloquent speeches of his career. That night, Wilson felt ill. He returned to Washington, and on October 2, his wife found him lying unconscious on the floor of the White House, the victim of a stroke that had paralyzed his left side.

After the stroke, Wilson could not work more than an hour or two at a time, and he saw very few people. He did not meet with the cabinet for seven months. When he learned that Secretary of State Lansing had convened cabinet meetings, Wilson forced the man to resign. Focusing his waning energy on the fight over the treaty, Wilson lost touch with other issues, and critics charged that his wife, Edith Bolling Wilson, was running the government.

Humanity is the accuser, the U.S. Senate is the assassin, and the Treaty of Versailles is the victim in this commentary on the Senate's rejection of the treaty. Isolationists, who wanted to keep the United States out of European affairs, opposed the treaty because it included the Covenant for the League of Nations. ❖

On November 6, 1919, Lodge finally reported the treaty out of committee, along with "Fourteen Reservations," one for each of Wilson's points. The most important reservation stipulated that implementation of Article X, Wilson's key article, required the action of Congress in each case.

Even though the Democrats could not pass the treaty without reservations, Wilson refused to compromise. When Mrs. Wilson urged her husband to accept the Lodge reservations, he said, "Better a thousand times to go down fighting than to dip your colors to dishonorable compromise."

On November 19, the treaty—with the Lodge reservations—failed, 39 to 55. Following Wilson's instructions, the Democrats voted against it. A motion to approve without the reservations lost 38 to 53, with only one Republican voting in favor. Neither Wilson nor Lodge would compromise. When the treaty with reservations again came up for vote on March 19, 1920, twenty-one Democrats defied Wilson and voted for it. But by a vote of 49 to 35, seven votes short of the necessary two-thirds majority, the treaty was defeated.

CHRONOLOGY

1901	Hay-Paunceforte Treaty empowers United States to build an isthmian canal
1904	Theodore Roosevelt introduces his Corollary to the Monroe Doctrine
1904–1905	Russo-Japanese War is fought
1905	Taft-Katsura Agreement recognizes Japanese power in Korea
1908	Root-Takahira Agreement vows to maintain the status quo in the Pacific ❖ Roosevelt sends the fleet around the world
1911	Revolution begins in Mexico
1913–1914	Bryan negotiates "cooling-off" treaties to end the war
1914	World War I begins ❖ U.S. Marines take Veracruz, Mexico ❖ Panama Canal is completed
1915	Japan issues Twenty-One Demands to China (January) ❖ Germany declares the waters around the British Isles a war zone (February) ❖ *Lusitania* torpedoed (May) ❖ Bryan resigns; Robert Lansing becomes secretary of state (June) ❖ *Arabic* pledge restricts submarine warfare (September)
1916	Germany issues *Sussex* pledge (March) ❖ General John J. Pershing leads a punitive expedition into Mexico to seize Pancho Villa (April) ❖ Wilson wins reelection (November)
1917	Wilson calls for "peace without victory" (January) ❖ Germany resumes unrestricted U-boat warfare (February) ❖ United States enters World War I (April) ❖ Congress passes the Selective Service Act (May) ❖ First American troops reach France (June) ❖ War Industries Board is established (July)
1918	Wilson outlines Fourteen Points for peace (January) ❖ Germany asks for peace (October) ❖ Armistice ends the war (November)
1919	Peace negotiations begin in Paris (January) ❖ Treaty of Versailles is defeated in the Senate
1920	Warren G. Harding is elected president

To Wilson, one chance remained: the presidential election of 1920. The Democrats nominated Governor James M. Cox of Ohio. Wilson called for "a great and solemn referendum" on the treaty. The Democratic platform endorsed the treaty but agreed to accept reservations to clarify the American role in the League.

On the Republican side, Senator Warren G. Harding of Ohio won the presidential nomination. Harding waffled on the treaty, but it made little difference. Voters wanted a change. Harding won in a landslide. Without a peace treaty, the United States remained technically at war, and it was not until July 1921, almost three years after the last shot was fired, that Congress passed a joint resolution ending the war.

Conclusion: Postwar Disillusionment

After 1919, disillusionment set in. World War I was feared before it started, popular while it lasted, and hated when it ended. To a whole generation that followed, it appeared futile—killing without a cause, sacrifice without benefit. Books, plays, and movies—such as Hemingway's *Farewell to Arms,* John Dos Passos's *Three Soldiers,* and Lawrence Stallings and Maxwell Anderson's *What Price Glory?*—depicted waste, horror, and death.

The war and its aftermath damaged the progressive, humanitarian spirit of the early years of the century. It killed "something precious and perhaps irretrievable in the hearts of thinking men and women." Progressivism survived well into the 1920s and the New Deal, but it no longer had its old conviction or broad popular support. Bruising fights over the war and the League drained people's energy and enthusiasm.

Woodrow Wilson died in Washington in 1924, three years after the new president, Harding, promised "not heroics but healing; not nostrums but normalcy; not revolution but restoration." Nonetheless, the "war to end all wars" and the spirit of Woodrow Wilson left an indelible imprint on the country.

Key Terms

Hay-Bunau-Varilla Treaty, p. 466
Roosevelt Corollary, p. 466
"dollar diplomacy", p. 468
moral diplomacy, p. 468
Selective Service Act, p. 474
Committee on Public Information (CPI), p. 476
Espionage Act, p. 477
Sedition Act, p. 477
War Industries Board (WIB), p. 477
Food Administration, p. 477
Fourteen Points, p. 479

Recommended Reading

American foreign policy between 1901 and 1921 has been the subject of considerable study. Richard W. Leopold, *The Growth of American Foreign Policy* (1962), is balanced and informed. Robert E. Osgood, *Ideals and Self-Interest in America's Foreign Relations* (1953), and William Appleman Williams, *Roots of the Modern American Empire* (1969), explore the forces underlying American foreign policy.

For American policy toward Latin America, see Dana G. Munro's detailed account, *Intervention and Dollar Diplomacy in the Caribbean, 1900–1920* (1964); Mary A. Renda, *Taking Haiti: Military Occupation and the Culture of U.S. Imperialism, 1915–1940* (2001); and Emily S. Rosenberg, *Financial Missionaries to the World: The Politics and Culture of Dollar Diplomacy, 1900–1930* (1999). Arthur S. Link examines Wilson's foreign policy in his exceptional five-volume biography, *Wilson* (1947–1965), and in *Woodrow Wilson: Revolution, War, and Peace* (1979).

Studies of events at home during the war include David M. Kennedy, *Over Here* (1980); Robert D. Cuff, *The War Industries Board* (1973); and Maurine W. Greenwald, *Women, War, and Work* (1980). Susan Zeiger, *In Uncle Sam's Service: Women Workers with the American Expeditionary Force, 1917–1919* (1999), and Kathleen Kennedy, *Disloyal Mothers and Scurrilous Citizens: Women and Subversion During World War I* (1999), look at the role of women; Jennifer D. Keene, *Doughboys, the Great War, and the Remaking of America* (2001), at the war's effects on the soldiers; and Mark Robert Schneider, *"We Return Fighting": The Civil Rights Movement in the Jazz Age* (2001), Mark Ellis, *Race, War, and Surveillance: African Americans and the United States Government during World War I* (2001), and Theodore Kornweibel, Jr., *"Investigate Everything": Federal Efforts to Compel Black Loyalty During World War I* (2002), at its impact on African Americans.

Arthur Walworth, *America's Moment, 1918: American Diplomacy at the End of World War I* (1977), examines Wilson's attempt to create a peaceful world order.

For a list of additional titles related to this chapter's topics, please see http://www.ablongman.com/divine.

Suggested Web Sites

Woodrow Wilson

http://www.ipl.org/ref/POTUS/wwilson.html
This page contains basic factual data about his election and presidency, speeches, and on-line biographies.

World War I Document Archive

http://www.lib.byu.edu/~rdh/wwi/
This archive contains sources about World War I in general, not just America's involvement.

World War One: Trenches on the Web

http://www.worldwar1.com/index.html
This site provides a mass of data concerning the prosecution of the world's first global war.

The Great Migration in Chicago

http://lcweb.loc.gov/exhibits/african/afam011.html
This site looks at the black experience in the Great Migration through the lens of one prominent destination.

The American Experience: Influenza

http://www.pbs.org/wgbh/pages/amex/influenza
This PBS site reveals the impact of the great flu epidemic of 1918.

Chapter 25

Transition to Modern America

Wheels for the Millions

The moving assembly line that Henry Ford developed in 1913 in Highland Park, Michigan, to manufacture the Model T marked only the first step toward full mass production and the beginning of America's worldwide industrial supremacy. Ford already had a vision of a vast industrial tract where machines, moving through a sequence of carefully arranged manufacturing operations, would transform raw materials into finished cars, trucks, and tractors. By the mid-1920s at River Rouge, his plant southeast of Detroit, his vision had been realized.

Ford expanded his industrial dream in 1919 when he built a blast furnace and foundry to make engine blocks for both the Model T and his tractors. By 1924, more than forty thousand workers were turning out nearly all the metal parts used in making Ford vehicles.

Visitors from all over the world came to marvel at River Rouge. Some were disturbed by the jumble of machines and the apparent congestion on the plant floor, but industrial experts recognized that the arrangement led to incredible productivity because "the work moves and the men stand still." As a whole, the plant was "one huge, perfectly timed, smoothly operating industrial machine."

In 1927, Ford closed the assembly line at Highland Park. For the next six months, his engineers worked on designing a more compact and efficient assembly line at River Rouge for the Model A, which went into production in November. By then, River Rouge had more than justified Ford's vision. For a generation of engineers, wrote historian Geoffrey Perrett, the River Rouge plant was "a monument."

Mass production, born in Highland Park in 1914 and perfected at River Rouge in the 1920s, became a hallmark of American industry. Soon Ford's emphasis on the flow of parts moving past stationary workers became the standard in nearly every American factory. The moving assembly line took away the last vestige of craftsmanship and turned workers into near robots. It also led to amazing efficiency that produced both high profits for manufacturers and low prices for buyers.

OUTLINE

The Second Industrial Revolution

City Life in the Jazz Age

The Rural Counterattack

Politics of the 1920s

Conclusion: The Old and the New

MOST IMPORTANT, MASS PRODUCTION CONTRIBUTED to a consumer goods revolution. American factories turned out a flood of automobiles, electrical appliances, and other items that made life easier and more pleasant for most Americans. The result was the creation of a distinctively modern America, one marked by the material abundance that has characterized American society ever since.

But the abundance came at a price. The 1920s have been portrayed as a decade of escape and frivolity, and for many Americans they were just that. But those years also were an era of transition: a time when the old America of individualistic rural values gave way to a new America of conformist urban values. The transition was often wrenching, and many Americans clung desperately to the old ways. Modernity finally won, but not without a struggle.

THE SECOND INDUSTRIAL REVOLUTION

The first Industrial Revolution in the late nineteenth century had catapulted the United States to the forefront of the world's richest and most highly developed nations. With the advent of the new consumer goods industries, the American people by the 1920s enjoyed the highest standard of living of any nation on earth. From 1922 to 1929, the economy boomed. American industrial output nearly doubled, and the gross national product rose by 40 percent. Most of this explosive growth took place in industries producing goods for consumers. Equally important, the national per capita annual income increased by 30 percent to $681 in 1929. American workers became the highest paid in history. Combined with the expansion of installment credit programs that allowed customers to buy now and pay later, this income growth allowed a purchasing spree unlike anything the nation had ever experienced.

The key to the new affluence was technology. Electric motors replaced steam engines as the basic source of energy in factories, and efficiency experts helped maximize labor's output. Production per worker-hour increased an amazing 75 percent in the 1920s.

The Automobile Industry

The effects of the consumer goods revolution can best be seen in the automobile industry, which became the nation's largest in the 1920s. Rapid growth was its distinguishing feature. In 1920, there were 10 million cars in the nation; by the end of the decade, 26 million were on the road.

Ford continued to lead the way, but General Motors and Chrysler Corporation offered stiff competition. Small manufacturers began to disappear, victims of the huge costs involved in mass production. *Oligopoly,* control of an industry by a few large companies, became the dominant pattern in all the consumer goods industries.

The automobile boom depended on the apparently insatiable American appetite for cars. But soon the market became saturated as more and more of the people who could afford the novel luxury had become car owners. Marketing became as crucial as production. Automobile makers began to rely heavily on advertising and annual model changes, seeking to make customers dissatisfied with their old vehicles and eager to order new ones. Installment buying also helped prolong the boom.

Despite these efforts, sales slumped in 1927 when Ford stopped making the Model T, picked up again the next year with the introduction of the Model A, and began to slide again in 1929. The automobile industry revealed a basic weakness in the consumer goods economy: once people bought an item with a long life, they were out of the market for years.

In the affluent 1920s, few observers recognized the signs of economic instability. They were too enthralled by the stimulating effect the automobile industry had on such industries as steel, rubber, paint, glass, and road construction. Filling stations, tourist cabins (forerunners of the modern motel), and drive-ins of all kinds began to dot the landscape along the major and minor highways. The auto changed the whole pattern of city life, fueling a suburban explosion as real estate developers built houses in ever wider concentric circles around the central cities.

Patterns of Economic Growth

Automobiles were the most conspicuous of the consumer products that flourished in the 1920s but certainly not the only ones. The electrical industry grew nearly as quickly. Two-thirds of all American families had electricity by the end of the decade, and they spent vast sums on washing machines, vacuum cleaners, refrigerators, and ranges. The new appliances eased the burdens of the housewife and ushered in an age of leisure.

Radio broadcasting and motion picture production also boomed in the 1920s. The early success of KDKA in Pittsburgh stimulated the growth of more than eight hundred independent radio stations, and by 1929, NBC had formed the first successful radio network. The film industry thrived in Hollywood, reaching its maturity in the mid-1920s. With the advent of the "talkies" in 1929, average weekly movie attendance climbed to nearly 100 million.

Other industries prospered as well. Production of light metals, chemicals, and synthetics grew into major businesses. Americans found a whole new spectrum of products to buy—cigarette lighters, wristwatches, heat-resistant glass cooking dishes, and rayon stockings were just a few.

The corporation continued to be the dominant business structure in the 1920s. Corporations now had hundreds of thousands of stockholders. The enormous profits the corporations generated provided ample funds to finance growth and expansion, freeing companies from their earlier dependence on investment bankers such as J. P. Morgan. Operating independent of outside restraint, corporate managers were accountable only to other managers.

Another wave of mergers accompanied the growth of corporations during the 1920s. By the end of the decade, the two hundred largest nonfinancial corporations owned almost half of the country's corporate wealth. The greatest abuses took place in public utilities, where promoters such as Samuel Insull built vast paper empires by gaining control of power companies and then draining them of their assets.

The most distinctive feature of the new consumer-oriented economy was the stress on advertising. Skillful practitioners such as Edward Bernays and Bruce Barton sought to control public tastes and consumer spending by identifying the good life with the possession of the latest product of American industry, be it a car, a refrigerator, or a cigarette.

Uniformity and standardization, the characteristics of mass production, now prevailed. Chain stores proliferated at the expense of small retail establishments. Kansas farmers bought the same items as Pennsylvania factory workers. Sectional differences in dress, food, and furniture began to disappear. Radio and films even threatened regional accents by promoting a standard national dialect devoid of any local flavor.

❖ A Look at the Past ❖

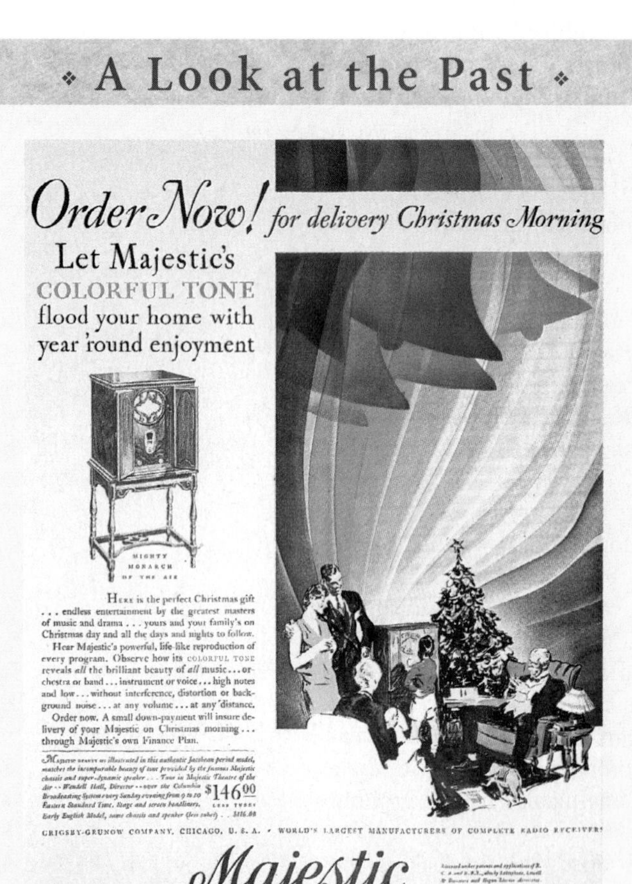

Radio

Radios became enormously popular during the 1920s and 1930s, giving people access to news and entertainment in their homes on demand. While some radios fit on table tops, other models were large, fine pieces of furniture suitable for covering with doilies and treasured photographs. What do such expensive, fancy models suggest about the place of radio in the home? Why would radios attain a privileged position in the home?

Economic Weaknesses

The New Era, as businessmen labeled the decade, was not as prosperous as it first appeared. The revolution in consumer goods disguised the decline of many traditional industries in the 1920s. Railroads suffered from poor management and from the competition of the growing trucking industry. Coal was being replaced by petroleum and natural gas. Cotton textiles declined with the development of rayon and other synthetic fibers.

Hit hardest of all was agriculture. American farmers had expanded production to meet the demands of World War I. After the war, farm prices and exports fell sharply. Throughout the 1920s, the farmers' share of the national income dropped until by 1929, per capita annual farm income was only $273, compared to the national average of $681.

Urban workers, although better off than farmers, did not share fully in the decade's affluence. The industrial labor force remained remarkably steady for a period of economic growth; the technical innovations meant that the same number of workers could produce far more than before. Most of the new jobs came in the lower-paying service industries. Although wages rose slowly, conditions of life for the worker did improve. Prices remained stable, so workers experienced a gain in real wages.

Organized labor proved unable to advance the interests of workers in the 1920s. Many businessmen used the injunction and "yellow dog" contracts, which forbade employees from joining unions, to establish open shops and deny workers the benefits of collective bargaining. Other employers wooed their workers away from unions using techniques of welfare capitalism, spending money to improve plant conditions and winning employee loyalty with pensions, paid vacations, and company cafeterias. The net result was a decline in union membership from a postwar high of five million to less than three million by 1929.

❖ A Look at the Past ❖

Glenwood Stove Ad

The Glenwood stove, fueled by wood, coal, or gas, reveals the unevenness of technological change. While some women were able to cook with convenient, clean natural gas, others still used dirty coal or carried armloads of wood. The Glenwood also demonstrated that consumers wanted to purchase fashionable, up-to-date, and labor-saving products even if such goods depended on wood rather than the modern fuel, gas. Why do you suppose standardization had become a goal for consumers as well as for producers?

Black workers remained on the bottom, both economically and socially. Many of the blacks who migrated northward during World War I found jobs only in menial service areas—collecting garbage, washing dishes, sweeping floors. Yet even these jobs offered them a better life than they found on the depressed southern farms, and so the migration continued. The black population in Chicago, New York, and other northern cities more than doubled during the 1920s.

Middle- and upper-class Americans were the groups who thrived in the decade. The rewards of the second Industrial Revolution went to the managers—the engineers, bankers, and executives—who directed the new industrial economy. These were the people who bought the fine new homes in the suburbs and who could afford more than one car. Their conspicuous consumption helped fuel the prosperity of the 1920s, but their disposable income eventually became greater than their material wants. The result was speculation, as men with idle money began to invest heavily in the stock market to reap gains from the industrial growth.

The economic trends of the decade had both positive and negative implications for the future. On the plus side, the growth of new consumer-based industries was solid. Automobiles and appliances were not passing fancies but part of the modern American way of life. The future pattern of American culture—cars and suburbs, shopping centers and skyscrapers—was set by the end of the 1920s.

But at the same time, there were ominous signs of danger. The unequal distribution of wealth, the growth of consumer debt, the saturation of the market for cars and appliances, and the rampant speculation all contributed to economic instability. The boom of the 1920s would end in a great crash; yet the achievements of the decade would survive even that dire experience.

City Life in the Jazz Age

The city replaced the countryside as the center of American life in the 1920s. The 1920 census revealed that for the first time, more than half the population lived in cities, defined broadly to include all places of more than 2,500 people. Between 1920 and 1930, cities with populations of 250,000 or more added some eight million people.

The skyscraper soon became the most visible feature of the city. Constrained by inflated land prices, builders built upward, developing a distinctively American architectural style in the process. By 1929, the United States had 377 buildings more than seventy stories tall. The skyscraper came to symbolize the new mass culture.

In the metropolis, life was different. The old community ties of home, church, and school were loosening, but there were important gains—new ideas, new creativity, new perspectives. Some city-dwellers became lost and lonely without the old institutions; others thrived in the urban environment.

Women and the Family

The urban culture of the 1920s witnessed important changes in the American family, which began to break down under the impact of economic and social change. A new freedom for women and children seemed to be emerging in its wake.

Although World War I accelerated the process by which women left the home for work, the postwar decade witnessed a return to the slower pace of the prewar years. During the 1920s there was no permanent gain in the number of working women. Two million more women were employed in 1930 than in 1920, but this represented an increase of only 1 percent. Most women workers, however, had lower-paying jobs, ranging from stenographers and retail store clerks to maids. For the most part, the professions were reserved for men, with women relegated to such stereotypical fields as teaching and nursing.

Women had won the right to vote in 1920, but the Nineteenth Amendment proved to have less impact than its proponents had hoped. It robbed women of a unifying cause, and the suffrage itself did little to change the prevailing gender roles. Men remained the principal breadwinners in the family; women cooked, cleaned, and reared the children.

The feminist movement, however, still showed signs of vitality. In 1923, the National Woman's party succeeded in having an Equal Rights Amendment (ERA) introduced in Congress. Other women's organizations opposed the amendment on the ground that women needed legal protection, especially laws guaranteeing them at least a minimum wage and limiting the maximum length of the workday. The drive for the ERA failed in the 1920s, but social feminists were more successful in pushing for such humanitarian reforms as the Sheppard-Towner Act of 1921, which provided federal aid to establish state programs for maternal and infant health care.

A generational change had a profound impact on feminism in the 1920s. Instead of crusading for social progress, young women concentrated on individual self-expression by rebelling against Victorian restraints. In the cities, some quickly adopted what critic H. L. Mencken called the "flapper" image. Cutting their hair short, raising their skirts above the knee, and binding their breasts, flappers set out to compete on equal terms with men on the golf course and in the speakeasy. Shocking to their elders, the flappers assaulted the traditional double standard in sex, demanding that equality with men should include sexual fulfillment before and during marriage. The new permissiveness led to a sharp rise in the divorce rate.

The sense of women's emancipation was heightened by a drop in the birthrate and the abundance of consumer goods. Yet appearances were deceptive. Many women could not enjoy the new laborsaving devices. The typical childless woman spent between forty-three and fifty hours a week on household duties; for mothers, the average workweek was fifty-six hours, far longer than that of their husbands. And despite the talk of the "new woman," traditional gender roles remained unshaken. As one historian has concluded, "In the 1920s, as in the 1790s, marriage was the only approved state for women."

The family, however, did change. It became smaller as easier access to effective birth control methods enabled couples to limit the number of their offspring. More and more married women took jobs outside the home. Young people, who had once joined the labor force when they entered their teens, now enjoyed adolescence as a stage of life devoted to school and leisure.

This prolonged adolescence led to new strains on the family in the form of youthful revolt. Freed of the traditional burden of earning a living at an early age, youth in the 1920s went on a great spree. Heavy drinking, casual sexual encounters, and a constant search for excitement became the hallmarks of the upper-class youth immortalized by F. Scott Fitzgerald. The theme of rebellion against parental authority, which runs through all aspects of the 1920s, was at the heart of the youth movement.

The Roaring Twenties

Excitement ran high in the cities as crime waves and highly publicized sports events flourished. Prohibition ushered in such distinctive features of the decade as speakeasies, bootleggers, and bathtub gin. Crime rose sharply as middle- and upper-class Americans willingly broke the law to gain access to alcoholic beverages. City streets became the scene of violent shoot-outs between rival bootleggers, and underworld czars such as Al Capone controlled illicit empires.

Sports became a national mania in the 1920s as people gained more leisure time. Golf boomed, with two million men and women playing the sport. Spectator sports attracted even more attention. Millions of Americans found drama in the exploits of boxer Jack Dempsey, footballer Red Grange, and baseball great Babe Ruth. Massive new stadiums had to be built to hold the growing numbers of sports fans.

In what Frederick Lewis Allen called "the ballyhoo years," the popular yearning for excitement led people to seek thrills in all kinds of ways—applauding Charles Lindbergh's solo flight across the Atlantic and flocking to such bizarre events as six-day bicycle races, dance marathons, and flagpole-sittings. Hero worship of sports and entertainment stars became an escape from the drabness of life on the assembly line.

Sex became another focal point in the 1920s as Victorian standards began to crumble. Sophisticated city-dwellers seemed to be intent on exploring a new freedom in sexual expression. Hollywood exploited the obsession with sex by producing movies with such provocative titles as *A Shocking Night* and *Women and Lovers.* Plays and novels focused on adultery, and the new urban tabloids delighted in telling their readers about love nests and kept women. Young people embraced the new permissiveness joyfully, with the automobile providing couples an easy means to escape parental supervision.

Sheik with Sheba *is the title of this John Held, Jr., drawing, which appeared on a 1925 cover of* Judge *magazine. Held's drawings define the image of the "flapper" era—the young woman with rolled-down stockings and rouged knees and the young man with cigarette and pocket flask at the wheel of his car.* ❖

There is considerable debate, however, over the extent of the sexual revolution in the 1920s. Actual changes in sexual behavior are beyond the historian's reach, hidden in the privacy of the bedroom, but the old Victorian prudery was a clear casualty of the 1920s. At least in urban areas, sex was no longer a taboo subject; men and women now could and did discuss it openly.

Flowering of the Arts

The greatest cultural advance of the 1920s was the outpouring of literature. The city gave rise to a new class of intellectuals—writers who commented on the new industrial society. Many were bewildered by the rapidly changing social patterns of the 1920s and appalled by the materialism of American culture. Some fled to Europe to live as expatriates. Others stayed at home, observing and condemning the excesses of a business civilization. All shared a sense of disillusionment and wrote pessimistically of the flawed promise of American life. Yet, ironically, their body of writing revealed a profound creativity that suggested that America was coming of age intellectually.

The exiles included the poet T. S. Eliot and the novelist Ernest Hemingway. In *The Waste Land,* which appeared in 1922, Eliot evoked images of fragmentation and sterility that had a powerful impact on the other disillusioned writers of the decade. Eliot reached the depths of despair in *The Hollow Men* (1925), a biting depiction of the emptiness of modern life. Hemingway sought redemption from the modern plight in the romantic individualism of his heroes. He wrote of men alienated from society who found a sense of identity in their own courage and quest for personal honor. His greatest impact on other writers came from his sparse, direct, clean prose style.

Writers who stayed home were equally critical of contemporary American life. In *The Great Gatsby* (1925), F. Scott Fitzgerald chronicled American high society, emphasizing its emptiness and lack of human concern. Sinclair Lewis became the most popular of the critical novelists. *Main Street* (1920) satirized the values of small-town America as dull, complacent, and narrow-minded, and *Babbitt* (1922) poked fun at the commercialism of the 1920s.

Most savage of all was H. L. Mencken, the Baltimore newspaperman and literary critic who founded *The American Mercury* in 1923. He mocked everything he found distasteful in America, from the Rotary Club to the Ku Klux Klan. A born cynic, he served as a zealous guardian of public integrity in an era of excessive boosterism.

The cultural explosion of the 1920s was surprisingly broad. It included novelists such as Sherwood Anderson and John Dos Passos—who described the way the new machine age undermined such traditional American values as craftsmanship and a sense of community—and playwrights such as Eugene O'Neill and Maxwell Anderson. Women writers were particularly effective in dealing with regional themes. Edith Wharton continued to write penetratingly about eastern aristocrats, and Willa Cather and Ellen Glasgow focused on the plight of women in the Midwest and the South, respectively. The greatest contribution to American music, imbuing it with a new vitality, came from the spread of jazz as blacks migrated northward. The form of jazz known as the blues became an authentic national folk music.

The cultural growth of the 1920s was the work of African Americans as well as whites. W. E. B. Du Bois became the intellectual voice of the African American community developing in New York City's Harlem. Along with James Weldon Johnson, a gifted poet, Du Bois became the leader of the **Harlem Renaissance.** The NAACP moved its headquarters to Harlem, and in 1923, the Urban League began publishing *Opportunity,* a magazine devoted to scholarly studies of racial issues.

Harlem Renaissance An African American cultural, literary, and artistic movement centered in Harlem, an area in New York City, in the 1920s. Harlem, the largest black community in the world outside Africa, was considered the cultural capital of African Americans.

Black literature blossomed. In stark images, Claude McKay in *White Shadows* (1922) expressed both his resentment against racial injustice and his pride in blackness. Countee Cullen and Langston Hughes won critical acclaim for the beauty of their poems and the eloquence of their portrayal of the black tragedy.

During Harlem's golden age, "almost everything seemed possible," wrote historian David Lewis. "You could be black and proud, politically assertive and economically independent, creative and disciplined—or so it seemed." Moreover, the mood of the Harlem Renaissance spread to black communities in other cities.

In retrospect, the literary flowering of the 1920s is strikingly paradoxical. Nearly all the writers, black and white, cried out against conformity and materialism. Few took any real interest in politics or in social reform. They retreated instead into individualism, seeking an escape from the prevailing business civilization in their art. Whether they went abroad or stayed home, the writers of the 1920s turned inward to avoid being swept up in the consumer goods revolution. Yet despite their withdrawal—indeed, perhaps because of it—they produced an astonishingly rich and varied body of work. American writing had a greater intensity and depth than in the past; American writers, for the first time, were taken seriously by Europeans.

The Rural Counterattack

Dominance by the urban centers triggered a response that showed the ugly side of the 1920s, the side where hate and intolerance flourished. For millions of Americans who lived in small towns and on farms, the city came to represent all that was evil in contemporary life. Largely Anglo-Saxon and steeped in traditional Protestantism, these rural folk condemned urban-centered crime, radicalism, and modernism, which they believed were threatening their way of life. Saloons, whorehouses, Little Italys and Little Polands, communist cells, free love, atheism—all were identified with the city. As the urban areas grew in population and influence, the countryside struck back in a deliberate if doomed attempt to restore a lost purity to American life.

Other factors contributed to the intensity of the rural counterattack. The war had unleashed a nationalistic spirit that craved unity and conformity. When the war was over, groups such as the American Legion tried to root out "un-American" behavior and insisted on cultural as well as political conformity. And the prewar progressive reform spirit added to the social tension. Stripped of much of its former idealism, progressivism focused on social problems such as drinking and illiteracy to justify repressive measures such as prohibition and immigration restriction. The result was tragic, for often it pitted rural America against urban America in ugly conflicts.

The Fear of Radicalism

Red Scare A wave of anticommunist, antiforeign, and antilabor hysteria that swept over America at the end of World War I. It resulted in the deportation of many alien residents and the violation of the civil liberties of many of its victims.

The first and most intense outbreak of national alarm, the **Red Scare,** came in 1919. The heightened nationalism of World War I found a new target in bolshevism. The Russian Revolution and the growth of communism in America frightened many Americans. Although the number of American Communists was never great, they were located in the cities, and their influence appeared to be magnified with the outbreak of widespread labor unrest.

A general strike in Seattle, a police strike in Boston, and a violent strike in the iron and steel industry thoroughly alarmed the American people in the spring and summer of 1919. A series of bombings and attempted bombings led to panic. On June 2, a bomb shattered the front of Attorney General A. Mitchell Palmer's home. Although the man who delivered it was blown to pieces, authorities quickly identified him as an Italian anarchist from Philadelphia.

In the public outcry that followed, Attorney General Palmer led the attack on the alien threat. In a series of raids that began on November 7, federal agents seized suspected anarchists and Communists and held them for deportation with no regard for due process of law. In December, 249 aliens were shipped to Russia. Nearly all were innocent of the charges against them. A month later, Palmer rounded up nearly four thousand suspected Communists in a single evening. Aliens rounded up were deported without hearings or trials.

For a time, it seemed that this Red Scare reflected the prevailing views of the American people. Instead of condemning their government's actions, citizens voiced their approval and even urged more drastic steps. In one particularly revolting episode, a group of war veterans in Centralia, Washington, dragged a radical from the town jail, castrated him, and hanged him from a railway bridge. The coroner's report stated that the victim "jumped off with a rope around his neck and then shot himself full of holes."

The very extremism of the Red Scare led to its rapid demise. Courageous government officials and prominent citizens spoke out against the government's violations of constitutional guarantees and the acts of terror. Finally, Palmer himself, with evident presidential ambition, went too far. In April 1920, he warned of a vast revolution to occur on May 1. When no bombings or violence took place on May Day, the public began to react against Palmer's hysteria, trying hard to forget their momentary loss of balance.

Yet the Red Scare exerted a continuing influence on American society in the 1920s. The foreign-born lived with the uneasy realization that they were viewed with hostility and suspicion. Two Italian aliens in Massachusetts, Nicola Sacco and Bartolomeo Vanzetti, were arrested in May 1920 for a payroll robbery and murder. They faced a prosecutor and jury who condemned them more for their ideas than for any evidence of criminal conduct and a judge who referred to them as "those anarchist bastards." Despite a worldwide effort that became the chief liberal cause of the 1920s, the two died in the electric chair on August 23, 1927. Their fate symbolized the bigotry and intolerance that lasted through the 1920s and made this decade one of the least admirable in American history.

Prohibition

In December 1917, Congress adopted the Eighteenth Amendment, prohibiting the manufacture and sale of alcoholic beverages. A little more than a year later, Nebraska became the necessary thirty-sixth state to ratify, and **prohibition** became the law of the land.

prohibition The ban of the manufacture, sale, and transportation of alcoholic beverages in the United States. The Eighteenth Amendment, adopted in 1918, established prohibition. It was repealed by the Twenty-first Amendment in 1933.

Beginning January 16, 1920, the Volstead Act, which implemented prohibition, banned most commercial production and distribution of beverages containing more than one-half of 1 percent of alcohol by volume. (Exceptions were made for medicinal and religious uses of wine and spirits. Production for one's own private use was also allowed.) Prohibition was the result of both a rural effort of the Anti-Saloon League and the urban progressive concern over the social disease of drunkenness. Although a number of states had already enacted prohibition laws by 1920, the real tragedy resulted from the effort to extend this "noble experiment" to the growing cities, where it was deeply resented by many ethnic groups and nearly totally disregarded by the well-to-do and the sophisticated.

Prohibition did in fact lead to a decline in drinking. The consumption of alcohol dropped sharply in rural areas and among the lower classes, who could not afford the high prices of bootleg liquor. Among the middle class and the wealthy, however, drinking became fashionable. Bootleggers supplied whiskey, which quickly replaced lighter spirits such as wine and beer. Despite the risk of illness or death from drinking the unregulated alcohol, Americans consumed some 150 million quarts of liquor a year in the 1920s as bootleggers took in nearly $2 billion annually, about 2 percent of the gross national product.

Urban resistance to prohibition finally led to its repeal in 1933. But in the intervening years, it damaged American society by breeding a profound disrespect for the law. In city after city, police openly tolerated the traffic in liquor, and judges and prosecutors agreed to let bootleggers pay token fines. The countryside felt vindicated, yet rural and urban America alike suffered from this overzealous attempt to legislate morals.

The Ku Klux Klan

The most ominous expression of rural protest against the city was the rebirth of the Ku Klux Klan. On Thanksgiving night in 1915, on Stone Mountain in Georgia, Colonel William J. Simmons and thirty-four followers founded the modern Klan. Only "native-born, white, gentile Americans" were permitted to join. Membership grew slowly during World War I but mushroomed after 1920. Across the South and the West, the Klan attracted men seeking to relieve their anxiety over a changing society.

The Klan of the 1920s was not just anti-black; the tensions and conflicts in American society, as Klansmen perceived it, came from aliens—Italians and Russians, Jews and Catholics. The Klan punished blacks who did not know their place, women who practiced the new morality, and aliens who refused to conform. Beatings, floggings, burning with acid, even murder were condoned. But they also

A 1925 Ku Klux Klan demonstration in Cincinnati, Ohio, attended by nearly thirty thousand robed members and marked by the induction of eight thousand young boys in the Junior Order. Only native-born, white Americans "who believe in the tenets of the Christian religion" were admitted into the Klan. The original Ku Klux Klan, formed during the Reconstruction era to terrorize and intimidate former slaves, disbanded in 1869. The Klan that formed in 1915 declined through the 1920s but did not officially disband until 1944. Two years later, a third Klan emerged, focusing on the civil rights movement and communism as its enemies. ❖

tried more peaceful methods of coercion, formulating codes of behavior and seeking communitywide support. In addition, the Klan entered politics, showing remarkable strength in Texas, Oklahoma, Oregon, and Indiana.

Its appeal lay in the sanctuary it offered to insecure and anxious people. It gave its members reassurance and an exotic world of titles and practices. Members found a sense of identity in the group activities, whether they were peaceful picnics, ominous parades in white robes, or fiery crosses blazing in the night. By the mid-1920s, the Klan boasted a membership of nearly five million, and it had separate orders for women, boys, and girls.

The Klan fell even more quickly than it rose. Its more violent activities began to offend the nation's conscience. Misuse of funds and sexual scandals among Klan leaders, notably in Indiana, repelled many of the rank and file. Membership declined sharply after 1925; by the end of the decade, the Klan had virtually disappeared. But the spirit lived on, testimony to the recurring demons of nativism and racist hatred that have surfaced periodically throughout the American experience.

Immigration Restriction

The nativism that permeated the Klan found its most successful outlet in the immigration legislation of the 1920s. The sharp increase in immigration in the late nineteenth century had led to a broad-based movement to restrict the flow of people from Europe. In 1917, over Wilson's veto, Congress enacted a literacy test that reduced the number of immigrants, and the war caused an even more drastic decline.

After armistice, however, rumors began to spread of an impending flood of people seeking to escape war-ravaged Europe. Worried members of Congress spoke of a "barbarian horde" that would inundate the United States with "dangerous and deadly enemies of the country." Even though the actual number of immigrants fell below the prewar yearly average, Congress in 1921 passed an emergency immigration act.

The 1921 act failed to satisfy the nativists. It still permitted more than half a million Europeans to come to the United States in 1923, nearly half of them from southern and eastern Europe. The declining percentage of Nordic immigrants alarmed writers such as Madison Grant, who warned the American people that the Anglo-Saxon stock that had founded the nation was about to be overwhelmed by lesser breeds with inferior genes. Psychologists, relying on primitive IQ tests used by the army in World War I, confirmed this judgment.

Responding to such theories, in 1924, Congress adopted the **National Origins Quota Act,** which limited immigration from Europe to 150,000 a year; allocated most of the places to immigrants from Great Britain, Ireland, Germany, and Scandinavia; and banned all Asian immigrants. The measure passed Congress with overwhelming rural support.

National Origins Quota Act This 1924 act established a quota system to regulate the influx of immigrants to America. The system restricted the "new" immigrants from southern and eastern Europe and Asia. It reduced the annual total of immigrants.

The new restrictive legislation marked the most enduring achievement of the rural counterattack. Unlike the Red Scare, prohibition, and the Klan, the quota system would survive until the 1960s. Yet even here, the rural victory was not complete. A growing tide of Mexican laborers, exempt from the quota act, flowed northward across the Rio Grande to fill the continuing need for unskilled workers on farms and in the service trades. The Mexican immigration marked the strengthening of an element in the national ethnic mosaic that would grow in size and influence until it became a major force in modern American society.

The Fundamentalist Challenge

The most significant—and, as it turned out, longest-lasting—challenge to the new urban culture was rooted in the traditional religious beliefs of millions of Americans who felt alienated from city life, from science, and from much of what modernization entailed. Sometimes this challenge was direct, as when Christian fundamentalists campaigned against the teaching of evolution in the public schools. Their success in Tennessee touched off a court battle, the **Scopes trial,** that drew the attention of the entire country to the small town of Dayton in the summer of 1925. There, William Jennings Bryan engaged in a crusade against the theory of evolution, appearing as a chief witness against John Scopes, a high school biology teacher who had deliberately violated a new Tennessee law that forbade the teaching of Darwin's theory.

Scopes trial Also called the "monkey trial," the 1925 Scopes trial was a contest between modern liberalism and religious fundamentalism. John Scopes was on trial for teaching Darwinian evolution in defiance of a Tennessee state law. He was found guilty and fined $100.

In the trial, Bryan testified under oath that he believed Jonah had been swallowed by a big fish and declared, "It is better to trust in the Rock of Ages than in the age of rocks." Chicago defense attorney Clarence Darrow succeeded in making Bryan look ridiculous. The court found Scopes guilty but let him off with a small fine; Bryan, exhausted by his efforts, died a few days later. H. L. Mencken, who covered the trial in person, rejoiced in believing that fundamentalism was dead.

Other aspects of the fundamentalist challenge were more subtle but no less important in countering the modernizing trend. Middle- and upper-class Americans drifted into a genteel Christianity that stressed good works and respectability, but the fervid evangelical denominations continued to hold on to the old faith, and more aggressive fundamentalist sects, such as the Jehovah's Witnesses, grew rapidly.

Many who came to the city in the 1920s brought their religious beliefs with them and found new outlets for their traditional ideas. Thus evangelist Aimee Semple McPherson enjoyed amazing success in Los Angeles with her "Four-Square

Gospel." Far from dying out, biblical fundamentalism remained remarkably strong in the cities as well as the country. The rural counterattack, though challenged by the city, did enable some older American values to survive in the midst of the new mass production culture.

Politics of the 1920s

The tensions between the city and the countryside also shaped the course of politics in the 1920s. On the surface, it was a Republican decade. The GOP controlled the White House from 1921 to 1933 and had majorities in both houses of Congress from 1919 to 1931. The Republicans halted further reform legislation and established a friendly relationship between government and business. Important shifts were taking place, however, in the American electorate. The Democrats, although divided into competing urban and rural wings, were laying the groundwork for the future by winning over millions of new voters, especially among the ethnic groups in the cities. The rising tide of urban voters indicated a fundamental shift away from the Republicans toward a new Democratic majority.

Harding, Coolidge, and Hoover

The Republicans regained the White House in 1920 with the election of Warren G. Harding of Ohio. Handsome and dignified, Harding reflected both the wholesomeness and the narrowness of small-town America. He was basically a genial man who lacked the capacity to govern and who delegated power broadly as president.

He made some good cabinet choices, notably Charles Evans Hughes as secretary of state and Herbert C. Hoover as secretary of commerce, but two corrupt officials sabotaged his administration. Attorney General Harry Daugherty became involved in a series of questionable deals that led ultimately to his forced resignation, and Secretary of the Interior Albert Fall was the chief figure in the **Teapot Dome scandal.** Two oil promoters gave Fall nearly $400,000 in loans and bribes; in return, he helped them secure leases on naval oil reserves in Elk Hills, California, and Teapot Dome, Wyoming. The scandal came to light after Harding's death from a heart attack in 1923. Fall eventually served a year in jail, and the reputation of the Harding administration never recovered.

Teapot Dome scandal Scandal in which Secretary of the Interior Albert Fall was convicted of accepting bribes in exchange for leasing government-owned oil lands in Wyoming (Teapot Dome) and California (Elks Hill) to private oil businessmen.

Vice President Calvin Coolidge assumed the presidency on Harding's death, and his honesty and integrity quickly reassured the nation. A reserved, reticent man of Yankee stock, Coolidge became famous for his epigrams, which contemporaries mistook for wisdom. "The business of America is business," he proclaimed. Consistent with his philosophy, he believed his duty was simply to preside benignly, not govern the nation. Satisfied with the prosperity of the mid-1920s, the people responded favorably. Coolidge was elected to a full term by a wide margin in 1924.

When Coolidge announced in 1927 that he did not "choose to run" for reelection, Herbert Hoover became the Republican choice to succeed him. By far the ablest GOP leader of the decade, Hoover epitomized the American legend of the self-made man. Orphaned as a boy, he had worked his way through Stanford University and had gained both wealth and fame as a mining engineer. Sober, intelligent, and immensely hardworking, Hoover embodied the nation's faith in individualism and free enterprise.

He used his office to help American manufacturers and exporters expand their overseas trade, and he strongly supported a trade association movement to encourage cooperation rather than cutthroat competition among smaller American companies. He saw business and government as partners, working together to achieve efficiency and affluence for all Americans.

Republican Policies

During the 1920 campaign, Harding had urged a return to "normalcy," a coined word that became the theme for the Republican administrations of the 1920s. Aware that the public was tired of zealous reform-minded presidents, Harding and his successors sought a return to traditional Republican policies. In some areas they were successful, but in others they were forced to adjust to the new realities of a mass production society.

The most obvious attempt to go back to the Republicanism of William McKinley came in tariff and tax policy. Fearful of a flood of postwar European imports, Congress passed an emergency tariff act in 1921 and followed it a year later with the protectionist Fordney-McCumber Tariff Act.

Secretary of the Treasury Andrew Mellon, a wealthy Pittsburgh banker and industrialist, worked hard to achieve a similar return to "normalcy" in taxation. He pressed for repealing excess-profits taxes on corporations and slashing personal rates on the very rich. He also reduced government spending from its wartime peak of $18 billion to just over $3 billion by 1925, creating a slight surplus. Congress cooperated by cutting the highest income tax bracket to a modest 20 percent.

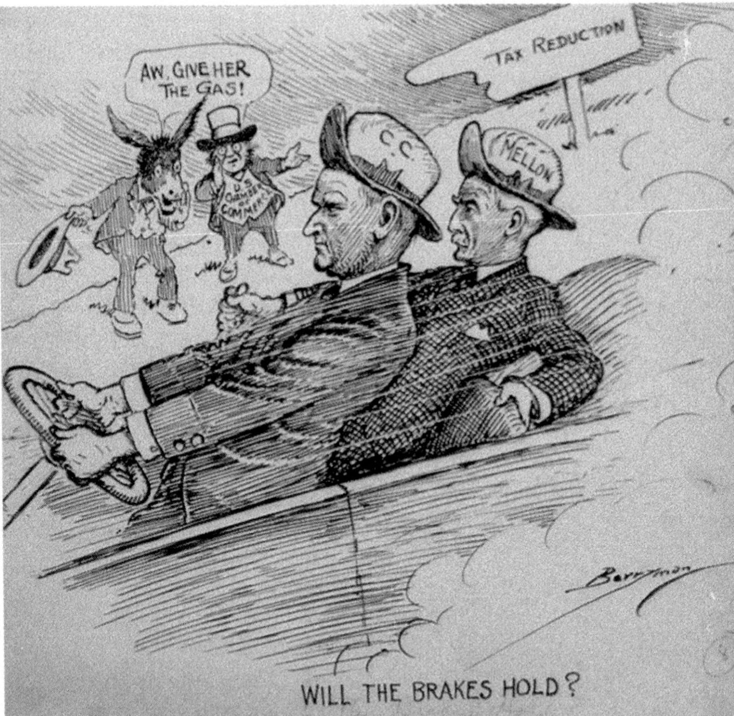

In this 1925 political cartoon, Clifford Berryman depicts Calvin Coolidge and Andrew Mellon in a car racing downhill to tax reductions. The wealthy benefited most from Mellon's tax reduction policies, paying as much as one third less in 1926 than they had paid in 1921. ◆

The growing crisis in American farming during the decade forced the Republican administrations to seek new solutions. The end of the war led to a sharp decline in farm prices and a return to the problem of overproduction. Southern and western lawmakers formed a farm bloc in Congress to press for special legislation for American agriculture. Although the farm bloc helped pass several laws, it failed to get at the root problem of overproduction. Farmers then supported more controversial measures designed to raise domestic crop prices by having the government sell the surplus overseas at low world prices. Coolidge vetoed the legislation on grounds that it involved unwarranted government interference in the economy.

Yet the government's role in the economy increased rather than lessened in the 1920s. Republicans widened the scope of federal activity and nearly doubled the ranks of government employees. Hoover led the way in the Commerce Department, establishing new bureaus to help make American industry more efficient in housing, transportation, and mining. Instead of going back to the laissez-faire tradition of the nineteenth century, the Republican administrations of the 1920s were pioneering a close relationship between government and private business.

The Divided Democrats

While the Republicans ruled in the 1920s, the Democrats seemed bent on self-destruction. The pace of the second Industrial Revolution and growing urbanization split the party in two. One faction centered in the rural South and West. Traditional Democrats who had supported Wilson stood for prohibition, fundamentalism, the Klan, and other aspects of the rural counterattack against the city. In contrast, a new breed of Democrat was emerging in the metropolitan areas of the North and Midwest. Immigrants and their descendants began to participate actively in the Democratic party. Primarily Catholics and Jews and strongly opposed to prohibition, they had little in common with their rural counterparts.

The split within the party surfaced dramatically at the national convention in New York in 1924. Held in Madison Square Garden, the convention soon degenerated into what one observer described as a "snarling, cursing, tenuous, suicidal, homicidal roughhouse." Urban and rural factions of the party opposed each other at every turn. The delegates divided between Alfred E. Smith, the governor of New York, and William G. McAdoo of California, Wilson's secretary of the treasury. When it became clear that neither the city nor the rural candidate could win a majority, both men withdrew; on the 103rd ballot, the weary Democrats finally chose John W. Davis as their compromise nominee. Senator Bob La Follette of Wisconsin ran on the independent Progressive party ticket. His campaign was ineffective; so was Davis's. Both were easily defeated by Coolidge.

Yet the Democrats were in far better shape than this setback indicated. Beginning in 1922, the party had made heavy inroads into the GOP majority in Congress. Even in 1924, the Republican vote in the nation's largest cities decline. In 1926, the Democrats came within one vote of controlling the Senate and had picked up more seats in the House. The largest cities were swinging clearly into the Democratic column; all the party needed was a charismatic leader who could fuse the older rural elements with the new urban voters.

The Election of 1928

The selection of Al Smith as the Democratic candidate in 1928 indicated the growing power of the city. Born on the Lower East Side of Manhattan of mixed Irish-German ancestry, Smith was the prototype of the urban Democrat. He was Catholic; he was associated with a big-city machine; he was a "wet" who wanted to end prohibition. Rejected by rural Democrats in 1924, he still had to prove that he could unite the South and West behind his leadership. His lack of education, poor grammar, and distinctive New York accent hurt him, as did his eastern provincialism.

The choice facing the American voter in 1928 seemed unusually clear-cut. Herbert Hoover was a Protestant, a "dry," and an old-stock American who stood for efficiency and individualism. Just as Smith appealed to new voters in the cities, so Hoover won the support of many old-line Democrats who feared the city and the pope.

Yet beneath the surface, as historian Allan J. Lichtman pointed out, there were "striking similarities between Smith and Hoover." Both were self-made men who

CHRONOLOGY	
1919	U.S. agents arrest 1,700 in Red Scare raids ❖ Congress passes Volstead Act over Wilson's veto
1920	Republican Warren G. Harding is elected president ❖ Nineteenth Amendment is passed, granting women the right to vote
1921	Congress enacts quotas for European immigrants
1923	Harding dies; Vice President Calvin Coolidge assumes the presidency ❖ Newspapers expose Ku Klux Klan graft, torture, murder
1924	Coolidge is elected to full term ❖ Senate probes Teapot Dome scandal
1925	John Scopes is convicted of teaching theory of evolution in violation of Tennessee law
1927	Charles Lindbergh completes the first nonstop transatlantic flight from New York to Paris ❖ Coolidge vetoes farm price control bill ❖ Sacco and Vanzetti are executed ❖ The movie *The Jazz Singer* features a soundtrack
1928	Republican Herbert Hoover defeats Democrat Al Smith for the presidency

embodied the American belief in freedom of opportunity and upward mobility. Neither advocated any significant degree of economic change or any redistribution of national wealth or power. Although Smith's religion hurt him the most, his failure to spotlight the growing cracks in prosperity and offer alternative economic policies ensured his defeat.

The 1928 election was a dubious victory for the Republicans. Hoover won easily, but Smith succeeded for the first time in winning a majority of votes for the Democrats in the nation's twelve largest cities. A new Democratic electorate was emerging, consisting of Catholics and Jews, Irish and Italians, Poles and Greeks. Now the task was to unite the traditional Democrats of the South and West with the urban, ethnic populations of the Northeast and Midwest.

Conclusion: The Old and the New

The election-night celebrations at Hoover campaign headquarters were muted by prohibition and by the president elect's natural reserve. Had Hoover known what lay just ahead for the country, and for his presidency, no doubt the party would have been even more somber.

During the 1920s, America struggled to enter the modern era. The economics of mass production and the politics of urbanization drove the country forward, but the persistent appeal of individualism and rural-based values held it back. Americans achieved greater prosperity than ever before, but the prosperity was unevenly distributed. Further, as the outbursts of nativism, ethnic and racial bigotry, and intolerance revealed, prosperity hardly guaranteed generosity or unity. Nor, for that matter, did it guarantee continued prosperity, even for those who benefited initially. As much as America changed during the 1920s, in one crucial respect the country remained as before. The American economy, for all its remarkable productive capacity, was astonishingly fragile. This was the message Hoover was soon to learn.

Key Terms

Harlem Renaissance, p. 493
Red Scare, p. 494
prohibition, p. 495
National Origins Quota Act, p. 497
Scopes trial, p. 497
Teapot Dome scandal, p. 498

Recommended Reading

William Leuchtenburg provides the best overview of the 1920s in *The Perils of Prosperity, 1914–1932* (1958). He stresses the theme of rural-urban conflict and claims that the achievements of the decade were more significant than its failures. Ellis Hawley, *The Great War and the Search for a Modern Order* (1979), and Donald McCoy, *Coming of Age* (1973), are also valuable as surveys of the period. Frederick Lewis Allen, *Only Yesterday: An Informal History of the 1920s* (1931), is a classic, and still delightfully readable. The changing political alignments of the 1920s are covered in David Burner, *The Politics of Provincialism* (1968). The essays in John Braeman, Robert H. Bremner, and David Brody, eds., *Change and Continuity in Twentieth-Century America: The 1920s* (1968), provide various perspectives on important facets of the period.

Economic developments of the 1920s are the subject of George Soule, *Prosperity Decade* (1947). Helen Lynd and Robert Lynd, *Middletown* (1929), examine the social and cultural trends of the decade. David J. Goldberg, *Discontented America* (1999), finds unhappiness beneath the apparent prosperity.

Edward J. Larson, *Summer for the Gods* (1998), is the most recent and accessible account of the Scopes trial. Lawrence Levine, *Defender of the Faith* (1965), covers the last ten years of William Jennings Bryan's life. The lives of other public figures of the 1920s are traced in David Levering Lewis, *W. E. B. Du Bois*, vol. 2 (2000); Terry Teachout, *The Skeptic* (2002), on H. L. Mencken; Elisabeth Israels Perry, *Belle Moskowitz* (2000); and Robert A. Slayton, *Empire Statesman* (2001), and Christopher M. Finan, *Alfred E. Smith* (2002), both on the leading Democrat of the 1920s.

For a list of additional titles related to this chapter's topics, please see http://www.ablongman.com/divine.

Suggested Web Sites

Automotive History at the Michigan Electronic Library

http://mel.org/business/autos-history.html
This page has several links to sites about automotive history in America.

Harlem 1900–1940: An African American Community

http://www.si.umich.edu/CHICO/Harlem/
The New York Public Library's Schomburg Center for Research in Black Culture hosts this site that includes a database, a timeline, and an exhibit.

William P. Gottlieb—Photographs from the Golden Age of Jazz

http://memory.loc.gov/ammem/wghtml/wghome.html
The Music Division of the Library of Congress has numerous images, audio, and scanned articles from the 1940s.

The Scopes Trial

http://www.law.umkc.edu/faculty/projects/ftrials/scopes/scopes.htm
This site provides a detailed discussion of the trial, biographies of the major figures, and excerpts from the trial transcript.

American Temperance and Prohibition

http://prohibition.history.ohio-state.edu/
This site looks at the temperance movement over time and contains many informative links.

National Arts and Crafts Archives

http://arts-crafts.com/archive/archive.shtml
This site serves as a guide to materials on the Arts and Crafts movement, which lasted roughly from 1890 to 1929.

The Jazz Age: Flapper Culture and Style

http://www.geocities.com/flapper_culture
This site contains many links to information about the popular culture of the 1920s with special reference to the flapper.

The Calvin Coolidge Experience

http://www.geocities.com/CapitolHill/4921/
This site is an unusual look at one of America's less colorful presidents.

Chapter 26

Franklin D. Roosevelt and the New Deal

The Struggle Against Despair

Oscar Heline never forgot the terrible waste of the Great Depression. "Grain was being burned," he told interviewer Studs Terkel. "It was cheaper than coal." Heline lived in Iowa, in the heart of the farm belt. "A county just east of here, they burned corn in their courthouse all winter. . . . You couldn't hardly buy groceries for corn." Farmers, desperate for higher prices, resorted to destruction. As Heline recalled, "People were determined to withhold produce from the market—livestock, cream, butter, eggs, what not. If they would dump the produce, they would force the market to a higher level. The farmers would man the highways, and cream cans were emptied in ditches and eggs dumped out. They burned the trestle bridge, so the trains wouldn't be able to haul grain."

Film critic Pauline Kael recounted a different memory of the 1930s. Kael was a college student in California during the Great Depression, and was struck by the number of students who were missing fathers. "They had wandered off in disgrace because they couldn't support their families. Other fathers had killed themselves, so the family could have the insurance. Families had totally broken down." Kael and many of her classmates struggled to stay in school. "There were kids who didn't have a place to sleep, huddling under bridges on the campus. I had a scholarship, but there were times when I didn't have any food. The meals were often three candy bars."

NO AMERICAN WHO LIVED THROUGH the Great Depression ever forgot the experience. As the stories of Heline and Kael show, the individual memories were of hard times, but also of determination, adaptation, and survival.

The depression decade had an equally profound effect on American institutions. To cope with the problems of poverty and dislocation, Americans looked to government as never before, and in doing so transformed American politics and public life. The agent of the transformation—the man America turned to in its moment of trial—was Franklin D. Roosevelt. His answer to the country's demands for action was an ambitious program of relief and reform called the **New Deal.**

Outline

The Great Depression

Fighting the Depression

Roosevelt and Reform

Impact of the New Deal

End of the New Deal

Conclusion: Evaluation of the New Deal

New Deal President Franklin Roosevelt's program of legislation to combat the Great Depression. The New Deal included measures aimed at relief, reform, and recovery. They achieved some relief and considerable reform but little recovery.

THE GREAT DEPRESSION

The depression of the 1930s came as a shock to Americans who had grown used to the prosperity of the 1920s. The consumer revolution of that earlier decade had fostered a general confidence that the American way of life would continue to improve. But following the collapse of the stock market in late 1929, factories closed, machines fell silent, and millions of Americans walked the streets looking for jobs that didn't exist.

The Great Crash

The consumer goods revolution contained the seeds of its own demise. The productive capacity of the automobile and appliance industries grew faster than the effective demand. At that point, production began to falter, and in 1927, the nation underwent a mild recession. The sale of durable goods declined, and construction of houses and buildings fell slightly. If corporate leaders had heeded these warning signs, they might have responded by raising wages or lowering prices, both effective ways to stimulate purchasing power and bolster sales. Or if government officials had recognized the danger signs and forced a halt in installment buying and slowed bank loans, the nation might have experienced a sharp but brief depression.

Neither government nor business leaders were so farsighted. The Federal Reserve Board lowered the discount rate, charging banks less for loans in an attempt to stimulate the economy. Much of this additional credit, however, went not into solid investment in factories and machinery but instead into the stock market, touching off a new wave of speculation that obscured the growing economic slowdown and ensured a far greater crash to come.

Individuals with excess cash began to invest heavily in the stock market, and the market moved upward. The strongest surge began in the spring of 1928, when investors ignored the declining production figures in the belief that they could make a living in the market. People bet their savings on speculative stocks. Corporations used their large cash reserves to supply money to brokers, who in turn loaned it to investors on margin.

Investors could now play the market on credit, buying stock listed at $100 a share with $10 down and $90 on margin (the broker's loan for the balance). If the stock advanced to $150, the investor could sell and reap a gain of 500 percent on the $10 investment; in the bull (rising) market climate of the 1920s, everyone was sure that the market would go up.

By 1929, it seemed that the whole nation was engaged in speculation. So great was the public's interest in the stock market that newspapers carried the stock averages on the front pages. Although more people were spectators than speculators, the bull market became a national obsession, assuring everyone that the economy was healthy and preventing any serious analysis of its underlying flaws.

And then things changed, almost overnight. On October 24—later known as Black Thursday—the rise in stock prices faltered, and when it did investors nervously began to sell. Such leading stocks as RCA and Westinghouse plunged, losing nearly half their value in a single day. Speculators panicked as their creditors demanded new collateral, and the panic caused prices to plummet still further. Within weeks the gains of the previous two years had vanished.

The great crash of the stock market soon spilled over into the larger economy. Banks and other financial institutions suffered heavy losses in the market and were forced to curtail lending for consumer purchases. As consumers came up short, factories cut back production, laying off some workers and reducing hours for others. The layoffs and cutbacks lowered purchasing power even further, so fewer people bought cars and appliances. More factory layoffs resulted, and plants closed entirely, leading to even less money for the purchase of consumer goods.

UNEMPLOYMENT, 1929–1942

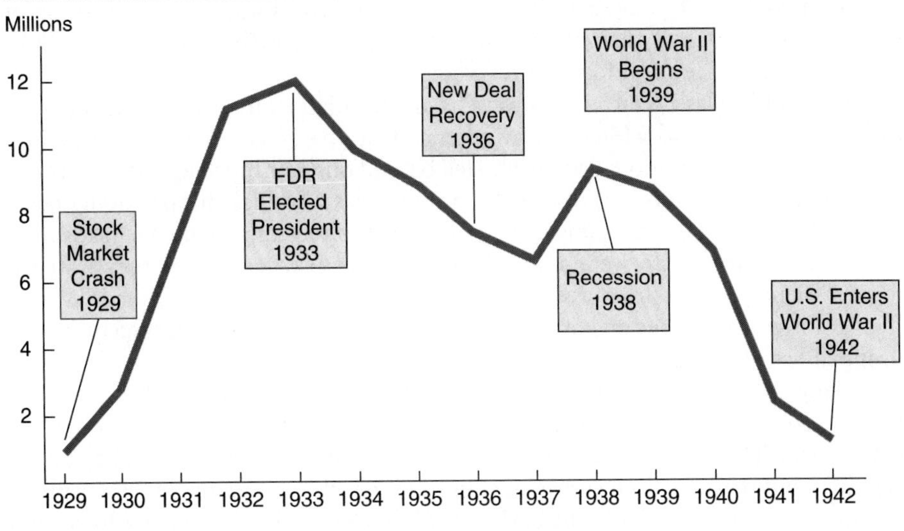

The downward economic spiral continued for four years. By 1932, unemployment had swelled to 25 percent of the workforce. Steel production was down to 12 percent of capacity, and the gross national product fell to two-thirds of the 1929 level. The bright promise of mass production had ended in a nightmare.

The basic explanation for the Great Depression lies in the fact that U.S. factories produced more goods than the American people could consume. There were other contributing causes—unstable economic conditions in Europe, the agricultural decline since 1919, corporate mismanagement, and excessive speculation—but at bottom people simply did not have enough money to buy the consumer products coming off the assembly lines.

The failure of the new economic system to distribute wealth more broadly was the chief difficulty. Too much money had gone into profits, dividends, and industrial expansion and not enough into the hands of the workers, who were also consumers. Factory productivity had increased 43 percent during the decade, but the wages of industrial workers had gone up only 11 percent. If the billions that went into stock market speculation had been used instead to increase wages—which would then have increased consumer purchasing power—production and consumption could have been brought into balance. Unfortunately for the prophets and pioneers of the New Era, it took the bitter experience of the Great Depression to teach them the true dynamics of the consumer goods economy.

Effect of the Depression

It is difficult to measure the human cost of the Great Depression. The material hardships were bad enough. Families lived in lean-tos made of scrap wood and metal and went without meat and fresh vegetables for months, existing on soup and beans. The psychological burden was even greater: Americans suffered through years of grinding poverty with no letup in sight. The unemployed stood in line for hours waiting for a relief check; veterans sold apples or pencils on street corners, their image as heroes and family providers now in question. In the country, crops rotted in the fields because prices were too low to make harvesting worthwhile.

Few Americans escaped the suffering. Blacks were often the first to lose their jobs. Mexican Americans were deported in droves, now that citizens were willing to labor in the fields and lay track on the railroads. The poor of all hues survived because they knew better than most Americans how to exist in poverty. They stayed in bed in cold weather, both to keep warm and to avoid unnecessary burning of calories. They patched their shoes with rubber from old tires, heated only their kitchens, and ate scraps of food others would reject.

The middle class, which had always lived with high expectations, was hit hard. Many professional and white-collar workers refused to ask for charity even as their families went without food. People who fell behind on their mortgage payments lost their homes, and health care declined as middle-class families stopped going regularly to doctors and dentists, unable to make the required cash payments in advance.

Even the well-to-do were affected, weighed down with guilt as they watched former friends and business associates join the ranks of the impoverished. "My father lost everything" became an all-too-familiar refrain among young people who dropped out of college.

Many Americans sought new vistas. Men and boys, and some women, rode the rails in search of jobs, hopping freight trains to move south in the winter or west in the summer. Those who became tramps had to keep on the move to avoid arrest for vagrancy, but they did find a sense of community in the "hobo jungles" that sprang up along the major railroad routes. Here the homeless could find a place to eat and sleep and people with whom to share their misery.

Fighting the Depression

The Great Depression presented an enormous challenge for American political leadership. The inability of the Republicans to overcome the economic catastrophe provided the Democrats with the chance to regain power. Although they failed to achieve full economic recovery before the outbreak of World War II, the Democrats did succeed in alleviating the suffering and establishing their political dominance.

Hoover and Voluntarism

Herbert Hoover was the Great Depression's most prominent victim. Expressing complete faith in the American economic system, he relied primarily on voluntary cooperation with business to halt the slide. He called the leaders of industry to the White House and secured their agreement to maintain prices and wages at high levels. Yet within a few months, employers were reducing wages and cutting prices in a desperate effort to survive.

Hoover also believed in voluntary efforts to relieve the human suffering brought about by the depression. He called on private charities and local governments to help feed and clothe those in need. But when these resources were exhausted, he rejected all requests for direct federal relief, asserting that such handouts would undermine the character of proud American citizens.

As the depression deepened, Hoover reluctantly began to move beyond voluntarism to undertake more sweeping governmental measures. The new Federal Farm Board loaned money to aid cooperatives and bought up surplus crops in the open market in a vain effort to raise farm prices. At Hoover's request, Congress cut taxes and adopted a few federal public works projects. To help imperiled banks and insurance companies, Hoover proposed and Congress established the Reconstruction Finance Corporation. The RFC loaned money to financial institutions to save them from bankruptcy. Hoover's critics, however, pointed out that while he favored aid to business, he still opposed measures such as direct relief and massive public works that would help the millions of unemployed.

By 1932, Hoover's efforts to overcome the depression had clearly failed. His public image suffered its sharpest blow in the summer of 1932 when he ordered

General Douglas MacArthur to clear out the **bonus army.** This group of ragged World War I veterans who had marched on Washington in a vain effort to get a bill granting them bonuses passed in Congress. Mounted troops drove the bonus marchers out of their shanties in Anacostia Flats along the Potomac River, blinding the veterans with tear gas and burning their shacks.

bonus army In June 1932, a group of unemployed World War I veterans marched on Washington, D.C., to demand immediate payment of their war pensions. Congress rejected their demands, and President Hoover had them forcibly removed from their encampment.

Meanwhile, the nation's banking structure approached collapse. Bank customers responded to rumors of bankruptcy by rushing in to withdraw their deposits, thereby causing bank failures to rise steadily. Everywhere, Americans longed for a new president.

The Emergence of Roosevelt

The man who came forward to meet this national need was Franklin D. Roosevelt, a distant cousin of the Republican Teddy. Born into a wealthy New York family, he enjoyed a privileged life of private tutors and trips to Europe. Well educated and supremely secure, he had served in a number of elected and appointed offices. In 1921, he suffered an attack of polio. Refusing to give in, he fought back bravely, and though he never again walked unaided, he was elected governor of New York in 1928.

Roosevelt's dominant trait was his ability to persuade and convince other people. He possessed a marvelous voice, deep and rich; a winning smile; and a buoyant confidence that was contagious. His bout with polio gave him both an understanding of human suffering and broad political appeal as a man who had faced heavy odds and overcome them. A master politician with an agile mind, he had little patience with philosophical nuances. He dealt with the appearance of issues, not their deepest substance, and he displayed a flexibility toward political principles that often dismayed even his warmest admirers.

Roosevelt took advantage of the political opportunity offered by the Great Depression. With the Republicans discredited, he united the Democratic party. After winning the party's nomination in 1932, he broke with tradition by flying to Chicago and accepting in person, telling the cheering delegates, "I pledge myself to a new deal for the American people."

In the fall, he defeated Herbert Hoover in a near landslide for the Democrats. Roosevelt not only met the challenge of the depression but also solidified the shift to the Democratic party that would dominate American politics for a half century.

The Hundred Days

When Franklin Roosevelt took the oath of office on March 4, 1933, the nation's economy was on the brink of collapse. Unemployment stood at nearly thirteen million—one-fourth the labor force—and banks were closed in thirty-eight states. Speaking from the steps of the capitol, FDR declared boldly, "First of all, let me assert my firm belief that the only thing we have to fear is fear itself—nameless, unreasoning, unjustified terror." Then he announced that he would call Congress into special session and request "broad executive power to wage a war against the emergency, as great as the power that would be given to me if we were in fact invaded by a foreign foe."

Within the next ten days, Roosevelt won his first great New Deal victory by saving the nation's banks. First he closed all the banks; then he presented new banking legislation to Congress, which it promptly passed. The measure provided for government supervision and aid to the banks. Strong ones would be reopened with federal support, weak ones closed, and those in difficulty bolstered by government loans.

On March 12, FDR addressed the nation by radio in the first of his "fireside chats." In conversational tones, he told the public what he had done. He assured

Americans that the government now stood behind the banks. The next day, March 13, the nation's largest and strongest banks opened their doors; at the end of the day, customers had deposited more cash than they withdrew. The banking crisis was over.

"Capitalism was saved in eight days," boasted one of Roosevelt's advisers. Most surprising was the conservative nature of FDR's action. Instead of nationalizing the banks, he had simply thrown the government's resources behind them and preserved private ownership. Though some other New Deal measures would be more radical, Roosevelt set the tone in the banking crisis. He was out to reform and restore the American economy system, not change it drastically.

For the next three months, Congress responded to a series of presidential initiatives. During the Hundred Days, Roosevelt sent fifteen major requests to Congress and obtained fifteen pieces of legislation. One of these, the **Tennessee Valley Authority (TVA),** was one of the most ambitious of Roosevelt's New Deal measures. This innovative effort at regional planning resulted in the building of a series of dams in seven states along the Tennessee River to control floods, ease navigation, and produce electricity. Although critics lamented the cost of the project and its impact on the environment and certain local communities, it went far toward bringing one of the most underdeveloped parts of the country into the modern era.

Tennessee Valley Authority (TVA) A New Deal effort at regional planning created by Congress in 1933, this agency built dams and power plants on the Tennessee River. Its programs for flood control, soil conservation, and reforestation helped raise the standard of living of millions in the Tennessee River Valley.

Other New Deal agencies were temporary, designed to meet the specific economic problems of the depression. None was completely successful; the depression would continue for another six years. But psychologically, the nation turned the corner in the spring of 1933. Under FDR, the government seemed to be responding to the economic crisis, enabling people to look to the future with hope for the first time since 1929.

Roosevelt and Recovery

Two major New Deal programs launched during the Hundred Days were aimed at industrial and agricultural recovery. The first was the **National Recovery Administration (NRA),** FDR's attempt to achieve economic advance through planning and cooperation among government, business, and labor. Businessmen were intent on stabilizing production and raising prices for their goods. Spokesmen for labor were equally determined to spread gainful work by setting maximum hours and minimum wages.

National Recovery Administration (NRA) New Deal federal agency created in 1933 to promote economic recovery and revive industry during the Great Depression.

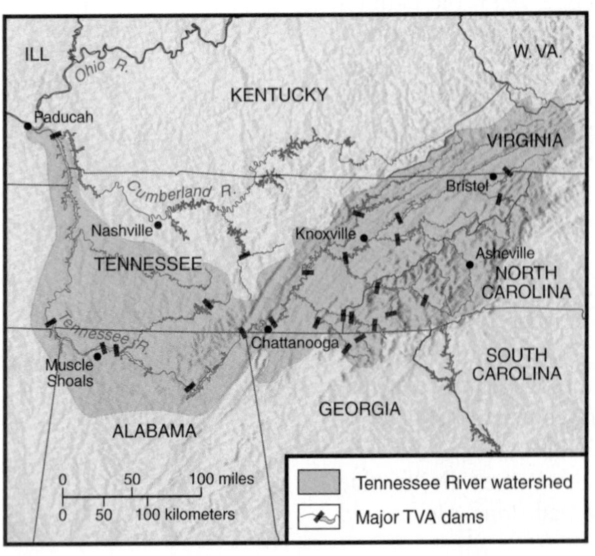

TENNESSEE VALLEY AUTHORITY *The Tennessee Valley Authority (TVA) served a seven-state region in the Southeast. Developing such a vast project required federal funding and management, both of which were provided through a federally owned corporation. The TVA expanded the hydroelectric plants at Muscle Shoals, Alabama, and built dams, power plants, and transmission lines to service the surrounding area.* ❖

The NRA hoped to achieve both goals by permitting companies in each major industry to cooperate in writing codes of fair competition that would set realistic limits on production, allocate percentages to individual producers, and set firm guidelines on prices. Section 7a of the enabling act mandated protection for labor in all the codes by establishing maximum hours, minimum wages, and the guarantee of collective bargaining by unions. No company could be compelled to join, but the New Deal sought complete participation by appealing to patriotism. Each firm that took part could display a blue eagle and stamp the symbol on its products. Led by Hugh Johnson, the NRA quickly enrolled the nation's leading companies and unions.

The NRA soon bogged down in a huge bureaucratic morass. The codes proved difficult to enforce and favored big business at the expense of smaller competitors. In addition, labor quickly became disenchanted with Section 7a. By 1934, more and more businessmen were complaining about the new agency. When the Supreme Court finally invalidated the NRA in 1935 on constitutional grounds, few mourned its demise. The idea of trying to overcome the depression by relying on voluntary cooperation between competing businessmen and labor leaders had collapsed in the face of individual self-interest and greed.

The New Deal's attempt at farm recovery fared a little better. Henry A. Wallace, FDR's secretary of agriculture, came up with an answer to the farmer's old dilemma of overproduction. The government would act as a clearinghouse for producers of major crops, arranging for them to set production limits for wheat, cotton, corn, and other leading crops. Under the **Agricultural Adjustment Administration (AAA),** the government would allocate acreage among individual farmers, encouraging them to take land out of production by paying them subsidies.

Agricultural Adjustment Administration (AAA) Created by Congress in 1933 as part of the New Deal, this agency attempted to restrict agricultural production by paying farmers subsidies to take land out of production.

After initial problems in 1933, the AAA program worked better in 1934 and 1935 as land removed from production led to smaller harvests and rising farm prices. Farm income rose for the first time since World War I. Most of the gain came from the subsidy payments themselves rather than from higher market prices.

On the whole, large farmers benefited most from the program. Possessing the capital to buy machinery and fertilizer, they were able to farm more efficiently than before on fewer acres of land. Small farmers, tenants, and sharecroppers did not fare as well, receiving little of the government payments and often being driven off the land as owners took acreage previously cultivated by tenants and sharecroppers out of production. In the long run, the New Deal reforms improved the efficiency of American agriculture, but at a real human cost.

The Supreme Court eventually found the AAA unconstitutional in 1936, but Congress reenacted it in modified form that year and again in 1938. The system of allotments became a standard feature of the farm economy. In another effort to assist the rural poor, the Farm Security Administration (FSA) loaned tenant farmers and sharecroppers money to buy their own land. But congressional appropriations were so modest that only about 2 percent obtained loans. The result of the New Deal for American farming was to hasten its transformation into a business in which only the efficient and well capitalized would thrive.

Roosevelt and Relief

The New Deal was far more successful in meeting the most immediate problem of the 1930s, relief for the millions of unemployed and destitute citizens. Roosevelt never shared Hoover's distaste for direct federal support; in May 1933, Congress authorized the Reconstruction Finance Corporation to distribute $500 million to the states to help individuals and families in need.

Roosevelt brought in former social worker Harry Hopkins to direct the relief program. By the end of 1933, Hopkins had cut through red tape to distribute money to nearly one-sixth of the American people. The relief payments were modest, but they enabled millions to avoid starvation and stay out of humiliating breadlines.

❖ A Look at the Past ❖

FSA Photos

"Migrant Mother" (left) is one of the best-known photographs commissioned by the Farm Security Administration (FSA) during the 1930s. The FSA used photographs to document rural problems and to build support for its resettlement program. Roy Stryker, the project's director, wanted the photographs to convince the public that rural Americans faced difficulties but with help were capable of overcoming those troubles. Rural Americans had to appear deserving. Photographers such as Dorothea Lange, who took these photographs, experimented with compositions in an effort to capture artistically pleasing images that provoked the reactions Stryker wanted. Compare Lange's famous image to the one she never intended to publish. Why would the photograph on the right fail to meet Stryker's demands? What emotions do the photograph on the left evoke? How does the image on the left meet Stryker's requirements?

An imaginative early effort was the **Civilian Conservation Corps (CCC),** which enrolled young males from city families on relief and sent them to work on the nation's public lands, cutting trails, planting trees, building bridges, and paving roads. The program contributed both to their families' incomes and to the nation's welfare.

Civilian Conservation Corps (CCC) One of the most popular New Deal programs, the CCC was created by Congress to provide government jobs to young men between 18 and 25 in reforestation and other conservation projects.

Hopkins realized the need to do more than just keep people alive, and he soon became an advocate of work relief. Hopkins argued that the government should put the jobless to work, not just to encourage self-respect but also to enable them to earn enough to purchase consumer goods and thus stimulate the entire economy. The Public Works Administration (PWA), headed by Secretary of the Interior Harold Ickes, had been authorized in 1933, but Ickes failed to put many people to work.

Works Progress Administration (WPA) Congress created this New Deal agency in 1935 to provide work relief for the unemployed. Federal works projects included building roads, bridges, and schools, but the WPA also funded projects for artists, writers, and young people.

The final commitment to the idea of work relief came in 1935 when Roosevelt established the **Works Progress Administration (WPA)** to spend nearly $5 billion authorized by Congress for emergency relief. The WPA put the unemployed on the federal payroll so that they could earn enough to meet their basic needs and help stimulate the stagnant economy. The WPA provided work for skilled and unskilled alike. It also tried to preserve the skills of American artists, actors, and writers by paying them to practice their craft.

The WPA helped ease the burden for the unemployed, but it failed to overcome the depression. Rather than spending too much, as his critics charged, Roosevelt's greatest failure was not spending enough to prime the American economy by increasing consumer purchasing power. By responding to basic human needs, Roosevelt had made the depression bearable, but the New Deal's failure to go beyond relief to achieve prosperity led to growing frustration and prompted more radical alternatives that challenged the conservative nature of the New Deal and forced FDR to shift to the left.

Roosevelt and Reform

In 1935, the focus of the New Deal shifted from relief and recovery to reform. During his first two years in office, FDR had concentrated on fighting the depression by shoring up the sagging American economy. He was developing a "broker state" concept of government, responding to pressures from organized elements such as corporations, labor unions, and farm groups while ignoring the needs and wants of the dispossessed who had no clear political voice.

The continuing depression and the high unemployment built pressures for more sweeping changes. Roosevelt faced the choice of either exploring more radical programs designed to end historical inequities in American life or deferring to others' solutions. Bolstered by an impressive Democratic victory in the 1934 congressional elections, FDR responded by embracing a reform program that marked the climax of the New Deal.

Challenges to FDR

The signs of discontent were visible everywhere by 1935. In the upper Midwest, progressives and agrarian radicals, led by Minnesota Governor Floyd Olsen, were demanding substantial changes to raise farmers' and workers' incomes. Textile plant strikes shut down mills in twenty states. The most serious challenge to Roosevelt's leadership, however, came from three demagogues who captured national attention in the mid-1930s.

The first was Father Charles Coughlin, a Roman Catholic priest from Detroit who had originally supported FDR. Speaking to a rapt nationwide radio audience, Coughlin appealed to the discontented with a strange mix of crank monetary schemes and anti-Semitism. He broke with the New Deal in late 1934, calling for monetary inflation and nationalization of the banking system.

A more benign but equally threatening figure appeared in California. Dr. Francis Townsend, a 67-year-old physician, came forward in 1934 with a scheme to assist the elderly, who were suffering greatly during the depression. The Townsend Plan proposed giving everyone over the age of 60 a monthly pension of $200 with the provision that it must be spent within thirty days. It would thus provide an old-age pension and stimulate the economy. Although impractical, more than ten million people signed petitions endorsing the Townsend Plan.

A third new voice of protest was that of Huey Long, a flamboyant senator from Louisiana. An early New Deal supporter, Long turned against FDR and by 1935 had become a major political threat to the president. In 1934, he announced a nationwide "Share the Wealth" movement. He spoke grandly of taking from the rich to make "Every Man a King," guaranteeing each American a home worth $5,000 and an annual income of $2,500. To finance the plan, Long advocated seizing all fortunes of more than $5 million and levying a tax of 100 percent on income over $1 million. Millions of Americans responded favorably to Long's plan. Threatening to run as a third-party candidate in 1936, Long generated fear among Democratic leaders that he might attract three or four million votes, possibly enough to swing the election to the Republicans. Although he was assassinated in 1935, his popularity showed the need for the New Deal to do more to help those still in distress.

Social Security

When the new Congress met in January 1935, Roosevelt was ready to support a series of reform measures designed to take the edge off national dissent. Many of the Democrats in Congress were to the left of Roosevelt, favoring increased spending and more sweeping federal programs. Congress was prepared to enact virtually any proposal that Roosevelt offered.

Social Security Act This 1935 New Deal legislation established a system of old age, unemployment, and survivors' insurance funded by wage and payroll taxes. It did not include health insurance and did not originally cover many of the most needy groups and individuals.

The most significant reform enacted in 1935 was the **Social Security Act.** Unlike other modern industrial nations, the United States had never developed a welfare system to aid the aged, the disabled, and the unemployed. FDR's plan had three major parts. First, it provided for old-age pensions financed by a tax on employers and workers, with no government contributions. Second, it set up a system of unemployment compensation on a federal-state basis, with employers paying a payroll tax and each state setting the benefit levels and administering the program locally. Finally, it provided for direct federal grants to the states, on a matching basis, for welfare payments to the blind, handicapped, needy elderly, and dependent children. Despite some criticism from the right and the left, Congress overwhelmingly passed the Social Security Act.

Since its passage, critics have pointed out its shortcomings. The old-age pensions and grants to the handicapped and dependent children were paltry, and not everyone was covered. People who needed the most protection in their old age, such as farmers and domestic servants, were not included. The regressive feature of the act was even worse. All participants, regardless of income or economic status, paid in at the same rate, with no supplement from the general revenue. The trust fund also took out of circulation money that was desperately needed to stimulate the economy in the 1930s.

The conservative nature of the legislation reflected Roosevelt's own fiscal orthodoxy, but even more it was a product of his political realism. Despite the severity of the depression, he realized that establishing a system of federal welfare went against deeply rooted American convictions. He insisted on a tax on participants to give those involved in the pension plan a vested interest in Social Security. He wanted them to feel that they had earned their pensions and that in the future no one would dare take them away. Above all, FDR had succeeded in establishing the principle of governmental responsibility for the aged, the handicapped, and the unemployed. Whatever the defects of the legislation, Social Security stood as a landmark of the New Deal, creating a system to provide for the welfare of individuals in a complex industrial society.

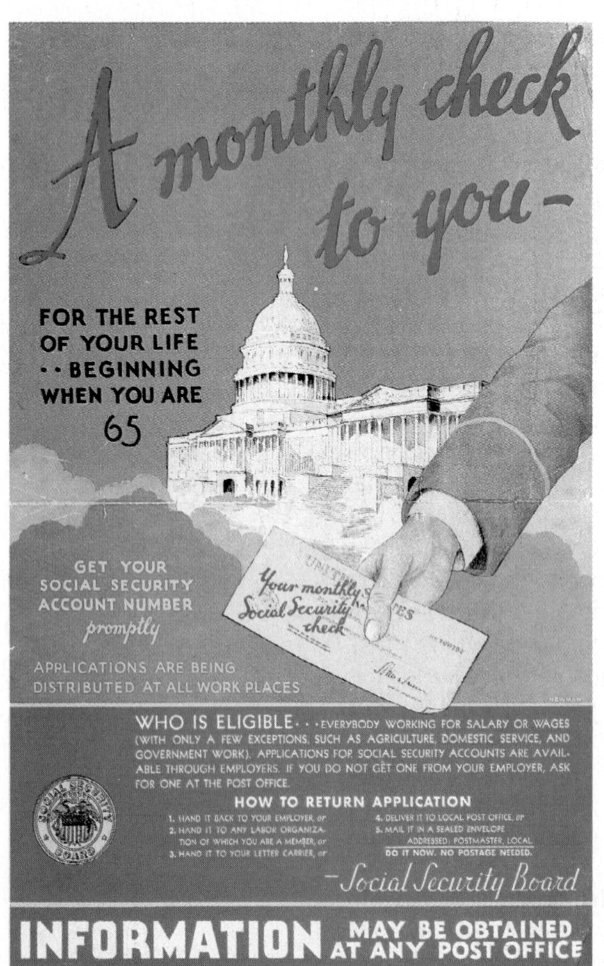

Despite the administration's boosterism, many believed that Social Security could not fulfill its promises. ❖

Labor Legislation

The other major reform achievement in 1935 was passage of the National Labor Relations Act or the **Wagner Act,** as it became known. Senator Robert Wagner of New York introduced legislation in 1934 to outlaw company unions and other unfair labor practices in order to ensure collective bargaining for unions. Although initially opposed by Roosevelt, the bill gained support in Congress and was signed into law in July 1935.

Wagner Act Formally known as the National Labor Relations Act, this New Deal legislation enacted in 1935 created the National Labor Relations Board to supervise union elections and designate winning unions as official bargaining agents. The board could also issue cease-and-desist orders to employers who dealt unfairly with their workers.

The Wagner Act created the National Labor Relations Board to preside over labor-management relations and enable unions to engage in collective bargaining with federal support. The act outlawed a variety of union-busting tactics and in its key provision decreed that whenever the majority of a company's workers voted for a union to represent them, management would be compelled to negotiate with the union on all matters of wages, hours, and working conditions. With this unprecedented government sanction, labor unions could now proceed to recruit the large number of unorganized workers throughout the country. The Wagner Act, the most far-reaching of all New Deal measures, led to the revitalization of the American labor movement and a permanent change in labor-management relations.

Three years later, Congress passed a second law that had a lasting impact on American workers, the Fair Labor Standards Act. A long-sought goal of the New Deal, the measure aimed to establish both minimum wages and maximum hours of work per week. The act was aimed at unorganized workers and met with only grudging support from unions. Southern conservatives opposed it strongly, both on ideological grounds and because it threatened the very low wages in the South that had attracted northern industry since Reconstruction.

Roosevelt finally succeeded in winning passage of the Fair Labor Standards Act in 1938, but only at the cost of exempting many key industries from its coverage. Despite its loopholes, the legislation did lead to pay raises for the twelve million workers earning less than the newly set minimum wage of 40 cents an hour. More important, like Social Security, it set up a system on which Congress could build in the future to reach more generous and humane levels.

All in all, Roosevelt's record in reform was similar to that in relief and recovery—modest success but no sweeping victory. A cautious and pragmatic leader, FDR moved far enough to the left to overcome the challenges of Coughlin, Townsend, and Long without venturing too far from the mainstream. His reforms improved the quality of life in America significantly, but he made no effort to correct all the nation's social and economic wrongs.

Impact of the New Deal

The New Deal had a broad influence on the quality of life in the United States in the 1930s. Government programs reached into areas hitherto untouched. Many of them brought about long overdue improvements, but others failed to make any significant dent in historic inequities. The most important advances came with the dramatic growth of labor unions; conditions for working women and minorities showed no comparable advance.

Rise of Organized Labor

Trade unions were weak at the onset of the Great Depression, with a membership of fewer than three million workers. Most were in the American Federation of Labor (AFL), a collection of craft unions that served the needs of skilled workers. The nation's basic industries, including steel and automobiles, were unorganized; the great mass of unskilled workers thus fared poorly in terms of wages and working conditions.

In some cases, striking union members met with brute force. Philip Evergood's 1937 painting, The American Tragedy, *recounts the violence of the Republic Steel strike.* ❖

John L. Lewis, head of the United Mine Workers, took the lead in organizing unskilled workers in mass production industries by forming the Committee on Industrial Organization (CIO) in 1935. Dynamic and ruthless, Lewis first battled with the conservative leadership of the AFL, and then, after being expelled, he renamed his group the Congress of Industrial Organizations and announced in 1936 that he would use the Wagner Act to extend collective bargaining to the nation's auto and steel industries.

Within five years, Lewis had scored a remarkable series of victories. The big steel companies, led by U.S. Steel, surrendered without a fight in 1937; the smaller firms engaged in violent resistance, as did the automobile industry. When General Motors resisted, members of the newly created United Automobile Workers (UAW) simply sat down in the factory, refusing to leave until the company recognized their union and threatening to destroy the valuable tools and machines if they were removed forcibly. General Motors conceded defeat and signed a contract with the UAW. Chrysler quickly followed suit, and after a hard fight, so did Ford.

By the end of the 1930s, the CIO had some five million members, slightly more than the AFL. The successes were remarkable; organizers for the CIO and the AFL had been successful in the automaking, steel, textile, rubber, electrical, and metal industries. For the first time, unskilled as well as skilled workers were unionized. Because women and blacks made up a substantial proportion of the unskilled workforce, they too benefited from the creation of the CIO.

Yet despite the impressive gains, only 28 percent of all Americans (excluding farmworkers) belonged to unions in 1940. Employer resistance and traditional hostility to unions blocked further progress, as did the aloof attitude of President Roosevelt. The Wagner Act had helped open the way, but labor leaders deserved most of the credit for the gains that were achieved.

The New Deal Record on Help to Minorities

The Roosevelt administration's attempts to aid the downtrodden were least effective among African Americans and other racial minorities. The Great Depression had hit blacks with special force. The fall in the price of cotton had ruined many sharecroppers and tenant farmers, and by 1933, more than 50 percent of urban blacks were unemployed. To make matters worse, hard times exacerbated racial prejudice.

The New Deal helped blacks survive the depression, but it never tried to confront the racial injustice built into federal relief programs. Although the programs served blacks as well as whites, in the South, the weekly payments blacks received were much smaller. Neither the minimum wage nor Social Security covered the 65 percent of all black workers who worked as farmers or domestic servants. In almost every agency, including the TVA, the interests of blacks counted little, if at all.

Despite this bleak record, African Americans rallied behind Roosevelt's leadership, abandoning their historic ties to the Republican party. In part, this switch came in response to Roosevelt's appointment of a number of prominent blacks to high-ranking government positions. The president's wife, Eleanor Roosevelt, spoke out eloquently throughout the decade against racial discrimination. But perhaps the most influential factor in the blacks' political switch was the color-blind policy of Harry Hopkins. He had more than one million African Americans working for the WPA by 1939. Uneven as his record was, Roosevelt had still done more to aid this oppressed minority than any previous president since Lincoln.

The New Deal did far less for Mexican Americans. Engaged primarily in agricultural labor, these people found their wages in the California fields dropping steadily. The Roosevelt administration cut off any further influx from Mexico, and local authorities rounded up and shipped migrants back to Mexico to reduce the welfare rolls. Despite a few benefits from New Deal relief programs, the overall pattern was one of very great economic hardship and relatively little federal assistance for Mexican Americans.

Native Americans, after decades of neglect, fared slightly better under the New Deal. Roosevelt appointed John Collier, a social worker who championed Indian rights, to serve as commissioner of Indian affairs. In 1934, Congress passed the Indian Reorganization Act, a reform measure designed to stress tribal unity and autonomy instead of attempting (as previous policy had done) to transform Indians into self-sufficient farmers by granting them small plots of land. Modest gains also occurred in education, but more than 300,000 Native Americans remained the nation's most impoverished citizens.

Women at Work

The decade witnessed a continued decline in the status of American women. Since men were considered the major breadwinners, women were often fired first. A Gallup poll revealed that 82 percent of the people disapproved of working wives, with 75 percent of the women polled agreeing.

Many of the working women in the 1930s were either single or the sole support of an entire family. Yet their wages remained lower than those for men, and their unemployment rate ran higher than 20 percent throughout the decade. The New Deal offered little encouragement. NRA codes sanctioned lower wages for women. The minimum wage did help women employed in industry, but too many worked as maids and waitresses, jobs not covered by the law. The percentage of women in the workforce was no higher in 1940 than it had been in 1910, and the sexist inequities in the marketplace were as great as ever.

The one area of advance in the 1930s came in government. Eleanor Roosevelt set an example that encouraged millions of American women. She traveled continually around the country, always eager to uncover wrongs and bring them to the president's attention. Frances Perkins, the secretary of labor, became the first woman cabinet member; FDR appointed women as ambassadors and federal judges for the first time; and women were elected to the Senate and the House of Representatives. But overall, a decade that was grim for most Americans was especially hard on American women.

End of the New Deal

The New Deal reached its high point in 1936, when Roosevelt was overwhelmingly reelected and the Democratic party strengthened its hold on Congress. But this political triumph was deceptive. In the next two years, Roosevelt met with a series of defeats in Congress. Yet despite these setbacks, he remained a popular political leader who had restored American self-confidence as he attempted to meet the challenges of the Great Depression.

The Election of 1936

Roosevelt enjoyed his finest political hour in 1936. A man who loved the give-and-take of politics, FDR faced challenges from both the left and the right as he sought reelection. Father Coughlin and Gerald L. K. Smith organized the Union party, with North Dakota Progressive Congressman William Lemke heading the ticket. At the other extreme, a group of wealthy industrialists formed the Liberty League to fight what they saw as the New Deal's assault on property rights. In 1936, the Liberty League endorsed the Republican presidential candidate, Governor Alfred M. Landon of Kansas. A moderate, colorless figure, Landon disappointed his backers by refusing to campaign for repeal of the popular New Deal reforms.

Roosevelt ignored Lemke and the Union party, focusing attention instead on the assault from the right. Democratic spokesmen condemned the Liberty League as a "millionaires' union" and reminded the American people of how much Roosevelt had done for them in fighting unemployment and providing relief. In his speeches, FDR said he welcomed the hatred of the "economic royalists." This frank appeal to class sympathies proved enormously successful, and Roosevelt scored an easy victory at the polls.

Equally important, the election marked the stunning success of a new political coalition that would dominate American politics for the next three decades. FDR, building on the inroads into the Republican majority that Al Smith had begun in 1928, carried urban areas by impressive margins, held on to the traditional Democratic votes in the South and West, and added to them by appealing strongly to the diverse religious and ethnic groups in the northern cities. The strong support of labor and blacks indicated that the nation's new alignment followed economic as well as cultural lines. The poor and the oppressed became attached to the Democratic party, leaving the GOP in a minority position, limited to the well-to-do and to rural and small-town Americans of native stock.

The Supreme Court Fight

FDR proved far more adept at winning elections than at achieving his goals in Congress. In 1937, he attempted to use his recent success to overcome the one obstacle remaining in his path, the Supreme Court. During his first term, the Court had declared several New Deal programs unconstitutional. The justices were elderly men who were generally hostile to New Deal measures; one, Willis Van Devanter, even postponed retirement to be able to express his strong opposition.

When Congress convened in 1937, the president offered a startling proposal to thwart the Court's threat to the New Deal. Declaring that the Court was falling behind schedule because of the age of its members, he asked Congress to appoint a new justice for each member of the Court over the age of 70, up to a maximum of six.

Although the **"Court-packing" scheme,** as critics quickly dubbed it, was perfectly legal, it outraged not only conservatives but liberals as well, who realized that it could set a dangerous precedent for the future. Republicans wisely kept silent, letting prominent Democrats lead the fight against Roosevelt's plan. Despite all-out pressure from the White House, resistance in the Senate blocked early action on the proposal.

"Court-packing" scheme Concerned that the conservative Supreme Court might declare all his New Deal programs unconstitutional, President Roosevelt asked Congress to allow him to appoint additional justices to the Court. Both Congress and the public rejected this "Court-packing" scheme, and it was defeated.

The Court defended itself well, pointing out that it was not behind schedule. The Court then surprised observers with a series of rulings approving such controversial New Deal measures as the Wagner Act and Social Security. In the midst of the struggle, Justice Van Devanter resigned, enabling FDR to make his first appointment to the Court since taking office in 1933. Feeling that he had proved his point, FDR allowed his Court-packing plan to die in the Senate.

Although Roosevelt made four more appointments during the next few years, the Court fight had weakened his relations with Congress and with members of his own party. Many senators and representatives, mostly Southerners, who had voted reluctantly for Roosevelt's measures during the depths of the depression now felt free to oppose any further New Deal reforms.

The New Deal in Decline

The legislative record during Roosevelt's second term was meager. Aside from the minimum wage and a maximum hour law passed in 1938, Congress did not extend the New Deal into any new areas. Disturbed by growing congressional resistance, Roosevelt set out in the spring of 1938 to defeat a number of conservative Democratic congressmen and senators. His efforts were unsuccessful, however, and the failure of this attempted purge further underscored Roosevelt's strained relations with Congress.

The worst blow came in the economic sector. The slow but steady improvement in the economy suddenly gave way to a sharp recession in the late summer of 1937. In the next ten months, industrial production fell by one-third, and nearly four million workers lost their jobs. Critics of the New Deal quickly labeled the downturn the "Roosevelt recession."

The criticism was overblown but not without basis. In an effort to reduce expanding budget deficits, Roosevelt had cut back sharply on WPA and other government programs after the election. This led to a reduction in consumer spending. Urged by economists, Roosevelt finally requested a \$3.75 billion relief appropriation in April 1938, and the economy began to revive. But the president's premature attempt to balance the budget meant two more years of hard times and marred his reputation as the energetic warrior of the depression.

The political result of the attempted purge and the recession was a strong Republican upsurge in the 1938 elections. In addition, after 1938, anti–New Deal Southerners voted more and more often with Republican conservatives to block social and economic reform measures. Not only was the New Deal over by the end of

MAJOR NEW DEAL LEGISLATION AND AGENCIES

Year Created	Act or Agency	Provisions
1933	Agricultural Adjustment Administration (AAA)	Attempted to regulate agricultural production through farm subsidies; reworked after the Supreme Court ruled its key regulatory provisions unconstitutional in 1936; coordinated agricultural production during World War II, after which it was disbanded.
	Banking Act of 1933 (Glass-Steagall Act)	Prohibited commercial banks from selling stock or financing corporations; created FDIC.
	Civilian Conservation Corps (CCC)	Young men between the ages of 18 and 25 volunteered to be placed in camps to work on regional environmental projects, mainly west of the Mississippi; they received $30 a month, of which $25 was sent home; disbanded during World War II.
	Civil Works Administration (CWA)	Emergency work relief program put more than four million people to work during the extremely cold winter of 1933–1934, after which it was disbanded.
	Federal Deposit Insurance Corporation (FDIC)	A federal guarantee of savings bank deposits initially of up to $2,500, raised to $5,000 in 1934, and frequently thereafter; continues today with a limit of $100,000.
	Federal Emergency Relief Administration (FERA)	Combined cash relief to needy families with work relief; superseded in early 1935 by the extensive work relief projects of the WPA and unemployment insurance established by Social Security.
	National Recovery Administration (NRA)	Attempted to combat the Great Depression through national economic planning by establishing and administering a system of industrial codes to control production, prices, labor relations, and trade practices among leading business interests; ruled unconstitutional by the Supreme Court in 1935.
	Public Works Administration (PWA)	Financed more than 34,000 federal and nonfederal construction projects at a cost of more than $6 billion; initiated the first federal public housing program, made the federal government the nation's leading producer of power, and advanced conservation of the nation's natural resources; discontinued in 1939 due to its effectiveness at reducing unemployment and promoting private investment.
	Tennessee Valley Authority (TVA)	An attempt at regional planning. Included provisions for environment and recreational design; architectural, educational, and health projects; and controversial public power projects; continues today to meet the Tennessee Valley's energy and flood-control needs.

1938, but a new bipartisan conservative coalition that would prevail for a quarter century had formed in Congress.

CONCLUSION: EVALUATION OF THE NEW DEAL

The New Deal lasted a brief five years, and most of its measures came in two legislative bursts in the spring of 1933 and the summer of 1935. Yet its impact on American life was enduring. Nearly every aspect of economic, social, and political development in the decades that followed bore the imprint of Roosevelt's leadership.

The least impressive achievement of the New Deal came in the economic realm. Whatever credit Roosevelt is given for relieving human suffering in the depths of the Great Depression must be balanced against his failure to achieve recovery in the 1930s. His modest programs produced only slow and halting improvement. Although much of the advance came as a result of government spending, FDR never embraced the concept of planned deficits, striving instead for a balanced budget. As a result, the nation had barely reached the 1929 level of production a decade later, and nearly ten million men and women were still unemployed.

Year Created	Act or Agency	Provisions
1934	Federal Communications Commission (FCC)	Regulatory agency with wide discretionary powers established to oversee wired and wireless communication; reflected growing importance of radio in everyday lives of Americans during the Great Depression; continues to regulate television as well as radio.
	Federal Housing Administration (FHA)	Expanded private home ownership among moderate-income families through federal guarantees of private mortgages, the reduction of down payments from 30 to 10 percent, and the extension of repayment from 20 to 30 years; continues to function today.
	Securities and Exchange Commission (SEC)	Continues today to regulate trading practices in stocks and bonds according to federal laws.
1935	National Labor Relations Board (NLRB); established by Wagner Act	Greatly enhanced power of American labor by overseeing collective bargaining; continues to arbitrate labor-management disputes today.
	National Youth Administration (NYA)	Established by the WPA to reduce competition for jobs by supporting education and training of youth; paid grants to more than 2 million high school and college students in return for work performed in their schools; also trained another 2.6 million out-of-school youths as skilled labor to prepare them for later employment in the private sector; disbanded during World War II.
	Rural Electrification Administration (REA)	Transformed American rural life by making electricity available at low rates to American farm families in areas that private power companies refused to service; closed the cultural gap between rural and urban everyday life by making modern amenities, such as radio, available in rural areas.
	Social Security Act	Guaranteed retirement payments for enrolled workers beginning at age 65; set up federal-state system of unemployment insurance and care for dependent mothers and children, the handicapped, and public health; continues today.
	Works Progress Administration (WPA)	Massive work relief program funded projects ranging from construction to acting; disbanded by FDR during World War II.
1937	Farm Security Administration (FSA)	Granted loans to small farmers and tenants for rehabilitation and purchase of small-sized farms; Congress slashed its appropriations during World War II when many poor farmers entered the armed forces or migrated to urban areas.
1938	Fair Labor Standards Act	Established a minimum wage of 40 cents an hour and a maximum workweek of 40 hours for businesses engaged in interstate commerce.

Equally important, Roosevelt refused to make sweeping changes in the American economic system. Aside from the TVA program of dam construction and electrification, he promoted no broad experiments in regional planning and no attempts to alter free enterprise beyond imposing limited forms of governmental regulation. The New Deal did nothing to alter the basic distribution of wealth and power in the nation. The outcome was the preservation of the traditional capitalist system with a thin overlay of federal control.

More significant change occurred with the adoption of Social Security. The government acknowledged for the first time a responsibility to provide for the welfare of citizens unable to care for themselves in an industrial society. The Wagner Act helped stimulate the growth of labor unions to balance corporate power, and the minimum wage law provided a much needed floor for many workers. Yet the New Deal tended to help only the more vocal and organized groups, such as union members and commercial farmers. People without effective voices or political clout received scant help from the New Deal. Roosevelt did little more than Hoover in responding to the long-term needs of the dispossessed.

The most lasting impact of the Roosevelt leadership came in politics. FDR forged a new coalition. He united rural and urban Democrats and attracted new

CHRONOLOGY

1932	Franklin D. Roosevelt is elected president (November)
1933	Emergency Banking Relief Act is passed in one day (March) ❖ Twenty-First Amendment repeals prohibition (December)
1934	Securities and Exchange Commission is authorized (June)
1935	Workers Program Administration (WPA) hires unemployed (April) ❖ Wagner Act grants workers collective bargaining (July) ❖ Congress passes Social Security Act (August)
1936	FDR wins second term as president (November)
1937	Auto workers' sit-down strike forces General Motors contract (February) ❖ FDR loses Court-packing battle (July) ❖ "Roosevelt recession" begins (August)
1938	Congress sets minimum wage at 40 cents an hour (June)

groups to the Democratic party, principally blacks and organized labor. His political success led to a major realignment that lasted long after he left the scene.

His political achievement also reveals the true nature of Roosevelt's success. He was a brilliant politician who recognized the essence of leadership in a democracy—appealing directly to the people and infusing them with a sense of purpose. Thus despite his limitations as a reformer, Roosevelt proved to be the man the American people needed in the 1930s, the leader who gave them the psychological lift that helped them endure and survive the Great Depression.

Key Terms

New Deal, p. 504
bonus army, p. 507
Tennessee Valley Authority (TVA), p. 508
National Recovery Administration (NRA), p. 508
Agricultural Adjustment Administration (AAA), p. 509
Civilian Conservation Corps (CCC), p. 510
Works Progress Administration (WPA), p. 510
Social Security Act, p. 512
Wagner Act, p. 513
"Court-packing" scheme, p. 517

Recommended Reading

The best overall account of political developments in the 1930s is William Leuchtenburg, *Franklin D. Roosevelt and the New Deal* (1963). Leuchtenburg offers a balanced treatment but concludes by defending Roosevelt's record. For a more critical view, see James MacGregor Burns, *Roosevelt: The Lion and the Fox* (1956), which portrays FDR as an overly cautious political leader; and Robert A. McElvaine, *The Great Depression: America, 1929–1941* (1984), which laments the New Deal's failure to make more sweeping changes in American life. Gene Smiley, *Rethinking the Great Depression* (2002), succinctly challenges conventional wisdom on the subject.

David M. Kennedy provides a comprehensive portrait of American life during both the Great Depression and World War II in *Freedom from Fear* (1999). More succinct is Gerald D. Nash, *The Crucial Era: The Great Depression and World War II, 1929–1945* (1992). For a sympathetic examination of the New Deal through 1936, see Arthur M. Schlesinger, Jr., *The Age of Roosevelt,* 3 vols. (1957–1960); Paul Conkin offers a brief but provocative critique of Roosevelt's policies in *The New Deal* (1967). George McJimsy, *The Presidency of Franklin Delano Roosevelt* (2000), is the most recent and best-balanced account.

John Kenneth Galbraith, *The Great Crash, 1929* (1961), has long been the standard treatment of that stomach-churning event, but Maury Klein, *Rainbow's End* (2001), may displace it. Alan Brinkley, *Voices of Protest* (1982), assesses the challenges to Roosevelt from the left and the right. Lizabeth Cohen, *Making a New Deal: Industrial Workers in Chicago, 1919–1939* (1990), examines the effects of the Great Depression and the New Deal on the working class. Blanche Wiesen Cook's continuing biography, *Eleanor Roosevelt,*

2 vols. to date (1992–), shows the transformation of the first lady into an advocate of the poor and dispossessed. Franklin Roosevelt's troubles with the Supreme Court are traced in William Leuchtenburg, *The Supreme Court Reborn* (1995); and Barry Cushman, *Rethinking the New Deal Court* (1998). The waning of the New Deal is the theme of Alan Brinkley, *The End of Reform* (1995).

For a list of additional titles related to this chapter's topics, please see http://www.ablongman.com/divine.

Suggested Web Sites

Voices from the Dust Bowl: The Charles L. Todd and Robert Sonkin Migrant Worker Collection, 1940–1941

http://memory.loc.gov/ammem/afctshtml/tshome.html
Farm Security Administration (FSA) studies of migrant work camps in central California in 1940 and 1941 are the bulk of this site. The collection includes audio recordings, photographs, manuscript materials, and publications.

New Deal Network

http://newdeal.feri.org/
This database includes photographs, political cartoons, and texts—including speeches, letters, and other historic documents—from the New Deal period.

Franklin Delano Roosevelt

http://www.ipl.org/ref/POTUS/fdroosevelt.html
This site provides information about FDR, the only president to serve more than two terms.

A New Deal for the Arts

http://www.archives.gov/exhibit_hall/new_deal_for_the_arts/index.html
Artworks, documents, and photographs recount the federal government's efforts to fund artists in the 1930s in this National Archives site.

America from the Great Depression to World War II: Photographs from the FSA and OWI, ca. 1935–1945

http://memory.loc.gov/ammem/fsowhome.html
These images in the Farm Security Administration-Office of War Information Collection show Americans from all over the nation experiencing everything from despair to triumph in the 1930s and 1940s.

Chapter 27

America and the World, 1921–1945

A Pact Without Power

On August 27, 1928, U.S. Secretary of State Frank B. Kellogg, French Foreign Minister Aristide Briand, and representatives of twelve other nations met in Paris to sign a pact outlawing war. Spectators watched and photographers recorded the historic ceremony. In the United States, a senator called the **Kellogg-Briand Pact** "the most telling action ever taken in human history to abolish war."

In reality, the Pact of Paris was the result of a determined American effort to avoid involvement in the European alliance system. In June 1927, Briand had sent a message to the American people inviting the United States to join with France in signing a pact to outlaw war between the two nations. The invitation struck a sympathetic response, but the State Department feared correctly that Briand's true intention was to establish a close tie between France and the United States. France believed that an antiwar pact with the United States would at least ensure American sympathy, if not involvement, in case of another European war. Kellogg outmaneuvered Briand by proposing that the pledge against war not be confined to just France and the United States, but instead be extended to all nations. An unhappy Briand had no choice but to agree, and so the diplomatic charade finally culminated in the elaborate signing ceremony in Paris.

Eventually, the signers of the Kellogg-Briand Pact included nearly every nation in the world, but the effect was negligible. All promised to renounce war as an instrument of national policy, except in matters of self-defense. The pact relied solely on the moral force of world opinion.

UNFORTUNATELY, THE KELLOGG-BRIAND PACT was symbolic of American foreign policy in the years immediately following World War I. Instead of asserting the role of world leadership its resources and power commanded, the United States retreated from involvement with other nations. America went its own way, extending trade and economic dominance but refusing to take the lead in maintaining world order. This retreat from responsibility seemed unimportant in the 1920s when the very exhaustion from World War I ensured relative peace and tranquillity. But in the 1930s, when threats to world order arose in Europe and Asia, the American people retreated even deeper, searching for an isolationist policy that would spare them the agony of another great war.

OUTLINE

Retreat, Reversal, and Rivalry

Isolationism

The Road to War

Turning the Tide Against the Axis

The Home Front

Victory

Conclusion: The Transforming Power of War

There was no place to hide in the modern world. The Nazi onslaught in Europe and the Japanese expansion in Asia finally convinced America to reverse its isolationist stance and become involved in World War II in late 1941, at a time when the chances for an Allied victory seemed most remote. With incredible swiftness, the nation mobilized its military and industrial strength. American armies were soon fighting on three continents, the U.S. Navy controlled the world's oceans, and the nation's factories were sending a vast stream of war supplies to more than twenty Allied countries.

When Allied victory came in 1945, the United States was by far the most powerful nation in the world. But instead of the enduring peace that might have permitted a return to a less active foreign policy, the onset of the Cold War with the Soviet Union brought on a new era of tension and rivalry. This time the United States could not retreat from responsibility. World War II was a coming of age for American foreign policy.

Kellogg-Briand Pact Also called the Pact of Paris, this 1929 agreement pledged its signatories, eventually including nearly all nations, to shun war as an instrument of policy. Derided as an "international kiss," it had little effect on the actual conduct of world affairs.

Retreat, Reversal, and Rivalry

Bitter disillusionment ran through every aspect of American foreign policy in the 1920s. Wilsonian idealism was gone. American diplomats made loans, negotiated treaties and agreements, and pledged the nation's good faith, but they were careful not to make any binding commitments on behalf of world order. The result was neither isolation nor involvement but rather a cautious middle course that managed to alienate friends and encourage foes.

Retreat in Europe

The United States emerged from World War I the richest nation on earth, displacing Britain from its prewar position of economic primacy. Each year of the 1920s saw the nation increase its economic lead as the balance of trade tipped heavily in America's favor. The war-ravaged countries of Europe borrowed enormous amounts from American bankers to rebuild their economies, and American exports and overseas investments far exceeded prewar levels.

The European nations could no longer compete on equal terms. The high American tariff, first imposed in 1922 and raised again in 1930, frustrated attempts by Britain, France, and a defeated Germany to earn the dollars necessary to meet their American financial obligations. Although the Allied partners in World War I asked Washington to cancel $10 billion in war debts, American leaders from Wilson to Hoover indignantly refused.

Only a continuing flow of private American capital to Germany allowed the payment of reparations to the Allies and the partial repayment of war debts in the 1920s. The financial crash of 1929 halted the flow of dollars across the Atlantic and led to subsequent default on the debt payments, with accompanying bitterness on both sides of the ocean.

Political relations fared little better. The United States never joined the League of Nations, nor did it take part in the attempts by Britain and France to negotiate European security treaties. The Republican administrations of the 1920s refused to compromise American freedom of action by embracing collective security, the principle on which the League was founded. And FDR made no effort to renew Wilson's futile quest. Remaining aloof from the European balance of power, the United States refused to stand behind the increasingly shaky Versailles settlement.

The United States ignored the Soviet Union throughout the 1920s. American businessmen, however, actively traded with the Soviets and pressed for diplomatic recognition of the Bolshevik regime. In 1933, Roosevelt finally signed an agreement opening up diplomatic relations between the two countries.

Cooperation in Latin America

United States policy in the Western Hemisphere was both more active and more enlightened than in Europe. The State Department sought new ways in the 1920s to pursue traditional goals of political dominance and economic advantage in Latin America. Both Republican and Democratic administrations worked hard to limit American military involvement and to extend American trade and investment in the nations to the South. Under Harding, Coolidge, and Hoover, American marines were withdrawn from Haiti, the Dominican Republic, and Nicaragua. Renewed unrest in Nicaragua in 1925, however, led to a second intervention that lasted until the early 1930s.

Showing a new sensitivity, the State Department in 1930 released the Clark Memorandum, a policy statement repudiating the controversial Roosevelt Corollary to the Monroe Doctrine. The United States had no right to intervene in neighboring states under the Monroe Doctrine, declared Undersecretary of State J. Reuben Clark, although he asserted a traditional claim to protect American lives and property under international law.

When FDR took office in 1933, relations with Latin America were far better than they had been under Wilson, but American trade in the hemisphere had fallen drastically as the Great Depression worsened. Roosevelt moved quickly to solidify the improved relations and gain economic benefits. He proclaimed a **Good Neighbor policy** and then proceeded to win goodwill by renouncing the imperialism of the past.

Good Neighbor policy
President Franklin D. Roosevelt's administration initiated a new approach to Western hemispheric relations with a policy declaring America's intention to use cooperation and friendship in place of threats and armed intervention in its dealings with Latin America.

Starting in 1933, Roosevelt's secretary of state, Cordell Hull, moved toward a policy of nonintervention. A year later, the United States loosened its grip on Cuba (renouncing the Platt Amendment) and Panama. By 1936, American troops were no longer occupying any Latin American nation. But the United States had not changed its basic goal of political and economic dominance in the hemisphere. Rather, the new policy of benevolence reflected Roosevelt's belief that cooperation and friendship were more effective tactics than threats and armed intervention.

The Good Neighbor policy opened up new trade opportunities. American commerce with Latin America increased fourfold in the 1930s, and investment rose substantially from its Great Depression low. Most important, FDR succeeded in forging a new policy of regional collective security between the nations of the Western Hemisphere and the United States.

Rivalry in Asia

In the years following World War I, the United States and Japan were on a collision course in the Pacific. The Japanese, lacking the raw materials to sustain their developing industrial economy, were determined to expand onto the Asian mainland. They had taken Korea by 1905 and during World War I had extended their control over the mines, harbors, and railroads of Manchuria, the industrial region of northeastern China. The American Open Door policy remained the primary obstacle to complete Japanese domination over China. The United States thus faced the clear-cut choice of either abandoning China or forcefully opposing Japan's expansion. American efforts to avoid making this painful decision postponed the eventual showdown but not the growing rivalry.

The first attempt at a solution came in 1921 when the United States convened the Washington Conference. The major objective was a political settlement of the tense Asian situation, but the most pressing issue was a dangerous naval race between Japan and the United States. Projected construction indicated that both countries would overtake the British navy by the end of the decade. Japan, spending nearly one-third of its budget on naval construction, was eager for an agreement; in the United States, too, growing congressional concern over appropriations suggested the need for slowing the naval buildup.

Secretary of State Charles Evans Hughes outlined a specific plan for naval disarmament. After three months of discussion, the delegates signed the Five Power Treaty limiting capital ships (battleships and aircraft carriers) in a ratio of 5:5:3 for the United States, Britain, and Japan, respectively, and 1.67:1.67 for France and Italy. Japan agreed to the lower ratio only in return for an American pledge not to fortify Pacific bases such as the Philippines and Guam. The treaty cooled off the naval race even though it did not cover cruisers, destroyers, or submarines.

The Washington Conference also produced the Nine Power Treaty, which pledged the signatories to uphold the Open Door policy, and the Four Power Treaty, which created a new Pacific security pact. Neither document contained any enforcement provision beyond a promise to consult in case of violation. In essence, the Washington treaties formed a parchment peace, a pious set of pledges that attempted to freeze the status quo in the Pacific.

This compromise lasted less than a decade. In September 1931, Japanese forces overran Manchuria in a brutal act of aggression. The United States, paralyzed by the Great Depression, responded feebly. In January 1932, Secretary of State Henry L. Stimson vowed that the United States would not recognize the legality of the Japanese seizure of Manchuria. Despite ultimate concurrence by the League of Nations on nonrecognition, the Japanese ignored the American moral sanction and incorporated the former Chinese province into their expanding empire.

Aside from the Good Neighbor approach in the Western Hemisphere, American foreign policy faithfully reflected the prevailing disillusionment with world power that gripped the country after World War I. The United States avoided taking any constructive steps toward preserving world order, preferring instead the empty symbolism of the Washington treaties and the Kellogg-Briand Pact.

Isolationism

The retreat from an active world policy in the 1920s turned into a headlong flight back to isolationism in the 1930s. Two factors were responsible. First, the Great Depression made foreign policy seem remote and unimportant to most Americans. Second, the danger of war abroad, when it did finally penetrate the American consciousness, served only to strengthen the desire to escape involvement.

Three powerful and discontented nations were on the march in the 1930s—Germany, Italy, and Japan. In Germany, Adolf Hitler came to power in 1933 as the head of the National Socialist, or Nazi, movement. A shrewd and charismatic leader, Hitler capitalized on both domestic discontent and bitterness over Germany's defeat in World War I. Blaming the Jews and the Communists for all of Germany's ills and asserting the supremacy of the "Aryan" race of blond, blue-eyed Germans, he quickly imposed a totalitarian dictatorship in which the Nazi party ruled and the *Führer* (leader) was supreme. As he consolidated his power, his ultimate threat to world peace became clear. Hitler took Germany out of the League of Nations, reoccupied the Rhineland, and formally denounced the Treaty of Versailles.

In Italy, another dictator, Benito Mussolini, had come to power in 1922. Emboldened by Hitler's success, he embarked on an aggressive foreign policy in 1935. His invasion of Ethiopia led its emperor, Haile Selassie, to call on the League of Nations for support. The League's halfway measures utterly failed to halt Mussolini's conquest. Collective security had failed its most important test.

Japan formed the third element in the threat to world peace. Militarists began to dominate the government in Tokyo by the mid-1930s, using tactics of fear and even assassination against their liberal opponents. By 1936, Japan had left the League of Nations and had repudiated the Washington treaties. A year later, its armies began an invasion of China that signified the beginning of the Pacific phase of World War II.

The resurgence of militarism in Germany, Italy, and Japan undermined the Versailles settlement and threatened to destroy the existing balance of power. In 1937, the three totalitarian nations signed a pact creating a Berlin-Rome-Tokyo axis. The alliance of the **Axis Powers** ostensibly was aimed at the Soviet Union, but in fact it threatened the entire world. Only a determined American response could unite the other nations against the Axis threat. Unfortunately, the United States deliberately abstained from assuming this role of leadership until it was nearly too late.

Axis Powers During World War II, the alliance between Germany, Italy, and Japan was known as the Berlin-Rome-Tokyo axis, and the three members were called the Axis Powers. They fought against the Allied Powers, led by the United States, Britain, and the Soviet Union.

The Lure of Pacifism and Neutrality

The growing danger of war abroad led to a rising American desire for noninvolvement. Memories of the horrors of World War I contributed heavily. Historians began to treat the Great War as a mistake, criticizing Wilson for failing to preserve American neutrality and claiming that the clever British had duped the United States into entering the war.

American youth made clear their determination not to repeat the mistakes of their elders. Pacifism swept college campuses. In April 1934, students and professors walked out of class to attend massive antiwar rallies, which became an annual rite of spring in the 1930s. Pacifist orators urged students to sign a pledge not to support their country "in any war it might conduct."

The pacifist movement found a scapegoat in the munitions industry. The publication of several books exposing the unsavory business tactics of the large arms dealers such as Krupps in Germany and Vickers in Britain led to the demand to curb these "merchants of death." Senator Gerald Nye of North Dakota headed a special Senate committee that spent two years investigating the dealings that brought enormous profits to munitions firms such as Du Pont. Nye went further, charging that bankers and munitions makers were responsible for American intervention in 1917. Although he offered no proof, the public—prepared to believe the worst of business during the Great Depression—accepted the merchants-of-death thesis.

The Nye Committee's revelations culminated in neutrality legislation aimed at avoiding involvement in European conflicts. In August 1935, Congress passed the first of three **neutrality acts.** The 1935 law banned the sale of arms to nations at war and warned American citizens not to sail on belligerent ships. In 1936, a second act added a ban on loans, and in 1937, a third neutrality act made these prohibitions permanent and required, on a two-year trial basis, that all trade other than munitions be conducted on a cash-and-carry basis.

neutrality acts Reacting to their disillusionment with World War I and absorbed in the domestic crisis of the Great Depression, Americans backed Congress's three neutrality acts in the 1930s. The 1935 and 1936 acts forbade selling munitions or lending money to belligerents in a war. The 1937 act required that all remaining trade be conducted on a cash-and-carry basis.

President Roosevelt played a passive role in the adoption of the neutrality legislation. Privately, he expressed some reservations, but publicly he bowed to the prevailing isolationism. Yet FDR did take a few steps to try to limit the nation's retreat into isolationism. His failure to invoke the neutrality act after the Japanese invasion of China in 1937 enabled the hard-pressed Chinese to continue buying arms from the United States. In January 1938, he used his influence to block a proposal by Indiana Congressman Louis Ludlow to require a nationwide referendum before Congress could declare war. FDR's strongest public statement came earlier, in Chicago in October 1937, when he denounced "the epidemic of world lawlessness" and called for an international effort to "quarantine" this disease.

War in Europe

The neutrality legislation played directly into the hands of Adolf Hitler. Bent on the conquest of Europe, he could now proceed without worrying about American interference. In March 1938, he seized Austria in a bloodless coup. Six months later, he was demanding the Sudetenland, a province of Czechoslovakia with a large German population. When British and French leaders approved Hitler's move at their Munich conference, FDR gave his tacit consent.

Within six months of the meeting at Munich, Hitler violated his promises by seizing nearly all of Czechoslovakia. In the United States, the State Department, with FDR's approval, pressed for neutrality revision, hoping to place *all* trade with belligerents, including munitions, on a cash-and-carry basis. The House, however, rejected the proposal, aware that it would favor Britain and France, who controlled the sea.

In July 1939, Roosevelt finally abandoned his aloof position and met with Senate leaders to plead for reconsideration. Even with the threat of war in Europe, strong isolationist sentiment prevailed. Congressional leaders refused to alter the neutrality acts.

On September 1, 1939, Hitler began World War II by invading Poland. Britain and France responded two days later by declaring war. The Soviets had played a key role by signing a nonaggression treaty with Hitler in late August. The Nazi-Soviet pact enabled Germany to avoid a two-front war; the Russians were rewarded with a generous slice of eastern Poland.

President Roosevelt reacted to the outbreak of war by proclaiming American neutrality, but the successful aggression by Nazi Germany brought into question the isolationist assumption that American well-being did not depend on the European balance of power. Strategic as well as ideological considerations began to undermine the earlier belief that the United States could safely pursue a policy of neutrality and noninvolvement. Americans came to realize that their own democracy and security were at stake in the European war.

Hitler sent his armies into Poland with tremendous force and firepower, devastating the country. Here German troops observe as the German Luftwaffe *bombs Warsaw in September 1939 destroying the city and forcing its inhabitants to surrender.* ❖

THE ROAD TO WAR

For two years, the United States tried to remain at peace while war raged in Europe and Asia. In contrast to Wilson's attempt to be impartial during most of World War I, however, the American people displayed an overwhelming sympathy for the Allies and total distaste for Germany and Japan. Roosevelt made no secret of his preference for an Allied victory, but a fear of isolationist criticism compelled him to move slowly, and often deviously, in adopting a policy of aid for Britain and France short of actually entering the war.

From Neutrality to Undeclared War

Two weeks after the outbreak of war in Europe, Roosevelt called Congress into special session to revise the neutrality legislation. His aim was to repeal the arms embargo in order to supply weapons to Britain and France, but he refused to state this openly. Instead he asked Congress to replace the arms embargo with cash-and-carry regulations. Congress passed the revised neutrality policy by heavy margins in early November 1939.

A series of dramatic German victories had a profound impact on American opinion. In the spring of 1940, Germany seized Denmark and Norway and unleashed the *Blitzkrieg* ("lightning war") on the western front. Using tanks, armored columns, and dive bombers in close coordination, the German army drove the British off the continent in three weeks; three weeks later, France fell to Hitler's victorious armies.

Americans were stunned. Hitler had taken only six weeks to achieve what Germany had failed to do in four years of fighting in World War I. Suddenly they realized that they did have a stake in the outcome; if Britain fell, Hitler might well gain control of the British navy and the Atlantic, opening the New World to German penetration.

Roosevelt responded by invoking a policy of all-out aid to the Allies short of war. Denouncing Germany and Italy as representing "the gods of force and hate," he pledged American support for Britain and its allies. In early September, FDR announced the transfer of fifty old destroyers to Britain in exchange for rights to build air and naval bases on eight British possessions in the Western Hemisphere. Giving warships to a belligerent nation was clearly a breach of neutrality, but Roosevelt stressed the importance of the United States' guarding its Atlantic approaches.

Isolationists protested against this departure from neutrality. Roosevelt's opponents in the Midwest formed the America First Committee to oppose the drift toward war. Such diverse individuals as aviator-hero Charles Lindbergh, conservative Senator Robert A. Taft, and socialist leader Norman Thomas condemned FDR for involving the United States in a foreign conflict that they claimed in no way threatened America.

To support the administration's policies, moderate New Dealers, eastern seaboard Anglophiles, and liberal Republicans joined forces to organize the Committee to Defend America by Aiding the Allies. Kansas newspaper editor William Allen White served as chairman of this interventionist organization, which advocated unlimited assistance to the British short of war. Above all, the interventionists challenged the isolationist premise that events in Europe did not affect American security. As White declared, "The future of western civilization is being decided upon the battlefield of Europe."

In the ensuing debate, the American people gradually came to agree with the interventionists. Frightened by the events in Europe, Congress approved large sums for preparedness, increasing the defense budget from $2 billion to $10 billion during 1940. Roosevelt courageously asked for a peacetime draft, the first in American history, to build up the army, and Congress consented.

The sense of crisis affected domestic politics. Roosevelt ran for an unprecedented third term in 1940 because of the war; the Republicans nominated Wendell Willkie, who shared FDR's commitment to aid for Britain. Roosevelt's decisive victory made it clear that the nation supported his departure from neutrality.

After the election, FDR took his boldest step. Responding to British Prime Minister Winston Churchill's warning that his nation was running out of money, the president asked Congress to approve a new program to lend and lease goods and weapons to countries fighting against aggressors. Roosevelt's call for America to become "the great arsenal of democracy" seemed straightforward enough, but he acted somewhat deviously by naming the program **Lend-Lease** and by comparing it to loaning a garden hose to put out a fire.

Lend-Lease Plan approved by Congress in 1941 that allowed the United States to sell, lend, lease, or transfer war materials to any country whose defense the president declared as vital to that of the United States.

Isolationists angrily denounced Lend-Lease as both unnecessary and untruthful. In March 1941, however, Congress voted by substantial margins to authorize the president to "sell, transfer title to, exchange, lease, lend, or otherwise dispose of" war supplies to "any country the president deems vital to the defense of the United States." The accompanying $7 billion appropriation ended the "cash" part of cash-and-carry and ensured full British access to American war supplies.

The "carry" problem still remained. German submarines were sinking more than 500,000 tons of shipping a month. Britain desperately needed the help of the American navy in escorting convoys across the U-boat-infested waters of the North Atlantic. Roosevelt responded with naval patrols as far east as Iceland. Hitler placed his submarine commanders under strict restraints to avoid drawing America into the European war. Nevertheless, incidents were bound to occur.

Undeclared naval war quickly followed. A German submarine damaged the U.S. destroyer *Kearney,* and another sank the *Reuben James.* FDR issued orders for the destroyers to shoot U-boats on sight. At Roosevelt's request, Congress repealed the "carry" section of the neutrality laws and permitted American ships to deliver supplies to Britain. Now American merchant ships as well as destroyers would become targets for German attacks. By December 1941, war with Germany seemed inevitable.

In leading the nation to the brink of war in Europe, Roosevelt opened himself to criticism from both sides in the domestic debate. Interventionists believed he was too cautious; isolationists claimed that he had misled the American people by professing peace while plotting for war. Roosevelt was certainly less than candid, relying on executive discretion to engage in highly provocative acts in the North Atlantic. Although he clearly saw the threat that Germany represented, he was also aware that most Americans wanted to stay out of another war. Realizing that leading a divided nation into war would be disastrous, FDR played for time, inching the country toward war while waiting for the Axis nations to make the ultimate move. Japan finally obliged at Pearl Harbor.

Showdown in the Pacific

Japan had taken advantage of the war in Europe to expand in Asia. The defeat of France and the Netherlands in 1940 left French and Dutch colonial possessions in the East Indies and Indochina vulnerable and defenseless. Japan now set out to incorporate these territories—rich in oil, tin, and rubber—into what was called the Greater East Asia Co-Prosperity Sphere.

The Roosevelt administration countered with economic pressure. Japan depended heavily on the United States for petroleum and scrap iron and steel. In July 1940, FDR signed an order setting up a licensing and quota system for the export of these crucial materials to Japan and banned the sale of aviation gasoline altogether. The United States was now employing economic sanctions to block Japanese expansion in Southeast Asia.

Tokyo appeared unimpressed. In early September 1940, Japanese troops occupied strategic bases in the northern part of French Indochina. Later in the month, Japan signed the Tripartite Pact with Germany and Italy, a defensive treaty that confronted the United States with a possible two-ocean war and a global totalitarian threat. Roosevelt and his advisers, however, saw Germany as the primary danger; thus they pursued a policy of all-out aid to Britain while hoping that economic measures alone would deter Japan.

The embargo on aviation gasoline, extended to include scrap iron and steel, was a burden Japan could bear, but a possible ban on all oil shipments was a different matter. Entirely dependent on oil imports from the United States and the Dutch East Indies, Japan tried to negotiate with the United States, but these talks broke down. Tokyo wanted nothing less than a free hand in China and an end to American sanctions, while the United States insisted on an eventual Japanese evacuation of all China.

In July 1941, Japan invaded southern Indochina, beginning the chain of events that led to war. Washington knew of this aggression before it occurred. Naval intelligence experts had broken the Japanese diplomatic code and were intercepting and reading all messages between Tokyo and the Japanese embassy in Washington. FDR responded on July 25, 1941, with an order freezing all Japanese assets in the United States. Trade with Japan, including the vital oil shipments, came to a complete halt. When the Dutch government-in-exile took similar actions, Japan faced a dilemma: to have oil shipments resumed, Tokyo would have to end its aggression; the alternative would be to seize the needed petroleum supplies in the Dutch East Indies, an action that would mean war.

With General Hideki Tojo, an army militant, as the premier of Japan, the Tokyo government moved toward war. To mask its war preparations, Tokyo sent yet another envoy to Washington with new peace proposals, a mission both Japan and the United States knew was futile. Army and navy leaders urged FDR to seek a temporary settlement with Japan to give them time to prepare American defenses in the Pacific. Secretary of State Hull, however, refused to allow any concessions, sending a stiff ten-point reply to Tokyo that included a demand for Japanese withdrawal from China.

Two weeks later, on the evening of December 6, 1941, the first thirteen parts of the Japanese reply to Hull's note arrived in Washington. After reading the decoded text late that night, President Roosevelt said, "This means war."

The fourteenth part of Japan's reply arrived the next day, December 7, revealing Japan's complete rejection of the American position. Officials in Washington tried to warn American bases in the Pacific, but they were too late. Just before 1 P.M. Washington time, squadrons of Japanese carrier-based planes caught the American fleet at **Pearl Harbor,** Hawaii, totally by surprise. In a little more than an hour, the Japanese crippled the American Pacific fleet and destroyed its base at Pearl Harbor, sinking eight battleships and killing more than 2,400 American sailors.

Pearl Harbor On December 7, 1941, Japanese warplanes attacked U.S. naval forces at Pearl Harbor, Hawaii, sinking several ships and killing more than 2,400 American sailors. The event marked America's entrance into World War II.

Speaking before Congress the next day, President Roosevelt termed December 7 "a date which will live in infamy" and asked for a declaration of war against Japan. With only one dissenting vote, both chambers consented. On December 11, Germany and Italy declared war against the United States; the nation was now fully involved in World War II.

The whole country united behind Roosevelt's leadership to seek revenge for Pearl Harbor and to defeat the Axis threat to American security. After the war, however, critics charged that FDR had entered the conflict by a back door, claiming that the president had deliberately exposed the Pacific fleet to attack. Subsequent investigations uncovered negligence in both Hawaii and Washington but no evidence to support the conspiracy charge. Both military experts and FDR had badly underestimated the daring and skill of the Japanese, but there was no plot. Perhaps the most frightening aspect of the whole episode is that it took the shock of the Japanese

American ships were destroyed in the surprise attack on Pearl Harbor, December 7, 1941. Caught completely off guard, U.S. forces still managed to shoot down twenty-nine enemy planes. ❖

sneak attack to make the American people aware of the full extent of the Axis threat to their well-being and persuade them out of the long fruitless effort to stay out of the war.

Turning the Tide Against the Axis

In the first few months after the United States entered the war, the outlook for victory was bleak. In Europe, Hitler's armies controlled virtually the entire continent, from Norway in the north to Greece in the south. Despite the nonaggression pact, German armies had penetrated deep into the Soviet Union after an initial invasion in June 1941. In North Africa, General Erwin Rommel's Afrika Korps had pushed the British back into Egypt and threatened the Suez Canal.

The situation was no better in Asia. The Pearl Harbor attack had enabled the Japanese to move unopposed across Southeast Asia. Within three months, they had conquered Malaya and the Dutch East Indies, with its valuable oil fields, and were pressing the British back in both Burma and New Guinea. American forces under General Douglas MacArthur had tried but failed to block the Japanese conquest of the Philippines. With the American navy still recovering from the devastation at Pearl Harbor, Japan controlled the western half of the Pacific.

It took the United States and its allies two years to halt the German and Japanese offensives. Then they faced the difficult process of driving back the enemy, freeing the vast conquered areas, and defeating the Axis powers on their home territory. It was a difficult and costly struggle requiring great sacrifice and heavy losses; World War II tested American will and resourcefulness to the hilt.

Wartime Partnerships

The greatest single advantage that the United States and its partners possessed was their willingness to form a genuine coalition to bring about the defeat of the Axis powers. In striking contrast was the behavior of Germany and Japan, each fighting a separate war without any attempt at cooperation.

The United States and Britain achieved a complete wartime partnership. Prewar military talks led to the formation of the Combined Chiefs of Staff, which directed Anglo-American military operations. The close cooperation between FDR and Prime Minister Churchill ensured a common strategy. The leaders decided at the outset that a German victory posed the greater danger and thus gave priority to the European theater in the conduct of the war.

Relations with the other members of the coalition in World War II were not quite so harmonious. The decision to defeat Germany first displeased the Chinese, who had been at war with Japan since 1937. Roosevelt tried to appease Chiang Kai-shek with a trickle of supplies. France posed a more delicate problem. FDR virtually ignored the Free French government in exile under General Charles de Gaulle. Roosevelt preferred to deal with the Vichy regime, despite its collaboration with Germany, because it still controlled the French fleet and retained France's overseas territories.

The greatest strain of all within the wartime coalition was with the Soviet Union. Although Roosevelt had ended the long period of nonrecognition in 1933, close ties had failed to develop. The great Russian purge trials and the temporary Nazi-Soviet alliance from 1939 to 1941, along with deep-seated cultural and ideological differences, made wartime cooperation difficult.

Ever the pragmatist, Roosevelt tried hard to break down the old hostility and establish a more cordial relationship with the Soviets during the war. He was quick to give Lend-Lease aid to the USSR, and in May 1942, he promised a visiting Russian diplomat that the United States would create a second front in Europe by the end of that year, a pledge he could not fulfill. In January 1943, Roosevelt and Churchill met in Casablanca, Morocco, to declare a policy of unconditional surrender, vowing that the Western Allies would fight on until the Axis nations were completely defeated.

Despite the promises, the Soviet Union bore the brunt of the battle against Hitler in the early years of the war. The United States and Britain, grateful for the respite to build up their forces, could do little more than offer promises of future help and send Lend-Lease supplies. The result was a rift that never fully healed—one that did not prevent the defeat of Germany but did ensure future tensions and uncertainties between the Soviet Union and the Western nations.

Halting the German Blitz

From the outset, the United States favored an invasion across the English Channel as the key to victory in Europe. Roosevelt and his leading military advisers were convinced that such a frontal assault would be the quickest way to win the war. Army Chief of Staff George C. Marshall placed his protégé, Dwight D. Eisenhower, in charge of drawing up and implementing the invasion.

But the British preferred a perimeter approach, with air and naval attacks around the edge of the continent, until Germany was softened up for the final invasion. Roosevelt temporarily consented to this plan, and in November 1942, American and British troops landed on the Atlantic and Mediterranean coasts of Morocco and Algeria.

The British launched an attack against Rommel at El Alamein in Egypt and soon forced the Afrika Korps to retreat across Libya to Tunisia. American forces then hit Rommel in Tunisia. After a humiliating defeat at the Kasserine Pass, General George Patton rallied the demoralized American soldiers, and by May 1943, Germany had been driven from Africa, leaving behind nearly 300,000 troops. During these same months, the Red Army broke the back of German military power after Hitler poured in division after division in what was ultimately a critical defeat at the battle of Stalingrad.

At Churchill's insistence, FDR agreed to follow up the North African victory with the invasion first of Sicily and then Italy in the summer of 1943. Italy dropped out of the war when Mussolini fled to Germany, but the Italian campaign proved to be a strategic dead end. Germany sent in enough divisions to establish a strong defensive line in the mountains south of Rome; American and British troops were forced to fight their way slowly up the peninsula, suffering heavy casualties.

More important, these Mediterranean operations delayed the second front, postponing it eventually to the spring of 1944. Meanwhile, the Soviets began to push the Germans out and looked forward to the liberation of Poland, Hungary, and Romania, where they could establish "friendly" Communist regimes. Having borne the brunt of the fighting against Nazi Germany, Stalin was ready to claim his reward—the postwar domination of eastern Europe.

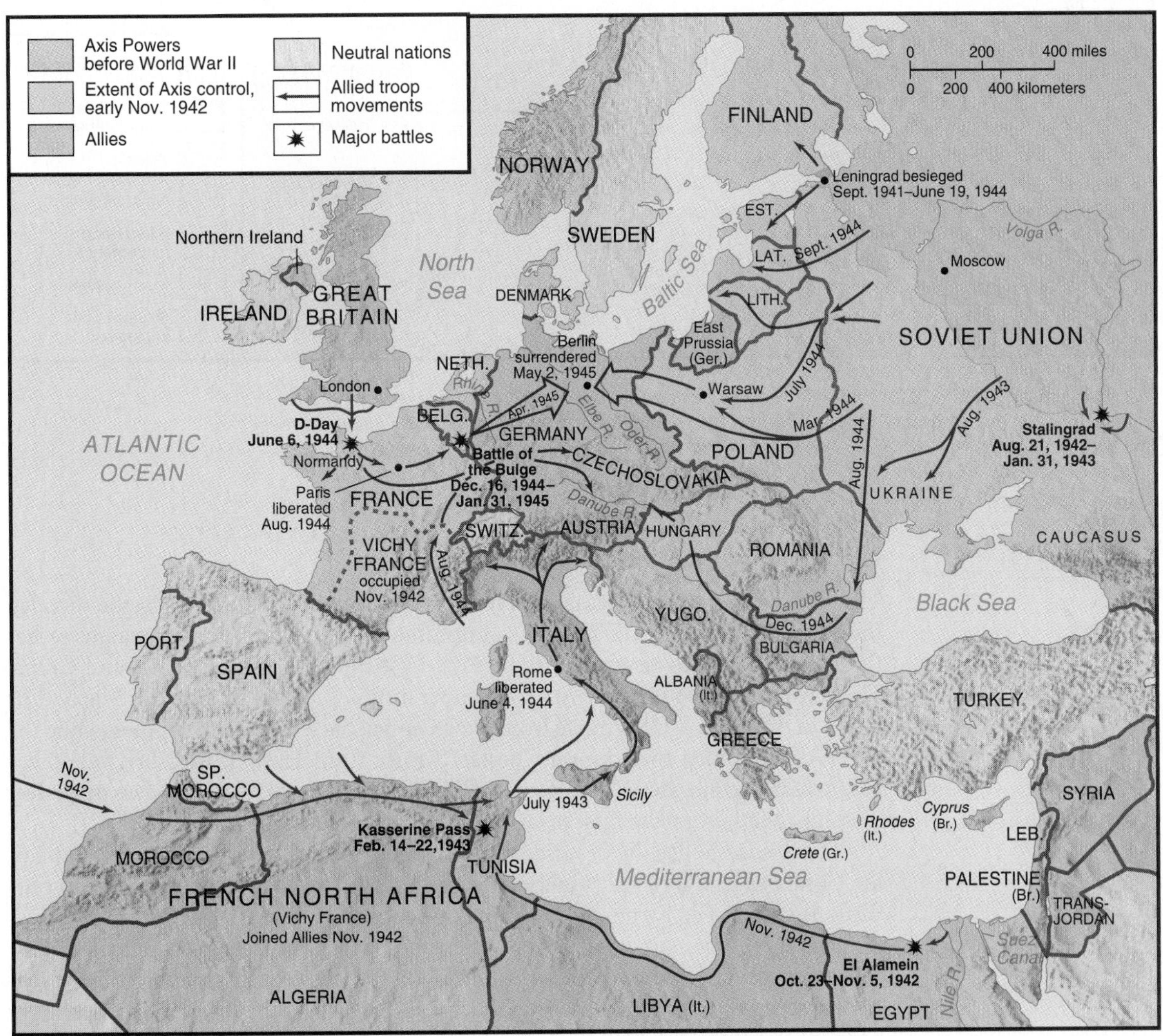

WORLD WAR II IN EUROPE AND NORTH AFRICA *The tide of battle shifted in this theater of war during the winter of 1942–1943. The massive German assault on the eastern front was turned back by the Russians at Stalingrad, and the Allied forces recaptured North Africa.* ❖

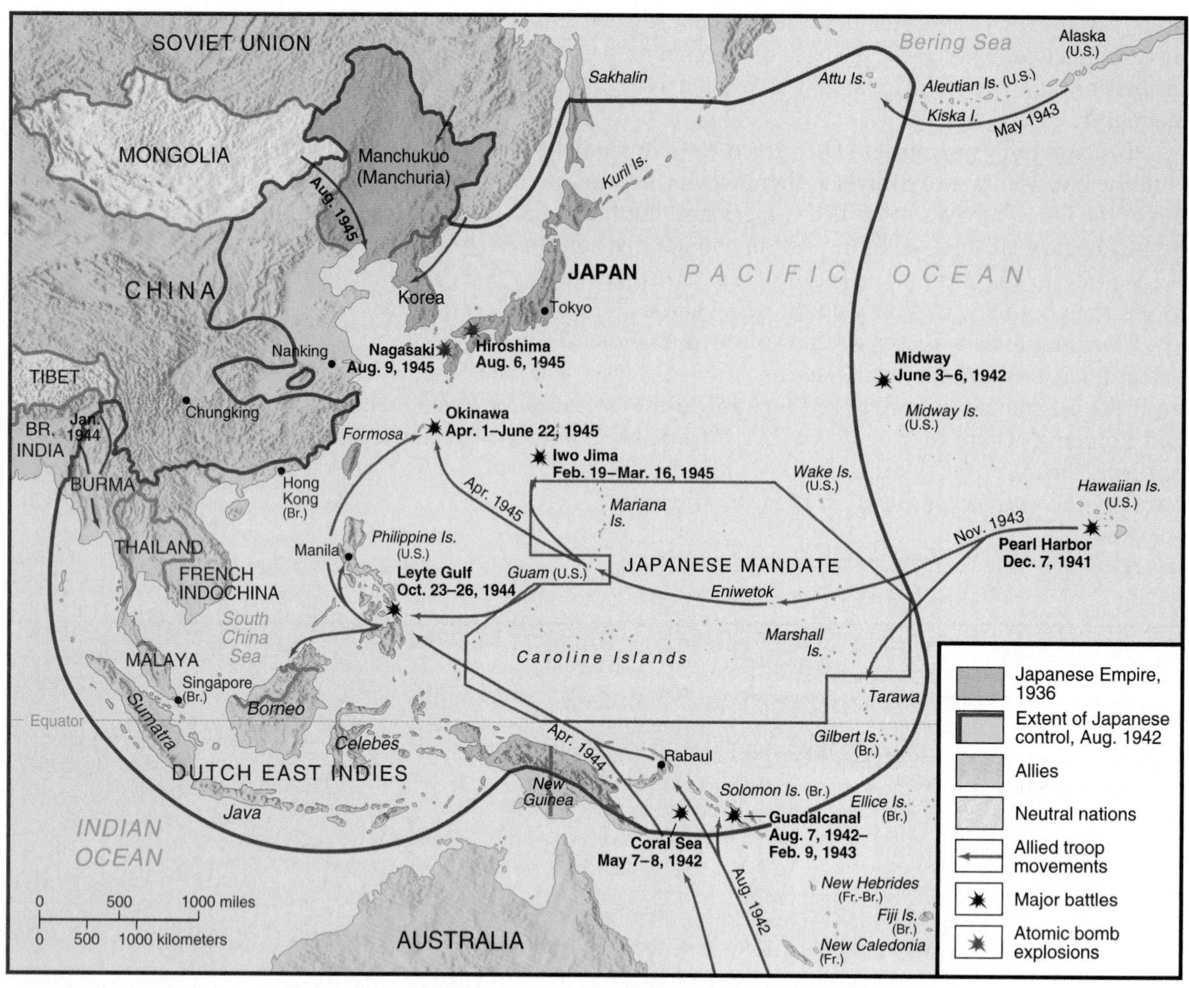

WORLD WAR II IN THE PACIFIC *The tide of battle turned in the Pacific the same year as in Europe. The balance of sea power shifted back to the United States from Japan after the naval victories of 1942.* ❖

Checking Japan in the Pacific

The decision to defeat Germany first and the vast expanses of the Pacific dictated the nature of the war against Japan—amphibious, island-hopping campaigns rather than any attempt to reconquer the Dutch East Indies, Southeast Asia, and China. There would be two separate American operations. One, led by Douglas MacArthur based in Australia, would move from New Guinea back to the Philippines, while the other, commanded by Admiral Chester Nimitz from Hawaii, was directed at key Japanese islands in the central Pacific. The original plan called for the two offensives to come together for the final invasion of the Japanese home islands.

Success in the Pacific depended above all on control of the sea. In the battle of the Coral Sea in May 1942, American naval forces blocked a Japanese thrust to outflank Australia. The turning point came one month later at Midway. In this important battle, superior American air power enabled Nimitz's forces to engage the enemy at long range. The battle of Midway ended with the loss of four Japanese aircraft carriers compared to just one American. It was the first defeat the modern Japanese navy had ever suffered, and it left the United States in control of the central Pacific.

Encouraged by the victory, American forces launched their first Pacific offensive in the Solomon Islands, east of New Guinea, in August 1942. Six months later, the last Japanese were driven from the key island of Guadalcanal. At the same time, MacArthur began the long, bloody job of driving the Japanese back along the north coast of New Guinea.

By early 1943, the defensive phase of the war with Japan was over. The enemy surge had been halted in both the central and the southwestern Pacific, and the United States was ready to move back toward the Philippines. Just as Soviet Russia had broken German power in Europe, the United States had halted the Japanese. And like the Soviet plans for eastern Europe, America expected to reap the rewards of victory by dominating the Pacific in the future.

❖ A Look at the Past ❖

WWII Ration Stamps

Ration stamps became necessary during World War II when gasoline, tires, selected foodstuffs, and other products became scarce. Stamps with patriotic or military symbolism suggest that rationing was an honorable sacrifice, not a hardship. How effective was the tactic of using such symbols? If Americans accepted rationing as their duty, what does that suggest about attitudes toward the war effort and government?

The Home Front

World War II had a greater impact than the Great Depression on American life. While American soldiers and sailors fought abroad, the nation underwent sweeping social and economic changes at home. American industry worked to capacity to meet the need for war materials. Increased production in both industry and agriculture benefited workers and farmers alike. The expansion of war-related industries encouraged many people to move to where new jobs had sprung up. Women moved out of the home into the paid workforce; rural dwellers relocated to urban areas, and northerners and easterners sought new opportunities and new homes in the South and West. Another beneficiary of the return to prosperity brought on by the war was FDR, who had seen the nation through the dark days of the depression. The nation's economic recovery helped him win reelection to the presidency for a fourth term in 1944.

The Arsenal of Democracy

American industry made the nation's single most important contribution to victory. The manufacturing plants that had run at half capacity through the 1930s now hummed with activity. In Detroit, automobile assembly lines were converted to produce tanks and airplanes with the same efficiency as they had once turned out cars. Shipmakers were just as productive. In part, America won the battle of the Atlantic by building ships faster than German U-boats could sink them.

The vast industrial expansion, however, created many problems. In 1942, FDR appointed Donald Nelson to head the War Production Board (WPB). An easygoing man, Nelson was soon outmaneuvered by the army and the navy, which preferred to negotiate directly with large corporations. Shortages of such critical materials as steel, aluminum, and copper led to an allocation system based on military priorities. However, through tax incentives for industrialists and rationing of import products, American industries were able to meet the needs of the military. All in all, the nation's factories turned out twice as many goods as the German and Japanese industries combined.

Roosevelt revealed the same tendency toward compromise in directing the economic mobilization as he had in shaping the New Deal. When administrators clashed, FDR worked toward a consensus and fair settlements. The president was also forced to compromise with Congress, which pared down the administration's requests for large tax increases. Half the cost of the war was financed by borrowing; the other half came from revenues. A $7 billion revenue increase in 1942 included so many first-time taxpayers that in the following year, the Treasury Department instituted a new practice—withholding income taxes from workers' wages.

The result of this wartime economic explosion was growing affluence. Despite the federal incentives to business, heavy excess-profit taxes and a 94 percent tax rate for the very rich kept the wealthy from benefiting unduly. The huge increase in federal spending, from $9 billion in 1940 to $98 billion in 1944, spread through American society. A government agreement with labor unions in 1943 held wage rates to a 15 percent increase, but the long hours of overtime doubled and sometimes tripled the weekly paychecks of factory workers. Farmers shared in the new prosperity as their incomes quadrupled between 1940 and 1945. Most important, this rising income ensured postwar prosperity. Workers and farmers saved their money, channeling much of it into government war bonds, waiting for the day when they could buy the cars and home appliances they could not have obtained during the long years of depression and war.

A Nation on the Move

The war led to a vast migration of the American population. Young men left their homes for training camps and then for service overseas. Defense workers and their families moved to the new booming shipyards, munitions factories, and aircraft plants. Rural areas lost population while coastal regions, especially along the Pacific and the Gulf of Mexico, drew millions of people. California had the greatest gains, adding nearly two million to its population in less than five years.

The movement of people caused severe social problems. Housing was in short supply. Migrating workers crowded into house trailers and boardinghouses, bringing unexpected windfalls to landlords. Family life suffered under these crowded living conditions; an increase in the number of marriages was offset by a rising divorce rate. In addition, schools and other social agencies were hard pressed to service the remarkable baby boom that began during the war.

The demand for workers led to a dramatic rise in female employment. Women entered industries once viewed as exclusively male; by the end of the war, they worked alongside men tending blast furnaces in steel mills and welding hulls in shipyards. The wartime experience helped undermine the concept that woman's only proper place was in the home.

African Americans shared in the wartime migration, but racial prejudice limited their social and economic gains. Nearly one million served in the armed forces, but few saw combat. The army placed blacks in segregated units and used them for service and construction tasks. The navy was even worse, relegating them to menial jobs until late in the war.

Black civilians fared a little better. In 1941, black labor leader A. Philip Randolph threatened a massive march on Washington to force Roosevelt to end racial discrimination in defense industries and government employment and to integrate the armed forces. FDR compromised, persuading Randolph to call off the march and drop his integration demand in return for an executive order creating the Fair Employment Practices Committee (FEPC) to ban racial discrimination in war industries. As a result, black employment by the federal government rose sharply; the FEPC proved less successful in the private sector. The nationwide shortage of labor was more influential than the FEPC in the rise in black employment during wartime. Blacks moved from the rural South to northern and western cities, finding occupations in the automobile, aircraft, and shipbuilding industries.

A Look at the Past

Service Star

Households with members enlisted in the armed forces earned the privilege to display service stars in their windows. Each blue star represented one family member, whether male or female, active in the armed services. A gold star was displayed (sometimes covering a blue star) when the family member was killed in action or died in service. Why would the federal government issue service stars? How would displaying service stars aid the war effort? How might families with no family members eligible for serving in the military have felt about having no service stars?

The movement of an estimated 700,000 people helped transform black-white relations from a regional issue into a national concern that could no longer be ignored. The limited housing and recreational facilities for both black and white war workers created tensions that led to urban race riots. The worst riot took place in Detroit in June 1943; twenty-three blacks and nine whites died in the fighting. These outbursts of racial violence fueled the resentments that would grow into the postwar civil rights movement. For most blacks, despite the economic gain, World War II was a reminder of the inequality of American life.

One-third of a million Mexican Americans served in the armed forces and shared some of the same experiences as blacks. At home, Spanish-speaking people left the rural areas of the Southwest for jobs in the cities. Despite low wages and union resistance, they managed to improve their economic position substantially. But they still faced discrimination based both on skin color and language, most notably in the Los Angeles "zoot suit" riots in 1943, when white servicemen attacked

Mexican American youths dressed in their distinctive long jackets and pegged trousers. The racial prejudice heightened feelings of ethnic identity and led returning Mexican American veterans to form organizations to press for equal rights in the future.

A tragic counterpoint to the voluntary movement of American workers in search of jobs was the forced relocation of 120,000 Japanese Americans from the West Coast. Responding to racial fears in California after Pearl Harbor, FDR approved an army order in February 1942 to move both the Issei (Japanese Americans who had emigrated from Japan) and the Nisei (people of Japanese ancestry born in the United States and therefore U.S. citizens) to "detention centers" in the interior. Forced to dispose of their farms and businesses at distress prices, the Japanese Americans lost not only their liberty but also most of their worldly goods. Herded into detention centers, they lived as prisoners in tar-papered barracks behind barbed wire, guarded by armed troops.

Appeals to the Supreme Court proved fruitless; the justices upheld relocation on the grounds of national security in wartime. Beginning in 1943, individual Japanese Americans could win release by pledging their loyalty and finding a job away from the West Coast, but the detention centers were not closed down until March 1946. Although the Japanese Americans never experienced the torture and mass death of the German concentration camps, their treatment was a disgrace to a nation fighting for freedom and democracy.

Win-the-War Politics

Roosevelt used World War II to strengthen his leadership and maintain Democratic political dominance. As war brought about prosperity and removed the economic discontent that had sustained the New Deal, FDR announced that "Dr. New Deal" had given way to "Dr. Win-the-War." Congress, already controlled by a conservative coalition of southern Democrats and northern Republicans, had almost slipped into GOP hands in 1942. With very low voter turnout, the Republicans won forty-four new seats in the House and nine in the Senate.

In 1944, Roosevelt responded to the Democratic slippage by dropping Henry Wallace, his liberal vice president, for Harry Truman, a moderate and down-to-earth Missouri senator who was acceptable to all factions of the Democratic party. Equally important, FDR received increased political support from organized labor.

The Republicans nominated Thomas E. Dewey, a moderate from New York who made Roosevelt's age and health the primary issues, along with the charge that the Democrats were soft on communism. His foreign policy statements were far more internationalist than previous Republican policy. Indeed, Dewey pioneered a bipartisan approach to foreign policy. He accepted wartime planning for the future United Nations and kept the issue of an international organization out of the campaign.

FDR's vitality impressed the voters, however, and in November 1944, he swept back into office for a fourth term. But the war years had taken their toll. The president, suffering from high blood pressure and congestive heart failure, would lead the nation for only a few months more.

Victory

World War II ended with surprising swiftness. Once the Axis tide had been turned in Europe and Asia, it did not take long for the Soviet Union, the United States, and Britain to mount the offensives that drove Germany and Japan back across the vast areas they had conquered and set the stage for their final defeat.

The long-awaited second front finally came on June 6, 1944. For two years, the United States and Britain had concentrated on building up an invasion force of nearly three million troops and a vast armada of ships and landing craft to carry them across the English Channel. In hopes of catching Hitler by surprise, Eisenhower chose the Normandy peninsula, where the absence of good harbors had justified light German fortifications.

D-Day was originally set for June 5, but bad weather forced a delay. At dawn on June 6, the British and American troops fought their way ashore along a 40-mile stretch of beach, encountering stiff German resistance at several points. By the end of the day, however, Eisenhower had won his beachhead; a week later, more than 300,000 men were slowly pushing back the German forces through the hedgerows of Normandy. The breakthrough came on July 25 at Saint-Lô, opening a gap for General George Patton's Third Army. Soon American forces liberated Paris and reached the Rhine River, but a shortage of supplies, especially gasoline, forced a three-month halt.

D-Day The day Allied troops crossed the English Channel and opened a second front in western Europe, June 6, 1944. The "D" stands for "disembarkation": to leave a ship and go ashore.

Hitler took advantage of this breathing spell to deliver a daring counterattack. In mid-December, the remaining German armored divisions burst through a weak point in the Allied lines in the Ardennes Forest, planning to cut off nearly one-third of Eisenhower's forces. The gamble, however, failed. By committing nearly all his reserves to this effort, known as the Battle of the Bulge, Hitler had delayed Eisenhower's advance into Germany, but he had fatally weakened German resistance in the west.

The end came quickly. During the spring of 1945, Soviet and American troops moved separately toward Berlin. A massive Soviet offensive began in mid-January and swept across the Oder River. General Bradley's troops crossed the Rhine, and Allied forces captured the industrial Ruhr basin. In April, the two armies met at the Elbe River. With the Red Army already in the suburbs of Berlin, Adolf Hitler committed suicide on April 30. A week later, on May 7, 1945, Eisenhower accepted the unconditional surrender of all German forces. Just eleven months and a day after the landing in Normandy, the Allied forces had brought the war in Europe to a successful end.

After they entered Germany, American troops found horrifying evidence of the holocaust—Hitler's eradication of 6 million European Jews. American soldiers were shocked at the conditions within the German concentration camps—lethal gas chambers, huge ovens for cremation, bodies stacked like cords of wood, and, most vivid of all, the emaciated, skeleton-like survivors with their blank stares. These awful discoveries removed any doubt in the minds of the American people about the evil nature of the Nazi regime they had just helped to destroy.

Two survivors at the Mittlebau Dora camp at Nordhausen, Germany, lie among hundreds of dead on the barrack floors. Photos of the death camps made the almost unimaginable atrocities of the Führer*'s regime real to Americans at home.* ❖

War Aims and Wartime Diplomacy

The American contribution to Hitler's defeat was relatively minor compared to the damage inflicted by the Soviet Union. As his armies overran Poland and the Balkan countries, Joseph Stalin was determined to retain control over this region, which had been the historic pathway for western invaders into Russia. Delay in opening the second front and an innate distrust of the West convinced the Soviets that they should maximize their territorial gains by imposing communist regimes on eastern Europe.

American postwar goals were quite different. Now believing that the failure to join the League of Nations in 1919 had laid the groundwork for World War II, the American people and their leaders vowed to put their faith in a new attempt at collective security. At Moscow in 1943, Secretary of State Hull won Soviet agreement to participate in a future world organization at the war's end. In the first wartime Big Three conference, held at Teheran, Iran, in late 1943, Stalin reaffirmed his commitment and also indicated to FDR that the USSR would enter the war against Japan once Germany was defeated.

Yalta Conference Yalta, a city in the Russian Crimea, hosted this wartime conference of the Allies in February 1945 in which the Allies agreed to final plans for the defeat of Germany and the terms of its occupation. The Soviets agreed to allow free elections in Poland, but the elections were never held.

By the time the Big Three met again in February 1945 at the **Yalta Conference,** the military situation favored the Soviets. Stalin drove a series of hard bargains. He refused to give up his plans for communist domination of Poland and the Balkans, although he did agree to hold free elections in eastern Europe. More important for the United States, Stalin promised to enter the Pacific war three months after Germany surrendered. In return, Roosevelt offered extensive concessions in Asia, including Soviet control over Manchuria. Although neither a sellout nor a betrayal, Yalta was, as some critics have charged, a diplomatic victory for the Soviets, reflecting their major contribution to victory in Europe.

For the president, the long journey to Yalta proved too much. In early April 1945, FDR left Washington for Warm Springs, Georgia, where he had always been able to relax. He was sitting for his portrait at midday on April 12, 1945, when he suddenly complained of a "terrific headache," then slumped forward and died. The nation mourned a man who had gallantly met the challenges of depression and global war but had not lived to see the final victory. Unfortunately, he had taken no steps to prepare his successor for the difficult problems that lay ahead.

The defeat of Nazi Germany dissolved the bond between the United States and the Soviet Union in World War II. With very different histories, cultures, and ideologies, the two nations had little in common beyond their enmity toward Hitler. It was now up to the inexperienced Harry Truman to deal with the growing rift that was destined to develop into the Cold War.

Triumph and Tragedy in the Pacific

The total defeat of Germany in May 1945 turned all eyes toward Japan. The American forces were moving swiftly; by the end of 1944, they had secured bases for further advances and were building airfields for American B-29s to begin a deadly bombardment of the Japanese home islands. In addition, by the end of the year, General MacArthur had retaken the Philippines. The Japanese navy, in a Pacific version of the Battle of the Bulge, launched a daring three-pronged attack on the American invasion fleet in Leyte Gulf. The U.S. Navy rallied to blunt all three Japanese thrusts, sinking four carriers and ending any further Japanese naval threat.

The defeat of Japan was now only a matter of time. The United States had three ways to proceed. Diplomats suggested a negotiated peace, urging that the United States modify the unconditional-surrender formula to permit Japan to retain the institution of the emperor. The military favored a full-scale invasion and estimated that it would suffer hundreds of thousands of casualties.

Manhattan Project In early 1942, Franklin Roosevelt, alarmed by reports that German scientists were working on an atomic bomb, authorized a crash program to build the bomb first. The Manhattan Project, named for the Corps of Engineers district originally in charge, spent $2 billion and produced the weapons that devastated Hiroshima and Nagasaki in 1945.

The third possibility involved the highly secret **Manhattan Project.** Since 1939, the United States had spent $2 billion to develop an atomic bomb based on the fission of radioactive uranium and plutonium. Scientists, many of them refugees from Europe, worked at the University of Chicago; at Oak Ridge, Tennessee; at Hanford, Washington; and at a remote laboratory in Los Alamos, New Mexico, to perfect this deadly new weapon. On July 16, 1945, they successfully tested the first atomic bomb in the New Mexico desert, creating a fireball brighter than several suns and a telltale mushroom cloud that rose 40,000 feet above an enormous crater in the desert floor.

When informed of the achievement, President Truman authorized the army air force to use the atomic bomb against Japan. He followed the recommendation of a committee headed by Secretary of War Henry L. Stimson to drop the bomb on a Japanese city without any prior warning. Both Truman and Stimson viewed the decision as a legitimate wartime measure, one designed to save the hundreds of thousands of American and Japanese lives that would be lost in a full-scale invasion.

CHRONOLOGY

1922	Washington Naval Conference limits tonnage
1928	Kellogg-Briand Pact outlaws war ❖ Clark Memorandum repudiates Roosevelt Corollary (issued publicly in 1930)
1931	Japan occupies China's Manchuria province
1933	FDR extends diplomatic recognition to the USSR
1936	Hitler's troops reoccupy the Rhineland
1937	FDR signs permanent neutrality act ❖ FDR urges quarantine of aggressor nations
1938	Munich Conference appeases Hitler
1939	Germany invades Poland; World War II begins
1941	Japanese attack Pearl Harbor; United States enters World War II
1942	U.S. defeats Japanese at Midway ❖ Allies land in North Africa
1943	Soviets smash Nazis at Stalingrad
1944	Allies land on Normandy beachheads
1945	Big Three meet at Yalta ❖ FDR dies; Harry Truman becomes president ❖ Germany surrenders unconditionally ❖ United States drops atomic bombs on Hiroshima and Nagasaki; Japan surrenders

Weather conditions on the morning of August 6 dictated the choice of Hiroshima as the bomb's target. The explosion incinerated 4 square miles of the city and killed more than sixty thousand people instantly. Two days later, the Soviet Union entered the war against Japan, and the next day, August 9, the United States dropped a second bomb on Nagasaki. No more atomic bombs were available, but no more were needed. Japan surrendered unconditionally on August 14, 1945. Three weeks later, Japan signed a formal capitulation agreement on the decks of the battleship *Missouri* in Tokyo Bay to bring World War II to its official close.

Conclusion: The Transforming Power of War

The second great war of the twentieth century has had a lasting impact on American life. For the first time, the nation's military potential had been reached; in 1945, it was unquestionably the strongest country on the earth. In the future, the United States would be involved in all parts of the world. And despite its enormous strength in 1945, the nation's new world role would encompass failure and frustration as well as power and dominion.

The legacy of war was equally strong at home. Four years of fighting brought about industrial recovery and unparalleled prosperity. The old pattern of unregulated free enterprise was as much a victim of the war as of the New Deal; big government and huge deficits had now become the norm as economic control passed from New York and Wall Street to Washington and Pennsylvania Avenue. The war led to far-reaching changes in American society that would become apparent decades later. Such distinctive patterns of recent American life as the baby boom and the growth of the Sunbelt can be traced back to wartime origins. The war was a watershed in twentieth-century America, ushering in a new age of global concerns and domestic upheaval.

KEY TERMS

Kellogg-Briand Pact, p. 523
Good Neighbor policy, p. 524
Axis Powers, p. 526
neutrality acts, p. 526
Lend-Lease, p. 529
Pearl Harbor, p. 530
D-Day, p. 539
Yalta Conference, p. 540
Manhattan Project, p. 540

RECOMMENDED READING

The best general account of American attitudes toward the world in the 1920s can be found in Warren I. Cohen, *Empire Without Tears* (1987). Robert Dallek provides a thorough account of FDR's diplomacy in *Franklin D. Roosevelt and American Foreign Policy, 1932–1945* (1979). For a more critical view, see Robert A. Divine, *Roosevelt and World War II* (1969). David M. Kennedy, *Freedom from Fear* (1999), sets Roosevelt's foreign and wartime policies against the background of domestic politics.

Two good books on the continuing controversy over Pearl Harbor are Roberta Wohlstetter, *Pearl Harbor: Warning and Decision* (1962), and Gordon W. Prange, *At Dawn We Slept* (1981). Both authors deny the charge that Roosevelt deliberately exposed the naval base to attack.

In his brief overview of wartime diplomacy, *American Diplomacy During the Second World War,* 2nd ed. (1985), Gaddis Smith stresses the tensions within the victorious coalition. So does Mark Stoler in *Allies and Adversaries* (2000). Kenneth S. Davis, *FDR: The War President* (2000); Thomas Fleming, *The New Dealers' War* (2001); and Michael Beschloss, *The Conquerors* (2002), portray American leadership during the war. Williamson Murray and Allan R. Millett, *A War to Be Won* (2000), and Carlo D'Este, *Eisenhower: A Soldier's Life* (2002), focus on the fighting. Robert S. Norris, *Racing for the Bomb* (2002), and Gregg Herken, *Brotherhood of the Bomb* (2002), describe the Manhattan Project and what it led to.

The best accounts of the home front are Kennedy, *Freedom from Fear;* Richard Polenberg, *War and Society* (1972); John M. Blum, *V Was for Victory* (1976); and Doris Kearns Goodwin, *No Ordinary Time* (1995). Daniel Kryder, *Divided Arsenal* (2000); Ronald Takaki, *Double Victory* (2000); and Greg Robinson, *By Order of the President* (2001), trace the war's effects on racial and ethnic minorities in the United States.

For a list of additional titles related to this chapter's topics, please see http://www.ablongman.com/divine.

SUGGESTED WEB SITES

A People at War

http://www.archives.gov/exhibit_hall/a_people_at_war.html
This National Archives Exhibit takes a close look at the contributions millions of Americans made to the war effort.

Powers of Persuasion—Poster Art of World War II

http://www.archives.gov/exhibit_hall/powers_of_persuasion_home.html
These powerful posters at the National Archives were part of the battle for the hearts and minds of the American people.

America from the Great Depression to World War II: Photographs from the FSA and OWI, ca. 1935–1945

http://memory.loc.gov/ammem/fsowhome.html
These images in the Farm Security Administration–Office of War Information Collection show Americans from all over the nation experiencing everything from despair to triumph in the 1930s and 1940s.

A-Bomb WWW Museum

http://www.csi.ad.jp/ABOMB/
This site offers information about the impact of the first atomic bomb as well as the background and context of weapons of total destruction.

The United States Holocaust Memorial Museum

http://www.ushmm.org/
This is the official site of the Holocaust Museum in Washington, D.C.

Tuskegee Airmen

http://www.wpafb.af.mil/museum/history/prewwii/ta.htm
The Air Force Museum at Wright-Patterson Air Force Base maintains this site about the African American pilots of World War II.

Abraham Lincoln Brigade Archives

http://www.alba-valb.org
This Brandeis University site has posters and photographs from the Spanish civil war and the unit of American volunteers who fought in it.

World War II Resources: Primary Source Materials on the Web

http://www.ibiblio.org/pha/index.html
This site has a large number of searchable primary texts from all aspects of World War II.

Chapter 28

The Onset of the Cold War

The Potsdam Summit

I am getting ready to go see Stalin and Churchill," President Truman wrote to his mother in July 1945, "and it is a chore." On board the cruiser *Augusta,* the new president continued to complain about the trip to Potsdam in his diary. Halfway around the world, Joseph Stalin left Moscow a day late because of a slight heart attack. Obsessed with security and hating to fly, he traveled to Potsdam, a suburb of Berlin, by rail. He was ready to claim the spoils of war.

The two men, one the veteran revolutionary who had been in power for two decades, the other an untested leader in office barely three months, symbolized the enormous differences that now separated the wartime allies. Stalin was above all a realist. Brutal in securing total control at home, he was more flexible in his foreign policy, bent on exploiting the Soviet Union's victory in World War II rather than aiming at world domination. Cunning and caution were the hallmarks of his diplomatic style. Truman, in contrast, personified traditional Wilsonian idealism. Lacking Roosevelt's guile, the new president placed his faith in international cooperation. Like many Americans, he believed implicitly in his country's innate goodness. Self-assured to the point of cockiness, he came to Potsdam clothed in the armor of self-righteousness.

Truman accepted Stalin at face value, believing that he could deal with the Soviet leader. Together with Winston Churchill and his replacement, Clement Attlee, whose Labour party had just triumphed in British elections, Truman and Stalin clashed over such difficult issues as reparations, the Polish border, and the fate of eastern Europe. Truman tried to move the agenda along briskly, and he was upset by the constant delays. In an indirect way, he informed Stalin of the existence of the atomic bomb, tested successfully in the New Mexico desert just before the conference began. Stalin's only comment was that he hoped the United States would make "good use of it against the Japanese."

Reparations proved to be the crucial issue at the **Potsdam Conference.** The Soviets wanted to rebuild their war-ravaged economy with German industry; the United States feared it would be saddled with the entire cost of caring for the defeated Germans. A compromise was finally reached. Each side would take reparations primarily from its own occupation zone, a solution that unwittingly set the stage for the future division of Germany. "Because they could not agree on 'how to govern Europe,'" wrote historian Daniel Yergin, Truman and Stalin "began to divide it."

Outline

The Cold War Begins

Containment

The Cold War Expands

The Cold War at Home

Eisenhower Wages the Cold War

Conclusion: The Continuing Cold War

Potsdam Conference The final wartime meeting of the leaders of the United States, Great Britain, and the Soviet Union was held at Potsdam, outside Berlin, in July 1945. Truman, Churchill, and Stalin discussed the future of Europe, but their failure to reach meaningful agreements soon led to the onset of the Cold War.

THE CONFERENCE THUS ENDED on an apparent note of harmony; beneath the surface, however, the bitter antagonism of the Cold War was already festering. The United States and the Union of Soviet Socialist Republics, each distrustful of the other, were preparing for a long and bitter confrontation. A dozen years later, Truman reminisced to an old associate about Potsdam. He recalled his innocence and Stalin's duplicity. Then he added ruefully, "And I liked the little son of a bitch."

Potsdam marked the end of the wartime alliance. America and Russia, each distrustful of the other, began to engage in a long and bitter confrontation. For the next decade, the two superpowers would vie for control of postwar Europe, and later clash over the spread of communism to Asia. By the time Truman's and Stalin's successors met for the next summit conference, at Geneva in 1955, the Cold War was at its height.

THE COLD WAR BEGINS

The conflict between the United States and the Soviet Union began gradually. For two years, the nations tried to adjust their differences—over the division of Europe, postwar economic aid, and the atomic bomb—through discussion and negotiation. The Council of Foreign Ministers provided the forum. Beginning in London in the fall of 1945 and meeting with their Soviet counterparts in Paris, New York, and Moscow, American diplomats searched for a way to live in peace with a suspicious Soviet Union.

The Division of Europe

The fundamental disagreement was over who would control postwar Europe. In the east, the Red Army had swept over Poland and the Balkans, laying the basis for Soviet domination there. American and British forces had liberated western Europe, from Scandinavia to Italy. The Russians were intent on imposing communist governments loyal to Moscow in the Soviet sphere. The United States insisted on national self-determination. The Soviets regarded this demand for free elections as subversive. Suspecting American duplicity, Stalin brought down what Churchill characterized as an **Iron Curtain** from the Baltic to the Adriatic as he set up a series of satellite governments.

Iron Curtain British Prime Minister Winston Churchill coined the phrase "Iron Curtain" to refer to the boundary in Europe that divided Soviet-dominated eastern and central Europe from western Europe, which was free from Soviet control.

Germany was the key. The temporary zones of occupation gradually hardened into permanent lines of division. Ignoring the Potsdam Conference agreement that the country be treated as an economic unit, the United States and Great Britain by 1946 were refusing to permit the Soviets to take reparations from the industrial western zones. The United States and England merged their zones and championed the idea of the unification of all Germany. Russia, fearing a resurgence of German military power, responded by intensifying the communization of its zone, which included the jointly occupied city of Berlin. By 1947, Britain, France, and the United States were laying plans to transfer their authority to an independent West Germany.

The Soviet Union consolidated its grip on eastern Europe in 1946 and 1947. One by one, communist governments took power in Poland, Hungary, Romania, and Bulgaria, each ultimately controlled by Stalin. The climax came in March 1948 when a coup in Czechoslovakia overthrew a democratic government and gave the Soviets a strategic foothold in central Europe.

The division of Europe was an inevitable outgrowth of World War II. Both sides were intent on imposing their values—the Soviets stood in eastern Europe, and the United States and Britain were present in Germany, France, and Italy. A

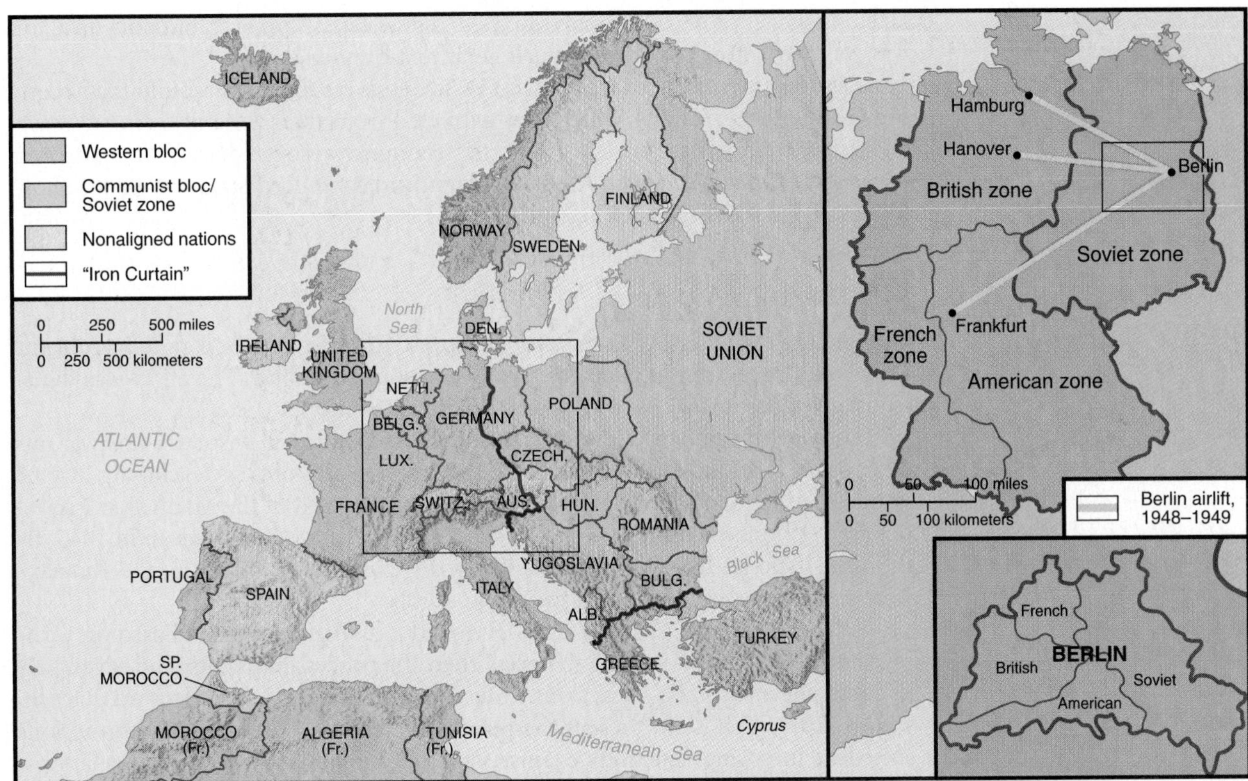

EUROPE AFTER WORLD WAR II *The heavy red line splitting Germany shows in graphic form the division of Europe between the Western and Soviet spheres of influence. The two power blocs faced each other across an "Iron Curtain."* ❖

frank recognition of competing spheres of influence might have avoided further escalation of tension. But the Western nations, remembering Hitler's aggression in the 1930s, began to see Stalin as an equally dangerous threat to their well-being. Instead of accepting him as a cautious leader bent on protecting Russian security, they perceived him as an aggressive dictator leading a communist drive for world domination.

Withholding Economic Aid

The Second World War had inflicted enormous damage on the USSR in terms of lost lives, destroyed factories, and torn-up railroad track. The industrialization that Stalin had achieved at great sacrifice in the 1930s had been badly set back; even agricultural production had fallen by half during the war. Outside aid and assistance were vital for the reconstruction of the Soviet Union. American leaders knew of the Soviets' plight and hoped to use it to good advantage. Truman was convinced that economically "we held all the cards and the Russians had to come to us."

There were two possible forms of postwar assistance—loans and Lend-Lease. In January 1945, the Soviets requested a $6 million loan to finance postwar reconstruction. Despite initial American encouragement, FDR deferred action on this request; as relations cooled, the chances for action dimmed. By the war's end, the loan request, though never formally turned down, was dead.

Lend-Lease proved no more successful. On May 11, 1945, Truman terminated all Lend-Lease shipments to the Soviet Union, including those already at sea. The State Department saw the action as applying "leverage"; Stalin termed it "brutal."

Heeding Soviet protests, Truman resumed Lend-Lease shipments, but only until the war was over in August. After that, all Lend-Lease ended.

Deprived of American assistance, the Soviets were forced to rebuild their economy through reparations, which they extracted from their zone of Germany, eastern Europe, and Manchuria. Slowly, the economy recovered from the war, but bitterness over the American refusal to extend aid convinced Stalin of Western hostility and deepened the growing antagonism.

The Atomic Dilemma

Overshadowing all else was the atomic bomb. The new weapon raised problems that would have been difficult for friendly nations to resolve. The effect was disastrous, given the uneasy state of Soviet-American relations.

The wartime policy followed by Roosevelt and Churchill ensured a postwar nuclear arms race. Instead of informing their major ally of the developing atomic bomb, they kept it a closely guarded secret. Stalin learned of the Manhattan Project through espionage and responded by starting a Soviet atomic program in 1943. By the time Truman told Stalin of the weapon's existence at Potsdam, the Russians were well on the way to making their own bomb.

After the war, the United States developed a disarmament plan based on turning first control of fissionable material, then the processing plants, and ultimately its stockpile of bombs over to an international agency. Later, Bernard Baruch, whom Truman chose to present the plan to the United Nations, added provisions aimed at imposing sanctions against violators and exempting the international agency from the UN veto. Ignoring scientists who pleaded for a more cooperative position, Baruch followed instead the advice of Army Chief of Staff Dwight D. Eisenhower, who cited the rapid demobilization of American armed forces to argue that "we cannot at this time limit our capability to produce or use this weapon." In effect, the **Baruch Plan,** with its multiple stages and emphasis on inspection, would preserve the American atomic monopoly for the indefinite future.

Baruch Plan In 1946, Bernard Baruch presented an American plan to control and eventually outlaw nuclear weapons. The plan called for UN control of nuclear weapons in three stages before the United States gave up its stockpile. Soviet insistence on immediate nuclear disarmament without inspection doomed the Baruch Plan and led to a nuclear arms race between the United States and the Soviet Union.

The Soviets responded predictably. They called for a total ban on the production and use of the new weapon as well as the destruction of all existing bombs. This proposal was founded on the same perception of national self-interest as the American plan. The Red Army was still relatively strong, and Soviet leaders wanted to use its conventional strength to the utmost by outlawing the atomic bomb.

No agreement was possible. Neither the United States nor the Soviet Union could abandon its position without surrendering a vital national interest. America stressed the need for inspection and control; Russia advocated immediate disarmament. The two superpowers agreed to disagree. Trusting neither each other nor any form of international cooperation, each concentrated on taking maximum advantage of its wartime gains. Thus the Soviets exploited the territory they had conquered in Europe while the United States retained its economic and strategic advantages over the Soviet Union. The result was the Cold War.

Containment

A major departure in American foreign policy occurred in January 1947 when General George C. Marshall became secretary of state. He had the capacity to think in broad, strategic terms. An extraordinarily good judge of ability, he relied on gifted subordinates to handle the day-to-day implementation of his policies. In the months after taking office, he came to rely on two exceptionally gifted men in particular.

Dean Acheson, an experienced Washington lawyer and bureaucrat, was appointed undersecretary of state and given free rein by Marshall to conduct American diplomacy. An ardent Anglophile, he wanted to see the United States take over a faltering Britain's role as the supreme arbiter of world affairs. Recalling the lesson taught by the Munich Conference of 1938, he opposed appeasement and advocated a policy of negotiating only from strength.

Marshall's other mainstay was George Kennan, the Soviet expert who headed the newly created Policy Planning Staff. A career foreign service officer, he had served in Moscow, where he developed a profound distrust for the Soviet regime. He believed that only strong and sustained resistance could halt the outward flow of Soviet power. In the spring of 1947, a sense of crisis impelled Marshall, Acheson, and Kennan to set out on a new course in American diplomacy: "a long-term, patient but firm containment of Russian expansionist tendencies." The new **containment** policy both consolidated America's evolving postwar anticommunism and established guidelines that would shape the nation's role in the world for the next two decades.

containment First proposed by George Kennan in 1947, containment became the basic strategy of the United States throughout the Cold War. Kennan argued that firm American resistance to Soviet expansion would eventually compel Moscow to adopt more peaceful policies.

The Truman Doctrine

The initial step came in response to an urgent British request. On February 21, 1947, the British informed the United States that they could no longer afford to aid the anticommunist governments in Greece or Turkey. Believing that the Soviets were responsible for the strife in Greece (in fact they were not), Marshall, Acheson, and Kennan quickly decided that the United States would have to take over Britain's role in the eastern Mediterranean.

Attempting to secure congressional support for their policy, Acheson warned that if Greece went communist, it would threaten Iran, all the Mideast, Africa, Italy, and France. The bipartisan group of congressional leaders was deeply impressed. Finally, Republican Senator Arthur M. Vandenberg spoke up, saying he would support the president but adding that to ensure public backing, Truman would have to "scare hell" out of the American people.

The president followed Vandenberg's advice. On March 12, 1947, he asked Congress for $400 million for military and economic assistance to Greece and Turkey. He made clear that more was involved than just these two countries, that America must aid free peoples resisting subjugation. After a brief debate, both the House and the Senate approved the program.

The **Truman Doctrine** marked an informal declaration of "cold war" against the Soviet Union. Truman used the crisis in Greece to secure congressional approval and build a national consensus for the policy of containment. In less than two years, the civil war in Greece ended, but the American commitment to oppose communist expansion, whether by internal subversion or external aggression, placed the United States on a collision course with the Soviet Union around the globe.

Truman Doctrine In 1947, President Truman asked Congress for money to aid the Greek and Turkish governments that were then threatened by communist rebels. Arguing for the appropriations, Truman asserted his doctrine that the United States was committed to support free people everywhere who were resisting subjugation by communist attack or rebellion.

The Marshall Plan

By 1947, many Americans believed that western Europe, far more vital to U.S. interests than the eastern Mediterranean, was vulnerable to Soviet penetration. The problem was economic. World War II had taken a terrible toll on Britain, France, Italy, and other European countries. Food was scarce, industrial machinery was broken and obsolete, and workers were demoralized by years of depression and war. Resentment and discontent led to growing communist voting strength, especially in Italy and France. Unless the United States could do something to reverse the process, it seemed as though all Europe might drift into the communist orbit.

Acheson believed that it was time to extend American "economic power" in Europe both "to call an effective halt to the Soviet Union's expansionism" and "to create a basis for political stability and economic well-being." The experts drew up a plan for the massive infusion of American capital to finance the economic recovery of Europe. In a commencement speech at Harvard on June 5, 1947, Marshall

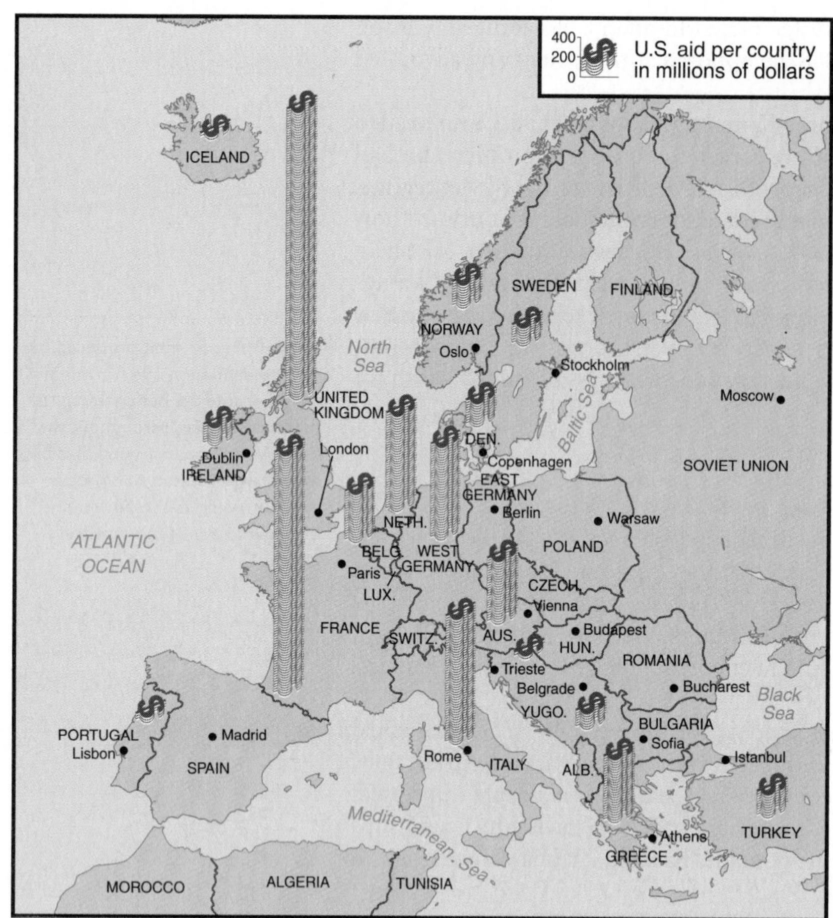

MARSHALL PLAN AID TO EUROPE, 1948–1952 *The Marshall Plan, also known as the European Recovery Program, provided aid totaling $13 billion to European countries following World War II. Most of the money went to former allies Great Britain and France, but former enemies Italy and West Germany also received substantial aid. To receive the grants, countries pledged to control inflation and lower tariffs.* ❖

proposed American aid to foster the "political and social conditions in which free institutions can exist."

Marshall Plan In 1947, Secretary of State George Marshall proposed a massive economic aid program to rebuild the war-torn economies of western European nations. The plan was motivated by both humanitarian concern for the conditions of those nations' economies and fear that economic dislocation would promote communism in western Europe.

The fate of the **Marshall Plan** depended on the reaction of the Soviet Union and the U.S. Congress. Marshall had taken a gamble by including the USSR in his offer of aid. At a meeting of the European nations in Paris in July 1947, the Soviet foreign minister ended the suspense by abruptly withdrawing. Neither the USSR nor its satellites would take part, apparently because Moscow saw the Marshall Plan as an American attempt to weaken Soviet control over eastern Europe. The other European countries then made a formal request for $17 billion in assistance over the next four years.

Congress responded cautiously to this proposal. The administration lobbied vigorously, pointing out that the Marshall Plan would help the United States by stimulating trade with Europe as well as checking Soviet expansion. It was the latter argument, however, that proved decisive, especially after the Czech coup in March 1948. Congress approved the Marshall Plan by heavy majorities. The United States quickly put forth loans that generated a broad industrial revival in western Europe that became self-sustaining by the 1950s. The threat of communist domination faded, and Europe's return to prosperity proved to be a bonanza for American farmers, miners, and manufacturers.

North Atlantic Treaty Organization (NATO) In 1949, the United States, Canada, and ten European nations formed this military mutual-defense pact. In 1955, the Soviet Union countered NATO with the formation of the Warsaw Pact, a military alliance among those nations within its own sphere of influence.

The Western Military Alliance

The final phase of containment came in 1949 with the establishment of the **North Atlantic Treaty Organization (NATO).** NATO grew out of European fears of Soviet military aggression. Recalling Hitler's tactics in the 1930s, the people of western Europe wanted assurance that the United States would protect them from attack as they began to achieve economic recovery.

In January 1949, Truman called for a defense pact; ten European nations joined the United States and Canada in signing the North Atlantic Treaty. This historic departure from the traditional policy of isolation caused extensive debate, but the Senate ratified it in July 1949.

There were two main features of NATO. First, the United States committed itself to the defense of Europe in case of an attack. In effect, the United States was extending its atomic shield over Europe. The second feature was designed to reassure worried Europeans that the United States would honor this commitment. In late 1950, Truman appointed General Eisenhower to the post of NATO supreme commander and authorized the stationing of four American divisions in Europe to serve as the nucleus of the NATO army. Now any assault would automatically involve American troops, a fact that would deter the Soviet Union.

The Western military alliance escalated the developing Cold War. It represented an overreaction to the Soviet danger. Americans and Europeans alike were attempting to apply the lesson of Munich to the Cold War. But there was no evidence of any Soviet plan to invade western Europe, and in the face of the American atomic bomb, none was likely. All NATO did was intensify Russian fears of the West and thus increase the level of international tension. The USSR and its satellites responded to NATO with the Warsaw Pact, a defense community of their own.

The Berlin Blockade

The main Soviet response to containment came in 1948 at the West's most vulnerable point. American, British, French, and Soviet troops each occupied a sector of Berlin, but the city was located more than 100 miles inside the Soviet zone of Germany. Stalin decided to test his opponents' resolve by cutting off all rail and highway traffic to Berlin on June 20, 1948.

The timing was very awkward for Truman, who was locked in a tight presidential race. Immersed in election-year politics, he was caught unprepared by the Berlin blockade. The alternatives were not very appealing. The United States could withdraw its forces and lose not just the city but the confidence of all Europe; it could try to send in reinforcements and fight for Berlin; or it could sit tight and attempt to find a diplomatic solution. Truman decided to fight to save Berlin.

The administration adopted a two-phase policy. The first part was a massive airlift of food, fuel, and supplies for both the troops and civilians in Berlin. Then, to guard against Soviet interruption of the **Berlin airlift,** Truman transferred sixty American B-29s, planes capable of delivering atomic bombs, to bases in England. The president was bluffing; the B-29s were not equipped with atomic bombs, but at the time the threat was effective.

Berlin airlift In 1948, in response to a Soviet land blockade of Berlin, the United States carried out a massive effort to supply the 2 million Berlin citizens with food, fuel, and other goods by air for more than six months, forcing the Soviets to end the blockade in 1949.

For a few weeks, the world teetered on the edge of war. Stalin did not attempt to disrupt the flights to Berlin, but he rejected all American diplomatic initiatives. At any time the Soviets could have halted the airlift by jamming radar or shooting down the defenseless cargo planes. For Truman, the tension was fierce. He feared that America was dreadfully close to war.

Slowly, the tension eased. The Russians did not shoot down any planes, and Truman was reelected, in part because the Berlin crisis had rallied the nation behind his leadership. In early 1949, the Soviets gave in, ending the blockade in return for another meeting of the Council of Foreign Ministers on Germany—a conclave that proved as unproductive as all the earlier ones.

The Berlin crisis marked the end of the initial phase of the Cold War. The airlift had given the United States a striking political victory, showing the world the triumph of American ingenuity over Russian stubbornness. Yet it could not disguise the fact that the Cold War had cut Europe in two. A divided Europe—politically, economically, and now militarily—was a far cry from the wartime hopes for a peaceful world. Such was the bitter legacy of World War II.

The Cold War Expands

The rivalry between the United States and the Soviet Union grew in the late 1940s and the early 1950s. Both sides began to rebuild their military forces with new methods and advanced weapons. Equally significant, the diplomatic competition spread from Europe to Asia as each of the superpowers sought to enhance its influence in the East. By the time Truman left office in early 1953, the Cold War had taken on global proportions.

The Military Dimension

After World War II, American leaders were intent on reforming the nation's military system in light of the wartime experience. Two goals were uppermost. First, nearly everyone agreed in the aftermath of Pearl Harbor that the armed services should be unified into an integrated military system. The developing Cold War reinforced this decision. Equally important, planners realized the need for new institutions to coordinate military and diplomatic strategy so that the nation could cope effectively with threats to its security.

National Security Act
Congress passed the National Security Act in 1947 in response to perceived threats from the Soviet Union after World War II. It established the Department of Defense and created the Central Intelligence Agency and National Security Council.

In 1947, Congress passed the **National Security Act,** which established the Department of Defense. In addition, the act created the Central Intelligence Agency (CIA) to coordinate the intelligence-gathering activities of various government agencies. Finally, the act established the National Security Council (NSC) to advise the president on all matters regarding the nation's security.

Despite the appearance of equality among the services, the newly created air force quickly emerged as the dominant power in the atomic age. Both Truman and Congress allotted more money to the air force than to the army or the navy.

American military planners received a great boost in the fall of 1949 when the Soviet Union exploded its first atomic bomb. President Truman appointed a high-level committee to explore mounting an all-out effort to build a hydrogen bomb to maintain American nuclear supremacy.

Some scientists had technical objections to the H-bomb; others opposed the new weapon on moral grounds, claiming that its enormous destructive power (one

The explosion of a U.S. test bomb over an uninhabited island in the Pacific on November 1, 1952, demonstrated to the world the fearsome power of the hydrogen bomb. This early H-bomb was capable of destroying a city the size of Washington, D.C. Over the next decade, both the United States and the Soviet Union developed far more powerful bombs. ❖

thousand times greater than the atomic bomb) made it unthinkable. But Dean Acheson—who succeeded Marshall as secretary of state in early 1949—believed it was imperative that the United States develop the hydrogen bomb before the Soviet Union did. When Acheson presented the committee's favorable report to the president in January 1950, Truman took only seven minutes to decide to go ahead with the new bomb.

At the same time, Acheson ordered the Policy Planning Staff to draw up a new statement of national defense policy. **NSC-68,** as the document eventually became known, was based on the premise that the Soviet Union sought "to impose its absolute authority over the rest of the world" and thus "mortally challenged" the United States. Paul Nitze, who headed the Policy Planning Staff, advocated a massive expansion of American military power so that the United States could halt and overcome the Soviet threat. NSC-68 stood as a symbol of the Truman administration's determination to win the Cold War regardless of cost.

NSC-68 National Security Council planning paper No. 68 redefined America's national defense policy. Adopted in 1950, it committed the United States to a massive military buildup to meet the challenge posed by the Soviet Union.

The Cold War in Asia

The Soviet-American conflict developed more slowly in Asia. At Yalta, the two superpowers had agreed to a Far Eastern balance of power, with the USSR dominating northeastern Asia and the United States in control of the Pacific, including Japan and its former island empire.

The United States moved quickly to consolidate its sphere of influence. General Douglas MacArthur, in charge of Japanese occupation, denied the Soviet Union any role in the reconstruction of Japan. Instead, he supervised the transition of the Japanese government into a constitutional democracy in which communists were barred from all government posts. The Japanese willingly renounced war in their new constitution, relying instead on American forces to protect their security. In addition, the United States held full control over the Marshall, Mariana, and Caroline Islands.

As defined at Yalta, China lay between the Soviet and American spheres. When World War II ended, the country was torn between Chiang Kai-shek's Nationalists in the south and Mao Tse-tung's Communists in the north. Although Chiang received American political and economic backing, his regime was corrupt, and a raging inflation rate devastated the Chinese middle classes and thus eroded his base of power. Mao used tight discipline and patriotic appeals to strengthen his hold on the peasantry and extend his influence. When the Soviets abruptly vacated Manchuria

The Soviet view of the Cold War, as depicted in this Soviet cartoon, shows the United States stretching out long arms to take hold of Korea, Iran, Turkey, Taiwan, and Vietnam. ❖

in 1946, Mao inherited control of this rich northern province. Ignoring American advice, Chiang rushed north to occupy Manchurian cities, overextending his supply lines and exposing his forces to Communist counterattack.

American policy aimed at averting a Chinese civil war by encouraging Chiang and Mao to form a coalition government. The policy failed. By 1947, as China plunged into full-scale civil war, the Truman administration had given up any serious effort to influence the outcome. Political mediation had failed, military intervention was out of the question, and a policy of continued American economic aid served only to appease domestic supporters of Chiang; 80 percent of the military supplies ended up in Communist hands.

The climax came at the end of the decade. Mao's forces drove the Nationalists out of Manchuria in late 1948 and advanced across the Yangtze River by mid-1949. Acheson released a lengthy report justifying American policy in China on the grounds that the civil war there "was beyond the control of the government of the United States." Republican senators, however, disagreed, blaming American diplomats for sabotaging the Nationalists. While the domestic debate raged over responsibility for the loss of China, Chiang's forces fled the mainland for sanctuary on Formosa (Taiwan) in December 1949. Two months later, Mao and Stalin signed a Sino-Soviet treaty of mutual assistance that clearly placed China in the Russian orbit.

The American response to the Communist triumph in China was twofold. First, the State Department refused to recognize the legitimacy of the new regime in Peking (Beijing), maintaining instead formal diplomatic relations with the Nationalists on Formosa. Then, to compensate for the loss of China, the United States focused on Japan as its main ally in Asia. The State Department encouraged the buildup of Japanese industry, and the Pentagon expanded American bases on the Japanese home islands and Okinawa. As it had done in Europe, the Cold War had now split Asia in two.

The Korean War

The showdown between the United States and the Soviet Union in Asia came in Korea, which had been divided at the 38th parallel in 1945. The Soviets occupied the industrial North, installing a Communist government under the leadership of Kim Il-Sung. In the agrarian South, Syngman Rhee emerged as the American-sponsored ruler. The two superpowers pulled out most of their occupation forces by 1949. The Soviets, however, helped train a well-equipped army in the North, while the United States gave much more limited military assistance to South Korea.

On June 25, 1950, the North Korean army suddenly crossed the 38th parallel in great strength. We now know that Stalin had approved this act of aggression in advance. In January 1950, the Soviet leader had told Mao Tse-tung that he was ready to overthrow the Yalta settlement in the Far East. In April, when Kim Il-Sung came to Moscow to gain approval for the assault on South Korea, Stalin gave it willingly, apparently in the belief that the United States was ready to abandon Syngman Rhee. But the ever cautious Stalin warned Kim not to count on Soviet assistance, saying, "If you should get kicked in the teeth, I shall not lift a finger. You have to ask Mao for all the help." Despite expressing some reservations, in May, Mao also approved the planned North Korean aggression.

Both Stalin and Mao had badly miscalculated the American response. President Truman saw the invasion as a clear-cut case of Soviet aggression reminiscent of the 1930s. "Communism was acting in Korea just as Hitler, Mussolini, and the Japanese had acted ten, fifteen, and twenty years earlier," he commented in his memoirs. Following Acheson's advice, the president convened the UN Security Council and, taking advantage of a temporary Soviet boycott, secured a resolution condemning North Korea as an aggressor and calling on the member nations to engage in a collective security action. Within a few days, American troops from Japan were in

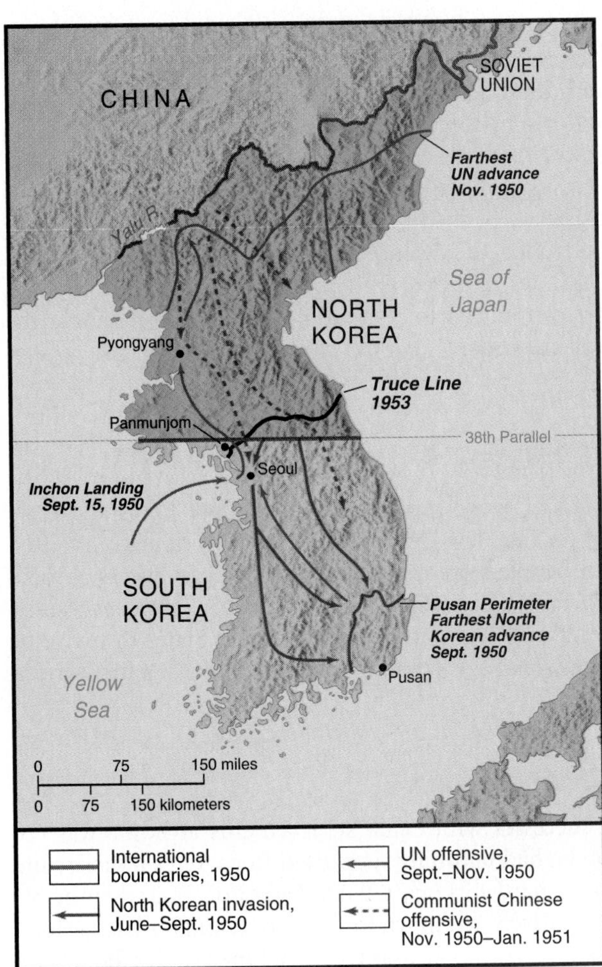

THE KOREAN WAR, 1950–1953 *After a year of rapid movement up and down the Korean peninsula, the fighting stalled just north of the 38th parallel. The resulting truce line has divided North and South Korea ever since the July 1953 armistice.* ❖

combat in South Korea. The conflict, which would last for more than three years, was technically a police action fought under UN auspices; in reality, the United States was at war with a Soviet satellite in Asia.

In the beginning, the fighting went badly as the North Koreans continued to drive down the peninsula. But by August, American forces had halted the Communist advance near Pusan. In September, General MacArthur changed the whole complexion of the war by carrying out a brilliant amphibious assault at Inchon, on the waist of Korea, cutting off and destroying most of the North Korean army in the South. Encouraged by this victory, Truman began to shift from his original goal of restoring the 38th parallel to a new one: reunification of Korea by military force.

The administration ignored warnings from Peking, sent by way of India, against an American invasion of North Korea. Both Acheson and MacArthur advised Truman that the Chinese would not enter the conflict. Rarely has an American president received worse advice. The UN forces crossed the 38th parallel in October, advanced confidently to the Yalu River in November, and then were completely routed by a massive Chinese counterattack that drove them out of all North Korea by December. MacArthur finally stabilized the fighting near the 38th parallel, but when Truman decided to give up his attempt to unify Korea, the general protested to Congress, calling for a renewed offensive and proclaiming, "There is no substitute for victory."

Truman courageously relieved the popular hero of the Pacific of his command on April 11, 1951. The Korean War then settled into a stalemate near the 38th parallel as truce talks with the Communists bogged down for the rest of Truman's term in office. The president could take heart from the fact that he had achieved his primary goals, defense of South Korea and the principle of collective security. Yet by taking the gamble to reunify Korea by force, he had confused the American people and humiliated the United States in the eyes of the world.

In the last analysis, the most significant result of the Korean conflict was massive American rearmament. The war led to the implementation of NSC-68—the army expanded to 3.5 million troops, the defense budget increased to $50 billion a year by 1952, and the United States acquired military bases in distant quarters of the world. America was now committed to waging a global contest against the Soviet Union with arms as well as words.

The Cold War at Home

The Cold War cast a long shadow over American life in the late 1940s and early 1950s. Truman tried to carry on the New Deal reform tradition he had inherited from FDR, but the American people were more concerned about events abroad. The Republican party used growing dissatisfaction with both postwar economic adjustment and fears of communist penetration of the United States to revive its sagging fortunes and regain control of the White House in 1952 for the first time in twenty years.

Truman's Troubles and Vindication

Matching his foreign policy successes with equal achievements at home was not easy for Truman. As a senator, he had faithfully supported Roosevelt's policies, and he had earned a reputation as a hardworking, reliable legislator. But when he assumed the presidency, he was relatively unknown to the public, and his background as a Missouri county judge associated with Kansas City machine politics did not inspire confidence in his leadership abilities. Surprisingly well read, Truman possessed sound judgment, the ability to reach decisions quickly, and a fierce and uncompromising sense of right and wrong.

Two weaknesses marred his performance in the White House. One was his fondness for old friends, which resulted in the appointment of many Missouri and Senate cronies to high office. These men brought little credit to his administration. Truman's other serious limitation was his lack of political vision. He tried to perpetuate FDR's New Deal, but he engaged in a running battle with Congress rather than pursuing a coherent legislative program.

The fact that the postwar mood was not conducive to a new outburst of reform, of course, handicapped Truman's performance. Not only were the American people enjoying material prosperity, but the Cold War also diverted attention from domestic problems. Congress did pass the Employment Act of 1946, which asserted the principle that the government was responsible for the state of the economy and created the Council of Economic Advisers to guide the president. But the original goal of mandatory federal planning to achieve full employment failed to survive the legislative process.

After the Republican victory in 1946, relations between the president and Congress became increasingly stormy. Truman successfully vetoed two GOP measures to give large tax cuts to the wealthy, but Congress overrode his veto of the **Taft-Hartley Act** in 1947. Designed to redress the imbalance in labor-management relations created by the Wagner Act, the Taft-Hartley Act outlawed specific union practices, and it permitted the president to invoke an eighty-day cooling-off period to delay strikes that might endanger national health or safety.

Taft-Hartley Act This 1947 anti-union legislation outlawed the closed shop and secondary boycotts. It also authorized the president to seek injunctions to prevent strikes that posed a threat to national security.

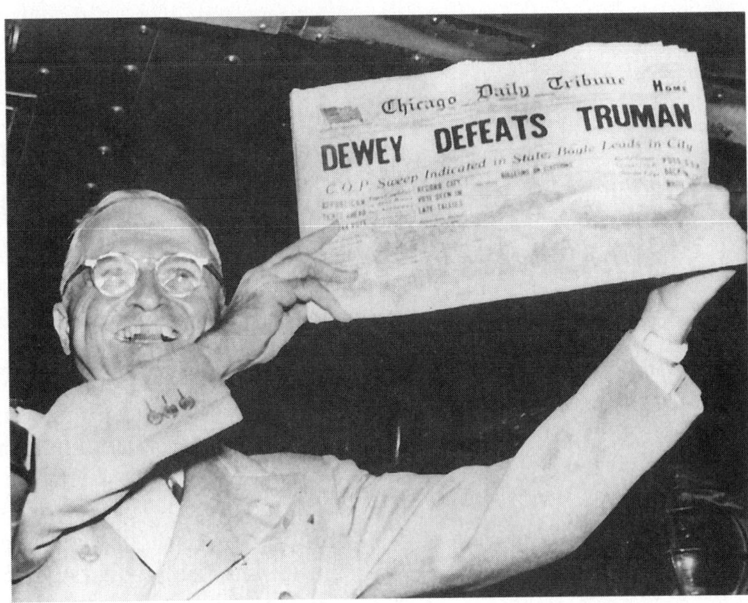

A jubilant Harry Truman, on the morning after his 1948 election win, displays the headline blazoned on the front page of the Chicago Daily Tribune*—a newspaper that believed the pollsters.* ❖

Truman's political fortunes reached their lowest ebb in early 1948. Former Vice President Henry A. Wallace announced his third-party (Progressive) candidacy in the presidential contest that year. Although Truman was renominated by the Democratic party, his prospects for victory looked dim, especially after disgruntled Southerners, alarmed by Truman's civil rights advocacy, bolted the Democratic party to nominate Strom Thurmond, the governor of South Carolina, on the States' Rights party ticket.

The defection of the **Dixiecrats** in the South and Wallace's liberal followers in the North led political experts to predict an almost certain victory for the Republican candidate, Governor Thomas E. Dewey of New York. While Dewey waged a cautious, uninspired campaign, Truman barnstormed around the country denouncing the "do-nothing" Republican Eightieth Congress. To the amazement of the pollsters, Truman won a narrow victory in November. The old Roosevelt coalition—farmers, organized labor, urban ethnic groups, and blacks—had held together, enabling Truman to remain in the White House and the Democrats to gain control of Congress.

Dixiecrats A group of southern Democrats who bolted from their party in 1948 and supported Governor Strom Thurmond of South Carolina as the presidential candidate of the States' Rights party.

There was one more reason for Truman's win in 1948. During the election, held at the height of the Berlin crisis, the GOP failed to challenge Truman's conduct of the Cold War. Locked in a tense rivalry with the Soviet Union, the American people saw no reason to reject a president who had countered aggression overseas with the Truman Doctrine and the Marshall Plan. Until the Republicans found a way to challenge Truman's Cold War policies, they had little chance to regain the White House.

The Loyalty Issue

Despite Truman's surprise victory in 1948, there was one area on which the Democrats were vulnerable. The fear of communism abroad that had led to the bipartisan containment policy could be used against them at home by politicians who were more willing to exploit the public's deep-seated anxiety.

Fear of radicalism has been a recurrent feature of American life since the early days of the republic. The Cold War heightened the traditional belief that subversion from abroad endangered the nation. Bold rhetoric from members of the Truman administration, portraying the men in the Kremlin as inspired revolutionaries bent on world conquest, frightened the American people. They viewed the Soviet Union as a successor of Nazi Germany—a totalitarian police state that threatened the basic liberties of free people.

House Un-American Activities Committee (HUAC) This congressional committee played a prominent role in attempting to uncover and punish those suspected of aiding the communist cause in the early years of the Cold War.

A series of revelations of communist espionage activities reinforced these fears, sparking a second "Red Scare." A Soviet spy ring was uncovered in Canada in 1946, and the **House Un-American Activities Committee (HUAC)** held hearings that indicated that communist agents had flourished in government departments in the 1930s. Although Truman tried to dismiss the loyalty issue as a "red herring," he felt compelled to take protective measures, thus lending substance to the charges of subversion. In March 1947, he had initiated a loyalty program, ordering security checks on government employees to root out communists. Originally intended to remove subversives for whom "reasonable grounds exist for belief that the person involved is disloyal," within four years the Loyalty Review Board was dismissing workers as security risks if there was "reasonable doubt" of their loyalty. Thousands of government workers lost their jobs, charged with guilt by association with radicals or with membership in left-wing organizations.

The most famous disclosure came in August 1948 when Whittaker Chambers, a repentant communist, accused Alger Hiss, once a prominent State Department official, of having been a Soviet spy in the 1930s. When Hiss denied the charges, Chambers produced microfilms of confidential government documents that he claimed Hiss had given him in the late 1930s. Although the statute of limitations prevented a charge of treason against Hiss, he was convicted of perjury in January 1950 and sentenced to a five-year prison term.

Events abroad intensified the sense of danger. The Communist triumph in China in the fall of 1949 came as a shock; soon there were charges that "fellow travelers" in the State Department were responsible for "the loss of China." In September 1949, when the Truman administration announced that the USSR had detonated its first atomic bomb, the loss of America's nuclear monopoly was blamed on Soviet espionage. In early 1950, Klaus Fuchs, a British scientist who had worked on the wartime Manhattan Project, admitted giving the Soviets vital information about the A-bomb.

A few months later, the government charged American Communists Ethel and Julius Rosenberg with conspiracy to transmit atomic secrets to the Soviet Union. They were found guilty of treason in 1951 and, despite their claims of innocence and worldwide appeals for clemency on their behalf, were executed in 1953. Thus by the early 1950s, nearly all the ingredients were at hand for a new outburst of hysteria—fear of communism, evidence of espionage, belief in a vast conspiracy. The only element missing was a leader to focus this new wave of intolerance.

McCarthyism in Action

On February 12, 1950, Senator Joseph R. McCarthy of Wisconsin delivered a routine speech in Wheeling, West Virginia. A little known Republican, he suddenly attracted national attention when he declared, "I have here in my hand a list of 205—a list of names that were made known to the secretary of state as being members of the Communist party and who nevertheless are still working and shaping policy in the State Department." Although he never substantiated his charge, McCarthy's speech triggered a four-and-a-half-year crusade to hunt down alleged communists in government. The stridency and sensationalism of the senator's accusations soon won the name **McCarthyism.**

McCarthyism In 1950, Senator Joseph R. McCarthy began a sensational campaign against communists in government that led to more than four years of charges and counter-charges, ending when the Senate censured him in 1954. McCarthyism became the contemporary name for the red scare of the 1950s.

McCarthy's basic technique was the multiple untruth. He leveled a bevy of charges of treasonable activities in government. While officials were refuting his initial accusations, he brought forth a steady stream of new ones so that the corrections never caught up. He failed to unearth a single confirmed communist in government, but he kept the Truman administration in turmoil. He exploited the press with great skill, combining current accusations with promises of future disclosures to guarantee headlines.

The secret of McCarthy's power was the fear he engendered among his Senate colleagues. They believed McCarthy's opposition would doom their chances for reelection. McCarthy delighted in making sweeping, startling charges of communist sympathies against prominent public figures. A favorite target was aristocratic Secretary of State Dean Acheson, but General George Marshall and even fellow Republicans were also named in his charges.

The attacks on the wealthy, famous, and privileged won McCarthy a devoted national following, although the public opinion polls indicated his approval rating never rose above 50 percent. He drew a disproportionate backing from working-class Catholics and ethnic groups who usually voted Democratic. He offered a simple solution to the complicated Cold War: defeat the enemy at home rather than continue to engage in costly foreign aid programs and entangling alliances abroad. Above all, McCarthy appealed to conservative Republicans in the Midwest who shared his right-wing views and felt cheated by Truman's upset victory in 1948. Even GOP leaders who viewed McCarthy's tactics with distaste quietly encouraged him to attack vulnerable Democrats.

The Republicans in Power

In 1952, the GOP capitalized on a growing sense of national frustration to capture the presidency. The stalemate in Korea and the second Red Scare at home created the desire for change; revelations of scandals by several individuals close to Truman intensified the feeling that someone needed to clean up "the mess in Washington." In Dwight D. Eisenhower, the Republican party found the perfect candidate to explore what one senator called K_1C_2—Korea, communism, and corruption.

A war hero with an amiable manner and a winning smile, Eisenhower seemed to have the gifts to unite a divided nation. While his running mate, Senator Richard M. Nixon of California, hammered away at the Democrats on communism and corruption, "Ike" promised that once elected, he would go to Korea if necessary to bring "an early and honorable end" to the war. In the November election, Eisenhower handily defeated Illinois governor Adlai Stevenson.

Once elected, Eisenhower moved quickly to fulfill his campaign pledge. He went to Korea, assessed the battlefield options, ruled out a new offensive, and turned his attention to a diplomatic settlement, even hinting to China that he might use nuclear weapons to break the stalemated peace talks. That threat, together with the death of Joseph Stalin in early March, finally led to the signing of an armistice on July 27, 1953, which ended the fighting but left Korea divided, as it had been before the war, near the 38th parallel.

Eisenhower was less effective in dealing with the problem raised by Senator McCarthy. McCarthy did not end his crusade with the Republican victory in 1952. Instead, he used his new position as chairman of the Senate Committee on Government Operations as a base for ferreting out suspected communists on the federal payroll. Eisenhower's advisers urged the president to use his own great prestige to stop McCarthy. But Ike refused such a confrontation, saying, "I will not get into a pissing contest with that skunk."

The Wisconsin senator finally overreached himself. In 1954, he uncovered an army dentist suspected of disloyalty and proceeded to attack the upper echelons of the U.S. Army. The controversy culminated in the televised Army-McCarthy hearings. For six weeks, the senator revealed his crude, bullying behavior to the American people. Viewers were repelled by his frequent outbursts and by his attempt to slur the reputation of a young lawyer associated with army counsel Joseph Welch. This last maneuver led Welch to condemn McCarthy for his "reckless cruelty" and ask rhetorically, as millions watched on television, "Have you no sense of decency, sir?"

Courageous Republicans, such as Margaret Chase Smith of Maine, joined with Democrats to bring about Senate censure of McCarthy in December 1954. The vote was 67 to 22. Rebuked, McCarthy fell quickly from prominence. He died three years later virtually unnoticed and unmourned.

Yet his influence was profound. Not only did he paralyze national life with shameful activities, but he also helped impose a political and cultural conformity that froze dissent for the rest of the 1950s. Long after McCarthy's passing, the nation tolerated loyalty oaths for teachers, the banning of left-wing books in public libraries, and the blacklisting of entertainers in radio, television, and films. Freedom of expression was inhibited, and the opportunity to try out new ideas and approaches was lost as the United States settled into a sterile Cold War consensus.

Although Eisenhower could claim that his policy of giving McCarthy enough rope to hang himself had worked, it is possible that a bolder and more forthright presidential attack on the senator might have spared the nation some of the excesses of the second Red Scare.

Eisenhower Wages the Cold War

Dwight D. Eisenhower came to the presidency in 1952 unusually well prepared to lead the nation at the height of the Cold War. His long years of military service had exposed him to a wide variety of international issues and a broad array of world leaders. His gifts were political and diplomatic as well as military. He was blessed with a sharp, pragmatic mind and a genius for organization that enabled him to plan and carry out large enterprises. And he had serene confidence in his own ability.

Eisenhower chose John Foster Dulles as his secretary of state. The myth soon developed that Ike gave Dulles free rein to conduct American diplomacy. Such was not the case. Eisenhower let Dulles make the public speeches and appearances before congressional committees, but Dulles carefully consulted with the president before every appearance. Ike respected Dulles's opinions, but he made all the major decisions himself.

From the outset, Eisenhower was determined to bring the Cold War under control. Ideally, he wanted to end it, but as a realist, he would settle for a relaxation of tensions with the Soviet Union. In part, he was motivated by a deeply held budgetary concern; Ike was convinced that the nation was in danger of going bankrupt unless military spending was reduced. As president, he inaugurated a "new look" for American defense, cutting back on the army and navy and relying even more heavily than Truman had on the air force and its nuclear striking power. As a result, the defense budget dropped from $50 billion to $40 billion annually. In 1954, Dulles announced reliance on **massive retaliation**—actually a continuation of Truman's policy of deterrence. Rather than becoming involved in limited wars as in Korea, the United States would consider the possibility of using nuclear weapons to halt any communist aggression that threatened vital U.S. interests anywhere in the world.

massive retaliation The "new look" defense policy of the Eisenhower administration in the 1950s was to threaten "massive retaliation" with nuclear weapons in response to any act of aggression by a potential enemy.

While he permitted Dulles to make his veiled nuclear threats, Eisenhower's fondest dream was to end the arms race. Sobered by the development of the hydrogen bomb, the president began a new effort at disarmament with the Soviets. Yet before this initiative could take effect, Ike had to weather a series of crises around the world that tested his skill and patience to the utmost.

Entanglement in Indochina

Dien Bien Phu In 1954, Vietminh rebels besieged a French garrison at Dien Bien Phu, deep in the interior of northern Vietnam. In May, after the United States refused to intervene, Dien Bien Phu fell to the communists.

The first crisis facing the new president came in Indochina. Since 1950, the United States had been giving France military and economic aid in a war in Indochina against communist guerrillas led by Ho Chi Minh. The Chinese increased their support to Ho's forces, known as the Vietminh, after the Korean War ended; by the spring of 1954, the French were on the brink of defeat. The Vietminh had surrounded nearly ten thousand French troops at **Dien Bien Phu** deep in the interior of northern Indochina; in desperation, France turned to the United States for help. Admiral Arthur Radford, chairman of the Joint Chiefs of Staff, proposed an American air strike to lift the siege. Although the other Joint Chiefs had strong objections to involving American forces in another Asian war so soon after Korea, hawkish Republican senators were clamoring for action.

Eisenhower decided against Radford's bold proposal, but he killed it in his typically indirect fashion. Fearful that an air attack would lead inevitably to the use of ground troops, Ike insisted that both Congress and American allies in Europe approve the strike in advance. Congressional leaders, recalling the recent Korean debacle, were reluctant to agree; the British were appalled and ruled out any joint action. The president used these objections to reject intervention in Indochina in 1954.

Cartoonist Herblock, a sharp critic of Dulles's hard line, depicts him in a Superman suit pushing Uncle Sam to the brink of nuclear war. ❖

Dien Bien Phu fell to the Vietminh in May 1954. At an international conference held in Geneva a few weeks later, Indochina was divided at the 17th parallel. Ho gained control of North Vietnam, while the French continued to rule in the South, with provision for a general election within two years to unify the country. The election was never held, largely because Eisenhower feared it would result in an overwhelming mandate for Ho. Instead, the United States gradually took over from the French in South Vietnam, sponsoring a new government in Saigon headed by Ngo Dinh Diem, a Vietnamese nationalist from a northern Catholic family. While Eisenhower can be given credit for refusing to engage American forces on behalf of French colonialism in Indochina, his determination to resist communist expansion had committed the United States to a long and eventually futile struggle to prevent Ho Chi Minh from achieving his long-sought goal of a unified, independent Vietnam.

Containing China

The Communist government in Peking posed a serious challenge to the Eisenhower administration. Senate Republicans blamed the Democrats for the "loss" of China. They viewed Mao as a puppet of the Soviet Union and insisted that the United States recognize the Nationalists on Formosa as the only legitimate government of China. While State Department experts realized that there were underlying tensions between China and the Soviet Union, Mao's intervention in the Korean War had convinced most Americans that the Chinese Communists were an integral part of a larger communist effort at world domination. Thus Truman and Acheson had abandoned any hope of trying to exploit differences between Mao and Stalin by wooing China away from the Soviet Union.

Eisenhower and Dulles chose to accentuate the potential conflict between China and the Soviet Union. They adopted a strong line, hoping to please congressional hawks and show China that the Soviet Union could not protect China's interests. Eisenhower and Dulles hoped that a policy of firmness would contain Communist Chinese expansion and drive a wedge between Moscow and Peking.

A crisis in the Formosa Straits provided the first test of the new policy. In the fall of 1954, the mainland government threatened to seize islands off the coast of China occupied by the Nationalists. Fearful that this would be the first step toward an invasion of Formosa, Eisenhower committed the United States to defend Formosa. Once he received congressional support for his action, he and Dulles started to hint that they were prepared to use nuclear weapons to protect Formosa.

The Chinese leaders, unsure whether Eisenhower was bluffing, decided not to test American resolve.

The apparent refusal of the Soviet Union to come to China's aid in the crisis contributed to the growing rift between the two communist nations, but the Eisenhower administration failed to take full advantage of it.

Turmoil in the Middle East

The gravest crisis came in the Middle East when Egyptian leader Gamal Nasser seized the Suez Canal in July 1956. Britain and France were ready to use force immediately; their citizens owned the canal company, and their economies were dependent on the canal for the flow of oil from the Persian Gulf. Eisenhower, however, was staunchly opposed to intervention, preferring to seek a diplomatic solution with Nasser, who kept the canal running smoothly. The European allies nevertheless decided to take a desperate gamble—invade Egypt and seize the canal while relying on the United States to prevent any Soviet interference.

When Britain and France launched their attack in early November, Eisenhower was furious. Unhesitatingly, he instructed Dulles to sponsor a UN resolution calling for the two nations' withdrawal from Egypt. Yet when the USSR supported the proposal and went further, threatening rocket attacks on British and French cities and offering to send "volunteers" to fight in Egypt, Ike made it clear that he would not allow Soviet interference.

Just after noon on election day, November 6, 1956, British Prime Minister Anthony Eden called the president to inform him that Britain and France were ending their invasion. Eisenhower breathed a sigh of relief. American voters rallied behind Ike, electing him to a second term. As a result of the **Suez crisis,** the United States replaced Britain and France as the main Western influence in the Middle East. With the Soviets strongly backing Egypt and Syria, the Cold War had found yet another battleground.

Suez crisis Egyptian leader Gamal Nasser nationalized the Suez Canal in 1956 when the United States withdrew promised aid to build the Aswan Dam on the Nile. Britain and France, dependent on Middle East oil that was transported through the Suez Canal, launched an armed attack to regain control. President Eisenhower protested the use of force and persuaded Britain and France to withdraw their troops.

Two years later, Eisenhower found it necessary to intervene in the strategic Middle Eastern country of Lebanon. Political power in this neutral nation was divided between Christian and Muslim elements. When the outgoing Christian president, Camille Chamoun, broke with tradition by seeking a second term, Muslim groups (aided by Egypt and Syria) threatened to launch a rebellion. After some hesitation, Ike decided to intervene to uphold the U.S. commitment to political stability in the Middle East.

American marines moved swiftly ashore on July 15, 1958, securing the Beirut airport and preparing the way for a force of some fourteen thousand troops. Lebanese political leaders quickly agreed on a successor to Chamoun, and American soldiers left the country before the end of October. This restrained use of force achieved Eisenhower's primary goal of quieting the explosive Middle East. It also served, as Dulles pointed out, "to reassure many small nations that they could call on us in a time of crisis."

Covert Actions

Amid these dangerous crises, the Eisenhower administration worked behind the scenes in the 1950s to expand the nation's global influence. In 1953, the CIA was instrumental in overthrowing a popularly elected government in Iran and placing the shah in full control of that country. American oil companies were rewarded with lucrative concessions, and Eisenhower believed that he had gained a valuable ally on the Soviet border. But these short-run gains created a deep-seated animosity among Iranians that would haunt the United States in the years to come.

Closer to home in Latin America, Ike once again relied on covert action. In 1954, the CIA masterminded the overthrow of a leftist regime in Guatemala. The immediate advantage was in denying the Soviets a possible foothold in the Western Hemisphere, but Latin Americans resented the thinly disguised interference of the United States in their internal affairs. More important, when Fidel Castro seized power in Cuba in 1959, the Eisenhower administration adopted a hard line that helped drive Cuba into the Soviet orbit and led in turn to covert action against Castro.

Eisenhower's record as a cold warrior was thus mixed. His successful ending of the Korean War and his peacekeeping efforts in Indochina and Formosa and in the Suez crisis are all to his credit. Yet his reliance on coups and subversion directed by the CIA in Iran and Guatemala reveal Ike's corrupting belief that the end justified the means. Nevertheless, he could boast, as he did in 1962, of his ability to keep the peace.

❖ A Look at the Past ❖

Fallout Shelter

Fallout shelters caught the interest and attention of both private citizens and entire communities during the early years of the Cold War. Directions for constructing and stocking the shelters appeared in official government documents as well as magazines such as *Popular Mechanics*. Whether specially constructed, elaborate shelters or merely a protected corner of the basement as shown here, fallout shelters revealed how seriously Americans viewed the threat of nuclear war. The shelters also indicated that people believed it possible to survive a nuclear war. Contrast those attitudes to ours. Do we consider nuclear war to be a real threat or survivable if it did occur? Examine the design and furnishings of this shelter. Was this designed only to meet standards for survival? Could this be used for other purposes? What do the supplies shown here suggest about how long people expected to remain in the shelter in the event of a nuclear attack?

Waging Peace

Eisenhower hoped to ease Cold War tensions by ending the nuclear arms race. The development of the hydrogen bomb and long-range ballistic missiles raised the stakes considerably. By the mid-1950s, peace, as Winston Churchill noted, depended on a balance of terror.

Throughout the 1950s, Eisenhower sought a way out of the nuclear dilemma. In April 1953, shortly after Stalin's death, he called on the Soviets to join him in a new effort at disarmament. They ignored this appeal, but Eisenhower kept trying. He outlined an atoms-for-peace plan whereby both the United States and the Soviet Union would donate fissionable material to be used for peaceful purposes, and at the Geneva summit conference in 1955 he suggested an "open skies" program of mutual aerial surveillance. Unfortunately, the Soviets rebuffed both of Eisenhower's overtures.

After his reelection in 1956, the president renewed efforts toward nuclear arms control. Concern over atmospheric fallout from nuclear testing led both Eisenhower and Nikita Khrushchev, who had emerged as Stalin's successor, to seek a ban on such experiments. In October 1958, Eisenhower and Khrushchev each voluntarily suspended further weapons tests pending the outcome of a conference held at Geneva to work out a test ban treaty. Although the Geneva Conference failed to make progress, neither the United States nor the Soviet Union resumed testing for the remainder of Ike's term.

The suspension of testing halted the pollution of the world's atmosphere, but it did not lead to the improvement in Soviet-American relations that Eisenhower sought. In the late 1950s, Khrushchev took advantage of the Soviet feat in launching ***Sputnik,*** the first artificial satellite to orbit the earth, to intensify the Cold War. Playing on Western fears that the Soviets had made a breakthrough in missile technology, the Russian leader began to issue threats, proclaiming, "We will bury capitalism." The most serious threat of all came in November 1958, when Khrushchev declared that within six months he would sign a separate peace treaty with East Germany, thereby ending American, British, and French occupation rights in Berlin.

Sputnik In October 1957, the Soviet Union surprised the world by launching this first artificial satellite to orbit the earth. The resulting outcry in the United States, especially fears that the Soviets were ahead in both space exploration and military missiles, forced the Eisenhower administration to increase defense spending and accelerate America's space program.

CHRONOLOGY

1945	Truman meets Stalin at Potsdam Conference (July) ❖ World War II ends with Japanese surrender (August)
1946	Winston Churchill gives "Iron Curtain" speech
1947	Truman Doctrine announced to Congress (March) ❖ George Marshall outlines Marshall Plan (June) ❖ Truman orders loyalty program for government employees (March)
1948	Soviets begin blockade of Berlin (June) ❖ Truman scores upset victory in presidential election
1949	NATO treaty signed in Washington (April) ❖ Soviet Union tests its first atomic bomb (August)
1950	Truman authorizes building of hydrogen bomb (January) ❖ Senator Joseph McCarthy claims communists in government (February) ❖ North Korea invades South Korea (June)
1951	Truman recalls MacArthur from Korea
1952	Dwight D. Eisenhower elected president
1953	Julius and Ethel Rosenberg executed for atomic-secrets spying (June) ❖ Korean War truce signed at Panmunjom (July)
1954	Fall of Dien Bien Phu to the Vietminh ends French control of Indochina
1956	England and France touch off Suez crisis
1957	Russia launches *Sputnik* satellite
1959	Fidel Castro takes power in Cuba
1960	American U-2 spy plane shot down over Russia

Eisenhower refused to abandon Berlin, however, and prudent diplomacy convinced Khrushchev not to act on his threat.

In 1959, Khrushchev visited the United States and agreed to attend a summit conference in Paris in May 1960. This much heralded meeting never took place. On May 1, the Soviets shot down an American U-2 plane piloted by Francis Gary Powers. The United States had been overflying the Soviet Union since 1956 in these high-altitude spy planes, gaining vital information about the Soviet missile program. When Eisenhower belatedly took full responsibility for the Powers overflight, Khrushchev responded with a scathing personal denunciation and a refusal to meet with Eisenhower.

Conclusion: The Continuing Cold War

The breakup of the Paris summit marked the end of Eisenhower's attempt to moderate the Cold War. The disillusioned leader told an aide that the "stupid U-2 mess" had destroyed all his efforts for peace. Before he left office, however, Eisenhower made one final effort. He delivered a farewell address in which he gave a somber warning about the danger of massive military spending. "In the councils of government, we must guard against the acquisition of unwarranted influence, whether sought or unsought, by the military-industrial complex," he declared. "The potential for the disastrous rise of misplaced power exists and will persist."

military-industrial complex In his farewell address in January 1961, President Eisenhower used this phrase to warn about the danger of massive defense spending and the close relationship between the armed forces and industrial corporations that supplied their weapons.

Rarely has an American president been more prophetic. In the years that followed, the level of defense spending skyrocketed as the Cold War escalated. The **military-industrial complex** reached its acme of power in the 1960s when the

United States realized the full implications of Truman's doctrine of containment. Eisenhower had succeeded in keeping the peace for eight years, but he had failed to halt the momentum of the Cold War he had inherited from Truman. Ike's efforts to ease tension with the Soviet Union were dashed by his own distrust of communism and by Khrushchev's belligerent rhetoric and behavior. Still, he had begun the process of relaxing tensions that would survive the troubled 1960s and, after a few false starts, would finally begin to erode the Cold War by the end of the 1980s.

Key Terms

Potsdam Conference, p. 544
Iron Curtain, p. 544
Baruch Plan, p. 546
containment, p. 547
Truman Doctrine, p. 547
Marshall Plan, p. 548
North Atlantic Treaty Organization (NATO), p. 548
Berlin airlift, p. 549
National Security Act, p. 550
NSC-68, p. 551
Taft-Hartley Act, p. 554
Dixiecrats, p. 555
House Un-American Activities Committee (HUAC), p. 556
McCarthyism, p. 556
massive retaliation, p. 558
Dien Bien Phu, p. 558
Suez crisis, p. 560
Sputnik, p. 561
military-industrial complex, p. 562

Recommended Reading

The Cold War spawned a vast array of books, some enduring in nature and many that are already outdated. The best general guide to American diplomacy since World War II is Walter LaFeber, *America, Russia and the Cold War, 1945–2000,* 9th ed. (2002). On the much-debated question of the origins of the Cold War, the most balanced account is Daniel Yergin, *Shattered Peace* (1977); for a dissenting view, see Thomas G. Paterson, *On Every Front* (1979). John Lewis Gaddis, *We Now Know* (1997), integrates new disclosures from Soviet and Chinese archives to provide the best rounded account of the Cold War through the early 1960s.

The classic account of containment is still the lucid recollection of its chief architect, George Kennan, *Memoirs, 1925–1950* (1967). John Lewis Gaddis uses Kennan's ideas as a point of departure for his account of the changing nature of American Cold War policy in *Strategies of Containment* (1982). Melvyn P. Leffler offers a full account of the development of containment in *A Preponderance of Power* (1992); Arnold A. Offner is more critical of Truman's policies in *Another Such Victory* (2002). For developments in the Far East, consult the perceptive book by Akira Iriye, *The Cold War in Asia* (1974). On the Korean conflict, see Burton Kaufman, *The Korean War,* 2nd ed. (1997), and Bruce Cumings, *The Origins of the Korean War,* 2 vols. (1981 and 1991).

The best book on the Truman period is Alonzo L. Hamby, *Man of the People* (1995), which provides a balanced portrait of a controversial leader. Richard M. Fried offers a perceptive overview of the postwar anticommunist crusade in *Nightmare in Red: The McCarthy Era in Perspective* (1990); the best biography of McCarthy is David Oshinsky, *A Conspiracy So Immense* (1983).

Stephen A. Ambrose evaluates Dwight D. Eisenhower positively in the second volume of his biography, *Eisenhower: The President* (1985). For an equally favorable analysis, see Robert A. Divine, *Eisenhower and the Cold War* (1981). Richard H. Immerman provides a balanced portrait of Eisenhower's secretary of state in *John Foster Dulles* (1999).

For a list of additional titles related to this chapter's topics, please see http://www.ablongman.com/divine.

Suggested Web Sites

Harry S Truman

http://www.ipl.org/ref/POTUS/hstruman.html
This page contains basic factual data about his election and presidency, speeches, and on-line biographies.

Harry S Truman Library and Museum

http://www.trumanlibrary.org
This presidential library site has numerous photos and various important primary documents relating to Truman.

Cold War

http://cnn.com/SPECIALS/cold.war/
This is the companion site to the CNN Perspectives series on the Cold War. It contains information including interactive timelines and a quiz.

Korean War Project

http://www.koreanwar.org
This site has information about the Korean War and is a guide to resources on the struggle.

NATO at 50

http://www.cnn.com/SPECIALS/1999/nato/
This site from CNN has an excellent timeline and images telling the history of the North Atlantic Treaty Organization.

Senator Joe McCarthy—A Multimedia Celebration

http://webcorp.com/mccarthy/
This webcorp site includes audio and visual clips of McCarthy's speeches.

Chapter 29

Affluence and Anxiety

Levittown: The Flight to the Suburbs

On May 7, 1947, William Levitt announced plans to build two thousand houses in a former potato field on Long Island, 30 miles from midtown Manhattan. Using mass production techniques he had learned while erecting navy housing during the war, Levitt quickly built four thousand homes. In 1948, he began offering his houses for sale for a small amount down and a low monthly payment. Young couples, crowded in city apartments or still living with their parents, rushed out to buy Levitt's houses. By the time **Levittown** was completed in 1951, it contained more than seventeen thousand homes.

Levitt eventually built two more Levittowns, one in Pennsylvania and one in New Jersey. Each contained the same curving streets, neighborhood parks and playgrounds, and community swimming pools as the first development. Levitt's houses were ideal for young people just starting out in life. They were cheap, comfortable, and efficient, and each house came with a refrigerator, range, and washing machine. Despite the conformity of the houses, the three Levittowns were surprisingly diverse communities; residents had a wide variety of religious, ethnic, and occupational backgrounds. Blacks, however, were rigidly excluded. In time, as the more successful families moved on to larger homes in more exclusive neighborhoods, the Levittowns became enclaves for lower-middle-class families.

LEVITTOWN SYMBOLIZED THE MOST SIGNIFICANT social trend of the postwar era in the United States—the flight to the suburbs. While central cities remained relatively stagnant during the decade, suburbs grew by 46 percent; by 1960, one-third of the nation lived in the suburbs. This massive shift in population from the central city was accompanied by a **baby boom** that started during World War II. Young married couples began to have three, four, even five children, and these larger families led to a 19 percent growth in the nation's population between 1950 and 1960, the greatest increase in growth rate since 1910.

The economy soared along with residential construction. A multitude of new consumer products—ranging from frozen foods to filtered cigarettes, from high-fidelity phonographs to cars equipped with automatic transmissions and tubeless tires—appeared in stores and showrooms. And in the suburbs, the supermarket replaced the corner grocer.

Although a new affluence for most Americans replaced the poverty and hunger of the Great Depression, the haunting memories of the 1930s remained vivid. The absorption of material goods took on an almost desperate quality, as if a profusion of houses, cars, and home appliances could guarantee that the nightmare of economic depression would never return. Critics were quick to condemn the conformity, charging the newly affluent with forsaking traditional American individualism

Outline

The Postwar Boom
The Good Life?
Farewell to Reform
The Struggle over Civil Rights
Conclusion: Restoring National Confidence

Levittown In 1947, William Levitt used mass production techniques to build inexpensive homes in suburban New York to help relieve the postwar housing shortage. Levittown became a symbol of the movement to the suburbs in the years after World War II.

baby boom Post-World War II Americans idealized the family. The booming birth rate after the war led children born to this generation to be commonly referred to as "baby boomers."

to live in identical houses, drive look-alike cars, and accumulate the same material possessions.

Events abroad added to the feeling of anxiety in the postwar years. Nuclear war became a frighteningly real possibility. The rivalry with the Soviet Union had led to the second Red Scare, with charges of treason and disloyalty being leveled at loyal Americans. Many Americans joined Senator Joseph McCarthy in searching for the communist enemy at home rather than abroad. Loyalty oaths and book burning revealed how insecure Americans had become in the era of the Cold War. The 1950s also witnessed a growing demand by African Americans for equal opportunity in an age of abundance. The civil rights movement, along with strident criticism of the consumer culture, revealed that beneath the bland surface of suburban affluence forces for change were at work.

The Postwar Boom

For fifteen years following World War II, the nation witnessed a period of unparalleled economic growth. Pent-up demand for consumer goods fueled a steady industrial expansion, and heavy government spending during the Cold War added an extra stimulus to the economy, offsetting brief recessions in 1949 and 1953 and moderating a steeper one in 1957–1958. By the end of the 1950s, the majority of the population had achieved an affluence that finally dimmed lingering fears of the Great Depression.

Postwar Prosperity

The economy began to move forward as the result of two long-term factors. First, American consumers, after being held in check by depression and then by wartime scarcities, finally had a chance to indulge their suppressed appetites for material goods. Initially, American factories could not turn out enough automobiles and appliances to satisfy the hordes of buyers, whose personal savings at war's end stood at $37 billion. By 1950, however, production had finally caught up with demand.

The Cold War provided the extra stimulus the economy needed when postwar expansion slowed. The Marshall Plan and other foreign aid programs financed a heavy export trade. The Korean War helped overturn a brief recession and ensure continued prosperity as the government spent massive amounts on guns, planes, and munitions.

In the 1950s, the baby boom and the spectacular growth of suburbia served as great stimulants to the consumer goods industries. Manufacturers turned out an ever-increasing number of refrigerators, washing machines, and dishwashers to equip the kitchens in the houses that were being built across America. The automobile industry thrived with suburban expansion as two-car families became more and more common. The electronics industry took off. Customers were especially eager to acquire the latest marvel of home entertainment, the television set.

Yet the economic abundance of the 1950s was not without its problems. While some sections of the nation (notably the emerging Sunbelt areas of the South and West) benefited enormously from the growth of the aircraft and electronics industries, older manufacturing regions did not fare as well. The steel industry fell behind the rate of national growth, agriculture did not share in the general affluence, and unemployment persisted despite the boom. Moreover, the rate of economic growth slowed in the second half of the decade, causing concern about the continuing vitality of the American economy.

None of these flaws, however, could disguise the fact that the nation was prospering to an extent no one dreamed possible a decade or two earlier. The gross national product more than doubled its 1940 level. More important, workers now labored less than forty hours a week; they rarely worked on Saturdays, and nearly all enjoyed a two-week paid vacation each year. By the mid-1950s, the average American family had twice as much real income to spend as its counterpart had possessed in the boom years of the 1920s. The American people, in one generation, had moved from poverty and depression to the highest standard of living the world had ever known.

Life in the Suburbs

Rather than forming a homogeneous social group, the suburbs contained a surprising variety of people from all social classes. Doctors and lawyers, shoe salesmen and master plumbers often lived in the same developments. The traditional distinctions of ancestry, education, and size of residence no longer differentiated people so easily.

Yet suburbs could vary widely, from working-class communities clustered near factories built in the countryside to old, elitist areas such as Scarsdale, New York, and Shaker Heights, Ohio. Most were almost exclusively white and Christian; a few enabled Jews and blacks to join in the flight from the inner city.

Life in these suburban communities depended on the automobile. Highways and expressways allowed husbands to commute to jobs in the cities. Wives drove to the shopping centers that spread across the countryside by the mid-1950s. Children rode buses to school, then were driven to piano lessons and Little League ball games.

❖ A Look at the Past ❖

Western-themed Toys

Following World War II, westerns enjoyed enormous popularity. TV and movie westerns provided inspiration to both children and manufacturers. Plastic cowboys and Indians, miniature frontier towns, ranches, and forts invited children to reenact western dramas. Western-themed toys, with heroes adults approved of, enabled children to extend screen fantasies into their lives. Westerns permitted adults to escape their worries and experience a world where good and evil were clearly defined and good always triumphed. Why do you think westerns and their associated goods appealed so strongly to Americans during the postwar period?

The home became the focus for activities and aspirations. Men and women who moved to the suburbs prized the new kitchens, extra bedrooms, large garages, and small, neat lawns. *Togetherness* became the byword of the 1950s. Families did things together—gathering around the TV sets that dominated living rooms, attending community activities, or going on vacations or outings in the huge station wagons of the era.

Emphasis on family life did little to encourage the advancement of feminism. The end of the war saw many women who had entered the workforce return to the home, where the role of wife and mother continued to be viewed as the ideal one for women in the 1950s. Trends toward getting married earlier and having larger families reinforced the tendency of women to devote all their efforts to housework and child rearing rather than acquiring professional skills and pursuing careers outside the home. Dr. Benjamin Spock's 1946 best-seller *Baby and Child Care* became a fixture in millions of homes, and the traditional women's magazines such as *McCall's* and *Good Housekeeping* thrived by featuring articles and inspirational pieces such as "Homemaking Is My Vocation."

Nevertheless, the number of working wives doubled between 1940 and 1960. The heavy expenses involved in rearing and educating children led wives and mothers to seek ways to augment the family income, unintentionally preparing the way for a new demand for equality in the 1960s.

The Good Life?

Consumerism was the dominant social theme of the 1950s. Yet even with an abundance of creature comforts and added hours of leisure time, the quality of life left many Americans anxious and dissatisfied.

Areas of Greatest Growth

Organized religion flourished in the climate of the 1950s. Church and synagogue attendance rose, but some observers condemned the bland, secular nature of suburban churches, which seemed to be part of the consumer society. Yet the emergence of neo-orthodoxy in Protestant seminaries and the rapid spread of radical forms of fundamentalism (such as the Assemblies of God) indicated that millions of Americans were searching for inner faith.

The growth of the new suburban communities caused major problems for schools. The unprecedented increase in the number of school-age children overwhelmed the resources of many local districts, leading to demands for federal aid. Except for programs set up in reaction to Soviet scientific advances in space during the late 1950s, Congress and the Eisenhower administration provided only limited assistance to schools.

An important controversy arose over the nature of education in the 1950s. Critics of "progressive" education called for sweeping educational reforms and a new stress on traditional academic subjects. This issue often split suburban communities. The one thing all seemed to agree on was the desirability of a college education, and the number of young people attending college more than doubled between 1940 and 1960.

The largest growth area was the exciting new mass medium of television. From a shaky start just after the war, TV blossomed in the 1950s. By 1957, three national networks controlled the airways, reaching forty million sets over nearly five hundred stations. Advertisers soon took charge of the new medium, using many of the techniques first pioneered in radio, including pretaped commercials, quiz shows, and soap operas.

At first, the insatiable demand for programs encouraged a burst of creativity. Playwrights such as Reginald Rose, Rod Serling, and Paddy Chayefsky wrote notable dramas for *Playhouse 90, Studio One,* and the *Goodyear Television Playhouse.* Broadcast live from cramped studios, these productions thrived on tight dramatic structures, movable scenery, and frequent close-ups of the actors.

Advertisers, however, quickly became disillusioned with the live anthology programs, which usually dealt with controversial subjects or focused on ordinary people and events. Sponsors wanted shows that stressed excitement, glamour, and success. Westerns and situation comedies soon prevailed; a fling with quiz shows ended in scandal. Despite its early promise of innovation, television soon became a technologically sophisticated but unadventurous conveyor of the consumer culture.

Critics of the Consumer Society

One striking feature of the 1950s was the abundance of self-criticism. A number of widely read books explored the flaws in the new suburbia, criticizing the movement toward conformity and the obsession with material goods. The most sweeping indictment came in William H. Whyte's book *The Organization Man* (1956), delineating the change from the old Protestant ethic, with its emphasis on hard work and personal responsibility, to a new social ethic, where everything centered on "the team" and the ultimate goal was "belongingness." The result was a stifling conformity and a loss of personal identity.

Harvard sociologist David Riesman was the most influential social critic of the 1950s. His book, *The Lonely Crowd,* appeared in 1950 and set the tone for intellectual commentary about suburbia for the rest of the decade. Riesman described the shift from the "inner-directed" American of the past, who had relied on such traditional values as self-denial and frugality, to the "other-directed" American of the consumer society, who constantly adapted his behavior to conform to social pressures. The consequence—a decline in individualism and a tendency for people to become acutely sensitive to the expectations of others—produced a bland and tolerant society of consumers short on creativity and daring. More caustically, in *White Collar* (1951) and *The Power Elite* (1956), C. Wright Mills attacked the modern corporation for depriving workers of their own identities and imposing an impersonal discipline through manipulation and propaganda.

The disenchantment with the consumer culture was expressed most eloquently by the **beats,** literary groups that rebelled against the materialism of the 1950s. The name came from the quest for beatitude, a state of inner grace that is sought in Zen Buddhism. Jack Kerouac's novel *On the Road* (1957) set the tone for the fledgling movement. Flouting the respectability of suburbia, the "beatniks," as middle-class America termed them and their followers, were easily identified by their long hair, bizarre clothing, and penchant for sexual promiscuity and drug experimentation. They were conspicuous dropouts from a society they found senseless. Yet as highly visible nonconformists in an era of stifling conformity, the beats demonstrated a style of social protest that would flower into the counterculture of the 1960s.

beats In the late 1950s, young poets and novelists such as Jack Kerouac became known as the beats or "beatniks" for their innovative writing and bizarre behavior. Calling themselves members of "the beat generation," they challenged the prevailing materialism of the consumer culture.

The Reaction to *Sputnik*

The profound insecurity that underlay American life throughout the 1950s surfaced in October 1957, when the Soviets sent the satellite *Sputnik* into orbit around the earth. The American public's reaction to this impressive scientific feat was panic. Declining economic growth, the recession of 1957–1958, the growing concern that American schools were lagging behind their Russian counterparts—all contributed to a conviction that the nation had somehow lost its previously unquestioned primacy in the world.

"All the News That's Fit to Print"

The New York Times.

LATE CITY EDITION

VOL. CVII..No. 36,414. NEW YORK, SATURDAY, OCTOBER 5, 1957. FIVE CENTS

SOVIET FIRES EARTH SATELLITE INTO SPACE; IT IS CIRCLING THE GLOBE AT 18,000 M. P. H.; SPHERE TRACKED IN 4 CROSSINGS OVER U. S.

HOFFA IS ELECTED TEAMSTERS' HEAD; WARNS OF BATTLE

Defeats Two Foes 3 to 1 —Says Union Will Fight 'With Every Ounce'

COURSE RECORDED

Navy Picks Up Radio Signals—4 Report Sighting Device

By WALTER SULLIVAN

560 MILES HIGH

Visible With Simple Binoculars, Moscow Statement Says

By WILLIAM J. JORDEN

The approximate orbit of the Russian earth satellite is shown by black line. The rotation of the earth will bring the United States under the orbit of Soviet-made moon.

Device Is 8 Times Heavier Than One Planned by U.S.

FAUBUS COMPARES HIS STAND TO LEE'S

Says He Will Remain Loyal to People of Arkansas— All Is Quiet at School

Flu Widens in City; 10% Rate Predicted; 200,000 Pupils Out

ARGENTINA TAKES EMERGENCY STEPS

State of Siege Proclaimed in Buenos Aires Region —Arrests Reported

SATELLITE SIGNAL BROADCAST HERE

Impulse Carried on Radio and TV—First Reported by Long Island Station

By ROY SILVER

Sputnik I *on its support stand before launching. The first news of* Sputnik *was not carried in Soviet newspapers until two days after the launch.* ❖

After *Sputnik,* the president and Congress moved to restore national confidence. In 1958, Congress created the National Aeronautics and Space Administration (NASA), appropriating vast sums to allow the agency to compete with the Russians in the space race. Soon a new group of heroes, the astronauts, began the training that led to suborbital flights and eventually to John Glenn's five-hour flight around the globe in 1962. Congress also sought to match Soviet educational advances by passing the **National Defense Education Act (NDEA).** This legislation authorized federal financing of scientific and foreign language programs in the nation's schools and colleges.

National Defense Education Act (NDEA) Passed in response to *Sputnik,* this 1958 legislation provided an opportunity and stimulus for college education for many Americans. It allocated funds for upgrading studies in the sciences, foreign languages, guidance services, and teaching innovation.

The belief persisted, however, that the faults lay deeper, that in the midst of affluence and abundance Americans had lost their competitive edge. Economists pointed to the higher rate of Soviet economic growth, and social critics bemoaned a supermarket culture that stressed consumption over production, comfort over hard work. It would take time for the American people to recover their traditional optimism and sense of national purpose after the shock of *Sputnik.*

Farewell to Reform

It is not surprising that the spirit of reform underlying the New Deal failed to flourish in the postwar years. Growing affluence took away the sense of grievance and the cry for change that was so strong in the 1930s. Eager to enjoy the new prosperity after years of want and sacrifice, the American people lost their enthusiasm for federal regulation and welfare programs.

Truman and the Fair Deal

After his 1948 victory, a triumphant Harry Truman announced his legislative program on January 5, 1949. He called for a **Fair Deal,** a reform package that comprised a new program of national medical insurance, federal aid to education, the Fair Employment Practices Commission (FEPC) to prevent economic discrimination against blacks, and an overhaul of the farm subsidy program.

Fair Deal A series of reform measures proposed by President Truman in 1949, including federal aid to education, civil rights measures, and national medical insurance. A bipartisan conservative coalition in Congress blocked this effort to move beyond the New Deal reforms of the 1930s.

The Fair Deal was never enacted. Except for raising the minimum wage and broadening Social Security, Congress refused to pass any of Truman's health, education, or civil rights measures. In part, Truman was to blame for trying to secure too much too soon. More important, however, was the fact that Congress remained under the control of a bipartisan conservative coalition of northern Republicans and southern Democrats.

Although his legislative failure became certain in 1950 when war once again subordinated domestic issues to foreign policy, Truman deserves credit for maintaining and consolidating the New Deal. His spirited leadership prevented any Republican effort to repeal the gains of the 1930s. Moreover, even though he failed to get any new measures enacted, he broadened the reform agenda and laid the groundwork for future advances in health care, aid to education, and civil rights.

Eisenhower's Modern Republicanism

Moderation was the keynote of the Eisenhower presidency. His major goal from the outset was to restore calm and tranquillity to a badly divided nation. Unlike FDR and Truman, he had no commitment to social change or economic reform, yet he had no plans to dismantle the social programs of the New Deal. He sought instead to work toward balancing the budget, to keep military spending in check, to encourage as much private initiative as possible, and to reduce federal activities to the bare minimum. Defining his position as **Modern Republicanism,** he claimed that he was "conservative when it comes to money and liberal when it comes to human beings."

Modern Republicanism President Eisenhower characterized his views as "Modern Republicanism." Claiming he was liberal toward people but conservative about spending public money, he helped balance the federal budget and lower taxes without destroying existing social programs.

On domestic issues, Eisenhower preferred to delegate authority and to play a passive role. He concentrated his own efforts on the Cold War abroad. The men he chose to run the nation reflected his preference for successful corporation executives. Eisenhower was equally reluctant to play an active role in dealing with Congress. A fervent believer in the separation of powers, Ike did not want to engage in intensive lobbying. Such skillful aides as Sherman Adams, the White House chief of staff, insulated Eisenhower from many of the nation's pressing domestic problems.

Republican losses in the midterm election of 1954 weakened Eisenhower's relations with Congress. The Democrats regained control of both houses and kept it throughout the 1950s. The president had to rely on two Texas Democrats, Senate Majority Leader Lyndon B. Johnson and House Speaker Sam Rayburn, for legislative action; at best, it was an awkward and uneasy relationship.

The result was a very modest legislative record. Eisenhower extended Social Security benefits and raised the minimum wage. He consolidated the administration of welfare programs by creating the Department of Health, Education, and Welfare in 1953. But Ike steadfastly opposed Democratic plans for compulsory health insurance and comprehensive federal aid to education. The lack of presidential support and the continuing grip of the conservative coalition in Congress blocked any further reform in the 1950s.

Highway Act of 1956 A significant legislative achievement of Eisenhower's presidency that created the interstate highway system. The system, built over twenty years, provided jobs in construction, shortened travel times, and increased dependence on the automobile while weakening the railroads.

The one significant legislative achievement of the Eisenhower years came with the passage of the **Highway Act of 1956.** After a twelve-year delay, Congress appropriated funds for a 41,000-mile interstate system of multilane divided expressways that would connect all the nation's major cities. Although the act hurt railroad interests, it pleased a variety of road users: the trucking industry, automobile clubs,

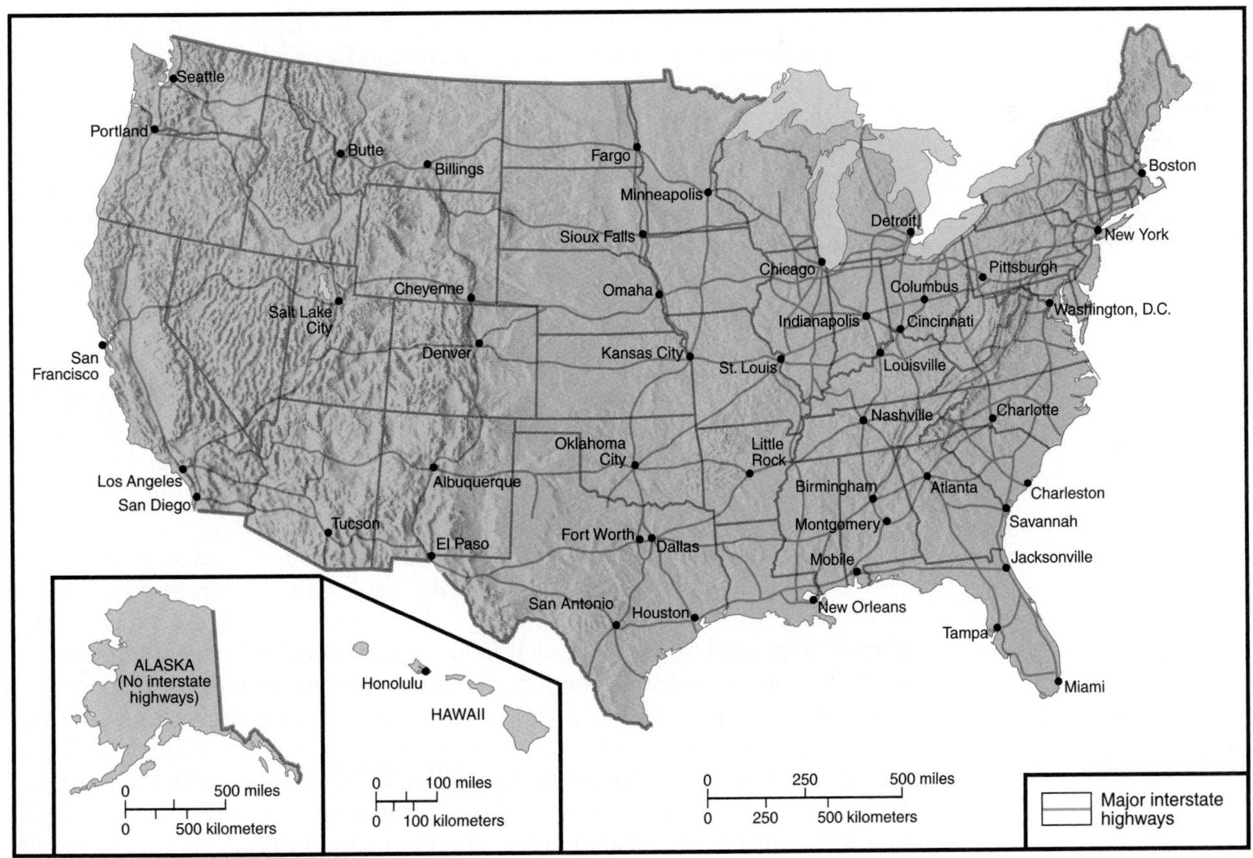

THE INTERSTATE HIGHWAY SYSTEM *The 1956 plan to create an interstate highway system drastically changed America's landscape and culture. Today, the system covers about 45,000 miles, only a few thousand more miles than called for in the original plan.* ❖

organized labor (eager for construction jobs), farmers, and state highway officials. Built over the next twenty years, the interstate system had a profound influence on American life. It stimulated the economy and shortened travel time dramatically while intensifying the nation's dependence on the automobile and distorting metropolitan growth patterns into long strips paralleling the new expressways.

Overall, the Eisenhower years marked an era of political moderation. The American people, enjoying the abundance of the 1950s, seemed quite content with legislative inaction. He was sensitive to the nation's economic health; when recessions developed in 1953 and 1957, he quickly abandoned his goal of a balanced budget in favor of a policy advocating government spending to restore prosperity. Thus Eisenhower maintained the New Deal legacy of federal responsibility for social welfare and the state of the economy while successfully resisting demands for more extensive government involvement in American life.

The Struggle over Civil Rights

Although the Cold War gave birth to the ugly loyalty issue, it had a more positive effect on another social problem, the denial of civil rights to African Americans. The contradiction between the denunciation of the Soviet Union for its human rights violations and the second-class status of African Americans began to arouse the national conscience. Fighting for freedom against communist tyranny abroad, Americans had to face the reality of the continued denial of freedom to a submerged minority at home.

Blacks had benefited economically from World War II, but they were still a seriously disadvantaged group. Those who moved for better opportunities to northern and western cities were concentrated in blighted and segregated neighborhoods, working at low-paying jobs, suffering economic and social discrimination, and failing to share fully in the postwar prosperity.

In the South, conditions were much worse. State laws forced blacks to live almost totally apart from white society. Blacks attended separate schools and were rigidly excluded from all public facilities. They were forced to use separate waiting rooms in train stations, separate seats on all forms of transportation, and separate rest rooms and drinking fountains. Segregation was enforced at all places of public entertainment and in hospitals, prisons, mental institutions, and nursing homes.

Civil Rights as a Political Issue

Truman was the first president to attempt to alter the historic pattern of racial discrimination in the United States. But southern resistance blocked any action by Congress, and the inclusion of a strong civil rights plank in the 1948 Democratic platform led to the walkout of some southern delegations and a separate States' Rights (Dixiecrat) ticket in several states of the South that fall.

Black voters in the North overwhelmingly backed Truman over Dewey in the 1948 election. In key states—California, Ohio, and Illinois—it was the black voters in Los Angeles, Cleveland, and Chicago that ensured the Democratic victory. Truman responded by including civil rights legislation in his Fair Deal program in 1949. Once again, however, determined southern opposition blocked congressional action on a permanent fair employment commission and an antilynching measure.

Even though Truman was unable to secure any significant legislation, he did succeed in adding civil rights to the liberal, Democratic agenda and used his executive power to assist blacks seeking redress of grievances in school and housing issues. He strengthened the civil rights division of the Justice Department, which aided black groups in these issues. Most important, in 1948, Truman issued an order calling for the desegregation of the armed forces. By the end of the 1950s, the military had become far more integrated than American society at large.

Desegregating the Schools

The nation's schools soon became the primary target of civil rights advocates. The NAACP concentrated first on the universities, successfully waging an intensive legal battle to win admission for qualified blacks to graduate and professional schools. Led by Thurgood Marshall, NAACP lawyers then took on the broader issue of segregation in the country's public schools. Challenging the 1896 Supreme Court decision in *Plessy* v. *Ferguson* that upheld the constitutionality of "separate but equal" public facilities, Marshall argued that even substantially equal but separate schools did profound psychological damage to black children and thus violated the Fourteenth Amendment.

A unanimous Supreme Court agreed in its 1954 decision in the case of ***Brown* v. *Board of Education of Topeka.*** Chief Justice Earl Warren wrote the landmark opinion, which flatly declared that "separate educational facilities are inherently unequal." Recognizing that it would be difficult to change historic patterns of segregation quickly, the Court ruled in 1955 that desegregation should proceed "with all deliberate speed" and left the details to the lower federal courts.

Brown v. *Board of Education of Topeka* In 1954, the Supreme Court reversed the *Plessy* v. *Ferguson* decision (1896) that established the "separate but equal" doctrine. The *Brown* decision found segregation in schools inherently unequal and initiated a long and difficult effort to integrate the nation's public schools.

"All deliberate speed" proved agonizingly slow. Southern states responded with a policy of massive resistance. Encouraged by a "southern manifesto" signed by 101 congressmen and senators, which denounced the *Brown* decision as "a clear abuse of judicial power," school boards found ways to evade the Court's ruling. By the end of the decade, fewer than 1 percent of the black children in the Deep South attended school with whites.

A conspicuous lack of presidential support further weakened the desegregation effort. Eisenhower was not a racist, but he believed that people's attitudes could not be changed by "cold lawmaking," only "by appealing to reason, by prayer, and by constantly working at it through our own efforts." Quietly and unobtrusively, he worked to achieve desegregation in federal facilities. Yet he refrained from endorsing the *Brown* decision.

Southern leaders mistook Ike's silence for tacit support of segregation. In 1957, however, Eisenhower corrected this misunderstanding. Backing the federal courts, he used federal troops to ensure the integration of Little Rock's Central High School. The troops remained there for the rest of the school year. Little Rock authorities then closed Central High School for two years; when it reopened, there were only three blacks in attendance.

Despite the snail's pace of school desegregation, the *Brown* decision led to other advances. In 1957, Eisenhower proposed and Congress passed a bill creating a permanent Commission for Civil Rights, one of Truman's original goals. It also provided for federal efforts aimed at "securing and protecting the right to vote." A second civil rights act in 1960 slightly strengthened the voting rights section.

Like the desegregation effort, the attempt to ensure black voting rights in the South was still largely symbolic. Southern registrars used a variety of devices, ranging from intimidation to unfair tests, to deny blacks the suffrage. Yet the actions of Congress and the Supreme Court marked a vital turning point in national policy toward racial justice.

Angry whites taunt Elizabeth Eckford, one of nine African American students who enrolled at Little Rock's Central High School in 1957. The Arkansas National Guard, acting on orders from the state's governor Orval Faubus, refused the students entry into the school. The students were finally able to enter the school under the escort of paratroopers from the 101st Airborne Division. ❖

The Beginnings of Black Activism

The most dynamic force for change came from blacks themselves. The shift from legal struggles in the courts to black protest in the streets began with an incident in Montgomery, Alabama. On December 1, 1955, Rosa Parks, a black seamstress who had been active in the local NAACP chapter, violated a city ordinance by refusing to give up her seat to a white person on a local bus. After her arrest, blacks gathered

In February 1960, black students from North Carolina A&T College staged a sit-in at a "whites only" Woolworth's lunch counter in Greensboro, North Carolina. Their act of nonviolent protest spurred similar demonstrations in public spaces across the South in an effort to draw national attention to racial injustice, to demand desegregation of public facilities, and to prompt the federal government to take a more active role to end segregation. At right, civil rights activists from Tougaloo College in Mississippi bear the verbal and physical abuse of white hecklers at a sit-in demonstration at a Woolworth's lunch counter on May 28, 1963. ❖

to protest and found a young, eloquent leader in Martin Luther King, Jr. He agreed to lead a massive boycott of the city's bus system, which depended heavily on black patronage.

Montgomery bus boycott In late 1955, African Americans led by Martin Luther King, Jr. boycotted the buses in Montgomery, Alabama, after seamstress Rosa Parks was arrested for refusing to move to the back of a bus. The boycott, which ended when the Supreme Court ruled in favor of the protesters, marked the beginning of a new, activist phase of the civil rights movement.

The **Montgomery bus boycott**'s goal was at first modest. King simply asked that seats be taken on a first-come, first-served basis, with blacks being seated from the back and whites from the front of each bus. The boycotters became more assertive as they endured both legal harassment and sporadic acts of violence. An effective system of car pools enabled the protesters to avoid the city buses. Soon they were insisting on a total end to segregated seating.

The boycott ended in victory a year later when the Supreme Court ruled the Alabama segregated-seating law unconstitutional. The protest movement had won far more than this limited dent in the wall of segregation, however. King had provided blacks with a new weapon to fight racial oppression: a policy of passive resistance that stressed nonviolence and goodwill.

Southern Christian Leadership Conference (SCLC) An organization founded by Martin Luther King, Jr. to direct the crusade against segregation. Its weapon was passive resistance that stressed nonviolence and love, and its tactic direct, though peaceful, confrontation.

Student Nonviolent Coordinating Committee (SNCC) A radical group advocating black power, the SNCC's leaders, scornful of integration and interracial cooperation, broke with Martin Luther King, Jr. to advocate greater militancy and acts of violence.

A year after the successful bus boycott, King founded the **Southern Christian Leadership Conference** (**SCLC**) to direct the crusade against segregation. Then in February 1960, another spontaneous event sparked a further advance for passive resistance. Four black students from North Carolina Agricultural and Technical College sat down at a dime-store lunch counter in Greensboro, North Carolina. After being denied service, they refused to move. Other students, both whites and blacks, joined in similar "sit-ins" across the South. By the end of the year, some fifty thousand young people had succeeded in desegregating public facilities in more than a hundred southern cities. Several thousand of the demonstrators were arrested and put in jail, but the movement gained strength, leading to the formation of the **Student Nonviolent Coordinating Committee** (**SNCC**) in April 1960. From this time on, SCLC and SNCC, with their tactics of direct peaceful confrontation would replace the NAACP, with its reliance on court action, in the forefront of the civil rights movement. The change would eventually lead to dramatic success, but it also ushered in a period of heightened tension and social turmoil in the 1960s.

CHRONOLOGY

1946	Republicans win control of both houses of Congress in November elections
1947	William Levitt announces first Levittown
1948	Truman orders end to segregation in armed forces
1949	Minimum wage raised from 40 to 75 cents an hour
1950	Gwendolyn Brooks becomes first African American woman to be awarded Pulitzer Prize
1951	Remington Rand unveils UNIVAC, the first electronic digital computer to be marketed commercially
1952	Edward R. Murrow inaugurates television news show *See It Now*
1953	McDonald's chooses golden arches design for its hamburger shops
1954	Supreme Court orders schools desegregated in *Brown* v. *Board of Education of Topeka*
1955	Dr. Jonas Salk reports success of antipolio vaccine (April) ❖ African Americans begin boycott of Montgomery, Alabama, bus company (December)
1956	Eisenhower signs legislation creating the interstate highway system
1957	Congress passes first Civil Rights Act since Reconstruction
1958	Charles Van Doren confesses to cheating on television quiz show *Twenty-one*
1960	African American college students stage sit-in in Greensboro, North Carolina

CONCLUSION: RESTORING NATIONAL CONFIDENCE

In 1959, disturbed by the criticism of American society sparked by *Sputnik*, President Eisenhower appointed a Commission on National Goals "to develop a broad outline of national objectives for the next decade and longer." The commission eventually issued a report that called for increased military spending abroad, greater economic growth at home, broader educational opportunities, and more government support for both scientific research and the advancement of the arts. The consensus seemed to be that rather than a change of direction, all the United States needed was a renewed commitment to the pursuit of excellence.

The 1950s ended with the national mood less troubled than when the decade began amid the turmoil of the second Red Scare and the Korean War, yet hardly as tranquil or confident as Eisenhower had hoped it would be. The American people felt reassured about the state of the economy, no longer fearing a return to the grim years of the Great Depression. At the same time, however, they were aware that abundance alone did not guarantee the quality of everyday life and realized that there was still a huge gap between American ideals and the reality of race relations, in the North as well as the South.

KEY TERMS

Levittown, p. 566

baby boom, p. 566

beats, p. 569

National Defense Education Act (NDEA), p. 570

Fair Deal, p. 570

Modern Republicanism, p. 570

Highway Act of 1956, p. 571

Brown v. *Board of Education of Topeka*, p. 573

Montgomery bus boycott, p. 574

Southern Christian Leadership Conference (SCLC), p. 574

Student Nonviolent Coordinating Committee (SNCC), p. 574

Recommended Reading

Two excellent books survey the social, cultural, and political trends in the United States during the postwar period. In *One Nation Divisible* (1980), Richard Polenberg analyzes class, ethnic, and racial changes; James T. Patterson offers a perceptive overview of American life from the end of World War II through the mid-1970s in *Grand Expectations* (1996).

Richard Pells provides a sweeping survey of the American intellectual community's response to the Cold War in *The Liberal Mind in a Conservative Age* (1985). The broadest account of American life during the decade is David Halberstam, *The Fifties* (1993). Other important books on social and cultural trends include Elaine Tyler May, *Homeward Bound: American Families in the Cold War Era* (1988); Kenneth A. Jackson, *Crabgrass Frontier* (1986); Lisabeth Cohen, *A Consumer's Republic* (2003); and Serge Guilbaut, *How New York Stole the Idea of Modern Art* (1983).

Charles Alexander provides a balanced view of the Eisenhower years in *Holding the Line* (1975), portraying the Republican president as an able chief executive who was well suited to the times. Fred Greenstein, *The Hidden Hand Presidency* (1982), explores Eisenhower's fondness for indirect leadership. For the impact of *Sputnik* and the space program, see Walter A. MacDougall, *The Heavens and the Earth* (1985) and Robert A. Divine, *The* Sputnik *Challenge* (1993).

Taylor Branch gives a comprehensive account of the genesis of the civil rights movement in *Parting the Waters: America in the King Years, 1954–1963* (1988). Three fine biographies—David L. Lewis's *King* (1970), Stephen B. Oates's *Let the Trumpet Sound* (1982), and David Garrow's *Bearing the Cross* (1986)—present perceptive portraits of Martin Luther King, Jr., the movement's most influential leader. On civil rights, see also Adam Fairclough, *To Redeem the Soul of America* (1987), Joanne Grant, *Ella Baker* (1999); and James T. Patterson, *Brown* v. *Board of Education* (2001).

For a list of additional titles related to this chapter's topics, please see http://www.ablongman.com/divine.

Suggested Web Sites

Fifties Web Site Home Page

http://www.fiftiesweb.com/

This entertaining site tells about and samples music and television from the 1950s. It also includes a related links page.

1950s America

http://www.english.upenn.edu/~afilreis/50/home.html

This site by Professor Al Filreis of the University of Pennsylvania contains a large array of 1950s literature and images in an alphabetical index.

Levittown: Documents of an Ideal American Suburb

http://www.uic.edu/~pbhales/Levittown/

The postwar boom in housing made suburban living the cultural norm in America and shaped a generation. The story of the classic suburb, Levittown, is told on this site in pictures and text.

Dwight David Eisenhower

http://www.ipl.org/ref/POTUS/ddeisenhower.html

This site contains basic factual data about Eisenhower's election and presidency, including speeches and other materials.

The Dwight D. Eisenhower Library and Museum

http://www.eisenhower.utexas.edu/

This site contains mainly photos of the presidents.

Chapter 30

The Turbulent Sixties

Kennedy versus Nixon: The First Televised Presidential Candidate Debate

On Monday evening, September 26, 1960, Senator John F. Kennedy and Vice President Richard M. Nixon faced each other in the nation's first televised debate between two presidential candidates. Kennedy, the relatively unknown Democratic challenger, had proposed the debates; Nixon, confident of his mastery of television, had accepted even though as the early front-runner in the election he had more to lose and less to gain.

Nixon arrived an hour early, looking tired and ill at ease. He was still recuperating from a knee injury that had slowed his campaign and left him pale and weak as he pursued a hectic catch-up schedule. Makeup experts offered to hide Nixon's heavy beard and soften his prominent jowls, but the GOP candidate declined. Kennedy, tanned from open-air campaigning in California and rested by a day spent nearly free of distracting activity, wore very light makeup and changed from a gray to a dark blue suit better adapted to the intense lighting on the set.

Before an audience estimated at 77 million, Kennedy led off, echoing Abraham Lincoln by saying that the nation faced the question of "whether the world will exist half-slave and half-free." Although the ground rules limited the first debate to domestic issues, Kennedy argued that foreign and domestic policy were inseparable. He accused the Republicans of letting the country drift at home and abroad. Nixon, caught off guard, seemed to agree with Kennedy's assessment of the nation's problems, but he contended that he had better solutions.

For the rest of the hour, the two candidates answered questions from a panel of journalists. Radiating confidence and self-assurance, Kennedy used a flow of statistics and details to create the image of a man deeply knowledgeable about all aspects of government. Nixon seemed nervous and unsure of himself.

Polls taken over the next few weeks revealed a sharp swing to Kennedy. Nixon suffered more from his less attractive physical image than from what he said; those who heard the debate on radio thought that the Republican candidate more than held his own. Nixon improved his appearance and strategy in the three additional debates, but the damage had been done. A postelection poll revealed that of four million voters who were influenced by the debates, three million voted for Kennedy.

THE TELEVISION DEBATES WERE ONLY ONE of many factors influencing the outcome of the 1960 election. During the fall campaign, Kennedy exploited the national mood of frustration that had followed *Sputnik*. At home, he promised to stimulate the lagging economy and implement long-overdue reforms in education, health care, and civil rights. Abroad, he pledged a renewed commitment to the Cold War, vowing that he would lead the nation to victory over the Soviet Union.

Outline

Kennedy Intensifies the Cold War

The New Frontier at Home

"Let Us Continue"

Johnson Escalates the Vietnam War

Years of Turmoil

The Return of Richard Nixon

Conclusion: The End of an Era

We Americans

Unintended Consequences: The Second Great Migration

The Democratic victory of 1960 was paper-thin. Kennedy's edge in the popular vote was only two-tenths of 1 percent. Yet even though he had no mandate, Kennedy's triumph did mark a sharp political shift. In contrast to the aging Eisenhower, Kennedy symbolized youth, energy, and ambition. His mastery of the new medium of television reflected his sensitivity to the changes taking place in American life. He came to office promising reform at home and advance abroad. Over the next eight years, he and his vice president, Lyndon Johnson, achieved many of their goals only to find the nation caught up in new and even greater dilemmas.

Kennedy Intensifies the Cold War

John F. Kennedy was determined to succeed where he believed Eisenhower had failed. Critical of his predecessor for holding down defense spending and apparently allowing the Soviet Union to open up a dangerous lead in intercontinental ballistic missiles (ICBMs), Kennedy sought to warn the nation of its peril and lead it to victory in the Cold War. In his inaugural address, he ignored domestic issues and warned the world that "we shall pay any price, bear any burden, meet any hardship, support any friend, oppose any foe, to assure the survival and success of liberty."

From the day he took office, Kennedy gave foreign policy top priority. In part, this decision reflected the perilous world situation, the immediate dangers ranging from a developing civil war in Vietnam to the emergence of Fidel Castro as a Soviet ally in Cuba. But it also corresponded to Kennedy's personal priorities. As a congressman and senator, he had been an intense cold warrior, supporting containment after World War II, lamenting the loss of China, and accusing the Eisenhower administration of allowing the USSR to open up a dangerous missile gap.

Kennedy's appointments reflected his determination to win the Cold War. His choice of Dean Rusk, an experienced but unassertive diplomat, to head the State Department indicated that Kennedy planned to be his own secretary of state. He surrounded himself with young, pragmatic advisers who prided themselves on toughness: McGeorge Bundy, dean of Harvard College, became national security adviser; Walt W. Rostow, an MIT economist, was Bundy's deputy; and Robert McNamara, the youthful president of the Ford Motor Company, took over as secretary of defense. These New Frontiersmen all shared a hard-line view of the Soviet Union and the belief that American security depended on superior force and the willingness to use it.

Flexible Response

The first goal of the Kennedy administration was to build up the nation's armed forces. During the 1960 campaign, Kennedy had claimed that the Soviets were opening a missile gap. In fact, the United States had a significant lead in nuclear striking power by early 1961. Paying little heed to Eisenhower's somber farewell warning about the danger of massive military spending, the new administration, intent on putting the Soviets on the defensive, authorized the construction of an awesome nuclear arsenal that included one thousand Minuteman ICBMs. The United States thus opened a missile gap in reverse, creating the possibility of a successful American first strike.

At the same time, the Kennedy administration reinforced its conventional military strength. Secretary of Defense McNamara developed plans to add five combat-ready army divisions, three tactical air wings, and a ten-division strategic reserve. The president took a personal interest in counterinsurgency. He expanded the Special Forces unit at Fort Bragg, North Carolina, and insisted, over army objections, that it adopt a distinctive green beret as a symbol of its elite status.

The purpose of this buildup was to create an alternative to Eisenhower's policy of massive retaliation. Instead of responding to communist moves with nuclear threats, the United States could now call on a wide spectrum of force, ranging from ICBMs to Green Berets. The danger of this new strategy of **flexible response,** however, was that the existence of such a powerful arsenal would tempt the new administration to test its strength against the Soviet Union.

flexible response The Kennedy administration rejected the Eisenhower strategy of massive retaliation in favor of flexible response, which emphasized the use of conventional as well as nuclear weapons in meeting threats to American security.

Crisis over Berlin

The first test came in Germany. Since 1958, Soviet Premier Khrushchev had been threatening to sign a peace treaty that would put access to the isolated western zones of Berlin under the control of East Germany. The steady flight of skilled workers to the West through the Berlin escape route weakened the East German regime dangerously, and the Soviets believed they had to resolve this issue quickly.

At a summit meeting in Vienna in June 1961, Kennedy and Khrushchev focused on Berlin as the key issue. In a series of meetings, the two leaders failed to find a solution. During their last session, the failure to reach agreement took on an ominous tone. "I want peace," Khrushchev declared, "but if you want war, that is your problem." "It is you, not I," the young president replied, "who wants to force a change." When the Soviet leader said he would sign a German peace treaty by December, Kennedy added, "It will be a cold winter."

The climax came sooner than either man expected. On July 25, Kennedy delivered an impassioned televised address to the American people in which he called the defense of Berlin "essential" to "the entire Free World." He took the unprecedented step of calling more than 150,000 reservists and National Guardsmen to active duty. Above all, he sought to convince Khrushchev of his determination and resolve.

Aware of superior American nuclear striking power, Khrushchev settled for a stalemate. On August 13, the Soviets sealed off their zone of the city. They began the construction of the **Berlin Wall** to stop the flow of brains and talent to the West. For a brief time, Russian and American tanks maneuvered within sight of each other at Checkpoint Charlie, but the tension gradually eased. The Soviets signed the separate peace treaty; Berlin—like Germany and, indeed, all Europe—remained divided between the East and the West. Neither side could claim a victory, but Kennedy believed that at least he had proved America's willingness to honor its commitments.

Berlin Wall In 1961, the Soviet Union built a high barrier to seal off its sector of Berlin in order to stop the flow of refugees out of the Soviet zone of Germany.

Containment in Southeast Asia

Two weeks before Kennedy's inaugural, Khrushchev gave a speech in Moscow in which he declared Soviet support for "wars of national liberation." His words were actually aimed more at China than the United States, but Kennedy concluded that the United States and the Soviet Union were now locked in a struggle for the hearts and minds of the uncommitted in Asia, Africa, and Latin America.

Calling for a new policy of nation building, Kennedy advocated financial and technical assistance designed to help Third World nations achieve economic modernization and stable, pro-Western governments. Measures ranging from the formation of the idealistic Peace Corps to the creation of the ambitious Alliance for Progress—a massive economic aid program for Latin America—were part of this effort. Unfortunately, Kennedy relied even more on counterinsurgency and the Green Berets to beat back the communist challenge.

Southeast Asia offered the gravest test. The American decision to back Ngo Dinh Diem had prevented the holding of elections throughout Vietnam in 1956, as called for in the Geneva accords. Instead, Diem sought to establish a separate government in the South with large-scale American economic and military aid. By the time Kennedy entered the White House, however, the Communist government in North Vietnam, led by Ho Chi Minh, was directing the efforts of Viet Cong rebels in the South.

Flames engulf a Buddhist monk, the Reverend Quang Duc, who set himself afire at an intersection in Saigon, Vietnam, to protest persecution of Buddhists by Vietnam president Ngo Dinh Diem and his government. Other monks placed themselves in front of the wheels of nearby fire trucks to prevent them from reaching Duc. ❖

As the guerrilla war intensified in the fall of 1961, Kennedy sent two trusted advisers, Walt Rostow and General Maxwell Taylor, to South Vietnam. They returned favoring the dispatch of eight thousand American combat troops. General Taylor described the risks of "backing into" a major Asian war by way of South Vietnam as "present but not impressive."

Kennedy decided against sending in combat troops in 1961, but he authorized substantial increases not only in economic aid to Diem but also in the size of the military mission in Saigon. The number of American advisers grew from fewer than a thousand in 1961 to more than sixteen thousand by late 1963. American aid slowed the Communists' momentum, but by 1963, the situation had again become critical. Diem had failed to win the support of his own people; Buddhist monks set themselves aflame in public protests, and even Diem's own generals plotted his overthrow.

President Kennedy was in a quandary. He realized that the fate of South Vietnam would be determined not by Americans but by the Vietnamese. But at the same time, he was not prepared to accept the possible loss of all Southeast Asia. Although aides later claimed he planned to pull out after the 1964 election, Kennedy raised the stakes by tacitly approving a coup that led to Diem's overthrow and death on November 1, 1963. The resulting power vacuum in Saigon made further American involvement in Vietnam almost certain.

Containing Castro: The Bay of Pigs Fiasco

Kennedy's determination to check global communist expansion reached a peak of intensity in Cuba. In the 1960 presidential campaign, pointing to the growing ties between the Soviet Union and Fidel Castro's regime, he had accused the Republicans of permitting a "Communist satellite" to arise on "our very doorstep." Kennedy had even issued a statement backing "anti-Castro forces in exile."

In reality, the Eisenhower administration had been training a group of Cuban exiles in Guatemala since March 1960 as part of a CIA plan to topple the Castro regime. Many of Kennedy's advisers had tactical and moral doubts about the proposed invasion, but the president, committed by his own campaign rhetoric and assured of success by the military, decided to go ahead.

On April 17, 1961, fourteen hundred Cuban exiles moved ashore at the **Bay of Pigs** on the southern coast of Cuba. Even though the United States had masterminded the entire operation, Kennedy insisted on covert action, even canceling at the last minute a planned American air strike on the beachhead. With air superiority, Castro's well-trained forces had no difficulty quashing the invasion.

Bay of Pigs In April 1961, a group of Cuban exiles organized and supported by the CIA landed on the southern coast of Cuba in an effort to overthrow Fidel Castro. When the invasion ended in disaster, President Kennedy took full responsibility for the failure.

Aghast at the swiftness of the defeat, Kennedy took personal responsibility for the failure. In his address to the American people, however, he showed no remorse for arranging the violation of a neighboring country's sovereignty, only regret at the outcome. Above all, he expressed renewed defiance, asserting that the United States would resist "Communist penetration" in the Western Hemisphere. For the remainder of his presidency, Kennedy continued to harass the Castro regime.

Containing Castro: The Cuban Missile Crisis

The climax of Kennedy's crusade came in October 1962 with the **Cuban missile crisis.** Throughout the summer and early fall, the Soviets engaged in a massive arms buildup in Cuba, ostensibly to protect Castro from an American invasion. Although Kennedy had warned the Soviets against the introduction of any offensive weapons, Khrushchev secretly took a daring gamble and started to build missile sites in Cuba. Later he claimed that his purpose was purely defensive, but most likely he was responding to the pressures from his own military to close the enormous strategic gap in nuclear striking power that Kennedy had opened.

Cuban missile crisis In October 1962, the United States and the Soviet Union came close to nuclear war when President Kennedy insisted that Nikita Khrushchev remove the forty-two missiles he had secretly deployed in Cuba. The Soviets eventually did so, nuclear war was averted, and the crisis ended.

On October 14, 1962, American U-2 planes finally discovered the missile sites, which were nearing completion. As soon as he learned what Khrushchev had done, Kennedy decided to seek a showdown. Insisting on absolute secrecy, he convinced a special group of advisers to come up with a response.

Weighing his alternatives, Kennedy decided on a two-step procedure. He would proclaim a quarantine of Cuba to prevent the arrival of new missiles and threaten a nuclear strike to force the removal of those already there. If the Soviets did not cooperate, the United States would invade Cuba and dismantle the missiles by force.

On the evening of October 22, Kennedy informed the nation of the existence of the Soviet missiles and his plans to remove them. He spared no words in blaming Khrushchev, and he made it clear that any missile attack from Cuba would lead to "a full retaliatory response upon the Soviet Union."

For the next six days, the world hovered on the brink of nuclear catastrophe. Khrushchev replied defiantly, and some sixteen Soviet ships continued on course toward Cuba. While the U.S. Navy deployed to intercept those ships 500 miles from the island, American troops assembled in Florida in preparation for an invasion.

The first break came at midweek when the Soviet ships suddenly halted to avert a confrontation at sea. Kennedy felt better on Friday when Khrushchev sent him a long, rambling letter offering a face-saving way out: the Soviets would remove the missiles in return for an American promise never to invade Cuba. Kennedy was ready to accept when a second Russian message raised the stakes by insisting that American missiles be withdrawn from Turkey. Attorney General Robert Kennedy—the president's brother and most trusted adviser—suggested that he ignore the second Russian message and accept the original offer.

On Saturday night, October 27, Robert Kennedy met with the Soviet ambassador, Anatoly Dobrynin, to make it clear that this was the last chance to avert nuclear conflict. The next morning, Khrushchev agreed to remove the missiles in return for Kennedy's promise not to invade Cuba. The crisis was over.

On the surface, Kennedy appeared to have won a stunning personal and political victory. His party successfully overcame the Republican challenge in the November elections, and his own popularity reached new heights in the polls. The American people, on the defensive since *Sputnik,* suddenly felt that they had proved their superiority over the Soviets.

The Cuban missile crisis had more substantial results as well. Shaken by their close call, Kennedy and Khrushchev agreed to install a "hot line" to speed direct communication between Washington and Moscow in an emergency. Long-stalled negotiations over the reduction of nuclear testing suddenly resumed, leading to the limited test ban treaty of 1963, which outlawed tests in the atmosphere while still permitting them underground. Above all, Kennedy displayed a new maturity as a result of the crisis. He shifted from the rhetoric of confrontation to that of conciliation.

Despite these hopeful signs, the missile crisis also had an unfortunate consequence. Policymakers who believed that the Soviets understood only the language of force were confirmed in their penchant for a hard line. Hawks who had backed Kennedy's military buildup felt that events had justified a policy of nuclear superiority. The Soviet leaders drew similar conclusions. "Never will we be caught like this again," vowed one Russian official. After 1962, the Soviets embarked on a crash program to build up their navy and to overtake the American lead in nuclear missiles. Kennedy's moment of triumph thus ensured the escalation of the arms race. His legacy was one of short-term success and long-term anxiety.

The New Frontier at Home

The election of John F. Kennedy marked the arrival of a new generation of leadership. For the first time, people born in the twentieth century who had entered political life after World War II were in charge of national affairs. Kennedy himself had been elected to Congress in 1946 at the age of twenty-nine and had won a Senate seat in 1952. Although he had not sponsored any significant legislation as a senator, he championed the traditional Democratic reforms during his presidential campaign, under the banner of the **New Frontier.** More important was his criticism of the Republicans for allowing sluggish economic growth and failing to deal with such pressing social problems as health care and education. His call to get the nation moving again was particularly attractive to young people, who had shunned political involvement during the Eisenhower years.

New Frontier The campaign program advocated by John F. Kennedy in the 1960 election. He promised to revitalize the stagnant economy and enact reform legislation in education, health care, and civil rights.

The new administration reflected Kennedy's aura of youth and energy. The most controversial cabinet choice was Robert F. Kennedy, the president's brother, as attorney general. Critics scoffed at his lack of legal experience, but the president prized his brother's loyalty and shrewd political advice. As important as his cabinet appointments were his White House staff appointments. Like their counterparts in foreign policy, these New Frontiersmen prided themselves on being tough-minded and pragmatic. In contrast to Eisenhower, Kennedy relied heavily on academics and intellectuals to help him infuse the nation with energy and a new sense of direction.

Kennedy's greatest asset was his personality. A cool, handsome, and intelligent man, he possessed a sense of style that endeared him to the American public. He seemed to be a new Lancelot, bent on calling forth the best in national life; admirers likened his inner circle to King Arthur's court at Camelot. Reporters loved him, both for his fact-filled and candid press conferences and for his witty comments.

The Congressional Obstacle and Economic Advance

Neither Kennedy's wit nor his charm proved strong enough to break the logjam in Congress. Since the late 1940s, a series of reform bills ranging from health care to federal aid to education had been stalled on Capitol Hill. Although Kennedy embraced these Democratic measures, he was hurt by the loss of twenty seats in the House and two in the Senate. The conservative coalition of northern Republicans and southern Democrats opposed all efforts at reform.

The situation was especially critical in the House, where 101 southern representatives held the balance of power between 160 northern Democrats and 174

Republicans. Aided by Speaker Sam Rayburn, Kennedy was able to enlarge the Rules Committee and overcome a conservative roadblock, but the narrow vote, 217 to 212, revealed how difficult it would be to enact his education and health care proposals. Thus the composition of Congress, coupled with Kennedy's distaste for legislative infighting, caused the New Frontier to languish.

Kennedy gave a higher priority to the sluggish American economy. He was determined to recover quickly from the recession he had inherited and to stimulate the economy to achieve a much higher rate of long-term growth. In part, he wanted to redeem his campaign pledge to get the nation moving again; he also believed that the United States had to surpass the Soviet Union in economic vitality.

Rejecting the idea of massive spending on public works, Kennedy sided with the experts who claimed that the problem was essentially technological and urged training and redevelopment programs to modernize American industry. The actual stimulation of the economy, however, came not from such social programs but from greatly increased appropriations for defense and space. By 1962, more than half the federal budget was devoted to space and defense; aircraft and computer companies in the South and West benefited, but unemployment remained uncomfortably high in the older industrial areas of the Northeast and Midwest.

The administration's desire to keep the inflation rate low led to a serious confrontation with the business community. Kennedy relied on informal wage and price guidelines to hold down the cost of living. But in April 1962, just after the president had persuaded the steelworker's union to accept a new contract with no wage increases, U.S. Steel head Roger Blough informed Kennedy that his company was raising steel prices by $6 a ton. Outraged, Kennedy publicly criticized the action. Privately, he confided to aides, "My father always told me that all businessmen were sons-of-bitches, but I never believed it till now."

Threatened with a cutoff in Pentagon steel orders and an antitrust suit, Blough reconsidered. When several smaller steel companies refused to raise their prices in the hope of expanding their share of the market, U.S. Steel capitulated and rolled back its prices. But the business community deeply resented the president's action.

Troubled by his strained relations with business and by the continued lag in economic growth, Kennedy decided to adopt a more unorthodox approach in 1963. Walter Heller, chairman of the Council of Economic Advisers, had long urged a major cut in taxes to stimulate consumer spending and give the economy the jolt it needed. The idea of a tax cut and resulting deficits during a period of prosperity went against economic orthodoxy, but Kennedy finally gave his approval. When enacted by Congress in 1964, the massive tax cut ($13.5 billion) led to one of the longest sustained economic advances in American history.

Kennedy's economic policy was far more successful than his legislative efforts. Although the rate of economic growth doubled to 4.5 percent by the end of 1963 and unemployment was reduced substantially, the cost of living rose only 1.3 percent a year. Personal income went up 13 percent in the early 1960s, but the greatest gains came in corporate profits, up 67 percent in this period. Critics pointed out that the Kennedy administration failed to close the glaring loopholes in the tax law that benefited the rich and that it made no effort to help those at the bottom by forcing a redistribution of national wealth. And in spite of the overall economic growth, the public sector remained neglected. Ecological and social problems continued to grow at an alarming rate.

Moving Slowly on Civil Rights

Kennedy faced a genuine dilemma over the issue of civil rights. During the 1960 campaign, he had promised to launch an attack on segregation in the Deep South, but fear of alienating the large bloc of southern Democrats, however, forced him to play down civil rights legislation.

The president's solution was to defer congressional action in favor of executive leadership in this area. He directed his brother, Attorney General Robert Kennedy, to continue and expand the Eisenhower administration's efforts to achieve voting rights for southern blacks. Working with the civil rights movement, the Justice Department labored to register previously disfranchised blacks. But the attorney general could not force the FBI to provide protection for the civil rights volunteers who risked their lives by encouraging blacks to register. Kennedy's other efforts to improve the conditions for blacks in America had limited results.

freedom ride A freedom ride, sponsored by the Congress of Racial Equality (CORE), was a bus trip taken by both black and white civil rights advocates in the 1960s. They rode buses through the South to test the enforcement of federal regulations that prohibited segregation in interstate public transportation.

The civil rights movement refused to accept the administration's indirect approach. In May 1961, the Congress of Racial Equality (CORE) sponsored a **freedom ride** in which a biracial group attempted to test a 1960 Supreme Court decision outlawing segregation in all bus and train stations used in interstate commerce. When they arrived in Birmingham, Alabama, the freedom riders were attacked by a mob of angry whites. The attorney general quickly dispatched several hundred federal marshals to protect the freedom riders, but the president was more upset at the distraction the protesters created. Deeply involved in the Berlin crisis, Kennedy directed an aide to get in touch with CORE leaders. "Tell them to call it off," he demanded. "Stop them."

In September, after the attorney general finally convinced the Interstate Commerce Commission to issue an order banning segregation in interstate terminals and buses, the freedom rides ended. The Kennedy administration then sought to prevent further confrontations by involving civil rights activists in its voting drive.

A pattern of belated reaction to southern racism marked the basic approach of the Kennedys. When James Meredith courageously sought admission to the all-white University of Mississippi in 1962, the president and the attorney general worked closely with Mississippi Governor Ross Barnett to avoid violence. But despite Barnett's later promise of cooperation, the night before Meredith enrolled at the University of Mississippi, a mob attacked the federal marshals and National Guard troops sent to protect him. The violence left two dead and 375 injured, but Meredith attended the university and eventually graduated.

"I Have a Dream"

Martin Luther King, Jr., finally forced President Kennedy to abandon his cautious tactics and come out openly in behalf of racial justice. In the spring of 1963, King began a massive protest in Birmingham, one of the South's most segregated cities. Public marches and demonstrations aimed at integrating public facilities and opening up jobs for blacks quickly led to police harassment and many arrests, including that of King himself. Police Commissioner Eugene "Bull" Connor was determined to crush the civil rights movement; King was equally determined to prevail.

Connor played directly into King's hands. On May 3, as six thousand children marched in place of the jailed protesters, authorities broke up a demonstration with clubs, snarling police dogs, and high-pressure hoses. With a horrified nation watching scene after scene of this brutality on television, the Kennedy administration quickly intervened to arrange a settlement with the Birmingham civil leaders that ended the violence and granted most of the blacks' demands.

March on Washington In August 1963, civil rights leaders organized a massive rally in Washington to urge passage of President Kennedy's civil rights bill. The high point came when Martin Luther King, Jr., gave his "I Have a Dream" speech to more than two hundred thousand marchers in front of the Lincoln Memorial.

More important, Kennedy finally ended his long hesitation and sounded the call for action. Calling the problem a "moral issue," he sponsored civil rights legislation providing equal access to all public accommodations as well as an extension of voting rights for blacks.

Despite pleas from the government for an end to demonstrations and protests, the movement's leaders decided to keep pressure on the administration. On August 28, 1963, more than 200,000 marchers gathered in the nation's capital for a daylong rally in front of the Lincoln Memorial, where they listened to hymns, speeches, and prayers for racial justice. The climax of the **March on Washington** was King's eloquent description of his dream for a united America.

By the time of Kennedy's death in November 1963, his civil rights legislation was well on its way to passage in Congress. Yet even this achievement did not fully satisfy his critics. They pointed to his failure to issue an executive order to end housing discrimination and to make good on his other campaign promises. For many, Kennedy had raised hopes for racial equality that he never fulfilled.

But unlike Eisenhower, he had provided presidential leadership for the civil rights movement. His emphasis on executive action gradually paid off, especially in extending voting rights. By early 1964, some 40 percent of southern blacks had the franchise. Moreover, Kennedy's sense of caution and restraint, painful and frustrating as it was to black activists, had proved well founded. Avoiding an early, and possibly fatal, defeat in Congress, he had waited until a national consensus emerged and then had carefully channeled it behind effective legislation. Behaving very much the way Franklin Roosevelt did in guiding the nation into World War II, Kennedy chose to be a fox rather than a lion on civil rights.

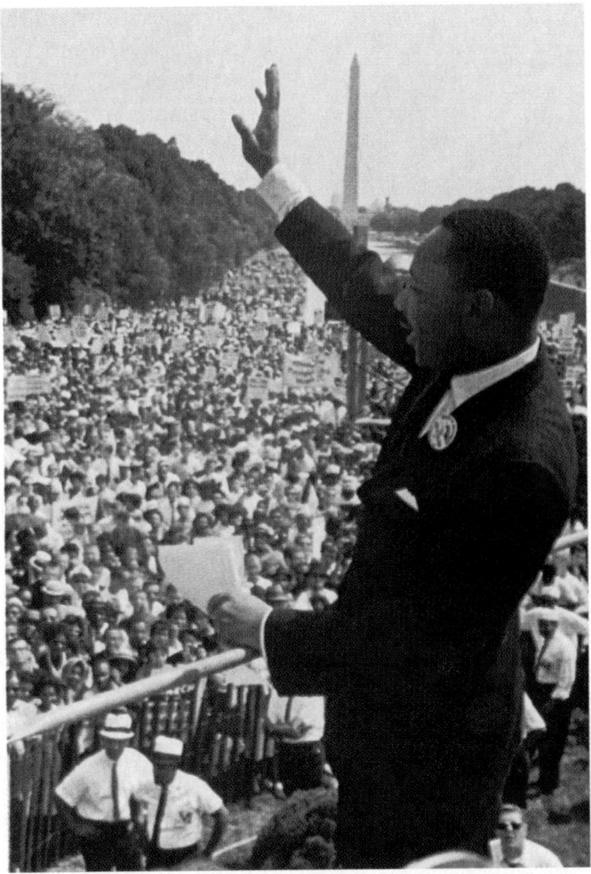

Reverend Martin Luther King, Jr., addresses the crowd at the March on Washington in August 1963. The largest single demonstration of the early 1960s, the march reflected the spirit and determination of many devoted to the cause of equality for African Americans. In his speech, King recounted the difficulties of blacks' struggle for freedom, then stirred the crowd with the description of his dream for America: "I have a dream that one day this nation will rise up and live out the true meaning of its creed—we hold these truths to be self-evident, that all men are created equal." ❖

The Supreme Court and Reform

The most active impulse for social change in the early 1960s came from a surprising source: the usually staid and conservative Supreme Court. Under the leadership of Earl Warren, the Court ventured into new areas. A group of liberal judges—especially William O. Douglas, Hugo Black, and William J. Brennan, Jr.—argued for social reform, while advocates of judicial restraint (such as Felix Frankfurter) fought stubbornly against the new activism.

In addition to ruling against segregation, the Warren Court in the Eisenhower years had angered conservatives by protecting the constitutional rights of victims of McCarthyism. In *Yates* v. *United States* (1956), the judges reversed the conviction of fourteen communist leaders, claiming that government prosecutors had failed to prove that the accused had actually organized a plot to overthrow the government. Mere advocacy of revolution, the Court said, did not justify conviction.

The resignation of Felix Frankfurter in 1962 enabled Kennedy to appoint Arthur Goldberg, a committed liberal, to the Supreme Court. With a clear majority now favoring judicial intervention, the Warren Court issued a series of landmark decisions designed to extend to state and local jurisdictions the traditional rights afforded the accused in federal courts. The Court in *Gideon* v. *Wainwright* (1963), *Escobedo* v. *Illinois* (1964), and *Miranda* v. *Arizona* (1966) decreed that defendants had to be provided lawyers, had to be informed of their constitutional rights, and could not be interrogated or induced to confess to a crime without defense counsel present. In effect, the Court extended to the poor and the ignorant constitutional guarantees that had always been available to the rich and the knowledgeable.

The most far-reaching Warren Court decisions came in the area of legislative reapportionment. In *Baker* v. *Carr* (1962), the Court required Tennessee to redistrict its legislative seats to redress rural overrepresentation in its state government. The Court proclaimed that places in all legislative bodies be allocated on the basis of "people, not land or trees or pastures." The principle of "one man, one vote" greatly increased the political power of cities at the expense of rural areas.

The activism of the Supreme Court stirred up a storm of criticism. The rulings that extended protection to criminals and subversives led some Americans to charge that the Court was encouraging crime and weakening national security. Decisions banning school prayers and permitting pornography incensed many conservative Americans who saw the Court as undermining moral values. Legal scholars worried more about the weakening of the Court's prestige as it became more directly involved in the political process. On balance, however, the Warren Court helped achieve greater social justice by protecting the rights of the underprivileged and by permitting dissent and free expression to flourish.

"Let Us Continue"

The New Frontier came to a sudden and violent end on November 22, 1963, when Lee Harvey Oswald assassinated John F. Kennedy as the president rode in a motorcade in downtown Dallas. The shock of losing the young leader, who had become a symbol of hope and promise for a whole generation, stunned the world. The American people were bewildered by the rapid sequence of events: the brutal killing of their beloved president; the slaying of Oswald by Jack Ruby, captured on TV; and the hurried Warren Commission report, which identified Oswald as the lone assassin.

President Lyndon B. Johnson moved quickly to fill the vacuum left by Kennedy's death. He soon met with a stream of world leaders to reassure them of American political stability. Five days after the tragedy in Dallas, Johnson spoke eloquently to a special joint session of Congress. Asking Congress to enact Kennedy's tax and civil rights bills as a tribute to the fallen leader, LBJ concluded, "Let us here highly resolve that John Fitzgerald Kennedy did not live or die in vain."

Johnson in Action

Johnson suffered in the inevitable comparison with his younger and more stylish predecessor. LBJ was acutely aware of his own lack of polish, but his assets—an intimate knowledge of Congress and incredible energy and determination to succeed—more than compensated. His ego was legendary. When a young marine officer tried to direct him to the proper helicopter, saying, "This one is yours," Johnson responded, "Son, they are all my helicopters."

LBJ's height and intensity gave him a powerful presence; he dominated any room he entered. Yet he found it impossible to project his intelligence and vitality to large audiences. Unlike Kennedy, he wilted before the camera, turning his televised speeches into stilted and awkward performances. Johnson, trying to belie his reputation as a riverboat gambler, came across like a foxy grandpa, clever and calculating and not to be trusted.

Whatever his shortcomings in style, however, Johnson possessed far greater ability than Kennedy in dealing with Congress. He entered the White House with more than thirty years' experience in Washington as a legislative aide, congressman, and senator. His encyclopedic knowledge of the legislative process and his shrewd manipulation of individual senators had enabled him to become the most influential Senate majority leader in history.

Above all, Johnson sought consensus. Indifferent to ideology, he had moved easily from New Deal liberalism to oil-and-gas conservatism as his career advanced. He could work comfortably with southern conservatives or liberals. Suddenly thrust into power, Johnson used his gifts wisely. Citing his favorite scriptural passage from Isaiah, "Come now, and let us reason together, saith the Lord," he concentrated on securing passage of Kennedy's tax and civil rights bills in 1964.

The tax cut came first. In February, after skillful maneuvering by Johnson, Congress reduced personal income taxes by more than $10 billion, touching off a sustained economic boom. Consumer spending increased by an impressive $43 billion in the next eighteen months, and new jobs opened up at the rate of one million a year.

Johnson was even more influential in passing the Kennedy civil rights measure. Staying in the background, he encouraged liberal amendments that strengthened the bill in the House. With Hubert Humphrey leading the floor fight in the Senate, Johnson refused all efforts at compromise, counting on growing public pressure to force northern Republicans to abandon their traditional alliance with southern Democrats. After a fifty-five-day filibuster failed, Johnson won the fight.

The 1964 Civil Rights Act, signed on June 2, outlawed the segregation of blacks in public facilities, established the Fair Employment Practices Committee to lessen racial discrimination in employment, and protected the voting rights of blacks. An amendment sponsored by segregationists in an effort to weaken the bill added gender to the prohibition of discrimination in Title VII of the act; in the future, women's groups would use this clause to secure government support for greater equality in employment and education.

The Election of 1964

Passage of two key Kennedy measures within six months did not satisfy Johnson. Having established the theme of continuity, he now set out to win the presidency in his own right. Acutely aware of Kennedy's narrow victory in 1960, he hoped to win by a great landslide.

Searching for a cause of his own, LBJ found one in the issue of poverty. Beginning in the late 1950s, economists had warned that the prevailing affluence masked a persistent and deep-seated problem of poverty. In 1962, Michael Harrington's book *The Other America* attracted national attention. Writing with passion and eloquence, Harrington claimed that nearly one-fifth of the nation lived in poverty.

Three groups predominated among the poor—blacks, the aged, and households headed by women. The problem, Harrington contended, was that the poor were invisible, living in slums or depressed areas such as Appalachia and cut off from the educational facilities, medical care, and employment opportunities afforded more affluent Americans. Moreover, poverty was a vicious circle. The children of the poor were trapped in the same culture of poverty as their parents.

Johnson quickly took over proposals that Kennedy had been developing and made them his own. In his State of the Union address in January 1964, LBJ announced, "This administration, today, here and now, declares unconditional war on poverty in America." Over the next eight months, Johnson fashioned a comprehensive poverty program.

The new Office of Economic Opportunity (OEO) set up a wide variety of programs, ranging from Head Start for preschoolers to the Job Corps for high school dropouts in need of vocational training. The emphasis was on self-help, with the government providing money and know-how, but the level of funding was never high enough to meet the OEO's ambitious goals. Nevertheless, the **War on Poverty,** along with the economic growth provided by the tax cut, helped reduce the ranks of the poor by nearly ten million between 1964 and 1967.

For Johnson, the new program established his reputation as a reformer in an election year. The man he faced in the election had a different sort of reputation. Senator Barry Goldwater, the Republican candidate, was an outspoken conservative from Arizona. A dignified and articulate man, Goldwater openly advocated a rejection of the welfare state and a return to unregulated free enterprise. He spoke out boldly against the Tennessee Valley Authority, denounced Social Security, and advocated a hawkish foreign policy.

Johnson stuck carefully to the middle of the road, embracing the liberal reform program—which he now called the **Great Society**—while stressing his concern for

War on Poverty President Johnson declared war on poverty in his 1964 State of the Union address. A new Office of Economic Opportunity (OEO) oversaw a variety of programs to help the poor, including the Job Corps and Head Start.

Great Society President Johnson called his version of the Democratic reform program the Great Society. In 1965, Congress passed many Great Society measures, including Medicare, civil rights legislation, and federal aid to education.

balanced budgets and fiscal orthodoxy. On election day, LBJ did even better than FDR had in 1936, receiving 61.1 percent of the popular vote and sweeping the electoral college 486 to 52. The Democrats also achieved huge gains in Congress. Kennedy's legacy and Goldwater's candor had enabled Johnson to break the conservative grip on Congress for the first time in a quarter of a century.

The Triumph of Reform

Medicare The 1965 Medicare Act provided Social Security funding for hospitalization insurance for people over 65 and a voluntary plan to cover doctor bills paid in part by the federal government.

LBJ moved quickly to secure his legislative goals. He gave two traditional Democratic reforms, health care and education, top priority. Aware of strong opposition to a comprehensive medical program, LBJ settled for **Medicare,** which mandated health insurance under the Social Security program for Americans over age 65, with a supplementary Medicaid program for the indigent.

On education, LBJ overcame the religious hurdle by supporting a child benefit approach, allocating federal money to advance the education of students in parochial as well as public schools. The Elementary and Secondary Education Act of 1965 provided more than $1 billion in federal aid. During his administration, federal aid to education increased sharply.

Civil rights proved to be the most difficult test of Johnson's leadership. Martin Luther King, Jr., concerned that three million southern blacks were still denied the right to vote, in early 1965 chose Selma, Alabama, as a test case. The white authorities in Selma, led by Sheriff James Clark, used cattle prods and bullwhips to break up the demonstrations and jailed more than two thousand blacks. Johnson intervened in March, ordering the Alabama National Guard to federal duty to protect the demonstrators. He also had the Justice Department draw up a new voting rights bill and personally addressed Congress on civil rights.

AFRICAN AMERICAN VOTER REGISTRATION BEFORE AND AFTER THE VOTING RIGHTS ACT OF 1965

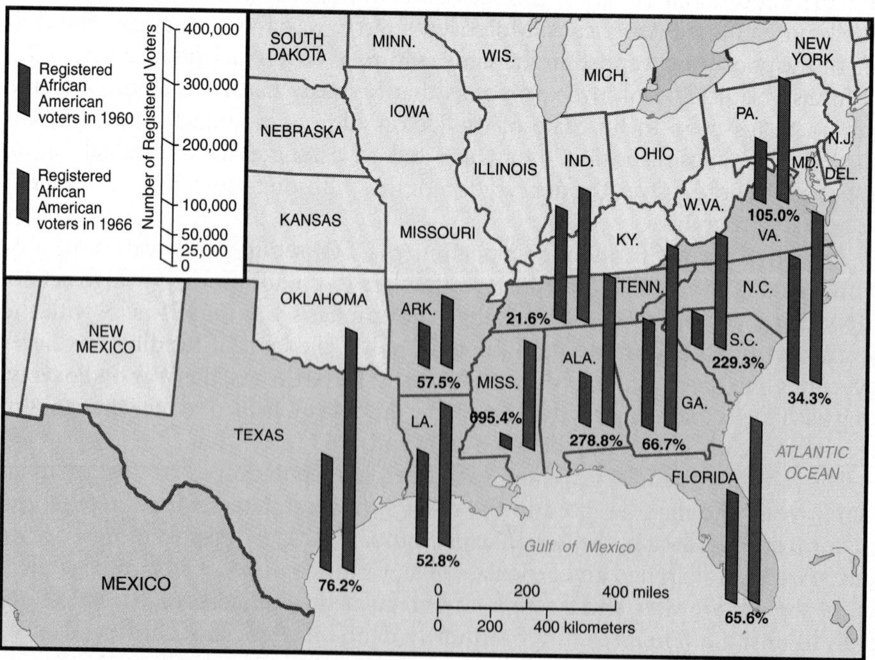

The percentages shown on the map indicate the increase in African American voter registration between 1960 and 1966.

Five months later, Congress passed the **Voting Rights Act of 1965.** The act banned literacy tests in states and counties in which less than half the population had voted in 1964 and provided for federal registrars in these areas to ensure blacks the franchise. The results were dramatic. For the first time since Reconstruction, blacks were playing an active and effective role in southern politics.

Voting Rights Act of 1965
This law effectively banned literacy tests for voting rights and provided for federal registrars to ensure the franchise to minority voters. Within a few years, a majority of African Americans had become registered voters in the southern states.

Before the eighty-ninth Congress ended its first session in the fall of 1965, it had passed eighty-nine bills. These measures ranged from ensuring clean air and water to improving education and housing. In nine months, Johnson had enacted the entire Democratic reform agenda, moving the nation beyond the New Deal by mandating federal concern for health, education, and the quality of life in both city and countryside.

The man responsible for this great leap forward, however, had failed to win the public adulation he so deeply desired. The people did not respond to Johnson's leadership with the warmth and praise they had showered on Kennedy, and reporters continued to portray him as a crude wheeler-dealer. No one was more aware of this lack of affection than LBJ himself. When foreign policy problems soon eroded his popularity, few remembered his remarkable legislative achievement at home. Yet in one brief outburst of reform, he had accomplished more than any president since FDR.

Johnson's Great Society had a lasting impact on American life. Federal aid to education, the enactment of Medicare and Medicaid, and the civil rights acts of 1964 and 1965 changed the nation irrevocably. The aged and the poor now were guaranteed access to medical care, communities saw an infusion of federal funds to improve local education, and African Americans could now attend integrated schools, enjoy public facilities, and gain political power by exercising the right to vote. But even at this moment of triumph for liberal reform, new currents of dissent and rebellion were brewing.

Johnson Escalates the Vietnam War

Lyndon Johnson stressed continuity in foreign policy just as he had in enacting Kennedy's domestic reforms. Not only had he inherited the policy of containment from Kennedy, but he also had the same Cold War beliefs and convictions. Feeling less confident about dealing with international issues, he tended to rely on Kennedy's advisers—notably Secretary of State Rusk, Secretary of Defense McNamara, and McGeorge Bundy, the national security adviser until he was replaced in 1966 by the even more hawkish Walt Rostow.

Although Johnson had had broad exposure to national security affairs, he fully accepted the common assumptions of Americans influenced by the "lessons" of World War II. Like many people of his generation, he believed that weakness, not strength, led to war. And he had also seen the devastating political impact of the communist triumph in China on the Democratic party in the 1940s. "I am not going to lose Vietnam," he told the American ambassador to Saigon just after taking office in 1963. "I am not going to be the president who saw Southeast Asia go the way China went."

Aware of the problem Castro had caused John Kennedy, LBJ moved firmly to contain communism in the Western Hemisphere. When a military junta overthrew a leftist regime in Brazil, Johnson offered covert aid and open encouragement. In 1965, to block the possible emergence of a Castro-type government, LBJ sent twenty thousand American troops to the Dominican Republic. His flimsy justification served only to alienate liberal critics in the United States. The intervention ended in 1966 with the election of a conservative government. But the cost of Johnson's victories was substantial. Such liberals as Senate Foreign Relations Committee Chairman William Fulbright deserted LBJ. The more Johnson struggled to uphold the traditional Cold War policies he had inherited from Kennedy, the more he found himself under attack from Congress, the media, and the universities.

The Vietnam Dilemma

It was Vietnam rather than Latin America that became Lyndon Johnson's obsession and led ultimately to his political downfall. He inherited the Civil War in South Vietnam and the American commitment to Diem's regime in Saigon from Eisenhower and Kennedy.

The situation in Vietnam plagued Johnson from the outset. He took office only three weeks after the coup that had removed Diem and left a vacuum of power. In 1964, seven different governments ruled South Vietnam, and the mood in Saigon was tense and restless. Resisting pressure from the Joint Chiefs of Staff for direct American military involvement, LBJ simply continued Kennedy's policy of economic and technical assistance. He insisted it was still up to the Vietnamese themselves to win the war. At the same time, he expanded American support for covert operations, including amphibious raids on the North.

The undercover activities led directly to the Gulf of Tonkin affair. On August 2, 1964, North Vietnamese torpedo boats attacked the *Maddox,* an American destroyer engaged in electronic intelligence gathering in the Gulf of Tonkin, in the belief that the American ship had been involved in a South Vietnamese raid nearby. The *Maddox* escaped unscathed, but to show American resolve, the navy sent in another destroyer, the *C. Turner Joy.* On the evening of August 4, the two destroyers, responding to sonar and radar contacts, opened fire on North Vietnamese gunboats in the area. Later investigation suggested that the North Vietnamese gunboats had not attacked the American ships, but Johnson ordered retaliatory air strikes on North Vietnamese naval bases.

The next day, the president asked Congress to pass a resolution authorizing him to take "all necessary measures to repel any armed attack against the forces of the United States and to prevent further aggression." Later, critics charged that LBJ wanted a blank check from Congress to carry out the future escalation of the Vietnam War, but such a motive is unlikely. In part, he wanted the **Gulf of Tonkin Resolution** to demonstrate to North Vietnam the American determination to defend South Vietnam at any cost. He also wanted to preempt the Vietnam issue from his Republican opponent, Barry Goldwater, who had been advocating a tougher policy. By taking a firm stand on the Gulf of Tonkin incident, Johnson could both impress the North Vietnamese and outmaneuver a political rival at home. Later, after the incident had served its purpose, Johnson dismissed the attack with "Hell, I think we may have fired at a whale."

Gulf of Tonkin Resolution
After a North Vietnamese attack on an American destroyer in the Gulf of Tonkin in 1964, President Johnson persuaded Congress to pass a resolution giving him the authority to use armed force in Vietnam.

Congress responded with alacrity. The House acted unanimously, and only two senators, both Democrats, voted against the Gulf of Tonkin Resolution. Johnson appeared to have won a spectacular victory, and his approval rating in the polls shot up from 42 to 72 percent.

In the long run, however, the easy victory proved costly. Once having used force against North Vietnam, LBJ was more likely to do so in the future, and the congressional resolution was phrased broadly enough to enable him to use whatever level of force he wanted—including unlimited military intervention. Above all, when he did wage war in Vietnam, he left himself open to the charge of deliberately misleading Congress. Presidential credibility proved to be Johnson's Achilles heel; in that sense, his political downfall began with the Gulf of Tonkin Resolution.

Escalation

The full-scale American involvement in Vietnam began in 1965 in a series of steps designed primarily to prevent a North Vietnamese victory. With the political situa-

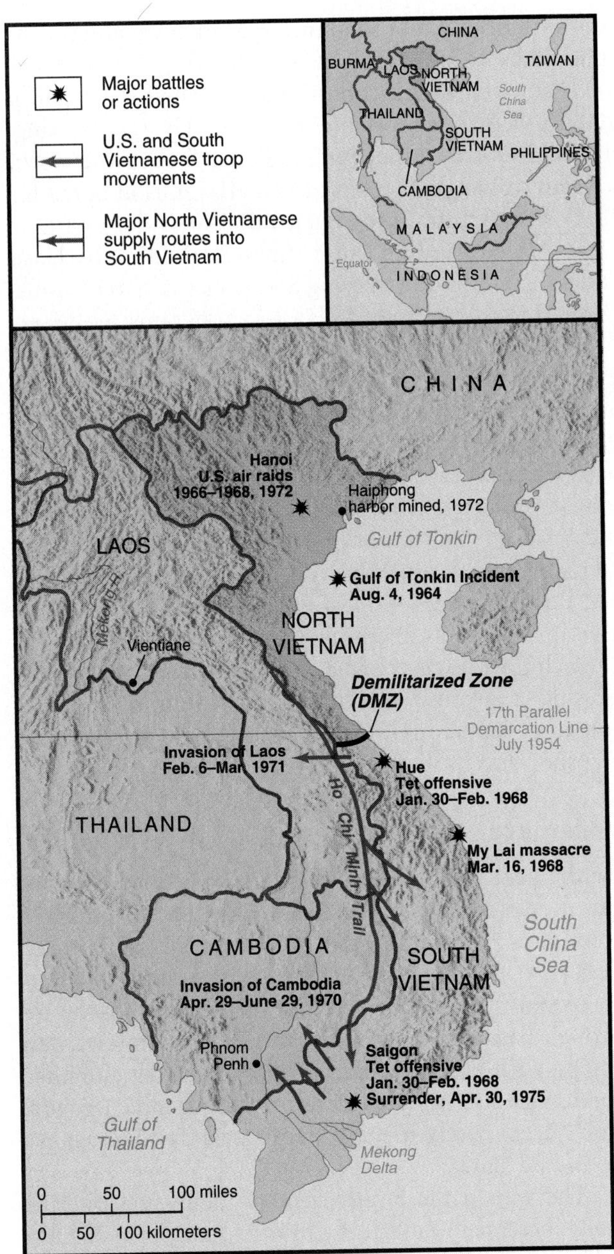

SOUTHEAST ASIA AND THE VIETNAM WAR
American combat forces in South Vietnam rose from 16,000 in 1963 to 500,000 in 1968, but a successful conclusion to the conflict was no closer. ❖

tion in Saigon growing more hopeless every day, the president's advisers urged the bombing of the North as the only conceivable solution. American air attacks would serve several purposes: they would block North Vietnamese infiltration routes, make Hanoi pay a heavy price for its role, and lift the sagging morale of the South Vietnamese. Most important, they would save South Vietnam from utter defeat. Johnson responded in February 1965 by ordering a long-planned aerial bombardment of selected North Vietnamese targets.

The air strikes proved ineffective. In April, Johnson authorized the use of American ground forces in South Vietnam, but he restricted them to defensive operations intended to protect American air bases. Rejecting the clear-cut alternatives of withdrawal or the massive use of force, LBJ settled for a steady military escalation designed to compel Hanoi to accept a diplomatic solution. In July, the president permitted a gradual increase in the bombing of North Vietnam and allowed American ground commanders to conduct combat operations in the South. Most ominously, he approved the immediate dispatch of fifty thousand troops to Vietnam and the future commitment of fifty thousand more.

The July decisions formed "an open-ended commitment to employ American military forces as the situation demanded," wrote historian George Herring. Convinced that withdrawal would destroy American credibility before the world and that an invasion of the North would lead to World War III, Johnson opted for large-scale but limited military intervention. Moreover, LBJ feared the domestic consequences of either extreme. A pullout could cause a massive political backlash at home as conservatives condemned him for betraying South Vietnam to communism. All-out war, however, would mean the end of his social programs. So he settled for a limited war, committing a half million American troops to battle in Southeast Asia, all the while pretending it was a minor engagement and refusing to ask the American people for the support and sacrifice required for victory.

Johnson was not solely responsible for the Vietnam War. He inherited a policy that assumed that Vietnam was vital to the national interest and a deteriorating situation that demanded a more active American role. Truman, Eisenhower, and Kennedy had taken the United States deep into the Vietnam maze; it was Johnson's fate to have to find a way out. But LBJ assumed full responsibility for the way he tried to resolve his dilemma. Failing to acknowledge the stark choices involved, insisting on secrecy and deceit, refusing to acknowledge that he had committed the nation to a dangerous military involvement—these were Johnson's sins in Vietnam.

U.S. TROOP LEVELS IN VIETNAM (DECEMBER 31 OF EACH YEAR)

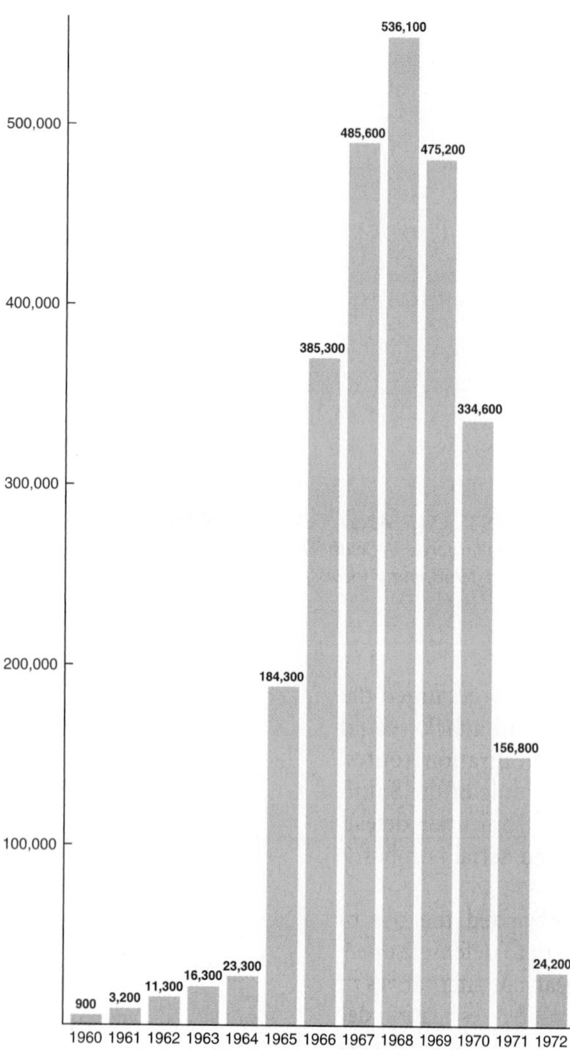

Source: U.S. Department of Defense

Stalemate

For the next three years, Americans waged an intensive war in Vietnam and succeeded only in preventing a Communist victory. Bombing of North Vietnam proved ineffective, failing either to damage its essentially agrarian economy or to block the flow of supplies southward through Laos and Cambodia. In fact, the American air attacks, with their resultant civilian casualties, supplied North Vietnam with a powerful propaganda weapon, which it effectively used to sway world opinion against the United States.

The war in the South went no better. Despite the steady increase in American ground forces, from 184,000 in late 1965 to more than 500,000 in early 1968, the Viet Cong still controlled much of the countryside. The search-and-destroy tactics employed by the Americans proved ill suited. The Viet Cong waged a war of insurgency, avoiding fixed positions and striking from ambush. In a vain effort to destroy the enemy, General William Westmoreland used superior American firepower wantonly, devastating the countryside, causing civilian casualties, and driving the peasantry into the arms of the guerrillas.

The main premise of Westmoreland's strategy was to wage a war of attrition that would finally reach a "crossover point" when communist losses each month would be greater than the number of new troops they could recruit. He hoped to lure the Viet Cong and the North Vietnamese regulars into pitched battles in which

American firepower would inflict heavy casualties. But soon it was the communists who were deciding where and when the fighting would take place, provoking American attacks in remote areas of South Vietnam that favored the defenders and made Westmoreland pay heavily in American lives for the communist losses. By the end of 1967, the nearly half million American troops Johnson had sent to Vietnam had failed to defeat the enemy. At best, LBJ had only achieved a bloody stalemate that gradually turned the American people against a war they had once eagerly embraced.

Years of Turmoil

The Vietnam War became the focal point for a growing movement of youthful protest that made the 1960s the most turbulent decade of the twentieth century. Disenchantment with conventional middle-class values, a rapid increase in college enrollments as a result of the post–World War II baby boom, a reaction against the crass materialism of the affluent society—with its endless suburbs and shopping malls—all led American youth to embrace an alternative lifestyle based on the belief that people are "sensitive, searching, poetic, and capable of love." They were ready to create a counterculture.

The agitation of the 1960s was at its height from 1965 to 1968, the years that marked the escalation of the Vietnam War. Disturbances that began on college campuses quickly spread to infect the entire society, from the ghettos of the cities to the lettuce fields of the Southwest. All who felt disadvantaged and dissatisfied—students, blacks, browns, women, hippies—took to the streets to give vent to their feelings.

The Student Revolt

The first sign of student rebellion came in the fall of 1964 at the prestigious University of California at Berkeley. A small group of radical students resisted university efforts to deny them a place to solicit volunteers and funds for off-campus causes. Forming the Free Speech Movement, they struck back by occupying administration buildings and blocking the arrest of a nonstudent protester. For the next two months, the campus was in turmoil.

In the end, the protesters won the rights of free speech and association that they championed, and youth everywhere had a new model for effective direction. The hero was Mario Savio, a student who had eloquently summed up the cause by likening the university to a great machine and telling others "You've got to put your bodies upon the gears, and upon the wheels, upon the levers, upon all the apparatus, and you've got to make it stop."

The Free Speech Movement at Berkeley offered many insights into the causes of campus unrest. It was fueled in part by student suspicion of the older depression-born generation that viewed affluence as the answer to all problems. Unable to exert much influence on the power structure that directed the consumer society, the students turned on the university, which they viewed as the faithful servant of the corporate and political elite as it trained hordes of technicians to operate the new computers, harbored the research laboratories that perfected dreadful military weapons, and regimented its students with IBM punch cards.

Student protest found its full expression in the explosive growth of the **Students for a Democratic Society (SDS).** Founded in Port Huron, Michigan, in 1962, the radical organization wanted to rid American society of poverty, racism, and violence. Although the SDS embraced many traditional liberal reforms, such as expanded public housing and comprehensive health insurance, its founders advocated a new approach called participatory democracy. In contrast to both liberalism and old-style socialism, the SDS sought salvation through the individual rather

Students for a Democratic Society (SDS) Founded in 1962, the SDS was a popular college student organization that protested shortcomings in American life, notably racial injustice and the Vietnam War. It led thousands of campus protests before it split apart at the end of the 1960s.

than the group. Personal control of one's life and destiny, not the creation of new bureaucracies, was the hallmark of the New Left.

In the next few years, the SDS grew phenomenally. Spurred on by the Vietnam War and massive campus unrest, the SDS could count more than a hundred thousand followers and was responsible for disruptions at nearly a thousand colleges in 1968. Yet its very emphasis on the individual and its fear of bureaucracy left it leaderless and subject to division and disunity. By 1970, a split between factions, some of which were given to violence, led to its complete demise.

The meteoric career of the SDS symbolized the turbulence of the 1960s. For a brief time, it seemed as though the nation's youth had gone berserk, indulging in a wave of experimentation with drugs, sex, and rock music. Older Americans believed that all the nation's traditional values, from the Puritan work ethic to the family, were under attack. Not all American youth joined in the cultural insurgency; the rebellion was generally limited to children of the upper middle class. But like the flappers of the 1920s, the protesters set the tone for an entire era and left a lasting impression on American society.

❖ A Look at the Past ❖

Army Fatigue Jacket

Gray flannel suits with conservative ties and dresses with tightly fitted bodices represented the standard uniform during the years of 1950s conformity. By the late 1960s, American youth had cast aside those conservative clothes and instead wore tie-dyed shirts, jeans, and clothes made from Indian print fabrics. Many young people, especially anti-war protesters, also wore military surplus clothing such as this army fatigue jacket. Why do you think civilians protesting the Vietnam War chose to adopt military attire? Can you think of other examples of clothing used for political or social protest?

Protesting the Vietnam War

The most dramatic aspect of the youthful rebellion came in opposing the Vietnam War. The first student "teach-ins" began at the University of Michigan in March 1965; soon they spread to campuses across the nation.

One of the great ironies of the Vietnam War was the system of student draft deferments, which enabled students enrolled in college to avoid military service. As a result, the children of the well-to-do, who were more likely to attend college, were able to escape the draft. Those too poor to attend college served in Vietnam in much larger numbers. One survey revealed that men from disadvantaged families, including a disproportionately large number of blacks and Hispanics, were twice as likely to be drafted and sent into combat in Vietnam as those from more privileged backgrounds. Consequently, a sense of guilt led many college activists, safe from Vietnam because of their student status, to take the lead in denouncing an unjust war.

As the fighting in Southeast Asia intensified in 1966 and 1967, the protests grew larger and the slogans more extreme. "Hey, hey, LBJ, how many kids have you killed today?" chanted students. At the Pentagon in October 1967, more than 100,000 demonstrators confronted a cordon of military policemen guarding the heart of the nation's war machine. From the windows above, Secretary of Defense McNamara and his generals looked down on the angry protesters.

The climax came in the spring of 1968. Driven both by opposition to the war and concern for social justice, the SDS and black radicals at Columbia University joined forces in April. They seized five buildings, effectively paralyzing one of the country's leading colleges. After eight days of tension, the New York City police regained control. The brutal repression quickened the pace of protest elsewhere. Sit-ins, violent marches, and arrests became common.

The students failed to stop the war, but they did succeed in gaining a voice in their education. University administrations allowed undergraduates to sit on faculty committees to plan the curriculum and gave up their once rigid control of dormitory and social life. But the students' greatest impact lay outside politics and the campus. They spawned a cultural uprising that transformed the manners and mores of America.

The Cultural Revolution

In contrast to the political revolt of the elitist SDS, the cultural rebellion by youth in the 1960s was pervasive. Led by college students, young people challenged the prevailing adult values, in clothing, hairstyles, sexual conduct, work habits, and music. Blue jeans and love beads took the place of business suits and pearl necklaces, and family life gave way to communes for the "flower children" of the 1960s.

Music became the touchstone of the new departure. Folksingers such as Joan Baez and Bob Dylan, popular for their songs of social protest in the mid-1960s, gave way to rock groups such as the Beatles, whose lyrics were often suggestive of drug use, and finally to "acid rock" as symbolized by the Grateful Dead. The climactic event of the decade came at an outdoor concert near Woodstock, New York, when 400,000 young people indulged in a three-day orgy of rock music, drug experimentation, and sexual activity.

The cultural revolution was heavily influenced by the drug scene. Former Harvard psychology professor Timothy Leary invited youth to "tune in, turn on, drop out," literally, as they experimented with marijuana, LSD, and other drugs. Its ultimate expression of insurgency was the Yippie movement, led by such men as Jerry Rubin and Abbie Hoffman. The Yippies mocked the consumer culture and delighted in capitalizing on the mood of social protest to win attention. They succeeded in revealing the hypocrisy in American society, but in the process they fragmented the protest movement; serious radicals dismissed them as parasites.

"Black Power"

The civil rights movement, which had conceived the mood of protest in the 1960s, fell on hard times. The legislative triumphs of 1964 and 1965 were relatively easy victories over southern bigotry. Now the movement faced the far more complex problem of achieving economic equality in the cities of the North. Mired in poverty, crowded into ghettos, blacks had actually fallen further behind whites in disposable income since the beginning of the integration effort. The civil rights movement had raised the expectations of urban African Americans; frustration mounted as they failed to experience any significant economic gain.

❖ A Look at the Past ❖

WOODSTOCK MUSIC & ART FAIR
presents
AN AQUARIAN EXPOSITION
in
WHITE LAKE, N.Y.*

3 DAYS of PEACE & MUSIC

WITH
Joan Baez
Arlo Guthrie
Tim Hardin
Richie Havens
Incredible String Band
Ravi Shankar
Sly And The Family Stone
Bert Sommer
Sweetwater
Keef Hartley
Canned Heat
Creedence Clearwater
Grateful Dead
Janis Joplin
Jefferson Airplane
Mountain
Quill
Santana
The Who
The Band
Jeff Beck Group
Blood, Sweat and Tears
Joe Cocker
Crosby, Stills and Nash
Jimi Hendrix
Iron Butterfly
Ten Years After
Johnny Winter
FRI. AUG. 15
SAT. AUG. 16
SUN. AUG. 17
All programs subject to change without notice
*White Lake, Town of Bethel, Sullivan County, N.Y.

Woodstock Brochure

The dove and guitar on this brochure for the 1969 Woodstock Music Festival graphically present Woodstock's purpose: peaceful, joyful coexistence. More than 400,000 revelers ignored bad weather and poor conditions to listen to folk and rock music. The age of Aquarius, when peace and harmony would triumph, had seemingly arrived. How do you explain the contradiction between the call for peace and harmony and the growing violence of the 1960s?

The first sign of trouble came in the summer of 1964, when black teenagers in Harlem and Rochester, New York, rioted. The next summer, a massive outburst of rage and destruction swept the Watts neighborhood of Los Angeles as the inhabitants burned buildings and looted stores. In 1967, the worst riots yet took place in Newark and Detroit, where forty-three people were killed and hundreds injured.

The civil rights coalition fell apart, a victim of both its legislative success and its economic failure. Black militants took over the leadership of the Student Nonviolent Coordinating Committee (SNCC); they disdained white help and even reversed Martin Luther King's insistence on nonviolence. SNCC's new leader, Stokely Carmichael, told blacks that they should seize power in those parts of the South where they outnumbered whites. "I am not going to beg the white man for anything I deserve," he said, "I'm going to take it." Soon his calls for "black power" became a rallying cry for more militant African Americans who advocated the need for blacks to form their "own institutions, credit unions, co-ops, [and] political parties" and even write their "own history."

Others went further than calls for ethnic separation. H. Rap Brown, who replaced Carmichael as the leader of SNCC in 1967, told a black crowd in Cambridge, Maryland, to "get your guns" and "burn this town down," while Huey Newton, one of the founders of the militant Black Panther party, proclaimed that "political power comes through the barrel of a gun."

King suffered most from this extremism. His denunciation of the Vietnam War cost him the support of the Johnson administration and the more conservative civil rights groups such as the NAACP and the Urban League. Radical blacks rejected his nonviolent approach to change. King finally seized on poverty as the proper enemy for attack, but before he could lead his Poor People's March on Washington in 1968, he was assassinated in Memphis in early April.

Both blacks and whites realized that the nation had lost its most eloquent spokesman for racial harmony. His tragic death elevated King to the status of a martyr, but it also led to one last outbreak of widespread urban violence. Blacks exploded in angry riots in 125 cities across the nation; in Chicago and Baltimore, army units were needed to restore order in the ghettos. The worst rioting took place in Washington, D.C., where buildings were set on fire within a few blocks of the White House.

Yet there was a positive side to the emotions engendered by black nationalism. Spokespersons began to urge blacks to take pride in their ethnic heritage, to embrace their blackness as a positive value. Blacks began to wear bushy "Afro" hairstyles and take interest in their African roots. The word *Negro*—identified with white supremacy of the past—virtually disappeared from usage overnight, replaced by *Afro-American* or *black.* Singer James Brown best expressed the sense of racial identity: "Say It Loud—I'm Black and I'm Proud."

Ethnic Nationalism

Other groups quickly emulated the black phenomenon. Native Americans decried the callous use of their identity as football mascots; Puerto Ricans demanded that their history be included in school and college texts; and Polish, Italian, and Czech groups insisted on respect for their nationalities. Congress acknowledged these demands with passage of the Ethnic Heritage Studies Act of 1972, which recognized ethnicity as a positive force in American society and appropriated money to subsidize ethnic studies courses.

Mexican Americans were in the forefront of the ethnic groups that became active in the 1970s. The primary impulse came from the efforts of César Chávez to organize the poorly paid grape pickers and lettuce workers in California into the National Farm Workers Association (NFWA). Chávez appealed to ethnic nationalism in mobilizing Mexican American field hands to strike against grape growers in the San Joaquin Valley in 1965. Once Chávez had won the attention of the media, a national boycott of grapes by Mexican Americans and their sympathizers among the young people of the country led to a series of hard-fought victories over the growers. The five-year struggle brought union victory in 1970, but at an enormous cost—95 percent of the farmworkers had lost their homes and their cars. Undaunted, Chávez turned next to the lettuce fields, and although he met with strong resistance, he succeeded in raising the hourly wage of farmworkers in California to $3.53 by 1977 (it had been $1.20 in 1965).

Chávez's efforts helped spark an outburst of ethnic consciousness among Mexican Americans that swept through the urban barrios of the Southwest. Aware that a majority of their compatriots were functionally illiterate as a result of language difficulties and inferior schools, Mexican American leaders campaigned for bilingual programs and improved educational opportunities. Young activists began to call themselves Chicanos, which had previously been a derogatory term, and to take pride in their cultural heritage; in 1968, they succeeded in establishing the first Mexican American studies program at California State College at Los Angeles. In addition, student protests in several leading southwestern cities led to significant reforms, such as the introduction of bilingual programs in grade schools and the hiring of more Chicano teachers at all levels.

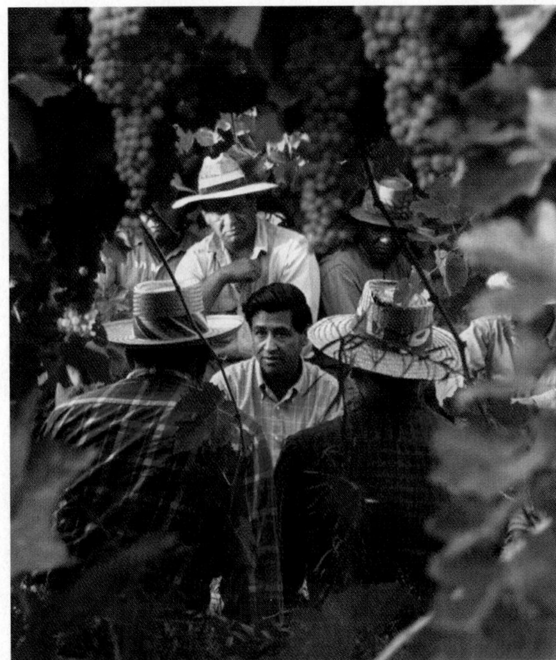

In March 1966, César Chávez, shown here talking with workers, led striking grape pickers on a 250-mile march from Delano, California, to the state capital at Sacramento to dramatize the plight of the migrant farmworkers. With the slogan "God is beside you on the picket line," the march took on the character of a religious pilgrimage. ❖

Women's Liberation

Active as they were in the civil rights and antiwar movements, women soon learned that the male leaders of protest causes were little different from corporate executives—they expected women to fix the food and type the communiqués while the men made the decisions. Women soon realized that they could achieve respect and equality only by mounting their own protest.

In some ways, the position of women in American society was worse in the 1960s than it had been in the 1920s. After forty years, there was a lower percentage of women enrolled in the nation's colleges and professional schools, and women with college degrees earned only half as much as similarly trained men. Women were still relegated to stereotypical occupations such as nursing and teaching. And gender roles, as portrayed in the media, continued to call for the husband to be the breadwinner and the wife to be the homemaker.

Betty Friedan was the first to put into words the sense of grievance and discrimination that developed among women in the 1960s in her 1963 book *The Feminine Mystique.* Calling the American home "a comfortable concentration camp," she attacked the prevailing view that women were completely contented with their housekeeping and child-rearing tasks, claiming that housewives had no self-esteem and no sense of identity.

The 1964 Civil Rights Act helped women attack economic inequality head-on by making it illegal to discriminate in employment on the basis of gender. Women filed suit for equal wages, demanded (with little success) that companies provide day care for their infants and preschool children, and entered politics to lobby against laws that were unfair to women. As the women's liberation movement grew, its advocates began to attack laws banning abortion and waged a campaign to toughen the enforcement of rape laws.

National Organization for Women (NOW) Founded in 1966, this organization called for equal employment opportunity and equal pay for women. NOW also championed the legalization of abortion and passage of the Equal Rights Amendment to the Constitution.

The women's movement met with many of the same obstacles as other protest groups in the 1960s. The moderate leadership of the **National Organization for Women (NOW),** founded by Friedan in 1966, was soon challenged by members with more extreme views. The harsh rhetoric and militancy of the extremists

Betty Friedan poses with a copy of her groundbreaking book, The Feminine Mystique. *In the work, Friedan castigated advertisers, educators, and others for promoting what she labeled the feminine mystique—the idea that women could find fulfillment only in their roles as wives and mothers. Friedan helped spark the modern feminist movement, which had its roots in the nineteenth-century women's rights movement and built on the efforts of earlier activists such as Susan B. Anthony, Lucretia Mott, and Elizabeth Cady Stanton.* ❖

repelled many women who expressed satisfaction with their lives. But despite these disagreements, most women—and a great many men—supported the effort to achieve equal status, and in 1972, Congress responded by approving the Equal Rights Amendment to the Constitution. This measure, first introduced in Congress in 1923, now faced a vote in the state legislatures, the final step toward ratification.

The Return of Richard Nixon

The turmoil of the 1960s reached a crescendo in 1968 as the American people responded to the two dominant events of the decade—the war in Vietnam and the cultural insurgency at home. In an election marked by a series of bizarre events, including riots and an assassination, Richard Nixon staged a remarkable comeback to win the post denied him in 1960.

Vietnam Undermines Lyndon Johnson

The climax of the war in Vietnam came in late January 1968 when the Viet Cong, aided by North Vietnamese regulars, launched an offensive during Tet, the lunar New Year, recklessly attacking the South Vietnamese cities and provincial capitals. American and government troops quickly beat back the **Tet offensive,** but at home, television viewers were shocked by scenes of Viet Cong fighting within the walls of the American embassy compound in Saigon. The outcome was a tactical defeat for the Communists but a decided political setback for the United States. President Johnson had been hammering away at the idea that the war was almost over; suddenly it appeared to be nearly lost.

Tet offensive In February 1968, the Viet Cong launched a major offensive in the cities of South Vietnam. Although caught by surprise, American and South Vietnamese forces successfully quashed this attack, yet the Tet offensive was a blow to American public opinion and led President Johnson to end the escalation of the war and seek a negotiated peace.

Johnson reluctantly came to the conclusion that the war would end in a stalemate. In mid-March, he decided to limit the bombing of North Vietnam in an effort to open up peace negotiations with Hanoi. In a speech to the nation on Sunday evening, March 31, 1968, Johnson outlined his plans for a new effort at ending the war peacefully and concluded by saying, as proof of his sincerity, "I shall not seek, and I will not accept, the nomination of my party for another term as your president." Thus a stunned nation learned that LBJ had become the first major political casualty of the Vietnam War.

In the fourteen years since the siege of Dien Bien Phu, American policy had gone full circle in Vietnam. Even though Eisenhower had decided against using force to rescue the French, his commitment to the Diem regime in Saigon had led eventually to American military involvement on a massive scale. Three years of inconclusive fighting and a steadily mounting loss of American lives had disillusioned the American people and finally cost Lyndon Johnson the presidency. And the full price the nation would have to pay for its folly in Southeast Asia was still unknown—the Vietnam experience would continue to cast a shadow over American life for years to come.

The failure in Vietnam reflected the difficulty the United States faced in pursuing containment on a global scale. Policies that had worked well in Europe in the 1940s had little relevance to the very different situation in Southeast Asia. Intent on halting the spread of communism, American leaders never grasped the political realities in Vietnam. The United States ended up backing a series of corrupt regimes in Saigon while the Viet Cong won the struggle for the hearts and minds of the Vietnamese people. More than anything else, the Vietnam War revealed the need for a thorough reexamination of the basic premises of American foreign policy in the Cold War.

Democrats Divided

Lyndon Johnson's withdrawal from the presidential race after the Tet offensive set the tone for the 1968 election. LBJ's decision had come in response to political as well as military realities. By 1966, the antiwar movement had spread from the college campuses to Capitol Hill. Former supporters such as Senator William Fulbright began to question the conflict. Housewives and middle-class professionals were attending the antiwar rallies. Johnson felt like a prisoner in the White House, since in his infrequent public appearances he was hounded by larger and larger gatherings of antiwar demonstrators.

The essentially leaderless protest against the war had taken on a new quality on January 3, 1968, when Senator Eugene McCarthy, a Democrat from Minnesota, announced that he would challenge LBJ for the party's presidential nomination. Cool, aloof, almost arrogant, McCarthy was an intellectual motivated primarily by a belief that Kennedy and Johnson had abused the power of the presidency. McCarthy's idealism proclaimed, "Whatever is morally necessary must be made politically possible." His stance against the war attracted the support of American youth. In the New Hampshire primary in early March, the nation's earliest political test, McCarthy shocked the political experts by coming within a few thousand votes of defeating Johnson.

McCarthy's strong showing in New Hampshire led Robert Kennedy to enter the presidential race. Despite the obvious charge of opportunism he faced, Kennedy had a much better chance than McCarthy to defeat LBJ and win in the fall. Unlike McCarthy, whose appeal was largely limited to upper-middle-class whites and college students, Kennedy attracted strong support among blue-collar workers, blacks, Chicanos, and other minorities who formed the nucleus of the continuing New Deal coalition.

LBJ's dramatic withdrawal caused an uproar in the Democratic party. With Johnson's tacit backing and strong support from party regulars and organized labor, Vice President Hubert H. Humphrey, a classic Cold War liberal who had worked equally hard for social reform at home and American expansion abroad, declared his candidacy. The antiwar movement, however, considered him totally unacceptable. Accordingly, he decided to avoid the primaries and work for nomination within the framework of the party.

Kennedy and McCarthy, the two antiwar candidates, were thus left to contest the spring primaries, causing agonizing choices among voters who sought change. Kennedy won everywhere except in Oregon, but his narrow victory in California ended in tragedy when a Palestinian immigrant, Sirhan Sirhan, assassinated him in a Los Angeles hotel.

With his strongest opponent struck down, Humphrey had little difficulty turning back the challenges from McCarthy and from George McGovern at the Chicago convention. Backed by party leaders, including Chicago's political boss, Mayor Richard Daley, Humphrey supporters defeated an antiwar resolution and won the nomination on the first ballot.

Humphrey's triumph was marred by violence outside the heavily guarded convention hall. Radical groups had urged their members to come to Chicago to agitate; the turnout was relatively small but included many who were ready to provoke the authorities in their despair over the convention's outcome. Epithets and cries of "pigs" brought about a savage response from Daley's police, who shared their mayor's contempt for the protesters.

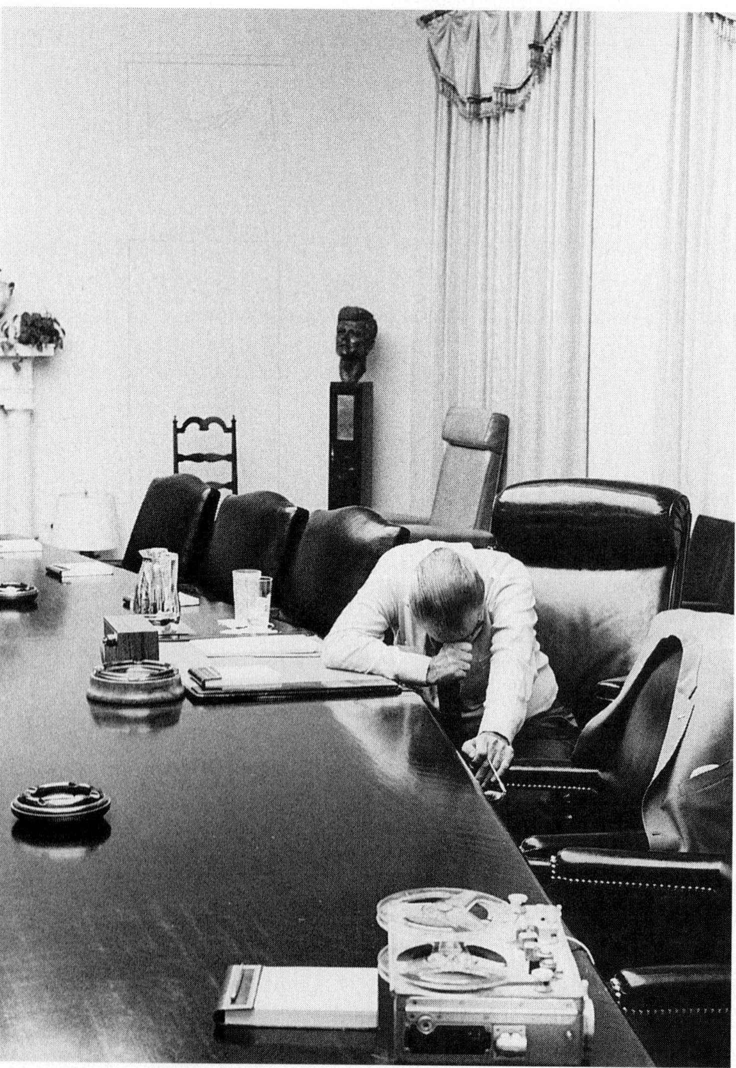

President Johnson, alone in the Cabinet room, rests his head on his hand as he listens to a tape from his son-in-law Marine Captain Charles Robb recounting his combat experiences in Vietnam. Johnson stunned the nation with his announcement on March 31, 1968, that he would not seek reelection. Poor results in the March primaries and public opinion polls indicated that support for LBJ was eroding. ❖

The bitter fumes of tear gas hung in the streets for days afterward; the battered heads and bodies of demonstrators and innocent bystanders alike flooded the city's hospital emergency rooms. What an official investigation later termed a "police riot" marred Humphrey's nomination and made a sad mockery of his call for "the politics of joy." The Democratic party itself had become a victim of the Vietnam War.

The Republican Resurgence

The primary beneficiary of the Democratic debacle was Richard Nixon. Written off as politically dead after his unsuccessful race for governor of California in 1962, Nixon had slowly rebuilt his place within the party. Positioning himself squarely in the middle, he quickly became the front-runner for the Republican nomination. At the GOP convention in Miami Beach, Nixon won an easy first-ballot nomination and chose Maryland Governor Spiro Agnew as his running mate.

In the fall campaign, Nixon opened up a wide lead by avoiding controversy and reaping the benefit of discontent with the Vietnam War. He played the peace issue shrewdly, appearing to advocate an end to the conflict without ever taking a definite stand. Above all, he chose the role of reconciler for a nation torn by emotion, a leader who promised to bring a divided country together again.

Humphrey, in contrast, found himself hounded by antiwar demonstrators who heckled him constantly. He walked a tightrope, desperate for the continued support of Johnson but handicapped by LBJ's stubborn refusal to end all bombing of North Vietnam. His campaign gradually gained momentum, however, as he picked up support from union leaders and from blacks who remembered his strong stand on civil rights. When he broke with Johnson in late September by announcing that if elected, he would "stop the bombing of North Vietnam as an acceptable risk for peace," he began to close in on Nixon.

Unfortunately for Humphrey, a third-party candidate cut deeply into the usual Democratic majority. George Wallace had first gained attention as the racist governor of Alabama whose motto was "Segregation now, segregation tomorrow, segregation forever." His appeal was to blue-collar workers and white ethnics who believed that many of the gains made by blacks during the 1960s had come at their expense.

Running on the ticket of the American Independent party, Wallace was a close third in the September polls, but as the election neared, his following declined. Humphrey continued to gain, especially after Johnson agreed in late October to end all bombing of North Vietnam. By the first week in November, the outcome was too close for the experts to call.

Nixon won the election by just 500,000 votes—and with the smallest share of the popular vote of any winning candidate since 1916—but scored a clear-cut victory in the electoral college, sweeping a broad band of states from Virginia and the Carolinas through the Midwest to the Pacific. As expected, Humphrey did well in the urban Northeast, and Wallace made a strong showing in the Deep South.

Conclusion: The End of an Era

The election marked a repudiation of the politics of protest and the cultural insurgency of the mid-1960s. The combined popular vote for Nixon and Wallace, 56.5 percent of the electorate, signified that there was a "silent majority" that was fed up with violence and confrontation. A growing concern over psychedelic drugs, rock music, lack of decorum in dress and behavior, and sexual permissiveness offset the usual Democratic advantage on economic issues and led to the election of a Republican president. By voting for Nixon and Wallace, the American people were sending out a message: they wanted a return to traditional values and an end to the war in Vietnam.

CHRONOLOGY

1961	JFK establishes Peace Corps (March) ❖ U.S.-backed Bay of Pigs invasion crushed by Cubans (April)
1962	Astronaut John H. Glenn, Jr., becomes first American to orbit the earth (February) ❖ President Kennedy forces U.S. Steel to roll back price hike (April) ❖ Cuban missile crisis takes world to brink of nuclear war (October)
1963	United States, Great Britain, and USSR sign Limited Nuclear Test Ban Treaty (August) ❖ JFK assassinated; Lyndon B. Johnson sworn in as president (November)
1964	President Johnson declares war on poverty (January) ❖ Congress overwhelmingly passes Gulf of Tonkin Resolution (August) ❖ Johnson wins presidency in landslide (November)
1965	LBJ commits fifty thousand American troops to combat in Vietnam (July) ❖ Congress enacts Medicare and Medicaid (July)
1966	National Organization for Women (NOW) formed
1967	Israel wins Six Day War in Middle East (June) ❖ Riots in Detroit kill forty-three, injure two thousand, leave five thousand homeless (July)
1968	Vietcong launch Tet offensive (January) ❖ Johnson announces he will not seek reelection (March) ❖ Martin Luther King, Jr., assassinated in Memphis (April) ❖ Robert Kennedy assassinated in Los Angeles (June)

At the election of Richard Nixon, an era came to an end with the passing of two concepts that had guided American life since the 1930s. First, the liberal reform impulse, which reached its zenith with the Great Society legislation in 1965, had clearly run its course. Civil rights, Medicare, and federal aid to education would continue in place, but Nixon's triumph signaled a strong reaction against the growth of federal power. At the same time, the Vietnam fiasco spelled the end of activist foreign policy that had begun with American entry into World War II. Containment, so successful in protecting western Europe against the Soviet threat, had proved a disastrous failure when applied on a global scale. The last three decades of the twentieth century would witness a struggle to replace outmoded liberal internationalism with new policies at home and abroad.

KEY TERMS

flexible response, p. 579
Berlin Wall, p. 579
Bay of Pigs, p. 581
Cuban missile crisis, p. 581
New Frontier, p. 582
freedom ride, p. 584
March on Washington, p. 584
War on Poverty, p. 587
Great Society, p. 587
Medicare, p. 588
Voting Rights Act of 1965, p. 589
Gulf of Tonkin Resolution, p. 590
Students for a Democratic Society (SDS), p. 593
National Organization for Women (NOW), p. 597
Tet offensive, p. 598

RECOMMENDED READING

The best general account of the 1960s is Jim F. Heath, *Decade of Disillusionment* (1975), which stresses the continuity in policy between the Kennedy and Johnson administrations. Arthur M. Schlesinger, Jr., *A Thousand Days* (1965) is the classic history of the Kennedy administration; for a more balanced view, see Richard Reeves, *President Kennedy* (1993). The best study of Kennedy's foreign policy is Michael R. Beschloss, *The Crisis Years: Kennedy and*

Khrushchev, 1960–1963 (1991); for the Cuban missile crisis, consult Graham Allison and Philip Zelikow, *Essence of Decision,* 2nd ed. (1999).

Victor S. Navasky offers a critical view of Robert Kennedy as attorney general in *Kennedy Justice* (1971). The best overview of civil rights developments in the 1960s is Hugh Davis Graham, *The Civil Rights Era, 1960–1972* (1990).

Robert Dallek offers a balanced view of Johnson's presidential years in *Flawed Giant* (1998). The best one-volume biography of Lyndon Johnson is Irwin Unger and Debi Unger, *LBJ* (1999); John A. Andrew III provides a concise account of LBJ's domestic program in *Lyndon Johnson and the Great Society* (1998). For the impact of the 1965 immigration legislation, see Hugh Davis Graham, *Collision Course* (2002). For LBJ's foreign policy, see H. W. Brands, *The Wages of Globalism* (1995). The best introduction to the Vietnam War is the balanced survey by George Herring, *America's Longest War,* 4th ed. (2002). For contrasting views of Johnson's responsibility for the Vietnam conflict, see Fredrik Logevall, *Choosing War* (1999), highly critical, and Lloyd Gardner, *Pay Any Price* (1995), more understanding.

The most comprehensive account of the student protests is Terry Anderson, *The Movement and the Sixties* (1995), but see also Todd Gitlin, *The Sixties* (1987), more sympathetic to the youthful protesters; W. J. Rorabaugh, *Berkeley at War* (1989); and Rhodri Jeffrey-Jones, *Peace Now!* (1999).

Garry Wills provides the most revealing portrait of Richard Nixon's character and prepresidential career in *Nixon Agonistes* (1970). The best account of the 1968 election is Lewis L. Gould, *1968: The Election That Changed America* (1993).

For a list of additional titles related to this chapter's topics, please see http://www.ablongman.com/divine.

Suggested Web Sites

The Avalon Project: The Cuban Missile Crisis

http://www.yale.edu/lawweb/avalon/diplomacy/forrel/cuba/cubamenu.htm

Part of the foreign relations series of the Avalon Project at Yale Law School, this site includes a collection of on-line documents pertaining to the Cuban Missile Crisis and its aftermath.

John Fitzgerald Kennedy

http://www.ipl.org/ref/POTUS/jfkennedy.html

This site contains basic factual data about Kennedy's election and presidency, speeches, and on-line biographies.

The Kennedy Assassination

http://mcadams.posc.mu.edu/home.htm

This well-organized site has images, essays, and photos on the assassination.

Lyndon B. Johnson

http://www.ipl.org/ref/POTUS/lbjohnson.html

This page contains basic factual data about his election and presidency, speeches, and on-line biographies.

Lyndon B. Johnson Library and Museum

http://www.lbjlib.utexas.edu/

This presidential library contains images and on-line exhibits.

National Aeronautics and Space Administration

http://www.hq.nasa.gov/office/pao/History/histsub.htm

NASA's Office of Policy and Plans History Office maintains this site about NASA and its history.

Investigating the Vietnam War

http://www.spartacus.schoolnet.co.uk/vietintro.htm

This site from Spartacus Educational Publishing, U.K., has an excellent list of annotated links to the best Vietnam-related sites.

Vietnam War Bibliography

http://hubcap.clemson.edu/~eemoise/bibliography.html

Edwin Moise of Clemson University maintains this extensive bibliography of print works about Vietnam and the Vietnam War.

Vietnam On-line

http://www.pbs.org/wgbh/pages/amex/vietnam/index.html

From PBS and the American Experience, this site contains a detailed, interactive timeline of the war, interpretive essays, and autobiographical reflections.

My Lai Courts Martial (1970)

http://www.law.umkc.edu/faculty/projects/ftrials/mylai/mylai.htm

This site contains images, chronology, and court and official documents maintained by Dr. Doug Linder at University of Missouri—Kansas City Law School.

JFK Assassination Web Page

http://ourworld.compuserve.com/homepages/MGriffith_2/jfk.htm

This is a personal page but a very thorough one that is a guide to the best Internet resources for the assassination.

Martin Luther King, Jr., Papers Project

http://www.stanford.edu/group/King/

This site at Stanford University has links and selected digital documents by and concerning Martin Luther King, Jr.

National Civil Rights Museum

http://www.mecca.org/~crights/nc2.html

This site provides a virtual tour of the museum with its interpretive exhibits.

The Digger Archives

http://www.diggers.org/

This site provides information about The San Francisco Diggers who became one of the legendary groups in the Haight-Ashbury district during the years 1966 to 1968.

Free Speech Movement: Student Protest—U.C. Berkeley, 1964–65

http://www.lib.berkeley.edu/BANC/FSM/

The Bancroft Library at U.C.-Berkeley houses this exhibit with oral histories, a chronology, and documents.

Voices of the Civil Rights Era

http://www.webcorp.com/civilrights/index.htm

Webcorp provides audio clips from prominent figures of the Civil Rights era including Martin Luther King, Jr., and Malcolm X.

Martin Luther King, Jr.

http://www.seattletimes.com/mlk/

This site from the *Seattle Times* has several articles about King and the civil rights movement.

The Sixties Project

http://lists.village.virginia.edu/sixties/

This University of Virginia site has extensive exhibits, documents, and personal narratives from the 1960s.

Civil Rights Oral History Bibliography

http://www-dept.usm.edu/~mcrohb/

This University of Southern Mississippi site includes complete transcripts of the selected oral resources.

1969 Woodstock Festival and Concert

http://www.woodstock69.com/index.htm

This site provides pictures and lists of songs from the famous rock festival.

United States v. *Cecil Price et al.* (The "Mississippi Burning" Trial) 1967

http://www.law.umkc.edu/faculty/projects/ftrials/price&bowers/price&bowers.htm

This site contains images, chronology, and court and official documents maintained by Dr. Doug Linder at University of Missouri-Kansas City Law School.

UNINTENDED CONSEQUENCES

The Second Great Migration

"This is not a revolutionary bill," President Lyndon Johnson declared when he signed the Immigration Act of 1965 into law. Rarely has a president been so wrong. The changes Congress made in American immigration policy led a second great migration, larger and even more diverse than the first, which took place in the thirty years before World War I. By the end of the century, the second great wave of immigration had profoundly altered the ethnic composition of the United States.

The political leaders responsible for changing immigration policy in the 1960s had very different intentions. Focused on removing long-standing inequities in the law, they sought to replace the national origins system, adopted in the 1920s, which favored people from western Europe, with a new set of criteria designed to bring in newcomers with economic skills the United States needed and to reunite broken families. Above all, the architects of change wanted to end the unfair race-based quotas for people of Asian extraction and the evident discrimination against applicants from eastern and southern Europe. Attorney General Robert Kennedy called the national origins quotas "a standing affront to many Americans and to many countries." At the height of the Cold War, realism seemed to join with idealism in the effort to end a discriminatory immigration policy that smacked of racism.

The legislative process, however, often works in mysterious ways. The bill passed by Congress did end the national origins system, as its framers desired, but reversed the new priorities, giving highest preference to family reunification and less emphasis to job skills and asylum for refugees. As enacted and later amended, the 1965 Immigration Act set an annual limit of 170,000 for immigrants from Europe, Asia, and Africa, and 120,000 for those from Western Hemisphere countries, with a ceiling of 20,000 for immigrants from any one country. The total of 290,000, would be only slightly higher than the number admitted under the old system.

By the end of the 1970s, it was clear that the family preferences, which made up nearly 70 percent of the allotted visas, were allowing recent immigrants to bring in large numbers of relatives, instead of reuniting immigrants who had been in the United States for years with their families. The figure, "The Second Great Migration: A Theoretical Example," shows how one postgraduate student with a nonimmigrant visa, by adroit use of the available family preferences, could easily gain the admission of eighteen relatives in just a decade. Moreover, once resident aliens became citizens, they could bring in "immediate relatives"—spouses, children under 21, and parents—without regard to visa limits.

Two significant developments flowed directly from the Great Society's immigration policy. First, annual immigration increased steadily from an average of 250,000 in the 1950s to at least 1 million by the end of the century. In 1990, in an effort to place "immediate relatives" under an effective limit, Congress approved an overall ceiling of just under 700,000 immigrants a year, except for refugees. But other legislation allowing undocumented workers to gain legal status, as well as an estimated 300,000 illegal immigrants a year, swelled the actual total to more than 1 million. In effect, the 1965 legislation had led to a quadrupling of newcomers entering the United States every year.

The other unintended consequence of the 1965 Immigration Act was a rapid shift in the source of the new immigrants. Europe, the traditional place of origin for immigrants, fell from providing 70 percent of newcomers in the 1950s, to just 16 percent by the mid-1990s. Latin American immigrants rose from 25 to 49 percent of the total, while Asia supplied 32 percent by the end of the century, up from just 6 percent in the 1950s. This change in the countries of origin was as striking as the similar shift from western to eastern Europe in the first great migration. Where once Germany, Great Britain, and Ireland had furnished the majority of newcomers, by 1989 it was Mexico, the Philippines, and Vietnam that led the list, with no European country among the top ten.

The result was a growing diversity that promised to make the United States a truly multiethnic society in the twenty-first century. By the 1990s, the number of foreign-born Americans had more than doubled to 10 percent of the population. Hispanic Americans were the most rapidly growing segment, replacing African Americans as the nation's largest minority in 2001. Asian Americans, although much smaller in number, grew at a fast pace and had greater success economically than any other ethnic group.

THE SECOND GREAT MIGRATION: A THEORETICAL EXAMPLE

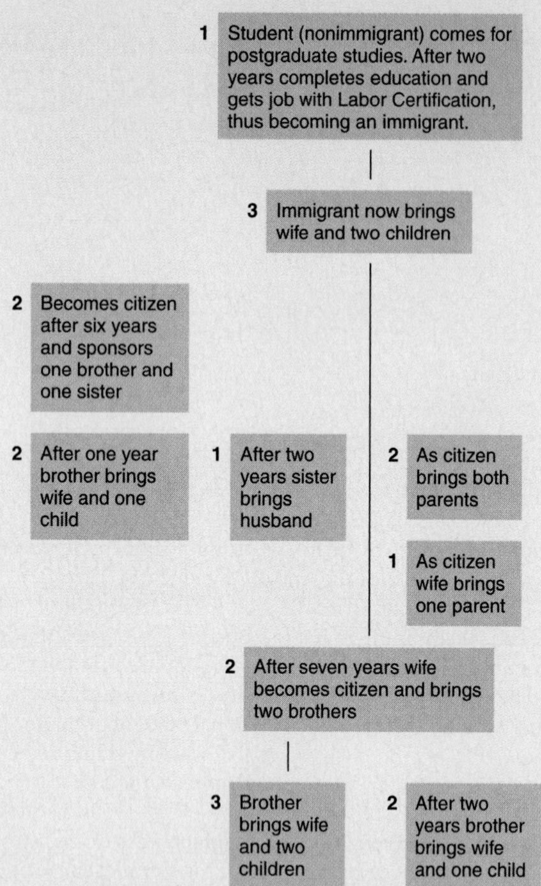
1 Student (nonimmigrant) comes for postgraduate studies. After two years completes education and gets job with Labor Certification, thus becoming an immigrant.
3 Immigrant now brings wife and two children
2 Becomes citizen after six years and sponsors one brother and one sister
2 After one year brother brings wife and one child
1 After two years sister brings husband
2 As citizen brings both parents
1 As citizen wife brings one parent
2 After seven years wife becomes citizen and brings two brothers
3 Brother brings wife and two children
2 After two years brother brings wife and one child

Note: Total is nineteen after original student arrived for postgraduate education ten years earlier. Adapted from David M. Reimer, *Still the Golden Door,* 2d ed. (New York: Columbia University Press, 1992), p. 95.

REGION OF BIRTH OF FOREIGN BORN, 2000

Region	Number
Latin America	16,086,974
Asia	8,226,254
Europe	4,915,557
Africa	881,300
North America	829,442
Australia, New Zealand, and Pacific Islands	168,046

Source: Associated Press, June 9, 2002.

By the end of the century it was clear that the Immigration Act of 1965 had led to a major shift in the racial and ethnic composition of the United States. The effort to erase past discriminatory and race-based quotas resulted in an unexpected flow of people from Asia and Latin America that ensured the end of traditional European dominance. By 2050, according to Census Bureau projections, the country will be almost evenly divided between non-Hispanic whites and minorities. Social harmony in the twenty-first century will depend on whether the melting pot continues to melt, blending ethnic groups into mainstream America, or whether these groups, as their numbers grow, will shape the society into one that political leaders of the 1960s such as Lyndon Johnson and Robert Kennedy could never have foreseen.

Chapter 31

A Crisis in Confidence, 1969–1980

The Watergate Break-In

On the evening of June 17, 1972, five men broke into the headquarters of the Democratic National Committee in the Watergate complex in Washington, D.C. They wore surgical gloves and carried cans of Mace, lock-picking tools, camera equipment, and telephone bugging devices. Busy filming documents and checking on electronic bugs planted two weeks before, the burglars were caught by police after an alert security guard discovered they had carelessly left doors taped open.

The leader of the group, James McCord, a former CIA employee, was working for CREEP (the Committee to Re-Elect the President), and police quickly found the telephone number of White House aide E. Howard Hunt in his address book. Despite the obvious tie to the Nixon administration, presidential press secretary Ron Ziegler denied any White House involvement in the Watergate break-in, dismissing it as "a third-rate burglary attempt."

In fact, the criminal act was a direct outgrowth of the paranoia that characterized the Nixon presidency. Aware that he had won office by a very narrow margin in 1968, Nixon was determined to do everything possible to ensure his reelection in 1972. Concerned about leaks from the White House, he authorized wiretaps on the telephones of both reporters and key aides. After the *New York Times* and the *Washington Post* began publishing the **Pentagon Papers,** a compilation of secret documents on the Vietnam War, Nixon took drastic measures to plug any further leaks of secret documents. His aides created a self-styled "plumbers" unit within the White House directed by G. Gordon Liddy, a former FBI agent, and E. Howard Hunt, a veteran of the CIA. Charged with preserving secrecy and discrediting those who spoke to the press, Hunt and Liddy set out to embarrass Daniel Ellsberg, the Defense Department official who had leaked the Pentagon Papers, going so far as to break into his psychiatrist's office in search of damning information.

Convinced that people throughout society were working for his defeat in 1972, Nixon ordered aides John Dean and Charles Colson to prepare an "enemies list." They eventually compiled a roster of several hundred prominent citizens, ranging from movie stars such as Jane Fonda and Paul Newman to journalists and educators such as columnist James Reston and Kingman Brewster, president of Yale University, as well as twelve African American congressmen. The plan was to direct the IRS and other government agencies to target these "enemies" for audits and investigations, or, as John Dean put it, to use "the available federal machinery to screw our political enemies." Operating under a siege mentality, the Nixon White House was prepared to do anything necessary to defeat its opponents, who were thought to include the media, the intellectual community, and virtually all minority groups.

Outline

- Nixon in Power
- The Crisis of Democracy
- Energy and the Economy
- Private Lives—Public Issues
- Politics After Watergate
- From Détente to Renewed Cold War
- Conclusion: A Failed Presidency

Pentagon Papers A secret Defense Department study of the Vietnam War. Publication of the papers in 1971 revealed how civilian and military leaders had misled the American people about the nation's role in Vietnam.

The president's greatest concern was guaranteeing his reelection. He appointed Attorney General John Mitchell to head CREEP and gave him access to extensive funds and the use of men like Liddy and Hunt. Specialists in political "dirty tricks" harassed Democratic contenders, while Liddy developed an elaborate plan to disrupt the Democratic convention in Miami and to spy on party activities. The bungled Watergate break-in, directed by Liddy and Hunt, was thus the culmination of abuses of power that grew directly out of Nixon's personal insecurity.

The president probably did not have any advance knowledge of the break-in, but he committed a criminal act by authorizing a far-reaching cover-up. On June 23, he ordered his aides to instruct the FBI to defer to the CIA in regard to the Watergate burglary, invoking nonexistent national security concerns to block an investigation that might expose White House involvement. Determined to contain the damage, Nixon told John Mitchell, "I want you to stonewall it, let them plead the Fifth Amendment, cover up, or anything else." Putting John Dean in charge, Nixon successfully covered up the Watergate affair while winning reelection in 1972, only to have the whole matter later unravel and drive him from office.

WATERGATE WAS BUT THE FIRST of a series of shocks in the 1970s that shook the confidence of the American people. War in the Middle East led to a sharp increase in the price of oil and waves of inflation that devastated the economy. Revolutions in Nicaragua and Iran added to the dilemmas confronting the nation's leaders. By the end of the decade, the American people were beginning to question the validity of traditional American values and institutions as they tried to cope with difficult challenges at home and abroad.

Nixon in Power

Before Watergate cast its long shadow over his presidency, Nixon dealt ably with a wide range of issues at home and abroad. While his domestic policies had only limited success, he proved both skillful and effective in the international arena, achieving a significant, though temporary, reduction in Cold War tensions.

The man who took office as the thirty-sixth president of the United States on January 26, 1969, seemed to be a new Nixon. Gone was the fiery rhetoric and the penchant for making enemies. In their place, observers found an air of moderation and restraint. He appeared to have his emotions under firm control. But beneath the surface, he remained bitter, hurt, and sensitive to criticism.

An innately shy man, Nixon hoped to enjoy the power of the presidency in splendid solitude. He assembled a powerful White House staff whose main task was to isolate him from Congress, the press, and even his own cabinet. Loyal subordinates such as H. R. Haldeman and John Ehrlichman took charge of domestic issues, often making decisions without even consulting Nixon. Foreign policy was Nixon's great passion, and here he relied heavily on Henry Kissinger, his national security adviser, to formulate policy, leaving Secretary of State William Rogers to keep the State Department bureaucrats busy with minor details.

The Nixon White House soon could be likened to a fortress under siege. Distrusting everyone, Nixon sought to preside without help from either Congress or his cabinet. In his quest for privacy, Nixon cut himself off from the nation and thus sowed the seeds of his downfall.

Reshaping the Great Society

Beginning his first term on a hopeful note, Nixon promised the nation peace and respite from the chaos of the 1960s. Rejecting the divisions that had split Americans asunder, he pledged in his inaugural address to "bring us together."

Nixon's moderation indicated a return to the politics of accommodation that had characterized the Eisenhower era. Faced with a Democratic Congress, Nixon, like Ike, appeared ready to accept the main outlines of the welfare state. Instead of any massive overthrow of the Great Society, he focused on making the federal bureaucracy function more efficiently.

Nixon was successful with his efforts to shift responsibility for social problems from Washington to state and local authorities. He developed the concept of revenue sharing, by which federal funds would be dispersed to state, county, and city agencies to meet local needs. In 1972, Congress approved a measure to share $30.1 billion with local governments over a five-year period. An accompanying ceiling of $2.5 billion a year on federal welfare payments, however, meant that much of the revenue-sharing payments had to be allocated by cities and states to programs previously paid for by the federal government.

In the area of civil rights, Nixon made a shrewd political move. Action by Congress and the outgoing Johnson administration had ensured that massive desegregation of southern schools would finally begin just as Nixon took office. Nixon and his attorney general, John Mitchell, decided to shift the responsibility for the process to the courts. When the courts ordered action, the Nixon administration complied. But in the minds of southern white voters, it was the hated Supreme Court, not Richard Nixon, who had forced them to integrate their schools.

Nixon used similar tactics in his attempt to reshape the Supreme Court along more conservative lines. His appointment of Warren Burger, an experienced federal judge with moderate views, to replace the retiring Earl Warren as chief justice, met with little objection. But liberal Democrats succeeded in blocking the nomination first of Clement Haynesworth of South Carolina and then of G. Harrold Carswell of Florida. Nixon denounced the liberals for insulting "millions of Americans who live in the South." Once again, Nixon had used the Supreme Court to enhance his political appeal to Southerners.

Nixon finally filled the Court position with Harry Blackmun, a reputable conservative from Minnesota, who easily won confirmation. Subsequently, the president appointed Lewis Powell and William Rehnquist. Surprisingly, the Burger Court, despite its more conservative makeup, did not overturn the Warren Court's decisions. It continued to uphold the legality of desegregation, ruling in 1971 that busing was a necessary and proper way to achieve integrated schools.

The moderation of the Supreme Court and the legislative record of the Nixon administration demonstrated that the nation was not yet ready to abandon the reforms adopted in the 1960s. The pace of change slowed down in areas such as civil rights and welfare, but the commitment to social justice remained.

Nixonomics

The economy posed a more severe test for Richard Nixon. He inherited a rising inflation rate, the product of LBJ's unsuccessful attempt to wage the Vietnam War without raising taxes. Strongly opposed to the idea of federal controls, Nixon opted for a reduction in government spending while encouraging the Federal Reserve Board to curtail the money supply, forcing up interest rates and slowing the rate of business expansion.

The result was disastrous. Inflation continued, reaching nearly 6 percent by the end of 1970, the highest rate since the Korean War. At the same time, the economy underwent its first major recession since 1958. The stock market tumbled, the sharpest drop in thirty years; unemployment rose; business failures jumped alarmingly. Democrats quickly coined a new word, ***Nixonomics,*** to describe the disaster.

Nixonomics A word used by Democrats critical of President Nixon's economic policies, in particular the inability to curb inflation at a time of high unemployment and recession.

Conditions seemed to worsen in 1971. Inflation continued unabated, and the nation's balance of trade became negative as imports exceeded exports by a substantial margin. In mid-August, Nixon acted suddenly and boldly to halt the economic

Economic problems tested President Nixon soon after he took office in 1969. The cost of living rose as the government attempted to pay for the Vietnam War and Great Society programs with massive deficit spending. At the same time, declines in manufacturing and industrialization contributed to rising unemployment. ❖

decline. Abandoning his earlier resistance to controls, he announced a ninety-day freeze on wages and prices, to be followed by federally imposed guidelines in both areas. He also ordered a devaluation of the dollar, which, along with a 10 percent surtax on all imports, led to a greatly improved balance of trade. The sudden Nixon economic reversal quickly ended the recession.

Building a Republican Majority

"The Great Nixon Turnaround," as historian Lloyd Gardner termed it, came too late to help the Republicans in the 1970 congressional elections. From the time he took office in 1969, Nixon was obsessed with the fact that he had received only 43 percent of the popular vote. The Republicans were still a minority party, and to be re-elected in 1972, Nixon would need to win over southern whites and blue-collar workers who had followed George Wallace out of the Democratic party.

Attorney General John Mitchell devised a southern strategy to help achieve a Republican majority by 1972. The administration's well-publicized objection to school desegregation in the South and the attempt to put Haynesworth and Carswell on the Court were part of this design. Advisers urged the Nixon administration to direct its appeal to "middle Americans"—southern whites, Catholic ethnic groups, blue-collar workers, and the new suburbanites of the South and West.

Nixon unleashed his vice president, Spiro Agnew, in an attempt to exploit the social issue in the 1970 election. Blaming all social concerns from sexual permissiveness to crime in the streets on Democratic liberals and their allies in the media, Agnew delivered a series of scathing speeches. He denounced intellectuals as "an effete corps of impudent snobs" and damned the press as "nattering nabobs of negativism." Despite howls of protest, Agnew proved to be an effective political weapon.

The Democrats decided to change their tactics. Democratic candidates were careful to stress economic issues, blaming the Republicans for both inflation and recession. On social issues, they joined the chorus against crime, pornography, and drugs.

The outcome was a standoff. Agnew's attacks helped the GOP limit the usual off-year losses in the House to nine seats, and the Republicans actually gained two votes in the Senate. But the Democrats did well in state elections and proved once again that economic issues were crucial in American politics. Nixon and the Republicans still did not command a national majority.

In Search of Détente

Nixon gave foreign policy top priority, and he proved surprisingly adept at it. In Kissinger, he had a White House specialist who had devoted his life to the study of diplomacy. Nixon and Kissinger approached foreign policy from a similar realistic perspective. "They recognized a cold and logical world without fated allies or enemies—only interested parties," commented one close observer. Instead of viewing the Cold War as an ideological struggle for survival with communism, they saw it as a traditional great-power rivalry, one to be managed and controlled rather than won.

Kissinger and Nixon had a grand design. Realizing that recent events, especially the Vietnam War and the rapid Soviet arms buildup of the 1960s, had eroded

America's position of primacy in the world, they planned a strategic retreat. There were five major centers of power by the 1970s—the United States, the Soviet Union, China, Japan, and the NATO countries of western Europe. The USSR had great military strength, but its economy was weak and it had a dangerous rival in China. Kissinger planned to use American trade—notably grain and high technology—to induce Soviet cooperation while at the same time improving U.S. relations with China. With the Soviets neutralized, the United States would then focus on its economic rivalry with Japan and the countries of western Europe.

Nixon and Kissinger shrewdly played the China card as their first step toward achieving **détente**—a relaxation of tension—with the Soviet Union. After preliminary negotiations, Nixon traveled to China in February 1972. During his well-publicized tour, he met with the Communist leaders and ended more than two decades of Sino-American hostility. The problem of Formosa (Taiwan) prevented full-scale diplomatic relations, but Nixon agreed to establish an American liaison mission in Peking as a first step toward ultimate recognition.

détente President Nixon and Henry Kissinger pursued a policy of détente, a French word meaning a relaxation of tension, with the Soviet Union as a way to lessen the possibility of nuclear war in the 1970s.

The Soviets, who viewed China as a dangerous adversary, responded by agreeing to negotiate an arms control pact with the United States. The **Strategic Arms Limitation Talks (SALT)** had been under way since 1969. During a visit to Moscow in May 1972, Nixon signed two vital documents with Soviet leader Leonid Brezhnev. The first limited the two superpowers to two hundred antiballistic missiles (ABMs) apiece; the second froze the number of offensive ballistic missiles for a five-year period.

Strategic Arms Limitation Talks (SALT) In 1972, the United States and the Soviet Union culminated four years of Strategic Arms Limitation Talks by signing a treaty limiting the deployment of antiballistic missiles (ABM) and an agreement to freeze the number of offensive missiles for five years.

The SALT I agreements were most important as a symbolic first step toward control of the nuclear arms race. They signified that the United States and Russia were trying to achieve a settlement of their differences by peaceful means.

Ending the Vietnam War

Vietnam remained the one foreign policy challenge that Nixon could not meet. He had a three-part plan to end the conflict: renewed bombing, a hard line in negotiations with Hanoi, and the gradual withdrawal of American troops. The last tactic, known as Vietnamization, proved the most successful. As South Vietnamese troops began to take over the major combat role, the number of American soldiers in Vietnam dropped from 543,000 in 1968 to 29,000 by 1972, and domestic opposition to the war declined.

Renewed bombing proved the most controversial part of the plan. As early as the spring of 1969, Nixon secretly ordered raids on Communist supply lines in neutral Cambodia. Then in April 1970, he ordered both air and ground strikes into Cambodia. These relieved pressure on hard-pressed South Vietnamese forces but caused a massive outburst of antiwar protests at home. Tragedy struck at Kent State University in Ohio in early May. After rioters had fire-bombed an army training building, the governor sent in National Guard troops, who were taunted by irate students. The Guardsmen opened fire, killing four students and wounding eleven more. A week later, two black students were killed at Jackson State College in Mississippi. Soon there were riots and protests on more than four hundred campuses across the country.

Nixon had little sympathy for the demonstrators, describing them as "bums" intent on "blowing up the campuses." The silent majority to whom he appealed seemed to agree. An Honor America Day program, held in Washington, D.C., on July 4 attracted 250,000 people who heard Billy Graham and Bob Hope endorse the president's policies. Nixon's Cambodian invasion did little to shorten the Vietnam War, but the public reaction stiffened his resolve not to surrender.

The third tactic, negotiation with Hanoi, finally proved successful. Beginning in the summer of 1969, Kissinger held a series of secret meetings with North Vietnam's foreign minister, Le Duc Tho. By the fall of 1972, the two sides were near

The renewed bombing of North Vietnam and invasion of Cambodia ordered by Nixon in hopes of ending the conflict precipitated student protests at many campuses. At Kent State University in Ohio, demonstrators and bystanders were shot by National Guardsmen. ❖

agreement, but South Vietnamese objections blocked a settlement before the 1972 elections. When the North Vietnamese tried to make last-minute changes, Nixon ordered a series of savage B-52 raids on Hanoi that finally led to the signing of a truce on January 27, 1973. In return for the release of all American prisoners of war, the United States agreed to remove troops from South Vietnam in sixty days. The political clauses allowed the North Vietnamese to keep troops in the South, thus virtually guaranteeing future control over all of Vietnam by the Communists.

The agreement was, in fact, a disguised surrender, but finally the American combat role in Vietnam was over, after eight years of fighting, more than 57,000 Americans killed, and more than $150 billion expended. The war ranks as America's second most expensive and fourth deadliest armed conflict. Yet even as the fighting wound down, the nation was already deeply enmeshed in another crisis, what Gerald R. Ford termed "the long national nightmare" of Watergate.

The Crisis of Democracy

The June 1, 1972, break-in at the Democratic National Committee offices came back to haunt Richard Nixon in 1973 and 1974. His determination to stonewall the press on any White House involvement in the burglary—including instructions to his aides to lie under oath—proved successful in the short run, but eventually the cover-up led to his downfall.

The Election of 1972

The irony of the Watergate break-in was that by the time it occurred, Nixon's election was assured. Aided by Republican dirty tricks, the Democrats destroyed themselves. First Edmund Muskie, the front-runner, replying in the New Hampshire primary to a letter accusing him of prejudice against New Englanders of French Canadian descent, lost his composure—and his following. Then an assassin shot and seriously wounded George Wallace. Paralyzed, Wallace was forced to drop out of the race, leaving Nixon with a complete monopoly over the political right.

Senator George McGovern of South Dakota emerged with the Democratic nomination. He ran on a platform that advocated a negotiated settlement in Vietnam, the right to abortion, and tolerance of diverse lifestyles. The platform was perceived as "antiestablishment" by many middle-class Americans and greatly strengthened Nixon's appeal.

Nixon shrewdly let McGovern's apparent extremism and New Left support become the main issue in the campaign, rather than the president's own record in office. Nixon's chances were further strengthened by the recent improvement in the economy and his foreign policy triumphs with China and the Soviet Union.

The result was a stunning victory for Nixon. He won a popular landslide with 60.8 percent of the vote—second only to LBJ'S record in 1964—and an even more decisive sweep of the electoral college. The voting patterns did suggest the beginning of a major political realignment, as only blacks, Jews, and low-income voters continued to vote overwhelmingly Democratic. The GOP made significant gains in the South and West and showed the emerging strength of the Sunbelt.

The Watergate Scandal

Only Richard Nixon knew how fragile his victory was in 1972. He was deeply implicated in the attempt to cover up the involvement of White House aides in the original burglary. On June 23, only six days after the crime, he ordered the CIA to keep the FBI off the case, on the specious grounds that it involved national security. And he urged his aides to lie under oath if necessary.

In the short run, the cover-up, directed by White House counsel John Dean, worked. Hunt and Liddy were convicted for their roles in the Watergate break-in, but they carefully avoided implicating either CREEP or Nixon's inner circle of advisers.

The first thread unraveled when federal judge John Sirica sentenced the burglars to long jail terms. James McCord was the first to crack, informing Sirica that he had received money from the White House and had been promised a future pardon in return for his silence. By April 1973, Nixon was forced to fire John Dean, who refused to become the scapegoat for the cover-up, and to allow Haldeman and Ehrlichman, who were deeply implicated, to resign. The Senate then appointed a special committee to investigate the **Watergate scandal.** In a week of dramatic testimony, Dean revealed Nixon's personal involvement in the cover-up. Still Nixon hoped to weather the storm, since it was basically the word of the president of the United States against Dean's.

Watergate scandal A break-in at the Democratic National Committee offices in the Watergate complex in Washington was carried out under the direction of White House employees. Disclosure of the White House involvement in the break-in and subsequent cover-up forced President Nixon to resign in 1974 to avoid impeachment.

The existence of tapes of conversations in the Oval Office, recorded regularly since 1970, finally brought Nixon down. At first, the president tried to invoke executive privilege to withhold the tapes. But his tactics merely delayed action; they did not end the matter. The Supreme Court ruled unanimously in June 1974 that the tapes had to be turned over to Judge Sirica.

By that time, the House Judiciary Committee, acting on evidence uncovered by the Senate committee, voted three articles of impeachment, charging Nixon with obstruction of justice, abuse of power, and contempt of Congress. Facing the release of tapes that directly implicated him in the cover-up, Nixon finally chose to resign on August 9, 1974.

Nixon's resignation proved to be the climax of the Watergate scandal. The entire episode revealed both the weaknesses and strengths of the American political system. Most regrettable was the abuse of presidential authority, a reflection of both the growing power of the modern presidency and the fatal flaws in Richard Nixon's character. Unlike such previous executive branch scandals as the Whiskey Ring and Teapot Dome, Watergate involved a lust for power rather than for money.

But Watergate also demonstrated the vitality of a democratic society. The press showed how investigative reporting could unlock even the most closely guarded executive secrets. Judge Sirica proved that an independent judiciary was still the best bulwark for individual freedom. And Congress rose to the occasion, both by carrying out a successful investigation of executive misconduct and by following a scrupulous and nonpartisan impeachment process that left Nixon with no chance to escape his ultimate fate.

The nation survived the shock of Watergate with its institutions intact. Congress, in decline since Johnson's administration, was rejuvenated, with its members now intent on expanding congressional authority into all areas of American life.

Energy and the Economy

In the midst of Watergate, the outbreak of war in the Middle East threatened a vital national interest—the supply and price of the fuel on which the American way of life was based. In the course of the 1970s, the resulting energy crisis helped touch off an inflationary impulse that had a profound impact on the national economy.

The October War

On October 6, 1973, Egypt and Syria launched a surprise attack on Israel. The fighting caught American leaders completely off guard. After recovering from the initial shock, President Nixon and Henry Kissinger expected Israel to repel the Arab invaders and display the same military dominance it had used to win the Six-Day War in 1967. In that conflict, Israel had devastated its Arab neighbors, taking possession of the Golan Heights from Syria, the Sinai peninsula from Egypt, and Jerusalem and the West Bank from Jordan. Instead of increasing Israel's security, however, these conquests had added to Middle East tensions. They unified the Arab countries, who now called for the return of their lands.

Henry Kissinger used the October War as an opportunity to shift American policy from its traditional pro-Israeli position to the more neutral stance of honest broker between Israel and its Arab neighbors. At first, Nixon and Kissinger had to approve a massive resupply in mid-October to help Israel stem the Egyptian and Syrian offensives. But when the Israelis quickly routed their opponents, the United States intervened diplomatically to prevent a victory for Israel that would preclude American mediation. The fighting finally ended in late October with neither side gaining a complete victory.

Organization of Petroleum Exporting Countries (OPEC) A cartel of oil-exporting nations. In late 1973, OPEC took advantage of the October War and an oil embargo by its Arab members to quadruple the price of oil. This huge increase had a devastating impact on the American economy.

Kissinger's apparent diplomatic triumph, however, was offset by an unforeseen consequence of the October War. On October 17, the Arab members of the **Organization of Petroleum Exporting Countries (OPEC)** announced a 5 percent cut in oil production, with additional cuts of 5 percent each month until Israel gave up the lands it had seized in 1967. President Nixon announced a $2.2 billion aid package for Israel on October 19, and the next day, Saudi Arabia cut off oil shipments to the United States.

The Arab oil embargo had a disastrous impact on the American economy. First, it produced a worldwide shortage of oil. Arab producers cut production by 25 percent from the September 1973 level, leading to a curtailment of 10 percent in the world supply. For the United States, which imported one-third of its daily consumption, this meant a loss of nearly 2 million barrels a day. Long lines formed at service stations as motorists kept filling their tanks in fear of running out of gas.

A dramatic increase in oil prices proved to be a far more significant result of the embargo. After the Arab embargo began, OPEC raised crude oil prices fourfold. In the United States, gasoline prices at the pumps nearly doubled in a few weeks' time, and the cost of home heating fuel rose even more sharply.

President Nixon responded with a series of temporary measures, including pleas to turn down thermostats in homes and offices, close service stations on weekends to curb pleasure driving, and reduce automobile speed limits to 50 miles per hour. When the Arab oil embargo ended in March, after Kissinger negotiated an

Israeli pullback in the Sinai, the American public relaxed. Gasoline once again became plentiful, thermostats were raised, and people resumed their love affair with the automobile.

The energy crisis, however, did not end with the lifting of the embargo. The Arab action marked the beginning of a new era in American history. The United States, with only 6 percent of the world's population, had been using nearly 40 percent of the earth's energy supplies. A nation that based its way of life on abundance and expansion was forced to face up to the reality of limited resources and economic stagnation.

The Oil Shocks

Cheap energy propelled the amazing growth of the American economy after World War II. The gross national product had more than doubled between 1950 and 1973; the American people had based their way of life on gasoline prices that averaged about 35 cents a gallon. The huge gas-guzzling cars, the flight to the suburbs, the long drive to work each day, the detached houses heated by fuel oil and natural gas and cooled by central air-conditioning all assumed plentiful and inexpensive energy that everyone took for granted.

The first great oil shock of the 1970s came with the October War and the resulting Arab oil embargo. Global demand for oil, intensified by the explosive economic development of western Europe and Japan as well as the United States, had caught up with oil production.

The effect on the American economy was devastating. Gasoline prices jumped from 35 to 65 cents a gallon; the cost of manufacturing went up proportionately, and utility rates rose sharply as a result of the higher cost of fuel oil and natural gas. Suddenly the American people faced drastic and unexpected increases in such everyday expenses as driving to work and heating their homes.

The result was a sharp decline in consumer spending and the worst recession since World War II. The GNP dropped by 6 percent in 1974 and unemployment rose to over 9 percent, the highest level since the Great Depression of the 1930s. Detroit was hit the hardest. Reacting to the high cost of gasoline, Americans turned away from big cars with low gas mileage.

President Gerald R. Ford, who followed Richard Nixon into the White House, responded belatedly to the economic crisis by proposing a tax cut to stimulate consumer spending. Congress passed a $22.8 billion reduction in taxes in 1975. With this stimulus, the economy gradually recovered by 1976, but the resulting budget deficits helped keep inflation above 5 percent and prevented a return to full economic health.

Jimmy Carter, who succeeded Ford, had little more success in achieving a rapid rate of economic growth. Continued federal deficits and relatively high interest rates kept the economy sluggish throughout 1977 and 1978. Then in 1979, the outbreak of the Iranian Revolution and the overthrow of the shah touched off another oil shock. The members of the OPEC cartel took advantage of the situation to raise prices to $30 a barrel—a staggering $21-a-barrel increase over the next eighteen months. Gasoline prices climbed to more than $1 a gallon at American service stations, and an even greater wave of inflation than the 1973 increase occurred.

The American people panicked. Gas lines formed as automobile drivers started filling their tanks every day or two. The long lines frustrated American drivers; incidents of violence began to mount, and the public took out its fury on the Carter administration.

By the fall of 1979, world supply had caught up with demand, and the oil scare ended. But the price of gasoline remained above $1 a gallon, and the inflation rate began to reach double-digit levels again. The twin oil shocks of the 1970s had left the economy battered and had undermined the average American's faith in the future.

The Search for an Energy Policy

The oil shocks of 1973 and 1979 were but two symptoms of a much deeper energy crisis. Put simply, the United States was running out of the fossil fuels on which it had relied for its economic growth in the past. Domestic oil production peaked in 1970 and declined every year thereafter. Natural gas, another nonrenewable resource, would also exhaust its supply eventually. American political leaders had to devise a national policy to meet the temporary shortfalls of the 1970s and also the long-term energy problem inherent in past reliance on fossil fuels.

The success of the environmental movement in the late 1960s and early 1970s compounded the problem. Efforts to protect the environment and curtail pollution of the nation's air and water had led to significant legislative restrictions on American industry. Congress created the **Environmental Protection Agency (EPA)** in 1970 to monitor industry and passed a Clean Air Act that encouraged public utilities to shift from using coal, which polluted the atmosphere, to clean-burning fuel oil and natural gas to generate electricity.

Environmental Protection Agency (EPA) Congress created this agency in 1970 as part of a broader effort to protect the environment and curb the pollution of the nation's air and water.

The energy crunch pitted the environmentalists and advocates of economic growth in direct confrontation. Those who put ecology first lost out. In the mid-1970s, Congress authorized construction of an Alaskan pipeline over environmentalists' objections and ordered public utilities to resume burning coal to produce electricity. During the rest of the decade, the government gradually relaxed environmental regulations to permit strip-mining of coal and offshore oil drilling.

The nation's leaders had an even more difficult time devising a coherent and workable long-term national energy policy. The Republicans advocated removing price controls on oil and natural gas to give wildcatters the incentive to bring in new supplies of these fuels. Greater production of coal, expanded nuclear power plants, and new technology to explore the possibilities of synthetic fuels and solar energy were all parts of the Republican approach to the energy problem.

The Democrats, in contrast, stressed price controls and conservation. They wanted to continue an elaborate system of price controls instituted by Nixon in 1973, and they favored stand-by plans for gas rationing as a better way to allocate scarce supplies than relying on the marketplace.

The nation failed to adopt either the Republican or the Democratic energy plan; instead, Congress tried to muddle through with elements of both approaches. Thus President Ford, who favored expanded production, was able to win approval for building the Alaskan pipeline. President Carter placed a strong emphasis on reviving the lagging American coal industry. In late 1975, Congress extended the price controls on domestic oil for another forty months and, in its most significant step toward conservation, mandated annual increases in automobile gasoline mileage that forced Detroit to produce more fuel-efficient cars.

The overall outcome, however, was a patchwork that fell far short of a coherent national strategy for solving the energy problem. Oil imports actually increased by 50 percent between 1973 and 1979, rising from 6 million to 9 million barrels a day, an amount nearly half of the nation's daily petroleum usage.

❖ A Look at the Past ❖

Locking Gas Cap

The energy crisis of the 1970s brought rationing and long lines at gas stations. As gas became increasingly difficult to obtain and rose in expense, consumers took many measures to deal with their fuel problems. Some bought fuel-efficient Japanese cars. The market for protective devices such as this locking gas cap grew as reports circulated about siphoning gasoline out of cars. Before long, locking gas caps became standard on most cars. What do the reports and the caps suggest about the depth of consumer fears? Do you think the widespread use of locking caps reflected an enduring change in public confidence and willingness to trust fellow Americans?

The Great Inflation

The gravest consequence of the oil shocks was inflation. The startling increase in price levels in the 1970s stemmed from many causes. The Vietnam War, particularly President Johnson's early attempts to avoid a tax increase to pay for the fighting, created huge budget deficits. A worldwide shortage of food triggered a 20 percent rise in American food prices in 1973 alone. But above all else, it was the sixfold increase in petroleum prices, which raised the cost of every economic activity, that was the primary source of the great inflation of the 1970s.

The impact on consumers was staggering. The price of an automobile jumped 72 percent between 1973 and 1978, and the prices of houses and food increased just as rapidly. Corresponding wage increases merely kept most Americans even. For the first time since World War II, real wages did not increase in the 1970s, and in 1980, the real income of the average American family fell by 5.5 percent.

Curbing inflation proved to be beyond the power of the federal government. Neither Ford's nor Carter's efforts could abate the rise in inflation. Finally, in October 1979, the Federal Reserve Board began a sustained effort to halt inflation by mandating increased bank reserves to curtail the supply of money in circulation. But the new tight-money policy served only to heighten inflation in the short run by driving interest rates up to record levels. By the spring of 1980, the prime interest rate reached 20 percent.

The Shifting American Economy

Inflation and the oil shocks helped bring about significant changes in American business and industry in the 1970s. The most obvious result was the slowing of the rate of economic growth. More important, American industry began to lose its position of primacy in world markets. In all major industrial sectors except aerospace, U.S. corporations had declined between 1959 and 1976 in relation to Japanese and western European competitors.

The most serious losses came in the heavy industries where the United States had once led the world. New steel producers in western Europe, Japan, and the Third World, using more advanced technology and aided by government subsidies, were producing steel far more efficiently than their American counterparts. As a result, by the end of the 1970s, American firms were closing down their obsolete mills in the East and Midwest, idling thousands of workers.

Foreign competition did even more damage in the automobile industry. The oil shocks led to a consumer demand for small, efficient cars. German and Japanese automakers seized the opportunity to expand their once small volume of sales in the United States. By 1977, imported cars had captured 18.3 percent of the American market, with Japan leading the way. In response, Detroit spent $70 billion retooling to produce a new fleet of smaller, lighter, front-wheel-drive cars; but American manufacturers barely survived the foreign invasion.

In other areas, American corporations fared much better. Such multinationals as IBM and Pepsi-Cola continued to prosper all over the globe. The growth of high-technology industries proved to be the most profitable new trend of the 1970s. Computer companies and electronics firms grew at a rapid rate, especially after the development of the silicon chip, a small, wafer-thin microprocessor that could perform complex calculations almost instantly. The result was a geographic shift of American industry from the East and Midwest to the Sunbelt. At the same time, the decline of the steel and auto industries was leading to massive unemployment and economic stagnation in the northern industrial heartland.

The overall pattern was one of an economy in transition. The oil shocks had caused serious problems of inflation, slower economic growth, and rising unemployment rates. But American business still displayed the enterprise and the ability to develop new technologies that held the promise of continued economic vitality in the 1980s.

Private Lives—Public Issues

Sweeping changes in the private lives of the American people began in the 1970s and continued for the rest of the century. The traditional American family, with the husband as wage earner and the wife as homemaker, gave way to much more diverse living arrangements. The number of working women, including wives and mothers, increased sharply; the wage gap between the sexes narrowed, but women still lagged noticeably behind men in earnings. Then, in the years following 1970 came the emergence of an active gay rights movement as more and more homosexuals began to disclose their sexual identities and demand an end to discrimination.

The Changing American Family

The traditional nuclear family of the 1950s no longer prevailed in America by the end of the twentieth century. The number of married couple households with children dropped from 30 percent in the 1970s to 23.5 percent by 2000. The number of unmarried couples doubled in the 1990s, while adults living alone surpassed the number of married couples with children for the first time in American history.

The divorce rate, which doubled between the mid-1960s and the late 1970s, leveled off for the rest of the century. Nevertheless, half of all first marriages still ended in divorce. After a sharp fall in the 1970s, the birthrate climbed again as the baby boom generation began to mature. There was a marked increase in the number of births to women over age 30, as well as a very high proportion of children born to single mothers, who composed 7 percent of all households by 2000, a 25 percent increase since 1990. Conservatives, alarmed by the decline of the nuclear family, called for change. "We need to discourage people from living together outside of marriage," observed Bridget Maher of the Family Research Council, "and encourage them to have children within marriage."

For better or worse, the American family structure changed significantly in the last three decades of the twentieth century, with a large number of people either never marrying or postponing marriage until late in the childbearing period. The traditional family unit, with the working father and the mother rearing the children at home, rapidly declined. Most mothers worked outside the home, and many were the sole support for their children. The proportion of children living with only one parent doubled in twenty years. Women without partners headed more than one-third of all impoverished families, and children made up 40 percent of the nation's poor. Although politicians, especially Republicans, refer to family values during campaigns, the fact remains that the American family underwent great stress due to social changes in the last third of the twentieth century, and children have suffered disproportionately.

Gains and Setbacks for Women

American women experienced significant changes in their way of life and their place in society in the last quarter of the twentieth century. The prevailing theme concerned the increasing percentage of working women. There was a rapid movement of women into the labor force in the 1970s; six million more married women held jobs by the end of the decade as two incomes became increasingly necessary to keep up with inflation. The trend continued through the 1980s. Fully 61 percent of the nearly nineteen million new jobs created during the decade were filled by women; many of the new jobs, however, were entry-level or low-paying service positions.

Women scored some impressive breakthroughs. They began to enter corporation boardrooms, became presidents of major universities, and were admitted to West Point and Annapolis. Women entered blue-collar, professional, and small-business fields traditionally dominated by men. Reagan's appointment of Sandra Day O'Connor to the Supreme Court in 1981 marked a historic first; Clinton doubled the number of women on the Court with his selection of Ruth Bader Ginsburg.

Yet at the same time, women encountered a great deal of resistance. Most women continued to work in female-dominated fields—as nurses, secretaries, teachers, and waitresses. Those who entered such "male" areas as management and administration soon encountered the so-called glass ceiling, which kept them from advancing beyond mid-level executive status. In 1990, only 4.3 percent of corporate officers were women. Most in business worked at the middle and lower rungs of management with staff jobs in personnel and public relations, not key operational positions in sales and marketing that would lead to the boardroom; women held fewer than 3 percent of the top jobs in Fortune 500 companies. The economic boom of the 1990s, however, led to a steady increase in the number of women executives; in 1998, there was an increase of 514,000.

Even with these gains, however, by 2002 women's wages still averaged only 77.5 percent of men's earnings. A college education helped close the gap, but a woman with a degree made only $600 a year more on the average than a man with a high school diploma. Younger women did best; those between 16 and 24 earned almost 90 cents for every dollar paid to a male in the same age group. Older women, who often had no other source of support, fared poorly; those over the age of 50 earned only 64 percent as much as men their age. Feminists had once hoped to close the gender gap by the year 2000, but experts predicted women would not reach pay equity with men until 2018.

The most encouraging development for women came in business ownership. Often blocked by the glass ceiling and seeking flexible schedules, more and more women went into business for themselves. The number of female business owners increased 40 percent between 1987 and 1992, twice the national rate of business growth. A women's trade group estimated that in 1996, women owned almost eight million businesses, employing more than eighteen million workers—one out of four American workers. A speaker at the first National Women's Economic Summit in 1996 exaggerated only slightly in crediting her group with restoring prosperity, claiming that "the American economy has been revitalized in good measure because of the participation of and contributions of women business owners."

Beyond economic opportunity, the women's movement had two goals in recent years. The first was ratification of the **Equal Rights Amendment (ERA).** Approved by Congress in 1972, the ERA stated simply, "Equality of rights under the law shall not be denied or abridged by the United States or any state on account of sex." Within a year, twenty-two states had approved the amendment, but the efforts gradually faltered just three states short of ratification. The opposition came in part from working-class women who feared, as one union leader explained, that those employed as "maids, laundry workers, hospital cleaners, or dishwashers" would lose the protection of state laws that regulated wages and hours of work for women. Right-wing activist Phyllis Schlafly led an organized effort to defeat the ERA, claiming the amendment would lead to unisex toilets, homosexual marriages, and the drafting of women. The National Organization for Women (NOW) fought back, persuading Congress to extend the time for ratification by three years and waging intense campaigns for approval in Florida and Illinois. But the deadline for ratification finally passed on June 30, 1982, with the ERA forces still three states short. NOW leader Eleanor Smeal vowed a continuing struggle: "The crusade is not over. We know that we are the wave of the future."

Equal Rights Amendment (ERA) In 1972, Congress approved this constitutional amendment, a measure designed to guarantee women equal treatment under the law. Despite a three-year extension in the time allowed for ratification by the states, ERA supporters fell three states short of winning adoption.

VOTING ON THE EQUAL RIGHTS AMENDMENT

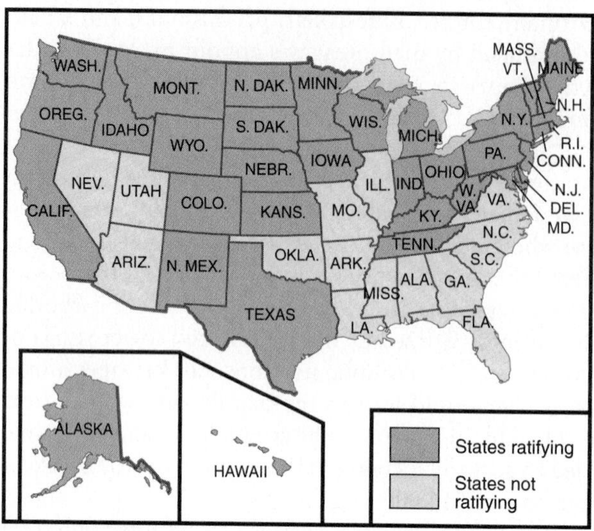

By the end of 1974, thirty-four states had ratified the ERA; Indiana finally approved the amendment in 1977, but the remaining fifteen states held out, leaving ratification three states short of the required three-fourths majority.

Roe v. *Wade* In 1973, the Supreme Court ruled in *Roe* v. *Wade* that women had a constitutional right to abortion during the early stages of pregnancy. The decision provoked a vigorous right-to-life movement that opposed abortion.

The women's movement focused even more of its energies in protecting a major victory it had won in ***Roe* v. *Wade*** in 1973. "Right-to-life" groups, consisting of mainly orthodox Catholics, fundamentalist Protestants, and conservatives, fought back. In 1978, with strong support from President Carter, Congress passed the Hyde amendment, which denied the use of federal funds to pay for abortions for poor women. Nevertheless, prochoice groups organized privately funded family planning agencies and abortion clinics to give more women a chance to exercise their constitutional right to abortion.

As Presidents Reagan and Bush appointed more conservative judges to the Court, however, prochoice groups began to fear the future overturn of *Roe* v. *Wade.* The Court avoided a direct challenge, contenting itself with lesser actions that upheld the rights of states to regulate abortion clinics, impose a 24-hour waiting period, and require the approval of one parent or a judge before a minor could have an abortion. Abortion became an issue in presidential contests, with the Republicans upholding a prolife position and the Democrats taking a prochoice stand. Clinton's election and appointment of Ruth Bader Ginsburg to the Court appeared to end the danger to *Roe* v. *Wade,* but in 2000 the Court margin in rejecting a Nebraska law forbidding certain late-term abortions fell to a bare majority, 5–4. And even the exercise of the right to abortion proved difficult and sometimes dangerous in view of the often violent protests of prolife groups outside abortion clinics. For women, abortion was a hard-won right they still had to struggle to protect.

The Gay Liberation Movement

On the evening of July 29, 1969, a squad of New York policemen raided the Stonewall Inn, a Greenwich Village bar frequented by drag queens and lesbians. As the patrons were being herded into vans, a crowd of gay onlookers began to jeer and taunt the police. A riot quickly broke out. "Beer cans and bottles were heaved at the windows and a rain of coins descended on the cops," reported the *Village Voice.* "Almost by signal the crowd erupted into cobblestone and bottle heaving." The next night, more than four hundred policemen battled two thousand gay demonstrators through the streets of Greenwich Village. The two-day "Stonewall riots" marked the beginning of the modern **gay liberation movement.** Refusing to play the role of victims any longer, gays decided to affirm their sexual orientation and demand an end to discrimination against homosexuals.

gay liberation movement In the 1970s, homosexuals began an effort to win social and legal acceptance and to encourage all gays and lesbians to affirm their sexual identity.

Within a few days, two new organizations were formed in New York, the Gay Liberation Front and the Gay Activist Alliance, with branches and offshoots quickly appearing in cities across the country. The basic theme of gay liberation was to urge all homosexuals to come "out of the closet" and affirm with pride their sexual identity. Instead of shame, they would find freedom and self-respect in the very act of coming out. "Come Out for Freedom! Come Out Now!" proclaimed the Gay Liberation Front's newspaper. "Come Out of the Closet Before the Door Is Nailed Shut!"

In the course of the 1970s, hundreds of thousands of gays and lesbians responded to the call. They formed more than a thousand local clubs and organizations and won a series of notable victories. In 1974, the American Psychiatric Association stopped classifying homosexuality as a mental disorder, and by the end of the decade, half the states had repealed their sodomy statutes. Gays fought hard in cities and states for laws forbidding discrimination against homosexuals in housing and employment, and in 1980 they finally succeeded in getting a gay rights plank in the Democratic national platform.

In the 1980s, the onset of the AIDS epidemic forced the gay liberation movement on the defensive. Stung by the accusation that AIDS was a "gay disease," male homosexuals faced new public condemnation at a time when they were trying desperately to care for the growing number of victims of the disease within their ranks. The gay organizations formed in the 1970s to win new rights now had to channel their energies into caring for the ill, promoting safe sexual practices, and fighting for greater public funding to help conquer AIDS. In 1986, ACT UP (AIDS Coalition to Unleash Power) began a series of violent demonstrations in which members disrupted public meetings, chained themselves to a New York Stock Exchange balcony, and spray-painted outlines of corpses on the streets of San Francisco to call attention to the plight of people dying of AIDS.

The movement also continued to stimulate gay consciousness in the 1980s. In 1987, an estimated 600,000 gays and lesbians took part in a march on Washington on behalf of gay rights. Every year afterward, gay groups held a National Coming Out Day in October to encourage homosexuals to proclaim their sexual identity. In a more controversial move, some gay leaders encouraged "outing"—releasing the names of prominent homosexuals, primarily politicians and movie stars, in an effort to make the nation aware of how many Americans were gay or lesbian. Gay leaders claimed there were more than twenty million gays and lesbians in the nation, basing this estimate on a Kinsey report that had announced in the late 1940s that one in ten American males had engaged in homosexual behavior. A sociological survey released in the spring of 1993 contradicted these numbers, finding only 1.1 percent of American males exclusively homosexual. Whatever the actual number, it was clear by the 1990s that gays and lesbians formed a significant minority that had succeeded in forcing the nation, however grudgingly, to respect its rights.

There was one battle, however, in which victory eluded the gay liberation movement. In the 1992 election, gays and lesbians had strongly backed Democratic candidate Bill Clinton, who had promised if elected to end the ban on homosexuals in the military. In his first days in office, however, President Clinton stirred up great resistance in the Pentagon and Congress when he tried to issue an executive order forbidding such discrimination. The Joint Chiefs of Staff and many Democrats, led by Georgia Senator Sam Nunn, warned that acceptance of gays and lesbians would destroy morale and seriously weaken the armed forces. Clinton finally settled for the Pentagon's compromise "don't ask, don't tell" policy, which would permit homosexuals to continue serving in the military as they had in the past as long as they did not reveal their sexual orientation. However disappointed gays and lesbians were in Clinton's retreat, their leaders realized that the real problem was the resistance of mainstream America to full acceptance of homosexuality.

Public attitudes toward gays and lesbians seemed to be changing in the 1990s, but the growing tolerance had definite limits. In a 1996 poll, 85 percent of those questioned believed that gays should be treated equally in the workplace, up from 76 percent in 1992. Violence against gays, however, continued, most notably in the 1998 fatal beating of Matthew Shepard, a 21-year-old gay college student, in Wyoming. The brutal attack spurred calls for hate-crime legislation and the judge in the case, banning a so-called gay-panic defense, sentenced Shepard's assailants to two consecutive terms of life imprisonment.

The issue of same-sex marriage came to a head at the end of the century. In 1996, President Clinton signed the Defense of Marriage Act, which decreed that states did not have to recognize same-sex marriages performed elsewhere. But in 2000, following a state supreme court ruling, the Vermont legislature legalized "civil unions" between individuals of the same sex, enabling gays and lesbians to receive all the legal benefits available to married couples. Whether sanctioned by law or not, the number of gay and lesbian households steadily increased; the 2000 census revealed that there were nearly 600,000 homes in America headed by same sex couples. While nearly one-quarter were in California and New York, there was at least one gay or lesbian couple living in 99 percent of the nation's counties.

Politics After Watergate

The energy crisis and the economic dislocations of the mid-1970s could not have come at a worse time. Watergate had a paralyzing effect on the American political system. Awareness that the Cold War had led to an imperial presidency created a growing demand to weaken the power of the president and strengthen congressional authority. The result was increasing tension between the White House and Capitol Hill, which prevented the kind of strong, effective leadership needed to meet the unprecedented problems of the 1970s.

The Ford Administration and the 1976 Campaign

Gerald R. Ford had the distinction of being the first president who had not been elected to national office. Richard Nixon had appointed him to the vice presidency after Spiro Agnew resigned to avoid prosecution for accepting bribes while he was governor of Maryland. The amiable Ford was a popular choice, and he seemed ready to restore public confidence in the presidency when he replaced Nixon in August 1974. As his vice president, Ford appointed Nelson Rockefeller, former governor of New York.

Ford's honeymoon lasted only a month. On September 8, 1974, he shocked the nation by announcing he had granted Richard Nixon a full and unconditional pardon for all federal crimes he "committed or may have committed or taken part in" during his presidency. Ford's intent was to end the bitterness over Watergate, but his gesture backfired, eroding public confidence in his judgment and making him seem somehow complicit in the scandal.

Ford soon found himself fighting an equally difficult battle on behalf of the beleaguered CIA. The Watergate scandal and the Vietnam fiasco had destroyed the public's trust in the government and lent credibility to a startling series of disclosures about past covert actions. The president allowed the CIA to confirm some of these charges and then he made things worse by blurting out to the press the juiciest item of all: the CIA had been involved in plots to assassinate foreign leaders.

Senate and House select committees appointed to investigate the CIA now focused on the assassination issue, eventually charging that the agency was involved in no less than eight separate attempts to kill Fidel Castro. In late 1975, Ford moved to limit the damage to the CIA. He appointed a respected former congressman, George Bush, as the new CIA director and issued an executive order outlawing assassination as an instrument of American foreign policy. Congress also increased its own surveillance of the CIA.

Ford proved less successful in his dealings with Congress on other issues. As a congressman, he had opposed virtually every Great Society measure, and he proved far more conservative than Nixon in the White House. In a little more than a year, he vetoed thirty-nine separate bills. He supported "maximum freedom for private enterprise."

Ford's weak record and the legacy of Watergate made the Democratic nomination a prize worth fighting for in 1976. A large field of candidates entered the contest, but a virtual unknown, former Georgia governor James Earl ("Jimmy") Carter, quickly became the front-runner. Aware of the voters' disgust with politicians of both parties, Carter ran as an outsider who was untainted by Washington.

Appearing refreshingly candid and honest, Carter swept through the primaries and won the Democratic nomination easily. Victory in November seemed assured. The polls gave Carter a 33-point lead over Ford when the campaign began, but he quickly lost ground as he began to hedge on the issues. Ford, however, also made costly mistakes, reinforcing his image as a bumbler. In a televised debate, responding to a question about Iron Curtain countries, he declared, "There is no Soviet domination of eastern Europe."

Carter won an extremely narrow victory in 1976. Ford swept nearly the entire West, but Carter carried the South and key northern industrial states such as New York and Ohio. Far more than in most recent elections, the outcome turned on class and racial factors. The poor and especially the black vote clinched the victory for the Democrats.

Disenchantment with Carter

The new president, described by an associate as "superficially self-effacing but intensely shrewd," was an ambitious and intelligent politician. He was especially adept at using symbols. He emerged from airplanes carrying his own garment bag and acted like an ordinary citizen who happened to be elected president. The substance, however, failed to match the style. He sought the White House convinced he was brighter and better than his competitors, but once there, he had no clear sense of direction, no discernible political philosophy.

The makeup of his administration reflected the conflicting tendencies that would eventually prove destructive. In the White House, he surrounded himself with close associates from Georgia. Yet he picked establishment Democrats such as Cyrus Vance and Joseph Califano for key cabinet positions. In the lower ranks, he selected followers of McGovern, Senator Edward M. ("Ted") Kennedy, and Ralph Nader, liberal activists who were intent on regulating business and preserving the environment. The result was bound to be tension and conflict, as the White House staff and the federal bureaucracy worked at cross-purposes.

President Carter strove hard for a balanced budget but was forced to accept mounting deficits. Federal agencies fought to save the environment and help consumers but served only to anger industry. Carter's unwillingness to take the political risks involved in revamping the overburdened Social Security system by reducing benefits and raising the retirement age blocked the efforts of Joseph Califano, head of the Department of Health, Education, and Welfare. Califano finally gave up his attempt to draw up a workable national health insurance plan.

Informed by his pollsters in 1979 that he was losing the nation's confidence, Carter sought desperately to redeem himself. He tried to pin responsibility for his failure on the American people's "crisis of confidence" and then on his advisers, but neither attempt could hide the fact that Carter, despite his good intentions and hard work, had failed to provide the bold leadership the nation needed.

From Détente to Renewed Cold War

America's political position in the world declined sharply in the 1970s. In part, the fault was internal. The Vietnam War left the American people convinced that the nation should never again intervene abroad, and Watergate discredited strong presidential leadership, shifting power over foreign policy to Congress. The new national consensus was symbolized by the War Powers Act, passed in 1973, which required the president to consult with Congress before sending American troops into action overseas. At the same time, external events and developments, notably the control over oil exercised by OPEC and the threats posed by revolutionary nationalism in the Middle East and Latin America, further weakened American foreign policy. No longer able to dominate the international scene, the United States began to play the role of spectator and at times even of victim.

Retreat in Asia

It was Ford's fate to reap where Nixon had sown. Once American aid stopped, the South Vietnamese government was unable to halt the April 1975 North Vietnamese offensive. American forces concentrated on evacuating 150,000 loyal South Vietnamese, but many more were left behind when the last helicopter left the roof of the embassy in Saigon. After a quarter century of futile effort, the United States finally had to admit defeat in the nation's longest and most humiliating foreign war.

Less than a month later, Ford had a chance to remind the world of American power. The communist Khmer Rouge government of Cambodia seized an American freighter, the *Mayaguez,* and imprisoned its crew. When the communists ignored the initial American protest, Ford authorized an armed attack on Cambodia by two thousand marines from bases in Thailand. By the time the American forces landed on a small offshore island, Cambodia had freed the crewmen. The nation took pride in the president's resort to force, but forty Americans paid for his decision with their lives.

Accommodation in Latin America

President Carter was more successful than Ford in adjusting to the growing nationalism in the world, particularly in Central America, where the United States had imposed order for most of the twentieth century by backing reactionary regimes.

The first test came in Panama. Resentment over American ownership of the Panama Canal had led Lyndon Johnson to enter into negotiations aimed at the eventual return of the waterway to Panama. Carter completed the long diplomatic process in 1977 by signing two treaties. One restored sovereignty in the canal zone to Panama; the other provided for gradual Panamanian responsibility for operating the canal, with appropriate safeguards for its use and defense by the United States. In 1978, after a bitter struggle, the Senate ratified the treaties.

Carter was less successful, however, in dealing with a growing problem of left-wing uprisings in Central America. In mid-1979, dictator Anastasio Somoza fell before the rebel Sandinista forces in Nicaragua. Despite American attempts to moderate the Sandinista revolution, the new regime moved steadily to the left, developing close ties with Castro's Cuba. In El Salvador, a growing leftist insurgency against a repressive regime put the United States in an awkward position. Unable to find a workable alternative between the extremes of reactionary dictatorship and radical revolution in Central America, Carter tried to use American economic aid to encourage the military junta in El Salvador to carry out democratic reforms. But after the guerrillas launched a major offensive in January 1981, he authorized large-scale military assistance to the government for its war against the insurgents, setting a precedent for the future.

The Quest for Peace in the Middle East

The inconclusive results of the 1973 October War gave Henry Kissinger the opportunity to play the role of peacemaker in the troubled Middle East. In arranging a pullback of Israeli forces in both the Sinai and the Golan Heights, he demonstrated that the United States could be a neutral mediator between Israelis and Arabs. Equally important, he had detached Egypt from dependence on the Soviet Union, thereby weakening the Soviets' influence in the Middle East.

In November 1977, Egyptian president Anwar Sadat stunned the world by traveling to Jerusalem in an effort to reach agreement directly with Israel. The next year, Carter invited both Sadat and Israeli Prime Minister Menachem Begin to negotiate under his guidance at Camp David. Eventually, the talks led to the ambiguous **Camp David Accords**—a framework for negotiations rather than an actual peace settlement. In 1979, Israel and Egypt signed a peace treaty that provided for the gradual return of the entire Sinai to Egypt but left the fate of the Palestine Arabs up in the air. By excluding both the Palestine Liberation Organization (PLO) and the Soviet Union from the negotiations, the United States alienated Egypt from the other Arab nations and drove the more radical states closer to the Soviet Union.

A highlight of Carter's presidency was his role in helping negotiate the Camp David Accords between Israeli Prime Minister Menachem Begin (right) and Egyptian President Anwar Sadat (left). The agreements set the stage for a peace treaty between Israel and Egypt. ❖

Any sense of progress in the Middle East as a result of Camp David was quickly offset in 1979 with the outbreak of the Iranian Revolution. Under Nixon and Kissinger, the United States had come to depend heavily on the shah and his powerful army for defense of the vital Persian Gulf. Carter continued the close relationship with the shah, despite growing signs of domestic discontent with his leadership. When the exiled Ayatollah Ruholla Khomeini led a fundamentalist Muslim revolt against the shah in 1978, the Carter administration misjudged the nature of the Iranian Revolution.

Camp David Accords In 1978, President Carter mediated a peace agreement between the leaders of Egypt and Israel at Camp David, a presidential retreat near Washington, D.C. The next year, Israel and Egypt signed a peace treaty based on the Camp David Accords.

At first, the United States encouraged the shah to remain in Iran, but when he decided to leave the country in January 1979, Carter tried to work with a moderate successor regime rather than encourage an army coup. With Khomeini's return from exile, Muslim militants quickly seized power in Teheran. In October 1979, Carter permitted the exiled shah to enter the United States for medical treatment. Incensed mobs in Iran denounced the United States, and on November 4, militant students seized the U.S. embassy in Teheran and took fifty-three Americans prisoner.

The prolonged **Iranian hostage crisis** revealed the extent to which American power had declined in the 1970s. Neither Carter's diplomatic efforts nor economic sanctions nor the concentration of U.S. naval forces in the Indian Ocean had any effect on the Iranian government. In his State of the Union message in January 1980, the president enunciated a new Carter Doctrine, telling the world the United States would fight to protect the vital oil supplies of the Persian Gulf.

Iranian hostage crisis In 1979, Iranian fundamentalists seized the American embassy in Tehran and held fifty-three American diplomats hostages for over a year. The Iranian hostage crisis weakened the Carter presidency; the hostages were finally released on January 20, 1981, the day Ronald Reagan became president.

Carter was unable to back up the brave words with meaningful action. In April 1980, the president authorized a desperate rescue mission that ended in failure when several helicopters broke down in the Iranian desert. The mission was aborted, an accident cost the lives of eight crewmen, and Secretary of State Cyrus Vance, who had opposed the rescue attempt, resigned in protest. The hostage crisis dragged on through the summer and fall of 1980, a symbol of American weakness that proved a powerful political handicap to Carter in the upcoming presidential election.

The Cold War Resumes

The policy of détente was already in trouble when Carter took office in 1977. Congressional refusal to relax trade restrictions on the Soviet Union had doomed Kissinger's attempts to win political concessions from the Soviets through economic incentives. The Kremlin's repression of the growing dissident movement and its harsh policy restricting the emigration of Soviet Jews had caused many Americans to doubt the wisdom of seeking accommodation with the Soviet Union.

Carter's emphasis on human rights struck the Soviets as a direct repudiation of détente. For Carter, his "absolute" commitment to human rights was easier said than done. He did withhold aid from authoritarian governments in Chile and Argentina, but equally repressive regimes in South Korea and the Philippines continued to receive generous American support. Human rights proved, in the words of one presidential aide, "absolute in principle but flexible in application." The Soviets, however, were disturbed by the principle, particularly after Carter received Soviet exiles in the White House.

Secretary of State Vance concentrated on continuing the main pillar of détente, the strategic arms limitation talks (SALT). In 1974, President Ford had met with Brezhnev and reached tentative agreement on the outline of SALT II, which sought to limit each side to 2,400 nuclear launchers. In March 1977, Vance went to Moscow to propose a drastic reduction in this level; the Soviets, already angry over human rights, rejected the American proposal. In 1980, however, Carter signed a SALT II agreement with the USSR that did lower the ceiling on nuclear delivery systems to 2,250 launchers.

Zbigniew Brzezinski, Carter's national security adviser, worked from the outset to reverse the policy of détente. He favored confrontation with the Kremlin. Toward this end, he prevailed on the president to advocate adoption of the new MX missile to replace the existing Minuteman ICBMs, which some experts thought were now vulnerable to a Soviet first strike. The new weapons system, together with the planned Trident submarine, ensured that regardless of SALT, the nuclear arms race would be sped up in the 1980s.

Brzezinski was also successful in persuading the president to use China to outmaneuver the Soviets. On January 1, 1979, the United States and China exchanged ambassadors, completing the reconciliation that Nixon had begun in 1971. The new relationship between China and the United States presented the Soviet Union with the problem of defending itself against two distinct enemies.

The Cold War, in abeyance for nearly a decade, resumed with full fury in December 1979 when the Soviet Union invaded Afghanistan. Although the move was designed to ensure an Afghani regime friendly to the Soviet Union, many observers took it as the beginning of a Soviet thrust toward the Indian Ocean and the Persian Gulf. Carter responded to this aggression with a series of stern measures. The United States banned the sale of high technology to the Soviets, embargoed the export of grain, resumed draft registration, and even boycotted the 1980 Moscow Olympics. These American actions did not halt the invasion of Afghanistan, but they doomed détente. Carter, who had come into office hoping to advance human rights and control the nuclear arms race, now found himself a victim of the renewed Cold War.

CHRONOLOGY

1966	National Organization for Women (NOW) is formed
1967	Riots in Detroit kill forty-three, injure two thousand, leave five thousand homeless
1968	Martin Luther King, Jr., is assassinated in Memphis, Tennessee ❖ Robert F. Kennedy is assassinated in Los Angeles, California
1970	U.S. forces invade Cambodia ❖ Ohio National Guardsmen kill four students at Kent State University
1972	President Nixon visits China ❖ United States and USSR sign the SALT I accords in Moscow ❖ White House "plumbers" unit breaks into Democratic headquarters in the Watergate complex ❖ Richard Nixon wins reelection in a landslide victory over George McGovern
1973	United States and North Vietnam sign truce ❖ Arab oil embargo creates an energy crisis in the United States
1974	Supreme Court orders Nixon to surrender the White House tapes ❖ Nixon resigns the presidency
1975	Last evacuation helicopter leaves the roof of the U.S. embassy in Saigon, South Vietnam
1977	President Carter signs Panama Canal treaties restoring sovereignty to Panama
1979	Iranian militants take fifty-three Americans hostage in the U.S. embassy in Teheran ❖ Soviet invasion of Afghanistan leads to U.S. withdrawal from the 1980 Moscow Olympics

CONCLUSION: A FAILED PRESIDENCY

National frustration over the hostages in Iran and the Soviet invasion of Afghanistan, coupled with anxiety over the energy crunch and rampant inflation, eroded public confidence in the Carter administration. A leader who had benefited from Vietnam and Watergate had now been betrayed by events. By mid-1980, the president's overall approval rating fell to 23 percent in the polls—and a mere 18 percent in foreign policy. The American people, disillusioned by the failures of Nixon, Ford, and Carter, yearned for new political leadership to meet the challenges at home and abroad.

KEY TERMS

Pentagon Papers, p. 608

Nixonomics, p. 609

détente, p. 611

Strategic Arms Limitation Talks (SALT), p. 611

Watergate scandal, p. 613

Organization of Petroleum Exporting Countries (OPEC), p. 614

Environmental Protection Agency (EPA), p. 616

Equal Rights Amendment (ERA), p. 619

Roe v. *Wade,* p. 620

gay liberation movement, p. 621

Camp David Accords, p. 625

Iranian hostage crisis, p. 625

RECOMMENDED READING

The most comprehensive account of Nixon's political career and presidency is the three-volume biography by Stephen E. Ambrose, *Nixon* (1987–1992). Melvin Small offers a balanced assessment of Nixon's White House years in *The Presidency of Richard Nixon* (1999); for a more detailed view, see Richard Reeves, *President Nixon* (2001). Stanley Kutler provides a thorough account of the scandal that drove Nixon from office in *The Wars of Watergate* (1990).

H. W. Brands offers a good survey of American foreign policy from the mid-1970s through the mid-1990s in *Since Vietnam* (1995). For foreign policy under Nixon, see William P. Bundy, *A Tangled Web* (1998), and Jeffrey Kimball, *Nixon's Vietnam War* (1998). Raymond L. Garthoff, *Détente and Confrontation* (1985) covers relations with the Soviet Union in the 1970s. The best biography of Henry Kissinger is Walter Isaacson, *Kissinger* (1989). James Bamford, *Body of Secrets* (2001), deals with the highly secretive National Security Agency.

In *The Prize* (1991), Daniel Yergin puts the energy crisis of the 1970s in historical perspective. Richard Barnet gives a thorough description of the impact of the energy crisis and foreign competition on the American economy in the 1970s in *The Lean Years* (1980). For economic policy under Carter, see W. Carl Biven, *Jimmy Carter's Economy* (2002).

Two books survey popular culture in the 1970s: David Frum, *How We Got Here: The 70's* (2000) and Bruce J. Schulman, *The Seventies* (2001).

For the Ford and Carter administrations, see John R. Greene, *The Presidency of Gerald R. Ford* (1995), and Burton I. Kaufman, *The Presidency of Jimmy Carter* (1993). Gaddis Smith surveys Carter's foreign policy in *Morality, Reason, and Power* (1985). For the crisis with Iran, see Barry Rubin, *Paved with Good Intentions* (1980).

For a list of additional titles related to this chapter's topics, please see http://www.ablongman.com/divine.

SUGGESTED WEB SITES

May 4, 1970: Twenty-Five Years of Remembrance

http://www.library.kent.edu/exhibits/4may95/index.html
This site commemorates the twenty-fifth anniversary of the shootings at Kent State University with a detailed chronology and other information.

Documents from the Women's Liberation Movement

http://scriptorium.lib.duke.edu/wlm/
Primary documents on-line from the Special Collections Library at Duke University provide firsthand information about the women's liberation movement.

Constitutional Issues: Watergate and the Constitution

http://www.nara.gov/education/teaching/watergate/watergat.html
From the National Archives' teaching materials, this site has a good chronology of Watergate and a 1974 memorandum from the Watergate Special Prosecution Force weighing the pros and cons of seeking an indictment against former President Richard Nixon.

CNN 1970s Interactive Timeline

http://cnn.com/SPECIALS/1999/century/episodes/08/
CNN has a series of interactive timelines with several interesting sites. This one covers the years from 1970 to 1979.

Richard Milhous Nixon

http://www.ipl.org/ref/POTUS/rmnixon.html
This site contains basic factual data about Nixon's election and presidency, speeches, and on-line biographies.

Watergate 25

http://www.washingtonpost.com/wp-srv/national/longterm/watergate/front.htm
This site features a chronology, images, searchable articles, and a good deal of background information about the burglary and its consequences.

Gerald Rudolph Ford

http://www.ipl.org/ref/POTUS/grford.html
This site contains basic factual data about Ford's election and presidency, speeches, and on-line biographies.

James Earl Carter, Jr.

http://www.ipl.org/ref/POTUS/jecarter.html
This site contains basic factual data about Carter's election and presidency, speeches, and on-line biographies.

Giant Leap

http://cnn.com/TECH/specials/apollo/
This CNN site commemorates the thirtieth anniversary of the 1969 moonwalk and tells the story of NASA and the ongoing space program.

Chapter 32

The Republican Resurgence, 1980–1992

Reagan and the Rise of Conservatism

The Republican National Committee sponsored a televised address by Hollywood actor Ronald Reagan on behalf of Barry Goldwater's presidential candidacy in October 1964. In contrast to Goldwater's strident rhetoric, Reagan used relaxed, confident, and persuasive terms to put forth the case for a return to individual freedom. Instead of the usual choice between increased government activity and less government involvement, Reagan presented the options of either going up or down—"up to the maximum of human freedom consistent with law and order, or down to the ant heap of totalitarianism."

Although this speech did not rescue Goldwater's unpopular candidacy, it marked the beginning of Ronald Reagan's remarkable political career. A year later, a group of wealthy friends persuaded him, largely on the basis of the success of "the speech," to run for the California governorship. Reagan proved a formidable candidate. His friendly, relaxed manner and his mastery of television enabled him to present his strongly conservative message without appearing to be a rigid ideologue of the right. He won handily. Reagan's views addressed rising middle-class suburban resentment over high taxes, expanding welfare programs, and bureaucratic regulation.

In two terms as governor, Reagan displayed a natural ability as a political leader. Rather than insisting on implementing all of his conservative policies, he proved surprisingly flexible. Dealing with a Democratic legislature, he yielded on raising taxes and increasing state spending while managing to trim the welfare rolls.

By the time Reagan left the governor's office in 1974, many signs pointed to a gathering conservative mood across the nation. In a popular rebellion against escalating property taxes in 1978, California's voters passed Proposition 13, which called for a 57 percent cut in taxes and resulted in a gradual reduction in social services. Concern over greater acceptance of homosexuality in society and rising abortion and divorce rates impelled religious groups to engage in political activity to defend traditional family values. Jerry Falwell, a successful Virginia radio and television evangelist, founded the **Moral Majority**, a fundamentalist group dedicated to preserving the "American way of life."

The population shift of the 1970s, especially to the Sunbelt region in the South and West (see Chapter 33), added momentum to the conservative upsurge. People moving to the Sunbelt tended to be white, middle- and upper-class suburbanites—skilled workers, young professionals, and business executives who were attracted both by economic opportunity and by a political climate stressing low taxes, less

Outline

Reagan in Power

Reaganomics

Reagan and the World

Social Dilemmas

Passing the Torch to Bush

Conclusion: Republican Economic Woes

Moral Majority In 1979, the Reverend Jerry Falwell founded the Moral Majority to combat "amoral liberals," drug abuse, "coddling" of criminals, homosexuality, communism, and abortion. The Moral Majority represented the rise of political activism among organized religion's radical right.

Neoconservatism Former liberals who advocated a strong stand against communism abroad and free market capitalism at home became known as neoconservatives. These intellectuals stressed the positive values of American society in contrast to liberals who emphasized social ills.

government regulation, and more reliance on the marketplace. The political impact of population shifts from East to West and North to South during the 1970s was reflected in the congressional gains by the Sunbelt and Far West states after the 1980 census.

Conservatives also succeeded, for the first time since World War II, in making their cause intellectually respectable. Scholars and academics on the right flourished in new "think tanks." Writer William F. Buckley and economist Milton Friedman advocated conservative causes in print and on television. **Neoconservatism** became fashionable among many intellectuals who were former liberal stalwarts. They denounced liberals for being too soft on the communist threat abroad and too willing to compromise high standards at home in the face of demands for equality from African Americans, women, and the disadvantaged. They called for a reaffirmation of capitalism and a new emphasis on what was right about America rather than an obsessive concern with social ills.

BY THE END OF THE 1970S, Ronald Reagan was recognized as the nation's most effective spokesman for the conservative resurgence. His personal charm softened the hard edges of his right-wing call to arms, and his conviction that America could regain its traditional self-confidence by reaffirming basic ideals had a broad appeal to a nation shaken by inflation at home and humiliation abroad. He easily won the 1980 GOP presidential nomination.

In his acceptance speech at the Republican convention in Detroit, he set forth the themes that endeared him to conservatives—less government, balanced budget, family values, and peace through increased military spending. Reagan offered reassurance and hope for the future. He spoke of restoring to the federal government "the capacity to do the people's work without dominating their lives." As historian Robert Dallek has pointed out, Reagan "assured his listeners that he was no radical idealist courting defeat, but a sensible, thoroughly likable American with a surefire formula for success that would please everyone." In Ronald Reagan, the Republicans had found the perfect candidate to exploit both the American people's frustration with the domestic and foreign policy failures of the 1970s and the more conservative mood of the nation.

In the White House, Reagan would have a lasting impact on American life. At home, his success in reducing taxes and cutting spending on social programs reversed the trend toward greater reliance on the federal government that had prevailed since the New Deal. Yet his economic policies, along with a sharp increase in defense spending, created unprecedented budget deficits that would plague his successors through the mid-1990s. Abroad, Reagan was successful in rebuilding American military power and compelling the Soviet Union to choose diplomacy rather than confrontation, culminating in the dramatic end of the Cold War during the presidency of George Bush. Yet even this unexpected victory led not to a new era of peace in the world, but rather to dangerous crises in the Middle East and the Balkans. For better or worse, President Reagan left an enduring legacy.

Reagan in Power

The liberal Democratic political coalition, originally forged by Franklin D. Roosevelt in the Great Depression, finally split apart by the end of the 1970s. The Watergate scandal gave the Democrats a brief reprieve, but by the end of the decade, the Republicans were using the conservative upsurge to make inroads into such normally Democratic groups of voters as Jews, Southerners, and blue-collar workers. Yet the continuing appeal of the New Deal legacy prevented a total political realignment.

The Reagan Victory

In 1980, Jimmy Carter found himself in trouble. Inflation, touched off by the second oil shock of the 1970s, reached double-digit figures. The Federal Reserve Board's effort to shrink the money supply had led to a recession, with unemployment reaching 7.8 percent by July 1980. What Ronald Reagan dubbed the "misery index," the combined rate of inflation and unemployment, hit 28 percent early in 1980.

Foreign policy almost hurt Carter. The Soviet invasion of Afghanistan dashed hopes for continued détente; the hostage crisis in Iran highlighted the nation's helplessness in the face of flagrant violations of its sovereignty. In the short run, Carter used that crisis to beat back the challenge to his renomination by fellow Democrat Edward Kennedy. The Democrats rallied behind Carter, although the delegates to the party's convention displayed a notable lack of enthusiasm in renominating him.

Reagan, and his running mate, George Bush, hammered away at the state of the economy and the world. Reagan scored heavily among traditionally Democratic blue-collar groups by blaming Carter for inflation, which robbed workers of any gain in real wages. Reagan also accused Carter of allowing the Soviets to outstrip the United States militarily and promised a massive buildup of American forces if he were elected. The Iranian situation helped Reagan by accentuating U.S. weakness in the world. Carter's position was further hurt by the independent candidacy of liberal Republican John Anderson of Illinois, who appealed to voters disenchanted with Carter but not yet ready to embrace Reagan.

The president struck back by claiming that Reagan was too reckless to conduct American foreign policy in the nuclear age. Carter tried to portray his Republican challenger as a warmonger. The attack backfired. In a televised debate, Reagan assured the American people of his devotion to peace, leaving Carter with the onus of trying to land a low blow. Reagan scored impressively when he summed up the country's dire economic condition by suggesting that voters ask themselves simply, "Are you better off now than you were four years ago?"

On election day, the American people answered with a resounding "no." Reagan carried forty-four states and gained 51 percent of the popular vote. Reagan clearly benefited from the growing political power of the Sunbelt. Even more impressive

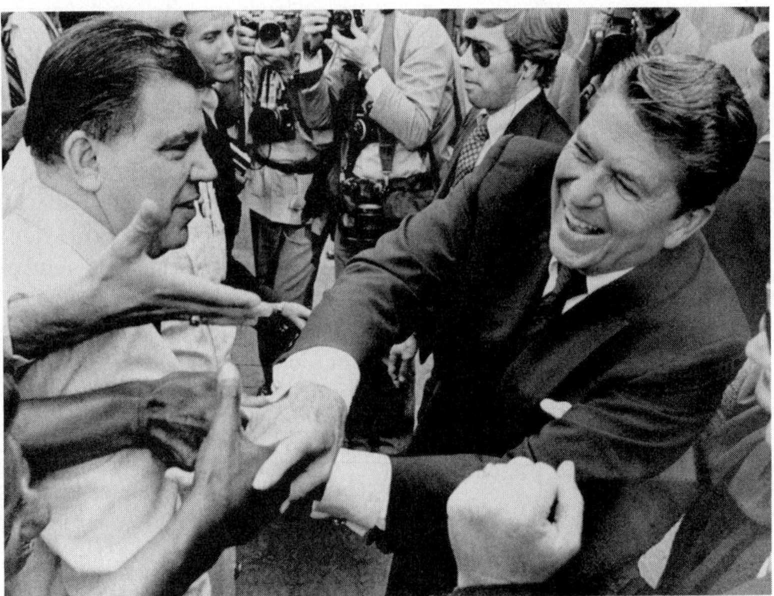

Republican presidential candidate Ronald Reagan greets supporters in Cincinnati during his 1980 campaign. Reagan won the election, carrying all but six states. ❖

were Reagan's inroads into the old New Deal coalition. Reagan received 50.5 percent of the blue-collar vote and 46 percent of the Jewish vote, the best showing by a Republican since 1928. Only one group remained loyal to Carter: African American voters gave him 85 percent of their ballots.

Even more surprising were the Republican gains in Congress. For the first time since 1954, the GOP gained control of the Senate, 53 to 46, and the party picked up thirty-three seats in the House to narrow the Democratic margin from 114 to 50. Liberals were the chief losers in Congress.

The meaning of the election was less clear than its outcome. Nearly all observers agreed that voters had rendered an adverse judgment on the Carter administration. But most experts did not assess the outcome to be as major a realignment in American politics as the Democratic victory of Franklin Roosevelt in 1932. Voters in 1980 expressed a distaste for current economic conditions, not a strongly held ideological preference. Political scientist Walter Dean Burnham termed the result "a conservative revitalization," but one that stopped short of making the GOP the dominant party.

Journalist Theodore White disagreed, viewing the outcome as a repudiation of the Democratic coalition that had dominated American politics since the days of FDR and the New Deal. White may well have been right. The movement of the populations from the Northeast and Midwest to the South and West, along with the flight from the city, helped the Republicans far more than the Democrats. The Reagan victory in 1980 signaled a partial political realignment, ending a half century of Democratic dominance.

Cutting Spending and Taxes

When Ronald Reagan took office in January 1981, the ravages of inflation had devastated the economy. Interest rates hovered near 20 percent, while the value of the dollar, compared to 1960, had dropped to just 36 cents. The new president blamed what he termed "the worst economic mess since the Great Depression" on high federal spending and excessive taxation. "Government is not the solution to our problems," Reagan announced in his inaugural address, "government is the problem."

supply-side economics
Advocates of supply-side economics claimed that tax cuts would stimulate the economy by giving individuals a greater incentive to earn more money, which would lead to greater investment and eventually larger tax revenues at a lower rate. Critics replied that supply-side economics would only burden the economy with larger government deficits.

The president embraced the concept of **supply-side economics** as the proper remedy for the nation's economic ills. Supply-side economists believed that the private sector, freed of the ever-increasing burden of government spending, would shift its resources from tax shelters to productive investments, leading to an economic boom that would provide enough new income to offset the lost revenue. Although many other economists worried that the 30 percent cut in income taxes that Reagan favored would lead to staggering deficits, the president was confident that his program would both stimulate the economy and reduce the role of government.

The president made spending the first target. Quickly deciding not to attack such popular middle-class entitlement programs as Social Security and Medicare and sparing critical social services for the "truly deserving needy," the so-called safety net, they concentrated on slashing $41.4 billion from the budget by cutting heavily into such other social services as food stamps and by reducing public service jobs, student loans, and support for urban mass transit. Appearing before a joint session of Congress only weeks after an attempt on his life, Reagan won a commanding 253-to-176 margin of victory for his budget in the House and an even more lopsided vote of 78 to 20 in the Senate in May. Reagan thus emerged from the budget struggle victorious.

The president proved equally successful in reducing taxes. He advocated a cut of 10 percent in personal income taxes for three consecutive years. When the Democrats countered with a two-year plan that would reduce taxes by only 15 percent, Reagan compromised with a proposal to cut taxes by 5 percent the first year but insisted on the full 10 percent reduction for the second and third years.

Although some critics feared that the loss of revenue might result in a huge deficit, the president once again overcame Democratic resistance in Congress, demonstrating beyond any doubt his ability to wield presidential power effectively.

Limiting the Role of Government

Reagan met with only mixed success in his other efforts to restrict government activity and reduce federal regulation of the economy. Cutting back on the scope of federal agencies and limiting their impact on American business was a central tenet of the president's political philosophy. The goal of **deregulation** led to the appointment of men and women who shared his belief in relying on the marketplace rather than the bureaucracy to direct the nation's economy. Thus Secretary of the Interior James Watt outraged environmentalists by opening up federal land to coal and timber production, halting the growth of national parkland, and making more than a billion acres available for offshore oil drilling. Though Watt was eventually forced to resign, the Reagan administration continued its policy of reducing government intervention in business long after Watt's departure.

deregulation Process of cutting back on the scope of federal agencies and relying instead on the free market to keep prices of consumer goods and services low and quality high. Ronald Reagan continued the deregulation process begun by Jimmy Carter.

The most effective cabinet member in the administration's first two years was Transportation Secretary Drew Lewis. He helped relieve the troubled American automobile industry of many of the regulations adopted in the 1970s to reduce air pollution and increase passenger safety. At the same time, he played a key role in the behind-the-scenes negotiations that led Japan to agree in the spring of 1981 to restrict its automobile exports to the United States for the next three years. This unilateral Japanese action enabled the Reagan administration to help Detroit's carmakers without openly violating its free market position by endorsing protectionist measures.

The Reagan administration was less successful in trying to cut back on the entitlement programs that it viewed as the primary cause of the growing budget deficits. Social Security was the greatest offender. A 500 percent increase in Social Security benefits in the 1970s threatened to bankrupt the system's trust fund by the end of the century. Reagan, overconfident from his budget victory, met a sharp rebuff when he tried to make substantial cuts in future benefits. The president then appointed a bipartisan commission to recommend ways to protect the system's endangered trust fund. In March 1983, Congress approved a series of changes that guaranteed the solvency of Social Security by gradually raising the retirement age, delaying cost-of-living increases for six months, and taxing pensions paid to the well-to-do elderly.

The administration's record in dealing with civil rights and women's concerns proved clumsy and divisive. Although feminist groups were disappointed by the administration's strong rhetorical attacks on legalized abortion, the appointment of Sandra Day O'Connor, the first woman to sit on the Supreme Court, pleased them. By this one shrewd move, Reagan was able to both fulfill a campaign pledge and make a symbolic gesture to women. At the same time, the president also buttressed the conservative tilt of the Court.

The administration's civil rights record proved especially revealing. Aware of how few African Americans had supported the GOP in 1980, Reagan made no effort to reward this group with government jobs or favors. Instead, the Justice Department actively opposed busing to achieve school integration and affirmative action measures that resulted in minority hiring quotas.

Chief Justice Warren Burger swears in Sandra Day O'Connor, the first woman to serve on the U.S. Supreme Court, in September 1981. ❖

REAGANOMICS

The sweeping reductions in domestic spending and income taxes that Reagan achieved in 1981 gave rise to conflicting economic expectations. Supply-side economists believed that the tax relief granted to investors would lead to rapid business growth, which would raise more than enough new revenue to offset the lower rates. The administration's critics, by contrast, were sure that heavy defense spending coupled with tax reductions would create massive deficits and result in economic stagnation.

Recession and Recovery

The supply-side theory became the first economic casualty of the 1980s. The naive belief that a combination of cuts in social spending and sharply reduced taxes could unleash an economic boom that would avoid huge deficits was the victim of both Reagan's insistence on huge increases in defense spending and the Federal Reserve Board's tight money policy. It was the latter that touched off a recession that began in the fall of 1981 and grew steadily worse throughout 1982; factory utilization fell to under 70 percent and unemployment reached a postwar high of 10.4 percent in October 1982.

Reagan refused to give up his income tax cuts, but he proved flexible in other ways, slightly moderating the defense buildup, accepting fewer cuts in social programs than he proposed, and finally agreeing to a $98 billion increase in miscellaneous federal taxes. He refused, however, to cancel the final 10 percent cut in income taxes due in mid-1983. Instead he declared that all signs pointed to "a strong recovery."

Whether by design or good luck, the president's optimism proved justified. In the second quarter of 1983, the economy came to life. The final 10 percent tax cut in July stimulated consumer spending, along with moderating inflation, which kept prices from rising so quickly. The long-depressed automobile industry, helped by Japan's voluntary quotas on car exports, began to boom. The American people went on a great buying spree; consumer installment debt increased as much in the first six months of 1983 as in all of 1982.

Best of all, inflation remained under control as the economy expanded. At the same time, interest rates, which had been hovering around 16.5 percent in 1982, fell and remained below 11 percent, enabling consumers to buy goods and corporations to expand their inventories much more easily. A combination of long-term Federal Reserve policy, the impact of the recession, and a worldwide decline in energy and food prices enabled the Reagan administration to take credit for solving the problem that had proved fatal for Carter and the Democrats.

The Growing Deficit

A problem emerged in the mid-1980s to cloud Reagan's claims of economic recovery: the growing federal budget deficit. As the economy weakened and unemployment increased, tax revenues fell below projections while government spending on unemployment insurance and other social programs climbed. The deficit reached $207.8 billion in 1983, nearly triple the pre-Reagan high of $70.5 billion in 1976.

Some economists were predicting that at current spending and tax rates, the deficit would rise to more than $300 billion a year by the end of the decade. The result, many feared, would be soaring interest rates as the government competed with the private sector for the limited amount of investment capital in the nation. In fact, a slumping world economy led to a massive infusion of foreign investment, which kept the prime rate from rising above 11 percent.

When the deficit continued to climb during the economic recovery of the mid-1980s, Congress finally came forward with what appeared to be a drastic solution.

Republican senators Phil Gramm of Texas and Warren Rudman of New Hampshire joined with Democrat Ernest Hollings of South Carolina to set a series of budgetary ceilings designed to eliminate the deficit entirely by 1991, through automatic, across-the-board spending cuts. After the Supreme Court invalidated the compulsory feature, the revised Gramm-Rudman-Hollings Balanced Budget Act did succeed in halting the deficit spiral. As altered by Congress in 1986 and 1987, **Gramm-Rudman,** as it became known, stretched out the goal of ending the deficit until 1993. The president and Congress were able to lower the deficit from a peak of $221 billion in 1986 to a more manageable $155 billion by 1988. Even more important, the deficit as a percentage of the GNP fell from over 5 percent to close to 3 percent, a level common in many industrial nations.

Gramm-Rudman The Gramm-Rudman-Hollings Balanced Budget Act of 1985, popularly known as Gramm-Rudman, revised federal budgeting procedures. It authorized the president to impose automatic spending reductions to meet annual deficit limits.

In essence, Gramm-Rudman was a political compromise. The price Reagan had to pay for Democratic help in resolving his budgetary crisis was to stop the increase in defense spending. But at the same time, by agreeing to sizable budget deficits for the next few years, the Democrats, who controlled Congress, had to give up any hope of expanding existing social programs or enacting new ones, such as a comprehensive national health plan.

Another alarming deficit—in the balance of overseas trade—also became an important issue in the mid-1980s. American exports had been falling steadily since the 1970s as a result of the decline in traditional manufacturing industries—iron and steel, electronics, and automobiles. The Japanese had been the biggest gainers as they dominated the American market in consumer goods.

In the 1980s, the American people had begun living beyond their means. Just as the government incurred large deficits rather than raising taxes to pay for the huge defense buildup, so consumers had cut back on personal saving in order to buy imported cars, television sets, and VCRs, encouraging further foreign investment. Reaganomics had succeeded in continuing America's traditional high standard of living, but at a very high price—massive borrowing that mortgaged the nation's future.

The Rich Grow Richer

There were both gains and losses in the Reagan years. Inflation fell from double-digit levels by 1982 and averaged about 4 percent for the rest of the decade. A sharp drop in the world price of oil in late 1985 helped lower the trade deficit and brought inflation down to less than 2 percent, although cheap oil had a devastating impact on oil-producing states such as Texas, Louisiana, and Oklahoma.

After the end of the 1982 recession, employment grew steadily; by 1990, there were nearly nineteen million more Americans working than in 1980. There were losers as well, however. Blue-collar jobs declined as American industry, notably steel and auto, streamlined operations by closing obsolete plants, switching to automated production, and farming out manufacturing to foreign producers with far lower labor costs. Companies that specialized in labor-intensive consumer products, such as Eastman Kodak and General Electric, virtually stopped all manufacturing in the United States, concentrating instead on marketing and distributing goods made abroad to their specifications.

At the same time, however, the service sector expanded rapidly, especially the financial, transportation, and health care industries. Accountants, lawyers, and technicians flourished, with women especially benefiting from the change from blue- to white-collar jobs. Union membership no longer guaranteed a high-wage job; education and technical training were the keys to success in the postindustrial economy. By 1990, nearly one in three workers was an executive, technician, or professional; only one in five worked in factories. Labor unions were especially hard hit; union membership dropped from 23 percent of the workforce in 1980 to 15.5 percent by 1992.

The most striking change in the decade was the growing inequality of wealth in America. In the five income categories used by the Census Bureau, the lowest 20 percent of Americans dropped 6 percent in pretax income in the 1980s; the three middle groups gained about 5 percent; and the top fifth increased their incomes by 20 percent over the decade. The top 1 percent, the truly rich, did best of all, doubling their after-tax income in ten years. By 1989, the top fifth made as much money as the other 80 percent combined, while the top 1 percent alone earned as much as the middle fifth of the population. This income disparity was the product of both economic restructuring and Republican tax policy. The decline in manufacturing meant that many assembly line workers had lost their jobs and were working for little more than the minimum wage in the service sector. At the same time, the income tax cuts and adjustments reduced the top rate from 70 percent to 31 percent. A parallel increase in Social Security payroll taxes meant that by the end of the decade, the tax burden for a middle-class family was 37.3 cents of every dollar earned, compared to 35 cents for the wealthy.

The economic inequities of the 1980s were most clearly reflected in the transfer of actual wealth—housing, property, stocks, savings, and retirement accounts. Between 1983 and 1989, family wealth increased from $13.6 trillion to $16.1 trillion; 55 percent of the gain in the net assets went to the top 0.5 percent of the population. The poor and the lower middle class actually lost $256 billion in wealth during this boom period. As a result, wealth became even more concentrated than income in the 1980s. By the end of the decade, the top fifth of the population owned 80 percent of the nation's entire household wealth.

The economic changes of the 1980s hit the middle class particularly hard. Median family income, which had doubled between 1947 and 1973, remained stagnant for the next twenty years. Middle-class fathers responded by working longer hours and their wives left the home for the workplace in increasing numbers in order to maintain a decent standard of living for their families.

By the 1990s, middle-class Americans came to believe that their children would not fare as well as they had. This feeling of diminished expectations came for several reasons. In part, people began to realize that the rapid expansion and prosperity of the 1950s and 1960s was a happy accident unlikely to occur again. The inflation in real estate values by the 1980s added greatly to the net worth of an older generation but made it very difficult for their children to benefit from the same kind of appreciation. Above all, the baby boom generation took affluence for granted and expected to continue to enjoy all the blessings of an abundant society. Yet their parents feared that while their children would be able to live a life envied by most of the world's population, they would not share fully in the American dream.

Reagan Affirmed

"Are you better off now than you were four years ago?" Reagan had asked voters at the end of his 1980 debate with Jimmy Carter. By the mid-1980s, he appeared to have delivered on his implicit promise to stem inflation and revive the stagnant American economy.

Despite the growing gap between the rich and the poor, Reagan could boast of impressive economic gains after weathering the 1982 recession. The recovery led to 16 million new jobs as the unemployment rate dropped back under 6 percent. Inflation remained low and even median family income, although still below the post–World War II peak reached in the early 1970s, moved steadily upward.

The economic boom that began in 1983 came at just the right time for the Republican party. By early 1984, with personal income rising and unemployment shrinking rapidly, Democratic prospects dimmed for the 1984 election. After a long and bruising primary battle, Walter Mondale, former Minnesota senator and Carter's vice president, won the Democratic nomination. In a bold break with tradition, he chose a woman as a running mate, Congresswoman Geraldine Ferraro of New York.

When the Republicans renominated Reagan and Bush, the campaign quickly came down to one issue—leadership. The GOP claimed Reagan had overcome the problems that overwhelmed Carter, notably inflation at home and disrespect abroad. The president told voters if they reelected him, "you ain't seen nothin' yet."

Mondale and Ferraro, in contrast, accused Reagan of helping the rich at the expense of the poor, saddling future generations with huge deficits, and risking war in the Middle East and Central America. In a surprise move, the Democratic candidate announced he intended to raise taxes to curb the deficit and then accused Reagan of harboring a "secret plan" to increase taxes himself.

The tactics failed; the outcome was an even greater Reagan landslide than in 1980. With a solid base in the South and West, the president cut deeply into the normally Democratic states of the Northeast and the swing states of the Midwest to take the electoral votes of all but Minnesota and the District of Columbia. Exit surveys revealed that economic issues were uppermost in the minds of voters; in the midst of a strong economic recovery, Reagan won a majority among all voters earning more than $12,500 a year. More than two-thirds of the white males in the nation voted for Reagan; he even won a majority of the blue-collar and women's vote. Of all the traditional Democratic groups, only African Americans proved loyal to the party.

The 1984 election was far more a triumph for Reagan than for his party. The GOP made only small gains in the House and actually lost two seats in the Senate. Despite minor gains at the state level, the GOP failed to achieve the party realignment it sought. The nation seemed to be dividing politically along economic lines, with the wealthy and affluent who fared best from Reagan's economic policies supporting the president while a growing underclass of African Americans, Hispanics, and the working poor were voting solidly Democratic. Middle-class Americans who held the balance revealed their mixed feelings by backing a Republican for president and Democratic candidates for the House and Senate.

Reagan and the World

Ronald Reagan was even more determined to reverse the course of American policy abroad than at home. He believed that under Carter, American prestige and standing in the world had dropped to an all-time low. Intent on restoring traditional American pride and self-respect, Reagan's mission was to strengthen America's defenses and recapture world supremacy from the Soviet Union.

In reality, the new president was simply continuing the hard line that Carter had begun to take after the invasion of Afghanistan. The Democrats had begun a massive military buildup in 1979 that included plans for cruise missiles in Europe, a rapid deployment force in the Middle East, and a 5 percent increase in the defense budget.

Under Reagan, the Pentagon flourished. Secretary of Defense Caspar Weinberger, once known as a budget cutter, presented a plan that would more than double defense spending. The emphasis was on new weapons, ranging from the B-1 bomber and the controversial MX nuclear missile to the expansion of the navy from 456 to 600 ships. Despite growing opposition in Congress, by 1985 the defense budget grew to more than $300 billion at the very time the administration was cutting back on domestic spending.

The president scored his first foreign policy victory on the day he took office, thanks again to efforts begun under Carter. On January 20, 1981, Iran released the fifty-three Americans held hostage and thus enabled Reagan to begin his presidency on a positive note.

After some initial difficulty, Reagan proved more successful than Carter in bringing harmony and order to the conduct of American foreign policy. The appointment of Alexander Haig to head the State Department was a clear attempt to restore the dominant role of the secretary of state. Haig, a former general, NATO commander, Kissinger aide, and White House chief of staff under Nixon, was a well-known and forceful figure but soon proved too outspoken and domineering for Reagan's White House staff. Finally, in mid-1982, Reagan replaced Haig as secretary of state with George Shultz, a professional economist with extensive government experience, whose low-key, relaxed style brought an air of calm reassurance to the conduct of American foreign policy.

Despite the steady increase in defense spending and the formation of a smoothly functioning foreign policy team, Reagan soon found his diplomatic goals more difficult to achieve than the budgetary and tax measures he had pushed so speedily through Congress. Yet in the long run, he could claim credit for a goal that had eluded his predecessors in the White House—the end of the Cold War.

Challenging the "Evil Empire"

The belief that the Soviet Union was a deadly enemy that threatened the well-being and security of the United States was the central tenet of Reagan's approach to foreign policy. He saw the Soviets as bent on world revolution, ready "to commit any crime, to lie, to cheat" to advance their cause. Citing what he called a "record of tyranny," Reagan denounced them before the United Nations in 1982, claiming that "Soviet-sponsored guerrillas and terrorists are at work in Central and South America, in Africa, the Middle East, in the Caribbean and in Europe, violating human rights and unnerving the world with violence."

Given the view of the USSR as "the focus of evil in the modern world," it is not surprising the new president pursued Carter's hard line. Abandoning détente, Reagan proceeded to implement a 1979 decision to place 572 Pershing II and cruise missiles in western Europe within range of Moscow and other Soviet population centers to match Soviet deployment of medium-range missiles aimed at NATO countries. Despite strong protests from the Soviet Union, as well as growing uneasiness in Europe and an increasingly vocal nuclear freeze movement at home, the United States began putting these weapons in bases in Great Britain and Germany in November 1983. The Soviets responded by breaking off disarmament negotiations in Geneva.

Strategic Defense Initiative (SDI) Popularly known as "Star Wars," President Reagan's Strategic Defense Initiative (SDI) proposed the construction of an elaborate computer-controlled, antimissile defense system capable of destroying enemy missiles in outer space. Critics claimed SDI could never be perfected.

The nuclear arms race had now reached a more dangerous level than ever before. The United States stepped up research and development of the **Strategic Defense Initiative (SDI),** an antimissile system based on the use of lasers and particle beams to destroy incoming missiles in outer space. SDI was promptly dubbed "Star Wars" by the media. Although critics charged that SDI would increase the arms race, the Reagan administration defended "Star Wars" as a legitimate attempt to free the United States from the deadly trap of deterrence, with its reliance on the threat of nuclear retaliation to keep the peace. Meanwhile, the Soviet Union kept deploying larger and more accurate land-based ICBMs. Although both sides continued to observe the unratified SALT II agreements, the fact remained that between them the two governments had nearly fifty thousand warheads in their nuclear arsenals.

Turmoil in the Middle East

Reagan tried to continue Carter's basic policy in the turbulent Middle East. In April 1982, the Israelis honored a Camp David pledge by making their final withdrawal from the Sinai. Reagan hoped to achieve the other Camp David objective of providing a homeland for the Palestinian Arabs on the West Bank, but Israel instead continued to build Jewish settlements in this disputed area. The threat of the Palestine

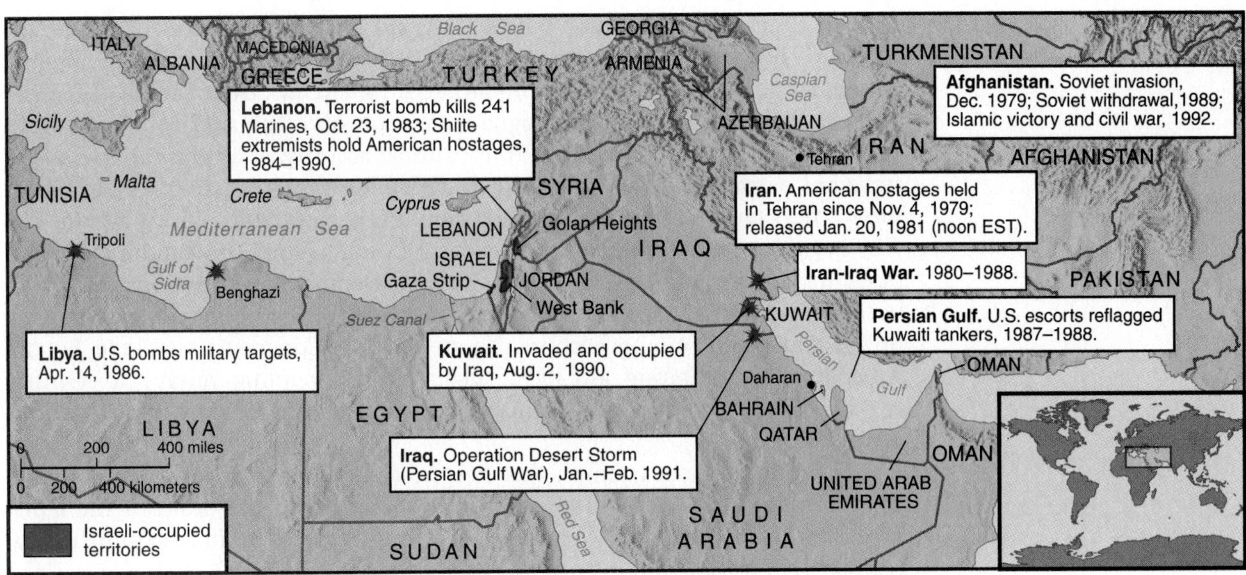

TROUBLE SPOTS IN THE MIDDLE EAST, 1979–1992 *Armed conflict and territorial attacks in this region intensified in the early and mid-1980s.* ❖

Liberation Organization (PLO), based in southern Lebanon and frequently raiding across the border into Israel, seemed to be the major obstacle to further progress.

On June 6, 1982, with tacit American encouragement, Israel invaded southern Lebanon in order to secure Israel's northern border and destroy the PLO. The Reagan administration made no effort to halt this offensive but did join with France and Italy in sending a multinational force to permit the PLO to evacuate to Tunisia. Unfortunately, the United States soon became enmeshed in the Lebanese civil war, raging since 1975. American marines, sent to Lebanon as part of the multinational force to restore order, were caught up in the renewed hostilities between Muslim and Christian militias. The Muslims perceived the marines as aiding the Christian-dominated government of Lebanon instead of acting as neutral peacekeepers and began firing on the vulnerable American troops.

In the face of growing congressional demands for the withdrawal of the marines, Reagan declared they were there to protect Lebanon from the designs of Soviet-backed Syria. But finally, after terrorists drove a truck loaded with explosives into the American barracks, killing 241 marines, the president had no choice but to pull out. Despite his good intentions, Reagan had experienced a humiliation similar to Carter's in Iran, one that left Lebanon in shambles and the Arab-Israeli situation worse than ever.

Confrontation in Central America

Reagan faced a difficult situation in Central America. In an area marked by great extremes of wealth, the United States sought moderate middle-class regimes to support. Washington usually ended up backing repressive right-wing dictatorships rather than the more leftist groups who raised the radical issues of land reform and redistribution of wealth. Yet it was often oppression by U.S.-supported regimes that drove those seeking political change to embrace revolutionary tactics.

This is precisely what happened in Nicaragua, where the leftist Sandinista coalition finally succeeded in overthrowing the repressive Somoza regime in 1979. In an effort to strengthen the many middle-class elements in the original Sandinista government and to avoid forcing Nicaragua into the Cuban and Soviet orbit, Carter extended American economic aid.

The Reagan administration quickly reversed the policy. Alexander Haig cut off all aid to Nicaragua in the spring of 1981. The new policy became self-fulfilling as Nicaragua became even more dependent on Cuba and the Soviet Union.

The United States and Nicaragua were soon on a collision course. In April 1983, the president declared that "the national security of all the Americas is at stake in Central America," but Congress, fearful of repeating the Vietnam fiasco, proved reluctant to seek a military solution. Reagan opted for covert action. The CIA began supplying the Contras, exiles fighting against the Sandinistas from bases in Honduras and Costa Rica. Despite Democratic objections, the U.S.-backed rebels tried to disrupt the Nicaraguan economy, raiding villages, blowing up oil tanks, and mining harbors. Then, in 1984, Congress passed the Boland Amendment prohibiting any U.S. agency from spending money in Central America. The withdrawal of U.S. financial backing left the Contras in a precarious position.

The only clear-cut triumph that Reagan achieved in the hemisphere came in the Caribbean. In October 1983, a military coup led to the death of the leftist prime minister of Grenada, who was subsequently replaced by an even more radical regime. The Reagan administration, already upset by Grenada's close ties to Cuba and the construction of a large airfield on the small Caribbean island, decided to intervene to prevent the communists from acquiring a strategic military base.

Nearly two thousand U.S. marines invaded Grenada on October 25, 1983. After brief but spirited resistance from eight hundred Cuban workers and troops on the island, the American forces claimed a victory that cost eighteen lives. Reagan proudly pointed to the Grenada invasion as one of his successes in Latin America.

Aside from Grenada, however, the Reagan administration had little to show for its massive military buildup. In the Middle East, its well-intentioned use of marines

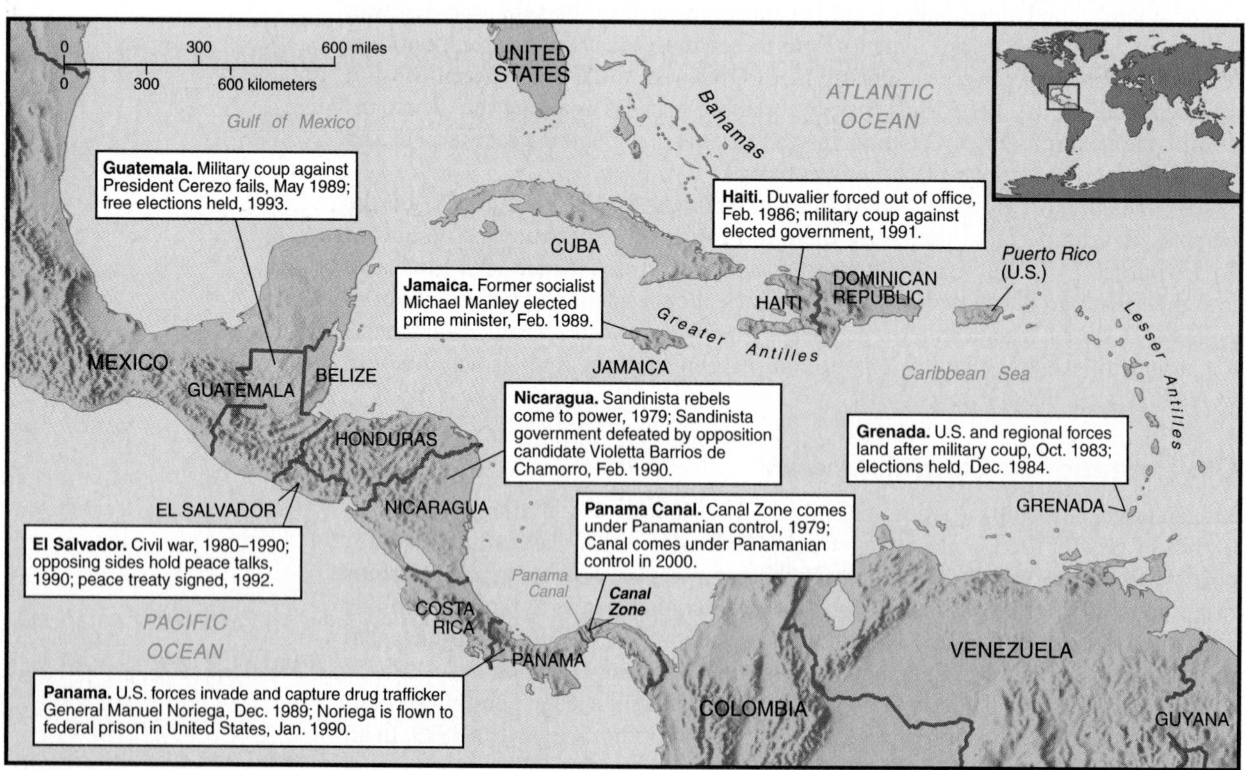

TROUBLE SPOTS IN CENTRAL AMERICA AND THE CARIBBEAN *U.S. involvement in Central American trouble spots intensified in the 1980s.* ❖

had ended in disaster, and its determined opposition to left-wing groups in Central America had at best achieved a stalemate. Relations with the Soviet Union had fallen into one of the deepest chills of the entire Cold War, and the nuclear arms race was more intense than ever.

Trading Arms for Hostages

The Reagan administration's policies in the Middle East and Central America reached a tragic convergence in the **Iran-Contra affair.** In mid-1985, Robert McFarlane, Reagan's national security adviser, began a new initiative designed to restore American influence in the troubled Middle East. Concerned over the fate of six Americans held hostage in Lebanon by groups thought to be loyal to the Ayatollah Khomeini, McFarlane proposed trading American antitank missiles to Iran in return for the hostages' release. Although he realized that the president was primarily concerned with the fate of the hostages, one of whom was CIA officer William Buckley, McFarlane's main goal in proposing the exchange was to establish good relations with moderate elements in Iran, anticipating the aged Khomeini's death. The Iranians, desperate for weapons in the war they had been waging against Iraq since 1980, seemed willing to comply.

Iran-Contra affair The Iran-Contra affair involved officials high in the Reagan administration secretly selling arms to Iran and using the proceeds to finance the Contra rebels in Nicaragua. This illegal transaction usurped the congressional power of the purse.

McFarlane soon found himself in over his head. He relied heavily on a young marine lieutenant colonel assigned to the National Security Council (NSC), Oliver North, and North in turn sought the assistance of CIA director William Casey. Casey soon took charge. By early 1986, when John Poindexter, a naval officer with little political experience, replaced a burned-out McFarlane as national security adviser, Casey was able to persuade the president to go ahead with shipments of both antitank missiles and antiaircraft missiles to Iran.

The concept of trading arms for hostages was fatally flawed. The Reagan administration, in an effort to help end the war between Iran and Iraq, had imposed an arms embargo on Iran and had tried to prevent U.S. allies from sending weapons there. In addition, no sooner was one hostage released than several more Americans were taken hostage. As one observer commented, "As soon as Iran realized how highly we valued getting those hostages back, they apparently kept a good supply of hostages to ensure that we would do their bidding."

The arms deal with Iran was bad policy, but what came next was criminal. Ever since the Boland Amendment in late 1984 had cut off congressional funding, the Reagan administration had been searching for ways to supply the Contras. Oliver North was put in charge of soliciting donations from wealthy right-wing Americans. In early 1986, North had what he later described as a "neat idea" (apparently shared by Casey)—he could use the enormous profits from the sale of weapons to Iran to finance the Contras. North's ploy was clearly not only illegal but also unconstitutional, since it meant usurping the congressional power of the purse.

Unlike the policy of trading arms for hostages, the diversion of the profits to the Contras was a closely held secret. Apparently only North, Casey, and Poindexter were aware of the illegal activity until November 1986, when the press finally learned of the Iranian arms sales. While Attorney General Edwin Meese conducted an internal investigation, North hurriedly destroyed most of the incriminating documents but overlooked one key memo that revealed the Contra diversion.

The political fallout was heavy. The administration, having learned from the Watergate cover-up, tried to control the damage by breaking the bad news itself. But the subsequent investigations led to the dismissal of Poindexter and North, and Donald Regan was forced to resign. Although every effort was made to protect Reagan himself, a poll taken in December 1986 revealed that his popularity had dropped from 67 percent to 46 percent in just a month, the steepest decline ever recorded.

The vital question of whether Ronald Reagan had approved of the Contra diversion was never answered satisfactorily. Public opinion polls indicated that most Americans suspected that the president was at least aware of the Contra diversion. In the absence of firm evidence, however, they were willing to give Reagan the benefit of the doubt, and a protracted congressional hearing in the summer of 1987 did little to clear up the confusion.

While he escaped from the Iran-Contra affair without being held fully responsible for it, Reagan's presidency was in serious trouble. In Congress, the Democrats, who gained control of the Senate as well as the House in the 1986 elections, began to override his vetoes, reject his nominees, and bring a total halt to even humanitarian aid to the Contras. Reagan was still in the White House, but his reliance on others to conduct the affairs of state had robbed him of his power to lead the nation.

Reagan the Peacemaker

By the end of 1987, Reagan made a remarkable recovery. Stepping into the foreign affairs arena, Reagan shed his image as a hawk and set out to reverse the course of Soviet-American relations.

A momentous change in leadership in the Soviet Union proved fortunate. Mikhail Gorbachev, a young and dynamic Soviet leader, had a new vision for his country. Gorbachev was equally intent on improving relations with the United States as part of his new policy of *perestroika* (restructuring the Soviet economy) and *glasnost* (political openness). Soviet economic performance had been deteriorating steadily and the war in Afghanistan had become a major liability. Gorbachev needed a breathing spell in the arms race and a reduction in Cold War tensions to carry out his sweeping changes at home.

The first meeting between Reagan and Gorbachev, at Geneva in 1985, had gone well but had not led to any significant agreements. A hurried summit at Reykjavik, Iceland, in October 1986, just before the Iran-Contra affair had become public, nearly led to a historic breakthrough. The two men reached general agreement on the long-disputed issue of intermediate nuclear forces (INF) in Europe and then discussed the abolition of all nuclear weapons over the next decade. Although the two leaders could reach no agreement, it was clear that the Soviet Union was eager to curtail the arms race.

The apparent failure at Reykjavik, however, did not halt the new momentum toward peace; both leaders needed a foreign policy triumph too much not to continue the dialogue. Throughout 1987, experts worked out the details of an **Intermediate Nuclear Forces agreement** that promised to become the most significant achievement in disarmament since SALT I in 1972. Meeting in Washington in December 1987, Reagan and Gorbachev agreed to remove and destroy all intermediate-range missiles and to permit on-site inspections to verify the process.

Intermediate Nuclear Forces agreement Signed by President Reagan and Soviet President Gorbachev in Washington in late 1987, this agreement provided for the destruction of all intermediate-range nuclear missiles and permitted on-site inspection for the first time during the Cold War.

Another Reagan-Gorbachev summit in Moscow in mid-1988 did not achieve any further progress toward the goal of reducing the nuclear arsenals, but the pictures of Reagan and Gorbachev strolling amiably about Red Square in front of Lenin's tomb, saluting tourists, and taking turns kissing babies gave rise to the hope that an end to the Cold War was finally in sight.

Reagan's popularity soared to 70 percent, higher than it had been before the Iran-Contra affair. He had succeeded in making a major breakthrough in the nuclear arms race, and he could claim that his policies had moderated Soviet behavior. During the president's last year in office, the Soviets cooperated with the United States in pressuring Iran and Iraq to end their long war. Most impressive of all, Gorbachev moved to end the invasion of Afghanistan that had renewed the Cold War in 1979. By the time Reagan left office in January 1989, he had scored a series of foreign policy triumphs that offset his dismal Iran-Contra fiasco and thus helped redeem his presidency.

Social Dilemmas

Two complex social issues arose in the 1980s that went against the grain of the general sense of well-being in the Reagan and Bush years. A massive viral epidemic and a new drug crisis threatened the social fabric of the United States, yet the government failed to respond promptly or effectively to either one.

The AIDS Epidemic

The outbreak of **AIDS** (acquired immune deficiency syndrome) in the early 1980s took most Americans by surprise. Even health experts had difficulty grasping the nature and extent of the new public health threat. Doctors first noticed a few cases of a rare form of pneumonia and an unusual type of skin cancer in male patients in New York and San Francisco in 1981, but it was several years before researchers finally identified it as a hitherto unknown virus that had spread from Central Africa by way of Haiti and had found its first American victims primarily among gay men.

AIDS Acquired immune deficiency syndrome (AIDS) is a disease of the immune system transmitted through blood especially by sexual contact or contaminated needles. AIDS reached epidemic proportions in the United States in the 1980s before it was gradually contained in the 1990s.

Initially, AIDS was perceived as a threat only to gay men. With a growing sense of urgency as the death toll mounted, gay men began to practice safer sex, using condoms and confining themselves to trusted partners. It soon became clear, however, that AIDS could not be so easily contained. It began to appear among intravenous (IV) drug users who shared the same needles and eventually among hemophiliacs and others receiving frequent blood transfusions. The threat of a contaminated national blood supply terrified middle-class America, as did the possibility of the spread of AIDS to heterosexuals.

Scientists tried to reassure the public by explaining that the virus could be spread only by the exchange of bodily fluids, primarily blood and semen, and not by casual contact. The death of movie star Rock Hudson in the summer of 1985 intensified the sense of national panic. Controversy soon developed over proposals for mandatory blood tests for suspected carriers and the segregation of AIDS victims. The integrity of hospital blood supplies caused the most realistic concern; in 1985, a new test finally gave reassurance that transfusions could be performed safely.

The Reagan administration proved slow and halting in its approach to the AIDS epidemic. Lack of sympathy for gays and a need to reduce the deficit worked against any large increase in health spending; what little money was devoted to AIDS went almost entirely for research rather than for educational measures to slow its spread. The only real leadership came from Surgeon General C. Everett Koop, who surprised his conservative backers in 1986 by coming out boldly with proposals for sex education, the use of condoms to ensure "safer sex," and confidential blood testing to help contain the disease.

While the administration dallied, the grim toll mounted. Since the average time between the initial infection and the first symptoms was five years and could be as long as fourteen years, efforts at prevention had little immediate impact. In November 1983, there were 2,803 known cases and 1,416 deaths; by the time Rock Hudson died in mid-1985, more than 12,000 cases and more than 6,000 deaths had been reported.

Growing public concern finally led to action. In 1987, President Reagan appointed a special presidential commission headed by Admiral James Watkins, a former chief of naval operations, to study the AIDS epidemic. The Watkins report in 1988 criticized the administration's AIDS efforts as "inconsistent" and recommended a new effort that included antidiscrimination legislation and explicit prevention education. Koop responded by sending out a pamphlet titled *Understanding AIDS* to 107 million households, and that fall, Congress voted to spend $1.3 billion to fight AIDS, with much of the money going for confidential testing and counseling and home care for victims.

❖ A Look at the Past ❖

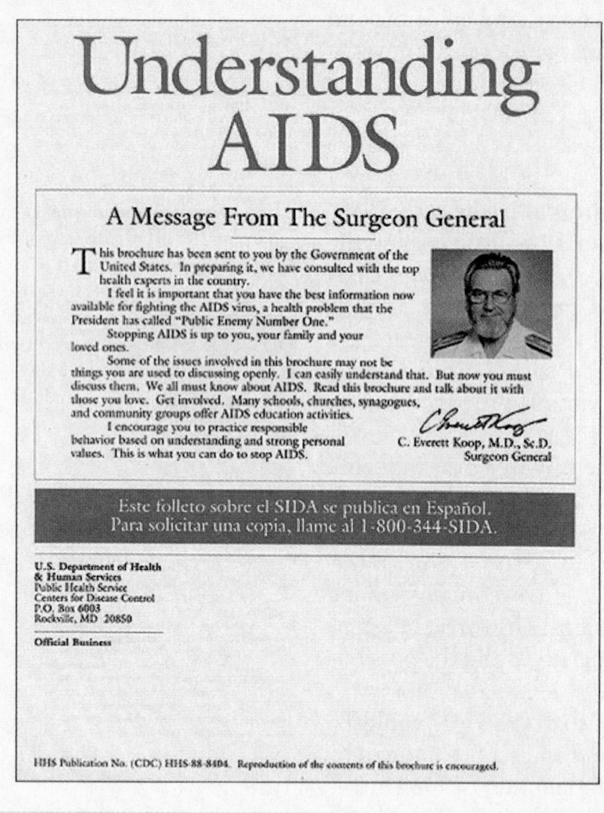

Understanding AIDS

A Message From The Surgeon General

This brochure has been sent to you by the Government of the United States. In preparing it, we have consulted with the top health experts in the country.

I feel it is important that you have the best information now available for fighting the AIDS virus, a health problem that the President has called "Public Enemy Number One."

Stopping AIDS is up to you, your family and your loved ones.

Some of the issues involved in this brochure may not be things you are used to discussing openly. I can easily understand that. But now you must discuss them. We all must know about AIDS. Read this brochure and talk about it with those you love. Get involved. Many schools, churches, synagogues, and community groups offer AIDS education activities.

I encourage you to practice responsible behavior based on understanding and strong personal values. This is what you can do to stop AIDS.

C. Everett Koop, M.D., Sc.D.
Surgeon General

Este folleto sobre el SIDA se publica en Español.
Para solicitar una copia, llame al 1-800-344-SIDA.

U.S. Department of Health
& Human Services
Public Health Service
Centers for Disease Control
P.O. Box 6003
Rockville, MD 20850

Official Business

HHS Publication No. (CDC) HHS-88-8404. Reproduction of the contents of this brochure is encouraged.

AIDS Brochure

In response to the rapid spread of AIDS in the 1980s and the growing public concern about the new and deadly disease, Surgeon General C. Everett Koop wrote an eight-page brochure titled *Understanding AIDS* that was mailed out by the Public Health Service in 1988 to all 107 million U.S. households. It was the largest public health mailing ever done. Shown here is the first page of the booklet with a message from the surgeon general. Note the availability of a Spanish version of the publication. Why do you think the government sponsored a mass mailing on AIDS? According to this brochure, what is one chief weapon in stopping the AIDS epidemic? Why do you suppose many people at the time found the mailing controversial? Do you think it would still be considered controversial if it were mailed today?

Despite the new efforts, the epidemic continued to grow. In 1987, there were 50,000 cases; by mid-1989, the count had reached 100,000. The U.S. Centers for Disease Control in Atlanta reported more than 200,000 cases at the end of 1991; the toll had increased to more than 500,000 by mid-1996.

The number of those infected with HIV appeared to be stabilizing by the mid-1990s at between 650,000 and 900,000. Yet what was once known as the "gay disease" had spread far beyond that one group in society by the end of the century. Minorities and the young were at greatest risk. African American youths made up two-thirds of the new HIV cases among people under 25. "The disease is disappearing from the mainstream," claimed a Washington, D.C., clinic director, "and becoming a disease of kids who are disenfranchised anyway."

The most encouraging development was a fall-off in the death rate from AIDS that began in the mid-1990s. Health officials attributed the decline to heavier spending on treatment and prevention and, above all, to powerful new drug combinations. By 2001, however, the drop in new cases and deaths from AIDS began to level off. "The latest data," commented one expert in August 2001, "suggest that the era of dramatic declines is now over." There was a particularly alarming increase in the number of new cases among young gay men who apparently believed that the new treatment had made the disease manageable. But unfortunately the so-called AIDS cocktail was very expensive, running as high as $15,000 a year, and did not work for everyone. And even more disturbing was the growing realization that AIDS was threatening to decimate the population of Third World countries, especially in sub-Sahara Africa.

The War on Drugs

The 1980s witnessed the rapid spread of cocaine use in America, leading to a growing sense of social crisis by the end of the decade. Cocaine had long been viewed as a relatively harmless recreational drug used by only a few people—rock musicians, Hollywood producers, and the very wealthy. By the end of the 1970s, the snorting of cocaine had spread beyond these groups. The "illusion of instant happiness" came at a high price—$100 for a few snorts and the danger of brain damage or death from an overdose. Nevertheless, the number of users exceeded four million by 1982.

By the mid-1980s, however, cocaine suddenly was perceived as a danger to American society. The deaths of several celebrities from cocaine overdoses alarmed the public. More ominous was the emergence of crack, a cheap cocaine derivative that could be smoked in a pipe to give a very intense high. Dealers sold this new form of cocaine for as little as $10 a dose, opening up a vast new market among the poor in the urban ghettos. By 1986, an estimated 5.8 million people were using cocaine at least once a month and more than 600,000 were confirmed addicts.

Despite its relatively low cost, crack led to an explosion of urban crime. The brief but intense high lasted only a few minutes, leading users to keep smoking more, desensitizing their nervous systems and thus forcing them to use still larger amounts to achieve euphoria. Needing as much as $1,000 of crack each day to sustain their habits, users resorted to crime sprees to gain the necessary funds. By 1987, more than 70 percent of all suspects arrested for burglary in Manhattan tested positive for cocaine.

The Reagan administration tried several approaches to the problem posed by cocaine. In 1982, First Lady Nancy Reagan chose drug education as her special project. Using the slogan "Just Say No," she urged schools, churches, and civic groups to inform young people about the dangers of cocaine. Her program helped educate the middle class but had little impact on the crack smokers in the ghetto.

In the mid-1980s, the administration began to place greater emphasis on interdiction, using agents of the Drug Enforcement Agency (DEA, a body created by President Nixon in 1973), the Customs Bureau, and the Coast Guard to try to seal off the nation's borders. An international cartel of drug dealers, led by a group of Colombians, overcame this effort by saturating the nation with cocaine, losing only a fraction to the hard-pressed DEA. In reality, the Reagan administration was unwilling to devote the personnel and resources that truly effective interdiction would require; with one eye on the deficit, Washington was content with a few highly publicized skirmishes in what it termed the War on Drugs.

The very nature of the cocaine industry frustrated a third, and potentially most promising, countermeasure, wiping out the coca fields and processing plants in South America. The administration relied on diplomatic efforts in cooperation with the governments of Colombia, Bolivia, and Peru to curb the trade in cocaine, with little success. For many South American farmers, no alternative existed outside growing coca, the plant from whose leaves cocaine was derived.

The efforts of the Bush administration proved no more successful than the Reagan program. An ambitious "Andean strategy," funded at more than $2 billion, pledged American support for antidrug programs in Colombia, Bolivia, and Peru. Yet by 1992, coca leaf production had reached the record level of 336,300 tons, nearly three times what it was in 1984.

The Clinton administration proved equally unsuccessful in its two-part approach to the drug problem. One aspect of the new Democratic strategy was to focus primarily on trying to curtail drug use in the United States. But a reduced budget and the inherent difficulty in attacking the causes of drug addiction blocked any progress. By 1996, the number of Americans engaging in illicit drug use, primarily marijuana, had dropped to twelve million, but the number of heroin and cocaine users remained stable at about three million.

The Clinton administration's other approach to the drug war was to focus its overseas efforts primarily on eradicating the source of cocaine in Colombia, Bolivia, and Peru. A presidential directive issued in November 1993 targeted foreign drug cartels as a "national security threat." Although the new policy led to the arrest of eight major cartel chieftains in Colombia, the flow of drugs into the United States continued unabated, with Mexico becoming the new pipeline, funneling an estimated 210 tons of cocaine to the United States in 1995. By the turn of the century, it was clear that there was no end in sight to the war on drugs.

Passing the Torch to Bush

Reagan's triumphal reelection in 1984 raised Republican hopes they had achieved a major political realignment in 1980. The economic boom that had begun after the 1982 recession, along with the promise of the end of the Cold War, reinforced this trend and enabled George Bush to replace Ronald Reagan in the White House.

The Changing Palace Guard

Ronald Reagan had always been especially dependent on aides and assistants. He saw his own role as standing above the heat of bureaucratic battle, providing the nation with a set of goals and a vision of the future. As the "Great Communicator," he built the public consensus and let others manage the more mundane task of turning his dreams into reality.

His initial success depended heavily on the very effective White House team of James Baker, Edwin Meese, and Michael Deaver. Baker, a Texan with extensive Washington experience, became chief of staff, managing the White House and directing legislative strategy. But Ronald Reagan's laid-back style was misleading. Although it is true that he preferred to be presented with solutions rather than problems, it was Reagan's determination to cut taxes, reduce domestic spending, and rebuild America's defenses that gave shape and coherence to his administration's policies. In the White House, he thrived on the interplay among Baker, Meese, and Deaver, letting them present various alternatives and then instinctively suggesting compromises. Neither brilliant nor well read, Reagan had a quick mind and a remarkable feel for the public's emotions that enabled him to perform effectively as a detached but charismatic chief executive.

An abrupt change in the White House staff in 1985 nearly proved disastrous for Reagan. Tired of the constant infighting, Baker agreed to Secretary of the Treasury Regan's suggestion that the two men swap jobs. A self-made Wall Street operator, Regan possessed a confident, abrasive manner and a determination to assert his authority as White House chief of staff. When Meese became attorney general and Deaver left the government later in 1985, Regan took advantage of the president's passive nature, extending his own control and thus ending the give-and-take in the Oval Office that had allowed Reagan to shape policy choices during his first term.

At first, Regan and Baker were able to score a major victory. Intent on lowering taxes on the wealthy still more while capitalizing on growing congressional demands for a simpler and fairer revenue system, the two men pressed for a major overhaul of the income tax. Working with Congress, they hammered out the 1986 Tax Reform Act, which cut the top rate from 50 to 28 percent while wiping out most shelters by severely restricting tax breaks for losses in real estate ventures and many other speculative enterprises. The new rates exempted six million people at the lower end from paying taxes while an alternative minimum tax prevented the rich from escaping their fair share. Although designed to bring in the same total revenue, the new act led to short-term increases in business taxes that kept the federal deficit from growing any larger.

The administration had only partial success in another area—appointing conservative federal judges who would simply follow the law and leave policy issues to Congress and state legislatures. In 1986, after a brief skirmish with the Senate, he succeeded in replacing outgoing Chief Justice Warren Burger with the Supreme Court's strongest conservative, William Rehnquist. Equally conservative appeals court judge Antonin Scalia joined the Supreme Court at the same time. But in 1987, when the president nominated Robert Bork, an outspoken opponent of judicial activism, to fill the next vacancy, Democrats drew the line. Opposition from labor and civil rights groups finally led the Senate to reject Bork's nomination by a vote of 58 to 42. It was a bittersweet victory, however, as Reagan responded by appointing the moderately conservative, but far more diplomatic, Anthony Kennedy to the Court.

George Bush, Reagan's successor in the White House, made two appointments to the Supreme Court. His first choice, David H. Souter of New Hampshire, reflected the president's desire to avoid the kind of controversy stirred by the Bork nomination. Souter, dubbed "the stealth nominee" because of his unknown views on controversial issues, won Senate approval easily in 1991, but then, to the dismay of conservatives, sided consistently with the liberal minority on the Court. Bush's second choice, Clarence Thomas, proved far more controversial. Picked in 1991 to replace Thurgood Marshall, Thomas was an African American conservative who opposed affirmative action. Despite his race, civil rights groups opposed his nomination on ideological grounds. The Senate Judiciary Committee hearings became explosive when University of Oklahoma law school professor Anita Hill accused Thomas of sexual harassment when she had been employed by him in a government agency a decade earlier. Thomas denied the charges and defended himself by accusing the Judiciary Committee of conducting "a high tech lynching of an uppity black who in any way deigns to think for himself." The Senate finally confirmed Thomas by a vote of just 52 to 48, the narrowest margin ever for a Supreme Court appointment. The American people, however, had fewer reservations about Thomas, as polls showed 58 percent believing him and only 24 percent finding Hill's charges credible. On the Court, Thomas regularly voted in tandem with Justice Antonin Scalia, leader of the conservative bloc, and thus, despite Souter's defection, his appointment ensured that the Court would continue to champion free market principles over increased governmental regulation.

The Election of 1988

The Democrats approached the 1988 election with growing optimism. They had regained control of the Senate in 1986. Ronald Reagan would not be on the ballot. The Iran-Contra and the looming budget deficit all appeared to place the GOP on the defensive. Michael Dukakis, the successful governor of Massachusetts, emerged from the grueling primary contests the clear-cut winner. With the selection of moderate Texas Senator Lloyd Bentsen as his vice presidential running mate, Dukakis left the convention at Atlanta confident of victory, with polls showing him ahead by 17 points.

The republican nominee, Vice President George Bush, proved to be a much stronger candidate than anyone had expected. Despite the controversial choice of Indiana Senator Dan Quayle as his running mate, Bush quickly regained the lead. The Republicans waged a ruthless attack on Dukakis, portraying him as soft on crime and defense. Above all, the GOP candidate repeatedly promised not to raise taxes, reiterating his favorite line: "Read my lips—no new taxes."

The election's outcome confirmed the pollsters' projections. Bush won overwhelmingly in the South, carried most of the West, and defeated Dukakis in such key industrial states as Michigan and Pennsylvania. His victory reflected the continuing GOP dominance of the electoral college, as well as the natural advantage of an incumbent at a time when the economy was healthy and the world at relative peace. The Democrats, however, increased their margins in both the House and the Senate.

The election of 1988 indicated that, at least on the presidential level, a significant change had taken place in American politics in 1980. Bush consolidated the GOP's grip on the electoral college, winning in the Sunbelt states of the South and West and cementing much of Reagan's inroads into the working-class vote. At the same time, racial polarization in politics continued, with Dukakis getting 88 percent of the African American vote and 69 percent of the Hispanic ballots. The Democrats, despite their success in Congress, faced the challenge of trying to regain the support of white middle-class voters for their presidential candidates.

Bush's Domestic Agenda

Many people expected the Bush administration to reflect the reputation of the new president—bland and cautious, lacking in vision but safely predictable. At home, he lived up to his reputation, sponsoring few initiatives in education, health care, and environmental protection while continuing the Reagan theme of limiting federal interference in the everyday lives of American citizens. He vetoed family leave legislation, refused to sponsor meaningful health care reform, and watered down civil rights proposals in Congress. The one exception was the **Americans with Disabilities Act (ADA),** passed by Congress in 1991, which prohibited discrimination against the disabled in hiring, transportation, and public accommodations.

Americans with Disabilities Act (ADA) Passed by Congress in 1991, the ADA banned discrimination against the disabled in employment and mandated easy access to all public and commercial buildings.

Most of Bush's time was taken up with two pressing domestic problems. First, the nation's savings and loan industry, based on U.S. government–insured deposits, was in grave trouble as a result of lax regulation and unwise, even possibly fraudulent, loan policies. After record losses of $13.4 billion in 1988, more than 250 S&Ls had been forced to close. The continuing budget deficit provided an even greater challenge. The nation simply spent beyond its means, with deficits still running more than $150 billion a year.

The president and Congress finally reached agreement on both issues. In August 1989, Congress passed an administration bill to close or merge more than seven hundred ailing S&Ls at a cost of $157 billion over a ten-year period. Financial institutions would pay about two-thirds of the total, the federal government the remaining $50 billion. The proposal included a restructuring of the federal regulatory system and bond provisions to keep the thrift bailout from adding to the deficit. A new federal agency, the Resolution Trust Corporation (RTC), closed more than five hundred S&Ls, primarily in the Sunbelt states, and took over the properties on which developers had secured loans many times their actual value and gradually sold them off at discount prices. By the time the RTC expired in 1992, the initial cost to the government was more than $150 billion, and the eventual bill for the S&L cleanup, including interest, was estimated at between $500 and $700 billion.

Action on the budget proved even more difficult. Facing a Gramm-Rudman goal of $110 billion for the 1991 budget, Bush finally got Congress to accept a deficit of $105 billion in late 1989. The following year, facing a deficit of more than $200 billion, George Bush finally agreed to break his "no new taxes" pledge and support a budget that included both new taxes on the wealthy and substantial spending cuts, mainly for the military. The resulting agreement projected a savings of $500 billion over five years, half from reduced spending and half from new taxes.

Unfortunately for the president, the budget deal coincided with the beginning of a slow but painful recession that ended the Republican prosperity of the 1980s (see Chapter 33). Not only did Bush face recriminations from voters for breaking his "read my lips" pledge, but the economic decline led to greatly reduced government revenues. As a result, the deficit continued to soar. Instead of reducing the deficit by $500 billion, the 1990 budget agreement had led to an increase of more than $1 trillion in the national debt during Bush's presidency.

The End of the Cold War

Abroad, the Bush administration faced an unprecedented year of change that marked the end of the post–World War II era. In country after country, communism gave way to freedom as the Cold War seemed to melt away more quickly than anyone had dared hope.

The first attempt at internal liberation proved tragically abortive. In May 1989, students in China began a monthlong demonstration for freedom in Peking's Tiananmen Square that attracted worldwide attention. Americans were fascinated to see Chinese students call for democracy with a hunger strike and a handcrafted replica of the Statue of Liberty. But on the evening of June 4, the Chinese leaders sent tanks and troops to the square to quash the demonstration. The next day, full-scale repression swept over China. Chinese leaders imposed martial law to quell the dissent and shatter any hope for a democratic China.

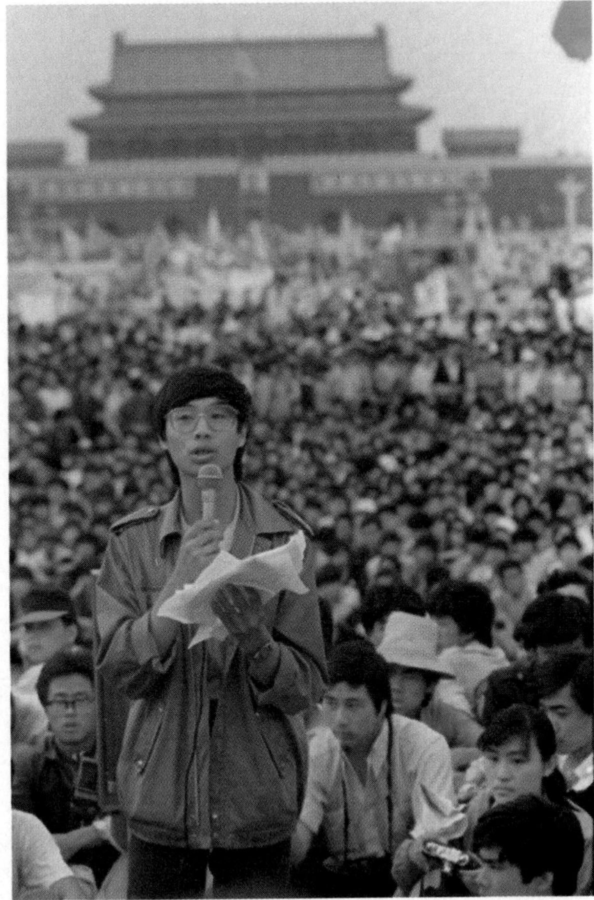

Fed up with the corruption that accompanied the economic benefits of Chinese leader Deng Xiaoping's reforms, Chinese students demonstrated for democracy in the spring of 1989. Their nonviolent protest in Beijing's Tiananmen Square at first evoked a surprisingly passive government response. Here, student leader Wang Dan, standing before a large crowd in Tiananmen Square on May 27, calls for a citywide march. In early June, military action was called for to break the students' resistance. Tanks, armored personnel carriers, and trucks cleared the square after firing on the unarmed students. ❖

President Bush responded cautiously. He wanted to preserve American influence with the Chinese government. So despite official statements denouncing the crackdown, Bush permitted National Security Adviser Brent Scowcroft to undertake a secret mission to Peking to maintain a working relationship with the Chinese leaders.

A far more promising trend toward freedom began in Europe in mid-1989. In June, Lech Walesa and his Solidarity movement came to power in free elections in Poland. Soon the winds of change were sweeping over the former Iron Curtain countries. One by one, the repressive governments of Hungary, East Germany, Czechoslovakia, Bulgaria, and Romania fell. The most heartening scene of all took place in East Germany in early November when the new Communist leaders suddenly announced the opening of the Berlin Wall. Workers quickly demolished a 12-foot-high section of the despised physical symbol of the Cold War, joyously singing a German version of "For He's a Jolly Good Fellow."

Most people realized that Mikhail Gorbachev was responsible for the liberation of eastern Europe. In late 1988, he signaled the spread of his reforms to the Soviet satellites by announcing that the Brezhnev Doctrine, which called for Soviet control of eastern Europe, was now replaced with "the Sinatra doctrine," which meant that the people of this region could now do things "their way." It was Gorbachev's refusal to use armed force to keep repressive regimes in power that permitted the long-delayed liberation of the captive peoples of central and eastern Europe.

Yet by the end of 1991, both Gorbachev and the Soviet Union had become victims of the demise of communism. On August 19, 1991, eight right-wing plotters placed Gorbachev under arrest while he was vacationing in the Crimea and attempted to seize control of the government in Moscow. Boris Yeltsin, the newly

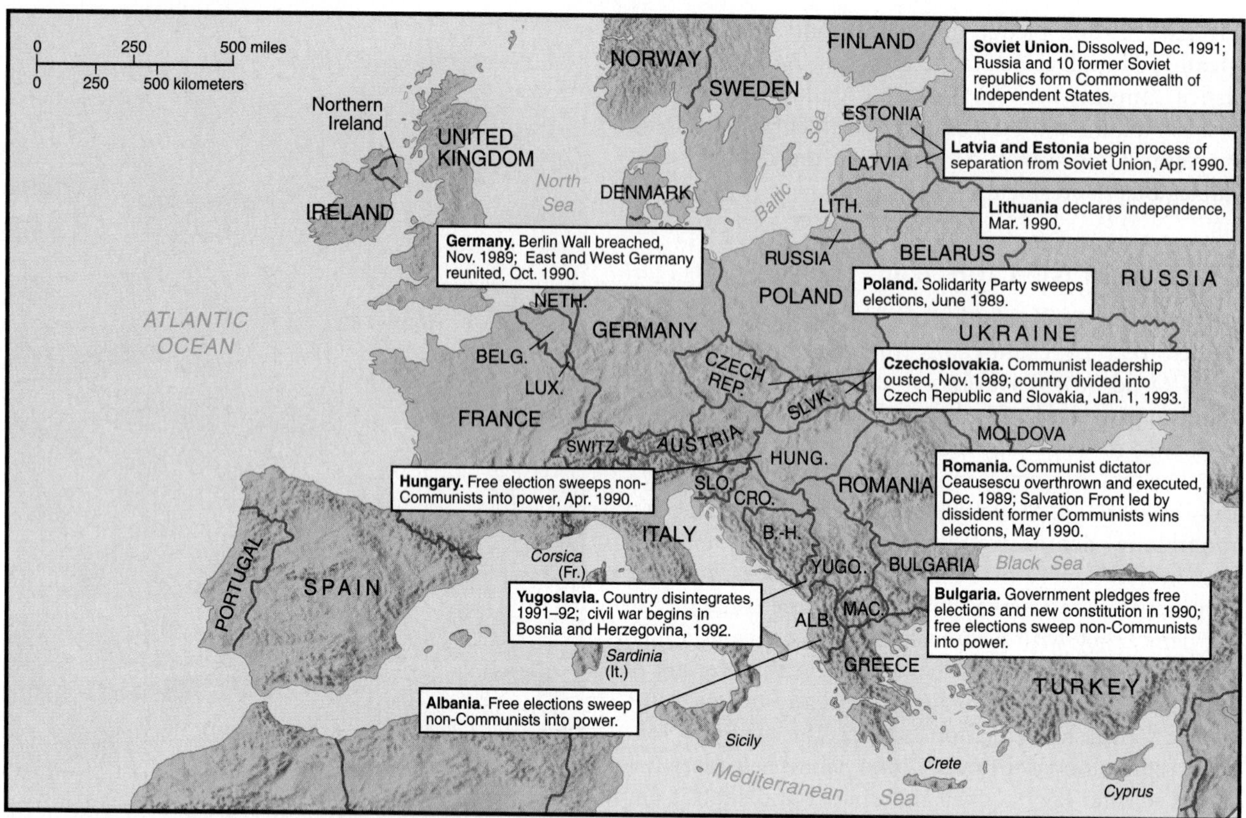

THE END OF THE COLD WAR *Free elections in Poland in June 1989 triggered the domino effect in the fall of communism in eastern Europe and the former Soviet Union. Changes in policy came quickly, but the restructuring of social and economic institutions continues to take time.* ✧

elected president of the Russian Republic, however, broke up the coup by mounting a tank in Moscow and demanding Gorbachev's release. The Red Army rallied to Yeltsin's side. The coup failed, and Gorbachev was released, only to resign in December 1991 after the fifteen republics dissolved the Soviet Union.

Russia, by far the largest and most powerful of the former Soviet republics, took the lead in joining with ten others to form a loose alignment called the Commonwealth of Independent States (CIS). Yeltsin then disbanded the Communist party and continued the reforms begun by Gorbachev to establish democracy and a free market system in Russia. The Bush administration, although criticized for its cautious approach, welcomed the demise of communism and offered economic assistance to Russia and the other members of the new CIS. The most important steps came in the critical area of nuclear weapons. In 1991, Bush and Gorbachev signed several agreements that reduced nuclear warheads, eliminated land missiles with multiple warheads, and curtailed the number of nuclear weapons to a level not seen since the mid-1960s. Bush could claim that by the time he left office in January 1993, the Cold War was over.

Waging Peace

The end of the Cold War, however, did not bring about a world free of violence. In December 1989, twenty-seven thousand American troops invaded Panama and quickly installed a new government friendly to the United States in the largest American military operation since the Vietnam War. Despite the death of twenty-three Americans and several hundred Panamanians, this action won approval from the people of both countries when it resulted in the capture of drug-trafficking General Manuel Noriega. By taking such bold and decisive action in Panama, Bush was able to shake his reputation for caution. But critics noted that the president, in the best tradition of the Cold War, had waged war without consulting Congress.

For three decades the Berlin Wall stood as the most visible symbol of the division between East and West in the Cold War. Dismantling of the wall in November 1989 marked the beginning of the end of the Cold War. ❖

Eight months later, Bush suddenly faced a much graver challenge. On August 2, 1990, Saddam Hussein, the dictatorial ruler of Iraq, stunned the world by invading defenseless Kuwait and threatening Saudi Arabia and the oil-rich Persian Gulf region. The president responded firmly, despite an earlier balance-of-power policy of supporting Iraq against Iran. He accused Saddam of naked aggression and carefully built up a UN coalition to uphold what he termed "a new world order." Equally important, he quickly persuaded Saudi Arabia to accept a huge American troop buildup, dubbed Desert Shield. With the United States importing nearly half of the oil the American people used every day, there was a compelling strategic need to prevent the bulk of the world's oil reserves from falling under the sway of Saddam Hussein. Whatever the appeal of the president's call for a "new world order," control of the Persian Gulf was clearly a vital national interest.

Debate raged, however, on the best way to meet the Iraqi threat. Many Democrats in Congress supported Bush's efforts to place international economic sanctions on Iraq but opposed the use of force. Bush had clearly opted for a different solution by November. Operation Desert Shield was giving way to **Operation Desert Storm.** After securing UN support and winning a vote in Congress, Bush on January 17, 1991, unleashed a devastating aerial assault on Iraq. The overwhelming American advantage in modern weaponry softened up Saddam's forces; when the ground offensive began on February 24, it took only a hundred hours to bring about the collapse of Iraq's military forces.

Operation Desert Storm Desert Storm was the code name used by the United States and its coalition partners in waging war against Iraq in early 1991 to liberate Kuwait.

Desert Storm brought mixed blessings. It was a great personal victory for George Bush, who saw his approval rating climb to an unprecedented level.

Antiaircraft fire lights up the sky over Baghdad, Iraq, during the 1991 Persian Gulf War. A month of strikes on Iraqi targets was followed by a ground offensive that lasted only one hundred hours before Iraqi troops began to surrender and President Bush ordered a cease-fire. Critics of Bush's decision argued that stopping the advance allowed an unvanquished Saddam Hussein to remain in power in Iraq. ❖

CHRONOLOGY

1980	Ronald Reagan wins the presidency in a landslide
1981	American hostages in Iran are released after 444 days in captivity (January) ❖ Sandra Day O'Connor becomes the first woman U.S. Supreme Court justice (September)
1982	Equal Rights Amendment fails state ratification (June) ❖ Unemployment reaches a postwar record high of 10.4 percent (October)
1983	Soviets shoot down Korean airliner (September) ❖ United States invades Grenada (October)
1984	Russia boycotts summer Olympics in Los Angeles (July) ❖ Ronald Reagan is reelected president (November)
1985	Mikhail Gorbachev becomes leader of the Soviet Union (March)
1986	Space shuttle *Challenger* explodes, killing seven astronauts (January) ❖ Iran-Contra affair is made public (November)
1987	Reagan and Gorbachev sign INF treaty at Washington summit
1988	George Bush defeats Michael Dukakis decisively in the presidential election
1989	*Exxon Valdez* oil spill pollutes more than 500 square miles of Alaskan waters (March) ❖ San Francisco rocked by massive earthquake (October) ❖ Berlin Wall crumbles (November)
1990	Saddam Hussein invades Kuwait (August) ❖ Bush breaks his "no new taxes" campaign pledge, supports $500 billion budget deal (November)
1991	Operation Desert Storm frees Kuwait and crushes Iraq (January–February) ❖ Soviet Union dissolved, replaced by Commonwealth of Independent States (December)

American military leaders believed that they had finally atoned for Vietnam, a sentiment widely shared by a euphoric public. Best of all, the price of gasoline, which had climbed to a record $1.34 a gallon in October, fell back to just over $1 a gallon. At the same time, however, Saddam Hussein continued to rule in Baghdad, persecuting Kurds in northern Iraq and Shi'ite Muslims in the south. Most alarming of all, the Persian Gulf War had halted a slow recovery from the lingering recession and revived growing fears for America's economic health in the post–Cold War years.

Conclusion: Republican Economic Woes

In the long run, the Persian Gulf War may have damaged George Bush more than it helped him politically. It was his concentration on the Gulf crisis that led him to enter into the budget deal with congressional Democrats in the fall of 1990—a deal that alienated conservative Republicans and left him open to the charge of violating his 1988 campaign pledge not to raise taxes. Most damaging of all for Bush, the Gulf War had halted a slow recovery from the lingering recession and revived fears over America's economic health in the post–Cold War era. For twelve years, the Republicans had relied on a robust economy to enact their programs and consolidate their power—now the Democrats finally had a chance to accuse the GOP of endangering the nation's economic health.

Key Terms

Moral Majority, p. 630
Neoconservatism, p. 630
supply-side economics, p. 632
deregulation, p. 633
Gramm-Rudman, p. 635
Strategic Defense Initiative (SDI), p. 638
Iran-Contra affair, p. 641
Intermediate Nuclear Forces agreement, p. 642
AIDS, p. 643
Americans with Disabilities Act (ADA), p. 648
Operation Desert Storm, p. 651

Recommended Reading

A British observer, Godfey Hodgson, gives a perceptive and balanced analysis of the conservative movement that led to Reagan's election in *The World Turned Right Side Up* (1996). The most detailed account of the Reagan presidency is the second volume of journalist Lou Cannon's biography, *President Reagan* (1991). Bob Schieffer and Gary Paul Gates offer a critical overview of the Reagan administration in *The Acting President* (1989), which focuses on Reagan's detached style of leadership.

Michael Schaller, *Reckoning with Reagan* (1992), and Haynes Johnson, *Sleepwalking Through History* (1991), offer critical accounts of the Reagan administration. For a more positive view by a Reagan aide, see Martin Anderson, *Revolution* (1988). Thomas Ferguson and Joel Rogers analyze the political realignment of the 1980s in *Right Turn* (1985).

For Reagan's foreign policy, the most complete account is by his secretary of state, George Shultz, *Turmoil and Triumph* (1992). Frances Fitzgerald provides a critical analysis of the Strategic Defense Initiative in *Way Out There in the Blue* (2000). The two best accounts of how the Cold War ended are Don Oberdorfer, *The Turn* (1991), and Raymond L. Garthoff, *The Great Transition* (1994). Jay Winik, *On the Brink* (1996), gives the Reagan administration full credit for winning the Cold War.

John Robert Greene provides a balanced view of the Bush administration in *The Presidency of George Bush* (2000); the best biography of the president is Herbert Parmet, *George Bush* (1997). For foreign policy, see George Bush and Brent Scowcroft, *A World Transformed* (1998). Bob Woodward traces the decisions leading to the Gulf War in *The Commanders* (1991); the best overview of the military operations is Michael R. Gordon and Bernard F. Trainor, *The Generals' War* (1995).

For a list of additional titles related to this chapter's topics, please see http://www.ablongman.com/divine.

Suggested Web Sites

The 80s Server
http://www.80s.com/
This site has a variety of sources of information about the 1980s, but the best parts are open to members only.

The Gulf War
http://www.pbs.org/pages/frontline/gulf/index.html
This Frontline and PBS site combines personal accounts with a chronology and general information about the war.

Ronald Wilson Reagan
http://www.ipl.org/ref/POTUS/rwreagan.html
This site contains basic factual data about Reagan's election and presidency, speeches, and on-line biographies.

George Herbert Walker Bush
http://www.ipl.org/ref/POTUS/ghwbush.html
This site contains basic factual data about Bush's election and presidency, speeches, and on-line biographies.

In Their Own Words: NIH Online AIDS History Project
http://aidshistory.nih.gov
National Institutes of Health site documenting the early years of HIV/AIDS. Resources include oral histories of AIDS researchers, a timeline of key events in AIDS history from 1981–1988, document and image archives, and a links page.

Chapter 33

America in Flux

The Buck Starts Here

The two men who met in Little Rock, Arkansas, on December 2, 1992, could not have been more different. Bill Clinton, the president-elect, was gregarious and charming; his guest, Federal Reserve Chairman Alan Greenspan, was shy, gloomy, and reserved. Alan Greenspan was also a genius at statistical analysis and a successful businessman. A lifelong Republican with libertarian instincts such as a strong belief in free markets and the power of the individual, Greenspan had served as chairman of the Council of Economic Advisers in the Ford administration and Ronald Reagan had appointed him chairman of the Federal Reserve Board in 1987. Reappointed to a second four-year term in 1991 by George Bush, Greenspan oversaw the nation's fiscal policy from a modest Washington office dominated by a wall plaque proclaiming, "The Buck Starts Here."

Despite their personal and political differences, Clinton and Greenspan shared a common goal: To rein in the alarming growth of the federal deficit while stimulating the expansion of the stagnant economy. George Bush's $500 billion deal with Congress in 1990 to cut spending and raise taxes had failed to reduce the deficit because of declining government revenues in the recession of 1990–1991. Already over $200 billion a year, the shortfall was expected to reach $400 billion by the end of Clinton's first term. As a result, the interest on the ever-expanding national debt would continue to grow, threatening to surpass defense spending as the government's largest single expense. Even though Clinton had focused on economic revitalization during the campaign, promising a middle-class tax cut and job creation, he realized he would have to give deficit reduction his highest priority.

Greenspan preached the benefits of deficit reduction and lower bond rates. A drop in the cost of borrowing money, both for businesses that were expanding and for home mortgages, could lead to rapid economic growth. And renewed economic growth would create jobs and thus help lower the 6 percent unemployment rate that was hurting American workers.

Greenspan's argument hit home with Clinton. To the dismay of his liberal advisers, Clinton followed Greenspan's advice and made deficit reduction the centerpiece of his economic policy. The president made public the crucial decision in his first State of the Union address on February 17, 1993. Striking a bipartisan note, President Clinton outlined a bold plan to reduce the deficit by more than $500 billion over four years, half by cutting spending and half by raising taxes, mainly on the wealthy.

The applause for Clinton's economic plan reverberated far beyond the halls of Congress and caused his popularity in the polls to rise. More important, in less than two weeks interest rates on 30-year bonds dropped below 7 percent for the first time ever. Greenspan was proved right and Clinton had won his biggest gamble.

Outline

The Changing American Population

Democratic Revival

Clinton and the World

The End of the Century

The New Millennium

Conclusion: The American Century?

Over the next seven years, the Clinton-Greenspan partnership paid off handsomely. The economy boomed with the creation of 20 million new jobs, the stock market soared to new highs year after year, and unemployment fell to an all-time low of 4 percent. Moreover, rising government revenues wiped out the deficit and even produced a $100 billion surplus in 2000. And the future promised to be even brighter.

THE BOOM OF THE 1990S owed its success to more than just wise fiscal policy. An enormous increase in productivity, made possible by new technology, especially computers, enabled workers to turn out more goods without increasing costs, which kept inflation in check. Continued declines in defense spending with the end of the Cold War helped, as did the increases in American exports as a result of new trade policies and agreements. American consumers were the real heroes, buying vast numbers of cars, computers, and household goods in pursuit of the good life. Best of all, even though the wealthy continued to reap the greatest rewards, prosperity reached every level, with those at the bottom making real, if modest, advances.

American life at the turn of the century consisted of more than just material abundance. The population shift to the Sunbelt that began in the 1970s continued through the end of the century, though at a somewhat slower pace. The equally important flow of immigrants from Latin America and Asia, made possible by the Immigration Act of 1965, remained strong, helping to transform the United States into a more ethnically diverse country.

The most surprising development came overseas as the end of the Cold War led not to a peaceful world but rather spawned a series of crises in Africa, the Balkans, and the Middle East that led to frequent American military involvement. Yet even these traditional foreign policy challenges proved minor compared to the threat of international terrorism engendered by America's world supremacy. Attacks on the World Trade Center in 1993 and American embassies in East Africa in 1998 were but the forerunners of the tragic events of September 11, 2001. The hijacking and suicide mission that used American airliners to destroy the twin towers of the World Trade Center and damage the Pentagon shocked the nation and made September 11 a day of infamy equal to December 7, 1941, the day of the Japanese attack on Pearl Harbor.

Bill Clinton, whose second term was marred by his affair with a White House intern, left office in early 2001, replaced by George W. Bush, son of the former President Bush. In his last year in office, Clinton appointed Alan Greenspan to a fourth term as Fed chairman, but a downturn in the economy in early 2001 soon wiped out the projected budget surplus and tarnished Greenspan's reputation for economic wizardry.

The new president, however, faced an even greater challenge than a declining economy as he waged war against the campaign of terrorism conducted by al Qaeda and Osama bin Laden. It was ironic that Clinton, despite his economic success, had never faced in his eight years in office the kind of challenge that gives rise to claims of presidential greatness. Yet President Bush was presented with such an opportunity in only his first year in the White House.

THE CHANGING AMERICAN POPULATION

From the *Mayflower* to the covered wagon, movement has always characterized the American people. The last three decades of the twentieth century witnessed two significant shifts in the American population: movement internally to the Sunbelt region of the South and West and a remarkable influx of immigrants from developing nations. These changes led to increased urbanization, greater ethnic diversity, and growing social unrest.

A People on the Move

Sunbelt This region consists of a broad band of states running across the South from Florida to Texas, extending west and north to include California and the Pacific Northwest. Beginning in the 1970s, this area experienced rapid economic growth and major gains in population.

The most striking finding in the 1980 census was that for the first time in American history, more than half the people lived in the South and West. The **Sunbelt,** a broad band running across the country below the 37th parallel from the Carolinas to southern California, had begun to flourish with the buildup of military bases and defense plants during World War II. Rapid population growth continued with the stimulus of heavy Cold War defense spending and accelerated in the 1970s when both new high-technology firms and more established industries were attracted by lower labor costs and the favorable climate of the Sunbelt states. In the next decade, the flow continued, but at a slower rate. The South, particularly Florida, continued to boom, and cities throughout the Sunbelt thrived. By 1990, Los Angeles had displaced Chicago as the nation's second largest city, and Houston had passed Philadelphia to take fourth position. Eight of the nation's cities now had more than one million residents; four were in the Sunbelt, and of the rest, only New York gained in population in the 1980s.

The increasing urbanization of America had both positive and negative aspects. People living in the large metropolitan areas were both more affluent and better educated than their rural counterparts, but they also had to deal with rising crime rates, longer commutes in heavy traffic, and higher living costs. Nevertheless, the big cities and their suburbs continued to thrive, accounting for 80 percent of all Americans by 2000.

Another striking population trend was the nationwide rise in the number of the elderly. At the beginning of the century, only 4.1 percent of the population was age 65 or older; by 1997, Americans over 65 made up 13 percent of the population, with the nearly 4 million over 85 the fastest-growing group of all. Six of every ten of these older Americans were women, and they tended to have a higher rate of chronic disease and to be worse off economically than younger Americans. Many of those over 85 lived in nursing homes and accounted for one-third of all Medicaid

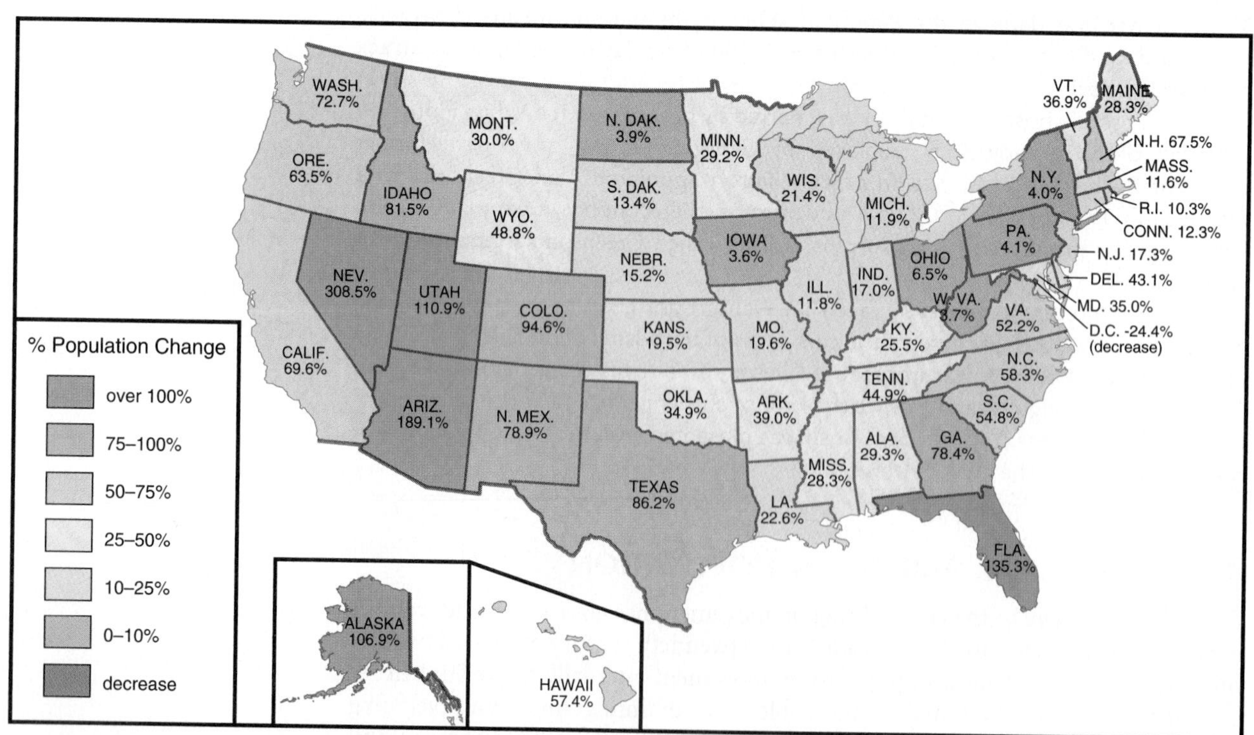

POPULATION SHIFTS, 1970–2000 *Although all fifty states experienced some population growth between 1970 and 2000, states in the West and the South saw the largest percentage increases.* ❖

payments, but annual cost-of-living increases in Social Security payments spared them the worst ravages of inflation. The average family income of those over 65 was just under $20,000 a year in 1985, and three out of four owned their own homes. Most impressive of all was their political power: 65 percent of those over 65 voted regularly, compared to just 46 percent of the entire population. The American Association of Retired Persons (AARP), with more than thirty million members, proved very effective at protecting the interests of the elderly in Washington.

The Revival of Immigration

The flow of immigrants into the United States reached record proportions in the 1990s as a result of the new policies adopted in 1965. (See "Unintended Consequences: The Second Great Migration," pp. 605–606.) The number of new arrivals peaked at more than 2 million in 2001, but then fell back to 1.2 million in 2002 as a result of tighter immigration controls following the September 11 terrorist attacks. By 2002, there was a record high of 32.2 million foreign-born residents of the United States, 11.5 percent of the total population.

The new wave of immigrants came mainly from Latin America and Asia. By 2002, just over half the foreign-born population of the United States came from Latin America, slightly more than one-quarter from Asia, and only 15 percent from Europe. The new immigrants tended to settle in urban areas in six states—California, Texas, New York, Florida, Illinois, and New Jersey. In California, the influx of immigrants from Asia and Mexico created growing pressure on public services, especially during the recession of the early 1990s.

The arrival of more than 26 million immigrants in three decades was bound to lead to controversy over whether immigrants were a benefit or a liability to American society. A study by the National Academy of Sciences in 1997 reported that while government services used by immigrants—schools, welfare, health clinics—cost more initially than was collected from them in taxes, in the long run, immigrants and their families more than paid their way. One scholar estimated that in 1992 immigrants who had entered the country since 1970 had contributed $27 million more in taxes than the cost of social services they had used. In regard to employment, immigrants tended to help consumers and employers by working for relatively low wages in restaurants, the textile industry, and farming, but they hurt low-skilled U.S. workers, notably high school dropouts and many African Americans, by keeping wages low. Economist George J. Borjas, himself a refugee from Cuba, claimed that immigrants from developing counties lacked the education and job skills needed to achieve the level of prosperity attained by newcomers in the past; instead of entering the mainstream of American life, they were likely to remain a permanent underclass.

Public attitudes began to shift toward the end of the century. Legislation adopted in 1996 dropped restrictions on legal immigrants in favor of provisions aimed at illegal aliens—more money to guard the nation's borders and a ban on social services for illegal immigrants. A 1997 poll showed that the number of people who believed immigrants were bad for the nation had dropped from 60 percent in 1993 to 42 percent, with 43 percent affirming the benefits of immigration for the country. The booming economy, with resulting low unemployment, made newcomers willing to do the hard jobs shunned by the native-born appear to be a blessing rather than a threat.

The Surging Hispanics

People of Hispanic origin became the nation's largest ethnic group in 2002, surpassing African Americans for the first time. The rapidly growing Hispanic population had climbed to nearly 39 million, a rise of more than 60 percent, accounting for 13 percent of the nation's population. "It doesn't surprise me," commented the leader of the League of Latin American Citizens. "Anybody that travels around . . . can see Latinos everywhere, working everywhere, trying to reach the American dream."

The Census Bureau identified four major Hispanic categories: Mexican Americans, Puerto Ricans, Cuban Americans, and "other Hispanics," consisting mainly of the original Hispanic population and recent immigrants from Central America. These Hispanic groups were relatively youthful, tended to be relatively poor, were generally employed in low-paying positions. Although the position of Hispanics had improved considerably in the boom years of the 1980s and 1990s, the poverty rate among Hispanics was twice the national average

Lack of education was a key factor in preventing economic progress for Hispanics. The American Council on Education released a report in 1991 that found Hispanics "are grossly under-represented at every rung of the educational ladder." Fewer Hispanics graduated from high school than other minorities and their school dropout rate was the nation's highest at more than 50 percent. Hispanic leaders warned that these figures boded ill not just for their own group, but for society as a whole. "You either educate us," claimed a San Antonio activist, "or you pay for building more jails or for more welfare."

undocumented aliens Once derisively called "wetbacks," undocumented aliens are illegal immigrants, mainly from Mexico and Central America.

The entry of several million illegal immigrants from Mexico, once derisively called "wetbacks" and now known as **undocumented aliens,** created a substantial social problem for the nation and especially for the Southwest. Critics argued that the aliens took jobs away from U.S. citizens, kept wages artificially low, and received extensive welfare and medical benefits that strained budgets in states such as Texas and California. Defenders of the undocumented aliens, however, contended that the nation gained from the abundant supply of workers who were willing to do the backbreaking jobs in fields and factories shunned by most Americans and that these illegal entrants usually paid sales and withholding taxes but rarely used government services for fear of being deported. Whichever view was correct, an exploited class of illegal aliens was living on the edge of poverty.

Concern over economic competition from an estimated four million Mexican "illegals" led Congress to pass legislation in 1986 that penalized employers who hired undocumented workers. Congress permitted those aliens who could show that they were living in the United States before 1982 to become legal residents; nearly three million accepted this offer of amnesty to become legal residents. The reform effort, however, failed to stem the continued flow of undocumented workers northward from Mexico in the 1990s—perhaps as many as 500,000 a year. While experts debated the exact number, the Immigration and Naturalization Service estimated in 1997 that 5 million foreigners, mainly from Mexico and Central America, were living illegally in the United States—two million in California alone.

Despite stepped-up border enforcement efforts after the September 11 attacks, illegal immigrants continued to move northward from Mexico and Central America in the early years of the twenty-first century. The trip was not without hazards. Mexican experts estimated that more than 2000 migrants lost their lives attempting to enter the United States illegally between 1997 and 2003. Yet the movement continued. As one rural Mexican official commented, "There are great problems in the countryside. And that famous American dream keeps calling."

Advance and Retreat for African Americans

African Americans formed the second largest of the nation's ethnic minorities. In 2002, there were just over 38 million blacks in the United States, 12.8 percent of the population. Although the heaviest concentration of African Americans was in northern cities, notably New York and Chicago, there was a significant movement back to the South. This shift, which began in the 1970s and accelerated in the 1990s, meant that by 2000 nearly 54 percent of those identifying themselves as black for the census lived in the sixteen states of the Sunbelt. Family ties and a search for ancestral roots helps explain this movement, but it also reflects the same economic incentives that drew so many Americans to this region in the last three decades of the twentieth century.

Middle-class African Americans had made some gains during the 1970s and 1980s. By 1976, one-third of all black workers held white-collar jobs—double the rate of 1960. Education proved the key to African American advances. Black graduates of the nation's colleges and universities had relatively easy entry into higher-paying jobs in banks, corporations, and government agencies. Black college enrollment increased by 43 percent between 1970 and 2000, giving more African Americans the opportunity for a middle-class lifestyle.

Yet despite these gains, there were setbacks as well for African Americans. In *Bakke* v. *Regents of the University of California,* the Supreme Court ruled against racial quotas for blacks at the University of California's medical school at Davis, although the ruling did permit universities to consider race as "simply one element" in efforts to select a diverse student body. In subsequent decisions, the Court upheld an affirmative action program designed by Kaiser Aluminum to help advance minority workers and ordered American Telephone and Telegraph to hire more African Americans and women to make up for past discrimination.

Affirmative action yielded only mixed results for blacks. For those able to gain university admission, such programs proved helpful, but even blacks who graduated from college did not do as well economically as their white counterparts. For blacks without education, the situation was much worse. Even in the boom years of the 1980s, unemployment rates for African Americans remained over 10 percent, and among black teenagers, the level was a staggering 40 percent. Nor did blacks share equally in the economic recovery of the 1990s. More than two million black families were living below the poverty line in 1998; the poverty rate for blacks was nearly double that for white Americans.

Rodney King became the symbol of black frustration in the United States. In April 1991, a bystander videotaped four Los Angeles policemen brutally beating King, who had been stopped for a traffic violation. The pictures of the rain of blows on King shocked the nation. Nearly a year later, when an all-white jury acquitted the four officers of charges of police brutality, rioting erupted in South Central Los Angeles that for a time threatened the entire city when the police failed to respond promptly. Looting stores at will, attacking and injuring passing motorists, and setting businesses on fire, the rioters focused the nation's attention on the plight of urban blacks. In the aftermath of the riot, government and state agencies promised new efforts to help the ghetto dwellers, but urban blacks saw little hope for improvement. For black youth in Los Angeles, accustomed to gang warfare and drive-by shootings, their only aspiration was simply to stay alive.

Americans from Asia and the Middle East

Asian Americans were the fasting-growing minority group at the end of the century. In 2000, there were more than 12 million Americans of Asian or Pacific Island descent. Although they represented only 4 percent of the total population, they were increasing at seven times the national rate, and future projections indicated that by 2050 one in ten Americans would be of Asian ancestry. The Chinese formed the largest single group of Asian Americans, followed by Filipinos, Japanese, Indians, Koreans, and Vietnamese. Immigration was the primary reason for the rapid growth of all these groups except the Japanese; in the 1980s, Asia provided 46 percent of all immigrants to the United States.

Compared to other minorities, Asian Americans are relatively well educated and affluent. Three out of four Asian youths graduate from high school, compared to less than one out of two for blacks and Hispanics. Asian Americans also have the highest percentage of college graduates and recipients of doctoral degrees of any minority group; in fact, they are better represented in colleges and universities than the white majority. Many Asians have entered professional fields, and as a result, the median income for Asian American families is more than $4,000 higher than the 1998 national level.

Not all Asian Americans have fared well, however. Refugees from Southeast Asia have experienced both economic hardship and persecution. The median family income for Vietnamese Americans in the mid-1980s was $8,000 below that for whites. Nearly half the Laotian refugees living in Minnesota were unemployed because they had great difficulty learning to read and write English. Vietnamese fishermen who settled on the Gulf Coast experienced repeated attacks on their livelihood in Texas and Louisiana. In the Los Angeles riots in 1992, Korean stores and shops became a main target for looting and firebombing.

But the overall experience of Asian Americans has been a positive one. They came to America seeking economic opportunity, or as many put it, "to climb the mountain of gold." "People are looking for a better life," a Chinese spokeswoman explained. "It's as simple as that, and we will continue to come here, especially if the situations over there [in Asia] stay tight, or get worse."

The number of Americans from the Middle East grew almost as fast as the number of those from Asia in the 1990s. The 2000 census counted 1.5 million Americans of Middle Eastern ancestry, up from only 200,000 thirty years earlier. Most came from Arab countries, as well as Israel and Iran. Concentrated in California, New York, and Michigan, Middle Eastern Americans were well-educated, with nearly half having college degrees.

Melting Pot or Multiethnic Diversity?

"Cultural diversity probably accelerated more in the 1980s than any other decade," noted demographer Carl Haub. The influx of people from all around the world, not just from Europe, had profound implications for American culture. Traditionally, the favorite American self-image was the melting pot, the title of Israel Zangwill's play written in 1908, at the height of European immigration into the nation. "America is God's crucible, the great Melting-Pot where all the races of Europe are melting and re-forming," one of his characters proclaimed. "Germans and Frenchmen, Irishmen and Englishmen, Jews and Russians—into the Crucible with you all! God is making the American!"

The melting pot image carried with it the concept of stripping newcomers of their culture and national traits and casting them into an Anglo-Saxon mold. Seeing that each ethnic group has proudly retained its separate identity, this analogy has seemed irrelevant to Third World migrants to America in recent times. Instead of reforming immigrants into an American type, immigration could better be seen as broadening the diversity that has always characterized the United States.

The new awareness of ethnic diversity manifested itself in many ways. In public education, blacks led a crusade against Eurocentric curriculum and demanded a new emphasis on the influence of African culture; on college campuses, the call for multicultural courses and separate departments for African American and Hispanic studies created controversy. Citing the forecasts of a declining Anglo dominance and the rise of minority groups in the next century, ethnic leaders advocated cultural pluralism.

Many Americans found themselves perplexed and uncertain of their cultural identity by the end of the twentieth century. A Census Bureau survey, asking people to state their ancestry, revealed that fully one-fourth of Americans listed German first, with Irish and English a distant second and third. Some Hispanics and people of Arab descent found the census classifications meaningless, since neither group considered the racial classifications of black, Asian–Pacific Islander, white, or American Indian applicable to them. Horace Kallen, one of the early critics of

Zangwill's melting pot analogy, offered a more appealing image of the nation's diverse heritage. He likened the United States to a symphony orchestra, in which each nationality and ethnic group contributed its "own specific timbre and tonality" to create "a multiplicity in a unity, an orchestration of mankind." As Americans wrestle with the continuing dilemma embodied in the national motto, "*E pluribus unum*," the image of a great symphony in which all groups blend together harmoniously offers a way to balance the pride individuals find in ethnic identity with the need for national unity.

Democratic Revival

The Democrats, victims of the runaway inflation of the 1970s, became the beneficiaries of the lingering recession of the early 1990s. Moving away from its traditional liberal reliance on big government, the party regained strength by choosing moderate candidates and tailoring its programs to appeal to the hard-pressed middle class. The new tactics enabled the Democrats to regain the White House in 1992 and retain it in 1996, despite a Republican sweep of Congress in 1994. The key figure in this political shift was Bill Clinton, who overcame some early setbacks to reap the rewards of a sustained economic boom.

The Election of 1992

The persistence of the recession that had begun two years earlier became the dominant political reality of 1992. As Bush's popularity plummeted, two men sought to capitalize on this bleak outlook. First, Arkansas Governor Bill Clinton defeated a field of five other challengers for the Democratic nomination by becoming the champion of economic renewal. Forgoing traditional liberal appeals to interest groups, Clinton stressed the need for investment in the nation's future—rebuilding roads and bridges, training workers for high-tech jobs, and solving the growing national health care crisis. One key statistic gave his message a vital appeal—in 1991, workers' wages failed to keep pace with inflation.

Despite victories in the Democratic primaries, however, Clinton faced a new rival in H. Ross Perot. An eccentric Texas billionaire, Perot singled out the deficit as the nation's gravest problem and decided to run as an independent candidate in response to a grassroots movement (which he financed himself).

When Clinton succeeded in unifying the Democratic party and gaining agreement on a moderate platform promising economic change, Perot stunned his supporters by suddenly dropping out of the race in July. Clinton immediately became the front-runner, leaving Bush far behind. With unemployment continuing unabated and the economy faltering, the American people turned their backs on George Bush and the Reagan revolution. Even GOP assaults on Clinton's character, notably his evasion of the draft during the Vietnam War, failed to halt the Democratic momentum. The message that Clinton's political advisers tacked up at the Democratic candidate's headquarters in Little Rock—"It's the economy, stupid"—provided the key to victory in November. Even though Perot reentered the race, Clinton won.

For political scientists, 1992 was a clear case of a negative referendum. Voters had rejected the Reagan-Bush programs decisively. Troubled both by the frightening deficit and the sluggish economy, they had chosen Clinton's program of economic renewal over Perot's call for short-term sacrifice to achieve long-term prosperity. Clinton maintained the Democratic grip on ethnic minorities, winning 83 percent support from African Americans and 62 percent from Hispanics; gained back both the elderly and the blue-collar Reagan Democrats; and cut deeply into the crucial middle class.

THE ELECTION OF 1992

Candidate	Party	Popular Vote	Electoral Vote
Bill Clinton	Democratic	44,908,232	370
George Bush	Republican	39,102,282	168
H. Ross Perot	Independent	19,725,433	—
	Minor Parties	773,161	—
		104,509,108	538

Most important, Clinton had broken the GOP's grip on the South and West. When the boom of the 1980s collapsed, the Sunbelt states proved as receptive as the rest of the nation to the call for change. Yet while there was no doubt about the rejection of Bush, there remained a question of precisely what change the electorate actually wanted—responsible budgetary policies to reduce the deficit or federal spending programs to achieve jobs and economic growth.

Economic Recovery

In the White House, Bill Clinton proved to be the most adept politician since Franklin Roosevelt. Born William Jefferson Clinton in Hope, Arkansas, in 1946, he weathered a difficult childhood with an alcoholic stepfather by developing skills at dealing with people and using personal charm to achieve his goals. Educated at Georgetown University, law school at Yale, with a two-year stint as a Rhodes scholar at Oxford, he entered politics after teaching law briefly at the University of Arkansas and won election first as Arkansas attorney general and then as governor. Defeated after his first term in 1980, Clinton won the nickname "Comeback Kid" by regaining the governor's office in 1982, using it to earn a reputation as one of the nation's most successful young political leaders over the next ten years.

Bill Clinton's political gifts centered on the easy way in which he was able to reconcile what biographer Martin Walker called "the ambivalence between the bubba and the brains, between the redneck and [the] Rhodes scholar." Empathy, charm, and understanding, combined with a genuine desire to serve, made him a formidable political leader. Unfortunately, serious flaws marred his political gifts. His eagerness to please undercut his devotion to principle. He wanted so much to prevail that he often ignored the cost of winning. Despite his apparently sincere devotion to causes such as civil rights and equality for women, even those who voted for Clinton had doubts about his personal integrity.

What often saved Clinton from his own worst faults was his loyal wife, Hillary Rodham Clinton. An accomplished attorney, she rescued his candidacy in 1992 by defending him against charges of adultery. But more important, from the outset she was his political partner, sharing in the strategic planning that won him the presidency. They made a formidable political team.

In his first months of office, Bill Clinton's political skills appeared to evaporate as he had difficulty in making the transition from governor of a small state to president of the nation, a position under intense media scrutiny. His inept handling of the "gays in the military" issue, made worse by his own draft evasion during the Vietnam War and several botched cabinet appointments, robbed him of the usual honeymoon period new presidents enjoy. He reacted with bitter indignation to the ensuing media criticism.

In appointing his cabinet, Clinton did try to live up to his pledges of ethnic and gender diversity. Hazel O'Leary, a black woman, served as secretary of energy, while Janet Reno, a political unknown, became attorney general. The cabinet also included two Hispanics and two African Americans, but diversity ended there. Fourteen of the eighteen cabinet members were lawyers, and most were wealthy. Secretary of Labor Robert Reich, a Harvard professor, was one of the few advocates for working-class Americans. Beyond the cabinet, two-thirds of the Clinton administration appointees were white men.

Clinton's most important appointments came in the economic realm. Senator Lloyd Bentsen, a fiscal conservative, became secretary of the Treasury, with Robert Rubin, a Wall Street bond trader, serving as special assistant for economic policy; former Congressman Leon Panetta, a longtime deficit hawk, took on the key job of White House budget director. By choosing such a conservative team to guide economic policy, Clinton was risking the fate of his administration on the single issue of deficit reduction.

Newly elected President Clinton meets with Federal Reserve Board Chair Alan Greenspan in the Oval Office in 1993. ❖

These advisers helped the president shape the economic program calling for tax increases and spending cuts to achieve a balanced budget that he presented to Congress and the nation on February 17, 1993. Despite the warm reception for his State of the Union address, Clinton still had to wage a long and determined fight to complete his economic program. It took all-out arm-twisting from the White House to get Congress to approve the final budget terms—$241 billion in new taxes and $255 billion in spending cuts, for a total reduction of $496 billion over four years. In late August, the House approved the budget by just two votes, and in the Senate, Vice President Gore cast his vote to break a 50 to 50 deadlock.

Despite the narrow margin, it was a major achievement. Clinton stood firm on deficit reduction, compromising on details but insisting on a program that promised to cut the deficit in half within four years. Moreover, he succeeded in winning approval for some of his education and job-training programs while increasing income tax rates on the wealthy from 33 to 39.6 percent. At the same time, he secured passage of the earned income tax credit for the working poor. And best of all, lower interest rates created by action of the Federal Reserve Board and the growing confidence of financial markets led to a steadily expanding economy that made Clinton's deficit reduction goals realistic. Unlike George Bush in 1990, who sealed his political doom by reneging on his promise not to raise taxes, a healthier economy enabled Clinton both to raise taxes and to win respect by standing on principle. He did, however, risk the same fate as Bush since Republicans were quick to call the budget deal "the biggest tax increase in the history of the world."

President versus Congress

Deficit reduction marked only the beginning of Bill Clinton's struggles with Congress. For the next four years, he engaged in a series of confrontations, winning some and losing some with first Democratic and then Republican majorities in the two houses.

His most important triumph came when Congress approved the **North American Free Trade Agreement (NAFTA)** in the fall of 1993. NAFTA, initiated and nearly completed by Bush, was a free trade plan that combined 250 million Americans with 90 million Mexicans and 27 million Canadians into a common market without tariff barriers. Although Clinton had muted his support for NAFTA

North American Free Trade Agreement (NAFTA) A free trade plan initiated in the Bush administration and enacted by a narrow vote in Congress in the early months of the Clinton administration. It established a common market without tariff barriers between the United States, Canada, and Mexico.

during the 1992 campaign, once elected, he saw it as the first step in creating similar free trade associations with Asia and Europe that would enable the United States to dominate global markets.

Critics of NAFTA did not share Clinton's optimism. Representing both ends of the political spectrum, they warned that free trade would undermine small American companies and send millions of American jobs to exploited and underpaid workers in third world countries. The issue of free trade divided the Democratic party, with many liberals and labor union members strongly opposed. Ross Perot, the defeated 1992 third-party candidate, became the best known critic, especially with his vivid claim about the loud "sucking sound" that would signal the flushing of American jobs down the drain.

The toughest fight came in the House, but 102 Democrats finally joined with 132 Republicans to approve NAFTA by a 34-vote margin, giving Clinton a solid victory there. The Senate added its consent by a vote of 61 to 38. Thus Clinton triumphed over key elements within his own party to achieve a significant goal.

At the height of the debate over NAFTA, President Clinton allowed his wife to make public his administration's massive plan for health reform in an unprecedented appearance before the House Ways and Means Committee. "I am here as a mother, as a wife, a daughter, a sister, a woman, as an American citizen concerned about the health of her family and the health of her nation," Hillary Clinton told the startled representatives as she presented the 1,364-page health care reform plan.

When he first took office, Bill Clinton had signaled the importance of this issue by appointing his wife to head a task force to find a comprehensive solution to the nation's health care problem. Clinton had two primary objectives. The first was an all-embracing health care system that would include the thirty-seven million Americans who lacked health insurance. At the same time, the president was committed to reduce the skyrocketing cost of health care. Medicare was one of the prime culprits—the cost of medical services to the elderly had risen to more than one-fifth of all federal revenues by 1991. The trick would be to devise a system that would reduce costs while extending medical insurance to everyone in the nation, without raising taxes or adding to the deficit. The only possible solution involved rationing health care by having someone in authority place limits on the medical services each American could receive—a strategy that was political dynamite.

The plan that Hillary Clinton presented to the House Ways and Means Committee in October 1993 had two key features. First, it required large companies to offer a generous health care package to all workers, with employers paying 80 percent of the estimated $4,200 annual cost per family. The second feature dealt with small businesses, which were required to form large health alliances so that they could purchase equally generous benefit packages from insurance companies. The task force believed that these mandatory health alliances would have enough clout to bargain for competitive rates, thereby sharply reducing health costs.

The initial public reception was favorable. When Congress began studying the details, however, attitudes started to change. Opponents, primarily Republicans and representatives of small business, counterattacked, claiming that it would deprive Americans of the right to choose their own doctors. The tactic of embracing the concept of reform but questioning the specifics of the Clinton plan proved highly effective.

By January 1994, the administration's health care plan was in deep trouble. The longer congressional committees debated the plan, the lower support for it fell in the polls. By midsummer, only 39 percent of the American people expressed confidence in the administration's health proposal. When Democrats were unable to round up sixty votes to break a Republican filibuster on procedural issues in late August 1994, the Senate dropped the issue, effectively killing the Clinton health plan.

In retrospect, it seems evident that the incompatible goals of reducing costs while striving for universal coverage had doomed the plan from the outset. Shrewder political maneuvering by the Clintons might have enabled them to salvage a scaled-down health reform. Instead, by insisting on a sweeping overhaul of the American health system rather than accepting incremental changes, Clinton would have to pay a heavy political price.

Contract with America

Clinton's failure to deliver on his health care promise helped fuel a dramatic Republican resurgence. A young maverick congressman from Georgia, Newton Leroy "Newt" Gingrich, had been leading a Republican attack against the House Democratic leadership. Using a well-funded political action committee, GOPAC, Gingrich supported other young, conservative Republicans who waged constant war against the Democratic leadership. Sensing that the nation was ready for change, Gingrich believed that a vulnerable Clinton made 1994 the right year for an all-out effort to capture control of both houses of Congress.

In an attempt to transform 435 separate races into one national contest, Gingrich asked all GOP candidates to sign a ten-point **Contract with America.** The Contract consisted of familiar conservative goals, including a balanced budget amendment to the Constitution, term limits for members of Congress, a line-item veto for the president, and a middle-class tax cut. For the first time in recent political history, a party sought to win Congress on ideological issues rather than relying on individual personalities.

Contract with America In the 1994 congressional election, Congressman Newt Gingrich had Republican candidates sign a "contract" in which they pledged their support for such things as a balanced budget amendment, term limits for members of Congress, and a middle-class tax cut.

A series of embarrassing disclosures involving Bill Clinton's character made the tactic particularly effective in 1994. During the 1992 campaign, the *New York Times* had raised questions about a bankrupt Arkansas land development called Whitewater in which the Clintons had lost a modest investment. In late 1993, the Resolution Trust Corporation, charged with cleaning up the savings and loan debacle of the 1980s, began exploring Hillary Clinton's relationship with Madison Guaranty, a failed financial institution that had loaned the Clintons money for their Whitewater investment. Republicans were quick to charge that, in effect, American taxpayers were left holding the bill for a corrupt Arkansas bank that had close ties to the Clintons. Although there was no evidence of illegal acts, at the president's request, Attorney General Janet Reno appointed a special prosecutor to investigate the Whitewater affair.

Additional scandals cropped up over activities that had taken place after Clinton was elected president. Travelgate was the name given to the firing, apparently at the urging of Hillary Clinton, of several career White House employees who arranged travel for the press covering the president. Then in early 1994, Paula Jones, a former Arkansas state employee, charged that in 1991, then-Governor Clinton had exposed himself to her in a Little Rock hotel room and asked for oral sex.

Republicans used these episodes to revive earlier questions about Bill Clinton's character. More important, they were able to make more substantial attacks on the president, pointing to his failure to enact health care reform and, above all, reminding voters that in 1993 Clinton had enacted "the biggest tax increase" of all time.

The outcome of the November 1994 vote stunned political observers. The Republicans won both houses, gaining 9 seats in the Senate and an astonishing 53 in the House to take control for the first time in forty years. The GOP extended its sweep into the states, winning 32 governorships, including those of New York, California, and Texas, where George W. Bush, the son of the man whom Clinton beat in 1992, won handily.

There were two ways to view the remarkable about-face. Claiming that voters endorsed their Contract with America, the GOP hailed the outcome as a mandate to dismantle the welfare state and government in general in favor of free market economics. Clinton and some of his advisors, however, noted that the 1994 election was hardly representative of the country as a whole. The turnout was low—less than

40 percent, compared to 56 percent when Clinton won the presidency just two years before. Nationally, barely more than half of those voting supported Republicans, so that in effect just 20 percent of the electorate had determined the outcome.

The most striking statistic lay in the gender breakdown. Women voted for Democratic candidates by a margin of 53 to 47 percent, while men went Republican by a much bigger differential, 57 to 43. In effect, it was an outpouring of "angry white males" who believed that Clinton was unfit to be president who determined the outcome. The lesson for Clinton was clear. He could not convert the diehard opponents, but if he could win back the women and minorities who had voted for him in 1992 but stayed home in 1994, he had a chance to play the part of Comeback Kid once more.

The Clinton Rebound

After Clinton's surprising victory in 1992, the slogan in his Little Rock war room—"It's the economy, stupid"—became the easiest way to explain the outcome. Four years later, the same pithy commentary proved even more apt. The candidate who had accused his opponent of ignoring the economic suffering accompanying the recession of 1990–1991 now became the beneficiary of the recovery that had actually begun before the 1992 election.

The scope of the prosperity that spread throughout America in the 1990s was astonishing. Leaner American corporations, benefiting from downsizing—the ruthless firing of employees to achieve greater efficiency—now found they could compete on favorable terms with Japanese and German rivals. Productivity shot up, keeping labor costs down, while technological advances, especially in microprocessors, made American products the envy of the world. By 1996, Clinton could boast that nine million new jobs had been created since he took office and that the United States now led all other nations in the export of manufactured goods.

Clinton not only could claim credit for this remarkable resurgence, but he had the political skill to assuage the heavy human costs involved. In persuading Congress to pass the Family and Medical Leave Act in 1993 and increasing the minimum wage in 1996, the president was able to present himself as a caring leader concerned about the welfare of all Americans, not just the rich and powerful.

The Republicans, fresh from their sweeping victory in Congress, ironically became the vehicle for Clinton's political rehabilitation. Mistaking a negative referendum against Clinton for a ringing endorsement of his Contract with America, Newt Gingrich played directly into the president's hands. In 1995, despite majorities in both houses, the GOP enacted only four minor parts of the Contract.

The president found Gingrich and his followers a perfect foil. When they demanded a balanced budget by early in the next century, Clinton agreed in principle, but then refused to accept GOP plans to slash programs such as Medicare and Medicaid. Portraying himself as the defender of the downtrodden, Clinton claimed that the Republican cuts in education, college loans, and health care would hurt children, ambitious young people, and the elderly.

The GOP leadership in Congress then made a gross miscalculation by threatening to close down the government to force Clinton to give way. The president stood firm, aware that Gingrich's negative ratings were higher than his own. Twice the Republicans shut down all but the most vital of federal services. The public outcry, however, directed almost entirely against Gingrich and the GOP, finally forced the Republicans to relent. They accepted a compromise in early 1996 that promised a balanced budget in seven years. Clinton was thus able to begin the campaign year by taking credit for balancing the budget while making the Republicans appear to be the enemies of Medicare and Social Security.

Once he had regained the initiative, Clinton pursued a policy of "triangulation," in which he distanced himself from both conservative Republicans and liberal

THE ELECTION OF 1996

Candidate	Party	Popular Vote	Electoral Vote
Bill Clinton	Democratic	47,401,185	379
Robert Dole	Republican	39,197,469	159
H. Ross Perot	Independent	8,085,294	—
		94,683,948	538

Democrats and took the center position. He signed new welfare legislation that turned the welfare program over to the states, funded by scaled-down federal grants, and required recipients to find work within two years or lose their benefits.

While Republican hopefuls fought each other in a series of grueling and expensive party primaries, Clinton began raising huge sums to conduct a massive television campaign. Throughout the spring and summer, the airwaves were filled with 30-second commercials picturing the Republicans as trying to weaken Medicare and deny social services to those in need while Clinton fought to preserve the heritage of the New Deal and the Great Society. By the time the GOP nominated Bob Dole, the respected but dour Senate majority leader from Kansas, the contest was all but over. Having used up nearly all his federal matching funds in the primaries, Dole was unable to counter Clinton's TV blitz.

The ensuing fall campaign turned out to be anticlimactic. Everything Dole tried proved ineffective. On election day, the president won his expected victory. A low turnout (10 million fewer voters than in 1992) and the third-party candidacy of Ross Perot (only a nuisance factor in 1996) prevented Clinton from winning a clear majority of the popular vote. But he carried 31 states with 379 electoral votes, for a decisive victory over Dole. Clinton's strategy of winning back the vote of women and minorities with his stress on education, health care, and providing opportunities for the young paid off handsomely. If the angry white male was the symbol of the GOP congressional victory in 1994, then "soccer moms"—suburban middle-class women concerned about social issues—proved the key to Clinton's comeback in 1996.

In winning a second term, Clinton was both skillful and lucky. He benefited from the powerful economic growth that surpassed even his own expectations. With the deficit falling faster than either Clinton or Greenspan had estimated, the economy had proved to be his greatest ally. But Clinton was also fortunate in the men who opposed him. Gingrich and Dole were experienced and able congressional leaders, but neither possessed the charisma or the public sensitivity that enabled Clinton to connect with the voter.

Yet it took both political skill and daring to weather the rejection Clinton experienced in 1994 and to adapt to the changing mood of the American people. Even though the president probably had little to do with the underlying causes of the economic boom, his willingness to adopt Greenspan's fiscal strategy and stake everything on deficit reduction gave him a reasonable claim to some of the credit. Most important, Clinton won in large measure because, unlike his opponents in 1992 and 1996, he seemed to embody, in the words of a British observer, "all the characteristics of his generation, distilled to an intensity that matched his ambition."

CLINTON AND THE WORLD

American foreign policy underwent notable changes in the 1990s. Unlike his predecessor, Bill Clinton gave top priority to domestic issues rather than international affairs. And where Bush had viewed the world largely in geopolitical terms, stressing

American strategic interests, Clinton gave economics top consideration, seeking markets abroad to stimulate the dormant American economy. Yet there was one similarity—under Clinton American foreign policy continued to drift, lacking direction in the confusing post–Cold War world.

In choosing his foreign policy team, Clinton wisely went with experienced professionals to whom he could delegate foreign policy while he carried out his domestic agenda. Secretary of State Warren M. Christopher, who had served under Jimmy Carter, pursued a cautious, lawyerly approach to world problems, while National Security Advisor Anthony Lake carefully kept a low profile. These veteran diplomats, and their second-term replacements, Madeleine Albright and Sandy Berger, worked skillfully on the international issues confronting the nation, but they were hampered by the lack of any overarching principle to guide them.

Global Tensions in the Post–Cold War Era

Clinton's greatest challenge was in dealing with America's old Cold War rivals, Russia and China. Inheriting the chaos left by the breakup of the Soviet Union, the president concentrated on two issues. First, he followed Bush's lead in backing Russian President Boris Yeltsin to the hilt. In 1993, Clinton persuaded Congress to provide a $2.5 billion aid package to help Yeltsin carry out his free market reforms of the devastated Russian economy. The Clinton administration strongly supported Yeltsin and his successor, Vladimir V. Putin, despite Russia's continuing brutal war with Chechnya. Although American policy created tension, the Clinton administration succeeded in maintaining good relations with Russia and especially in signing new agreements to reduce both nations' nuclear arsenals.

The president's policy toward China was more questionable. Clinton ignored China's dismal human rights record and continued Bush's policy of extending most favored nation status to Beijing. The growing importance of trade with China, whose economic output in 1993 exceeded Britain's, led Clinton to overlook China's many human rights violations. As trade with China began to rival that with Japan, the president announced a policy of "constructive engagement." It was better, he and his spokespeople declared, to keep talking, and trading, with China than to harden Chinese resentment against the West by harping on moral issues.

The Chinese, however, proved to be less than cooperative. China ignored U.S. protests over its exports of missiles to Iran and nuclear technology to Pakistan and continued to stifle dissent at home. Constructive engagement clearly had its limitations.

In other parts of the world, the Middle East proved as perplexing for Clinton as it had for his predecessors. The administration continued the efforts to broker a peace between Israel and the Palestinian Arabs. Despite a promising beginning at a meeting between Yasir Arafat and Yitzhak Rabin in Washington in 1993, Clinton was unable to overcome the implacable ethnic and religious tensions that blocked the path to peace in the Middle East.

In Iraq, Clinton met the continued defiance of Saddam Hussein by twice ordering American cruise missile attacks on Iraqi military targets and by expanding the no-fly zone to cover two-thirds of the country. U.S. relations with Iran failed to improve, even with the election of a more moderate prime minister in 1997. Saudi Arabia remained a staunch ally, despite strains from a terrorist attack that killed nineteen American air force personnel in 1996. More worrisome was the increasingly heavy U.S. reliance on Persian Gulf oil as a result of Americans' love affair with gas-guzzling vans, pick-up trucks, and sport utility vehicles. A sharp increase in the price of oil in early 2000 brought howls of protest from angry motorists and highlighted the danger of continuing American dependence on foreign oil.

Intervening in Somalia and Haiti

The most difficult foreign policy decisions for the Clinton administration concerned the question of whether to use American troops to intervene abroad. The absence of the Cold War threat, with its implicit need to counter communist rivals, made it much more difficult for the president and his advisers to decide when the national interest required sending American men and women into harm's way. Between 1993 and 1999, Clinton opted for foreign intervention in four areas—Somalia, Haiti, Bosnia, and Kosovo—with decidedly mixed results.

Clinton inherited the Somalian venture. In December 1992, George Bush had sent twenty-five thousand American troops to that starving county on a humanitarian mission. Under Clinton, however, the original aim of using troops to protect the flow of food supplies and relief workers fighting the ravages of famine gradually shifted to supporting a UN effort at nation building. Tragedy struck in October 1993 when eighteen American soldiers died in a botched attempt to capture a local warlord in Mogadishu. When television cameras recorded the naked corpse of a U.S. helicopter pilot being dragged through the streets of Somalia's capital, an angry Congress demanded a quick end to the intervention. American forces left Somalia by the end of March 1994 in what was unquestionably the low point of Clinton's foreign policy.

The lack of clear criteria governing intervention that had brought on the disaster in Somalia almost led to another fiasco in Haiti. Seeking to halt the flow into Florida of thousands of Haitians fleeing both poverty and tyranny, Clinton worked to compel the military rulers of Haiti to abdicate in favor of the man they had overthrown in 1991, Jean-Bertrand Aristide.

After nearly a year of trade sanctions and increasing diplomatic pressure, the president prepared to use force to remove the generals. At the last minute, a three-member peace mission led by former President Jimmy Carter worked out a compromise that allowed U.S. troops to land unopposed in late September 1994. Aristide returned to Haiti to take power in mid-October, but he could do little either to restore democracy or achieve economic progress in view of his country's bankrupt treasury, devastated economy, and deep political divisions. By the time Aristide turned over the presidency to his elected successor in 1996, Haiti remained mired in hopeless poverty. The reality of Haiti's plight had frustrated Clinton's effort to use American power righteously.

Halting Civil War in Bosnia

Bosnia provided an even more stern test for the president's foreign policy. The breakup of Yugoslavia in 1991 led the Muslim president of Bosnia to ask the European Community to recognize the independence of Bosnia-Herzegovina. Bosnia's ethnic and religious makeup—44 percent Muslim, 31 percent Serb, and 17 percent Croat—quickly led to civil war by the spring of 1992. The Bosnian Serbs, aided by their allies in Serbia, used the guns and heavy weaponry of the former Yugoslavian army to seize more than 70 percent of Bosnian territory. The Muslim and Croatian forces, hampered by an international arms embargo, were unable to mount effective resistance as the Serbs began a policy of "ethnic cleansing," driving Muslims and Croats from their ancestral homes and farms and beginning a lethal bombardment of the capital, Sarajevo.

Although Clinton had criticized Bush's failure to stop the fighting in Bosnia during the campaign, the new president followed an equally cautious policy at first. When the Serbs rejected his peace proposal in the spring of 1993, the president fell back on using American air power to patrol no-fly zones over Bosnia designed to protect UN peacekeeping efforts and six "safe areas" created to shelter the Muslim victims of ethnic cleansing. Meanwhile, Serb artillery continued to pour a withering fire on the civilian population of Sarajevo, and journalists reported a series of brutal atrocities in which Serb troops slaughtered thousands of Muslim men.

Clinton finally acted in 1995. After allowing former U.S. military officers to help Croatia rebuild its army and permitting Middle Eastern countries to send arms to both the Croatian and the Muslim forces in Bosnia, Clinton unleashed American air power. In the summer of 1995, American planes under NATO auspices began a series of air strikes on the Serb forces shelling Sarajevo from the surrounding mountains.

The air campaign, which lasted for two weeks, along with a major counteroffensive by better equipped Croatian and Muslim forces, finally led to a cease-fire in mid-October 1995. The three warring factions sent delegations to discuss a settlement at Wright-Patterson Air Force Base in Dayton, Ohio. After three weeks of talks, U.S. mediator Richard Holbrooke secured their agreement to create a weak central government for all Bosnia at Sarajevo but divide the rest of the country into two parts—a Muslim-Croatian federation with 51 percent of the territory and a Serbian enclave with 49 percent. The Dayton plan called for free elections, the return of refugees to their former homes, and a NATO force to oversee the peace process.

Clinton took a calculated risk in sponsoring the Dayton settlement. The division of Bosnia into two competing halves meant only a temporary halt to the fighting rather than an end to the struggle for control of the country. But in halting the fighting at least temporarily, and especially in lifting the siege of Sarajevo, Clinton could take credit for a major humanitarian achievement. He displayed uncharacteristic political courage in agreeing to commit twenty thousand American troops to the International Force (IFOR) that would undertake the dangerous task of supervising the implementation of the Dayton accords. The fact that there was no clear-cut American national interest at stake, beyond the desire to save human life, made it an even more impressive achievement.

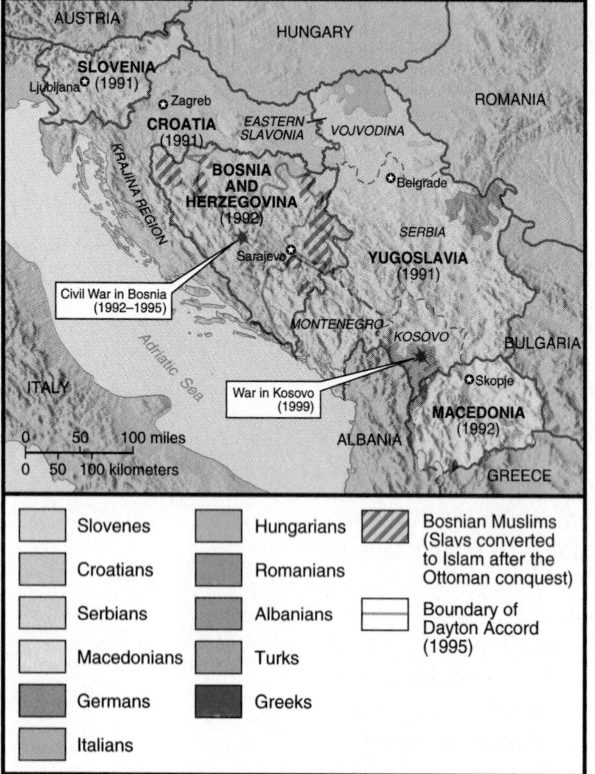

THE BREAKUP OF YUGOSLAVIA/CIVIL WAR IN BOSNIA *With the end of the Communist regime in Yugoslavia in the early 1990s, the country broke apart into ethnically distinct regions. In Bosnia, Muslims, Croatians, and Serbians fought a bloody civil war rife with atrocities on all sides over the issue of ethnic cleansing.* ❖

The American troops, originally scheduled to leave by late 1996, stayed on in reduced number when the original departure date was postponed indefinitely. Few refugees were able to return to their original farms and villages, and suspected war criminals remained at large in the Serbian enclave. British, French, and U.S. members of IFOR faced tense confrontations with angry Serb mobs. Yet, the net result was an uneasy truce without fighting and without peacekeeping casualties. Clinton had not only been brave; he had been lucky as well.

Saving Kosovo

President Clinton faced an even more serious challenge in another Balkan troublespot—Kosovo. Serbian leader Slobodan Milosevic had ended the province's autonomy within Yugoslavia and imposed Serbian rule in 1989, even though 90 percent of the population was ethnic Albanian. When these people, who called themselves Kosovars, resisted by waging guerrilla war against the Serbian police, Milosevic responded with a campaign of repression and ethnic cleansing that outraged world opinion. After diplomatic efforts failed in 1998 and early 1999, the United States and NATO began an aerial assault on Serbia on March 24, 1999, in an effort to end the persecution of the Kosovars.

At first it appeared that Clinton and his outspoken secretary of state, Madeleine Albright, had miscalculated. The initial air attacks, largely directed at empty barracks and remote military bases, failed to persuade Milosevic to seek peace. Instead, he stepped up the ethnic cleansing in Kosovo, forcing hundreds of thousands of Kosovars to leave their homes and flee to neighboring Albania and Macedonia. Even worse, when Clinton ordered more intense bombing of Serbia, some of the strikes led to heavy civilian casualties; the most embarrassing incident was the accidental bombing of the Chinese embassy in Belgrade in early May 1999.

Clinton, despite his reputation as an opportunist, stayed the course in Kosovo. He explained to the American people his devotion to a humanitarian cause. "It is perhaps the first conflict ever fought where no one wanted any land, or money, or geopolitical advantage," he declared. "We just wanted to stop and reverse ethnic cleansing."

His perseverance paid off. Unable to strike effectively at the Serbian army in Kosovo, NATO planes concentrated on the infrastructure of Serbia, targeting bridges, oil refineries, and, most important of all, power stations. By the end of May, Serbia had lost 60 percent of its electrical capacity and the domestic pressure on Milosevic began to mount. With Russian diplomats acting as go-betweens, Milosevic finally agreed to end his attempts to purge Kosovo of its Albanian inhabitants. An agreement signed on June 10, 1999, called for the withdrawal of all Serb forces and placed Kosovo under UN supervision, with NATO troops acting as peacekeepers.

The conflict over Kosovo revealed both the strengths and weaknesses of the United States in the turbulent post–Cold War world. American military power, while great, was limited by the need to work with allies and by a strong desire to avoid risking American lives. When the fighting ended, the Kosovars returned to their devastated homeland and soon NATO troops had the thankless task of preventing the Albanians from seeking revenge against the Serbian minority in Kosovo.

The Clinton record abroad highlights the dilemma facing the United States in the post–Cold War world. Lacking the central focus of rivalry with another super power, the United States has to decide when and where to bring its great power to bear without exhausting itself in endless adventures overseas. Clinton failed in Somalia and achieved only limited success in Haiti, but he could claim credit for ending a bloody civil war in Bosnia and for rescuing the Kosovars from Milosevic's ethnic cleansing. Like his predecessor, however, Clinton was unable to define a clear international mission for post-Cold War America. As a result, instead of setting the global agenda, the United States remained the prisoner of events abroad.

The End of the Century

It was the best of times; it was the worst of times. The 1990s witnessed an unparalleled burst of economic growth that clearly established the United States as the world's richest nation. Yet in the same decade, violence in the form of angry protests from both the extreme right and the extreme left, as well as a senseless series of school shootings, shocked the nation. Waco, Oklahoma City, Seattle, Littleton—these scenes of devastation revealed deep flaws in American society. And even the man who claimed credit for the prosperity, Bill Clinton, nearly lost the presidency over a sexual affair with a young White House intern.

From Deficit to Surplus

In early 2000, the boom of the 1990s officially became the longest sustained period of economic growth in American history. Since March 1991, the economy had expanded by an incredible 64 percent, creating 20 million new jobs. Unemployment dropped below 5 percent in 1997 and stayed there for the rest of the decade. Best of all, inflation remained low, averaging just over 2 percent a year and thus enabling family income not only to recover from the 1990–1991 recession, but even to surpass the previous all-time high of the early 1970s. The wealthy continued to make the greatest gains, but prosperity reached every level, with those at the bottom making real, if modest, advances.

Economists had difficulty explaining this happy situation. The primary factor appeared to be continued increases in productivity, which allowed the economy to expand without creating inflationary pressures. Businesses invested heavily not just in new plants and machinery, but in new technology—especially computers and sophisticated software—that enabled workers to increase their output steadily. While the growth in exports that Clinton fought for acted as a stimulus, it was the American consumer who was the real hero. Any doubt about the domestic roots of the boom were dispelled with the Asian crash of 1997–1998, which, despite sparking a brief downturn in the stock market, failed to halt the American economic advance.

Federal Reserve Chairman Alan Greenspan helped sustain the boom by keeping inflation in check. He shrewdly lowered interest rates in late 1997 to stimulate the economy during the Asian turmoil. Then he began to raise them in 1999 and 2000 to the highest level of the decade to slow down the economy and prevent surging world oil prices from leading to a repetition of the great inflation of the 1970s.

The greatest benefit of this remarkable economic boom was the transformation of the federal budget. The worrisome deficits of the early 1990s disappeared, replaced to the delight of both Democrats and Republicans, with surpluses, at first modest, but then substantial. But the two parties could not agree on how to spend the unexpected bonanza. Republicans called for across-the-board tax reductions, while Democrats wanted to shore up the faltering Social Security and Medicare programs. Clinton's veto of congressional tax cuts led to a deadlock that actually seemed to accomplish what most Americans preferred—paying off the national debt which had grown so large from past deficits.

The optimistic forecasts all depended on sustaining an unprecedented economic expansion. A recession, the normal pattern in the business cycle of the past, would make the debate over whether to reduce taxes or shore up social programs irrelevant. Those who won control of the White House and Congress in 2000, therefore, would face the challenge not only of spending the surplus wisely, but also of ensuring its very existence.

❖ A Look at the Past ❖

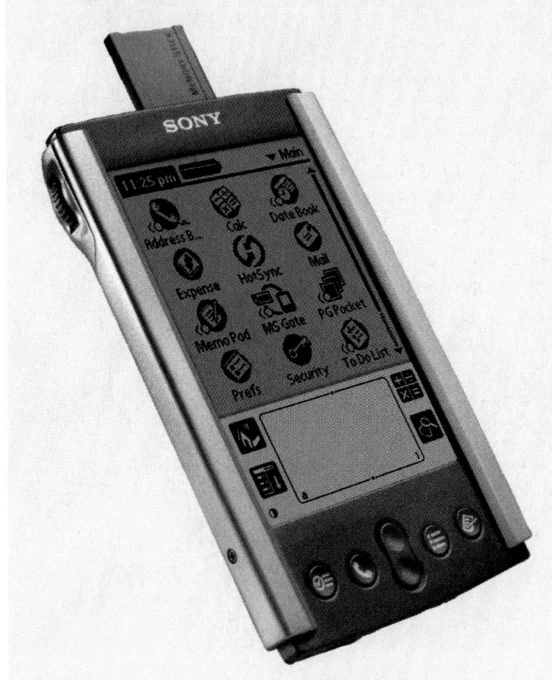

Handheld Computer

During the 1980s, personal computers became available and affordable. Desktop computers soon became standard office equipment and in high demand both at home and at school. Computers revolutionized office work and almost every other kind of work. By the 1990s, desktop computers no longer met consumer processing requirements and powerful, portable laptops entered the market. A decade later, the even more portable and affordable handheld computers, such as the personal digital assistant (PDA) shown here, allowed users to do work or send email from almost anywhere. The speed at which new computer technology becomes dated suggests that even devices we use today may be historical artifacts tomorrow. Why do you think the trend has been for computers to get smaller? Why would someone need a portable computer rather than a desktop version? What does such a portable computer suggest about business and work practices? What other products suggest similar work patterns?

Violence in the 1990s

Amid the unprecedented prosperity, a series of violent episodes disturbed the nation in the last decade of the century. Across the political spectrum, those who feared the loss of personal freedom resorted to force to express their discontent.

On the right, a militia movement accelerated after a shoot-out at Ruby Ridge, Idaho, in August 1992. Trying to arrest Christian survivalist Randy Weaver for illegal arms sales, federal agents shot and killed Weaver's wife and son during an eleven-day siege. Ruby Ridge became the rallying cry for right-wing activists who expressed their hatred for blacks, homosexuals, abortionists, and above all, the federal government, which they saw as a threat to individual freedom.

A second tragic incident—the siege and destruction of the Branch Davidian compound in Waco, Texas, in 1993—intensified the militia impulse. What began in January as an attempt to arrest charismatic leader David Koresh on gun-dealing charges finally ended in April with the death of 75 Branch Davidians. As a stunned nation tried to understand what had happened at Waco, many dissidents had a ready explanation. An evil government, part of an international conspiracy to create a new world order at the expense of traditional American liberties, was responsible. Across the nation, citizens began joining the nearly 150 militia units that sprang up in thirty-three states. Many did not share the racist and bigoted views of some of the militia organizers; the majority were middle-class citizens who felt threatened by an encroaching federal government.

On April 19, 1995, the second anniversary of the Waco tragedy, Timothy McVeigh, who shared the viewpoint of the movement but was not a member of any militia unit, set off a powerful bomb in a rented truck in the street next to the federal building in Oklahoma City. Caught by chance less than a hundred miles away, McVeigh would eventually die for his crime. Yet he showed no remorse, believing innocent people had to die to end "the system."

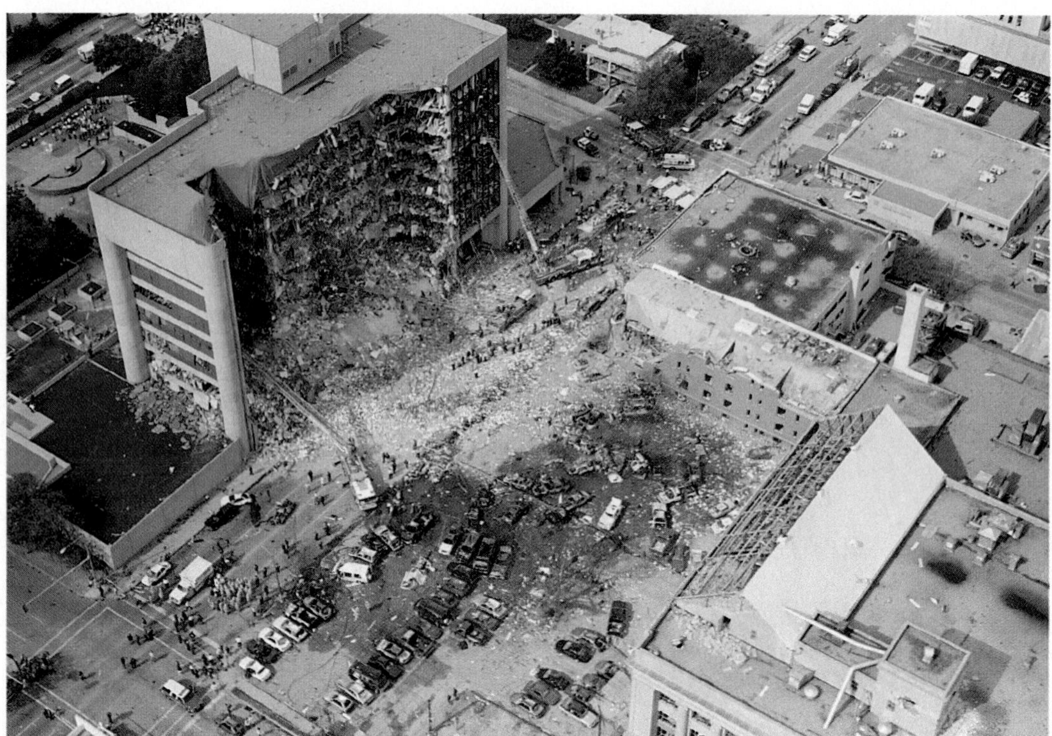

An aerial view of the destroyed Alfred P. Murrah Federal Building in Oklahoma City suggests the extent of the physical damage caused by the bomb blast on April 19, 1995, but cannot come close to expressing the human tragedy of the loss of 169 lives and the hundreds of injuries. ❖

The hatred of corporate America was as strong on the far left as on the far right. Its most dramatic expression came from the Unabomber—an unknown enemy of the global economy who sent sixteen bombs through the mail to corporation executives and university professors between 1978 and 1995, killing three people and injuring twenty-three others. In 1995, the *Washington Post* published the Unabomber's "manifesto," a 35,000-word polemic in which he blamed modern technology for all of humanity's ills.

Nearly a year later, in April 1996, federal agents arrested Theodore J. Kaczynski at a remote cabin in Montana. Kaczynski had earned a Ph.D. in mathematics at Harvard and held a tenure-track teaching position at the University of California in Berkeley, but in 1969 he resigned in order to live in seclusion without modern conveniences. After refusing to agree to an insanity defense, Kaczynski pled guilty to thirteen federal charges and was sentenced to prison for life without the possibility of parole. While few condoned his violent acts, some sympathized with Kaczynski's resentment over the degree to which technology encroached on individual privacy and curtailed personal freedom.

World Trade Organization (WTO) Global international organization that deals with rules of trade between nations. It became a target for demonstrations in the late 1990s by protesters claiming that global corporations exploited workers and damaged the environment.

The clearest expression of unhappiness with the global economy of the 1990s came at the **World Trade Organization (WTO)** meeting in Seattle in late 1999. More than forty thousand protestors gathered to denounce what they believed to be the secret and autocratic way that the WTO encouraged the exploitation of both low-paid workers and natural resources in developing countries. At first, orderly marches led by organized labor and environmental groups drew large crowds and sent an important message of dissent. But then more violent demonstrators began smashing windows, spray-painting graffiti on Nike and Gap stores, and trashing Starbucks coffee-bars. The police reacted, using tear gas, nightsticks, and rubber bullets to clear the streets and arrest more than 500 demonstrators. Despite the violence, the protestors succeeded not only in interrupting the WTO meeting, which adjourned without reaching any new trade agreements, but also in gaining worldwide attention for their grievances.

Even more perplexing were the series of senseless school shootings that occurred in the late 1990s. The first was in Pearl, Mississippi, on October 1, 1997, when a 16-year-old boy stabbed his mother to death and then fatally shot two girls and wounded seven other high school students. Similar outbursts at West Paducah, Kentucky; Jonesboro, Arkansas; and Springfield, Oregon, in the 1997–1998 school year saw angry teenagers kill nine of their classmates and three adults, as well as wounding a score of others. The culmination came at Columbine High School in Littleton, Colorado, in April 1999. Eric Harris and Dylan Klebold used automatic weapons to slaughter twelve fellow students and a teacher, then killed themselves, in the worst incident of school violence in American history.

The youthful killers had much in common. They all were white, above average in intelligence, attended nonurban schools, came from middle-class families, and were deeply alienated. All appeared to hold grudges against classmates they felt had ostracized them. Luke Woodham of Pearl explained that he acted "because people like me are mistreated every day."

Explanations for the violent behavior ranged from easy access to guns to the violence of pop culture. Parents were criticized for leading such busy lives that they neglected their emotionally fragile children. In all five cases it was clear afterward that those who committed the crimes gave ample warning that something was very wrong.

Critics called for tighter gun controls, greater parental supervision of teenagers, and restrictions on the extreme lyrics of popular music and the violent nature of video games. If nothing else, the school shootings revealed that beneath the veneer of prosperity there were deep flaws in both family structure and popular culture at the end of the century.

Shadow on the White House

"CLINTON ACCUSED OF URGING AIDE TO LIE," read the headline in the *Washington Post* on the morning of January 21, 1998. For the first time, the American people learned that Kenneth Starr, the special prosecutor appointed in 1994 to probe the Whitewater affair, was investigating charges that President Clinton had conducted a clandestine affair with a young White House intern, Monica Lewinsky. For the next year, the Lewinsky scandal dominated national attention as Bill Clinton fought hard to save his presidency.

Clinton's relationship with the twenty-two-year-old intern began in November 1995 and continued into early 1997, before the president terminated the relationship in April. The affair came to light in January 1998 when Linda Tripp, a co-worker of Lewinsky at the Pentagon, handed tapes of telephone conversations to the special prosecutor on which the intern described her sexual encounters with the president. When Starr's office leaked this development to the media, reporters besieged Clinton. On January 26, 1998, the president flatly denied the charges, saying, "I did not have sexual relations with that woman, Miss Lewinsky."

For the next six months, the president stoutly maintained his innocence, aided greatly by Hillary Clinton who stood by her husband and charged that Starr's investigation was part of a "vast right-wing conspiracy" designed to drive him from the White House. Many Americans withheld judgment. Indeed, with the economy booming, Clinton's approval rate in the polls went from the low 60s to more than 70 percent.

Matters finally came to a head in August. With a new legal team, Lewinsky reached agreement with Starr's office. She gave a detailed account of her ten sexual encounters with the president and provided crucial physical evidence implicating Clinton. At the same time, she cast doubt on obstruction of justice charges against

Clinton and his associates by denying that they had tried to buy her silence with job offers.

Realizing that he could no longer deny the affair, the president sought to limit the damage. He agreed to appear before Starr's grand jury. On August 17 he admitted having "inappropriate intimate contact" with Lewinsky, but insisted that he had not engaged in a sexual relationship. That evening Clinton spoke briefly to the nation. Still claiming that he had given "legally accurate" answers, the president for the first time admitted to a relationship with Lewinsky that was "not appropriate" and "wrong." He said he regretted misleading the people and especially his wife, but refused to apologize for his behavior or his false denials.

Clinton's fate hung in the balance. For the first time, some Democrats began to denounce the president's behavior as "disgraceful" and "immoral." But just when Clinton was most vulnerable, the special prosecutor rescued him. In early September, Starr sent a 452-page report to Congress outlining eleven possible impeachment charges against Clinton. The key one was perjury, and Starr believed he had to go into excruciating detail on all ten sexual encounters between Clinton and Lewinsky to prove that the president had lied when he denied engaging in sexual relations with the intern.

The American people responded by condemning Starr rather than the president. Shocked by the sordid details, they blamed the prosecutor for exposing families to distasteful sexual practices on the evening news. When a stunned Hillary Clinton continued to support her husband, much of the public concluded that however bad the president's conduct, it was a private matter, one to be settled between a husband and a wife, not in the pubic arena.

Republican leaders ignored this sentiment and pressed ahead with impeachment proceedings. The clearest warning sign came in November, when the Democrats surprised the nation by gaining 5 seats in the House of Representatives and narrowed the GOP margin to six votes. In December the House voted on four articles of impeachment, rejecting two, but approving two others, perjury and obstruction of justice, by small margins in nearly straight party-line votes.

The final showdown in the Senate was anticlimatic. With a two-thirds vote required to find the president guilty and remove him from office, there was no chance of conviction in the high-charged partisan mood that prevailed. The evidence against Clinton was strongest on the perjury charge, but on February 12, 1999, the GOP was unable to muster even a majority, with 45 in favor and 55 opposed. After a second, closer vote, 50 to 50, on obstruction of justice, the presiding officer, Chief Justice William Rehnquist, declared, "Acquitted of the charges."

Clinton had survived the Monica Lewinsky affair because once again he proved to be a far more skillful politician than his Republican opponents. With his wife's unflagging public support, he was able to persuade the American people that his political opponents were waging a vendetta against him.

Yet Bill Clinton emerged from the ordeal with his presidency badly damaged. People forgave him his personal failings during an era of unrivaled prosperity, but they no longer held him in high esteem. His final two years in office would be devoted to a concerted effort to restore his damaged reputation. Desperate for a legacy to mark his White House years, Clinton failed to realize that he had already created an enduring one—he would always be remembered as the president who dishonored his office by his unseemly affair with a young intern.

The New Millennium

The eve of the twenty-first century was for many a time of anxiety as well as celebration. Since the mid-1990s, experts had warned of what became known as the Year 2000, or Y2K, problem—the likely failure of computers because they had been programmed with only the last two digits for each year of the twentieth century.

Concern that the entire technology-based modern way of life would crash as computers confused 2000 with 1900 led to a massive effort to reprogram financial and public service systems. Consumers responded by stockpiling canned goods, generators, and survival gear. The billions spent in preparing for Y2K helped sustain the boom of the 1990s, but proved unnecessary as the United States made the transition to the new millennium without interruptions in basic services.

Yet the new age did bring unforeseen challenges. A close and controversial election resulted in Republican control of the White House and Congress. In 2001, the boom collapsed with the crash of the technology laden Nasdaq stock market. A brief recession and a sluggish recovery led to a steadily rising unemployment rate despite extensive tax cuts which helped unbalance the federal budget. Then on September 11, 2001, terrorist attacks on the World Trade Center and the Pentagon ushered in a new age of fear and reprisal. Efforts to protect the homeland clashed with traditional civil liberties, while abroad the war on terrorism led to the invasion of Afghanistan and Iraq, yet failed to eliminate completely the terrorist threat to the United States. The world of the twenty-first century thus proved to be not only different but dangerous.

The Disputed Election of 2000

Two dominant trends shaped the election of 2000. The first, which favored the Democrats, was the economic boom that had erased the budget deficit and brought prosperity to nearly all Americans in the 1990s. At the same time, however, many voters felt a sense of disappointment and even betrayal because of Clinton's personal failings. The conflict between material abundance and moral values resulted in the closest election in more than a century.

The two candidates, Governor George W. Bush of Texas and Vice President Al Gore of Tennessee, had little in common beyond being the sons of successful political fathers. Gore had spent eighteen years in Washington as a congressman, senator, and vice president. Somewhat stiff and aloof in manner, he had mastered the intricacies of all the major policy issues. Bush, in contrast, had pursued a business career before winning the governorship of Texas in 1994. Personable and outgoing, Bush had the temperament for leadership but lacked not only experience but a full grasp of national issues.

The conventional political wisdom pointed to an easy win for Al Gore in the fall election, but two factors reduced his chances. In the past, the candidate of a party in power during prosperous times had a clear advantage. A perceived need to separate himself from Clinton's scandals, however, led Gore to run as his own man and fail to capitalize on the president's glowing economic record. The decision of consumer advocate Ralph Nader to run for president on the Green party ticket further complicated Gore's campaign and forced him to move to the left, enabling Bush to appeal more effectively to moderate independents.

In the fall campaign, the candidates presented American voters with a clear choice. Bush called for limiting the role of government and relying instead on the free market. The centerpiece of his campaign was a proposed across-the-board tax cut. He also favored partial privatization of Social Security and placed greater weight on the private sector in his prescription drug plan and other reform proposals. Gore, in contrast to Clinton's efforts to move the Democratic party to the center in 1992 and 1996, became the advocate of government action, calling for an expanded federal role in education and health care.

The race for the White House, to the delight of the media, proved to be close and exciting. Until the end of the campaign, the parties ran neck and neck and were too close for the polls to accurately predict a winner. The early returns on election night proved that the polls were right in stressing the closeness of the presidential race. Gore seemed the likely winner when the networks mistakenly predicted a

Democratic victory in Florida. When the TV analysts put Florida back in the undecided column, Bush began to forge ahead, sweeping the rest of the South, including the Clinton-Gore home states of Arkansas and Tennessee. After midnight, when the networks again mistakenly called Florida, this time for Bush, the vice president telephoned the governor to concede, only to recant an hour later when it became clear that the Bush margin in Florida was paper thin.

For the next five weeks, all eyes were on the outcome in Florida. Gore had a lead nationwide in the popular vote and 267 electoral votes, yet Bush, with 246 votes in the Electoral College, could win the presidency with Florida's 25. Both sides sent phalanxes of lawyers to Florida. Bush's team, working with Florida's Republican secretary of state, sought to certify the results that showed the governor with a lead of 930 votes out of nearly 6 million cast. Citing many voting problems disclosed by the media, Gore asked for a recount in three heavily Democratic counties in south Florida. All three used antiquated punch card machines that resulted in some ballots not being clearly marked for any presidential candidate when the chads, the bits of paper removed when a card is punched, were not completely detached from the cards. For weeks the results in Florida, and hence of the entire election, appeared to depend on how one divined the intent of a voter based on hanging, dimpled, or bulging chads.

The decision finally came in the courts. Democrats appealed the initial attempt to certify Bush as the victor to the Florida Supreme Court, where the majority of judges had been appointed by Democratic governors. The Florida court twice ordered recounts, the second time for all counties in the state, but Bush's lawyers appealed to the United States Supreme Court. On December 12, five weeks after the election, the Court overruled the state court's call for a recount in a 5 to 4 decision that reflected a long-standing ideological divide among the nine justices. The next day, Gore conceded, and Bush finally became president-elect.

When the electoral college finally voted on December 18, there were 271 votes cast for Bush and 266 for Gore (one District of Columbia Gore elector abstained). Nearly complete election totals showed that Gore had received more than 500,000 more popular votes than Bush. The governor had carried more states, thirty to twenty, but the vice president had won in the large states with major metropolitan areas such as California, New York, and Illinois.

Bush's narrow victory revealed deep divisions in American life at the end of the twentieth century. The rural West and South went for Bush, along with a few key Midwest and border states, while Gore won the urban states along both coasts. There was an equally strong divide along economic lines, with the poor voting for Gore, the rich for Bush, and the middle class dividing evenly between the two candidates. Gore continued to benefit from the gender gap, winning 54 percent of the women's vote, and he won an even larger share of the black vote, 90 percent, than Clinton in 1996. Bush succeeded in narrowing the Democratic margin among Hispanic voters, taking 35 percent, compared to only 28 percent for Dole four years earlier. The two

The Election of 2000

Candidate	Party	Popular Vote	Electoral Vote
George W. Bush	Republican	50,456,167	271
Al Gore	Democratic	50,996,064	266*
Ralph Nader	Green	2,864,810	—
	Other	448,750	—
		104,765,791	537

*One District of Columbia Gore elector abstained.

candidates split the suburban vote evenly and Bush succeeded in recapturing the lead among Catholic voters.

Exit polls confirmed the underlying split in the electorate. More than 60 percent of voters surveyed said issues were more important than personality. Yet Bush was the overwhelming choice of those who placed primary emphasis on character and values. It was clear that Bush, who ended every campaign speech with a promise to restore dignity and honor to the White House, had used Clinton's foibles to counter Democratic claims of achieving prosperity. By the narrowest of margins, the American people appeared to have placed values ahead of material well-being in the election of 2000.

Bush's Domestic Agenda

George W. Bush's first few months in office provided a demanding test of the inexperienced president's leadership qualities. In Washington, he faced urban, liberal Democrats who resisted his efforts at conciliation out of a determination to stand up for their constituencies, mainly organized labor, environmental activists, and civil rights groups. With only a narrow Republican majority in the House and just a one-vote margin in the Senate, the president faced a difficult task. The result was a mixed record—some sweeping victories but also several stinging setbacks.

Before battling with Congress, Bush had to organize his administration. Like most modern presidents, he relied heavily on past associates in staffing the White House. Colin Powell, the former chairman of the Joint Chiefs of Staff, became secretary of state, where he belied his military background by becoming an advocate for cooperation with other nations, urging diplomacy over the use of force. In contrast, Donald Rumsfeld, the new secretary of defense (a post he had held in the Ford administration) was intent on streamlining the armed forces in order to enable the United States to fulfill its post–Cold War position of world preeminence. Along with Vice President Cheney, Rumsfeld was on a collision course with Powell, leaving the delicate task of reconciling the ensuing conflict to National Security Adviser Condoleezza Rice.

Bush's most controversial choice was former senator John Ashcroft of Missouri for attorney general. A staunch conservative and favorite of the Christian right, Ashcroft stirred fears among Democrats of using the Justice Department to restrict traditional religious and civic freedoms. His former Senate colleagues finally confirmed him by a narrow margin.

The first order of business was the tax cut, which required intense lobbying from the White House. Through adroit maneuvering, Bush finally succeeded in persuading Congress to pass legislation in early June that cut taxes by a staggering $1.35 trillion over a ten-year period. Many of the cuts would only take effect in future years, but Congress offered an immediate stimulus to the economy by authorizing rebate payments to taxpayers: $600 for couples and $300 for individuals earning more than $6,000 a year. While critics saw this measure as a betrayal of the long effort to balance the budget, Bush contended that future budget surpluses would more than make up for the loss of tax revenue.

The slowing American economy, which soon turned the projected budget surplus into annual deficits, failed to halt the Bush administration's tax cut momentum. In 2003, arguing that a further reduction in taxes would stimulate the stalled economy, Bush prevailed upon Congress to adopt another $350 billion in cuts. Like the 2001 cuts, the new reductions were temporary in order to preserve the possibility of a balanced budget by 2010. Opponents charged that if a future Congress made these tax cuts permanent, as seemed likely, the total cost would rise to nearly $1 trillion. While Clinton had favored a policy of eliminating the deficit, Bush made tax reduction the centerpiece of his economic policy.

Although it took six months longer, the president also succeeded in getting Congress to enact his education reform program in December 2001. Borrowing the label "No Child Left Behind" from liberal Democrats, the administration pushed hard for a new policy requiring states to give annual performance tests to all elementary school students. Democrats countered with demands for increased federal funding of public education to assist states and local school boards in raising their standards. Bush shrewdly cultivated the support of Senator Ted Kennedy, a leading liberal Democrat, to forge a bipartisan consensus. The final measure increased federal aid to education by $4 billion and mandated state tests in reading and math for all students in grades three through eight, and at least once during grades ten to twelve.

The new administration's successes in cutting taxes and in educational reform were balanced by setbacks in the Senate and in the economy. On May 24, 2001, Senator James M. Jeffords, a Republican moderate from Vermont, surprised the GOP by announcing that he was leaving the party. By becoming an independent and aligning himself with the Democrats, Jeffords reduced the number of Republicans to 49 in the Senate, thus giving the Democrats control of the upper chamber. The new majority leader, Senator Tom Daschle of South Dakota, quickly asserted his authority to block a number of administration initiatives, including a proposal to drill for oil in environmentally sensitive areas of the Arctic National Wildlife Refuge in Alaska. The Democratic leadership prevented a Senate vote on several key Bush judicial appointees and served notice they would insist on a moderate nominee for the next Supreme Court vacancy.

In the spring of 2001 the American economy experienced its first recession in ten years. A glut of unsold goods forced manufacturers to curtail production and lay off workers. Unemployment rose to 6 percent by 2002, despite the efforts of the Federal Reserve to stem the decline by cutting interest rates eleven times in 2001. The tax rebates authorized by Congress helped stimulate recovery in the summer, but then the September 11 attacks led to a further decline. In 2002, the economy once again began to recover, only to be stalled late in the year by concern over potential war with Iraq.

One of the most troubling aspects of the economic downturn was the collapse of several major corporations and the subsequent revelation of shocking financial practices. WorldCom, Inc., a major telecommunications company, became the largest corporation in American history to declare bankruptcy, while a New York grand jury charged executives of Tyco International, a large electronics company, with stealing more than $600 million from shareholders through stock fraud, false expense reports, and unauthorized bonuses. Enron, a Houston energy company, failed in late 2001 as the result of astonishingly corrupt business practices, including fraudulent accounting and private partnerships designed to inflate profits and hide losses. When the company declared bankruptcy, shareholders lost more than $50 billion, while rank-and-file employees lost not only their jobs but much of their retirement savings.

The public disclosures of the corrupt practices of these major corporations further weakened public confidence in American business and served to slow recovery from the recession of 2001. President Bush contended that the tax cut he had pushed through Congress would provide the necessary stimulus for full recovery. The stock market began to rally in the spring of 2003 after three straight years of losses, and consumer spending helped drive the economy's growth rate to over 7 percent in the third quarter of the year. But unemployment continued to rise, going over 6 percent by mid-2003 as companies kept trimming their payrolls to cut costs and become profitable again. The political outlook for George W. Bush, very much aware of the way a sluggish economy had made his father a one-term president, depended on how quickly the recovering economy could produce new jobs and thus restore the confidence of voters in the party in power.

Terrorism: Attack and Counterattack

On the morning of September 11, 2001, nineteen Islamic militant terrorists hijacked four U.S. airliners and turned them to attack targets in New York City and Washington, D.C. The hijackers took over two planes flying out of Boston's Logan Airport en route to California, and flew them into the World Trade Center (WTC) in New York. One plane slammed into the north tower just before 9 A.M. and the second hit the south tower only twenty minutes later. Within two hours, both towers had collapsed, taking the lives of nearly 3,000 victims trapped in the buildings or crushed by the debris and more than 300 firefighters and other rescue workers who attempted to save them.

In Washington, an American Airlines flight that left Dulles Airport bound for Los Angeles met a similar fate. Taken over by five terrorists, the Boeing 757 plowed into the Pentagon, destroying one wing of the building and killing 189 military personnel and civilian workers. The terrorists had seized a fourth plane, United Airlines flight 93, scheduled to fly from Newark, New Jersey, to San Francisco. Over Pennsylvania, as the hijackers attempted to turn the plane toward the nation's capital, the passengers fought to regain control of the plane. They failed to do so, but did succeed in preventing the plane from hitting another target in Washington—perhaps the White House or the Capitol Building. Flight 93 crashed in southern Pennsylvania, killing all 44 passengers and crew as well as the hijackers.

President Bush met the crisis with a display of leadership and determination that few suspected he possessed. "None of us will forget this day," he told the American people in a televised speech on the evening of September 11. "Yet we go forward to defend freedom and all that is good and just in the world." In a key sentence, the president had strengthened the vague wording in the original speechwriter's draft to insist that the United States would not only pursue the terrorists responsible for the assault, but any person or nation that assisted them. In declaring a **war on terrorism,** Bush vowed, "We will make no distinction between those who planned these acts and those who harbor them."

war on terrorism Initiated by President George W. Bush after the attacks of September 11, 2001, the broadly defined war on terrorism aimed to weed out terrorist operatives and their supporters throughout the world.

Bush spoke later to a joint session of Congress on September 20—a speech that 80 million Americans watched on television. In it the president promised to pursue those responsible for September 11: "Our grief has turned to anger and anger to resolution. Whether we bring our enemies to justice or bring justice to our enemies, justice will be done." And the counterattack, he cautioned, would take time.

As rescue efforts continued in the rubble of the World Trade Center, President Bush toured the site on September 14, 2001. In CNN's televised coverage of the visit, Bush is shown here addressing rescue workers through a bullhorn. Firefighter Bob Beckwith stands beside him. ❖

"Americans should not expect one battle but a lengthy campaign, unlike any other we have ever seen." The outcome, however, would never be in doubt. "I will not yield; I will not rest," Bush declared to thunderous applause. "I will not relent in waging this struggle for freedom and security for the American people."

It would take far more than words to avenge September 11 and end the terrorist threat to the United States. It soon became evident that Osama bin Laden, a wealthy Saudi, and his terrorist organization, al Qaeda ("the Base" in Arabic), had planned and carried out the attacks. Bin Laden had originally been part of the international Muslim resistance to the Soviet invasion of Afghanistan that had received support and weapons from the CIA in the 1980s. He turned against the United States at the time of the 1991 Gulf War, outraged by the presence of large numbers of American troops in his native Saudi Arabia. Earlier, in the late 1980s, he had formed al Qaeda as a determined group of Islamic fundamentalists intent on restoring orthodox religion in the Arab world and cleansing it of foreign influence, especially American. The CIA had evidence linking bin Laden and al Qaeda to the bombing of two American embassies in East Africa in 1998 and the attack on the American destroyer *USS Cole* in Yemen in 2000. And bin Laden soon released video tapes gloating over the September 11 attacks.

The United States had been trying to neutralize al Qaeda for at least a decade without any success. Ordered out of Saudi Arabia in 1991, bin Laden had sought refuge, first in the Sudan and later in Afghanistan, after the Taliban, another extremist Muslim group, had taken over that country. In Afghanistan, bin Laden set up camps to train hundreds of would-be terrorists, mainly from Arab countries but including recruits from the Philippines, Indonesia, and Central Asia. After the embassy bombings, President Clinton ordered cruise missile attacks on several of these camps in the hope of killing bin Laden. The al Qaeda leader survived, though, leaving one of the targets only a few hours before the strike.

Bush's determination to go after those harboring terrorists made Afghanistan the prime target for the American counterattack. The president ordered the Pentagon and the CIA, which already had agents on the scene, to launch an invasion of Afghanistan to destroy the Taliban, wipe out al Qaeda, and capture or kill Osama bin Laden.

In early October, the CIA and Army Special Forces began the operation, relying on the Northern Alliance, an Afghan political coalition still resisting the Taliban. Using a variety of methods, ranging from substantial bribes of local warlords to frequent air strikes, American forces quickly routed the Taliban and by December had installed a U.S.-friendly regime in Kabul. Most of Afghanistan, however, remained in chaos, and despite extensive efforts and several near misses, bin Laden had avoided capture, apparently taking refuge in the rugged mountain areas along the Pakistan border.

The quick victory in Afghanistan marked only the beginning of the war on terrorism waged by the Bush administration. With help from a broad international coalition including a cooperative government in Pakistan, the CIA and FBI were able to capture a number of high-ranking al Qaeda officials. Other Muslim countries, notably Egypt and Jordan, also proved invaluable in interrogating suspected terrorists and helping foil their plans for new attacks against the United States. The CIA gained a rich harvest of intelligence data in Afghanistan and received additional useful information from several hundred terrorists imprisoned at the American naval base in Guantanamo, Cuba.

While waging the war abroad, the Bush administration also focused on the problem of securing the United States from any further terrorist assaults. The president favored the creation of a new Department of Homeland Security, combining Customs, the Coast Guard, the Immigration and Naturalization Service (INS), and other government bureaus into one central agency to protect the nation.

In November 2002, Congress approved the new Department of Homeland Security, to be headed by Tom Ridge, former governor of Pennsylvania.

The difficulty in protecting the nation from terrorist attack was highlighted by an anthrax scare in the fall of 2001. Several employees of a Florida newspaper publishing company became ill in October with the anthrax bacteria, one dying after inhaling the spores in an envelope that came through the mail. Later in the month, a secretary at NBC News in New York City was exposed to the deadly white powder while opening a letter addressed to anchorman Tom Brokaw. In November, similar envelopes arrived in Washington addressed to members of Congress. After the deaths of two postal workers forced authorities to close the central mail processing facility in the nation's capital, letters filled with anthrax were found addressed to Senators Tom Daschle and Patrick Leahy. There were no further anthrax incidents, but the episode showed how vulnerable the nation was to biological attack.

The homeland security department faced a particularly hard task in policing the nation's borders and alerting the public to potential threats. With more than 1 million immigrants and 42 million more visitors entering the United States each year, neither the Immigration and Naturalization Service (INS)—later replaced by the Bureau of Citizenship and Immigration Services (BCIS)—nor the customs service could guarantee that they had prevented any terrorist from slipping into the country. Ridge's office stepped up patrols of such likely targets as nuclear power plants and public water supply systems. Using a color-coded chart, from time to time homeland security raised the nation's alert status from yellow (elevated risk) to orange (high risk), just one level below red (highest risk). By the spring of 2003, the public tended to ignore these danger signals as nearly two years had passed without a further terrorist attack on American soil.

A primary focus of homeland security was on ensuring the safety of airline travel in the wake of the September 11 hijackings. In November 2001, President Bush signed legislation replacing private companies with government employees at all airport screening stations. The understandable public fear of flying after September 11 had a devastating effect on the airline industry, forcing the cancellation of many flights and the laying off of thousands of pilots and other workers. Despite a $15 billion government bailout approved in late September 2001, the airlines continued to experience heavy losses. Although air travel began to revive slowly in 2002, the industry, along with other forms of tourism, continued to be a drag on an already sluggish economy.

The war on terrorism raised an even more fundamental question than economic stagnation. Attorney General John Ashcroft, using new powers granted by Congress, conducted a broad crackdown on possible terrorists, detaining many Muslim Americans on flimsy evidence and insisting that concern for national security outweighed traditional civil liberties. Opponents quickly challenged Ashcroft, arguing that the terrorists would win their greatest victory if the United States violated its own historic principles of individual freedom in the name of fighting terrorism. It was a debate that troubled many Americans who had difficulty reconciling the need for security with respect for civil liberties.

The real winner in the war against terrorism, at least in the short run, was George W. Bush. His resolute stand against terrorism and his determination to avenge the September 11 attacks struck a responsive chord among the American people. His approval rating, a respectable 53 percent before September 11, shot up to over 90 percent in the weeks following the attack, and then settled into the 65 to 75 percent range, extraordinarily high for a first-term president. The way the American people had rallied around his leadership helped offset growing doubts about his tax cuts and the stalled economy. The attacks on the Twin Towers and the Pentagon had transformed his presidency and gave him a good chance of winning a second term in the White House.

The New American Empire?

The terrorist attacks on the United States were the catalyst for a major change in direction for American foreign policy. Not only did the Bush administration wage an intensive effort to avenge September 11 and prevent further attacks, it initiated a new global policy of American preeminence. For the first time since the end of the Cold War, the United States had a clear, if controversial, blueprint for international affairs.

The new administration rejected traditional forms of international cooperation. The president was outspoken in refusing to expose American military personnel to the jurisdiction of the International Criminal Court for possible crimes committed in worldwide peacekeeping efforts.

The new direction of American foreign policy became clear on January 29, 2002, when Bush delivered his second State of the Union address to Congress and the nation. Not only did he repeat his vow to punish all nations sponsoring terrorism, but he became specific. In a memorable phrase, he accused Iraq, Iran, and North Korea of forming "an axis of evil." Nine months later, in September 2002, the Bush administration released a fully developed statement of its new world policy, "National Security Strategy (NSS) of the United States." The goal of American policy, Bush's NSS statement declared, was to "extend the peace by encouraging free and open societies on every continent."

unilateralism A national policy of acting alone without consulting others.

There were two main components of the new strategy, which critics quickly called **unilateralism.** The first was to accept fully the role the nation had been playing since the end of the Cold War—that of global police. The United States would not shrink from its responsibility to defend freedom anywhere in the world—with allies if possible, by itself if necessary. To implement this policy, the NSS statement asserted that the Bush administration would maintain "military strength beyond challenge." "Our forces," the statement declared, "will be strong enough to dissuade potential adversaries from pursuing a military buildup in hopes of surpassing, or equaling, the power of the United States."

In playing the role of world police, Bush and his advisers asserted the right to the preemptive use of force. Learning from September 11, the NSS statement continued, "We cannot let our enemies strike first." Although promising to seek the support of the international community before using force, the NSS statement said, "we will not hesitate to act alone, if necessary, to exercise our right of self-defense." In other words, the Bush administration, aware that the United States was far stronger militarily and economically than any other nation, accepted its new role as final arbiter of all international disputes.

The new strategy reflected the triumph of Rumsfeld and Cheney over Colin Powell. Instead of the traditional reliance on diplomacy and international cooperation that Powell and the State Department favored, the United States would act on its own. The result, in the eyes of both its critics and defenders, would be a new American empire.

weapons of mass destruction (WMD) Biological, chemical, and nuclear weapons capable of widespread destruction.

Iraq quickly became the test case for this new shift in American foreign policy. After his "axis of evil" speech in January, President Bush focused on what he and his Pentagon advisers called **weapons of mass destruction (WMD)** that they claimed Saddam Hussein had been secretly amassing in large quantities. The United States demanded that Iraq permit UN inspectors (forced out of the country in 1998) to search for such weapons. Iraq had promised the UN it would allow such searches in 1991 at the end of the Gulf War. In August 2002, more than ten years later, Bush agreed to allow Secretary of State Colin Powell to work to ensure that the UN resume its weapons inspection and force Saddam to disarm. The Pentagon, meanwhile, made its own plans for a unilateral American military solution.

Slowly, but inevitably, the United States moved toward war with Iraq in late 2002 and early 2003. Congress approved a resolution in October authorizing the president to use force against Saddam Hussein's regime. A month later, the UN Security Council voted unanimously to send its team of inspectors back into Iraq, warning Saddam of "severe consequences" if he failed to comply. Despite the failure of the international inspectors to find any evidence of chemical, biological, or nuclear weapons in Iraq, the Bush administration kept pressing for a Security Council resolution authorizing the use of force to compel Saddam to disarm. When France and Russia vowed to veto any such measure, Bush and his advisers decided to ignore the world body and proceed on their own. Preemption would have its first real test.

The ensuing war with Iraq surprised both the backers and the critics of unilateralism. On March 18, two days before the planned start of hostilities, President Bush made a last-minute decision to launch a cruise missile and laser bomb air strike on a bunker in Baghdad, in the belief that Saddam was inside. The results were unknown, but the next day, 24 hours earlier than planned, three columns of American troops, a total of 65,000, began to execute a two-pronged invasion of Iraq from bases in Kuwait. Britain, the only major power to join the United States in the fighting, helped by besieging the city of Basra and taking control of southern Iraq. After a week of rapid advance and only light casualties, the main American thrust seemed to bog down less than 100 miles from Baghdad. Unexpected attacks by guerrilla forces necessitated a pause while newly arriving American troops destroyed these irregular units and increased patrols to protect the long supply line.

But victory was within sight. The turning point came on March 25 when the three columns of American troops resumed their advance northward. Saddam sent elite units of the Republican Guard to engage the Americans south of Baghdad only to see them decimated by air strikes and then overrun by American armor. Within a week, the army had captured the Baghdad international airport, and on April 8, just three weeks after the fighting had begun, marines marched virtually unopposed into the heart of the city. The American people watched the televised scene of joyous Iraqis toppling a statue of Saddam in Fardos Square. An Iraqi major summed up the enormity of his country's defeat: "Losing a war is one thing, but losing Baghdad is another," he explained. "It was like losing the dearest thing in life."

The war was essentially over by April 8, although sporadic resistance continued north of Baghdad until early May, when President Bush formally declared an end to

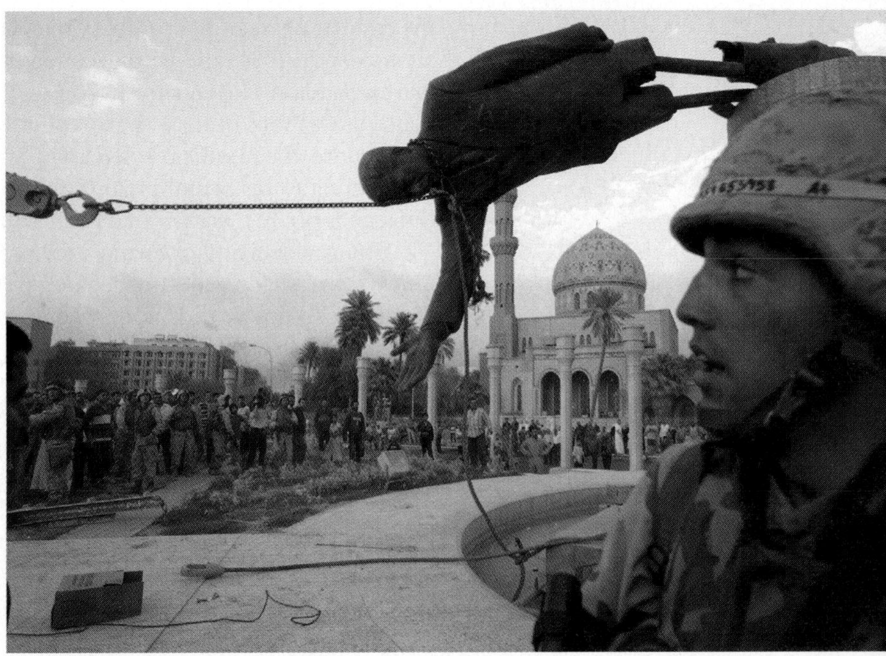

In a memorable image from the war in Iraq, Iraqi civilians and U.S. soldiers pull down a statue of Saddam Hussein in Baghdad on April 9, 2003. Eight months later, U.S. soldiers captured the former Iraqi president near Tikrit. ❖

CHRONOLOGY

1992	Riots devastate South Central Los Angeles after verdict in Rodney King case (May) ❖ Bill Clinton elected president (November)
1993	General Motors announces loss of $23.4 billion, the largest one-year loss in U.S. corporate history
1994	Former football star O. J. Simpson charged with killing ex-wife Nicole Brown Simpson and her friend Ronald Goldman (June) ❖ Republicans gain control of both houses of Congress (November)
1995	U.S. troops arrive in Bosnia as part of international peacekeeping force (December)
1996	FBI arrests Theodore Kaczynski, suspected Unabomber, in Montana ❖ Clinton signs major welfare reform measure (August)
1997	Federal jury gives Timothy McVeigh death sentence for Oklahoma City bombing
1998	Terrorists bomb American embassies in Kenya and Tanzania
1999	Senate acquits Clinton of impeachment charges (February) ❖ Dow Jones Industrial Average exceeds 10,000 for first time (March)
2000	Y2K furor proves unfounded ❖ George W. Bush wins contested presidential election
2001	American economy goes into recession, ending the longest period of expansion in U.S. history (March) ❖ Terrorist attacks on World Trade Center and the Pentagon (September 11) ❖ Anthrax spores found in mail (October) ❖ United States military action against the Taliban regime in Afghanistan (October–December)
2002	Police arrest suspected D.C. snipers who killed ten and wounded three residents of the metro area (October) ❖ Department of Homeland Security created (November)
2003	U.S. troops invade Iraq and overthrow Saddam Hussein's regime (March–April) ❖ Saddam Hussein captured (December)

the combat phase of the conflict. In less than half the time that it had taken to liberate Kuwait in 1991, and with even fewer American casualties, the United States had driven Saddam Hussein from power. But the subsequent failure to find any evidence of weapons of mass destruction led critics to question the validity of the war. In response, the president's defenders stressed the importance of deposing Saddam by pointing to his brutal prisons and to the killing fields south of Baghdad where thousands of Shi'ite rebels had been slaughtered in 1991.

The problems of restoring order and rebuilding the shattered Iraqi economy quickly overshadowed the debate over the war's legitimacy. Daily attacks on American troops in the Sunni triangle north of Baghdad began in the summer of 2003 and increased in intensity during the fall, killing an average of three American soldiers each week. By October, more troops had died from these attacks than had been killed during the combat phase in March and April. Widespread looting, sabotage of oil pipelines, and the difficulty in repairing and operating outdated power plants and oil facilities made economic recovery very slow and halting. U.S. efforts to involve occupation forces from other UN members yielded only a few troops. In the fall of 2003, a group of wealthier nations led by Japan pledged $13 billion for Iraq's reconstruction; Congress, after considerable debate, finally authorized another $18.6 billion to help rebuild Iraq, along with $51 billion to support the American army of occupation.

The capture of Saddam Hussein in December 2003 helped boost President Bush's approval rating, which had begun to sag as problems persisted in postwar Iraq. The situation in Iraq, however, still remained troubling after Saddam's capture. Despite slow but steady progress in restoring public services such as electric power and the gradual recovery of the Iraqi oil industry, the armed insurrection continued. Mortar attacks on Baghdad hotels, roadside bombs aimed at American armored convoys, and hand-held missile attacks on American helicopters made Iraq a very dangerous place. Equally disturbing, conflicts of interest between Shi'ite and Sunni Muslims, as well as the Kurdish population's demand for autonomy, threatened the American goal of creating a stable Iraqi government. George W. Bush, bolstered by a reviving economy, still faced a likely campaign attack by Democrats in 2004 on his handling of the war with Iraq.

Conclusion: The American Century?

On the eve of American entry into World War II, Henry Luce, founder of the *Time-Life* publishing empire, predicted that the 1900s would become known in history as the American century. The onset of the Cold War made Luce's prediction premature. But the demise of the Soviet Union in 1991, leaving the United States as the world's sole superpower, and the subsequent assertion of American preeminence by the George W. Bush administration suggest that the next one hundred years may well be the real American century. The United States, despite a slow recovery from the 2001 recession and hostile world opinion, remains by far the strongest nation on the globe. Its military power is unrivaled and its economy is still the engine driving the world's markets.

Yet daunting challenges face the United States in the twenty-first century. History has repeatedly shown how brief a time most nations have to enjoy their moment of world supremacy. Like the empires of Greece and Rome, or even of Great Britain in more recent times, the United States must guard against the powerful force of imperial decay. In a world suspicious of American motives, the challenge facing the United States is to convince its own citizens, as well as those of other nations, that the American mission of spreading democracy, of being a beacon of liberty to all peoples, remains a worthwhile and attainable goal.

Key Terms

Sunbelt, p. 656
undocumented aliens, p. 658
North American Free Trade Agreement (NAFTA), p. 663
Contract with America, p. 665
World Trade Organization (WTO), p. 674
war on terrorism, p. 681
unilateralism, p. 684
weapons of mass destruction (WMD), p. 684

Recommended Reading

Bob Woodward offers the fullest account of the Clinton-Greenspan effort to end the budget deficits in two books, *The Agenda* (1994), on Clinton's economic policy, and *Maestro* (2000), on Greenspan's service as chairman of the Federal Reserve Board.

The best book on recent immigration from developing countries is David Reimers, *Still the Golden Door,* 2nd ed. (1992). Peter Skerry provides a thoughtful survey of the largest single Hispanic group in *Mexican-Americans* (1993). For the role of blacks in politics since World War II, see Steven F. Lawson, *Running for Freedom* (1991).

British journalist Martin Walker gives a balanced account of Clinton's first term in *The President We Deserve* (1996). For the first lady's perspective, see Hillary Clinton,

Living History (2003). Two books cover the Monica Lewinsky scandal and the ensuing impeachment proceedings: Michael Isikoff, *Uncovering Clinton* (2000), and Richard A. Posner, *An Affair of State* (1999).

Haynes Johnson traces the boom years of the 1990s in *The Best of Times* (2001). For the stock market bubble, see John Cassidy, *dot.com: The Greatest Story Ever Sold* (2002).

The best survey of foreign policy in the Clinton years is David Halberstam, *War in a Time of Peace* (2001). For Bosnia, see Richard Holbrooke, *To End a War* (1998); David Fromkin deals with the other Balkan crisis in *Kosovo Crossing* (1999).

In *Gathering Storm* (1996), Morris Dees and James Corcoran offer a somber assessment of the militia movement from the Ruby Ridge shootout to the Oklahoma City bombing.

The most balanced account of the disputed 2000 election is Howard Gillman, *The Votes that Counted* (2001). For contrasting opinions, see Richard A. Posner, *Breaking the Deadlock* (2001), in support of the Supreme Court decision, and Alan M. Dershowitz, *Supreme Injustice* (2001), sharply critical.

The first memoir to come out of the George W. Bush White House is David Frum, *The Right Man* (2003), favorable to the president but not entirely uncritical. On the events of September 11 and their aftermath, see Richard Bernstein, et al., *Out of the Blue* (2002), based on *New York Times* reporting; and Steven Brill, *After* (2003), on the way people came to terms with the tragedy. For the war on terrorism, see Paul Pillar, *Terrorism and U.S. Foreign Policy* (2001), and Victor Davis Hanson, *An Autumn of War* (2002), essays supportive of Bush's efforts.

Williamson Murray and Robert H. Scales, Jr., survey the fighting that led to the defeat of Saddam Hussein's regime in *The Iraq War* (2003).

For a list of additional titles related to this chapter's topics, please see http://www.ablongman.com/divine.

Suggested Web Sites

American Identities
http://xroads.virginia.edu/~YP/ethnic.html
This site suggests resources for studying America's multiple ethnic identities.

Census 2000
http://www.census.gov/main/www/cen2000.html
U.S. Census Bureau gateway to 2000 census information and data.

William Jefferson Clinton
http://www.ipl.org/ref/POTUS/wjclinton.html
This site contains basic factual data about Clinton's election and presidency, speeches, and on-line biographies.

Investigating the President: The Trial
http://www.cnn.com/ALLPOLITICS/resources/1998/lewinsky
This site from CNN provides information and documents about the scandals surrounding President Clinton and his impeachment.

A Brief History of the Internet, Version 3.1
http://www.isoc.org/internet-history/
The Internet Society puts out this site that explores the development and impact of the Internet.

The Computer Museum History Center
http://computerhistory.org
This site for the Computer Museum History Center features on-line archives and exhibits tracing five decades of computer history.

George Walker Bush
http://www.ipl.org/ref/POTUS/gwbush.html
This site contains basic factual data about Bush's election and presidency, speeches, and on-line biographies.

September 11, 2001: Attack on America
http://www.yale.edu/lawweb/avalon/sept_11/sept_11.htm
The Avalon Project at Yale Law School sponsors this collection of documents relating to the September 11 terrorist attacks.

War in Iraq
http://www.cnn.com/SPECIALS/2003/Iraq
A CNN special report on the war, including interactive maps, headlines, video, and topical information.

Appendix

The Declaration of Independence

The Articles of Confederation

The Constitution of the United States of America

Amendments to the Constitution

Presidential Elections

For additional reference material, go to
www.ablongman.com/divine/appendix
The on-line appendix includes the following:

The Declaration of Independence
The Articles of Confederation
The Constitution of the United States of America
Amendments to the Constitution
Presidential Elections
Vice Presidents and Cabinet Members by Administration
Supreme Court Justices
Presidents, Congresses, and Chief Justices, 1789–2001
Territorial Expansion of the United States (map)
Admission of States of the Union
U.S. Population, 1790–2000
Ten Largest Cities by Population, 1700–1900
Birthrate, 1820–2000 (chart)
Death Rate, 1900–2000 (chart)
Life Expectancy, 1900–2000 (chart)
Urban/Rural Population, 1750–1900 (chart)
Women in the Labor Force, 1890–1990
United States Physical Features (map)
United States Native Vegetation (map)
Ancient Native American Communities (map)
Native American Peoples, c. 1500 (map)
Present-Day United States (map)

THE DECLARATION OF INDEPENDENCE

In Congress, July 4, 1776

The Unanimous Declaration of the Thirteen United States of America,

When, in the course of human events, it becomes necessary for one people to dissolve the political bonds which have connected them with another, and to assume, among the powers of the earth, the separate and equal station to which the laws of nature and of nature's God entitle them, a decent respect to the opinions of mankind requires that they should declare the causes which impel them to the separation.

We hold these truths to be self-evident: That all men are created equal; that they are endowed by their Creator with certain unalienable rights; that among these are life, liberty, and the pursuit of happiness; that, to secure these rights, governments are instituted among men, deriving their just powers from the consent of the governed; that whenever any form of government becomes destructive of these ends, it is the right of the people to alter or to abolish it, and to institute new government, laying its foundation on such principles, and organizing its powers in such form, as to them shall seem most likely to effect their safety and happiness. Prudence, indeed, will dictate that governments long established should not be changed for light and transient causes; and accordingly all experience hath shown that mankind are more disposed to suffer, while evils are sufferable, than to right themselves by abolishing the forms to which they are accustomed. But when a long train of abuses and usurpations, pursuing invariably the same object, evinces a design to reduce them under absolute despotism, it is their right, it is their duty, to throw off such government, and to provide new guards for their future security. Such has been the patient sufferance of these colonies; and such is now the necessity which constrains them to alter their former systems of government. The history of the present King of Great Britain is a history of repeated injuries and usurpations, all having in direct object the establishment of an absolute tyranny over these states. To prove this, let facts be submitted to a candid world.

He has refused his assent to laws, the most wholesome and necessary for the public good.

He has forbidden his governors to pass laws of immediate and pressing importance, unless suspended in their operation till his assent should be obtained; and, when so suspended, he has utterly neglected to attend to them.

He has refused to pass other laws for the accommodation of large districts of people, unless those people would relinquish the right of representation in the legislature, a right inestimable to them, and formidable to tyrants only.

He has called together legislative bodies at places unusual, uncomfortable, and distant from the depository of their public records, for the sole purpose of fatiguing them into compliance with his measures.

He has dissolved representative houses repeatedly, for opposing, with manly firmness, his invasions on the rights of the people.

He has refused for a long time, after such dissolutions, to cause others to be elected; whereby the legislative powers, incapable of annihilation, have returned to the people at large for their exercise; the state remaining, in the mean time, exposed to all the dangers of invasions from without and convulsions within.

He has endeavored to prevent the population of these states; for that purpose obstructing the laws for naturalization of foreigners; refusing to pass others to encourage their migration hither, and raising the conditions of new appropriations of lands.

He has obstructed the administration of justice, by refusing his assent to laws for establishing judiciary powers.

He has made judges dependent on his will alone, for the tenure of their offices, and the amount and payment of their salaries.

He has erected a multitude of new offices, and sent hither swarms of officers to harass our people and eat out their substance.

He has kept among us, in times of peace, standing armies, without the consent of our legislatures.

He has affected to render the military independent of, and superior to, the civil power.

He has combined with others to subject us to a jurisdiction foreign to our constitution, and unacknowledged by our laws, giving his assent to their acts of pretended legislation:

For quartering large bodies of armed troops among us;

For protecting them, by a mock trial, from punishment for any murder which they should commit on the inhabitants of these states;

For cutting off our trade with all parts of the world;

For imposing taxes on us without our consent;

For depriving us, in many cases, of the benefits of trial by jury;

For transporting us beyond seas, to be tried for pretended offenses;

For abolishing the free system of English laws in a neighboring province, establishing therein an arbitrary government, and enlarging its boundaries, so as to render it at once an example and fit instrument for introducing the same absolute rule into these colonies;

For taking away our charters, abolishing our most valuable laws, and altering fundamentally the forms of our governments;

For suspending our own legislatures, and declaring themselves invested with power to legislate for us in all cases whatsoever.

He has abdicated government here, by declaring us out of his protection and waging war against us.

He has plundered our seas, ravaged our coasts, burned our towns, and destroyed the lives of our people.

He is at this time transporting large armies of foreign mercenaries to complete the works of death, desolation, and tyranny already begun with circumstances of cruelty and perfidy scarcely paralleled in the most barbarous ages, and totally unworthy the head of a civilized nation.

He has constrained our fellow-citizens, taken captive on the high seas, to bear arms against their country, to become the executioners of their friends and brethren, or to fall themselves by their hands.

He has excited domestic insurrection among us, and has endeavored to bring on the inhabitants of our frontiers the merciless Indian savages, whose known rule of warfare is an undistinguished destruction of all ages, sexes, and conditions.

In every stage of these oppressions we have petitioned for redress in the most humble terms; our repeated petitions have been answered only by repeated injury. A prince, whose character is thus marked by every act which may define a tyrant, is unfit to be the ruler of a free people.

Nor have we been wanting in our attentions to our British brethren. We have warned them, from time to time, of attempts by their legislature to extend an unwarrantable jurisdiction over us. We have reminded them of the circumstances of our emigration and settlement here. We have appealed to their native justice and magnanimity; and we have conjured them, by the ties of our common kindred, to disavow these usurpations, which would inevitably interrupt our connections and correspondence. They, too, have been deaf to the voice of justice and of consanguinity. We must, therefore, acquiesce in the necessity which denounces our separation, and hold them, as we hold the rest of mankind, enemies in war, in peace friends.

We, therefore, the representatives of the United States of America, in General Congress assembled, appealing to the Supreme Judge of the world for the rectitude of our intentions, do, in the name and by the authority of the good people of these colonies, solemnly publish and declare, that these United Colonies are, and of right ought to be, FREE AND INDEPENDENT STATES; that they are absolved from all allegiance to the British crown, and that all political connection between them and the state of Great Britain is, and ought to be, totally dissolved; and that, as free and independent states, they have full power to levy war, conclude peace, contract alliances, establish commerce, and do all other acts and things which independent states may of right do. And for the support of this declaration, with a firm reliance on the protection of Divine Providence, we mutually pledge to each other our lives, our fortunes, and our sacred honor.

John Hancock

Button Gwinnett
Lyman Hall
Geo. Walton
Wm. Hooper
Joseph Hewes
John Penn
Edward Rutledge
Thos. Heyward, Junr.
Thomas Lynch, Junr.
Arthur Middleton
Samuel Chase
Wm. Paca
Thos. Stone
Charles Carroll of Carrollton
George Wythe
Richard Henry Lee
Th. Jefferson
Benj. Harrison
Thos. Nelson, Jr.

Francis Lightfoot Lee
Carter Braxton
Robt. Morris
Benjamin Rush
Benja. Franklin
John Morton
Geo. Clymer
Jas. Smith
Geo. Taylor
James Wilson
Geo. Ross
Caesar Rodney
Geo. Read
Tho. M'kean
Wm. Floyd
Phil. Livingston
Frans. Lewis
Lewis Morris
Richd. Stockton

Jno. Witherspoon
Fras. Hopkinson
John Hart
Abra. Clark
Josiah Bartlett
Wm. Whipple
Saml. Adams
John Adams
Robt. Treat Paine
Elbridge Gerry
Step. Hopkins
William Ellery
Roger Sherman
Sam'el Huntington
Wm. Williams
Oliver Wolcott
Matthew Thornton

THE ARTICLES OF CONFEDERATION

Between the States of New Hampshire, Massachusetts Bay, Rhode Island and Providence Plantations, Connecticut, New York, New Jersey, Pennsylvania, Delaware, Maryland, Virginia, North Carolina, South Carolina, Georgia

ARTICLE 1

The stile of this confederacy shall be "The United States of America."

ARTICLE 2

Each State retains its sovereignty, freedom and independence, and every power, jurisdiction, and right, which is not by this confederation expressly delegated to the United States, in Congress assembled.

ARTICLE 3

The said states hereby severally enter into a firm league of friendship with each other for their common defence, the security of their liberties and their mutual and general welfare; binding themselves to assist each other against all force offered to, or attacks made upon them, or any of them, on account of religion, sovereignty, trade, or any other pretence whatever.

ARTICLE 4

The better to secure and perpetuate mutual friendship and intercourse among the people of the different states in this union, the free inhabitants of each of these states, paupers, vagabonds, and fugitives from justice excepted, shall be entitled to all privileges and immunities of free citizens in the several states; and the people of each State shall have free ingress and regress to and from any other State, and shall enjoy therein all the privileges of trade and commerce, subject to the same duties, impositions, and restrictions, as the inhabitants thereof respectively; provided, that such restrictions shall not extend so far as to prevent the removal of property, imported into any State, to any other State of which the owner is an inhabitant; provided also, that no imposition, duties, or restriction, shall be laid by any State on the property of the United States, or either of them.

If any person guilty of, or charged with treason, felony, or other high misdemeanor in any State, shall flee from justice and be found in any of the United States, he shall, upon demand of the governor or executive power of the State from which he fled, be delivered up and removed to the State having jurisdiction of his offence.

Full faith and credit shall be given in each of these states to the records, acts, and judicial proceedings of the courts and magistrates of every other State.

ARTICLE 5

For the more convenient management of the general interests of the United States, delegates shall be annually appointed, in such manner as the legislature of each State shall direct, to meet in Congress, on the 1st Monday in November in every year, with a power reserved to each State to recall its delegates, or any of them, at any time within the year, and to send others in their stead for the remainder of the year.

No State shall be represented in Congress by less than two, nor by more than seven members; and no person shall be capable of being a delegate for more than three years in any term of six years; nor shall any person, being a delegate, be capable of holding any office under the United States, for which he, or any other for his benefit, receives any salary, fees, or emolument of any kind.

Each State shall maintain its own delegates in a meeting of the states, and while they act as members of the committee of the states.

In determining questions in the United States, in Congress assembled, each State shall have one vote.

Freedom of speech and debate in Congress shall not be impeached or questioned in any court or place out of Congress: and the members of Congress shall be protected in their persons from arrests and imprisonments, during the time of their going to and from, and attendance on Congress, except for treason, felony, or breach of the peace.

ARTICLE 6

No State, without the consent of the United States, in Congress assembled, shall send any embassy to, or receive any embassy from, or enter into any conference, agreement, alliance, or treaty with any king, prince, or state; nor shall any person, holding any office of profit or trust under the United States, or any of them, accept of any present, emolument, office or title, of any kind whatever, from any king, prince, or foreign state; nor shall the United States, in Congress assembled, or any of them, grant any title of nobility.

No two or more states shall enter into any treaty, confederation, or alliance, whatever, between them, without the consent of the United States, in Congress assembled, specifying accurately the purposes for which the same is to be entered into, and how long it shall continue.

No State shall lay any imposts or duties which may interfere with any stipulations in treaties entered into by the United States, in Congress assembled, with any king, prince, or state, in pursuance of any treaties already proposed by Congress to the courts of France and Spain.

No vessels of war shall be kept up in time of peace by any State, except such number only as shall be deemed necessary by the United States, in Congress assembled, for the defence of such State or its trade; nor shall any body of forces be kept up by any State, in time of peace, except such number only as, in the judgment of the United States, in Congress assembled, shall be deemed requisite to garrison the forts necessary for the defence of such State; but every State shall always keep up a well regulated and disciplined militia, sufficiently armed and accoutred, and shall provide, and constantly have ready for use, in public stores, a due number of field pieces and tents, and a proper quantity of arms, ammunition and camp equipage.

No State shall engage in any war without the consent of the United States, in Congress assembled, unless such State be actually invaded by enemies, or shall have received certain advice of a resolution being formed by some nation of Indians to invade such State, and the danger is so imminent as not to admit of a delay till the United States, in Congress assembled, can be consulted; nor shall any State grant commissions to any ships or vessels of war, nor letters of marque or reprisal, except it be after a declaration of war by the United States, in Congress assembled, and then only against the kingdom or state, and the subjects thereof, against which war has been so declared, and under such regulations as shall be established by the United States, in Congress assembled, unless such States be infested by pirates, in which case vessels of war may be fitted out for that occasion, and kept so long as the danger shall continue, or until the United States, in Congress assembled, shall determine otherwise.

ARTICLE 7

When land forces are raised by any State for the common defence, all officers of or under the rank of colonel, shall be appointed by the legislature of each State respectively, by whom such forces shall be raised, or in such manner as such State shall direct; and all vacancies shall be filled up by the State which first made the appointment.

ARTICLE 8

All charges of war and all other expences, that shall be incurred for the common defence or general welfare, and allowed by the United States, in Congress assembled, shall be defrayed out of a common treasury, which shall be supplied by the several states, in proportion to the value of all land within each State, granted to or surveyed for any person, as such land and the buildings and improvements thereon shall be estimated according to such mode as the United States, in Congress assembled, shall, from time to time, direct and appoint.

The taxes for paying that proportion shall be laid and levied by the authority and direction of the legislatures of the several states, within the time agreed upon by the United States, in Congress assembled.

ARTICLE 9

The United States, in Congress assembled, shall have the sole and exclusive right and power of determining on peace and war, except in the cases mentioned in the 6th article; of sending and receiving ambassadors; entering into treaties and alliances, provided that no treaty of commerce shall be made, whereby the legislative power of the respective states shall be restrained from imposing such imposts and duties on foreigners as their own people are subjected to, or from prohibiting the exportation or importation of any species of goods or commodities whatsoever; of establishing rules for deciding, in all cases, what captures on land or water shall be legal, and in what manner prizes, taken by land or naval forces in the service of the United States, shall be divided or appropriated; of granting letters of marque and reprisal in times of peace; appointing courts for the trial of piracies and felonies committed on the high seas, and establishing courts for receiving and determining, finally, appeals in all cases of captures; provided, that no member of Congress shall be appointed a judge of any of the said courts.

The United States, in Congress assembled, shall also be the last resort on appeal in all disputes and differences now subsisting, or that hereafter may arise between two or more states concerning boundary, jurisdiction or any other cause whatever; which authority shall always be exercised in the manner following: whenever the legislative or executive authority, or lawful agent of any State, in controversy with another, shall present a petition to Congress, stating the matter in question, and praying for a hearing, notice thereof shall be given, by order of Congress, to the legislative or executive authority of the other State in controversy, and a day assigned for the appearance of the parties by their lawful agents, who shall then be directed to appoint, by joint consent, commissioners or judges to constitute a court for hearing and determining the matter in question; but, if they cannot agree, Congress shall name three persons out of each of the United States, and from the list of such persons each party shall alternately strike out one, in the petitioners beginning, until the number shall be reduced to thirteen; and from that number not less than seven, nor more than nine names, as Congress shall direct, shall, in the presence of Congress, be drawn out by lot; and the persons whose names shall be drawn, or any five of them, shall be commissioners or judges to hear and finally determine the controversy, so always as a major part of the judges who shall hear the cause shall agree in the determination; and if either party shall neglect to attend at the day appointed, without shewing reasons which Congress shall judge sufficient, or, being present, shall refuse to strike, the Congress shall proceed to nominate three persons out of each State, and the secretary of Congress shall strike in behalf of such party absent or refusing; and the judgment and sentence of the court to be appointed, in the manner before prescribed, shall be final and conclusive; and if any of the parties shall refuse to submit to the authority of such court, or to appear or defend their claim or cause, the court shall nevertheless proceed to pronounce sentence or judgment, which shall, in like manner, be final and decisive, the judgment or sentence and other proceedings being, in either case, transmitted to Congress, and lodged among the acts of Congress for the security of the parties concerned: provided, that every commissioner, before he sits in judgment, shall take an oath, to be administered by one of the judges of the supreme or superior court of the State where the cause shall be tried, "well and truly to hear and determine the matter in question, according to the best of his judgment, without favour, affection, or hope of reward": provided, also, that no State shall be deprived of territory for the benefit of the United States.

All controversies concerning the private right of soil, claimed under different grants of two or more states, whose jurisdictions, as they may respect such lands and the states which passed such grants, are adjusted, the said grants, or either of them, being at the same time claimed to have originated antecedent to such settlement of jurisdiction, shall, on the petition of either party to the Congress of the United States, be finally determined, as near as may be, in the same manner as is before prescribed for deciding disputes respecting territorial jurisdiction between different states.

The United States, in Congress assembled, shall also have the sole and exclusive right and power of regulating the alloy and value of coin struck by their own authority, or by that of the respective states; fixing the standard of weights and measures throughout the United States; regulating the trade and managing all affairs with the Indians not members of any of the states; provided that the legislative right of any State within its own limits be not infringed or violated; establishing and regulating post offices from one State to another throughout all the United States, and exacting such postage on the papers passing through the same as may be requisite to defray the expences of the said office; appointing all officers of the land forces in the service of the United States, excepting regimental officers; appointing all the officers of the naval forces, and commissioning all officers whatever in the service of the United States; making rules for the government and regulation of the said land and naval forces, and directing their operations.

The United States, in Congress assembled, shall have authority to appoint a committee to sit in the recess of Congress, to be denominated "a Committee of the States," and to consist of one delegate from each State, and to appoint such other committees and civil officers as may be necessary for managing the general affairs of the United States, under their direction; to appoint one of their number to preside; provided that no person be allowed to serve in the office of president more than one year in any term of three years; to ascertain the necessary sums of money to be raised for the service of the United States, and to appropriate and apply the same for defraying the public expences; to borrow money or emit bills on the credit of the United States, transmitting, every half year, to the respective states, an account of the sums of money so borrowed or emitted; to build and equip a navy; to agree upon the number of land forces, and to make requisitions from each State for its quota, in proportion to the number of white inhabitants in such State; which requisitions shall be binding; and, thereupon, the legislature of each State shall appoint the regimental officers, raise the men, and cloathe, arm, and equip them in a soldier-like manner, at the expence of the United States; and the officers and men so cloathed, armed, and equipped, shall march to the place appointed and within the time agreed on by the United States, in Congress assembled; but if the United States, in Congress assembled, shall, on consideration of circumstances, judge proper that any State should not raise men, or should raise a smaller number than its quota, and that any other State should raise a greater number of men than the quota thereof, such extra number shall be raised, officered, cloathed, armed, and equipped in the same manner as the quota of such State, unless the legislature of such State shall judge that such extra number cannot be safely spared out of the same, in which case they shall raise, officer, cloathe, arm, and equip as many of such extra number as they judge can be safely spared. And the officers and men so cloathed, armed, and equipped, shall march to the place appointed and within the time agreed on by the United States, in Congress assembled.

The United States, in Congress assembled, shall never engage in a war, nor grant letters of marque and reprisal in time of peace, nor enter into any treaties or alliances, nor coin money, nor regulate the value thereof, nor ascertain the sums and expences necessary for the defence and welfare of the United States, or any of them: nor emit bills, nor borrow money on the credit of the United States, nor appropriate money, nor agree upon the number of vessels of war to be built or purchased, or the number of land or sea forces to be raised, nor appoint a commander in chief of the army or navy, unless nine states assent to the same; nor shall a question on any other point, except for adjourning from day to day, be determined, unless by the votes of a majority of the United States, in Congress assembled.

The Congress of the United States shall have power to adjourn to any time within the year, and to any place within the United States, so that no period of adjournment be for a longer duration than the space of six months, and shall publish the journal of their proceedings monthly, except such parts thereof, relating to treaties, alliances or military operations, as, in their judgment, require secrecy; and the yeas and nays of the delegates of each State on any question shall be entered on the journal, when it is desired by any delegate; and the delegates of a State, or any of them, at his, or their request, shall be furnished with a transcript of the said journal, except such parts as are above excepted, to lay before the legislatures of the several states.

ARTICLE 10

The committee of the states, or any nine of them, shall be authorized to execute, in the recess of Congress, such of the powers of Congress as the United States, in Congress assembled, by the consent of nine states, shall, from time to time, think expedient to vest them with; provided, that no power be delegated to the said committee for the exercise of which, by the articles of confederation, the voice of nine states, in the Congress of the United States assembled, is requisite.

ARTICLE 11

Canada acceding to this confederation, and joining in the measures of the United States, shall be admitted into and entitled to all the advantages of this union; but no other colony shall be admitted into the same, unless such admission be agreed to by nine states.

ARTICLE 12

All bills of credit emitted, monies borrowed and debts contracted by, or under the authority of Congress before the assembling of the United States, in pursuance of the present confederation, shall be deemed and considered as a charge against the United States, for payment and satisfaction whereof the said United States and the public faith are hereby solemnly pledged.

ARTICLE 13

Every State shall abide by the determinations of the United States, in Congress assembled, on all questions which, by this confederation, are submitted to them. And the articles of this confederation shall be inviolably observed by every State, and the union shall be perpetual; nor shall any alteration at any time hereafter be made in any of them, unless such alteration be agreed to in a Congress of the United States, and be afterwards confirmed by the legislatures of every State.

These articles shall be proposed to the legislatures of all the United States, to be considered, and if approved of by them, they are advised to authorize their delegates to ratify the same in the Congress of the United States; which being done, the same shall become conclusive.

THE CONSTITUTION OF THE UNITED STATES OF AMERICA

PREAMBLE

We the People of the United States, in Order to form a more perfect Union, establish Justice, insure domestic Tranquility, provide for the common defence, promote the general Welfare, and secure the Blessings of Liberty to ourselves and our Posterity, do ordain and establish this Constitution for the United States of America.

ARTICLE I

Section 1

All legislative Powers herein granted shall be vested in a Congress of the United States, which shall consist of a Senate and House of Representatives.

Section 2

The House of Representatives shall be composed of Members chosen every second Year by the People of the several States, and the Electors in each State shall have the Qualifications requisite for Electors of the most numerous Branch of the State Legislature.

No Person shall be a Representative who shall not have attained to the Age of twenty five Years, and been seven Years a Citizen of the United States, and who shall not, when elected, be an inhabitant of that State in which he shall be chosen.

Representatives and direct Taxes shall be apportioned among the several States which may be included within this Union, according to their respective Numbers, *which shall be determined by adding to the whole Number of free Persons, including those bound to Service for a Term of Years, and excluding Indians not taxed, three fifths of all other Persons.** The actual Enumeration shall be made within three Years after the first Meeting of the Congress of the United States, and within every subsequent Term of ten Years, in such Manner as they shall by Law direct. The Number of Representatives shall not exceed one for every thirty Thousand, but each State shall have at Least one Representative; *and until such enumeration shall be made, the State of New Hampshire shall be entitled to chuse three, Massachusetts eight, Rhode-Island and Providence Plantations one, Connecticut five, New York six, New Jersey four, Pennsylvania eight, Delaware one, Maryland six, Virginia ten, North Carolina five, South Carolina five, and Georgia three.*

When vacancies happen in the Representation from any State, the Executive Authority thereof shall issue Writs of Election to fill such Vacancies.

The House of Representatives shall chuse their Speaker and other Officers; and shall have the sole Power of Impeachment.

*Passages no longer in effect are printed in italic type.

Section 3

The Senate of the United States shall be composed of two Senators from each State, *chosen by the Legislature thereof,* for six Years; and each Senator shall have one Vote.

Immediately after they shall be assembled in Consequence of the first Election, they shall be divided as equally as may be into three Classes. The Seats of the Senators of the first Class shall be vacated at the Expiration of the second Year, of the second Class at the Expiration of the fourth Year, and of the third Class at the Expiration of the sixth Year so that one third may be chosen every second Year; and if Vacancies happen by Resignation, or otherwise, during the Recess of the Legislature of any state, the Executive thereof may make temporary Appointments until the next Meeting of the Legislature, which shall then fill such Vacancies.

No Person shall be a Senator who shall not have attained to the Age of thirty Years, and been nine Years a Citizen of the United States, and who shall not, when elected, be an Inhabitant of that State for which he shall be chosen.

The Vice President of the United States shall be President of the Senate, but shall have no Vote, unless they be equally divided.

The Senate shall chuse their other Officers, and also a President *pro tempore,* in the Absence of the Vice President, or when he shall exercise the Office of President of the United States.

The Senate shall have the sole Power to try all Impeachments. When sitting for that Purpose, they shall be on Oath or Affirmation. When the President of the United States is tried the Chief Justice shall preside: And no Person shall be convicted without the Concurrence of two thirds of the Members present.

Judgment in Cases of Impeachment shall not extend further than to removal from Office, and disqualification to hold and enjoy any Office of honor, Trust or Profit under the United States: but the Party convicted shall nevertheless be liable and subject to Indictment, Trial, Judgment and Punishment, according to Law.

Section 4

The Times, Places and Manner of holding Elections for Senators and Representatives, shall be prescribed in each State by the Legislature thereof; but the Congress may at any time by Law make or alter such Regulations, except as to the Places of chusing Senators.

The Congress shall assemble at least once in every Year, *and such Meeting shall be on the first Monday in December, unless they shall by Law appoint a different Day.*

Section 5

Each House shall be the Judge of the Elections, Returns and Qualifications of its own Members, and a Majority of each shall constitute a Quorum to do Business; but a smaller Number may adjourn from day to day, and may be authorized to compel the Attendance of absent Members, in such Manner, and under such Penalties as each House may provide.

Each House may determine the Rules of its Proceedings, punish its Members for disorderly Behaviour, and, with the Concurrence of two thirds, expel a Member.

Each House shall keep a Journal of its Proceedings, and from time to time publish the same, excepting such Parts as may in their Judgment require Secrecy; and the Yeas and Nays of the Members of either House on any question shall, at the Desire of one fifth of those Present, be entered on the Journal.

Neither House, during the Session of Congress, shall, without the Consent of the other, adjourn for more than three days, nor to any other Place than that in which the two Houses shall be sitting.

Section 6

The Senators and Representatives shall receive a Compensation for their Services, to be ascertained by Law, and paid out of the Treasury of the United States. They shall in all Cases, except Treason, Felony and Breach of the Peace, be privileged from Arrest during their Attendance at the Session of their respective Houses, and in going to and returning from the same; and for any Speech or Debate in either House, they shall not be questioned in any other Place.

No Senator or Representative shall, during the Time for which he was elected, be appointed to any civil Office under the Authority of the United States, which shall have been created, or the Emoluments whereof shall have been encreased during such time, and no Person holding any Office under the United States, shall be a Member of either House during his Continuance in Office.

Section 7

All Bills for raising Revenue shall originate in the House of Representatives; but the Senate may propose or concur with Amendments as on other Bills.

Every Bill which shall have passed the House of Representatives and the Senate, shall, before it become a Law, be presented to the President of the United States; If he approve he shall sign it, but if not he shall return it, with his Objections to the House in which it shall have originated, who shall enter the Objections at large on their Journal, and proceed to reconsider it. If after such Reconsideration two thirds of that House shall agree to pass the Bill, it shall be sent, together with the Objections, to the other House, by which it shall likewise be reconsidered, and if approved by two thirds of that House, it shall become a Law. But in all such Cases the Votes of both Houses shall be determined by yeas and Nays, and the Names of the Persons voting for and against the Bill shall be entered on the Journal of each House respectively. If any Bill shall not be returned by the President within ten Days (Sundays excepted) after it shall have been presented to him, the Same shall be a Law, in like Manner as if he had signed it, unless the Congress by their Adjournment prevent its Return, in which Case it shall not be a Law.

Every Order, Resolution, or Vote to which the Concurrence of the Senate and House of Representatives may be necessary (except on a question of Adjournment) shall be presented to the President of the United States; and before the Same shall take Effect, shall be approved by him, or being disapproved by him, shall be repassed by two thirds of the Senate and House of Representatives, according to the Rules and Limitations prescribed in the Case of a Bill.

Section 8

The Congress shall have Power To lay and collect Taxes, Duties, Imposts and Excises, to pay the Debts and provide for the common Defence and general Welfare of the United States; but all Duties, Imposts and Excises shall be uniform throughout the United States;

To borrow Money on the credit of the United States;

To regulate Commerce with foreign Nations, and among the several States, and with the Indian Tribes;

To establish an uniform Rule of Naturalization, and uniform Laws on the subject of Bankruptcies throughout the United States;

To coin Money, regulate the Value thereof, and of foreign Coin, and fix the Standard of Weights and Measures;

To provide for the Punishment of counterfeiting the Securities and current Coin of the United States;

To establish Post Offices and post Roads;

To promote the Progress of Science and useful Arts, by securing for limited Times to Authors and Inventors the exclusive Right to their respective Writings and Discoveries;

To constitute Tribunals inferior to the supreme Court;

To define and punish Piracies and Felonies committed on the high Seas, and Offences against the Law of Nations;

To declare War, grant Letters of Marque and Reprisal, and make Rules concerning Captures on Land and Water;

To raise and support Armies, but no Appropriation of Money to that Use shall be for a longer Term than two Years;

To provide and maintain a Navy;

To make Rules for the Government and Regulation of the land and naval Forces;

To provide for calling forth the Militia to execute the Laws of the Union, suppress Insurrections and repel Invasions;

To provide for organizing, arming, and disciplining, the Militia, and for governing such Part of them as may be employed in the Service of the United States, reserving to the States respectively, the Appointment of the Officers, and the Authority of training the Militia according to the discipline prescribed by Congress;

To exercise exclusive Legislation in all Cases whatsoever, over such District (not exceeding ten Miles square) as may, by Cession of particular States, and the Acceptance of Congress, become the Seat of the Government of the United States, and to exercise like Authority over all Places purchased by the Consent of the Legislature of the State in which the Same shall be, for the Erection of Forts, Magazines, Arsenals, dock-Yards, and other needful Buildings;—And

To make all Laws which shall be necessary and proper for carrying into Execution the foregoing Powers, and all other Powers vested by this Constitution in the Government of the United States, or in any Department of Officer thereof.

Section 9

The Migration or Importation of such Persons as any of the States now existing shall think proper to admit, shall not be prohibited by the Congress prior to the Year one thousand eight hundred and eight, but a Tax or duty may be imposed on such Importation, not exceeding ten dollars for each Person.

The Privilege of the Writ of Habeas Corpus shall not be suspended, unless when in Cases of Rebellion or Invasion the public Safety may require it.

No Bill of Attainder or ex post facto Law shall be passed.

No Capitation, or other direct, Tax shall be laid, unless in Proportion to the Census or Enumeration herein before directed to be taken.

No Tax or Duty shall be laid on Articles exported from any State.

No Preference shall be given by any Regulation of Commerce or Revenue to the Ports of one State over those of another: nor shall Vessels bound to, or from, one State, be obliged to enter, clear, or pay Duties in another.

No Money shall be drawn from the Treasury, but in Consequence of Appropriations made by Law; and a regular Statement and Account of the Receipts and Expenditures of all public Money shall be published from time to time.

No Title of Nobility shall be granted by the United States: And no Person holding any Office of Profit or Trust under them, shall, without the Consent of the Congress, accept of any present, Emolument, Office, or Title, of any kind whatever, from any King, Prince, or foreign State.

Section 10

No State shall enter into any Treaty, Alliance, or Confederation; grant Letters of Marque and Reprisal; coin Money; emit Bills of Credit; make any Thing but gold and silver Coin a Tender in Payment of Debts; pass any Bill of Attainder, ex post facto Law, or Law impairing the obligation of Contracts, or grant any Title of Nobility.

No State shall, without the Consent of the Congress, lay any Imposts or Duties on Imports or Exports, except what may be absolutely necessary for executing its inspection Laws: and the net Produce of all Duties and Imposts, laid by any State on Imports or Exports, shall be for the Use of the Treasury of the United States; and all such Laws shall be subject to the Revision and Controul of the Congress.

No State shall, without the Consent of Congress, lay any Duty of Tonnage, keep Troops, or Ships of War in time of Peace, enter into any Agreement or Compact with another State, or with a foreign Power, or engage in War, unless actually invaded, or in such imminent Danger as will not admit of delay.

ARTICLE II

Section 1

The executive Power shall be vested in a President of the United States of America. He shall hold his Office during the Term of four Years, and, together with the Vice President, chosen for the same Term, be elected, as follows:

Each State shall appoint, in such Manner as the Legislature thereof may direct, a Number of Electors, equal to the whole Number of Senators and Representatives to which the State may be entitled in the Congress: but no Senator or Representative, or Person holding an Office of Trust or Profit under the United States, shall be appointed an Elector.

The Electors shall meet in their respective States, and vote by Ballot for two Persons, of whom one at least shall not be an Inhabitant of the same State with themselves. And they shall make a List of all the Persons voted for, and of the Number of Votes for each; which List they shall sign and certify, and transmit sealed to the Seat of the Government of the United States, directed to the President of the Senate. The President of the Senate shall, in the Presence of the Senate and House of Representatives, open all the Certificates, and the Votes shall then be counted. The Person having the greatest Number of Votes shall be the President, if such Number be a Majority of the whole number of Electors appointed; and if there be more than one who have such Majority, and have an equal Number of Votes, then the House of Representatives shall immediately chuse by Ballot one of them for President; and if no Person have a Majority, then from the five highest on the List the said House shall in like Manner chuse the President. But in chusing the President, the Votes shall be taken by States, the Representation from each State having one Vote; A quorum for this Purpose shall consist of a Member or Members from two thirds of the States, and a Majority of all the States shall be necessary to a Choice. In every Case, after the Choice of the President, the Person having the greatest Number of Votes of the Electors shall be the Vice President. But if there should remain two or more who have equal Votes, the Senate shall chuse from them by Ballot the Vice President.

The Congress may determine the time of chusing the Electors, and the Day on which they shall give their Votes; which Day shall be the same throughout the United States.

No person except a natural born Citizen, *or a Citizen of the United States, at the time of the Adoption of this Constitution,* shall be eligible to the Office of President; neither shall any Person be eligible to that Office who shall not have attained to the Age of thirty five Years, and been fourteen Years a Resident within the United States.

In Case of the Removal of the President from Office, or of his Death, Resignation, or Inability to discharge the Powers and Duties of the said Office, the Same shall devolve on the Vice President, and the Congress may by Law provide for the Case of Removal, Death, Resignation or Inability, both of the President and Vice President, declaring what Officer shall then act as President, and such Officer shall act accordingly, until the Disability be removed, or a President shall be elected.

The President shall, at stated Times, receive for his Services, a Compensation, which shall neither be encreased nor diminished during the Period for which he shall have been elected, and he shall not receive within that period any other Emolument from the United States, or any of them.

Before he enter on the Execution of his Office, he shall take the following Oath or Affirmation:—"I do solemnly swear (or affirm) that I will faithfully execute the Office of President of the United States, and will to the best of my Ability, preserve, protect and defend the Constitution of the United States."

Section 2

The President shall be Commander in Chief of the Army and Navy of the United States, and of the Militia of the several States, when called into the actual Service of the United States; he may require the Opinion, in writing, of the principal Officer in each of the executive Departments, upon any Subject relating to the Duties of their respective Offices, and he shall have Power to grant Reprieves and Pardons for Offences against the United States, except in Cases of Impeachment.

He shall have Power, by and with the Advice and Consent of the Senate, to make Treaties, provided two thirds of the Senators present concur; and he shall nominate, and by and with the Advice and Consent of the Senate, shall appoint Ambassadors, other public Ministers and Consuls, Judges of the supreme Court, and all other Officers of the United States, whose Appointments are not herein otherwise provided for, and which shall be established by Law: but the Congress may by Law vest the Appointment of such inferior Officers, as they think proper in the President alone, in the Courts of Law, or in the Heads of Departments.

The President shall have Power to fill up all Vacancies that may happen during the Recess of the Senate, by granting Commissions which shall expire at the End of their next Session.

Section 3

He shall from time to time give to the Congress Information of the State of the Union, and recommend to their Consideration such Measures as he shall judge necessary and expedient; he may, on extraordinary Occasions, convene both Houses, or either of them, and in Case of disagreement between them, with Respect to the Time of Adjournment, he may adjourn them to such Time as he shall think proper; he shall receive Ambassadors and other public Ministers; he shall take Care that the Laws be faithfully executed, and shall Commission all the officers of the United States.

Section 4

The President, Vice President and all civil Officers of the United States, shall be removed from Office on Impeachment for, and Conviction of, Treason, Bribery or other high Crimes and Misdemeanors.

ARTICLE III

Section 1

The judicial Power of the United States, shall be vested in one supreme Court, and in such inferior Courts as the Congress may from time to time ordain and establish. The Judges, both of the supreme and inferior Courts, shall hold their offices during good Behaviour, and shall, at stated Times, receive for their Services, a Compensation, which shall not be diminished during their Continuance in Office.

Section 2

The judicial Power shall extend to all Cases, in Law and Equity, arising under this Constitution, the Laws of the United States, and Treaties made, or which shall be made, under their Authority;—to all Cases affecting Ambassadors, other public Ministers and Consuls;—to all Cases of admiralty and maritime Jurisdiction;—to Controversies to which the United States shall be a Party;—to Controversies between two or more States;—*between a State and Citizens of another State;*—between Citizens of different States;—between Citizens of the same State claiming Lands under Grants of different States, and between a State, or the Citizens thereof, and foreign States, Citizens or Subjects.

In all Cases affecting Ambassadors, other public Ministers and Consuls, and those in which a State shall be Party, the supreme Court shall have original Jurisdiction. In all the other Cases before mentioned, the supreme Court shall have appellate Jurisdiction, both as to Law and Fact, with such Exceptions, and under such Regulations as the Congress shall make.

The Trial of all Crimes, except in Cases of Impeachment, shall be by Jury; and such Trial shall be held in the State where the said Crimes shall have been committed, but when not committed within any State, the Trial shall be at such Place or Places as the Congress may by Law have directed.

Section 3

Treason against the United States, shall consist only in levying War against them, or in adhering to their Enemies, giving them Aid and Comfort. No person shall be convicted of Treason unless on the Testimony of two Witnesses to the same overt Act, or on Confession in open Court.

The Congress shall have Power to declare the Punishment of Treason, but no Attainder of Treason shall work Corruption of Blood, or Forfeiture except during the Life of the Person attainted.

ARTICLE IV

Section 1

Full Faith and Credit shall be given in each State to the public Acts, Records, and judicial Proceedings of every other State. And the Congress may by general Laws prescribe the Manner in which such Acts, Records and Proceedings shall be proved, and the Effect thereof.

Section 2

The Citizens of each State shall be entitled to all Privileges and Immunities of Citizens in the several States.

A Person charged in any State with Treason, Felony, or other Crime, who shall flee from Justice, and be found in another State, shall on Demand of the executive Authority of the State from which he fled, be delivered up, to be removed to the State having Jurisdiction of the Crime.

No Person held to Service or Labour in one State, under the Laws thereof, escaping into another, shall, in Consequence of any Law or Regulation therein, be discharged from such Service or Labour, but shall be delivered up on Claim of the Party to whom such Service or Labour may be due.

Section 3

New States may be admitted by the Congress into this Union; but no new State shall be formed or erected within the Jurisdiction of any other State; nor any State be formed by the Junction of two or more States, or Parts of States, without the Consent of the Legislatures of the States concerned as well as of the Congress.

The Congress shall have Power to dispose of and make all needful Rules and Regulations respecting the Territory or other Property belonging to the United States; and nothing in this Constitution shall be so construed as to Prejudice any Claims of the United States, or of any particular States.

Section 4

The United States shall guarantee to every State in this Union a Republican Form of Government, and shall protect each of them against Invasion; and on Application of the Legislature, or of the Executive (when the Legislature cannot be convened) against domestic violence.

ARTICLE V

The Congress, whenever two thirds of both Houses shall deem it necessary, shall propose Amendments to this Constitution, or, on the Application of the Legislatures of two thirds of the several States, shall call a Convention for proposing Amendments, which, in either Case, shall be valid to all Intents and Purposes, as Part of this Constitution, when ratified by the Legislatures of three fourths of the several States, or by Conventions in three fourths thereof, as the one or the other Mode of Ratification may be proposed by the Congress; Provided *that no Amendment which may be made prior to the Year One thousand eight hundred and eight shall in any Manner affect the first and fourth Clauses in the Ninth Section of the first Article;* and that no State, without its Consent, shall be deprived of its equal Suffrage in the Senate.

ARTICLE VI

All Debts contracted and Engagements entered into, before the Adoption of this Constitution, shall be as valid against the United States under this Constitution, as under the Confederation.

This Constitution, and Laws of the United States which shall be made in Pursuance thereof; and all Treaties made, or which shall be made, under the Authority of the United States, shall be the supreme Law of the Land; and the Judges in every State shall be bound thereby, any Thing in the Constitution or Laws of any State to the Contrary notwithstanding.

The Senators and Representatives before mentioned, and the Members of the several State Legislatures, and all executive and Judicial Officers, both of the United States and of the several States, shall be bound by Oath or Affirmation, to support this Constitution; but no religious Test shall ever be required as a Qualification to any Office of public Trust under the United States.

ARTICLE VII

The Ratification of the Conventions of nine States, shall be sufficient for the Establishment of this Constitution between the States so ratifying the Same.

Done in Convention by the Unanimous Consent of the States present the Seventeenth Day of September in the Year of our Lord one thousand seven hundred and Eighty seven and of the Independence of the United States of America the Twelfth* IN WITNESS whereof We have hereunto subscribed our Names,

George Washington
President and Deputy from Virginia

Delaware
George Read
Gunning Bedford, Jr.
John Dickinson
Richard Bassett
Jacob Broom

Maryland
James McHenry
Daniel of St. Thomas Jenifer
Daniel Carroll

Virginia
John Blair
James Madison, Jr.

North Carolina
William Blount
Richard Dobbs Spraight
Hugh Williamson

South Carolina
John Rutledge
Charles Cotesworth Pinckney
Charles Pinckney
Pierce Butler

Georgia
William Few
Abraham Baldwin

New Hampshire
John Langdon
Nicholas Gilman

Massachusetts
Nathaniel Gorham
Rufus King

Connecticut
William Samuel Johnson
Roger Sherman

New York
Alexander Hamilton

New Jersey
William Livingston
David Brearley
William Paterson
Jonathan Dayton

Pennsylvania
Benjamin Franklin
Thomas Mifflin
Robert Morris
George Clymer
Thomas FitzSimons
Jared Ingersoll
James Wilson
Gouverneur Morris

*The Constitution was submitted on September 17, 1787, by the Constitutional Convention, was ratified by the Convention of several states at various dates up to May 29, 1790, and became effective on March 4, 1789.

AMENDMENTS TO THE CONSTITUTION

AMENDMENT I

Congress shall make no law respecting an establishment of religion, or prohibiting the free exercise thereof; or abridging the freedom of speech, or of the press; or the right of the people peaceably to assemble, and to petition the Government for a redress of grievances.

AMENDMENT II

A well regulated Militia being necessary to the security of a free State, the right of the people to keep and bear Arms, shall not be infringed.

AMENDMENT III

No Soldier shall, in time of peace be quartered in any house, without the consent of the Owner, nor in time of war, but in a manner to be prescribed by law.

AMENDMENT IV

The right of the people to be secure in their persons, houses, papers, and effects, against unreasonable searches and seizures, shall not be violated, and no Warrants shall issue, but upon probable cause, supported by Oath or affirmation, and particularly describing the place to be searched, and the persons or things to be seized.

AMENDMENT V

No person shall be held to answer for a capital, or otherwise infamous crime, unless on a presentment or indictment of a Grand Jury, except in cases arising in the land or naval forces, or in the Militia, when in actual service in time of War or public danger; nor shall any person be subject for the same offense to be twice put in jeopardy of life or limb; nor shall be compelled in any criminal case to be a witness against himself, nor be deprived of life, liberty, or property, without due process of law; nor shall private property be taken for public use, without just compensation.

AMENDMENT VI

In all criminal prosecutions, the accused shall enjoy the right to a speedy and public trial, by an impartial jury of the State and district wherein the crime shall have been committed, which district shall have been previously ascertained by law, and to be informed of the nature and cause of the accusation; to be confronted with the witnesses against him; to have compulsory process for obtaining witnesses in his favor, and to have the Assistance of Counsel for his defence.

AMENDMENT VII

In Suits at common law, where the value in controversy shall exceed twenty dollars, the right of trial by jury shall be preserved, and no fact tried by a jury, shall be otherwise reexamined in any Court of the United States, than according to the rules of the common law.

AMENDMENT VIII

Excessive bail shall not be required, nor excessive fines imposed, nor cruel and unusual punishments inflicted.

AMENDMENT IX

The enumeration in the Constitution, of certain rights, shall not be construed to deny or disparage others retained by the people.

AMENDMENT X*

The powers not delegated to the United States by the Constitution, nor prohibited by it to the States, are reserved to the States respectively, or to the people.

AMENDMENT XI [ADOPTED 1798]

The Judicial power of the United States shall not be construed to extend to any suit in law or equity, commenced or prosecuted against one of the United States by Citizens of another State, or by Citizens or Subjects of any Foreign State.

AMENDMENT XII [ADOPTED 1804]

The Electors shall meet in their respective states, and vote by ballot for President and Vice President, one of whom, at least, shall not be an inhabitant of the same state with themselves; they shall name in their ballots the person voted for as President, and in distinct ballots the person voted for as Vice President, and they shall make distinct lists of all persons voted for as President, and of all persons voted for as Vice President, and of the number of votes for each, which lists they shall sign and certify, and transmit sealed to the seat of the government of the United States, directed to the President of the Senate;—The President of the Senate shall, in the presence of the Senate and House of Representatives, open all the certificates and the votes shall then be counted;—The person having the greatest number of votes for President, shall be the President, if such number be a majority of the whole number of Electors appointed; and if no person have such majority, then from the persons having the highest numbers not exceeding three on the list of those voted for as President, the House of Representatives shall choose immediately, by ballot, the President. But in choosing the President, the votes shall be taken by states, the representation from each state having one vote; a quorum for this purpose shall consist of a member or members from two-thirds of the states, and a majority of all the states shall be necessary to a choice. And if the House of Representatives shall not choose a President whenever the

*The first ten amendments (the Bill of Rights) were ratified and their adoption was certified on December 15, 1791.

right of choice shall devolve upon them, before *the fourth day of March* next following, then the Vice President shall act as President, as in the case of the death or other constitutional disability of the President.—The person having the greatest number of votes as Vice President, shall be the Vice President, if such number be a majority of the whole number of Electors appointed, and if no person have a majority, then from the two highest numbers on the list, the Senate shall choose the Vice President; a quorum for the purpose shall consist of two-thirds of the whole number of Senators, and a majority of the whole number shall be necessary to a choice. But no person constitutionally ineligible to the office of President shall be eligible to that of Vice President of the United States.

AMENDMENT XIII [ADOPTED 1865]

Section 1

Neither slavery nor involuntary servitude, except as a punishment for crime whereof the party shall have been duly convicted, shall exist within the United States, or any place subject to their jurisdiction.

Section 2

Congress shall have power to enforce this article by appropriate legislation.

AMENDMENT XIV [ADOPTED 1868]

Section 1

All persons born or naturalized in the United States, and subject to the jurisdiction thereof, are citizens of the United States and of the State wherein they reside. No State shall make or enforce any law which shall abridge the privileges or immunities of citizens of the United States; nor shall any State deprive any person of life, liberty, or property, without due process of law; nor deny to any person within its jurisdiction the equal protection of the laws.

Section 2

Representatives shall be apportioned among the several States according to their respective numbers, counting the whole number of persons in each State, excluding Indians not taxed. But when the right to vote at any election for the choice of electors for President and Vice President of the United States, Representatives in Congress, the Executive and Judicial officers of a State, or the members of the Legislature thereof, is denied to any of the male inhabitants of such State, being twenty-one years of age, and citizens of the United States, or in any way abridged, except for participation in rebellion, or other crime, the basis of representation therein shall be reduced in the proportion which the number of such male citizens shall bear to the whole number of male citizens twenty-one years of age in such State.

Section 3

No person shall be a Senator or Representative in Congress, or elector of President and Vice President, or hold any office, civil or military, under the United States, or under any State, who, having previously taken an oath, as a member of Congress, or as an officer of the United States, or as a member of any State legislature, or as an executive or judicial officer of any State, to support the Constitution of the United States, shall have engaged in insurrection or rebellion against the same, or given aid or comfort to the enemies thereof. But Congress may by a vote of two-thirds of each House, remove such disability.

Section 4

The validity of the public debt of the United States, authorized by law, including debts incurred for payment of pensions and bounties for services in suppressing insurrection or rebellion, shall not be questioned. But neither the United States nor any State shall assume or pay any debt or obligation incurred in aid of insurrection or rebellion against the United States, or any claim for the loss or emancipation of any slave; but all such debts, obligations and claims shall be held illegal and void.

Section 5

The Congress shall have power to enforce, by appropriate legislation, the provisions of this article.

AMENDMENT XV [ADOPTED 1870]

Section 1

The right of citizens of the United States to vote shall not be denied or abridged by the United States or by any State on account of race, color, or previous condition of servitude.

Section 2

The Congress shall have power to enforce this article by appropriate legislation.

AMENDMENT XVI [ADOPTED 1913]

The Congress shall have power to lay and collect taxes on incomes, from whatever source derived, without apportionment among the several States, and without regard to any census or enumeration.

AMENDMENT XVII [ADOPTED 1913]

The Senate of the United States shall be composed of two Senators from each State, elected by the people thereof, for six years; and each Senator shall have one vote. The electors in each State shall have the qualifications requisite for electors of the most numerous branch of the State legislatures.

When vacancies happen in the representation of any State in the Senate, the executive authority of such State shall issue writs of election to fill such vacancies: *Provided,* That the legislature of any State may empower the executive thereof to make temporary appointments until the people fill the vacancies by election as the legislature may direct.

This amendment shall not be so construed as to affect the election or term of any Senator chosen before it becomes valid as part of the Constitution.

AMENDMENT XVIII [ADOPTED 1919, REPEALED 1933]

Section 1

After one year from the ratification of this article the manufacture, sale, or transportation of intoxicating liquors within, the importation thereof into, or the exportation thereof from the United States and all territory subject to the jurisdiction thereof for beverage purposes is hereby prohibited.

Section 2

The Congress and the several States shall have concurrent power to enforce this article by appropriate legislation.

Section 3

This article shall be inoperative unless it shall have been ratified as an amendment to the Constitution by the legislatures of the several States, as provided in the Constitution, within seven years from the date of the submission hereof to the States by the Congress.

AMENDMENT XIX [ADOPTED 1920]

The right of citizens of the United States to vote shall not be denied or abridged by the United States or by any State on account of sex.

Congress shall have power to enforce this article by appropriate legislation.

AMENDMENT XX [ADOPTED 1933]

Section 1

The terms of the President and Vice President shall end at noon on the 20th day of January, and the terms of Senators and Representatives at noon on the 3d day of January, of the years in which such terms would have ended if this article had not been ratified and the terms of their successors shall then begin.

Section 2

The Congress shall assemble at least once in every year, and such meeting shall begin at noon on the 3d day of January, unless they shall by law appoint a different day.

Section 3

If, at the time fixed for the beginning of the term of the President, the President elect shall have died, the Vice President elect shall become President. If a President shall not have been chosen before the time fixed for the beginning of his term, or if the President elect shall have failed to qualify, then the Vice President elect shall act as President until a President shall have qualified; and the Congress may by law provide for the case wherein neither a President elect nor a Vice President elect shall have qualified, declaring who shall then act as President, or the manner in which one who is to act shall be selected, and such person shall act accordingly until a President or Vice President shall have qualified.

Section 4

The Congress may by law provide for the case of the death of any of the persons from whom the House of Representatives may choose a President whenever the right of choice shall have devolved upon them, and for the case of the death of any of the persons from whom the Senate may choose a Vice President whenever the right of choice shall have devolved upon them.

Section 5

Sections 1 and 2 shall take effect on the 15th day of October following the ratification of this article.

Section 6

This article shall be inoperative unless it shall have been ratified as an amendment to the Constitution by the legislatures of three fourths of the several States within seven years from the date of its submission.

AMENDMENT XXI [ADOPTED 1933]

Section 1

The eighteenth article of amendment to the Constitution of the United States is hereby repealed.

Section 2

The transportation or importation into any State, Territory, or possession of the United States for delivery or use therein of intoxicating liquors in violation of the laws thereof, is hereby prohibited.

Section 3

This article shall be inoperative unless it shall have been ratified as an amendment to the Constitution by conventions in the several States, as provided in the Constitution, within seven years from the date of the submission hereof to the States by the Congress.

AMENDMENT XXII [ADOPTED 1951]

Section 1

No person shall be elected to the office of the President more than twice, and no person who has held the office of President, or acted as President, for more than two years of a term to which some other person was elected President shall be elected to the office of the President more than once. But this Article shall not apply to any person holding the office of President when this Article was proposed by the Congress, and shall not prevent any person who may be holding the office of President, or acting as President, during the term within which this Article becomes operative from holding the office of President or acting as President during the remainder of such term.

Section 2

This article shall be inoperative unless it shall have been ratified as an amendment to the Constitution by the legislatures of three-fourths of the several States within seven years from the date of its submission to the States by the Congress.

AMENDMENT XXIII [ADOPTED 1961]

Section 1

The District constituting the seat of Government of the United States shall appoint in such manner as the Congress shall direct:

A number of electors of President and Vice President equal to the whole number of Senators and Representatives in Congress to which the District would be entitled if it were a State, but in no event more than the least populous State; they shall be in addition to those appointed by the States, but they shall be considered, for the purposes of the election of President and Vice President, to be electors appointed by a State; and they shall meet in the District and perform such duties as provided by the twelfth article of amendment.

Section 2

The Congress shall have power to enforce this article by appropriate legislation.

AMENDMENT XXIV [ADOPTED 1964]

Section 1

The right of citizens of the United States to vote in any primary or other election for President or Vice President, for electors for President or Vice President, or for Senator or Representative in Congress, shall not be denied or abridged by the United States or any state by reason of failure to pay any poll tax or other tax.

Section 2

The Congress shall have the power to enforce this article by appropriate legislation.

AMENDMENT XXV [ADOPTED 1967]

Section 1

In case of the removal of the President from office or his death or resignation, the Vice President shall become President.

Section 2

Whenever there is a vacancy in the office of the Vice President, the President shall nominate a Vice President who shall take the office upon confirmation by a majority vote of both houses of Congress.

Section 3

Whenever the President transmits to the President pro tempore of the Senate and the Speaker of the House of Representatives his written declaration that he is unable to discharge the powers and duties of his office, and until he transmits to them a written declaration to the contrary, such powers and duties shall be discharged by the Vice President as Acting President.

Section 4

Whenever the Vice President and a majority of either the principal officers of the executive departments or of such other body as Congress may by law provide, transmit to the President pro tempore of the Senate and the Speaker of the House of Representatives their written declaration that the President is unable to discharge the powers and duties of his office, the Vice President shall immediately assume the powers and duties of the office as Acting President.

Thereafter, when the President transmits to the President pro tempore of the Senate and the Speaker of the House of Representatives his written declaration that no inability exists, he shall resume the powers and duties of his office unless the Vice President and a majority of either the principal officers of the executive department or of such other body as Congress may by law provide, transmit within four days to the President pro tempore of the Senate and the Speaker of the House of Representatives their written declaration that the President is unable to discharge the powers and duties of his office. Thereupon Congress shall decide the issue, assembling within 48 hours for that purpose if not in session. If the Congress, within 21 days after receipt of the latter written declaration, or, if Congress is not in session, within 21 days after Congress is required to assemble, determines by two-thirds vote of both houses that the President is unable to discharge the powers and duties of his office, the Vice President shall continue to discharge the same as Acting President; otherwise, the President shall resume the powers and duties of his office.

AMENDMENT XXVI [ADOPTED 1971]

Section 1

The right of citizens of the United States, who are 18 years of age or older, to vote shall not be denied or abridged by the United States or any state on account of age.

Section 2

The Congress shall have the power to enforce this article by appropriate legislation.

AMENDMENT XXVII [ADOPTED 1992]

No law, varying the compensation for the services of the Senators and Representatives shall take effect, until an election of Representatives shall have intervened.

Presidential Elections

Year	Candidates	Parties	Popular Vote	Electoral Vote	Voter Participation
1789	**George Washington**		*	69	
	John Adams			34	
	Others			35	
1792	**George Washington**		*	132	
	John Adams			77	
	George Clinton			50	
	Others			5	
1796	**John Adams**	Federalist	*	71	
	Thomas Jefferson	Democratic-Republican		68	
	Thomas Pinckney	Federalist		59	
	Aaron Burr	Dem.-Rep.		30	
	Others			48	
1800	**Thomas Jefferson**	Dem.-Rep.	*	73	
	Aaron Burr	Dem.-Rep.		73	
	John Adams	Federalist		65	
	C. C. Pinckney	Federalist		64	
	John Jay	Federalist		1	
1804	**Thomas Jefferson**	Dem.-Rep.	*	162	
	C. C. Pinckney	Federalist		14	
1808	**James Madison**	Dem.-Rep.	*	122	
	C. C. Pinckney	Federalist		47	
	George Clinton	Dem.-Rep.		6	
1812	**James Madison**	Dem.-Rep.	*	128	
	De Witt Clinton	Federalist		89	
1816	**James Monroe**	Dem.-Rep.	*	183	
	Rufus King	Federalist		34	
1820	**James Monroe**	Dem.-Rep.	*	231	
	John Quincy Adams	Dem.-Rep.		1	
1824	**John Quincy Adams**	Dem.-Rep.	108,740 (30.5%)	84	26.9%
	Andrew Jackson	Dem.-Rep.	153,544 (43.1%)	99	
	William H. Crawford	Dem.-Rep.	46,618 (13.1%)	41	
	Henry Clay	Dem.-Rep.	47,136 (13.2%)	37	
1828	**Andrew Jackson**	Democratic	647,286 (56.0%)	178	57.6%
	John Quincy Adams	National Republican	508,064 (44.0%)	83	

*Electors selected by state legislatures.

Year	Candidates	Parties	Popular Vote	Electoral Vote	Voter Participation
1832	**Andrew Jackson**	Democratic	687,502 (55.0%)	219	55.4%
	Henry Clay	National Republican	530,189 (42.4%)	49	
	John Floyd	Independent		11	
	William Wirt	Anti-Mason	33,108 (2.6%)	7	
1836	**Martin Van Buren**	Democratic	765,483 (50.9%)	170	57.8%
	William Henry Harrison	Whig		73	
	Hugh L. White	Whig	739,795 (49.1%)	26	
	Daniel Webster	Whig		14	
	W. P. Magnum	Independent		11	
1840	**William Henry Harrison**	Whig	1,274,624 (53.1%)	234	80.2%
	Martin Van Buren	Democratic	1,127,781 (46.9%)	60	
	J. G. Birney	Liberty	7069	—	
1844	**James K. Polk**	Democratic	1,338,464 (49.6%)	170	78.9%
	Henry Clay	Whig	1,300,097 (48.1%)	105	
	J. G. Birney	Liberty	62,300 (2.3%)	—	
1848	**Zachary Taylor**	Whig	1,360,967 (47.4%)	163	72.7%
	Lewis Cass	Democratic	1,222,342 (42.5%)	127	
	Martin Van Buren	Free-Soil	291,263 (10.1%)	—	
1852	**Franklin Pierce**	Democratic	1,601,117 (50.9%)	254	69.6%
	Winfield Scott	Whig	1,385,453 (44.1%)	42	
	John P. Hale	Free-Soil	155,825 (5.0%)	—	
1856	**James Buchanan**	Democratic	1,832,955 (45.3%)	174	78.9%
	John C. Frémont	Republican	1,339,932 (33.1%)	114	
	Millard Fillmore	American	871,731 (21.6%)	8	
1860	**Abraham Lincoln**	Republican	1,865,593 (39.8%)	180	81.2%
	Stephen A. Douglas	Democratic	1,382,713 (29.5%)	12	
	John C. Breckinridge	Democratic	848,356 (18.1%)	72	
	John Bell	Union	592,906 (12.6%)	39	
1864	**Abraham Lincoln**	Republican	2,213,655 (55.0%)	212*	73.8%
	George B. McClellan	Democratic	1,805,237 (45.0%)	21	
1868	**Ulysses S. Grant**	Republican	3,012,833 (52.7%)	214	78.1%
	Horatio Seymour	Democratic	2,703,249 (47.3%)	80	
1872	**Ulysses S. Grant**	Republican	3,597,132 (55.6%)	286	71.3%
	Horace Greeley	Dem.; Liberal Republican	2,834,125 (43.9%)	66†	
1876	**Rutherford B. Hayes‡**	Republican	4,036,298 (48.0%)	185	81.8%
	Samuel J. Tilden	Democratic	4,300,590 (51.0%)	184	
1880	**James A. Garfield**	Republican	4,454,416 (48.5%)	214	79.4%
	Winfield S. Hancock	Democratic	4,444,952 (48.1%)	155	

*Eleven secessionist states did not participate.
†Greeley died before the electoral college met. His electoral votes were divided among the four minor candidates.
‡Contested result settled by special election.

Year	Candidates	Parties	Popular Vote	Electoral Vote	Voter Participation
1884	**Grover Cleveland**	Democratic	4,874,986 (48.5%)	219	77.5%
	James G. Blaine	Republican	4,851,981 (48.2%)	182	
1888	**Benjamin Harrison**	Republican	5,439,853 (47.9%)	233	79.3%
	Grover Cleveland	Democratic	5,540,309 (48.6%)	168	
1892	**Grover Cleveland**	Democratic	5,556,918 (46.1%)	277	74.7%
	Benjamin Harrison	Republican	5,176,108 (43.0%)	145	
	James B. Weaver	People's	1,041,028 (8.5%)	22	
1896	**William McKinley**	Republican	7,104,779 (51.1%)	271	79.3%
	William Jennings Bryan	Democratic People's	6,502,925 (47.7%)	176	
1900	**William McKinley**	Republican	7,207,923 (51.7%)	292	73.2%
	William Jennings Bryan	Dem.-Populist	6,358,133 (45.5%)	155	
1904	**Theodore Roosevelt**	Republican	7,623,486 (57.9%)	336	65.2%
	Alton B. Parker	Democratic	5,077,911 (37.6%)	140	
	Eugene V. Debs	Socialist	402,283 (3.0%)	—	
1908	**William H. Taft**	Republican	7,678,908 (51.6%)	321	65.4%
	William Jennings Bryan	Democratic	6,409,104 (43.1%)	162	
	Eugene V. Debs	Socialist	420,793 (2.8%)	—	
1912	**Woodrow Wilson**	Democratic	6,293,454 (41.9%)	435	58.8%
	Theodore Roosevelt	Progressive	4,119,538 (27.4%)	88	
	William H. Taft	Republican	3,484,980 (23.2%)	8	
	Eugene V. Debs	Socialist	900,672 (6.0%)	—	
1916	**Woodrow Wilson**	Democratic	9,129,606 (49.4%)	277	61.6%
	Charles E. Hughes	Republican	8,538,221 (46.2%)	254	
	A. L. Benson	Socialist	585,113 (3.2%)	—	
1920	**Warren G. Harding**	Republican	16,152,200 (60.4%)	404	49.2%
	James M. Cox	Democratic	9,147,353 (34.2%)	127	
	Eugene V. Debs	Socialist	919,799 (3.4%)	—	
1924	**Calvin Coolidge**	Republican	15,725,016 (54.0%)	382	48.9%
	John W. Davis	Democratic	8,386,503 (28.8%)	136	
	Robert M. La Follette	Progressive	4,822,856 (16.6%)	13	
1928	**Herbert Hoover**	Republican	21,391,381 (58.2%)	444	56.9%
	Alfred E. Smith	Democratic	15,016,443 (40.9%)	87	
	Norman Thomas	Socialist	267,835 (0.7%)	—	
1932	**Franklin D. Roosevelt**	Democratic	22,821,857 (57.4%)	472	56.9%
	Herbert Hoover	Republican	15,761,841 (39.7%)	59	
	Norman Thomas	Socialist	881,951 (2.2%)	—	
1936	**Franklin D. Roosevelt**	Democratic	27,751,597 (60.8%)	523	61.0%
	Alfred M. Landon	Republican	16,679,583 (36.5%)	8	
	William Lemke	Union	882,479 (1.9%)	—	
1940	**Franklin D. Roosevelt**	Democratic	27,244,160 (54.8%)	449	62.5%
	Wendell L. Willkie	Republican	22,305,198 (44.8%)	82	
1944	**Franklin D. Roosevelt**	Democratic	25,602,504 (53.5%)	432	55.9%
	Thomas E. Dewey	Republican	22,006,285 (46.0%)	99	

Year	Candidates	Parties	Popular Vote	Electoral Vote	Voter Participation
1948	**Harry S Truman**	Democratic	24,105,695 (49.5%)	304	53.0%
	Thomas E. Dewey	Republican	21,969,170 (45.1%)	189	
	J. Strom Thurmond	State-Rights Democratic	1,169,021 (2.4%)	38	
	Henry A. Wallace	Progressive	1,156,103 (2.4%)	—	
1952	**Dwight D. Eisenhower**	Republican	33,936,252 (55.1%)	442	63.3%
	Adlai E. Stevenson	Democratic	27,314,992 (44.4%)	89	
1956	**Dwight D. Eisenhower**	Republican	35,575,420 (57.6%)	457	60.6%
	Adlai E. Stevenson	Democratic	26,033,066 (42.1%)	73	
	Other	—	—	1	
1960	**John F. Kennedy**	Democratic	34,227,096 (49.9%)	303	62.8%
	Richard M. Nixon	Republican	34,108,546 (49.6%)	219	
	Other	—	—	15	
1964	**Lyndon B. Johnson**	Democratic	43,126,506 (61.1%)	486	61.7%
	Barry M. Goldwater	Republican	27,176,799 (38.5%)	52	
1968	**Richard M. Nixon**	Republican	31,770,237 (43.4%)	301	60.6%
	Hubert H. Humphrey	Democratic	31,270,533 (42.7%)	191	
	George Wallace	American Indep.	9,906,141 (13.5%)	46	
1972	**Richard M. Nixon**	Republican	47,169,911 (60.7%)	520	55.2%
	George S. McGovern	Democratic	29,170,383 (37.5%)	17	
	Other	—	—	1	
1976	**Jimmy Carter**	Democratic	40,828,587 (50.0%)	297	53.5%
	Gerald R. Ford	Republican	39,147,613 (47.9%)	241	
	Other	—	1,575,459 (2.1%)	—	
1980	**Ronald Reagan**	Republican	43,901,812 (50.7%)	489	52.6%
	Jimmy Carter	Democratic	35,483,820 (41.0%)	49	
	John B. Anderson	Independent	5,719,722 (6.6%)	—	
	Ed Clark	Libertarian	921,188 (1.1%)	—	
1984	**Ronald Reagan**	Republican	54,455,075 (59.0%)	525	53.3%
	Walter Mondale	Democratic	37,577,185 (41.0%)	13	
1988	**George H. W. Bush**	Republican	48,886,000 (53.4%)	426	57.4%
	Michael S. Dukakis	Democratic	41,809,000 (45.6%)	111	
1992	**William J. Clinton**	Democratic	43,728,375 (43%)	370	55.0%
	George H. W. Bush	Republican	38,167,416 (38%)	168	
	H. Ross Perot	Independent	19,237,247 (19%)	—	
1996	**William J. Clinton**	Democratic	45,590,703 (50%)	379	48.8%
	Robert Dole	Republican	37,816,307 (41%)	159	
	Ross Perot	Reform	7,866,284		
2000	**George W. Bush**	Republican	50,456,167 (47.88%)	271	51.2%
	Al Gore	Democratic	50,996,064 (48.39%)	266*	
	Ralph Nader	Green	2,864,810 (2.72%)	—	
	Other		834,774 (less than 1%)	—	

*One District of Columbia Gore elector abstained.

Credits

Unless otherwise credited, all photographs are the property of Pearson Education, Inc. Page abbreviations are as follows: **T** *top,* **C** *center,* **B** *bottom,* **L** *left,* **R** *right.*

CHAPTER 1

3 Courtesy of the National Museum of the American Indian, Smithsonian Institution, S2578 5/2981. Photo by Carmelo Guadagno **6** The Granger Collection, New York **9** Clement N'Taye/AP/Wide World Photos **18** © The British Museum

CHAPTER 2

25 Courtesy of the Association for the Preservation of Virginia Antiquities **26** The Granger Collection, New York **31** © Paul Skillings **35** The Library Company of Philadelphia

CHAPTER 3

45L Worcester Art Museum, Worcester, Mass., Gift of Mr. and Mrs. Albert W. Rice **45R** Worcester Art Museum, Worcester, Mass., Sarah C. Garver Fund **51** Abby Aldrich Rockefeller Folk Art Center, Williamsburg, Va. **54** © Shelburne Museum, Shelburne, Vt.

CHAPTER 4

61 *Pa. German Painted Wooden Box* by Elmer G. Anderson. Index of American Design, © 2005 Board of Trustees, National Gallery of Art, Washington, D.C. **63** © Richard Cummins/Corbis **66** Courtesy of Westover **69** By courtesy of the National Portrait Gallery, London **74** Courtesy of the Trustees of the British Library **81** © Stephen M. Bailey

CHAPTER 5

84 Courtesy of the John Carter Brown Library at Brown University **87** *Stamp Act Repeal'd,* English, 1766. Cream colored earthenware, lead-glazed and hand painted. Photograph by Mark Sexton. Peabody Essex Museum **89** The Library of Congress **96** The Historical Society of Pennsylvania/Atwater Kent Museum

CHAPTER 6

107 The Library Company of Philadelphia **114** Smithsonian Institution **119** Samuel Jennings, *Liberty Displaying the Arts and Sciences,* The Library Company of Philadelphia

CHAPTER 7

128 From the Collections of the Henry Ford Museum & Greenfield Village **138** Courtesy Lilly Library, Indiana University, Bloomington, Ind. **140** The Library of Congress **145** National Museum of American History, Smithsonian Institution

CHAPTER 8

152 Peabody Museum of Archaeology and Ethnology, Harvard University **156** Abby Aldrich Rockefeller Folk Art Museum, Williamsburg, Va. **158** Collection of The New-York Historical Society. Negative number 7278 **162** Collection of Davenport West, Jr.

CHAPTER 9

169 The Library of Congress **172** The Granger Collection, New York **173** © John Eastcott/YVA Momatiuk/Photo Researchers, Inc. **175** American Textile History Museum, Lowell, Mass.

CHAPTER 10

187 *General Andrew Jackson,* 1845, oil on canvas, 97 $\frac{1}{4} \times 61 \frac{1}{2}$ inches. In the collection of The Corcoran Gallery of Art, Gift of William Wilson Corcoran **188** *Rustic Dance After a Sleigh Ride* by William Sidney Mount, 1830, oil on canvas, 22 $\frac{1}{8} \times 27 \frac{1}{8}$ inches. Museum of Fine Arts, Boston, Bequest of Martha C. Karolik for the M. and M. Karolik Collection of American Paintings, 1815–1865, 48.458. Reproduced with Permission. © 2005 Museum of Fine Arts, Boston. All Rights Reserved **193** Courtesy of The Newberry Library, Chicago **196** Collection of The New-York Historical Society, Negative number 42459 **199** Collection of David J. and Janice L. Frent **201** The Saint Louis Art Museum, Gift of Bank of America

CHAPTER 11

206 The Library of Congress **208** North Carolina Museum of Art, Raleigh. Purchased with funds from the State of North Carolina **213** The Museum of the Confederacy, Richmond, Va. Photography by Katherine Wetzel **219** The Library of Congress **225** Fair Street Pictures

CHAPTER 12

228 Laurie Platt Winfrey **230** Fruitlands Museums, Harvard, Mass. **233** © Susan Oristaglio/Esto Photographics, Inc. **234** Photograph Courtesy Peabody Essex Museum. Photo by Mark Sexton **236** © Bettmann/Corbis **238** National Portrait Gallery, Smithsonian Institution/Art Resource, NY

CHAPTER 13

250 *Handcart Pioneers* by CCA Christensen. © by Intellectual Reserve, Inc. Courtesy of Museum of Church History and Art. Used by Permission **254** © Bettmann/Corbis **259** Agriculture Department, Smithsonian Institution

CHAPTER 14

273L New York Public Library, Astor, Lenox and Tilden Foundations **273R** Maryland Historical Society, Baltimore, Md. **276** From the Bella C. Landauer Collection of Business and Advertising Art. Collection of The New-York Historical Society. Negative number 38219 **281** The Library of Congress **285** Alexander Edouart, *Blessing of the Enrequita Mine,* 1860. Bancroft Library, University of California, Berkeley

CHAPTER 15

291 The Library of Congress **295L** National Museum of American History, Smithsonian Institution **295R** The Museum of the Confederacy, Richmond, Va. Photography by Katherine Wetzel **298–302** The Library of Congress **304** *Harper's Weekly*

CHAPTER 16

314 The Library of Congress **315** The New York Public Library **319** Collection of The New-York Historical Society. Negative number 50475 **321** © Bettmann/Corbis **324** *Harper's Weekly* **327** © Corbis

CHAPTER 17

336 From *A Pictographic History of the Oglala Sioux* by Amos Bad Heart Bull, text by Helen Blish, University of Nebraska Press **340** Used by permission from the Union Pacific Museum Collection **343** Californio Vaquero Trousers, Wool, Cotton, Silver, 1834. Autry Museum of

Western Heritage, Los Angeles. Acquisition made possible by the Ramona Chapter, Native Sons of the Golden West **346** Joseph H. Bailey © National Geographic Society **351** Montana Historical Society, Helena

CHAPTER 18

354 *Treasures of Art, Industry, and Manufacture Represented in the American Centennial Exhibition at Philadelphia,* 1876. Plate 35: The Corliss Engine. Publisher: Cosack & Co., Buffalo, N.Y., 1877. The Thomas J. Watson Library, The Metropolitan Museum of Art. Photograph © 1981 The Metropolitan Museum of Art **357** Culver Pictures **359** The Granger Collection, New York **360** *Puck,* 1901 **363** From the Collections of the Henry Ford Museum and Greenfield Village **365** The Granger Collection, New York

CHAPTER 19

374 New York Public Library, Astor, Lenox and Tilden Foundations **376** Collection of David J. and Janice L. Frent **379** The Advertising Archive **382** University of Michigan Medical School records, Bentley Historical Library, University of Michigan. J. Jefferson Gibson, Photographer **384** © The Museum of the City of New York, The Byron Collection **389** Hulton Archive/Getty Images

CHAPTER 20

391 National Museum of American History, Smithsonian Institution **395** The Kansas State Historical Society, Topeka, Kans. **398** The Granger Collection, New York **402** Culver Pictures **404** *Puck,* 1900

CHAPTER 21

409 The State Historical Society of Wisconsin **414** The Granger Collection, New York **419** New York Public Library, Astor, Lenox and Tilden Foundations **422** Culver Pictures

CHAPTER 22

427 Culver Pictures **428** New York Public Library, Astor, Lenox and Tilden Foundations **435** Walter Reuther Library, Wayne State University **436** The Granger Collection, New York **438** George Wesley Bellows (United States, 1882–1925), *Cliff Dwellers,* 1913. Los Angeles County Museum of Art, Los Angeles County Fund. Photograph © 2005 Museum Associates/LACMA

CHAPTER 23

447 Culver Pictures **452** The Granger Collection, New York **454** Smithsonian Institution **457** Museum of American Political Life, University of Hartford **460B** Walter P. Reuther Library, Wayne State University **460T** National Archives

CHAPTER 24

467 *Puck,* 1901 **470** © Bettmann/Corbis **476** *The Argonne* by Harvey Dunn/National Museum of American History, Smithsonian Institution **478** Courtesy of the American Legion **482** The Granger Collection, New York

CHAPTER 25

488 The Granger Collection, New York **489** Gaslight Advertising Archives **492** The Granger Collection, New York **496** © Bettmann/Corbis **499** The Library of Congress

CHAPTER 26

510–512 The Library of Congress **514** Mrs. Philip Evergood/ACA Galleries

CHAPTER 27

527 Bildarchiv Preussischer Kulturbesitz/Art Resource, NY **531** Official U.S. Navy Photograph **537** Courtesy of Military Antiques, Petaluma, Ca. **539** U.S. Army Photo

CHAPTER 28

550 National Archives **551** The Fotomas Index **555** © Bettmann/Corbis **559** from Herblock's *Special for Today* (Simon & Schuster, 1958). Originally appeared in The Washington Post **561** The National Archives

CHAPTER 29

567 © Christie's Images **569L** Sovfoto **569R** Copyright © 1957 by The New York Times Co. Reprinted by permission **573–574L** © Bettmann/Corbis **574R** AP/Wide World Photos

CHAPTER 30

580–585 AP/Wide World Photos **594** Courtesy of Vintage Trends.com **595** Archive Photos/Blank Archive/Getty Images **597** Getty Images **598** © Nancy Ellison/Sygma/Corbis **600** Lyndon Baines Johnson Library

CHAPTER 31

610 Courtesy of the *Louisville Courier,* Culver Pictures **612** Kent State University **616** Courtesy of Stant Manufacturing Inc. **625** Bill Fitz-Patrick/The White House

CHAPTER 32

631 © Bettmann/Corbis **633** Michael Evans/The White House **644** U.S. Department of Health & Human Services **649** Mark Avery/AP/Wide World Photos **651T** © R. Bossu/Sygma/Corbis **652B** © Sygma/Corbis

CHAPTER 33

663 AP/Wide World Photos **673** AP/Wide World Photos/Sony Corporation **674** © Paul Kregger/Sygma/Corbis **681** Jeff Greenberg/PhotoEdit **685** Jerome Delay/AP/Wide World Photos

Index

Key terms and the text page on which the term and definition appear are highlighted in boldface type.

A

AARP. *See* American Association of Retired Persons (AARP)
A&Ps, 362
Abenaki Indians, 4
ABMs. *See* Antiballistic missiles (ABMs)
Abolition and abolitionists: African Americans as, 238–239; American Colonization Society and, 236–237; Civil War as anti-slavery crusade, 300; dissension and, 237–238; evaluation of, 238–239; Fugitive Slave Law of 1850 and, 270; Jacksonian-era politics and, 190; literary, 276; radical antislavery movement and, 237–239; after Revolution, 106; slavery in Mexican cession and, 267; Underground Railroad and, 238; women's rights and, 238, 239. *See also* specific abolitionists
Abortion: in antebellum era, 234; clinics, 620
Absenteeism: in workplace, 434
Acheson, Dean, 546–547; H-bomb and, 551; Korean War and, 552; McCarthy and, 557
Acid rock, 595
Acquired immune deficiency syndrome. *See* AIDS
Activism: black, 573–574; Mexican American, 596–597; of Supreme Court, 585–586; of woman suffrage movement, 446. *See also* specific groups and issues
ACT UP, 621
Adams, Abigail, 107
Adams, Charles Francis, 299, 390
Adams, Henry, 396
Adams, John, 90, 91, 126; Congress and, 93; Constitution (U.S.) and, 117; death of, 163; election of 1796 and, 137; France and, 138, 141; midnight appointments by, 141, 153; Treaty of Paris and, 99–100
Adams, John Quincy, 191; East Florida and, 166; election of 1824 and, 190–191; election of 1828 and, 191–192, 199; Monroe Doctrine and, 180–181; presidency of, 181–182, 190–191; as secretary of state, 177
Adams, Louisa Catherine Johnson, 191
Adams, Samuel, 89–90, 91; republicanism and, 104
Adams, Samuel Hopkins, 453
Adams, Sherman, 571
Adamson Act (1916), 461
Adams-Onís Treaty, 166, 245, 253 (illus.)
Adaptations, 2
Addams, Jane, 418, 434, 470; Hull House of, 385
Adding machine, 361
Adena peoples, 3
Admiralty system, 52
Adolescence, 491. *See also* Youth
Adventures of Huckleberry Finn, The (Twain), 400
Advertising, 488, 488 (illus.), 489 (illus.); growth of, 362; in national and international markets, 409 (illus.); on television, 568
AEF. *See* American Expeditionary Force (AEF)
Affirmative action, 659
Affluence, 487; in 1950s, 565; in World War II, 536. *See also* Prosperity; Second Industrial Revolution; Wealth
Afghanistan, 637; Soviet invasion of, 626, 631, 642; Taliban in, 682
AFL. *See* American Federation of Labor (AFL)
Africa: colonies in, 421 (illus.); customs from, 51 (illus.); as market, 408; slaves from, 48–50, 49 (illus.); sub-Sahara, AIDS in, 644; West African cultures and, 8–9
African Americans: as abolitionists, 238–239; affirmative action and, 659; African Methodist Episcopal (AME) Church and, 209; Black Codes and, 313–314, 318–319; Black Power movement and, 595–596; as buffalo soldiers, 351–352; civil rights and, 566, 572; in Civil War, 301; convict lease system and, 329; as cowboys, 343, 343 (illus.); Cult of Domesticity and, 232; in Democratic party, 515; economic status of, 489; in election of 1980, 632; as Exodusters, 345; Farmers' Alliance and, 395; in Great Depression, 505; Harlem Renaissance and, 493; higher education for, 381–382; hotel boom and, 184; identity of, 50; illiteracy of, 381; impact of Civil War on, 305–306; in Jacksonian era, 190; Jim Crow laws and, 328–329; Ku Klux Klan and, 323; labor unions and, 366; life expectancy in 1880, 377; lynchings of, 322, 327 (illus.), 328, 478; March on Washington (1963) and, 584, 585 (illus.); National Association for the Advancement of Colored People and, 432; national women's organization for, 445; Native Americans and, 210; New Negro and, 478; Niagara Movement and, 432; in 1990s, 658–659; northern migration of, 478, 479 (illus.); occupations of, 364; as officeholders, 320; poverty among, 587; during Reconstruction, 310–311; after Revolution, 106–107; Second Seminole War and, 210; segregated schools for, 380–381; in southern governments, 320; Spanish-American War and, 352, 415–416, 424; stereotyping of, 225; on Supreme Court, 647; Supreme Court and civil rights of, 328 (illus.); as tenant farmers, 431; Tocqueville on, 202; Voting Rights Act (1965) and, 588 (illus.), 589; voting rights of, 107, 391, 394; as western farmers, 345; white norms and, 321; women as workers and, 431; during World War I, 474, 478; zoning laws and segregation of, 436. *See also* Freedpeople; Slaves and slavery; specific individuals
African Methodist Episcopal (AME) Church, 107, **209,** 322
Africans: in Virginia, 49. *See also* Slaves and slavery
Afrika Korps, 531, 532
Afro-American: use of term, 596
Aged: Medicare and, 588; population of, 656–657; poverty among, 587
Agencies, 461; in New Deal, 517–518; during World War I, 477. *See also* specific agencies
Agnew, Spiro, 601, 610
Agrarianism: Tertium Quids and, 154
Agricultural Adjustment Administration (AAA, 1933), **509,** 518
Agricultural colleges: land for, 306, 381
Agricultural experiment stations, 346
Agricultural Revolution, 3
Agriculture: commercial, 173–174; of Confederacy, 294; contract labor in, 318; cotton and, 218–220, 219 (illus.); crop lien system and, 327–328; crops from West, 347; diversification and, 218; immigration and, 259–260; industrialization and, 354; irrigation and, 332, 339, 340; labor in, 175; merino sheep and, 173 (illus.); in New England, 46; in 1920s, 489, 499; reaper and, 258 (illus.), 259; Roosevelt, Franklin D., and, 509; sharecropping and, 318; shipping and, 171; steel plow and, 258 (illus.), 259, 259 (illus.); tobacco and, 216–217; vacuum evaporator and, 258 (illus.); in West, 169; after World War II, 566. *See also* Crops; Farms and farming; specific crops
Aguinaldo, Emilio, 420, 421
AIDS, 643–644; epidemic of, 621
Airlines: after September 11, 2001, 683. *See also* Aviation
Air pollution, 589; auto industry and, 633; energy policy and, 616
Aix-la-Chapelle, Treaty of, 73
Alabama: annexation of, 166; secession of, 289; segregated schools in, 381; steel industry in, 359
Alabama claims, 410
Alamo, 248
Alaska: oil pipeline in, 616; purchase of, 410; territorial status for, 421–422
Albania: Kosovars and, 671
Albany: as Fort Orange, 32
Albany Plan, 74
Albany Regency, 191
Albermarle, 36
Albright, Madeleine, 668, 671

Alcohol and alcoholism: in cities, 373; Indians and, 8, 337; in 1920s, 491; Prohibition and, 495; purity crusade and, 445; temperance movement and, 230–231, 230 (illus.)
Aldrich, Nelson, 455
Alexander I (Russia): Pacific Coast and, 180
"Alexander's Ragtime Band" (Berlin), 437
Alfred P. Murrah Federal Building: bombing of, 673, 674 (illus.)
Alger, Horatio, 365
Algiers, 8
Algonquian Indians: death rates among, 8
Algonquian-speaking peoples, 4
Alien and Sedition Acts (1798), **139**
Alienation: in literature, 493
Alien Enemies Law (1798), 139
Alien Law (1798), 139
Aliens: deportation of, 494; Klan and, 495–495. *See also* Immigrants and immigration
Allen, Frederick Lewis, 491
Allen, Richard, 107–108; African Methodist Episcopal (AME) Church and, 209
Alliance(s): with France, 96–97; NATO as, 548–549; Washington on, 136. *See also* specific alliances
Alliance, Treaty of (France), 97
Alliance for Progress, 579
Alliance movement, 394, 395–396
Allies (Allied Powers, World War I), 470, 471; alliances, battlefronts, and (1914-1917), 473 (illus.); U.S. trade and loans and, 471; war debts of, 523
Allies (Second World War): U.S. aid to, 528
All Mexico movement, 255
al Qaeda, 655, 682
Alternating current: high-voltage, 362
Alton, Illinois: lynching in, 237
Amalgamated Iron and Steel Workers, 367
Amendments: Reconstruction, 316 (illus.); Tallmadge, 178. *See also* Bill of Rights; specific Amendments
America First Committee, 528
American Association of Retired Persons (AARP), 657
American Bible Society, 230
American Board of Customs Commissioners, 87
American Colonization Society, 215, 236–237
American Council on Education: on Hispanics, 658
American Crisis (Paine), 95
American Economic Association, 384
American empire, 420 (illus.). *See also* Empire(s); Imperialism
American Expeditionary Force (AEF), 474, 476 (illus.)
American Federation of Labor (AFL), 366, 434, 513
American identity, 80–81
American Independent party: election of 1968 and, 601
Americanization: of colonies, 59; of immigrants, 433
American Medical Association (AMA), 444
American party, 273, 275. *See also* Know-Nothing party
American Psychiatric Association: homosexuality classified by, 621
American Railway Union (ARU), 397, 448
American Revolution, 82–101, 92 (illus.), 93–98; equality during, 82; events leading to, 85–91; French alliance in, 96–97; as imperial war, 97; Loyalists in, 98–99; opening of, 91–93; peace settlement after, 99–101; society after, 104–109; in South, 97–98
American Rights Committee, 472
Americans with Disabilities Act (ADA) (1991), **648**
American system (Clay), **176,** 200
American Telephone and Telegraph: affirmative action at, 659
American Temperance Society, 231
American Tobacco Company, 452, 457
American Tragedy, The (Evergood), 514 (illus.)
American Woman Suffrage Association, 446
Americas: migration to, 2–3; naming of, 11; Spanish borderlands and, 62–64
Amherst, Jeffrey, 75
Amity and Commerce, Treaty of (France), 97
Amos Bad Heart Bull, 336 (illus.)
Anaconda policy, 293
Anarchists: Haymarket Riot and, 367; McKinley's assassination by, 404; in 1920s, 494
Anasazi culture, 3
Andean strategy: for drug war, 645
Anderson, Alexander, 158 (illus.)
Anderson, John, 631
Anderson, Maxwell, 483, 493
Anderson, Sherwood, 493
Andros, Edmund, 54
Anesthetics, 377
Anglicans. *See* Church of England
Anglicization: of 18th-century culture, 53; process of, 81
Anglo-American Convention: of 1818, 166; Treaty of 1848 and, 253 (illus.)
Anglo-Americans: as cowboys, 343 (illus.); in Hispanic America, 285–286; in New Mexico, 340
Anglo-Dutch rivalry: in New York, 32–34
Anglo-Saxons: racism and, 409, 497
Animals: in Americas, 2; in Columbian Exchange, 6
Annapolis: capital in, 116
Annexation: of Hawaii, 411; of Midway Islands, 410; Philippines and, 418; of Samoan Islands, 411–412
Anthony, Susan B., 380, 598 (illus.)
Anthrax scare, 683
Antiballistic missiles (ABMs): controls of, 611
Anti-Catholicism, 274; new immigrants and, 374
Anticolonialism: Mexican-American War settlement and, 255
Antidraft riots: in Civil War, 301
Antiestablishment platform: in 1972, 613
Antietam: battle of, 298
Antifederalists, 120–121
Anti-German sentiment: during World War I, 476
Anti-immigrant bias, 274
Anti-imperialism: after Spanish-American War, 418–419
Anti-Imperialist League, 419
Anti-Masonic party: Whigs and, 197–198
Antinomianism, 31
Anti-Saloon League, 445
Anti-Semitism: new immigrants and, 374. *See also* Jews and Judaism
Antislavery societies, 107
Anti-Slavery Society: Garrison, William Lloyd, and, 238; women's rights and, 238
Antitrust movement, 360, 394
Antiwar movement, 594–595; during Civil War, 302; election of 1968 and, 599–601; Kent State, Jackson State, and, 611
Antiwar rallies: before World War II, 526
Apache Indians, 331, 332–333
Appalachian Mountains: lands west of, 110–112, 111 (illus.)
Appeal . . . to the Colored Citizens of the World (Walker), 238
Appleton, Nathan, 175
Appliances: laborsaving, 491; manufacturing of, 566; in 1920s, 488
Applied psychology: labor unrest and, 435
Appomattox Courthouse: Lee's surrender at, 305
Apportionment: census of 1790 and, 144
Apprenticeship system: in Black Codes, 321
Arabic (passenger liner), 464–465, 471
Arab-Israeli wars: October War (1973) and, 614; Six-Day War (1967) and, 614
Arab oil embargo, 614–615
Arafat, Yasir, 668
Arapaho Indians, 331, 333, 351
Architecture: Gothic Revival, 233 (illus.); in Jacksonian era, 188; skyscrapers and, 372, 490
Arctic National Wildlife Refuge: Bush, George W., and, 680
Ardennes Forest: Battle of the Bulge in, 539
Argonne Forest: battle at, 475, 476 (illus.)
Aristocracy: natural, 185
Arizona: acquisition of, 255
Arkansas, 289; Clinton as governor of, 662; secession of, 291; Unionist government in, 312
Arkansas National Guard: school integration and, 573 (illus.)
Armada (Spain), 16
Armed forces: African Americans in, 301; British, in Northwest Territory, 132; Continental Army as, 93; desegregation of, 572; Kennedy and, 578–579; nationalists and, 115; provisional, 138–139; in Spanish-American War, 415; under Washington, 94. *See also* Marines (U.S.); Military; Navy (U.S.); Soldiers
Armistice: for World War I, 475
Armor: in Virginia, 25
Arms and armaments: embargo in World War II, 528; neutrality acts in 1930s and, 526; right to bear, 123. *See also* Weapons
Arms control: Eisenhower and, 561
Arms dealers: before World War II, 526
Arms race. *See* Nuclear arms race
Armstrong, Louis "Satchmo," 437
Army Corps of Engineers, 150
Army-McCarthy hearings, 557
Army of Northern Virginia, 298
Army of the Potomac, 298
Army War College, 465
Art(s): Ashcan School in, 438 (illus.), 439; and democracy, 188–189; experimentation in, 438–440; in Jacksonian era, 188–189; New York Armory show and, 439; in 1920s, 492–493; WPA and, 511. *See also* Culture; specific arts
Arthur, Chester A., 393
Articles of Capitulation, 33

Articles of Confederation, 110; Constitution compared with, 121; critiques of, 113–115; revision of, 117
Article X: of League of Nations, 481, 482
Artifacts: Native American, 152 (illus.)
Artisans, 174; of Philadelphia, 65
Aryans: Hitler on, 525
Ashburton (Lord): Webster-Ashburton Treaty and, 245
Ashcan School, 438 (illus.), **439**
Ashcroft, John, 679; after September 11, 2001, 683
Asia: Cold War in, 551–554; Columbus on, 11; economic crash in, 672; immigration from, 338, 605, 606, 655, 657; Japanese expansion in, 523; Korean War in, 552–554; as market, 408; U.S.-Japanese rivalry in, 524–525; in World War II, 531; Yalta concessions and, 540. *See also* Southeast Asia; specific countries
Asian Americans, 659–660
Asiatic Squadron, 416
Assassinations: CIA and, 622–623; of Garfield, 393, 410; of Kennedy, John F., 586; of Kennedy, Robert F., 600; of King, Martin Luther, Jr., 596; of Lincoln, 305; of McKinley, 404, 451
Assemblies: in Carolina, 36; colonial, 71–72; in Georgia, 40; in New York, 33–34
Assemblies of God, 568
Assembly: freedom of, 123
Assembly lines, 486; dissembly factories and, 361; technology and, 427, 428
Assimilationism: for Native Americans, 335–336
Assumption: Hamilton on, 131
Astor, John Jacob, 166–167
Astoria, Oregon, 166–167
Asylums, 235–236
Atlanta: Civil War in, 304 (illus.), 305; race riot in, 432
Atlanta Compromise (Booker T. Washington), 382
Atlantic empire. *See* British empire
Atlantic Ocean region: Algonquian-speaking peoples of, 4; Columbus in, 11; England and, 16; slave trade and, 9
Atlantic & Pacific Tea Company. *See* A&Ps
Atomic bomb: ban on, 546; Cold War and, 546; Soviets and, 543, 556; in World War II, 540–541
Atoms-for-peace program: of Eisenhower, 561
Attlee, Clement, 543
Attorney general: Randolph as, 128. *See also* specific individuals
Audiencia (judicial body), 12
Audiotapes: of Nixon, 613
Austin, Stephen F.: Texas Revolution and, 247
Australia: convict settlers in, 61
Austria: German annexation of, 526
Austria-Hungary: immigrants from, 374. *See also* World War I
Authority: of federal government, 113–116
Automation: in processed materials industries, 429
Automobiles and automobile industry: boom in, 634; Ford and, 405, 486; locking gas caps and, 616 (illus.); mass production in, 427; Model T, 427; oil shocks and, 615, 617; pollution controls and, 633; suburbs and, 567; after World War II, 566
Aviation: Lindbergh and, 491; Wright brothers flight and, 405. *See also* Airlines
Axis of evil: Bush, George W., on, 684
Axis powers (World War II), **526,** 531–535
Aztecs: culture of, 4

B

Babbitt (Lewis), 493
Babcock, Orville E., 325–326
Baby and Child Care (Spock), 567
Baby boom, 565, 566; affluence and diminished expectations of, 636
Backcountry, 58, **60,** 61
Back-to-Africa movements: American Colonization Society and, 236–237
Backus, John, 108
Bacon, Nathaniel, 53
Bacon's Rebellion, 53–54
Baer, George F., 452
Baez, Joan, 595
Baghdad, Iraq, 651 (illus.)
Bahamas: Columbus in, 11
Bailey, James A., 378
Baily v. *Drexel Furniture Company,* 446
Baker, James, 646
Baker v. *Carr,* 585
Bakke v. *Regents of the University of California,* 659
Balanced budget: Carter and, 623; Roosevelt, Franklin D., and, 518. *See also* Budget; Spending
Balance of government: in Carolina, 38
Balance of power: in Far East, 551
Balance of trade: Nixon and, 609, 610
Balkan region: Soviet armies in, 539. *See also* specific countries
Ballads: of late 19th century, 378
Ballinger, Richard A., 456
Ballinger-Pinchot affair, 456
Ballot box, 391 (illus.)
Baltimore: in Civil War, 295; riots in (1968), 596; in War of 1812, 161
Baltimore (Lords). *See* Calvert family
Baltimore and Ohio Railroad, 356
Band concerts, 437
Banking Act (1933). *See* Glass-Steagall Act (1933)
Banknotes, 174
Bank of the United States, 131; Bank War and, 195–197; Panic of 1819 and, 177; second (1816), 174, 176–177; Van Buren and, 198; Whigs and, 200
Banks and banking: commercial, 174; in Great Depression, 507; market economy and, 174; railroad industry and, 358; reform of, 458–459; Roosevelt, Franklin D., and, 507–508; Van Buren and, 198, 199
Bank War, 195–197, 196 (illus.)
Banneker, Benjamin, 107
Baptists, 276; evangelicalism and, 227; Second Great Awakening and, 227–228
Barbados: migrants to Carolina from, 38; slaves in, 49
Barbary War, 152
Barbed wire, 344, 345, 346
Barnett, Ross, 584
Barnum, P.T., 331, 378
Barrios, 479
Bartering, 174
Barton, Bruce, 488
Baruch, Bernard M., 477, 546
Baruch Plan, 546
Baseball, 378, 437, 491
Battle of Princeton (Mercer), 96 (illus.)
Battle of the standards, 343; election of 1896 as, 401
Battles: in American Revolution, 92 (illus.); in Vietnam War, 591 (illus.); in War of 1812, 160 (illus.). *See also* specific battles and wars
Battleships, 412
Bay Colony. *See* Massachusetts; Massachusetts Bay Colony
Bay of Pigs fiasco, 580–**581**
Beats (beatniks), **569**
Beaufort, South Carolina, 310
Beckwourth, Jim, 167
Beecher, Lyman: evangelical Calvinism and, 229; Finney, Charles G., and, 229; reform and, 230–231
Begin, Menachem, 625
Beijing, 552; student resistance in Tiananmen Square, 649, 649 (illus.)
Belgium: German invasion of, 471
Belknap, William E., 326
Bell, Alexander Graham, 353, 361
Bell, John, 281, 281 (illus.)
Bellamy, Edward, 384
Belleau Wood: battle at, 475
"Belligerency" status: for Confederacy, 299
Bellows, George, 438 (illus.)
Benevolent societies: Beecher, Lyman, and, 230; benevolent empire and, 231, 236–237; women and, 233
Bennington, battle at, 95
Bentsen, Lloyd, 647, 663
Berger, Sandy, 668
Beringia, 2
Berkeley, John (Lord), 34
Berkeley, William, 21; Bacon's Rebellion and, 53–54
Berkman, Alexander, 367
Berlin: crisis over, 579; Khrushchev and, 561–562; occupation of, 544; in World War II, 539
Berlin, Irving, 437
Berlin airlift, 549
Berlin blockade, 549–550
Berlin Decree (1806), 156
Berlin-Rome-Tokyo axis, 526
Berlin Wall, 579; destruction of, 649, 651 (illus.)
Bernays, Edward, 488
Bessemer, Henry, 358
Bessemer process, 258 (illus.), 358, 359 (illus.)
Bethel Church for Negro Methodists, 107
Bible: English, 15
Bicameral legislatures: in states, 109
Biddle, Nicholas: Bank War and, 195–197, 196 (illus.)
Big Bonanza strike, 341
Big business: antitrust legislation and, 394; in Progressive Era, 427; railroads as, 355; trusts, oligopolies, and, 428. *See also* Business
Big Foot (chief), 335, 352
"Big Four": at Paris Peace Conference, 481
Big-navy advocates, 412
"Big stick" diplomacy, 467 (illus.)
Big Three: at Teheran, 539–540; at Yalta, 540
Bilingual programs, 597
"Billion-Dollar Congress," 393–394

Bill of rights: absence from Constitution, 119; in territories, 113
Bill of Rights (U.S.), 122–**123**; ratification of, 123. *See also* specific Amendments
Billy the Kid, 340
Bingham, George Caleb, 201
Bin Laden, Osama, 655, 682
Biogenetic law (Haeckel), 409
Biological weapons: in Iraq, 685
Birds of passage, 433
Birmingham, Alabama: civil rights demonstrations in, 584; freedom riders in, 584
Birney, James G.: election of 1844 and, 252
Birth control, 431–432
Birth of a Nation, The (film), 437
Birthrate: of African Americans, 50; decline in, 431; in 1920s, 491; single mothers and, 618. *See also* Fertility rates
Bison. *See* Buffalo
Black(s): use of term, 596. *See also* African Americans; Africans; Slaves and slavery
Black, Hugo, 585
Black Codes, 313–314, 318–319; apprenticeship provisions in, 321
Blackfoot Indians, 333
Black Hawk, 168
Black Hills: Indian removal to, 334–335; Indians and gold rush in, 335, 341
Black Kettle (Chief), 333
Blacklisting: in McCarthy period, 558
Blackmun, Harry, 609
Black nationalism, 596
Black Panther party, 596
Black Power movement, 595–596
Black suffrage: presidential Reconstruction policies and, 313; Reconstruction Acts and, 315, 316. *See also* African Americans; Voting and voting rights
Black Thursday, 504
Blaine, James G., 393, 408, 410
Blair, Francis P.: election of 1828 and, 191
Bland-Allison Silver Purchase Act (1878), **393**
"Bleeding Kansas," 275
Blitzkrieg (lightning war), 528
Blockades: of American commerce, 93; in Barbary War, 152; of Berlin, 549–550; by Britain, 156; in Civil War, 293, 294, 295; economic, of Russia, 477; in World War I, 464, 471
Bloomer pants (clothing), 338
Blough, Roger, 583
Blue-collar jobs: decline in, 635
Blue laws, 230
Blues (music), 437, 493
Board of Special Inquiry: for immigrants, 389
Board of Trade (England), 52, 71
Bobbsey Twins stories, 438
Boland Amendment (1984), 640, 641
Bolden, Charles "Buddy," 437
Boleyn, Anne, 15
Bolivia, 645; cocaine sources in, 646
Bolsheviks: in Russia, 477, 523. *See also* Communism
Bombings: of North Vietnam, 591, 592, 598, 611, 612 (illus.). *See also* Atomic bomb
Bonanza farms, 346
Bonanza West. *See* West (region)
Bonus army, 507
Book of Mormon, 249
Books: banning of left-wing, 558. *See also* Literature
Booth, John Wilkes, 305
Bootleggers: in 1920s, 491
Borah, William E., 482
Borderlands: Spanish, 62–64, 64 (illus.)
Borders: treaties with Britain over, 166; after War of 1812, 167 (illus.). *See also* Boundaries; Frontier
Border states: secession and, 292
Borjas, George J., 657
Bork, Robert, 647
Borrowing: consumer, 635; Greenspan and, 654
Bosnia: civil war in, 669–671, 670 (illus.); Clinton and, 669; division of, 670
Bosnian Serbs, 669
Bosses: in political machines, 376
Boston: immigrant population in, 373; police strike in, 494
Boston Manufacturing Company, 175
Boston Massacre, 88, 89 (illus.)
Boston Tea Party, 90–91
Boundaries: extending, 166–168; of Indian land claims, 169 (illus.); for Indian tribes, 333; of Louisiana Purchase, 151; Pacific Ocean as, 166; after Revolution, 100; of slavery, 178; with Spain, 115–116; Texas-New Mexico dispute over, 269; Venezuela-British Guiana dispute, 410–411. *See also* Borders
Boxer Rebellion: Open Door Policy and, 423–424
Boxing (prize fighting), 379, 491
Boycotts: AFL and, 366; of British goods, 87–88; of grapes, 597; Montgomery bus boycott, 573–574
Bozeman Trail, 334
Braddock, Edward, 74
Bradford, William, 28
Bradley, Omar, 539
Branch Davidians: in Waco, 673
Brancusi, Constantin, 439
Brandeis, Louis D., 448, 459–460
Brandeis brief, 448
Brand names, 362
Brazil: Johnson, Lyndon B., and, 589; Portugal and, 11
Breckinridge, John, 280
Breed's Hill. *See* Bunker Hill, battle of
Brendan (Saint), 9
Brennan, William J., Jr., 585
Brent, Linda. *See* Jacobs, Harriet
Brer Rabbit stories, 210
Brewster, Kingman, 607
Brezhnev, Leonid: nuclear agreements with, 611; SALT talks and, 626
Brezhnev Doctrine, 649
Bridger, Jim, 167
Britain. *See* England (Great Britain)
British empire: in Atlantic region, 56–57; events leading to American Revolution, 85–91; imperial wars of, 72–77; loss of American colonies and, 83–84; mercantilism in, 51–53; Pitt and, 74–75; after Seven Years' War, 76
British Guiana: boundary dispute with Venezuela, 410–411
Broadway theater, 378
Brokaw, Tom: anthrax scare and, 683
Brook Farm, 241, 242
Brooklyn Bridge, 359
Brooks, Preston: caning of Sumner, 266
Brown, H. Rap, 596
Brown, James, 596
Brown, John: Harpers Ferry raid of, 279, 280 (illus.); in Kansas, 275
***Brown* v. *Board of Education of Topeka*, 573**
Bruce, Blanche K., 321 (illus.)
Bryan, Alfred, 470 (illus.)
Bryan, William Jennings, 418, 454; "Cross of Gold" speech of, 402, 402 (illus.); election of 1896 and, 402–403; election of 1900 and, 404, 420; Scopes trial and, 497; as secretary of state, 468, 471
Brzezinski, Zbigniew, 626
Buchanan, James, 275, 276; Mormons and, 250; Oregon question and, 253; secession and, 290
Buckley, William F., 630, 641
Buddhist monks: protests against Diem by, 580 (illus.)
Budget: Bush, George W., and, 679; Carter and, 623; of Clinton, 663; defense, 554; Jefferson and, 150; Kennedy and, 583; Reagan and, 632; Roosevelt, Franklin D., and, 518. *See also* Defense spending; Deficit(s); Spending; specific presidents
Buffalo, 332; extermination of, 336–337; Plains Indians and, 333
Buffalo Bill's Wild West Show. *See* Wild West Show
"Buffalo nickel," 337
Bulgaria: fall of government in, 649
Bulge, Battle of the, 539
Bull Moose party. *See* Progressive party, in 1912
Bull Run: first battle of, 297; second battle of, 298
Bundy, McGeorge, 578, 589
Bunker Hill, battle of, 91
Bureaucracy: Civil War and, 307; federal, 128, 499; Nixon and, 609
Bureau of Citizenship and Immigration Services (BCIS), 683
Bureau of Corporations, 451
Burger, Warren, 609, 647
Burgoyne, John, 95
Burial mounds: Indian, 3–4
Burke, Edmund, 90
Burma: in World War II, 531
Burnside, Ambrose E., 298–299
Burr, Aaron, 153, 154–155; Chase impeachment and, 154; election of 1800 and, 141; treason of, 155
Burwell family, 47
Bus boycott: in Montgomery, 573–574
Bush, George (father): Andean strategy for drug war and, 645; as CIA director, 623; domestic agenda of, 648–649; economic assistance to Russia, 650; economy and, 652; election of 1980 and, 631; election of 1988 and, 647–648; election of 1992 and, 661, 662 (illus.); end of Cold War and, 649–650; Operation Desert Storm (Persian Gulf War) and, 651–652; Panama invasion and, 650–651; Somalia and, 669; Supreme Court appointments of, 647; as vice president, 637
Bush, George W. (son), 655; airport screeners and, 683; approval ratings after September 11, 683; domestic policy of, 679–680; election of 2000 and, 677–678, 678 (illus.); September 11, 2001, and, 681–682, 681 (illus.); war on terrorism and, 681–682

Business: codes of fair competition in, 509; Coolidge on, 498; corporate fraud and, 680; female ownership of, 619; hotel boom and, 184; inventions for, 361; in 1920s, 488; in 1970s, 617; state regulation of, 450; transatlantic telegraph and, 361. *See also* Big business; Corporations
Business cycle: slave economy and, 219
Business organization: holding company, 361; trusts, 360, 361; vertical integration, 359
Busing, 609
Bute, earl of (John Stuart), 83
Butte, Montana: prowar vigilantism in, 476
Byrd, William II: journal of, 58
Byrd, William III: home of, 66 (illus.)
Byrd family, 47

C

Cabinet: of Adams, John, 137; of Carter, 623; of Clinton, 662–663; of Harding, 498; of Jackson, Andrew, 192; of Jefferson, 149–150; of Johnson, Lyndon B., 589; of Monroe, 177; of Reagan, 633; of Washington, 128; women in, 516
Cable: for telegraphs, 361
Cabot, John, 14
Cahokia, 3
Calhoun, John C.: Eaton affair and, 194; election of 1824 and, 190–191; election of 1828 and, 191; and Jackson, 194; nullification crisis and, 194–195; as secretary of war, 177; southern voting bloc and, 269; Texas annexation and, 251; as vice president, 195; as War Hawk, 159
Califano, Joseph, 623
California, 338; cession to U.S. of, 255; expansionism and, 246; gold rush and, 257, 341; immigrants in, 657; Mexican Americans in, 285, 340; Mexican-American War and, 254–255; as Mexican territory, 246; Reagan as governor of, 629; Spain and, 13, 63; statehood for, 268–269, 270 (illus.); undocumented aliens in, 658; in World War II, 536
California Indians, 333
California State College: Mexican American studies program at, 597
California Trail, 249 (illus.)
Californios, 340; gold discovery and treatment of, 285
Call of the Wild, The (London), 401
Calvert family: Cecilius, 27; Charles, 56; George, 27
Calvin, John, 14
Calvinism: in England, 15; Enlightenment and, 228–229; Great Awakening and, 68; neo-Calvinism and, 229; Second Great Awakening and, 228–229
Cambodia, 592; *Mayaguez* seizure by, 624; in Vietnam War, 611
Cambridge Agreement (1629), 29
Camden, battle at, 92 (illus.), 97
Camelot: Kennedy administration and, 582
Campaigns (political): for election of 1896, 401–403. *See also* Elections
Camp David Accords, 625, 625 (illus.), 638
Canada: annexation and, 409; boundary with, 166, 245, 253 (illus.); Britain and, 76, 159–160; France and, 13–14; NAFTA and, 663; Quebec Act and, 90; trade with, 157; War of 1812 and, 159, 160, 161
Canadian Southern Railway, 357 (illus.)
Canals, 171–173, 431; across isthmus of Central America, 465; building of Panama, 466
Canary Islands: Columbus in, 11
Canning, George, 180
Cannon, Joseph "Uncle Joe," 455
Cape Breton Island: Louisbourg and, 73
Cape Coast Castle: as slave trading post, 9 (illus.)
Cape Fear, 36, 37
Capital (city): lack of, 116; in Washington, 141, 149
Capital (financial): grants to railroads, 356; in postwar South, 318
Capitalism: factory production and, 175; industrialization and, 368
Capone, Al, 491
"Captains of industry," 355
Caravans: in West Africa, 8
Caribbean region: migrants from, 38 (illus.); slave empire in, 273; Spain and, 11; in Spanish-American War, 417 (illus.); Triangular trade and, 67; trouble spots in, 640 (illus.); U.S. activities in (1898–1930s), 469 (illus.). *See also* specific countries
Carib people, 8
Carlisle Indian School, 335–336
Carmichael, Stokely, 596
Carnegie, Andrew, 358–359, 365, 367, 418
Carolina(s), 22, 36–38, 38 (illus.); backcountry of, 61. *See also* North Carolina; South Carolina
Carpetbaggers, 320
Carranza, Venustiano, 469, 470
Carrington, Edward, 144–145
Carrying trade, 148–149
Cars. *See* Automobiles and automobile industry
Carson, Kit, 167
Carson River Valley: Comstock Lode in, 341
Carswell, G. Harrold, 609, 610
Carter, James Earl ("Jimmy"): assessment of, 627; Cold War and, 626; deregulation and, 633; election of 1976 and, 623; election of 1980 and, 631; energy crisis and, 615; Haiti and, 669; inflation and, 617; Iran and, 625; Latin America and, 624–625; military buildup under, 637; presidency of, 623–624; SALT II and, 626
Carter Doctrine, 625
Carteret, George, 34
Carter family, 47
Carthage, Illinois: lynching in, 250
Cartier, Jacques, 13
Cartoons. *See* Political cartoons
Casablanca meeting, 532
Cascade Mountains, 332
Case workers: social workers as, 385
Casey, William, 641
Cash-and-carry policy: in World War II, 528, 529
Cash register, 361, 363 (illus.)
Cass, Lewis, 268
Caste system: economic, in Spanish-Mexican society, 340
Cast-iron plow, 332
Castle Garden, 388
Castro, Fidel, 561, 578; Bay of Pigs fiasco and, 580–581; CIA assassination attempts against, 623; Cuban missile crisis and, 581–582
Casualties: of AIDS epidemic, 643, 644; of Civil War, 305, 306 (illus.); of Philippine-American War, 420; of Spanish-American War, 418; of World War I, 475
Cather, Willa, 493
Catherine of Aragon, 15
Catholics and Catholicism: in California in 1830s, 246; common school movement and, 235; Democratic party and, 200; in 1880s, 378; in England, 15–16; evangelicalism and, 227; of Ferdinand and Isabella, 10; of immigrants, 271, 273; in Ireland, 16; of James II (England), 22; of Mary I (England), 15; in Maryland, 26–27, 55–56; of new immigrants, 374, 375; Protestant Reformation and, 14–15; Quebec Act and, 90; slavery and, 246, 247; of Smith, Alfred E., 500; Spanish missionaries and, 12
Cato's Letters (Trenchard and Gordon), 70
Catt, Carrie Chapman, 446
Cattle, 343–345, 344 (illus.)
Cavalry (U.S.): buffalo soldiers in, 351–352
CCC. *See* Civilian Conservation Corps (CCC)
Cease-fire: in Bosnia, 670
Celia (slave), 225
Censorship: after Revolution, 103; slavery debate and, 216
Census: of 1810, 147; ethnic and racial classifications on, 660; of 1790, 144–145
Centennial Exposition (Philadelphia), 353, 354 (illus.)
Central America: Boland Amendment and, 640; canal across isthmus of, 465; Carter and, 624–625; immigrants from, 658; Indians of, 4; Reagan and intervention in, 639–641; trouble spots in, 640 (illus.). *See also* Latin America; specific countries
Central government: Madison on, 118
Central High School: integration of, 573
Central Intelligence Agency (CIA), 550; Afghanistan and, 682; assassination plots by, 622–623; Bay of Pigs fiasco and, 580–581; covert actions of, 560–561; in Nicaragua, 640; Watergate Scandal and, 613
Central Pacific Railroad: transcontinental railroad and, 357
Central Powers: in World War I, 470
Cervera, Pascual, 417, 418
Cézanne, 439
Chaco Canyon (New Mexico): Anasazi culture in, 3
Chacón, Albino, 286
Chacón, Rafael, 286
"Chain store," 362
Chambers, Whittaker, 556
Chamoun, Camille, 560
Champion's Hill: battle at, 304 (illus.)
Champlain, Samuel de, 13
Chancellorsville: battle of, 302
Charles I (England): execution of, 21; Massachusetts Bay and, 29; Parliament and, 84; Virginia and, 26
Charles II (England), 22; Carolina and, 36; charter to Duke of York from, 33; Pennsylvania charter and, 35; regulation of trade and, 52
Charleston. *See* Charles Town
Charles Town, 37; in American Revolution, 97

Charter(s): colonial, 21; for Connecticut, 32; for Georgia, 39; for Maryland, 27; for Massachusetts, 54; for Pennsylvania, 35; protection of, 179; for Virginia, 23, 24
Charter of Liberties (Pennsylvania), 36
Chase, Samuel, 154
Château-Thierry, battle at, 475
Chatham, earl of: Pitt as, 87
Chattanooga: battle of, 303
Chávez, César, 596–597, 597 (illus.)
Chechnya: Russian war with, 668
Checks and balances: in Constitution (U.S.), 113
Chemical weapons: in Iraq, 685
Chenaworth, Richard B.: cast-iron plow and, 258 (illus.)
Cheney, Dick, 679, 684
Cherokee Indians, 62, 168, 194 (illus.), 332; alphabet of, 193; Trail of Tears and, 193, 194 (illus.); way of life of, 193
Chesapeake (ship), 157
Chesapeake region, 22; colonies in 1640, 23 (illus.); Maryland and, 26–27; by 1700, 56; society in, 46–48; Virginia and, 23–26; in War of 1812, 161
Cheyenne Indians, 331, 333, 351; warfare with, 333
Chiang Kai-shek, 551; loss to Mao by, 552; World War II and, 532
Chicago, 372; African Americans in, 658; architecture of, 372; cattle and, 343; drinking establishments in, 373; Haymarket Riot in, 366, 367; Hull House in, 385; immigrants in, 373; industry in, 436; jazz in, 437; political machine in, 376; Pullman strike in, 397; race riot in, 478; riots of 1968 in, 596
"Chicago" (Sandburg), 440
Chicago, Burlington and Quincy railroads, 452
Chicanos: use of term, 597
Chickasaw Indians, 62, 168, 194 (illus.)
Chief Joseph, 335
Chief justice: Marshall as, 141
Child, Lydia Maria: *Incidents in the Life of a Slave Girl* (Jacobs) and, 225
Childbearing: in Chesapeake region, 47; in 1920s, 491
Child labor, 364, 366, 400, 431; during Industrial Revolution, 261; legislation regulating, 444, 446, 450, 461
Child rearing, 431; in Plains tribes, 333
Children: apprenticeship provisions for freed, 321; born to slaves, 50; changing family and, 618; corporal punishment of, 233, 235; discovery of, 233–234; education and, 234–235, 380–381; in immigrant families, 374; in late 19th century families, 379; in New England, 44, 44 (illus.), 45 (illus.); in 1950s, 567; on Overland Trail, 338; toys and, 234 (illus.); Victorian morality and, 377–378. *See also* Child labor; Families; Infant mortality
Children's Bureau, 456
China: Boxer Rebellion in, 423–424; Clinton and, 668; Communists in, 551–552, 556; containment of, 559–560; immigrants from, 431, 433, 659; Japan and, 524, 525, 534; Korean War and, 553–554, 559; Mao Tse-tung in, 551–552; Nixon in, 611; northwest passage to, 13; Open Door Policy and, 423–424; power in 1970s, 611; Soviet Union and, 559, 560; spheres of influence in, 422; Tiananmen Square protests and, 649, 649 (illus.); trade with, 175; trading ports and economic concessions in, 421 (illus.); U.S. ambassador to, 626; World War II and, 532
Chinese Exclusion Act (1882), 342, **364**
Chinese immigrants: discrimination against, 364; in mining camps, 342; transcontinental railroad and, 357
Chinook Indians, 332
Chippendale, Thomas, 65
Chivington, John M., 333
Chivington massacre. *See* Sand Creek massacre
Choctaw Indians, 62, 168, 194 (illus.)
Christensen, Carl Christian Anton, 250
Christianity: fundamentalism in, 497–498, 629; Indians and, 7; slavery and, 50, 206, 208–209, 215. *See also* Catholics and Catholicism; Protestantism; specific groups
Christian right: Ashcroft and, 679
Christopher, Warren M., 668
Christowe, Stoyan, 388, 389
Chrysler Corporation, 487
Church and state, 106–107
Churches: in 1880s, 378; in New England, 44; Old Ship Meetinghouse as, 31 (illus.); sectionalism in, 276
Churchill, Winston, 543; on Cold War, 561; on Iron Curtain, 544; in World War II, 532
Church of England, 15; disestablishment of, 106; Puritans and, 28–29
Church of Jesus Christ of Latter-day Saints. *See* Mormons
CIA. *See* Central Intelligence Agency (CIA)
Cimarron (Ferber), 347
Cincinnati, 147
Cincinnati Red Stockings, 378
Circular letter, 88
Circuses, 378
Cities and towns, 344; black migration to northern, 478, 479 (illus.); black population of, 489; as centers of trade, 149; city manager in, 449; commercial life in, 148–149; commission form of government in, 449; crime in, 373; depression of 1890s and, 385–386, 390; growth of, 436; immigrants in, 373–375, 375 (illus.); industrial, 175, 175 (illus.); lifestyle in 1920s, 490–493; linked by railroads, 355; in Massachusetts, 30; Mexican American migration to, 479; in Midwest, 169; New England families in, 44; political machines in, 375–376; pollution in, 373; population of, 371, 372, 386; provincial, 64–65; railroads and, 355; reform and, 383–386, 449–450; settlement houses in, 385; skyscrapers in, 372; slums in, 372, 385; social and cultural change and, 376–383; socioeconomic segregation in, 436; streetcars and, 372; in Sunbelt, 656; tenements and overcrowding in, 373; walking, 372; zoning in, 436. *See also* specific cities and towns
Citizenship, 315; for Hawaiian republic, 421; for Mexicans, 285; Naturalization Law (1798) and, 139
"City on a hill": Massachusetts Bay as, 29–30
Civic organizations, 386
Civic virtue, 85, 104
Civilian Conservation Corps (CCC), 509, 518
Civilization: European colonizing and, 1
Civil rights, 572–574; Johnson, Lyndon B., and, 587, 588–589; Kennedy and, 583–584; Marshall, John, and, 155; Nixon and, 609; Supreme Court, blacks, and, 328 (illus.); Truman and, 555; Warren Court and, 585
Civil Rights Act: of 1866, 314, 318; of 1964, 587, 597; of 1965, 589
Civil Rights Cases, 328 (illus.)
Civil rights movement, 566, 573–574; Black Power movement and, 595–596; freedom rides in, 584; March on Washington and, 584, 585 (illus.)
Civil service: reform of, 392, 393
Civil Service Commission, 393
Civil unions: between homosexuals, 622
Civil war(s): in Bosnia, 669–671, 670 (illus.); in China, 552; in England, 22, 36; in Kansas Territory, 275; in Lebanon, 639
Civil War (U.S.), 288; advantages and disadvantages of North and South, 292–293; African Americans in, 301, 302 (illus.), 351; anaconda policy in, 293; campaigns and battles (1861-1862), 296 (illus.), 297–299; campaigns and battles (1863-1865), 302–305, 302 (illus.), 304 (illus.); casualties of, 305, 306 (illus.); compromise proposals and, 290; diplomacy during, 299; effects of, 305–307; emancipation and, 300–301; events leading to, 287, 288–290; financing of, 294–295; Fort Sumter and, 290–292, 291 (illus.); home front mobilizations in, 293–295, 297; Lee's surrender at Appomattox and, 305; navies in, 293, 297; "On to Richmond" strategy, 296 (illus.) 297–298; organizational revolution and, 307–308; peninsula campaign and, 297–298; political leadership during, 295–297; seizure of military installations in seceded states, 290, 291; slavery vs. indivisibility of Union as reason for, 292; Smalls, Robert, in, 310; strategy in, 292–293, 293 (illus.); as total war, 292–299; wartime Reconstruction and, 312; women during, 305
Civil Works Administration (CWA, 1933), 518
Claiborne, William, 1
Clans: in West Africa, 8
Clarissa (Richardson), 107
Clark, J. Reuben, 524
Clark, William, 152
Clark Memorandum, 524
Classes: caste and, 205; in New England, 45–46. *See also* specific classes
Classical cultures: Renaissance rediscovery of, 10
Clay, Cassius M., 216
Clay, Henry: American system of, 176, 200, 251; Bank War and, 196–197; Compromise of 1850 and, 269; election of 1824 and, 190–191; election of 1828 and, 191, 192, 196–197; election of 1844 and, 252; Missouri Compromise and, 178; as War Hawk, 159
Clayton Act (1913), 435 (illus.)
Clayton Antitrust Act (1914), **459**
Clean Air Act, 616
Clemenceau, Georges, 481
Clemens, Samuel Langhorne. *See* Twain, Mark
Clement VII (Pope), 15

Clergy: lay leadership and, 186; Protestant Reformation and, 15
Clermont (steamboat), 171
Cleveland, Grover, 393, 393 (illus.), 413; election of 1894 and, 399; free silver and, 402; Latin American policy of, 410; Panic of 1893 and, 396; Pullman strike and, 397; Sherman Silver Purchase Act and, 399; Venezuela-British Guiana dispute and, 410–411
Cleveland, Ohio, 436
Cliff Dwellers (Bellows), 438 (illus.)
Climate: of Great Plains, 332
Clinton, De Witt, 159, 171–172
Clinton, Henry, 97
Clinton, Hillary Rodham, 662; health care reform and, 664; Lewinsky scandal and, 676; Whitewater and, 665
Clinton, William Jefferson ("Bill"), 654; cabinet of, 662–663; character of, 665; Defense of Marriage Act and, 622; drug policy of, 645–646; election of 1992 and, 661–662; election of 1994 and, 665–666; election of 1996 and, 667 (illus.); foreign policy of, 667–672; as governor of Arkansas, 662; Greenspan and, 654–655, 663 (illus.); Haiti and, 669; homosexuals in military and, 621; impeachment of, 676; Kosovo and, 671–672; Lewinsky and, 675–676; Somalia and, 669; Whitewater and, 665
Clothing: bloomer pants as, 338; colonial, 45 (illus.); of cowboys, 343 (illus.); mass production and ready-to-wear, 361, 435; of slaves, 213 (illus.); sporting fads and, 378, 379 (illus.); Victorian era middle-class, 378, 379 (illus.); of women on Overland Trail, 338; of youth movement, 594 (illus.)
Clubs: in Philadelphia, 65–66; political, 136
Coal and coal industry, 489; energy policy and, 616; from federal lands, 633; strikes against, 397–398, 452–453
Coaling stations, 412
Coalitions: in New Deal, 516, 518, 519–520, 632; in World War II, 532
"Coastwise" commerce, 67
Cocaine, 645
Codes of law: in Massachusetts Bay Colony, 31
Cody, William F. "Buffalo Bill," 337
Coercive (Intolerable) **Acts** (1774), **90,** 99 (illus.); resistance to, 91
Cold War, 543, 544; in Asia, 551–554; beginning of, 544–545; Berlin blockade and, 549–550; containment policy in, 546–550; economy and, 566; Eisenhower and, 558–562, 570–571; end of, 649–650, 650 (illus.); expansion of, 550–554; Gorbachev and, 642, 649; at home, 554–558; Johnson, Lyndon B., and, 589–593; Kennedy and, 577, 578; loyalty issue and, 555–556; massive retaliation policy in, 558; in Middle East, 560; Nixon and détente in, 610–611; resumption of, 626; Southeast Asia and, 579–580; Soviet view of, 551 (illus.); Truman Doctrine and, 547; waging peace during, 561–562. *See also* Vietnam War
Colfax, Schuyler, 325
Collective bargaining, 460
Collective security: after World War I, 523
Colleton, John, 36
Collier, John, 515
Colombia: drugs in, 645, 646; Panama Canal and, 466
Colonies and colonization: American identity and, 80–81; assemblies in, 71–72; Carolina as, 36–38; in Chesapeake region, 22–27; cities in, 64–65; coaling stations and, 412; consumer society in, 67–68; convict settlers in, 61; created from Massachusetts Bay Colony, 32; cultural convergence in, 42–43; culture of, 77; diversity of English, 22; Dutch, 32–33; English, 21–40; English regulation of, 50–53; Enlightenment in, 65–66; expansion of, 59; families in, 42; governing of, 70–72; growth and diversity of, 60–62; in Ireland, 16–17; Middle Colonies, 32–36; money for, 23; in New England, 27–32; Puritans in, 27–32; regulation of trade in, 51–53; Roanoke and, 17–18; in 1750, 73 (illus.); society in, 83–85; Spanish, 13, 63–64; Spanish-American War and, 413; on taxation without representation, 84–85; tensions with Britain, 99 (illus.); voluntary, of free blacks, 300; West and, 73–74; women in, 44–45; in World War II, 529. *See also* Back-to-Africa movements
Colorado: Mexican-American War and, 255
Colorado Fuel and Iron Company: strike against, 460, 460 (illus.)
Colored Farmers' National Alliance and Cooperative Union, 395
Colson, Charles, 607
Colt, Samuel: revolver and, 258 (illus.)
Columbian Exchange, 6
Columbian Star Dishes, 199 (illus.)
Columbia University, 381; student seizure of buildings at, 594–595
Columbine High School: shootings in, 675
Columbus, Christopher, 10–11; European exploration and, 1–2
Comanche Indians, 331, 333, 335, 351
Combined Chiefs of Staff: in World War II, 532
"Coming out of the closet," 621
Commander in chief: Washington as, 94
Commerce: banking for, 174; British blockade of, 93; in cities, 148–149; France and, 137, 141; Hamilton on, 129; Indians and, 7–8; intercoastal, 67; marketing and, 174; mercantilism and, 51; on rivers, 171. *See also* Interstate commerce; Navigation Acts; Trade
Commerce and Labor, Department of, 451
Commerce Court, 456
Commercial agriculture, 173–174
Commission for Civil Rights, 573
Commission on National Goals (1959), 575
Committee on Industrial Organization. *See* Congress of Industrial Organizations (CIO)
Committee on Public Information (CPI), 476
Committees of correspondence, 90, 91
Committee to Defend America by Aiding the Allies, 528
Common law: in England, 72
Common market: NAFTA as, 663–664
Common Sense (Paine), **93**
Commonwealthmen (England), 70, 88, 120
Commonwealth of Independent States (CIS), 650
Communication(s): among Indian groups, 4; internationalism and, 408; inventions in, 361; rotary printing press and, 258 (illus.); telegraph and, 256, 258 (illus.)
Communism: in Cambodia, 624; in eastern Europe, 533; fears of, 494; Japan and, 551; Johnson, Lyndon B., and, 589; loyalty issue and, 555–556; McCarthyism and, 556–557; in Southeast Asia, 599; Supreme Court and, 585; in Vietnam, 558–559, 580. *See also* Cold War; Soviet Union
Communist China, 551–552. *See also* China
Competition: antitrust legislation and, 394; in oil industry, 360; in railroad industry, 357–358; in steel industry, 359; tariff barriers to, 354
Compromise of 1850, 266, **269**–270, 270 (illus.)
Compromise of 1877, 326
Compulsory school attendance, 380, 400, 431
Computers, 673 (illus.); Year 2000 (Y2K) problem and, 676–677
Comstock, Anthony, 378
Comstock, Henry T. P., 341
Comstock Law (1873), 378, 432
Comstock Lode, 341, 343
Concentration policy, 333–334
Concord, battle at, 91, 92 (illus.)
Condoms: AIDS and use of, 643
Confederacies: Native American, 62
Confederacy (Civil War South): advantages and disadvantages of, 292–293; attempts at recognition for, 299; "belligerency" status for, 299; conscription in, 293; creation of, 289; diplomacy of, 299; food riots in, 294; Fort Sumter and, 291–292; resources of, 294; wealth of, 295. *See also* Civil War (U.S.)
Confederate Congress, 295, 297
Confederate Ordnance Bureau, 294
Confederate States of America. *See* Confederacy (Civil War South)
Conflict: ethnic, 61; with Native Americans, 62. *See also* Wars and warfare; specific types
Conformity: in 1950s, 565
Congregationalists: in Massachusetts, 30; in New England, 44; Old and New Lights and, 69; Second Great Awakening and, 228, 229
Congress (U.S.): African Americans in, 310; apportionment and, 144–145; under Articles, 110; "Billion-Dollar," 393–394; Bush, George W., and, 679, 680; caning of Sumner in, 266; Clinton and, 663, 665; farm bloc in, 499; First, 128, 144; Ford and, 622–623; Johnson, Andrew, and, 314; Johnson, Lyndon B., and, 586–587; Kennedy and, 582–583; leadership during Revolution, 91–93; power during 1877-1900, 392; state representation in, 118; Ten Percent Plan and, 312; wartime Reconstruction plan of, 312; in Watergate Scandal, 613–614; western lands and, 113; Wilson and, 459. *See also* Confederate Congress; Continental Congress
Congressional Medal of Honor: for black Spanish-American War troops, 416; for buffalo soldiers, 352
Congressional Reconstruction, 314–316
Congressional Union, 446
Congress of Industrial Organizations (CIO), 514–515
Congress of Racial Equality (CORE), 584

Conklin, Roscoe, 325
Connecticut, 30 (illus.), 32, 37 (illus.)
Connor, Eugene "Bull," 584
***Conquistadores*, 10,** 11–13
Conscience: freedom of, 27
Conscription. *See* Draft (military)
Conservation, 454; Taft and, 456; in West (to 1917), 430 (illus.)
Conservatism (political), 629–630
Consolidation: by railroads, 358; in steel industry, 359
Conspicuous consumption, 384
Constitution(s): of Confederacy, 289; in England, 70, 84; in Kansas, 275; Lecompton, 277; in Reconstruction South, 313–314; in states, 108–109
Constitution (ship), 160
Constitution (U.S.), 104; Articles of Confederation compared with, 121; bank controversy and, 131; Bill of Rights and, 122–123; framers of, 108; implied powers of, 131; Iran-Contra affair and, 641; loose construction of, 131; Marshall and, 179; ratification of, 120–121, 122 (illus.); signing of, 119–120; slavery and, 119–120, 267; strict construction of, 146–147
Constitutional convention: in California, 269; during Reconstruction, 310, 312, 313; in states, 109
Constitutional Convention (U.S.), 117–120
Constitutionality: of secession, 288, 312
Constitutional Union party, 281, 281 (illus.)
Constructive engagement policy: of Clinton, 668
Consumer goods market: Japan in, 635
Consumer installment debt: increase in, 634
Consumerism: and consumer culture in 1950s, 568–569; consumer revolution and, 486–487; rubber, vulcanization of, and, 259; toys and, 234 (illus.). *See also* Consumers and consumer society; Second Industrial Revolution; specific consumer goods and industries
Consumers and consumer society: advertising and, 488; in colonies, 67–68; critics of, 568–569; electrical products and, 488; inflation in 1970s and, 617; Navigation Acts and, 52–53; oil shocks, economy, and, 615; quality of life and, 567–568
Consumer spending, 363 (illus.)
Containment policy, 546–550, **547,** 563; toward China, 559–560; failure of, 602; Johnson, Lyndon B., and, 589; in Southeast Asia, 579–580
Continental Army, 93, 94–96, 97–98; Newburgh Conspiracy and, 115; at Valley Forge, 96. *See also* American Revolution
Continental Congress: First, 91; Second, 91–93, 108, 109–110
Continental paper money, 114, 114 (illus.)
Continental System (France), 156–157
Contraceptives. *See* Birth control
Contract(s): union, 489
Contract labor: freedpeople as, 301, 318
Contract with America, 665, 666
Contras (Nicaragua), 640, 641. *See also* Iran-Contra affair
Convention of Mortefontaine, 141
Conventions (political): Constitutional, 117; Democratic (1924), 500; Democratic (1968), 600–601; on secession, 288
Converse, Marion S. D., 224
Conversion: of Indians to Christianity, 7
Convicts: lease system for, 329; as settlers, 61
Coode, John, 55–56
Coolidge, Calvin, 498
"Cooling-off" treaties, 468
Cooper, Ashley Anthony (Earl of Shaftesbury), 37
Cooper, Peter: railroad locomotive and, 258 (illus.)
Cooperationists, 288
Copperheads, 302
Coral Sea, battle of, 534
CORE. *See* Congress of Racial Equality (CORE)
Corliss engine, 353, 354 (illus.)
Cornwallis, Charles (Lord), 95, 97–98
Coronado, Francisco Vásquez de, 13
Coronel, Don Antonio Franco, 285
Corporations: collapse of, 680; criticism of, 569; impact of Civil War and, 307; in 1920s, 488; protection of, 179; Unabomber and, 674
Corruption: corporate, 680; Grant and, 325–326, 392; Harding and, 498; Jefferson and Madison on, 131; in oil industry, 360; political machines and, 376; in politics, 378; railroads and, 356; in Reconstruction governments, 320; of Redeemer regimes, 327; in St. Louis, 426
Cortés, Hernán, 11
Cosmopolitan magazine, 426
Costa Rica, 640
Cost of living: in cities, 656; Nixon and, 610 (illus.)
Cotton and cotton industry: commercial agriculture in, 173–174; cotton gin and, 218, 253 (illus.); factories in, 175; society in Old South and, 205; spinning mills in, 149; synthetics and, 489. *See also* Textiles and textile industry
Cotton Belt, 205
Cotton famine: during Civil War, 299
Cotton gin, 218, 258 (illus.)
Cotton Kingdom, 212–213, 218–220
Coughlin, Charles, 511, 516
Council of Economic Advisers: Kennedy and, 583
Council of Foreign Ministers: meeting on Germany, 549
Council of National Defense, 478
Council of Nobles (Carolina), 37, 38
Council of the Indies (Spain), 12
Counterinsurgency: Kennedy and, 578, 579
County court: in Virginia, 26
County Election (Bingham), 201 (illus.)
Coups. *See* specific countries
Court(s): Adams' midnight appointments to, 141; desegregation and, 609; federal, 128; freedpeople's use of, 321–322; Jefferson and, 153–154; vice-admiralty, 52. *See also* Supreme Court (U.S.)
Court of Chancery (London), 54
"Court-packing" scheme: of Roosevelt, Franklin D., **517**
Covenant: with Puritans, 29
Coverdale, Miles, 15
Covert actions: under Eisenhower, 560–561; in Nicaragua, 640; in Vietnam, 590
Cowboys: clothing of, 343 (illus.); race and ethnicity of, 343–344
Cowpens, battle at, 92 (illus.), 97
Cow towns, 344
Cox, James M., 483
Coxey, Jacob S., 397
Coxey's Army, 397
Crack cocaine, 645
Craft unions: in Great Depression, 513. *See also* Labor unions; specific unions
Crane, Stephen, 401
Crash. *See* Stock market crash (1929)
Crawford, William C., 177; election of 1824 and, 190–191
Crazy Horse, 335
Creative adaptations, 2
Credit: commercial, 174; for consumer purchases, 67; Hamilton's system of, 130–131; installment, 487; Panic of 1873 and, 323; sharecropping and, 318; stock purchases with, 504
Crédit Mobilier scandal, 325, 356
Creditor nation: U.S. as, 479
Creek Indians, 62, 168, 194 (illus.)
Creel, George, 476
CREEP (Committee to Re-Elect the President), 607, 608, 613
Creoles, 50
Crime and criminals: asylums and, 235; in cities, 373, 656; convict settlers and, 61; crack use and, 645; in 1920s, 491; prisons and, 236; Supreme Court on rights of, 585
Crittenden, John, 290
Crittenden compromise, 290
Croats, 669
Cromwell, Oliver, 22
Crop lien system, 327–328
Crops: in Carolina, 38; in Columbian Exchange, 6; commercial, 174; from West, 347. *See also* specific crops
Croquet (game), 378
Crossroads of the Pacific: Hawaiian islands as, 411
Crow Indians, 333
Crown Point: surrender by French, 75
Cuba, 407; attempts to acquire, 272–273; Bay of Pigs fiasco, 580–581; Castro in, 561, 578; government of, 422; independence of, 410, 414, 418, 422; missile crisis in, 581–582; Platt Amendment and, 422; rebellion against Spain by, 413; reconcentration policy in, 413; Teller Amendment and, 414; U.S. intervention in, 466, 468
Cuban Americans, 658
Cuban missile crisis, 581–582
Cullen, Countee, 493
Cult of Domesticity, 232–233, 239
Cultural identity, 660–661
Culture: acculturation of immigrants and, 80–81; African American, 50, 51 (illus.); American vs. British, 70–72; Anglicization of, 53; Aztec, 4; boarding school for Indian children and, 335–336; clothing and, 186, 187; colonial, 42–43, 64–68, 77; Eastern Woodland, 4–5, 5 (illus.); European, 5–8, 64–68; European-Indian trade and, 6–7; of frontier, 169–170; Hispanic in Southwest, 340; of immigrants, 375; of Irish, 17; in Jacksonian era, 186–189; machine, 353; Native American, 3–5, 5 (illus.); new urban, 435–440; New World clash of, 1–2; Renaissance and, 9–10; republican, 104–105; revolution in 1960s, 595; section-

alism in, 276; and social change (1877-1900), 376–383; theater and, 103; trade and, 67–68; urban, 490–491; in West Africa, 8–9; of work, 364–365. *See also* Art(s); Diversity; Society; specific groups
Currency: greenbacks as, 322–323; standardized and reliable, 307. *See also* Money
Curriculum: in late 19th century higher education, 381; in late 19th century schools, 380
Currier and Ives: Fort Sumter bombardment lithograph and, 291 (illus.)
Custer, George A., 335, 341, 351
"Custer's Last Stand," 335, 336 (illus.)
Customs: African, 51 (illus.); expansion of, 52; Indian, 1, 7. *See also* Culture; Lifestyle; specific groups
Customs commissioners, 89
CWA. *See* Civil Works Administration (CWA)
Czech Americans, 596
Czechoslovakia: coup in (1948), 544, 548; fall of repressive government in, 649; German invasion of, 526, 527
Czolgosz, Leon, 404

D

Dakota Territory: Indian removal to, 334–335
Daley, Richard J.: Democratic convention of 1968 and, 600–601
Dallek, Robert, 630
Dalrymple, Oliver, 346
Dams, 431
Dance: experimentation in, 438; ragtime music and, 437
Darrow, Clarence, 383, 497
***Dartmouth College* v. *Woodward*, 179**
Darwin, Charles, 383, 408; evolution theory of, 497
Daschle, Tom, 680; anthrax scare and, 685
Daugherty, Harry, 498
Davies, John, 17
Davis, Jefferson, 303; leadership of, 292, 295–297; as president of Confederacy, 289
Davis, John W., 500
Dawes, William, 91
Dawes Severalty Act (1887), **336**
Dayton plan, 670
D-Day, 539
Deadwood, 341
Dean, John, 607, 608, 613
Dearborn, Henry, 150
Death camps: in World War II, 539, 539 (illus.)
Death rate. *See* Mortality rate
Deaver, Michael, 646
Debates: Kennedy-Nixon, 577; Lincoln-Douglas, 278
De Bow's Review, 220
Debs, Eugene V., 397, 442, 448, 453, 458; World War I repression and, 477
Debt: in Civil War, 295; pre-revolutionary, 101; for purchases of manufactured goods, 67; after Revolution, 114; after Seven Years' War, 85; state, 131; in West, 169; after World War I, 523. *See also* National debt
Decker, Sarah P., 445
Declaration of Independence, 93; fiftieth anniversary of, 163
Declaratory Act (1766), 99 (illus.)
Deep South: creation of Confederacy by, 289; secession of, 288–290. *See also* South
Deere, John: steel plow and, 258 (illus.), 259
Defense Department, 550
Defense of Marriage Act (1996), 622
Defense spending, 562; Kennedy and, 578, 583; in Korean War, 554; Reagan and, 630, 634, 635, 637
Defense workers: in World War II, 536
Deficit(s), 615; Bush, George, and, 648, 649; Clinton and, 654, 663; decline of, 672; energy crisis and, 615; Gramm-Rudman and, 635; Kennedy and, 583; in 1970s, 617; in overseas trade, 635; Reagan and, 634–635; reduction of, 667; Roosevelt, Franklin D., and, 518
Deflation: Specie Resumption Act and, 323
De Gaulle, Charles, 532
Deism: decline of, 227
Delaware, 32, 37 (illus.); in Civil War, 292; Three Lower Counties as, 35, 36
Delaware River, 35 (illus.); Washington and, 95
De La Warr (Lord), 24
De Leon, Don Martin, 285
De Lôme, Enrique Dupuy, 413–414
Demagogues: in Great Depression, 511–512
Democracy: along frontier, 113; Hamilton on, 129; in Japan, 551; in theory and practice, 185–190
Democratic-Conservatives: in South, 323–324
Democratic National Committee: break-in at, 612
Democratic party, 270, 271; convention of 1835 and, 198; convention of 1968 and, 600–601; in 1870s and 1880s, 391; election of 1852 and, 271; election of 1860 and, 280–281; election of 1894 and, 399; election of 1896 and, 401–403; election of 1968 and, 599–601; election of 1970 and, 610; election of 1984 and, 636–637; election of 1992 and, 661–662; election of 2000 and, 677–678; emancipation and, 301; establishment of, 191; New Deal coalition and, 516, 518, 519–520; in 1920s, 499–500; Redeemers and, 327; second party system and, 200–201; in South, 328; Young America and, 244
Demography: of blacks, 50; of Chesapeake region, 46–47; multiethnicity and, 660
Demonstrations: antiwar, 594–595, 611; civil rights, 584
Dempsey, Jack, 491
Deng Xiaoping, 649 (illus.)
Dentistry: nitrous oxide and, 377
Departments of government, 128. *See also* specific departments
Department stores, 362
Depressions: of 1870s, 346; of 1890s, 385, 390, 396–399; after Panic of 1819, 189, 195; after Panic of 1837, 198. *See also* Great Depression (1930s)
Deregulation, 633
Desegregation: of military, 572; Nixon and, 609; of public facilities, 574; of schools, 573
Deseret, 250
Desertions: from army (1865-1890), 352
Desert Land Act (1877), 339
Desktop computers, 673 (illus.)
Detective thrillers (popular fiction), 437–438
Détente policy, 610–**611,** 626; Reagan and, 638
Detention centers: for Japanese Americans, 538
Detroit: riots in, 537, 596
Detroit, Fort, 160
Dewey, George, 416, 416 (illus.)
Dewey, John, 447
Dewey, Thomas E.: election of 1944 and, 538; election of 1948 and, 555
Díaz, Porfirio, 468
Dickinson, John, 110; Constitution (U.S.) and, 117
Dictators and dictatorships: in Central America, 639; Hitler as, 525; Mussolini as, 525. *See also* specific countries and individuals
Diem, Ngo Dinh, 559, 579–580, 580 (illus.)
Dien Bien Phu, 558
Diet (food): changes in, 377; of Civil War soldiers, 295 (illus.); Columbian Exchange and, 6; in 1880s, 377; innovations in, 361; in Spanish-American War, 415. *See also* Food
Dime novels, 337
Dingley Tariff, 403, 456
Diphtheria, 377
Diplomacy: "big stick," 467 (illus.); during Civil War, 299; "dollar diplomacy," 467–468; with France, 133; King Cotton, 299; moral, 468; transatlantic telegraph and, 361; *Trent* incident and, 299; of Wilson, 472; in World War II, 539–540
Direct current: low-voltage, 362
Direct election: of senators, 457
Direct primary, 448
"Dirty tricks": in election of 1972, 612–613
Disabled people: Social Security and, 512. *See also* Americans with Disabilities Act (ADA) (1991)
Disappearing quorum rule, 393
Disarmament: naval, 524–525; Soviets and, 546
Discovery (ship), 23
Discrimination: against Mexican Americans, 537–538; against new immigrants, 374; against women in occupations and education, 431; in World War II, 536. *See also* African Americans; specific groups
Disease: in Columbian Exchange, 6; in Continental Army, 96; European impact on Native Americans, 6 (illus.), 8; farm-bred, 431; medical science revolution and, 377; smallpox and, 62; in Spanish-American War, 415, 418; in Virginia, 23–24, 26; from working conditions, 364; yellow fever, 422
Disestablishment: of state churches, 106–107
Disfranchisement: of blacks, 328, 432
Dissembly factories: in meatpacking industry, 361
Dissent: during Civil War, 295; crushing of, 138–139; in Massachusetts, 31–32
Distribution of wealth: Great Depression and, 505. *See also* Poverty; Wealth
District courts, 128
District of Columbia: abolition of slave trade in, 269; as capital, 149. *See also* Washington, D.C.
Diversity: in Clinton cabinet, 662–663; of colonists, 60–62; ethnic, 660–661; Franklin on, 80; immigration and, 605; in Middle Colonies, 32–34; in New York colony, 33
Divorce: grounds for, 108; of Henry VIII (England), 15; increase in, 431; in late 19th century, 380; in 1970s, 618; in World War II, 536

Dix, Dorothea, 236, 236 (illus.)
Dixiecrats, 555
Dobrynin, Anatoly, 581
Dodd, Samuel T. C., 360
Dole, Bob, 667
"Dollar diplomacy," 467–468
Dolliver, Jonathan P., 456
Domestic policy. *See* specific presidents
Dominican order, 12
Dominican Republic: Johnson, Lyndon B., and, 589; U.S. intervention in, 466, 468
Dominion of New England, 54, 55
Donelson, Fort, capture of, 297
"Don't ask, don't tell" policy: for gays in military, 621–622
Dos Passos, John, 483, 493
Douglas, Stephen A., 287, 291; Compromise of 1850 and, 269; debates with Lincoln, 278; election of 1860 and, 280–281; Freeport Doctrine of, 278; Kansas-Nebraska Act and, 271–272; Lecompton constitution and, 277–278
Douglas, William O., 585
Douglas Democrats, 281
Douglass, Charles and Lewis, 302 (illus.)
Douglass, Frederick, 238, 238 (illus.), 302 (illus.), 321 (illus.)
Dove, Arthur, 439
Downtowns, 436
Dowry, 44
Draft (military): in Civil War, 293, 301–302; in Vietnam War, 594; for World War I, 474; for World War II, 528
Drake, Edwin L., 360; oil well and, 258 (illus.)
Drake, Francis, 16; in Roanoke, 18
Dred Scott v. *Sandford*, 276–277, 278
Dreiser, Theodore, 401
Drinking. *See* Alcohol and alcoholism
Drug Enforcement Agency (DEA), 645
Drug industry: regulation of, 453–454
Drugs and drug use (illegal), 645–646. *See also* War on Drugs
Drug subculture, 595, 601
Dry farming, 346
Du Bois, W. E. B., 381, 382, 432, 478, 493
Dudley family, 46
Due process of law: in territories, 113
Dukakis, Michael, 647, 648
Duke's Laws, 33
Dulles, John Foster, 558, 559
Duncan, Isadora, 438
Dunmore (Lord), 93
Dunn, Harvey, 476 (illus.)
Du Pont Corporation, 428, 452, 526
Duquesne, Fort, 74, 75
Dutch: in New Netherland, 32–33
Dutch East Indies: Japan and, 531, 534; in World War II, 529, 530
Dutch Reformed Calvinists, 34
Dutch West India Company, 32
Duties: on trade, 52. *See also* Tariff(s); Taxation
Dwight, Timothy: Calvinism and, 228–229
Dylan, Bob, 595

E

Eagle: as patriotic symbol, 128 (illus.)
Earned income tax credit: for working poor, 663
Earp, Wyatt, 344
Earth: geography of, 11
East: steel plant closings in, 617
Eastern Europe: Gorbachev and liberation of, 649; immigrants from, 374; Marshall Plan and, 548; Stalin and, 533; after World War II, 544
Eastern front: in World War I, 473 (illus.)
Eastern Woodland cultures, 4–5, 5 (illus.)
East Florida, 166
East Germany, 579; Khrushchev and, 561–562; opening of Berlin Wall and, 649
East Indies. *See* Dutch East Indies
East Jersey, 34. *See also* New Jersey
Eastman Kodak, 428
East St. Louis: race riot in, 478
Easy-money factions, 322–323
Eaton, John, 192
Eaton, Peggy O'Neale, 192, 194
Eckford, Elizabeth, 573 (illus.)
Ecology: European settlement and, 7. *See also* Environment
Economic aid: after World War II, 545–546
Economic mobility: industrialization and, 365
Economic nationalism, 404
Economics: attack on classical, 383–384; supply-side, 634
Economy: under Articles of Confederation, 116; boom in 1990s, 655; Bush, George W., and, 679; of Carolina, 38; Clinton and, 654, 663; of Confederacy, 294; election of 1992 and, 661; farming and, 347; government role in, 499; Hamilton on, 129, 131–132; immigrants in, 657; Jefferson on, 129–130; Kennedy and, 583; market, 173–176; New Deal impact on, 518–519; in 1950s, 565, 572; in 1970s, 617–618; in 1990s, 666, 672; Nixon and, 609–610, 610 (illus.); *Nixonomics* and, 609–610; of North (Civil War), 294; oil shocks and, 615; patterns of growth in, 488; Persian Gulf War and, 652; post-World War II boom in, 566–567; railroads and, 257, 355; Reagan and, 631, 632–633, 636; recession and recovery of, 634; recession of 1937 and, 517; recovery in 1990s, 662–663; Roosevelt, Franklin D., and, 507–508; Soviet, 546; stock market crash (1929) and, 504–505; surplus in, 672; transformation of, 66–67; transportation and, 171; in Virginia, 24–25, 53; weaknesses in, 489–490; of West, 332; western mines and, 342–343; during World War II, 535–536
Eden, Anthony, 560
Edison, Thomas Alva, 353, 361–362
Edison Illuminating Company, 362
Education: of African Americans, 659; in antebellum era, 234–235; of Asian Americans, 659–660; Bush, George W., and, 680; in Chesapeake, 48; common school movement and, 234–235; compulsory, 235; debating societies and, 235; of elites, 46; for freedpeople, 322; of Hispanics, 658; Johnson, Lyndon B., and, 588; in late 19th century, 380–381; lyceums and, 188, 235; for Mexican Americans, 597; NDEA and, 570; in New England, 44; in Northwest Ordinance, 113; pragmatism and reform of, 447; southern nationalism and, 276; suburban development and, 568; techniques in late 19th century, 381; for women, 108, 431; women's earnings and, 619. *See also* Schools
Edward VI (England), 15
Edwards, Jonathan, 68
Efficiency: in workplace, 429
Effigy jars: Mississippian, 3 (illus.)
Egypt: Camp David Accords and, 625; October War and, 614; Suez crisis and, 560
Ehrlichman, John, 608, 613
Eighteenth Amendment, 445
Eight-hour workday, 365, 435, 446, 456, 478; on interstate railways, 461
Eisenhower, Dwight D.: Baruch Plan and, 546; Cold War and, 558–563; Commission on National Goals of, 575; Cuba and, 580; election of 1952 and, 557–558; election of 1956 and, 561; farewell address of, 562–563; Highway Act of 1956 and, 571–572; McCarthy and, 557–558; on military-industrial complex, 562–563; Modern Republicanism of, 570–572; as NATO supreme commander, 549; Normandy invasion and, 532, 539; school desegregation and, 573; Vietnam and, 558–559
El Alamein, battle at, 532
El Caney, Cuba: battle at, 417
Elderly. *See* Aged
Elect: Calvin on, 14; in New England, 44; Puritans as, 29
Elections, 201 (illus.); of 1788, 127–128; of 1796, 137; of 1800, 141; of 1804, 153; of 1808, 158; of 1812, 159; of 1816, 177; of 1824, 190–191; of 1826, 191; of 1828, 185, 191–192; of 1832, 196–197; of 1836, 198; of 1840, 199–200; of 1844, 244, 251–252; of 1848, 268, 287; of 1852, 271; of 1854, 274; of 1855, 274; of 1856, 275; of 1860, 280–281, 281 (illus.); of 1864, 303–305; of 1866, 314, 315; of 1868, 322, 323; of 1872, 323–324, 325, 380; of 1875, 325; of 1876, 311, 326, 392; between 1876–1892, 392; between 1876–1896, 391; of 1878, 311; of 1880, 311; of 1884, 393; of 1888, 392, 393; of 1890, 394, 396; of 1892, 396; of 1894, 399; of 1896, 343, 399, 401–403; of 1900, 404, 420, 448; of 1904, 448, 453; of 1908, 454; of 1910, 456; of 1912, 442–443, 448, 457–458; of 1914, 459; of 1916, 461, 472; of 1918, 480; of 1920, 477, 483, 498; of 1924, 498; of 1928, 498, 500–501; of 1932, 507; of 1934, 511; of 1936, 516; of 1938, 517; of 1942, 538; of 1944, 538; of 1948, 554, 554 (illus.); of 1952, 557–558; of 1956, 561; of 1960, 577–578; of 1964, 587; of 1968, 599–601; of 1970, 610; of 1972, 612–613; of 1976, 623; of 1980, 630, 631–632; of 1984, 636–637; of 1986, 642; of 1988, 647–648; of 1992, 661–662, 662 (illus.); of 1994, 665–666; of 1996, 667 (illus.); of 2000, 678 (illus.); deadlock in, 391–392; presidential debates and, 577; turnout for presidential, 448–449. *See also* Electoral college
Electoral college: election of 1796 and, 137; election of 1800 and, 141; election of 1824 and, 191; election of 2000 and, 678
Electoral votes, 118
Electorate: Democratic, 501; voting between 1876-1896, 391. *See also* Voting and voting rights
Electricity, 487; consumer products and, 488; Edison and, 362; leisure time and, 379;

signs and, 379; transportation and, 372; Westinghouse and, 362
Elementary and Secondary Education Act (1965), 588
Elevated rapid transit, 372
Elevators, 353, 372
Eliot, Charles W., 381
Eliot, T. S., 439, 492
Elites: in English politics, 70; Hamilton and, 129; housing of, 66 (illus.); in New England, 46
Elizabeth I (England), 14, 15; religion and, 15–16
Elkins Act (1903), 453
Ellis Island: immigrant experience on, 388–389
Ellsberg, Daniel, 607
El Salvador: leftists in, 624–625
Ely, Richard T., 383–384, 451
Emancipation, 267; backlash against, 301; in Tennessee, 313; Ten Percent Plan and, 312
Emancipation Proclamation, 300
Embargo: on arms sales in World War II, 528; Jeffersonian, 157–158; in World War II, 530
Embargo Act (1807), **157**–158
Emerson, Ralph Waldo, 276; on Civil War, 307–308; lyceums and, 188; transcendentalism and, 241; Young America and, 244
Empire(s): acquisition of, 418–424; American, 407, 420 (illus.), 687; French, 13–14; governing, 421–422; Portuguese, 11; Spanish, 11–13, 62–64, 64 (illus.); spirit of, 408–409; world colonial empires (1900), 421 (illus.); worldwide scramble for, 408. *See also* specific empires
Employees: federal, 499. *See also* Workers
Employers: iron law of wages and, 366; labor unions and, 365
Employers' liability laws, 450
Employment: of blacks, 536; Clinton and, 666; by 1990, 635; of women, 490, 618–619. *See also* Jobs; Unemployment; specific groups
Employment Act (1946), 554
Empresarios, 247
Encomienda system, **12**
"Enemies list": of Nixon, 607
Energy: electric, 487; steam engine and, 258 (illus.); worldwide race for, 412
Energy crisis, 614–616; energy policy and, 616; locking gas caps and, 616 (illus.); oil shocks in, 615
Engerman, Stanley, 221
Engineering: of Erie Canal, 172, 172 (illus.)
England (Great Britain): *Alabama* claims and, 410; American Revolution and, 93–96, 97–98; border conflicts with, 245, 253–254; borders in Canada and, 166; China and, 422; colonies and, 21–40, 59, 70–72, 73 (illus.), 99 (illus.); Confederate diplomacy and, 299; constitution in, 70; exploration by, 14; Fourteen Points and, 480; France and, 97, 132; Georgia and, 37 (illus.), 38 (illus.), 39–40; Hay-Pauncefote Treaty and, 465–466; immigrants in mining camps, 342; Indians and, 62; Irish colonization by, 16–17; Jay's Treaty with, 133; Latin America and, 181–182; Madison and, 158; mainland colonies of, 37 (illus.); nationalism in, 16; New Amsterdam and, 33; Open Door Policy and, 423; Oregon occupation with, 166; Protestantism in, 15–16; Protestant Reformation and, 15; renewed involvement in colonies, 50–53; Roanoke settlement by, 17–18; Samoa and, 412; Spanish Armada attack on, 16; Suez crisis and, 560; trade with, 158; Treaty of Ghent and, 161–163; U.S. shipping and, 133, 156, 158; Venezuela-British Guiana boundary dispute and, 410; voyages of exploration by, 12 (illus.); War of 1812 with, 159–163; Webster-Ashburton Treaty and, 245. *See also* British empire; World War I; World War II; specific rulers
English language: Bible in, 15
Enlightenment, 65–66, 228–229
Enrollment Act (1863), 301
Enron, 680
Entertainment: and leisure (1877-1900), 378–379; in Progressive Era, 437–438
Entitlement programs: Reagan and, 632
Entrepreneurs: industrialization and, 355; Jeffersonians on, 127
Enumerated goods, 51–52
Environment: ancient migration to Americas and, 2; of Chesapeake, 46; European settlement and, 7; of Great Plains, 332, 346; human behavior and, 446–447; human development and, 377; New World encounters and, 8; nuclear testing and, 561; Watt and, 633. *See also* Pollution
Environmental movement: energy policy and, 616
Environmental Protection Agency (EPA), 616
Epidemics: AIDS, 643–644. *See also* Disease
Episcopalians: Democratic party and, 200
Equality: for blacks, 318–319, 595–596; Civil Rights Act (1964) and, 587; for ethnic nationalities, 596–597; Fifteenth Amendment and, 323; Fourteenth Amendment and, 315; gay liberation movement and, 620–622; meaning of, 82; of Quakers, 34; after Revolution, 104; social behaviors and, 146; between states, 178; for women, 107–108, 107 (illus.), 567, 597–598, 618–620. *See also* Equal Rights Amendment (ERA); Liberty; Rights
Equal Rights Amendment (ERA), 619; of 1923, 598; of 1972, 598, 619, 620 (illus.)
Era of Good Feelings, 176, 182
Ericson, Leif, 9
Eric the Red, 9
Erie Canal, 171–172, 172 (illus.)
Erie Railroad, 356
Erskine, David M., 158
Escobedo v. *Illinois,* 585
Espionage Act (1917), **477**
Estates: in Virginia, 66 (illus.)
Ethiopia: Italian invasion of, 525
Ethnic Albanians: in Kosovo, 671
Ethnic cleansing: in Bosnia, 669–670; in Kosovo, 671
Ethnic groups and ethnicity: acculturation and, 80–81; in Bosnia-Herzegovina, 666; Catholic immigrants and, 273; of colonists, 60–62; diversity of, 660–661; of immigrants, 605–606; in mining camps, 342; of minorities, 605–606; in Pennsylvania, 61; social role of, 596; zoning laws and segregation of, 436. *See also* specific groups
Ethnic Heritage Studies Act (1972), 596
Ethnic nationalism, 596–597
Ethnocentrism: English, 17; of European explorers, 7
Eugenics, 433
Europe and Europeans: Adams, John Quincy, and, 180–181; before conquest of Americas, 9–11; ideas from, 64–68; Indian cultures and, 5–8; Indian relations with, 62; Marshall Plan and, 547–548, 548 (illus.); Monroe Doctrine and, 181; Napoleonic Wars in, 156–157; nation-states of, 9–10; New World and, 1–2, 10–11; religion and Reformation in, 14–15; after Treaty of Versailles, 481 (illus.); U.S. foreign policy and, 409; U.S. defense of, 549; U.S. military divisions in, 549; U.S. retreat from, 523; West African settlements and, 8, 9; World War I and, 473 (illus.); World War II and, 526–527, 533 (illus.), 538–539, 543, 544–545, 545 (illus.)
European Recovery Program. *See* Marshall Plan
Evangelicals and evangelicalism, 61; abolitionism and, 226; families and, 231–233; in Great Awakening, 68, 69 (illus.); in late 19th century, 378; middle class and, 283; missionary and benevolent societies and, 229–231; reform and, 229–231; revivals and, 226; rise of, 227–231; Second Great Awakening and, 227–231; of slaves, 208–209; utopianism and, 239–240; Whigs and, 198, 200
Evans, Oliver: steam engine and, 258 (illus.)
Evergood, Philip, 514
"Everybody Works but Father" (song), 400
Evolutionary theory: literature and, 400; Scopes Trial and, 497. *See also* Darwin, Charles
Excess-profit tax, 499
Executive: as president, 118; in Virginia Plan, 118; weak, 116
Executive departments, 128
Executive powers: Lincoln and, 295, 312
Ex-Federalists: Whigs and, 197
Exodusters, 345
Expansion and expansionism: All Mexico movement and, 255; borderlands of 1830s and, 245–246; California gold rush and, 257; costs of, 262; election of 1844 and, 251–252; to Far West, 245–251, 257; into Florida, 166; foreign (1867-1900), 409–411; internal, 256–262; Japanese, 523, 524, 529–530; Mexican-American War and, 255–256; by mid-nineteenth century, 246 (illus.); *Moby-Dick* and, 244; overseas, 407, 408; Pierce and, 272–273; railroads and, 257; after Spanish-American War, 418–424; Texas annexation and, 244, 251–252; after War of 1812, 166–170; Young America and, 244, 245. *See also* Westward movement
Expatriate writers: in 1920s, 492–493
"Experiment in Misery, An" (Crane), 401
Exploration and discovery: creative adaptations and, 2; by Dutch, 32–33; by England, 14; by France, 6, 13–14; by Lewis and Clark, 152; by Spain, 11–13; by Vikings, 9; voyages of, 12 (illus.); west of the Mississippi, 332
Exports: of agricultural products, 347; auto, 633; controls of, 114; foreign markets and, 408; regulation of, 52; to West Indies, 67

F

Factions: of Hamilton and Jefferson, 132; Madison on, 116; Washington on, 136. *See also* Political parties; specific parties
Factories: agricultural supplies to, 173 (illus.); discipline of, 364; in Great Depression, 504; mobility of labor supply for, 365; in textile manufacturing, 175; Triangle Shirtwaist Company fire and, 429; workers in large, 428
Factory inspection laws, 450
Factory system: status of housewives and, 379
Fair competition: business codes of, 509
Fair Deal, 570
Fair Employment Practices Commission (FEPC), 570
Fair Employment Practices Committee (FEPC), 536, 587
Fair Labor Standards Act (1938), 513
Fall, Albert, 498
Fallen Timbers, battle of, 134, 148 (illus.)
Falwell, Jerry, 629
Families: alcoholism and, 231; in antebellum era, 231–234; in Chesapeake region, 46–47; childhood and, 233–234; child labor and, 446; Cult of Domesticity and, 232–233; education of children and, 234–235; in English colonies, 42; focus on children, 431; of freedpeople, 321; along frontier, 169–170; of immigrants, 374–375; in late 19th century, 379; marriage for love and, 231; in Massachusetts Bay, 29; in middle class, 636; migration by, 605, 606 (illus.); in mining, 397; in New England, 43–44; in 1920s, 490–491; in 1950s, 567; in 1970s, 618; power in, 107; size of, 377; in slavery, 207–208; in World War II, 536
Family and Medical Leave Act (1993), 666
Family planning agencies, 620
Far East: Roosevelt, Theodore, and, 467
Farewell Address: of Eisenhower, 562; of Washington, **136**
Farewell to Arms (Hemingway), 483
Farmer's Alliance, 394, 395–396; Ocala Demands and, 395
Farmer's Alliance and Industrial Union, 395
Farm Labor Standards Act (1938), 519
Farms and farming: Alliance movement and, 394, 395–396; bonanza farms, 346; cattle ranching and, 344; commercialism, scientific methods, and, 347; credit for, 460; crop lien system and, 327–328; debt and, 169; depression of 1890s and, 390, 396; discontent and, 394–395; dry farming, 346; Exodusters as, 345; foreign markets for, 408; by German immigrants, 60; Grange and, 346–347; greenback movement and, 322–323; licensed warehouses for farm products, 461; by Native Americans, 336; in 1920s, 489, 499; planters and, 205, 212–214, 218–220; populism and, 394; in Progressive Era, 430–431; Roosevelt, Franklin D., and, 509; sharecropping and, 318, 319 (illus.), 432; Shays's Rebellion and, 117; tenant farmers and, 430–431; in West, 339, 345–347; Whiskey Rebellion and, 136; yeomen and, 46, 205, 214–215. *See also* Agricultural Revolution; Agriculture; Diet; Diet (food); Food
Farm Security Administration (FSA), 509, 510 (illus.), 519
Farmworkers: Mexican, 596–597, 597 (illus.); migrant and immigrant, 431
Far West: settlement of, 166–168
Faubus, Orval, 573 (illus.)
FDIC. *See* Federal Deposit Insurance Corporation (FDIC)
Federal agencies. *See* Agencies
Federal Aid Roads Act (1916), 427–428
Federal budget deficit. *See* Deficit(s)
Federal Bureau of Investigation (FBI): Watergate Scandal and, 613
Federal Communications Commission (FCC, 1934), 519
Federal Deposit Insurance Corporation (FDIC), 518
Federal elections bill (1890), 394
Federal Emergency Relief Administration (FERA), 518
Federal Farm Loan Act (1916), 460
Federal Farm Loan Board, 460
Federal government: authority of, 113–116. *See also* Government (U.S.)
Federal Housing Administration (FHA, 1934), 519
***Federalist, The,* 120**; No. 10, 117
Federalists, 120–121, 127, 132; Adams' appointment of, 141; Alien and Sedition Acts and, 139; decline of, 150, 154, 161; election of 1796 and, 137; election of 1808 and, 158; after War of 1812, 176; Washington's Farewell Address and, 136. *See also* Ex-Federalists
Federal judges: Reagan administration appointment of, 647. *See also* Judiciary
Federal regulatory system: restructuring of, 648
Federal Reserve Act (1913), **458**–459
Federal Reserve Board, 459, 631; Cinton and, 663; Great Depression (1930s), 504; Greenspan and, 654; inflation and, 617; tight money policy of, 634
Federal Trade Commission, 459
Federal Workmen's Compensation Act, 461
Female suffrage. *See* Woman suffrage
Feminine Mystique, The (Friedan), 597, 598 (illus.)
Feminism, 597–598, 598 (illus.); domestic, 233; in 1920s, 490–491; social-justice movement and, 445; after World War II, 567
Feminization of professions, 364
Femme couverte doctrine, 380
Fencing: barbed wire for, 346; of ranches, 345
FEPC. *See* Fair Employment Practices Commission (FEPC); Fair Employment Practices Committee (FEPC)
FERA. *See* Federal Emergency Relief Administration (FERA)
Ferber, Edna, 347
Ferdinand (Aragon) and Isabella (Castile), 10–11
Ferraro, Geraldine, 637
Fertility rates: decline in, 379
Fessenden, William Pitt, 314
Fetterman, William J., 334
Fetterman massacre, 334
Feudal system: in Maryland, 27
Fiction: popular, 437–438. *See also* Literature
Field, Cyrus W., 361
Field, Marshall, 362
Fifteenth Amendment, 316 (illus.), **323,** 328, 394
54th Massachusetts Colored Regiment, 302 (illus.)
Filipinos, 659. *See also* Philippines
Fillmore, Millard, 269, 275
Films. *See* Movies and movie industry
Finances: under Articles of Confederation, 114; Hamilton on, 130–132; after Revolution, 112
Financing: of Civil War, 294–295; for railroads, 356, 358; of World War II, 536
Finney, Charles G.: revivals and, 226, 229; teachings of, 229; Weld, Theodore Dwight, and, 237
Finney, Fort, 110
Fireside chats: of Roosevelt, Franklin D., 507–508
First Congress, 128, 144. *See also* Congress (U.S.)
First Continental Congress, 91
First Reconstruction Act (1867), 316
First United States Volunteer Cavalry (Rough Riders), 407
First World War. *See* World War I
Fish, Hamilton, 410
Fishing: Indians and, 18 (illus.)
Fiske, John, 409
Fisk University, 382
Fitch, John: steamboat and, 258 (illus.)
Fitzgerald, F. Scott, 491, 493
Fitzhugh, George: proslavery arguments and, 216
Five and ten cent store, 362
"Five civilized tribes": removal of, 168
$5 day, 435
Five Power Treaty, 525
"Flapper" era, 491, 492 (illus.)
Flatboats, 171
Fletcher v. *Peck,* 154
Flexible response, 578–579
Flight 93: on September 11, 2001, 681
Florida: boom in, 656; British control of, 76; election of 2000 and, 678; Georgia and, 39; Jefferson and, 150; obtaining, 166; after Revolution, 100; secession of, 289; Spain in, 13
Flower children: in 1960s, 595
Flu. *See* Influenza
Fogel, Robert, 221
Folk, Joseph W., 426
Folklore: of West, Indians in, 337
Folkways, 147; of workplace, 429
Fonda, Jane, 607
Food: regulation of industry, 453–454; in Virginia, 24. *See also* Agricultural Revolution; Agriculture; Diet (food); Farms and farming
Food Administration, 477, 478 (illus.)
Food riots: in Confederacy, 294
Football, 437, 491; intercollegiate, 378–379
Foraker Act (1900), **422**
Force Acts (1870-1871), **323**
Force Bill: of 1833, 195; of 1890, 394
Ford, Gerald R., 612; election of 1976 and, 623; foreign policy of, 623; inflation and, 617; oil shocks and, 615; presidency of, 622–623; SALT talks and, 626
Ford, Henry, 405, 435, 486
Ford Motor Company, 427, 487
Fordney-McCumber Tariff Act (1922), 499
Ford's Theater: Lincoln's assassination at, 305

Foreign aid: export trade and, 566; after World War II, 545–546
Foreign-born Americans: in 1920s, 494–495. *See also* Immigrants and immigration
Foreign investments: before World War I, 465
Foreign markets: Asian, 410; economic growth and, 408; industrialism and need for, 412
Foreign policy: Carter and, 631; of Clinton, 667–672; of Eisenhower, 558–562; end of activist, 602; under Ford, 623; global tensions after Cold War and, 668; isolationism as, 525–527; Japan and, 524–525; Jay's Treaty and, 133–134; of Jefferson, 157; of Johnson, Lyndon B., 589–593; of Kennedy, 578; in late 19th century, 409–411; of Madison, 158–159; Monroe Doctrine and, 180–181; neutrality in, 132–133; from 1901–1920, 465; Nixon and, 608; nontransfer principle in, 410; Open Door Policy toward China, 423–424; of Pierce, 272–273; Reagan and, 637–642; of Roosevelt, Franklin D., 526; of Roosevelt, Theodore, 465–466; Roosevelt Corollary and, 466–467; Spain and, 115–116; Washington and, 132–134, 136; of Wilson, 468–470; after World War I, 522; XYZ Affair and, 137–138
Foreign trade, 566; deficit in, 635. *See also* Trade
Forestation, 339
Forest preserve program, 454
Forest Service, 454
Formosa. *See* Taiwan
Formosa Straits: Chinese islands in, 559
Forts: in California, 63; in western lands, 110. *See also* specific forts
"40 acres and a mule," 318
Foster, John W., 411
Founders, 127
Fourier, Charles, 239
Fourierist phalanxes, 239–240, 240 (illus.)
"Four-minute men," 476
Four Power Treaty, 525
"Four-Square Gospel," 497–498
Fourteen Points, 479, 480, 480 (illus.)
Fourteenth Amendment, 314–315, 316 (illus.), 328; Reconstruction Acts and, 315; separate but equal schools and, 573
Fox, George, 34
Fox Indians, 168
Frame of Government (Penn), 35
Framers of Constitution. *See* Constitution (U.S.)
France: Adams, John, and, 141; American Revolution and, 96–97; British fighting with, 132; China and, 422; colonies of, 73 (illus.); Confederate diplomacy and, 299; exploration and settlement by, 13–14; fall to Hitler, 528; Fourteen Points and, 480; Free French and Vichy government in World War II, 532; immigrants in mining camps, 342; imperial wars and, 72–73; Indians and, 6, 62; Indochina and, 558–559; Louis XI in, 10; Louisiana Purchase from, 151–152; Madison and, 158; Napoleonic Wars and, 156–157; Normandy landing in, 539; Ohio Valley and, 74; Open Door Policy and, 423; in Southeast, 63; South Vietnam and, 559; Suez crisis and, 560; voyages of exploration by, 12 (illus.); in World War II, 529; XYZ Affair and, 137–138. *See also* Franco-American treaties; World War I
Franciscans, 12
Franco-American treaties, 97, 133
Frankfurter, Felix, 478, 585
Franklin, Benjamin: Albany Plan of, 74; antislavery societies and, 107; on colonial diversity, 80; Constitution and, 117, 124; Enlightenment and, 65; France and, 96; Treaty of Paris and, 99–100
Franz Ferdinand, 470
Fraternal societies: for new immigrants, 375
Fraud: corporate, 680
Freake, John and Elizabeth, 45 (illus.)
Fredericksburg: battle of, 298
Free blacks, 107–108; efforts at voluntary colonization of, 300; in Old South, 210–211; in Virginia, 107. *See also* African Americans
Free coinage of silver, 394
Freedmen's Bureau, 314, 318, 319; marriage of freedpeople and, 321; schools of, 322
Freedom(s): of African Americans, 107; in Bill of Rights, 123; McCarthyism and, 558; of religion, 113; terrorism and, 683. *See also* specific freedoms
"Freedom ride," 584
Freedom's Journal, 238
Freedpeople: Black Codes and, 313–314, 318–319, 321; contract labor of, 318; education for, 322; institutions of, 322; land for, 316, 318; marriage and, 321; public and private rights for, 320–322; regimentation within South, 301; sharecropping and, 318
Free French government: in World War II, 532
Free labor: slavery and, 268, 274
Free mail delivery, 363 (illus.)
Freemen: in Chesapeake, 48; in Massachusetts, 30; in Virginia, 53
Freeport Doctrine, 278
Free soil, 266
Free-Soilers, 267–268; in Kansas, 274–275
Free-Soil party, 268, 271
Free Speech movement: in 1960s, 593
Free states: Missouri Compromise and, 177–179
Freethinkers: evangelicalism and, 227
Free trade: NAFTA and, 663–664; U.S. and, 354
Frémont, John C., 254, 275
French and Indian War. *See* Seven Years' War
French empire, 13–14, 75
French Indochina: Japanese occupation of, 530
French Revolution, 132–133
Fresh Air Fund, 374
Frick, Henry Clay, 367
Friedan, Betty, 597, 598 (illus.)
Friedman, Milton, 630
Frontier, 135 (illus.); democracy along, 113; in 18th century, 58–59; imperial wars along, 72–73; people and culture of, 169–170; southwestern, 134; Spanish along, 63; Turner's thesis on, 347–348
Fronts. *See* specific wars
Frost, Robert, 440
FSA. *See* Farm Security Administration (FSA)
Fuchs, Klaus, 556
Fuels: energy policy and, 616
Fugitive Slave Law (1850), **269,** 270, 270 (illus.); Jacobs, Harriet, and, 225
Fugitive slaves: in Florida, 166
Führer (leader): Hitler as, 525
Fulbright, William, 589, 599
Fulton, Robert, 149, 171
Fundamental Constitutions of Carolina, 37
Fundamentalism: Christian, 568, 629; Islamic, 682; in 1920s, 497–498
Fundamental Orders (Connecticut), 32
Funding: Hamilton on, 130–131
Furniture: colonial, 65
Fur trade: Astor and, 166–167; French and, 6; French-Indian, 13

G

Gabriel's rebellion. *See* Prosser, Gabriel
Gadsden Purchase (1853), 255, 273
Gage, Thomas: American Revolution and, 91; as Massachusetts governor, 90
Gallatin, Albert, 149–150, 157
Galveston, Texas, 449
Games: in late 19th century, 378
Gangsters: in 1920s, 491. *See also* Crime and criminals
Gardner, Lloyd, 610
Gardoqui, Diego de, 116
Garfield, James A., 393, 408, 410
Garland, Hamlin, 395
Garrett, Pat, 340
Garrison, William Lloyd, 432; antislavery movement and, 237–238; attempted lynching of, 237; *Liberator, The* and, 237; Turner, Nat, and, 204; women's rights and, 238
Gasoline: energy crisis and, 614, 615; locking gas caps and, 616 (illus.)
Gates, Horatio, 95, 97
Gauguin, 439
Gay Activist Alliance, 621
Gay consciousness, 621
Gay Liberation Front, 621
Gay liberation movement, 618, 620–622, **621**
Gays and lesbians: AIDS and, 643, 644; in military, 621–622, 662; public attitudes toward, 622
Gender and gender roles: in Chesapeake region, 47; Cult of Domesticity and, 232–233; division of labor in Plains tribes, 333; marriage and, 231; of migrants to Spanish borderlands, 63; in New England, 29, 45 (illus.); in 1920s, 490; power and, 107; voting by, 666; women's liberation movement and, 597–598
Gender gap, 619
General Court (Massachusetts): Hutchinson and, 32
General Electric, 428
General Federation of Women's Clubs, 445
General Motors, 487
Genêt, Edmond, 133
Geneva: Reagan-Gorbachev summit in, 642
Geneva Conference (1958), 561
Geneva summit (1955), 544
Gentry: in Chesapeake, 48; public opinion and, 127
Geographic mobility: industrialization and, 365
George I (England), 72–73
George II (England), 74, 91
George III (England), 83, 84 (illus.)
George, Henry, 383
Georgia, 37 (illus.), 38 (illus.), 39–40; secession of, 289; western land claims of, 111–112
Germain, George (Lord), 95

German immigrants, 59, 60–61, 260, 273; acculturation of, 80; in mining camps, 342
German mercenaries. *See* Hessian mercenaries
Germantown, battle at, 96
Germany: automobiles from, 617; China and, 422; Open Door Policy and, 423; Paris Peace Conference and, 480, 481; peace with Russia, 477; reparations and, 481, 523; in Samoa, 412; submarine warfare by, 464–465, 472, 473; *Sussex* pledge and, 472; U.S. loans to, 523; Zimmerman telegram and, 473; zones in, 544. *See also* German immigrants; Nazi Germany; World War I
Germs. *See* Disease; Germ warfare; Medicine
Germ warfare: by British against Indians, 62
Geronimo (chief), 352
Gerry, Elbridge, 137
Gettysburg: battle of, 303, 304 (illus.)
Gettysburg Address (Lincoln), 288
Ghent, Treaty of, 161–163
Ghettos: riots in, 596
Ghost Dances, 335
***Gibbons* v. *Ogden*, 180**
Gideon v. *Wainwright*, 585
Gilbert, Humphrey: as military governor of Ireland, 17
Gilded Age: politics in, 391–393
Gilman, Charlotte Perkins, 380
Gingrich, Newton Leroy ("Newt"), 665, 666
Ginsburg, Ruth Bader, 619; *Roe* v. *Wade* and, 620
Glaciers, 2
Gladden, Washington, 385
Glasgow, Ellen, 493
Glasnost, 642
Glass ceiling, 619
Glass-Steagall Act (1933), 518
Glenn, John, 570
Glidden, Joseph, 346
Glorious Revolution, 22; in Bay Colony, 54–55; in England, 22; in Maryland, 55–56; in New York, 55
GNP. *See* Gross national product (GNP)
Godspeed (ship), 23
Golan Heights, 614
Gold: bond sales, 402; Comstock Lode, value of silver, and, 343; conquistadores and, 13; discoveries and removal of Indians, 333; discoveries in Australia and Alaska, 403; Sherman Act, silver coinage, and, 394, 399; from Spanish colonies, 13
Goldberg, Arthur, 585
Golden spike: transcontinental railroad and, 357
Gold Rush of 1849, 341; disease and, 333
Gold standard: Bland-Allison Silver Purchase Act and, 393–394
Gold Standard Act (1900), **404,** 404 (illus.)
Goldwater, Barry, 587, 590; Reagan and, 629
Golf, 491
Goliad massacre, 248
Gompers, Samuel, 366, 434, 459, 478
Good Housekeeping (magazine), 567
Good Neighbor Policy, 467, 524
Goods: enumerated, 51–52; in Triangular trade, 67. *See also* Consumer goods market
Goodyear, Charles: rubber and, 258 (illus.), 259
Gorbachev, Mikhail, 642
Gordon, Thomas, 70
Gore, Al: election of 2000 and, 677–678, 678 (illus.)
"Gospel of prosperity," 320
Gothic Revival architecture, 233 (illus.)
Gould, Jay, 357, 366
Government: Albany Plan and, 74; in Carolina, 36; city manager form, 449; of colonies, 70–72; commission form, 449; of Confederacy, 289; of Connecticut, 32; of Dominion of New England, 54; of Massachusetts, 30–31; Mayflower Compact and, 28; of Middle Colonies, 33–34; of New Jersey, 34; of New Spain, 12; of Pennsylvania, 35; political machines in city, 375–376; promotion of industry by, 354–355; republican, 104–105; after Revolution, 104; state, 108–109; of Virginia, 24–25, 26
Government (U.S.), 109–113; civil rights activism by, 573, 574; employment of blacks by, 536; establishment of, 127–128; implied powers of, 179–180; inflation in 1970s and, 617; Jefferson on, 140, 150; New Deal agencies of, 517; powers after Civil War, 306; Republican shutdown of, 666; role in economy, 499; supremacy over states, 306; western economies and, 332; western lands ceded to, 111–112
Governors: colonial, 71; reform, 450–451; of states, 109
Gradualist approach: of Washington, Booker T., 382, 432
Graduate school, 381
Graham, Billy, 611
Gramm-Rudman, 635
Gramm-Rudman-Hollings Balanced Budget Act. *See* Gramm-Rudman
Granada: Muslims in, 10
Grand Alliance (Europe), 180
Grandfather clause: voting and, 391
Grandparents: in Chesapeake region, 47; in New England, 43
Grange. *See* National Grange of the Patrons of Husbandry
Grange, Red, 491
Grant, Madison, 497
Grant, Ulysses S., 317; in Civil War, 297, 302, 303, 304 (illus.); corruption and, 325–326, 392; election of 1868 and, 322; expansionism of, 410; greenbacks and, 323; spoilsmen and, 325; violence in south and, 325
Grape boycott, 597, 597 (illus.)
Grasse (Comte de), 98
Grateful Dead, 595
"Great American Desert," 332
Great Awakening, 68–70
Great Britain. *See* England (Great Britain)
Great Depression (1930s), 503, 504–520; effect of, 505–506; fighting against, 506–507; isolationism during, 525–527; minorities during, 515; recession of 1937 and, 517; Roosevelt, Franklin D., in, 507–520; World War I debt payments and, 523. *See also* New Deal
Greater East Asia Co-Prosperity Sphere, 529
Great Gatsby, The (Fitzgerald), 493
Great Lakes: Erie Canal and, 171–172, 172 (illus.); naval forces in, 166; in War of 1812, 160
Great Northern Railroad, 452
Great Plains: environment of, 332, 346; farming on, 345–346. *See also* Plains Indians
Great Railroad strike of 1877, 366, 367 (illus.)
Great Society, 587–588, 602; immigration policy of, 605–606; Nixon and, 608–609
Great War. *See* World War I
Greece: immigrants from, 374; Truman Doctrine and, 547
Greeley, Horace, 325, 332
Greenbackers, 322
Greenback movement, 322–323
Green Berets: Kennedy and, 578
Greene, Nathanael, 97
Green party: in election of 2000, 677
Greensboro, North Carolina: sit-ins in, 574
Greenspan, Alan, 654; Clinton and, 654–655, 663 (illus.); economic boom and, 672
Greenville, Treaty of, 134
Greenwich Village: artists in, 438–439
Grenada: U.S. invasion of, 640
Grenville, George, 85; fall of, 87
Grenville, Richard, 18
Grierson, Benjamin H., 351
Griffith, D. W., 437
Grimké, Angelina, 239
Grimké, Sarah, 239
Grocery stores, 362
Gross national product (GNP): oil shocks and, 615; real, between 1865-1914, 355; after World War II, 567
Guadalcanal, battle at, 535
Guadalupe Hidalgo, Treaty of, 255, 285
Guam, 465; cession of, 418; naval control of, 422
Guatemala: CIA covert action in, 560–561
Guerrière (ship), 160
Guerrilla warfare: in Kansas, 275; in Philippines, 419–421
Guilford Courthouse, battle at, 92 (illus.), 97
Guillotine: in French Revolution, 132
Guiteau, Charles J., 393
Gulf of Mexico region: in World War II, 536
Gulf of Tonkin Resolution, 590
Gulf War. *See* Persian Gulf War
Guns: Indian trade for, 6; school violence and controls over, 675
Gurkin, Michael, 388

H

Habeas corpus, writ of: Lincoln's suspension of, 295
Haeckel, Ernst, 409
Haig, Alexander, 638, 640
Haile Selassie (Ethiopia), 525
Haiti: intervention in, 669; U.S. intervention in, 468
Hakluyt, Richard, 22; on New World, 18
Haldeman, H. R., 608, 613
Half-Way Covenant, 44
Hallam, Lewis, 103
Halleck, Henry W., 298
Hall v. *DeCuir*, 328 (illus.)
Hamilton, Alexander, 107; antislavery societies and, 107; Articles of Confederation and, 115; Burr and, 155; Constitution (U.S.) and, 117; on economic future of United States, 131–132; election of 1796 and, 137; *Federalist, The,* and, 120; financial plan of, 130–132; High Federalist followers of, 138;

ideology of, 129–130; party identification and, 126; provisional army and, 138–139; as Secretary of Treasury, 128; Whiskey Rebellion and, 136
Hamilton, Alice, 434
Hammer v. *Dagenhart,* 446
Hampton Normal and Industrial Institute, 381
Hancock, John, 89
Handcart (Christensen), 250 (illus.)
Handheld computer, 673 (illus.)
Handy, M. C., 437
Hanna, Marcus A., 401–402, 404–405
Hannibal and St. Joseph Railroad, 343
Hanoverian dynasty (England), 72–73. *See also* specific kings
Harding, Warren G., 483, 484, 498, 499
Hard-money factions, 322, 323
Harlem Renaissance, 493
Harpers Ferry, Virginia: John Brown's raid on, 279
Harper's Weekly, 324
Harrington, Michael, 587
Harris, Eric, 675
Harrison, Benjamin, 393, 393 (illus.), 394, 396, 408, 410, 411
Harrison, William Henry, 159; death of, 251; election of 1836 and, 198; election of 1840 and, 199
Harte, Bret, 357
Hartford Convention, 161
Harvard University, 381, 445
Hatch, Edward, 351
Hatch Act (1887), 346
Haub, Carl, 660
Hawaii, 410; as American protectorate, 411; annexation of, 411; Pearl Harbor attack and, 530–531, 531 (illus.); territorial status and citizenship for, 421
Hawkins, John, 16
Hawks: U.S. military and, 582
Hawthorne, Nathaniel, 188, 241–242
Hay, John, 414, 423, 465
Hay-Bunau-Varilla Treaty, 466
Hayes, Rutherford B., 326, 392–393
Hay-Herrán Convention (1903), 466
Haymarket Riot, 366, **367,** 367 (illus.)
Haynesworth, Clement, 609, 610
Hay-Pauncefote Treaty, 465–466
Headright system: in Carolina, 36; in Virginia, **25**
Head Start program, 587
Health: in Chesapeake region, 46–47; Clinton and health care reform, 664–665; in New England, 43
Health, Education, and Welfare Department, 571; Califano and, 623
Health care: Carter and, 623; in 1880, 377
Held, John, Jr., 492 (illus.)
Heline, Oscar, 503
Heller, Walter, 583
Hell's Kitchen, 384
Helper, Hinton Rowan, 216, 280
"Helperism," 280
Hemingway, Ernest, 483, 492–493
Hemophiliacs: AIDS and, 643
Henri, Robert, 439
Henry VII (England), 10; exploration and, 14
Henry VIII (England): Protestant Reformation and, 14, 15
Henry, Fort, capture of, 297
Henry, John, 103
Henry, Patrick, 86, 91; as Antifederalist, 121; Constitution (U.S.) and, 117
Henson, Josiah, 238
Hepburn Act (1906), **453**
Herblock, 559 (illus.)
Herrán, Thomas, 466
Herring,, George, 592
Hessian mercenaries, 93; at Trenton, 95
Hickok, Wild Bill, 344
Hierarchy: in New England society, 45–46
Higher education: in Chesapeake, 48; professional training emphasized in, 382. *See also* Universities and colleges
High Federalists, 138; secession plans of, 155
High Plains, 332
Highway Act (1956), 571–572
Highways. *See* Roads and highways
Hijackings. *See* September 11, 2001, terrorist attacks
Hill, Anita, 647
Hillsborough (Lord), 88
Hippies. *See* Flower children; Youth movement
Hiroshima: atomic bombing of, 541
Hispanic America and Americans, 657–658; after 1848, 285–286; categories of, 658; on southwestern frontier, 340
Hiss, Alger, 556
Historia de las Indias (Las Casas), 12
History and historiography: "new Western historians," 348; on sectional crisis leading to Civil War, 281–283; on Turner's thesis of the frontier, 347–348. *See also* specific historians
"History of the Standard Oil Company" (Tarbell), 426
Hitler, Adolf, 525; Austria, Czechoslovakia, and, 526–527; Battle of the Bulge and, 539; European control by, 531; Munich conference and, 526; suicide of, 539. *See also* Nazi Germany; World War II
HIV, 644. *See also* AIDS
Hobo jungles: in Great Depression, 506
Ho Chi Minh, 558, 579; in North Vietnam, 559
Hoe, Richard M.: rotary printing press and, 258 (illus.)
Hoffman, Abbie, 595
Hofstadter, Richard, 386
Holbrooke, Richard, 670
Holding company, 361
Holidays: Mother's Day as, 431. *See also* Thanksgiving
Holland: English migration to, 22; Scrooby Separatists in, 28; trade and, 32–33. *See also* Dutch entries
Holliday, Doc, 344
Hollings, Ernest, 635
Hollow Men, The (Eliot), 492
Holmes, Oliver Wendell, 188
Holocaust, 539
Holy Experiment: of Penn, 35–36
Home fronts: in Civil War, 293–295, 297; in World War II, 535–538
Homeland Security, department of, 682–683
Homelessness: in late 19th century, 384 (illus.)
Homemaking, 431
Home rule: for South, 326
Homestead Act (1862), 306, **339,** 391
Homestead Strike, 359, 367–**368,** 367 (illus.)
Homosexuals. *See* Gay liberation movement; Gays and lesbians
Honduras, 640
Hooker, Joseph, 302
Hooker, Thomas, 32
Hookworm disease, 431
Hoover, Herbert C.: bonus army and, 507; economy and, 499; election of 1928 and, 498, 500–501; election of 1932 and, 507; Food Administration and, 477; Great Depression and, 506–507; as secretary of commerce, 498
Hope, Bob, 611
Hopewell peoples, 3
Hopi Indians, 332
Hopkins, Harry, 509; African Americans and, 515
Horse: Plains Indians and, 333
Hospitals: in late 1800s, 377
Hostages: in Iran, 625–626, 637; Iran-Contra affair and, 641
Hotel boom, 184–185
"Hot line": between U.S. and Soviet Union, 582
Hourly wages: in 1920s, 487
"House divided" speech (Lincoln), 278
Households: changing family structure and, 618; female-headed, 587; freedpeople's rights in, 320–321; in New England, 44
House Judiciary Committee: Watergate and, 613
House of Burgesses (Virginia), **24**–25; Henry in, 86; after Revolution, 109
House of Commons (England), 70
House of Lords (England), 70
House of Representatives (U.S.), 118; membership in, 145; sectionalism in election of speaker, 280
House of Seven Gables, The (Hawthorne), 242
House Un-American Activities Committee (HUAC), 556
Housewives: factory system and status of, 379. *See also* Women
Housing: of elites, 66 (illus.); of freedpeople, 319 (illus.); Gothic Revival architecture and, 233 (illus.); Johnson, Lyndon B., and, 589; skyscrapers, 372; slums, 372; sod houses, 345–346; tenements, 373; in World War II, 536
Houston: growth of, 656
Houston, Sam: Republic of Texas and, 248
Howe, Elias: sewing machine and, 258 (illus.), 259
Howe, Frederick C., 470
Howe, William, 94–95, 97
Howells, William Dean, 400
How the Other Half Lives (Riis), 373
HUAC. *See* House Un-American Activities Committee (HUAC)
Hudson, Henry, 32
Hudson, Rock, 643
Hudson Bay region, 14
Hudson River Railroad, 357 (illus.)
Huerta, Victoriano, 469
Hughes, Charles Evans, 450, 472, 498, 525
Hughes, Langston, 493
Huitzilopochtli (god), 4
Hull, Cordell, 524, 530, 539
Hull, Isaac, 160

Hull House, 385
Human behavior: environment and, 446–447
Humanitarianism: of U.S. in Kosovo, 671
Human rights: Carter and, 626; in China, 668
Human sacrifice: by Aztecs, 4
Hume, David, 116
Humphrey, Hubert H., 587, 599–600
Hundred Days: of Roosevelt, Franklin D., 507–508
Hungary: fall of repressive government in, 649
Hunt, E. Howard, 607, 608, 613
Hunting: of buffalo, 337; in North America, 2–3
Huron Indians: Christianity and, 7
Hussein, Saddam, 651, 652; capture of, 687; Clinton and, 668; destruction of statue of, 685 (illus.); war with Iraq and, 684–686; WMD and, 684
Hutchinson, Anne, 31
Hutchinson, Thomas, 84, 89
Hyde amendment, 620
Hydrogen bomb (H-bomb), 550–551, 550 (illus.)

I

ICBMs. *See* Intercontinental ballistic missiles (ICBMs)
ICC. *See* Interstate Commerce Commission (ICC)
Ice Age: migration to Americas and, 2
Ice boxes, 377
Ickes, Harold, 510
Idaho, 332, 338
Identity: African American, 50; American, 80–81, 147; cultural, 660–661; ethnic, 596–597; racial, 596
Ideology: republican, 104, 116; sectional crisis and, 282; women and, 107–108
"I Didn't Raise My Boy to Be a Soldier" (Bryan and Piantadosi, song), 470 (illus.)
"I Have a Dream" speech (King), 584, 585 (illus.)
Iliff, John F., 339
Illegal aliens. *See* Undocumented aliens
Illinois, 110; Cahokia in, 3; immigrants in, 657; railroad regulation in, 392; slavery outlawed in, 113
Illiteracy: of African Americans, 381; of blacks (1900-1910), 432; decline in, 380
Illness. *See* Disease
Immigrant associations, 375
Immigrants and immigration: American identity and, 80–81; from Asia, 655, 659–660; attempts to limit, 433; as benefit or liability, 657; to Carolina, 38; Chinese Exclusion Act and, 364; in cities, 372, 373–375, 375 (illus.); in Civil War, 306; Democratic party and, 200; election of 1852 and, 271; Ellis Island and, 388–389; as farm workers, 431; federal control of, 388; first/second class vs. third class (steerage), 388; Hispanics and, 657–658; illegal, 657; industrialization and, 260–262, 354; in labor force, 432–433; from Latin America, 655; laws against, 389; to Maryland, 27; mass, 259–260; from Middle East, 659–660; in mining, 342, 397; nativism and, 273–274; new immigrants, 374, 432; in 1920s, 494–495; in 1990s, 657; to "old country," 433; policy toward, 605–606, 606 (illus.); railroad land and westward migration of, 339, 340 (illus.); restrictions on, 496–497; settlement houses and, 385; settlement patterns of, 433; slaves and, 9; sources of, 373–374; in thirteen colonies, 59 (illus.); urbanization and, 260; in West, 338; World War I and, 470–471, 497. *See also* Migration; specific groups
Immigration Act (1965), 605–606, 655
Immigration and Naturalization Service (INS), 658, 683
Impeachment: of Belknap, William E., 326; of Chase, Samuel, 154; of Clinton, 676; constitutional definition of, 154; of Johnson, Andrew, 316–317, 392; of Pickering, 153–154
Impending Crisis of the South, The (Helper), 216, 280
Imperialism, 408; election of 1900 and, 420; evolutionary theory and, 408; foreign markets and, 408; renunciation of, 524
Imperial Valley (California): farming in, 431
Imperial wars, 72–77; American Revolution and, 97
Implied powers: Hamilton on, 131; Supreme Court on, 179–180
Imports: from England, 67; of oil, 616; increase in (1816), 176; tax on, 128; Triangular trade and, 67
Impost of 1781, 115
Impressment: Treaty of Ghent and, 162, 163. *See also* Royal Navy
Inaugural address: of Lincoln (first), 290, 291
Inauguration: of Jefferson, 141, 149
Incandescent lamp, 362. *See also* Electricity
Incas, 4
Inchon, battle at, 553
Incidents in the Life of a Slave Girl (Jacobs), 225
Income: of Asian Americans, 660; increase in, 436; in 1929, 487; in 1970s, 617; after World War II, 567
Income tax: Johnson, Lyndon B., and, 586–587; in 1920s, 499; Reagan's cuts, 634; Sixteenth Amendment and, 456; withholding of, 536
Indentured servants, 25–26; in Chesapeake, 46–47, 48; convict settlers as, 61
Independence: Americanization of colonies and, 59; American Revolution and, 93–98; French recognition of U.S., 96–97; Treaty of Paris and, 100; vote for, 93. *See also* American Revolution
India: immigrants from, 659
Indiana, 110; slavery outlawed in, 113
Indian Country, 333; opening to white settlers, 347
Indian Intercourse Act (1834), 333
Indian policy: assimilation and, 335–336; concentration policy as, 333–334; "one big reservation" as, 333; peace policy and, 334–335, 351; small reservation policy as, 334–335
Indian removal, 333; during Jackson administration, 192–193, 194 (illus.); Tocqueville on, 202
Indian Reorganization Act (1934), 515
Indians: naming of, 11. *See also* Native Americans; Paleo-Indians; specific groups
Indian Territory: removal to, 335
Individualism: impact of Civil War on, 307–308; radical, 241
Indochina: Dien Bien Phu and, 558–559; division of, 559; in World War II, 529
Industrial capitalism: immigrants and, 374
Industrialization: carrying trade and, 149; early, 174–176. *See also* specific industries
Industrial psychology, 435
Industrial research laboratories, 428
Industrial Revolution, 257–262; agricultural labor force and, 175; second, 487–490
Industrial Workers of the World (IWW), 434, 435 (illus.)
Industry and industrialization, 353–369; automation and, 429; black workers and, 536–537; British, 67; child labor and, 261; costs and benefits of, 368–369; and culture of work, 364–365; decline in manufacturing industries, 635; development in, 354–355; factory mode of production and, 258–259; foreign markets for, 408; immigration and, 259–260; Industrial Revolution and, 257–262; inventions and, 361–362; labor and, 365–368, 367 (illus.); literature and, 400; marketing and advertising in, 362–363; mass production and, 258–259; in 1970s, 617; of North (Civil War), 294; oil industry and, 359–361; protective tariffs for, 176; railroads and, 355–358; shift to Sunbelt and, 617; slavery and, 220; in South, 327; steel industry and, 358–359; trusts in, 360; wage earners and, 363–368; after War of 1812, 175; women and, 261; during World War II, 535–536. *See also* Labor unions; Organized labor; specific industries
Inequality: in Jacksonian era, 185–186; of wealth, 636
Infant industries: after War of 1812, 175
Infant mortality, 436; in Chesapeake, 48; between 1877 and 1900, 377
Inflation, 177; under Articles of Confederation, 114; in Civil War, 294, 295; decline in, 635; Kennedy and, 583; in 1970s, 617; in 1980s, 631, 634; in 1990s, 672; Nixon and, 609; Reagan and, 632; in Spain, 13
Influence of Sea Power upon History, The, 1660–1783 (Mahan), 412
Influenza, 6, 8
Initiative, 450
Injunctions, 366; against Pullman strike, 397
Inner Light: of Quakers, 34
In re Debs, 366, 397
Installment credit, 487
Insull, Samuel, 488
Integration: of schools, 573. *See also* Civil rights; Civil rights movement; Desegregation
Intellectual societies: in Philadelphia, 65–66
Intellectual thought, 568–569; beats and, 569; conservatism and, 630; Enlightenment and, 65–66; impact of European, 64–68; in 1920s, 492–493; on poverty and wealth, 383–385; during Progressive Era, 446–448; in Renaissance, 10; social Darwinism, 383; Social Gospel, 385. *See also* Philosophy
Inter-American Conference (1889), 410
Intercoastal trade, 67
Intercollegiate Athletic Association, 437
Intercollegiate football, 378–379, 437
Intercontinental ballistic missiles (ICBMs), 578, 638
Interest groups, 449; Madison on, 116–117

Interest of America in Sea Power, The (Mahan), 412
Interest rates: Clinton and, 663; decline in, 634; in 1970s, 617; Shays's Rebellion and, 117
Interlocking directorates, 428, 459
Intermediaries: marketing and, 174
Intermediate nuclear forces (INF), 642
Intermediate Nuclear Forces agreement (1987), **642**
Internal improvements, 176, 177; in postwar South, 320; transportation revolution and, 170–173
International drug cartels, 645
International Force (IFOR): U.S. troops in, 670, 671
International Harvester Corporation, 433
Internationalism: in late 1800s, 408
Interracial marriage: European-Indian, 7, 13; in Latin America, 13
Interracial violence, 50
Interstate commerce: government regulation of, 180
Interstate Commerce Act (1887), 392
Interstate Commerce Commission (ICC), 392, 453; segregation banned by, 584
Interstate highway system, 571–572, 571 (illus.)
Interventionists: in World War II, 528
Intolerable Acts. *See* Coercive (Intolerable) Acts (1774)
Intravenous (IV) drug users: AIDS and, 643
Inventors and inventions: Franklin and, 65; industrialization and, 361–362; naval, 10; practical, 258 (illus.). *See also* Technology; specific inventors and inventions
Investment: foreign, 465; in industrial development, 354; in stock market, 504
Investment banking: control of railroad industry by, 358; in 1920s, 488
IQ tests: racism and, 497
Iran: covert action in, 560; hostage crisis in, 637; Revolution in (1979), 625
Iran-Contra affair, 641–642
Iranian hostage crisis, 625–626
Iraq: Clinton and, 668; fund for reconstruction of, 686; recovery in, 687; war with (2003), 680, 684–686
Ireland: English in, 16–17, 22; immigrants from, 260, 273; as model for English colonies, 17
Irish Americans: antidraft riot of, 301
Iron and iron industry: ore for steel industry, 359; strike in, 494
Iron Curtain, 544
Iron law of wages, 366
Iroquois Indians, 8
Irrigation, 332, 431; in West (to 1917), 430 (illus.); of western land, 339
Isabella of Castile, 10. *See also* Ferdinand (Aragon) and Isabella (Castile)
Islam: fundamentalism and, 682; in West Africa, 8
Isolationism, 408; after World War I, 525–527
Israel: Camp David Accords and, 625; Clinton and, 668; October war and, 614; PLO, Lebanon, and, 639; Six-Day War and (1967), 614; withdrawal from Sinai, 638
Issei: in World War II, 538
Isthmian Canal Commission, 466
Italian Americans, 596
Italy: Allied invasion of, 533; expansion by, 525; immigrants from, 373, 374; Mussolini in, 525; Open Door Policy and, 423
Itinerant preachers, 69
IWW. *See* Industrial Workers of the World (IWW)

J

Jackson, Andrew, 184; Bank War and, 195–197, 196 (illus.); battle of New Orleans and, 161; cabinet and Kitchen Cabinet of, 192; Calhoun, John C., and, 194; East Florida and, 166; Eaton affair and, 192, 194; election of 1824 and, 190–191; election of 1826 and, 191; election of 1828 and, 185, 191–192, 199; election of 1832 and, 196–197; Force Bill (1833) and, 195; historiography of, 185; inauguration of, 185; Indian removal and, 192–193, 194 (illus.); nullification crisis and, 193–195; as Old Hickory, 192; personality of, 192; Polk and, 252; portrait of, 187 (illus.); specie circular of, 198; spoils system and, 192
Jackson, Mississippi: battle at, 304 (illus.)
Jackson, Patrick Tracy, 175
Jackson, Rachel, 191
Jackson, Thomas J. "Stonewall," 298
Jacksonian Democracy, 190–195
Jackson State College: student killings at, 611
Jacobins: in French Revolution, 132
Jacobs, Harriet, 224–225
James, William, 377, 447
James I (England), 22; tobacco and, 24; Virginia as royal colony and, 26; Virginia colony and, 23
James II (England), 22; Massachusetts charter annulled by, 54; Middle Colonies and, 33; New Jersey and, 34
Jamestown, 18; society in, 26
Janson, Charles William, 146
Japan: in American consumer goods market, 635; atomic bombing of, 540–541; automobiles from, 617; China and, 422; defeat of, 540–541; expansion and, 467, 523, 525, 529–530; in Far East, 467; halting of, 534–535; immigrants from, 431, 433, 659; Manchuria seized by (1931), 525; militarism in, 525; navy of, 524; in 1970s, 611; Open Door Policy and, 423; Pearl Harbor attack by, 530–531, 531 (illus.); rivalry with, 524–525; surrender of, 541; as U.S. ally, 552; war with Russia, 467; after World War II, 551
Japanese Americans: detention in World War II, 538
Japanese immigrants: discrimination against, 364
Jay, John: antislavery societies and, 107; as chief justice, 128; *Federalist, The,* and, 120; Mississippi River navigation and, 116; Treaty of Paris and, 99–100
Jay's Treaty, 133–**134,** 137
Jazz (music), 437, 493
Jazz Age: arts in, 492–493; city life in, 490–493; as Roaring Twenties, 491–492
Jefferson, Thomas: Barbary War and, 152; census of 1790 and, 144, 145; Constitution (U.S.) and, 117; critics of, 153–156; death of, 163; Declaration of Independence and, 93; on disestablishment, 106; election of 1796 and, 137; election of 1800 and, 141; election of 1804 and, 153; Embargo Act of, 157–158; European wars and, 156–157; foreign policy of, 157–158; ideology of, 129–130; on Indians, 168; Kentucky Resolutions and, 140; Louisiana Purchase and, 150–152; on manufacturing, 132; Northwest Ordinance and, 112–113; party identification and, 126; presidency of, 149–153; as Secretary of State, 128; slave trade and, 155–156; as strict constructionist, 146–147; as vice president, 137
Jeffersonians, 127. *See also* Republicans (Jeffersonian)
Jeffords, James M., 680
Jennings, Samuel, 119 (illus.)
Jerseys, 33 (illus.). *See also* New Jersey
Jesuits: in Maryland, 27
Jews and Judaism: from eastern Europe, 375; holocaust and, 539, 539 (illus.); as immigrants, 373, 374; pogroms against, 373; in Soviet Union, 626; on Supreme Court, 459–460
Jim Crow laws, 328–329, 432
Jobs: for African Americans, 489, 659; Clinton and, 666; free vs. slave competition for, 107; Johnson, Lyndon B., and, 587; for women, 618–619. *See also* Employment; Occupations
Jobs Corps, 587
Johns Hopkins University, 381
Johnson, Andrew, 314 (illus.); Congress and, 314–315; impeachment of, 316–317, 392; Reconstruction policies of, 313–314; on slavery, 313
Johnson, Hiram, 456
Johnson, James Weldon, 493
Johnson, Lyndon B., 578; assumption of presidency by, 586–587; election of 1964 and, 587; election of 1968 and, 599; Great Society and, 587–588; on Immigration Act (1965), 605; reforms under, 588–589; as Senate Majority Leader, 571; Vietnam War and, 589–593, 598–599, 600 (illus.); War on Poverty and, 587
Johnson, Tom L., 449–450
Johnson Hiram, 450
Johnston, Joseph E., 298, 305
Joint Chiefs of Staff: on gays in military, 621
Joint-stock company, 23
Jones, Samuel M. "Golden Rule," 449
Jonesboro, Arkansas: school violence in, 675
Joplin, Scott, 378
Joseph (Chief), 335
Journalism: muckraking and, 426; transatlantic telegraph and, 361; yellow, 413. *See also* Press
Judicial review, 153
Judiciary: Marshall and, 179; in Watergate Scandal, 613. *See also* Court(s); Supreme Court (U.S.)
Judiciary Act (1798), 128; repeal of, 153
Jungle, The (Sinclair), 453, 454
Junta: in El Salvador, 624–625
Justice Department: civil rights division of, 572
"Just Say No" drug campaign, 645

K

Kaczynski, Theodore J.: as Unabomber, 674
Kael, Pauline: on 1930s, 503

Kaiser, The: Beast of Berlin (film), 476
Kaiser Aluminum: affirmative action at, 659
Kallen, Horace, 660
Kansas: African Americans in, 345
Kansas-Nebraska Act (1854), 271–273, **272,** 272 (illus.), 274, 287; extension of slavery and, 266
Kansas Territory, 266; Free-Soilers vs. slaveholders in, 274–275; Lecompton controversy and constitution in, 277–278; popular sovereignty in, 274–275
Kasserine Pass, battle at, 532
Kearney (ship), 529
Kearney, Fort, 338
Kearny, Stephen: Mexican-American War and, 254
Keating-Owen Act (1916), 446, 461
Kelley, Oliver H., 346
Kellogg, Frank B., 482, 522
Kellogg-Briand Pact (1928), **522,** 525
Kelly, William, 358; air-boiling process and, 258 (illus.)
Kendall, Amos: election of 1828 and, 191
Kennan, George, 547
Kennedy, Anthony, 647
Kennedy, Edward M. ("Ted"), 623, 631; Bush, George W., and, 680
Kennedy, John F.: assassination of, 586; Bay of Pigs fiasco and, 580–581; civil rights and, 583–584; Cuban missile crisis and, 581–582; election of 1960 and, 577–578; King and, 584; New Frontier and, 582–586; presidential debate by, 577
Kennedy, Robert F., 581; assassination of, 600; as attorney general, 582; election of 1968 and, 599, 600
Kent State University: student killings at, 611, 612 (illus.)
Kentucky, 110, 113, 166; in Civil War, 292, 297
Kentucky and Virginia Resolutions, 139–**140**
Kerosene, 360
Kerouac, Jack, 569
Key, Francis Scott, 161
Khmer Rouge: in Cambodia, 624
Khomeini, Ayatollah Ruholla, 625, 641
Khrushchev, Nikita, 561; Berlin crisis and, 579; Cuban missile crisis and, 581–582
Kickapoo Indians, 351
Kilrain, Jake, 379
Kim Il-Sung, 552
Kindergarten, 381
King, Martin Luther, Jr.: assassination of, 596; "I Have a Dream" speech of, 584, 585 (illus.); Kennedy and, 584; March on Washington and, 584, 585 (illus.); Montgomery bus boycott and, 574; SCLC and, 574; SNCC and, 596; voting rights and, 588–589
King, Rodney, 659
"King Cotton diplomacy," 299
King George's War, 73–74
King Hendrick. *See* Theyanoguin (King Hendrick)
King Philip. *See* Metacomet (Wampanoags)
King Philip's War, 72
Kings and kingdoms. *See* Monarchs and monarchies; specific rulers
Kings Mountain, battle at, 92 (illus.), 97
King William's War, 72
Kinsey report: homosexuality and, 621
Kinship: in Chesapeake region, 47; lineage structures in West Africa, 8; in New England, 44; slave, 50
Kiowa Indians, 331, 333, 335, 351
Kissinger, Henry, 608, 625; détente policy and, 610–611; October War and, 614; Vietnam negotiations by, 611–612
Kitchen Cabinet: of Jackson, Andrew, 192
Kitty Hawk, North Carolina: Wright brothers flight at, 405
Klan. *See* Ku Klux Klan
Klebold, Dylan, 675
Knights of Labor, 365–366
Know-Nothing party, 273–274
Knox, Henry, 128
Knox, Philander C., 467–468
Koop, C. Everett, 643, 644 (illus.)
Korea: division of, 552; immigrants from, 659, 660; Japan and, 467, 524
Korean War, 552–554, 553 (illus.), 566
Koresh, David, 673
Kosovo: Clinton and, 669, 671–672
Krupp, 526
Ku Klux Klan: in 1920s, 495–496, 496 (illus.); terrorism of, **323,** 324–325
Ku Klux Klan Acts. *See* Force Acts (1870–1871)
Kurds, 652; in Iraq, 687
Kurz and Allison: lithograph of 54th Massachusetts Colored Regiment, 302 (illus.)
Kuwait: Iraqi invasion of, 651

L

Labor: activists in, 175; African Americans and, 49, 515; in agriculture, 175; in Chesapeake, 46–47; domestic servants and, 186; *encomienda* system of, 12; free vs. slave, 107, 274; along frontier, 170; gender division in Plains tribes, 333; immigrants as, 432–433; immigration and, 262; indentured servants as, 25–26; Indian, 8; industrialization and, 354, 363–368; in Industrial Revolution, 261–262; Jacksonian-era politics and, 190; mobility of, 365; New Deal and, 513–515; in New England, 44, 46; in 1920s, 487; organized, 489; slaves as, 174; steel plant closings and, 617; Taft-Hartley Act and, 554; women as, 618; in World War I, 478–479. *See also* Labor unions; Strikes; Workers
Labor agents: to recruit immigrants, 433
Labor Department, 460
Labor force. *See* Labor; Workers
Labor-management relations: Wagner Act and, 513
Laborsaving devices, 491
Labor strikes. *See* Strikes
Labor unions: Clayton Act and, 435 (illus.); decline in, 635; development and growth of, 365–366; for farmworkers, 597; injunctions and, 366; membership of, 489; in New Deal, 513–515; in Progressive Era, 434; unskilled workers in, 514–515; in World War I, 478; in World War II, 536
Labor violence. *See* Strikes
Ladies' Home Journal, 362, 379 (illus.), 426
Lady's Magazine and Repository of Entertaining Knowledge, The, 107 (illus.)
Lafayette (Marquis de), 98, 165
La Follette, Robert, 455, 473; election of 1924 and, 500; "Wisconsin Idea" of, 450–451
Laissez-faire: attack on, 383; Redeemers and, 327; second party system and, 200–201; Van Buren and, 198–199
Lake, Anthony, 668
Lake Champlain, 166
Lake Erie: in War of 1812, 160
Lake Shore and Michigan Southern Railway, 357 (illus.)
Lake Superior: iron ore deposits near, 359
Land: cession of Indian, 134; confiscated in Civil War, 311; Dawes Act and, 336; for freedpeople, 318; in Georgia, 40; grants to railroads, 306, 339, 356; headright system of, 25; Homestead Act and, 336, 339; legislation for western, 339; marketing of western, 113; Mexican grants of, 340; Native Americans and, 336; in Ohio valley, 147; opening of Oklahoma to white settlers, 347; Radical Reconstruction and redistribution of, 316; speculation in, 168, 339; *Tejanos* and, 285–286; as voting requirement, 106; water issue in West and, 339; westward movement and, 338–340
Land bridge: Beringia as, 2
Land-grant colleges, 381; gender-segregated seating at, 382 (illus.)
Landon, Alfred M., 516
Land Ordinance (1785), 112 (illus.), 113
Lange, Dorothea, 510 (illus.)
Language(s): of Algonquian-speaking peoples, 4; creole, 50; of immigrants, 81; Indian, 3; in West Africa, 8
Lansing, Robert, 471, 472, 473, 482
Laos, 592; refugees from, 660
Laramie, Fort, 338
La Salle, René Robert Cavalier (Sieur de), 13
Las Casas, Bartolomé de, 12
Las Guasimas: battle of, 417
Lateen sail, 10
Lathrop, Julia, 434
Latin America: Alliance for Progress and, 579; Carter and, 624–625; covert action in, 560–561; immigration from, 605, 606, 655, 657; markets in, 408, 410; mining techniques of, 342; Monroe Doctrine and, 180–181; nontransfer principle and, 410; Roosevelt, Franklin D., and, 524; Roosevelt Corollary and, 466–467; Spanish-Indian intermarriage in, 13; Wilson and, 468. *See also* specific countries
Latinos. *See* Hispanic America and Americans; Latin America; specific groups
Laud, William, 29
Law(s): Anglicization of, 71–72; interpretation in Progressive Era, 448; legal precedent vs. environmental data, 448; state, regulatory, 450. *See also* specific laws
Law codes. *See* Codes of law
Lawrence, Kansas: sack of, 275
Lawrence, Massachusetts: IWW strike in, 434
Laws and Liberties, 31
Lawyers: criminal right to, 585
Layoffs: in Great Depression, 504
Lazarus, Emma, 388
Leach, Douglas, 54
Leadership: by African Americans, 310
Leadville, 341

League for the Protection of the Family, 400
League of Latin American Citizens, 658
League of Nations, 481, 482 (illus.); German withdrawal from, 525; Italian aggression and, 525; Japanese withdrawal from, 525; United States and, 523
Leahy, Patrick: anthrax scare and, 685
Lean Bear, 331
Leary, Timothy, 595
Lease, Mary E., 395, 395 (illus.), 430
Lebanon: civil war and U.S. intervention in, 639; Eisenhower's intervention in, 560; Iran-Contra affair and, 641; Israeli invasion of, 639
Lecompton constitution, 277
Lee, Alice. *See* Roosevelt, Alice Lee
Lee, Ivy L., 435
Lee, "Mother" Ann, 240
Lee, Richard Henry, 91
Lee, Robert E., 292, 298, 302, 303, 304 (illus.), 305
Leftists: in Central America, 624–625
Legal precedent: vs. environmental data, 448
Legal system: colonial and English, 72
Legislation: civil rights, 572, 584, 585; on immigration, 389, 605–606; in New Deal, 517–518. *See also* specific acts
Legislatures: House of Burgesses as, 24–25; in Massachusetts, 31; in Pennsylvania, 36; political representation in, 106; in state governments, 109; in Virginia Plan, 118
Leisler, Jacob, 55
Leisler's rebellion, 55
Leisure, 377; and entertainment (1877-1900), 378–379; feminine subculture and, 233; in Progressive Era, 437–438
Lemke, William, 516
Lend-Lease: for Soviet Union, 532; after World War II, 545; in World War II, **529**
Lenin, V. I., 477
Leopard (ship), 157
Lesbians. *See* Gay liberation movement; Gays and lesbians
Letters from a Farmer in Pennsylvania (Dickinson), 110
Leveling, democratic, 185–186
Levitt, William, 565
Levittown, 565, 566
Lewinsky, Monica, 675–676
Lewis, David, 493
Lewis, Drew, 633
Lewis, John L.: United Mine Workers and, 514
Lewis, Meriwether, 152
Lewis, Sinclair, 493
Lewis and Clark expedition, 151 (illus.), **152,** 335
Lexington, battle at, 91
Leyte Gulf, battle at, 540
Liberal internationalism: end of, 602
Liberal Republicans, 325
Liberator, The, 237, 238
Liberia, 215, 236
Libertarianism: Greenspan and, 654
Liberty: African American rights to, 107; order and, 104; protections of, 179
Liberty Displaying the Arts and Sciences (Jennings), 119 (illus.)
Liberty League, 516
Liberty of conscience: in Carolina, 36
Liberty party, 238, 252
Licensed warehouses: for farm products, 461
Liddy, G. Gordon, 607, 608, 613
Life expectancy: in Chesapeake, 47, 48; in 1880, 377; in England, 29; in New England, 43; rise in, 436
Life magazine, 426
Lifestyle: autos and, 487; in Chesapeake region, 46–48; of Eastern Woodland cultures, 4–5; in New England, 43–46; on Overland Trail, 337–338; of Plains Indians, 333; after Second World War, 567; in 2000, 655; urban, 148–149. *See also* Society
Lightning rod, 65
Liliuokalani (Hawaii), 411
Lincoln, Abraham, 298 (illus.), 331; assassination of, 305; biography of, 287; Civil War and, 297, 298; compromise proposals and, 290; election of 1860 and, 280–281; election of 1864 and, 303–305; emancipation and, 300–301; Emancipation Proclamation of, 300; Gettysburg Address of, 288; as "great emancipator," 301; inaugural address of (first), 290, 291; leadership of, 287, 288, 295; movement of family of, 170; policy of coercion of, 291; Ten Percent Plan of, 312; Thirteenth Amendment and, 301; two-front war of, 293; youth of, 235
Lincoln, Levi, 150
Lincoln-Douglas debates, 278
Lindbergh, Charles, 491; America First Committee and, 528
Lindsay, Vachel, 439
Lineage structures: in West Africa, 8
"Line of settlement." *See* Frontier
Literacy: Cherokee alphabet and, 193; in New England, 44; popular literature and, 187; slavery and, 216; test for immigrants, 496–497; as test for voting, 328, 391; among white male colonists, 85
Literary World, 244
Literature: of Brahmin poets, 188; in Jacksonian era, 187; mass market for, 187; naturalism in, 400–401; in 1920s, 492–493; popular fiction, 437–438; realism in, 400; romantic movement in, 187, 188; of rural disillusionment, 395; sectionalism in, 276; after World War I, 483; Young America and, 244. *See also* specific works and authors
Little, Frank, 476
Little Bighorn: battle of, 335, 336 (illus.), 351
Little League, 567
Little Rock: Central High School integration in, 573; federal troops in, 573
Littleton, Colorado: school violence in, 671, 675
Livingston, Robert, 151
Lloyd George, David, 481
Locke, John, 37
Lockport, New York: Erie Canal and, 172 (illus.)
Loco-Focos, 198
Locomotives, 356
Lodge, Henry Cabot, 480, 481
Logrolling, 191
London, Jack, 401
London Company: Virginia colony and, 23
Lonely Crowd, The (Riesman), 568–569
Long, Crawford W.: ether, use of, and, 258 (illus.)
Long, Huey, 511–512
Long, Stephen S., 167
Longfellow, Henry Wadsworth, 188
Longhorn cattle, 343
Long Island, 30 (illus.); battle in, 95
Looking Backward, 2000–1887 (Bellamy), 384
Looms: high-speed, 361
Loose construction: of Constitution, 131
Lords of Trade (England), 52
Los Alamos, New Mexico: atomic bomb and, 540
Los Angeles: growth of, 656; King, Rodney, and, 659; Korean immigrants in, 660; zoning in, 436; "zoot suit" riots in, 537–538
Los Angeles County: Spanish-speaking population in, 340
Lost colony, 18
Louis XI (France), 10
Louis XVI (France): American Revolution and, 97; in French Revolution, 132
Louisbourg: British attack on, 75; colonial capture of, 73
Louisiana: French in, 13; after Louisiana Purchase, 152; political violence in, 323; secession of, 289; segregated schools in, 381; as state, 166; Unionist government in, 312
Louisiana Purchase, 150–152, **151,** 151 (illus.); border with Canada, 166
Lovejoy, Elijah: lynching of, 237
"Love Song of J. Alfred Prufrock" (Eliot), 439
Lowell, Amy, 439
Lowell, Francis Cabot, 175
Lowell, James Russell, 188
Lowell, Massachusetts: as industrial town, 175, 175 (illus.)
Loyalists, 85; African American, 94; compensation after Revolution, 101; in Revolution, 97, 98–99; strongholds of, 98 (illus.)
Loyalty issue: oaths for teachers and, 558; Truman and, 555–556
Loyalty Review Board, 556
Luce, Henry, 687
Ludlow, Colorado: coal strike at, 460, 460 (illus.)
Ludlow, Louis, 526
Luftwaffe (Germany), 527
Lusitania (passenger liner): sinking of, 464–465, 471
Luther, Martin, 14
Lutherans: Democratic party and, 200
Luxury goods: demands for, 9–10
Lyceums, 188, 235
Lynchings, 322; attempted, of Garrison, 237; of black war veterans, 478; of Little, Frank, 476; of Lovejoy, Elijah, 237; of Smith, Joseph, 250; in South, 327 (illus.), 328; after Spanish-American War, 424; during World War I, 478
Lyon, Matthew, 139

M

MacArthur, Douglas: bonus army and, 507; Japan and, 551; in Korean War, 553; in Philippines, 531, 540; in World War II Pacific, 534, 535
Macedonia: Kosovars and, 671
Machines, 353; for farming, 346; vs. skilled artisans, 364; vs. workers, 429
Machines (political), 375–376; of African Americans, 310–311

Mackay, John W., 341
Macon's Bill Number Two, 158
Macune, Charles W., 395
Macy, R. H., 362
Maddox (ship), 590
Madero, Francisco, 469
Madison, James: Articles of Confederation and, 115; on Bill of Rights, 122; congressional apportionment and, 144; Constitution (U.S.) and, 117; election of 1808 and, 158; election of 1812 and, 159; *Federalist, The,* and, 117, 120; on Hamilton's funding ideas, 130–131; Marbury and, 153; on republican government, 116–117; as secretary of state, 149; on title for chief executive, 126; Virginia Plan and, 117–118; War of 1812 and, 159
Magazines: women's, 567
Mahan, Alfred Thayer, 412
Maher, Bridget, 618
Mail: parcel post, 430; rural free delivery (RFD) and, 430
Mail-order catalogs, 362, 436 (illus.)
Mail-order houses, 347
Maine, 33; border conflict with Britain and, 245; as free state, 178
Maine (battleship): sinking of, 413–414, 414 (illus.)
Mainland colonies: English, 37 (illus.). *See also* Colonies and colonization; specific colonies
Main Street (Lewis), 493
Maize, 6
Majority rule: Lincoln and, 290
Majority status: of Hispanics in New Mexico, 286; of Hispanics in Southern California, 285
Malaria, 418; rural, 431
Malaya: Japan and, 531
Mammals: in Americas, 2; human population and, 3
Management: in 1920s, 489
Manassas Junction, Virginia. *See* Bull Run
Manchuria: Japan and, 524, 525; Soviet departure from, 551–552
Mandan Indians: buffalo robe of, 152 (illus.)
Manhattan Project, 540
Manifest Destiny, 246 (illus.), **251**; attempts to revive, 272; coining of phrase and, 252; doctrine of, 252–253; internal expansion and, 257; Mexican-American War and, 251–256; Oregon and, 267; slavery in territories and, 271; Tyler, John, and, 251
Manila Bay: battle at, 418, 417
Mann, Horace: common school movement and, 234–235
Mann Act (1910), 445
Mann-Elkins Act (1910), 456
Manners and mores: in society (1877–1900), 377–378
Manufacturing: Bessemer process and, 258 (illus.); continuous process production and, 258, 262; decline in industries, 635, 636; factory mode of production and, 258–259; goods from England, 67; interior markets for, 171; machine tools and, 259; mass production and, 258–259; in 1970s, 617; putting-out system of, 175; sewing machine and, 258 (illus.), 259; of textiles, 259, 261; Townshend duties and, 88; after World War II, 566; during World War II, 535–536
Mao Tse-tung, 551–552; Korean War and, 552, 559
"Maple Leaf Rag" (Joplin), 378
Marbury, William, 153
***Marbury* v. *Madison,* 153**
"March King": Sousa as, 437
March on Washington, 584; for gay rights, 621; in 1941, 536; in 1963, 584, 585 (illus.)
Marcy, William, 272
Margin purchases, 504
Marian exiles, 15
Marin, John, 439
Marines (U.S.): in Grenada, 640; in Lebanon, 560, 639; terrorism against, 639; withdrawn from Latin America, 524
Market(s): immigrants and expansion of, 354; for western farmers, 176
Market economy, 173–176; industrialism and, 174–176; middle class and, 283
Marketing: commercial agriculture and, 173–174, 173 (illus.); industrialization and, 362. *See also* Advertising
Marne River: battle at, 474–475
Marquette, Jacques, 13
Marriage: age at, 618; in Chesapeake region, 47; European-Indian, 7, 13; of freedpeople, 321; of immigrants, 374; in late 19th century, 379; for love, 231; in New England, 43–44; in 1950s, 567; polygamy and, 250; same-sex, 622; in Virginia, 26; in World War II, 536
Marshall, George C., 532; McCarthy and, 557; as secretary or state, 546
Marshall, John, 137; on Burr's treason, 155; as chief justice, 141, 153; federal government and, 179
Marshall, Thurgood, 647; school desegregation and, 573
Marshall Plan, 547–548, 548 (illus.); export trade and, 566
Martha's Vineyard, 33
Martial law: antidraft riots and, 302; in border states, 292; Davis and, 297; Lincoln's declaration of, 295
Mary I (Tudor, England), 15
Mary II (England), 22, 54
Maryland, 26–27, 37 (illus.); Civil War in, 292, 298; culture clash in, 1; Glorious Revolution in, 55; as royal colony, 56. *See also* Chesapeake region
Mason, George: Bill of Rights and, 119, 122; Constitution (U.S.) and, 117
Mason, James M., 299
Mason family, 47
Massachusetts, 30 (illus.), 37 (illus.); charter annulled in, 54; circular letter in, 88; Coercive Acts and, 90–91; dissent in, 31–32; power of people in, 109; as separate colony, 32; Stamp Act Congress and, 86. *See also* New England
Massachusetts Bay Colony: as "city on a hill," 29–30; Glorious Revolution in, 54–55; Native Americans in, 21; Plymouth absorbed into, 28. *See also* Massachusetts
Massachusetts Institute of Technology (MIT), 381
Massacres. *See* specific massacres
Massasoit, 28
Mass consumption, 435
Massive retaliation, 558
Mass production, 363 (illus.), 428, 486; in automobile industry, 427; in clothing industry, 435
Mass transit systems, 372
Master, Edgar Lee, 440
Masterson, William B. (Bat), 344
Material culture: Navigation Acts and, 52–53
Materialism: criticisms of, 568–569
Mather, Cotton, 54, 56
Mather, Increase, 55
Matisse, 439
Mayaguez (ship): seizure of, 624
Mayan peoples, 4
Mayflower (ship), 27
Mayflower Compact, 28
Mayr, Christian, 208
McAdoo, William G., 500
McCall's (magazine), 567
McCarthy, Eugene, 599, 600
McCarthy, Joseph, 556–557, 566; Eisenhower and, 557–558. *See also* McCarthyism
McCarthyism, 556–557; Supreme Court and, 585
McClellan, George, 297–298, 298 (illus.), 305
McClure, Samuel S., 426
McClure's Magazine, 426, 427 (illus.)
McCord, James, 607, 613
McCormick, Cyrus: reaper and, 258 (illus.), 259
McCormick harvester works: strike at, 366–367
McCoy, Joseph G., 343
***McCulloch* v. *Maryland,* 179**–180
McDowell, Irvin, 297
McDowell, Mary, 434
McFarlane, Robert, 641
McGovern, George, 600, 613, 623
McGuffey's Eclectic Readers, 235, 380
McHenry, Fort, 161
McIntosh, Fort, 110
McKay, Claude, 493
McKinley, William: administration of, 403–404; assassination of, 404, 451; election of 1896 and, 401–403; election of 1900 and, 420; Hawaii annexation and, 411; Open Door Policy of, 423–424; Philippines and, 418, 420; Spanish-American War and, 413–415, 416, 417; Treaty of Paris (1898) and, 418, 419
McKinley Tariff Act (1890), 393, 410, 411
McNamara, Robert, 578, 589, 594
McPherson, Aimee Semple, 497–498
McVeigh, Timothy, 673
Meade, George, 303
Measles, 6, 8
Meat Inspection Act (1906), 453
Meatpacking industry: refrigerated rail cars and, 361; regulation of, 453
Mechanization: in Lowell mills, 175
Media. *See* specific media
Medicaid, 589; to elderly, 656–657
Medical examinations: of immigrants, 388–389
Medicare, 588, 632
Medicine: and ether, 258 (illus.); life expectancy and, 436; revolution in, 377
Mediterranean region: Barbary War and, 152; in World War II, 533

Meese, Edwin, 641, 646
Mellon, Andrew, 499
Melting pot: metaphor of, 386; population by 2050 and, 606; reality of, 660–661
Melville, Herman, 188, 244
Memphis: race riot in, 315
Men: in Chesapeake region, 47; clothing in Victorian era, 378; of Eastern Woodland cultures, 4; in late 19th century families, 379; in mining camps, 342; in New England, 43; on Overland Trail, 337–338; in Plains tribes, 333; in Spanish-Mexican society, 340; voting by, 106, 666. *See also* Families; Gender and gender roles
Mencken, H. L., 491, 497
Menéndez de Avilés, Pedro, 63
Mental illness: asylums and, 235–236
Mercantilism, 51
Mercenaries: in American Revolution, 93
Mercer, William, 96 (illus.)
Merchant marine, 148–149
"Merchants of death": arms dealers as, 526
Meredith, James, 584
Mergers and consolidations: in 1920s, 488; in Progressive Era, 428
Merino sheep, 173 (illus.)
Merrimack. See Virginia (*Merrimack,* ironclad)
Mescalero Apache Indians: warfare of, 352
Mestizos, 13
Metacomet (Wampanoags), 54 (illus.)
Methodists, 276; evangelicalism and, 227; Second Great Awakening and, 227
Metropolitan areas: population of, 656. *See also* Cities and towns; Urban areas
Meuse River: in World War I, 475, 476 (illus.)
Mexican Americans, 658; in California, 340; as cowboys, 343, 343 (illus.); in Great Depression, 505; in New Deal, 515; northern migration of, 479; protests by, 596–597; in Southwest, 433; World War I and, 478; World War II and, 537–538
Mexican-American War, 254–256, 256 (illus.), 287
Mexican cession: slavery issue in, 267; Taylor and, 268–269; Wilmot Proviso and, 267–268
Mexicans: in mining camps, 342; U.S. citizenship for, 285
Mexico: All Mexico movement and, 255; annexation and, 409; Aztecs of, 4; border conflicts with, 245–246; conquistadores in, 11–12; as drug pipeline, 646; immigration from, 338, 431, 433, 497, 605, 657; intervention in, 468–470; Mexican-American War and, 254–256; NAFTA and, 663; Republic of Texas and, 247–248; revolution of 1910 in, 433; slavery and, 247; Texas Revolution and, 247; trade with, 248; U.S. expansionism and, 244, 245–249; Zimmerman telegram and, 473
Michigan: slavery outlawed in, 113
Michilimackinac, Fort, 160
Middle Americans: Nixon and, 610
Middle class: African Americans in, 311, 659; families in late 19th century, 379; in Great Depression, 506; median family income of, 636; movement to, 365; in 1920s, 489; professionals in, 444; in suburbs, 372; tax burden for, 636; Victorian era dress of, 378; women in, 431; women in work place and, 636
Middle Colonies, 22, 33 (illus.); blacks in, 50; diversity in, 32–34
Middle East: Americans from, 659–660; Camp David Accords and, 625, 625 (illus.); Clinton and, 668; Reagan and, 638–639; Suez crisis and, 560; trouble spots in (1979–1992), 639 (illus.). *See also* Arab-Israeli wars; specific countries
Middle ground: Native Americans in, 61–62
Midnight appointments: of Adams, 141, 153
Midway Islands: annexation of, 410; battle at, 534
Midwest: land-grant colleges and coeducation in, 381; settlement of, 168–169; steel plant closings in, 617; violence in mining in, 397–398
Migrant farm workers, 431
"Migrant Mother" (Lange), 510 (illus.)
Migration: of blacks to North, 478, 479 (illus.); from England, 22; to Georgia, 39; of immigrants to old country, 433; to Ireland, 22; of Mexicans, 478–479; to New England, 43, 45–46; to New World from Spain, 13; to North America, 2; of Plains Indians, 333; to Sunbelt, South, and West, 655, 656–657, 656 (illus.); after War of 1812, 166–170; during World War II, 536–538. *See also* Immigrants and immigration
Milan Decree (1807), 156
Militarism: in Germany, Italy, and Japan, 525–526
Military: in American Revolution, 82; in Cold War, 550–551; desegregation of, 572; expansion of, 551; gays in, 621–622, 662; Hawks and, 582; Jefferson and, 150; Kennedy and, 578–579; maintenance after Seven Years' War, 85; redcoats in Boston, 88; in Vietnam, 591–592, 592 (illus.), 593. *See also* Armed forces; Marines (U.S.); Navy (U.S.); Soldiers
Military academy: at West Point, 150
Military alliance: NATO as, 548–549
Military bases: U.S. acquisition of, 554
Military districts: in Reconstruction South, 315 (illus.)
Military draft. *See* Draft (military)
Military-industrial complex, 562–563
Military rule: in South, 316, 319, 392
Militia: American Revolution and, 94; Jefferson and, 150; at Lexington, 91; in Ohio Valley, 74; at Ruby Ridge, Idaho, 673; in Waco, 673
Millennial Church (Shakers), 240
Miller, Arthur, 363
Miller, Lewis, 156 (illus.)
"Mill girls," 175
Mills: factory system in, 175
Mills, C. Wright, 569
Milosevic, Slobodan, 671
Mines and mining: Comstock Lode and, 341; depression of 1890s and violence in, 397–398; immigrants and, 397–398; mining camps and, 341–342; placer mining, 341; safety regulations for, 456; strikes and, 341; in West, 341–343, 342 (illus.)
Minimum age laws: for work, 431
Minimum wage, 513; Clinton and, 666; Roosevelt, Franklin D., and, 508
Minnesota: Laotian refugees in, 660
Minorities: AIDS and, 644; gays as, 621; Hispanic Americans as, 605–606; life expectancy in 1880, 377; during New Deal, 515; rights in states, 109. *See also* specific groups
Minor v. *Happersett,* 391
Minuteman ICBMs, 578, 626
Minutemen, 91
Miranda v. *Arizona,* 585
Misery index, 631
Missile gap: Kennedy on, 578
Missiles: Carter and, 626; in Cuba, 581; Iran-Contra affair and, 641; medium-range, 638; spy planes and, 562
Missions and missionaries: Beecher, Lyman, and, 230; in California, 63; in city slums, 385; foreign to civilize the world, 409; in Hawaii, 411; Spanish, 12, 63 (illus.)
Mississippi: Civil War in, 302; race riots in, 325; secession of, 289; segregated schools in, 381
Mississippian culture, 3, 3 (illus.)
Mississippi River region: Civil War in, 297, 302; commerce and, 147; England and, 76; French and, 13, 74; Indians in, 3; Native Americans in, 3; Pinckney's Treaty and, 134; settlement to, 168–169; Spanish closing of, 115; territories east of, 100
Mississippi Territory, 166
Missouri (ship): Japanese surrender on, 541
Missouri (state): in Civil War, 292; as slave state, 178
Missouri Compromise (1820), 177–**179,** 178 (illus.), 267; attempts to extend, 268, 290; constitutionality of, 277; repeal of, 272, 272 (illus.)
Missouri River region, 167
Mitchell, John (attorney general), 608, 610
Mitchell, John (union leader), 452
Mittlebau Dora camp: in holocaust, 539 (illus.)
Mobility (labor), 365
Mobility (social): in Massachusetts Bay, 32
Mobilization: for World War I, 474
Moby-Dick (Melville), 244
Model A Ford, 486
Model T Ford, 427, 486
"Modern Colossus of (Rail) Roads" (political cartoon), 357 (illus.)
Modernists, 439
Modern Republicanism: of Eisenhower, **570**–572
Molasses: Sugar Act and, 86
Monarchs and monarchies: English Stuart monarchs and, 22; European "new monarchs" and, 10. *See also* specific dynasties, monarchs, and countries
Mondale, Walter, 636–637
Money: Continentals as, 114, 114 (illus.); for long-distance commerce, 174
Money question: hard- vs. easy-money, 322–323
Monitor (ironclad), 297
Monopoly, 360. *See also* Trusts
Monroe, Harriet, 439
Monroe, James, 177; East Florida and, 166; election of 1808 and, 158; election of 1824 and, 190; Era of Good Feelings and, 176; internal improvements and, 170; Louisiana Purchase and, 151; Panic of 1819 and, 177; War of 1812 and, 159

Monroe Doctrine (1823), 180–**181**, 408, 468; North and South America and, 409; Roosevelt Corollary to, 466–467; Venezuela-British Guiana dispute and, 410–411
Monrovia, 215
Montana: Sioux War in, 334
Montcalm, marquis de, 75–76
Montesquieu (Baron de), 116
Montezuma (Mexico): Cortés and, 11
Montgomery, Alabama: Confederacy established in, 289
Montgomery bus boycott, 573–574
Montgomery Ward (store), 362
Monticello, 134
Montreal, 13; French surrender at, 76
Moody, Dwight L., 378
Moral diplomacy, 468
Morale: during Civil War, 301
Morality: Victorian, 377–378
Moral Majority, 629, 630
Morgan, J. P., and Company, 358, 452; interlocking directorates and, 428
Morgan, J. Pierpont, 358, 362, 452, 488; in steel industry, 359
Mormons, 337; evangelicalism and, 227; trek of, 249–250, 249 (illus.), 250 (illus.); in Utah, 250
Morrill Land Grant Act (1862), 381
Morris, Gouveneur, 119
Morris, Robert, 112; Articles of Confederation and, 115; Constitution (U.S.) and, 117
Morse, Samuel F. B.: telegraph and, 256, 258 (illus.)
Mortality rate: in Chesapeake, 46–47; decline in, 436
Morton, Ferdinand "Jelly Roll," 437
Moscow: Reagan-Gorbachev summit in, 642
Mothers: single, 618. *See also* Children; Families; Women
Mother's Day, 431
Motion pictures. *See* Movies and movie industry
Mott, Lucretia, 598 (illus.); Seneca Falls Convention and, 239
Moultrie, Fort, 291 (illus.)
Mound-building cultures, 3
Mount, William Sidney, 188
"Mountain men," 167
Movies and movie industry, 488; in early 20th century, 437; sex and, 491
Muckrakers, 426, 427, 427 (illus.), 453
Mugwumps, 378
Mulattoes, 13; in English colonies, 50
***Muller* v. *Oregon*, 448**
Multiethnic society, 660–661
Multinational companies: in 1970s, 617
Munich conference (1938), 526–527
Munn v. *Illinois*, 392
Munster (Ireland): English in, 17
Murder: in early Maryland, 1–2
Murrah Federal Building: bombing of, 673, 674 (illus.)
Murray, William Vans, 141
Music: acid rock, 595; black southern folk influences on, 437; blues, 437, 493; classical, 378; jazz, 437; in Jazz Age, 493; marches, 437; ragtime, 378, 437; sentimental ballads and, 378
Muskie, Edmund: election of 1972 and, 612–613
Muslims: in Bosnia, 669, 670; Iranian hostage crisis and, 625; in Lebanon, 560; in Spain, 10; war on terrorism and, 682. *See also* Islam
Mussolini, Benito, 525, 533
MX missile, 626

N

NAACP. *See* National Association for the Advancement of Colored People (NAACP)
Nader, Ralph, 623; election of 2000 and, 677, 678
NAFTA. *See* North American Free Trade Agreement (NAFTA)
Nagasaki: atomic bombing of, 541
Nantucket, 33
Napoleon I Bonaparte (France): Louisiana Purchase and, 151–152; U.S. trade and, 158
Napoleon III, 299
Napoleonic Wars, 156–157
Narragansett Indians, 4, 31
NASA. *See* National Aeronautics and Space Administration (NASA)
Nashoba, Tennessee, utopian community at, 239
Nashville (cruiser), 466
Nashville, Tennessee: battle at, 305; convention of southern states in, 269
Nasser, Gamal: Suez crisis and, 560
Nast, Thomas: attack on trusts (cartoon), 428 (illus.); "Worse Than Slavery" cartoon of, 324 (illus.)
National Aeronautics and Space Administration (NASA), 570
National American Woman Suffrage Association, 380, 446
National Association for the Advancement of Colored People (NAACP), 432, 493; black militants and, 596; school desegregation and, 573
National Association of Colored Women, 445
National Association of Manufacturers, 444
National bank, 176; of 1863, 307; Bank of the United States as, 131
National Child Labor Committee, 443
National Collegiate Athletic Association, 437
National Coming Out Day, 621
National Conference of Charities and Corrections, 444
National Conference of Social Work, 444
National conservation policy, 454
National Consumers' League, 448
National Council of Mothers, 445
National debt: under Articles of Confederation, 115; Hamilton on, 130; Jefferson and, 150; after Revolution, 115. *See also* Debt
National Defense Education Act (NDEA, 1958), **570**
National Education Association, 444
National Farm Bureau Federation, 444
National Farmers' Alliance and Industrial Union, 394, 395
National Farm Workers Association (NFWA), 596–597
National Federation of Settlements, 444
National government. *See* Government (U.S.)
National Grange of the Patrons of Husbandry, 346–347, 395
National Greenback party, 322, 323
National Guard, 415; blacks in, 415; at Kent State and Jackson State, 611, 612 (illus.)
National health insurance plan: Carter and, 623
Nationalism: black, 596; economic, 404; in England, 16; ethnic, 596–597; Monroe Doctrine and, 180–181; southern, 270, 276; Supreme Court and, 179–180; War of 1812 and, 162 (illus.), 165, 176
Nationalist China, 551, 559; Taiwan and, 552; U.S. defense of, 559–560
Nationalists, 115; Articles of Confederation and, 114–115
National Labor Relations Act. *See* Wagner Act (1935)
National Labor Relations Board (NLRB), 513, 519
National Labor Union, 365
National market: advertising in, 362; homogeneity of goods in, 363; railroads and, 355
National Municipal League, 449
National Organization for Women (NOW), 597–598, 619
National Origins Quota Act (1924), **497**
National parks and forests, 455 (illus.)
National Reclamation Act (Newlands Act) (1902), **339**
National Recovery Administration (NRA), 508–509, 516, 518
National Republicans: Whigs and, 197
National Road, 170, 177
National security: drug cartels and, 646; Johnson, Lyndon B., and, 589
National Security Act (1947), **550**
National Security Council (NSC), 641; NSC-68 and, 551
National Security Strategy (NSS), 684
National Socialism. *See* Nazi Germany
National societies and associations: in Progressive Era, 443
National Urban League, 432
National Woman Suffrage Association, 446
National Women's Economic Summit (1996), 619
National Youth Administration (NYA, 1935), 519
Nation building: politics of, 176–182; after War of 1812, 165–182
Nation-states: in Europe, 9–10
Native Americans: African Americans and, 210; assimilationism and, 335–336; Bacon's Rebellion and, 53–54; Black Hills gold rush and, 335; buffalo soldiers and, 351–352; in Caribbean region, 11; cession of land by, 134; cultures of, 1–2, 6–7; Dawes Act and, 336; Eastern Woodland cultures and, 4–5, 5 (illus.); *encomienda* system and, 12; end of tribal life, 335–337; England and, 74; before European conquest, 2–8; European diseases and, 6 (illus.), 8; European impact on cultures of, 5–8; extermination of buffalo and, 336–337; at Fallen Timbers, 134; of Far West, 246; final battles of Plains Indians, 335; fishing by, 18 (illus.); French and, 13; Ghost Dances and, 335; gold discoveries and removal of, 333; Indian Reorganization Act and, 515; Jeffersonians and, 148; King Philip's War and, 72; major groups and culture areas (1600s), 5 (illus.); major western battles and reservations, 334 (illus.); in Massachusetts Bay, 21; Metacomet and, 54; in Mexico and Central America, 4; in mid-

dle ground, 61–62; of Midwest, 168; by 1900, 337; nullification crisis and, 194; in Ohio valley, 147; organization of, 333; Paleo-Indians and, 2; Plains Indians lifestyle, 333; population of, 8, 332; removal and, 168, 192–193, 194 (illus.), 333; Sand Creek massacre and, 333–334; Santa Fe trail and, 248; Scots-Irish and, 81; Second Seminole War and, 210; in semislavery, 246; after Seven Years' War, 85; Spanish and, 12, 13; Theyanoguin (King Hendrick) and, 74 (illus.); Tocqueville on, 202; Trail of Tears and, 193, 194 (illus.); Virginia colony and, 24, 26; as wards of the state, 337; western lands of, 110–111; westward movement and, 135 (illus.), 331–332; *Worcester* v. *Georgia* and, 193; Wounded Knee Massacre of, 335. *See also* Indian policy; specific groups
Nativism, 271; Know-Nothings and, 273–274; in Progressive Era, 433; after World War I, 497
NATO. *See* North Atlantic Treaty Organization (NATO)
Nat Turner's Rebellion, 204
Natural gas, 616
Naturalism: in literature, 400–401
Naturalization Law (1798), 139
Natural resources: gold rush and, 258 (illus.); for industrial development, 354; oil wells and, 258 (illus.); rubber, vulcanization of, and, 258 (illus.), 259
Natural rights, 109
Nauvoo, Illinois: Mormons in, 250
Navajo Indians, 332–333
Naval bases: in Hawaii, 411
Naval War College, 416
Navigation: steamboat and, 171
Navigation Acts, 52; Bay Colony and, 54; colonial economy and, 66–67; punishment for not following, 89; of 1660, 51–52; of 1673, 52; of 1696, 52; Sugar Act and, 85
Navy (U.S.): advocates of big-navy, 412; in Civil War, 293, 297; as New Navy, 412; in Spanish-American War, 416–417, 416 (illus.), 417 (illus.); in War of 1812, 160; Washington Conference and, 524; world tour of, 467; in World War I, 474. *See also* World War II
Navy Department, 139
Nazi Germany, 523, 525; *Blitzkrieg* by, 528; halting, 532–533; invasion of Austria and Czechoslovakia by, 526–527; invasion of Poland by, 527, 527 (illus.); nonaggression pact with Soviet Union, 527. *See also* Germany; Hitler, Adolf
Nazi-Soviet pact, 527, 532
NBC, 488
Necessary and proper clause, 131
Necessity, Fort, 74
Negro: use of term, 596
Negro Convention movement and, 238
Nelson, Donald, 535
Neo-Calvinism, 229
Neoconservatism, 630
Neo-orthodoxy: Protestant, 568
Netherlands: in World War II, 529. *See also* Dutch; Holland
Neutrality: of American shipping, 156; during French Revolution, 132–133; Madison and, 158; Monroe and, 180; before World War I, 470–471; before World War II, 526, 527, 528
Neutrality acts (1935, 1936, 1937), **526,** 529
New Amsterdam, 32, 33. *See also* New York (city)
Newark: riots in (1967), 596
Newburgh Conspiracy (1783), 115
New Deal, 461, **503,** 504; decline of, 517–518; Eisenhower and, 572; end of, 516–518; evaluation of, 518–520; Hundred Days in, 507–508; impact of, 513–516; legislation in, 513, 517; minorities during, 515; political coalition in, 516, 518, 519–520; recession of 1937 and, 517; reforms in, 511–513; relief programs in, 509–511; Social Security in, 512; Truman and, 570; women in, 515–516
New England, 22, 30 (illus.); blacks in, 50; Dominion of, 54; families in, 43–44; Hartford Convention in, 161; Indian war against (1675), 21; manufacturing in, 175; Pilgrims in, 28; Puritans in, 28–32; society in, 43–46
New Era: in 1920s, 489
New France, 13–14; imperial wars and, 72
New Freedom, 457, 458–461
New Frontier, 578, **582**–586, 586
New Guinea: in World War II, 531, 534
New Hampshire, 30 (illus.), 37 (illus.), 332
New Harmony, Indiana, utopian community at, 239
New Haven colony, 30 (illus.); in Connecticut, 32
New immigrants, 374, 432
New Jersey, 32, 34, 37 (illus.); female suffrage repealed in, 108; immigrants in, 657; in Revolution, 95
New Jersey Plan, 118
Newlands Act. *See* National Reclamation Act (Newlands Act) (1902)
New Left: election of 1972 and, 613
New Lights, 69
Newman, Paul, 607
New Mexico: Anasazi in, 3; cession to U.S. of, 255; expansionism and, 245–246; Hispanics in, 286, 340; Mexican-American War and, 254–255; as Mexican territory, 246; statehood for, 269; Texas boundary and, 269
"New monarchs" (Europe), 10
New Nationalism, 457, 459–461
New Navy, 412
New Negro, 478
New Netherland, 32, 33
New Orleans, 13, 73 (illus.); access to, 134; battle of, 161; in Civil War, 296 (illus.), 297; closing to U.S. commerce, 151; desegregated schools of, 322; race riot in, 315; in War of 1812, 161
New Orleans (steamboat), 171
New Spain: government of, 12; missions in, 63 (illus.)
Newspapers, 391; advertising in, 362; political culture and, 135. *See also* Press
New Sweden, 37 (illus.)
Newton, Huey, 596
"New Western historians," 348
New woman: assertiveness of, 380; in 1920s, 491
New World: Columbus in, 11; culture clash in, 1; Europe and, 10–11; France and, 13–14; Hakluyt on, 18. *See also* Americas; Exploration and discovery; specific regions
New York (city), 372; African Americans in, 658; capital in, 116; draft riot in, 301; electric signs in, 379; Ellis Island in, 388–389; Greenwich Village in, 438–439; Hell's Kitchen in, 384; immigrants in, 373; industry in, 436; Salvation Army in, 384 (illus.); settlement houses in, 385; tenements and population density in, 373; theater in, 378; Tweed Ring in, 376. *See also* World Trade Center
New York (colony), 30 (illus.), 32–34, 37 (illus.); Glorious Revolution in, 55; New Jersey and, 34
New York (state): Erie Canal and, 171–172; federal troops sent to, 157; immigrants in, 657
New York Armory show, 439
New York Central Railroad, 356, 358
New York County Courthouse, 376
New York State Tenement House Commission, 444
New York Times: Pentagon Papers and, 607
Nez Percé Indians, 335
NFWA. *See* National Farm Workers Association (NFWA)
Niagara, Fort: surrender by French, 75
Niagara Movement, 432
Nicaragua: Sandinistas in, 624; U.S. intervention in, 468, 639–640
Nicolls, Richard, 33
Nimitz, Chester, 534
Niña (ship), 11
Nine Power Treaty, 525
Nineteenth Amendment, 446, 490
Ninth Cavalry, 351–352, 415
Nisei: in World War II, 538
Nitze, Paul, 551
Nixon, Richard M.: on antiwar protests, 611; election of 1960 and, 577–578; election of 1968 and, 601; election of 1972 and, 612–613; energy crisis and, 614–616; pardon of, 622; presidency of, 608–612; presidential debate with Kennedy, 577; resignation of, 613; Vietnam War and, 611–612; Watergate Scandal and, 607–608, 613–614. *See also* Economy; Foreign policy; Nixonomics; Watergate Scandal
***Nixonomics*, 609**–610
Noble and Holy Order of the Knights of Labor. *See* Knights of Labor
"No Child Left Behind," 680
Nomadic hunters, 2
Non-Intercourse Act (1809), 158
Nonintervention: of Britain and France during Civil War, 299; in Latin America, 524
Nontransfer principle, 410
Nonviolent protest: in civil rights movement, 574, 574 (illus.)
Norcom family: James, 224–225; Maria, 224–225; Mary Matilda, 225
Noriega, Manuel, 651
"Normalcy": Harding on, 499
Normal schools (teacher-training institutions), 381
Normandy invasion: in World War II, 532, 538–539
Norris, Frank, 401
Norsemen. *See* Vikings
North (Civil War): advantages and disadvantages of, 292–293; backlash against emancipation in, 301; draft and draft riots in, 301; resources of, 294. *See also* Civil War (U.S.)

North (region): abolitionism and, 267; black migration to, 478, 479 (illus.); black population of cities in, 489; caning of Sumner and, 266; cultural sectionalism in, 276; extinction of slavery in, 107; Missouri Compromise and, 178–179; view of South in, 283; zoning and ethnic segregation in, 436
North, Frederick (Lord), 88, 90, 93
North, Oliver, 641
North Africa: Barbary War and, 152; World War II in, 531, 532–533, 533 (illus.)
North America: in 1800, 148 (illus.); in 1819, 167 (illus.); migration to, 2; in 1750, 73 (illus.); after 1763, 76 (illus.); U.S. foreign policy and, 409
North American Free Trade Agreement (NAFTA), 663–664
North Atlantic Treaty Organization (NATO), 548–549; in Bosnia, 670; in Kosovo, 671
North Carolina, 37 (illus.), 289; Roanoke settlement in, 17–18; secession of, 291; segregated schools in, 381. *See also* Carolina(s)
North Carolina A&T College: sit-in by students from, 574, 574 (illus.)
Northeast: Civil War in, 303
Northern Pacific Railroad, 452
Northern Securities Company, 452
North Korea: Korean War and, 552–554. *See also* Korea
North Star, 238
North Vietnam: bombings of, 591, 592, 598, 611, 612 (illus.); Gulf of Tonkin Resolution against, 590; after Vietnam War, 623. *See also* Vietnam; Vietnam War
Northwestern Alliance, 395
Northwest Ordinance, 112–113
Northwest passage: Cabot and, 14; French search for, 13
Northwest Territory: British military in, 132; Indians in, 134
NOW. *See* National Organization for Women (NOW)
Noyes, John Humphrey, 240
NRA. *See* National Recovery Administration (NRA)
NSC-68, 551
NSS. *See* National Security Strategy (NSS)
Nuclear arms race, 546, 638; Carter and, 626; SALT I and, 611; Soviet Union and, 642
Nuclear families, 618; in New England, 43
Nuclear freeze movement, 638
Nuclear weapons: Cold War and, 546; H-bomb and, 550–551; reduction and curtailment of, 650. *See also* Atomic bomb; Nuclear arms race; specific treaties
Nullification, 193–195, **194**; Embargo Act and, 157; Jefferson on, 140
Nye Committee, 526

O

Oath of allegiance: to Union, for ex-Confederates, 312
Oberlin College: founding of, 237
Ocala Demands, 395, 396
Occupations: of women, 364, 400, 431. *See also* Professions; Women; Workers
O'Connor, Sandra Day, 619
October War (1973), 614; Middle East after, 625
Octopus, The (Norris), 401
Oder River: in World War II, 539
OEO. *See* Office of Economic Opportunity (OEO)
Officeholders: blacks as, 320; responsiveness of, 450
Office of Economic Opportunity (OEO), 587
Offshore oil, 616, 633
Oglethorpe, James, 39
Ograbme, 157, 158 (illus.)
Ohio, 110, 166; slavery outlawed in, 113; steel industry in, 359
Ohio-Mississippi river system, 171
Ohio River region: France and, 74; migration into, 147; Mississippi River transportation and, 115; Native Americans in, 3
Oil and oil industry: Alaskan pipeline and, 616; energy crisis and, 614–616; holding company in, 361; Japan and, 530; offshore drilling and, 616, 633; oligopoly in, 428; from Persian Gulf region, 668; price increases in, 617; Rockefeller and, 359–361; trusts in, 360
Oil embargo, 614–615
Oil shocks, 615; inflation and, 617
O'Keeffe, Georgia, 439
Okinawa, 552
Oklahoma: African Americans in, 345; Indian removal to, 335; oil in, 361; opening to white settlement, 347; removal of five civilized tribes to, 168. *See also* Indian Country
Oklahoma City: federal building bombing in, 671, 673, 674 (illus.)
Old-age pensions: Social Security and, 512; in Townsend Plan, 511
Older people: in 1900, 436. *See also* Aged
Old Hickory. *See* Jackson, Andrew
Old Lights, 69
Old Northwest: settlement of, 168–169
Old Plantation, 51 (illus.)
Olds, Ransom E., 427
Old Ship Meetinghouse, 31 (illus.)
Old South, 205; blacks in, 205–211; divided society of, 212–216; whites in, 212–216. *See also* South
O'Leary, Hazel, 662
Oligopoly, 428
Oliver Iron and Steel Company: IWW strike against, 435 (illus.)
Olney, Richard, 410
Olsen, Floyd, 511
Olympics: U.S. boycott in 1980, 626
Omaha convention: People's party formed at, 396
Omnibus bill, 269
Oñate, Juan de, 13
"One big reservation" policy, 333
Oneida community, 240
O'Neill, Eugene, 493
"One man, one vote" principle, 585
Onís, Luis de, 166
On the Road (Kerouac), 569
"On to Richmond" strategy, 296 (illus.) 297–298
OPEC. *See* Organization of Petroleum Exporting Countries (OPEC)
Open Door Policy, 423–424, 467, 524; "dollar diplomacy" and, 468; Nine Power Treaty and, 525
Open range: cattle ranching on, 343
"Open skies" program, 561
Operation Desert Shield, 651
Operation Desert Storm, 651–652
Opportunity (Urban League), 493
Orange, Fort (Albany), 32
Orcutt, Susan, 390
Orders in Council (England), 156
Ordinance of 1784, 113
Ordinance of 1787. *See* Northwest Ordinance
Oregon, 267; border conflict with Britain and, 245, 253–254, 253 (illus.); expansionism and, 244, 249, 252; Russia and, 180; territorial boundaries of, 245; U.S.-British joint occupation of, 166
Oregon Trail, 248–249, 249 (illus.)
Organizational revolution, 307–308
Organization Man, The (Whyte), 568
Organization of Petroleum Exporting Countries (OPEC), 614–615
Organizations: of freedpeople, 322; for women, 108
Organized crime: in 1920s, 491
Organized labor, 489; in New Deal, 513–515. *See also* Labor unions; Strikes
Organized mob violence: against black voters, 319; in South, 311
Organized religion: in 1950s, 568
Orlando, Vittorio, 481
Ostend Manifesto, 273
O'Sullivan, John L.: Manifest Destiny and, 252
Oswald, Lee Harvey, 586
Other America, The (Harrington), 587
Otis, Elisha G.: elevator and, 258 (illus.)
Otis, James, 86
Our Country: Its Possible Future and Its Present Crisis (Strong), 409
"Outing": of homosexuals, 621
Overbuilding: by railroads, 357
Overland Trail, 337–338
Overseas markets. *See* Foreign markets
Overseas trade. *See* Foreign trade; Trade
Ovington, Mary, 432
Owen, Robert: New Harmony and, 239
Owenite communities, 239–240, 240 (illus.)

P

Pacific Coast region, 332; discrimination against Japanese and Chinese in, 364; Russia and, 180; Spain and, 63; in World War II, 536
Pacific Northwest: Adams-Onís Treaty and, 245; boundary dispute over, 253–254, 253 (illus.)
Pacific Ocean: as boundary, 166; Japan and, 529–530, 531, 534–535; U.S.-Japanese rivalry in, 524–525; World War II and, 534 (illus.), 551–552
Pacific theater: in Spanish-American War, 416 (illus.)
Pacifism: before World War II, 526
Pact of Paris (1928). *See* Kellogg-Briand Pact (1928)
Padroni (labor agents), 433
Paine, Thomas, 93, 95
Painting: Ashcan School of, 438 (illus.), 439; modernist, 439; Postimpressionist, 439
Pakenham, Edward, 161
Paleo-Indians, 2–3
Palestine Liberation Organization (PLO), 625, 638–639

Palestinian Arabs, 625; Clinton and, 668
Palmer, A. Mitchell, 494
Pamela (Richardson), 107
Panama: Carter and, 624; independence of, 466; U.S. invasion of, 650–651; U.S. protectorate in, 466
Panama Canal, 465–466; return to Panama, 624
Pan-American Exposition, 404
Pan-Americanism, 409, 410
Pan-American Union, 410
Panetta, Leon, 663
Panics: of 1819, 177, 189, 195; **of 1837, 198,** 250; of 1873, 320, 322; of 1893, 358; of 1907, 454
Paper money: Continentals as, 114, 114 (illus.)
Parcel post, 420
Pardons: for ex-Confederates, 312; of Nixon, 622
Parents: in New England, 44, 44 (illus.). *See also* Families
Paris: Peace Conference at, 480–482; Peace of (1763), 76 (illus.); Treaty of (1783), 99–101, 115–116; **Treaty of** (1898), **418,** 420 (illus.)
Parish schools. *See* Parochial education
Parker, Alton B., 453
Parks, Rosa, 573–574
Parliament: in Carolina, 37–38
Parliament (England), 70; Charles I and, 29; English civil war and, 22; imperial legislation and, 51–52; loss of American colonies and, 83–85; Stamp Act repealed by, 87
Parliamentary sovereignty, 83, 84
Parochial education, 274, 375
Parties. *See* Political parties; specific parties
Partisan politics: Washington and, 128
Party politics, 126–142. *See also* Partisan politics
Passive resistance: in civil rights movement, 574
Pasteur, Louis, 377
Patent medicines: regulation of, 453–454, 454 (illus.)
Patents: issued in 1890, 361
Paterson, New Jersey: IWW strike in, 434
Patriotism: in Civil War, 291; eagle as symbol of, 128 (illus.); War of 1812 and, 162 (illus.)
Patriots: in American Revolution, 94
Patronage, 128; Jefferson on, 150
Patton, George, 532; Normandy invasion and, 539
Patuxt Indians, 28
Paul, Alice, 446
Pawnee Indians, 333
Payne-Aldrich Act (1909), 455–456
Peace commission: to end Sioux War, 334–335
Peace conference: after Russian-Japanese war, 467; after World War I, 480–482
Peace Corps, 579
Peacekeeping: in Bosnia, 669–670
Peace of Paris (1763), 76 (illus.)
Peace policy: for Indians, 334–335, 351
Peace settlement: after American Revolution, 99–101
"Peace without victory": Wilson and, 473
Pearl, Mississippi: school violence in, 675
Pearl Harbor: Japanese attack on, **530**–531, 531 (illus.)
Peking. *See* Beijing
Pendleton Act (1883), **393**
Peninsula campaign, 297–298
Penn, William, 32, 34–35; departure from colonies, 36
Pennsylvania, 32, 37 (illus.); abolition of slavery in, 107; backcountry of, 60; coal strike in, 452–453; German immigrants in, 60; prejudice in, 61; Quakers in, 34–36; September 11, 2001, plane crash in, 681; steel industry in, 359
Pennsylvania Dutch: German immigrants as, 60
Pennsylvania Main Line Canal, 172
Pennsylvania Railroad, 356, 358
Pensions: for army, 115; in Townsend Plan, 511
Pentagon: Kennedy and, 583; September 11, 2001, and, 655, 677, 681
Pentagon Papers, 607, 608
People, the: in Constitution, 119; power to, 109
People's (or Populist) party, 347, 396, **396,** 399; election of 1896 and, 401–403
People's Republic of China. *See* China; Communist China
Pepperrell, William, 73
Per capita income: in 1929, 487
Perestroika, 642
Perkins, Frances, 516
Perot, H. Ross: election of 1992 and, 661, 662 (illus.); on NAFTA, 664
Perrett, Geoffrey, 486
Perry, Oliver Hazard, 160
Pershing, John J. "Black Jack," 470, 474
Persian Gulf region: Carter Doctrine and, 625; U.S. reliance on oil from, 668
Persian Gulf War: economy and, 652. *See also* Operation Desert Storm
Personal computers, 673 (illus.)
Personal digital assistant (PDA), 673 (illus.)
Personal saving, 635
Personnel management: labor unrest and, 435
Peru, 645; cocaine sources in, 646; Incas in, 4; Spain and, 11
Petersburg: siege of, 303, 305
Petroleum. *See* Oil and oil industry
Philadelphia, 35 (illus.), 372; capital in, 116; Franklin n, 65–66; immigrant population in, 373; industry in, 436; political machine in, 376
Philadelphia (ship), 152
Philadelphia convention, 117–120
Philadelphia Negro, The (Du Bois), 382
Philanthropy, 307; of Carnegie, 359; higher education and, 381
Philip, King. *See* Metacomet (Wampanoags)
Philip II (Spain): Armada of, 16
Philippine-American War, 419–421
Philippine Commission. *See* Taft Commission
Philippines, 465, 467; immigration from, 605; independence for, 421; reconcentration-like policy of U.S. in, 420; Spanish-American War and, 416–417, 418; in World War II, 531, 540
Philosophy: of pragmatism, 400
Phonographs, 361–362, 437
Piantadosi, Al, 470 (illus.)
Picasso, 439
Pickering, John, 153–154
Picketing: Clayton Act and, 435 (illus.). *See also* Labor; Strikes
Piecework, 364
Pierce, Franklin, 271, 275; foreign policy of, 272–273
Pikes Peak: gold strike at, 341
Pilgrims: Separatists as, 27–28
Pinchot, Gifford, 442, 454, 456
Pinckney, Charles Cotesworth: election of 1796 and, 137; election of 1800 and, 141; election of 1804 and, 153
Pinckney, Thomas, 134, 137
Pinckney's Treaty. *See* San Lorenzo, Treaty of
Pinta (ship), 11
Pipeline: Alaskan, 616
Pirates: Barbary, 152; English Sea Dogs as, 16
Pit, The (Norris), 401
Pitt, William, 74–75, 76, 87
Pittsburgh, 147; Fort Duquesne and, 74; steel industry in, 359
Pius V (Pope): Elizabeth I and, 16
Placer mining, 341
Plains Indians, 333–335
Plantation duty, 52
Planter (steamship), 310
Planters and plantations: in Carolina, 38; in Chesapeake society, 47–48; Johnson, Andrew, and, 313; in Maryland, 27; slaves and, 49, 107; in Virginia, 23
Plants: in Columbia Exchange, 6
Platt Amendment, 422, 466
Plattsburg, battle at, 161
Playwrights: in 1920s, 493; for television, 568
Plessy* v. *Ferguson, 328 (illus.), **380,** 573
PLO. *See* Palestine Liberation Organization (PLO)
Plunkitt, George Washington, 376
Pluralistic society, 386
Plymouth Colony, 30 (illus.), 37 (illus.); Pilgrims in, 28
Pneumonia, 377
Pocahontas, 24
Pocket-veto: by Lincoln, 312
Poe, Edgar Allan, 189, 276
Poetry (magazine), 439
Poets and poetry: in Progressive Era, 439–440; realism in, 400. *See also* specific poets
Pogroms, 373
Poindexter, John, 641
Poison gas: in World War I, 474
Poland: immigrants from, 374; Nazi invasion of, 527, 527 (illus.); Solidarity movement in, 649; Soviet armies in, 539
Polish Americans, 596
Polish National Alliance, 375
Political cartoons: anti-Know-Nothings, 273 (illus.); on Bryan's "Cross of Gold" speech, 402 (illus.); on Dulles' hard line, 559 (illus.); on election of 1860, 281; on George III, 84 (illus.); on gold standard, 404 (illus.); on Know-Nothing charges of election stealing by immigrants, 273 (illus.); "Modern Colossus of (Rail) Roads," 357 (illus.); Nast on trusts, 428 (illus.); on new immigrants, 374 (illus.); Ograbme and, 158 (illus.); on Reconstruction, 314 (illus.); on Rockefeller, John D., 360 (illus.); on Roosevelt, Theodore, 452 (illus.); on Treaty of Versailles, 482 (illus.); on U.S. acquisitions, 419 (illus.); on U.S. preservation of China sovereignty, 422 (illus.); "World's Constable, The" (Roosevelt Collary), 467 (illus.); "Worse Than Slavery" (Nast), 324 (illus.)

Political clubs, 136
Political coalition: in New Deal, 516, 518, 519–520
Political culture: American vs. British, 70–72; popular, 135–136; after Revolution, 103–104
Political leadership: during Civil War, 295–297
Political machines. *See* Machines (political)
Political organization: mining frontier and western, 343
Political parties: deadlock between, 391–392; public opinion and, 127; sectional, 271; after War of 1812, 176. *See also* Party politics; specific parties
Political power: of southern blacks, 311
Political systems: in West Africa, 8
Politics and politicians, 377; Alliance movement and, 395–396; British, 70–71; civil rights and, 572; corruption in, 378; of 1890s, 390–405; extremism in, 142; federal government, role of, and, 190; hotel boom and, 185; among Indian groups, 4; in Jacksonian era, 189–195; Jay's Treaty and, 135; logrolling and, 191; loyal opposition and, 189; machines and, 191; mass democracy and, 191; of nation building, 176–182; nativism and, 273–274; in 1920s, 498–501; party system and, 189, 191; presidential debates and, 577; realignment in, 630; reforms of, 105–106; before Revolution, 83–84; second party system and, 195, 197–200, 200–201; solid South and, 198; special interests and, 191; of stalemate, 391–393; after Watergate, 622–624; in World War II, 538
Polk, James K., 267; election of 1844 and, 244, 251–252; Jackson, Andrew, and, 252; Mexican-American War and, 254–256; Oregon question and, 253–254; Texas annexation and, 251–252; youth of, 244
Polk, Leonidas, 395
Poll tax, 432; voting and, 391
Pollution: in cities, 373; Johnson, Lyndon B., and, 589; suspension of nuclear testing and, 561. *See also* Environment
Polygamy: among Indians, 7; among Mormons, 250
Pontiac (Ottawa): uprising by, 85
Pools (business): in steel industry, 359
Poor: immigration experience of, 388–389; studies of, 385–386; wealth inequality and, 636. *See also* Poverty
Poor People's March on Washington (King, 1968), 596
Pope, John, 298
Popes and papacy: Henry VIII (England) and, 15. *See also* specific popes
Popular culture: political, 135–136
Popular fiction, 437–438
Popular religion: in Great Awakening, 68–69. *See also* Religion(s)
Popular sovereignty, 268, 287; civil war and, 278; Compromise of 1850 and, 269; constitutionality of, 277; in Kansas, 274–275; Kansas-Nebraska Act and, 272 (illus.)
Population: African American, 50, 489, 658–659; baby boom and, 565; of British colonies, 72; in census of 1790, 144–145; changing nature of, 655–661; characteristics by 2050, 606; of Chesapeake region, 47; in cities, 64–65, 371, 372, 490; of colonies, 59; density in cities, 373; in 1877, 377; growth of, 147; immigrants in, 354, 373; Indian loss of, 8; median age (in 1920), 436; of New England, 43; of New France, 14; racial and ethnic composition of, 605–606; of reservations, 337; shift in 1970s, 629–630; in Sunbelt, 655; of Tenochtitlán, 4; trends in, 656–657; of unmarried women after Civil War, 305; of Virginia, 25; in West, 345
Populist party. *See* People's (or Populist) party
Port Gibson: battle at, 304 (illus.)
Port Huron, Michigan: SDS and, 593
Portolá, Gaspar de, 63
Port Royal, 36, 37
Portsmouth, New Hampshire: peace conference at, 467
Portugal: division of New World by, 11; voyages of exploration by, 12 (illus.); West Africa and, 8, 9
Portuguese empire, 11
Postimpressionists, 439
Potsdam conference, 543
Pound, Ezra, 439
Poverty, 384; among blacks, 659; in cities, 373; in Great Depression, 505–506; in Haiti, 669; hotel boom and, 184; immigration and, 260; of Indians, 515; institutionalization and, 235–236; of Native Americans, 337; as root of crime proposition, 383; in United States, 587; women without partners and, 618. *See also* Poor
Powderly, Terence V., 365, 366
Powell, Colin, 679; loss of influence by, 684
Powell, Lewis, 609
Power: in family, 107; by 1970s, 611; in states, 109; state vs. federal government, 288; virtue and, 85
Power (energy). *See* Energy
Power Elite, The (Mills), 569
Powers, Francis Gary, 562
Powhatan Indians, 4
Pragmatism, 400, **447**
Pragmatism (James), 447
Prairie du Chien, Wisconsin: Native Americans at, 169 (illus.)
Prairie Plains, 332
Preachers: in Great Awakening, 68–69
Predatory wealth, 384
Predestination: Calvin on, 15; Quakers and, 34
Preemption right: for public lands, 169
Preparedness campaign: for World War I, 472
Presbyterians: Finney, Charles G., and, 226, 229; Second Great Awakening and, 228
Prescott, Samuel, 91
Presidency: authority of, 392; Force Bill (1833) and, 195; Jackson's use of power and, 195–197; under Washington, 128
President: executive as, 118; states of origin, 392; title for, 126. *See also* specific presidents
Presidential debates: by Kennedy and Nixon, 577
Presidential elections. *See* Elections
Presidential pardon: for ex-Confederates, 312; for Nixon, 622
Presidential power, 448; attempts to limit, 316; reestablishing, 392–393
Presidios (forts): in California, 63
Press: freedom of, 123; in Jacksonian era, 186; printing press and, 258 (illus.). *See also* Journalism; Newspapers
Price, The (play), 363
Price controls: on oil and natural gas, 616
Price freeze: by Nixon, 610
Princeton: battle at, 95, 96 (illus.); capital in, 116
Principall Navigations, Voyages, and Discoveries of the English Nation, The (Hakluyt), 18
Printing: in Chesapeake, 48; printing press and, 258 (illus.)
Private enterprise: federal government and, 306–307
Privateers: of Confederacy, 299; in War of 1812, 160
Prochoice groups, 620
Proclamation of 1763, 85
Proclamation of neutrality (1793), 133
Production: consumer society and, 67
Productivity: increases in, 672; in 1990s, 666; in workplace, 429
Professionalization: in Jacksonian era, 186
Professional societies, 444
Professions: Asian Americans in, 660; feminization of, 364; rise of, 443–444; training for, 382; women in, 364, 490, 619
Progress and Poverty (George), 383
Progressive education, 568
Progressive Era, 405, 426–440; African Americans in, 432; arts during, 438–440; children and, 431; cities in, 436; immigrants in labor force during, 432–433; industrialism in, 427–429; labor-oriented reforms of, 434; leisure in, 437–438; mass society in, 429–433; muckraking in, 426; pragmatism and, 447; professions in, 443–444; purity crusade during, 445; reform in cities and states during, 448–451; Roosevelt, Theodore, and, 451–454; socialism in, 448; social-justice movement in, 444–445; sociological jurisprudence and, 448; Taft and, 454–458; trusts in, 428; urban culture in, 435–440; Wilson and, 458–461; women and, 431, 445–446; workplace conflict during, 434–435
Progressive party: in 1912, 442, **457,** 461; in 1948, 555
Progressivism, 426–**427**; election of 1916 and, 461; historians' view of, 443; reshaping of country by, 440; Roosevelt, Theodore, Wilson, and, 426–427; spirit of, 443; after World War I, 484. *See also* Progressive Era
Prohibition, 495; Eighteenth Amendment and, 445
Prohibitory Act (1775), 93, 99 (illus.)
Promontory, Utah: transcontinental railroads meeting at, 357
Propaganda, 135; in Civil War, 302; during World War I, 476
Property: as voting requirement, 106; women and, 45
"Property Protected à la Françoise," 138 (illus.)
Prophet, the. *See* Tenskwatawa (the Prophet)
Proportional representation: in Virginia Plan, 118
Proposition 13 (California), 629
Proprietary colonies: Carolina as, 36–38; New Jersey as, 34
Prosperity: in 1920s, 498; in 1990s, 655, 666, 672; World War II and, 536, 566–567
Prosser, Gabriel, 209
Prostitution: attempts to get rid of, 445; in mining camps, 342

Protective tariffs, 403; of 1862, 306; American system as, 176; in 1920s, 499. *See also* Tariff(s)
Protectorate: Hawaii as, 411
Protest(s): antiwar, 611; against British taxation, 86–87; by gays, 620–621; by Mexican Americans, 596–597; in 1960s, 593–598; by People's party, 396; against Sugar Act, 86
Protestant Association (Maryland), 56
Protestant ethic, 235
Protestant Reformation, 14–**15**; Puritan movement and, 28–29
Protestants and Protestantism: Calvin and, 14; common school movement and, 235; in 1880s, 378; of Elizabeth I (England), 15–16; English colonization of Ireland and, 17; evangelical, 61; Luther and, 14; in Maryland, 27, 55–56; nativism and, 273; Protestant ethic and, 235; Reformation and, 14–15; sectionalism and, 276; of William and Mary (England), 22. *See also* Evangelicals and evangelicalism; Great Awakening
Providence, 31
Provisional governors: in Johnson's Reconstruction plan, 313
Psychedelic drugs, 601
Psychology, 377
Public morality: supervision of, 378
Public opinion, 127; advertising and, 488; on League of Nations, 481; on Reagan and Iran-Contra affair, 642
Public relations: corporate, 435
Public schools, 311; for Asian children in San Francisco, 467; in late 19th century, 380; in South, 320
Public Works Administration (PWA), 510, 518
Public works projects: in Great Depression, 506; Kennedy and, 583
Puck cartoons. *See* Political cartoons
Pueblo Indians: whites and, 63, 64
Pueblos: of Anasazi culture, 3
Puerto Ricans, 658; nationalism of, 596
Puerto Rico, 465; cession of, 418; Spanish-American War in, 418; territorial status and citizenship for, 422
Puget Sound: acquisition of, 254
Pullman, George M.: passenger car and, 258 (illus.)
Pullman Palace Car Company, 397
Pullman strike, 366, 367 (illus.), **397,** 398, 448
Pure Food and Drug Act (1906), 453–454
Puritanism: Second Great Awakening and, 228–229
Puritans, 28–32; England and, 56; Native Americans and, 21; women and, 44–45
Purity crusade, 445
Putin, Vladimir V., 668
Put-in-Bay, battle at, 160
Putting-out system, 175
PWA. *See* Public Works Administration (PWA)
Pynchon family, 46

Q

al Qaeda. *See* al Qaeda
Quakers, 34–36; in Jerseys, 33 (illus.), 34; in Pennsylvania, 32, 34–36; on theater, 103
Quang Duc (Buddhist monk): self-immolation of, 579 (illus.)
Quartering Act (1765), 99 (illus.)
Quasi-War, 137–138
Quayle, Dan, 647
Quebec, 73 (illus.); founding of, 13; French defeat at, 76
Quebec Act (1774), 90
Queen Anne's War, 72–73
Queens. *See* specific rulers
Quetzalcoatl (god), 11
Quinine: in Civil War, 295 (illus.)
Quitrents: in Carolina, 36; in Pennsylvania, 36
Quotas: on exports to Japan, 529; on immigration, 497

R

Rabin, Yitzhak, 668
Race and racism: affirmative action and, 659; antiabolitionist violence and, 237; Black Codes and, 313–314, 318–319, 321; against black Spanish-American War troops, 415–416; *Californios* and, 285; in cavalry, 351; in Chesapeake society, 47; emancipation and, 300, 301; equality and, 146–147; expansionism and, 254–255; Harlem Renaissance and, 493; in Jacksonian era, 190; Jim Crow laws and, 328–329; Meredith, James, and, 584; Mexican-American War settlement and, 255; in mining camps, 342; in movies, 437; Native Americans and, 193; New Deal and, 515; against new immigrants, 433; in 1920s, 497; proslavery arguments and, 216; Roosevelt, Theodore, and, 451; in South, 107; Tocqueville on, 202; of Wilson, 459; in World War II, 536–538. *See also* African Americans; Civil rights; Civil rights movement; Slaves and slavery
Race riots: in Atlanta, 432; against black Spanish-American War troops, 416; in East St. Louis, 478; in Memphis, 315; in Mississippi, 325; in New Orleans, 315; in 1919, 478; in Springfield, Illinois, 432; in World War II, 537. *See also* Riot(s)
Radcliffe, 381
Radford, Arthur, 559
Radical individualism, 241
Radical Reconstruction, 315–316, 319, 320, 326
Radical Republicans, 300, 305, **312,** 314; Johnson's Reconstruction policies and, 313
Radicals and radicalism: black, 596; fears of (1920s), 494–495; at First Continental Congress, 91; Haymarket Riot and, 367. *See also* Communism
Radio, 488, 488 (illus.); networks on, 488; Roosevelt, Franklin D., and, 507–508
Ragtime (music), 378, 437
Railroads, 172; air brake for, 353; bankers' financing and control of, 358; as big business, 355; cattle and, 343; consolidation by, 358; economy and, 257, 259, 355; eight-hour workday on interstate, 461; expansion of, 256, 257; growth problems for, 357–358; innovations in, 355; land grants to, 306, 339, 356; linking cities, 354; locomotive and, 258 (illus.); in 1920s, 489; oligopoly in, 428; Panic of 1893 and, 358; Pullman passenger car and, 258 (illus.); rate wars between, 358; regulation of, 392, 453, 456; safety of workers on, 364; safety regulations for, 456; in South, 320; strikes against, 366, 397; subsidies for, 332; technology of, 257; transcontinental, 357; transportation of goods by, 363 (illus.); trunk lines and, 356; in westward movement and, 338
Rainey, Gertrude "Ma," 437
Rain-in-the-Face, 335
Raleigh, Walter, 17–18; second colony of, 18
Rancheros, 246
Ranching. *See* Cattle
Randolph, A. Philip: march on Washington (1941) and, 536
Randolph, Edmund, 117; as attorney general, 128; Bill of Rights and, 122
Randolph, John, 154, 158
Randolph, Thomas Mann, 82
Ratification: of Bill of Rights, 123; of Constitution (U.S.), 120–121, 122 (illus.)
Rationing: in World War I, 477; in World War II, 535
Rations: in Civil War, 295 (illus.)
Rauschenbusch, Walter, 384
Rayburn, Sam: as House Speaker, 571, 583
Reading. *See* Illiteracy; Literacy
Readmission to Union: of former Confederate states, 316. *See also* Reconstruction
Reagan, Nancy: "Just Say No" drug campaign of, 645
Reagan, Ronald, 630; AIDS epidemic and, 643–644; assessment of administration, 646–647; cabinet of, 633; as California governor, 629; Central America and, 639–641, 641; conservatism and, 629–630, 630; defense spending by, 634, 635, 637; deficit and, 634–635; deregulation and, 633; election of 1980 and, 630, 631–632, 631 (illus.); election of 1984 and, 637; foreign policy of, 637–642; Grenada invasion and, 640; income tax cuts of, 634; Iran-Contra affair and, 641–642; Middle East and, 638–639, 640–641; New Deal coalition and, 632; Soviet Union and, 638, 642; Supreme Court appointments of, 647; war on drugs and, 645; wealthy under, 636
Reaganomics, 634–637
Realism: in literature, 400; in painting, 439
Rearmament: in Korean War, 554
Rebates: in railroad industry, 358
Rebecca of Sunnybrook Farm (Wiggins), 437
Rebellions. *See* Revolts and rebellions
Recall, 450
Recession: election of 1992 and, 661; of 1937, 517; in 1949 and 1953, 566; in 1980s, 631; of 1981, 634; of 1990–1991, 648, 654; in 2001, 680; Nixon and, 609–610
Reciprocity treaties, 411; trade and, 410
Reconcentration policy: in Cuba, 413
Reconstruction, 310–329, 315 (illus.); Compromise of 1877 and, 326; congressional, 314–316; end of, 326; minimal vs. radical policy proponents, 311–312; presidential (Johnson), 313–314; Radical, 315–316, 319, 320, 326; retreat from, 322–326; reunion and the New South, 326–329; southern society during, 317–322; Ten Percent Plan, 312; as "unfinished revolution," 311, 329; wartime, 312
Reconstruction Acts (1867), 315, 316, 317

Reconstruction Amendments. *See* Fifteenth Amendment; Fourteenth Amendment; Thirteenth Amendment
Reconstruction Finance Corporation (RFC), 506, 509
Records (phonograph), 362
Recovery programs: of Roosevelt, Franklin D., 508–509, 518
Red Army, 650; in eastern Europe, 544; in World War II, 533
Red Badge of Courage, The (Crane), 401
Red Cloud, 334, 334 (illus.)
Redcoats: at Boston Massacre, 88, 89 (illus.); under Braddock, 74; at Lexington, 91. *See also* American Revolution
Redeemers, 326–327, 328
Red River War, 335, 351–352
Red Scare: McCarthyism and, 556–557, 566; in 1919, 477, 479; in 1920s, 494–495; after World War II, 556
Reed, Ester DeBerdt, 108
Reed, Thomas B., 393
Reed, Walter, 422
Referendum, 450
Reform and reform movements: Alliance movement, 394, 395–396; antitrust, 360; asylums and, 235–236; banking reform, 458–459; benevolent empire and, 231, 236–237; in cities, 449–450; civil service reform, 392, 393; counterpoint on, 241–242; of courts, 153; education and, 234–235, 447; end of liberal, 602; of health care, 664; institutional, 234–236; in Jacksonian era, 186; Jeffersonian, 150; Johnson, Lyndon B., and, 588–589; in late 19th century, 378, 383–385; muckrakers and, 426, 427; Mugwumps and, 378; political, 105–106; political machines and, 376; radical, 236–241; revivals and, 229–231; Roosevelt, Franklin D., and, 511–513; Roosevelt, Theodore, and, 453; Second Great Awakening and, 226, 228–231; after Second World War, 570–574; settlement houses and, 385; social, 105; social-justice movement, 444–445; in South, 320; in states, 450–451; temperance and, 378
Reformation, 14–15
Refrigerated railroad cars, 356, 361
Refrigeration: cattle ranching and, 344
Refugees: Indians as, 8; from Southeast Asia, 660
Regan, Donald, 641, 646
Regions: in English colonies, 42; identification with, 147. *See also* specific regions
Regulation: of industrialism, 403; of interstate commerce, 180; of railroads, 392; by Roosevelt, Theodore, 453–454; by states, 450; of steamboats, 171
Regulation movement, 450
Rehnquist, William, 609, 647; Clinton impeachment and, 676
Reich, Robert, 663
Reign of Terror: in French Revolution, 132
Relief programs: of Roosevelt, Franklin D., 509–511, 517
Religion(s): African American, 50; in Bosnia-Herzegovina, 666; Christian fundamentalism and, 497–498, 629; Elizabeth I (England) and, 15–16; in ethnic communities, 61; freedom of, 123; Great Awakening and, 68–70; Indians and, 7; Islamic fundamentalism and, 682; Luther and, 14; in Maryland, 26–27, 55–56; in Massachusetts Bay, 31–32; in New England, 44; of "new monarchs," 10; in 1920s, 497–498; in 1950s, 568; popular, 68–69; Protestant Reformation and, 14–15; sectionalism in, 276; social justice and, 384, 385; in West Africa, 8. *See also* specific groups
Religious freedom, 106–107, 113
Religious schools: of eastern European Jews, 375
Religious toleration: in Maryland, 27; in New York, 33; in Rhode Island, 32
Relocation: of Japanese Americans, 538
Removal. *See* Indian removal
Renaissance, 9
Reno, Janet, 662; Whitewater and, 665
Reparations: for Germany, 481; after World War I, 523; after World War II, 543
Report on Manufactures (Hamilton), 131–132
Report on the Public Credit (Hamilton), 130
Representation: in legislatures, 106
Repression: under Alien and Sedition Acts, 139
Republicanism, 103–124, **104**; Articles of Confederation and, 116–117; culture of, 104–105; of Jefferson and Hamilton, 129–130; Madison on, 116–117; Montesquieu on, 116; in states, 108–109; Washington and, 128; women and, 107–108
Republican party, 271, **274**–275; and "Billion-Dollar Congress," 393–394; Contract with America and, 665; in 1824, 190; in 1870s and 1880s, 391; election of 1894 and, 399; election of 1896 and, 401–403; election of 1952 and, 557–558; election of 1968 and, 601; election of 1984 and, 637; election of 2000 and, 677–678; as first sectional party, 282–283; impeachment of Andrew Johnson and, 317; Klan violence against, 323, 324–325; Lincoln in, 287; Modern Republicanism and, 570–572; in 1920s, 498–501; Nixon and, 610; program cuts and, 666; progressives in, 456; radical wing of, 266; in South, 319–320, 323–325. *See also* Liberal Republicans
Republicans (Jeffersonian), 132; dissension among, 154; election of 1796 and, 137; Jay's Treaty and, 134; after War of 1812, 176; Whiskey Rebellion and, 136
Republic of Texas, 247–248
Republic Steel strike, 514 (illus.)
Reservations (Indian): population of, 337; removal to, 334–335; in West, 332–333
Resistance: of Native Americans, 334, 335
Resolution Trust Corporation (RTC), 648, 665
Reston, James, 607
Restoration (England), 36; intervention in colonies after, 50–53
Reuben James (ship), 529
Revels, Hiram R., 321 (illus.)
Revenue Act (1764). *See* Sugar Act (1764)
Revenue-sharing payments: Nixon and, 609
Revenue stamps: protests against, 86–87
Revere, Paul, 91; etching of Boston Massacre, 89 (illus.)
Revivalism: Finney, Charles G., and, 226, 229; in Great Awakening, 68–70; in late 19th century, 378; reform and, 229–231, 237; Second Great Awakening and, 227–228, 228 (illus.), 229
Revolts and rebellions: Bacon's Rebellion, 53–54; Boxer Rebellion and, 423–424; by Leisler, 55; by Pontiac, 85; Shays's, 117; Stono Uprising as, 50. *See also* American Revolution
Revolution(s): agricultural, 3; cultural (1960s), 595; Glorious (England), 22; in Hawaii, 411; in Iran (1979), 625; in medicine, 377; in Mexico, 469; in transportation, 170–173
Revolutionary War in America. *See* American Revolution
Reykjavik, Iceland: Reagan-Gorbachev summit in, 642
RFC. *See* Reconstruction Finance Corporation (RFC)
Rhee, Syngman, 552
Rhode Island, 32, 37 (illus.); Providence in, 31
Rice, Condoleezza, 679
Rice and rice plantations, 38; slaves and, 50
Richardson, Samuel, 107
Richmond, Virginia: capture of, 304 (illus.), 305; in Civil War, 296 (illus.)
Ridge, Tom, 683
Riesman, David, 568–569
Rights: of African Americans, 106–107; to bear arms, 123; in Bill of Rights, 122–123; in state constitutions, 109; of women, 107–108. *See also* specific rights and groups
Riis, Jacob, 373
Rillieux, Norbert: vacuum evaporator and, 258 (illus.)
Rio Grande region: Spain and, 63
Riot(s): at Democratic convention (Chicago, 1968), 600–601; food, in Confederacy, 294; New York City draft riot, 301; Stonewall, 620–621. *See also* Race riots
Ripley, George, 241
River Rouge Ford plant, 486
Rivers: in Plains, 332; as transportation network, 171. *See also* specific river regions
Roads and highways, 170–171, 177; Federal Aid Roads Act and, 427–428; Highway Act of 1956 and, 571–572, 571 (illus.); planned highway system and, 428
Roanoke (beads), 1
Roanoke colony, 17–18
Roaring Twenties, 491–492
Robb, Charles, 600 (illus.)
Robber barons, 355
Robins, Margaret Dreier, 434
Rochambeau (Comte de), 98
Rochester, New York, 436
Rochester Theological Seminary, 384
Rockefeller, John D., 359–361, 381
Rockefeller, Nelson, 622
Rockefeller Sanitary Commission, 431
Rockingham, Charles Watson-Wentworth (Lord), 87
Rocky Mountain Fur Company, 167
Rocky Mountains, 332; "mountain men" in, 167; South Pass through, 338
***Roe v. Wade*, 620**
Rogers, William, 608
Roman Catholic Church. *See* Catholics and Catholicism
Romania: fall of repressive government in, 649
Rommel, Erwin, 531, 532

Roosevelt, Alice Lee, 377
Roosevelt, Eleanor: African Americans and, 515; women's rights and, 516
Roosevelt, Franklin D., 461; challenges to, 511–512; Churchill and, 532; death of, 540; election of 1932 and, 507; election of 1936 and, 516; foreign policy of, 526; Good Neighbor Policy and, 524; Hundred Days of, 507–508; League of Nations and, 523; minorities and, 515; neutrality legislation and, 526; New Deal and, 503; recovery and, 508–509; reform and, 511–513; relief programs of, 509–511; Social Security and, 512; Soviet Union and, 532; Supreme Court and, 517; World War II and, 527, 529; World War II home front and, 535–536; World War II politics and, 538; at Yalta, 540
Roosevelt, Theodore, 377, 408, 437, 444, 452 (illus.); assumption of presidency, 404; coal miners' strike and, 452–453; conservation of, 454; election of 1912 and, 457–458; expansion of presidency and, 461; foreign policy of, 465–466; muckrakers term and, 426; New Nationalism of, 457; as New York governor, 424; Panama Canal and, 465–466; progressivism and, 426; reform program and regulatory measures of, 453–454; and Rough Riders, 407; in Spanish-American War, 417; Taft and, 442, 456; trusts and, 451–452; as vice president, 404, 424; Washington, Booker T., and, 451; World War I and, 472
Roosevelt Corollary, 466–467, 468; in 1930s, 524
Root, Elihu, 465
Root, John, 372
Root-Takahira Agreement, 467
Rosenberg, Ethel and Julius, 556
Rostow, Walt W., 578, 580, 589
Rotary press, 362
Rotogravure illustrations, 362
Rough Riders, 407, 416, 417
Rover Boys series, 438
Roxbury, Massachusetts: Brook Farm and, 241
Royal African Company, 49
Royal colonies: governors in, 71; in Maryland, 56; North and South Carolina as, 38; Virginia as, 26
Royal Navy (England): seizures of U.S. ships by, 156, 158; slave trade and, 156
Rubin, Jerry, 595
Rubin, Robert, 663
Ruby, Jack, 586
Ruby Ridge, Idaho: militia movement at, 673
Rudman, Warren, 635
Rule Britannia (song), 77
"Rule of reason": for restraint of trade cases, 457
Rum: in Georgia, 39, 40
Rumsfeld, Donald, 679; NSS and, 684
Rural areas: blacks in, 432; depression of 1890s and, 390; entertainment in, 378; factory-made goods in, 363 (illus.); free coinage of silver and, 401; mail delivery in, 430; mail order and, 362, 430, 436 (illus.); migration from, 430; in 1920s, 493–498; "one man, one vote" principle and, 585; population in, 377; separation from urban areas, 149
Rural Electrification Administration (REA, 1935), 519
Rural free delivery (RFD), 347, 430, 436 (illus.)
Rush-Bagot Agreement (1817), 166
Rusk, Dean, 578, 589
Russia: Alaska sale by, 410; China and, 422; Clinton and, 668; immigrants from, 374; Lenin and Bolsheviks in, 477; Open Door Policy and, 423; Pacific Coast and, 63; peace with Germany, 477; reforms and free market system in, 650; war with Japan, 467. *See also* Soviet Union; World War I; World War II
Russian Republic: Yeltsin as president of, 649–650
Russian Revolution, 477
Rustic Dance After a Sleigh Ride (Mount), 188 (illus.)
Ruth, Babe, 491
Ryswick, Treaty of, 72

S

Sacagawea (Shoshoni), 152
Sacco, Nicola, 495
Sac Indians, 168
Sack of Lawrence, 275
Sacramento Valley, 338
Sacrifice: by Aztecs, 4
Sadat, Anwar, 625
Safer sex: AIDS and, 643
Safety: airline, 683; in automobiles, 633; standards for workers, 364; of workers, 429; in workplace, 429
Sahara desert: trade and, 8
Saigon, 580; Buddhist protests in, 580 (illus.); fall of, 624. *See also* Vietnam; Vietnam War
Sailing: innovations in, 10
St. Augustine, 13; Spain and, 63
St. Denis, Ruth, 438
St. Lawrence River region: French and, 13; Louisbourg and, 73
Saint-Lô, France, 539
St. Louis, 167; corruption in, 426
"St. Louis Blues" (Handy), 437
St. Mary's (Maryland), 27
St.-Mihel salient, 475
Salem Village: witchcraft and, 55
Salisbury, Lord, 410
SALT II, 638
Salvation: Calvin on, 14; Puritans on, 29
Salvation Army, 384 (illus.)
Samoan Islands: annexation of, 411–412; naval control in, 422
Sampson, William T., 417
Sandburg, Carl, 440
Sand Creek massacre, 333–334
Sandinistas: in Nicaragua, 624, 639, 640
Sandys, Edwin, 24–25
San Francisco: Asian children in public schools, 467; political machine in, 376
Sanger, Margaret: birth control and, 432
Sanitation: in cities, 373
San Jacinto, battle of, 248
San Juan Hill, battle at, 416, 417; buffalo soldiers and, 352
San Lorenzo, Treaty of, 134
Santa Anna, Antonio López de: Mexican-American War and, 255; Texas and, 247–248
Santa Fe Trail, 248–249, 249 (illus.)
Santa Maria (ship), 11
Santiago, 417; battle at, 352, 418
Santo Domingo, 151
Sarajevo, 669, 670
Saratoga, battle at, 92 (illus.)
Satellites (space): Sputnik as, 561, 569–570, 569 (illus.)
Satellite states: Soviet, 544
Saudi Arabia, 651
"Savages": Indians as, 168
Savannah: in American Revolution, 97; Civil War in, 304 (illus.), 305
Savings and loan industry crisis, 648
Savio, Mario, 593
Sawyer, Samuel Tredwell, 225
Scalia, Antonin, 647
Scandals. *See* specific scandals
Scandinavia: Vikings from, 9
Scarlet Letter, The (Hawthorne), 242
Schools: in Chesapeake, 48; desegregation of, 573; for freedpeople, 322; Jewish religious schools, 375; for Native Americans, 335–336; parochial, 274, 375; segregated, 572; suburban development and, 568; violence in 1990s, 673–675. *See also* Education
School shootings, 671
Schurz, Carl, 325
Scientific labor management: in workplace, 429
SCLC. *See* Southern Christian Leadership Conference (SCLC)
Scool Kill (Schuylkill) river, 35 (illus.)
Scopes, John, 497
Scopes trial, 497
Scots-Irish immigrants, 59, 60–61; acculturation of, 80
Scott, Dred, 277
Scott, Thomas A., 359
Scott, Winfield, 271, 297; Mexican-American War and, 254–255
Scowcroft, Brent, 649
Scripture: family and, 43; Hutchinson and, 31; Puritans and, 29
Scrooby Manor: Pilgrims from, 27–28
SDI. *See* Strategic Defense Initiative (SDI)
SDS. *See* Students for a Democratic Society (SDS)
Sea Dogs, 16
Searches: prohibition of unreasonable, 123
Sears, Roebuck and Company, 362; catalog of, 436 (illus.)
Seattle: strike in, 494; WTO protests in, 671, 674–675
Sea Wolf, The (London), 401
Secession, 289 (illus.); constitutional theory behind, 288; of Deep South, 288–290; election of 1860 and, 281; High Federalist plans for, 155; Kentucky and Virginia Resolutions and, 140; Lincoln's election and, 287; New England and, 161
Second Bank of the United States, 174, 176–177, 195
Second Child Labor Act (1919), 446
Second Continental Congress, 91–93; national government and, 109–110; state constitutions and, 108
Second front (World War II), 532, 538–539; Soviets and, 539

Second Great Awakening, 227, 228 (illus.); frontier phase of, 227–228; in North, 228–229; reform movements and, 228–231, 236, 237
Second great migration, 605–606, 657
Second Industrial Revolution, 487–490
Second party system, 200; Compromise of 1850 and, 270–271; Kansas-Nebraska Act and demise of, 272
Second Seminole War, 210
Second War of Independence: War of 1812 as, 163
Second World War. *See* World War II
Sectional crisis: historians on cause of, 281–283
Sectionalism, 267; Civil War and, 288; in Congress, 266; cultural, 276; between 1857 and 1860, 275–281; in election of 1856, 275; Kansas-Nebraska Act and, 272–273; Missouri Compromise and, 178; Republican party and, 288
Securities and Exchange Commission (SEC, 1934), 519
Security: Homeland Security Department and, 682–683
Security Council (UN): Korean War and, 552–553
Security treaties: after World War I, 523
Sedition Act (1918), **477**
Segregation: of African Americans, 572; in army, 351; of Asian children in San Francisco public schools, 467; of black Spanish-American War troops, 416; *Brown* decision and, 573; freedom rides and, 584; Jim Crow laws and, 328–329; socioeconomic in cities, 436; in southern schools, 380–381; of southwestern Mexicans, 433; after Spanish-American War, 424; Wallace on, 601; Warren Court against, 585
Selective Service Act (1917), **474**
Self-determination principle, 480
Selma, Alabama: voter registration in, 588
Seminole Indians, 166, 168, 194 (illus.)
Senate (U.S.), 118; African Americans in, 321 (illus.); caning of Seward in, 266
Senators: direct election of, 457
Seneca Falls Convention, 239
Senegambia, 8
Separate but equal facilities, 380, 572, 573
Separate sphere of domesticity: in late 19th century, 379
Separation of powers: Eisenhower and, 571
Separatists: as Pilgrims, 28
September 11, 2001, terrorist attacks, 655, 677, 681–682; immigration controls after, 657
Sequin, Juan, 285
Sequoyah, 193
Serbia, 669; bombing of, 671; Milosevic and, 671
Serbs: in Bosnia-Herzegovina, 666
Serra, Junípero, 63
Servants. *See* Indentured servants
Service sector: expansion of, 635, 636
Service stars: in World War II, 537 (illus.)
Settlement: between Appalachians and Mississippi, 166; by convicts, 61; creative adaptations and, 2; English, 21–40; European, 7; of Far West, 166–168, 248–249; by France, 13–14; along frontier, 169–170; reasons for, 22; at Roanoke, 17–18. *See also* Colonies and colonization; Frontier; specific colonies
Settlement houses, 385
Seven Cities of Cibola, 13
Seven Pines: battle of, 298
Seventh Cavalry, 351
Seven Years' War, 74–77; colonies after, 84–85
Seward, William H., 271, 280, 299; expansive foreign policy of, 409–410
"Seward's Folly," 410
Sewing machines, 361
Sex and sexuality: Clinton scandals and, 675–676; gay liberation movement and, 620–622; in 1920s, 491–492; Victorian morality and, 377
Sex education: AIDS and, 643
Sexual harassment: Hill-Thomas issue, 647; slavery and, 224
Shaftesbury, Earl of. *See* Cooper, Anthony Ashley (Earl of Shaftesbury)
Shah of Iran, 625
Shakers, 240, 240 (illus.)
"Shame of Minneapolis, The" (Steffens), 426
Sharecropping, 318, 319 (illus.), 432; in Great Depression, 509
"Share the Wealth" movement: of Long, 511–512
Sharpsburg. *See* Antietam
Shasta Indians, 332
Shawnee Indians, 62; Tecumseh and, 147–148
Shays, Daniel, 117
Shays's Rebellion, 117
Sheep, 345; merino, 173 (illus.)
Sheik with Sheba (Held), 492 (illus.)
Shell shock, 474
Shenandoah Valley, 61; Civil War in, 298
Shepard, Matthew, 622
Sherman, John, 280
Sherman, William T., 303, 304 (illus.), 305
Sherman Antitrust Act, 394, 452
Sherman Silver Purchase Act (1890), **394,** 399
Shi'ite Muslims, 652; in Iraq, 687
Shiloh: battle of, 297
Ships and shipping, 10, 147–148; canals and, 171–173; during Civil War, 299; English seizures of, 16; during French Revolution, 133; limitations on, 525; neutrality in, 156; for New Navy, 412; at Pearl Harbor, 531 (illus.); rivers and, 171; *Sussex* pledge and, 472; during World War I, 464–465; in World War II, 535. *See also* Navy (U.S.)
Shultz, George, 638
Sicily: Allied invasion of, 533
Sierra Nevada Mountains, 332, 338; transcontinental railroad and, 357
Silent majority: election of 1968 and, 601
Silver: coinage and Sherman Act, 394, 399; Comstock Lode, value of gold, and, 343; election of 1896 and, 401–403; election of 1900 and, 420; free coinage of, 401; Gold Standard Act and, 404; from Spanish colonies, 13
Silver Democrats, 399
Simmons, William J., 495
Simms, William Gilmore, 276
Simpson, Jeremiah, 395
Sims, William S., 474
Sin: Quakers and, 34
Sinai peninsula, 614; return to Egypt, 625
Sinclair, Upton, 453, 454
Singer Sewing Machine Company, 409 (illus.)
Single mothers, 618
Single-tax clubs, 383
Sioux Indians, 333, 351
Sioux War, 334, 335
Sirhan, Sirhan, 600
Sirica, John, 613
Sister Carrie (Dreiser), 401
Sit-ins, 574 (illus.)
Sitting Bull, 335, 337
Six-Day War (1967), 614
Sixteenth Amendment, 456–457
Skilled artisans, 364
Skilled labor, 365
Skliris, Leonidas G., 433
Skyscrapers, 359, 372, 490
Slater, Samuel, 149
Slave codes, 49–50
Slave factories, 9 (illus.)
Slaveholders: in Kansas, 275
Slave plantation system: entrenchment in South, 283. *See also* Planters and plantations
Slave power, 266, 274, 275, 277
Slaves and slavery: American Revolution and, 94; in antebellum era, 205–210; in Carolina, 38, 38 (illus.); in Chesapeake, 48; clothing of, 213 (illus.); community and, 207–208, 208 (illus.); concentration of, 217 (illus.), 218 (illus.); constitutional compromise over, 119–120, 119 (illus.); cotton economy and, 174; Cotton Kingdom and, 218–220, 219 (illus.); daily life of, 206–207; divided society in Old South and, 205; emancipation and, 300–301; Emancipation Proclamation and, 300; family life and, 206 (illus.), 207–208, 208 (illus.); Force Bill (1833) and, 195; vs. free labor, 274; Fugitive Slave Law of 1850 and, 269; in Georgia, 39, 40; immigration of, 59; Indians and, 7, 8, 246; industry and, 207, 220; in Jacksonian era, 186, 190; labor of, 206–207, 206 (illus.); Lincoln and, 287; Lincoln-Douglas debates and, 278; Mexican-American War and, 254–255; Mexican cession and, 267; Missouri Compromise and, 178–179; North and, 213; origins and destinations of African slaves, 49 (illus.); outlawed in West, 113; paternalism and, 213–214; planters and, 212–214; popular sovereignty and, 268; profitability issue and, 220–221; prohibitions on, 107, 178; proslavery arguments and, 215–216; rape and, 214, 224–225; rebellion encouraged by British, 93; religion and, 206, 208–209; resistance and rebellion and, 204, 206, 209–210, 211 (illus.); after Revolution, 106–107; roots of, 48–50; sectionalism and, 266; small slaveholders and, 214; social status and, 146; in South, 107, 216–221; Stono Uprising and, 50; Texas and, 247, 248, 251; Thirteenth Amendment and, 301; Tocqueville on, 202; Turner's Rebellion and, 204; underground economy and, 207; Underground Railroad and, 210, 218 (illus.), 238; urban, 207; yeoman farmers and, 215. *See also* Abolitionists and abolitionists; Free blacks; Slave trade
Slave states: Missouri Compromise and, 177–179
Slave trade, 49, 119; abolition in District of Columbia, 269; illegal commerce in, 156,

156 (illus.); internal, 216–218; outlawing of, 155–156, 156 (illus.); Portuguese, 9
Slidell, John, 299; Mexican-American War and, 254
Sloughter, Henry, 55
Slums: religious missions in, 385
Smallpox, 6, 6 (illus.), 8; contamination of blankets for Indians, 62. *See also* Disease
Small reservation policy, 334–335
Smalls, Robert, 310–311, 328
Smeal, Eleanor, 619
Smith, Adam, 51
Smith, Alfred E., 516; election of 1924 and, 500; election of 1928 and, 500–501
Smith, Bessie "Empress of the Blues," 437
Smith, Gerald L. K., 516
Smith, Jedediah, 167
Smith, John, 23, 24
Smith, Joseph: lynching of, 250; Mormon trek and, 249–250
Smith, Margaret Chase: McCarthy and, 558
Smith, Robert, 150
Smith College, 381
"Smoked Yankees," 415–416
Smoking: Virginia and, 24. *See also* Tobacco and tobacco industry
Smythe, Thomas, 23
SNCC. *See* Student Nonviolent Coordinating Committee (SNCC)
Social control: asylums and, 235–236
Social Darwinism, 383
Social Gospel, 385
Socialism: before First World War, 448; World War I repression and, 477
Socialist party, 442; membership increase in, 448
Social-justice movement, 444–445; purity crusade and, 445; women and woman suffrage in, 445–446, 447 (illus.)
Social mobility: industrialization and, 365
Social salvation, 385
Social Security, 512, 512 (illus.), 519; Bush, George W., and, 677; Carter and, 623; Medicare and, 588; payroll taxes, increase in, 636; Reagan and, 632; Roosevelt, Franklin D., and, 512
Social Security Act (1935), **512,** 519
Social welfare: crisis in, 385–386
Social workers: in late 19th century, 385; national organization for, 444–445; professional schools for, 445
Society: in backcountry, 58; changes during World War I, 479; in Chesapeake, 47–48; after Civil War, 311; colonial, 60–62, 83–85; community of consumers in, 363; in Confederacy, 301; of frontier lands, 169–170; impact of World War II on, 541; industrial, 353–369; mass, in Progressive Era, 429–433; multiethnic, 660–661; in New England, 43–46; planter, 47–48; pluralistic, 386; racially mixed in Latin America, 13; railroads and, 355; reconstructing southern, 317–322; reforms of, 105; after Revolution, 104–109; rural, 493–498; social and cultural change in (1877–1900), 376–383; social behaviors and, 146; Spanish-Mexican heritage and, 340; standardization in, 488; Supreme Court and (1960s), 585–586; Victorian morality and, 377–378; in Western Europe, 10; in World War II, 536–538
"Society" (Howells), 400
Society for the Suppression of Vice, 378
Society of Friends. *See* Quakers
Socioeconomic segregation: in cities, 436
Sociological jurisprudence, 448
Sociology: studies of poor in, 385–386
Sod houses, 345–346
Sodomy laws, 621
Soldiers: African Americans as, 301, 351; in American Revolution, 94; in Bosnia, 670, 671; in Civil War, 295 (illus.); in railroad strike of 1877, 366; in Spanish-American War, 415; in Vietnam, 591–592, 592 (illus.), 593; in World War I, 474–475. *See also* Armed forces; Military
Solidarity movement, 649
Solomon Islands, battle at, 534
Somalia: intervention in, 669
Somoza, Anastasio, 624, 639
Sons of Liberty, 86; boycotts by, 87–88
Soto, Hernando de, 6, 13
Souls of Black Folk, The (Du Bois), 432
Sousa, John Philip, 437
Souter, David H., 647
South: African American Loyalists in, 94; African American migration to, 658–659; American Revolution in, 97–98; backcountry of, 60; Black Codes in, 318–319; blacks at turn of 20th century in, 432; black Spanish-American War troops in, 415–416; Brooks' caning of Sumner and, 266; child labor in, 400; class and caste in, 205; convict lease system in, 329; cooperationists in, 288; cotton industry in, 173–174; crisis of fear in, 278–280; cultural sectionalism in, 276; divided society in, 205; economy of, 216–221; education in, 380–381; election of 1992 and, 662; Fourteenth Amendment and, 315; home rule and end of Reconstruction in, 326; Indian removal in, 168; Jim Crow laws in, 328–329; Ku Klux Klan in, 323, 324–325; land and labor reorganization in, 317–318; Lincoln's election and, 287; lynchings in, 328; migration of blacks from, 478; military districts in, 315 (illus.); military rule in, 316; Missouri Compromise and, 178–179; nationalism of, 270; Nixon and, 609, 610; Panic of 1873 and, 320; peonage of blacks in, 432; population shift to, 655, 656–657, 656 (illus.); racial segregation and zoning in, 436; railroad consolidation in, 356; Reconstruction in, 315 (illus.), 317–322; Redeemer regimes in, 326–327; Republican party in, 319–320; school desegregation in, 573; segregated schooling in, 380–381; settlements in, 113; slavery in, 107; slave trade and, 155–156; on tariff of 1789, 128; tenant farming in, 430–431; view of North, 283; violence against blacks in, 319; women of households in, 224–225. *See also* Civil War (U.S.), Confederacy (Civil War South); Reconstruction; Slaves and slavery; Sunbelt; specific states and colonies
South America: coca in, 645; Native American migration to, 2–3; U.S. foreign policy and, 409. *See also* Central America; Latin America
South Carolina, 37 (illus.); secession of, 288; segregated schools in, 381; Stono Uprising in, 50; Witherspoon family in, 42. *See also* Carolina(s)
Southeast: France and Spain in, 63; Soto in, 13
Southeast Asia: communism in, 599; containment in, 579–580; Japan and, 529, 531, 534; refugees from, 660; Vietnam War and, 591 (illus.). *See also* Vietnam; Vietnam War; specific countries
Southern Alliance, 395. *See also* National Farmers' Alliance and Industrial Union
Southern Christian Leadership Conference (SCLC), 574
Southern Europe: immigrants from, 374
Southern manifesto: school desegregation and, 573
Southern rights, 275
South Korea: Korean War and, 552–554. *See also* Korea
South Vietnam: Kennedy and, 579, 580; after Vietnam War, 623. *See also* Vietnam; Vietnam War
Southwest: Indians in, 3; Kiowa and Comanche Indians in, 335; Mexican Americans in, 537; Mexican immigrants in, 433; migration of Mexicans to, 478–479; Spanish explorers in, 13; Spanish-speaking population in, 340
Sovereignty: parliamentary, 83, 84. *See also* Popular sovereignty
Soviet Union: Afghanistan invasion and, 626, 642; Arab-Israeli negotiations and, 625; arms race and, 642; atomic bomb of, 556; beginning of Cold War and, 544–545; Berlin and, 539, 549–550, 579; China and, 559, 560; Cold War view of, 551 (illus.); Cuba and, 561, 581–582; demise of communism in, 649; dissolution of, 650; eastern Europe and, 544–545; German invasion of, 531; Gorbachev and, 642, 649–650; human rights issues in, 626; Jews in, 626; Kennedy and, 578; Nixon and, 610–611; nonaggression treaty with Hitler and, 527; NSC-68 and, 551; power in 1970s, 611; Reagan and, 638, 642; *Sputnik* and, 561, 569–570, 569 (illus.); Stalingrad battle and, 533; Suez crisis and, 560; United States and, 523; wartime coalition with, 532; weapons buildup in, 582; after World War II, 546. *See also* Russia
Space exploration: Kennedy and, 583; space race and, 570; *Sputnik* and, 561, 569–570, 569 (illus.)
Spain: Armada of, 16; attempts to acquire Cuba from, 272–273; borderlands of 18th century, 62–64, 64 (illus.); division of New World by, 11; exploration and settlement by, 11–13; Ferdinand and Isabella of, 10; Florida and, 166; Georgia and, 39; Louisiana and, 151; migration to New World from, 13; Mississippi River region, 134; postrevolutionary diplomacy with, 115–116; Treaty of Paris and, 418; voyages of exploration by, 12 (illus.). *See also* Spanish-American War
Spanish-American War, 404, 407, 413–418; buffalo soldiers in, 352; Caribbean theater, 417 (illus.); casualties of, 418; course of, 416–418; Hawaii annexation and, 411; *Maine* and, 413–414, 414 (illus.); Navy in, 416–417; Pacific theater of, 416 (illus.); "smoked Yankees" (blacks) in, 415–416; as splendid little war, 415; yellow journalism and, 413

Spanish empire, 11–13, 62–64, 64 (illus.)
Spanish-speaking people: in Southwest, 340
Speaker of the House: sectionalism in election of, 280
Special Forces: Kennedy and, 578
Special interests. *See* Interest groups
Specie, 174; under Articles of Confederation, 114
Specie circular, 198
Specie Resumption Act (1875), 323
Spectator (journal), 65
Spectator sports: in late 19th century, 378–379; in 1920s, 491
Spectral evidence, 55
Speculation: Indian lands and, 336; in land, 168; in 1920s, 489; in railroads, 357; stock market crash (1929) and, 504; in western lands, 113, 339
Speech: freedom of, 123
Spencer, Herbert, 383
Spending: Clinton and, 654; Kennedy and, 583; Reagan and, 630, 632–633; on social reforms, 588; in World War II, 536. *See also* Budget; Defense spending
Spheres of influence: in China, 422; in Pacific region, 551
Spies and spying: during Red Scare, 556; U-2 incident and, 562; during World War I, 477
Spinning mills, 149
Spock, Benjamin, 567
Spoilsmen (politicos): in Republican party, 325
Spoils system: Jackson, Andrew, and, 192
Sports: clothing and, 378; in late 19th century, 378–379; in 1920s, 491; in Progressive Era, 437
Springfield, Illinois: race riot in, 432
Springfield, Oregon: school violence in, 675
***Sputnik*, 561**; reactions to, 569–570, 569 (illus.)
Squanto (Patuxt Indians), 28
Square Deal (Roosevelt, Theodore), 452–453
Squatters, 168–169
Squatter sovereignty, 268. *See also* Popular sovereignty
Stalin, Joseph: in eastern Europe, 533; Korean War and, 552; at Potsdam, 543; in World War II, 539–540
Stalingrad, battle at, 533, 533 (illus.)
Stallings, Lawrence, 483
Stamp Act (1765), 86–87, 87 (illus.), 99 (illus.)
Stamp Act Congress, 86–87
Standardization, 488; by railroads, 356; of typewriter keyboard, 365
Standard of living: in 1920s, 487; under Reagan, 635. *See also* Lifestyle
Standard Oil Company, 360, 361, 428, 452, 457
Stanford, Leland, 381
Stanford University, 381
Stanton, Edwin, 317
Stanton, Elizabeth Cady, 598 (illus.); Seneca Falls Convention and, 239
Stanwix, Fort, 110
Starr, Kenneth, 675–676
"Stars and Stripes Forever, The" (Sousa), 437
"Star-Spangled Banner, The," 161
"Starving time": in Virginia, 24
"Star Wars." *See* Strategic Defense Initiative (SDI)
State(s): between Appalachians and Mississippi, 166; under Articles of Confederation, 110; debt after Revolution, 130; experiments in, 392; federal assumption of debt of, 131; Know-Nothings and, 274; in Midwest, 168; Nixon and, 609; "one man, one vote" principle and, 585; reform in, 450–451; representation in Congress, 118; republicanism in, 108–109; Social Security grants to, 512; sodomy laws in, 621; supremacy of federal government over, 306; western land claims by, 110–112, 111 (illus.)
State Department, 128; Red Scare and, 556
Statehood: qualifications for, 113; in West, 343. *See also* specific states
State income tax, 451
State laws: Supreme Court on, 154
States' rights, 147; Force Bill (1833) and, 195; Indian removal and, 193; Jefferson on, 140; nullification crisis and, 193–195; Republicans and, 176; Whigs and, 197
States' Rights (Dixiecrats) party. *See* Dixiecrats
Statue of Liberty, 388
Status: inequality between men and women in work, 364; social equality and, 146. *See also* Classes
Steamboats, 171, 258 (illus.); Fulton and, 149
Steam engine: invention of, 258 (illus.)
Steel and steel industry, 359 (illus.); Bessemer process for, 358; Carnegie and, 358–359; in Great Depression, 504; Kennedy and, 583; losses by, 617; strike in, 494; after World War II, 566
Steerage, 388
Steffens, Lincoln, 426
Stephen, Alexander: as vice president of Confederacy, 289
Stephens, Uriah S., 365
Stevens, John L., 411
Stevens, Thaddeus, 314 (illus.), 316
Stimson, Henry L., 525, 540
"Stinking weed": tobacco as, 26 (illus.)
Stock: for railroads, 358
Stockholders: in 1920s, 488
Stock market crash (1929), 504–505
Stock ticker, 361
Stonewall riots, 620–621
Stono Uprising (1739), 50
Stores: chain, 362; department, 362; grocery, 362
Stove: Franklin, 65
Stowe, Harriet Beecher, 214, 276
Straight, Willard, 468
Strategic Arms Limitation Talks (SALT), 611, 626; SALT I and, 611; SALT II and, 626
Strategic Defense Initiative (SDI), 638
Stratemeyer, Edward, 438
Streetcars, 372
Street gangs, 373
Street railways, 436
Strict construction: of Constitution, 146–147
Strikes: AFL and, 366; by black cotton pickers, 395; against coal industry, 397–398, 452–453; between 1870-1890, 367 (illus.); in 1894, 397; Great Railroad strike of 1877, 366, 367 (illus.); Haymarket Riot and, 366, 367; Homestead, 359, 367–368; increase after 1910, 434; injunctions and, 366; by IWW, 434; Knights of Labor and, 365; Ludlow coal strike, 460; McCormick harvester works strike, 366–367; by migrant farmworkers, 597, 597 (illus.); in 1920s, 494; Pullman, 366, 397, 448; against railroads, 366; violence in, 514 (illus.)
Strong, Josiah, 409
Stryker, Roy, 510 (illus.)
Stuart monarchs (England), 22, 29; Parliament and, 84; restoration of, 36. *See also* specific rulers
Student Nonviolent Coordinating Committee (SNCC), 574; black militant control of, 596
Student revolt: in 1960s, 593
Students for a Democratic Society (SDS), 593–594
Stuyvesant, Peter, 33
Submarines, 465; in World War I, 471–472, 473; in World War II, 529
Sub-Saharan Africa: cultures of, 8–9
Subsidies: for railroads, 320, 332; to steel industry, 617
Subtreasury system (government warehouses): of Alliance movement, 395
Suburbs, 656; growth of, 372; in 1950s, 565, 566; schools and, 568; wealthy, 436
Subversives: Red Scare and, 556
Sudetenland: German invasion of, 526
Suez Canal, 357; in World War II, 531
Suez crisis, 560
Suffolk Resolves, 91
Sugar Act (1764), 85–86, 99 (illus.)
Sugar and sugar industry: Hawaii and, 411
Sugar islands: slaves in, 49
Suicides: in cities, 373
Sullivan, John L., 379
Sullivan, Louis H., 372
Summit meetings. *See* specific meetings
Sumner, Charles, 266, 316
Sumner, William Graham, 383
Sumter, Fort: attack on, 291–292, 291 (illus.)
Sunbelt, 629–630, **656**; African American migration to, 658–659; population shift to, 655, 656–657, 656 (illus.); shift of industry to, 617; after World War II, 566
Sunni Muslims: in Iraq, 687
Superpowers: after World War II, 546. *See also* Cold War; Soviet Union
Supply-side economics, 632, 634
Supreme Court (U.S.), 128; on antitrust legislation, 394; black civil rights and, 328 (illus.), 329; Bush, George W., and, 680; Bush, George H. W., and, 647; on child labor limitations, 446; *Dred Scott* case and, 276–277; on governing American Empire, 421; injunctions and, 366, 397; Jefferson and, 153–154; Jews on, 459–460; judicial review and, 153; under Marshall, 179–180; Nixon and, 609; on Northern Securities trust suit, 452; on railroad regulation, 392; Reagan and, 647; restraint of trade and, 457; Roosevelt, Franklin D., and, 517; on separate but equal facilities, 380; social change (1960s) and, 585–586; on state laws, 154; on vote for women, 391; women on, 619; on working hours for women, 448
Surgery: anesthetic use in, 377
Surplus: in economy, 672; farm, 499

Survey, The (magazine), 445
Surveying: of western lands, 113
Susan Constant (ship), 23
Sussex (steamer), 472
Sussex pledge, 472
Swift, Gustavus F., 361
Sylvis, William H., 365
Synagogues: of eastern European Jews, 375
Synthetic fibers, 489
Syria, 560; October War and, 614

T

Tadman, Michael, 217
Taft, Robert A.: World War II and, 528
Taft, William Howard, 433, 461; Ballinger-Pinchot controversy and, 456; "dollar diplomacy" of, 467–468; election of 1908 and, 454; election of 1912 and, 457–458; in Philippines, 421, 454; presidency of, 455–457; progressives and, 456–457; Roosevelt, Theodore, and, 442; as secretary of war, 467; trusts and, 452, 457
Taft Commission: in Philippines, 421
Taft-Hartley Act (1947), **554**
Taft-Katsura Agreement, 467
Taiwan, 559; Nationalist Chinese on, 552; Nixon and, 611
Taliban, 682
"Talkies," 488. *See also* Movies and movie industry
Talleyrand-Périgord, Charles-Maurice de, 141
Tallmadge, James, 178
Tammany Hall, 376
Tampa, Florida: race riot in, 416
Taney, Roger B., 277; Bank War and, 197
Tangier, 8
Tarbell, Ida, 426
Tariff(s), 176, 393; competition and, 354; Dingley, 403, 456; of 1816, 176; manufacturing protection and, 175; McKinley Tariff Act, 393; in 1920s, 499; nullification crisis and, 193–195; Payne-Aldrich Act, 455–456; protective (1862), 306; of 1789, 128; Underwood, 458; Wilson-Gorman, 410; after World War I, 523. *See also* specific tariffs
Tariff of abominations, 191, 194
Tariff reciprocity, 410
Task forces, 386
Taxation: apportionment of, 145; under Articles of Confederation, 110, 114; Bush, George, and, 648; Bush, George W., and, 677, 679; in California, 629; Clinton and, 654, 663; colonial protests against, 87; Ford and, 615; income, 456; Jefferson and, 150; Johnson, Lyndon B., and, 586–587; Kennedy and, 583; Long on, 512; new forms of, 404; in 1920s, 499; Reagan and, 630, 632–633, 634; after Seven Years' War, 85; Sixteenth Amendment and, 456; Social Security and, 512; state income tax, 451; on whiskey, 136; in World War II, 536. *See also* Tariff(s)
Taxation without representation: colonies on, 84–85, 86–87
Tax Reform Act (1986), 646–647
Taylor, Frederick Winslow: efficiency methods in workplace, 429
Taylor, John, 139–140, 154
Taylor, Maxwell, 580
Taylor, Nathaniel: neo-Calvinism and, 229
Taylor, Zachary, 287; election of 1848 and, 268; Mexican-American War and, 254–255; plan on slavery in Mexican cession, 268–269
Tea Act (1773), 99 (illus.)
Teacher-training institutions, 381
Teach-ins: as antiwar protests, 594
Teapot Dome scandal, 498
Technology: in 1890s, 405; for farming, 346; industrial development and, 354; machine tools and, 259; naval, 10; personal freedom and, 674; for railroads, 356; second Industrial Revolution and, 487; Y2K and, 677. *See also* Inventors and inventions
Tecumseh (Shawnee), 147, 158–159; death of, 160
Teheran conference (1943), 539–540
Tejanos, 248; after Mexican-American War, 285–286
Telegraph, 354; transatlantic, 361
Telephone, 353, 354, 361
Television: in 1950s, 567, 568; presidential debates on, 577
Teller, Henry M., 414
Teller Amendment (1898), **414**
Temperance movement, 230, 230 (illus.); Eighteenth Amendment and, 445; in late 19th century, 378; Second Great Awakening and, 230–231; split in, 236; Temperance Society and, 236
Tenant farmers, 430–431; in Great Depression, 509
Tenement house laws, 444
Tenements, 371, 373
Tennent, Gilbert, 69
Tennessee, 166, 289; Civil War in, 297; redistricting in, 585; Scopes trial in, 497; secession of, 291
Tennessee Coal and Iron Company, 452, 457
Tennessee Valley Authority (TVA), 508, 508 (illus.), 518
Tenochtitlán, 4
Ten Percent Plan, 312
Tenskwatawa (the Prophet), 147
Tenth Amendment, 123
Tenth Cavalry, 351–352, 415
Tenure of Office Act, 316, 317
Terkel, Studs, 503
Territories: Kansas-Nebraska Act and, 271–273; overseas, acquisition of, 408; slave labor vs. free labor and, 268; slavery issue and, 267, 278–279; in West, 113, 339–340. *See also* specific territories
Terrorism: anthrax scare and, 685; attack on Marines in Lebanon, 639; against freedpeople, 319; Homeland Security Department and, 682–683; of Ku Klux Klan, 323, 324–325; risk status and, 683; of September 11, 2001, 655, 677, 681–682; war on, 681–682
Tertium Quids, 154, 158
Tesla, Nikola, 362
Tet offensive, 598
Teton Sioux Indians, 335
Texas: annexation of, 244, 251–252; boundary dispute with New Mexico, 269; immigrants in, 657; oil in, 361; Republic of, 247–248, 254; secession of, 289; Spain and, 13; *Tejanos* in, 285–286; Texas Revolution and, 247; Tyler, John, and, 251; undocumented aliens in, 658
Texas and Pacific Railroad, 366
Texas Panhandle, 343
Textiles and textile industry, 149; cotton famine in, 299; industrialization and, 174–176; innovations in, 361
Thames River, battle of the, 160
Thanksgiving, 28
Theater: American culture and, 103; in Jacksonian era, 188; in late 19th century, 378
Theory of the Leisure Class, The (Veblen), 384
Theyanoguin (King Hendrick), 74 (illus.)
Think tanks, 630
Third parties. *See* specific parties
Third World: AIDS in, 644; Kennedy and, 579
Thirteenth Amendment, 301, **313,** 316 (illus.)
Tho, Le Duc, 611
Thomas, Clarence, 647
Thomas, J. Edgar, Steel Works, 359
Thomas, Lorenzo, 317
Thomas, Norman: World War II and, 528
Thomson, James, 77
Thoreau, Henry David, 276; transcendentalism and, 241
Three-fifths clause: Northerners and, 161, 178; slaves and, 155
Three Lower Counties: as Delaware, 35, 36
Three Soldiers (Dos Passos), 483
Thurmond, Strom: election of 1948 and, 555
Tiananmen Square: student resistance in, 649, 649 (illus.)
Ticonderoga, Fort, 75
Tidewater region: planters in, 58
Tight-money policy: in 1970s, 617
Tilden, Samuel J., 326
Timber: from federal lands, 633
Timber and Stone Act (1878), 339
Timber Culture Act (1873), 339
Time zones: railroads and, 356
Tippecanoe, battle of, 159
Tippecanoe and Tyler, Too, 199
Title: of president, 126
Title VII (Civil Rights Act of 1964), 587
Titusville, Pennsylvania: oil well at, 360
Tobacco and tobacco industry: Chesapeake society and, 47–48; in Maryland, 27; Native Americans and, 21; plantation crops and, 216–217; in Virginia, 24–25, 26 (illus.)
Tocqueville, Alexis de: wisdom of, 201–202
Togetherness: in 1950s, 567
Tojo, Hideki, 530
Toleration: in Maryland, 27
Toll roads, 171
Toltec peoples, 4
Tombstone (town), 341
Tom Swift series, 438
Tordesillas, Treaty of, 11
Tories: Loyalists as, 85, 99
Total war: Civil War as, 292–299
Tougaloo College: sit-in by students of, 573
Towns. *See* Cities and towns
Townsend, Francis, 511
Townsend Plan, 511
Townshend, Charles, 87–88
Townshend Revenue Acts (1767), 87–88, 99 (illus.)
Townships: in West, 113
Toys, 393 (illus.); mechanical bank, 376 (illus.); western-themed, 567

Track width (gauge): standard, of railroads, 356
Tracy, Benjamin F., 412
Trade: under Articles of Confederation, 114; carrying trade and, 148–149; with China, 175; deficit in, 635; Dutch, 32–33; Embargo Act of 1807 and, 157–158; with England, 158; in Far West, 248–249; with France, 159; Hamilton on, 129; Indians and, 3–4, 6, 7–8; intercoastal, 67; mercantilism and, 51; Napoleon's Continental System and, 156–157; Native American, 62; Nixon and, 609; reciprocity treaties and, 410; regulation of colonial, 51–53; triangular, 67; in West Africa, 8–9; before World War I, 465. *See also* Commerce; Foreign trade
Trade cards, 409 (illus.)
Trade deficit: decline in, 635
Trading posts: slave, 9 (illus.)
Traffic: in cities, 656
Trail of Tears, 193, 194 (illus.)
Trails: Bozeman, 334; cattle, 343–344, 344 (illus.); western, 248–249, 249 (illus.)
Trans-Appalachian west: settlement in, 166, 168–169
Transatlantic cable: for telegraphs, 361
Transcendentalism, 240
Transcontinental railroad, 306, 357; extermination of buffalo and, 336
Transcontinental Treaty. *See* Adams-Onís Treaty
Transportation: on canals, 171–173; under Madison and Monroe, 177; revolution in, 170–173; on rivers, 171; on roads and highways, 170–171; rural-urban separation and, 149; steamboat and, 258 (illus.); suburbs and innovations in, 372. *See also* Automobiles and automobile industry; Railroads; Roads and highways; specific types
Transportation Act (1718), 61
Trash: on Overland Trail, 338
Travel: by railroads, 355. *See also* Transportation
Treason: of Burr, 155
Treasury Department, 128
Treaties: after American Revolution, 99–101; of arbitration ("cooling-off" treaties), 468; over borders, 166; end of treaty making with Indian tribes, 335; with Panama, 624; reciprocity, 410, 411. *See also* specific treaties
Treaty of 1848 (Anglo-American Convention), 253 (illus.)
Treaty of Guadalupe Hidalgo. *See* Guadalupe Hidalgo, Treaty of
Trenchard, John, 70
Trench warfare: in World War I, 474–475
Trent (steamer), 299
Trenton, battle at, 92 (illus.), 95
Trial by jury, 123; in territories, 113
Triangle Shirtwaist Company fire, 429
Triangular trade, 67
Triangulation policy: of Clinton, 666
Tripartite Pact, 530
Tripoli, 8, 152
Tripp, Linda, 675
Trist, Nicholas P.: Mexican-American War and, 255
Troops. *See* Armed forces; Military; Soldiers
Trucking industry, 489
Truman, Harry: Berlin blockade and, 549–550; civil rights issues and, 572; Cold War at home and, 554–558; election of 1944 and, 538; election of 1948 and, 554, 554 (illus.); Fair Deal of, 570; Korean War and, 552–554; lend-lease and, 545–546; at Potsdam, 543; World War II and, 540–541
Truman Doctrine, 547
Trunk lines, 356
Trusts, 360, 361; in Progressive Era, 428; Roosevelt, Theodore, and, 451–452; Taft and, 452; Wilson and, 459
Tuberculosis, 377
Tubman, Harriet, 238
Tudor dynasty (England), 14, 16. *See also* specific monarchs
Tunis, 8
Tunisia: in World War II, 532
Turkey: Cuban missile crisis and, 581–582; Truman Doctrine and, 547. *See also* World War I
Turner, Frederick Jackson, 347
Turner, Nat, rebellion of, 204, 210
Turner Joy, C. (ship), 590
Turner's thesis, 347–348
Turnpikes, 170–171
Tuskegee Institute, 381
Tutuila (Samoa): naval control of, 422
TVA. *See* Tennessee Valley Authority (TVA)
Twain, Mark, 400, 418
Tweed, William M., 376, 376 (illus.)
"Tweed Days in St. Louis" (Steffens), 426
Tweed Ring, 376
Twelfth Amendment, 141
Twenty-Fourth and Twenty-Fifth Infantry, 415, 417
Tyco International, 680
Tyler, John: election of 1840 and, 199; election of 1844 and, 251–252; Manifest Destiny and, 251; Texas annexation and, 251
Tyndale, William, 15
Typewriter, 353, 361, 365
Typhoid, 377, 418
Typhus, 6

U

UAW. *See* United Automobile Workers (UAW)
U-boats: in World War I, 464, 471–472. *See also* Submarines
Ulster (Ireland): English in, 17
Unabomber, 674
Uncle Tom's Cabin (Stowe), 214, 276, 280
Unconditional surrender: Casablanca policy for, 532
Underclass: immigrants as, 657
Underground Railroad, 210, 218 (illus.); black abolitionists and, 238
Understanding AIDS, 643, 644 (illus.)
Underwood Tariff Act (1913), **458**
Undocumented aliens, 657, **658**
Unemployment: of blacks, Black Codes and, 319; Bush, George W., and, 680; decline in, 636; during depression of 1890s, 396; in Great Depression, 504, 505 (illus.), 518; Kennedy and, 583; of Native Americans, 337; in 1933, 507; in 1970s, 617; in 1980s, 631; in 1982, 634; in 1990s, 672; Social Security and, 512; of women, 516; after World War II, 566
Unicameral legislatures: in Pennsylvania, 36; in states, 109
Unilateralism, 684; war with Iraq and, 685–686
Union (Civil War). *See* Civil War (U.S.); North (Civil War)
Unionists: in South, 290; wartime Reconstruction and, 312
Union of Soviet Socialist Republics. *See* Soviet Union
Union Pacific Railroad, 339; Crédit Mobilier scandal and, 325; transcontinental railroad and, 357
Union party, 516
Unitarians: evangelicalism and, 227
United Automobile Workers (UAW): General Motors strike by, 514
United Fruit, 428
United Mine Workers, 397–398, 398 (illus.), 452, 460
United Nations (UN), 538; Bosnia peacekeeping and, 669–670; coalition in Persian Gulf War, 651; Korean War and, 552–553; Powell and, 684; Suez crisis and, 560
United Society of Believers (Shakers), 240
United States: activities in Caribbean (1898–1930s), 469 (illus.); as creditor nation, 479; economic primacy of, 523; power in 1970s, 611; as strongest nation on earth, 687; unilateral foreign actions of, 683–687; as world power, 404, 407; World War II and, 528–541. *See also* Cold War
U.S. Centers for Disease Control, 644
U.S. Chamber of Commerce, 444
U.S. Patent Office, 361
U.S. Public Health Service, 431
U.S. Steel Corporation, 359, 428, 452, 457; CIO and, 514
United States v. *E. C. Knight Co.,* 394
United States v. *Harris,* 328 (illus.)
Universal education, 380
Universities and colleges: for African Americans, 381–382; agricultural, 306; Asian Americans in, 659–660; education as field of study in, 381; football at, 378–379, 437; land-grant institutions, 381; in 19th century, 381–383; in 1950s, 568; professional schools of social work at, 445; during Reconstruction, 322; student protests in, 593, 594; for women, 381
University of California: *Bakke* case and, 659; Berkeley Free Speech movement at, 593
University of Chicago, 381, 445
University of Michigan, 382 (illus.)
University of Mississippi: Meredith, James, in, 584
University of Pennsylvania, 382
University of South Carolina: black and white students at, 322
Unskilled labor, 364; in CIO, 514–515
Upper class: in Great Depression, 506; in 1920s, 489
Upper South: secession and, 289
Urban areas: commercial life in, 148–149; increased population in, 354; lifestyle in 1920s, 490–493; Native American, 3; "one man, one vote" principle and, 585. *See also* Cities and towns; Suburbs
Urbanization, 656; between 1877 and 1900, 371–386; elevator and, 258 (illus.); immigration and, 260; Jefferson on, 132

Urban League: black militants and, 596; in 1920s, 493
Urban reform league, 449
USSR. *See* Soviet Union
Utah, 332, 338; acquisition of, 255; Mormons in, 250, 337; organization of, 269; as U.S. territory, 250
Utah Copper Company: immigrant workers provided for, 433
Ute Indians, 332
Utilities: public ownership of, 450
Utopianism, 239–241, **240,** 240 (illus.)
Utrecht, Treaty of, 72
U-2 spy plane: Cuban missile crisis and, 581; shooting of, 562

V

Vagrancy laws: Black Codes and, 319
Valley Forge: Continental Army at, 96
Values: religious and patriotic in Victorian era, 378; return to traditional (1968), 601
Van Buren, Martin, 268; Bank War and, 195, 196 (illus.), 197; election of 1828 and, 191; election of 1836 and, 198; election of 1840 and, 199; election of 1844 and, 251–252; as Jackson's successor, 194, 198; party system and, 189; Peggy Eaton affair and, 192, 194; rise and fall of, 198–200
Vance, Cyrus, 623, 626
Vandenberg, Arthur M., 547
Vanderbilt, Alfred G., 464
Vanderbilt, Cornelius (Commodore), 356, 357 (illus.)
Van Devanter, Willis, 517
Van Gogh, 439
Van Vorst, Bessie, 368
Vanzetti, Bartolomeo, 495
Vassar, 381
Vaudeville, 437
Veblen, Thorstein, 384
Veiller, Lawrence, 444
Venezuela: boundary dispute with British Guiana, 410–411
Veracruz, 469
Vermont: slavery prohibited in, 107
Verrazanno, Giovanni da: Indians and, 7
Versailles, Treaty of, 479–483; Europe after, 481 (illus.); German reparations in, 481; Germany and, 525; U.S. rejection of, 482–483
Vertical integration: of oil industry, 360; of steel industry, **359**
Vesey, Denmark, rebellion of, 209–210
Vespucci, Amerigo, 11
Veterans: in Great Depression, 507
Veto: executive power of, 118; by Johnson, Andrew, 314; of Polk, 267; in states, 109
Vice: attempts at suppression of, 378
Vice-admiralty courts, 52
Vice president: election of, 118. *See also* specific vice presidents
Vichy France, 532
Vickers (arms dealer), 526
Vicksburg: siege of, 296 (illus.), 302, 303, 304 (illus.)
Victorian morality, 377–378
Vienna summit meeting (1961), 579
Viet Cong, 579, 592, 599; Tet Offensive and, 598
Vietminh: at Dien Bien Phu, 558, 559
Vietnam: France and, 558–559; immigrants from, 605, 659; Kennedy and, 579–580; negotiation with, 611–612; after Vietnam War, 623. *See also* Vietnam War
Vietnam War, 578; ending of, 611–612; escalation of, 590–592; Johnson, Lyndon B., and, 589–593, 598–599; King and, 596; national policy in, 599; politicians and, 599; protests against, 593–595; SDS and, 594; stalemate in, 592–593. *See also* Vietnam
View of the Great Treaty Held at Prairie du Chien, 169 (illus.)
Vigilantism: against radical antiwar figures, 476
Vikings, 9
Villa, Francisco "Pancho," 469–470
Villard, Oswald Garrison, 432
Violence: in Birmingham, 584; Boston Massacre and, 88; against gays, 622; interracial, 50; in labor strikes, 514 (illus.); in 1990s, 673–675; against southern blacks, 319, 432; at University of Mississippi, 584
Virginia, 21, 23–26, 37 (illus.), 289; American Revolution in, 97–98; backcountry of, 61; Bacon's Rebellion in, 53; black people in, 49; Civil War in, 303; lands ceded by, 111; Raleigh in, 18; regulation of trade in, 52; as royal colony, 26; secession of, 291; segregated schools in, 381; tobacco in, 24–25; western land claims of, 111–112. *See also* Chesapeake region
Virginia (*Merrimack,* ironclad), 297
Virginia City, 341
Virginia Company (London), 24, 26
Virginia dynasty, 177
Virginia Plan, 117–118
Virginia Resolution, 140
Virginia Resolves, 86
Virtue: American clothing and, 88; civic, 71, 104; power tempered by, 85
Vittum, Harriet, 371
Volstead Act (1920), 495
Voltaire: Wheatley, Phillis, and, 107
Voluntarism: Hoover and, 506–507
Volunteers: for Spanish-American War, 415
Voting and voting rights, 588–589; African Americans and, 311, 323, 328, 572, 585; apathy in 1850s, 271; in Congress under Articles of Confederation, 110; decline in voter turnout and, 448–449; direct primary and, 448; disenfranchisement of blacks and, 328; election methods and, 189; in election of 1972, 613; in England, 70; free blacks and, 107; in Gilded Age, 391; organized mob violence and, 319; political machines and, 376; property requirement for, 106; in South, 323–325, 573; as visible, public act, 391 (illus.); of white males, 189; for women, 490. *See also* Electoral college; Woman suffrage
Voting Rights Act (1965), 588 (illus.), **589**
Voting trust: for railroads, 358
Voyages of exploration, 12 (illus.)

W

Wabash, St. Louis & Pacific Railway Co. v. *Illinois,* 392
Waco, Texas: Branch Davidians in, 671, 673
Wade-Davis Bill (1864), **312**
Wage earners. *See* Workers
Wage freeze: by Nixon, 610
Wage gap, 618
Wages: in industrial society, 363–364; inequality between men and women, 364, 431; iron law of, 366; in 1970s, 617; reduction in miners', 397; in textile industry, 175; of women, 619; in World War II, 536
Wagner, Fort, battle of, 302 (illus.)
Wagner, Robert, 513
Wagner Act (1935), **513,** 514, 515, 519
Wagon trains, 337–338
Wald, Lillian, 385, 448, 470
Walden (Thoreau), 241
Walesa, Lech, 649
Walker, David, 238
Walker, Martin, 662
Walking cities, 372
Wallace, George: assassination attempt on, 612; election of 1968 and, 601
Wallace, Henry A.: as Progressive party candidate (1948), 555; as secretary of agriculture, 509
Walling, William E., 432
Wampanoag Indians: Metacomet and, 54 (illus.)
Wanamaker, John, 362
Wang Dan, 649 (illus.)
War Committee on Labor, 478
War debts: after World War I, 523
War Department, 128, 472
Warehouse Act, 461
War Hawks, 159
War Industries Board (WIB), 477
War Labor Board (WLB), 478
War of 1812, 159–163, 160 (illus.); nation building after, 176–182; patriotism and, 162 (illus.); Treaty of Ghent after, 161–163; War Hawks and, 159; Washington, D.C., in, 161
War of Independence. *See* American Revolution
War of the Austrian Succession. *See* King George's War
War of the League of Augsburg. *See* King William's War
War of the Spanish Succession. *See* Queen Anne's War
War on Drugs, 645
War on Poverty, 587
War on terrorism, 681–682
War Production Board (WPB), 535
Warren, Earl: *Brown* decision and, 573; Supreme Court under, 585–586
Warren Commission: report by, 585
Wars and warfare: Civil War as total war, 292–299; imperial, 72–77; between Indians, 333; renunciation of, 522; 1689-1763, 75 (illus.). *See also* specific wars
Warsaw Pact, 548, 549
Wartime Reconstruction, 312
Washington (state): boundaries of, 245
Washington, Booker T., 381–382, 432, 451
Washington, D.C.: British burning of, 161; as capital, 149; capitol in, 141; Coxey's Army march on, 397; riots in (1968), 596
Washington, George: in American Revolution, 94; bank controversy and, 131; Constitution (U.S.) and, 117; Continental Army and, 93; Farewell Address of, 136; at First Continental Congress, 91; foreign affairs under, 132–134; Newburgh Conspiracy and, 115; in Ohio Valley, 74; as president, 127–128; provisional army and, 138; second term of, 132–134; title for, 126

Washington, Thomas: census of 1790 and, 144
Washington, Treaty of (1871), 410
Washington Conference (1921), 524–525
Washington Post: Pentagon Papers and, 607
WASPS, 377
Waste Land, The (Eliot), 492
Water: in cities, 373; and irrigation in West, 431; as western issue, 339
Watergate Scandal, 607–608, **613**–614; politics after, 622–624
Watkins, James, 643
Watkins report: on AIDS, 643
Watt, James, 633
Watts: riot in (1964), 596
Wayne, Anthony, 134
Wealth: from Americas, 11, 22; in Confederacy, 295; of elites, 46; inequality of, 636; in 1920s, 488; predatory, 384; after Revolution, 104; of South after Civil War, 318
Wealthy: in cities, 65; immigration experience of, 388
Weapons: Indian trade for, 6; revolver and, 258 (illus.); suspension of tests, 561; in World War I, 474. *See also* Arms and armaments; Missiles; Nuclear arms race; specific weapons
Weapons of mass destruction (WMD), 684
Weaver, James B., 396
Weaver, Randy, 673
Weber, Max, 439
Webster, Daniel: election of 1836 and, 198
Webster-Ashburton Treaty (1842), **245**
Webster's Spellers, 380
Weights and measures: uniform system of, 181
Weinberger, Caspar, 637
Welch, Joseph, 557
Weld, Theodore Dwight: revivalism, abolitionism, and, 237
Welfare capitalism, 489
Welfare system: Nixon and, 609; Social Security and, 512, 519
Wellesley, 381
"We Owe Allegiance to No Crown," 162 (illus.)
West (region): anti-British sentiment in, 158–159; buffalo soldiers in, 351–352; cattle in, 343–345, 344 (illus.); Civil War in, 297, 302; as colonial empire, 332; conquest of, 135 (illus.); election of 1992 and, 662; expansion into, 147–148; farming in, 345–347; folklore of, 337; Homestead Act of 1862 and, 306, 339; imperial wars over, 72–74; irrigation in, 430 (illus.), 431; land claims in, 110–112, 111 (illus.); land in, 338–339; mining in, 341–343, 342 (illus.); Native Americans in, 332–337; new states in, 331; Northwest Ordinance and, 112–113; Overland Trail and, 337–338; population shift to, 655, 656–657, 656 (illus.); settlement of, 337–340; steamships and, 149; territories in, 339–340; trans-Appalachian, 166; Turner's thesis and, 347–348; in War of 1812, 160. *See also* Westward movement
West Africa: societies and trade of, 8–9
West Bank, 638
Western Europe: medium-range missiles in, 638; power in 1970s, 611; society in, 10; after World War II, 544. *See also* specific countries
Western front: in World War I, 473 (illus.), 475 (illus.)
Western Hemisphere: U.S. policy in, 524
Western Pacific Railroad: immigrant workers provided for, 433
Western Reserve, 147
Westerns: popular fiction as, 437; on television, 568; after World War II, 567 (illus.)
West Germany, 579
West Indies: colonial exports to, 67; French in, 151
Westinghouse: railroad air brake of, 353
Westinghouse, George, 362
West Jersey, 34. *See also* New Jersey
Westmoreland, William: Vietnam War and, 592–593
Westover (house), 66 (illus.)
West Paducah, Kentucky: school violence in, 675
West Point military academy, 150
Westward movement, 147–148; British constraints on, 85; by Germans and Scots-Irish, 61; Native Americans and, 331–332; North American in 1800, 148 (illus.); Overland Trail and, 337–338
Weyler y Nicolau, Valeriano, 413
Wharton, Edith, 493
What Price Glory? (Stallings and Anderson), 483
Wheatley, Phillis, 107
Whigs (England), **83**
Whigs (U.S.), **197,** 270, 271; disintegration of, 272; election of 1836 and, 198; election of 1840 and, 199–200; election of 1844 and, 252; election of 1852 and, 271; emergence of, 197–198; Lincoln in, 287; Mexican-American War and, 255; second party system and, 200–201; Tyler, John, and, 251
Whiskey Rebellion, 136
"Whiskey Ring," 325–326
White, George H., 328
White, Hugh Lawson: election of 1836 and, 198
White, John, 18; on Indian fishing, 18 (illus.)
White, William Allen, 528
White Collar (Mills), 569
White-collar jobs: increase in, 635
Whitefield, George, 68–69, 69 (illus.)
Whites: free blacks and, 107; in Old South, 205, 212–216; as planters, 212–214; in population (1877), 377; Pueblo Indians and, 63; after Revolution, 104; as small slaveholders, 214; as yeoman farmers, 214–215
White Shadows (McKay), 493
White supremacy, 311; Alliance movement and, 395; Redeemers and, 327
Whitewater scandal, 665
Whitman, Walt, 189, 244, 355
Whitney, Eli: inventions of, 218, 258 (illus.)
Whyte, William H., 568
Wicomess Indians: Europeans and, 1
Wiggins, Kate Douglas, 437
Wild West Show: of Buffalo Bill Cody, 337, 343 (illus.), 378
Wiley, Harvey W., 453
Wilkinson, James, 155
William III (England), 52. *See also* William and Mary (England)
William and Mary (England), 22, 54–55; King Philip's War and, 72
Williams, Roger, 31
Williamsburg: Byrd in, 58
Williams v. *Mississippi,* 328 (illus.)
Wilmot, David, 267, 268
Wilmot Proviso (1846), 267–**268,** 269
Wilson, Edith Bolling, 482
Wilson, William B., 460
Wilson, Woodrow, 389, 433, 442, 450; child labor and, 446; death of, 484; diplomacy of, 464, 465, 472; election of 1912 and, 457–458; election of 1916 and, 472; foreign policy of, 468–470; Fourteen Points of, 479, 480, 480 (illus.); labor movement and, 460–461; League of Nations and, 481; Mexico and, 468–470; neutrality policy of, 470–471; New Freedom of, 457, 458–461; New Nationalism and, 459–461; at Paris Peace Conference, 480–482; peace efforts of, 472–473; progressivism and, 427; stroke of, 482; trusts and, 459; Versailles Treaty and, 482; World War I repression and, 476–477. *See also* World War I
Wilson-Gorman Tariff Act (1894), 399, 410
Winthrop, John, 21, 54, 56; Puritans and, 29, 30
Winthrop family, 46
Wisconsin: slavery outlawed in, 113
"Wisconsin Idea," 450–451
Witchcraft: in Salem Village, 55
Witherspoon family, 42
Withholding taxes: in World War II, 536
Wives: in Spanish-Mexican society, 340. *See also* Families; Women
WLB. *See* War Labor Board (WLB)
WMD. *See* Weapons of mass destruction (WMD)
Wobblies. *See* Industrial Workers of the World (IWW)
Wolfe, James, 75
Wolsey, Thomas, 15
Woman suffrage, 108, 380, 391, 445–446, 447 (illus.), 461; in New Jersey, 108; before 1920, 446 (illus.)
Women: abolition movement and, 238, 239; abortion rights for, 620; assertiveness of new woman, 380; benevolent societies and, 233; birth control and, 234, 431–432; as business owners, 619; in Chesapeake region, 47; Civil Rights Act (1964) and, 597; during Civil War, 305, 306 (illus.); clothing in Victorian era, 378; Cult of Domesticity and, 232–233, 239; divorce and, 224; earnings of, 618; of Eastern Woodland cultures, 4; education of, 108; farming by Indian, 336; feminine subculture and, 233; *femme couverte* doctrine and, 380; along frontier, 169; Garrison, William Lloyd, and, 238; glass ceiling and, 619; higher education for, 381; hotel boom and, 184; Hutchinson and, 31; in immigrant associations, 375; improved working conditions for, 444; in industrial occupations, 261; Jacksonian-era politics and, 190; in labor force, 232, 618; labor unions and, 366, 434, 435 (illus.); in late 19th century families, 379; leisure and, 233; marriage and, 231; in middle class, 431; as mill workers, 175, 175 (illus.); in mining camps, 342; motherhood and, 233;

national organizations of, 445; in New Deal, 515–516; in New England, 43, 44–45; in 1970s, 618–620; Nineteenth Amendment and, 446; in 1920s, 490–491; as older Americans, 656–657; on Overland Trail, 337–338; in Plains tribes, 333; as plantation mistresses, 212; poverty among, 587; prostitution and, 230, 232, 445; rape and, 214, 224–225; Seneca Falls Convention and, 239; as settlement workers, 385; in social-justice movement, 445–446; of southern households, 224–225; in Spanish-Mexican society, 340; support of revenue boycott by, 88; on Supreme Court, 619; unmarried, after Civil War, 305; as vice presidential candidate, 637; voting by, 666; white-collar jobs and, 635; WLB and wages of, 478; women's sphere and, 233; as workers, 364, 368, 400, 431; during World War I, 478; after World War II, 567; in World War II, 536; as writers, 493; yeoman, 214. *See also* Women's liberation movement

Women and Economics (Gilman), 380

Women's Christian Temperance Union (WCTU), 378, 445; black chapters of, 322

Women's liberation movement, 597–598

Women's rights: after Revolution, 107–108

Women's Trade Union League (WTUL), 434, 445

Wood, Leonard, 422

Woodham, Luke, 675

Woods, Robert, 385

Woodside, John Archibald, Jr., 162 (illus.)

Woodstock Music Festival, 595, 595 (illus.)

Woolworth, F. W., 362

Woolworth stores: sit-ins at, 574 (illus.)

Worcester v. *Georgia,* 193

Workday: eight-hour, 365, 435, 456, 461, 478; for women, 446

Workers: adjustments to factory age, 366; bias in workplace and, 364; children as, 364; compensation for government employees, 461; culture of, 364–365; impersonality of, 364–365; in large-scale factories, 429; in 1920s, 487; piecework and, 364; safety and, 364; speed and product vs., 428; steel plant closings and, 617; wages for, 363–364; women and, 364, 536. *See also* Labor

Workers, The (Wyckoff), 386

Workers' compensation laws, 450

Working class: antidraft riots and, 301; in cities, 372; Civil War and white, 306; compulsory education and, 235; Cult of Domesticity and, 232; employment of women and children from, 400; families in late 19th century, 379; movement to middle class, 365; new, 260–262

Working women: depression of 1890s and, 400; in New Deal, 515–516; in 1920s, 490; after World War II, 567. *See also* Labor; Women; Workers

Workplace: conflict in, 433–434; control of, 429; folkways of, 429; scientific labor management in, 429; women in, 618

Works Progress Administration (WPA), 510–511, 515, 519

Workweek: decline in hours, 437; maximum, 508; for women, 491

World colonial empires (1900), 421 (illus.)

WorldCom, Inc., 680

"World's Constable, The": political cartoon on Roosevelt Corollary, 467 (illus.)

World Trade Center: attack on (1993), 655; September 11, 2001, attacks and, 655, 677, 681

World Trade Organization (WTO): Seattle protests against, 671, 674–675

World War I: armistice for, 475; casualties of, 475; disillusionment after, 483–484; European alliances and battlefronts (1914–1917), 473 (illus.); European events leading to, 470; home front during, 476–477; labor in, 478–479; mobilization for, 474; neutrality policy of U.S., 470–471; preparedness campaign for, 472; repression during, 476–477; Treaty of Versailles and, 479–482; U-boats in, 471–472, 473, 474; United States after, 522, 523–524; U.S. entry into, 474; warfare in, 474–475, 475 (illus.). *See also* specific countries and battles

World War II: aims and diplomacy of, 539–540; Axis powers in, 526, 531–535; coalitions in, 532; division of Europe after, 543, 544–545; end of, 538–539; Europe and, 526–527, 533 (illus.), 545 (illus.); financing of, 536; holocaust in, 539, 539 (illus.); home front in, 535–538; impact of, 541; North Africa and, 532–533, 533 (illus.); opening of, 527, 527 (illus.); in Pacific, 525, 534 (illus.); Pearl Harbor attack in, 530–531, 531 (illus.); postwar boom and, 566–567; Potsdam conference after, 543; reforms after, 570–574; service stars in, 537 (illus.); Truman and, 540–541; U.S. road to war in, 528–531. *See also* specific countries and battles

"Worse Than Slavery" (Nast), 324 (illus.)

Wounded Knee Massacre, 335, 352

WPA. *See* Works Progress Administration (WPA)

WPB. *See* War Production Board (WPB)

Wright, Frances: Nashoba community and, 239

Wright, Frank Lloyd, 372

Wyckoff, Walter, 385–386

Wyoming: Mexican-American War and, 255

Wyoming Stock Growers' Association, 344

X

XYZ Affair, 137–**138**

Y

Yale, 381

Yalta Conference (1945), **540**; Far East and, 551

Yalu River, battle at, 553

YamaSee War, 7

Yates v. *United States,* 585

Yazoo controversy, 154

Year 2000 (Y2K) problem, 676–677

Yellow dog contracts, 489

Yellow fever, 418, 422

Yellow journalism, 413, 414 (illus.)

Yeltsin, Boris, 649–650, 668

Yeoman, 204; after Civil War, 319; in northern colonies, 46; in the Old South, 214–215

Yergin, Daniel, 543

Yippies, 595

York, Duke of. *See* James II (England)

Yorktown, battle at, 92 (illus.), 98

Young, Brigham: Mormon trek and, 250

Young America, 244; expansionism and, 244–245; Manifest Destiny and, 252–253

Youth: AIDS and, 644

Youth movement: clothing in 1960s, 594 (illus.); in 1920s, 491; in 1960s, 593–595

Yugoslavia: breakup of, 670 (illus.)

Yugoslavia (former): Bosnian fighting and, 669–671; Kosovo and, 671

Z

Zangwill, Israel: melting pot analogy of, 660, 661

Zen Buddhism, 569

Ziegler, Ron, 607

Zimmermann, Arthur, 473

Zimmerman telegram, 473

Zones: in Germany, 544

Zoning: in cities, 436

"Zoot suit" riots, 537–538

Zuni Indians, 332

PRESENT DAY WORLD

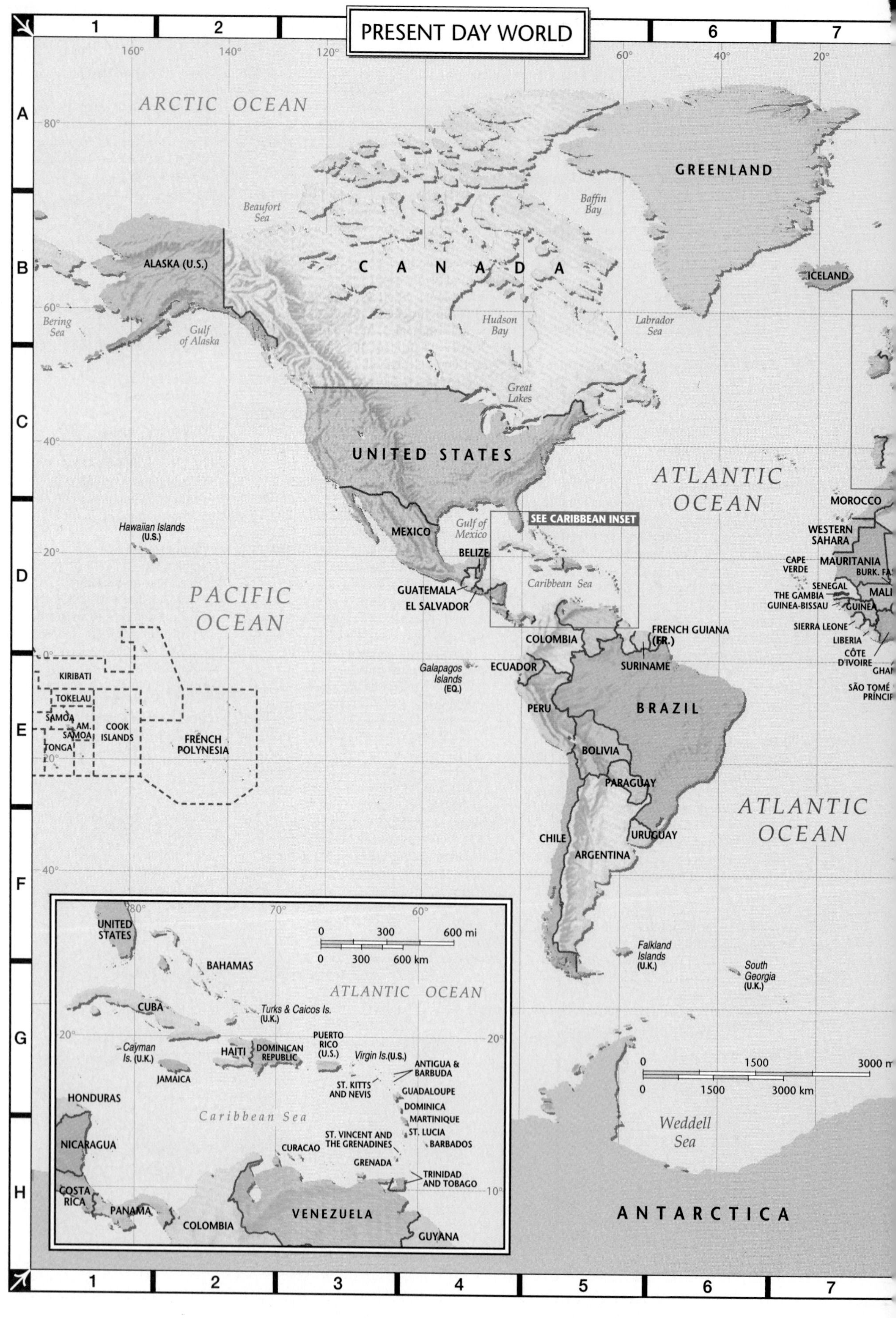

ARCTIC OCEAN
GREENLAND
Beaufort Sea
Baffin Bay
ALASKA (U.S.)
CANADA
ICELAND
Bering Sea
Gulf of Alaska
Hudson Bay
Labrador Sea
Great Lakes
UNITED STATES
ATLANTIC OCEAN
MOROCCO
SEE CARIBBEAN INSET
Hawaiian Islands (U.S.)
MEXICO
Gulf of Mexico
WESTERN SAHARA
BELIZE
CAPE VERDE
MAURITANIA
Caribbean Sea
SENEGAL
MALI
THE GAMBIA
GUINEA-BISSAU
GUINEA
PACIFIC OCEAN
GUATEMALA
EL SALVADOR
FRENCH GUIANA (FR.)
SIERRA LEONE
LIBERIA
COLOMBIA
CÔTE D'IVOIRE
Galapagos Islands (EQ.)
ECUADOR
SURINAME
KIRIBATI
TOKELAU
SAMOA
AM. SAMOA
COOK ISLANDS
TONGA
FRENCH POLYNESIA
PERU
BRAZIL
BOLIVIA
PARAGUAY
ATLANTIC OCEAN
CHILE
URUGUAY
ARGENTINA
Falkland Islands (U.K.)
South Georgia (U.K.)
UNITED STATES
BAHAMAS
0 300 600 mi
0 300 600 km
ATLANTIC OCEAN
CUBA
Turks & Caicos Is. (U.K.)
Cayman Is. (U.K.)
HAITI
DOMINICAN REPUBLIC
PUERTO RICO (U.S.)
Virgin Is.(U.S.)
ANTIGUA & BARBUDA
JAMAICA
ST. KITTS AND NEVIS
GUADALOUPE
HONDURAS
DOMINICA
Caribbean Sea
MARTINIQUE
ST. LUCIA
ST. VINCENT AND THE GRENADINES
BARBADOS
NICARAGUA
CURACAO
GRENADA
TRINIDAD AND TOBAGO
COSTA RICA
PANAMA
VENEZUELA
COLOMBIA
GUYANA
0 1500 3000 mi
0 1500 3000 km
Weddell Sea
ANTARCTICA

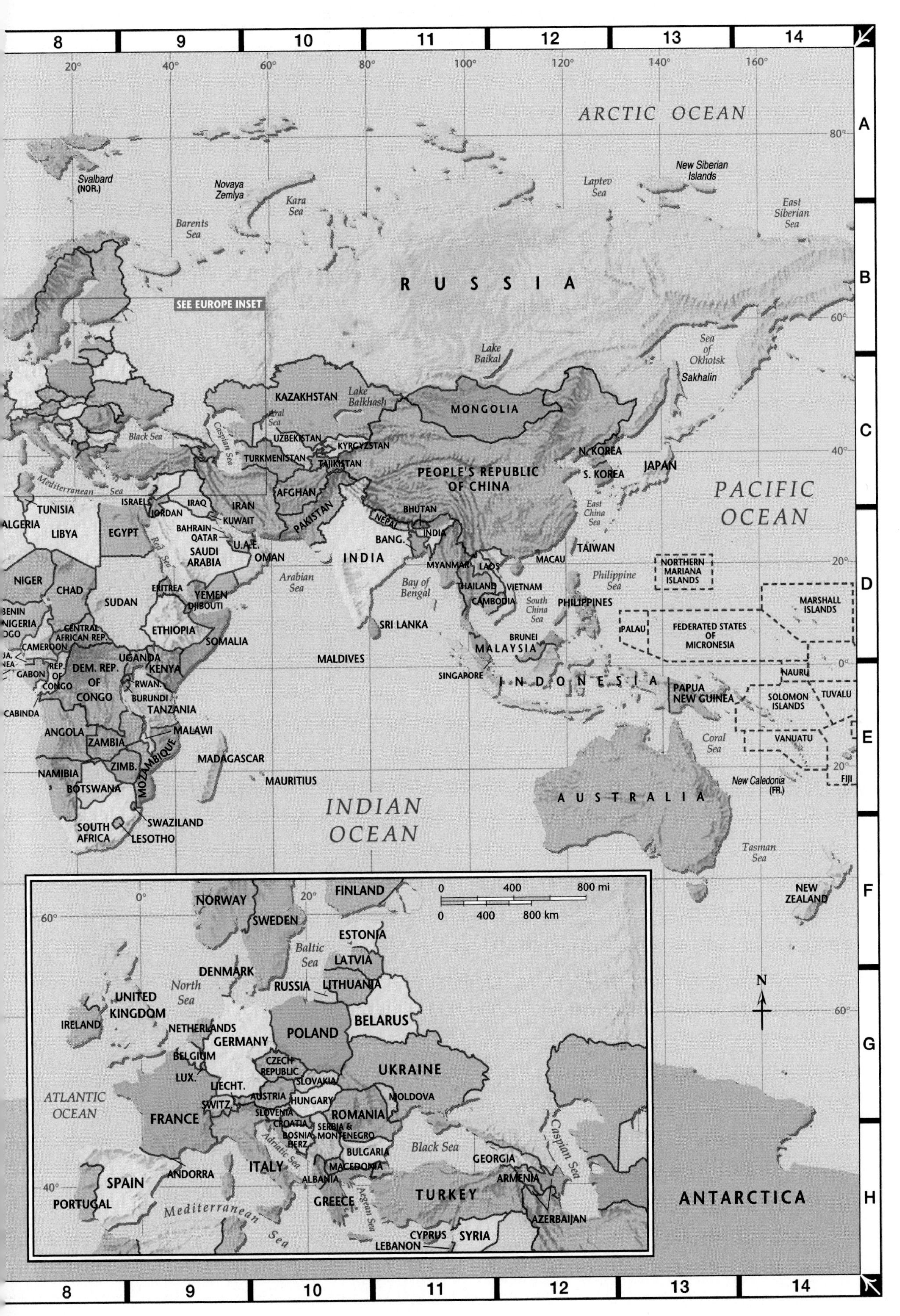

ARCTIC OCEAN
Svalbard (NOR.)
Novaya Zemlya
Barents Sea
Kara Sea
Laptev Sea
New Siberian Islands
East Siberian Sea
RUSSIA
SEE EUROPE INSET
Lake Baikal
Sea of Okhotsk
Sakhalin
KAZAKHSTAN
Lake Balkhash
MONGOLIA
Aral Sea
Caspian Sea
Black Sea
UZBEKISTAN
KYRGYZSTAN
TURKMENISTAN
TAJIKISTAN
N. KOREA
S. KOREA
JAPAN
PEOPLE'S REPUBLIC OF CHINA
PACIFIC OCEAN
Mediterranean Sea
TUNISIA
ISRAEL
IRAQ
IRAN
AFGHAN.
JORDAN
KUWAIT
PAKISTAN
BHUTAN
NEPAL
INDIA
ALGERIA
LIBYA
EGYPT
BAHRAIN
QATAR
U.A.E.
Red Sea
SAUDI ARABIA
OMAN
BANG.
East China Sea
TAIWAN
MACAU
NIGER
CHAD
SUDAN
ERITREA
YEMEN
DJIBOUTI
Arabian Sea
Bay of Bengal
MYANMAR
LAOS
THAILAND
VIETNAM
CAMBODIA
South China Sea
Philippine Sea
PHILIPPINES
NORTHERN MARIANA ISLANDS
MARSHALL ISLANDS
BENIN
NIGERIA
CENTRAL AFRICAN REP.
ETHIOPIA
SOMALIA
SRI LANKA
BRUNEI
MALAYSIA
PALAU
FEDERATED STATES OF MICRONESIA
CAMEROON
UGANDA
KENYA
MALDIVES
GABON
REP. OF CONGO
DEM. REP. OF CONGO
RWAN.
BURUNDI
TANZANIA
SINGAPORE
INDONESIA
NAURU
PAPUA NEW GUINEA
SOLOMON ISLANDS
TUVALU
CABINDA
ANGOLA
ZAMBIA
MALAWI
Coral Sea
VANUATU
ZIMB.
MOZAMBIQUE
MADAGASCAR
NAMIBIA
BOTSWANA
MAURITIUS
New Caledonia (FR.)
FIJI
AUSTRALIA
INDIAN OCEAN
SOUTH AFRICA
SWAZILAND
LESOTHO
Tasman Sea
NEW ZEALAND
ANTARCTICA
NORWAY
FINLAND
SWEDEN
0 400 800 mi
0 400 800 km
ESTONIA
Baltic Sea
LATVIA
DENMARK
North Sea
RUSSIA
LITHUANIA
UNITED KINGDOM
IRELAND
NETHERLANDS
GERMANY
POLAND
BELARUS
BELGIUM
CZECH REPUBLIC
UKRAINE
LUX.
LIECHT.
SLOVAKIA
ATLANTIC OCEAN
AUSTRIA
HUNGARY
MOLDOVA
SWITZ.
SLOVENIA
ROMANIA
FRANCE
CROATIA
BOSNIA HERZ.
SERBIA & MONTENEGRO
Adriatic Sea
BULGARIA
Black Sea
GEORGIA
Caspian Sea
ITALY
MACEDONIA
ARMENIA
SPAIN
ANDORRA
ALBANIA
Aegean Sea
TURKEY
PORTUGAL
GREECE
AZERBAIJAN
Mediterranean Sea
CYPRUS
SYRIA
LEBANON
N